UNIVERSITY CASEBOOK SERIES®

THE FIRST AMENDMENT AND RELATED STATUTES

PROBLEMS, CASES AND POLICY ARGUMENTS

SIXTH EDITION

EUGENE VOLOKH

Gary T. Schwartz Professor of Law
UCLA School of Law

FOUNDATION
PRESS

University Casebook Series is a trademark registered in the U.S. Patent and Trademark Office.

© 2001 FOUNDATION PRESS
© 2005, 2008, 2011 THOMSON REUTERS/FOUNDATION PRESS
© 2014 LEG, Inc. d/b/a West Academic
© 2016 LEG, Inc. d/b/a West Academic
      444 Cedar Street, Suite 700
      St. Paul, MN 55101
      1-877-888-1330

Printed in the United States of America

ISBN: 978-1-63460-510-6

To my parents, Anne and Vladimir,

who taught me by their example

about the importance of freedom—and of courage;

and to Leslie, Benjamin, and Samuel.

*

Introduction—Unusual Features of This Book

This textbook is structured differently from traditional law school casebooks in five important ways:

1. The Problem Method. Rather than using the traditional case method, this book is focused around problems.

The best way to understand the principles that a case sets forth is by applying them to concrete situations. This is what you'll do in real life, on the bar exam, and probably on the exam for this class. Thus, you should read the problem first (this is why the problems usually precede the cases in the casebook), read the cases with an eye towards solving the problem, and then reread the problem. After you get through the doctrinal analysis of the problem, you might ask whether the result makes policy sense.

2. Summary of the Law. To make it easier to learn the basic rules, this book includes a *rough summary* of the substantive law. This of course is a *supplement* to the cases and the class discussion, not a substitute. (Among other things, to properly understand what the tests actually mean, you have to know how they've been applied by the cases.) To make it easier to absorb the structure of the rules, the summary is written as an outline rather than as traditional prose.

3. The Pervasive Method. While some problems only ask you to apply what you've learned in the particular unit for which they're assigned, other problems require you to think back to other units you've studied throughout the semester. This, too, makes the problems more like the exam, like the bar, and like real life.

4. Explicit Focus on the Structure of Policy Arguments. This book aims to describe in detail the various kinds of free speech policy arguments and the common counterarguments, more explicitly than they are usually explained in most casebooks and classes. These explanations aren't meant to persuade you which arguments are right and which are wrong; rather, they're meant to illustrate the rhetoric of First Amendment law, rhetoric that you can use in your client's interest.

Each policy section gives the basic structure of an argument and of the standard counterarguments and counter-counterarguments. It also gives examples from various sources. Each example could work for you in two ways. First, by showing you concrete instances in which the argument has been given, it can help you make similar arguments of your own. Second, it may also help you make a counterargument to the claim that the example illustrates, by helping you show the dangers of this sort of claim.

Say, for instance, that one of the examples of a "Constitutional Tension" argument (an argument that speech restrictions may be justified by some other constitutional value) shows this sort of argument being used to justify censoring antiwar speech, on the theory that such censorship is authorized by Congress's constitutionally established war power. You can then respond to other kinds of Constitutional Tension arguments by saying "Oh, that argument is a Constitutional Tension argument, and it's dangerous because it can equally well be used—and has in fact been used—to suppress antiwar speech."

The policy sections intentionally include arguments that apply to various substantive areas of First Amendment law; thus, for instance, the No-Value or Low-Value Speech section gives examples from obscenity, libel, commercial speech, and other areas. This is done to show how arguments made in one context can be adapted to other contexts, and how accepting an argument in one sort of case may have implications for other cases.

Please read carefully through the policy sections, and consider how you can adapt the arguments given there to the particular problems that you're assigned.

5. A Bit More History. Though this book primarily focuses on the law as it is (or as it could have been), it also includes more historical materials than other books do, in places where those materials remain relevant to modern debates. Thus, for example, it includes a case applying the Sedition Act of 1798, and discusses Abraham Lincoln's defense of speech restrictions during the Civil War alongside the Court's defense of speech restrictions during World War I. Also, quite a few of the policy argument examples are drawn from late 1700s and 1800s cases and commentators, including James Madison, Joseph Story, John Stuart Mill, and others. This should help avoid the "1919 effect," in which many students of free speech implicitly (but erroneously) learn that free speech discourse burst full-grown from the heads of Holmes and Brandeis in 1919.

A WORD ABOUT EDITED CASES

Until I started writing this casebook, I didn't fully appreciate just how drastically many cases needed to be edited in order to fit into a casebook. This isn't just a question of casebook size, but also of the amount of attentive reading that students are likely to do. My goal has been to keep all cases at 10 pages or fewer, and I've generally succeeded; but this means that, just to give one example, *Texas Monthly v. Bullock* had to be edited down from 14,750 words to under 2,750.

Some of this editing can be done by eliminating citations, discussions of issues that are unrelated to why the case is included, less significant facts and procedural details, and tangential footnotes. But often the only way to suitably trim the case is by excluding some substantive arguments, both from the majority opinion and from the concurrences and dissents.

When I've had to do this, I've generally tried to start by trimming discussions of some of the precedents on which the case relies, but which aren't included in the readings. These discussions may have been quite important to the Justices, and may still be important to lawyers who practice in the field, but they tend to be (and I emphasize that this is only a tendency) less significant to understanding the core of the Court's holding or reasoning. I've also, when necessary, edited out some of the repetition that the Justices often included for rhetorical effect. Finally, I have sometimes edited out the arguments that seem the most tangential, that seem related to debates that raged at the time but that haven't remained important, or that were rejected in later cases.

I generally mark all omissions with ellipses ("..."), except for omissions of footnotes and citations; I mark changes or additions with brackets ("[" and "]"); I mark moved text with braces ("{" and "}"). I have also felt free to delete and insert paragraph breaks to make the material more readable. When a case quotes another case and adopts the other case's reasoning, I often omit the citation to that other case; such citations are often distracting, and are not really important when the citing case is adopting the quoted reasoning as its own. I also changed "Mr. Justice" in pre-1981 opinions to "Justice," to make the references consistent.

The risk, of course, is that the editing process may weaken the persuasive force of the opinions, and may thus be unfair to the opinions' authors and supporters. I have tried hard to avoid this, but I am sure that I've at times failed, especially since the judgment about which arguments are "tangential" and even what is "repetition" are so subjective. I apologize in advance for that, and hope that readers find the edits to be generally fair despite my inevitable lapses.

Epigraphs

Some chapters begin with epigraphs, generally excerpts from poems or other writings that I think say interesting things (though not always things with which I fully agree) about law, speech, or something else. They are sometimes specifically focused on the materials in the chapter, and sometimes just provide a possibly intriguing or amusing perspective on the class—or on law—generally. I'm always looking for good new epigraphs; please e-mail me suggestions at *volokh@law.ucla.edu*.

Acknowledgements

Many thanks to Stuart Banner, Alan Brownstein, Michael Kent Curtis, Rick Garnett, Sandy Levinson, Brett McDonnell, Dan Polsby, and Jim Weinstein for their thoughtful comments on drafts of this book; and to my own First Amendment teacher and current colleague Ken Karst. Thanks also to Laura Cadra, Kevin Gerson, Donna Gulnac, Jennifer Lentz, and John Wilson at the UCLA Law Library for their indispensable research assistance; to Jim Coates and Steve Errick for their help with the publication process; to Diane LeCover for all her work on the manuscript and the galleys; to Steve Cademartori and Hanah Metchis Volokh for their careful source-checking; to Garth Bostic, Sabrina Larson, Arvin Tseng for many helpful corrections; and to Khaled Abou El Fadl, Rabbi Yitzchok Adlerstein, Joan Del Fattore, David Fischer, Gideon Kanner, Leslie Pereira, Sasha Volokh, and Kit Winter for their answers to various questions. Thanks also to the First Amendment Online Primary Sources site, http://1stam.umn.edu/ (founded by Adam Samaha), from which I took some of the illustrations.

ABOUT THE AUTHOR

Eugene Volokh is Gary T. Schwartz Professor of Law at UCLA School of Law, where he teaches First Amendment law, criminal law, and academic legal writing. Before going into teaching, he clerked for Ninth Circuit Judge Alex Kozinski and for Justice Sandra Day O'Connor. He is the author of the following law review articles on the First Amendment (arranged in rough correspondence to the chapters of the book), as well as articles on a variety of other topics, and the *Academic Legal Writing* book; the list below also includes appellate cases that he has orally argued:

- Free speech generally: *Cheap Speech and What It Will Do*, 104 Yale L.J. 1805 (1995), reprinted in *First Amendment Law Handbook*, 1996-97, at 53 (Swanson ed.), and 1 Comm. Rev. 261 (1996).

- Free speech generally: *How the Justices Voted in Free Speech Cases, 1994 to 2000*, 48 UCLA L. Rev. 1191 (2001).

- Free speech generally: *Pragmatism vs. Ideology in Free Speech Cases*, 99 Nw. U. L. Rev. 33 (2004).

- Free speech generally: *The Freedom of Speech and Bad Purposes*, 63 UCLA L. Rev. __ (forthcoming 2016).

- II.A.4.d, II.A.4.e, II.B.4.d, II.E.3.k: *The Trouble with "Public Discourse" as a Limitation on Free Speech Rights*, 96 Va. L. Rev. 567 (2011).

- II.A.3.d: *In Defense of the Marketplace of Ideas / Search for Truth as a Theory of Free Speech Protection*, 96 Va. L. Rev. 595 (2011).

- II.A.4.i: *Freedom of Speech and the Constitutional Tension Method*, 3 U. Chi. Roundtable 223 (1996).

- II.B: *Tort Liability and the Original Meaning of the Freedom of Speech, Press, and Petition*, 96 Iowa L. Rev. 249 (2010).

- II.B: *Levitt v. Felton* (Mich. Ct. App. 2016).

- II.B: *State v. Turner*, 864 N.W.2d 204 (Minn. Ct. App. 2015).

- II.B.5.c: *Thomas Cooper, Early American Public Intellectual*, 4 NYU J. of Law & Liberty 372 (2009).

- II.B.5.c: *Elizabeth Ryland Priestley, Early American Author on Free Speech*, 4 NYU J. of Law & Liberty 382 (2009).

- II.B.6: *Amicus Curiae Brief: Boundaries of the First Amendment's "False Statements of Fact" Exception*, 6 Stan. J. Civ. Rts. & Civ. Libs. 343 (2010), reprinting an amicus brief filed in *United States v. Strandlof*, 746 F. Supp. 2d 1183 (D. Colo. 2010).

- II.B.7: *Freedom for the Press as an Industry, or for the Press as a Technology? From the Framing to Today*, 160 U. Pa. L. Rev. 459 (2012).

- II.B.7: *Obsidian Finance Group, LLC v. Cox*, 740 F.3d 1284 (9th Cir. 2014).

- II.B.8: *Dillon v. Seattle Deposition Reporters* (Wash. 2014).
- II.C: *Freedom of Speech, Shielding Children, and Transcending Balancing*, 1997 Sup. Ct. Rev. 141.
- II.D.3: *The "Speech Integral to Criminal Conduct" Exception*, 101 Cornell L. Rev. __ (forthcoming 2016).
- II.D.3: *Speech as Conduct: Generally Applicable Laws, Illegal Courses of Conduct, "Situation-Altering Utterances," and the Uncharted Zones*, 90 Cornell L. Rev. 1277 (2005).
- II.E: *Gruesome Speech*, 100 Cornell L. Rev. 901 (2015).
- II.E: *State v. Drahota*, 280 Neb. 267 (2010).
- II.E.3: *One-to-One Speech vs. One-to-Many Speech, Criminal Harassment Laws, and "Cyberstalking,"* 107 Nw. U. Rev. 731 (2013).
- II.E.3: *Chan v. Ellis*, 770 S.E.2d 851 (Ga. 2015).
- II.E.3.k: *Freedom of Speech and the Intentional Infliction of Emotional Distress Tort*, 2010 Cardozo L. Rev. de•novo 300.
- II.E.3.m: *The Mechanisms of the Slippery Slope,* 116 Harv. L. Rev. 1026 (2003) (discussing free speech alongside other matters).
- II.E.4: *Symbolic Expression and the Original Meaning of the First Amendment*, 97 Georgetown L.J. 1057 (2009).
- II.F: *Brewington v. State*, 7 N.E.3d 946 (Ind. 2014).
- II.F: *Ex Parte Perry*, __ S.W.3d __ (Tex. Ct. Crim. App. 2016).
- II.G: *Freedom of Speech and Independent Judgment Review in Copyright Cases*, 107 Yale L.J. 2431 (1998) (with Brett McDonnell).
- II.G: *Freedom of Speech and Intellectual Property: Some Thoughts After Eldred, 44 Liquormart, and Bartnicki*, 40 U. Hous. L. Rev. 697 (2003).
- II.G: *Freedom of Speech and the Right of Publicity,* 40 U. Hous. L. Rev. 903 (2003).
- II.G: *Amicus Brief of Michael Crichton[, Larry David, Jeremiah Healy, Elmore Leonard, Harry Shearer, Ron Shelton, Scott Turow, Paul Weitz, and the Authors Guild, Inc.]*, 11 UCLA Enter. L. Rev. 1 (2004), reprinting an amicus brief filed in *McFarlane v. Twist*, 540 U.S. 1006 (2003).
- II.G: *Amicus Brief of the Electronic Frontier Foundation and the ACLU of Virginia in Radiance Foundation, Inc. v. NAACP*, 4 NYU J. Intell. Prop. & Ent. L. 95 (2015) (with Mairead Dolan), reprinting an amicus brief filed in 786 F.3d 316 (4th Cir. 2015).
- II.H: *Tracy Rifle & Pistol LLC v. Harris*, __ F. App'x __ (9th Cir. 2016).
- II.H.2.c: *Speech Restrictions That Don't Much Affect the Autonomy of Speakers*, 28 Const. Comm. 347 (2011).
- III: *Freedom of Speech, Permissible Tailoring and Transcending Strict Scrutiny*, 144 U. Pa. L. Rev. 2417 (1996).
- III.B.c: *A Penumbra Too Far*, 106 Harv. L. Rev. 1639 (1993) (with Judge

Alex Kozinski).

- III.C.1: *Crime-Facilitating Speech*, 57 Stan. L. Rev. 1095 (2005).

- III.C.3: *Freedom of Speech and Information Privacy: The Troubling Implications of a Right to Stop People from Speaking About You*, 52 Stan. L. Rev. 1049 (2000), excerpted in Daniel J. Solove & Marc Rotenberg, *Information Privacy Law* (2003) and Richard C. Turkington & Anita L. Allen, *Privacy Law* 418-20 (2d ed. 2002).

- III.C.4: *Freedom of Speech and Appellate Review in Workplace Harassment Cases*, 90 Nw. U. L. Rev. 1009 (1996).

- III.C.4: *Freedom of Speech and Workplace Harassment*, 39 UCLA L. Rev. 1791 (1992), cited in *Avis Rent A Car System, Inc. v. Aguilar*, 529 U.S. 1138 (2000) (Thomas, J., concurring in the judgment), and excerpted in Judi Greenberg, Dorothy Roberts & Martha Minow, *Women and the Law Casebook* 287-95 (2d ed. 1998), and *Women and Work* 33-45 (Greenberg, Roberts & Frug eds. Supp. 1997).

- III.C.4: *Freedom of Speech, Cyberspace, Harassment Law, and the Clinton Administration*, 63 L. & Contemp. Prob. 299 (2000).

- III.C.4: *How Harassment Law Restricts Free Speech*, 47 Rutgers L.J. 561 (1995).

- III.C.4: *Thinking Ahead About Freedom of Speech and "Hostile Work Environment" Harassment*, 17 Berk. J. Emp. & Labor L. 305 (1996).

- III.C.4: *What Speech Does "Hostile Work Environment" Harassment Law Restrict?*, 85 Geo. L.J. 627 (1997), excerpted in *Ethical Theory and Business* 369-74 (Tom L. Beauchamp & Norman E. Bowie eds. 2003).

- III.C.5: *Parent-Child Speech and Child Custody Speech Restrictions*, 81 N.Y.U. L. Rev. 631 (2006).

- V.E.2: *First Amendment Protection for Search Engine Results*, 8 J. L. & Econ. Pol'y (2012) (with Donald M. Falk) (reprint of paper commissioned by Google, Inc.).

- V.C.2.f, II.D.2: *Crime Severity and Constitutional Line-Drawing*, 90 Va. L. Rev. 1957 (2004).

- V.D: *Freedom of Speech and Speech About Political Candidates*, 24 Harv. J.L. & Pub. Pol. 47 (2000).

- V.D: *Why Buckley v. Valeo Is Basically Right*, 34 Ariz. St. L.J. 1095 (2003).

- V.E.3: *Amicus Curiae Brief: Elane Photography, LLC v. Willock*, 8 N.Y.U. J. L. & Liberty 116 (2013), reprinting amicus brief filed in 309 P.3d 53 (N.M. 2013).

- V.E.3, VI.B: *Frudden v. Pilling*, 742 F.3d 1199 (9th Cir. 2014).

- V.F: *Gerawan Farming, Inc. v. California Agricultural Labor Relations Bd.* (Cal. Ct. App. pending).

- V.F: *Ex Parte Thompson*, 442 S.W.3d 325 (Tex. Ct. Crim. App. 2014).

- VI.A: *Lawson v. Gault* (4th Cir. pending).

- VI.B: *O'Brien v. Welty*, __ F.3d __ (9th Cir. 2016).

- VI.D.2.f: *Freedom of Expressive Association and Government Subsidies*, 58 Stan. L. Rev. 1919 (2006), cited in *Christian Legal Society v. Martinez*, 561 U.S. 661 (2010) (majority and concurrence).

- VII.B, II.G: *Freedom of Speech and Injunctions in Intellectual Property Cases*, 48 Duke L.J. 147 (1998) (with Mark Lemley).

- VIII, II.E, II.B.9, III.C.4.c: *Freedom of Speech in Cyberspace from the Listener's Perspective*, 1996 U. Chi. Legal Forum 377.

- VIII: *Deterring Speech: When Is It "McCarthyism"? When Is It Proper?*, 92 Calif. L. Rev. 1413 (2005).

- VIII.B.2: *Private Employees' Speech and Political Activity: Statutory Protection Against Employer Retaliation*, 16 Tex. Rev. L. & Pol. 295 (2012).

- XII.A: *Equal Treatment Is Not Establishment*, 13 Notre Dame J. Law, Ethics & Pub. Pol. 341 (1999).

- XIII.A: *A Common-Law Model for Religious Exemptions*, 46 UCLA L. Rev. 1465 (1999).

- XIII.A: *Intermediate Questions of Religious Exemptions—A Research Agenda with Test Suites*, 21 Cardozo L. Rev. 595 (1999).

- XIII.A: *Religious Law (Especially Islamic Law) in American Courts*, 66 Oklahoma L. Rev. 431 (2014).

- XIII.A: *The Priority of Law: A Response to Michael Stokes Paulsen*, 39 Pepp. L. Rev. 1223 (2013).

- XIV, III.C.4: *Freedom of Speech, Religious Harassment Law, and Religious Accommodation Law*, 33 Loy. U. Chi. L.J. 57 (2001).

SUMMARY OF CONTENTS

TABLE OF CONTENTS

TABLE OF SOURCES

Other Authorities

Amar, Foreword: The Document and the Doctrine, 114 Harv. L. Rev. 26 (2000), 897

Baker, Commercial Advertising: A Problem in the Theory of Freedom, 62 Iowa L. Rev. 1 (1976), 267

Bittker, Churches, Taxes and the Constitution, 78 Yale L.J. 1285 (1969), 949

Bollinger, Free Speech and Intellectual Values, 92 Yale L.J. 438 (1983), 41

Borden, Jews, Turks, and Infidels (1984), 830

Bork, Neutral Principles and Some First Amendment Problems, 47 Ind. L.J. 1 (1971), 35, 39

Browne, Title VII as Censorship, 52 Ohio St.

UNIVERSITY CASEBOOK SERIES®

THE FIRST AMENDMENT AND RELATED STATUTES

PROBLEMS, CASES AND POLICY ARGUMENTS

SIXTH EDITION

"Congress shall make no law respecting an establishment of religion, or prohibiting the free exercise thereof; or abridging the freedom of speech, or of the press; or the right of the people peaceably to assemble, and to petition the Government for a redress of grievances."

I. FREE SPEECH: A GENERAL OVERVIEW

> And now, perhaps, I ought to have done. But I know that some spirit of fire will feel that his main question has not been answered.
>
> He will ask, What is all this to my soul? ... What have you said to show that I can reach my own spiritual possibilities through such a door as this? How can the laborious study of a dry and technical system, the greedy watch for clients and practice of shopkeepers' arts, the mannerless conflicts over often sordid interests, make out a life?
>
> Gentlemen, I admit at once that these questions are not futile, that they may prove unanswerable, that they have often seemed to me unanswerable. And yet I believe there is an answer. They are the same questions that meet you in any form of practical life. If a man has the soul of Sancho Panza, the world to him will be Sancho Panza's world; but if he has the soul of an idealist, he will make—I do not say find—his world ideal.
>
> Of course, the law is not the place for the artist or poet. The law is the calling of thinkers. But to those who believe with me that not the least godlike of man's activities is the large survey of causes, that to know is not less than to feel, I say—and I say no longer with any doubt—that a man may live greatly in the law as well as elsewhere; that there as well as elsewhere his thought may find its unity in an infinite perspective; that there as well as elsewhere he may wreak himself upon life, may drink the bitter cup of heroism, may wear his heart out after the unattainable.
>
> —Oliver Wendell Holmes, Jr., Lecture to Harvard University Undergraduates

The free speech materials in this textbook are organized in what I hope will be a helpful analytical structure; the Part numbers in the book mirror (except for Part I) the numbers below.

I. Start by asking whether the speech restriction is imposed by *the government*. If the restriction is not imposed by the government, we have no state action and the U.S. Constitution doesn't apply. Recall that the First Amendment starts by saying "*Congress* shall make no law ..." and the Fourteenth Amendment, which has been read as applying the First Amendment to the states, says "No *state* shall...." Private parties can retaliate based on people's speech through private means (*e.g.*, firing an employee, boycotting a speaker, and so on) without violating the First Amendment. Part VIII.A discusses this, and notes an exception; Part VIII.B then discusses some statutes and state constitutional provisions that may indeed protect speech from private retaliation.

II. Ask then whether the speech fits within one of the exceptions from full protection, such as the exceptions for incitement, false statements of fact, threats, and the like. If the speech does fall within such an exception, then the restriction is generally valid (unless it impermissibly discriminates based on the content of the speech, see Part III.B).

III. But even if the restricted speech is outside the exceptions—if it's "fully protected speech"—it's really only presumptively protected. This presumption could be rebutted if the restriction passes *strict scrutiny,* a very demanding test but still one that can be met if the court concludes that the restriction is necessary enough.

IV. If the government is restricting speech—or expressive conduct—for reasons *unrelated to its communicative impact* (for instance, because the speech is too noisy, obstructs traffic, and the like), then apply the special (fairly relaxed) test applicable to such restrictions.

V. Ask whether the restriction may interfere with speech through means other than direct speech suppression.

B. Consider whether the government is interfering with speech by interfering with the *expressive associations* that produce speech, especially by forcing them to admit members that they don't want to admit.

C. Consider whether the government is deterring speech or association by preventing *anonymity*—i.e., by coercing the disclosure of speakers', members', or contributors' identities.

D. Consider whether the government is interfering with speech or association by *restricting the spending of money* on such activities.

E. Consider whether the government is *compelling speech,* which may interfere with the compelled person's or entity's other speech (or may be improper even without such interference).

F. Consider whether the government is *restricting the gathering of information,* and thus blocking people from further communicating such information.

VI. Ask whether the government is acting *in a special capacity,* such as employer, landlord, public school educator, and the like, rather than acting as sovereign (exercising its powers to control everyone's conduct). If so, a lower level of scrutiny may be applicable, even if the speech would be protected against the government acting as sovereign.

VII. Consider whether the *prior restraint* doctrine is applicable.

This, of course, is only a very rough outline.

II. EXCEPTIONS FROM FULL PROTECTION

We begin with the exceptions from protection (plus commercial advertising, a zone of diminished protection). If a restriction only restricts speech that falls within these exceptions, then the restriction is generally constitutional (but see Part III.B). These are generally traditionally recognized exceptions, which (mostly) rest on a historical judgment that certain speech (e.g., false statements of fact) is not very valuable or that certain kinds of restrictions on speech are justified.

If the restricted speech is outside those exceptions, then the restriction might still be constitutional if it passes strict scrutiny (Part III). But strict scrutiny is usually a very hard test to pass.

A. INCITEMENT

> They never told the [raging] crowd to [flay] a woman's hide,
> They never marked a man for death—what fault of theirs he died?—
> They only said "intimidate," and talked and went away—
> By God, the boys that did the work were braver men than they!
> Their sin it was that fed the fire—small blame to them that heard—
> The boys get drunk on rhetoric, and madden at a word— ...
> If words are words, or death is death, or powder sends the ball,
> [They] spoke the words that sped the shot—the curse be on [them] all.
> —Rudyard Kipling, *"Cleared"*

1. CURRENT LAW

a. *Summary*

Rule—Incitement: "Advocacy of the use of force or of law violation" is *constitutionally unprotected incitement* when it is

1. "directed to inciting or producing"

2. "imminent lawless action"

— which probably means action within hours or at most several days, but certainly excludes advocacy of illegal action "at some indefinite future time," see *Hess v. Indiana* (1973) (p. 7),

3. "and is likely to incite or produce such action." *Brandenburg v. Ohio* (1969) (p. 5).

Rule—Solicitation: A "proposal to engage in illegal activity," especially when focused on "a particular piece" of contraband, as opposed to "the abstract advocacy of illegality," is *constitutionally unprotected solicitation*. *United States v. Williams* (2008) (p. 9).

Possible exception: *Dennis v. United States* (1951) (p. 45) and *Yates v. United States* (1957) (p. 53), the Communist advocacy cases, are not consistent with the *Brandenburg* test; they allowed restrictions on advocacy of concrete action (rather than just of abstract doctrine) even when the action

3

wasn't imminent. Most scholars think these cases are no longer good law, and *Brandenburg* now governs, but keep in mind that *Dennis* and *Yates* have not been formally overruled.

Policy explanation for absence of protection:

1. What's the perceived harm that justifies the suppression of speech in these cases? The risk that people will be persuaded to violate the law, and the consequent damage that this violation will cause.

2. If the likely harm is really imminent (the mob will burn someone's house down), then the cost of allowing the speech is just too great.

Policy explanation for narrowness of unprotected area:

1. Advocacy of illegal conduct may persuade the public that the law (and social attitudes) should be changed.

2. A lot of important political advocacy has some element of praise—and perhaps even urging—of illegal conduct.

Policy arguments inferable from this:

1. Even evil, dangerous speech—speech that might persuade people to do some very bad things—is protected.

2. The government generally can't restrict speech just because the speech has a tendency, even a strong tendency, to change people's views in such a way that they'll commit crimes in the future.

3. Speech that's about to lead to imminent harm might be restrictable.

b. *Problem: "Abortionists Are Murderers"*

John Doe is speaking in a park and says, "Abortion is murder, which means abortionists are murderers. But because the law can't touch them, it's up to each of us to save the lives of the unborn by any means necessary." Mary Moe hears Doe and is persuaded that he's right; a month later she shoots a doctor who performs abortions. Doe is indicted for murder under a statute that says

> Any person who counsels the commission of a criminal act shall be liable to the same extent as the person who actually commits the act.

Is the prosecution of Doe constitutionally permissible? Imagine yourself as Doe's lawyer and make the best arguments you can for his position; then imagine yourself as the prosecutor, and make the best arguments you can for the prosecution.

c. *Problem: "Cop Killer"*

Ice-T's "Cop Killer" contains the following lines:

I got my black shirt on
I got my black gloves on
I got my ski mask on
This shit been too long.
I got my 12-gauge sawed off.
I got my headlights turned off.

I'm about to bust some shots off.
I'm about to dust some cops off.
    (Chorus:)   Cop killer, it's better you than me.
                Cop killer, fuck police brutality.
                Cop killer, I know your family's grievin'
                Fuck'em!
Cop Killer, but tonight we get even.
I got my brain on hype.
Tonight'll be your night.
I got this long-assed knife,
and your neck looks just right.
My adrenaline's pumpin'.
I got my stereo bumpin'.
I'm about to kill me somethin'.
A pig stopped me for nuthin'!
    (Chorus)
Die, die, die, pig, die!
Fuck the police! [repeated several times]

Radio station KXYZ broadcasts this song; prosecutor Elaine Smith charges the DJ with inciting people to commit murder, under a statute that implements the *Brandenburg v. Ohio* test. "Hundreds of thousands of people listen to KXYZ every day in their cars," says Ms. Smith: "Some are angry, some are on drugs, some are armed; any one of them might be pulled over by the police just as he's been listening to this song. If the song provokes even a few of them to pick a fight, and causes the death of even one police officer—or for that matter one angry kid—that's one death too many."

Can the DJ be convicted, despite the Free Speech Clause? Assume for purposes of this problem that radio broadcasts get as much constitutional protection as any other medium of communication.

Cf. *Lee Sheriff Wants Sedition Charge Over "Cop Killer,"* Orlando Sentinel Tribune, July 7, 1992, at D6 (a somewhat different claim than the one being argued here); *Davidson v. Time Warner, Inc.,* 1997 WL 405907 (S.D. Tex.) (involving a lawsuit brought by the family of a police officer who was murdered by someone who had been listening to Tupac Shakur's "Crooked Ass Nigga," a song with lyrics much like those in "Cop Killer").

d. *Brandenburg v. Ohio, 395 U.S. 444 (1969)*

Per curiam.

The appellant, a leader of a Ku Klux Klan group, was convicted under the Ohio Criminal Syndicalism statute for "advocat[ing] ... the duty, necessity, or propriety of crime, sabotage, violence, or unlawful methods of terrorism as a means of accomplishing industrial or political reform" and for "voluntarily assembl[ing] with any society, group, or assemblage of persons formed to teach or advocate the doctrines of criminal syndicalism." He was fined $1,000 and sentenced to one to 10 years' imprisonment....

The record shows that ... appellant[] telephoned an announcer-reporter on the staff of a Cincinnati television station and invited him to come to a

Ku Klux Klan "rally" to be held at a farm in Hamilton County. With the cooperation of the organizers, the reporter and a cameraman attended the meeting and filmed the events. Portions of the films were later broadcast on the local station and on a national network.

The prosecution's case rested on the films and on testimony identifying the appellant as the person who communicated with the reporter and who spoke at the rally. The State also introduced into evidence several articles appearing in the film, including a pistol, a rifle, a shotgun, ammunition, a Bible, and a red hood worn by the speaker in the films.

One film showed 12 hooded figures, some of whom carried firearms. They were gathered around a large wooden cross, which they burned. No one was present other than the participants and the newsmen who made the film. Most of the words uttered during the scene were incomprehensible when the film was projected, but scattered phrases could be understood that were derogatory of Negroes and, in one instance, of Jews.[1] Another scene on the same film showed the appellant, in Klan regalia, making a speech. The speech, in full, was as follows:

> This is an organizers' meeting. We have had quite a few members here today which are—we have hundreds, hundreds of members throughout the State of Ohio. I can quote from a newspaper clipping from the Columbus, Ohio Dispatch, five weeks ago Sunday morning. The Klan has more members in the State of Ohio than does any other organization. We're not a revengent organization, but if our President, our Congress, our Supreme Court, continues to suppress the white, Caucasian race, it's possible that there might have to be some revengeance taken.
>
> We are marching on Congress July the Fourth, four hundred thousand strong. From there we are dividing into two groups, one group to march on St. Augustine, Florida, the other group to march into Mississippi. Thank you.

The second film showed six hooded figures one of whom, later identified as the appellant, repeated a speech very similar to that recorded on the first film. The reference to the possibility of "revengeance" was omitted, and one sentence was added: "Personally, I believe the nigger should be returned to Africa, the Jew returned to Israel." Though some of the figures in the films carried weapons, the speaker did not....

In 1927, this Court sustained the constitutionality of California's Criminal Syndicalism Act, the text of which is quite similar to that of the laws of Ohio. *Whitney v. California*.... But *Whitney* has been thoroughly discredited by later decisions. See *Dennis v. United States*. These later decisions have fashioned the principle that the constitutional guarantees of free speech and free press do not permit a State to forbid or proscribe advocacy of the use of

---

[1] ... "How far is the nigger going to—yeah." "This is what we are going to do to the niggers." "A dirty nigger." "Send the Jews back to Israel." "Let's give them back to the dark garden." "Save America." "Let's go back to constitutional betterment." "Bury the niggers." "We intend to do our part." "Give us our state rights." "Freedom for the whites." "Nigger will have to fight for every inch he gets from now on."

force or of law violation except where such advocacy is directed to inciting or producing imminent lawless action and is likely to incite or produce such action.

{It was on the theory that the Smith Act embodied such a principle and that it had been applied only in conformity with it that this Court sustained the Act's constitutionality. *Dennis v. United States*. That this was the basis for *Dennis* was emphasized in *Yates v. United States*, in which the Court overturned convictions for advocacy of the forcible overthrow of the Government under the Smith Act, because the trial judge's instructions had allowed conviction for mere advocacy, unrelated to its tendency to produce forcible action.} *[This textbook uses braces—{ and }—to indicate moved text.—ed.]* ... "[T]he mere abstract teaching ... of the moral propriety or even moral necessity for a resort to force and violence, is not the same as preparing a group for violent action and steeling it to such action."

A statute which fails to draw this distinction impermissibly intrudes upon the freedoms guaranteed by the First and Fourteenth Amendments. It sweeps within its condemnation speech which our Constitution has immunized from governmental control. Measured by this test, Ohio's Criminal Syndicalism Act cannot be sustained. The Act ... [baldly defines] the crime in terms of mere advocacy not distinguished from incitement to imminent lawless action ....

Justice Douglas, concurring....

I see no place in the regime of the First Amendment for any "clear and present danger" test .... When one reads the opinions closely and sees when and how the "clear and present danger" test has been applied, great misgivings are aroused. First, the threats were often loud but always puny and made serious only by judges so wedded to the status quo that critical analysis made them nervous. Second, the test was so twisted and perverted in *Dennis v. United States* as to make the trial of those teachers of Marxism an all-out political trial ....

The line between what is permissible and not subject to control and what may be made impermissible and subject to regulation is the line between ideas and overt acts. The example usually given by those who would punish speech is the case of one who falsely shouts fire in a crowded theatre. This is, however, a classic case where speech is brigaded with action. They are indeed inseparable and a prosecution can be launched for the overt acts actually caused. Apart from rare instances of that kind, speech is, I think, immune from prosecution....

e.   *Hess v. Indiana, 414 U.S. 105 (1973)*

Per curiam.

The events leading to Hess' conviction [for disorderly conduct] began with an antiwar demonstration on the campus of Indiana University. In the course of the demonstration, approximately 100 to 150 of the demonstrators moved onto a public street and blocked the passage of vehicles. When the demonstrators did not respond to verbal directions from the sheriff to clear the street, the sheriff and his deputies began walking up the street, and the demonstrators in their path moved to the curbs on either side, joining a large number of spectators who had gathered.

Hess[, who] was standing off the street[,] ... [was arrested for saying] "We'll take the fucking street later," or "We'll take the fucking street again." Two witnesses ... testified ... that Hess did not appear to be exhorting the crowd to go back into the street, that he was facing the crowd and not the street when he uttered the statement, that his statement did not appear to be addressed to any particular person or group, and that his tone, although loud, was no louder than that of the other people in the area....

[The trial court found] that Hess' statement "was intended to incite further lawless action on the part of the crowd in the vicinity of appellant and was likely to produce such action." At best, however, the statement could be taken as counsel for present moderation; at worst, it amounted to nothing more than advocacy of illegal action at some indefinite future time. This is not sufficient to permit the State to punish Hess' speech.... *Brandenburg v. Ohio*. Since the uncontroverted evidence showed that Hess' statement was not directed to any person or group of persons, it cannot be said that he was advocating, in the normal sense, any action. And since there was no evidence, or rational inference from the import of the language, that his words were intended to produce, and likely to produce, *imminent* disorder, those words could not be punished by the State on the ground that they had "a 'tendency to lead to violence.'" ...

Justice Rehnquist, with whom [Chief Justice Burger] and Justice Blackmun join, dissenting...

Surely the sentence "We'll take the fucking street later (or again)" is susceptible of characterization as an exhortation, particularly when uttered in a loud voice while facing a crowd. The opinions of two defense witnesses cannot be considered proof to the contrary, since the trial court was perfectly free to reject this testimony if it so desired. Perhaps, as these witnesses and the majority opinion seem to suggest, appellant was simply expressing his views to the world at large, but that is surely not the only rational explanation.

The majority also places great emphasis on appellant's use of the word "later," even suggesting at one point that the statement "could be taken as counsel for present moderation." The opinion continues: "[A]t worst, it amounted to nothing more than advocacy of illegal action at some indefinite future time." From that observation, the majority somehow concludes that the advocacy was not directed towards inciting imminent action. But whatever other theoretical interpretations may be placed upon the remark, there are surely possible constructions of the statement which would encompass more or less immediate and continuing action against the harassed police. They should not be rejected out of hand because of an unexplained preference for other acceptable alternatives....

f.   United States v. Williams, 553 U.S. 285 (2008)

[This case discusses solicitation of crime generally, but also deals with child pornography, a subject that isn't covered until Part II.D.2. Here is what you need to know now about child pornography prosecutions:

1. Child pornography—a visual depiction (such as a photograph or a video) of an actual minor engaging in sexual conduct—is constitutionally unprotected. Possessing it and distributing it are serious crimes.

2. But prosecuting people for distributing child pornography can be difficult: The government must prove an actual child (not just a young-looking adult, or an entirely computer generated image) was involved.

3. Because of this, the government sometimes prosecutes people for offering to provide child pornography, or asking people to provide it. Such prosecutions may happen even when no actual child pornography is involved, just as prosecutions for soliciting murder can happen even if no murder ultimately takes place, and prosecutions for soliciting sale of drugs can happen even if the drugs used in an undercover police sale are fake.

4. The question in this case is whether such offers or solicitations are constitutionally unprotected. This is relevant to offers or solicitations related to a wide range of criminal conduct (such as murder, drug crimes, and more) beyond just child pornography.—ed.]

Justice Scalia delivered the opinion of the Court.

[A.] [18 U.S.C. § 2252A(a)(3)(B) provides for criminal punishment of 5 to 20 years in prison for] "Any person who ... knowingly ... advertises, promotes, presents, distributes, or solicits ... in interstate or foreign commerce ... any material or purported material in a manner that reflects the belief, or that is intended to cause another to believe, that the material or purported material ... contains ... a visual depiction of an actual minor engaging in sexually explicit conduct ...." ...

[R]espondent Michael Williams, using a sexually explicit screen name, signed in to a public Internet chat room. A Secret Service agent had also signed in to the chat room under the moniker "Lisa n Miami." The agent noticed that Williams had posted a message that read: "Dad of toddler has 'good' pics of her an [sic] me for swap of your toddler pics, or live cam." The agent struck up a conversation with Williams, leading to an electronic exchange of nonpornographic pictures of children. (The agent's picture was in fact a doctored photograph of an adult.) Soon thereafter, Williams messaged that he had photographs of men molesting his 4-year-old daughter.

Suspicious that "Lisa n Miami" was a law-enforcement agent, before proceeding further Williams demanded that the agent produce additional pictures. When he did not, Williams posted the following public message in the chat room: "HERE ROOM; I CAN PUT UPLINK CUZ IM FOR REAL—SHE CANT." Appended to this declaration was a hyperlink that, when clicked, led to seven pictures of actual children, aged approximately 5 to 15, engaging in sexually explicit conduct and displaying their genitals. The Secret Service then obtained a search warrant for Williams's home, where agents seized two hard drives containing at least 22 images of real children engaged in sexually explicit conduct ....

Williams was charged with one count of pandering child pornography under § 2252A(a)(3)(B) and one count of possessing child pornography .... He pleaded guilty to both counts but reserved the right to challenge the constitutionality of the pandering conviction....

[B.] The statute's definition of the material or purported material that may not be pandered or solicited precisely tracks the material held constitutionally proscribable in *New York v. Ferber* ...: ... material depicting actual children engaged in sexually explicit conduct....

[T]he statute's string of operative verbs—"advertises, promotes, presents, distributes, or solicits"—is reasonably read to have a transactional connotation. That is to say, the statute penalizes speech that accompanies or seeks to induce a transfer [whether or not commercial] of child pornography—via reproduction or physical delivery—from one person to another.... [Statutory construction discussion omitted.—ed.]

[C.] Offers to engage in illegal transactions are categorically excluded from First Amendment protection. *Giboney v. Empire Storage & Ice Co.*... [O]ffers to give or receive what it is unlawful to possess have no social value and thus ... enjoy no First Amendment protection. Many long established criminal proscriptions—such as laws against conspiracy, incitement, and solicitation—criminalize speech (commercial or not) that is intended to induce or commence illegal activities. Offers to provide or requests to obtain unlawful material, whether as part of a commercial exchange or not, are similarly undeserving of First Amendment protection. It would be an odd constitutional principle that permitted the government to prohibit offers to sell illegal drugs, but not offers to give them away for free.

To be sure, there remains an important distinction between a proposal to engage in illegal activity and the abstract advocacy of illegality. See *Brandenburg v. Ohio*. The Act before us does not prohibit advocacy of child pornography, but only offers to provide or requests to obtain it. {[T]he term "promotes" does not refer to abstract advocacy, such as the statement "I believe that child pornography should be legal" or even "I encourage you to obtain child pornography." It refers to the recommendation of a particular piece of purported child pornography with the intent of initiating a transfer.... There is no doubt that this prohibition falls well within constitutional bounds....}

[Nor does] the fact that the statute could punish a "braggart, exaggerator, or outright liar" render[] it unconstitutional.... [W]e have held that the government can ban *both* fraudulent offers, see, *e.g., Illinois ex rel. Madigan v. Telemarketing Associates, Inc.,* 538 U.S. 600 (2003), *and* offers to provide illegal products[. There is no basis for] forbid[ding] the government from punishing *fraudulent offers to provide illegal products....* [I]f anything, such statements are doubly excluded from the First Amendment....

Offers to deal in illegal products or otherwise engage in illegal activity

[also] do not acquire First Amendment protection when the offeror is mistaken about the factual predicate of his offer.... As with ... [the crime of attempt,] ... impossibility of completing the crime [of pandering and solicitation] because the facts were not as the defendant believed is not a defense. "All courts are in agreement that what is usually referred to as 'factual impossibility' is no defense to a charge of attempt." (... [A]n example [is] "the intended sale of an illegal drug [that] actually involved a different substance.") ...

Justice Souter, with whom Justice Ginsburg joins, dissenting....

[I agree that] Congress may criminalize [solicitation of child pornography and offers to provide child pornography] unrelated to any extant image. I part ways from the Court, however, on the regulation of proposals made with regard to specific, existing representations [which are inaccurately promoted as if actual children were depicted].... [A] transaction in [representations in which no actual children are depicted] could not be prosecuted consistently with the First Amendment, and I believe that maintaining the First Amendment protection of expression we have previously held to cover fake child pornography requires a limit to the law's criminalization of pandering proposals.... [Further details, which are specific to child pornography, and thus say little about the constitutional status of offers and solicitations more broadly, omitted.—ed.]

First Amendment doctrine ... tolerates speech restriction not on mere general tendencies of expression, or the private understandings of speakers or listeners, but only after a critical assessment of practical consequences.... *Brandenburg v. Ohio* unmistakably insists that any limit on speech be grounded in a realistic, factual assessment of harm.

This is a far cry from the Act before us now, which rests criminal prosecution for proposing transactions in expressive material on nothing more than a speaker's statement about the material itself, a statement that may disclose no more than his own belief about the subjects represented or his desire to foster belief in another....

2. THE OVERBREADTH DOCTRINE

In constitutional cases that don't involve free speech claims, the enforcement of a law can be held unconstitutional only if the challenger's own conduct (which the law prohibits) is constitutionally protected. A challenger whose conduct is constitutionally unprotected can't challenge the law on the grounds that the law also bars *someone else's* constitutionally protected conduct.

For example, say a statute lets the police search houses with probable cause but without a warrant. Such searches generally violate the Fourth Amendment, but there is an exception for "exigent circumstances," such as when the police are chasing a fleeing felon. The government searches your house without a warrant, but in a situation where exigent circumstances are present; you sue, claiming the whole statute is unconstitutional. You'll lose: Though the law is unconstitutional as applied to someone whose house is searched without exigent circumstances, it's constitutional as applied to you, since exigent circumstances were present.

But in free speech cases, you can challenge an entire law on its face, on the grounds that it's substantially overbroad: If the law unconstitutionally restricts a substantial amount of other people's speech, the law (and your conviction under it) will be invalidated even if my speech was constitutionally unprotected.

Brandenburg is a good illustration of this. The Court didn't have to decide whether Brandenburg's speech was outside the incitement exception. Rather, the Court held that the statute was itself unconstitutional because it went substantially beyond just unprotected incitement.

Some important limitations:

a. The overbreadth must be *substantial. New York v. Ferber* (1982) (p. 168).

b. The question is what's covered by the law *as construed by the courts*, not necessarily as written. Indeed, in the very case in which the law is challenged, a court might provide a narrowing construction (saying, for instance, that a ban on "promoting crime" should be read as only covering unprotected incitement). If so, the law would not be overbroad.

3. EVOLUTION: SPEECH THAT INTERFERES WITH A WAR EFFORT

a. *Problem: Advocacy in Wartime*

What, if anything, is wrong with the test applied in *Schenck, Debs, Abrams,* and *Gilbert*? Why not let speech be punished if it is likely to persuade others to violate the law, and is intended to do so (intention plus likelihood, but with no imminence requirement)? Why not let it be punished even if it is just likely to persuade others to violate the law, and the speaker knows that it was likely to do so (knowledge plus likelihood)?

b. *Abraham Lincoln on the Arrest of Clement Vallandigham*

In 1863, Clement Vallandigham—a prominent Democratic politician and former Congressman—was arrested for making an anti-Civil-War speech, and tried before a military court on the charge of:

> Publicly expressing, in violation of General Orders No. 38 ... sympathy for those in arms against the Government of the United States, and declaring disloyal sentiments and opinions, with the object and purpose of weakening the power of the Government in its efforts to suppress an unlawful rebellion.

The specific allegation was that Vallandigham

> did publicly address a large meeting of citizens, and did utter sentiments in words, or in effect, as follows, declaring the present war "a wicked, cruel, and unnecessary war;" "a war not being waged for the preservation of the Union;" "a war for the purpose of crushing out liberty and erecting a despotism;" "a war for the freedom of the blacks and the enslavement of the whites;" stating "that if the Administration had so wished, the war could have been honorably terminated months ago;" that "peace might have been

honorably obtained by listening to the proposed intermediation of France;"
... charging "that the Government of the United States was about to appoint
military marshals in every district, to restrain the people of their liberties,
to deprive them of their rights and privileges;" characterizing General Orders No. 38 ... "as a base usurpation of arbitrary authority," inviting his
hearers to resist the same, by saying, "the sooner the people inform the min-
ions of usurped power that they will not submit to such restrictions upon
their liberties, the better;" ...

All of which opinions and sentiments he well knew did aid, comfort, and
encourage those in arms against the Government, and could but induce in
his hearers a distrust of their own Government, sympathy for those in arms
against it, and a disposition to resist the laws of the land.

Vallandigham was convicted, and sentenced to be imprisoned for the duration of the war. Three days later, Lincoln changed his punishment to ban-
ishment to the Confederacy.

Vallandigham's trial excited much opposition from those who believed
that the prosecution violated the freedom of speech. Lincoln's response to
these criticisms was as follows:

> It is asserted ... that Mr. Vallandigham was, by a military commander,
> seized and tried "for no other reason than words addressed to a public meet-
> ing, in criticism of the course of the Administration, and in condemnation of
> the Military orders of the General." ... But the arrest, as I understand, was
> made for a very different reason. Mr. Vallandigham avows his hostility to
> the war on the part of the Union; and his arrest was made because he was
> laboring, with some effect, to prevent the raising of troops; to encourage de-
> sertions from the army; and to leave the rebellion without an adequate mil-
> itary force to suppress it.... [H]e was damaging the army, upon the existence
> and vigor of which the life of the nation depends....
>
> [My critics support] suppressing the rebellion by military force—by ar-
> mies. Long experience has shown, that armies cannot be maintained unless
> desertions shall be punished by the severe penalty of death.... Must I shoot
> a simple-minded soldier boy who deserts, while I must not touch a hair of a
> wily agitator who induces him to desert? This is none the less injurious
> when effected by getting a father, or brother, or friend into a public meeting,
> and there working upon his feelings till he is persuaded to write the soldier
> boy that he is fighting in a bad cause, for a wicked administration of a con-
> temptible government, too weak to arrest and punish him if he shall desert.
> I think that, in such a case, to silence the agitator and save the boy is not
> only constitutional, but withal a great mercy....
>
> Nor am I able to appreciate the danger ... that the American people will
> by means of military arrests during the rebellion lose the right of public
> discussion, the liberty of speech and the press, the law of evidence, trial by
> jury, and habeas corpus throughout the indefinite peaceable future which I
> trust lies before them, any more than I am able to believe that a man could
> contract so strong an appetite for emetics during temporary illness as to
> persist in feeding upon them during the remainder of his healthful life.
>
> [In a later letter:] I certainly do not know that Mr. V. has specifically,
> and by direct language, advised against enlistments, and in favor of deser-
> tion, and resistance to drafting, [but that was the effect of his words] .... This

hindrance, of the military, including maiming and murder, is due to the course in which Mr. V. has been engaged, in a greater degree than to any other cause; and [to Vallandigham personally] in a greater degree than to any other one man....

See Michael Kent Curtis, *Free Speech, "The People's Darling Privilege"* 300-18 (2000), the leading work on mid-1800s U.S. free speech debates.

c.   *Schenck v. United States, 249 U.S. 47 (1919)*

Justice Holmes delivered the opinion of the Court....

The [indictment] charges a conspiracy to violate the Espionage Act of June 15, 1917, by causing and attempting to cause insubordination, &c., in the military and naval forces of the United States, and to obstruct the recruiting and enlistment service of the United States, when the United States was at war with the German Empire, to-wit, that the defendants wilfully conspired to have printed and circulated to men who had been called and accepted for military service ... a document set forth and alleged to be calculated to cause such insubordination and obstruction.... The defendants were found guilty on all the counts....

Schenck ... was general secretary of the Socialist party and had charge of the Socialist headquarters from which the documents were sent. He identified a book found there as the minutes of the Executive Committee of the party. The book showed a resolution of August 13, 1917, that 15,000 leaflets should be printed on the other side of one of them in use, to be mailed to men who had passed exemption boards, and for distribution. Schenck personally attended to the printing.... [C]opies were proved to have been sent through the mails to drafted men....

The document in question upon its first printed side recited the first section of the Thirteenth Amendment, said that the idea embodied in it was violated by the Conscription Act and that a conscript is little better than a convict. In impassioned language it intimated that conscription was despotism in its worst form and a monstrous wrong against humanity in the interest of Wall Street's chosen few. It said, "Do not submit to intimidation," but in form at least confined itself to peaceful measures such as a petition for the repeal of the act.

The other and later printed side of the sheet was headed "Assert Your Rights." It stated reasons for alleging that any one violated the Constitution when he refused to recognize "your right to assert your opposition to the draft," and went on "If you do not assert and support your rights, you are helping to deny or disparage rights which it is the solemn duty of all citizens and residents of the United States to retain."

It described the arguments on the other side as coming from cunning politicians and a mercenary capitalist press, and even silent consent to the conscription law as helping to support an infamous conspiracy. It denied the power to send our citizens away to foreign shores to shoot up the people of other lands, and added that words could not express the condemnation such cold-blooded ruthlessness deserves, &c., &c., winding up "You must do your share to maintain, support and uphold the rights of the people of this country."

Of course the document would not have been sent unless it had been intended to have some effect, and we do not see what effect it could be expected to have upon persons subject to the draft except to influence them to obstruct the carrying of it out. The defendants do not deny that the jury might find against them on this point.

But it is said, suppose that that was the tendency of this circular, it is protected by the First Amendment to the Constitution.... [I]n many places and in ordinary times the defendants in saying all that was said in the circular would have been within their constitutional rights. But the character of every act depends upon the circumstances in which it is done. The most stringent protection of free speech would not protect a man in falsely shouting fire in a theatre and causing a panic. It does not even protect a man from an injunction against uttering words that may have all the effect of force. *Gompers v. Buck's Stove & Range Co.*, 221 U.S. 418, 439 (1911) [(upholding an injunction against newspaper articles that urged a labor boycott)].

The question in every case is whether the words used are used in such circumstances and are of such a nature as to create a clear and present danger that they will bring about the substantive evils that Congress has a right to prevent. It is a question of proximity and degree. When a nation is at war many things that might be said in time of peace are such a hindrance to its effort that their utterance will not be endured so long as men fight and that no Court could regard them as protected by any constitutional right.

It seems to be admitted that if an actual obstruction of the recruiting service were proved, liability for words that produced that effect might be enforced. The statute ... punishes conspiracies to obstruct as well as actual obstruction. If the act, (speaking, or circulating a paper,) its tendency and the intent with which it is done are the same, we perceive no ground for saying that success alone warrants making the act a crime....

d. *Debs v. United States, 249 U.S. 211 (1919)*

[Note: Eugene V. Debs was the Socialist Party leader and frequent Presidential candidate; he got 6% of the vote in 1912, and then 3% in 1920 while he was in prison for the conduct described in this case.—ed.]

Justice Holmes delivered the opinion of the Court.

This is an indictment under the Espionage Act of June 15, 1917, [alleging that Eugene V. Debs] obstructed and attempted to obstruct the recruiting and enlistment service of the United States.... The defendant was found guilty and was sentenced to ten years' imprisonment....

The main theme of the speech [that Debs gave, and that formed the basis for the indictment,] was Socialism, its growth, and a prophecy of its ultimate success. With that we have nothing to do, but if a part or the manifest intent of the more general utterances was to encourage those present to obstruct the recruiting service and if in passages such encouragement was directly given, the immunity of the general theme may not be enough to protect the speech.

The speaker began by saying that he had just returned from a visit to the workhouse in the neighborhood where three of their most loyal comrades were paying the penalty for their devotion to the working class—these being Wagenknecht, Baker and Ruthenberg, who had been convicted of aiding and abetting another in failing to register for the draft. He said that he had to be prudent and might not be able to say all that he thought, thus intimating to his hearers that they might infer that he meant more, but he did say that those persons were paying the penalty for standing erect and for seeking to pave the way to better conditions for all mankind.

Later he added further eulogies and said that he was proud of them. He then expressed opposition to Prussian militarism in a way that naturally might have been thought to be intended to include the mode of proceeding in the United States.... [Later still], he took up the case of Kate Richards O'Hare, convicted of obstructing the enlistment service, praised her for her loyalty to socialism and otherwise, and said that she was convicted on false testimony, under a ruling that would seem incredible to him if he had not had some experience with a Federal Court....

The defendant spoke of other cases, and then, after dealing with Russia, said that the master class has always declared the war and the subject class has always fought the battles—that the subject class has had nothing to gain and all to lose, including their lives; that the working class, who furnish the corpses, have never yet had a voice in declaring war and never yet had a voice in declaring peace....

The defendant next mentioned Rose Pastor Stokes, convicted of attempting to cause insubordination and refusal of duty in the military forces of the United States and obstructing the recruiting service. He said that she went out to render her service to the cause in this day of crises, and they sent her to the penitentiary for ten years; that she had said no more than the speaker had said that afternoon; that if she was guilty so was he, and that he would not be cowardly enough to plead his innocence; but that her message that opened the eyes of the people must be suppressed, and so after a mock trial before a packed jury and a corporation tool on the bench, she was sent to the penitentiary for ten years.

There followed personal experiences and illustrations of the growth of socialism, a glorification of minorities, and a prophecy of the success of the international socialist crusade, with the interjection that "you need to know that you are fit for something better than slavery and cannon fodder." The rest of the discourse had only the indirect though not necessarily ineffective bearing on the offences alleged that is to be found in the usual contrasts between capitalists and laboring men, sneers at the advice to cultivate war gardens, attribution to plutocrats of the high price of coal, &c., with the implication running through it all that the working men are not concerned in the war, and a final exhortation, "Don't worry about the charge of treason to your masters; but be concerned about the treason that involves your-selves."

The defendant addressed the jury himself, and while contending that his speech did not warrant the charges said, "I have been accused of ob-structing the war. I admit it. Gentlemen, I abhor war. I would oppose the war if I stood alone." The statement was not necessary to warrant the jury in finding that one purpose of the speech, whether incidental or not does not matter, was to oppose not only war in general but this war, and that the opposition was so expressed that its natural and intended effect would be to obstruct recruiting.

If that was intended and if, in all the circumstances, that would be its probable effect, it would not be protected by reason of its being part of a general program and expressions of a general and conscientious belief. [The defendant's First Amendment defense has been] disposed of in *Schenck v. United States* ....

There was introduced also an "Anti-War Proclamation and Program" adopted at St. Louis in April, 1917, coupled with testimony that about an hour before his speech the defendant had stated that he approved of that platform in spirit and in substance.... This document contained the usual suggestion that capitalism was the cause of the war and that our entrance into it "was instigated by the predatory capitalists in the United States." It alleged that the war of the United States against Germany could not "be justified even on the plea that it is a war in defence of American rights or American 'honor.'" It said "We brand the declaration of war by our Govern-ments as a crime against the people of the United States and against the nations of the world. In all modern history there has been no war more un-justifiable than the war in which we are about to engage."

Its first recommendation was, "continuous, active, and public opposition to the war, through demonstrations, mass petitions, and all other means within our power." Evidence that the defendant accepted this view and this declaration of his duties at the time that he made his speech is evidence that if in that speech he used words tending to obstruct the recruiting service he meant that they should have that effect.... We should add that the jury were most carefully instructed that they could not find the defendant guilty for advocacy of any of his opinions unless the words used had as their natural tendency and reasonably probable effect to obstruct the recruiting service, &c., and unless the defendant had the specific intent to do so in his mind.... [T]he verdict ... must be sustained....

e.   *Abrams v. United States, 250 U.S. 616 (1919)*

Justice Clarke delivered the opinion of the Court....

[D]efendants[] were convicted of conspiring to violate provisions of the Espionage Act .... [The third count of the indictment] charged the defend-ants with conspiring, when the United States was at war with the Imperial Government of Germany, to unlawfully utter, print, write and publish ... language "intended to incite, provoke and encourage resistance to the

United States in said war." The charge in the fourth count was that the defendants conspired "when the United States was at war with the Imperial German Government, ... unlawfully and willfully, by utterance, writing, printing and publication to urge, incite and advocate curtailment of production of things and products, to wit, ordnance and ammunition, necessary and essential to the prosecution of the war." The offenses were charged in the language of the Act ....

It was admitted on the trial that the defendants had united to print and distribute the described circulars and that 5,000 of them had been printed and distributed about the 22d day of August, 1918.... The circulars were distributed, some by throwing them from a window of a building ... in New York City.... The claim chiefly elaborated upon by the defendants in the oral argument and in their brief is that there is no substantial evidence in the record to support the judgment upon the verdict of guilty....

The first of the two articles attached to the indictment is conspicuously headed, "The Hypocrisy of the United States and her Allies." After denouncing President Wilson as a hypocrite and a coward because troops were sent into Russia, it proceeds to assail our government in general, saying: "His [the President's] shameful, cowardly silence about the intervention in Russia reveals the hypocrisy of the plutocratic gang in Washington and vicinity." It continues: "He [the President] is too much of a coward to come out openly and say: 'We capitalistic nations cannot afford to have a proletarian republic in Russia.'" Among the capitalistic nations Abrams testified the United States was included.

Growing more inflammatory as it proceeds, the circular culminates in:

The Russian Revolution cries: Workers of the World! Awake! Rise! Put down your enemy and mine!

Yes! friends, there is only one enemy of the workers of the world and that is CAPITALISM.

This is clearly an appeal to the "workers" of this country to arise and put down by force the government of the United States which they characterize as their "hypocritical," "cowardly" and "capitalistic" enemy....

The second of the articles was printed in the Yiddish language and in the translation is headed, "Workers—Wake Up." After referring to "his Majesty, Mr. Wilson, and the rest of the gang, dogs of all colors!" it continues:

Workers, Russian emigrants, you who had the least belief in the honesty of [the United States] Government ... must now throw away all confidence, must spit in the face the false, hypocritic, military propaganda which has fooled you so relentlessly, calling forth your sympathy, your help, to the prosecution of the war.

The purpose of this obviously was to persuade the persons to whom it was addressed to turn a deaf ear to patriotic appeals in behalf of the Government of the United States, and to cease to render it assistance in the prosecution of the war. It goes on:

With the money which you have loaned, or are going to loan them, they will make bullets not only for the Germans, but also for the Workers Soviets of

Russia. *Workers in the ammunition factories, you are producing bullets, bayonets, cannon, to murder not only the Germans, but also your dearest, best, who are in Russia and are fighting for freedom.*

It will not do to say ... that the only intent of these defendants was to prevent injury to the Russian cause. Men must be held to have intended, and to be accountable for, the effects which their acts were likely to produce. Even if their primary purpose and intent was to aid the cause of the Russian Revolution, the plan of action which they adopted necessarily involved, before it could be realized, defeat of the war program of the United States, for the obvious effect of this appeal, if it should become effective, as they hoped it might, would be to persuade [listeners] not to aid government loans and not to work in ammunition factories, where their work would produce "bullets, bayonets, cannon" and other munitions of war, the use of which would cause the "murder" of Germans and Russians.

Again, the spirit becomes more bitter as it proceeds to declare that—

America and her Allies have betrayed (the Workers). Their robberish aims are clear to all men. The destruction of the Russian Revolution, that is the politics of the march to Russia.
Workers, our reply to the barbaric intervention has to be a general strike! An open challenge only will let the Government know that not only the Russian Worker fights for freedom, but also *here in America lives the spirit of Revolution.*

This is not an attempt to bring about a change of administration by candid discussion, for no matter what may have incited the outbreak on the part of the defendant anarchists, the manifest purpose of such a publication was to create an attempt to defeat the war plans of the Government of the United States, by bringing upon the country the paralysis of a general strike, thereby arresting the production of all munitions and other things essential to the conduct of the war.

This purpose is emphasized in the next paragraph, which reads: "Do not let the Government scare you with their wild punishment in prisons, hanging and shooting. We must not and will not betray the splendid fighters of Russia. *Workers, up to fight.*" ...

That the interpretation we have put upon these articles, circulated in the greatest port of our land, from which great numbers of soldiers were at the time taking ship daily, and in which great quantities of war supplies of every kind were at the time being manufactured for transportation overseas, is not only the fair interpretation of them, but that it is the meaning which their authors consciously intended should be conveyed by them to others is further shown by the additional writings found in the meeting place of the defendant group and on the person of one of them. [More excerpts, all focusing on the goal of "creat[ing] so great a disturbance" that the allies couldn't intervene in Russia, omitted.—ed.]

These excerpts sufficiently show, that while the immediate occasion for this particular outbreak of lawlessness ... may have been resentment caused by our Government sending troops into Russia as a strategic operation against the Germans on the eastern battle front, yet the plain purpose of their propaganda was to excite, at the supreme crisis of the war, disaffection, sedition, riots, and, as they hoped, revolution, in this country for the purpose of embarrassing and if possible defeating the military plans of the Government in Europe....

[T]he language of these circulars was obviously intended to provoke and to encourage resistance to the United States in the war, [and] ... plainly urged and advocated a resort to a general strike of workers in ammunition factories for the purpose of curtailing the production of ordnance and munitions necessary and essential to the prosecution of the war .... Thus it is clear not only that some evidence but that much persuasive evidence was before the jury tending to prove that the defendants were guilty ....

Justice Holmes [joined by Justice Brandeis], dissenting....

[A.] [T]he suggestion to workers in the ammunition factories that they are producing bullets to murder their dearest, and the further advocacy of a general strike ... do urge curtailment of production of things necessary to the prosecution of the war within the meaning of the [Espionage Act]. But to make the conduct criminal that statute requires that it should be "with intent by such curtailment to cripple or hinder the United States in the prosecution of the war." It seems to me that no such intent is proved....

[T]he word intent as vaguely used in ordinary legal discussion means no more than knowledge at the time of the act that the consequences said to be intended will ensue. Even less than that will satisfy the general principle of civil and criminal liability. A man may have to pay damages, may be sent to prison, at common law might be hanged, if at the time of his act he knew facts from which common experience showed that the consequences would follow, whether he individually could foresee them or not.

But, when words are used exactly, a deed is not done with intent to produce a consequence unless that consequence is the aim of the deed. It may be obvious, and obvious to the actor, that the consequence will follow, and he may be liable for it even if he regrets it, but he does not do the act with intent to produce it unless the aim to produce it is the proximate motive of the specific act, although there may be some deeper motive behind.

It seems to me that this statute must be taken to use its words in a strict and accurate sense. They would be absurd in any other. A patriot might think that we were wasting money on aeroplanes, or making more cannon of a certain kind than we needed, and might advocate curtailment with success, yet even if it turned out that the curtailment hindered and was thought by other minds to have been obviously likely to hinder the United States in the prosecution of the war, no one would hold such conduct a crime....

[B.] [B]y the same reasoning that would justify punishing persuasion to murder, the United States constitutionally may punish speech that produces or is intended to produce a clear and imminent danger that it will bring about forthwith certain substantive evils that the United States constitutionally may seek to prevent. [*Schenck*; *Debs*.] The power undoubtedly is greater in time of war than in time of peace because war opens dangers that do not exist at other times.

But as against dangers peculiar to war, as against others, the principle of the right to free speech is always the same. It is only the present danger of immediate evil or an intent to bring it about that warrants Congress in setting a limit to the expression of opinion where private rights are not concerned.

Congress certainly cannot forbid all effort to change the mind of the country. Now nobody can suppose that the surreptitious publishing of a silly leaflet by an unknown man, without more, would present any immediate danger that its opinions would hinder the success of the government arms or have any appreciable tendency to do so. Publishing those opinions for the very purpose of obstructing, however, might indicate a greater danger and at any rate would have the quality of an attempt. So I assume that the second leaflet if published for the purposes alleged in the fourth count might be punishable.

But it seems pretty clear to me that nothing less than that would bring these papers within the scope of this law. An actual intent in the sense that I have explained is necessary to constitute an attempt, where a further act of the same individual is required to complete the substantive crime.... It is necessary where the success of the attempt depends upon others because if that intent is not present the actor's aim may be accomplished without bringing about the evils sought to be checked. An intent to prevent interference with the revolution in Russia might have been satisfied without any hindrance to carrying on the war in which we were engaged.

I do not see how anyone can find the intent required by the statute in any of the defendants' words. The second leaflet is the only one that affords even a foundation for the charge, and there, without invoking the hatred of German militarism expressed in the former one, it is evident from the beginning to the end that the only object of the paper is to help Russia and stop American intervention there against the popular government—not to impede the United States in the war that it was carrying on. To say that two phrases taken literally might import a suggestion of conduct that would have interference with the war as an indirect and probably undesired effect seems to me by no means enough to show an attempt to produce that effect.

I return for a moment to the third count. That charges an intent to provoke resistance to the United States in its war with Germany. Taking the clause in the statute that deals with that in connection with the other elaborate provisions of the act, I think that resistance to the United States means some forcible act of opposition to some proceeding of the United States in pursuance of the war.

I think the intent must be the specific intent that I have described and for the reasons that I have given I think that no such intent was proved or existed in fact. I also think that there is no hint at resistance to the United States as I construe the phrase.

In this case sentences of twenty years imprisonment have been imposed for the publishing of two leaflets that I believe the defendants had as much right to publish as the Government has to publish the Constitution of the United States now vainly invoked by them. Even if I am technically wrong and enough can be squeezed from these poor and puny anonymities to turn the color of legal litmus paper; I will add, even if what I think the necessary intent were shown; the most nominal punishment seems to me all that possibly could be inflicted, unless the defendants are to be made to suffer not for what the indictment alleges but for the creed that they avow—a creed that I believe to be the creed of ignorance and immaturity[,] ... but which ... no one has a right even to consider in dealing with the charges before the Court.

[C.] Persecution for the expression of opinions seems to me perfectly logical. If you have no doubt of your premises or your power and want a certain result with all your heart you naturally express your wishes in law and sweep away all opposition. To allow opposition by speech seems to indicate that you think the speech impotent, as when a man says that he has squared the circle, or that you do not care whole-heartedly for the result, or that you doubt either your power or your premises.

But when men have realized that time has upset many fighting faiths, they may come to believe even more than they believe the very foundations of their own conduct that the ultimate good desired is better reached by free trade in ideas—that the best test of truth is the power of the thought to get itself accepted in the competition of the market, and that truth is the only ground upon which their wishes safely can be carried out.

That at any rate is the theory of our Constitution. It is an experiment, as all life is an experiment. Every year if not every day we have to wager our salvation upon some prophecy based upon imperfect knowledge. While that experiment is part of our system I think that we should be eternally vigilant against attempts to check the expression of opinions that we loathe and believe to be fraught with death, unless they so imminently threaten immediate interference with the lawful and pressing purposes of the law that an immediate check is required to save the country....

Only the emergency that makes it immediately dangerous to leave the correction of evil counsels to time warrants making any exception to the sweeping command, "Congress shall make no law ... abridging the freedom of speech." Of course I am speaking only of expressions of opinion and exhortations, which were all that were uttered here ....

f.   *Gilbert v. Minnesota, 254 U.S. 325 (1920)*

Justice McKenna delivered the opinion of the Court.

A statute of Minnesota [states that] ... "It shall be unlawful for any person in any public place, or at any meeting where more than five persons are assembled, to advocate or teach by word of mouth or otherwise that men should not enlist in the military or naval forces of the United States ..." [and] ... "It shall be unlawful for any person to teach or advocate by any written or printed matter whatsoever, or by oral speech, that the citizens of this state should not aid or assist the United States in prosecuting or carrying on war with the public enemies of the United States." ...

The indictment charged that Gilbert ... under the conditions prohibited by [the law], the United States being then and there at war with ... Germany, used the following language:

> We are going over to Europe to make the world safe for democracy, but I tell you we had better make America safe for democracy first. You say, what is the matter with our democracy? I tell you what is the matter with it: Have you had anything to say as to who should be President? Have you had anything to say as to who should be Governor of this state? Have you had anything to say as to whether we would go into this war?
>
> You know you have not. If this is such a good democracy, for Heaven's sake why should we not vote on conscription of men? We were stampeded into this war by newspaper rot [*sic*] to pull England's chestnuts out of the fire for her. I tell you if they conscripted wealth like they have conscripted men, this war would not last over forty-eight hours....

[The freedom of speech] is not absolute; it is subject to restriction and limitation.... [T]he curious spectacle [is] presented of the Constitution of the United States being invoked to justify the activities of anarchy or of the enemies of the United States, and by a strange perversion of its precepts [being] adduced against itself. [We rejected this contention.]

Gilbert's speech had the purpose [the law] denounce[s]. The nation was at war with Germany, armies were recruiting, and the speech was the discouragement of that—its purpose was necessarily the discouragement of that. It was not an advocacy of policies or a censure of actions that a citizen had the right to make.

The war was flagrant; it had been declared by the power constituted by the Constitution to declare it, and in the manner provided for by the Constitution. It was not declared in aggression, but in defense, in defense of our national honor, in vindication of the "most sacred rights of our Nation and our people."

This was known to Gilbert for he was informed in affairs and the operations of the Government, and every word that he uttered in denunciation of the war was false, was deliberate misrepresentation of the motives which impelled it, and the objects for which it was prosecuted. He could have had no purpose other than that of which he was charged. It would be a travesty on the constitutional privilege he invokes to assign him its protection.

Justice Holmes concurs in the result.

The Chief Justice ... dissents [on non-free-speech grounds]....

Justice Brandeis, dissenting. [Omitted.—ed.]

4.   More Evolution: Speech Advocating Crime

a.   *Problem: Murder Advocacy Exception*

Consider the following proposed free speech exception: "Speech that advocates or defends the propriety of unlawful killing shall not be constitutionally protected." Identify the kinds of speech that you think this exception will definitely cover and the kinds that you think it might cover, depending on how it's interpreted.

Then, armed with this sense of the exception's scope, go through each policy argument genre discussed below, and give an argument from that genre for or against this exception, and a matching counterargument.

b. *Gitlow v. New York, 268 U.S. 652 (1925)*

Justice Sanford delivered the opinion of the Court.

[A.] Benjamin Gitlow was ... sentenced to imprisonment [under a statute that criminalized] "advocat[ing] ... the ... propriety of overthrowing ... organized government by force or violence, or by assassination ... of any of the executive officials of government, or by any unlawful means ..." ....

The defendant is a member of the Left Wing Section of the Socialist Party, a dissenting branch or faction of that party formed in opposition to its dominant policy of "moderate Socialism." ... The Left Wing Section was organized nationally at a conference in New York City in June, 1919, attended by ninety delegates from twenty different States. The conference elected a National Council, of which the defendant was a member, and left to it the adoption of a "Manifesto." This was published in The Revolutionary Age, the official organ of the Left Wing.

The defendant ... arranged for the printing of the paper and took to the printer the manuscript of the first issue which contained the Left Wing Manifesto, and also a Communist Program and a Program of the Left Wing that had been adopted by the conference. Sixteen thousand copies were printed, which ... were paid for by the defendant, as business manager of the paper.... There was no evidence of any effect resulting from the publication and circulation of the Manifesto....

[The Manifesto] condemned the dominant "moderate Socialism" for its recognition of the necessity of the democratic parliamentary state; ... and advocated, in plain and unequivocal language, the necessity of accomplishing the "Communist Revolution" by a militant and "revolutionary Socialism," based on "the class struggle" and mobilizing the "power of the proletariat in action," through mass industrial revolts developing into mass political strikes and "revolutionary mass action" [giving as examples two then-recent political strikes—ed.], for the purpose of conquering and destroying the parliamentary state and establishing in its place, through a "revolutionary dictatorship of the proletariat," the system of Communist Socialism....

[B.] The statute does not penalize the utterance or publication of abstract "doctrine" or academic discussion having no quality of incitement to any concrete action. It is not aimed against mere historical or philosophical essays. It does not restrain the advocacy of changes in the form of government by constitutional and lawful means.

What it prohibits is language advocating ... the overthrow of organized government by unlawful means. These words imply urging to action.... It is not the abstract "doctrine" of overthrowing organized government by unlawful means which is denounced by the statute, but the advocacy of action for the accomplishment of that purpose....

The Manifesto, plainly, is neither the statement of abstract doctrine nor, as suggested by counsel, mere prediction that industrial disturbances and revolutionary mass strikes will result spontaneously in an inevitable process of evolution in the economic system. It advocates and urges in fervent language mass action which shall progressively foment industrial disturbances and through political mass strikes and revolutionary mass action overthrow and destroy organized parliamentary government....:

> The proletariat revolution and the Communist reconstruction of society— *the struggle for these*—is now indispensable.... The Communist International calls the proletariat of the world to the final struggle! ...

The means advocated for bringing about the destruction of organized parliamentary government, namely, mass industrial revolts usurping the functions of municipal government, political mass strikes directed against the parliamentary state, and revolutionary mass action for its final destruction, necessarily imply the use of force and violence, and in their essential nature are inherently unlawful in a constitutional government of law and order.... [T]he jury were warranted in finding that the Manifesto advocated not merely the abstract doctrine of overthrowing organized government by force, violence and unlawful means, but action to that end ....

[C.] That a State in the exercise of its police power may punish those who abuse [the freedom of speech and of the press] by utterances inimical to the public welfare, tending to corrupt public morals, incite to crime, or disturb the public peace, is not open to question.... And, for yet more imperative reasons, a State may punish utterances endangering the foundations of organized government and threatening its overthrow by unlawful means. These imperil its own existence as a constitutional State.

Freedom of speech and press ... does not protect disturbances to the public peace or the attempt to subvert the government. It does not protect publications or teachings which tend to subvert or imperil the government or to impede or hinder it in the performance of its governmental duties. It does not protect publications prompting the overthrow of government by force; the punishment of those who publish articles which tend to destroy organized society being essential to the security of freedom and the stability of the state.... "The safeguarding and fructification of free and constitutional institutions is the very basis and mainstay upon which the freedom of the press rests, and that freedom, therefore, does not and cannot be held to include the right virtually to destroy such institutions."

By enacting the present statute the State has determined, through its legislative body, that utterances advocating the overthrow of organized government by force, violence and unlawful means, are so inimical to the general welfare and involve such danger of substantive evil that they may be penalized in the exercise of its police power. That determination must be given great weight....

That utterances inciting to the overthrow of organized government by unlawful means, present a sufficient danger of substantive evil to bring their punishment within the range of legislative discretion, is clear. Such utterances, by their very nature, involve danger to the public peace and to the security of the State. They threaten breaches of the peace and ultimate revolution.

And the immediate danger is none the less real and substantial, because the effect of a given utterance cannot be accurately foreseen. The State cannot reasonably be required to measure the danger from every such utterance in the nice balance of a jeweler's scale. A single revolutionary spark may kindle a fire that, smouldering for a time, may burst into a sweeping and destructive conflagration.

It cannot be said that the State is acting arbitrarily or unreasonably when in the exercise of its judgment as to the measures necessary to protect the public peace and safety, it seeks to extinguish the spark without waiting until it has enkindled the flame or blazed into the conflagration. It cannot reasonably be required to defer the adoption of measures for its own peace and safety until the revolutionary utterances lead to actual disturbances of the public peace or imminent and immediate danger of its own destruction; but it may, in the exercise of its judgment, suppress the threatened danger in its incipiency....

[D.] It is clear that the question in such cases is entirely different from that involved in those cases where the statute merely prohibits certain acts involving the danger of substantive evil, without any reference to language itself, and it is sought to apply its provisions to language used by the defendant for the purpose of bringing about the prohibited results. There, ... it must necessarily be found, as an original question, without any previous determination by the legislative body, whether the specific language used involved such likelihood of bringing about the substantive evil as to deprive it of the constitutional protection.... [The *Schenck* clear-and-present-danger test] was manifestly intended ... to apply only in cases of this class, and has no application to those like the present, where the legislative body itself has previously determined the danger of substantive evil arising from utterances of a specified character....

Justice Holmes[, joined by Justice Brandeis,] dissenting....

[T]here was no present danger of an attempt to overthrow the government by force on the part of the admittedly small minority who shared the defendant's views. It is said that this manifesto was more than a theory, that it was an incitement. Every idea is an incitement. It offers itself for belief and if believed it is acted on unless some other belief outweighs it or some failure of energy stifles the movement at its birth.

The only difference between the expression of an opinion and an incitement in the narrower sense is the speaker's enthusiasm for the result. Eloquence may set fire to reason. But whatever may be thought of the redundant discourse before us it had no chance of starting a present conflagration.

If in the long run the beliefs expressed in proletarian dictatorship are destined to be accepted by the dominant forces of the community, the only meaning of free speech is that they should be given their chance and have their way.

If the publication of this document had been laid as an attempt to induce an uprising against government at once and not at some indefinite time in the future it would have presented a different question. The object would have been one with which the law might deal, subject to the doubt whether there was any danger that the publication could produce any result, or in other words, whether it was not futile and too remote from possible consequences. But the indictment alleges the publication and nothing more....

c.   *Whitney v. California, 274 U.S. 357 (1927)*

Justice Sanford delivered the opinion of the Court....

[Whitney was sentenced to imprisonment under the California Criminal Syndicalism Act, which made it a felony to organize or join "any ... group ... of persons organized or assembled to advocate, teach or aid and abet criminal syndicalism," defined as:—ed.]

> any doctrine ... advocating ... the commission of crime, sabotage (... meaning willful and malicious physical damage or injury to physical property), or unlawful acts of force and violence or unlawful methods of terrorism as a means of accomplishing a change in industrial ownership or control or effecting any political change....

[The defendant was involved in founding the Communist Labor Party.] In its "Platform and Program" the Party declared that it was in full harmony with "the revolutionary working class parties of all countries" and adhered to the principles of Communism ..., and that its purpose was ... organizing the workers as a class, in a revolutionary class struggle to conquer the capitalist state, for the overthrow of capitalist rule, [and] the conquest of political power[;] ... advocated, as the most important means of capturing state power, the action of the masses, ... the use of the political machinery of the capitalist state being only secondary; ... and recommended that strikes of national importance be supported and given a political character, and that propagandists and organizers be mobilized "who can not only teach, but actually help to put in practice the principles of revolutionary industrial unionism and Communism." ...

[A] State in the exercise of its police power may punish those who abuse [the freedom of speech] by utterances inimical to the public welfare, tending to incite to crime, disturb the public peace, or endanger the foundations of organized government and threaten its overthrow by unlawful means .... By enacting the provisions of the Syndicalism Act the State has declared, through its legislative body, that to knowingly be or become a member of or assist in organizing an association to advocate, teach or aid and abet the commission of crimes or unlawful acts of force, violence or terrorism as a means of accomplishing industrial or political changes, involves such danger to the public peace and the security of the State, that these acts should be penalized in the exercise of its police power. That determination must be given great weight. Every presumption is to be indulged in favor of the validity of the statute, and it may not be declared unconstitutional unless it is an arbitrary or unreasonable attempt to exercise the authority vested in the State in the public interest.

The essence of the offense denounced by the Act is the combining with others in an association for the accomplishment of the desired ends through the advocacy and use of criminal and unlawful methods. It partakes of the nature of a criminal conspiracy. That such united and joint action involves even greater danger to the public peace and security than the isolated utterances and acts of individuals is clear. We cannot hold that, as here applied, the Act is an unreasonable or arbitrary exercise of the police power of the State, unwarrantably infringing any right of free speech, assembly or association ....

Justice Brandeis [joined by Justice Holmes, concurring in the judgment]....

[A]lthough the rights of free speech and assembly are fundamental, they are not in their nature absolute. Their exercise is subject to restriction, if the particular restriction proposed is required in order to protect the state from destruction or from serious injury, political, economic or moral. That the necessity which is essential to a valid restriction does not exist unless speech would produce, or is intended to produce, a clear and imminent danger of some substantive evil which the state constitutionally may seek to prevent has been settled. See *Schenck v. United States.*

It is said to be the function of the legislature to determine whether at a particular time and under the particular circumstances the formation of, or assembly with, a society organized to advocate criminal syndicalism constitutes a clear and present danger of substantive evil; and that by enacting the law here in question the Legislature of California determined that question in the affirmative. Compare *Gitlow v. New York....* But where a statute is valid only in case certain condition exist, the enactment of the statute cannot alone establish the facts which are essential to its validity....

This Court has not yet fixed the standard by which to determine when a danger shall be deemed clear; how remote the danger may be and yet be deemed present; and what degree of evil shall be deemed sufficiently substantial to justify resort to abridgment of free speech and assembly as the means of protection. To reach sound conclusions on these matters, we must bear in mind why a state is, ordinarily, denied the power to prohibit dissemination of social, economic and political doctrine which a vast majority of its citizens believes to be false and fraught with evil consequence.

Those who won our independence believed that the final end of the state was to make men free to develop their faculties, and that in its government the deliberative forces should prevail over the arbitrary. They valued liberty both as an end and as a means. They believed liberty to be the secret of happiness and courage to be the secret of liberty.

They believed that freedom to think as you will and to speak as you think are means indispensable to the discovery and spread of political truth; that without free speech and assembly discussion would be futile; that with them, discussion affords ordinarily adequate protection against the dissemination of noxious doctrine; that the greatest menace to freedom is an inert people; that public discussion is a political duty; and that this should be a fundamental principle of the American government. {Compare Thomas Jefferson: "We have nothing to fear from the demoralizing reasonings of some, if others are left free to demonstrate their errors and especially when the law stands ready to punish the first criminal act produced by the false reasonings; these are safer corrections than the conscience of the judge." ... Also in [Jefferson's] Inaugural Address: "If there be any among us who would wish to dissolve this union or change its republican form, let them stand undisturbed as monuments of the safety with which error of opinion may be tolerated where reason is left free to combat it."}

They recognized the risks to which all human institutions are subject. But they knew that order cannot be secured merely through fear of punishment for its infraction; that it is hazardous to discourage thought, hope and imagination; that fear breeds repression; that repression breeds hate; that hate menaces stable government; that the path of safety lies in the opportunity to discuss freely supposed grievances and proposed remedies; and that the fitting remedy for evil counsels is good ones. Believing in the power of reason as applied through public discussion, they eschewed silence coerced by law—the argument of force in its worst form. Recognizing the occasional tyrannies of governing majorities, they amended the Constitution so that free speech and assembly should be guaranteed.

Fear of serious injury cannot alone justify suppression of free speech and assembly. Men feared witches and burnt women. It is the function of speech to free men from the bondage of irrational fears. To justify suppression of free speech there must be reasonable ground to fear that serious evil will result if free speech is practiced. There must be reasonable ground to believe that the danger apprehended is imminent. There must be reasonable ground to believe that the evil to be prevented is a serious one.

Every denunciation of existing law tends in some measure to increase the probability that there will be violation of it. Condonation of a breach enhances the probability. Expressions of approval add to the probability. Propagation of the criminal state of mind by teaching syndicalism increases it. Advocacy of lawbreaking heightens it still further.

But even advocacy of violation, however reprehensible morally, is not a justification for denying free speech where the advocacy falls short of incitement and there is nothing to indicate that the advocacy would be immediately acted on.... In order to support a finding of clear and present danger it must be shown either that immediate serious violence was to be expected or was advocated, or that the past conduct furnished reason to believe that such advocacy was then contemplated.

Those who won our independence by revolution were not cowards. They did not fear political change. They did not exalt order at the cost of liberty.

To courageous, self-reliant men, with confidence in the power of free and fearless reasoning applied through the processes of popular government, no danger flowing from speech can be deemed clear and present, unless the incidence of the evil apprehended is so imminent that it may befall before there is opportunity for full discussion.

If there be time to expose through discussion the falsehood and fallacies, to avert the evil by the processes of education, the remedy to be applied is more speech, not enforced silence. Only an emergency can justify repression. Such must be the rule if authority is to be reconciled with freedom. Such, in my opinion, is the command of the Constitution. It is therefore always open to Americans to challenge a law abridging free speech and assembly by showing that there was no emergency justifying it.

Moreover, even imminent danger cannot justify resort to prohibition of these functions essential to effective democracy, unless the evil apprehended is relatively serious. Prohibition of free speech and assembly is a measure so stringent that it would be inappropriate as the means for averting a relatively trivial harm to society. A police measure may be unconstitutional merely because the remedy, although effective as means of protection, is unduly harsh or oppressive.

Thus, a State might, in the exercise of its police power, make any trespass upon the land of another a crime .... It might, also, punish ... an incitement to commit the trespass. But it is hardly conceivable that this Court would hold constitutional a statute which punished as a felony the mere voluntary assembly with a society formed to teach that pedestrians had the moral right to cross uninclosed, unposted, waste lands and to advocate their doing so, even if there was imminent danger that advocacy would lead to a trespass.

The fact that speech is likely to result in some violence or in destruction of property is not enough to justify its suppression. There must be the probability of serious injury to the State. Among free men, the deterrents ordinarily to be applied to prevent crime are education and punishment for violations of the law, not abridgment of the rights of free speech and assembly....

Whether in 1919, when Miss Whitney did the things complained of, there was in California such clear and present danger of serious evil, might have been made the important issue in the case.... She claimed below that the statute as applied to her violated the Federal Constitution; but she did not claim that it was void because there was no clear and present danger of serious evil, nor did she request that the existence of these conditions of a valid measure thus restricting the rights of free speech and assembly be passed upon by the court of a jury....

[T]here was evidence on which the court or jury might have found that such danger existed.... [T]here was ... testimony which tended to establish the existence of a conspiracy, on the part of members of the International Workers of the World, to commit present serious crimes; and likewise to show that such a conspiracy would be furthered by the activity of the society of which Miss Whitney was a member. Under these circumstances the judgment of the state court cannot be disturbed....

d. Policy—Search for Truth / Marketplace of Ideas

Basic argument for protection: "This speech restriction will make it harder for people to discover the truth about _____, because _____."

Basic argument for restriction: "Allowing the speech will not advance the search for truth about _____—or will even interfere with this search for truth—because _____."

1 (for protection). "[W]hen men have realized that time has upset many fighting faiths, they may come to believe ... that the ultimate good desired is better reached by free trade in ideas—that the best test of truth is the power of the thought to get itself accepted in the competition of the market, and that truth is the only ground upon which their wishes safely can be carried out. That at any rate is the theory of our Constitution." *Abrams v. United States* (Holmes, J., dissenting).

"If in the long run the beliefs expressed in proletarian dictatorship are destined to be accepted by the dominant forces of the community, the only meaning of free speech is that they should be given their chance and have their way." *Gitlow v. New York* (Holmes, J., dissenting).

2a (for restriction). The market doesn't function well as to this speech.

"[T]he idea of the racial inferiority of nonwhites infects, skews, and disables the operation of a market .... It trumps good ideas that contend with it in the market. It is an epidemic that distorts the marketplace of ideas and renders it dysfunctional." Charles R. Lawrence III, *If He Hollers Let Him Go: Regulating Racist Speech on Campus,* in *Words That Wound* 77 (1993).

"Many people grow up to regard [the fundamental institutions of our society] not as institutions to be tested but as standards against which the correctness of new policies and institutions can be tested. When that happens, as is common, processes of critical judgment are short-circuited." Charles E. Lindblom, *Politics and Markets* 207 (1977), *quoted in* Steven H. Shiffrin & Jesse H. Choper, *The First Amendment* 14 (3d ed. 2001).

"Especially when the wealthy have more access to the most potent media of communication than the poor, how sure can we be that 'free trade in ideas' is likely to generate truth?" Laurence Tribe, *American Constitutional Law* (2d ed. 1988).

"[Advertisers] spend some sixty billion dollars per year.... Those who would oppose the materialist message must combat forces that have a massive economic advantage. Any confidence that we will know what is truth by seeing what emerges from such combat is ill placed." Steven H. Shiffrin, *The First Amendment and Economic Regulation,* 78 Nw. U. L. Rev. 1212, 1281 (1983).

2b (for restriction). We know this speech is wrong and thus doesn't advance the search for truth; no need to risk people being deluded by it.

"[There is] universal acceptance of the wrongness of the doctrine of racial supremacy. There is no nation left on this planet that submits as its national self-expression the view that Hitler was right.... At the universities, at the centers of knowledge of the international community, the doctrines of racial supremacy are again uniformly rejected. At the United Nations the same is true. We have fought wars and spilled blood to establish the universal acceptance of this principle. The universality of the principle, in a world bereft of agreement on many things, is a mark of collective human progress. The victim's perspective, one mindful of the lessons of history, thus accepts racist speech as sui generis and universally condemned." Mari Matsuda, *Public Response to Racist Speech: Considering the Victim's Story,* in *Words That Wound* 37 (1993).

"What do you want to sell in the marketplace? What idea? The idea of murder?" Erna Gans, a concentration camp survivor arguing against protecting Nazi speech, *quoted in* Fred W. Friendly & Martha J.H. Elliot, *The Constitution: That Delicate Balance* 83 (1984) *and* Shiffrin & Choper.

"[T]here is no constitutional value in false statements of fact[, because they do not] materially advanc[e] society's interest in 'uninhibited, robust, and wide-open' debate on public issues." *Gertz v. Robert Welch.*

"[T]he lewd and obscene, the profane, the libelous, and the insulting or 'fighting words' ... are no essential part of any exposition of ideas, and are of ... slight social value as a step to truth." *Chaplinsky v. New Hampshire.*

See also other examples given under *Policy—No-Value or Low-Value Speech* (p. 90).

3a (for protection). Response to 2a: Even if the marketplace doesn't do a perfect job of rejecting the bad speech, it will do a better job than the government will.

"[P]erhaps the worst umpires or referees of truth are the oppressive arms of government which will always attempt to impose an orthodoxy consonant with the frequently corrupt interests of the bureaucracy.... We maintain a strong version of the First Amendment not because the truth or usefulness of an idea ... cannot in many areas be ascertained to some degree of certainty.... [but] because we lack the capacity to distinguish areas of certainty, more or less, from areas where truth as we now see it is elusive and changeable in the future." Nicholas Wolfson, *Free Speech and Hateful Words,* 60 U. Cin. L. Rev. 1 (1991).

"If acceptance of an idea in the competition of the market is not the 'best test' [then what] is the alternative? It can only be acceptance of an idea by some individual or group narrower than that of the public at large. Thus, the alternative to competition in the market must be some form of elitism. It seems hardly necessary to enlarge on the dangers of that path." Melville Nimmer, *Nimmer on Freedom of Speech* 1-12 (1984).

3b (for protection). Response to 2b: This speech *does* help the search for truth, specifically by _____, and the marketplace *is* working.

"[M]uch linguistic expression ... conveys not only ideas capable of relatively precise, detached explication, but otherwise inexpressible emotions as well. In fact, words are often chosen as much for their emotive as their cognitive force.... [W]e cannot indulge the facile assumption that one can forbid particular words without also running a substantial risk of suppressing ideas in the process." *Cohen v. California.*

"Even a false statement may be deemed to make a valuable contribution to the public debate, since it brings about 'the clearer perception and livelier impression of truth, produced by its collision with error.'" *New York Times v. Sullivan.*

"[H]owever true [an opinion] may be, if it is not fully, frequently, and fearlessly discussed, it will be held as a dead dogma, not a living truth.... He who knows only his own side of the case, knows little of that.... [I]f he is ... unable to refute the reasons on the opposite side; if he does not so much as know what they are, he has no ground for preferring either opinion....

"This is illustrated in the experience of almost all ethical doctrines and religious creeds. They are all full of meaning and vitality to those who originate them, and to the direct disciples of the originators ... so long as the struggle lasts to give the doctrine or creed an ascendency over other creeds.... But when it has come to be an hereditary creed, and to be received passively ... there is a progressive tendency to forget all of the belief except the formularies ... until it almost ceases to connect itself at all with the inner life of the human being." John Stuart Mill, *On Liberty* (1859).

"It is this right, the right to err politically, which keeps us strong as a Nation. For no number of laws against communism can have as much effect as the personal conviction which comes from having heard its arguments and rejected them, or from having once accepted its tenets and later recognized their worthlessness." *Barenblatt v. United States* (Black, J., dissenting).

4 (for restriction). Response to 3a: We let the legal system decide what is true in various contexts, such as _____ (for instance, libel law or false advertising law); sure, there's a risk of error there, but it's a risk of error we accept because _____. Why not let courts determine historical truth or scientific truth or moral truth, too, at least within certain contexts where there's a truly broad consensus?

"[N]o forum is perfect, but that is not a justification for leaving whole classes of defamed individuals without redress or a realistic opportunity to clear their names. We entrust to juries and the courts the responsibility of decisions affecting the life and liberty of persons. It is perverse indeed to say that these bodies are incompetent to inquire into the truth of a statement of fact in a defamation case." *Dun & Bradstreet v. Greenmoss Builders* (White, J., concurring in the judgment).

e. *Policy—Self-Government*

Basic argument for protection: "Because we're a self-governing democracy, we as voters need to hear *all* views to decide which way we should vote.

The government, even if representative of the majority's will, may not shut off the flow of ideas that could lead the majority to change its mind. In particular, this speech may help the majority decide on _____."

Basic arguments for restriction: "This speech doesn't contribute to democracy and self-government (or actually interferes with them) because _____, and thus there's no free speech problem with restricting it."

"Sometimes, speech must be restricted, because there are other countervailing interests that must somctimes prevail. The question then is *who decides* when this happens. Legislatures and juries have their flaws, but courts have theirs, and we should let the democratically selected legislature (or jury) decide in this case because _____."

1 (for protection). "The Constitution supposes that [elected officials] .... may not discharge their trusts .... Hence, they are all made responsible to their constituents, [at elections or through impeachment].... [Whether the officials' conduct exhibits] such a violation of duty as to justify a contempt, a disrepute or hatred among the people, can only be determined by a free examination thereof, and a free communication among the people thereon." James Madison, *Report of the Virginia Legislature's Committee on the Sedition Act* (1799).

"Nor do I see how the people can exercise on rational grounds their elective franchise, if perfect freedom of discussion of public characters be not allowed." Cooper's address to the jury, in *United States v. Cooper.*

"[T]he will of the people is the foundation of all free government[;] ... to give effect to this will, free thought, free speech and a free press are absolutely indispensable.... [It is a] constitutional right of the people to discuss all measures of their Government, and to approve or disapprove ...; ... they have a like right to propose and advocate that policy which, in their judgment, is best ...; [and] these ... are their rights in time of war as well as in times of peace, and of far more value and necessity in war than in peace, for in peace, liberty, security, and property are seldom endangered, in war, they are ever in peril." Resolution of the Ohio Democratic Convention, June 1863, condemning the Lincoln Administration's arrest of Clement Vallandigham, a pro-Southern ex-congressman, *discussed in* Michael Kent Curtis, *Free Speech, "The People's Darling Privilege"* 324 (2000).

2a (for restriction). This speech undermines important institutions of self-government.

"The liberty of the press is, indeed, valuable—long may it preserve its lustre! ... [But] can it be tolerated in any civilized society that any should be permitted with impunity to tell falsehood to the people, with an express intention to deceive them, and lead them into discontent, if not into insurrection, which is so apt to follow? ... The necessity [of punishing libels against the government is even greater in a republic than in a monarchy], because in a republic more is dependent on thc good opinion of the people for its support .... Take away from a republic the confidence of the people, and the whole fabric crumbles into dust." *Case of Fries,* 9 F. Cas. 826, 838-39 (C.C. D. Pa. 1799) (Iredell, J., riding circuit).

"If a man attempts to destroy the confidence of the people in their officers, their supreme magistrate, and their legislature, he effectually saps the foundation of the government." *Cooper* (Chase, J., riding circuit).

"[In the campaign finance context,] both the first amendment and the law with which it is in potential conflict are designed to accomplish the same broad purpose, namely to advance the interests of democratic self-government." Martin Redish, *Campaign Spending Laws and the First Amendment,* 46 N.Y.U. L. Rev. 900, 907 (1971) (describing the argument but ultimately not endorsing it).

2b (for restriction). This speech promotes nondemocratic actions, rather than actions through the institutions of self-government.

"Speech advocating forcible overthrow of the government contemplates a group less than a majority seizing control of the monopoly power of the state when it cannot gain its ends through speech and political activity. Speech advocating violent overthrow is thus not 'political speech' as that term must be defined by a Madisonian system of government ... because it is not aimed at a new definition of political truth by a legislative majority. Violent overthrow of government breaks the premises of our system concerning the ways in which truth is defined, and yet those premises are the only reasons for protecting political speech." Robert Bork, *Neutral Principles and Some First Amendment Problems,* 47 Ind. L.J. 1, 31 (1971).

2c (for restriction): This speech promotes a certain policy, namely _____ (such as racism, Communism, violent revolution, and so on) that may not properly be implemented by a self-governing society, because _____. It is therefore no substantial burden on self-government to restrict speech that would promote such unjust laws.

"Political discourse extends only to those ideas and values that can legitimately play a role in the determination of our political obligations.... Racist and sexist values cannot participate in the shaping of political obligations because the legal obligations they generate do not have morally binding force." Alon Harel, *Bigotry, Pornography, and the First Amendment,* 65 So. Cal. L. Rev. 1887, 1887 (1992).

2d (for restriction): This speech is irrelevant to self-government.

"[Because the key principle behind the freedom of speech is preserving democracy and self-government, the First Amendment protects] only ... speech which bears, directly or indirectly, upon issues with which voters have to deal—only, therefore, to the consideration of matters of public interest." Alexander Meiklejohn, *Free Speech and Its Relation to Self-Government* 94 (1948).

"[The government should have more power to restrict speech in these circumstances:] First, the speech must be far afield from the central concern of the first amendment, which, broadly speaking, is effective popular control of public affairs.... Second, ... [s]peech that has purely noncognitive appeal will be entitled to less constitutional protection. Third, ... if the speaker is seeking to communicate a message, he will be treated more favorably than if he is not. Fourth, the various classes of low-value speech reflect judgments that in certain areas, government is unlikely to be acting for constitutionally impermissible reasons or producing constitutionally troublesome harms." Cass R. Sunstein, *Pornography and the First Amendment,* 1986 Duke L.J. 589, 603-04.

2e (for restriction): This speech restriction is the product of the democratic process, and courts shouldn't set it aside. (It helps if the argument also explains why this restriction should be treated this way, while other restrictions are struck down.)

"It is not for us to decide how we would adjust the clash of interests which this case presents were the primary responsibility for reconciling it ours. Congress has determined that the danger created by advocacy of overthrow justifies the ensuing restriction on freedom of speech." *Dennis v. United States* (Frankfurter, J., concurring).

"[T]emperate investigations of the nature and forms of government ... are proper for public information. [But when] malicious publications ... infect insidiously the public mind with a subtle poison, and produce the most mischievous and alarming consequences, by their tendency to anarchy, sedition, and civil war[, w]e cannot, consistently with our official duty, pronounce such conduct dispunishable....

"[I]t may not be easy in every instance, to draw the exact distinguishing line. To the jury, it peculiarly belongs to decide on the *intent* and *object* of the writing.... What is the meaning of the words 'being responsible for the abuse of that liberty' [in the Pennsylvania Constitution's free press clause], if the jury are interdicted from deciding on the case? Who else can constitutionally decide on it? ... The objection, that the determinations of juries may vary at different times, arising from their different political opinions, proves too much. The same matter may be objected against them, when party spirit runs high, in other criminal prosecutions." *Respublica v. Dennie,* 4 Yeates 267 (Pa. 1805) (paragraphs reordered).

"[T]he Court strikes down the [limit on independent expenditures], strangely enough claiming more insight as to what may improperly influence candidates than is possessed by the majority of Congress that passed this bill and the President who signed it. Those supporting the bill undeniably included many seasoned professionals who have been deeply involved in elective processes and who have viewed them at close range over many years.... I would take the word of those who know—that limiting independent expenditures is essential to prevent transparent and widespread evasion of the contribution limits." *Buckley v. Valeo* (White, J., concurring in part and dissenting in part).

3. Response to 2a-2d: Giving the government the power to decide what does or doesn't well serve self-government is bad, because _____.

"[A conclusion that] the Legislature is invested with authority to suppress whatever discussion or publication shall be deemed subversive of the public safety or peace ... would nullify the provisions of the Constitution, and place that discretionary power in legislators, which it was the manifest intent of the Constitution to withhold from them." *A Full Statement of the Reasons ... Why There Should Be No Penal Laws Enacted ... Respecting Abolitionists ...* 10 (1836), *cited in* Michael Kent Curtis, *The Curious History of Attempts to Suppress Antislavery Speech, Press, and Petition in 1835–37*, 89 Nw. U. L. Rev. 785 (1995).

"[A]ll sorts of different people think that all sorts of different speech is valueless or downright pernicious [citing advertising, television, *Lady Chatterley's Lover*, pornography, and Communist advocacy]. If all it takes to remove First Amendment protection from a given kind of speech is that a sufficiently large number of people finds the speech less valuable than other kinds, we may as well not have a First Amendment at all. Such an understanding of the First Amendment—according to which speech not valued by a majority receives no protection—throws all speech regulation questions back into the political arena." Judge Alex Kozinski & Stuart Banner, *The Anti-History and Pre-History of Commercial Speech,* 71 Tex. L. Rev 747 (1993).

3c. Rejoinder to 2c: No ideas, no matter how reprehensible or contrary to past or present enlightened opinion, may be taken off the table in a democracy, because _____; for true self-government, the majority must be able to discuss and consider implementing any policies, no matter how reprehensible they may seem, because _____.

3d. Rejoinder to 2d: This speech (for instance, art, advertising, or even pornography) *does* influence, albeit indirectly, people's attitudes to life, society, and so on, by _____, and thus does contribute to self-government.

"[T]he First Amendment ... forbids Congress to abridge the freedom of a citizen's speech ... whenever [the speech is] utilized for the governing of the nation.... [But] other activities [besides overtly political speech] ... must [also] be included within the scope of the First Amendment.... [T]here are many forms of thought and expression [*i.e.*, education, philosophy, science, literature, arts, and information and opinion bearing on public issues] within the range of human communications from which the voter derives the knowledge, intelligence, sensitivity to human values: the capacity for sane and objective judgment which, so far as possible, a ballot should express." Alexander Meiklejohn, *The First Amendment Is an Absolute*, 1961 Sup. Ct. Rev. 245, 255-57.

3e. Rejoinder to 2e: Those who are in power will often base speech restrictions on their own selfish desires, and not actually on the interests or the will of the majority, because _____. Elected officials may restrict criticism of themselves in order to get reelected, or restrict criticism of others in order to get those others' help in getting reelected; unelected judges may restrict speech in order to minimize criticism of themselves, the government that they serve, or the class to which they belong.

f.   Policy—Alternatives to Suppressing Speech

Argument: "The government may serve its interests effectively enough by doing _____ instead of by restricting speech."

Possible supplement: "True, this might not serve the interest as effectively as speech suppression would, but it would be effective enough, because _____; and the loss of effectiveness is worth it because _____."

1. "[T]he fitting remedy for evil counsels is good ones.... If there be time to expose through discussion the falsehood and fallacies, to avert the evil by the processes of education, the remedy to be applied is more speech, not enforced silence.... Among free men, the deterrents ordinarily to be applied to prevent crime are education and punishment for violations of the law, not abridgment of the rights of free speech and assembly ...." *Whitney v. California* (Brandeis, J., concurring in the judgment). [Note that this focuses on counterspeech as the only *permissible* alternative, and doesn't explicitly say that it will always be an *effective* alternative.—ed.]

"The breadth of this ... restriction of speech imposes an especially heavy burden on the Government to explain why a less restrictive provision would not be as effective as the CDA." *Reno v. ACLU.*

2. Response to 1: These alternatives might not be as effective as the speech restriction, because _____. Counterspeech, for instance, often can't undo most of the damage done by the speech itself. If someone urges a crowd to bomb draft offices or abortion clinics, and the next day someone else "counterspeaks," some of the initial listeners won't hear the second message, and others will hear it but will be more persuaded by the advocacy of violence than by the response urging peace. The goal of preventing violence is thus best served by preventing the bad speech in the first place.

"This apotheosis of Truth [emerging from speech and counterspeech], however, shows a blindness to the deadly fact that meantime the 'power of the thought' ... might 'get itself accepted in the competition of the market,' by munitions workers, so as to lose the war; in which case, the academic victory which Truth, 'the ultimate good,' might later secure in the market, would be too 'ultimate' to have any practical value for a defeated America." John H. Wigmore, *Freedom of Speech and Freedom of Thuggery in War-Time and Peace-Time,* 14 Ill. L. Rev. 539, 550-51 (1920).

"Appellants contend that the contribution limitations must be invalidated because bribery laws and narrowly drawn disclosure requirements constitute a less restrictive means of dealing with 'proven and suspected *quid pro quo* arrangements.' But laws making criminal the giving and taking of bribes deal with only the most blatant and specific attempts of those with money to influence governmental action.... Congress was surely entitled to conclude that disclosure [requirements were] only a partial measure, and that contribution ceilings were a necessary legislative concomitant to deal with the reality or appearance of corruption ...." *Buckley v. Valeo.*

g. *Policy—Relative Harm (or Not) of Speech/Utility (or Not) of Restriction*

Basic argument: "The speech restricted here is/isn't really that dangerous, because _____, and thus the restriction is necessary/unnecessary."

1 (for harmlessness of speech): "[N]obody can suppose that the surreptitious publishing of a silly leaflet by an unknown man, without more, would

present any immediate danger that its opinions would hinder the success of the government arms or have any appreciable tendency to do so." *Abrams v. United States* (Holmes, J., dissenting).

"[Communists] *as a political party* [in the U.S.] are of little consequence.... It is inconceivable that those who went up and down this country preaching the doctrine of revolution which petitioners espouse would have any success.... To believe that petitioners and their following are placed in such critical positions as to endanger the Nation is to believe the incredible." *Dennis v. United States* (Douglas, J., dissenting).

"[F]orbidding criminal punishment for conduct such as Johnson's will not endanger the special role played by our flag or the feelings it inspires.... [N]obody can suppose that this one gesture of an unknown man will change our Nation's attitude towards its flag." *Texas v. Johnson*.

2 (for harm of speech): The speech really is dangerous, because _____.

"Every denunciation of existing law tends in some measure to increase the probability that there will be violation of it. Condonation of a breach enhances the probability. Expressions of approval add to the probability. Propagation of the criminal state of mind by teaching syndicalism increases it. Advocacy of lawbreaking heightens it still further." *Whitney v. California* (Brandeis, J., concurring in the judgment, though concluding that the speech should be protected despite the harm).

"If [this speaker can make this statement] then others could lawfully do so; and a thousand disaffected [speakers] were ready and waiting to do so. Though this circular was 'surreptitious,' the next ones need not be so. If such urgings were lawful, every munitions factory in the country could be stopped by them. The relative amount of harm that one criminal act can effect is no measure of its criminality, and no measure of the danger of its criminality." John H. Wigmore, *Freedom of Speech and Freedom of Thuggery in War-Time and Peace-Time,* 14 Ill. L. Rev. 539, 550 (1920); see also Robert Bork, *Neutral Principles and Some First Amendment Problems,* 47 Ind. L.J. 1, 33 (1971).

"[T]he validity of this regulation need not be judged solely by reference to the demonstration at hand. Absent the prohibition on sleeping, there would be other groups who would demand permission to deliver an asserted message by camping ... as does CCNV, and the denial of permits to still others would present difficult problems for the Park Service." *Clark v. CCNV*.

"[Mr. Vallandigham's] arrest was made because he was laboring, with some effect, to prevent the raising of troops; to encourage desertions from the army; and to leave the Rebellion without an adequate military force to suppress it.... Long experience has shown, that armies cannot be maintained unless desertions shall be punished by the severe penalty of death.... Must I shoot a simple-minded soldier boy who deserts, while I must not touch a hair of a wily agitator who induces him to desert?" Lincoln on Vallandigham (p. 12).

"Pornography is neither harmless fantasy nor a corrupt and confused misrepresentation of an otherwise neutral and healthy sexual situation. It institutionalizes the sexuality of male supremacy, fusing the erotization of dominance and submission with the social construction of male and female.... Men treat women as who they see women as being. Pornography constructs who that is." Catherine MacKinnon, *Pornography, Civil Rights, and Speech,* 20 Harv. Civ. Rts.-Civ. Lib. L. Rev. 1 (1985).

"The train [of gunpowder] is laid, and a single spark may blow our Constitution into atoms, and scatter its blackened fragments to the winds. Unless measures are adopted to meet and repel the efforts of the abolitionists [including suppressing their proabolition advocacy], this country is inevitably doomed to be theatre of a civil ... war." *The Slave Question,* U.S. Telegraph, June 22, 1834, at 843, *cited in* Michael Kent Curtis, *Free Speech, "The People's Darling Privilege"* 136 (2000).

"'Words are bullets' and the communists know it and use them so. Whatever guarantees of sovereignty and freedom are enjoyed by this state and its citizens are certain to vanish if the United States of America is destroyed or taken over by the communists." "The danger of communist propaganda lies ... in the fact that it is a specific tool or weapon used by the communists for the express purpose of bringing about the forcible total destruction or subjugation of this state and nation and the total eradication of the philosophy of freedom upon which this state and nation were founded." Declaration of Public Policy in support of a ban on communist propaganda, La. Rev. Stat. tit. 14, § 390 (enacted 1962).

3. Response to 1: What's more, the true effects of this sort of speech are hard to forecast, because _____, and legislative forecasts should be given at least as much deference as judicial ones, because _____.

"To make validity of legislation depend on judicial reading of events still in the womb of time—a forecast, that is, of the outcome of forces at best appreciated only with knowledge of the topmost secrets of nations—is to charge the judiciary with duties beyond its equipment. We do not expect courts to pronounce historic verdicts on bygone events. Even historians have conflicting views to this day on the origins and conduct of the French Revolution .... It is as absurd to be confident that we can measure the present clash of forces and their outcome as to ask us to read history still enveloped in clouds of controversy." *Dennis* (Frankfurter, J., concurring).

"It is not within our competence to confirm or deny claims of social scientists as to the dependence of the individual on the position of his racial or religious group in the community. It would, however, be arrant dogmatism ... for us to deny that the Illinois Legislature may warrantably believe that a man's job and his educational opportunities and the dignity accorded him may depend as much on the reputation of the racial and religious group to which he willy-nilly belongs, as on his own merits. This being so, we are precluded from saying that speech concededly punishable when immediately directed at individuals cannot be outlawed if directed at groups with whose position and esteem in society the affiliated individual may be inextricably involved." *Beauharnais v. Illinois* (Frankfurter, J.).

4. Response to 1: And the restriction really might have a good chance of effectively combating this harm, because _____.

"Only those lacking responsible humility will have a confident solution for problems as intractable as the frictions attributable to differences of race, color or religion. This being so, it would be out of bounds for the judiciary to deny the legislature a choice of policy, provided it is not unrelated to the problem and not forbidden by some explicit limitation on the State's power." *Beauharnais.*

5. Response to 2: The harms caused by the speech can be prevented pretty much as well without restricting the speech, specifically by _____. See *Policy—Alternatives to Suppressing Speech,* p. 37.

6. Response to 2: The speech must be protected despite the harm it causes, because the harm of suppressing it is greater, since _____.

h. *Policy—Social Costs of Suppression and Benefits of Toleration*

Basic argument: "This speech restriction will actually be counterproductive, because it would lead to the following bad results: _____" (fill in the blank with something other than interference with the search for truth, the marketplace of ideas, or self-government).

Alternative formulation: "Allowing this speech will actually be beneficial, because it would lead to the following good results: _____."

1. "Those who won our independence ... knew that order cannot be secured merely through fear of punishment for its infraction; that it is hazardous to discourage thought, hope and imagination; that fear breeds repression; that repression breeds hate; that hate menaces stable government; that the path of safety lies in the opportunity to discuss freely supposed grievances and proposed remedies; and that the fitting remedy for evil counsels is good ones." *Whitney v. California* (Brandeis, J., concurring in the judgment).

"[T]he flag's deservedly cherished place in our community will be strengthened, not weakened, by our holding today. Our decision is a reaffirmation of the principles of freedom and inclusiveness that the flag best reflects, and of the conviction that our toleration of criticism such as Johnson's is a sign and source of our strength." *Texas v. Johnson.*

"[T]oleration [of offensive speech] can help [a society] establish or prove symbolically the arrival of [a capacity of security and control].... To think of freedom of speech in this way evokes Seneca's prescription on mercy—its primary value, when implemented by the ruler, is in what it bespeaks of the party who is merciful, his confidence and security and self-restraint in the face of challenges to that authority." Lee Bollinger, *Free Speech and Intellectual Values,* 92 Yale L.J. 438 (1983).

"[A]s to those murmurs or secret discontents [the liberty of the press] may occasion, it is better they should get vent in words, that they may come to the knowledge of the magistrate before it be too late, in order to his providing a remedy against them." David Hume, *Of the Liberty of the Press*

(1742).

"This normal give and take of democratic society provides dissenters with a range of peaceful methods to achieve their goals[: voting, petitioning, persuading fellow citizens, and] conduct[ing] peaceful protests and engag[ing] in other forms of nonviolent civil disobedience. These outlets function as a 'safety valve,' providing a range of nonviolent options for dissent and thus reducing the likelihood that a group will choose violence to achieve its goals." Mark L. Rienzi, *Safety Valve Closed: The Removal of Nonviolent Outlets for Dissent and the Onset of Anti-Abortion Violence,* 113 Harv. L. Rev. 1210 (2000).

2. Response to 1: These are contestable sociological claims, which may not be true here, because _____, and are in any event unprovable, because _____. Legislatures will do at least as well as judges at sorting them out.

"The [safety valve] argument is paternalistic; it says we are denying you what you say you want, and we are doing it for your own good. The [speech restrictions], which you think will help you, will really make matters worse. If you knew this, you would join us in opposing them.... [But in fact,] the psychological evidence suggests that permitting one person to say or do hateful things to another increases, rather than decreases, the chance that he or she will do so again the future. Moreover, others may believe it is permissible to follow suit.... Pressure valves may be safer after letting off steam; human beings are not." Richard Delgado & David H. Yun, *Pressure Valves and Bloodied Chickens: An Analysis of Paternalistic Objections to Hate Speech Regulation,* 82 Calif. L. Rev. 871 (1994).

3. Response to 1: If the speech does have these beneficial side effects, or if the restriction does have these harmful side effects, the legislature will have ample incentive to leave the speech alone, because _____.

i.   *Policy—Constitutional Tension Method*

Basic argument: "The Constitution itself embodies many values, besides just free speech. Because the speech here jeopardizes [name another constitutional value] by _____, the speech is not protected by the Constitution."

1. "[T]he curious spectacle [is] presented of the Constitution of the United States being invoked to justify [speech subversive of constitutional values], and by a strange perversion of its precepts [being] adduced against itself." *Gilbert v. Minnesota* (referring to the war power clauses).

"[The interest in speech, profoundly important as it is, is no more conclusive ... than other attributes of democracy." *Dennis v. United States* (Frankfurter, J., concurring).

"[Tolerating racist speech is] a reading of the first amendment that requires sacrificing rights guaranteed under the equal protection clause." Charles R. Lawrence III, *If He Hollers Let Him Go: Regulating Racist Speech on Campus,* in *Words That Wound* 81 (1993).

"Free speech is not so absolute or irrational a conception as to imply paralysis of the means for effective protection of all the freedoms secured by the Bill of Rights. In the cases before us, the claims on behalf of freedom of speech and of the press [to publish statements aimed at influencing pending cases] encounter claims on behalf of liberties no less precious [*i.e.*, the administration of justice by an impartial judiciary]." *Bridges v. California,* 314 U.S. 252, 282 (1941) (Frankfurter, J., dissenting).

See also *Terminiello v. City of Chicago,* 337 U.S. 1 (1949) (Jackson, J., dissenting) (referring to the constitutional interest in preserving democracy as a reason for restricting speech that might unintentionally lead to mob violence); *Kunz v. New York,* 340 U.S. 290 (1951) (Jackson, J., dissenting) (referring to free exercise of religion as a reason to restrict speech that harshly condemns religion).

2. Response to 1: The freedom of speech is not actually in tension with any of these values, because _____.

"One [can] read the various constitutional provisions [not] as setting up abstract values, values which may be in tension with one another[,] ... [but] as simply creating particular government powers or disabilities.... [And speech] can't literally take away government power, or an immunity from government action. Antiwar advocacy may make it harder to wage war, but it doesn't actually contradict Congress's war power .... Insulting Catholicism on the street corner may run contrary to the spirit of religious freedom, but it isn't the government 'mak[ing a] law ... prohibiting the free exercise [of religion].' If we accept this approach, then there is no constitutional tension. We can obey the Free Speech Clause without being untrue to any other constitutional provision." Eugene Volokh, *Freedom of Speech and the Constitutional Tension Method,* 3 U. Chi. Roundtable 223 (1996).

3. Response to 1: That Congress has the *power* to do something doesn't mean that it has the right to restrict speech in order to do it, because _____. All federal actions must rest on one or another grant of power; the Bill of Rights is meant to constrain the federal government even when it's acting within its Article I power grants.

"When the Constitution was adopted, many people strongly opposed it because the document contained no Bill of Rights to safeguard certain basic freedoms.... The amendments were offered to *curtail* and *restrict* the general powers granted ... two years before in the original Constitution. The Bill of Rights changed the original Constitution into a new charter under which no branch of government could abridge the people's freedoms of press, speech, religion, and assembly. Yet the Solicitor General argues ... that the general powers of the Government adopted in the original Constitution should be interpreted to limit and restrict the specific and emphatic guarantees of the Bill of Rights adopted later. I can imagine no greater perversion of history." *New York Times Co. v. United States* (Black, J., concurring).

4. Response to 1: The Constitution embodies so many values that the constitutional tension method, if accepted, would justify restricting a huge variety of speech: speech that in some measure works against democracy, equality, private property, federalism, separation of powers, or what have

you. Such a result would be undesirable, because _____, and the constitutional tension method should therefore be rejected.

5.   Still More Evolution: Communist Conspiracy

> Sam Goldwyn said, "How'm I gonna do decent pictures when all my good writers are in jail?" Then he added, the infallible Goldwyn, "Don't misunderstand me, they all ought to be hung."
> —Dorothy Parker, Interview, in *Writers at Work*

a.   *Problem: Extremist Muslim Conspiracy*

The U.S. has been fortunate in having little terrorism conducted by domestic Muslim extremists. The 9/11 attacks were conducted by terrorists from overseas (unlike the 7/7/2005 attacks in London, in which several English nationals were involved).

Imagine that a new movement aims to change that. The movement's leaders try to teach American Muslims that they have a religious duty to wage holy war against the United States. The holy war is to include suicide bombings aimed both at civilian and military targets, sabotage of power plants and other infrastructure, and especially the murder of nonextremist Muslims who cooperate with the civilian authorities. The goal of the holy war is to pressure the U.S. government into (1) withdrawing all support for Israel and for Arab governments that oppose extremist Islam, (2) withdrawing American soldiers from all majority-Muslim countries (even when the soldiers are there at the invitation of the government), (3) ending the war against ISIS, al Qaeda, and the Taliban, and not interfering with those movements' attempt to create states or rule existing states, (4) ending attempts to prevent the development of nuclear weapons by extremist Muslim regimes (such as Iran's or a Taliban-run Afghanistan's), and (5) punishing blasphemy against Islam (such as the publication of cartoons of Mohammed, or of blasphemous books such as the *Satanic Verses*).

The movement's leaders are careful not to participate in any planning conducted by people who are actually trying to commit sabotage and murder (since such participation would make the leaders punishable for conspiracy to commit sabotage and murder). Rather, they aim only to persuade others to engage in such acts.

The great majority of American Muslims oppose the movement. But the movement believes that if they can persuade even 5% of the Muslim population—including by persuading moderate Muslims that it's too dangerous to speak out against the movement—that could be enough to accomplish the movement's goals. (A Pew Forum on Religion & Public Life study estimates the Muslim population of the U.S. at about 1.8 million people, see http://religions.pewforum.org/affiliations.)

In response to this, the Congress revises subsection 3 the Smith Act to make it a crime "to organize or help to organize any society, group, or assembly of persons who teach, advocate, or encourage the overthrow or destruction of any government in the United States by force or violence, *or who teach, advocate, or encourage attempts to change the policy of the government of the United States by sabotage or killing*; or to be or become a member of, or affiliate with, any such society, group, or assembly of persons, knowing the purposes thereof" (amendment marked in italics). Would it be constitutional to prosecute the movement's leaders under this revised statute? Should it be?

b. *Dennis v. United States, 341 U.S. 494 (1951)*

Chief Justice Vinson announced ... an opinion in which Justice Reed, Justice Burton and Justice Minton join....

[Under the Smith Act, it is] "unlawful for any person[]"

(1) to knowingly or willfully advocate ... or teach the duty, necessity, desirability, or propriety of overthrowing ... any government in the United States by force or violence, or by the assassination of any officer of any such government; ...

[(2)] to organize or help to organize any ... group ... of persons who teach [or] advocate ... the overthrow ... of any government in the United States by force or violence;

[(3)] to be or become a member of, or affiliate with, any such ... group, ... knowing the purposes thereof....

[(4)] to attempt {or conspire} to commit ... any of the [above acts].

[T]he petitioners [were convicted of] wilfully and knowingly conspiring (1) to organize as the Communist Party ... a ... group ... of persons who teach and advocate the overthrow ... of the Government of the United States by force and violence, and (2) knowingly and wilfully to advocate and teach the duty and necessity of overthrowing ... the Government of the United States by force and violence....

[T]he Court of Appeals held that the record supports the following broad conclusions: ... [(1)] that the Communist Party is a highly disciplined organization, adept at infiltration into strategic positions, use of aliases, and double-meaning language; [(2)] that the Party is rigidly controlled; [(3)] that Communists, unlike other political parties, tolerate no dissension from the policy laid down by the guiding forces, but that the approved program is slavishly followed by the members of the Party; [(4)] that ... the general goal of the Party was, during the period in question, to achieve a successful overthrow of the existing order by force and violence....

The obvious purpose of the statute is to protect existing Government, not from change by peaceable, lawful and constitutional means, but from change by violence, revolution and terrorism.... Whatever theoretical merit there may be to the argument that there is a "right" to rebellion against dictatorial governments is without force where the existing structure of the government provides for peaceful and orderly change. We reject any principle of governmental helplessness in the face of preparation for revolution, which principle, carried to its logical conclusion, must lead to anarchy....

[Petitioners argue that the statute] prohibits academic discussion of the merits of Marxism-Leninism[and] that it stifles ideas .... [But the Smith

Act] is directed at advocacy, not discussion.

Thus, the trial judge properly charged the jury that they could not convict if they found that petitioners did "no more than pursue peaceful studies and discussions or teaching and advocacy in the realm of ideas." He further charged that it was not unlawful "to conduct in an American college and university a course explaining the philosophical theories set forth in the books which have been placed in evidence." ... Congress did not intend to eradicate the free discussion of political theories, to destroy the traditional rights of Americans to discuss and evaluate ideas without fear of governmental sanction. Rather Congress was concerned with the very kind of activity in which the evidence showed these petitioners engaged....

[T]he basis of the First Amendment is the hypothesis that speech can rebut speech, propaganda will answer propaganda, free debate on ideas will result in the wisest governmental policies.... [But] this is not an unlimited, unqualified right[;] ... the societal value of speech must, on occasion, be subordinated to other values and considerations....

Obviously, the words ["clear and present danger"] cannot mean that before the Government may act, it must wait until the *putsch* is about to be executed, the plans have been laid and the signal is awaited. If Government is aware that a group aiming at its overthrow is attempting to indoctrinate its members and to commit them to a course whereby they will strike when the leaders feel the circumstances permit, action by the Government is required....

[Even if the] Government is strong ... [and] may defeat the revolution with ease ...[,] an attempt to overthrow the Government by force, even though doomed from the outset because of inadequate numbers or power of the revolutionists, is a sufficient evil for Congress to prevent. The damage which such attempts create both physically and politically to a nation makes it impossible to measure the validity in terms of the probability of success, or the immediacy of a successful attempt.

In the instant case the trial judge charged the jury that they could not convict unless they found that petitioners intended to overthrow the Government "as speedily as circumstances would permit." This does not mean, and could not properly mean, that they would not strike until there was certainty of success. What was meant was that the revolutionists would strike when they thought the time was ripe. We must therefore reject the contention that success or probability of success is the criterion.

The situation with which Justices Holmes and Brandeis were concerned in *Gitlow v. New York* was a comparatively isolated event, bearing little relation in their minds to any substantial threat to the safety of the community.... They were not confronted with any situation comparable to the instant one—the development of an apparatus designed and dedicated to the overthrow of the Government, in the context of world crisis after crisis....

[We adopt this interpretation of the phrase "clear and present danger"]: "In each case (courts) must ask whether the gravity of the 'evil,' discounted by its improbability, justifies such invasion of free speech as is necessary to avoid the danger." ... [I]t is as succinct and inclusive as any other we might devise at this time. It takes into consideration those factors which we deem relevant, and relates their significances. More we cannot expect from words....

[We also affirm] the trial court's finding that the requisite danger existed. The mere fact that from the period 1945 to 1948 petitioners' activities did not result in an attempt to overthrow the Government by force and violence is of course no answer to the fact that there was a group that was ready to make the attempt. The formation by petitioners of such a highly organized conspiracy, with rigidly disciplined members subject to call when the leaders[—]these petitioners[—]felt that the time had come for action, coupled with the inflammable nature of world conditions, similar uprisings in other countries, and the touch-and-go nature of our relations with countries with whom petitioners were in the very least ideologically attuned, convince us that their convictions were justified on this score....

Justice Frankfurter, concurring in ... the judgment....

[A.] [The] conflict of interests [in this case] cannot be resolved by a dogmatic preference for one or the other, nor by a sonorous formula which is in fact only a euphemistic disguise for an unresolved conflict.... [W]e cannot escape a candid examination of the conflicting claims with full recognition that both are supported by weighty title-deeds....

The right of a government to maintain its existence—self-preservation—is the most pervasive aspect of sovereignty.... The most tragic experience in our history is a poignant reminder that the Nation's continued existence may be threatened from within. To protect itself from such threats, the Federal Government "is invested with all those inherent and implied powers which, at the time of adopting the Constitution, were generally considered to belong to every government ... as being essential to the exercise of its functions." ...

Just as there are those who regard as invulnerable every measure for which the claim of national survival is invoked, there are those who find in the Constitution a wholly unfettered right of expression. Such literalness treats the words of the Constitution as though they were found on a piece of outworn parchment instead of being words that have called into being a nation with a past to be preserved for the future....

The historic antecedents of the First Amendment preclude the notion that its purpose was to give unqualified immunity to every expression that touched on matters within the range of political interest. The Massachusetts Constitution of 1780 guaranteed free speech; yet there are records of at least three convictions for political libels obtained between 1799 and 1803. The Pennsylvania Constitution of 1790 and the Delaware Constitution of 1792 expressly imposed liability for abuse of the right of free speech. Madison's own State put on its books in 1792 a statute confining the abusive exercise of the right of utterance....

Jefferson did not rest his condemnation of the Sedition Act of 1798 on his belief in unrestrained utterance as to political matter. The First Amendment, he argued, reflected a limitation upon Federal power, leaving the right to enforce restrictions on speech to the States....

Free speech is subject to prohibition of those abuses of expression which a civilized society may forbid.... Absolute rules would inevitably lead to absolute exceptions, and such exceptions would eventually corrode the rules. The demands of free speech in a democratic society as well as the interest in national security are better served by candid and informed weighing of the competing interests, within the confines of the judicial process, than by announcing dogmas too inflexible for the non-Euclidean problems to be solved.

[B.] But how are competing interests to be assessed? Since they are not subject to quantitative ascertainment, the issue necessarily resolves itself into asking, who is to make the adjustment?—who is to balance the relevant factors and ascertain which interest is in the circumstances to prevail?

Full responsibility for the choice cannot be given to the courts. Courts ... are not designed to be a good reflex of a democratic society. Their judgment is best informed, and therefore most dependable, within narrow limits. Their essential quality is detachment, founded on independence.

History teaches that the independence of the judiciary is jeopardized when courts become embroiled in the passions of the day and assume primary responsibility in choosing between competing political, economic and social pressures. Primary responsibility for adjusting the interests which compete in the situation before us of necessity belongs to the Congress....

[C.] Bearing in mind that Justice Holmes regarded questions under the First Amendment as questions of "proximity and degree," *Schenck v. United States*, it would be a distortion, indeed a mockery, of his reasoning to compare the "puny anonymities" to which he was addressing himself in the *Abrams* case in 1919 or the publication that was "futile and too remote from possible consequences" in the *Gitlow* case in 1925 with the setting of events in this case in 1950....

The phrase "clear and present danger," in its origin, "served to indicate the importance of freedom of speech to a free society but also to emphasize that its exercise must be compatible with the preservation of other freedoms essential to a democracy and guaranteed by our Constitution." It were far better that the phrase be abandoned than that it be sounded once more to hide from the believers in an absolute right of free speech the plain fact that the interest in speech, profoundly important as it is, is no more conclusive in judicial review than other attributes of democracy or than a determination of the people's representatives that a measure is necessary to assure the safety of government itself....

Not every type of speech occupies the same position on the scale of values. There is no substantial public interest in permitting certain kinds of utterances: "the lewd and obscene, the profane, the libelous, and the insulting or 'fighting' words—those which by their very utterance inflict injury or tend to incite an immediate breach of the peace." *Chaplinsky v. New Hampshire*.... The defendants have been convicted of conspiring to organize a party of persons who advocate the overthrow of the Government by force and violence ... "by language reasonably and ordinarily calculated to incite persons to such action," and with the intent to cause the overthrow "as speedily as circumstances would permit." On any scale of values which we have hitherto recognized, speech of this sort ranks low....

[T]here is underlying validity in the distinction between advocacy and the interchange of ideas, and we do not discard a useful tool because it may be misused. That such a distinction could be used unreasonably by those in power against hostile or unorthodox views does not negate the fact that it may be used reasonably against an organization wielding the power of the centrally controlled international Communist movement.

The object of the conspiracy before us is so clear that the chance of error in saying that the defendants conspired to advocate rather than to express ideas is slight. Justice Douglas quite properly points out that the conspiracy before us is not a conspiracy to overthrow the Government. But it would be equally wrong to treat it as a seminar in political theory....

In 1947, it has been reliably reported, at least 60,000 members were enrolled in the Party. Evidence was introduced in this case that the membership was organized in small units, linked by an intricate chain of command, and protected by elaborate precautions designed to prevent disclosure of individual identity. There are no reliable data tracing acts of sabotage or espionage directly to these defendants. But a Canadian Royal Commission appointed in 1946 to investigate espionage reported that it was "overwhelmingly established" that "the Communist movement was the principal base within which the espionage network was recruited."

The most notorious spy in recent history [Klaus Fuchs—ed.] was led into the service of the Soviet Union through Communist indoctrination. Evidence supports the conclusion that members of the Party seek and occupy positions of importance in political and labor organizations. Congress was not barred by the Constitution from believing that indifference to such experience would be an exercise not of freedom but of irresponsibility.

[D.] On the other hand is the interest in free speech. The right to exert all governmental powers in aid of maintaining our institutions and resisting their physical overthrow does not include intolerance of opinions and speech that cannot do harm although opposed and perhaps alien to dominant, traditional opinion.... It is better for those who have almost unlimited power of government in their hands to err on the side of freedom. We have enjoyed so much freedom for so long that we are perhaps in danger of forgetting how much blood it cost to establish the Bill of Rights....

[S]peech is seldom restricted to a single purpose, and its effects may be manifold.... [C]oupled with [Communist] advocacy is criticism of defects in our society. Criticism is the spur to reform; and ... a healthy society must reform in order to conserve .... [T]here may be a grain of truth in the most uncouth doctrine, however false and repellent the balance may be.

Suppressing advocates of overthrow inevitably will also silence critics who do not advocate overthrow but fear that their criticism may be so construed. No matter how clear we may be that the defendants now before us are preparing to overthrow our Government at the propitious moment, it is self-delusion to think that we can punish them for their advocacy without adding to the risks run by loyal citizens who honestly believe in some of the reforms these defendants advance.... [T]ruth [cannot] be pursued in an atmosphere hostile to the endeavor or under dangers which are hazarded only by heroes....

[E.] It is not for us to decide how we would adjust the clash of interests which this case presents were the primary responsibility for reconciling it ours. Congress has determined that the danger created by advocacy of overthrow justifies the ensuing restriction on freedom of speech. The determination was made after due deliberation, and the seriousness of the congressional purpose is attested by the volume of legislation passed to effectuate the same ends....

We do not expect courts to pronounce historic verdicts on bygone events. Even historians have conflicting views to this day on the origins and conduct of the French Revolution .... It is as absurd to be confident that we can measure the present clash of forces and their outcome as to ask us to read history still enveloped in clouds of controversy....

Justice Jackson, concurring in affirmance of the judgment....

[A.] The Communist Party ... seeks members that are, or may be, secreted in strategic posts in transportation, communications, industry, government, and especially in labor unions where it can compel employers to accept and retain its members. It also seeks to infiltrate and control organizations of professional and other groups. Through these placements in positions of power it seeks a leverage over society that will make up in power of coercion what it lacks in power of persuasion....

The United States, fortunately, has experienced Communism only in its preparatory stages and for its pattern of final action must look abroad.... But Communist technique in the overturn of a free government was disclosed by the *coup d'etat* in which they seized power in Czechoslovakia [in 1948—ed.]. There the Communist Party during its preparatory stage claimed and received protection for its freedoms of speech, press, and assembly. Pretending to be but another political party, it eventually was conceded participation in government, where it entrenched reliable members chiefly in control of police and information services.

When the government faced a foreign and domestic crisis, the Communist Party had established a leverage strong enough to threaten civil war.... Communist officers of the unions took over transportation and allowed only persons with party permits to travel. Communist printers took over the newspapers and radio and put out only party-approved versions of events.

Possession was taken of telegraph and telephone systems and communications were cut off wherever directed by party heads. Communist unions took over the factories, and in the cities a partisan distribution of food was managed by the Communist organization. A virtually bloodless abdication by the elected government admitted the Communists to power, whereupon they instituted a reign of oppression and terror, and ruthlessly denied to all others the freedoms which had sheltered their conspiracy.

[B.] [Thus], either by accident or design, the Communist stratagem outwits the anti-anarchist pattern of statute aimed against "overthrow by force and violence" if qualified by the doctrine that only "clear and present danger" of accomplishing that result will sustain the prosecution.

The "clear and present danger" test ... [arose] before the era of World War II revealed the subtlety and efficacy of modernized revolutionary techniques used by totalitarian parties.... I would save [the test], unmodified, for application as a "rule of reason" in the kind of case for which it was devised. When the issue is criminality of a hot-headed speech on a street corner, or circulation of a few incendiary pamphlets, ... it is not beyond the capacity of the judicial process to gather, comprehend, and weigh the necessary materials for decision whether it is a clear and present danger of substantive evil or a harmless letting off of steam.... [T]he danger in such cases has matured by the time of trial or it was never present....

The formula in such cases favors freedoms that are vital to our society, and, even if sometimes applied too generously, the consequences cannot be grave. But its recent expansion has extended, in particular to Communists, unprecedented immunities. Unless we are to hold our Government captive in a judge-made verbal trap, we must approach the problem of a well-organized, nation-wide conspiracy ... as realistically as our predecessors faced the trivialities that were being prosecuted until they were checked with a rule of reason....

If we must decide that this Act and its application are constitutional only if we are convinced that petitioner's conduct creates a "clear and present danger" of violent overthrow, we must appraise imponderables, including international and national phenomena which baffle the best informed foreign offices and our most experienced politicians. We would have to foresee and predict the effectiveness of Communist propaganda, opportunities for infiltration, whether, and when, a time will come that they consider propitious for action, and whether and how fast our existing government will deteriorate. And we would have to speculate as to whether an approaching Communist coup would not be anticipated by a nationalistic fascist movement.

No doctrine can be sound whose application requires us to make a prophecy of that sort in the guise of a legal decision. The judicial process simply is not adequate to a trial of such far-flung issues. The answers given would reflect our own political predilections and nothing more.

The authors of the clear and present danger test never applied it to a case like this, nor would I. If applied as it is proposed here, it means that the Communist plotting is protected during its period of incubation; its preliminary stages of organization and preparation are immune from the law;

the Government can move only after imminent action is manifest, when it would, of course, be too late....

[I]t is not forbidden to put down force or violence, it is not forbidden to punish its teaching or advocacy, and the end being punishable, there is no doubt of the power to punish conspiracy for the purpose....

Justice Black, dissenting....

These petitioners were not charged with an attempt to overthrow the Government.... The charge was that they agreed to assemble and to talk and publish certain ideas at a later date ....

Undoubtedly, a governmental policy of unfettered communication of ideas does entail dangers. To the Founders of this Nation, however, the benefits derived from free expression were worth the risk....

I cannot agree that the First Amendment permits us to sustain laws suppressing freedom of speech and press on the basis of Congress' or our own notions of mere "reasonableness." Such a doctrine waters down the First Amendment so that it amounts to little more than an admonition to Congress. The Amendment as so construed is not likely to protect any but those "safe" or orthodox views which rarely need its protection....

Justice Douglas, dissenting.

[A.] If this were a case where those who claimed protection under the First Amendment were teaching the techniques of sabotage, the assassination of the President, the filching of documents from public files, the planting of bombs, the art of street warfare, and the like, I would have no doubts. The freedom to speak is not absolute; the teaching of methods of terror and other seditious conduct should be beyond the pale along with obscenity and immorality....

There comes a time when even speech loses its constitutional immunity. Speech innocuous one year may at another time fan such destructive flames that it must be halted in the interests of the safety of the Republic. That is the meaning of the clear and present danger test. When conditions are so critical that there will be no time to avoid the evil that the speech threatens, it is time to call a halt. Otherwise, free speech which is the strength of the Nation will be the cause of its destruction.

[B.] Yet free speech is the rule, not the exception. The restraint to be constitutional must be based on more than fear, on more than passionate opposition against the speech, on more than a revolted dislike for its contents. There must be some immediate injury to society that is likely if speech is allowed ... {Free speech—the glory of our system of government—should not be sacrificed on anything less than plain and objective proof of danger that the evil advocated is imminent.

On this record no one can say that petitioners and their converts are in such a strategic position as to have even the slightest chance of achieving their aims....} *[A]s a political party* [the Communists] are of little consequence. Communists in this country have never made a respectable or serious showing in any election.... Communism in the world scene is no bogey-man; but Communism as a political faction or party in this country plainly is.

Communism has been so thoroughly exposed in this country that it has been crippled as a political force. Free speech has destroyed it as an effective political party.... In days of trouble and confusion, when bread lines were long, when the unemployed walked the streets, when people were starving, the advocates of a short-cut by revolution might have a chance to gain adherents. But today ... [t]he country is not in despair; the people know Soviet Communism; the doctrine of Soviet revolution is exposed in all of its ugliness and the American people want none of it....

The political impotence of the Communists in this country does not, of course, dispose of the problem. Their numbers; their positions in industry and government; the extent to which they have in fact infiltrated the police, the armed services, transportation, stevedoring, power plants, munitions works, and other critical places—these facts all bear on the likelihood that their advocacy of the Soviet theory of revolution will endanger the Republic. But the record is silent on these facts.

If we are to proceed on the basis of judicial notice, it is impossible for me to say that the Communists in this country are so potent or so strategically deployed that they must be suppressed for their speech. I could not so hold unless I were willing to conclude that the activities in recent years of committees of Congress, of the Attorney General, of labor unions, of state legislatures, and of Loyalty Boards were so futile as to leave the country on the edge of grave peril. To believe that petitioners and their following are placed in such critical positions as to endanger the Nation is to believe the incredible.

It is safe to say that the followers of the creed of Soviet Communism are known to the F.B.I.; that in case of war with Russia they will be picked up overnight as were all prospective saboteurs at the commencement of World War II; that the invisible army of petitioners is the best known, the most beset, and the least thriving of any fifth column in history. Only those held by fear and panic could think otherwise....

The First Amendment makes confidence in the common sense of our people and in their maturity of judgment the great postulate of our democracy. Its philosophy is that violence is rarely, if ever, stopped by denying civil liberties to those advocating resort to force. The First Amendment reflects the philosophy of Jefferson "that it is time enough for the rightful purposes of civil government, for its officers to interfere when principles break out into overt acts against peace and good order." ...

c.   *Yates v. United States, 354 U.S. 298 (1957)*

Justice Harlan delivered the opinion of the Court....

These 14 petitioners stand convicted ... [of] conspiring (1) to advocate and teach the duty and necessity of overthrowing the Government of the United States by force and violence, and (2) to organize, as the Communist

Party of the United States, a society of persons who so advocate and teach, all with the intent of causing the overthrow of the Government by force and violence as speedily as circumstances would permit....

The indictment charged that in carrying out the conspiracy the defendants and their co-conspirators would (a) become members and officers of the Communist Party, with knowledge of its unlawful purposes, and assume leadership in carrying out its policies and activities; (b) cause to be organized units of the Party ...; (c) write and publish, in the "Daily Worker" and other Party organs, articles on the proscribed advocacy and teaching; (d) conduct schools for the indoctrination of Party members in such advocacy and teaching, and (e) recruit new Party members, particularly from among persons employed in the key industries of the nation.... Upon conviction each of the petitioners was sentenced to five years' imprisonment and a fine of $10,000....

We ... [hold, based on the Smith Act's legislative history, that the Act does not] prohibit[] advocacy and teaching of forcible overthrow as an abstract principle, divorced from any effort to instigate action to that end, so long as such advocacy or teaching is engaged in with evil intent.... We need not ... [decide this] in terms of constitutional compulsion, for our first duty is to construe this statute....

[I]ndoctrination of a group in preparation for future violent action, as well as exhortation to immediate action, by advocacy found to be directed to "action for the accomplishment" of forcible overthrow, to violence as "a rule or principle of action," and employing "language of incitement" is not constitutionally protected when the group is of sufficient size and cohesiveness, is sufficiently oriented towards action, and other circumstances are such as reasonably to justify apprehension that action will occur. [*Dennis.*] ... [But] mere doctrinal justification of forcible overthrow, ... even though uttered with the hope that it may ultimately lead to violent revolution, is too remote from concrete action to be regarded as the kind of indoctrination preparatory to action which was condemned in *Dennis*....

The essential distinction is that those to whom the advocacy is addressed must be urged to *do* something, now or in the future, rather than merely to *believe* in something.... We recognize that distinctions between advocacy or teaching of abstract doctrines, with evil intent, and that which is directed to stirring people to action, are often subtle and difficult to grasp, for in a broad sense, ... "Every idea is an incitement." But the very subtlety of these distinctions required the most clear and explicit instructions with reference to them, for they concerned an issue which went to the very heart of the charges against these petitioners.

The need for precise and understandable instructions on this issue is further emphasized by the equivocal character of the evidence in this record .... Instances of speech that could be considered to amount to "advocacy of action" are so few and far between as to be almost completely overshadowed by the hundreds of instances in the record in which overthrow, if mentioned at all, occurs in the course of doctrinal disputation so remote from action as to be almost wholly lacking in probative value. Vague references to "revolutionary" or "militant" action of an unspecified character, which are found in the evidence, might in addition be given too great weight by the jury in the absence of more precise instructions.... As to [some] petitioners ... we find no adequate evidence in the record which would permit a jury to find that they were members of ... a conspiracy [to advocate concrete action]....

There was testimony ... tying [other petitioners] to Party classes conducted in the San Francisco area during the year 1946, where there occurred what might be considered to be the systematic teaching and advocacy of illegal action which is condemned by the statute. It might be found that one of the purposes of such classes was to develop in the members of the group a readiness to engage at the crucial time, perhaps during war or during attack upon the United States from without, in such activities as sabotage and street fighting, in order to divert and diffuse the resistance of the authorities and if possible to seize local vantage points.

There was also testimony as to activities in the Los Angeles area, during the period covered by the indictment, which might be considered to amount to "advocacy of action," and with which [two petitioners] were linked. From the testimony of the witness Scarletto, it might be found that individuals considered to be particularly trustworthy were taken into an "underground" apparatus and there instructed in tasks which would be useful when the time for violent action arrived. Scarletto was surreptitiously indoctrinated in methods, as he said, of moving "masses of people in time of crisis." It might be found, under all the circumstances, that the purpose of this teaching was to prepare the members of the underground apparatus to engage in, to facilitate, and to cooperate with violent action directed against government when the time was ripe....

Justice Black, with whom Justice Douglas joins, concurring in part and dissenting in part. [Omitted.—ed.]

Justice Clark, dissenting. [Omitted.—ed.]

d. *Barenblatt v. United States, 360 U.S. 109 (1959) (Black, J., dissenting)*

[*Barenblatt* dealt chiefly with forced disclosure of expressive associations, rather than outright prohibition; but this excerpt from Justice Black's dissent, which was joined by Justice Douglas and Chief Justice Warren, is relevant to the debate in *Dennis.*—ed.]

[W]e cannot outlaw [the Communist Party], as a group, without endangering the liberty of all of us.... [M]ixed among those aims of communism which are illegal are perfectly normal political and social goals. And muddled with its revolutionary tenets is a drive to achieve power through the ballot, if it can be done.... To attribute to [all Communists], and to those who have left the Party, the taint of the group is to ignore both our traditions that guilt like belief is "personal and not a matter of mere association" and the obvious fact that "men adhering to a political party or other organization notoriously do not subscribe unqualifiedly to all of its platforms or asserted principles." ...

[O]nce we allow any group which has some political aims or ideas to be driven from the ballot and from the battle for men's minds because some of its members are bad and some of its tenets are illegal, no group is safe. Today we deal with Communists or suspected Communists. In 1920, instead, the New York Assembly suspended duly elected legislators on the ground that, being Socialists, they were disloyal to the country's principles. In the 1830's the Masons were hunted as outlaws and subversives, and abolitionists were considered revolutionaries of the most dangerous kind in both North and South. Earlier still, at the time of the universally unlamented alien and sedition laws, Thomas Jefferson's party was attacked [as subversive] ....

History should teach us then, that in times of high emotional excitement minority parties and groups which advocate extremely unpopular social or governmental innovations will always be typed as criminal gangs and attempts will always be made to drive them out. It was knowledge of this ... that caused the Founders of our land to enact the First Amendment as a guarantee that neither Congress nor the people would do anything to hinder or destroy the capacity of individuals and groups to seek converts and votes for any cause, however radical or unpalatable their principles might seem under the accepted notions of the time....

It is, sadly, no answer to say that this Court will not allow the trend to overwhelm us; that today's holding will be strictly confined to "Communists," as the Court's language implies. This decision can no more be contained than could the holding in *American Communications Ass'n v. Douds,* 339 U.S. 382 (1950)[, sustaining] ... an Act which required labor union officials to take an oath that they were not members of the Communist Party. The Court ... went to great lengths to explain that the Act held valid "touches only a relative handful of persons, leaving the great majority of persons of the identified affiliations and beliefs completely free from restraint." "[W]hile this Court sits," the Court proclaimed, no wholesale proscription of Communists or their Party can occur.

I dissented and said: "Under such circumstances, restrictions imposed on proscribed groups are seldom static .... [The Court's] reasoning would apply just as forcibly to statutes barring Communists and their respective sympathizers from election to political office, mere membership in unions, and in fact from getting or holding any job ...."

My prediction was all too accurate. Today, Communists or suspected Communists have been denied an opportunity to work as government employees, lawyers, doctors, teachers, pharmacists, veterinarians, subway conductors, industrial workers and in just about any other job. In today's holding they are singled out and, as a class, are subjected to inquisitions which the Court suggests would be unconstitutional but for the fact of "Communism." Nevertheless, this Court still sits!

{The record in this very case indicates how easily such restrictions spread. During the testimony of one witness an organization known as the Americans for Democratic Action was mentioned. Despite testimony that this organization did not admit Communists, one member of the Committee insisted that it was a Communist front because "it followed a party line, almost identical in many particulars with the Communist Party line." Presumably if this accusation were repeated frequently and loudly enough that organization, or any other, would also be called a "criminal gang."} ...

6.   A Note About Expressive Association

The Court has long recognized that the right to freedom of speech includes the right to expressive association. *See, e.g., Whitney v. California* (p. 27). To speak effectively, people generally need to organize into groups—political parties, advocacy groups (such as the ACLU, the NAACP, or the NRA), and the like—and therefore laws banning or restricting expressive association may unconstitutionally burden free speech. As *Dennis* illustrates, the Court has been willing to allow some constraints on expressive association, but it has always treated expressive association as a constitutionally protected aspect of freedom of speech.

Part V.B.a (p. 388) will discuss the scope of this right in more detail. But for now, just treat the right to associate for expressive purposes as an aspect of the free speech guarantee.

B.   False Statements of Fact

1.   Summary

a.   *Basic Theoretical Principles*

1.   "There is no constitutional value in false statements of fact." *Gertz v. Robert Welch* (1974) (p. 75).

2.   "Although the erroneous statement of fact is not worthy of constitutional protection, it is nevertheless inevitable in free debate. Punishment of error runs the risk of [making speakers unduly cautious, and reluctant to make even accurate allegations]. The First Amendment requires that we protect some falsehood in order to protect speech that matters." *Id.*

3.   "Under the First Amendment there is no such thing as a false idea." *Id.*

4.   The key question is just how much falsehood will be protected in order to protect "speech that matters"—and thus how much of the speech that matters can be put at risk in order to punish falsehood.

b.   *What False Statements Are Substantively Restrictable*

1.   False statements of fact can often lead to civil liability or even criminal punishment if they are said *with a sufficiently culpable mental state.*

2.   In particular, many categories of *knowingly false statements of fact (deliberate lies) or recklessly false statements of fact can almost always be punished.* (For more on what "recklessly" means here, see below.) This explains the constitutionality of:

— Libel law and slander law.

— The false light tort, which compensates people for the emotional injury of having false statements said about them that "would be highly offensive to a reasonable person," even when the statements don't damage the subject's reputation. *Time, Inc. v. Hill*, 385 U.S. 374 (1967).

— (Probably) trade libel law, which imposes liability for (at least) lies about other people's products. Cf. *Bose Corp. v. Consumers Union*, 466 U.S. 485 (1984) (assuming this, without deciding it).

— Statutes banning fraud, including fraudulent solicitation of charitable donations (though nonfraudulent solicitation of charitable donations is generally treated as fully protected speech). *Illinois ex rel. Madigan v. Telemarketing Associates, Inc.*, 538 U.S. 600 (2003).

— Criminal punishment of perjury and out-of-court lies to government officials (see, *e.g.*, 18 U.S.C. § 1001). See, *e.g.*, *Clipper Exxpress v. Rocky Mountain Motor Tariff Bureau, Inc.*, 690 F.2d 1240 (9th Cir. 1982).

— Likely, criminal punishment of false inducement of fear, as in the classic "falsely shouting fire in a theatre and causing a panic," *Schenck v. United States* (p. 14); *see also People v. Hanifin*, 2010 WL 4237709 (N.Y. App. Div.) (upholding prosecution of defendant for calling 911 and falsely reporting that he was going to set himself on fire).

3. Under some circumstances, *negligently false statements of fact may* also *lead to liability*, see *Gertz*. It's also possible that, where the speech is on matters of "private concern," speakers can be held *strictly liable* even for reasonable, nonnegligent mistakes, see *Dun & Bradstreet v. Greenmoss Builders* (1985) (p. 85).

4. Some false statements, however, *are not punishable even if they're deliberate lies*.

— The *United States v. Alvarez* (p. 103) plurality concluded that, while there are First Amendment exceptions for defamation, fraud, perjury, and likely false light invasion of privacy and impersonation of a government official, other knowing falsehoods are presumptively protected by the First Amendment, though they might still be restricted by laws that pass strict scrutiny (see Part III).

— The *Alvarez* concurrence concluded that speech outside these exceptions is likewise presumptively protected, but only under intermediate scrutiny (compare the lower protection offered to commercial advertising, see Part II.H) rather than strict scrutiny. It seems likely that the concurrence will be viewed as the controlling opinion on this score.

— *New York Times v. Sullivan* (p. 69) and *Rosenblatt v. Baer,* 383 U.S. 75 (1966), hold that the law can't punish even deliberate lies about *the government* (the traditional definition of "seditious libel"), so long as no particular person is defamed. Both the *Alvarez* plurality and the *Alvarez* concurrence are consistent with this holding.

— Both the *Alvarez* concurrence and the *Alvarez* dissent made clear that false statements about "philosophy, religion, history, the social sciences, the arts, and the like" are fully protected, and the logic of the *Alvarez* plurality seems consistent with that. Query to what extent this also extends to false statements about current events. See, *e.g.*, *Schaefer v. United States*, 251 U.S. 466, 494 (1920) (Brandeis, J., dissenting) (arguing that convictions for "willfully ... [publishing] false reports" during World War I "subject[] to new perils the constitutional liberty of the press," "will doubtless discourage criticism of the policies of the government," and thus should be set aside as unconstitutional).

5. Liability may be premised *only on statements of fact*, though statements that in context have a "provably false factual connotation"—implicit statements of fact—also count. *Gertz*; *Milkovich v. Lorain Journal*, 497 U.S. 1 (1990).

— For instance, "Joe deserves to die" may seem like a statement of opinion, but if it is said while describing a first-degree murder in which Joe is a suspect, it may imply a statement of fact—that Joe is the murderer. *Milkovich.*

— Conversely, saying that a real estate developer's negotiating position is "blackmail" might sound like a statement of fact—the developer is guilty of the crime of blackmail—but if in context it appears to just be a statement of opinion (the developer is behaving unreasonably and immorally), then it's not actionable. *Greenbelt Cooperative Publishing Ass'n v. Bresler*, 398 U.S. 6, 14 (1970).

c. *Mental State Required for False Statements to Be Unprotected*

Ask whether the statement is

(1) about a public figure/official and on a matter of public concern;

(2) about a private figure but on a matter of public concern; or

(3) on a matter of private concern.

1. False statements on matters of public concern that defame public figures/public officials are unprotected if

a. the speaker knows the statements to be false *or*

b. the speaker is reckless about their falsehood, *i.e.*, he is conscious of a high probability that the statements are false but publishes them nonetheless. *New York Times v. Sullivan.*

— This is often known as the "actual malice" test, but don't be fooled by the name—it has nothing to do with whether the speaker is acting maliciously. Think of it more as a "recklessness or worse" test, with "recklessness" (described in item (ii) above) meaning pretty much what it means in the Model Penal Code.

2. False statements on matters of public concern that defame private figures are unprotected if they are made negligently. *Gertz.*

3. False statements on matters of private concern—whether about public or private figures—might be unprotected even if they are nonnegligent. It's not clear what exactly the rule is here. *Dun & Bradstreet.*

4. Who are public figures or public officials?

a. Government officials are generally included, though perhaps sufficiently low-level government employees are not. The test seems to be whether the "position in government has such apparent importance that the public has an independent interest in the qualifications and performance of the person who holds it, beyond the general public interest in the qualifications and performance of all government employees," and whether "[t]he employee's position [is] one which would invite public scrutiny and discussion of the person holding it, entirely apart from the scrutiny and discussion occasioned by the particular charges in controversy." *Rosenblatt v. Baer,* 383 U.S. 75, 86, 87 n.13 (1966).

b. People who "have assumed an influential role in ordering society" are also public figures. *Gertz.*

— Mere involvement in community and professional affairs is not enough.

c. So are people who have "achieved ... pervasive fame or notoriety."

d. So are people who have "voluntarily inject[ed themselves] or [been] drawn into a particular public controversy."

— Such category (d) people are *limited-purpose public figures,* public figures only as to that controversy. *Id.*

— To fit within this category, the controversy must have been of some substantial public importance (beyond just being "of public concern").

— A high-profile divorce case, for instance, does not qualify. *Time, Inc. v. Firestone,* 424 U.S. 448, 454-55 (1976).

— Neither does a fairly minor, low-profile criminal prosecution. *Wolston v. Reader's Digest Ass'n,* 443 U.S. 157, 168-69 (1979).

5. What is "of public concern"?

a. The three-Justice lead opinion in *Dun & Bradstreet* provides some information, but not a lot.

— Speech "solely in the individual interest of the speaker and its specific business audience" distributed by a credit reporting service to a small audience ("five subscribers, who, under the terms of the subscription agreement, could not disseminate it further") is not on a matter of public concern, at least when it was "objectively verifiable" and "hardy and unlikely to be deterred by incidental state regulation."

— Allegations that a neighbor is a "whore" don't relate to matters of public concern.

b. "Anything which might touch on an official's fitness for office"—for instance, a claim that someone is a "former small-time bootlegger," even when the alleged misconduct is in the distant past—is of public concern. *Monitor Patriot Co. v. Roy,* 401 U.S. 265 (1971).

c. One might likewise argue that anything relevant to any other question of public importance, whether the question is factual or a value judgment, would be of public concern. Cf. Fed. R. Evid. 401 ("'Relevant evidence' means evidence having any tendency to make the existence of any fact that is of consequence to the determination of the action more probable or less probable than it would be without the evidence.").

d.   *Florida Star v. B.J.F.* (1989) (p. 286) suggests that the reference to a particular person (such as a rape victim) in an article that deals with broad questions (such as crime) is treated as speech on a matter of public concern. "[T]he news article [a brief account of a particular rape] concerned 'a matter of public significance' .... That is, the article generally, as opposed to the specific identity contained within it, involved a matter of paramount public import: the commission, and investigation, of a violent crime which had been reported to authorities." *See also Snyder v. Phelps* (2011) (p. 207).

e.   What is relevant to an issue will sometimes be hotly contested. For instance, is a candidate's homosexuality relevant to his fitness for office? Some readers (and voters) say yes, others say no. May a court decide, as a matter of law, that one set of readers is right and the other is wrong? Is it a question for a jury? Or is the statement treated as being on a matter of public concern so long as at least some people view it as relevant to a public issue, even if the court (or the majority of the public) disagrees?

f.   So it's often not clear whether a statement is on a matter of public concern. Your job is to make the best arguments you can on both sides.

g.   Theoretical difficulty: The Free Speech Clause is often seen as prohibiting the government from deciding what the public *should* be concerned about. How can this be reconciled with courts determining what is a matter of "public concern"? On the other hand, even Justices Black and Douglas—who generally took the most speech-protective positions of anyone on the Court—at times seemed to endorse a public concern/private concern distinction. Cf. Black's opinion in *New York Times*; Goldberg's opinion, joined by Douglas, in *New York Times*.

6.   What is "reckless disregard" of the facts?

a.   Publishing while "in fact entertain[ing] serious doubts as to the truth of the publication," *St. Amant v. Thompson*, 390 U.S. 727, 731 (1968).

b.   "Although failure to investigate will not alone support a finding of actual malice, purposeful avoidance of the truth"—"a deliberate decision not to acquire knowledge of facts that might confirm the probable falsity of [the] charges," *Harte-Hanks Communications, Inc. v. Connaughton*, 491 U.S. 657, 692 (1989)—would constitute actual malice.

d.   *Remedies and Procedures*

1.   *Punitive Damages*:

a.   Available in public concern cases—public figure or not—only if "actual malice" is proved (remember this is a term of art defined above). *Gertz*.

b.   Available in private concern cases even without a showing of "actual malice." *Dun & Bradstreet.*

c.   Same rule for "presumed damages," damages allowed by traditional libel law as a guess at compensatory damages. They are in principle compensatory, but don't require any specific evidence of the amount of tangible economic harm flowing from the defamation.

2.   *Criminal Liability:* Criminal libel penalties seem to be permissible, subject to the limitations imposed on civil suits, see *Garrison v. Louisiana* (1964) (p. 71). They appear to be uncommon in most places, but in some states they happen with some frequency. *See, e.g.,* David Pritchard, *Rethinking Criminal Libel: An Empirical Study,* 14 Comm. L. & Pol'y 303 (2009) (reporting about four criminal libel prosecutions per year in Wisconsin in 2000–2007)

3.   *Burden of Proof:* At least in public concern cases, the plaintiff must prove falsehood. Under the common law, the defendant had to prove truth. *Philadelphia Newspapers v. Hepps,* 475 U.S. 767, 776 (1986).

4.   *Quantum of Proof in Civil Cases:* At least in public figure/public concern cases, knowledge of falsehood or recklessness as to the possibility of falsehood has to be proven by clear and convincing evidence.

Summary of different kinds of false statements:

Said about	Topic	Mens rea required in this situation
Public figure	Public concern	"Actual malice" (*NYT*)
Private figure	Public concern	Compensatory damages: negligence; Other remedies: "actual malice" (*Gertz*)
The government	Public concern	All liability forbidden (*NYT*)
No particular person	Public concern	Sometimes, all liability forbidden (*Alvarez*); otherwise, "actual malice"
Any person	Private concern	Negligence enough (*Dun & Bradstreet*); strict liability might also be possible

e.   *Policy Explanations for the Existence of the Exception*

1.   What are the perceived harms that justify the suppression of false statements of fact?

a.   *Harm to subjects of the falsehood:* In the libel context, falsehoods can cause grave harm to particular people.

b.   *Harm to listeners and to society:* Falsehoods may hinder rather than help the search for truth.

c.   *Harm to quality of public participation in public affairs:* Pervasive scurrilous attacks can drive the victims away from participation in civic affairs, and deter others from getting involved in such affairs.

2.   False statements of fact are also less valuable, because they are less likely to contribute to the search for truth and to effective self-government.

Policy explanations for the limits on the exception:

1. The risk of liability might excessively "chill" even true statements.

2. Civil liability can deter speech, and therefore should be treated much the same as criminal liability for speech. (American courts have taken this view throughout American history, dating back at least to 1802. See Eugene Volokh, *Tort Liability and the Original Meaning of the Freedom of Speech, Press, and Petition*, 96 Iowa L. Rev. 249 (2010).)

Policy arguments inferable from this:

1. Some speech—such as false statements of fact—is widely agreed to be of low constitutional value, and therefore sometimes punishable.

2. Procedural requirements can be very important.

2. PUBLIC OFFICIALS/PUBLIC CONCERN

a. Problem: Governor v. Professor

Erik Jaffe hears on a radio talk show that the (male) Governor of his state has recently had sex with a 16-year-old girl, and he mentions this in one of the problems for a First Amendment Law class that he's teaching at the state university law school. He admits to a friend of his that he's actually motivated by malice: He doesn't like the Governor and enjoys saying nasty things about him. The Governor hears about this and sues Erik for slander. Assume that the constitutional rules for slander are the same as for libel. (Slander refers to oral defamation, libel to written defamation.) Will the Governor win? What remedies would he be able to get?

b. New York Times Co. v. Sullivan, 376 U.S. 254 (1964)

Justice Brennan delivered the opinion of the Court....

[A.] Respondent L. B. Sullivan is ... "Commissioner of Public Affairs and [his] duties are supervision of the Police Department, Fire Department, Department of Cemetery and Department of Scales" [of Montgomery, Alabama].... A jury [in a libel suit] ... awarded him damages of $500,000 ... against all the petitioners ....

Respondent's complaint alleged that he had been libeled by statements in a full-page advertisement that was carried in the New York Times ... [see http://www.law.ucla.edu/volokh/firstamendment/extra.pdf—ed.] ... [:]

> Third paragraph: In Montgomery, Alabama, after students sang "My Country, 'Tis of Thee" on the State Capitol steps, their leaders were expelled from school, and truckloads of police armed with shotguns and tear-gas ringed the Alabama State College Campus. When the entire student body protested to state authorities by refusing to re-register, their dining hall was padlocked in an attempt to starve them into submission....
>
> Sixth paragraph: Again and again the Southern violators have answered Dr. King's peaceful protests with intimidation and violence. They have bombed his home almost killing his wife and child. They have assaulted his person. They have arrested him seven times—for "speeding," "loitering" and similar "offenses." And now they have charged him with "perjury"—a *felony* under which they could imprison him for *ten years*....

[Respondent] contended that the word "police" in the third paragraph referred to him as the Montgomery Commissioner who supervised the Police Department, so that he was being accused of "ringing" the campus with police. He further claimed that the paragraph would be read as imputing to the police, and hence to him, the padlocking of the dining hall in order to starve the students into submission.

As to the sixth paragraph, he contended that since arrests are ordinarily made by the police, the statement "They have arrested [Dr. King] seven times" would be read as referring to him; he further contended that the "They" who did the arresting would be equated with the "They" who committed the other described acts.... Thus, he argued, the paragraph would be read as accusing the Montgomery police, and hence him, of answering Dr. King's protests with "intimidation and violence," bombing his home, assaulting his person, and charging him with perjury....

[S]ome of the statements contained in the two paragraphs were not accurate .... Although nine students were expelled by the State Board of Education, this was not for leading the demonstration at the Capitol, but for demanding service at a lunch counter in the Montgomery County Courthouse on another day. Not the entire student body, but most of it, had protested the expulsion, not by refusing to register, but by boycotting classes on a single day ....

The campus dining hall was not padlocked on any occasion, and the only students who may have been barred from eating there were the few who had neither signed a preregistration application nor requested temporary meal tickets. Although the police were deployed near the campus in large numbers on three occasions, they did not at any time "ring" the campus, and they were not called to the campus in connection with the demonstration on the State Capitol steps, as the third paragraph implied. Dr. King had not been arrested seven times, but only four; and although he claimed to have been assaulted some years earlier in connection with his arrest for loitering outside a courtroom, one of the officers who made the arrest denied that there was such an assault....

[R]espondent ... had not participated in the events described. Although Dr. King's home had in fact been bombed twice when his wife and child were there, both of these occasions antedated respondent's tenure as Commissioner, and the police were not only not implicated in the bombings, but had made every effort to apprehend those who were. Three of Dr. King's four arrests took place before respondent became Commissioner. Although Dr. King had in fact been indicted (he was subsequently acquitted) on two counts of perjury, ... respondent had nothing to do with procuring the indictment.

Respondent made no effort to prove that he suffered actual pecuniary loss as a result of the alleged libel. One of his witnesses, a former employer, testified that if he had believed the statements, he doubted whether he "would want to be associated with anybody who would be a party to such things that are stated in that ad," and that he would not re-employ respondent if he believed "that he allowed the Police Department to do the things that the paper say he did." But neither this witness nor any of the others testified that he had actually believed the statements in their supposed reference to respondent.

[T]he advertisement ... was published by the Times upon an order from a New York advertising agency acting for the signatory Committee. The agency submitted the advertisement with a letter from A. Philip Randolph, Chairman of the Committee, certifying that the persons whose names appeared on the advertisement had given their permission.

Mr. Randolph was known to the Times' Advertising Acceptability Department as a responsible person, and in accepting the letter as sufficient proof of authorization it followed its established practice.... The manager of the Advertising Acceptability Department testified that he had approved the advertisement for publication because he knew nothing to cause him to believe that anything in it was false, and because it bore the endorsement of "a number of people who are well known and whose reputation" he "had no reason to question." Neither he nor anyone else at the Times made an effort to confirm the accuracy of the advertisement, either by checking it against recent Times news stories relating to some of the described events or by any other means....

[B.] [W]e consider this case against the background of a profound national commitment to the principle that debate on public issues should be uninhibited, robust, and wide-open, and that it may well include vehement, caustic, and sometimes unpleasantly sharp attacks on government and public officials. The present advertisement, as an expression of grievance and protest on one of the major public issues of our time, would seem clearly to qualify for the constitutional protection. The question is whether it forfeits that protection by the falsity of some of its factual statements and by its alleged defamation of respondent....

[C]onstitutional protection does not turn upon "the truth, popularity, or social utility of the ideas and beliefs which are offered." As Madison said, "Some degree of abuse is inseparable from the proper use of every thing; and in no instance is this more true than in that of the press." ... [E]rroneous statement is inevitable in free debate, and ... must be protected if the freedoms of expression are to have the "breathing space" that they "need ... to survive." ...

"Cases which impose liability for erroneous reports of the political conduct of officials reflect the obsolete doctrine that the governed must not criticize their governors.... The interest of the public here outweighs the interest of appellant or any other individual. The protection of the public requires not merely discussion, but information.... Errors of fact, particularly in regard to a man's mental states and processes, are inevitable.... Whatever is added to the field of libel is taken from the field of free debate." {*See also* John Stuart Mill, *On Liberty*: "... [T]o argue sophistically, to suppress facts or arguments, to misstate the elements of the case, or misrepresent the opposite opinion ... all this, even to the most aggravated degree, is so continually done in perfect good faith, by persons who are not considered ... ignorant or incompetent, that it is rarely possible, on adequate grounds, conscientiously to stamp the misrepresentation as morally culpable; and still less could law presume to interfere with this kind of controversial misconduct."}

Injury to official reputation affords no more warrant for repressing speech that would otherwise be free than does factual error.... [Government officials] are to be treated as "men of fortitude, able to thrive in a hardy climate" .... Criticism of their official conduct does not lose its constitutional protection merely because it is effective criticism and hence diminishes their official reputations.

If neither factual error nor defamatory content suffices to remove the constitutional shield from criticism of official conduct, the combination of the two elements is no less inadequate. This is the lesson to be drawn from the great controversy over the Sedition Act of 1798, which first crystallized a national awareness of the central meaning of the First Amendment.

That statute made it a crime ... [to] "... write, print, utter or publish ... any false, scandalous and malicious writing or writings against the government of the United States, or either house of the Congress ..., or the President ..., with intent to defame ... or to bring them, or either of them, into contempt or disrepute; or to excite against them, or either or any of them, the hatred of the good people of the United States." The Act allowed the defendant the defense of truth, and provided that the jury were to be judges both of the law and the facts. Despite these qualifications, the Act was vigorously condemned as unconstitutional in an attack joined in by Jefferson and Madison.

In the famous Virginia Resolutions of 1798, the General Assembly of Virginia resolved that ... "... [the Sedition Act] exercises ... a power ... expressly and positively forbidden by [The First Amendment]—a power which, more than any other, ought to produce universal alarm, because it is levelled against the right of freely examining public characters and measures, and of free communication among the people thereon, which has ever been justly deemed the only effectual guardian of every other right." Madison prepared the Report in support of the protest....

Earlier, ... Madison had said: "If we advert to the nature of Republican Government, we shall find that the censorial power is in the people over the Government, and not in the Government over the people." Of the exercise of that power by the press, his Report said: "In every state, probably, in the Union, the press has exerted a freedom in canvassing the merits and measures of public men, of every description, which has not been confined to the strict limits of the common law. On this footing the freedom of the press has stood; on this foundation it yet stands...." The right of free public discussion of the stewardship of public officials was thus, in Madison's view, a fundamental principle of the American form of government.

{The Report on the Virginia Resolutions further stated: "[I]t is manifestly impossible to punish the intent to bring those who administer the government into disrepute or contempt, without striking at the right of freely discussing public characters and measures; ... which, again, is equivalent to a protection of those who administer the government, if they should at any time deserve the contempt or hatred of the people, against being exposed to it, by free animadversions on their characters and conduct.... [A] government thus intrenched in penal statutes against the just and natural effects of a culpable administration, will easily evade the responsibility which is essential to a faithful discharge of its duty.

"Let it be recollected, lastly, that the right of electing the members of the government constitutes more particularly the essence of a free and responsible government. The value and efficacy of this right depends on the knowledge of the comparative merits and demerits of the candidates for public trust, and on the equal freedom, consequently, of examining and discussing these merits and demerits of the candidates respectively."}

Although the Sedition Act was never tested in this Court, the attack upon its validity has carried the day in the court of history. Fines levied in its prosecution were repaid by Act of Congress on the ground that it was unconstitutional. Calhoun, reporting to the Senate [in] 1836, assumed that its invalidity was a matter "which no one now doubts." Jefferson, as President, pardoned those who had been convicted and sentenced under the Act and remitted their fines, stating: "I discharged every person under punishment or prosecution under the sedition law, because I considered, and now consider, that law to be a nullity, as absolute and as palpable as if Congress had ordered us to fall down and worship a golden image." ...

[C.] {[T]he proposition ... that "The Fourteenth Amendment is directed against State action and not private action" ... has no application to this case. Although this is a civil lawsuit between private parties, the Alabama courts have applied a state rule of law which petitioners claim to impose invalid restrictions on their constitutional freedoms of speech and press. It matters not that that law has been applied in a civil action and that it is common law only, though supplemented by statute. The test is not the form in which state power has been applied but, whatever the form, whether such power has in fact been exercised.}

What a State may not constitutionally bring about by means of a criminal statute is likewise beyond the reach of its civil law of libel. The fear of damage awards under a rule such as that invoked by the Alabama courts here may be markedly more inhibiting than the fear of prosecution under a criminal statute. Alabama, for example, has a criminal libel law ... which allows as punishment upon conviction a fine not exceeding $500 and a prison sentence of six months. Presumably a person charged with violation of this statute enjoys ordinary criminal-law safeguards such as the requirements of an indictment and of proof beyond a reasonable doubt.

These safeguards are not available to the defendant in a civil action. The judgment awarded in this case—without the need for any proof of actual pecuniary loss—was one thousand times greater than the maximum fine provided by the Alabama criminal statute, and one hundred times greater than that provided by the Sedition Act.

And since there is no double-jeopardy limitation applicable to civil lawsuits, this is not the only judgment that may be awarded against petitioners for the same publication. Whether or not a newspaper can survive a succession of such judgments, the pall of fear and timidity imposed upon those who would give voice to public criticism is an atmosphere in which the First Amendment freedoms cannot survive....

{That the Times was paid for publishing the advertisement is as immaterial in this connection as is the fact that newspapers and books are sold. Any other conclusion would discourage newspapers from carrying "editorial advertisements" of this type, and so might shut off an important outlet for the promulgation of information and ideas by persons who do not themselves have access to publishing facilities—who wish to exercise their freedom of speech even though they are not members of the press.}

[D.] The state rule of law is not saved by its allowance of the defense of truth.... A rule compelling the critic of official conduct to guarantee the truth of all his factual assertions—and to do so on pain of libel judgments virtually unlimited in amount—leads to ... "self-censorship." Allowance of the defense of truth, with the burden of proving it on the defendant, does not mean that only false speech will be deterred. {Even a false statement may be deemed to make a valuable contribution to public debate, since it brings about "the clearer perception and livelier impression of truth, produced by its collision with error." Mill, *On Liberty.*} ...

Under such a rule, would-be critics of official conduct may be deterred from voicing their criticism, even though it is believed to be true and even though it is in fact true, because of doubt whether it can be proved in court or fear of the expense of having to do so. They tend to make only statements which "steer far wider of the unlawful zone." The rule thus dampens the vigor and limits the variety of public debate....

The constitutional guarantees require, we think, a federal rule that prohibits a public official from recovering damages for a defamatory falsehood relating to his official conduct unless he proves that the statement was made with "actual malice"—that is, with knowledge that it was false or with reckless disregard of whether it was false or not.

[E.] Since respondent may seek a new trial, we ... review the evidence in the present record to determine whether it could constitutionally support a judgment for respondent. This Court's duty is not limited to the elaboration of constitutional principles; we must also in proper cases review the evidence to make certain that those principles have been constitutionally applied.... In cases where ["the line between speech unconditionally guaranteed and speech which may legitimately be regulated"] must be drawn, ... [w]e must "make an independent examination of the whole record," so as to assure ourselves that the judgment does not constitute a forbidden intrusion on the field of free expression.

[W]e consider that the proof presented to show actual malice lacks the convincing clarity which the constitutional standard demands, and hence that it would not constitutionally sustain the judgment for respondent under the proper rule of law.... [T]here was no evidence whatever that [the individual petitioners] were aware of any erroneous statements or were in any way reckless in that regard....

As to the Times, we similarly conclude that the facts do not support a finding of actual malice. The statement by the Times' Secretary that, apart from the padlocking allegation, he thought the advertisement was "substantially correct," affords no constitutional warrant for the Alabama Supreme Court's conclusion that it was a "cavalier ignoring of the falsity of the advertisement [from which] the jury could not have but been impressed with the bad faith of The Times, and its maliciousness inferable therefrom." The statement does not indicate malice at the time of the publication; even if the advertisement was not "substantially correct"—although respondent's own proofs tend to show that it was—that opinion was at least a reasonable one, and there was no evidence to impeach the witness' good faith in holding it....

Finally, there is evidence that the Times published the advertisement without checking its accuracy against the news stories in the Times' own files. The mere presence of the stories in the files does not, of course, establish that the Times "knew" the advertisement was false, since the state of mind required for actual malice would have to be brought home to the persons in the Times' organization having responsibility for the publication of the advertisement.

With respect to the failure of those persons to make the check, the record shows that they relied upon their knowledge of the good reputation of many of those whose names were listed as sponsors of the advertisement .... We think the evidence against the Times supports at most a finding of negligence in failing to discover the misstatements, and is constitutionally insufficient to show the recklessness that is required for a finding of actual malice.

[F.] We also think the evidence was constitutionally defective in another respect: it was incapable of supporting the jury's finding that the allegedly libelous statements were made "of and concerning" respondent.... There was no reference to respondent in the advertisement, either by name or official position.... [I]t is plain that these statements could not reasonably be read as accusing respondent of personal involvement in the acts in question.... [Detailed explanation omitted.—ed.] ... [T]o the extent that some of [respondent's] witnesses thought respondent to have been charged with ordering or approving the [police] conduct or otherwise being personally involved in it, they based this notion ... solely on the unsupported assumption that, because of his official position, he must have been [involved]....

[The Alabama Supreme Court reasoned that] "... the average person knows that municipal agents, such as police and firemen, and others, are under the control and direction of the city governing body, and more particularly under the direction and control of a single commissioner. In measuring the performance or deficiencies of such groups, praise or criticism is usually attached to the official in complete control of the body."

This proposition has disquieting implications for criticism of governmental conduct. For good reason, "no court of last resort in this country has ever held, or even suggested, that prosecutions for libel on government have any place in the American system of jurisprudence." The present proposition would sidestep this obstacle by transmuting criticism of government, however impersonal it may seem on its face, into personal criticism, and hence potential libel, of the officials of whom the government is composed.... We hold that [the] proposition ... may not constitutionally be utilized to establish that an otherwise impersonal attack on governmental operations was a libel of an official responsible for those operations....

Justice Black, with whom Justice Douglas joins, concurring [in the judgment]....

"Malice," even as defined by the Court, is an elusive, abstract concept, hard to prove and hard to disprove. The requirement that malice be proved provides at best an evanescent protection for the right critically to discuss public affairs and certainly does not measure up to the sturdy safeguard embodied in the First Amendment....

The half-million-dollar verdict ... give[s] dramatic proof ... that state libel laws threaten the very existence of an American press virile enough to publish unpopular views on public affairs and bold enough to criticize the conduct of public officials.... The scarcity of testimony to show that Commissioner Sullivan suffered any actual damages at all suggests that [local] feelings of hostility [to Northern advocates of integration] had at least as much to do with rendition of this half-million-dollar verdict as did an appraisal of damages....

In my opinion the Federal Constitution has dealt with this deadly danger to the press in the only way possible without leaving the free press open to destruction—by granting the press an absolute immunity for criticism of the way public officials do their public duty. Stopgap measures like those the Court adopts are in my judgment not enough. This record certainly does not indicate that any different verdict would have been rendered here whatever the Court had charged the jury about "malice," "truth," "good motives," "justifiable ends," or any other legal formulas which in theory would protect the press. Nor does the record indicate that any of these legalistic words would have caused the courts below to set aside or to reduce the half-million-dollar verdict ....

This Nation, I suspect, can live in peace without libel suits based on public discussions of public affairs and public officials. But I doubt that a country can live in freedom where its people can be made to suffer physically or financially for criticizing their government, its actions, or its officials. "For a representative democracy ceases to exist the moment that the public functionaries are by any means absolved from their responsibility to their constituents; and this happens whenever the constituent can be restrained in any manner from speaking, writing, or publishing his opinions upon any public measure, or upon the conduct of those who may advise or execute it." An unconditional right to say what one pleases about public affairs is what I consider to be the minimum guarantee of the First Amendment....

Justice Goldberg, with whom Justice Douglas joins, concurring in the result....

[Justice Goldberg echoed Justice Black's arguments, but added:—ed.]

This is not to say that the Constitution protects defamatory statements directed against the private conduct of a public official or private citizen.... Purely private defamation has little to do with the political ends of a self-governing society....

{In most cases, as in the case at bar, there will be little difficulty in distinguishing defamatory speech relating to private conduct from that relating to official conduct. I recognize, of course, that there will be a gray area. The difficulties of applying a public-private standard are, however, certainly, of a different genre from those attending the differentiation between a malicious and nonmalicious state of mind. If the constitutional standard is to be shaped by a concept of malice, the speaker takes the risk not only that the jury will inaccurately determine his state of mind but also that the injury will fail properly to apply the constitutional standard set by the elusive concept of malice.} ...

c. *Garrison v. Louisiana, 379 U.S. 64 (1964)*

[This case is included only for its explanation of why any libel liability should be allowed, even when "actual malice" is shown.—ed.]

Justice Brennan delivered the opinion of the Court....

Although honest utterance, even if inaccurate, may further the fruitful exercise of the right of free speech, it does not follow that the lie, knowingly and deliberately published about a public official, should enjoy a like immunity. At the time the First Amendment was adopted, as today, there were those unscrupulous enough and skillful enough to use the deliberate or reckless falsehood as an effective political tool to unseat the public servant or even topple an administration....

[T]he use of the known lie as a tool is at once at odds with the premises of democratic government and with the orderly manner in which economic, social, or political change is to be effected. Calculated falsehood falls into that class of utterances which "are no essential part of any exposition of ideas, and are of such slight social value as a step to truth that any benefit that may be derived from them is clearly outweighed by the social interest in order and morality...." *Chaplinsky v. New Hampshire....*

d. *Dun & Bradstreet v. Greenmoss Builders, 472 U.S. 749 (1985) (White, J., concurring in the judgment)*

[Justice White joined the *New York Times v. Sullivan* majority, but soon became a forceful critic of the Court's libel jurisprudence.—ed.]

[A.] I have ... become convinced that the Court struck an improvident balance in the *New York Times* case between the public's interest in being fully informed about public officials and public affairs and the competing interest of those who have been defamed in vindicating their reputation.... Criticism and assessment of the performance of public officials and of government in general ... are not at all served by circulating false statements of fact about public officials. On the contrary, erroneous information frustrates these values. They are even more disserved when the statements falsely impugn the honesty of those men and women and hence lessen the confidence in government....

Yet in *New York Times v. Sullivan* cases, ... [t]he lie will [often] stand, and the public continue to be misinformed about public matters ... because the putative plaintiff's burden is so exceedingly difficult to satisfy and can be discharged only by expensive litigation. Even if the plaintiff sues, he frequently loses on summary judgment [or on appeal] ... because of insufficient proof of malice.... [And] when the plaintiff loses [before a jury], the jury will likely return a general verdict and there will be no judgment that the publication was false ....

The public is left to conclude that the challenged statement was true after all. Their only chance of being accurately informed is measured by the public official's ability himself to counter the lie, unaided by the courts. That is a decidedly weak reed to depend on for the vindication of First Amendment interests—"it is the rare case where the denial overtakes the original charge. Denials, retractions, and corrections are not 'hot' news, and rarely receive the prominence of the original story."

{It might be suggested that courts, as organs of the government, cannot be trusted to discern what the truth is. But the logical consequence of that view is that the First Amendment forbids all libel and slander suits, for in each such suit, there will be no recovery unless the court finds the publication at issue to be factually false.

Of course, no forum is perfect, but that is not a justification for leaving whole classes of defamed individuals without redress or a realistic opportunity to clear their names. We entrust to juries and the courts the responsibility of decisions affecting the life and liberty of persons. It is perverse indeed to say that these bodies are incompetent to inquire into the truth of a statement of fact in a defamation case.}

[B.] Also, by leaving the lie uncorrected, the *New York Times* rule plainly leaves the public official without a remedy for the damage to his reputation. Yet the Court has observed that the individual's right to the protection of his own good name is a basic consideration of our constitutional system, reflecting "our basic concept of the essential dignity and worth of every human being—a concept at the root of any decent system of ordered liberty." The upshot is that the public official must suffer the injury, often cannot get a judgment identifying the lie for what it is, and has very little, if any, chance of countering that lie in the public press....

[C.] [I]f protecting the press from intimidating damages liability that might lead to excessive timidity was the driving force behind *New York Times*[,] ... the Court engaged in severe overkill.... [I]nstead of escalating the plaintiff's burden of proof to an almost impossible level, we could have achieved our stated goal by limiting the recoverable damages to a level that would not unduly threaten the press. Punitive damages might have been scrutinized ... or perhaps even entirely forbidden. Presumed damages to reputation might have been prohibited, or limited, as in *Gertz v. Robert Welch, Inc....*

[T]he defamed public official, upon proving falsity, could at least have had a judgment to that effect. His reputation would then be vindicated; and to the extent possible, the misinformation circulated would have been countered. He might have also recovered a modest amount, enough perhaps to pay his litigation expenses.

At the very least, the public official should not have been required to satisfy the actual malice standard where he sought no damages but only to clear his name. In this way, both First Amendment and reputational interests would have been far better served....

It could be suggested that even without the threat of large presumed and punitive damages awards, press defendants' communication will be unduly chilled by having to pay for the actual damages caused to those they defame. But other commercial enterprises in this country not in the business of disseminating information must pay for the damage they cause as a cost of doing business, and it is difficult to argue that the United States did not have a free and vigorous press before the rule in *New York Times* was announced....

e. Policy—Chilling Effect

Basic argument: "The speech restriction at issue here will deter people from certain speech that the restriction doesn't even ostensibly cover, such as _____, because _____."

A true chilling effect argument claims that the restriction chills speech *that isn't formally covered* by the restriction. An argument that, for instance, "a ban on anti-government speech is bad because it would deter anti-government speech" is not a chilling effect argument. Rather, it's an argument that the law on its face applies to speech that for some reason (self-government, search for truth, etc.) should be protected.

1. "[C]ompelling the critic of official conduct to guarantee the truth of all his factual assertions—... on pain of libel judgments virtually unlimited in amount—leads to ... 'self-censorship.' Allowance of the defense of truth, with the burden of proving it on the defendant, does not mean that only false speech will be deterred.... [Speakers would] tend to make only statements which 'steer far wider of the unlawful zone.'" *New York Times v. Sullivan.*

"Uncertain meanings [of vague statutes] inevitably lead citizens to 'steer far wider of the unlawful zone' ... than if the boundaries of the forbidden areas were clearly marked.'" *Grayned v. City of Rockford.*

[As to rules requiring that certain statements be proven using hard-to-get original documents]: "If such strictness of testimony is required, there is an end at once of all political conversation .... The time, the labour, the difficulty, the expense, the harassment and fatigue ... which such doctrine would occasion to every citizen whom a corrupt administration might determine to ruin, would be ... itself sufficiently powerful to establish a perfect despotism over the press ...." Argument of defendant, *United States v. Cooper* (not included in the portion of the case excerpted in this book).

2. Response to 1: This speech restriction will not in fact have much of a chilling effect, because _____.

"The press today is vigorous and robust. To me, it is quite incredible to suggest that threats of libel suits from private citizens are causing the press to refrain from publishing the truth. I know of no hard facts to support that proposition, and the Court furnishes none." *Gertz v. Robert Welch, Inc.* (White, J., dissenting).

"Since advertising is the *sine qua non* of commercial profits, there is little likelihood of its being chilled by proper regulation and foregone entirely.... [This] may make it less necessary to tolerate inaccurate statements for fear of silencing the speaker." *Virginia State Bd. of Pharmacy v. Virginia Citizens Consumer Council.*

"The sort of chill envisioned here is far more attenuated and unlikely than that contemplated in traditional 'overbreadth' cases. We must conjure up a vision of a ... citizen suppressing his unpopular bigoted opinions for fear that if he later commits an offense covered by the statute, these opinions will be offered at trial to establish that he selected his victim on account of the victim's protected status, thus qualifying him for penalty enhancement.... This is simply too speculative a hypothesis to support Mitchell's overbreadth claim." *Wisconsin v. Mitchell*, 508 U.S. 476, 488-89 (1993) (upholding sentencing enhancements for hate-motivated assaults).

"Other professional activity of great social value is carried on under a duty of reasonable care and there is no reason to suspect the press would be less hardy than medical practitioners or attorneys for example." *Time, Inc. v. Hill*, 385 U.S. 374 (1967) (Harlan, J., concurring in part and dissenting in part).

3. Response to 1: All speech restrictions have *some* chilling effect; there's always some uncertainty as to the law (exactly what will qualify as a punishable threat or copyright infringement?) and as to the facts (will the jury conclude I knew the statement was false?). So we must endure some chilling effect; here, the chilling effect will be no greater than it was in those other cases where it was found to be tolerable, because _____.

"[The university] argues that the First Amendment is infringed by disclosure of peer review materials [in lawsuits about tenure cases] because disclosure undermines the confidentiality which is central to the peer review process, and this in turn is central to the tenure process, which in turn is the means by which petitioner seeks to exercise its asserted academic-freedom right of choosing who will teach. To verbalize the claim is to recognize how distant the burden is from the asserted right. Indeed, if the University's attenuated claim were accepted, many other generally applicable laws might also be said to infringe the First Amendment." *University of Penn. v. EEOC* (1990) (p. 433).

3. PRIVATE INDIVIDUALS/PUBLIC CONCERN

a. *Gertz v. Robert Welch, Inc., 418 U.S. 323 (1974)*

   i. *Generally*

Justice Powell delivered the opinion of the Court....

[A.] In 1968 a Chicago policeman named Nuccio shot and killed a youth named Nelson. The state authorities prosecuted Nuccio for the homicide and ultimately obtained a conviction for murder in the second degree. The Nelson family retained petitioner Elmer Gertz, a reputable attorney, to represent them in civil litigation against Nuccio.

Respondent publishes *American Opinion*, a monthly outlet for the views of the John Birch Society. Early in the 1960's the magazine began to warn of a nationwide conspiracy to discredit local law enforcement agencies and create in their stead a national police force capable of supporting a Communist dictatorship. As part of the continuing effort to alert the public to this assumed danger, the managing editor of *American Opinion* commissioned an article on the murder trial of Officer Nuccio[,] ... [which, as published, purported] to demonstrate that the testimony against Nuccio at his criminal trial was false and that his prosecution was part of the Communist campaign against the police....

[The article] contained serious inaccuracies. The implication that petitioner had a criminal record was false.... There was also no basis for the charge that petitioner was a "Leninist" or a "Communist-fronter." And he had never been a member of the "Marxist League for Industrial Democracy" or the "Intercollegiate Socialist Society." The managing editor of *American Opinion* made no effort to verify or substantiate the charges against petitioner.... [Gertz sued; the jury awarded him $50,000.—ed.] ...

[B.] Under the First Amendment there is no such thing as a false idea. However pernicious an opinion may seem, we depend for its correction not on the conscience of judges and juries but on the competition of other ideas.

But there is no constitutional value in false statements of fact. Neither the intentional lie nor the careless error materially advances society's interest in "uninhibited, robust, and wide-open" debate on public issues. They belong to that category of utterances which "are no essential part of any exposition of ideas, and are of such slight social value as a step to truth that any benefit that may be derived from them is clearly outweighed by the social interest in order and morality." *Chaplinsky v. New Hampshire.*

Although the erroneous statement of fact is not worthy of constitutional protection, it is nevertheless inevitable in free debate. As James Madison pointed out in the Report on the Virginia Resolutions of 1798: "Some degree of abuse is inseparable from the proper use of every thing; and in no instance is this more true than in that of the press." And punishment of error runs the risk of inducing a cautious and restrictive exercise of the constitutionally guaranteed freedoms of speech and press.

Our decisions recognize that a rule of strict liability that compels a publisher or broadcaster to guarantee the accuracy of his factual assertions may lead to intolerable self-censorship.... "Allowance of the defense of truth, with the burden of proving it on the defendant, does not mean that only false speech will be deterred." The First Amendment requires that we protect some falsehood in order to protect speech that matters.

The need to avoid self-censorship by the news media is, however, not the only societal value at issue. If it were, this Court would have embraced long ago the view that publishers and broadcasters enjoy an unconditional and indefeasible immunity from liability for defamation.... [Yet we would not lightly require the State to abandon] the compensation of individuals for the harm inflicted on them by defamatory falsehood.... [T]he individual's right to the protection of his own good name "reflects no more than our basic concept of the essential dignity and worth of every human being—a concept at the root of any decent system of ordered liberty...." ...

[C.] Because an *ad hoc* resolution of the competing interests at stake in each particular case is not feasible, we must lay down broad rules of general application. Such rules necessarily treat alike various cases involving differences as well as similarities. Thus it is often true that not all of the considerations which justify adoption of a given rule will obtain in each particular case decided under its authority.

[1.] With that caveat we have no difficulty in distinguishing among defamation plaintiffs. The first remedy of any victim of defamation is self-help—using available opportunities to contradict the lie or correct the error and thereby to minimize its adverse impact on reputation. Public officials and public figures usually enjoy significantly greater access to the channels of effective communication and hence have a more realistic opportunity to counteract false statements than private individuals normally enjoy. Private individuals are therefore more vulnerable to injury, and the state interest in protecting them is correspondingly greater.

{[R]ebuttal seldom suffices to undo harm of defamatory falsehood.... [T]he truth rarely catches up with a lie. But the fact that the self-help remedy of rebuttal, standing alone, is inadequate to its task does not mean that it is irrelevant to our inquiry.}

[2.] More important ..., there is a compelling normative ... distinction between public and private defamation plaintiffs. An individual who decides to seek governmental office must accept certain necessary consequences of that involvement in public affairs. He runs the risk of closer public scrutiny than might otherwise be the case.

And society's interest in the officers of government is not strictly limited to the formal discharge of official duties.... [T]he public's interest extends to "anything which might touch on an official's fitness for office.... Few personal attributes are more germane to fitness for office than dishonesty, malfeasance, or improper motivation, even though these characteristics may also affect the official's private character."

Those classed as public figures stand in a similar position. Hypothetically, it may be possible for someone to become a public figure through no purposeful action of his own, but the instances of truly involuntary public figures must be exceedingly rare.

For the most part those who attain this status have assumed roles of especial prominence in the affairs of society. Some occupy positions of such persuasive power and influence that they are deemed public figures for all purposes. More commonly, those classed as public figures have thrust themselves to the forefront of particular public controversies in order to influence the resolution of the issues involved. In either event, they invite attention and comment.

Even if the foregoing generalities do not obtain in every instance, the communications media are entitled to act on the assumption that public officials and public figures have voluntarily exposed themselves to increased risk of injury from defamatory falsehood concerning them. No such assumption is justified with respect to a private individual. He has not accepted public office or assumed an "influential role in ordering society." He has relinquished no part of his interest in the protection of his own good name, and consequently he has a more compelling call on the courts for redress of injury inflicted by defamatory falsehood. Thus, private individuals are not only more vulnerable to injury than public officials and public figures; they are also more deserving of recovery.

[D.] For these reasons we conclude that the States should retain substantial latitude in their efforts to enforce a legal remedy for defamatory falsehood injurious to the reputation of a private individual. The extension of the *New York Times* test proposed [to all statements on matters of public or general concern] would abridge this legitimate state interest to a degree that we find unacceptable. And it would occasion the additional difficulty of forcing state and federal judges to decide on an *ad hoc* basis which publications address issues of "general or public interest" and which do not—to determine ... "what information is relevant to self-government." We doubt the wisdom of committing this task to the conscience of judges....

We hold that, so long as they do not impose liability without fault, the States may define for themselves the appropriate standard of liability for a publisher or broadcaster of defamatory falsehood injurious to a private individual. This approach ... recognizes the strength of the legitimate state interest in compensating private individuals for wrongful injury to reputation, yet shields the press and broadcast media from the rigors of strict liability for defamation....

Justice Douglas, dissenting....

Discussion of public affairs is often marked by highly charged emotions, and jurymen, not unlike us all, are subject to those emotions.... With [an] amalgam of controversial elements pressing upon the jury, a jury determination, unpredictable in the most neutral circumstances, becomes for those who venture to discuss heated issues, a virtual roll of the dice separating them from liability for often massive claims of damage.

It is only the hardy publisher who will engage in discussion in the face of such risk, and the Court's preoccupation with proliferating standards in the area of libel increases the risks.... It matters little whether the standard be articulated as "malice" or "reckless disregard of the truth" or "negligence," for jury determinations by any of those criteria are virtually unreviewable.... The standard announced today [lets states adopt] ... the simple negligence standard as an option, with the jury free to impose damages upon a finding that the publisher failed to act as "a reasonable man." With such continued erosion of First Amendment protection, I fear that it may well be the reasonable man who refrains from speaking....

Justice Brennan, dissenting....

[A.] Matters of public or general interest do not "suddenly become less so merely because a private individual is involved, or because in some sense the individual did not 'voluntarily' choose to become involved." ...

"While the argument that public figures need less protection because they can command media attention to counter criticism may be true for some very prominent people, even then it is the rare case where the denial overtakes the original charge. Denials, retractions, and corrections are not 'hot' news, and rarely receive the prominence of the original story. When the public official or public figure is a minor functionary, or has left the position that put him in the public eye ..., the argument loses all of its force.

"In the vast majority of libels involving public officials or public figures, the ability to respond through the media will depend on the same complex factor on which the ability of a private individual depends: the unpredictable event of the media's continuing interest in the story. Thus the unproved, and highly improbable, generalization that an as yet [not fully defined] class of 'public figures' involved in matters of public concern will be better able to respond through the media than private individuals also involved in such matters seems too insubstantial a reed on which to rest a constitutional distinction."

Moreover, the argument that private persons should not be required to prove *New York Times* knowing-or-reckless falsity because they do not assume the risk of defamation by freely entering the public arena "bears little relationship either to the values protected by the First Amendment or to the nature of our society." Social interaction exposes all of us to some degree of public view. This Court has observed that "[t]he risk of this exposure is an essential incident of life in a society which places a primary value on freedom of speech and of press." Therefore, "[v]oluntarily or not, we are all 'public' men to some degree." ...

[B.] Adoption, by many States, of a reasonable-care standard in cases where private individuals are involved in matters of public interest—the probable result of today's decision—will likewise lead to self-censorship since publishers will be required carefully to weigh a myriad of uncertain factors before publication. The reasonable-care standard ... saddles the press with "the intolerable burden of guessing how a jury might assess the reasonableness of steps taken by it to verify the accuracy of every reference to a name, picture or portrait."

Under a reasonable-care regime, publishers and broadcasters will have to make pre-publication judgments about juror assessment of such diverse considerations as the size, operating procedures, and financial condition of the newsgathering system, as well as the relative costs and benefits of instituting less frequent and more costly reporting at a higher level of accuracy.... And, most hazardous, the flexibility which inheres in the reasonable-care standard will create the danger that a jury will convert it into "an instrument for the suppression of those 'vehement, caustic, and sometimes unpleasantly sharp attacks,' ... which must be protected if the guarantees of the First and Fourteenth Amendments are to prevail...."

[C.] On the other hand, the uncertainties which the media face under today's decision are largely avoided by the *New York Times* standard. I reject the argument that [applying *New York Times* to all speech that is on a matter of public concern] improperly commits to judges the task of determining what is and what is not an issue of "general or public interest." ... [T]he courts, the ultimate arbiters of all disputes concerning clashes of constitutional values, would only be performing one of their traditional functions in undertaking this duty.... The public interest is necessarily broad; any residual self-censorship that may result from the uncertain contours of the "general or public interest" concept should be of far less concern to publishers and broadcasters than that occasioned by state laws imposing liability for negligent falsehood....

Justice White, dissenting[, in an opinion with which Chief Justice Burger largely agreed—ed.]....

[A.] [U]ntil relatively recently, the consistent view of the Court was that libelous words constitute a class of speech wholly unprotected by the First Amendment .... The Court does not contend, and it could hardly do so, that those who wrote the First Amendment intended to prohibit the Federal Government, within its sphere of influence in the Territories and the District of Columbia, from providing the private citizen a peaceful remedy for damaging falsehood.... Scant, if any, evidence exists that the First Amendment was intended to abolish the common law of libel [of private citizens] ....

The debates in Congress and the States over the Bill of Rights are unclear and inconclusive on any articulated intention of the Framers as to the free press guarantee. We know that Benjamin Franklin, John Adams, and William Cushing favored limiting freedom of the press to truthful statements, while others such as James Wilson suggested a restatement of the Blackstone standard [that only prior restraints are unconstitutional].

{Franklin, for example, observed: "If by the *Liberty of the Press* were understood merely the Liberty of discussing the Propriety of Public Measures and political opinions, let us have as much of it as you please: But if it means the Liberty of affronting, calumniating, and defaming one another, I, for my part, own myself willing to part with my Share of it when our Legislators shall please so to alter the Law, and shall cheerfully consent to exchange my *Liberty* of Abusing others for the *Privilege* of not being abus'd myself."}

Jefferson endorsed Madison's formula that "Congress shall make no law ... abridging the freedom of speech or the press" only after he suggested: "The people shall not be deprived of their right to speak, to write, or otherwise to publish anything but false facts affecting injuriously the life, liberty or reputation of others...." {Jefferson's noted opposition to public prosecutions for libel of government figures did not extend to depriving them of private libel actions. There is even a strong suggestion that he favored state prosecutions.}

Doubt has been expressed that the Members of [the First] Congress envisioned the First Amendment as reaching even this far.... {Given this rich background of history and precedent and because we deal with fundamentals when we construe the First Amendment, we should proceed with care and be presented with more compelling reasons before we jettison the settled law of the States to an even more radical extent.} ...

The central meaning of *New York Times*, and for me the First Amendment as it relates to libel laws, is that seditious libel—criticism of government and public officials—falls beyond the police power of the State. In a democratic society such as ours, the citizen has the privilege of criticizing his government and its officials. But neither *New York Times* nor its progeny suggests that the First Amendment intended in all circumstances to deprive the private citizen of his historic recourse to redress published falsehoods damaging to reputation or that, contrary to history and precedent, the Amendment should now be so interpreted....

[B.] The Court evinces a deep-seated antipathy to "liability without fault." ... [Yet] the Court appears to be addressing those libels and slanders that are defamatory on their face and where the publisher is no doubt aware from the nature of the material that it would be inherently damaging to reputation. He publishes notwithstanding, knowing that he will inflict injury. With this knowledge, he must intend to inflict that injury, his excuse being that he is privileged to do so—that he has published the truth.

But as it turns out, what he has circulated to the public is a very damaging falsehood. Is he nevertheless "faultless"? Perhaps it can be said that the mistake about his defense was made in good faith, but the fact remains that it is he who launched the publication knowing that it could ruin a reputation.

In these circumstances, the law has heretofore put the risk of falsehood on the publisher where the victim is a private citizen and no grounds of special privilege are invoked. The Court would now shift this risk to the victim, even though he has done nothing to invite the calumny, is wholly innocent of fault, and is helpless to avoid his injury....

{It is difficult for me to understand why the ordinary citizen should himself carry the risk of damage and suffer the injury in order to vindicate First

Amendment values by protecting the press and others from liability for circulating false information. This is particularly true because such statements serve no purpose whatsoever in furthering the public interest or the
search for truth but, on the contrary, may frustrate that search and at the
same time inflict great injury on the defenseless individual. The owners of
the press and the stockholders of the communications enterprises can much
better bear the burden. And if they cannot, the public at large should somehow pay for what is essentially a public benefit derived at private expense....}

[C.] The press today is vigorous and robust. To me, it is quite incredible
to suggest that threats of libel suits from private citizens are causing the
press to refrain from publishing the truth. I know of no hard facts to support
that proposition, and the Court furnishes none.

The communications industry has increasingly become concentrated in
a few powerful hands operating very lucrative businesses reaching across
the Nation and into almost every home. Neither the industry as a whole nor
its individual components are easily intimidated, and we are fortunate that
they are not. Requiring them to pay for the occasional damage they do to
private reputation will play no substantial part in their future performance
or their existence.

{I fail to see how the quality or quantity of public debate will be promoted by further emasculation of state libel laws for the benefit of the news
media. "A great many forces in our society operate to determine the extent
to which men are free in fact to express their ideas. Whether there is a privilege for good faith defamatory misstatements on matters of public concern
or whether there is strict liability for such statements may not greatly affect
the course of public discussion. How different has life been in those states
which heretofore followed the majority rule imposing strict liability for misstatements of fact defaming public figures from life in the minority states
where the good faith privilege held sway?"

If anything, this trend may provoke a new and radical imbalance in the
communications process. It is not at all inconceivable that virtually unrestrained defamatory remarks about private citizens will discourage them
from speaking out and concerning themselves with social problems. This
would turn the First Amendment on its head. David Riesman, writing in
the midst of World War II on the fascists' effective use of defamatory attacks
on their opponents, commented: "Thus it is that the law of libel ... becomes
suddenly important for modern democratic survival."}

In any event, if the Court's principal concern is to protect the communications industry from large libel judgments, it would appear that its new
requirements with respect to general and punitive damages would be ample
protection. Why it also feels compelled to escalate the threshold standard of
liability I cannot fathom, particularly when this will eliminate in many instances the plaintiff's possibility of securing a judicial determination that
the damaging publication was indeed false, whether or not he is entitled to
recover money damages....

[D.] This case ultimately comes down to the importance the Court attaches to society's "pervasive and strong interest in preventing and redressing attacks upon reputation." From all that I have seen, the Court has miscalculated and denigrates that interest at a time when escalating assaults on individuality and personal dignity counsel otherwise. At the very least, the issue is highly debatable, and the Court has not carried its heavy burden of proof to justify tampering with state libel laws....

Freedom and human dignity and decency ... cannot survive without each other. Both exist side-by-side in precarious balance, one always threatening to overwhelm the other....

One of the mechanisms seized upon by the common law to accommodate these forces was the civil libel action tried before a jury of average citizens. And it has essentially fulfilled its role. Not because it is necessarily the best or only answer, but because "the juristic philosophy of the common law is at bottom the philosophy of pragmatism. Its truth is relative, not absolute. The rule that functions well produces a title deed to recognition."

In our federal system, there must be room for allowing the States to take diverse approaches to these vexing questions.... Finding no evidence that they have shirked this responsibility, particularly when the law of defamation is even now in transition, I would await some demonstration of the diminution of freedom of expression before acting....

ii. Presumed and Punitive Damages

Justice Powell delivered the opinion of the Court....

[W]e endorse [a lower mens rea threshold for liability] in recognition of the strong and legitimate state interest in compensating private individuals for injury to reputation. But this countervailing state interest extends no further than compensation for actual injury.... States may not permit recovery of presumed or punitive damages ... when liability is not based on a showing of knowledge of falsity or reckless disregard for the truth.

The common law of defamation is an oddity of tort law, for it allows recovery of purportedly compensatory damages without evidence of actual loss.... The largely uncontrolled discretion of juries to award damages where there is no loss unnecessarily compounds the potential of any system of liability for defamatory falsehood to inhibit the vigorous exercise of First Amendment freedoms. Additionally, the doctrine of presumed damages invites juries to punish unpopular opinion rather than to compensate individuals for injury sustained by the publication of a false fact. More to the point, the States have no substantial interest in securing for plaintiffs such as this petitioner gratuitous awards of money damages far in excess of any actual injury....

It is necessary to restrict defamation plaintiffs who do not prove knowledge of falsity or reckless disregard for the truth to compensation for actual injury [including] ... out-of-pocket loss[,] ... impairment of reputation and standing in the community, personal humiliation, and mental anguish and suffering. Of course, juries must be limited by appropriate instructions, and all awards must be supported by competent evidence concerning the injury, although there need be no evidence which assigns an actual dollar value to the injury....

Like the doctrine of presumed damages, jury discretion to award punitive damages unnecessarily exacerbates the danger of media self-censorship, but, unlike the former rule, punitive damages are wholly irrelevant to the state interest that justifies a negligence standard for private defamation actions. They are not compensation for injury. Instead, they are private fines levied by civil juries to punish reprehensible conduct and to deter its future occurrence. In short, the private defamation plaintiff who establishes liability under a less demanding standard than that stated by *New York Times* may recover only such damages as are sufficient to compensate him for actual injury....

Justice White, dissenting[, in an opinion with which Chief Justice Burger largely agreed—ed.].

[A.] [As to presumed damages,] courts and legislatures literally for centuries have thought that in the generality of cases, libeled plaintiffs will be seriously shortchanged if they must prove the extent of the injury to their reputations.... [D]amage to reputation is recurringly difficult to prove and ... requiring actual proof would repeatedly destroy any chance for adequate compensation.... {"The harm resulting from an injury to reputation ... may involve subtle differences in the conduct of the recipients toward the plaintiff[,] and ... the recipients, the only witnesses able to establish the necessary causal connection, may be reluctant to testify that the publication affected their relationships with the plaintiff...."}

The Court fears uncontrolled awards of damages by juries, but that not only denigrates the good sense of most jurors—it fails to consider the role of trial and appellate courts in limiting excessive jury verdicts where no reasonable relationship exists between the amount awarded and the injury sustained. Available information tends to confirm that American courts have ably discharged this responsibility.

The new rule with respect to general damages appears to apply to all libels or slanders, whether defamatory on their face or not, except, I gather, when the plaintiff proves intentional falsehood or reckless disregard.... Why a defamatory statement is more apt to cause injury if the lie is intentional than when it is only negligent, I fail to understand....

[B.] [As to punitive damages,] I see no constitutional difference between publishing with reckless disregard for the truth, where punitive damages will be permitted [under the majority view], and negligent publication where they will not be allowed. It is difficult to understand what is constitutionally wrong with assessing punitive damages to deter a publisher from departing from those standards of care ordinarily followed in the publishing industry, particularly if common-law malice is also shown.

I note also the questionable premise that "juries assess punitive damages in wholly unpredictable amounts bearing no necessary relation to the actual harm caused." ... While a jury award in any type of civil case may certainly be unpredictable, trial and appellate courts have been increasingly vigilant in ensuring that the jury's result is "based upon a rational consideration of the evidence and the proper application of the law." ... "The danger ... of immoderate verdicts, is certainly a real one, and the criterion to be applied by the judge in setting or reducing the amount is concededly a vague and subjective one. Nevertheless the verdict may be twice submitted by the complaining defendant to the common sense of trained judicial minds, once on motion for new trial and again on appeal, and it must be a rare instance when an unjustifiable award escapes correction."

The Court points to absolutely no empirical evidence to substantiate its premise. For my part, I would require something more substantial than an undifferentiated fear of unduly burdensome punitive damages awards before retooling the established common-law rule and depriving the States of the opportunity to experiment with different methods for guarding against abuses.

Even assuming the possibility that some verdicts will be "excessive," I cannot subscribe to the Court's remedy. On its face it is a classic example of judicial overkill. Apparently abandoning the salutary *New York Times* policy of case-by-case "independent examination of the whole record ... so as to assure ourselves that the judgment does not constitute a forbidden intrusion on the field of free expression," the Court substitutes an inflexible rule barring recovery of punitive damages absent proof of constitutional malice.... For almost 200 years, punitive damages and the First Amendment have peacefully coexisted. There has been no demonstration that state libel laws as they relate to punitive damages necessitate the majority's extreme response....

iii. Determining Whether Plaintiff Is a Public Figure

Justice Powell delivered the opinion of the Court....

Several years prior to the present incident, petitioner had served briefly on housing committees appointed by the mayor of Chicago, but at the time of publication he had never held any remunerative governmental position. Respondent admits this but argues that petitioner's appearance at the coroner's inquest rendered him a "de facto public official." ... Respondent's suggestion would sweep all lawyers under the *New York Times* rule as officers of the court and distort the plain meaning of the "public official" category beyond all recognition. We decline to follow it.

Respondent's characterization of petitioner as a public figure raises a different question. That designation may rest on either of two alternative bases. In some instances an individual may achieve such pervasive fame or notoriety that he becomes a public figure for all purposes and in all contexts. More commonly, an individual voluntarily injects himself or is drawn into a particular public controversy and thereby becomes a public figure for a limited range of issues. In either case such persons assume special prominence in the resolution of public questions.

Petitioner has long been active in community and professional affairs. He has served as an officer of local civic groups and of various professional organizations, and he has published several books and articles on legal subjects. Although petitioner was consequently well known in some circles, he had achieved no general fame or notoriety in the community.

None of the prospective jurors called at the trial had ever heard of petitioner prior to this litigation, and respondent offered no proof that this response was atypical of the local population. We would not lightly assume that a citizen's participation in community and professional affairs rendered him a public figure for all purposes. Absent clear evidence of general fame or notoriety in the community, and pervasive involvement in the affairs of society, an individual should not be deemed a public personality for all aspects of his life.

It is preferable to reduce the public-figure question to a more meaningful context by looking to the nature and extent of an individual's participation in the particular controversy giving rise to the defamation. In this context it is plain that petitioner was not a public figure. He played a minimal role at the coroner's inquest, and his participation related solely to his representation of a private client. He took no part in the criminal prosecution of Officer Nuccio.

Moreover, he never discussed either the criminal or civil litigation with the press and was never quoted as having done so. He plainly did not thrust himself into the vortex of this public issue, nor did he engage the public's attention in an attempt to influence its outcome....

4. PRIVATE INDIVIDUALS/PRIVATE CONCERN

a. *Problem: Professor v. Governor*

The Governor hears that Erik Jaffe, the First Amendment law professor from the previous problem, recently had sex with a 16-year-old girl, and cheerfully mentions this in a radio address. Erik sues the Governor for libel. Will Erik win? What remedies would he be able to get?

b. *Problem: Proposed Private Figure Libel Amendment*

Rep. Chris Newman introduces the following constitutional amendment on the floor of Congress: "The First Amendment shall not be interpreted as affecting liability for false, defamatory statements of fact made about private figures." What arguments can you make in favor of and against this amendment? (Assume, as we do throughout, that the First Amendment binds state governments via the Fourteenth Amendment.)

c. *Dun & Bradstreet v. Greenmoss Builders, 472 U.S. 749 (1985)*

Justice Powell ... delivered an opinion, in which Justice Rehnquist and Justice O'Connor joined....

[A.] Dun & Bradstreet, a credit reporting agency, provides subscribers with financial and related information about businesses. All the information is confidential; under the terms of the subscription agreement the subscribers may not reveal it to anyone else. On July 26, 1976, petitioner sent a report to five subscribers indicating that respondent, a construction contractor, had filed a voluntary petition for bankruptcy. This report was false and grossly misrepresented respondent's assets and liabilities.

That same day, while discussing the possibility of future financing with its bank, respondent's president was told that the bank had received the defamatory report. He immediately called petitioner's regional office, explained the error, and asked for a correction.

In addition, he requested the names of the firms that had received the false report in order to assure them that the company was solvent. Petitioner promised to look into the matter but refused to divulge the names of those who had received the report. After determining that its report was indeed false, petitioner issued a corrective notice on or about August 3, 1976, to the five subscribers who had received the initial report. The notice stated that one of respondent's former employees, not respondent itself, had filed for bankruptcy and that respondent "continued in business as usual." Respondent told petitioner that it was dissatisfied with the notice, and it again asked for a list of subscribers who had seen the initial report. Again petitioner refused to divulge their names....

[T]he error in petitioner's report had been caused when one of its employees, a 17-year-old high school student paid to review Vermont bankruptcy pleadings, had inadvertently attributed to respondent a bankruptcy petition filed by one of respondent's former employees. Although petitioner's representative testified that it was routine practice to check the accuracy of such reports with the businesses themselves, it did not try to verify the information about respondent before reporting it.

[Greenmoss Builders sued, and] the jury ... awarded ... $50,000 in compensatory or presumed damages and $300,000 in punitive damages....

[B.] [N]ot all speech is of equal First Amendment importance. {Obscene speech and "fighting words" long have been accorded no protection. In the area of protected speech, the most prominent example of reduced protection for certain kinds of speech concerns commercial speech. Such speech, we have noted, occupies a "subordinate position in the scale of First Amendment values." It also is more easily verifiable and less likely to be deterred by proper regulation. Accordingly, it may be regulated in ways that might be impermissible in the realm of noncommercial expression.}

It is speech on "matters of public concern" that is "at the heart of the First Amendment's protection." ... In contrast, speech on matters of purely private concern is of less First Amendment concern....

[T]he role of the Constitution in regulating state libel law is far more limited when the concerns that activated *New York Times v. Sullivan* and *Gertz v. Robert Welch, Inc.* are absent. In such a case, "[t]here is no threat to the free and robust debate of public issues; there is no potential interference with a meaningful dialogue of ideas concerning self-government; and there is no threat of liability causing a reaction of self-censorship by the press...."

While such speech is not totally unprotected by the First Amendment, see *Connick v. Myers,* its protections are less stringent. In *Gertz*, we found that the state interest in awarding presumed and punitive damages was not "substantial" in view of their effect on speech at the core of First Amendment concern. This interest, however, *is* "substantial" relative to the incidental effect these remedies may have on speech of significantly less constitutional interest.

The rationale of the common-law rules has been the experience and judgment of history that "proof of actual damage will be impossible in a great many cases where ... it is all but certain that serious harm has resulted in fact." As a result, courts for centuries have allowed juries to presume that some damage occurred from many defamatory ... publications.... In light of the reduced constitutional value of speech involving no matters of public concern, we hold that the state interest adequately supports awards of presumed and punitive damages—even absent a showing of "actual malice."

{The dissent's [approach] ... would lead to the protection of all libels—no matter how attenuated their constitutional interest. If the dissent were the law, a woman of impeccable character who was branded a "whore" by a jealous neighbor would have no effective recourse unless she could prove "actual malice" by clear and convincing evidence.... The dissent would, in effect, constitutionalize the entire common law of libel.} ...

[C.] "[W]hether ... speech addresses a matter of public concern must be determined by [the expression's] content, form, and context ... as revealed by the whole record." *Connick*. These factors indicate that petitioner's credit report concerns no public issue. It was speech solely in the individual interest of the speaker and its specific business audience. This particular interest warrants no special protection when—as in this case—the speech is wholly false and clearly damaging to the victim's business reputation.

Moreover, since the credit report was made available to only five subscribers, who, under the terms of the subscription agreement, could not disseminate it further, it cannot be said that the report involves any "strong interest in the free flow of commercial information." There is simply no credible argument that this type of credit reporting requires special protection to ensure that "debate on public issues [will] be uninhibited, robust, and wide-open."

In addition, the speech here, like advertising, is hardy and unlikely to be deterred by incidental state regulation. It is solely motivated by the desire for profit, which, we have noted, is a force less likely to be deterred than others.

Arguably, the reporting here was also more objectively verifiable than speech deserving of greater protection. In any case, the market provides a powerful incentive to a credit reporting agency to be accurate, since false credit reporting is of no use to creditors. Thus, any incremental "chilling" effect of libel suits would be of decreased significance. {[W]hile most States provide a qualified privilege against libel suits for commercial credit reporting agencies, in those States that do not there is a thriving credit reporting business and commercial credit transactions are not inhibited.} ...

{[Not] all credit reporting [will be] subject to reduced First Amendment protection. The protection to be accorded a particular credit report depends on whether the report's "content, form, and context" indicate that it concerns a public matter. We also do not hold ... that the report is subject to reduced constitutional protection because it constitutes economic or commercial speech. We discuss such speech, along with advertising, only to show how many of the same concerns that argue in favor of reduced constitutional protection in those areas apply here as well.} ...

Chief Justice Burger, concurring in the judgment.... [Chief Justice Burger agreed with much of the Powell opinion's analysis, and its conclusion that the speech was on a matter of private concern, but stressed that he thought *Gertz* was mistaken.—ed.]

Justice White, concurring in the judgment.... [Justice White took the same view as Chief Justice Burger, but also criticized the actual malice standard even as to public figures, see p. 71 above.—ed.]

Justice Brennan, with whom Justice Marshall, Justice Blackmun, and Justice Stevens join, dissenting....

[A.] The five Members of the Court voting to affirm the damages award in this case have provided almost no guidance as to what constitutes a protected "matter of public concern." ... Justice Powell adumbrates a rationale that would appear to focus primarily on subject matter[,] ... [*i.e.*, that] the speech is predominantly in the realm of matters of economic concern.... [But] this Court has consistently rejected the argument that speech is entitled to diminished First Amendment protection simply because it concerns economic matters or is in the economic interest of the speaker or the audience.... [F]reedom of expression is not only essential to check tyranny and foster self-government but also intrinsic to individual liberty and dignity and instrumental in society's search for truth....

[T]he choices we make when we step into the voting booth may well be the products of what we have learned from the myriad of daily economic and social phenomenon that surround us.... "Freedom of discussion, if it would fulfill its historic function in this nation, must embrace all issues about which information is needed or appropriate to enable the members of society to cope with the exigencies of their period." {[E]ven pure advertising may well be affected with a public interest, ... [because] "the free flow of commercial information is indispensable ... to the formation of intelligent opinions as to how [our economic] system ought to be regulated or altered." ... The greater state latitude for regulating commercial advertising is ... a function of "greater objectivity and hardiness" [rather than of any judgment that advertising is not speech on a matter of public concern].}

{[I]t may be that Justice Powell thinks this particular expression could not contribute to public welfare because the [communication was limited and confidential and thus the] public generally does not receive it.... [But] Dun & Bradstreet doubtless provides thousands of credit reports to thousands of subscribers who receive the information pursuant to the same strictures imposed on the recipients in this case. As a systemic matter, therefore, today's decision diminishes the free flow of information because Dun & Bradstreet will generally be made more reticent in providing information to all its subscribers.}

The credit reporting of Dun & Bradstreet falls within any reasonable definition of "public concern" consistent with our precedents.... [S]peech loses none of its constitutional protection "even though it is carried in a form that is 'sold' for profit." More importantly, an announcement of the bankruptcy of a local company is information of potentially great concern to residents of the community where the company is located; like the labor dispute at issue in *Thornhill*, such a bankruptcy "in a single factory may have economic repercussions upon a whole region."

And knowledge about solvency and the effect and prevalence of bankruptcy certainly would inform citizen opinions about questions of economic regulation. It is difficult to suggest that a bankruptcy is not a subject matter of public concern when federal law requires invocation of judicial mechanisms to effectuate it and makes the fact of the bankruptcy a matter of public record....

[**B.**] Even if the subject matter of credit reporting were properly considered ... as purely a matter of private discourse, this speech would fall well within the range of valuable expression for which the First Amendment demands protection. Much expression that does not directly involve public issues receives significant protection....

Our economic system is predicated on the assumption that human welfare will be improved through informed decisionmaking. In this respect, ensuring broad distribution of accurate financial information comports with the fundamental First Amendment premise that "the widest possible dissemination of information from diverse and antagonistic sources is essential to the welfare of the public." The economic information Dun & Bradstreet disseminates in its credit reports makes an undoubted contribution to this private discourse essential to our well-being....

The credit reports of Dun & Bradstreet bear few of the earmarks of commercial speech that might be entitled to somewhat less rigorous protection.... Credit reports are not commercial advertisements for a good or service or a proposal to buy or sell such a product. We have been extremely chary about extending the "commercial speech" doctrine beyond this narrowly circumscribed category of advertising because often vitally important speech will be uttered to advance economic interests and because the profit motive making such speech hardy dissipates rapidly when the speech is not advertising....

[**C.**] Even if ... [the credit report were treated as] the equivalent of commercial speech[,] ... this does not justify the elimination of restrictions on presumed and punitive damages.... [T]he regulatory means [even as to commercial speech must] be narrowly tailored so as to avoid any unnecessary chilling of protected expression....

Gertz specifically held that unrestrained presumed and punitive damages were "unnecessarily" broad in relation to the legitimate state interests. Indeed, *Gertz* held that in a defamation action punitive damages, designed to chill and not to compensate, were "*wholly irrelevant*" to furtherance of any valid state interest.... What was "irrelevant" in *Gertz* must still be irrelevant, and the requirement that the regulatory means be no broader than necessary is no less applicable even if the speech is simply the equivalent of commercial speech. Thus, unrestrained presumed and punitive damages for this type of speech must run afoul of First Amendment guarantees....

[D.] {Justice Powell has chosen a particularly inapt set of facts as a basis for urging a return to the common law. Though the individual's interest in reputation is certainly at the core of notions of human dignity, the reputational interest at stake here is that of a corporation.

Similarly, that this speech is solely commercial in nature undercuts the argument that presumed damages should be unrestrained in actions like this one because actual harm will be difficult to prove. If the credit report is viewed as commercial expression, proving that actual damages occurred is relatively easy. For instance, an alleged libel concerning a bank's customer may cause the bank to lower the credit limit or raise the interest rate charged that customer.... At worst the commercial damages caused by such action should be no more difficult to ascertain than many other traditional elements of tort damages.}

d. *Policy—No-Value or Low-Value Speech*

Basic argument: "The speech in this case has no First Amendment value, or at least lower value than does other speech, because the First Amendment protects speech that _____ [helps the search for truth / constitutes self-expression / is part of democratic self-government], and this speech lacks value for this purpose because _____."

Note: The value of speech may heavily depend on the underlying theory of why the First Amendment protects speech. If, for instance, one is arguing that speech is protected because it helps the search for truth, then speech is of "low value" if it doesn't much help the search for truth. If one is arguing that speech is protected because it's self-expression, then speech is of "low value" if it isn't really self-expressive. This is why no-value/low-value speech arguments explicitly or implicitly rely on some underlying "the First Amendment protects speech that _____" argument.

The most broadly persuasive "low-value speech" arguments, of course, are ones that show that the speech lacks value under a variety of different free speech theories.

1. "[T]here is no constitutional value in false statements of fact[, because they do not] materially advance[] society's interest in 'uninhibited, robust, and wide-open' debate on public issues." *Gertz v. Robert Welch.*

"Preventing unlimited display or distribution of obscene material, which by definition lacks any serious literary, artistic, political, or scientific value as communication is distinct from a control of reason and the intellect."

Paris Adult Theatre I v. Slaton.

"[T]he lewd and obscene, the profane, the libelous, and the insulting or 'fighting words' ... are no essential part of any exposition of ideas, and are of ... slight social value as a step to truth ...." *Chaplinsky v. New Hampshire.*

"The value of permitting live performances and photographic reproductions of children engaged in lewd sexual conduct is exceedingly modest, if not *de minimis*." *New York v. Ferber.*

"[S]ociety's interest in protecting [erotic materials] is of a wholly different, and lesser, magnitude than the interest in untrammeled political debate .... [F]ew of us would march our sons and daughters off to war to preserve the citizen's right to see 'Specified Sexual Activities' exhibited in the theaters of our choice." *Young v. American Mini Theatres, Inc.,* 427 U.S. 50, 70 (1976) (Stevens, J., writing for four Justices). *Obscenity*

"[C]ommercial speech ... [occupies a] subordinate position in the scale of First Amendment values ...." *Ohralik v. Ohio State Bar Ass'n.*

"[T]he public burning of the American flag by Johnson was no essential part of any exposition of ideas .... Far from being a case of 'one picture being worth a thousand words,' flag burning is the equivalent of an inarticulate grunt or roar ...." *Texas v. Johnson* (Rehnquist, C.J., dissenting).

"[There is] universal acceptance of the wrongness of the doctrine of racial supremacy.... The universality of the principle, in a world bereft of agreement on many things, is a mark of collective human progress. The victim's perspective, one mindful of the lessons of history, thus accepts racist speech as sui generis and universally condemned." Mari Matsuda, *Public Response to Racist Speech: Considering the Victim's Story,* in *Words That Wound* 37 (1993).

2. Response to 1: By making this assumption, you are neglecting an important way in which this speech is indeed valuable, namely _____.

"The Court's approach necessarily assumes that some works will be deemed obscene—even though they clearly have *some* social value—because the State was able to prove that the value, measured by some unspecified standard, was not sufficiently 'serious' to warrant constitutional protection.... Before today, the protections of the First Amendment have never been thought limited to expressions of *serious* literary or political value." *Paris Adult Theatre* (Brennan, J., dissenting).

Look back at the examples in item 3b, Policy—Search for Truth, p. 32.

3. Response to 1: Courts ought not determine whether this speech is valuable or not, for instance whether it has "serious" value or whether it is an "essential part of the exposition of ideas." (A) These decisions are too subjective to be intelligently made, because _____. (B) It should be up to speakers and listeners, not the government, to decide what speech is valuable and what is not, because _____.

"Art and literature reflect tastes; and tastes, like musical appreciation, are hardly reducible to precise definitions. That is one reason I have always *Obscenity* felt that 'obscenity' was not an exception to the First Amendment. For matters of taste, like matters of belief, turn on the idiosyncrasies of individuals. They are too personal to define and too emotional and vague to apply ...." *Paris Adult Theatre* (Douglas, J., dissenting).

Obscenity

"[D]ifferent people think that all sorts of different speech is valueless or downright pernicious [citing advertising, television, *Lady Chatterley's Lover*, pornography, and Communist advocacy]. If all it takes to remove First Amendment protection from a given kind of speech is that a sufficiently large number of people finds the speech less valuable than other kinds, we may as well not have a First Amendment at all. Such an understanding of the First Amendment—according to which speech not valued by a majority receives no protection—throws all speech regulation questions back into the political arena." Judge Alex Kozinski & Stuart Banner, *The Anti-History and Pre-History of Commercial Speech,* 71 Tex. L. Rev 747 (1993).

4. Rejoinder to 3: Unless all speech is equally protected—which can't be true, given the need to exclude threats, false advertising, and other generally uncontroversial exceptions—courts must draw distinctions between valuable speech and valueless speech, and the distinction here is unproblematic because _____.

"To require a parity of constitutional protection for commercial speech and noncommercial speech could invite dilution, simply by a leveling process, of the force of the Amendment's guarantee with respect to the latter kind of speech.... [We should] instead ... afford commercial speech a limited measure of protection, commensurate with its subordinate position in the scale of First Amendment values, while allowing modes of regulation that might be impermissible in the realm of [other] expression." *Ohralik v. Ohio State Bar Ass'n.*

e. Policy—Countervailing Private Rights

Basic argument: "This sort of speech doesn't just hurt broad social interests; it also infringes particular people's rights to _____ [live/not be injured/be happy/etc.]. Your free speech rights don't justify infringing my rights."

1. "That [the First A]mendment was intended to secure to every citizen an absolute right to speak, or write, or print, whatever he might please, without any responsibility ... is a supposition too wild to be indulged by any reasonable man. That would be, to allow every citizen a right to destroy, at his pleasure, the reputation, the peace, the property, and even the personal safety of every other citizen." Justice Joseph Story, *A Familiar Exposition of the Constitution of the United States* § 445 (1840).

"The right of a man to the protection of his own reputation from unjustified invasion and wrongful hurt reflects no more than our basic concept of the essential dignity and worth of every human being—a concept at the root of any decent system of ordered liberty. The protection of private personality, like the protection of life itself, is left primarily to the individual States .... But this does not mean that the right is entitled to any less recognition by this Court as a basic of our constitutional system." *Rosenblatt v. Baer*, 383 U.S. 75, 92 (1966) (Stewart, J., concurring).

"I do not believe that whatever is in words ... is beyond the reach of the law, no matter how heedless of others' rights .... I do not believe that the First Amendment precludes effective protection of the right of privacy—or ... an effective law of libel. I do not believe that we must or should ... strike down all state action, however circumspect, which penalizes the use of words as instruments of aggression and personal assault." *Time, Inc. v. Hill*, 385 U.S. 374 (1967) (Fortas, J., dissenting).

"'[F]airly defined areas of privacy must have the protection of law if the quality of life is to continue to be reasonably acceptable.'" *Florida Star v. B.J.F.* (White, J., dissenting).

"To enforce freedom of speech in disregard of the rights of others would be harsh and arbitrary in itself. That more people may be more easily and cheaply reached by sound trucks, perhaps borrowed without cost from some zealous supporter, is not enough to call forth constitutional protection for what those charged with public welfare reasonably think is a nuisance when easy means of publicity are open." *Kovacs v. Cooper*, 336 U.S. 77, 88-89 (1949).

2. The things that you say are countervailing private rights aren't really true rights, because _____: You don't really have a right to control what others know or think about you (cf. libel law and privacy law), or a right to be free from offense or even from noise, because _____.

3. Free speech sometimes includes the right to say things that *do* harm others' rights and interests, for instance inflict emotional distress on them (*Snyder v. Phelps*), reveal embarrassing facts about them (*Gertz*), interfere with their business relations (*NAACP v. Claiborne Hardware*), and so on, because _____. This is the price that all of us have to pay for First Amendment protection.

5. FACTS VS. OPINIONS—HISTORY

a. *Problem: Sedition Act*

Do you think the result in *United States v. Cooper* was constitutionally sound? If not, why not—because the Sedition Act should be considered unconstitutional, or because it was improperly applied?

b. *Sedition Act of 1798*

[It shall be illegal—on pain of up to a $2000 fine and 2 years in prison—to write or publish] any false, scandalous and malicious writing or writings against the government of the United States, or either house of the Congress ..., or the President ..., with intent to

[a] defame the said government, or either house of the said Congress, or the said President, or to bring them ... into contempt or disrepute;

[b] or to excite against them, or either or any of them, the hatred of the good

people of the United States,

[c] or to stir up sedition within the United States, or to excite any unlawful combinations therein, for opposing or resisting any law of the United States, or any [lawful] act of the President ..., or to resist, oppose, or defeat any such law or act,

[d] or to aid, encourage or abet any hostile designs of any foreign nation against the United States, their people or government....

[The Act was written to expire on March 3, 1801, the last day of the Presidential term in which it was enacted. This meant that the Act protected only the party that enacted it: The Act was enacted when both the Congress and the Presidency were in Federalist hands, the majority Federalists supported it, and the opposition Republicans opposed it.

But in early 1801, right before the Republicans took over the Presidency and the Congressional majority as a result of the 1800 election, the lame-duck Federalists nonetheless tried to reenact the Act, so that it would have protected their political enemies. The bill was defeated in the House by a 53-49 vote; nearly all Federalists voted for it, and all Republicans voted against it. The four Federalists who voted against the renewal consisted of one who voted against the 1798 Act, two who weren't in the House for the 1798 vote, and one who didn't cast a vote in 1798.—ed.]

c.   *United States v. Cooper, 25 F. Cas. 631 (C.C.D. Pa. 1800)*

[The libelous matter complained of was:] ... At that time [Mr. Adams] had just entered into office. He was hardly in the infancy of political mistake. Even those who doubted his capacity thought well of his intentions. Nor were we yet saddled with the expense of a permanent navy, or threatened, under his auspices, with the existence of a standing army. Our credit was not yet reduced so low as to borrow money at eight per cent. in time of peace, while the unnecessary violence of official expressions might justly have provoked a war.

Mr. Adams had not yet ... interfered, as president of the United States, to influence the decisions of a court of justice—a stretch of authority which the monarch of Great Britain would have shrunk from—an interference without precedent, against law and against mercy. This melancholy case of Jonathan Robbins, a native citizen of America, forcibly impressed by the British, and delivered up, with the advice of Mr. Adams, to the mock trial of a British court-martial, had not yet astonished the republican citizens of this free country; a case too little known, but of which the people ought to be fully apprised, before the election, and they shall be.

[The prosecutor] opened the case to the jury substantially as follows: ... Government should not encourage the idea, that they would not prosecute such atrocious conduct; for if this conduct was allowed to pass over, the peace of the country would be endangered. Error leads to discontent, discontent to a fancied idea of oppression, and that to insurrection, of which the two instances which had already happened were alarming proofs, and well-known to the jury.... [T]he jury, as citizens, must determine whether, from publications of this kind, the prosperity of the country was not endangered ... and show, that these kinds of attacks on the government of the country were not to be suffered with impunity.

[The defendant, acting as his own lawyer, argued:] ... I acknowledge ... the necessity of a certain degree of confidence in the executive government of the country. But this confidence ought not to be unlimited, and need not be paid up in advance; let it be earned before it be reposed; let it be claimed by the evidence of benefits conferred, of measures that compel approbation, of conduct irreproachable. It cannot be exacted by the guarded provisions of sedition laws, by attacks on the freedom of the press, by prosecutions ... [of] those who boldly express the truth, or who may honestly and innocently err in their political sentiments....

[I]n the present state of affairs, the press is open to those who will praise, while the threats of the law hang over those who blame the conduct of the men in power.... [S]urely this anxiety to protect public character must arise from fear of attack. That conduct which will not bear investigation will naturally shun it; and whether my opinions are right or wrong, ... I cannot help thinking they would have been better confuted by evidence and argument then by indictment. Fines and imprisonment will produce conviction neither in the mind of the sufferer nor of the public.

Nor do I see how the people can exercise on rational grounds their elective franchise, if perfect freedom of discussion of public characters be not allowed....

Chase, Circuit Justice (charging jury)....

It is my duty to state to you the law on which this indictment is preferred, and the substance of the accusation and defence....

There is no civilized country that I know of, that does not punish [seditious libels]; and it is necessary to the peace and welfare of this country, that these offences should meet with their proper punishment, since ours is a government founded on the opinions and confidence of the people.... If a man attempts to destroy the confidence of the people in their officers, their supreme magistrate, and their legislature, he effectually saps the foundation of the government.

A republican government can only be destroyed in two ways; the introduction of luxury, or the licentiousness of the press. This latter is the more slow, but most sure and certain, means of bringing about the destruction of the government....

Now we will consider this libel as published by the defendant, and observe what were his motives. You will find the [defendant] speaking of the president in the following words: "Even those who doubted his capacity, thought well of his intentions." ... [This] was in substance saying of the president, "You may have good intentions, but I doubt your capacity."

He then goes on to say: "Nor were we yet saddled with the expense of a permanent navy, nor threatened, under his (the president's) auspices, with the existence of a standing army. Our credit was not yet reduced so low as to borrow money at eight per cent. in time of peace."

Now, gentlemen, if these things were true, can any one doubt what effect they would have on the public mind? ... What! the president of the United States saddle us with a permanent navy, encourage a standing army, and borrow money at a large premium? And are we told, too, that this is in time of peace? If you believe this to be true, what opinion can you, gentlemen, form of the president? ...

The president is further charged for that "the unnecessary violence of his official expressions might justly have provoked a war." This is a very serious charge indeed. What, the president, by unnecessary violence, plunge this country into a war! ... I say, gentlemen, again, if you believe this, what opinion can you form of the president? Certainly the worst you can form: [Y]ou would certainly consider him totally unfit for the high station which he has so honorably filled, and with such benefit to his country.

[Discussion of the "borrow money" statement:] The [defendant] states that, under the auspices of the president, "our credit is so low that we are obliged to borrow money at eight per cent. in time of peace." I cannot suppress my feelings at this gross attack upon the president.... Are we now in time of peace? Is there no war? No hostilities with France? Has she not captured our vessels and plundered us of our property to the amount of millions? Has not the intercourse been prohibited with her? Have we not armed our vessels to defend ourselves, and have we not captured several of her vessels of war?

Although no formal declaration of war has been made, is it not notorious that actual hostilities have taken place? And is this, then, a time of peace? The very expense incurred, which rendered a loan necessary, was in consequence of the conduct of France. The [defendant], therefore, has published an untruth, knowing it to be an untruth.

[Discussion of the Robbins statement:] [T]he [defendant] charges the president with having influenced the judiciary department ... [and] says that this interference was a stretch of authority that the monarch of Great Britain would have shrunk from; an interference without precedent, against law and against mercy. Is not this an attack, and a most serious attack on the character of the president?

The [defendant] goes on thus: "This melancholy case of Jonathan Robbins, a native of America, forcibly impressed by the British, and delivered, with the advice of Mr. Adams, to the mock trial of a British court-martial, had not yet astonished the republican citizens of this free country,—a case too little known, but of which the people ought to be fully apprised before the election, and they shall be." ...

I can scarcely conceive a charge can be made against the president of so much consequence, or of a more heinous nature.... It appears then that this is a charge on the president, not only false and scandalous, but evidently made with intent to injure his character .... If this charge were true, there is not a man amongst you but would hate the president....

In [defendant's] allusion to Jonathan Robbins he expressly tells you this is "a case too little known, but of which the people ought to be fully apprised before the election, and they shall be." Here, then, the evident design of the [defendant] was, to arouse the people against the president so as to influence their minds against him on the next election. I think it right to explain this to you, because it proves, that the [defendant] was actuated by improper motives to make this charge against the president. It is a very heavy charge, and made with intent to bring the president into contempt and disrepute, and excite against him the hatred of the people of the United States....

I am clearly of opinion that the president could not refuse to deliver [Jonathan Robbins] up. This same Jonathan Robbins, whose real name appears to have been Nash, was charged with murder committed on board the Hermione, British ship of war. This Nash being discovered in America, the British minister made a requisition to the president that he should be delivered up....

By the twenty-seventh article of the treaty with Great Britain, it is stipulated, "that either of the contracting parties will deliver up to justice all persons who, being charged with murder or forgery committed within the jurisdiction of either, shall seek an asylum within any of the countries of the other ...." If the president, therefore, by this treaty, was bound to give this Nash up to justice, he was so bound by law; for the treaty is the law of the land: if so, the charge of interference to influence the decisions of a court of justice, is without foundation....

Now a dispute has arisen whether murder committed on board such a ship of war, was committed within the jurisdiction of Great Britain. I have no doubt as to the point. All vessels, whether public or private, are part of the territory and within the jurisdiction of the nation to which they belong. This is according to the law of nations.... Were it not so, crimes committed on board vessels of war would go unpunished; for no other country can claim jurisdiction.... [Thus, b]y the constitution, (since the treaty is the law of the land,) America was bound to give [Nash] up ....

Was this, then, an interference on the part of the president with the judiciary without precedent, against law and against mercy; for doing an act which he was bound by the law of the land to carry into effect, and over which a court of justice had no jurisdiction? Surely not; neither has it merited to be treated in the manner in which the [defendant] has done ....

[Discussion of the "standing army" statement:] Take this publication in all its parts, and it is the boldest attempt I have known to poison the minds of the people. [The defendant] asserts that Mr. Adams has countenanced a navy, that he has brought forward measures for raising a standing army in the country. The [defendant] is certainly a scholar, and has shown himself a man of learning, and has read much on the subject of armies. But to assert, as he has done, that we have a standing army in this country, betrays the most egregious ignorance, or the most wilful intentions to deceive the public.

We have two descriptions of armies in this country—we have an army which is generally called the Western army, enlisted for five years only—can this be a standing army? Who raises them? Congress. Who pays them? The people. We have also another army, called the provisional army, which is enlisted during the existence of the war with France—neither of these can, with any propriety, be called a standing army.

In fact, we cannot have a standing army in this country, the constitution having expressly declared that no appropriation shall be made for the support of an army longer than two years. Therefore, as congress may appropriate money for the support of the army annually, and are obliged to do it only for two years, there can be no standing army in this country until the constitution is first destroyed.

There is no subject on which the people of America feel more alarm, than the establishment of a standing army. Once persuade them that the government is attempting to promote such a measure, and you destroy their confidence in the government. Therefore, to say, that under the auspices of the president, we were saddled with a standing army, was directly calculated to bring him into contempt with the people, and excite their hatred against him.... This publication is evidently intended to mislead the ignorant, and inflame their minds against the president, and to influence their votes on the next election....

[What the defendant is required to show in order to prove the truth of his statements:] ... [T]he [defendant] in his defence must prove every charge he has made to be true; he must prove it to the marrow. If he asserts three things, and proves but one [or two], he fails .... [T]hough he should prove to your satisfaction, that the president had interfered to influence the decisions of a court of justice, that he had delivered up Jonathan Robbins without precedent, against law and against mercy, this would not be sufficient, unless he proved at the same time, that Jonathan Robbins was a native American, and had been forcibly impressed, and compelled to serve on board a British ship of war.

If he fails, therefore, gentlemen, in this proof, you must then consider whether his intention in making these charges against the president were malicious or not.... If you believe that he has published it without malice, or an intent to defame the president of the United States, you must acquit him. If he has proved the truth of the facts asserted by him, you must find him not guilty.

[Cooper was convicted, fined, and sentenced to prison. Forty years later, the Congress, concluding the Sedition Act was unconstitutional, directed that Cooper's fine be repaid with interest to his heirs. For more on Cooper—himself an early commentator on free speech, and later a legal academic, public intellectual, and overall troublemaker—and on his occasional coauthor Elizabeth Ryland Priestley, see Eugene Volokh, *Thomas Cooper, Early American Public Intellectual*, 4 NYU J. Law & Lib. 372 (2009), and Eugene Volokh, *Elizabeth Ryland Priestley, Early American Author on Free Speech*, 4 NYU J. Law & Lib. 382 (2009).—ed.]

d. Problem: Beauharnais, Jr.

Beauharnais' grandson makes the same speech that Beauharnais made in his day. A black person sues him for libel under a statute that's just like the Illinois law in *Beauharnais v. Illinois*, but that provides a civil right of action. The plaintiff argues that Beauharnais' speech falsely accuses him, as well as other blacks, of various crimes. What result under modern libel law?

e. Beauharnais v. Illinois, 343 U.S. 250 (1952)

Justice Frankfurter delivered the opinion of the Court.

[A.] The petitioner was convicted ... of violating § 224a of Division 1 of the Illinois Criminal Code ...:

> It shall be unlawful for any person, firm or corporation [(i)] to [distribute or present] in any public place ... [(ii)] any lithograph, moving picture, play, drama or sketch, [(iii)] which ... portrays depravity, criminality, unchastity, or lack of virtue [(iv)] of a class of citizens, of any race, color, creed or religion [(v)] ... [and] exposes [such citizens] to contempt, derision, or obloquy [(vi)] or which is productive of breach of the peace or riots....

The lithograph complained of was a leaflet setting forth a petition calling on the Mayor and City Council of Chicago "to halt the further encroachment, harassment and invasion of white people, their property, neighborhoods and persons, by the Negro...." Below was a call for "One million self respecting white people in Chicago to unite...." with the statement added that "If persuasion and the need to prevent the white race from becoming mongrelized by the negro will not unite us, then the aggressions ... rapes, robberies, knives, guns and marijuana of the negro, surely will." This, with more language, similar if not so violent, concluded with an attached application for membership in the White Circle League of America, Inc....

[B.] No one will gainsay that it is libelous falsely to charge another with being a rapist, robber, carrier of knives and guns, and user of marijuana.... [I]f an utterance directed at an individual may be the object of criminal sanctions, we cannot deny to a State power to punish the same utterance directed at a defined group, unless we can say that this a wilful and purposeless restriction unrelated to the peace and well-being of the State.

Illinois did not have to look beyond her own borders or await the tragic experience of the last three decades to conclude that wilful purveyors of falsehood concerning racial and religious groups promote strife and tend powerfully to obstruct the manifold adjustments required for free, ordered life in a metropolitan, polyglot community. From the murder of the abolitionist Lovejoy in 1837 to the Cicero riots of 1951, Illinois has been the scene of exacerbated tension between races, often flaring into violence and destruction. In many of these outbreaks, utterances of the character here in question, so the Illinois legislature could conclude, played a significant part.

The law was passed on June 29, 1917, at a time when the State was struggling to assimilate vast numbers of new inhabitants, as yet concentrated in discrete racial or national or religious groups—foreign-born brought to it by the crest of the great wave of immigration, and Negroes attracted by jobs in war plants and the allurements of northern claims. Nine years earlier, in the very city where the legislature sat, what is said to be the first northern race riot had cost the lives of six people, left hundreds of Negroes homeless and shocked citizens into action far beyond the borders of the State. [More examples of race riots omitted.—ed.] ...

In the face of this history and its frequent obligato of extreme racial and religious propaganda, we would deny experience to say that the Illinois legislature was without reason in seeking ways to curb false or malicious defamation of racial and religious groups, made in public places and by means calculated to have a powerful emotional impact on those to whom it was presented....

[C.] It may be argued, and weightily, that this legislation will not help matters; that tension and on occasion violence between racial and religious groups must be traced to causes more deeply embedded in our society than the rantings of modern Know-Nothings. Only those lacking responsible humility will have a confident solution for problems as intractable as the frictions attributable to differences of race, color or religion. This being so, it would be out of bounds for the judiciary to deny the legislature a choice of policy, provided it is not unrelated to the problem and not forbidden by some explicit limitation on the State's power.

That the legislative remedy might not in practice mitigate the evil, or might itself raise new problems, would only manifest once more the paradox of reform. It is the price to be paid for the trial-and-error inherent in legislative efforts to deal with obstinate social issues....

It would ... be arrant dogmatism, quite outside the scope of our authority in passing on the powers of a State, for us to deny that the Illinois legislature may warrantably believe that a man's job and his educational opportunities and the dignity accorded him may depend as much on the reputation of the racial and religious group to which he willy-nilly belongs, as on his own merits. This being so, we are precluded from saying that speech concededly punishable when immediately directed at individuals cannot be outlawed if directed at groups with whose position and esteem in society the affiliated individual may be inextricably involved.

[D.] We are warned that the choice open to the Illinois legislature here may be abused, that the law may be discriminatorily enforced; prohibiting libel of a creed or of a racial group, we are told, is but a step from prohibiting libel of a political party. {[But i]f a statute sought to outlaw libels of political parties, quite different problems not now before us would be raised. For one thing, the whole doctrine of fair comment as indispensable to the democratic political process would come into play. Political parties, like public men, are, as it were, public property.}

Every power may be abused, but the possibility of abuse is a poor reason for denying Illinois the power to adopt measures against criminal libels sanctioned by centuries of Anglo-American law. "While this Court sits" it retains and exercises authority to nullify action which encroaches on freedom of utterance under the guise of punishing libel. Of course discussion cannot be denied and the right, as well as the duty, of criticism must not be stifled....

As to the defense of truth, Illinois in common with many States requires a showing not only that the utterance state the facts, but also that the publication be made "with good motives and for justifiable ends." ... The teaching of a century and a half of criminal libel prosecutions in this country would go by the board if we were to hold that Illinois was not within her rights in making this combined requirement. Assuming that defendant's offer of proof directed to a part of the defense was adequate, it did not satisfy the entire requirement which Illinois could exact.

Libelous utterances not being within the area of constitutionally protected speech, it is unnecessary, either for us or for the State courts, to consider the issues behind the phrase "clear and present danger." ...

Justice Black, with whom Justice Douglas concurs, dissenting....

We are told that freedom of petition and discussion are in no danger "while this Court sits." ... [But if] those who peacefully petition for changes in the law are not to be protected "while this Court sits," who is?

I do not agree that the Constitution leaves freedom of petition, assembly, speech, press or worship at the mercy of a case-by-case, day-by-day majority of this Court. I had supposed that our people could rely for their freedom on the Constitution's commands, rather than on the grace of this Court on an individual case basis.

To say that a legislative body can, with this Court's approval, make it a crime to petition for and publicly discuss proposed legislation seems as farfetched to me as it would be to say that a valid law could be enacted to punish a candidate for President for telling the people his views. I think the First Amendment ... "absolutely" forbids such laws without any "ifs" or "buts" or "whereases." ...

Justice Douglas, dissenting.

Hitler and his Nazis showed how evil a conspiracy could be which was aimed at destroying a race by exposing it to contempt, derision, and obloquy.... [S]uch conduct directed at a race or group in this country could be made an indictable offense. For such a project would be more than the exercise of free speech. Like picketing, it would be free speech plus....

[E]ven without the element of conspiracy there might be times and occasions when the legislative or executive branch might call a halt to inflammatory talk, such as the shouting of "fire" in a school or a theatre.... [But] if in any case other public interests are to override the plain command of the First Amendment, the peril of speech must be clear and present, leaving no room for argument, raising no doubts as to the necessity of curbing speech in order to prevent disaster....

Today a white man stands convicted for protesting in unseemly language against our decisions invalidating restrictive covenants. Tomorrow a negro will be hailed before a court for denouncing lynch law in heated terms. Farm laborers in the west who compete with field hands drifting up from Mexico; whites who feel the pressure of orientals; a minority which finds employment going to members of the dominant religious group—all of these are caught in the mesh of today's decision....

Intemperate speech is a distinctive characteristic of man.... The Framers ... knew human nature as well as we do. They too had lived in dangerous days; they too knew the suffocating influence of orthodoxy and standardized thought. They weighed the compulsions for restrained speech and thought against the abuses of liberty. They chose liberty.

That should be our choice today no matter how distasteful to us the pamphlet of Beauharnais may be.... [Today's decision] represents a philosophy at war with the First Amendment—a constitutional interpretation which puts free speech under the legislative thumb.

It reflects an influence moving ever deeper into our society. It is notice to the legislatures that they have the power to control unpopular blocs. It is a warning to every minority that when the Constitution guarantees free speech it does not mean what it says.

Justice Jackson, dissenting....

[N]either the court nor jury found or were required to find any injury to any person, or group, or to the public peace, nor to find any probability, let alone any clear and present danger, of injury to any of these. Even though no individuals were named or described as targets of this pamphlet, if it resulted in a riot or caused injury to any individual Negro, such as being refused living quarters in a particular section, house or apartment, or being refused employment, certainly there would be no constitutional obstacle to imposing civil or criminal liability for actual results. But in this case no actual violence and no specific injury was charged or proved. The leaflet was simply held punishable as criminal libel *per se* irrespective of its actual or probable consequences....

Punishment of printed words, based on their *tendency* either to cause breach of the peace or injury to persons or groups, in my opinion, is justifiable only if the prosecution survives the "clear and present danger" test. It is the most just and workable standard yet evolved for determining criminality of words whose injurious or inciting tendencies are not demonstrated by the event but are ascribed to them on the basis of probabilities.... One of the merits of the clear and present danger test is that the triers of fact would take into account the realities of race relations and any smouldering fires to be fanned into holocausts. Such consideration might well warrant a conviction here when it would not in another and different environment....

Justice Reed, with whom Justice Douglas joins, dissenting. [This dissent argued that the terms "virtue," "derision," and "obloquy" were unconstitutionally vague as to group libel.—ed.]

6. One "False Statements of Fact" Exception, or Several Narrower Exceptions (for Libel, Fraud, etc.)?

a. *Problem: False Statements in Election Campaigns*

Assume that a state statute provides,

> It shall be a misdemeanor to make any knowingly false statement of fact during an election campaign, when the statement is reasonably likely to affect the views of one or more voters, whether the statement is (1) said about a candidate by that very candidate, (2) said about any person by some person other than the speaker, or (3) said about any other matter.

Would such a statute be constitutional? Is there a potential difference between the statements in categories 1, 2, and 3? *Compare Pestrak* v. *Ohio Elections Comm'n*, 926 F.2d 573 (6th Cir. 1991); *In re Chmura*, 608 N.W.2d 31 (Mich. 2000); *State v. Davis*, 27 Ohio App. 3d 65 (1985), *with 281 Care Comm. v. Arneson*, 638 F.3d 621 (8th Cir. 2011); *State ex rel. Public Disclosure Comm'n v. 119 Vote No! Comm.*, 135 Wash. 2d 618 (1998).

b. *United States v. Alvarez, 132 S. Ct. 2537 (2012)*

i. *What Rule Should Apply?*

Justice Kennedy announced the judgment of the Court and delivered an opinion, in which the Chief Justice, Justice Ginsburg, and Justice Sotomayor join....

[A.] In 2007, respondent [Xavier Alvarez] attended his first public meeting as a board member of the Three Valley Water District Board.... He introduced himself as follows: "I'm a retired marine of 25 years. I retired in the year 2001. Back in 1987, I was awarded the Congressional Medal of Honor. I got wounded many times by the same guy."

None of this was true. For all the record shows, respondent's statements were but a pathetic attempt to gain respect that eluded him. The statements do not seem to have been made to secure employment or financial benefits or admission to privileges reserved for those who had earned the Medal.

Respondent was indicted under the Stolen Valor Act[, 18 U.S.C. § 704(b)–(c):]

> Whoever falsely represents himself or herself ... to have been awarded any [U.S. military] decoration or medal ... shall be fined ..., imprisoned not more than six months [or one year for a Medal of Honor], or both....

[There was no dispute among the Justices that the law was limited to knowingly false statements of fact, and not honest errors, obvious jokes, statements made in works of fiction, and the like.—ed.]

[B.] "[A]s a general matter, the First Amendment means that government has no power to restrict expression because of its message, its ideas, its subject matter, or its content." *Ashcroft v. ACLU*.... In light of the substantial and expansive threats to free expression posed by content-based restrictions, this Court has rejected as "startling and dangerous" a "free-floating test for First Amendment coverage ... [based on] an ad hoc balancing of relative social costs and benefits." *United States v. Stevens.*

Instead, content-based restrictions on speech have been permitted, as a general matter, only when confined to the few "historic and traditional categories [of expression] long familiar to the bar." Among these categories are advocacy intended, and likely, to incite imminent lawless action, obscenity, defamation, speech integral to criminal conduct, so-called "fighting words," child pornography, fraud, true threats, and speech presenting some grave and imminent threat the government has the power to prevent, although a restriction under the last category is most difficult to sustain....

Absent from those few categories ... is any general exception to the First Amendment for false statements.... [S]ome false statements are inevitable if there is to be an open and vigorous expression of views in public and private conversation, expression the First Amendment seeks to guarantee.... [Statements in past opinions that knowing or reckless falsehoods generally lack constitutional value] all derive from cases discussing defamation, fraud [including fraud in seeking employment], or some other legally cognizable harm associated with a false statement, such as an invasion of privacy or the costs of vexatious litigation....

[Title 18 U.S.C §] 1001's prohibition on false statements made to Government officials, in communications concerning official matters, does not lead to the broader proposition that false statements are unprotected when made to any person, at any time, in any context. The same point can be made about what the Court has confirmed is the "unquestioned constitutionality of perjury statutes[]" .... Perjury undermines the function and province of the law and threatens the integrity of judgments that are the basis of the legal system. Unlike speech in other contexts, testimony under oath has the formality and gravity necessary to remind the witness that his or her statements will be the basis for official governmental action, action that often affects the rights and liberties of others....

Statutes that prohibit falsely representing that one is speaking on behalf of the Government, or that prohibit impersonating a Government officer, also protect the integrity of Government processes, quite apart from merely restricting false speech.... Even if [the government employee impersonation] statute may not require proving an "actual financial or property loss" resulting from the deception, the statute is itself confined to "maintain[ing] the general good repute and dignity of ... government ... service itself." ...

[T]he First Amendment stands against any "freewheeling authority to declare new categories of speech outside the scope of the First Amendment[.]" ... Before exempting a category of speech from the normal prohibition on content-based restrictions, ... the Court must be presented with "persuasive evidence that a novel restriction on content is part of a long (if heretofore unrecognized) tradition of proscription," *Brown v. Entertainment Merchants Assn.* The Government has not demonstrated that false statements generally should constitute a new category of unprotected speech on this basis.

[C.] The probable, and adverse, effect of the Act on freedom of expression illustrates ... the reasons for the law's distrust of content-based speech prohibitions.... Here the lie was made in a public meeting, but the statute would apply with equal force to personal, whispered conversations within a home.... Permitting the government [based on the interest in truthful discourse alone] to decree this speech to be a criminal offense, whether shouted from the rooftops or made in a barely audible whisper, would endorse government authority to compile a list of subjects about which false statements are punishable.

That governmental power has no clear limiting principle. Our constitutional tradition stands against the idea that we need Oceania's Ministry of Truth. See G. Orwell, *Nineteen Eighty–Four*.... The mere potential for the exercise of [such] power casts a chill, a chill the First Amendment cannot permit if free speech, thought, and discourse are to remain a foundation of our freedom.

Orwell

Justice Breyer, with whom Justice Kagan joins, concurring in the judgment....

[A.] As the dissent points out, "there are broad areas in which any attempt by the state to penalize purportedly false speech would present a grave and unacceptable danger of suppressing truthful speech." Laws restricting false statements about philosophy, religion, history, the social sciences, the arts, and the like raise such concerns, and in many contexts have called for strict scrutiny. But this case does not involve such a law. The dangers of suppressing valuable ideas are lower where, as here, the regulations concern false statements about easily verifiable facts that do not concern such subject matter.

Such false factual statements are less likely than are true factual statements to make a valuable contribution to the marketplace of ideas. And the government often has good reasons to prohibit such false speech.

[B.] But its regulation can nonetheless threaten speech-related harms.... False factual statements can serve useful human objectives, for example: in social contexts, where they may prevent embarrassment, protect privacy, shield a person from prejudice, provide the sick with comfort, or preserve a child's innocence; in public contexts, where they may stop a panic or otherwise preserve calm in the face of danger; and even in technical, philosophical, and scientific contexts, where (as Socrates' methods suggest) examination of a false statement (even if made deliberately to mislead) can promote a form of thought that ultimately helps realize the truth.

Moreover, as the Court has often said, the threat of criminal prosecution for making a false statement can inhibit the speaker from making true statements, thereby "chilling" a kind of speech that lies at the First Amendment's heart. Hence, the Court emphasizes mens rea requirements that provide "breathing room" for more valuable speech by reducing an honest speaker's fear that he may accidentally incur liability for speaking.

Further, the pervasiveness of false statements, made for better or for worse motives, made thoughtlessly or deliberately, made with or without

accompanying harm, provides a weapon to a government broadly empowered to prosecute falsity without more. And those who are unpopular may
fear that the government will use that weapon selectively, say by prosecuting a pacifist who supports his cause by (falsely) claiming to have been a
war hero, while ignoring members of other political groups who might make
similar false claims....

[C.] {Those circumstances lead me to apply what the Court has termed
"intermediate scrutiny" here.} {In determining whether a statute violates
the First Amendment, this Court has often found it appropriate to examine
the fit between statutory ends and means. In doing so, ... it has taken account of the seriousness of the speech-related harm the provision will likely
cause, the nature and importance of the provision's countervailing objectives, the extent to which the provision will tend to achieve those objectives,
and whether there are other, less restrictive ways of doing so. Ultimately
the Court has had to determine whether the statute works speech-related
harm that is out of proportion to its justifications.

Sometimes the Court has referred to this approach as "intermediate
scrutiny[]" ... [And] some such approach is necessary if the First Amendment is to offer proper protection in the many instances in which a statute
adversely affects constitutionally protected interests but warrants neither
near-automatic condemnation (as "strict scrutiny" implies) nor near-automatic approval (as is implicit in "rational basis" review). See, *e.g.*, *Turner
Broadcasting System v. FCC* ([content-neutral] "must-carry" cable regulations); *Central Hudson Gas & Elec. Corp. v. Public Serv. Comm'n* (nonmisleading commercial speech); *Burdick v. Takushi*, 504 U.S. 428 (1992) (election regulation); *Pickering v. Bd. of Ed.*, 391 U.S. 563 (1968) (government
employee speech); *United States v. O'Brien* (application of generally applicable laws to expressive conduct).}

[D.] [Many prohibitions on false statements, such as bans on fraud, defamation, the false light tort, and the intentional infliction of emotional distress tort,] tend to be narrower than the statute before us, in that they limit
the scope of their application, sometimes by requiring proof of specific harm
to identifiable victims; sometimes by specifying that the lies be made in contexts in which a tangible harm to others is especially likely to occur; and
sometimes by limiting the prohibited lies to those that are particularly
likely to produce harm....

Statutes forbidding lying to a government official ... are typically limited
to circumstances where a lie is likely to work particular and specific harm
by interfering with the functioning of a government department, and those
statutes also require a showing of materiality [as do perjury statutes]. Statutes prohibiting false claims of terrorist attacks, or other lies about the commission of crimes or catastrophes, require proof that substantial public
harm be directly foreseeable, or, if not, involve false statements that are
very likely to bring about that harm. Statutes forbidding impersonation of
a public official typically focus on acts of impersonation, not mere speech,
and may require a showing that, for example, someone was deceived into

following a "course [of action] he would not have pursued but for the deceitful conduct."

Statutes prohibiting trademark infringement present, perhaps, the closest analogy to the present statute. Trademarks identify the source of a good; and infringement causes harm by causing confusion among potential customers (about the source) and thereby diluting the value of the mark to its owner, to consumers, and to the economy. Similarly, a false claim of possession of a medal or other honor creates confusion about who is entitled to wear it, thus diluting its value to those who have earned it, to their families, and to their country.

But trademark statutes are focused upon commercial and promotional activities that are likely to dilute the value of a mark. Indeed, they typically require a showing of likely confusion, a showing that tends to assure that the feared harm will in fact take place....

[Such] limitations help to make certain that the [law] does not allow its threat of liability or criminal punishment to roam at large, discouraging or forbidding the telling of the lie in contexts where harm is unlikely or the need for the prohibition is small.

[E.] The statute before us lacks any such limiting features.... [It] applies in family, social, or other private contexts, where lies will often cause little harm. It also applies in political contexts, where although such lies are more likely to cause harm, the risk of censorious selectivity by prosecutors is also high.

Further, given the potential haziness of individual memory along with the large number of military awards covered (ranging from medals for rifle marksmanship to the Congressional Medal of Honor), there remains a risk of chilling that is not completely eliminated by mens rea requirements; a speaker might still be worried about being prosecuted for a careless false statement, even if he does not have the intent required to render him liable. And so the prohibition may be applied where it should not be applied, for example, to bar stool braggadocio or, in the political arena, subtly but selectively to speakers that the Government does not like....

Justice Alito, with whom Justice Scalia and Justice Thomas join, dissenting.

[A.] Only the bravest of the brave are awarded the Congressional Medal of Honor, but the Court today holds that every American has a constitutional right to claim to have received this singular award.... [T]he Stolen Valor Act of 2005 ... was enacted to stem an epidemic of false claims about military decorations. These lies, Congress reasonably concluded, were undermining our country's system of military honors and inflicting real harm on actual medal recipients and their families....

Congress responded to this problem by crafting a narrow statute that presents no threat to the freedom of speech. The statute reaches only knowingly false statements about hard facts directly within a speaker's personal knowledge. These lies have no value in and of themselves, and proscribing them does not chill any valuable speech. [And] {Congress was entitled to conclude that falsely claiming to have won the Medal of Honor is qualitatively different from even the most prestigious civilian awards and that the misappropriation of that honor warrants criminal sanction.}

[B.] By holding that the First Amendment nevertheless shields these lies, the Court breaks sharply from a long line of cases recognizing that the right to free speech does not protect false factual statements that inflict real harm and serve no legitimate interest.... [M]any kinds of false factual statements have long been proscribed without "'rais[ing] any Constitutional problem.'"

Laws prohibiting fraud, perjury, and defamation, for example, were in existence when the First Amendment was adopted, and their constitutionality is now beyond question.... The right to freedom of speech has been held to permit recovery for the intentional infliction of emotional distress by means of a false statement, see *Hustler Magazine, Inc. v. Falwell*, 485 U.S. 46 (1988), even though that tort did not enter our law until the late 19th century. And in *Time, Inc. v. Hill*, 385 U.S. 374 (1967), the Court concluded that the free speech right allows recovery for the even more modern tort of false-light invasion of privacy.

In line with these holdings, it has long been assumed that the First Amendment is not offended by prominent criminal statutes with no close common-law analog.... [Title] 18 U.S.C. § 1001 ... makes it a crime to "knowingly and willfully" make any "materially false, fictitious, or fraudulent statement or representation" in "any matter within the jurisdiction of the executive, legislative, or judicial branch of the Government of the United States." Unlike perjury, § 1001 is not limited to statements made under oath or before an official government tribunal. Nor does it require any showing of "pecuniary or property loss to the government." ...

Still other statutes make it a crime to falsely represent that one is speaking on behalf of, or with the approval of, the Federal Government. See, *e.g.*, 18 U.S.C. § 912 (making it a crime to falsely impersonate a federal officer). [This statute], like § 1001, does not require a showing of pecuniary or property loss[;]... its purpose is to "'maintain the general good repute and dignity'" of Government service.

These examples amply demonstrate that false statements of fact merit no First Amendment protection in their own right. {Respondent and his supporting amici attempt to limit this rule to certain subsets of false statements, but the examples described above belie that attempt. These examples show that the rule at least applies to (1) specific types of false statements that were neither illegal nor tortious in 1791 (the torts of intentional infliction of emotional distress and false-light invasion of privacy did not exist when the First Amendment was adopted); (2) false speech that does not cause pecuniary harm (the harm remedied by the torts of defamation, intentional infliction of emotional distress, and false-light invasion of privacy is often nonpecuniary in nature, as is the harm inflicted by statements that are illegal under §§ 912 and 1001); (3) false speech that does not cause detrimental reliance (neither perjury laws nor many of the federal false statement statutes require that anyone actually rely on the false statement); (4) particular false statements that are not shown in court to have caused specific harm (damages can be presumed in defamation actions involving knowing or reckless falsehoods, and no showing of specific harm is required in prosecutions under many of the federal false statement statutes); and (5) false speech that does not cause harm to a specific individual (the purpose of many of the federal false statement statutes is to protect government processes).}

[C.] It is true, as Justice Breyer notes, that many in our society either approve or condone certain discrete categories of false statements, including false statements made to prevent harm to innocent victims and so-called "white lies." But respondent's false claim to have received the Medal of Honor did not fall into any of these categories.... Respondent's claim, like all those covered by the Stolen Valor Act, served no valid purpose.

Respondent and others who join him in attacking the Stolen Valor Act take a different view. Respondent's brief features a veritable paean to lying. According to respondent, his lie about the Medal of Honor was nothing out of the ordinary for 21st-century Americans. "Everyone lies," he says [in his brief]. "We lie all the time." "[H]uman beings are constantly forced to choose the persona we present to the world, and our choices nearly always involve intentional omissions and misrepresentations, if not outright deception." An academic amicus tells us that the First Amendment protects the right to construct "self-aggrandizing fabrications such as having been awarded a military decoration."

This radical interpretation of the First Amendment is not supported by any precedent of this Court. The lies covered by the Stolen Valor Act have no intrinsic value and thus merit no First Amendment protection unless their prohibition would chill other expression that falls within the Amendment's scope. I now turn to that question.

[D.] While we have repeatedly endorsed the principle that false statements of fact do not merit First Amendment protection for their own sake, we have recognized that it is sometimes necessary to "exten[d] a measure of strategic protection" to these statements in order to ensure sufficient "'breathing space'" for protected speech. *Gertz.* [For example], in order to prevent the chilling of truthful speech on matters of public concern, we have held that liability for the defamation of a public official or figure requires proof that defamatory statements were made with knowledge or reckless disregard of their falsity....

[T]here are [also other] broad areas in which any attempt by the state to penalize purportedly false speech would present a grave and unacceptable danger of suppressing truthful speech. Laws restricting false statements about philosophy, religion, history, the social sciences, the arts, and other matters of public concern would present such a threat. The point is not that there is no such thing as truth or falsity in these areas or that the truth is always impossible to ascertain, but rather that it is perilous to permit the state to be the arbiter of truth.

Even where there is a wide scholarly consensus concerning a particular matter, the truth is served by allowing that consensus to be challenged without fear of reprisal. Today's accepted wisdom sometimes turns out to be mistaken. And in these contexts, "[e]ven a false statement may be deemed to make a valuable contribution to public debate, since it brings about 'the clearer perception and livelier impression of truth, produced by its collision with error.'"

Allowing the state to proscribe false statements in these areas also opens the door for the state to use its power for political ends. Statements about history illustrate this point. If some false statements about historical events may be banned, how certain must it be that a statement is false before the ban may be upheld? And who should make that calculation? While our cases prohibiting viewpoint discrimination would fetter the state's power to some degree, see *R.A.V. v. City of St. Paul* (explaining that the First Amendment does not permit the government to engage in viewpoint discrimination under the guise of regulating unprotected speech), the potential for abuse of power in these areas is simply too great.

In stark contrast to hypothetical laws prohibiting false statements about history, science, and similar matters, the Stolen Valor Act presents no risk at all that valuable speech will be suppressed. The speech punished by the Act is not only verifiably false and entirely lacking in intrinsic value, but it also fails to serve any instrumental purpose that the First Amendment might protect....

[E.] The plurality additionally worries that a decision sustaining the Stolen Valor Act might prompt Congress and the state legislatures to enact laws criminalizing lies about "an endless list of subjects." ... This concern is likely unfounded. With very good reason, military honors have traditionally been regarded as quite different from civilian awards....

In any event, if the plurality's concern is not entirely fanciful, it falls outside the purview of the First Amendment. The problem that the plurality foresees—that legislative bodies will enact unnecessary and overly intrusive criminal laws—applies regardless of whether the laws in question involve speech or nonexpressive conduct.

If there is a problem with, let us say, a law making it a criminal offense to falsely claim to have been a high school valedictorian, the problem is not the suppression of speech but the misuse of the criminal law, which should be reserved for conduct that inflicts or threatens truly serious societal harm. The objection to this hypothetical law would be the same as the objection to a law making it a crime to eat potato chips during the graduation ceremony at which the high school valedictorian is recognized.

The safeguard against such laws is democracy, not the First Amendment. Not every foolish law is unconstitutional....

ii. Applying the Rule

Justice Kennedy announced the judgment of the Court and delivered an opinion, in which the Chief Justice, Justice Ginsburg,

and Justice Sotomayor join....

[Because the plurality viewed knowingly false claims about having gotten a medal as being outside any First Amendment exception, and thus fully protected, it evaluated the law under "strict scrutiny" (see Part II.I of the casebook). The heart of its reasoning was this:—ed.]

[A.] In periods of war and peace alike public recognition of valor and noble sacrifice by men and women in uniform reinforces the pride and national resolve that the military relies upon to fulfill its mission.... The Government's interest in protecting the integrity of the Medal of Honor is beyond question.

But [under strict scrutiny,] ... the Government's chosen restriction on the speech at issue [must] be "actually necessary" to achieve its interest. There must be a direct causal link between the restriction imposed and the injury to be prevented. The link between the Government's interest in protecting the integrity of the military honors system and the Act's restriction on the false claims of liars like respondent has not been shown.... The Government points to no evidence to support its claim that the public's general perception of military awards is diluted by false claims such as those made by Alvarez....

The Government has [also] not shown, and cannot show, why counter-speech would not suffice to achieve its interest. The facts of this case indicate that the dynamics of free speech, of counterspeech, of refutation, can overcome the lie.

Respondent lied at a public meeting. Even before the FBI began investigating him for his false statements "Alvarez was perceived as a phony." Once the lie was made public, he was ridiculed online, his actions were reported in the press, and a fellow board member called for his resignation. There is good reason to believe that a similar fate would befall other false claimants....

In addition, when the Government seeks to regulate protected speech, the restriction must be the "least restrictive means among available, effective alternatives." There is, however, at least one less speech-restrictive means by which the Government could likely protect the integrity of the military awards system. A Government-created database could list Congressional Medal of Honor winners. Were a database accessible through the Internet, it would be easy to verify and expose false claims. It appears some private individuals have already created databases similar to this, and at least one database of past winners is online and fully searchable....

Justice Breyer, joined by Justice Kagan, concurring in the judgment....

[The concurrence concluded that restrictions on knowing lies should generally be evaluated under intermediate scrutiny, see casebook Parts II.H (discussing intermediate scrutiny of commercial speech restrictions) and III.A (discussing intermediate scrutiny of content-neutral speech restrictions), and therefore applied such intermediate scrutiny.—ed.]

[In my view,] it is possible substantially to achieve the Government's objective in less burdensome ways.... As is indicated by the limitations on the scope of the many other kinds of statutes regulating false factual speech, *supra*, it should be possible significantly to diminish or eliminate these remaining risks by enacting a similar but more finely tailored statute. For example, not all military awards are alike. Congress might determine that some warrant greater protection than others. And a more finely tailored statute might, as other kinds of statutes prohibiting false factual statements have done, insist upon a showing that the false statement caused specific harm or at least was material, or focus its coverage on lies most likely to be harmful or on contexts where such lies are most likely to cause harm.

I recognize that in some contexts, particularly political contexts, such a narrowing will not always be easy to achieve. In the political arena a false statement is more likely to make a behavioral difference (say, by leading the listeners to vote for the speaker) but at the same time criminal prosecution is particularly dangerous (say, by radically changing a potential election result) and consequently can more easily result in censorship of speakers and their ideas. Thus, the statute may have to be significantly narrowed in its applications. Some lower courts have upheld the constitutionality of roughly comparable but narrowly tailored statutes in political contexts. *See, e.g., United We Stand America, Inc. v. United We Stand, America New York, Inc.*, 128 F.3d 86 (2d Cir. 1997) (upholding against First Amendment challenge application of Lanham Act to a political organization); *Treasurer of the Committee to Elect Gerald D. Lostracco v. Fox*, 389 N.W.2d 446 (Mich. Ct. App. 1986) (upholding under First Amendment statute prohibiting campaign material falsely claiming that one is an incumbent).

Without expressing any view on the validity of those cases, I would also note, like the plurality, that in this area more accurate information will normally counteract the lie. And an accurate, publicly available register of military awards, easily obtainable by political opponents, may well adequately protect the integrity of an award against those who would falsely claim to have earned it....

Justice Alito, joined by Justice Scalia and Justice Thomas, dissenting.

[The dissent reasoned that the law need not be subjected either to intermediate scrutiny or strict scrutiny, because knowing lies are generally constitutionally unprotected, but nonetheless also argued that the law served an important interest, and that less restrictive alternatives proposed by the plurality and the concurrence would be inadequate.—ed.]

[A.] Congress passed the Stolen Valor Act in response to a proliferation of false claims concerning the receipt of military awards. For example, in a single year, more than 600 Virginia residents falsely claimed to have won the Medal of Honor. An investigation of the 333 people listed in the online edition of Who's Who as having received a top military award revealed that fully a third of the claims could not be substantiated. [More details omitted.—ed.] ...

It is well recognized in trademark law that the proliferation of cheap imitations of luxury goods blurs the "'signal' given out by the purchasers of the originals." In much the same way, the proliferation of false claims about military awards blurs the signal given out by the actual awards by making them seem more common than they really are, and this diluting effect harms the military by hampering its efforts to foster morale and esprit de corps. Surely it was reasonable for Congress to conclude that the goal of preserving the integrity of our country's top military honors is at least as worthy as that of protecting the prestige associated with fancy watches and designer handbags.

[B.] Congress had ample reason to believe that alternative approaches [for preserving the integrity of military honors] would not be adequate.... [Publishing a] comprehensive list or database of actual medal recipients ..., unfortunately, will not work. The Department of Defense has explained that the most that it can do is to create a database of recipients of certain top military honors awarded since 2001. {In addition, since the Department may not disclose the Social Security numbers or birthdates of recipients, this database would be of limited use in ascertaining the veracity of a claim involving a person with a common name.}

Because a sufficiently comprehensive database is not practicable, lies about military awards cannot be remedied by what the plurality calls "counterspeech." ... In addition, a steady stream of stories in the media about the exposure of imposters would tend to increase skepticism among members of the public about the entire awards system. This would only exacerbate the harm that the Stolen Valor Act is meant to prevent.

The plurality and the concurrence also suggest that Congress could protect the system of military honors by enacting a narrower statute[, for instance focused on] ... lies that are intended to "secure moneys or other valuable considerations." ... But much damage is caused, both to real award recipients and to the system of military honors, by false statements that are not linked to any financial or other tangible reward. Unless even a small financial loss—say, a dollar given to a homeless man falsely claiming to be a decorated veteran—is more important in the eyes of the First Amendment than the damage caused to the very integrity of the military awards system, there is no basis for distinguishing between the Stolen Valor Act and the alternative statutes that the plurality and concurrence appear willing to sustain.

Justice Breyer also proposes narrowing the statute so that it covers a shorter list of military awards, but he does not provide a hint about where he thinks the line must be drawn. Perhaps he expects Congress to keep trying until it eventually passes a law that draws the line in just the right place....

7. Special Protection for the Institutional Media?

a. *Generally*

The Supreme Court has generally interpreted the First Amendment as providing no special protection to the institutional media as compared to other speakers. In *New York Times v. Sullivan*, for instance, the defendants were both the newspaper (part of the institutional media) and the activists who placed the advertisement in the newspaper (not part of the institutional media); the Court treated both the same way. In *Dun & Bradstreet*, five Justices (the dissenters and Justice White) expressly rejected the argument that nonmedia defendants (such as Dun & Bradstreet) should get lesser First Amendment protections. This view reflects a largely unbroken American tradition from the Framing to now. *See* Eugene Volokh, *Freedom for the Press as an Industry, or for the Press as a Technology?—From the Framing to Today*, 160 U. Pa. L. Rev. 459 (2012).

Nonetheless, in some libel cases, including some after *Dun & Bradstreet*, the Court has reserved the question whether the institutional media should have greater First Amendment rights than other speakers. *See, e.g.*, *Milkovich v. Lorain Journal Co.*, 497 U.S. 1, 20 n.6 (1990). And while most lower court opinions considering the question hold that the institutional media have the same First Amendment rights as do others who use mass communications technology, about a dozen lower court cases take a different view. *See, e.g.*, *Fleming v. Moore*, 275 S.E.2d 632 (Va. 1981) (holding that *Gertz* doesn't apply to speakers who are not part of the institutional media, such as people who buy political advertisements); *Wheeler v. Green*, 593 P.2d 777 (Ore. 1979) (same, as to authors of letters to the editor). The question thus still remains open, though the weight of authority is against any special First Amendment rights for the institutional media.

Note that this all relates to *First Amendment* rights. Some additional statutory protections, not required by the First Amendment, are indeed limited to the institutional media—see, for instance, the journalist privilege provisions noted at p. 432.

b. *Lovell v. City of Griffin, 303 U.S. 444 (1938)*

Chief Justice Hughes delivered the opinion of the Court....

[The Court struck down an ordinance that gave city authorities broad power to bar leafletting, reasoning in part:—ed.]

The liberty of the press is not confined to newspapers and periodicals. It necessarily embraces pamphlets and leaflets.... The press in its historic connotation comprehends every sort of publication which affords a vehicle of information and opinion....

c. *Branzburg v. Hayes, 408 U.S. 665 (1972)*

Opinion of the Court by Justice White ....

[The Court rejected a claim of a special newsman's privilege to resist subpoenas related to confidential sources, reasoning in part that any such privilege couldn't be limited to a narrow category of professional journalists:—ed.]

The administration of a constitutional newsman's privilege would [also] present practical and conceptual difficulties of a high order. Sooner or later, it would be necessary to define those categories of newsmen who qualified for the privilege, a questionable procedure in light of the traditional doctrine that liberty of the press is the right of the lonely pamphleteer ... just as much as of the large metropolitan publisher .... The informative function asserted by representatives of the organized press ... is also performed by lecturers, political pollsters, novelists, academic researchers, and dramatists. Almost any author may quite accurately assert that he is contributing to the flow of information to the public, that he relies on confidential sources of information, and that these sources will be silenced if he is forced to make disclosures before a grand jury....

d. *Citizens United v. FEC, 558 U.S. 310 (2010)*

[The question in *Citizens United*, a case you'll see discussed in much more detail in Part V.D, was whether the government could restrict corporate and union speech supporting or opposing political candidates. Of course, most media outlets—newspapers, magazines, cable television channels—are owned by corporations. One common argument in this debate therefore goes like this:

Supporters of restrictions on corporate speech: Corporate speech supporting or opposing candidates should be restricted to prevent corruption, diminish inequality, or protect shareholders.

Supporters of protection for corporate speech: But under your theory, Congress and state legislatures could likewise restrict such speech by corporate-owned newspapers, magazines, and cable channels. That can't be right. Therefore, corporate speech must remain protected.

Supporters of restrictions on corporate speech: No, our theory is that the First Amendment *does* protect media corporations (perhaps because the Free Press Clause specially protects the institutional media), but doesn't protect other corporations, at least in this situation.

Supporters of protection for corporate speech: No, there's no basis for reading the First Amendment as setting up different levels of protection for media corporations and nonmedia corporations.

Of course, not all participants in campaign finance debates make these arguments, but many do, as you can see below.—ed.]

Justice Kennedy delivered the opinion of the Court....

[The antidistortion rationale for restricting corporate speech would let Congress] ban political speech of media corporations. Cf. *Miami Herald Co. v. Tornillo* (alleging the existence of "vast accumulations of unreviewable power in the modern media empires"). Media corporations are now exempt from § 441b's ban on corporate expenditures [because of the statutory exemption for "any news story, commentary, or editorial distributed through the facilities of any broadcasting station, newspaper, magazine, or other periodical publication."—ed.]. Yet media corporations accumulate wealth with the help of the corporate form, the largest media corporations have "immense aggregations of wealth," and the views expressed by media corporations often "have little or no correlation to the public's support" for those views. Thus, under the Government's reasoning, wealthy media corporations could have their voices diminished to put them on par with other media entities....

The media exemption discloses further difficulties with the law now under consideration.... "We have consistently rejected the proposition that the institutional press has any constitutional privilege beyond that of other speakers." See *Dun & Bradstreet, Inc. v. Greenmoss Builders, Inc.* (Brennan, J., joined by Marshall, Blackmun, and Stevens, JJ., dissenting); *id.* (White, J., concurring in judgment). With the advent of the Internet and the decline of print and broadcast media, moreover, the line between the media and others who wish to comment on political and social issues becomes far more blurred.

The law's exception for media corporations is, on its own terms, all but an admission of the invalidity of the antidistortion rationale. And the exemption results in a further, separate reason for finding this law invalid: Again by its own terms, the law exempts some corporations but covers others, even though both have the need or the motive to communicate their views. The exemption applies to media corporations owned or controlled by corporations that have diverse and substantial investments and participate in endeavors other than news.

So even assuming the most doubtful proposition that a news organization has a right to speak when others do not, the exemption would allow a conglomerate that owns both a media business and an unrelated business to influence or control the media in order to advance its overall business interest. At the same time, some other corporation, with an identical business interest but no media outlet in its ownership structure, would be forbidden to speak or inform the public about the same issue....

Chief Justice Roberts, with whom Justice Alito joins, concurring...

If taken seriously, [the antidistortion] logic would apply most directly to newspapers and other media corporations. They have a more profound impact on public discourse than most other speakers.

These corporate entities are, for the time being, not subject to § 441b's otherwise generally applicable prohibitions on corporate political speech. But this is simply a matter of legislative grace. The fact that the law currently grants a favored position to media corporations is no reason to overlook the danger inherent in accepting a theory that would allow government restrictions on their political speech.... [The antidistortion logic thus] threatens to undermine our First Amendment jurisprudence and the nature of public discourse more broadly ....

Justice Scalia, [with whom Justices Thomas and Alito join in relevant part], concurring.

The dissent ... interpret[s] the Freedom of the Press Clause to refer to the institutional press .... It is passing strange to interpret the phrase "the freedom of speech, or of the press" to mean, not everyone's right to speak or publish, but rather everyone's right to speak or the institutional press's right to publish. No one thought that is what it meant. Patriot Noah Webster's 1828 dictionary contains, under the word "press," the following entry:

> *Liberty of the press,* in civil policy, is the free right of publishing books, pamphlets, or papers without previous restraint; or the unrestrained right which every citizen enjoys of publishing his thoughts and opinions, subject only to punishment for publishing what is pernicious to morals or to the peace of the state.

As the Court's opinion describes, our jurisprudence agrees with Noah Webster and contradicts the dissent. "The liberty of the press is not confined to newspapers and periodicals. It necessarily embraces pamphlets and leaflets.... The press in its historical connotation comprehends every sort of publication which affords a vehicle of information and opinion." *Lovell v. City of Griffin*.

Justice Stevens, with whom Justice Ginsburg, Justice Breyer, and Justice Sotomayor join, ... dissenting in [relevant] part....

Justice Scalia ... would seemingly read out the Free Press Clause [from the First Amendment]: How else could he claim that my purported views on newspapers must track my views on corporations generally? {In fact, the Free Press Clause might be turned against Justice Scalia, for two reasons. First, we learn from it that the drafters of the First Amendment did draw distinctions—explicit distinctions—between types of "speakers," or speech outlets or forms.

Second, the Court's strongest historical evidence all relates to the Framers' views on the press, yet while the Court tries to sweep this evidence into the Free Speech Clause, the Free Press Clause provides a more natural textual home. The text and history highlighted by our colleagues suggests why one type of corporation, those that are part of the press, might be able to claim special First Amendment status ....} ...

The press plays a unique role not only in the text, history, and structure of the First Amendment but also in facilitating public discourse; ... "media corporations differ significantly from other corporations in that their resources are devoted to the collection of information and its dissemination to the public."

Our colleagues have raised some interesting and difficult questions about Congress' authority to regulate electioneering by the press, and about how to define what constitutes the press. *But that is not the case before us.* Section 203 does not apply to media corporations, and even if it did, Citizens United is not a media corporation. There would be absolutely no reason to consider the issue of media corporations if the majority did not ... invent the theory that legislatures must eschew all "identity"-based distinctions and treat a local nonprofit news outlet exactly the same as General Motors....

8. ANTI-SLAPP STATUTES

a. Anti-SLAPP Statutes as an Additional Statutory Protection for Speech

In recent decades, over a dozen states—including California, Florida, and New York—have enacted so-called "anti-SLAPP statutes," which try to decrease the "chilling effect" of certain kinds of libel litigation and other speech-restrictive litigation.

"SLAPP" stands for "Strategic Lawsuit Against Public Participation." The term has generally referred to lawsuits brought by some entities to deter political opposition to their projects. A classic SLAPP scenario involves a real estate developer suing neighbors who oppose its projects, though such lawsuits have also been brought by disability rights advocates who want to set up group homes for the disabled, and by others.

Because even an unfounded suit by a relatively rich entity against a person of modest means can cause the person to quickly surrender, even meritless SLAPPs may deter public debate. Anti-SLAPP statutes seek to prevent such unfounded suits by making them easier to dismiss early, and by making plaintiffs pay defendants' attorney fees if the suit is dismissed.

Anti-SLAPP statutes are not constitutionally required, and many states don't have them. They are an example of an "optional speech protection" that goes beyond the minimum that the First Amendment commands. Other examples involve state journalists' shield laws (see p. 432 below) and statutes that diminish publishers' libel liability if the publisher promptly prints a retraction.

b. Problem: Corporate Publicity

A manufacturer, the Snoopy Newman Pajama Company, produces a 7-minute film about its efforts to improve living conditions in Djibouti, where one of its factories is located. The Company agrees to sponsor a 37-minute long cable television documentary about Djibouti, on the condition that the company-produced film be included as part of the broadcast, with a suitable disclaimer disclosing the deal to viewers. The cable network broadcasts the resulting 44-minute film, together with the normal commercials that the network would sell during such a program.

A competitor sues the Company under a statute prohibiting false and misleading advertising. The competitor claims that the Company-produced film contained some false statements and some misleading ones. The statute allows a successful plaintiff to get an injunction against future repetitions of the false and misleading advertising, and to collect attorney fees and court costs.

The Company wants to file an anti-SLAPP motion. Does the anti-SLAPP statute apply to this litigation? If it does, what remedies would the Company be entitled to, and under what circumstances?

c.   Cal. Code Civ. Proc. §§ 425.16, 425.17

§ 425.16 (enacted 1992): (a) The Legislature finds ... that there has been a disturbing increase in lawsuits brought primarily to chill the valid exercise of the constitutional rights of freedom of speech and petition for the redress of grievances. The Legislature finds ... that it is in the public interest to encourage continued participation in matters of public significance, and that this participation should not be chilled through abuse of the judicial process. To this end, this section shall be construed broadly.

(b)(1) A cause of action against a person arising from any act of that person in furtherance of the person's right of petition or free speech ... in connection with a public issue shall be subject to a special motion to strike, unless the court determines that the plaintiff has established that there is a probability that the plaintiff will prevail on the claim.

(2) In making its determination, the court shall consider the pleadings, and supporting and opposing affidavits stating the facts upon which the liability or defense is based....

(c) In any action subject to subdivision (b), a prevailing defendant ... shall be entitled to recover his or her attorney's fees and costs. If the court finds that a special motion to strike is frivolous or is solely intended to cause unnecessary delay, the court shall award costs and reasonable attorney's fees to a plaintiff prevailing on the motion ....

(d) This section shall not apply to [enforcement actions brought by the government] ....

(e) As used in this section, "act in furtherance of a person's right of petition or free speech ... in connection with a public issue" includes [testimony and other statements in government proceedings, and] ...

(3) any written or oral statement or writing made in a place open to the public or a public forum in connection with an issue of public interest;

(4) or any other conduct in furtherance of the exercise of the constitutional right of petition or the constitutional right of free speech in connection with a public issue or an issue of public interest.

(f) The special motion ... shall be noticed for hearing not more than 30 days after service ....

(g) All discovery proceedings in the action shall be stayed [while the motion is pending, unless the court orders otherwise] ....

§ 425.17 (enacted 2003): ... (b) Section 425.16 does not apply to any action brought solely in the public interest or on behalf of the general public if all of the following conditions exist:

(1) The plaintiff does not seek any relief greater than or different from the relief sought for the general public or a class of which the plaintiff is a member. A claim for attorney's fees, costs, or penalties does not constitute greater or different relief for purposes of this subdivision.

(2) The action, if successful, would enforce an important right affecting

the public interest, and would confer a significant benefit, whether pecuniary or nonpecuniary, on the general public or a large class of persons.

(3) Private enforcement is necessary and places a disproportionate financial burden on the plaintiff in relation to the plaintiff's stake in the matter.

(c) Section 425.16 does not apply to any cause of action brought against a person primarily engaged in the business of selling or leasing goods or services ... arising from any statement or conduct by that person if ...:

(1) The statement or conduct consists of representations of fact about that person's or a business competitor's business operations, goods, or services, that is made for the purpose of obtaining approval for, promoting, or securing ... commercial transactions [in] the person's goods or services, or the statement or conduct was made in the course of delivering the person's goods or services [and]

(2) The intended audience is an actual or potential ... customer, or a person likely to repeat the statement to, or otherwise influence, an actual or potential ... customer, or the statement or conduct arose out of or within ... a regulatory approval process, proceeding, or investigation ....

(d) Subdivisions (b) and (c) do not apply to any of the following:

(1) Any [journalist or publisher, as defined in Cal. Const. art. I, § 2 (p. 432 below)] or any person engaged in the dissemination of ideas or expression in any book or academic journal, while engaged in the gathering, receiving, or processing of information for communication to the public.

(2) Any action against any person or entity based upon the creation, dissemination, exhibition, advertisement, or other similar promotion of any dramatic, literary, musical, political, or artistic work, including, but not limited to, a motion picture or television program, or an article published in a newspaper or magazine of general circulation.

(3) Any nonprofit organization that receives more than 50 percent of its annual revenues from ... government grants ... or reimbursements ....

9. Publishing or Distributing Others' False Statements

a. Summary

The First Amendment allows defamation liability to be imposed not just on the original authors of false statements of fact, but also on those who republish or redistribute the statements (subject to the First Amendment limitations discussed above). But this is constrained by certain common-law and statutory rules, see items 4–6 below.

1. First, let's distinguish three kinds of potential libel defendants:

(a) *Publishers*, such as newspapers, magazines, and broadcast stations, which themselves print or broadcast material submitted by others. This also includes authors, such as bloggers, writing their own work, even when they quote other sources.

(b) *Distributors*, such as bookstores, newsstands, and libraries, which distribute copies that have been printed by others.

(c) *Internet forum providers*, such as (i) Internet Service Providers (*e.g.*, America Online) that let users post to discussion groups on the ISPs' computers, (ii) ISPs that let users put up Web pages, (iii) Web discussion group operators that let users post items to a Web page, and (iv) blog operators that let users post comments.

2. All these defendants are liable under respondeat superior for false statements prepared by their employees, if the *employee-author* has the proper mens rea for liability. Since the employer's liability is derivative of the employee's, the employee's mens rea is the important issue.

3. Publishers are liable for nonemployees' false statements that they publish—for instance, op-eds by independent columnists, letters to the editor, or advertisements—if the *publisher* (which is to say the employee of the publisher who selected the items) has the proper mens rea for liability. *See* Restatement (Second) of Torts § 578.

4. Distributors, however, are liable only if they know the defamatory character of the material, or have "reason to know" it (*i.e.*, know facts from which a reasonable person would infer that the material is defamatory)—for instance, because the target of the defamation alerted the distributor, and pointed to evidence that the material is indeed false. Distributors have no duty to read through all the material they carry to see whether the materials might contain something defamatory. *See* Restatement (Second) of Torts § 581; *Janklow v. Viking Press*, 378 N.W.2d 875 (S.D. 1985).

— The distributor/publisher distinction was much more important before *New York Times Co. v. Sullivan* (1964) (p. 65), when libel law was generally based on strict liability. Publishers were subject to strict liability, but distributors were subject to know-or-reason-to-know liability, which was less demanding than "actual malice" but more demanding than negligence (because of the narrow definition of "reason to know"). After *Sullivan* and *Gertz v. Robert Welch, Inc.* (1974) (p. 77), the distributor/publisher distinction is

(a) basically unimportant for public figure/public concern statements (where the "actual malice" constitutional standard equally protects both publishers and distributors), and

(b) not hugely important for private figure/public concern statements (where the negligence constitutional standard provides protection to publishers that's not that far from what the know-or-reason-to-know standard gives distributors), but

(c) still potentially quite important for private concern statements in those jurisdictions that impose strict liability on publishers based on such statements.

5. Internet forum providers are *categorically immune* from defamation liability for things posted by their users. *See* 47 U.S.C. § 230 (enacted

1996), as interpreted by various lower court cases.

— This is true whether or not the forum provider exercises some editorial control over the users' posts. Defendants are immune even if they delete certain posts, only approve certain posts for distribution, edit out certain words or phrases, or manually copy users' submissions onto their Web site. See, *e.g.*, *Batzel v. Smith*, 333 F.3d 1018 (9th Cir. 2003). (Of course, if the material became defamatory because of the forum provider's edits—for instance if the provider edits the obviously hyperbolic "Volokh kills his students by assigning them too much reading" into the purportedly factual "Volokh kills his students"—the provider may be liable because his edits are themselves defamatory.)

— It is true even when the defendant actually knows that the statement is false, for instance when the libeled person has given the defendant evidence of the falsehood.

— Section 230 also preempts civil liability under a wide range of other state laws (such as the invasion of privacy tort), but doesn't affect intellectual property laws or federal criminal laws.

— The statute was preceded by two trial court decisions, *Cubby v. Compuserve, Inc.*, 776 F. Supp. 135 (S.D.N.Y. 1991), and *Stratton Oakmont, Inc. v. Prodigy Services Co.*, 1995 WL 805178 (N.Y. Sup. Ct.). *Cubby* held that Internet Service Providers (such as Compuserve) were entitled to be treated as distributors, not publishers. *Stratton Oakmont* held that only ISPs that exercised no editorial control over publicly posted materials would get distributor treatment, and ISPs that exercised some editorial control would be treated as publishers. This gave ISPs an incentive not to police their public areas for profanity, insults, and even defamation.

47 U.S.C. § 230 was intended to reverse *Stratton Oakmont*, but was written broadly enough that it could be interpreted as providing categorical immunity, even beyond the more limited immunity that distributors had enjoyed under Restatement (Second) of Torts § 581. That is in fact how § 230 has been interpreted by nearly all the courts that have considered it.

6. Let's return to publishers, when they quote others' statements. Say Alan writes, "Betty alleges Charlie committed armed robbery." Alan's statement is literally true: Betty did make the allegation. But the statement he is reporting on (Betty's statement) is false, and Alan has the requisite mens rea as to it (for instance, he entertained serious doubts about the truth of Betty's allegation, which is enough to make him liable for recklessness, even if Charlie is a public figure).

a. The general "republication rule" is that a publisher is responsible for the factual assertions in others' statements (subject to the mens rea and other requirements discussed in previous sections), even when he expressly attributes the statements to others. The accuracy of Alan's statement is evaluated as to the allegation it repeats (Betty's report), and not only as to the assertion it literally makes (that Betty reported it). Restatement (Second) of Torts § 578. And this is generally true even if Alan distances himself from the allegation, for instance by saying that Charlie has denied the statement, or that Betty has reason to lie. The principle is that "Tale bearers are as bad as tale makers."

b. Some recent cases disagree, and evaluate the statement's truth based on whether the allegation had been made, not based on whether the allegation (which the statement reports) is true. See, *e.g.*, *KTRK Television v. Felder*, 950 S.W.2d 100 (Tex. App. 1997); *In re United Press Int'l*, 106 Bankr. 323 (D.D.C. 1989). This, though, is a minority view; the view mentioned in (a) remains dominant.

c. But say a reporter is covering a trial, in which witnesses are making assertions that the reporter knows are false, or knows are likely false; or say a reporter is reporting on some official government report. The law has long recognized that such speech must in some measure be immune from liability, even when under the general rule (see 6.a above) the reporter's speech would be actionable. Under the common-law *fair report* privilege, the reporter and the newspaper are protected against liability for evenhanded and substantially accurate reports of government proceedings. In many states, this is an absolute privilege, applicable *even when* the reporter knows that the statements within those proceedings are false (or are likely to be false).

In the other states, though, this privilege is merely a "qualified" privilege, which means it can be lost when the reporter is acting with "actual malice." Such a qualified privilege still offers some protection, for instance when the statements are about a private figure and would thus be actionable if said negligently—the reporter would then get the benefit of the "actual malice" test under the qualified privilege, rather than just the negligence test that would be applicable without the privilege. But if the reporter knows the statement in the government proceeding is false (or is reckless about the possibility), he and his employer can be held liable.

The Court has never decided whether an absolute fair report privilege is constitutionally mandated.

d. What if the reported-on statement is outside a government proceeding? Consider this incident, from *Norton v. Glenn*, 860 A.2d 48 (Pa. 2004): "[City councilman Glenn] claimed that [council president Norton] and [city mayor] Wolfe were homosexuals and ... strongly impl[ied] that Glenn considered Norton and Wolfe to be 'queers and child molesters.' ... Glenn [also] asserted that Norton had made homosexual advances toward Glenn which escalated to Norton grabbing Glenn's penis ...." A newspaper published an article accurately describing the charges, and quoting Norton's unequivocal denial; the newspaper didn't adopt or concur in Glenn's statements. Norton and Wolfe sued both the newspaper and Glenn. The jury in the lawsuit against Glenn found that the statements were false.

Some courts would hold that the newspaper would nonetheless be protected under a First Amendment "neutral reportage" privilege, because the charges themselves were newsworthy even if they were false. (Why might that be?) "[W]hen a responsible, prominent organization ... makes serious charges against a public figure, the First Amendment protects the accurate and disinterested reporting of those charges," even when the reporter has serious doubts about the accuracy of the charges. *Edwards v. National Audubon Soc'y*, 556 F.2d 113 (2d Cir. 1977). Some later cases have extended this to certain charges on matters of public concern against private figures, and to statements made not just by responsible, prominent organizations but by any public figure, or even by any nonanonymous source.

Other courts, however, have rejected the neutral reportage privilege. In *Norton*, for instance, the Pennsylvania Supreme Court held that Norton's and Wolfe's lawsuit against the paper could go forward, and the paper could be held liable if it published Glenn's statements knowing of a high probability they were false. The case eventually settled for an undisclosed amount.

b. *Problem: Electronic Employment Services*

Electronic Employment Services provides a Web site for employers who are looking for workers and employees who are looking for work (think of it as an employment dating service). EES would like to set up some discussion groups in which jobhunters can discuss their experiences working for various companies. The plan is that any of EES's jobhunting customers can access the Web site and post messages that would then be readable by all the other jobhunters; the others could then respond to them, and so on until the conversation is exhausted.

EES is concerned, however, that it may be held liable for libelous statements in the messages. How would this have come out under the Restatement framework? How would this come out under 47 U.S.C. § 230? What would you advise EES to do?

c. *Restatement (Second) of Torts §§ 578, 581 (1977)*

§ 578. *Liability of Republisher*: Except [as provided by § 581], one who repeats or otherwise republishes defamatory matter is subject to liability as if he had originally published it....

Illustrations: 1. A newspaper feature syndicate supplies a defamatory article to each of its subscribing newspapers. Each paper that prints the article ... is separately subject to liability....

§ 581. *Transmission of Defamation Published by Third Person*: ... [O]ne who only delivers [*e.g.*, sells] or transmits defamatory matter published by a third person is subject to liability if, but only if, he knows or has reason to know of its defamatory character [except if the transmission is via radio or television, in which case § 578 applies].

Comment: ... b.... [N]either ["delivers" nor "transmits"] applies to one who merely makes available to another equipment or facilities that he may use himself for general communication purposes. This is true of the supplier of a typewriter ... [and] of a telephone company [which are generally immune from liability—ed.].

d.... [A] news dealer [or bookstore owner or library operator] is not liable for defamatory statements appearing in the [material] that he sells if he neither knows nor has reason to know of the defamatory [item]. The dealer is under no duty to examine the various publications that he offers for sale to ascertain whether they contain any defamatory items.

Unless there are special circumstances that should warn the dealer that a particular publication is defamatory, he is under no duty to ascertain its innocent or defamatory character. On the other hand, when a dealer offers for sale a particular paper or magazine that notoriously persists in printing scandalous items, the vendor may do so at the risk that any particular issue may contain defamatory language.... [Likewise, if] a particular author or a particular publisher has frequently published notoriously sensational or scandalous books, a shop or library that offers to the public such literature may take the risk of becoming liable to any one who may be defamed by them.

g.... [R]adio and television broadcasting companies ... are publishers more nearly analogous to a newspaper or the publisher of a book than to a telegraph company.... [T]hey initiate, select and put upon the air their own programs; or by contract they permit others to make use of their facilities to do so, and they cooperate actively in the publication. Their activity is similar to that of a newspaper, which employs its own reporters or writers to prepare matter to be published, or by contract agrees to publish matter, such as advertisements, prepared and controlled by others....

d.   47 U.S.C. § 230 (enacted 1996)

(a) ... The Congress finds the following: ...

(3) The Internet and other interactive computer services offer a forum for a true diversity of political discourse, unique opportunities for cultural development, and myriad avenues for intellectual activity.

(4) The Internet and other interactive computer services have flourished, to the benefit of all Americans, with a minimum of government regulation....

(b) ... It is the policy of the United States—

(1) to promote the continued development of the Internet and other interactive computer services and other interactive media; ...

(4) to remove disincentives for the development and utilization of blocking and filtering technologies that empower parents to restrict their children's access to objectionable or inappropriate online material ....

(c) Protection for "Good Samaritan" blocking and screening of offensive material.

(1) ... No provider or user of an interactive computer service shall be

treated as the publisher or speaker of any information provided by another information content provider.

(2) ... No provider or user of an interactive computer service shall be held liable on account of ... any action voluntarily taken in good faith to restrict access to or availability of material that the provider or user considers to be obscene, lewd, lascivious, filthy, excessively violent, harassing, or otherwise objectionable, whether or not such material is constitutionally protected ....

(e) ... (1) ... Nothing in this section shall be construed to impair the enforcement of ... [any] Federal criminal statute.

(2) ... Nothing in this section shall be construed to limit or expand any law pertaining to intellectual property.

(3) ... No cause of action may be brought and no liability may be imposed under any State or local law that is inconsistent with this section.

(f) ... (2) ... The term "interactive computer service" means any information service, system, or access software provider that provides or enables computer access by multiple users to a computer server, including specifically a service or system that provides access to the Internet ....

(3) ... The term "information content provider" means any person or entity that is responsible, in whole or in part, for the creation or development of information provided through the Internet or any other interactive computer service.

C. Obscenity

1. Current Law

a. *Summary*

Rule: Speech is unprotected if

1. "the [a] average person, [b] applying contemporary community standards, would find that the work, [c] taken as a whole, [d] appeals to the prurient interest," and

2. "the work depicts or describes, [a] in a patently offensive way [under [b] contemporary community standards, *Smith v. United States*, 431 U.S. 291 (1977)], [c] sexual conduct specifically defined by the applicable state law," and

3. "the work, [a] taken as a whole, [b] lacks serious [c] literary, artistic, political, or scientific value." *Miller v. California* (1973) (p. 128).

Subsidiary rules:

1. While distribution of obscene material, and even transportation of it for one's own private use, may be outlawed, see *United States v. Orito*, 413 U.S. 139 (1973), private possession at home may not be. *Stanley v. Georgia*, 394 U.S. 557 (1969).

2. The phrase "appeals to the prurient interest" is limited to speech appealing to a "shameful or morbid interest in sex." Speech appealing to "normal" interests in sex—"material that, taken as a whole, does no more than arouse 'good, old fashioned, healthy' interest in sex"—is not included. *Brockett v. Spokane Arcades, Inc.*, 472 U.S. 491 (1985).

— *United States v. Stevens* (2010) (p. 145) and *Brown v. Entertainment Merchants Ass'n* (2011) (p. 150) show that a sexual interest is indeed required. An interest in violence, for instance, even if seen as "shameful or morbid" by legislators and juries, doesn't qualify unless there is a sexual component to it.

3. "Where the material is designed for and primarily disseminated to a clearly defined deviant sexual group, ... the prurient-appeal requirement ... is satisfied if the dominant theme of the material taken as a whole appeals to the prurient interest in sex of the members of that group." *Mishkin v. New York*, 383 U.S. 502 (1966).

4. The serious value prong looks to whether "a reasonable person would find [serious] value in the material," not to whether "an ordinary member of any given community" would find such value. *Pope v. Illinois*, 481 U.S. 497 (1987).

5. A defendant can be punished only if he knows (or, possibly, has reason to know) the contents of the material. Reasonable ignorance is certainly a defense, *Smith v. California*, 361 U.S. 147 (1959); it's not clear whether negligent ignorance is a defense.

6. But a defendant needn't know the material is actually obscene; mistake of law is no defense. *Hamling v. United States*, 418 U.S. 87 (1974).

7. The government may also bar people from

— selling to customers whom they know to be (or perhaps should know to be) *minors*

— works that fit a special "obscene as to minors" test—the standard obscenity test but with "to minors" added at the end of each prong:

   a. the average person, applying contemporary community standards, would find the work, taken as a whole and with respect to minors, is designed to appeal to, or is designed to pander to, the prurient interest;

   b. the work depicts or describes, in a manner patently offensive with respect to minors, sexual conduct specifically defined by applicable state law; and

   c. the work taken as a whole, lacks serious literary, artistic, political, or scientific value for minors.

— *Ginsberg v. New York*, 390 U.S. 629 (1968), a pre-*Miller* case, upheld a law that implemented the then-current obscenity test with "to minors" added at the end of each prong; most lower courts and commentators have assumed that *Ginsberg* plus *Miller* justify laws that implement the *Miller*-based test given above.

Policy explanations for the exception:

1. Obscenity has "a tendency to exert a corrupting and debasing impact leading to antisocial behavior." *Paris Adult Theatre I v. Slaton* (1973) (p. 133). The concern isn't that any one particular obscene work will cause someone to do something bad (as with incitement). Rather, it's that the aggregate of such works will slowly change a consumer's attitudes—and therefore his behavior—for the worse. (Compare some of the arguments being made with regard to violence on television.)

2. How does obscenity differ from other speech that can lead to antisocial behavior—for instance, advocacy of violence—but that is nonetheless protected? Because it "by definition lacks any serious literary, artistic, political, or scientific value as communication," and therefore control of obscenity "is distinct from a control of reason and the intellect." *Slaton.*

3. Also, obscenity laws have a long tradition in American law, which *Roth* concluded extends to the time the First Amendment was drafted.

4. In recent years, the obscenity exception has in practice been narrow.

Policy arguments inferable from the existence of the exception:

1. It sometimes is permissible to restrict speech because of its long-term tendency to influence listeners to do bad things.

2. The law may permissibly sort material that has "serious value" from material that doesn't, and punish the latter but not the former.

Arguments for why this exception is unsound:

1. It shouldn't be up to the government to decide what's seriously valuable and what's not.

2. The test is too vague to provide adequate guidance to people, and might therefore lead them to overconstrain themselves.

3. Sexually explicit material necessarily communicates certain viewpoints—that sex (or the particular kind of sex being depicted) is good—and thus does have political value.

Query: Does sexually explicit material communicate in a different way than other material? Does its power to cause arousal make it different from other material that can cause bad ideas or, eventually, bad actions?

b. *Problem: Mafiosi in Love*

An Ohio statute says "The distribution, purchase, and rental of any material that's obscene under the standards of *Miller v. California* is prohibited." Martin Scorsese's new movie, *Mafiosi in Love*, has four extremely arousing sexual scenes that are more explicit than anything seen in Hollywood studio productions to date. When Cathy Seipp rents a video of *Mafiosi*, both she and the video store owner (Mitch Gunzler) are prosecuted. Will their Free Speech Clause defenses succeed?

c. *Miller v. California, 413 U.S. 15 (1973)*

Chief Justice Burger delivered the opinion of the Court....

[A.] Appellant ... was convicted of ... knowingly distributing obscene matter ... [for] causing five unsolicited advertising brochures to be sent [as part of a mass mailing] in an envelope addressed to a restaurant in Newport Beach, California. The envelope was opened by the manager of the restaurant and his mother. They had not requested the brochures; they complained to the police.

The brochures advertise four books entitled "Intercourse," "Man-Woman," "Sex Orgies Illustrated," and "An Illustrated History of Pornography," and a film entitled "Marital Intercourse." While the brochures contain some descriptive printed material, primarily they consist of pictures and drawings very explicitly depicting men and women in groups of two or more engaging in a variety of sexual activities, with genitals often prominently displayed.

[B.] [S]ince the Court now undertakes to formulate standards more concrete than those in the past, it is useful for us to focus on two of the landmark cases in the somewhat tortured history of the Court's obscenity decisions. In *Roth v. United States,* ... [f]ive Justices joined in the opinion stating:

> All ideas having even the slightest redeeming social importance—unorthodox ideas, controversial ideas, even ideas hateful to the prevailing climate of opinion—have the full protection of the [First Amendment] guaranties, unless excludable because they encroach upon the limited area of more important interests. But implicit in the history of the First Amendment is the rejection of obscenity as utterly without redeeming social importance.... *"[S]uch utterances are no essential part of any exposition of ideas, and are of such slight social value as a step to truth that any benefit that may be derived from them is clearly outweighed by the social interest in order and morality...."* ...

[Handwritten margin note: have full Protection unless excludable because they encroach upon the limited area of more important interest]

Nine years later, in *Memoirs v. Massachusetts,* 383 U.S. 413 (1966), the Court veered sharply away from the *Roth* concept and, with only three Justices in the plurality opinion, articulated a new test of obscenity. The plurality held that [for material to be obscene] ... "... it must be established that (a) the dominant theme of the material taken as a whole appeals to a prurient interest in sex; (b) the material is patently offensive because it affronts contemporary community standards relating to the description or representation of sexual matters; and (c) the material is utterly without redeeming social value." ...

While *Roth* presumed "obscenity" to be "utterly without redeeming social importance," *Memoirs* required that to prove obscenity it must be affirmatively established that the material is "*utterly* without redeeming social value." Thus, even as they repeated the words of *Roth*, the *Memoirs* plurality produced a drastically altered test that called on the prosecution to prove a negative, *i.e.*, that the material was "*utterly* without redeeming social value"—a burden virtually impossible to discharge under our criminal standards of proof.... Apart from the initial formulation in the *Roth* case, no majority of the Court has at any given time been able to agree on a standard to determine what constitutes obscene, pornographic material subject to regulation under the States' police power....

[C.] This much has been categorically settled by the Court, that obscene material is unprotected by the First Amendment.... We acknowledge, however, the inherent dangers of undertaking to regulate any form of expression. State statutes designed to regulate obscene materials must be carefully limited....

The basic guidelines for the trier of fact must be: (a) whether "the average person, applying contemporary community standards" would find that the work, taken as a whole, appeals to the prurient interest; (b) whether the work depicts or describes, in a patently offensive way, sexual conduct specifically defined by the applicable state law; and (c) whether the work, taken as a whole, lacks serious literary, artistic, political, or scientific value.... If a state law that regulates obscene material is thus limited, as written or construed, the First Amendment values ... are adequately protected by the ultimate power of appellant courts to conduct an independent review of constitutional claims when necessary....

{We do not adopt as a constitutional standard the "*utterly* without redeeming social value" test of *Memoirs* .... "A quotation from Voltaire in the flyleaf of a book will not constitutionally redeem an otherwise obscene publication ...." We also reject, as a constitutional standard, the ambiguous concept of "social importance."}

[I]t is not our function to propose regulatory schemes for the States. That must await their concrete legislative efforts. It is possible, however, to give a few plain examples of what a state statute could define for regulation under part (b) of the standard announced in this opinion:

(a) Patently offensive representations or descriptions of ultimate sexual acts, normal or perverted, actual or simulated.

(b) Patently offensive representation or descriptions of masturbation, excretory functions, and lewd exhibition of the genitals....

[D.] Under a National Constitution, fundamental First Amendment limitations on the powers of the States do not vary from community to community, but this does not mean that there are, or should or can be, fixed, uniform national standards of precisely what appeals to the "prurient interest" or is "patently offensive." These are essentially questions of fact, and our Nation is simply too big and too diverse for this Court to reasonably expect that such standards could be articulated for all 50 States in a single formulation, even assuming the prerequisite consensus exists.

When triers of fact are asked to decide whether "the average person, applying contemporary community standards" would consider certain materials "prurient," it would be unrealistic to require that the answer be based on some abstract formulation. The adversary system, with lay jurors as the usual ultimate factfinders in criminal prosecutions, has historically permitted triers of fact to draw on the standards of their community, guided always by limiting instructions on the law. To require a State to structure obscenity proceedings around evidence of a *national* "community standard" would be an exercise in futility....

It is neither realistic nor constitutionally sound to read the First Amendment as requiring that the people of Maine or Mississippi accept public depiction of conduct found tolerable in Las Vegas, or New York City. People in different States vary in their tastes and attitudes, and this diversity is not to be strangled by the absolutism of imposed uniformity....

{In *Jacobellis v. Ohio*, 378 U.S. 184 (1964), two Justices argued that application of "local" community standards would run the risk of preventing dissemination of materials in some places because sellers would be unwilling to risk criminal conviction by testing variations in standards from place to place. The use of "national" standards, however, necessarily implies that materials found tolerable in some places, but not under the "national" criteria, will nevertheless be unavailable where they are acceptable. Thus, in terms of danger to free expression, the potential for suppression seems at least as great in the application of a single nationwide standard as in allowing distribution in accordance with local tastes ....}

[T]he primary concern with requiring a jury to apply the standard of "the average person, applying contemporary community standards" is to be certain that, so far as material is not aimed at a deviant group, it will be judged by its impact on an average person, rather than a particularly susceptible or sensitive person—or indeed a totally insensitive one. We hold that the requirement that the jury evaluate the materials with reference to "contemporary standards of the State of California" serves this protective purpose and is constitutionally adequate.

Justice Douglas, dissenting. [Omitted.—ed.]

Justice Brennan, with whom Justice Stewart and Justice Marshall join, dissenting.

In my dissent in *Paris Adult Theatre I v. Slaton*, ... I note[] that I [have] no occasion to consider the extent of state power to regulate the distribution of sexually oriented material to juveniles or the offensive exposure of such material to unconsenting adults. In the case before us, appellant was convicted of distributing obscene matter ... on the basis of evidence that he had caused to be mailed unsolicited brochures advertising various books and a movie. I need not now decide whether a statute might be drawn to impose, within the requirements of the First Amendment, criminal penalties for the precise conduct at issue here.... [T]he statute under which the prosecution was brought [which banned all distribution of obscenity, whether the recipients are willing or unwilling, and adults or children,] is unconstitutionally overbroad, and therefore invalid on its face.

2. POLICY ARGUMENTS

a. *Problem: The Montana Constitution*

The Montana Constitution, Art. II, § 7, provides that

No law shall be passed impairing the freedom of speech or expression. Every person shall be free to speak or publish whatever he will on any subject, being responsible for all abuse of that liberty. In all suits and prosecutions for libel or slander the truth thereof may be given in evidence; and the jury, under the direction of the court, shall determine the law and the facts.

Your boss, Montana Supreme Court Justice Hanah Metchis, is considering whether this provision should be interpreted to have an obscenity exception, or whether even obscene speech should be protected under it. She asks you, her law clerk, to give her the best arguments on both sides.

b. Problem: Character Overlay Software

Within a few decades, there will probably be consumer-usable software that can easily overlay people's photographs and voices onto movies that depict someone else. The program would automatically and seamlessly alter multiple scenes in which the character is shown from different angles, with different facial expressions, doing different things. (One can already do this in some measure with photos, but this hypothetical program would be much more sophisticated.)

The program's user would give it (1) a file containing a movie, (2) files containing photographs of the person who is to be included in the movie, and, optionally, (3) recordings of the person's voice. The program would automatically replace all of a given character's appearances with the new person, and would adjust the character's words to simulate the new person's voice. The program would guess how the new person's features would likely move, or what the unphotographed parts of the person's body look like. It would also let the user provide input about such unknown items, and let the user modify the person's appearance in other ways.

A filmmaker could thus easily replace a stuntman's image with the star's. Parodists and artists could merge politicians', celebrities', or actors' faces and voices into existing footage (as in _Zelig_ or _Forrest Gump_). Parents could place their children and children's friends into kids' movies, which may make the movies more fun for the children. Similar technology could embed human actors into computer-generated movies.

But the most common use of the program would probably be pornography. Consumers would pay to download the program; separately buy a pornographic movie; get nonpornographic photographs and possibly voice recordings of celebrities or of acquaintances; run the program to merge the photographs and voices with the movie; and then watch pornography that "stars" whomever they lust after. Some such merged movies might be sold, but many will be made at home, to fit the user's own preferences.

Naturally, many people, famous or not, will be unhappy knowing that they are depicted without their permission in others' home sex movies. Imagine that Congress therefore decides to prohibit the distribution and use of the computer program that allows such movies to be made.

How would such a law be different for First Amendment purposes from normal obscenity legislation? Do you think the law should be upheld (even if that means changing First Amendment law), and on what grounds?

If you think the law should be struck down, what about laws that

(1) prohibit the *use* of the software to make such pornographic movies without the photographed person's consent,

(2) prohibit the *noncommercial distribution* of the movies, whether to a small group of friends or on the Internet, or

(3) prohibit the *commercial distribution* of the movies?

Don't limit yourself to considering whether such laws are constitutional under existing obscenity doctrine. Consider also whether you think there should be an obscenity exception at all, and whether you think it should be broader or narrower than it now is.

c. *Roth v. United States, 354 U.S. 476 (1957)*

Justice Brennan delivered the opinion of the Court.

[A.] The dispositive question is whether obscenity is utterance within the area of protected speech and press.... The guaranties of freedom of expression in effect in 10 of the 14 States which by 1792 had ratified the Constitution gave no absolute protection for every utterance. Thirteen of the 14 States provided for the prosecution of libel, and all of those States made either blasphemy or profanity, or both, statutory crimes. As early as 1712, Massachusetts made it criminal to publish "any filthy, obscene, or profane song, pamphlet, libel or mock sermon" in imitation or mimicking of religious services. Thus, profanity and obscenity were related offenses. In light of this history, it is apparent that the unconditional phrasing of the First Amendment was not intended to protect every utterance....

The protection given speech and press was fashioned to assure unfettered interchange of ideas for the bringing about of political and social changes desired by the people. This objective was made explicit as early as 1774 in a letter of the Continental Congress to the inhabitants of Quebec:

> The last right we shall mention, regards the freedom of the press. The importance of this consists, besides the advancement of truth, science, morality, and arts in general, in its diffusion of liberal sentiments on the administration of Government ....

All ideas having even the slightest redeeming social importance—unorthodox ideas, controversial ideas, even ideas hateful to the prevailing climate of opinion—have the full protection of the guaranties, unless excludable because they encroach upon the limited area of more important interests. But implicit in the history of the First Amendment is the rejection of obscenity as utterly without redeeming social importance. This rejection for that reason is mirrored in the universal judgment that obscenity should be restrained, reflected in the international agreement of over 50 nations, in the obscenity laws of all of the 48 States, and in the 20 obscenity laws enacted by the Congress from 1842 to 1956.... We hold that obscenity is not within the area of constitutionally protected speech or press.... [And], in light of our holding that obscenity is not protected speech, ... "... it is unnecessary ... to consider the issues behind the phrase 'clear and present danger.'" ...

[B.] However, sex and obscenity are not synonymous. Obscene material is material which deals with sex in a manner appealing to prurient interest. The portrayal of sex, *e.g.,* in art, literature and scientific works, is not itself sufficient reason to deny material the constitutional protection of freedom of speech and press. Sex, a great and mysterious motive force in human life, has indisputably been a subject of absorbing interest to mankind through the ages; it is one of the vital problems of human interest and public concern.... It is therefore vital that the standards for judging obscenity safeguard the protection of freedom of speech and press for material which does not treat sex in a manner appealing to prurient interest....

Justice Douglas, with whom Justice Black concurs, dissenting.

[A.] When we sustain these convictions, we make the legality of a publication turn on the purity of thought which a book or tract instills in the mind of the reader.... [P]unishment is inflicted for thoughts provoked, not for overt acts nor antisocial conduct. This test cannot be squared with our decisions under the First Amendment....

If we were certain that impurity of sexual thoughts impelled to action, we would be on less dangerous ground in punishing the distributors of this sex literature. But it is by no means clear that obscene literature, as so defined, is a significant factor in influencing substantial deviations from the community standards. [Factual argument omitted.—ed.] ... The absence of dependable information on the effect of obscene literature on human conduct should make us wary. It should put us on the side of protecting society's interest in literature, except and unless it can be said that the particular publication has an impact on action that the government can control....

{Freedom of expression can be suppressed if, and to the extent that, it is so closely brigaded with illegal action as to be an inseparable part of it. *Giboney v. Empire Storage & Ice Co.* As a people, we cannot afford to relax that standard. For the test that suppresses a cheap tract today can suppress a literary gem tomorrow. All it need do is to incite a lascivious thought or arouse a lustful desire. The list of books that judges or juries can place in that category is endless.}

[B.] [T]he trial judge ... charged the jury in the alternative that the federal obscenity statute outlaws literature dealing with sex which offends "the common conscience of the community." ... Certainly that standard would not be an acceptable one if religion, economics, politics or philosophy were involved. How does it become a constitutional standard when literature treating with sex is concerned?

Any test that turns on what is offensive to the community's standards is too loose, too capricious, too destructive of freedom of expression to be squared with the First Amendment.... [The test] creates a regime where in the battle between the literati and the Philistines, the Philistines are certain to win. If experience in this field teaches anything, it is that "censorship of obscenity has almost always been both irrational and indiscriminate." The test adopted here accentuates that trend....

[C.] Unlike the law of libel, ... there is no special historical evidence that literature dealing with sex was intended to be treated in a special manner by those who drafted the First Amendment. In fact, the first reported court decision in this country involving obscene literature was in 1821.

I reject too the implication that problems of freedom of speech and of the press are to be resolved by weighing against the values of free expression, the judgment of the Court that a particular form of that expression has "no redeeming social importance." The First Amendment, its prohibition in terms absolute, was designed to preclude courts as well as legislatures from weighing the values of speech against silence.... I have the same confidence in the ability of our people to reject noxious literature as I have in their capacity to sort out the true from the false in theology, economics, politics, or any other field....

d. *Paris Adult Theatre I v. Slaton, 413 U.S. 49 (1973)*

i. *Generally*

Chief Justice Burger delivered the opinion of the Court.

[This companion case to *Miller* involved adult movie theatres.—ed.]

[A.] [T]here are legitimate state interests at stake in stemming the tide of commercialized obscenity, even assuming it is feasible to enforce effective safeguards against exposure to juveniles and to passersby. {It is conceivable that an "adult" theater can ... prevent the exposure of its obscene wares to juveniles. An "adult" bookstore, dealing in obscene books, magazines, and pictures [which can be redistributed outside the bookstore], cannot realistically make this claim....}

Rights and interests "other than those of the advocates are involved." These include the interest of the public in the quality of life and the total community environment, the tone of commerce in the great city centers, and, possibly, the public safety itself.... [T]here is at least an arguable correlation between obscene material and crime. Quite apart from sex crimes, however, there remains one problem of large proportions ...:

> It concerns the tone of the society, ... the style and quality of life, now and in the future. A man may be entitled to read an obscene book in his room, or expose himself indecently there.... We should protect his privacy. But if he demands a right to obtain the books and pictures he wants in the market, and to foregather in public places—discreet, if you will, but accessible to all—with others who share his tastes, *then to grant him his right is to affect the world about the rest of us, and to impinge on other privacies.* Even supposing that each of us can, if he wishes, effectively avert the eye and stop the ear (which, in truth, we cannot), what is commonly read and seen and heard and done intrudes upon us all, want it or not....

[B.] But, it is argued, there are no scientific data which conclusively demonstrate that exposure to obscene material adversely affects men and women or their society. It is urged on behalf of the petitioners that, absent such a demonstration, any kind of state regulation is "impermissible." We reject this argument. It is not for us to resolve empirical uncertainties underlying state legislation, save in the exceptional case where that legislation plainly impinges upon rights protected by the Constitution itself....

From the beginning of civilized societies, legislators and judges have acted on various unprovable assumptions. Such assumptions underlie much lawful state regulation of commercial and business affairs. The same is true of the federal securities and antitrust laws and a host of federal regulations.

On the basis of these assumptions both Congress and state legislatures have, for example, drastically restricted associational rights by adopting antitrust laws, and have strictly regulated public expression by issuers of and dealers in securities, ... commanding what they must and must not publish and announce. Understandably those who entertain an absolutist view of the First Amendment find it uncomfortable to explain why rights of association, speech, and press should be severely restrained in the marketplace of goods and money, but not in the marketplace of pornography.

Likewise, when legislatures and administrators act to protect the physical environment from pollution and to preserve our resources of forests, streams, and parks, they must act on such imponderables as the impact of a new highway near or through an existing park or wilderness area.... [T]hat a congressional directive reflects unprovable assumptions about what is good for the people, including imponderable aesthetic assumptions, is not a sufficient reason to find that statute unconstitutional.

If we accept the unprovable assumption that a complete education requires the reading of certain books, and the well nigh universal belief that good books, plays, and art lift the spirit, improve the mind, enrich the human personality, and develop character, can we then say that a state legislature may not act on the corollary assumption that commerce in obscene books, or public exhibitions focused on obscene conduct, have a tendency to exert a corrupting and debasing impact leading to antisocial behavior? "Many of these effects may be intangible and indistinct, but they are nonetheless real."

Justice Cardozo said that all laws in Western civilization are "guided by a robust common sense...." The sum of experience, including that of the past two decades, affords an ample basis for legislatures to conclude that a sensitive, key relationship of human existence, central to family life, community welfare, and the development of human personality, can be debased and distorted by crass commercial exploitation of sex. Nothing in the Constitution prohibits a State from reaching such a conclusion and acting on it legislatively simply because there is no conclusive evidence or empirical data.

[C.] It is argued that individual "free will" must govern, even in activities beyond the protection of the First Amendment and other constitutional guarantees of privacy, and that government cannot legitimately impede an individual's desire to see or acquire obscene plays, movies, and books.... Most exercises of individual free choice—those in politics, religion, and expression of ideas—are explicitly protected by the Constitution.

Totally unlimited play for free will, however, is not allowed in our or any other society.... [F]or example, ... neither the First Amendment nor "free will" precludes States from having "blue sky" laws to regulate what sellers of securities may write or publish about their wares. Such laws are to protect the weak, the uninformed, the unsuspecting, and the gullible from the exercise of their own volition.... States are told by some that they must await a "laissez-faire" market solution to the obscenity-pornography problem, paradoxically "by people who have never otherwise had a kind word to say for laissez-faire," particularly in solving urban, commercial, and environmental pollution problems....

It is also argued that the State has no legitimate interest in "control [of] the moral content of a person's thoughts," and we need not quarrel with this. But we reject the claim that the State of Georgia is here attempting to control the minds or thoughts of those who patronize theaters. Preventing unlimited display or distribution of obscene material, which by definition lacks any serious literary, artistic, political, or scientific value as communication, is distinct from a control of reason and the intellect....

[From Chief Justice Burger's majority opinion in *Miller*:]

[D.] [T]o equate the free and robust exchange of ideas and political debate with commercial exploitation of obscene material demeans the grand conception of the First Amendment and its high purposes in the historic struggle for freedom.... There is no evidence, empirical or historical, that the stern 19th century American censorship of public distribution and display of material relating to sex in any way limited or affected expression of serious literary, artistic, political, or scientific ideas. On the contrary, it is beyond any question that the era following Thomas Jefferson to Theodore Roosevelt was an "extraordinarily vigorous period," not just in economics and politics, but in *belles lettres* and in "the outlying fields of social and political philosophies." We do not see the harsh hand of censorship of ideas—good or bad, sound or unsound—and "repression" of political liberty lurking in every state regulation of commercial exploitation of human interest in sex....

Moreover, state regulation of hard-core pornography so as to make it unavailable to nonadults, a regulation which Justice Brennan finds constitutionally permissible, has all the elements of "censorship" for adults; indeed even more rigid enforcement techniques may be called for with such dichotomy of regulation. One can concede that the "sexual revolution" of recent years may have had useful byproducts in striking layers of prudery from a subject long irrationally kept from needed ventilation. But it does not follow that no regulation of patently offensive "hard core" materials is needed or permissible; civilized people do not allow unregulated access to heroin because it is a derivative of medicinal morphine....

Justice Douglas, dissenting.... [Omitted.—ed.]

Justice Brennan, with whom Justice Stewart and Justice Marshall join, dissenting [back in *Paris Adult Theatre v. Slaton*].

[A.] Obscenity laws have a long history in this country.... This history caused us to conclude in *Roth* "that the unconditional phrasing of the First Amendment ... was not intended to protect every utterance" [and in particular not obscenity]....

[Post-*Roth* opinions] reflected our emerging view that ... state interests in protecting children and in protecting unconsenting adults may [justify obscenity laws].... It may well be, as one commentator has argued, that "exposure to [erotic material] is for some persons an intense emotional experience. A communication of this nature, imposed upon a person contrary to his wishes, has all the characteristics of a physical assault.... [And it] constitutes an invasion of his privacy...." But cf. *Cohen v. California*. Similarly, if children are "not possessed of that full capacity for individual choice which is the presupposition of the First Amendment guarantees," then the State may have a substantial interest in precluding the flow of obscene materials even to consenting juveniles.

[B.] But, whatever the strength of the state interests in protecting juveniles and unconsenting adults from exposure to sexually oriented materials, those interests cannot be asserted in defense of [a ban on obscenity for willing adults].... "[T]here appears to be little empirical basis for" the assertion that "exposure to obscene materials may lead to deviant sexual behavior or crimes of sexual violence." In any event, ... "if the State is only concerned about printed or filmed materials inducing antisocial conduct, ... in the context of private consumption of ideas and information we should adhere to the view that '[a]mong free men, the deterrents ordinarily to be applied to prevent crime are education and punishment for violations of the law....' *Whitney v. California* (Brandeis, J., concurring)."

Moreover, ... [under] "... the philosophy of the First Amendment," ... there is [no] legitimate state concern in the "control [of] the moral content of a person's thoughts," and ... a State "cannot constitutionally premise legislation on the desirability of controlling a person's private thoughts." ... If, as the Court today assumes, "a state legislature may ... act on the ... assumption that commerce in obscene books, or public exhibitions focused on obscene conduct, have a tendency to exert a corrupting and debasing impact leading to antisocial behavior," then it is hard to see how state-ordered regimentation of our minds can ever be forestalled. For if a State, in an effort to maintain or create a particular moral tone, may prescribe what its citizens cannot read or cannot see, then it would seem to follow that in pursuit of that same objective a State could decree that its citizens must read certain books or must view certain films. However laudable its goal—and that is obviously a question on which reasonable minds may differ—the State cannot proceed by means that violate the Constitution....

Recognizing these principles, we have held that so-called thematic obscenity—obscenity which might persuade the viewer or reader to engage in "obscene" conduct—is not outside the protection of the First Amendment:

> It is contended that the State's action was justified because the motion picture attractively portrays [an adulterous] relationship[,] which is contrary to the moral standards, the religious precepts, and the legal code of its citizenry. This argument misconceives what it is that the Constitution protects. Its guarantee is not confined to the expression of ideas that are conventional or shared by a majority. It protects advocacy of the opinion that adultery may sometimes be proper, no less than advocacy of socialism or the single

tax. And in the realm of ideas it protects expression which is eloquent no less than that which is unconvincing.

Even a legitimate, sharply focused state concern for the morality of the community cannot, in other words, justify an assault on the protections of the First Amendment. Where the state interest in regulation of morality is vague and ill defined, interference with the guarantees of the First Amendment is even more difficult to justify.

In short, while I cannot say that the interests of the State—apart from the question of juveniles and unconsenting adults—are trivial or nonexistent, I am compelled to conclude that these interests cannot justify the substantial damage to constitutional rights and to this Nation's judicial machinery that inevitably results from state efforts to bar the distribution even of unprotected material to consenting adults....

ii. Vagueness

Chief Justice Burger delivered the opinion of the Court [in *Miller v. California*].

In resolving the inevitably sensitive questions of fact and law [in obscenity cases], we must continue to rely on the jury system, accompanied by the safeguards that judges, rules of evidence, presumption of innocence, and other protective features provide, as we do with rape, murder, and a host of other offenses against society and its individual members. {The mere fact juries may reach different conclusions as to the same material does not mean that constitutional rights are abridged.... "[I]t is common experience that different juries may reach different results under any criminal statute. That is one of the consequences we accept under our jury system."}

Paradoxically, [Justice Brennan] indicates that suppression of unprotected obscene material is permissible to avoid exposure to unconsenting adults, as in this case, and to juveniles, although he gives no indication of how the division between protected and nonprotected materials may be drawn with greater precision for these purposes than for regulation of commercial exposure to consenting adults only. Nor does he indicate where in the Constitution he finds the authority to distinguish between a willing "adult" one month past the state law age of majority and a willing "juvenile" one month younger.

Under the holdings announced today, no one will be subject to prosecution for the sale or exposure of obscene materials unless these materials depict or describe patently offensive "hard core" sexual conduct specifically defined by the regulating state law, as written or construed. We are satisfied that these specific prerequisites will provide fair notice to a dealer in such materials that his public and commercial activities may bring prosecution. {"... '... [T]he Constitution does not require impossible standards'; all that is required is that the language 'conveys sufficiently definite warning as to the proscribed conduct when measured by common understanding and practices....' ... That there may be marginal cases in which it is difficult to determine the side of the line on which a particular fact situation falls is no sufficient reason to hold the language too ambiguous to define a criminal offense...."} If the inability to define regulated materials with ultimate, god-like precision altogether removes the power of the States or the Congress to regulate, then "hard core" pornography may be exposed without limit to the juvenile, the passerby, and the consenting adult alike, as, indeed, ... Justice Douglas contends....

[N]o amount of "fatigue" should lead us to adopt a convenient "institutional" rationale—an absolutist, "anything goes" view of the First Amendment—because it will lighten our burdens. "Such an abnegation of judicial supervision in this field would be inconsistent with our duty to uphold the constitutional guarantees." Nor should we remedy "tension between state and federal courts" by arbitrarily depriving the States of a power reserved to them under the Constitution, a power which they have enjoyed and exercised continuously from before the adoption of the First Amendment to this day. "Our duty admits of no 'substitute for facing up to the tough individual problems of constitutional judgment involved in every obscenity case.'"

Justice Brennan, with whom Justice Stewart and Justice Marshall join, [and with whom Justice Douglas largely agreed—ed.], dissenting [back in *Paris Adult Theatre v. Slaton*].

[A.] [A]fter 16 years of experimentation and debate I am reluctantly forced to the conclusion that none of the available formulas [defining obscenity], including the one announced today, can reduce the vagueness [of the obscenity test] to a tolerable level while at the same time striking an acceptable balance between the protections of the First and Fourteenth Amendments, on the one hand, and on the other the asserted state interest in regulating the dissemination of certain sexually oriented materials.

Test Too Vague

Any effort to draw a constitutionally acceptable boundary on state power must resort to such indefinite concepts as "prurient interest," "patent offensiveness," "serious literary value," and the like. The meaning of these concepts necessarily varies with the experience, outlook, and even idiosyncrasies of the person defining them. Although we have assumed that obscenity does exist and that we "know it when [we] see it," we are manifestly unable to describe it in advance except by reference to concepts so elusive that they fail to distinguish clearly between protected and unprotected speech....

No Notice

In addition to problems that arise when any criminal statute fails to afford fair notice of what it forbids, a vague statute in the areas of speech and press creates a second level of difficulty. We have indicated that "stricter standards of permissible statutory vagueness may be applied to a statute having a potentially inhibiting effect on speech; a man may the less be required to act at his peril here, because the free dissemination of ideas may be the loser." ...

[A third set of problems] ... concern the institutional stress that inevitably results where the line separating protected from unprotected speech is excessively vague. In *Roth v. United States,* we conceded that "there may be marginal cases in which it is difficult to determine the side of the line on which a particular fact situation falls...." Our subsequent experience demonstrates that almost every case is "marginal." And since the "margin" marks the point of separation between protected and unprotected speech, we are left with a system in which almost every obscenity case presents a constitutional question of exceptional difficulty.... As a result of our failure to define standards with predictable application to any given piece of material, there is no probability of regularity in obscenity decisions by state and lower federal courts.... The number of obscenity cases on our docket gives ample testimony to the burden that has been placed upon this Court....

The severe problems arising from the lack of fair notice, from the chill on protected expression, and from the stress imposed on the state and federal judicial machinery persuade me that a significant change in direction is urgently required. I turn, therefore, to the alternatives that are now open.

[B.] [1.] The approach requiring the smallest deviation from our present course would be to draw a new line between protected and unprotected speech .... In my view, clarity cannot be obtained pursuant to this approach except by drawing a line that resolves all doubt in favor of state power and against the guarantees of the First Amendment.

We could hold, for example, that any depiction or description of human sexual organs, irrespective of the manner or purpose of the portrayal, is outside the protection of the First Amendment .... But such a standard would be appallingly overbroad, permitting the suppression of a vast range of literary, scientific, and artistic masterpieces.... Yet short of that extreme it is hard to see how any choice of words could reduce the vagueness problem to tolerable proportions, so long as we remain committed to the view that some class of materials is subject to outright suppression ....

[2.] The alternative adopted by the Court today ... permits suppression if the government can prove that the materials lack "*serious* literary, artistic, political or scientific value." ... [But this] necessarily assumes that some works will be deemed obscene—even though they clearly have *some* social value—because the State was able to prove that the value, measured by some unspecified standard, was not sufficiently "serious" to warrant constitutional protection. That result is ... an invitation to widespread suppression of sexually oriented speech. Before today, the protections of the First Amendment have never been thought limited to expressions of *serious* literary or political value. See, *e.g., Cohen v. California*....

In any case, ... the Court's approach ... can have no ameliorative impact on the [unfairness to distributors, lack of guidance to law enforcement, chill on protected expression, and burden on the Court] that grow out of the vagueness of our current standards.... [T]he mere formulation of a "[specific sexual] conduct" test is no assurance that it can be applied with any [adequate] facility....

[3.] I have also considered the possibility of reducing our own role, and the role of appellate courts generally, in determining whether particular matter is obscene. Thus, we might conclude that juries are best suited to determine obscenity *vel non* and that jury verdicts in this area should not be set aside except in cases of extreme departure from prevailing standards. Or, more generally, we might adopt the position that where a lower federal or state court has conscientiously applied the constitutional standard, its finding of obscenity will be no more vulnerable to reversal by this Court than any finding of fact....

[T]he First Amendment[, however,] requires an independent review by appellate courts of the constitutional fact of obscenity.... [Deference to trial court decisions] would inevitably lead to even greater uncertainty and the consequent due process problems of fair notice. And the approach would expose much protected, sexually oriented expression to the vagaries of jury determinations....

[4.] Finally, I have considered the view ... that the First Amendment bars the suppression of any sexually oriented expression.... [But this would strip] the States of power to an extent that cannot be justified by the commands of the Constitution [when it comes to protecting children and unconsenting adults], at least so long as there is available an alternative approach that strikes a better balance between the guarantee of free expression and the States' legitimate interests....

e. Policy—Self-Expression (as argument for speech protection)

Basic argument: "This speech should be protected because the speaker is entitled to express himself, and this speech expresses _____."

1. It doesn't matter whether the speech enriches the marketplace of ideas or does other good things; the freedom to engage in this speech—for instance, art or music—is valuable by itself, not just as a means to an end.

"The right to speak and the right to refrain from speaking are complementary components of the broader concept of 'individual freedom of mind.' ... [By forcing the Maynards to display a license plate containing the words 'Live Free or Die,'] the State 'invades the sphere of intellect and spirit which it is the purpose of the First Amendment to our Constitution to reserve from all official control." *Wooley v. Maynard,* quoting *W. Va. State Bd. of Ed. v. Barnette.*

"The individual's interest in self-expression is a concern of the First Amendment separate from the concern for open and informed discussion, although the two often converge." *First Nat'l Bank of Boston v. Bellotti.*

2. Response to 1: This speech causes harms, direct or indirect, to others, specifically _____; this person's desire to express himself shouldn't justify his interfering with the happiness of others, because _____.

f. Policy—Tradition

Basic argument: This proposal is constitutional/unconstitutional because it comports with/contradicts longstanding American tradition, and that's relevant because _____ (e.g., tradition is evidence of original meaning, tradition is a source of collective national judgment that isn't to be lightly overturned, the absence of bad consequences flowing from the traditional acceptance of this practice shows we needn't worry about the slippery slope, or a practice's being traditional changes how people are likely to perceive it).

1. "The existence from the beginning of the Nation's life of a practice, ... [while] not conclusive of its constitutionality ...[,] is a fact of considerable import in the interpretation of abstract constitutional language. On its face, the Establishment Clause is reasonably susceptible of different interpretations regarding [property tax exemptions for churches]. This Court's interpretation of the clause, accordingly, is appropriately influenced by the reading it has received in the practices of the Nation.... '[A] page of history is worth a volume of logic.' The more longstanding and widely accepted a practice, the greater its impact upon constitutional interpretation." *Walz v. Tax Comm'n,* 397 U.S. 664, 681 (1970) (Brennan, J., concurring).

"What is relevant ... here is not the history of an established church in sixteenth century England or in eighteenth century America, but the history of the religious traditions of our people, reflected in countless practices of the institutions and officials of our government.... [Religious invocations and school prayers do not establish religion, but merely] recognize and ... follow the deeply entrenched and highly cherished spiritual traditions of our Nation—traditions which come down to us from those who almost two hundred years ago avowed their 'firm Reliance on the Protection of divine Providence' when they proclaimed the freedom and independence of this brave new world." *Engel v. Vitale* (Stewart, J. dissenting).

"In light of the unambiguous and unbroken history of more than 200 years, there can be no doubt that the practice of opening legislative sessions with prayer has become part of the fabric of our society. To invoke Divine guidance on a public body entrusted with making the laws is not, in these circumstances, an 'establishment' of religion or a step toward establishment; it is simply a tolerable acknowledgment of beliefs widely held among the people of this country." *Marsh v. Chambers.*

"Although the controversy over religious exercises in the public schools continued into this century, the opponents of subsidy to sectarian schools had largely won their fight by 1900. In fact, after 1840, no efforts of sectarian schools to obtain a share of public school funds succeeded.... Thus for more than a century, the consensus, enforced by legislatures and courts with substantial consistency, has been that public subsidy of sectarian schools constitutes an impermissible involvement of secular with religious institutions...." *Lemon v. Kurtzman* (Brennan, J., concurring).

"[T]he 'history and ubiquity' of a practice [such as nonsectarian legislative prayer] is relevant because it provides part of the context in which a reasonable observer evaluates whether a challenged governmental practice conveys a message of endorsement of religion." *County of Allegheny v. ACLU,* 492 U.S. 573, 630 (1989) (O'Connor, J., concurring in part and concurring in the judgment).

"'From 1791 to the present,' ... the First Amendment has 'permitted re-strictions upon the content of speech in a few limited areas,' and has never 'include[d] a freedom to disregard these traditional limitations.' ... [But] new categories of unprotected speech may not be added to the list by a legislature that concludes certain speech is too harmful to be tolerated.... [W]ithout per-suasive evidence that a novel restriction on content is part of a long ... tra-dition of proscription, a legislature may not revise the 'judgment [of] the American people,' embodied in the First Amendment, 'that the benefits of its restrictions on the Government outweigh the costs.'" *Brown v. Entertain-ment Merchants Ass'n* (Scalia, J.).

"The provisions of the Bill of Rights were designed to restrain transient majorities from impairing long-recognized personal liberties. They did not create by implication novel individual rights overturning accepted political norms. Thus, when a practice not expressly prohibited by the text of the Bill of Rights bears the endorsement of a long tradition of open, widespread, and unchallenged use that dates back to the beginning of the Republic, we have no proper basis for striking it down.

"Such a venerable and accepted tradition is not to be laid on the exam-ining table and scrutinized for its conformity to some abstract principle of First Amendment adjudication devised by this Court. To the contrary, such traditions are themselves the stuff out of which the Court's principles are to be formed. They are, in these uncertain areas, the very points of reference by which the legitimacy or illegitimacy of *other* practices is to be figured out.... I know of no other way to formulate a constitutional jurisprudence that reflects, as it should, the principles adhered to, over time, by the Amer-ican people, rather than those favored by the personal (and necessarily shift-ing) philosophical dispositions of a majority of this Court." *Rutan v. Repub-lican Party,* 497 U.S. 62 (1990) (Scalia, J., dissenting).

2. Response to 1: The Constitution embodies certain principles, such as _____; even if a tradition develops that is contrary to these principles, the general principles should prevail over the specific tradition.

"The tradition that is relevant in these cases is the American commit-ment to examine and reexamine past and present practices against the basic principles embodied in the Constitution.... Whatever traditional support may remain for [patronage systems] ..., it is plainly an illegitimate excuse for [such systems]." *Id.* at 92 (Stevens, J., concurring).

"I argue for the role of tradition in giving content only to *ambiguous* constitutional text; no tradition can supersede the Constitution. In my view, the Fourteenth Amendment's requirement of 'equal protection of the laws,' combined with the Thirteenth Amendment's abolition of the institution of black slavery, leaves no room for doubt that laws treating people differently because of their race are invalid." *Id.* at 95-96 n.1 (Scalia, J., dissenting).

3. Response to 1: This supposedly unchallenged tradition was in fact quite contested, specifically in the following ways, _____, and thus should not be given the deference we give to uncontested traditions.

"[E]ven if one does not regard the Fourteenth Amendment as crystal clear [in banning race discrimination], a tradition of *unchallenged* validity did not exist with respect to the practice in *Brown v. Board of Ed.* To the contrary, in the 19th century, the principle of 'separate-but-equal' had been vigorously opposed on constitutional grounds, ... and upheld only over the dissent of one of our historically most respected Justices." *Id.* (Scalia, J., dissenting).

"With respect to Justice Scalia's view that, until *Elrod v. Burns* was decided in 1976, it was unthinkable that patronage could be unconstitutional, it seems appropriate to point out ... [that] '... at least [since 1947], this Court has made clear that even though a person has no 'right' to a valuable governmental benefit and even though the government may deny him the benefit for any number of reasons, there are some reasons upon which the government may not act.'" *Id.* at 84-86 (Stevens, J., concurring).

g.   *Policy—No-Value or Low-Value Speech, see p. 90*

3.   THE LIMITS OF ANALOGIES TO OBSCENITY

a.   *United States v. Stevens, 559 U.S. 460 (2010)*

Chief Justice Roberts delivered the opinion of the Court....

[A.] {[18 U.S.C. § 48 provides,]

(a) ... Whoever knowingly creates, sells, or possesses a depiction of animal cruelty with the intention of placing that depiction in interstate or foreign commerce for commercial gain, shall be fined ... or imprisoned not more than 5 years, or both.

Animal Cruelty

(b) ... Subsection (a) does not apply to any depiction that has serious religious, political, scientific, educational, journalistic, historical, or artistic value.

(c) ... "[D]epiction of animal cruelty" means any visual or auditory depiction ... in which a living animal is intentionally maimed, mutilated, tortured, wounded, or killed, if such conduct is illegal under Federal law or the law of the State [defined to include the District of Columbia or United States territory, commonwealth, or possession—ed.] in which the creation, sale, or possession takes place, regardless of whether the maiming, mutilation, torture, wounding, or killing took place in the State ....}

The legislative background of § 48 focused primarily on the interstate market for "crush videos[," which] ... feature the intentional torture and killing of helpless animals, including cats, dogs, monkeys, mice, and hamsters. Crush videos often depict women slowly crushing animals to death "with their bare feet or while wearing high heeled shoes," sometimes while "talking to the animals in a kind of dominatrix patter" over "[t]he cries and squeals of the animals, obviously in great pain." Apparently these depictions "appeal to persons with a very specific sexual fetish)who find them sexually arousing or otherwise exciting." The acts depicted in crush videos are typically prohibited by the animal cruelty laws enacted by all 50 States and the District of Columbia. But crush videos rarely disclose the participants' identities, inhibiting prosecution of the underlying conduct.

This case, however, involves an application of § 48 to depictions of animal fighting. Dogfighting, for example, is unlawful in all 50 States and the District of Columbia, and has been restricted by federal law since 1976. Respondent Robert J. Stevens ran a business, "Dogs of Velvet and Steel," and an associated Web site, through which he sold videos of pit bulls engaging in dogfights and attacking other animals.

Among these videos were Japan Pit Fights and Pick-A-Winna: A Pit Bull Documentary, which include contemporary footage of dogfights in Japan (where such conduct is allegedly legal) as well as footage of American dogfights from the 1960's and 1970's. {The Government contends that these dogfights were unlawful at the time they occurred, while Stevens disputes the assertion.} A third video, Catch Dogs and Country Living, depicts the use of pit bulls to hunt wild boar, as well as a "gruesome" scene of a pit bull attacking a domestic farm pig. On the basis of these videos, Stevens was indicted on three counts of violating § 48....

[B.] "[A]s a general matter, the First Amendment means that government has no power to restrict expression because of its message, its ideas, its subject matter, or its content." ... "From 1791 to the present," however, the First Amendment has "permitted restrictions upon the content of speech in a few limited areas," and has never "include[d] a freedom to disregard these traditional limitations." These "historic and traditional categories long familiar to the bar"—including obscenity, defamation, fraud, incitement, and speech integral to criminal conduct, *Giboney v. Empire Storage & Ice Co.*—are "well-defined and narrowly limited classes of speech, the prevention and punishment of which have never been thought to raise any Constitutional problem." *Chaplinsky v. New Hampshire.*

The Government argues that "depictions of animal cruelty" should be added to the list. It contends that depictions of "illegal acts of animal cruelty" that are "made, sold, or possessed for commercial gain" necessarily "lack expressive value," and may accordingly "be regulated as *unprotected* speech." The claim is not just that Congress may regulate depictions of animal cruelty subject to the First Amendment, but that these depictions are outside the reach of that Amendment altogether ....

As the Government notes, the prohibition of animal cruelty itself has a long history in American law, starting with the early settlement of the Colonies. But we are unaware of any similar tradition excluding *depictions* of animal cruelty from "the freedom of speech" codified in the First Amendment, and the Government points us to none.

The Government contends ... that categories of speech may be exempted from the First Amendment's protection without any long-settled tradition of subjecting that speech to regulation. Instead, the Government points to Congress's "legislative judgment that ... depictions of animals being intentionally tortured and killed [are] of such minimal redeeming value as to render [them] unworthy of First Amendment protection,'" and asks the Court to uphold the ban on the same basis. The Government thus proposes that a claim of categorical exclusion should be considered under a simple balancing test: "Whether a given category of speech enjoys First Amendment protection depends upon a categorical balancing of the value of the speech against its societal costs."

Gov suggests balancing to

As a free-floating test for First Amendment coverage, that sentence is startling and dangerous. The First Amendment's guarantee of free speech does not extend only to categories of speech that survive an ad hoc balancing of relative social costs and benefits. The First Amendment itself reflects a judgment by the American people that the benefits of its restrictions on the Government outweigh the costs. Our Constitution forecloses any attempt to revise that judgment simply on the basis that some speech is not worth it. The Constitution is not a document "prescribing limits, and declaring that those limits may be passed at pleasure." ...

*§48
Too Broad*

[C.] [T]he constitutionality of § 48 hinges on how broadly it is construed.... We read § 48 to create a criminal prohibition of alarming breadth. To begin with, the text of the statute's ban on a "depiction of animal cruelty" nowhere requires that the depicted conduct be cruel. That text applies to "any ... depiction" in which "a living animal is intentionally maimed, mutilated, tortured, wounded, or killed." "[M]aimed, mutilated, [and] tortured" convey cruelty, but "wounded" or "killed" do not suggest any such limitation.

The Government [and dissent] contend[] that the terms in the definition should be read to require the additional element of "accompanying acts of cruelty."... [Indeed,] an ambiguous term may be "given more precise content by the neighboring words with which it is associated."... But the phrase "wounded ... or killed" at issue here contains little ambiguity.... Nothing about [its] meaning requires cruelty.

While not requiring cruelty, § 48 does require that the depicted conduct be "illegal." But ... [many] laws concerning the proper treatment of animals ... are not designed to guard against animal cruelty. Protections of endangered species, for example, restrict even the humane "wound[ing] or kill[ing]" of "living animal[s]."

Livestock regulations are often designed to protect the health of human beings, and hunting and fishing rules (seasons, licensure, bag limits, weight requirements) can be designed to raise revenue, preserve animal populations, or prevent accidents. The text of § 48(c) draws no distinction based on the reason the intentional killing of an animal is made illegal, and includes, for example, the humane slaughter of a stolen cow. {[The dissent argues] that hunting is not covered by animal cruelty laws. But the reach of § 48 is ... not restricted to depictions of conduct that violates a law specifically directed at animal cruelty. It simply requires that the depicted conduct be "illegal."}

What is more, the application of § 48 to depictions of illegal conduct extends to conduct that is illegal in only a single jurisdiction.... A depiction of entirely lawful conduct runs afoul of the ban if that depiction later finds its way into another State where the same conduct is unlawful. This provision greatly expands the scope of § 48, because although there may be "a broad societal consensus" against cruelty to animals, there is substantial disagreement [among jurisdictions] on what types of conduct are properly regarded as cruel....

In the District of Columbia, for example, all hunting is unlawful. Other jurisdictions permit or encourage hunting, and there is an enormous national market for hunting-related depictions in which a living animal is intentionally killed. Hunting periodicals have circulations in the hundreds of thousands or millions, and hunting television programs, videos, and Web sites are equally popular. The demand for hunting depictions exceeds the estimated demand for crush videos or animal fighting depictions [more than a hundredfold]. Nonetheless, because the statute allows each jurisdiction to export its laws to the rest of the country, § 48(a) extends to *any* magazine or video depicting lawful hunting, so long as that depiction is sold within the Nation's Capital.

Those seeking to comply with the law thus face a bewildering maze of regulations from at least 56 separate jurisdictions. Some States [such as Georgia and Virginia] permit hunting with crossbows, while others [such as Oregon] forbid it, or restrict it only to the disabled [as in New York]. Missouri allows the "canned" hunting of ungulates held in captivity, but Montana restricts such hunting to certain bird species. The sharp-tailed grouse may be hunted in Idaho, but not in Washington.

The disagreements among the States ... extend well beyond hunting. State agricultural regulations permit different methods of livestock slaughter in different places or as applied to different animals. California has recently banned cutting or "docking" the tails of dairy cattle, which other States permit. Even cockfighting, long considered immoral in much of America, is legal in Puerto Rico, and was legal in Louisiana until 2008. An otherwise-lawful image of any of these practices, if sold or possessed for commercial gain within a State that happens to forbid the practice, falls within the prohibition of § 48(a).

[D.] The only [statutory provision] standing between defendants who sell such depictions and five years in federal prison ... [is the exemption for] "any depiction that has serious religious, political, scientific, educational, journalistic, historical, or artistic value." The Government argues that this clause substantially narrows the statute's reach: News reports about animal cruelty have "journalistic" value; pictures of bullfights in Spain have "historical" value; and instructional hunting videos have "educational" value. Thus, the Government argues, § 48 reaches only crush videos, depictions of animal fighting (other than Spanish bullfighting), and perhaps other depictions of "extreme acts of animal cruelty."

The Government's attempt to narrow the statutory ban, however, requires an unrealistically broad reading of the exceptions clause. As the Government reads the clause, any material with "redeeming societal value," "'at least some minimal value,'" or anything more than "scant social value," is excluded under § 48(b).

But the text says "serious" value, and "serious" should be taken seriously. We decline the Government's invitation ... to regard as "serious" anything that is not "scant." (Or, as the dissent puts it, "'trifling.'") ... "[S]erious" ordinarily means a good bit more. The District Court's jury instructions required value that is "significant and of great import," and the Government defended these instructions as properly relying on "a commonly accepted meaning of the word 'serious.'" ...

[To be covered by § 48(b),] speech must also fall within one of the enumerated categories. Much speech does not. Most hunting videos, for example, are not obviously instructional in nature, except in the sense that all life is a lesson.... [M]any popular videos "have primarily entertainment value" and are designed to "entertai[n] the viewer, marke[t] hunting equipment, or increas[e] the hunting community." ...

The Government offers no principled explanation why these depictions of hunting or depictions of Spanish bullfights would be *inherently* valuable while those of Japanese dogfights are not. The dissent contends that hunting depictions must have serious value because hunting has serious value, in a way that dogfights presumably do not. But § 48(b) addresses the value of the *depictions*, not of the underlying activity. There is simply no adequate reading of the exceptions clause that results in the statute's banning only the depictions the Government would like to ban....

[T]he language of § 48(b) was largely drawn from our opinion in *Miller v. California*, which excepted from its definition of obscenity any material with "serious literary, artistic, political, or scientific value." ... In *Miller* we held that "serious" value shields depictions of sex from regulation as obscenity.... We did not, however, determine that serious value could be used as a general precondition to protecting *other* types of speech in the first place. *Most* of what we say to one another lacks "religious, political, scientific, educational, journalistic, historical, or artistic value" (let alone serious value), but it is still sheltered from government regulation. Even "[w]holly neutral futilities ... come under the protection of free speech as fully as do Keats' poems or Donne's sermons." ...

Thus, the protection of the First Amendment presumptively extends to many forms of speech that do not qualify for the serious-value exception of § 48(b), but nonetheless fall within the broad reach of § 48(c).

[E.] Not to worry, the Government says: The Executive Branch construes § 48 to reach only "extreme" cruelty, and it "neither has brought nor will bring a prosecution for anything less." ... But the First Amendment protects against the Government; it does not leave us at the mercy of *noblesse oblige*. We would not uphold an unconstitutional statute merely because the Government promised to use it responsibly.

This prosecution is itself evidence of the danger in putting faith in government representations of prosecutorial restraint. When this legislation was enacted [in 1999], the Executive Branch announced that it would interpret § 48 as covering only depictions "of wanton cruelty to animals designed to appeal to a prurient interest in sex." No one suggests that the videos in this case fit that description. The Government's assurance that it will apply § 48 far more restrictively than its language provides is pertinent only as an implicit acknowledgment of the potential constitutional problems with a more natural reading....

[F.] [We] need not and do not decide whether a statute limited to crush videos or other depictions of extreme animal cruelty would be constitutional. We hold only that § 48 is ... substantially overbroad, and therefore invalid under the First Amendment....

Justice Alito, dissenting.... [See p. 178 below.—ed.]

b. *Brown v. Entertainment Merchants Ass'n, 564 U.S. 786 (2011)*

Justice Scalia delivered the opinion of the Court....

[A.] Cal. Civ. Code Ann. §§ 1746–1746.5 ["the Act"—ed.] prohibits the sale or rental of "violent video games" to minors, and requires their packaging to be labeled "18." The Act covers games "in which the range of options available to a player includes killing, maiming, dismembering, or sexually assaulting an image of a human being, if those acts are depicted" in a manner that [1] "[a] reasonable person, considering the game as a whole, would find appeals to a deviant or morbid interest of minors," that [2] is "patently offensive to prevailing standards in the community as to what is suitable for minors," and that [3] "causes the game, as a whole, to lack serious literary, artistic, political, or scientific value for minors." Violation of the Act is punishable by a civil fine of up to $1,000....

[margin handwritten note: Like Miller]

[B.] [V]ideo games qualify for First Amendment protection. The Free Speech Clause exists principally to protect discourse on public matters, but we have long recognized that it is difficult to distinguish politics from entertainment, and dangerous to try. "Everyone is familiar with instances of propaganda through fiction. What is one man's amusement, teaches another's doctrine." *Winters v. New York,* 333 U.S. 507 (1948).

Like the protected books, plays, and movies that preceded them, video games communicate ideas—and even social messages—through many familiar literary devices (such as characters, dialogue, plot, and music) and through features distinctive to the medium (such as the player's interaction with the virtual world). That suffices to confer First Amendment protection. Under our Constitution, "esthetic and moral judgments about art and literature ... are for the individual to make, not for the Government to decree, even with the mandate or approval of a majority."

And whatever the challenges of applying the Constitution to ever-advancing technology, "the basic principles of freedom of speech and the press, like the First Amendment's command, do not vary" when a new and different medium for communication appears. The most basic of those principles is this: "[A]s a general matter, ... government has no power to restrict expression because of its message, its ideas, its subject matter, or its content."

{California claims that video games present special problems because they are "interactive," in that the player participates in the violent action on screen and determines its outcome. The latter feature is nothing new: ...

[Y]oung readers of choose-your-own-adventure stories have been able to make decisions that determine the plot by following instructions about which page to turn to.

As for the argument that video games enable participation in the violent action, that seems to us more a matter of degree than of kind.... [A]ll literature is interactive. "[T]he better it is, the more interactive. Literature when it is successful draws the reader into the story, makes him identify with the characters, invites him to judge them and quarrel with them, to experience their joys and sufferings as the reader's own."}

[C.] There are of course exceptions [to First Amendment protection].... These limited areas—such as obscenity, incitement, and fighting words— represent "well-defined and narrowly limited classes of speech, the prevention and punishment of which have never been thought to raise any Constitutional problem." *Chaplinsky v. New Hampshire*....

[I]n *United States v. Stevens,* we held that new categories of unprotected speech may not be added to the list by a legislature that concludes certain speech is too harmful to be tolerated.... [Courts may not] apply[] a "simple balancing test" that weighs the value of a particular category of speech against its social costs and then punishes that category of speech if it fails the test.... [W]ithout persuasive evidence that a novel restriction on content is part of a long ... tradition of proscription, a legislature may not revise the "judgment [of] the American people," embodied in the First Amendment, "that the benefits of its restrictions on the Government outweigh the costs."

That holding controls this case.... California has tried to make violent-speech regulation look like obscenity regulation by appending a saving clause required for the latter. That does not suffice.... [T]he obscenity exception to the First Amendment does not cover whatever a legislature finds shocking, but only depictions of "sexual conduct." ...

In *Winters,* we considered a New York criminal statute "forbid[ding] the massing of stories of bloodshed and lust in such a way as to incite to crime against the person[, which was defended as analogous to obscenity law] .... [But we concluded] that violence is not part of the obscenity that the Constitution permits to be regulated....

{Justice Alito recounts [various] disgusting video games in order to disgust us—but disgust is not a valid basis for restricting expression. And the same is true of Justice Alito's description of ... video games ... that have a racial or ethnic motive for their violence .... Justice Alito's argument highlights the precise danger posed by the California Act: that the *ideas* expressed by speech—whether it be violence, or gore, or racism—and not its objective effects, may be the real reason for governmental proscription.}

[D.] Because speech about violence is not obscene, it is of no consequence that California's statute mimics the New York statute regulating obscenity-for-minors that we upheld in *Ginsberg v. New York*, 390 U.S. 629 (1968). That case approved a prohibition on the sale to minors of *sexual* material that would be obscene from the perspective of a child .... We held that the legislature could "adjus[t] the definition of obscenity 'to social realities by permitting the appeal of this type of material to be assessed in terms of the sexual interests ...' of ... minors." ...

The California Act is something else entirely. It does not adjust the boundaries of an existing category of unprotected speech to ensure that a definition designed for adults is not uncritically applied to children.... Instead, [California] wishes to create a wholly new category of content-based regulation that is permissible only for speech directed at children.

That is unprecedented and mistaken. "[M]inors are entitled to a significant measure of First Amendment protection, and only in relatively narrow and well-defined circumstances may government bar public dissemination of protected materials to them." No doubt a State possesses legitimate power to protect children from harm, but that does not include a free-floating power to restrict the ideas to which children may be exposed....

California's argument would fare better if there were a longstanding tradition in this country of specially restricting children's access to depictions of violence, but there is none. Certainly [children's] *books* ... contain no shortage of gore. Grimm's Fairy Tales, for example, are grim indeed. As her just deserts for trying to poison Snow White, the wicked queen is made to dance in red hot slippers "till she fell dead on the floor, a sad example of envy and jealousy." Cinderella's evil stepsisters have their eyes pecked out by doves. And Hansel and Gretel (children!) kill their captor by baking her in an oven.

High-school reading lists are full of similar fare. Homer's Odysseus blinds Polyphemus the Cyclops by grinding out his eye with a heated stake.... "Even so did we seize the fiery-pointed brand and whirled it round in his eye, and the blood flowed about the heated bar. And the breath of the flame singed his eyelids and brows all about, as the ball of the eye burnt away, and the roots thereof crackled in the flame[."] In the Inferno, Dante and Virgil watch corrupt politicians struggle to stay submerged beneath a lake of boiling pitch, lest they be skewered by devils above the surface. And Golding's Lord of the Flies recounts how a schoolboy called Piggy is savagely murdered *by other children* while marooned on an island.

{[P]laying violent video games ... [is indeed "]different in 'kind'" from reading violent literature ..., but not in a way that causes the provision and viewing of violent video games, unlike the provision and reading of books, not to be expressive activity and hence not to enjoy First Amendment protection. Reading Dante is unquestionably more cultured and intellectually edifying than playing Mortal Kombat. But these cultural and intellectual differences are not *constitutional* ones.

Crudely violent video games, tawdry TV shows, and cheap novels and magazines are no less forms of speech than The Divine Comedy, and restrictions upon them must survive strict scrutiny—a question to which we devote our attention [below]. Even if we can see in them "nothing of any possible value to society ..., they are as much entitled to the protection of free speech as the best of literature."}

[E.] {[Justice Thomas argues] that parents have traditionally had the power to control what their children hear and say. This is true enough. And it perhaps follows from this that the state has the power to *enforce* parental prohibitions—to require, for example, that the promoters of a rock concert exclude those minors whose parents have advised the promoters that their children are forbidden to attend.

But it does not follow that the state has the power to prevent children from hearing or saying anything *without their parents' prior consent.* The latter would mean, for example, that it could be made criminal to admit persons under 18 to a political rally without their parents' prior written consent—even a political rally in support of laws against corporal punishment of children, or laws in favor of greater rights for minors. And what is good for First Amendment rights of speech must be good for First Amendment rights of religion as well: It could be made criminal to admit a person under 18 to church, or to give a person under 18 a religious tract, without his parents' prior consent....

[Yet such laws would be] obviously an infringement upon the religious freedom of young people and those who wish to proselytize young people. Such laws do not enforce *parental* authority over children's speech and religion; they impose *governmental* authority, subject only to a parental veto. In the absence of any precedent for state control, uninvited by the parents, over a child's speech and religion (Justice Thomas cites none), and in the absence of any justification for such control that would satisfy strict scrutiny, those laws must be unconstitutional.} ...

[Once the majority concluded that violent video games distributed to minors were as protected as other speech, it then had to decide whether the restriction could still be upheld under "strict scrutiny"—whether it was narrowly tailored to compelling government interests in (1) preventing harm to children and (2) protecting parents' ability to control what games their children played. That discussion is excerpted in the Strict Scrutiny unit, see p. 292. The discussion in this section focuses on the threshold question: Is such strict scrutiny unnecessary, because the restriction should be seen as an extension of the existing obscenity exception?—ed.]

Justice Alito, with whom the Chief Justice joins, concurring in the judgment....

[Justice Alito concluded that the California statute was unconstitutionally vague, but disagreed with the majority about whether a more precisely defined statute would be constitutional:—ed.]

[T]he experience of playing video games (and the effects on minors of playing violent video games) may be very different from anything that we have seen before. {The Court acts prematurely in dismissing this possibility out of hand.} ... Today's most advanced video games create [strikingly] realistic alternative worlds in which millions of players immerse themselves for hours on end... [I]n the near future video-game graphics may be virtually indistinguishable from actual video footage ... [and before long] will be seen in three dimensions.

It is also forecast that video games will soon provide sensory feedback.

By wearing a special vest or other device, a player will be able to experience physical sensations supposedly felt by a character on the screen. Some *amici* who support respondents foresee the day when "virtual-reality shoot-'em-ups" will allow children to "actually feel the splatting blood from the blown-off head" of a victim.

Persons who play video games also have an unprecedented ability to participate in the events that take place in the virtual worlds that these games create. Players can create their own video-game characters and can use photos to produce characters that closely resemble actual people. A person playing a sophisticated game can make a multitude of choices and can thereby alter the course of the action in the game....

[And i]n some of these games, the violence is astounding. Victims by the dozens are killed with every imaginable implement, including machine guns, shotguns, clubs, hammers, axes, swords, and chainsaws. Victims are dismembered, decapitated, disemboweled, set on fire, and chopped into little pieces. They cry out in agony and beg for mercy. Blood gushes, splatters, and pools. Severed body parts and gobs of human remains are graphically shown. In some games, points are awarded based, not only on the number of victims killed, but on the killing technique employed.

It also appears that there is no antisocial theme too base for some in the video-game industry to exploit. There are games in which a player can take on the identity and reenact the killings carried out by the perpetrators of the murders at Columbine High School and Virginia Tech. The objective of one game is to rape a mother and her daughters; in another, the goal is to rape Native American women. There is a game in which players engage in "ethnic cleansing" and can choose to gun down African-Americans, Latinos, or Jews. In still another game, players attempt to fire a rifle shot into the head of President Kennedy as his motorcade passes by the Texas School Book Depository.

If the technological characteristics of the sophisticated games that are likely to be available in the near future are combined with the characteristics of the most violent games already marketed, the result will be games that allow troubled teens to experience in an extraordinarily personal and vivid way what it would be like to carry out unspeakable acts of violence....

[And video] games are "far more concretely interactive[" than literature.] ... [T]hink of a person who reads the passage in Crime and Punishment in which Raskolnikov kills the old pawn broker with an axe. Compare that reader with a video-game player who creates an avatar that bears his own image; who sees a realistic image of the victim and the scene of the killing in high definition and in three dimensions; who is forced to decide whether or not to kill the victim and decides to do so; who then pretends to grasp an axe, to raise it above the head of the victim, and then to bring it down; who hears the thud of the axe hitting her head and her cry of pain; who sees her split skull and feels the sensation of blood on his face and hands. For most people, the two experiences will not be the same.

{[T]here are a few children's books that ask young readers to step into the shoes of a character and to make choices that take the stories along one of a very limited number of possible lines. But the very nature of the print medium makes it impossible for a book to offer anything like the same number of choices as those provided by a video game.} ...

Justice Thomas, dissenting....

[A.] The history [of the Colonies and the Revolutionary and post-Revolutionary era] clearly shows a founding generation that believed parents to have complete authority over their minor children and expected parents to direct the development of those children. [Details omitted.—ed.] In light of this history, ... the founding generation would not have understood "the freedom of speech" to include a right to speak to children without going through their parents. As a consequence, I do not believe that laws limiting such speech—for example, by requiring parental consent to speak to a minor— "abridg[e] the freedom of speech" within the original meaning of the First Amendment....

[B.] [T]he notion that parents have authority over their children and that the law can support that authority persists today. For example, at least some States make it a crime to lure or entice a minor away from the minor's parent. Every State in the Union still establishes a minimum age for marriage without parental or judicial consent. Individuals less than 18 years old cannot enlist in the military without parental consent. And minors remain subject to curfew laws across the country, and cannot unilaterally consent to most medical procedures....

The Court's constitutional jurisprudence "historically has reflected Western civilization concepts of the family as a unit with broad parental authority over minor children." Under that case law, "legislature[s] [can] properly conclude that parents and others, teachers for example, who have ... primary responsibility for children's well-being are entitled to the support of laws designed to aid discharge of that responsibility."

This is because "the tradition of parental authority is not inconsistent with our tradition of individual liberty; rather, the former is one of the basic presuppositions of the latter." ... "Legal restrictions on minors, especially those supportive of the parental role, may be important to the child's chances for the full growth and maturity that make eventual participation in a free society meaningful and rewarding[."] ...

Justice Breyer, dissenting....

[A.] [Justice Breyer argued that the law only modestly burdened speech, by simply imposing a parental permission requirement. He added:—ed.] Nor is the statute, if upheld, likely to create a precedent that would adversely affect other media, say films, or videos, or books. A typical video game involves a significant amount of physical activity. And pushing buttons that achieve an interactive, virtual form of target practice (using images of human beings as targets), while containing an expressive component, is not just like watching a typical movie....

[B.] {Since the Court in *Ginsberg* specified that the statute's prohibition applied to material that was *not* obscene [for adults], I cannot dismiss *Ginsberg* on the ground that it concerned obscenity.} *Ginsberg* makes clear that a State can prohibit the sale to minors of depictions of nudity; today the Court makes clear that a State cannot prohibit the sale to minors of the most violent interactive video games. But what sense does it make to forbid selling to a 13-year-old boy a magazine with an image of a nude woman, while protecting a sale to that 13-year-old of an interactive video game in which he actively, but virtually, binds and gags the woman, then tortures and kills her? What kind of First Amendment would permit the government to protect children by restricting sales of that extremely violent video game *only* when the woman—bound, gagged, tortured, and killed—is also topless?

Arbitrary line
Double standard

This anomaly is not compelled by the First Amendment. It disappears once one recognizes that extreme violence, where interactive, and *without literary, artistic, or similar justification,* can prove at least as, if not more, harmful to children as photographs of nudity. And the record here is more than adequate to support such a view. That is why I believe that *Ginsberg* controls the outcome here *a fortiori....*

This case is ultimately less about censorship than it is about education. Our Constitution cannot succeed in securing the liberties it seeks to protect unless we can raise future generations committed cooperatively to making our system of government work. Education, however, is about choices. Sometimes, children need to learn by making choices for themselves. Other times, choices are made for children—by their parents, by their teachers, and by the people acting democratically through their governments. In my view, the First Amendment does not disable government from helping parents make such a choice here—a choice not to have their children buy extremely violent, interactive video games, which they more than reasonably fear pose only the risk of harm to those children....

4. The Vagueness Doctrine

a. Summary

Rule

1. A speech restriction may be unconstitutionally vague if it fails to "provid[e] an ascertainable standard of conduct," *Baggett v. Bullitt*, 377 U.S. 360, 372 (1964).

2. "What renders a statute vague is not the possibility that it will sometimes be difficult to determine whether the incriminating fact it establishes has been proved; but rather the indeterminacy of precisely what that fact is. Thus, we have struck down statutes that tied criminal culpability to whether the defendant's conduct was 'annoying' or 'indecent'—wholly subjective judgments without statutory definitions, narrowing context, or settled legal meanings." *United States v. Williams* (2008) (p. 9).

3. On the other hand, the Court has upheld many restrictions that are indeed pretty vague; consider the definition of obscenity. If you can persuade a judge that the law you're defending is no more vague than those,

then the law will probably be upheld.

4. The rules are much more relaxed when the government is acting as subsidizer (*NEA v. Finley* (1998) (p. 626)) and controller of the military (*Parker v. Levy*, 417 U.S. 733 (1974)), and at least considerably relaxed when it's acting as employer (*Waters v. Churchill*, 511 U.S. 661, 671-72 (1994) (plurality)) and K-12 educator (*Bethel School Dist. No. 403 v. Fraser* (1986) (p. 600)).

5. Recall that in U.S. law, the meaning of a statute is determined by how courts have construed it, not just by what it says; the same applies in vagueness challenges. If courts have construed the terms of a vague law in a way that makes them less vague (called a "clarifying construction"), then a court considering a vagueness challenge would look to the law as construed by those other courts, not just as written. And the court that's faced with a vagueness challenge might itself create a clarifying construction, and uphold the statute on the basis of that construction, at least so long as the construction is not "unexpected" or "unforeseeable." *Marks v. United States*, 430 U.S. 188 (1977).

6. A challenger must generally show the law is vague as to the speech in which he engaged, and not just as to other speech. "[A] plaintiff whose speech is clearly proscribed cannot raise a successful vagueness claim ... for lack of notice. And he certainly cannot do so based on the speech of others." *Holder v. Humanitarian Law Project*, 561 U.S. 1 (2010).

   At the same time, a law's vagueness can expand the law's perceived breadth and so make it overbroad. "Given the vague contours of the coverage of the statute, it unquestionably silences [through fear that the speech may be punishable] some speakers whose messages would be entitled to constitutional protection." *Reno v. ACLU* (1997) (p. 163). "[Vague laws] lead citizens to 'steer far wider of the unlawful zone ... than if the boundaries of the forbidden areas were clearly marked.'" *Grayned v. City of Rockford* (1972) (p. 158).

7. A law's facial breadth may *lead it to be vague*: Because the law is so broad, no-one would really think of enforcing it literally, and enforcers will therefore in practice impose some limits that will ultimately prove vague. See *Board of Airport Comm'rs v. Jews for Jesus* (1987) (p. 162).

b. Problem: Telephone Harassment Law

A City of Bellevue telephone harassment makes it a crime to, among other things, "[1] with intent to disturb, embarrass, harass, intimidate, threaten or torment any other person, ... [2] make a telephone call to such other person ... [3] [w]ithout purpose of legitimate communication." Is this constitutional? Compare *City of Bellevue v. Lorang*, 992 P.2d 496 (Wash. 2000), with *Smith v. Martens*, 106 P.3d 28 (Kan. 2005).

c. Problem: Hostile Environment Harassment Law

Courts have interpreted Title VII and similar state and federal laws as imposing civil liability on employers when the employer, its employees, or its patrons engage in conduct or speech that is

    (a) "severe or pervasive" enough

    (b) to create a "hostile, abusive, or offensive work environment"

    (c) based on race, religion, sex, national origin, age, or disability

    (d) for the plaintiff and

    (e) for a reasonable person.

Courts have applied this both to speech said directly to the offended person and to speech (such as signs, e-mails, coworker conversations, and the like) seen or overheard by the person. Courts have generally said that the "severe or pervasive" requirement is usually not satisfied by a single instance of offensive speech, but can be satisfied by speech that happens several times over the span of weeks or months. Employers are generally liable when they know or have reason to know about the speech. As to speech by patrons, employers are liable only when they have the power to control the speech, for instance by instructing employees to eject offending patrons.

Is this law unconstitutionally vague? You will see the substantive parts of this problem discussed in the Captive Audiences problem (Part II.E.*3.e*, p. 192) and Part III.C.4.a (p. 333); but for now focus on whether the law is unconstitutionally vague.

    d.   *Grayned v. City of Rockford, 408 U.S. 104 (1972)*

    Justice Marshall delivered the opinion of the Court....

Grayned was tried and convicted of violating [a Rockford, Illinois ordinance that] ... reads, in pertinent part, as follows: "[N]o person, while on public or private grounds adjacent to any building in which a school or any class thereof is in session, shall willfully make or assist in the making of any noise or diversion which disturbs or tends to disturb the peace or good order of such school session or class thereof...." [Grayned was one of about 200 demonstrators who were protesting race discrimination at a Rockford, Illinois high school.—ed.] ...

[A.] It is a basic principle of due process that an enactment is void for vagueness if its prohibitions are not clearly defined. Vague laws offend several important values.

First, because we assume that man is free to steer between lawful and unlawful conduct, we insist that laws give the person of ordinary intelligence a reasonable opportunity to know what is prohibited, so that he may act accordingly. Vague laws may trap the innocent by not providing fair warning.

Second, if arbitrary and discriminatory enforcement is to be prevented, laws must provide explicit standards for those who apply them. A vague law impermissibly delegates basic policy matters to policemen, judges, and juries for resolution on an *ad hoc* and subjective basis, with the attendant dangers of arbitrary and discriminatory application.

Third, but related, where a vague statute "abut[s] upon sensitive areas of basic First Amendment freedoms," it "operates to inhibit the exercise of [those] freedoms." Uncertain meanings inevitably lead citizens to "'steer far wider of the unlawful zone' ... than if the boundaries of the forbidden areas were clearly marked."

[B.] Although the question is close, we conclude that the antinoise ordinance is not impermissibly vague.... [T]he court below did not elaborate on the meaning of the antinoise ordinance. In this situation, ... we must "extrapolate its allowable meaning."

Here, we are "relegated ... to the words of the ordinance itself," to the interpretations the court below has given to analogous statutes, and, perhaps to some degree, to the interpretation of the statute given by those charged with enforcing it. "Extrapolation," of course, is a delicate task, for it is not within our power to construe and narrow state laws.

[C.] With that warning, we find no unconstitutional vagueness in the antinoise ordinance. Condemned to the use of words, we can never expect mathematical certainty from our language. {It will always be true that the fertile legal "imagination can conjure up hypothetical cases in which the meaning of [disputed] terms will be in nice question."}

The words of the Rockford ordinance are marked by "flexibility and reasonable breadth, rather than meticulous specificity," but we think it is clear what the ordinance as a whole prohibits. Designed, according to its preamble, "for the protection of Schools," the ordinance forbids deliberately noisy or diversionary activity that disrupts or is about to disrupt normal school activities. It forbids this willful activity at fixed times—when school is in session—and at a sufficiently fixed place—"adjacent" to the school.

Were we left with just the words of the ordinance, we might be troubled by the imprecision of the phrase "tends to disturb." However, in [two earlier cases], the Supreme Court of Illinois construed a Chicago ordinance prohibiting, *inter alia*, a "diversion tending to disturb the peace," and held that it permitted conviction only where there was *imminent* threat of violence." Since [one case] was specifically cited in the opinion below, and it in turn drew heavily on [the other], we think it proper to conclude that the Supreme Court of Illinois would interpret the Rockford ordinance to prohibit only actual or imminent interference with the "peace or good order" of the school.

Although the prohibited quantum of disturbance is not specified in the ordinance, it is apparent from the statute's announced purpose that the measure is whether normal school activity has been or is about to be disrupted. We do not have here a vague, general "breach of the peace" ordinance, but a statute written specifically for the school context, where the prohibited disturbances are easily measured by their impact on the normal activities of the school.

Given this "particular context," the ordinance gives "fair notice to those to whom [it] is directed." Although the Rockford ordinance may not be as precise as the statute we upheld in *Cameron v. Johnson,* 390 U.S. 611 (1968)—which prohibited picketing "in such a manner as to obstruct or unreasonably interfere with free ingress or egress to and from" any court-house—we think that, as in *Cameron,* the ordinance here clearly "delineates its reach in words of common understanding."

Cox v. Louisiana, 379 U.S. 536 (1965), and *Coates v. Cincinnati,* 402 U.S. 611 (1971), on which appellant particularly relies, presented completely different situations. In *Cox,* a general breach of the peace ordinance had been construed by state courts to mean "to agitate, to arouse from a state of repose, to molest, to interrupt, to hinder, to disquiet." The Court correctly concluded that, as construed, the ordinance permitted persons to be punished for merely expressing unpopular views. {Similarly, in numerous other cases, we have condemned broadly worded licensing ordinances which grant such standardless discretion to public officials that they are free to censor ideas and enforce their own personal preferences.}

In *Coates,* the ordinance punished the sidewalk assembly of three or more persons who "conduct themselves in a manner annoying to persons passing by...." We held, in part, that the ordinance was impermissibly vague because enforcement depended on the completely subjective standard of "annoyance."

In contrast, Rockford's antinoise ordinance does not permit punishment for the expression of an unpopular point of view, and it contains no broad invitation to subjective or discriminatory enforcement. Rockford does not claim the broad power to punish all "noises" and "diversions." The vagueness of these terms, by themselves, is dispelled by the ordinance's requirements that (1) the "noise or diversion" be actually incompatible with normal school activity; (2) there be a demonstrated causality between the disruption that occurs and the "noise or diversion"; and (3) the acts be "willfully" done. "Undesirables" or their "annoying" conduct may not be punished.

The ordinance does not permit people to "stand on a public sidewalk ... only at the whim of any police officer." Rather, there must be demonstrated interference with school activities. As always, enforcement requires the exercise of some degree of police judgment, but, as confined, that degree of judgment here is permissible.

The Rockford City Council has made the basic policy choices, and has given fair warning as to what is prohibited. "[T]he ordinance defines boundaries sufficiently distinct" for citizens, policemen, juries, and appellate judges. It is not impermissibly vague....

e.   *Smith v. Goguen, 415 U.S. 566 (1974)*

[Note that, when this case was decided, it wasn't clear that the Court would strike down flag misuse bans (*e.g.,* a clear ban on wearing the flag on the seat of one's pants) on substantive grounds.   cd.]

Justice Powell delivered the opinion of the Court....

[A.] Goguen wore a small cloth version of the United States flag sewn to the seat of his trousers. The flag was approximately four by six inches and was displayed at the left rear of Goguen's blue jeans.... [He was prosecuted under a statute that] then read: "Whoever ... treats contemptuously the flag of the United States ... [is guilty of a misdemeanor]...." ...

[I]n a time of widely varying attitudes and tastes for displaying something as ubiquitous as the United States flag or representations of it, it could hardly be the purpose of the Massachusetts Legislature to make criminal every informal use of the flag.... The statutory language under which Goguen was charged, however, fails to draw reasonably clear lines between the kinds of nonceremonial treatment that are criminal and those that are not. Due process requires that all "be informed as to what the State commands or forbids," and that "men of common intelligence" not be forced to guess at the meaning of the criminal law. Given today's tendencies to treat the flag unceremoniously, those notice standards are not satisfied here.

We recognize that in a noncommercial context behavior as a general rule is not mapped out in advance on the basis of statutory language. In such cases, perhaps the most meaningful aspect of the vagueness doctrine is not actual notice, but the other principal element of the doctrine—the requirement that a legislature establish minimal guidelines to govern law enforcement. It is in this regard that the statutory language under scrutiny has its most notable deficiencies....

Statutory language of such a standardless sweep allows policemen, prosecutors, and juries to pursue their personal predilections. Legislatures may not so abdicate their responsibilities for setting the standards of the criminal law.... The aptness of his admonition is evident from appellant's candid concession during oral argument before the Court of Appeals ...:

> [A] war protestor who, while attending a rally at which it begins to rain, evidences his disrespect for the American flag by contemptuously covering himself with it in order to avoid getting wet, would be prosecuted under the Massachusetts statute. Yet a member of the American Legion who, caught in the same rainstorm while returning from an "America—Love It or Leave It" rally, similarly uses the flag, but does so regrettably and without a contemptuous attitude, would not be prosecuted.

Where inherently vague statutory language permits such selective law enforcement, there is a denial of due process.

[B.] [A]ppellant argues that ... the narrow subject matter of the statute ... "takes some of the vagueness away from the phrase, 'treats contemptuously ....' ... [If anyone] wants to stay clear of violating this statute, he just has to stay clear of doing something to the United States flag." ... [W]e fail to see how this alleged particularity resolves the central vagueness question—the absence of any standard for defining contemptuous treatment.

Appellant further argues that the Supreme Judicial Court [of Massachusetts] in Goguen's case has restricted the scope of the statute to intentional contempt.... [But] this holding still does not clarify what conduct constitutes contempt, whether intentional or inadvertent....

There are areas of human conduct where, by the nature of the problems presented, legislatures simply cannot establish standards with great precision. Control of the broad range of disorderly conduct that may inhibit a policeman in the performance of his official duties may be one such area, requiring as it does an on-the-spot assessment of the need to keep order.

But there is no comparable reason for committing broad discretion to law enforcement officials in the area of flag contempt. Indeed, because display of the flag is so common and takes so many forms, changing from one generation to another and often difficult to distinguish in principle, a legislature should define with some care the flag behavior it intends to outlaw. Certainly nothing prevents a legislature from defining with substantial specificity what constitutes forbidden treatment of United States flags....

Justice White, [whom Chief Justice Burger and Justices Rehnquist and Blackmun joined on this,] concurring in the judgment....

[T]here is a whole range of conduct that anyone with at least a semblance of common sense would know is contemptuous conduct and that would be covered by the statute if directed at the flag. In these instances, there would be ample notice to the actor and no room for undue discretion by enforcement officers. There may be a variety of other conduct that might or might not be claimed contemptuous by the State, but unpredictability in those situations does not change the certainty in others.

I am also confident that the statute was not vague with respect to the conduct for which Goguen was arrested and convicted. It should not be beyond the reasonable comprehension of anyone who would conform his conduct to the law to realize that sewing a flag on the seat of his pants is contemptuous of the flag.... [Goguen's] major argument is that wearing a flag patch on his trousers was conduct that "clearly expressed an idea, albeit unpopular or unpatriotic, about the flag or about the country it symbolizes .... Goguen may have meant to show that he believed that America was a fit place only to sit on, or the proximity to that portion of his anatomy might have had more vulgar connotations. Nonetheless, the strong and forceful communication of ideas is unmistakable." Goguen was under no misapprehension as to what he was doing and as to whether he was showing contempt for the flag of the United States....

[Justice White went on to conclude that, though laws "protect[ing] the physical integrity or to protect against acts interfering with the proper use of the flag" were constitutionally permissible, a broader ban on "contemptuous[]" treatment was an impermissibly viewpoint-based punishment "for communicating ideas about the flag unacceptable to the controlling majority in the legislature." Chief Justice Burger and Justices Blackmun and Rehnquist agreed with Justice White on the vagueness question, but dissented because they concluded that the "treats contemptuously" provision was substantively constitutional.—ed.]

f. Board of Airport Comm'rs v. Jews for Jesus, 482 U.S. 569 (1987)

Justice O'Connor delivered the opinion of the [unanimous] Court....

[A resolution of the Board of Airport Commissioners purports to ban all "First Amendment activities" in the Los Angeles airport.] The resolution [on

its face] prohibits even talking and reading, or the wearing of campaign buttons or symbolic clothing.... We think it obvious that such a ban cannot be
justified even if LAX were a nonpublic forum [*i.e.*, government property on
which the government as landlord generally has broad power to restrict
speech—ed.] because no conceivable governmental interest would justify
such an absolute prohibition of speech....

The petitioners suggest that the resolution is not substantially overbroad because it is intended to reach only expressive activity unrelated to
airport-related purposes.... [But] the vagueness of this suggested construction itself presents serious constitutional difficulty. The line between airport-related speech and nonairport-related speech is, at best, murky.

The petitioners, for example, suggest that an individual who reads a
newspaper or converses with a neighbor at LAX is engaged in permitted
"airport-related" activity because reading or conversing permits the travel-
ing public to "pass the time." We presume, however, that petitioners would
not so categorize the activities of a member of a religious or political organization who decides to "pass the time" by distributing leaflets to fellow travelers.

In essence, the result of this vague limiting construction would be to give
LAX officials alone the power to decide in the first instance whether a given
activity is airport related. Such a law that "confers on police a virtually unrestrained power to arrest and charge persons with a violation" of the resolution is unconstitutional because "[t]he opportunity for abuse, especially
where a statute has received a virtually open-ended interpretation, is self-
evident." ...

g. *Reno v. ACLU, 521 U.S. 844 (1997)*

Justice Stevens delivered the opinion of the Court....

[The Communications Decency Act of 1996 enacted two provisions:] 47
U.S.C. § 223(a) [makes punishable by up to two years in prison] ... "knowingly ... [conveying by means of a telecommunications device] any ... communication which is obscene or indecent, knowing that the recipient of the
communication is under 18 years of age ...." The second provision, § 223(d),
[makes punishable by up to two years in prison] ... "knowingly" "us[ing] any
interactive computer service" ... "to display in a manner available to a person under 18 years of age, any ... communication that, in context, depicts or
describes, in terms patently offensive as measured by contemporary community standards, sexual or excretory activities or organs ...."

[The Court ultimately struck down the CDA because it was too broad;
in the course of evaluating the CDA's breadth, it said the following:—ed.]

Regardless of whether the CDA is so vague that it violates the Fifth
Amendment, the many ambiguities concerning the scope of its coverage render it problematic for purposes of the First Amendment. For instance, each
of the two parts of the CDA uses a different linguistic form. The first uses
the word "indecent," while the second speaks of material that "in context,

depicts or describes, in terms patently offensive as measured by contemporary community standards, sexual or excretory activities or organs." Given the absence of a definition of either term, this difference in language will provoke uncertainty among speakers about how the two standards relate to each other and just what they mean.

{[Moreover, t]he statute does not indicate whether the "patently offensive" and "indecent" determinations should be made with respect to minors or the population as a whole. The Government asserts that the appropriate standard is "what is suitable material for minors." But [the members of the House-Senate conference committee deliberating on the bill] expressly rejected amendments that would have imposed such a "harmful to minors" standard. The Conferees also rejected amendments that would have limited the proscribed materials to those lacking redeeming value.}

Could a speaker confidently assume that a serious discussion about birth control practices, homosexuality, the First Amendment issues raised by the Appendix to our *FCC v. Pacifica Foundation* opinion, or the consequences of prison rape would not violate the CDA? This uncertainty undermines the likelihood that the CDA has been carefully tailored to the congressional goal of protecting minors from potentially harmful materials.

The vagueness of the CDA is a matter of special concern for two reasons. First, the CDA is a content-based regulation of speech. The vagueness of such a regulation raises special First Amendment concerns because of its obvious chilling effect on free speech.

Second, the CDA is a criminal statute.... The severity of criminal sanctions may well cause speakers to remain silent rather than communicate even arguably unlawful words, ideas, and images. As a practical matter, this increased deterrent effect, coupled with the "risk of discriminatory enforcement" of vague regulations, poses greater First Amendment concerns than those implicated by ... civil regulation ....

The Government argues that the statute is no more vague than the obscenity standard this Court established in *Miller v. California*.... Because the CDA's "patently offensive" standard (and, we assume, *arguendo*, its synonymous "indecent" standard) is one part of the three-prong *Miller* test, the Government reasons, it cannot be unconstitutionally vague.

The Government's assertion is incorrect as a matter of fact. The second prong of the *Miller* test—the purportedly analogous standard—contains a critical requirement that is omitted from the CDA: that the proscribed material be "specifically defined by the applicable state law." This requirement reduces the vagueness inherent in the open-ended term "patently offensive" as used in the CDA. Moreover, the *Miller* definition is limited to "sexual conduct," whereas the CDA extends also to include (1) "excretory activities" as well as (2) "organs" of both a sexual and excretory nature....

[Furthermore, j]ust because a definition including three limitations is not vague, it does not follow that one of those limitations, standing by itself, is not vague. {Even though the word "trunk," standing alone, might refer to luggage, a swimming suit, the base of a tree, or the long nose of an animal, its meaning is clear when it is one prong of a three-part description of a species of gray animals.} Each of *Miller's* additional two prongs—(1) that, taken as a whole, the material appeal to the "prurient" interest, and (2) that it "lac[k] serious literary, artistic, political, or scientific value"—critically limits the uncertain sweep of the obscenity definition.

The second requirement is particularly important because, unlike the "patently offensive" and "prurient interest" criteria, it is not judged by contemporary community standards. This "societal value" requirement, absent in the CDA, allows appellate courts to impose some limitations and regularity on the definition by setting, as a matter of law, a national floor for socially redeeming value....

In contrast to *Miller* and our other previous cases, the CDA thus presents a greater threat of censoring speech that, in fact, falls outside the statute's scope. Given the vague contours of the coverage of the statute, it unquestionably silences some speakers whose messages would be entitled to constitutional protection.

That danger provides further reason for insisting that the statute not be overly broad. The CDA's burden on protected speech cannot be justified if it could be avoided by a more carefully drafted statute....

[The Court went on to conclude that there were indeed less restrictive alternatives that would still achieve the government's goal, and the CDA thus failed strict scrutiny.—ed.]

D. "Speech Integral to [Unlawful] Conduct"

1. Summary

Since 2006, the Supreme Court has been reviving a long-dormant First Amendment exception: the exception for "speech integral to criminal [or tortious] conduct," first discussed in detail in *Giboney v. Empire Storage & Ice Co.* (1949) (p. 181). *United States v. Williams* (2008) (p. 9) relied heavily on *Giboney* in upholding restrictions on speech that solicits crime. *United States v. Stevens* (2010) (p. 178) cited it in recharacterizing the child pornography exception as a special case of the "speech integral to [unlawful] conduct" doctrine. Other recent cases, including *Rumsfeld v. FAIR* (2006) (p. 545), have relied on it as well. And in the 1940s, 1950s, and 1960s, the Court also treated the exceptions for threats, fighting words, and incitement as applications of this doctrine.

The scope of the "speech integral to [unlawful conduct] exception" isn't clear, but it appears that:

(a) When speech tends to cause, attempts to cause, or makes a threat to cause some illegal conduct (illegal conduct other than the prohibited speech itself)—such as murder, a fistfight, restraint of trade, child sexual abuse, discriminatory refusal to hire, and the like—this opens the door to possible restrictions on such speech.

(b) But the scope of such restrictions must still be narrowly defined, in order to protect speech that persuades or informs people who will not engage in illegal conduct. This is what has happened, for instance, with the incitement, fighting words, and child pornography exceptions.

Perhaps, then, the *Giboney* doctrine should be seen less as a single exception than as a guide to generating other exceptions (such as the solicitation exception, the child pornography exception, and the like). Still, the Court has recently articulated it as an exception, alongside incitement, libel, obscenity, and the like; we will treat it the same way.

2.   Child Pornography

a.   *Summary*

When *Ferber* was decided, it was generally understood as recognizing a new exception for child pornography. *See, e.g., Bose Corp. v. Consumers Union of U.S., Inc.*, 466 U.S. 485 (1984) (so describing the exception, alongside the familiar exceptions for incitement, libel, obscenity, and fighting words). But *United States v. Stevens* (2010) (p. 178) recharacterized child pornography as a special case of a broader exception for speech that is an "integral part" of criminal conduct.

Rule: Speech is unprotected if

1. It "visually depict[s]" children below the age of majority
2. "performing sexual acts or lewdly exhibiting their genitals." *New York v. Ferber* (1982) (p. 168).

a.   It does not matter whether the speech meets any of the prongs of the *Miller* test (*Ferber*).

b.   Something can be pornography about children, pornography that looks like it involves children (*Ashcroft v. Free Speech Coalition* (2002) (p. 172), pornography that people think is harmful when shown to children, or pornography that urges viewers to harm children, and yet not be child pornography.

Subsidiary rules:

1. *Osborne v. Ohio*, 495 U.S. 103 (1990): Private possession of child pornography may be outlawed.

2. A defendant may only be punished if he knows (or, possibly, has reason to know) that the material that he distributed or possessed involved an underage performer. A reasonable mistake of fact is a defense. *Ferber.* It's not clear whether negligent mistake of fact is a defense—*i.e.*, whether the mens rea required for liability is merely negligence as to age (which means only reasonable mistakes of fact are unpunishable) or recklessness as to age (which means all sincere mistakes of fact, including negligent ones, are protected).

Policy explanations for the exception:

1. Children are harmed in the production of the pornography, both in having to engage in the acts being displayed, and (in most cases) in having

the child pornography be a permanent record of those acts.

2. Distributing and possessing child pornography is an "integral part" of criminal activity.

3. Child pornography has "exceedingly modest, if not *de minimis*" expressive value, at least as a general rule.

b. *Problem: Morphed Images*

A producer takes an old sexually themed movie and replaces the adult actors' faces with photographs of the faces of real children. He then uses computer technology to animate the photographs, and to make the actors' bodies look like the bodies of real children. The producer photographs them when they're fully clothed, and not doing anything sexual.

May Congress ban distribution and possession of films made this way? Compare *United States v. Hotaling*, 2011 WL 677398 (2d Cir.) (answering yes); *United States v. Bach*, 400 F.3d 622 (8th Cir. 2005) (answering yes), with *State v. Zidel*, 940 A.2d 255 (N.H. 2008) (answering no).

c. *Problem: Affirmative Defense*

Your boss, Senator Michelle Boardman, is troubled by the outcome of *Ashcroft v. Free Speech Coalition*. She thinks that many people who distribute and possess real child pornography might indeed go free because they say "Oh, I thought it was virtual." Stories like this one make her worry that, even when these claims are false, prosecutors won't be able to convince jurors beyond a reasonable doubt that the defendant is lying, or may even have cases thrown out before trial:

> Charges were thrown out in two [Ohio child pornography] cases [based on the testimony of Dean Boland, a defense expert who testifies] about digital-imaging technology and the ways pornographers are using it to enhance and distribute their wares via the Internet.... "The majority of child pornography downloaded from the Internet ... really can't be determined to be actual children," Boland said. "It's very easy to fake these images, and prosecutors need to be required to authenticate their evidence." ...

James F. McCarty, *Ex-Prosecutor Now Toppling Porn Cases*, Cleveland Plain Dealer, June 25, 2004. The Senator would like to propose a version of CPPA that makes it harder for people to falsely use the "I thought it was virtual" argument. She thinks the solution might be to require the defendant to raise an affirmative defense (1) that the work wasn't made using real children, or (2) that even if it was so made, the defendant lacked the necessary mens rea about that fact.

But what mens rea should be required: Should the defendant have to show he didn't know the item was real child pornography? That he wasn't reckless about it? That he wasn't negligent? And what quantum of proof should the defendant have to meet: Should he have to show that the work wasn't child pornography, or that he lacked the relevant mens rea, by a preponderance of the evidence? By clear and convincing evidence? Should it suffice for him to introduce enough evidence to raise a reasonable doubt?

What options would you suggest to the Senator, and what would their pluses and minuses be, both constitutionally and practically?

 d. *New York v. Ferber, 458 U.S. 747 (1982)*

Justice White delivered the opinion of the Court....

[A.] [T]he exploitive use of children in the production of pornography has become a serious national problem.... In 1977, the New York Legislature enacted ... § 263.15, defining a ... felony: "A person is guilty of promoting a sexual performance by a child when, knowing the character and content thereof, he produces ... or promotes any performance which includes sexual conduct by a child less than sixteen years of age." ... {A "[s]exual performance" is defined as

> [(1)] any [play, motion picture, photograph, dance, or other visual representation exhibited before an audience] or part thereof
> [(2)] which includes [actual or simulated sexual intercourse, deviate sexual intercourse, sexual bestiality, masturbation, sado-masochistic abuse, or lewd exhibition of the genitals]
> [(3)] by a child less than sixteen years of age....}

Paul Ferber, the proprietor of a Manhattan bookstore specializing in sexually oriented products, sold two films to an undercover police officer. The films are devoted almost exclusively to depicting young boys masturbating. Ferber was [acquitted of] two counts of [distributing obscenity] and [found guilty of] two counts of violating § 263.15....

[B.] Like obscenity statutes, laws directed at the dissemination of child pornography run the risk of suppressing protected expression by allowing the hand of the censor to become unduly heavy. For the following reasons, however, we are persuaded that the States are entitled to greater leeway in the regulation of pornographic depictions of children.

First.... [A] State's interest in "safeguarding the physical and psychological well-being of a minor" is "compelling." ... [V]irtually all of the States and the United States have passed legislation proscribing the production of or otherwise combating "child pornography." The legislative judgment, as well as the judgment found in the relevant literature, is that the use of children as subjects of pornographic materials is harmful to the physiological, emotional, and mental health of the child. That judgment, we think, easily passes muster under the First Amendment.

Second. The distribution of photographs and films depicting sexual activity by juveniles is intrinsically related to the sexual abuse of children in at least two ways. First, the materials produced are a permanent record of the children's participation and the harm to the child is exacerbated by their circulation. Second, the distribution network for child pornography must be closed if the production of material which requires the sexual exploitation of children is to be effectively controlled. Indeed, there is no serious contention that the legislature was unjustified in believing that it is difficult, if not impossible, to halt the exploitation of children by pursuing only those who produce the photographs and movies.

While the production of pornographic materials is a low-profile, clandestine industry, the need to market the resulting products requires a visible apparatus of distribution. The most expeditious if not the only practical method of law enforcement may be to dry up the market for this material by imposing severe criminal penalties on persons selling, advertising, or otherwise promoting the product. Thirty-five States and Congress have concluded that restraints on the distribution of pornographic materials are required in order to effectively combat the problem, and there is a body of literature and testimony to support these legislative conclusions.

The *Miller v. California* standard ... does not reflect the State's particular and more compelling interest in prosecuting those who promote the sexual exploitation of children. Thus, the question under the *Miller* test of whether a work, taken as a whole, appeals to the prurient interest of the average person bears no connection to the issue of whether a child has been physically or psychologically harmed in the production of the work.

Similarly, a sexually explicit depiction need not be "patently offensive" in order to have required the sexual exploitation of a child for its production. In addition, a work which, taken on the whole, contains serious literary, artistic, political, or scientific value may nevertheless embody the hardest core of child pornography. "It is irrelevant to the child [who has been abused] whether or not the material ... has a literary, artistic, political or social value." We therefore cannot conclude that the *Miller* standard is a satisfactory solution to the child pornography problem.

Third. The advertising and selling of child pornography provide an economic motive for and are thus an integral part of the production of such materials, an activity illegal throughout the Nation. "It rarely has been suggested that the constitutional freedom for speech and press extends its immunity to speech or writing used as an integral part of conduct in violation of a valid criminal statute." *Giboney v. Empire Storage & Ice Co....* [W]ere the statutes outlawing the employment of children in these films and photographs fully effective, and the constitutionality of these laws has not been questioned, the First Amendment implications would be no greater than that presented by laws against distribution: enforceable production laws would leave no child pornography to be marketed.

Fourth. The value of permitting live performances and photographic reproductions of children engaged in lewd sexual conduct is exceedingly modest, if not *de minimis*. We consider it unlikely that visual depictions of children performing sexual acts or lewdly exhibiting their genitals would often constitute an important and necessary part of a literary performance or scientific or educational work....

[I]f it were necessary for literary or artistic value, a person over the statutory age who perhaps looked younger could be utilized. Simulation outside of the prohibition of the statute could provide another alternative. Nor is there any question here of censoring a particular literary theme or portrayal of sexual activity. The First Amendment interest is limited to that of rendering the portrayal somewhat more "realistic" by utilizing or photographing children.

Fifth... [I]t is not rare that a content-based classification of speech has been accepted because it may be appropriately generalized that within the confines of the given classification, the evil to be restricted so overwhelmingly outweighs the expressive interests, if any, at stake, that no process of case-by-case adjudication is required. When a definable class of material, such as that covered by § 263.15, bears so heavily and pervasively on the welfare of children engaged in its production, we think the balance of competing interests is clearly struck and that it is permissible to consider these materials as without the protection of the First Amendment.

More like cost/benefit

[**C.**] There are, of course, limits on the category of child pornography which, like obscenity, is unprotected by the First Amendment. As with all legislation in this sensitive area, the conduct to be prohibited must be adequately defined by the applicable state law, as written or authoritatively construed. Here the nature of the harm to be combated requires that the state offense be limited to works that *visually* depict sexual conduct by children below a specified age. The category of "sexual conduct" proscribed must also be suitably limited and described.

The test for child pornography is separate from the obscenity standard enunciated in *Miller* ...: A trier of fact need not find that the material appeals to the prurient interest of the average person; it is not required that sexual conduct portrayed be done so in a patently offensive manner; and the material at issue need not be considered as a whole.... As with obscenity laws, criminal responsibility may not be imposed without some element of scienter on the part of the defendant.

Section 263.15 ... comports with the above-stated principles. The forbidden acts to be depicted are listed with sufficient precision and represent the kind of conduct that, if it were the theme of a work, could render it legally obscene: "actual or simulated sexual intercourse, deviate sexual intercourse, sexual bestiality, masturbation, sado-masochistic abuse, or lewd exhibition of the genitals." The term "lewd exhibition of the genitals" is not unknown in this area and, indeed, was given in *Miller* as an example of a permissible regulation....

[T]he State is [also] not barred by the First Amendment from prohibiting the distribution of unprotected materials produced outside the State. {It is often impossible to determine where such material is produced.... In addition, States have not limited their distribution laws to material produced within their own borders because the maintenance of the market itself "leaves open the financial conduit by which the production of such material is funded and materially increases the risk that [local] children will be injured."}

[**D.**] It remains to address the claim that the New York statute is unconstitutionally overbroad because it would forbid the distribution of material with serious literary, scientific, or educational value or material which does not threaten the harms sought to be combated by the State....

Because of the wide-reaching effects of striking down a statute on its face at the request of one whose own conduct may be punished despite the First Amendment, we have recognized that the overbreadth doctrine is "strong medicine" and have employed it with hesitation, and then "only as a last resort." We have, in consequence, insisted that the overbreadth involved be "substantial" before the statute involved will be invalidated on its face.... While a sweeping statute, or one incapable of limitation, has the potential to repeatedly chill the exercise of expressive activity by many individuals, the extent of deterrence of protected speech can be expected to decrease with the declining reach of the regulation....

We consider this the paradigmatic case of a state statute whose legitimate reach dwarfs its arguably impermissible applications.... How often, if ever, it may be necessary to employ children to engage in conduct clearly within the reach of § 263.15 in order to produce educational, medical, or artistic works [such as medical textbooks or pictorials in the National Geographic] cannot be known with certainty. Yet we seriously doubt, and it has not been suggested, that these arguably impermissible applications of the statute amount to more than a tiny fraction of the materials within the statute's reach.

Nor will we assume that the New York courts will widen the possibly invalid reach of the statute by giving an expansive construction to the proscription on "lewd exhibition[s] of the genitals." Under these circumstances, § 263.15 is "not substantially overbroad and ... whatever overbreadth may exist should be cured through case-by-case analysis of the fact situations to which its sanctions, assertedly, may not be applied." ...

Justice O'Connor, concurring....

[The] Constitution might in fact permit New York to ban knowing distribution of works depicting minors engaged in explicit sexual conduct, regardless of the social value of the depictions. For example, a 12-year-old child photographed while masturbating surely suffers the same psychological harm whether the community labels the photograph "edifying" or "tasteless." The audience's appreciation of the depiction is simply irrelevant to New York's asserted interest in protecting children from psychological, emotional, and mental harm. An exception for depictions of serious social value, moreover, would actually increase opportunities for the content-based censorship disfavored by the First Amendment....

On the other hand, it is quite possible that New York's statute is overbroad because it bans depictions that do not actually threaten the harms identified by the Court. For example, clinical pictures of adolescent sexuality, such as those that might appear in medical textbooks, might not involve the type of sexual exploitation and abuse targeted by New York's statute. Nor might such depictions feed the poisonous "kiddie porn" market that New York and other States have attempted to regulate.

Similarly, pictures of children engaged in rites widely approved by their cultures, such as those that might appear in issues of the National Geographic, might not trigger the compelling interests identified by the Court.

It is not necessary to address these possibilities further today, however, because this potential overbreadth is not sufficiently substantial to warrant facial invalidation of New York's statute.

Justice Brennan, with whom Justice Marshall joins, concurring in the judgment....

[Justice Brennan generally agreed with the Court's decision to create a child pornography exception, but added this:—ed.] [I]n my view application of § 263.15 or any similar statute to depictions of children that in themselves do have serious literary, artistic, scientific, or medical value, would violate the First Amendment. As the Court recognizes, the limited classes of speech, the suppression of which does not raise serious First Amendment concerns, have two attributes. They are of exceedingly "slight social value," and the State has a compelling interest in their regulation.

The First Amendment value of depictions of children that are in themselves serious contributions to art, literature, or science, is, by definition, simply not "*de minimis.*" At the same time, the State's interest in suppression of such materials is likely to be far less compelling. For the Court's assumption of harm to the child resulting from the "permanent record" and "circulation" of the child's "participation" lacks much of its force where the depiction is a serious contribution to art or science. The production of materials of serious value is not the "low-profile, clandestine industry" that according to the Court produces purely pornographic materials. In short, it is inconceivable how a depiction of a child that is itself a serious contribution to the world of art or literature or science can be deemed "material outside the protection of the First Amendment." ...

e. Ashcroft v. Free Speech Coalition, 535 U.S. 234 (2002)

Justice Kennedy delivered the opinion of the Court....

[A.] [T]he Child Pornography Prevention Act of 1996 (CPPA) ... prohibits "any visual depiction, including any photograph, film, video, picture, or computer or computer-generated image or picture" that "is, or appears to be, of a minor engaging in sexually explicit conduct." The prohibition on "any visual depiction" does not depend at all on how the image is produced[, including on whether a real child was used in making the image].

The section captures a range of depictions, sometimes called "virtual child pornography," which include computer-generated images, as well as images produced by more traditional means. For instance, the literal terms of the statute embrace a Renaissance painting depicting a scene from classical mythology, a "picture" that "appears to be, of a minor engaging in sexually explicit conduct." The statute also prohibits Hollywood movies, filmed without any child actors, if a jury believes an actor "appears to be" a minor engaging in "actual or simulated ... sexual intercourse." ... [Respondents] challenged the statute in [federal court] ....

[B.] With [the CPPA's penalties of up to 15 years in prison for a first offense], few legitimate movie producers or book publishers, or few other

speakers in any capacity, would risk distributing images in or near the uncertain reach of this law. The Constitution gives significant protection from
overbroad laws that chill speech within the First Amendment's vast and
privileged sphere. Under this principle, the CPPA is unconstitutional on its
face if it prohibits a substantial amount of protected expression....

The CPPA ... extends to images that appear to depict a minor engaging
in sexually explicit activity without regard to the *Miller v. California* requirements. The materials need not appeal to the prurient interest. Any depiction of sexually explicit activity, no matter how it is presented, is proscribed. The CPPA applies to a picture in a psychology manual, as well as a
movie depicting the horrors of sexual abuse.

It is not necessary, moreover, that the image be patently offensive. Pictures of what appear to be 17-year-olds engaging in sexually explicit activity
do not in every case contravene community standards.

The CPPA prohibits speech despite its serious literary, artistic, political,
or scientific value. The statute proscribes the visual depiction of an idea—
that of teenagers engaging in sexual activity—that is a fact of modern society and has been a theme in art and literature throughout the ages. Under
the CPPA, images are prohibited so long as the persons appear to be under
18 years of age. This is higher than the legal age for marriage in many
States, as well as the age at which persons may consent to sexual relations.
It is, of course, undeniable that some youths engage in sexual activity before
the legal age, either on their own inclination or because they are victims of
sexual abuse.

Both themes—teenage sexual activity and the sexual abuse of children—have inspired countless literary works. William Shakespeare created
the most famous pair of teenage lovers, one of whom is just 13 years of age.
In the drama, Shakespeare portrays the relationship as something splendid
and innocent, but not juvenile. The work has inspired no less than 40 motion
pictures, some of which suggest that the teenagers consummated their relationship. Shakespeare may not have written sexually explicit scenes for
the Elizabethan audience, but were modern directors to adopt a less conventional approach, that fact alone would not compel the conclusion that the
work was obscene.

Contemporary movies pursue similar themes. [The Court offers some
examples, such as Traffic and American Beauty.—ed.] ... Whether or not the
films we mention violate the CPPA, they explore themes within the wide
sweep of the statute's prohibitions.

If these films, or hundreds of others of lesser note that explore those
subjects, contain a single graphic depiction of sexual activity within the statutory definition, the possessor of the film would be subject to severe punishment without inquiry into the work's redeeming value.... Under *Miller,* the
First Amendment requires that redeeming value be judged by considering
the work as a whole. Where [a single explicit] scene is part of the narrative,
the work itself does not for this reason become obscene, even though the

scene in isolation might be offensive.... [T]he CPPA [thus] cannot be read to prohibit obscenity ....

[C.] The Government [argues] that speech prohibited by the CPPA is virtually indistinguishable from child pornography, which may be banned without regard to whether it depicts works of value.... [But i]n contrast to the speech in *New York v. Ferber*, speech that itself is the record of sexual abuse, the CPPA prohibits speech that records no crime and creates no victims by its production.

Virtual child pornography is not "intrinsically related" to the sexual abuse of children, as were the materials in *Ferber*. While the Government asserts that the images can lead to actual instances of child abuse, the causal link is contingent and indirect. The harm does not necessarily follow from the speech, but depends upon some unquantified potential for subsequent criminal acts.

The Government says these indirect harms are sufficient because, as *Ferber* acknowledged, child pornography rarely can be valuable speech. This argument, however, suffers from two flaws.

First, *Ferber*'s judgment about child pornography was based upon how it was made, not on what it communicated. The case reaffirmed that where the speech is neither obscene nor the product of sexual abuse, it does not fall outside the protection of the First Amendment ....

[Second,] *Ferber* did not hold that child pornography is by definition without value. On the contrary, the Court recognized some works in this category might have significant value, but relied on virtual images—the very images prohibited by the CPPA—as an alternative and permissible means of expression: "[I]f it were necessary for literary or artistic value, ... [s]imulation outside of the prohibition of the statute could [be used]." ...

[D.] The CPPA, for reasons we have explored, is inconsistent with *Miller* and finds no support in *Ferber*. The Government seeks to justify its prohibitions in other ways.

[1.] It argues that the CPPA is necessary because pedophiles may use virtual child pornography to seduce children. There are many things innocent in themselves, however, such as cartoons, video games, and candy, that might be used for immoral purposes, yet we would not expect those to be prohibited because they can be misused.

The Government, of course, may punish adults who provide unsuitable materials to children, see *Ginsberg v. New York,* 390 U.S. 629 (1968), and it may enforce criminal penalties for unlawful solicitation. The precedents establish, however, that speech within the rights of adults to hear may not be silenced completely in an attempt to shield children from it. In *Butler v. Michigan,* 352 U.S. 380 (1957), the Court invalidated a statute prohibiting distribution of an indecent publication because of its tendency to "incite minors to violent or depraved or immoral acts." A unanimous Court agreed ... that the State could not "reduce the adult population ... to reading only what is fit for children." ...

Here, the Government wants to keep speech from children not to protect them from its content but to protect them from those who would commit other crimes. The principle, however, remains the same: The Government cannot ban speech fit for adults simply because it may fall into the hands of children.

The evil in question depends upon the actor's unlawful conduct, conduct defined as criminal quite apart from any link to the speech in question. This establishes that the speech ban is not narrowly drawn. The objective is to prohibit illegal conduct, but this restriction goes well beyond that interest by restricting the speech available to law-abiding adults.

[2.] The Government submits further that virtual child pornography whets the appetites of pedophiles and encourages them to engage in illegal conduct.... [But t]he mere tendency of speech to encourage unlawful acts is not a sufficient reason for banning it. The government "cannot constitutionally premise legislation on the desirability of controlling a person's private thoughts." ... The right to think is the beginning of freedom, and speech must be protected from the government because speech is the beginning of thought.... The government may not prohibit speech because it increases the chance an unlawful act will be committed "at some indefinite future time." The government may suppress speech for advocating the use of force or a violation of law only if "such advocacy is directed to inciting or producing imminent lawless action and is likely to incite or produce such action." *Brandenburg v. Ohio.*

There is here no attempt, incitement, solicitation, or conspiracy. The Government has shown no more than a remote connection between speech that might encourage thoughts or impulses and any resulting child abuse. Without a significantly stronger, more direct connection, the Government may not prohibit speech on the ground that it may encourage pedophiles to engage in illegal conduct.

[3.] The Government next argues that its objective of eliminating the market for pornography produced using real children necessitates a prohibition on virtual images as well. Virtual images, the Government contends, are indistinguishable from real ones; they are part of the same market and are often exchanged. In this way, it is said, virtual images promote the trafficking in works produced through the exploitation of real children.... [But i]f virtual images were identical to illegal child pornography, the illegal images would be driven from the market by the indistinguishable substitutes. Few pornographers would risk prosecution by abusing real children if fictional, computerized images would suffice....

[4.] Finally, the Government says that the possibility of producing images by using computer imaging makes it very difficult for it to prosecute those who produce pornography by using real children. Experts, we are told, may have difficulty in saying whether the pictures were made by using real children or by using computer imaging. The necessary solution, the argument runs, is to prohibit both kinds of images.

The argument, in essence, is that protected speech may be banned as a means to ban unprotected speech. This analysis turns the First Amendment upside down. The Government may not suppress lawful speech as the means to suppress unlawful speech. Protected speech does not become unprotected merely because it resembles the latter.

The Constitution requires the reverse. "[T]he possible harm to society in permitting some unprotected speech to go unpunished is outweighed by the possibility that protected speech of others may be muted ...." The overbreadth doctrine prohibits the Government from banning unprotected speech if a substantial amount of protected speech is prohibited or chilled in the process....

Affirmative defense

[5.] [T]he Government relies on an affirmative defense under the statute, which allows a defendant to avoid conviction for nonpossession offenses by showing that the materials were produced using only adults and were not otherwise distributed in a manner conveying the impression that they depicted real children. [But t]he Government raises serious constitutional difficulties by seeking to impose on the defendant the burden of proving his speech is not unlawful. An affirmative defense applies only after prosecution has begun, and the speaker must himself prove, on pain of a felony conviction, that his conduct falls within the affirmative defense.

In cases under the CPPA, the evidentiary burden is not trivial. Where the defendant is not the producer of the work, he may have no way of establishing the identity, or even the existence, of the actors. If the evidentiary issue is a serious problem for the Government, as it asserts, it will be at least as difficult for the innocent possessor. The statute, moreover, applies to work created before 1996, and the producers themselves may not have preserved the records necessary to meet the burden of proof. Failure to establish the defense can lead to a felony conviction.

We need not decide, however, whether the Government could impose this burden on a speaker. Even if an affirmative defense can save a statute from First Amendment challenge, here the defense is incomplete and insufficient, even on its own terms.... A defendant charged with possessing, as opposed to distributing, proscribed works may not defend on the ground that the film depicts only adult actors. So while the affirmative defense may protect a movie producer from prosecution for the act of distribution, that same producer, and all other persons in the subsequent distribution chain, could be liable for possessing the prohibited work.

Furthermore, the affirmative defense provides no protection to persons who produce speech by using computer imaging, or through other means that do not involve the use of adult actors who appear to be minors.... [T]he affirmative defense [thus] cannot save the statute, for it leaves unprotected a substantial amount of speech not tied to the Government's interest in distinguishing images produced using real children from virtual ones....

Justice Thomas, concurring in the judgment....

[The Government] points to no case in which a defendant has been acquitted based on a "computer-generated images" defense[, which is why Justice Thomas agreed the law is unconstitutional—ed.].... But if technological advances thwart prosecution of "unlawful speech," the Government may well have a compelling interest in barring or otherwise regulating some narrow category of "lawful speech" in order to enforce effectively laws against pornography made through the abuse of real children....

Justice O'Connor, with whom ... Chief Justice [Rehnquist] and Justice Scalia join as to Part [B], concurring in part and dissenting in part....

[A.] I agree ... that the CPPA's ban on [pornography depicting young-looking adults] is overbroad. The Court provides several examples of movies that, although possessing serious literary, artistic or political value and employing only adult actors ..., fall under the CPPA's proscription ....

[B.] [As to computer-generated images of fictional children, I would read] "appears to be ... of [a minor]" [to mean] "virtually indistinguishable from" .... [G]iven the rapid pace of advances in computer-graphics technology, the Government's concern [that defendants could evade liability by claiming that the images attributed to them are in fact computer-generated] is reasonable.... Moreover, this Court's cases do not require Congress to wait for harm to occur before it can legislate against it.

Although a content-based regulation may serve a compelling state interest, and be as narrowly tailored as possible while substantially serving that interest, the regulation may unintentionally ensnare speech that has serious literary, artistic, political, or scientific value or that does not threaten the harms sought to be combated by the Government. If so, litigants may challenge the regulation on its face as overbroad, but in doing so they bear the heavy burden of demonstrating that the regulation forbids a substantial amount of valuable or harmless speech....

Respondents provide no examples of films or other materials that are wholly computer-generated and contain images that "appea[r] to be ... of minors" engaging in indecent conduct, but that have serious value or do not facilitate child abuse. Their overbreadth challenge therefore fails....

Chief Justice Rehnquist, with whom Justice Scalia joins in [relevant] part, dissenting....

[S]erious First Amendment concerns would arise were the Government ever to prosecute someone for simple distribution or possession of a film with literary or artistic value, such as "Traffic" or "American Beauty." ... [But r]ead as a whole, ... I think the [CPPA] reaches only ... visual depictions of youthful looking adult actors engaged in *actual* sexual activity; mere *suggestions* of sexual activity, such as youthful looking adult actors squirming under a blanket ... fall outside the purview of the statute.... The reference to "simulated" conduct simply brings within the statute's reach depictions of hard core pornography that are "made to look genuine"—including the main target of the CPPA, computer generated images virtually indistinguishable from real children engaged in sexually explicit conduct.

Neither actual conduct nor simulated conduct, however, is properly construed to reach depictions such as those in a film portrayal of Romeo and Juliet .... This narrow reading ... is exactly how the phrase [has been] understood .... Indeed, had "sexually explicit conduct" been thought to reach the sort of material the Court says it does, then films such as "Traffic" and "American Beauty" would not have been made the way they were.... The chill felt by the Court ("[F]ew legitimate movie producers ... would risk distributing images in or near the uncertain reach of this law"), has apparently never been felt by those who actually make movies....

f.   Policy—Countervailing Private Rights, see p. 92

g.   Policy—No-Value or Low-Value Speech, see p. 90

3.   "Integral Part of Criminal Conduct"

a.   Problem: Publishing Leaked Classified Information

Steven Rosen receives from a government official "classified information relating to U.S. strategy pertaining to a certain Middle East country." The official committed a crime by revealing such information, because the information is classified for national security reasons, and because the official agreed—as part of his government employment—to keep such information secret. Punishing the official for such speech would be constitutional. *Snepp v. United States*, 444 U.S. 507, 509 n.3 (1980).

But Rosen is not a government official, and has not made any such agreement. He sends the information to a reporter, hoping the reporter will publish a story based on this information. Rosen is prosecuted for violating 18 U.S.C. § 793(e), which states

> Whoever having unauthorized ... access to ... information relating to the national defense which ... the possessor has reason to believe could be used to the injury of the United States or to the advantage of any foreign nation, willfully communicates ... the same to any person not entitled to receive it ... [s]hall be fined ... or imprisoned not more than ten years.

Assume that "[w]hoever having unauthorized ... access to ... information relating to the national defense" has been interpreted to include anyone who has gotten access to classified defense secrets, even without having a security clearance and therefore without having made any promises of confidentiality. Does the prosecution violate the First Amendment? *See United States v. Rosen*, 445 F. Supp. 2d 602 (E.D. Va. 2006).

b.   United States v. Stevens, 559 U.S. 460 (2010)

[We saw the case in the obscenity section, see p. 145; but the case also discussed the child pornography analogy, and the "integral part of criminal conduct" doctrine.—ed.]

Chief Justice Roberts delivered the opinion of the Court....

In *New York v. Ferber*, ... [w]e noted that the State of New York had a compelling interest in protecting children from abuse, and that the value of using children in these works (as opposed to simulated conduct or adult actors) was *de minimis*. But our decision did not rest on this "balance of competing interests" alone.

We made clear that *Ferber* presented a special case: The market for child pornography was "intrinsically related" to the underlying abuse, and was therefore "an integral part of the production of such materials, an activity illegal throughout the Nation." As we noted, "'[i]t rarely has been suggested that the constitutional freedom for speech and press extends its immunity to speech or writing used as an integral part of conduct in violation of a valid criminal statute.'" *Ferber* (quoting *Giboney v. Empire Ice & Storage Co.*). *Ferber* thus grounded its analysis in a previously recognized, long-established category of unprotected speech ....

Our construction of § 48 [see p. 147, part C—ed.] decides the constitutional question; the Government makes no effort to defend the constitutionality of § 48 as applied beyond crush videos and depictions of animal fighting. It argues that those particular depictions are intrinsically related to criminal conduct or are analogous to obscenity (if not themselves obscene), and that the ban on such speech is narrowly tailored to reinforce restrictions on the underlying conduct, prevent additional crime arising from the depictions, or safeguard public mores. But the Government nowhere attempts to extend these arguments to depictions of any other activities—depictions that are presumptively protected by the First Amendment but that remain subject to the criminal sanctions of § 48.

Nor does the Government seriously contest that the presumptively impermissible applications of § 48 (properly construed) far outnumber any permissible ones.... We therefore need not and do not decide whether a statute limited to crush videos or other depictions of extreme animal cruelty would be constitutional. We hold only that § 48 ... is ... substantially overbroad, and therefore invalid under the First Amendment....

Justice Alito, dissenting....

[A.] "When a federal court is dealing with a federal statute challenged as overbroad, it should, of course, construe the statute to avoid constitutional problems, if the statute is subject to such a limiting construction." Applying this canon, I would hold that § 48 does not apply to depictions of hunting. [Details, which focus on statutory interpretation, omitted.—ed.] [Likewise], nothing in the record suggests that anyone has ever created, sold, or possessed for sale a depiction of the slaughter of food animals or of the docking of the tails of dairy cows that would not easily qualify under the exception set out in § 48(b)....

The Court notes ... that cockfighting, which is illegal in all States, is still legal in Puerto Rico, and I take the Court's point to be that it would be impermissible to ban the creation, sale, or possession in Puerto Rico of a depiction of a cockfight that was legally staged in Puerto Rico. But assuming for the sake of argument that this is correct, this veritable sliver of unconstitutionality would not be enough to justify striking down § 48 *in toto*.... Invalidation for overbreadth is appropriate only if the challenged statute suffers from *substantial* overbreadth—judged not just in absolute terms, but in relation to the statute's "plainly legitimate sweep[]" {and consider[ing] a statute's application to real-world conduct, not fanciful hypotheticals} ... [And] § 48 has a substantial core of constitutionally permissible applications....

[B.] "[T]he primary conduct that Congress sought to address through its passage [of § 48] was the creation, sale, or possession of 'crush videos.'" ... [T]he *conduct* depicted in crush videos may constitutionally be prohibited. All 50 States and the District of Columbia have enacted statutes prohibiting animal cruelty.

But before the enactment of § 48, the underlying conduct depicted in crush videos was nearly impossible to prosecute.... [L]aw enforcement authorities often were not able to identify the parties responsible for the torture. In the rare instances in which it was possible to identify and find the perpetrators, ... "... the State [often] could not prove its jurisdiction over the place where the act occurred or that the actions depicted took place within the time specified in the State statute of limitations." ...

Congress [therefore] concluded that the only effective way of stopping the underlying criminal conduct was to prohibit the commercial exploitation of the videos of that conduct. And Congress' strategy appears to have been vindicated. We are told that "[b]y 2007, sponsors of § 48 declared the crush video industry dead. Even overseas Websites shut down in the wake of § 48. Now, after the [lower court's decision facially invalidating the statute], crush videos are already back online."

The First Amendment ... does not protect violent criminal conduct, even if engaged in for expressive purposes. Crush videos present a highly unusual free speech issue because they are so closely linked with violent criminal conduct. The videos record the commission of violent criminal acts, and it appears that these crimes are committed for the sole purpose of creating the videos. In addition, as noted above, Congress was presented with compelling evidence that the only way of preventing these crimes was to target the sale of the videos. Under these circumstances, I cannot believe that the First Amendment commands Congress to step aside and allow the underlying crimes to continue....

First, [as with the child pornography in *Ferber*,] the conduct depicted in crush videos is criminal in every State and the District of Columbia. Thus, any crush video made in this country records the actual commission of a criminal act that inflicts severe physical injury and excruciating pain and ultimately results in death. Those who record the underlying criminal acts are likely to be criminally culpable, either as aiders and abettors or conspirators. And in the tight and secretive market for these videos, some who sell the videos or possess them with the intent to make a profit may be similarly culpable. (For example, in some cases, crush videos were commissioned by purchasers who specified the details of the acts that they wanted to see performed.) To the extent that § 48 reaches such persons, it surely does not violate the First Amendment.

Second, [as in *Ferber*,] the criminal acts shown in crush videos cannot be prevented without targeting the conduct prohibited by § 48—the creation, sale, and possession for sale of depictions of animal torture with the intention of realizing a commercial profit....

#2 Targeted prevention

Finally, [as in *Ferber*,] the harm caused by the underlying crimes vastly outweighs any minimal value that the depictions might conceivably be thought to possess. Section 48 reaches only the actual recording of acts of animal torture; the statute does not apply to verbal descriptions or to simulations. And, unlike the child pornography statute in *Ferber* or its federal counterpart, § 48(b) provides an exception for depictions having any "serious religious, political, scientific, educational, journalistic, historical, or artistic value."... *like obscenity*

#3 Harm > Value of Depictions

[While] preventing the abuse of children is certainly much more important than preventing the torture of the animals used in crush videos[,] ... the Government also has a compelling interest in preventing the torture depicted in crush videos. The animals used in crush videos are living creatures that experience excruciating pain. Our society has long banned such cruelty, which is illegal throughout the country. In *Ferber*, the Court noted that "virtually all of the States and the United States have passed legislation proscribing the production of or otherwise combating 'child pornography,'" and the Court declined to "second-guess [that] legislative judgment." [We likewise should not] second-guess[] the legislative judgment about the importance of preventing cruelty to animals.

Section 48's ban on trafficking in crush videos also helps to enforce the criminal laws and to ensure that criminals do not profit from their crimes.... [T]aking the profit out of crime is a compelling interest....

Application of the *Ferber* framework also supports the constitutionality of § 48 as applied to depictions of brutal animal fights. [Details, which are much like those Justice Alito gives as to crush videos, omitted.—ed.]

c. *United States v. Williams, see p. 9*

d. *Giboney v. Empire Storage & Ice Co., 336 U.S. 490 (1949)*

Mr. Justice Black delivered the opinion of the Court.

[A.] {[Missouri law criminalizes] "... any ... combination ... or understanding ... in restraint of trade or competition in the ... transportation, manufacture, purchase or sale of any product or commodity ...."} This case ... raises questions concerning the constitutional power of a state to apply [this] law to labor union activities, and to enjoin union members from peaceful picketing carried on as an essential and inseparable part of a course of conduct which is in violation of the state law....

The appellants are members and officers of the Ice and Coal Drivers and Handlers Local Union No. 953, affiliated with the American Federation of

Labor. Its membership includes about 160 of 200 retail ice peddlers who drive their own trucks in selling ice from door to door in Kansas City. The union began efforts to induce all the nonunion peddlers to join. One objective of the organizational drive was to better wage and working conditions of peddlers and their helpers. Most of the nonunion peddlers refused to join the union.

To break down their resistance the union adopted a plan which was designed to make it impossible for nonunion peddlers to buy ice to supply their retail customers in Kansas City. Pursuant to the plan the union set about to obtain from all Kansas City wholesale ice distributors agreements that they would not sell ice to nonunion peddlers. Agreements were obtained from all distributors except ... Empire Storage and Ice Company....

The union thereupon informed Empire that it would use other means at its disposal to force Empire to come around to the union view. Empire still refused to agree. Its place of business was promptly picketed by union members although the only complaint registered against Empire, as indicated by placards carried by the pickets, was its continued sale of ice to nonunion peddlers.

Thus the avowed immediate purpose of the picketing was to compel Empire to agree to stop selling ice to nonunion peddlers. Missouri statutes make such an agreement a crime [and a basis for a lawsuit]....

About 85% of the truck drivers working for Empire's customers were members of labor unions. These union truck drivers refused to deliver goods to or from Empire's place of business. Had any one of them crossed the picket line he would have been subject to fine or suspension by the union of which he was a member.... [T]he picketing had an instantaneous adverse effect on Empire's business. It was reduced 85%.... [Empire sued, and a] court ... issued an injunction restraining the appellants from "placing pickets or picketing around or about the buildings" of Empire....

[B.] It is contended that the injunction against picketing adjacent to Empire's place of business is an unconstitutional abridgment of free speech because the picketers were attempting peacefully to publicize truthful facts about a labor dispute. But the record here does not permit this publicizing to be treated in isolation. For ... the sole immediate object of the publicizing adjacent to the premises of Empire, as well as the other activities of the appellants and their allies, was to compel Empire to agree to stop selling ice to nonunion peddlers.

Thus all of appellants' activities—their powerful transportation combination, their patrolling, their formation of a picket line warning union men not to cross at peril of their union membership, their publicizing—constituted a single and integrated course of conduct, which was in violation of Missouri's valid law. In this situation, the injunction did no more than enjoin an offense against Missouri law, a felony.

[We reject the contention] that the constitutional freedom for speech and press extends its immunity to speech or writing used as an integral part of

conduct in violation of a valid criminal statute.... [C]onduct otherwise unlawful is [not] always immune from state regulation because an integral
part of that conduct is carried on by display of placards by peaceful picketers.... No opinions relied on by petitioners assert a constitutional right in
picketers to take advantage of speech or press to violate valid laws designed
to protect important interests of society.

We think the circumstances here ... justify restraint of the picketing
which was done in violation of Missouri's valid law for the sole immediate
purpose of continuing a violation of law. In holding this, we are mindful of
the essential importance to our society of a vigilant protection of freedom of
speech and press. States cannot consistently with our Constitution abridge
those freedoms to obviate slight inconveniences or annoyances. But placards
used as an essential and inseparable part of a grave offense against an important public law cannot immunize that unlawful conduct from state control.

Nor can we say that the publication here should not have been restrained because of the possibility of separating the picketing conduct into
illegal and legal parts. For the placards were to effectuate the purposes of
an unlawful combination, and their sole, unlawful immediate objective was
to induce Empire to violate the Missouri law by acquiescing in unlawful demands to agree not to sell ice to nonunion peddlers.

It is true that the agreements and course of conduct here were as in most
instances brought about through speaking or writing. But it has never been
deemed an abridgement of freedom of speech or press to make a course of
conduct illegal merely because the conduct was in part initiated, evidenced,
or carried out by means of language, either spoken, written, or printed. See,
e.g., *Fox v. Washington*, 236 U.S. 273 (1915) [(upholding a conviction for
speech that "encourag[ed] an actual breach of law" by advocating nudism—
ed.)]; *Chaplinsky v. New Hampshire*. Such an expansive interpretation of
the constitutional guaranties of speech and press would make it practically
impossible ever to enforce laws against agreements in restraint of trade as
well as many other agreements and conspiracies deemed injurious to society.

[C.] The interest of Missouri in enforcement of its antitrust laws cannot
be classified as an effort to outlaw only a slight public inconvenience or annoyance. The Missouri policy against restraints of trade is of long standing
and is in most respects the same as that which the Federal Government has
followed for more than half a century. It is clearly drawn in an attempt to
afford all persons an equal opportunity to buy goods.

There was clear danger, imminent and immediate, that unless restrained, appellants would succeed in making that policy a dead letter insofar as purchases by nonunion men were concerned. Appellants' power with
that of their allies was irresistible. And it is clear that appellants were doing
more than exercising a right of free speech or press. They were exercising
their economic power together with that of their allies to compel Empire to
abide by union rather than by state regulation of trade....

{"Picketing by an organized group is more than free speech, since it involves patrol of a particular locality and since the very presence of a picket line may induce action of one kind or another, quite irrespective of the nature of the ideas which are being disseminated. Hence those aspects of picketing make it the subject of restrictive regulation." ... "... When to ... persuasion other things are added which bring about coercion, or give it that character, the limit of the right has been passed...." ... "... [O]nce [either an employer or employee] uses the economic power which he has over other men and their jobs to influence their action, he is doing more than exercising the freedom of speech protected by the First Amendment...."}

[T]he basic issue is whether Missouri or a labor union has paramount constitutional power to regulate and govern the manner in which certain trade practices shall be carried on in Kansas City, Missouri. Missouri has by statute regulated trade one way. The appellant union members have adopted a program to regulate it another way. The state has provided for enforcement of its statutory rule by imposing civil and criminal sanctions. The union has provided for enforcement of its rule by sanctions against union members who cross picket lines.

We hold that the state's power to govern in this field is paramount, and that nothing in the constitutional guaranties of speech or press compels a state to apply or not to apply its anti-trade-restraint law to groups of workers, businessmen or others....

E. Exceptions from Protection—Offensive Speech

1. Generally

a. Problem: Insulting a Widow

(1) Analyze the following:

A man, 31, was charged with harassment by mail, a misdemeanor, for allegedly sending an offensive card to the widow of a St. Louis police officer who was recently shot to death while making an arrest.

The card had a picture of a pig on the front and written on the inside was: "Sorry to hear about the dead piggy. No, really I am—I couldn't eat bacon for a week. Keep up the good job frisking those criminals. Rob." ...

When confronted, [the man] admitted that he sent the card and that it was meant to be offensive .... [He] told police that the [late husband's] shooting had received too much publicity and had taken attention away from the incident in Berkeley this summer in which two men were killed by narcotics officers ....

Bill Bryan, *Man Is Charged in Sending Letter to Widow of Officer,* St. Louis Post-Dispatch, Sept. 15, 2000, at C2.

(2) Same facts as above, but assume the card was sent to the mother of someone who had died of AIDS, and read "This is the way God punishes pigs who sin against his commandments—and those who raise their children to be pigs who flout God's law."

2. FIGHTING WORDS

a. *Summary: Fighting Words*

Speech is unprotected if it's "fighting words"—if it

1. "tend[s] to incite an immediate breach of the peace" by provoking a fight, *Chaplinsky v. New Hampshire* (1942) (p. 185),

2. is a "personally abusive epithet[] which, when addressed to the ordinary citizen, [is], as a matter of common knowledge, inherently likely to provoke violent reaction," *Cohen v. California* (1971) (p. 187), and

3. is "directed to the person of the hearer," and is thus likely to be seen as "a direct personal insult," *id.*

4. Possible limitation: *Chaplinsky* suggests that this exception might be limited only to "utterances [that] are no essential part of any exposition of ideas, and are of ... slight social value as a step to truth"—perhaps only epithets or vulgarities. On the other hand, *Texas v. Johnson* (1989) (p. 204) does not rely on such a limitation, thus leaving open the possibility that political statements such as flagburning might under the right circumstances constitute fighting words, too. *[handwritten: flagburning could be unprotected]*

Policy explanations for the exception:

1. What's the perceived harm that justifies the suppression of speech here? The risk of immediate violence. This doctrine is not ostensibly concerned with avoiding hurt feelings as such; it is focused on preventing fights.

2. Because the same ideas can be conveyed in a less provoking manner— because fighting words are "no *essential* part of any exposition of ideas"—the exception doesn't really seriously restrain speech.

Policy counter-arguments:

1. Why should we let the risk of an immediate fistfight justify suppressing speech when we don't let the risk of later, but more severe, violence justify it?

2. Why should a person's rights be restricted because of the risk of misbehavior by others?

3. Recall the "fighting words" in *Chaplinsky*—"fascist" and "racketeer," said to a police officer. Do they show that the fighting words doctrine is likely to suppress even important political speech?

4. Compare *Cohen v. California*, which suggests that harsh words often express thoughts in ways that gentle words can't match.

b. *Chaplinsky v. New Hampshire, 315 U.S. 568 (1942)*

> Trampas (Walter Huston): "When I want to know anything from you I'll tell you, you long-legged son-of-a——."
> Virginian (Gary Cooper) pulls out gun.
> Virginian: "If you want to call me that, smile."
> Trampas: "With a gun against my belly I—I always smile."
> —From *The Virginian* (movie based on the novel by Owen Wister)

Justice Murphy delivered the opinion of the Court.

[A.] Appellant ... was convicted [of] ... "... address[ing] any offensive, derisive or annoying word to any other person ... in any ... public place, [or] call[ing] him by any offensive or derisive name ...." The complaint charged that appellant, "... did unlawfully repeat ... to the complainant, ... 'You are a God damned racketeer' and 'a damned Fascist and the whole government of Rochester are Fascists or agents of Fascists' ...." ...

speech

Chaplinsky was distributing the literature of [the Jehovah's Witnesses] on the streets of Rochester on a busy Saturday afternoon. Members of the local citizenry complained to the City Marshal, Bowering, that Chaplinsky was denouncing all religion as a "racket." Bowering told them that Chaplinsky was lawfully engaged, and then warned Chaplinsky that the crowd was getting restless.

Some time later a disturbance occurred and the traffic officer on duty at the busy intersection started with Chaplinsky for the police station, but did not inform him that he was under arrest or that he was going to be arrested. On the way they encountered Marshal Bowering who had been advised that a riot was under way and was therefore hurrying to the scene. Bowering repeated his earlier warning to Chaplinsky who then addressed to Bowering the words set forth in the complaint.

Chaplinsky's version of the affair was slightly different. He testified that when he met Bowering, he asked him to arrest the ones responsible for the disturbance. In reply, Bowering cursed him and told him to come along. Appellant admitted that he said the words charged in the complaint with the exception of the name of the Deity....

[B.] [T]he right of free speech is not absolute at all times and under all circumstances. There are certain well-defined and narrowly limited classes of speech, the prevention and punishment of which has never been thought to raise any Constitutional problem. These include the lewd and obscene, the profane, the libelous, and the insulting or "fighting" words—those which by their very utterance inflict injury or tend to incite an immediate breach of the peace.

[S]uch utterances are no essential part of any exposition of ideas, and are of such slight social value as a step to truth that any benefit that may be derived from them is clearly outweighed by the social interest in order and morality. "Resort to epithets or personal abuse is not in any proper sense communication of information or opinion safeguarded by the Constitution, and its punishment as a criminal act would raise no question under that instrument."

The state statute here challenged comes to us authoritatively construed by the highest court of New Hampshire.... On the authority of its earlier decisions, the state court declared that the statute's purpose was to preserve the public peace, no words being "forbidden except such as have a direct tendency to cause acts of violence by the person to whom, individually, the remark is addressed." ... "... The statute, as construed, does no more than prohibit the face-to-face words plainly likely to cause a breach of the peace

statute

by the addressee, words whose speaking constitutes a breach of the peace by the speaker—including 'classical fighting words,' words in current use less 'classical' but equally likely to cause violence, and other disorderly words, including profanity, obscenity and threats."

We are unable to say that the limited scope of the statute as thus construed contravenes the constitutional right of free expression. It is a statute narrowly drawn and limited to define and punish specific conduct lying within the domain of state power, the use in a public place of words likely to cause a breach of the peace....

Nor can we say that the application of the statute to the facts disclosed by the record substantially or unreasonably impinges upon the privilege of free speech. Argument is unnecessary to demonstrate that the appellations "damn racketeer" and "damn Fascist" are epithets likely to provoke the average person to retaliation, and thereby cause a breach of the peace....

c. Cohen v. California, 403 U.S. 15 (1971)

[Another excerpt of the opinion will be given in the coming pages.—ed.]

Justice Harlan delivered the opinion of the Court....

[A.] Paul Robert Cohen was [sentenced to 30 days in jail for] ... "maliciously and willfully disturb[ing] the peace or quiet of any neighborhood or person ... by ... offensive conduct" ....

"On April 26, 1968, the defendant was [arrested in a courthouse corridor, outside a courtroom, for] wearing a jacket bearing the words 'Fuck the Draft' which were plainly visible. There were women and children present in the corridor.... The defendant testified that he wore the jacket knowing that the words were on the jacket as a means of informing the public of the depth of his feelings against the Vietnam War and the draft.

"The defendant did not engage in, nor threaten to engage in, nor did anyone as the result of his conduct in fact commit or threaten to commit any act of violence...."

In affirming the conviction the Court of Appeal held that "offensive conduct" means "behavior which has a tendency to provoke *others* to acts of violence or to in turn disturb the peace," and that the State had proved this element because, on the facts of this case, "[i]t was certainly reasonably foreseeable that such conduct might cause others to rise up to commit a violent act against the person of the defendant or attempt to forceably remove his jacket." ...

[B.] States are free to ban ... so-called "fighting words," those personally abusive epithets which, when addressed to the ordinary citizen, are, as a matter of common knowledge, inherently likely to provoke violent reaction. *Chaplinsky v. New Hampshire.* While the four-letter word displayed by Cohen in relation to the draft is not uncommonly employed in a personally provocative fashion, in this instance it was clearly not "directed to the person of the hearer." No individual actually or likely to be present could reasonably have regarded the words on appellant's jacket as a direct personal insult.

Nor do we have here an instance of the exercise of the State's police power to prevent a speaker from intentionally provoking a given group to hostile reaction. There is ... no showing that anyone who saw Cohen was in fact violently aroused or that appellant intended such a result....

The rationale of the California court {that [the] use [of this epithet] is inherently likely to cause violent reaction} is plainly untenable. At most it reflects an "undifferentiated fear or apprehension of disturbance [which] is not enough to overcome the right to freedom of expression." We have been shown no evidence that substantial numbers of citizens are standing ready to strike out physically at whoever may assault their sensibilities with execrations like that uttered by Cohen.

There may be some persons about with such lawless and violent proclivities, but that is an insufficient base upon which to erect, consistently with constitutional values, a governmental power to force persons who wish to ventilate their dissident views into avoiding particular forms of expression. The argument amounts to little more than the self-defeating proposition that to avoid physical censorship of one who has not sought to provoke such a response by a hypothetical coterie of the violent and lawless, the States may more appropriately effectuate that censorship themselves.

d. *Texas v. Johnson, 491 U.S. 397 (1989)*

[Two more excerpts of the opinion will be given in the coming pages, and the content-neutrality vs. content discrimination issue will be covered in Part IV.B.e, p. 363.—ed.]

Justice Brennan delivered the opinion of the Court....

[A.] While the Republican National Convention was taking place in Dallas in 1984, respondent Johnson participated in a political demonstration dubbed the "Republican War Chest Tour" ... to protest the policies of the Reagan administration and of certain Dallas-based corporations....

[During the demonstration, Johnson] accept[ed] an American flag handed to him by a fellow protestor who had taken it from a flagpole outside one of the targeted buildings.... The demonstration ended in front of Dallas City Hall, where Johnson unfurled the American flag, doused it with kerosene, and set it on fire. While the flag burned, the protestors chanted: "America, the red, white, and blue, we spit on you." ...

No one was physically injured or threatened with injury, though several witnesses testified that they had been seriously offended by the flag burning.... [Johnson was convicted of desecrating a venerated object, and sentenced to one year in prison and a $2,000 fine. The desecration statute outlawed] {"... intentionally or knowingly desecrat[ing] (1) a public monument; (2) a place of worship or burial; or (3) a state or national flag.... '[D]esecrate' means deface, damage, or otherwise physically mistreat in a way that the actor knows will seriously offend one or more persons likely to observe or discover his action...."} ...

[B.] Texas claims that its interest in preventing breaches of the peace justifies Johnson's conviction for flag desecration. However, no disturbance of the peace actually occurred or threatened to occur because of Johnson's burning of the flag.... The only evidence offered by the State at trial to show the reaction to Johnson's actions was the testimony of several persons who had been seriously offended by the flag burning.

The State's position, therefore, amounts to a claim that an audience that takes serious offense at particular expression is necessarily likely to disturb the peace and that the expression may be prohibited on this basis.... [But] a principal "function of free speech under our system of government is to invite dispute. It may indeed best serve its high purpose when it induces a condition of unrest, creates dissatisfaction with conditions as they are, or even stirs people to anger." It would be odd indeed to conclude *both* that "if it is the speaker's opinion that gives offense, that consequence is a reason for according it constitutional protection," *FCC v. Pacifica Foundation* (Stevens, J.), *and* that the government may ban the expression of certain disagreeable ideas on the unsupported presumption that their very disagreeableness will provoke violence.

Thus, we have not permitted the government to assume that every expression of a provocative idea will incite a riot, but have instead required careful consideration of the actual circumstances surrounding such expression, asking whether the expression "is directed to inciting or producing imminent lawless action and is likely to incite or produce such action." *Brandenburg v. Ohio*. To accept Texas' arguments that it need only demonstrate "the potential for a breach of the peace," and that every flag burning necessarily possesses that potential, would be to eviscerate our holding in *Brandenburg*. This we decline to do.

Nor does Johnson's expressive conduct fall within that small class of "fighting words" that are "likely to provoke the average person to retaliation, and thereby cause a breach of the peace." No reasonable onlooker would have regarded Johnson's generalized expression of dissatisfaction with the policies of the Federal Government as a direct personal insult or an invitation to exchange fisticuffs. We thus conclude that the State's interest in maintaining order is not implicated on these facts....

3. OFFENSIVE SPEECH THAT DOESN'T TEND TO CAUSE FIGHTS

a. *Summary: Infliction of Emotional Distress*
   Rule: Speech might be unprotected if
   1. it intentionally or recklessly inflicts
   2. severe emotional distress,
   3. through "extreme and outrageous" means,
   4. and is not on a matter of public concern, *Snyder v. Phelps* (2011) (p. 207). "Speech deals with matters of public concern when it can 'be fairly considered as relating to any matter of political, social, or other concern to

the community,' or when it 'is a subject of legitimate news interest; that is, a subject of general interest and of value and concern to the public.' The arguably 'inappropriate or controversial character of a statement is irrelevant to the question whether it deals with a matter of public concern.'"

— The Court did not squarely hold in *Snyder* that speech which satisfies these conditions is indeed unprotected. The Court held only that speech on matters of public concern is protected even if it inflicts severe emotional distress .

Policy explanations for this exception and the ones described in the next three subsections:

1. What's the perceived harm of offensive speech?

   a. The risk of offense/humiliation/emotional distress (especially cumulated among many offensive incidents perpetrated by many people).

   b. The deterioration of public spaces caused by people avoiding certain places in order to avoid being offended.

   c. A coarsening of the level of public discourse, which may make it harder for society to come to a consensus on important issues.

2. The restrictions would restrict only the mode of expression, not the ideas being expressed.

Policy counter-arguments:

1. Any "principle [outlawing certain offensive expressions] seems inherently boundless. How is one to distinguish [them] from any other offensive word[s]? ... [B]ecause governmental officials cannot make principled distinctions in this area[,] ... the Constitution leaves matters of taste and style ... to the individual." *Cohen v. California.*

2. Expression "conveys not only ideas capable of relatively precise, detached explication, but otherwise inexpressible emotions as well. In fact, words are often chosen as much for their emotive as their cognitive force.... [F]orbid[ding] particular words ... also run[s] a substantial risk of suppressing ideas in the process." *Cohen.*

b. *Summary: Unwanted Speech to a Particular Person*

   Rowan v. United States Post Office Dep't (1970) (p. 192) upheld a law that banned mailings to

1. a person's home when

2. the recipient specifically objected to the mailing, and

3. the recipient had the legal right to object to any mailing, with no content judgment by government enforcers (though the statute was limited to material that "the addressee in his sole discretion believes to be erotically arousing or sexually provocative," the Court stressed that the addressee could use this to block even "dry goods catalog[s]"), and

4. the ban left the speakers free to communicate to willing listeners in

other homes. *Rowan* didn't specifically stress this particular factor; but *Organization for a Better Austin v. Keefe* (1971) (p. 193) distinguished *Rowan* on the grounds that it involved only an "attempt[] to stop the flow of information into his own household," not "to the public."

— Query to what extent this precedent would justify laws in which some of these elements are absent. An example: Telephone harassment laws have long banned calls made with the intent to "abuse," "annoy," "harass," or "offend" the recipient (sometimes with the limitation that the calls must be repeated or anonymous). Many courts have upheld such statutes, though some have struck them down. The Supreme Court has not resolved this. *See Gormley v. Director*, 449 U.S. 1023 (1980) (White, J., dissenting from denial of certiorari) (noting the controversy); Eugene Volokh, *One-to-One Speech vs. One-to-Many Speech, Criminal Harassment Laws, and "Cyberstalking,"* 107 Nw. U. L. Rev. 731 (2013).

c. *Summary: Offensive Speech Over Broadcast Radio and Television*

FCC v. Pacifica Foundation (1978) (p. 197) held that the government may restrain vulgarity (and the same rule would likely apply to nudity)

1. on broadcast radio and television,

2. when the speech is offensive because of it form and not because of the opinions or viewpoints that it expresses.

The Court has expressly refused to extend *Pacifica* to other media, such as the Internet, *see Reno v. ACLU* (1997) (p. 203), dial-a-porn, see *Sable Communications v. FCC*, 492 U.S. 115 (1989), and cable television, *Turner Broadcasting System v. FCC* (1994) (p. 529).

d. *Summary: Abusive Words*

Speech *might* be unprotected if

1. it "by [its] very utterance inflict[s] injury" (presumably because it's so insulting), *Chaplinsky*.

2. Limitation: *Cohen v. California* (1971) (p. 195), *Texas v. Johnson* (1989) (p. 204), and *Snyder v. Phelps* (2011) (p. 207) all show that some very offensive speech is indeed protected. They don't articulate any clear rules that identify the boundaries of what's protected and what's not, but you can use them in arguing by analogy.

3. Limitation: One can argue based on *Chaplinsky* that this doctrine is limited only to "low-value speech"—statements that are indeed just personal insults and "no essential part of the exposition of ideas."

4. Many commentators, and some courts, believe that this doctrine is no longer good law. See, *e.g.*, *State v. Drahota*, 280 Neb. 267 (2010) (litigated by the author of this textbook); *Purtell v. Mason*, 527 F.3d 615, 624 (7th Cir. 2008). The Court has neither specifically overruled it nor reaffirmed it.

e. Problem: Captive Audiences

A common argument for protecting offensive speech is that people can just "avert their eyes" from the speech (an "alternatives to suppressing speech" argument). From this, some courts and commentators have inferred that when an audience is "captive" and unable to evade the offensive sights or sounds, the government may indeed restrict the speech based on its communicative impact.

The speech may still be constitutionally valuable, the argument would go, and it might be no more offensive than speech that's protected when said to a noncaptive audience—but the government has a stronger interest in shielding captive audiences than it does as to audiences who can just "avert their eyes." The Court has at times hinted that such a "captive audience exception" should exist, but has never definitively ruled on it.

Come up with a proposed definition of such an exception, or, if you prefer, an argument for why the exception shouldn't exist. The definition should contain (a) a test for distinguishing those audiences that are captive from those that are not, and (b) a test for determining whether, when the audience is indeed captive, a particular restriction is constitutional.

Test your proposal against the following hypotheticals:

1. Congress enacts a law prohibiting airplane passengers from saying offensive sexually themed, sexist, racist, or anti-religious things (even at a normal conversational volume) when such statements can be overheard by offended fellow passengers.

2. The California legislature enacts a law prohibiting profanity and epithets (such as "scab," "baby-killer," and the like) in signs on picket lines, whether the picketing is labor picketing, political picketing, antiabortion picketing, or anything else.

3. The California legislature enacts a law prohibiting sexually suggestive pictures on billboards.

4. Federal courts interpret Title VII as imposing civil liability on employers when private employees put up signs, send e-mail, or say things that (a) are sexually themed, sexist, racist, or religiously bigoted, and (b) are "severe or pervasive" enough to create a "hostile, abusive, or offensive work environment" for a reasonable coworker who sees the signs or overhears the statements. Prong (b) is interpreted by courts to exclude situations where the offensive speech happens only once, but to include situations where the offensive speech happens several times over the span of several weeks or months.

f. Rowan v. United States Post Office Dep't, 397 U.S. 728 (1970)

Chief Justice Burger delivered the [unanimous] opinion of the Court.

[Title 39 U.S.C. § 4009] ... provides a procedure whereby any householder may insulate himself from advertisements that offer for sale "matter which the addressee in his sole discretion believes to be erotically arousing or sexually provocative." ... [T]he Postmaster General, upon receipt of a notice from the addressee specifying that he has received advertisements found by him to be within the statutory category, [must] issue ... an order directing the sender ... to refrain from further mailings to the named addressee.... Subsection (e) grants to the district court jurisdiction to issue a compliance order upon application of the Attorney General.... Appellants [sued, claiming this provision] is unconstitutional....

Claim
← *(e)* *Uncon*

In today's complex society we are inescapably captive audiences for many purposes, but a sufficient measure of individual autonomy must survive to permit every householder to exercise control over unwanted mail.... Weighing the highly important right to communicate, but without trying to determine where it fits into constitutional imperatives, against the very basic right to be free from sights, sounds, and tangible matter we do not want, it seems to us that a mailer's right to communicate must stop at the mailbox of an unreceptive addressee....

Where right stops

In this case the mailer's right to communicate is circumscribed only by an affirmative act of the addressee giving notice that he wishes no further mailings from that mailer. To hold less would tend to license a form of trespass and would make hardly more sense than to say that a radio or television viewer may not twist the dial to cut off an offensive or boring communication and thus bar its entering his home.

→ *Addressee must affirmatively act*

Nothing in the Constitution compels us to listen to or view any unwanted communication, whatever its merit; we see no basis for according the printed word or pictures a different or more preferred status because they are sent by mail. The ancient concept that "a man's home is his castle" into which "not even the king may enter" has lost none of its vitality, and none of the recognized exceptions includes any right to communicate offensively with another.

Both the absoluteness of the citizen's right under § 4009 and its finality are essential; what may not be provocative to one person may well be to another. In operative effect the power of the householder under the statute is unlimited; he may prohibit the mailing of a dry goods catalog because he objects to the contents—or indeed the text of the language touting the merchandise. Congress provided this sweeping power not only to protect privacy but to avoid possible constitutional questions that might arise from vesting the power to make any discretionary evaluation of the material in a governmental official....

If this prohibition operates to impede the flow of even valid ideas, the answer is that no one has a right to press even "good" ideas on an unwilling recipient. That we are often "captives" outside the sanctuary of the home and subject to objectionable speech and other sound does not mean we must be captives everywhere. The asserted right of a mailer, we repeat, stops at the outer boundary of every person's domain....

g. *Organization for a Better Austin v. Keefe, 402 U.S. 415 (1971)*

[This case involves an injunction restricting speech because of its content, which is a "prior restraint," see Part VII, and thus especially likely to be unconstitutional. But the Court has relied on this case even in cases involving normal criminal or civil liability, *e.g.*, *Bolger v. Youngs Drug Products Corp.*, 463 U.S. 60 (1983).—ed.]

Chief Justice Burger delivered the opinion of the Court....

[A.] Organization for a Better Austin (OBA) is a racially integrated community organization in the Austin neighborhood of Chicago.... [OBA's] stated purpose is to "stabilize" the racial ratio in the Austin area....

It was the contention of OBA that respondent [a local real estate broker] had ... aroused the fears of the local white residents that Negroes were coming into the area and then ... was able to secure listings and sell homes to Negroes.... [M]embers of [OBA] distributed leaflets in Westchester[, where Keefe lived,] describing respondent's activities ... [and criticizing] respondent's real estate practices in the Austin neighborhood; one of the leaflets set out the business card respondent used to solicit listings, quoted him as saying "I only sell to Negroes," cited a Chicago Daily News article describing his real estate activities and accused him of being a "panic peddler." Another leaflet, of the same general order, stated that: "When he signs the agreement [promising to stop such practices], we stop coming to Westchester."

Two of the leaflets requested recipients to call respondent at his home phone number and urge him to sign the "no solicitation" agreement. On several days leaflets were given to persons in a Westchester shopping center. On two other occasions leaflets were passed out to some parishioners on their way to or from respondent's church in Westchester. Leaflets were also left at the doors of his neighbors.... One of the officers of OBA testified at trial that he hoped that respondent would be induced to sign the no-solicitation agreement by letting "his neighbors know what he was doing to us."

[At Keefe's request,] ... the trial court ... enjoin[ed] petitioners "from passing out pamphlets, leaflets or literature of any kind, and from picketing, anywhere in the City of Westchester, Illinois." ...

[B.] [T]he injunction operates, not to redress alleged private wrongs, but to suppress, on the basis of previous publications, distribution of literature "of any kind" in a city of 18,000.... The claim that the expressions were intended to exercise a coercive impact on respondent does not remove them from the reach of the First Amendment. Petitioners plainly intended to influence respondent's conduct by their activities; this is not fundamentally different from the function of a newspaper.... [S]o long as the means are peaceful, the communication need not meet standards of acceptability.

Any prior restraint on expression comes to this Court with a "heavy presumption" against its constitutional validity. Respondent thus carries a heavy burden of showing justification for the imposition of such a restraint. He has not met that burden.

No prior decisions support the claim that the interest of an individual in being free from public criticism of his business practices in pamphlets or leaflets warrants use of the injunctive power of a court. Designating the conduct as an invasion of privacy, the apparent basis for the injunction here, is not sufficient to support an injunction against peaceful distribution of informational literature of the nature revealed by this record. *Rowan* v. *United States Post Office Dept.* ... is not in point; the right of privacy involved in that case is not shown here. Among other important distinctions, respondent is not attempting to stop the flow of information into his own household, but to the public. Accordingly, the injunction issued by the Illinois court must be vacated....

h. *Cohen v. California, 403 U.S. 15 (1971)*

Justice Harlan delivered the opinion of the Court....

[See p. 187 above for the facts.—ed.]

[A.] Cohen was tried under a statute applicable throughout the entire State. Any attempt to support this conviction on the ground that the statute seeks to preserve an appropriately decorous atmosphere in the courthouse where Cohen was arrested must fail in the absence of any language in the statute that would have put appellant on notice that certain kinds of otherwise permissible speech or conduct would nevertheless, under California law, not be tolerated in certain places....

This is [also] not ... an obscenity case. Whatever else may be necessary to give rise to the States' broader power to prohibit obscene expression, such expression must be, in some significant way, erotic. It cannot plausibly be maintained that this vulgar allusion to the Selective Service System would conjure up such psychic stimulation in anyone likely to be confronted with Cohen's crudely defaced jacket....

[B.] [T]he mere presumed presence of unwitting listeners or viewers does not serve automatically to justify curtailing all speech capable of giving offense.... [G]overnment may properly act in many situations to prohibit intrusion into the privacy of the home of unwelcome views and ideas which cannot be totally banned from the public dialogue, *e.g., Rowan v. United States Post Office Dep't*[.] ... [But] "we are often 'captives' outside the sanctuary of the home and subject to objectionable speech." The ability of government, consonant with the Constitution, to shut off discourse solely to protect others from hearing it is, in other words, dependent upon a showing that substantial privacy interests are being invaded in an essentially intolerable manner. Any broader view of this authority would effectively empower a majority to silence dissidents simply as a matter of personal predilections.

In this regard, persons confronted with Cohen's jacket were in a quite different posture than, say, those subjected to the raucous emissions of sound trucks blaring outside their residences. Those in the Los Angeles courthouse could effectively avoid further bombardment of their sensibilities simply by averting their eyes. And, while it may be that one has a more substantial claim to a recognizable privacy interest when walking through a courthouse corridor than, for example, strolling through Central Park, surely it is nothing like the interest in being free from unwanted expression in the confines of one's own home....

[I]f Cohen's "speech" was otherwise entitled to constitutional protection, we do not think the fact that some unwilling "listeners" in a public building may have been briefly exposed to it can serve to justify this breach of the peace conviction where, as here, there was no evidence that persons powerless to avoid appellant's conduct did in fact object to it, and where that portion of the statute upon which Cohen's conviction rests evinces no concern, either on its face or as construed by the California courts, with the special plight of the captive auditor, but, instead, indiscriminately sweeps within its prohibitions all "offensive conduct" that disturbs "any neighborhood or person." ...

[C.] [Nor may states] punish[] public utterance of this unseemly expletive in order to maintain what they regard as a suitable level of discourse within the body politic.... The constitutional right of free expression is powerful medicine in a society as diverse and populous as ours. It is designed and intended to remove governmental restraints from the arena of public discussion, putting the decision as to what views shall be voiced largely into the hands of each of us, in the hope that use of such freedom will ultimately produce a more capable citizenry and more perfect polity and in the belief that no other approach would comport with the premise of individual dignity and choice upon which our political system rests.

To many, the immediate consequence of this freedom may often appear to be only verbal tumult, discord, and even offensive utterance. These are, however, within established limits, in truth necessary side effects of the broader enduring values which the process of open debate permits us to achieve. That the air may at times seem filled with verbal cacophony is, in this sense not a sign of weakness but of strength.

We cannot lose sight of the fact that, in what otherwise might seem a trifling and annoying instance of individual distasteful abuse of a privilege, these fundamental societal values are truly implicated. That is why "[w]holly neutral futilities come under the protection of free speech as fully as do Keats' poems or Donne's sermons," and why "so long as the means are peaceful, the communication need not meet standards of acceptability."

Against this perception of the constitutional policies involved, we discern certain more particularized considerations that peculiarly call for reversal of this conviction. First, the principle contended for by the State seems inherently boundless. How is one to distinguish this from any other offensive word?

Surely the State has no right to cleanse public debate to the point where it is grammatically palatable to the most squeamish among us. Yet no readily ascertainable general principle exists for stopping short of that result were we to affirm the judgment below. For, while the particular four-letter word being litigated here is perhaps more distasteful than most others of its genre, it is nevertheless often true that one man's vulgarity is another's lyric. Indeed, we think it is largely because governmental officials cannot make principled distinctions in this area that the Constitution leaves matters of taste and style so largely to the individual.

Additionally, ... much linguistic expression serves a dual communicative *(2)* function: it conveys not only ideas capable of relatively precise, detached explication, but otherwise inexpressible emotions as well. In fact, words are often chosen as much for their emotive as their cognitive force.

We cannot sanction the view that the Constitution, while solicitous of the cognitive content of individual speech has little or no regard for that emotive function which practically speaking, may often be the more important element of the overall message sought to be communicated.... "[O]ne of the prerogatives of American citizenship is the right to criticize public men and measures—and that means not only informed and responsible criticism but the freedom to speak foolishly and without moderation."

Finally, and in the same vein, we cannot indulge the facile assumption *(3)* that one can forbid particular words without also running a substantial risk of suppressing ideas in the process. Indeed, governments might soon seize upon the censorship of particular words as a convenient guise for banning the expression of unpopular views. We have been able, as noted above, to discern little social benefit that might result from running the risk of opening the door to such grave results....

Justice Blackmun, with whom ... Chief Justice [Burger] and Justice Black join, [dissenting]....

Cohen's absurd and immature antic, in my view, was mainly conduct and little speech. *See Giboney v. Empire Storage & Ice Co....* Further, the case appears to me to be well within the sphere of *Chaplinsky v. New Hampshire* .... As a consequence, this Court's agonizing over First Amendment values seems misplaced and unnecessary.... [The dissent gives no further First Amendment analysis.—ed.]

i.   FCC v. Pacifica Foundation, 438 U.S. 726 (1978)

Justice Stevens delivered the opinion of the Court [as to Parts A, D, and E] ... and an opinion in which ... Chief Justice [Burger] and Justice Rehnquist joined [as to Parts B and C]....

[A.] A satiric humorist named George Carlin recorded a 12-minute monologue entitled "Filthy Words[,"] ... about "the words you couldn't say on the public, ah, airwaves, um, the ones you definitely wouldn't say, ever." He ... repeat[ed those words] over and over again in a variety of colloquialisms. [See http://volokh.com/firstamendment/extra.pdf for a transcript.—ed.] ...

At about 2 o'clock in the afternoon on Tuesday, October 30, 1973, a New York radio station, owned by respondent Pacifica Foundation, broadcast the "Filthy Words" monologue. A few weeks later a man, who stated that he had heard the broadcast while driving with his young son, wrote a letter complaining to the Commission.... Pacifica ... was not aware of any other complaints about the broadcast.

On February 21, 1975, the Commission issued a declaratory order ...

holding that Pacifica "could have been the subject of administrative sanctions." The Commission did not impose formal sanctions, but it did state that the order would be "associated with the station's license file, and in the event that subsequent complaints are received, the Commission will then decide whether it should utilize any of the available sanctions ...." ...

[B.] Pacifica ... argues that the Commission's construction of the statutory language broadly encompasses so much constitutionally protected speech that reversal is required even if Pacifica's broadcast of the "Filthy Words" monologue is not itself protected by the First Amendment.... [But] our review is limited to the question whether the Commission has the authority to proscribe this particular broadcast.... [The Commission's] order was "issued in a specific factual context." That approach is appropriate for courts as well as the Commission when regulation of indecency is at stake, for indecency is largely a function of context—it cannot be adequately judged in the abstract....

It is true that the Commission's order may lead some broadcasters to censor themselves. At most, however, the Commission's definition of indecency will deter only the broadcasting of patently offensive references to excretory and sexual organs and activities. While some of these references may be protected, they surely lie at the periphery of First Amendment concern. {[And a] requirement that indecent language be avoided will have its primary effect on the form, rather than the content, of serious communication. There are few, if any, thoughts that cannot be expressed by the use of less offensive language.} ...

Invalidating any rule on the basis of its hypothetical application to situations not before the Court is "strong medicine" to be applied "sparingly and only as a last resort." We decline to administer that medicine to preserve the vigor of patently offensive sexual and excretory speech....

[C.] The question in this case is whether a broadcast of patently offensive words dealing with sex and excretion may be regulated because of its content. Obscene materials have been denied the protection of the First Amendment because their content is so offensive to contemporary moral standards. But the fact that society may find speech offensive is not a sufficient reason for suppressing it. Indeed, if it is the speaker's opinion that gives offense, that consequence is a reason for according it constitutional protection. For it is a central tenet of the First Amendment that the government must remain neutral in the marketplace of ideas.

{The monologue does present a point of view; it attempts to show that the words it uses are "harmless" and that our attitudes toward them are "essentially silly." The Commission objects, not to this point of view, but to the way in which it is expressed.}

If there were any reason to believe that the Commission's characterization of the Carlin monologue as offensive could be traced to its political content—or even to the fact that it satirized contemporary attitudes about four-letter words—First Amendment protection might be required. But that is simply not this case.

These words offend for the same reasons that obscenity offends. {"Obnoxious, gutter language describing these matters has the effect of debasing and brutalizing human beings by reducing them to their mere bodily functions...." Our society has a tradition of performing certain bodily functions in private, and of severely limiting the public exposure or discussion of such matters. Verbal or physical acts exposing those intimacies are offensive irrespective of any message that may accompany the exposure.} ... "[S]uch utterances are no essential part of any exposition of ideas, and are of such slight social value as a step to truth that any benefit that may be derived from them is clearly outweighed by the social interest in order and morality." *Chaplinsky* v. *New Hampshire*.

Although these words ordinarily lack literary, political, or scientific value, they are not entirely outside the protection of the First Amendment.... Nonetheless, the constitutional protection accorded to a communication containing such patently offensive sexual and excretory language need not be the same in every context.... It is a characteristic of speech such as this that both its capacity to offend and its "social value" ... vary with the circumstances. Words that are commonplace in one setting are shocking in another.

To paraphrase Justice Harlan, one occasion's lyric is another's vulgarity. Cf. *Cohen* v. *California*. {[T]he Court [in *Cohen*] ... noted that "there was no evidence that persons powerless to avoid [his] conduct did in fact object to it." In contrast, in this case the Commission was responding to a listener's strenuous complaint, and Pacifica does not question its determination that this afternoon broadcast was likely to offend listeners.... [And] the Commission imposed a far more moderate penalty on Pacifica than the state court imposed on Cohen. Even the strongest civil penalty at the Commission's command does not include criminal prosecution.}

In this case it is undisputed that the content of Pacifica's broadcast was "vulgar," "offensive," and "shocking." Because content of that character is not entitled to absolute constitutional protection under all circumstances, we must consider its context in order to determine whether the Commission's action was constitutionally permissible....

[D.] [E]ach medium of expression presents special First Amendment problems. And of all forms of communication, it is broadcasting that has received the most limited First Amendment protection. Thus, although other speakers cannot be licensed except under laws that carefully define and narrow official discretion, a broadcaster may be deprived of his license and his forum if the Commission decides that such an action would serve "the public interest, convenience, and necessity." Similarly, although the First Amendment protects newspaper publishers from being required to print the replies of those whom they criticize, it affords no such protection to broadcasters; on the contrary, they must give free time to the victims of their criticism. *FCC v. Red Lion Broadcasting*.

The reasons for these distinctions are complex, but two have relevance to the present case. First, the broadcast media have established a uniquely

(1) Pervasive in Home
└ Audience?

pervasive presence in the lives of all Americans. Patently offensive, indecent material presented over the airwaves confronts the citizen, not only in public, but also in the privacy of the home, where the individual's right to be left alone plainly outweighs the First Amendment rights of an intruder. *Rowan v. United States Post Office Dep't.* *Rowan*

Because the broadcast audience is constantly tuning in and out, prior warnings cannot completely protect the listener or viewer from unexpected program content. To say that one may avoid further offense by turning off the radio when he hears indecent language is like saying that the remedy for an assault is to run away after the first blow. One may hang up on an indecent phone call, but that option does not give the caller a constitutional immunity or avoid a harm that has already taken place. {The problem of harassing phone calls is hardly hypothetical. Congress has recently found it necessary to prohibit debt collectors from "plac[ing] telephone calls without meaningful disclosure of the caller's identity"; from "engaging any person in telephone conversation repeatedly or continuously with intent to annoy, abuse, or harass any person at the called number"; and from "us[ing] obscene or profane language or language the natural consequence of which is to abuse the hearer or reader."}

└ Outside the home

{Outside the home, the balance between the offensive speaker and the unwilling audience may sometimes tip in favor of the speaker, requiring the offended listener to turn away. As we noted in *Cohen:* "While this Court has recognized that government may properly act in many situations to prohibit intrusion into the privacy of the home of unwelcome views and ideas which cannot be totally banned from the public dialogue ..., we have at the same time consistently stressed that 'we are often "captives" outside the sanctuary of the home and subject to objectionable speech.'"}

(2) children

Second, broadcasting is uniquely accessible to children, even those too young to read. Although Cohen's written message might have been incomprehensible to a first grader, Pacifica's broadcast could have enlarged a child's vocabulary in an instant.... We held in *Ginsberg v. New York,* 390 U.S. 629 (1968), that the government's interest in the "well-being of its youth" and in supporting "parents' claim to authority in their own household" justified the regulation of otherwise protected expression [such as indecent books and motion pictures]. The ease with which children may obtain access to broadcast material, coupled with the concerns recognized in *Ginsberg,* amply justify special treatment of indecent broadcasting.

Gov interest like parents

{The Commission's action does not by any means reduce adults to hearing only what is fit for children. Adults who feel the need may purchase tapes and records or go to theaters and nightclubs to hear these words. In fact, the Commission has not unequivocally closed even broadcasting to speech of this sort; whether broadcast audiences in the late evening contain so few children that playing this monologue would be permissible is an issue neither the Commission nor this Court has decided.}

Timing?

[E.] It is appropriate, in conclusion, to emphasize the narrowness of our holding. This case does not involve a two-way radio conversation between a cab driver and a dispatcher, or a telecast of an Elizabethan comedy. We have not decided that an occasional expletive in either setting would justify any sanction or, indeed, that this broadcast would justify a criminal prosecution.

The Commission's decision rested entirely on a nuisance rationale under which context is all-important. The concept requires consideration of a host of variables. The time of day was emphasized by the Commission. The content of the program in which the language is used will also affect the composition of the audience[.] {Even a prime-time recitation of Geoffrey Chaucer's Miller's Tale would not be likely to command the attention of many children who are both old enough to understand and young enough to be adversely affected by passages such as: "And prively he caughte hire by the queynte."} ... [D]ifferences between radio, television, and perhaps closed-circuit transmissions, may also be relevant....

[A] "nuisance may be merely a right thing in the wrong place,—like a pig in the parlor instead of the barnyard." We simply hold that when the Commission finds that a pig has entered the parlor, the exercise of its regulatory power does not depend on proof that the pig is obscene....

Justice Powell, with whom Justice Blackmun joins, concurring in part [as to Parts A, D, and E] and concurring in the judgment....

I do not subscribe to the theory that the Justices of this Court are free generally to decide on the basis of its content which speech protected by the First Amendment ... is less "valuable" and hence deserving of less protection [or less coverage by the overbreadth doctrine].... This is a judgment for each person to make, not one for the judges to impose upon him.

The result turns instead on the unique characteristics of the broadcast media, combined with society's right to protect its children from speech generally agreed to be inappropriate for their years, and with the interest of unwilling adults in not being assaulted by such offensive speech in their homes. Moreover, I doubt whether today's decision will prevent any adult who wishes to receive Carlin's message in Carlin's own words from doing so, and from making for himself a value judgment as to the merit of the message and words....

{[And as] Justice Stevens points out, ... the Commission's order was limited to the facts of this case; "it did not purport to engage in formal rulemaking ...." In addition, since the Commission may be expected to proceed cautiously, as it has in the past, I do not foresee an undue "chilling" effect on broadcasters' exercise of their rights. I agree, therefore, that respondent's overbreadth challenge is meritless.}

Justice Brennan, with whom Justice Marshall joins, dissenting....

[A.] [A]n individual's actions in switching on and listening to communications transmitted over the public airways and directed to the public at large do not implicate fundamental privacy interests, even when engaged in within the home. Instead, because the radio is undeniably a public medium, these actions are more properly viewed as a decision to take part, if only as a listener, in an ongoing public discourse.... [T]he residual privacy interests [the listener] retains vis-à-vis the communication he voluntarily admits into his home are surely no greater than those of the people present in the corridor of the Los Angeles courthouse in *Cohen*....

[In any event,] unlike other intrusive modes of communication, such as sound trucks, "[t]he radio can be turned off"—and with a minimum of effort.... Whatever the minimal discomfort suffered by a listener who inadvertently tunes into a program he finds offensive during the brief interval before he can simply extend his arm and switch stations or flick the "off" button, it is surely worth the candle to preserve the broadcaster's right to send, and the right of those interested to receive, a message entitled to full First Amendment protection....

[B.] [The Court also] fails to accord proper weight to the interests of listeners who wish to hear broadcasts the FCC deems offensive. It permits majoritarian tastes completely to preclude a protected message from entering the homes of a receptive, unoffended minority....

Where the individuals constituting the offended majority may freely choose to reject the material being offered, we have never found their privacy interests of such moment to warrant the suppression of speech on privacy grounds.... Unlike the situation here, householders [in *Rowan*] who wished to receive the sender's communications were not prevented from doing so. Equally important, the determination of offensiveness *vel non* under the statute involved in *Rowan* was completely within the hands of the individual householder; no governmental evaluation of the worth of the mail's content stood between the mailer and the householder....

{Taken to their logical extreme, [the Commission's] rationales would support the cleansing of public radio of any "four-letter words" whatsoever, regardless of their context. The rationales could justify the banning from radio of [portions of the Bible; works] ... by the likes of Shakespeare, Joyce, Hemingway, Ben Jonson, Henry Fielding, Robert Burns, and Chaucer; [and] a good deal of political speech, such as the Nixon tapes ...

[Moreover,] the content [and impact] of a message ... can[not] be divorced from the words that are the vehicle for its expression .... A given word may have a unique capacity to capsule an idea, evoke an emotion, or conjure up an image.... [Cf.] *Cohen*. Moreover, even if an alternative phrasing may communicate a speaker's abstract ideas as effectively as those words he is forbidden to use, it is doubtful that the sterilized message will convey the emotion that is an essential part of so many communications....

[Nor can it be relevant that adults] "... may purchase tapes and records or go to theaters and nightclubs to hear [the tabooed] words." ... [T]hese alternatives involve the expenditure of money, time, and effort that many of those wishing to hear Mr. Carlin's message may not be able to afford[;] and ... in many cases the medium may well be the message.} ...

[C.] [T]he government unquestionably has a special interest in the well-being of children and consequently "can adopt more stringent controls on communicative materials available to youths than on those available to adults[."] But] the Court has accounted for this societal interest by adopting a "variable obscenity" standard that permits the prurient appeal of material available to children to be assessed in terms of the sexual interests of minors. *Ginsberg v. New York*.... Because the Carlin monologue is obviously not an erotic appeal to the prurient interests of children, the Court, for the first time, allows the government to prevent minors from gaining access to materials that are not obscene, and are therefore protected, as to them....

[P]arents, *not* the government, have the right to make certain decisions regarding the upbringing of their children.... [S]ome parents may actually find Mr. Carlin's unabashed attitude towards the seven "dirty words" healthy, and deem it desirable to expose their children to the manner in which Mr. Carlin defuses the taboo surrounding the words. Such parents may constitute a minority of the American public, but the absence of great numbers willing to exercise the right to raise their children in this fashion does not alter the right's nature or its existence....

{[A] narrowly drawn regulation prohibiting the use of offensive language on broadcasts directed specifically at younger children [might be legitimate].... This is so both because of the difficulties inherent in adapting the *Miller* formulation to communications received by young children, and because such children are "not possessed of that full capacity for individual choice which is the presupposition of the First Amendment guarantees."

I doubt ... that such a limited regulation amounts to a regulation of speech based on its content, since, by hypothesis, the only persons at whom the regulated communication is directed are incapable of evaluating its content. To the extent that such a regulation is viewed as a regulation based on content, it marks the outermost limits to which content regulation is permissible.}

Justice Stewart, with whom Justice Brennan, Justice White, and Justice Marshall join, dissenting. [This dissent argued that the FCC lacked statutory authority to restrict profanity.—ed.]

j. *Reno v. ACLU, 521 U.S. 844 (1997)*

Justice Stevens delivered the opinion of the Court[, which was in relevant part unanimous]....

[The Communication Decency Act] prohibits the knowing transmission of ... indecent messages [via telecommunications media, including the Internet and the Web] to any recipient under 18 years of age. [The Court struck down the law, but had to confront the argument that the restrictions was similar to that upheld in *Pacifica*.—ed.] ...

"[E]ach medium of expression ... may present its own problems." Thus, some of our cases have recognized special justifications for regulation of the broadcast media that are not applicable to other speakers, see *Red Lion Broadcasting Co. v. FCC*; *FCC v. Pacifica Foundation*. In these cases, the Court relied on the history of extensive Government regulation of the broadcast medium; the scarcity of available frequencies at its inception; and its "invasive" nature.

Those factors are not present in cyberspace. Neither before nor after the enactment of the CDA have the vast democratic forums of the Internet been subject to the type of government supervision and regulation that has attended the broadcast industry. {When *Pacifica* was decided, given that radio stations were allowed to operate only pursuant to federal license, and that Congress had ... prohibit[ed] licensees from broadcasting indecent speech, there was a risk that members of the radio audience might infer some sort of official or societal approval of whatever was heard over the radio. No such risk attends messages received through the Internet, which is not supervised by any federal agency.}

Moreover, the Internet is not as "invasive" as radio or television.... The District Court specifically found that "[c]ommunications over the Internet do not 'invade' an individual's home or appear on one's computer screen unbidden. Users seldom encounter content 'by accident.'" It also found that "[a]lmost all sexually explicit images are preceded by warnings as to the content," and cited testimony that "'odds are slim' that a user would come across a sexually explicit sight by accident."

[I]n *Sable Communications v. FCC*, 492 U.S. 115 (1989), ... [which struck down a ban] of indecent [dial-a-porn] telephone messages[,] ... [we similarly] distinguished our "emphatically narrow holding" in *Pacifica* because it did not involve a complete ban and because it involved a different medium of communication. We explained that "the dial-it medium requires the listener to take affirmative steps to receive the communication." "Placing a telephone call," we continued, "is not the same as turning on a radio and being taken by surprise by an indecent message."

Finally, unlike the conditions that prevailed when Congress first authorized regulation of the broadcast spectrum, the Internet can hardly be considered a "scarce" expressive commodity. It provides relatively unlimited, low-cost capacity for communication of all kinds.... Through the use of Web pages, mail exploders, and newsgroups, [any] individual can become a pamphleteer.... [O]ur cases provide no basis for qualifying the level of First Amendment scrutiny that should be applied to this medium....

k.   *Texas v. Johnson, 491 U.S. 397 (1989)*

Justice Brennan delivered the opinion of the Court....

[See p. 188 above for the facts.—ed.]

[A.] [T]he State emphasizes the "special place" reserved for the flag in our Nation [and argues] ... that it has an interest in preserving the flag as a symbol of *nationhood* and *national unity*, a symbol with a determinate range of meanings. According to Texas, if one physically treats the flag in a way that would tend to cast doubt on either the idea that nationhood and national unity are the flag's referents or that national unity actually exists, the message conveyed thereby is a harmful one and therefore may be prohibited.

If there is a bedrock principle underlying the First Amendment, it is that the government may not prohibit the expression of an idea simply because society finds the idea itself offensive or disagreeable.... [N]othing in our precedents suggests that a State may foster its own view of the flag by prohibiting expressive conduct relating to it. {Nor does *San Francisco Arts & Athletics, Inc. v. United States Olympic Comm.*, 483 U.S. 522 (1987), addressing the validity of Congress' decision to "authoriz[e] the United States Olympic Committee to prohibit certain commercial and promotional uses of the word 'Olympic,'" relied upon by the Chief Justice's dissent, even begin to tell us whether the government may criminally punish physical conduct towards the flag engaged in as a means of political protest.} ...

[And the] enduring lesson [of our prior decisions], that the government may not prohibit expression simply because it disagrees with its message, is not dependent on the particular mode in which one chooses to express an idea. If we were to hold that a State may forbid flag burning wherever it is likely to endanger the flag's symbolic role, but allow it wherever burning a flag promotes that role—as where, for example, a person ceremoniously burns a dirty flag—we would be saying that when it comes to impairing the flag's physical integrity, the flag itself may be used as a symbol—as a substitute for the written or spoken word or a "short cut from mind to mind"— only in one direction. We would be permitting a State to "prescribe what shall be orthodox" by saying that one may burn the flag to convey one's attitude toward it and its referents only if one does not endanger the flag's representation of nationhood and national unity....

To conclude that the government may permit designated symbols to be used to communicate only a limited set of messages would be to enter territory having no discernible or defensible boundaries. Could the government, on this theory, prohibit the burning of state flags? Of copies of the Presidential seal? Of the Constitution?

In evaluating these choices under the First Amendment, how would we decide which symbols were sufficiently special to warrant this unique status? To do so, we would be forced to consult our own political preferences, and impose them on the citizenry, in the very way that the First Amendment forbids us to do.

There is, moreover, no indication—either in the text of the Constitution or in our cases interpreting it—that a separate juridical category exists for the American flag alone. Indeed, we would not be surprised to learn that the persons who framed our Constitution and wrote the Amendment that we now construe were not known for their reverence for the Union Jack. The First Amendment does not guarantee that other concepts virtually sacred to our Nation as a whole—such as the principle that discrimination on the basis of race is odious and destructive—will go unquestioned in the marketplace of ideas. See *Brandenburg*. We decline, therefore, to create for the flag an exception to the joust of principles protected by the First Amendment.

{The Chief Justice's dissent appears to believe that Johnson's conduct may be prohibited and, indeed, criminally sanctioned, because "his act ... conveyed nothing that could not have been conveyed and was not conveyed

[Handwritten margin notes: "Dissent - could have done another way / └ BUT would water message"]

just as forcefully in a dozen different ways." ... [T]his assertion sit[s] uneasily next to the dissent's quite correct reminder that the flag occupies a unique position in our society[,] which demonstrates that messages conveyed without use of the flag are not "just as forcefu[l]" as those conveyed with it ....} ...

[T]he government has a legitimate interest in making efforts to "preserv[e] the national flag as an unalloyed symbol of our country." {"National unity as an end which officials may foster by persuasion and example is not in question...."} ... [But the government may not serve this interest by] criminally punish[ing] a person for burning a flag as a means of political protest.

[B.] We are fortified in today's conclusion by our conviction that forbidding criminal punishment for conduct such as Johnson's will not endanger the special role played by our flag or the feelings it inspires.... We are tempted to say, in fact, that the flag's deservedly cherished place in our community will be strengthened, not weakened, by our holding today. Our decision is a reaffirmation of the principles of freedom and inclusiveness that the flag best reflects, and of the conviction that our toleration of criticism such as Johnson's is a sign and source of our strength....

[Handwritten margin note: "counter speech!"]

The way to preserve the flag's special role is not to punish those who feel differently about these matters. It is to persuade them that they are wrong.... And, precisely because it is our flag that is involved, one's response to the flag burner may exploit the uniquely persuasive power of the flag itself. We can imagine no more appropriate response to burning a flag than waving one's own, no better way to counter a flag burner's message than by saluting the flag that burns, no surer means of preserving the dignity even of the flag that burned than by—as one witness here did—according its remains a respectful burial. We do not consecrate the flag by punishing its desecration, for in doing so we dilute the freedom that this cherished emblem represents....

Chief Justice Rehnquist, with whom Justice White and Justice O'Connor join, dissenting....

"[A] page of history is worth a volume of logic." For more than 200 years, the American flag has occupied a unique position as the symbol of our Nation, a uniqueness that justifies a governmental prohibition against flag burning in the way respondent Johnson did here [citing many examples of the use of the American flag as an inspirational symbol, such as the raising of the flag by American marines at Iwo Jima—ed.].

The American flag ... does not represent the views of any particular political party, and it does not represent any particular political philosophy. The flag is not simply another "idea" or "point of view" competing for recognition in the marketplace of ideas. Millions and millions of Americans regard it with an almost mystical reverence regardless of what sort of social, political, or philosophical beliefs they may have....

Only two Terms ago, in *San Francisco Arts & Athletics, Inc.*, the Court held that Congress could grant exclusive use of the word "Olympic" to the

United States Olympic Committee. The Court thought that this "restrictio[n] on expressive speech properly [was] characterized as incidental to the primary congressional purpose of encouraging and rewarding the USOC's activities." As the Court stated, "when a word [or symbol] acquires value 'as the result of organization and the expenditure of labor, skill, and money' by an entity, that entity constitutionally may obtain a limited property right in the word [or symbol]." Surely [the law] may recognize a similar interest in the flag....

[Moreover, a]s with "fighting words," so with flag burning, for purposes of the First Amendment: It is "no essential part of any exposition of ideas, and [is] of such slight social value as a step to truth that any benefit that may be derived from [it] is clearly outweighed" by the public interest in avoiding a probable breach of the peace.... Far from being a case of "one picture being worth a thousand words," flag burning is the equivalent of an inarticulate grunt or roar that, it seems fair to say, is most likely to be indulged in not to express any particular idea, but to antagonize others.... The Texas statute deprived Johnson of only one rather inarticulate symbolic form of protest—a form of protest that was profoundly offensive to many—and left him with a full panoply of other symbols and every conceivable form of verbal expression to express his deep disapproval of national policy....

Uncritical extension of constitutional protection to the burning of the flag risks the frustration of the very purpose for which organized governments are instituted. The Court decides that the American flag is just another symbol, about which not only must opinions pro and con be tolerated, but for which the most minimal public respect may not be enjoined. The government may conscript men into the Armed Forces where they must fight and perhaps die for the flag, but the government may not prohibit the public burning of the banner under which they fight. I would uphold the Texas statute as applied in this case.

Justice Stevens, dissenting....

[S]anctioning the public desecration of the flag will tarnish its value—both for those who cherish the ideas for which it waves and for those who desire to don the robes of martyrdom by burning it. That tarnish is not justified by the trivial burden on free expression occasioned by requiring that an available, alternative mode of expression—including uttering words critical of the flag—be employed.... If [the ideas of liberty and equality] are worth fighting for—and our history demonstrates that they are—it cannot be true that the flag that uniquely symbolizes their power is not itself worthy of protection from unnecessary desecration.

l.   Snyder v. Phelps, 562 U.S. 443 (2011)

Chief Justice Roberts delivered the opinion of the Court....

[**A.**] Marine Lance Corporal Matthew Snyder was killed in Iraq in the line of duty.... On the day of [his] memorial service, the Westboro congregation members [Fred W. Phelps and seven of his family members] picketed on public land adjacent to public streets near the Maryland State House, the United States Naval Academy, and Matthew Snyder's funeral.... [Their signs] stated, for instance: "God Hates the USA/Thank God for 9/11," "America is Doomed," "Don't Pray for the USA," "Thank God for IEDs," "Thank God for Dead Soldiers," "Pope in Hell," "Priests Rape Boys," "God Hates Fags," "You're Going to Hell," and "God Hates You." ...

The picketing took place within a 10- by 25-foot plot of public land adjacent to a public street, behind a temporary fence. That plot was approximately 1,000 feet from the church where the funeral was held. Several buildings separated the picket site from the church.

The Westboro picketers displayed their signs for about 30 minutes before the funeral began and sang hymns and recited Bible verses. None of the picketers entered church property or went to the cemetery. They did not yell or use profanity, and there was no violence associated with the picketing.

The funeral procession passed within 200 to 300 feet of the picket site. Although [plaintiff Albert Snyder, Matthew's father,] testified that he could see the tops of the picket signs as he drove to the funeral, he did not see what was written on the signs until later that night, while watching a news broadcast covering the event.

{A few weeks after the funeral, one of the picketers posted a message on Westboro's Web site discussing the picketing and containing religiously oriented denunciations of the Snyders, interspersed among lengthy Bible quotations. Snyder discovered the posting, referred to by the parties as the "epic," during an Internet search for his son's name. The epic is not properly before us and does not factor in our analysis.... Snyder never mentioned it in his petition for certiorari [and] ... devoted only one paragraph in the argument section of his opening merits brief to the epic.} ...

A jury found for Snyder on [his] intentional infliction of emotional distress [and] intrusion upon seclusion ... claims [against the Westboro picketers], and held Westboro liable for $2.9 million in compensatory damages and $8 million in punitive damages.... The District Court remitted the punitive damages award to $2.1 million ....

[B.] To succeed on a claim for intentional infliction of emotional distress in Maryland, a plaintiff must demonstrate that the defendant intentionally or recklessly engaged in extreme and outrageous conduct that caused the plaintiff to suffer severe emotional distress. The Free Speech Clause ... can serve as a defense in state tort suits, including suits for intentional infliction of emotional distress. {[T]here is "no suggestion that the speech at issue falls within one of the categorical exclusions from First Amendment protection, such as those for obscenity or fighting words."}

Whether the First Amendment prohibits holding Westboro liable for its speech in this case turns largely on whether that speech is of public or private concern, as determined by all the circumstances of the case.... "'[N]ot all speech is of equal First Amendment importance,'" ... and where matters of purely private significance are at issue, First Amendment protections are often less rigorous. *Dun & Bradstreet, Inc. v. Greenmoss Builders, Inc.* (opinion of Powell, J.); *Connick.* That is because restricting speech on purely private matters does not implicate the same constitutional concerns as limiting speech on matters of public interest ....

"[T]he boundaries of the public concern test are not well defined." ... [But] we have articulated some guiding principles, principles that accord broad protection to speech to ensure that courts themselves do not become inadvertent censors.

Speech deals with matters of public concern when it can "be fairly considered as relating to any matter of political, social, or other concern to the community," or when it "is a subject of legitimate news interest; that is, a subject of general interest and of value and concern to the public." The arguably "inappropriate or controversial character of a statement is irrelevant to the question whether it deals with a matter of public concern."

Our opinion in *Dun & Bradstreet,* on the other hand, provides an example of speech of only private concern. In that case we held, as a general matter, that information about a particular individual's credit report "concerns no public issue." The content of the report, we explained, "was speech solely in the individual interest of the speaker and its specific business audience." That was confirmed by the fact that the particular report was sent to only five subscribers to the reporting service, who were bound not to disseminate it further.

To cite another example, we concluded in *San Diego v. Roe,* 543 U.S. 77 (2004), that, in the context of a government employer regulating the speech of its employees, videos of an employee engaging in sexually explicit acts did not address a public concern; the videos "did nothing to inform the public about any aspect of the [employing agency's] functioning or operation." Deciding whether speech is of public or private concern requires us to examine the "'content, form, and context'" of that speech, ... including what was said, where it was said, and how it was said.

[C.] The "content" of Westboro's signs plainly relates to broad issues of interest to society at large, rather than matters of "purely private concern." ... While [the] messages may fall short of refined social or political commentary, the issues they highlight—the political and moral conduct of the United States and its citizens, the fate of our Nation, homosexuality in the military, and scandals involving the Catholic clergy—are matters of public import.

The signs certainly convey Westboro's position on those issues, in a manner designed, unlike the private speech in *Dun & Bradstreet,* to reach as broad a public audience as possible. And even if a few of the signs—such as "You're Going to Hell" and "God Hates You"—were viewed as containing messages related to Matthew Snyder or the Snyders specifically, that would not change the fact that the overall thrust and dominant theme of Westboro's demonstration spoke to broader public issues.... The fact that Westboro spoke in connection with a funeral, however, cannot by itself transform the nature of Westboro's speech....

There was no pre-existing relationship or conflict between Westboro and

Snyder that might suggest Westboro's speech on public matters was intended to mask an attack on Snyder over a private matter. Contrast *Connick* (finding public employee speech a matter of private concern when it was "no coincidence that [the speech] followed upon the heels of [a] transfer notice" affecting the employee)....

[D.] Snyder goes on to argue that Westboro's speech should be afforded less than full First Amendment protection "not only because of the words" but also because the church members exploited the funeral "as a platform to bring their message to a broader audience." There is no doubt that Westboro chose to stage its picketing at the Naval Academy, the Maryland State House, and Matthew Snyder's funeral to increase publicity for its views and because of the relation between those sites and its views—in the case of the military funeral, because Westboro believes that God is killing American soldiers as punishment for the Nation's sinful policies.

Westboro's choice to convey its views in conjunction with Matthew Snyder's funeral made the expression of those views particularly hurtful to many, especially to Matthew's father.... But Westboro conducted its picketing peacefully on matters of public concern at a public place adjacent to a public street. Such space occupies a "special position in terms of First Amendment protection." "[W]e have repeatedly referred to public streets as the archetype of a traditional public forum[.]" ...

[E.] That said, ... Westboro's choice of where and when to conduct its picketing ... is "subject to reasonable time, place, or manner restrictions" that are consistent with the standards announced in this Court's precedents. Maryland now has a law imposing restrictions on funeral picketing, as do 43 other States and the Federal Government. {The Maryland law prohibits picketing within 100 feet of a funeral service or funeral procession ....} To the extent these laws are content neutral, they raise very different questions from the tort verdict at issue in this case.... [W]e have no occasion to consider ... whether [such laws] are constitutional.

We have identified a few limited situations where the location of targeted picketing can be regulated under provisions ... determined to be content neutral. In *Frisby v. Schultz*, for example, we upheld a ban on such picketing "before or about" a particular residence. In *Madsen v. Women's Health Center, Inc.*, 512 U.S. 753 (1994), we approved an injunction requiring a buffer zone between protesters and an abortion clinic entrance. The facts here are obviously quite different, both with respect to the activity being regulated and the means of restricting those activities.

Simply put, the church members had the right to be where they were.... The picketing was conducted under police supervision some 1,000 feet from the church, out of the sight of those at the church. The protest was not unruly; there was no shouting, profanity, or violence.... [And] any distress occasioned by Westboro's picketing turned on the content and viewpoint of the message conveyed, rather than any interference with the funeral itself. A group of parishioners standing at the very spot where Westboro stood, holding signs that said "God Bless America" and "God Loves You," would not have been subjected to liability....

[F.] [Westboro's] speech cannot be restricted simply because it is upsetting or arouses contempt. "... [T]he government may not prohibit the expression of an idea simply because society finds the idea itself offensive or disagreeable." *Texas v. Johnson.* Indeed, "the point of all speech protection ... is to shield just those choices of content that in someone's eyes are misguided, or even hurtful."

The jury here was instructed that it could hold Westboro liable for intentional infliction of emotional distress based on a finding that Westboro's picketing was "outrageous." "Outrageousness," however, is a highly malleable standard with "an inherent subjectiveness about it which would allow a jury to impose liability on the basis of the jurors' tastes or views, or perhaps on the basis of their dislike of a particular expression." In a case such as this, a jury is "unlikely to be neutral with respect to the content of [the] speech," posing "a real danger of becoming an instrument for the suppression of ... 'vehement, caustic, and sometimes unpleasan[t]'" expression.

Such a risk is unacceptable; "in public debate [we] must tolerate insulting, and even outrageous, speech in order to provide adequate 'breathing space' to the freedoms protected by the First Amendment." ....

[G.] [Nor can there be] liability for intrusion upon seclusion [here, on the grounds that] Snyder was a member of a captive audience at his son's funeral.... "... [T]he burden normally falls upon the viewer to avoid further bombardment of [his] sensibilities simply by averting [his] eyes." ... "[T]he ability of government ... to shut off discourse solely to protect others from hearing it is ... dependent upon a showing that substantial privacy interests are being invaded in an essentially intolerable manner." *Cohen v. California.*

As a general matter, we have applied the captive audience doctrine only sparingly to protect unwilling listeners from protected speech. For example, we have upheld a statute allowing a homeowner to restrict the delivery of offensive mail to his home, see *Rowan v. Post Office Dept.*, and an ordinance prohibiting picketing "before or about" any individual's residence, *Frisby.*

Here, Westboro stayed well away from the memorial service. Snyder could see no more than the tops of the signs when driving to the funeral. And there is no indication that the picketing in any way interfered with the funeral service itself. We decline to expand the captive audience doctrine to the circumstances presented here....

[H.] Westboro believes that America is morally flawed; many Americans might feel the same about Westboro. Westboro's funeral picketing is certainly hurtful and its contribution to public discourse may be negligible. But Westboro addressed matters of public import on public property, in a peaceful manner, in full compliance with the guidance of local officials....

Speech is powerful. It can stir people to action, move them to tears of both joy and sorrow, and—as it did here—inflict great pain. On the facts before us, we cannot react to that pain by punishing the speaker. As a Nation we have chosen a different course—to protect even hurtful speech on public issues to ensure that we do not stifle public debate. That choice requires that we shield Westboro from tort liability for its picketing in this case....

Justice Breyer, concurring....

[T]he State is [not] always powerless to provide private individuals with necessary protection [against invasions of, *e.g.*, personal privacy] .... [But] Westboro's means of communicating its views consisted of picketing in a place where picketing was lawful and in compliance with all police directions. The picketing could not be seen or heard from the funeral ceremony itself. And Snyder testified that he saw no more than the tops of the picketers' signs as he drove to the funeral. To uphold the application of state law in these circumstances would [unconstitutionally] punish Westboro for seeking to communicate its views on matters of public concern without proportionately advancing the State's interest in protecting its citizens against severe emotional harm....

Justice Alito, dissenting....

[A.] Petitioner Albert Snyder is not a public figure. He is simply a parent whose son, Marine Lance Corporal Matthew Snyder, was killed in Iraq. Mr. Snyder wanted what is surely the right of any parent who experiences such an incalculable loss: to bury his son in peace. But respondents ... deprived him of that elementary right....

[T]he First Amendment ensures that [defendants] have almost limitless opportunities to express their views[, for instance, through articles, video recordings, and picketing in many places] .... It does not follow, however, that they may intentionally inflict severe emotional injury on private persons at a time of intense emotional sensitivity by launching vicious verbal attacks that make no contribution to public debate....

This Court has recognized that words may "by their very utterance inflict injury" and that the First Amendment does not shield utterances that form "no essential part of any exposition of ideas, and are of such slight social value as a step to truth that any benefit that may be derived from them is clearly outweighed by the social interest in order and morality." *Chaplinsky v. New Hampshire*. When grave injury is intentionally inflicted by means of an attack like the one at issue here, the First Amendment should not interfere with recovery....

The Westboro Baptist Church ... has devised a strategy [for getting publicity].... [C]hurch members have protested at nearly 600 military funerals. They have also picketed the funerals of police officers, firefighters, and the victims of natural disasters, accidents, and shocking crimes. And in advance of these protests, they issue press releases to ensure that their protests will attract public attention. This strategy works because it is expected that respondents' verbal assaults will wound the family and friends of the deceased and because the media is irresistibly drawn to the sight of persons who are visibly in grief. The more outrageous the funeral protest, the more publicity the Westboro Baptist Church is able to obtain....

Since respondents chose to stage their protest at Matthew Snyder's funeral and not at any of the other countless available venues, a reasonable person would have assumed that there was a connection between the messages on the placards and the deceased. Moreover, since a church funeral is an event that naturally brings to mind thoughts about the afterlife, some of respondents' signs—*e.g.*, "God Hates You," "Not Blessed Just Cursed," and "You're Going to Hell"—would have likely been interpreted as referring to God's judgment of the deceased....

After the funeral, the Westboro picketers reaffirmed the meaning of their protest. They posted an online account entitled "The Burden of Marine Lance Cpl. Matthew A. Snyder. The Visit of Westboro Baptist Church to Help the Inhabitants of Maryland Connect the Dots!" Belying any suggestion that they had simply made general comments about homosexuality, the Catholic Church, and the United States military, the "epic" addressed the Snyder family directly:

> God blessed you, Mr. and Mrs. Snyder, with a resource and his name was Matthew. He was an arrow in your quiver! In thanks to God for the comfort the child could bring you, you had a DUTY to prepare that child to serve the LORD his GOD—PERIOD! You did JUST THE OPPOSITE—you raised him for the devil....
>
> Albert and Julie RIPPED that body apart and taught Matthew to defy his Creator, to divorce, and to commit adultery. They taught him how to support the largest pedophile machine in the history of the entire world, the Roman Catholic monstrosity. Every dime they gave the Roman Catholic monster they condemned their own souls. They also, in supporting satanic Catholicism, taught Matthew to be an idolater....
>
> Then after all that they sent him to fight for the United States of Sodom, a filthy country that is in lock step with his evil, wicked, and sinful manner of life, putting him in the cross hairs of a God that is so mad He has smoke coming from his nostrils and fire from his mouth! How dumb was that?

While commentary on the Catholic Church or the United States military constitutes speech on matters of public concern, speech regarding Matthew Snyder's purely private conduct does not....

[B.] [I do not agree] that "the overall thrust and dominant theme of [their] demonstration spoke to" broad public issues ...; respondents' attack on Matthew was of central importance. But in any event, I fail to see why actionable speech should be immunized simply because it is interspersed with speech that is protected. The First Amendment allows recovery for defamatory statements that are interspersed with nondefamatory statements on matters of public concern, and there is no good reason why respondents' attack on Matthew Snyder and his family should be treated differently.

[T]he Court [also] suggests that respondents' personal attack on Matthew Snyder is entitled to First Amendment protection because it was not motivated by a private grudge, but I see no basis for the strange distinction that the Court appears to draw. Respondents' motivation—"to increase pub-

Reasonable to assume connection

Addressed family directly

Allows recovery for some speech

"private grudge"

licity for its views"—did not transform their statements attacking the character of a private figure into statements that made a contribution to debate on matters of public concern. Nor did their publicity-seeking motivation soften the sting of their attack....

[Finally,] the Court finds it significant that respondents' protest occurred on a public street, but this fact alone should not be enough to preclude IIED liability.... If the First Amendment permits the States to protect their residents from the harm inflicted by such attacks—and the Court does not hold otherwise—then the location of the tort should not be dispositive.... Neither classic "fighting words" nor defamatory statements are immunized when they occur in a public place, and there is no good reason to treat a verbal assault based on the conduct or character of a private figure like Matthew Snyder any differently.

[C.] [T]he enactment of {laws that restrict picketing within a specified distance of a funeral} ... is no substitute for the protection provided by the established IIED tort; according to the Court, the verbal attacks that severely wounded petitioner in this case complied with the new Maryland law regulating funeral picketing.... [But the enactment of the new laws] dramatically illustrates the fundamental point that funerals are unique events at which special protection against emotional assaults is in order. At funerals, the emotional well-being of bereaved relatives is particularly vulnerable. Exploitation of a funeral for the purpose of attracting public attention "intrud[es] upon their ... grief," and may permanently stain their memories of the final moments before a loved one is laid to rest. Allowing family members to have a few hours of peace without harassment does not undermine public debate.

I would therefore hold that, in this setting, the First Amendment permits a private figure to recover for the intentional infliction of emotional distress caused by speech on a matter of private concern....

m. Policy—Slippery Slope

> In other countries [than the American colonies], the people ... judge of an ill principle in government only by an actual grievance; here they anticipate the evil, and judge of the pressure of the grievance by the badness of the principle. They augur misgovernment at a distance and snuff the approach of tyranny in every tainted breeze.
> —Edmund Burke, Speech to Parliament, March 22, 1775

Basic argument: "If this speech restriction is accepted under this theory, then in the future some other speech restriction _____ might be accepted under the same theory using the following argument, _____, because these restrictions are similar in the following way: _____."

1. "[T]he principle contended for by the State seems inherently boundless. How is one to distinguish this from any other offensive word? Surely the State has no right to cleanse public debate to the point where it is grammatically palatable to the most squeamish among us. Yet no readily ascertainable general principle exists for stopping short of that result were we to affirm the judgment below. For, while the particular four-letter word being

litigated here is perhaps more distasteful than most others of its genre, it is nevertheless often true that one man's vulgarity is another's lyric." *Cohen v. California.*

"To conclude that the government may permit designated symbols to be used to communicate only a limited set of messages would be to enter territory having no discernible or defensible boundaries. Could the government, on this theory, prohibit the burning of state flags? Of copies of the Presidential seal? Of the Constitution? .... [To] decide which symbols were sufficiently special to warrant this unique status[,] ... we would be forced to consult our own political preferences, and impose them on the citizenry, in the very way that the First Amendment forbids us to do." *Texas v. Johnson.*

"[T]he caricature of respondent and his mother published in Hustler is at best a distant cousin of the political cartoons described [in the opinion], and a rather poor relation at that. If it were possible by laying down a principled standard to separate the one from the other, public discourse would probably suffer little or no harm. But we doubt that there is any such standard, and we are quite sure that the pejorative description 'outrageous' does not supply one." *Hustler Magazine, Inc. v. Falwell*, 485 U.S. 46 (1988).

"[T]he freedoms of speech, press, petition and assembly guaranteed by the First Amendment must be accorded to the ideas we hate or sooner or later they will be denied to the ideas we cherish. The first banning of an association because it advocates hated ideas—whether that association be called a political party or not—marks a fateful moment in the history of a free country." *Communist Party v. Subversive Activities Control Board*, 367 U.S. 1, 137 (1961) (Black, J., dissenting).

"[I]t is proper to take alarm at the first experiment on our liberties.... The freemen of America did not wait till usurped power had strengthened itself by exercise, and entangled the question in precedents. They saw all the consequences in the principle, and they avoided the consequences by denying the principle.... Who does not see that the same authority which can establish Christianity ... may establish with the same ease any particular sect of Christians ...? That the same authority which can force a citizen to contribute three pence only of his property for the support of any one [religious] establishment, may force him to conform to any other establishment in all cases whatsoever?" James Madison, *Memorial and Remonstrance Against Religious Assessments.*

"[I]n constitutional adjudication some steps, which when taken were thought to approach 'the verge,' have become the platform for yet further steps. A certain momentum develops in constitutional theory and it can be a 'downhill thrust' easily set in motion but difficult to retard or stop.... The dangers are increased by the difficulty of perceiving in advance exactly where the 'verge' of the precipice lies. As well as constituting an independent evil against which the Religion Clauses were intended to protect, involvement or entanglement between government and religion serves as a warning signal [of approach to this verge]." *Lemon v. Kurtzman.*

"Struggles to coerce uniformity of sentiment ... have been waged by many good as well as by evil men.... As first and moderate methods to attain unity have failed, those bent on its accomplishment must resort to an ever-increasing severity. As governmental pressure toward unity becomes greater, so strife becomes more bitter as to whose unity it shall be.... Those who begin coercive elimination of dissent soon find themselves exterminating dissenters.... [T]he First Amendment ... was designed to avoid these ends by avoiding these beginnings." *W. Va. State Bd. of Ed. v. Barnette.*

2. Response to 1: The slope is slippery both ways: If one rejects this speech restriction, then one would logically also have to reject other speech restrictions (such as _____), that all agree are sound, because _____.

3. Response to 1: Judges are quite capable of drawing sensible lines, because _____; constitutional law is full of slopes down which we haven't slipped, such as _____.

"[I]t has been said that it is dangerous to entrust any tribunal with power to judge of the mere tendency of acts or words.... [T]his argument proves merely that this, like all other human power, may be abused. But to prove that power may be abused, is not to prove that power does not exist. The same kind of reasoning would break down every useful institution of man." *State v. Chandler,* 2 Harr. 553 (Del. 1837) (upholding blasphemy law on the grounds that blasphemy tends to cause breaches of the peace).

"[When Chief Justice Marshall said] that the power to tax is the power to destroy[,] ... it was not recognized as it is today that most of the distinctions of the law are distinctions of degree. If the States had any power it was assumed that they had all power, and that the necessary alternative was to deny it altogether. But this Court ... can defeat an attempt to discriminate or otherwise go too far without wholly abolishing the power to tax. The power to tax is not the power to destroy while this Court sits." *Panhandle Oil Co. v. Mississippi ex. rel. Knox,* 277 U.S. 218, 223 (1928) (Holmes, J., dissenting), quoted as to free speech in *American Communications Ass'n v. Douds,* 339 U.S. 382 (1950).

"[T]here is underlying validity in the distinction between advocacy and the interchange of ideas, and we do not discard a useful tool because it may be misused. That such a distinction could be used unreasonably by those in power against hostile or unorthodox views does not negate the fact that it may be used reasonably against an organization wielding the power of the centrally controlled international Communist movement." *Dennis v. United States* (Frankfurter, J., concurring).

"We are warned that the choice open to the Illinois legislature here may be abused ...; prohibiting libel of a creed or of a racial group, we are told, is but a step from prohibiting libel of a political party. Every power may be abused, but the possibility of abuse is a poor reason for denying Illinois the power to adopt measures against criminal libels sanctioned by centuries of Anglo-American law. 'While this Court sits' it retains and exercises authority to nullify action which encroaches on freedom of utterance under the guise of punishing libel." *Beauharnais v. Illinois.*

"[G]reat consequences can grow from small beginnings, but the measure of constitutional adjudication is the ability and willingness to distinguish between real threat and mere shadow." *Abington School Dist. v. Schempp,* 374 U.S. 203 (1963) (Goldberg, J., concurring).

"Nor am I able to appreciate the danger ... that the American people will by means of military arrests during the rebellion lose the right of public discussion ... throughout the indefinite peaceable future which I trust lies before them, any more than I am able to believe that a man could contract so strong an appetite for emetics during temporary illness as to persist in feeding upon them during the remainder of his healthful life." Abraham Lincoln on the Arrest of Clement Vallandigham (p. 14).

4. Rejoinder to 3: But no principled lines are available, or, even if there might be some such lines, there's reason to doubt that the courts will find them, because _____.

"It is, sadly, no answer to say that this Court will not allow the trend to overwhelm us[and] that today's holding will be strictly confined to 'Communists' .... [In another case nine years ago,] the Court ... went to great lengths to explain that the Act held valid 'touches only a relative handful of persons, leaving the great majority of persons of the identified affiliations and beliefs completely free from restraint.' '[W]hile this Court sits,' the Court proclaimed, no wholesale proscription of Communists or their Party can occur.... [But t]oday, Communists or suspected Communists have been denied an opportunity to work as government employees, lawyers, doctors, teachers, pharmacists, veterinarians, subway conductors, industrial workers and in just about any other job.... Nevertheless, this Court still sits!

"{The record in this very case indicates how easily such restrictions spread. During the testimony of one witness an organization known as the Americans for Democratic Action was mentioned. Despite testimony that this organization did not admit Communists, one member of the Committee insisted that it was a Communist front because 'it followed a party line, almost identical in many particulars with the Communist Party line.' Presumably if this accusation were repeated frequently and loudly enough that organization, or any other, would also be called a 'criminal gang.'}" *Barenblatt v. United States* (Black, J., dissenting).

5. Response to 2: There is a particular principled place on this particular slope where one can draw a line, specifically _____, so if we accept this line, we won't be in danger of slipping further.

n. Policy—Alternative Channels Available to Speakers

Basic argument: "This speech restriction leaves the speaker with plenty of other opportunities to speak, such as _____; it therefore only mildly regulates the speech, rather than banning it or even seriously burdening it."

1. "[T]he public burning of the American flag by Johnson was no essential part of any exposition of ideas .... The Texas statute deprived Johnson of only one rather inarticulate symbolic form of protest—a form of protest that was profoundly offensive to many—and left him with a full panoply of other symbols and every conceivable form of verbal expression to express

2) Alt. Channels available to speaker

his deep disapproval of national policy." *Texas v. Johnson* (Rehnquist, C.J., dissenting).

"[C]opyright's idea/expression dichotomy 'strike[s] a definitional balance between the First Amendment and the Copyright Act by permitting free communication of facts while still protecting an author's expression.' No author may copyright his ideas or the facts he narrates.... [Respondent] possessed an unfettered right to use any factual information revealed in [the copyrighted work] for the purpose of enlightening its audience, but it can claim no need to 'bodily appropriate' ... 'expression' of that information by utilizing portions of the actual [work]." *Harper & Row v. Nation Enterprises.*

"The question is whether or not there is a real abridgment of the rights of free speech.... The right of free speech is guaranteed every citizen that he may reach the minds of willing listeners and to do so there must be opportunity to win their attention.... We do not think [a sound-truck ban] abridges that freedom.... There is no restriction upon the communication of ideas or discussion of issues by the human voice, by newspapers, by pamphlets, by [handbills]." *Kovacs v. Cooper,* 336 U.S. 77, 85, 87, 89 (1949).

2. Response to 1: The alternative channels are not in fact adequate for sufficiently serving the free speech value _____ (for instance, the search for truth or self-government), because _____.

"[W]e cannot indulge the facile assumption that one can forbid particular words without also running a substantial risk of suppressing ideas in the process. Indeed, governments might soon seize upon the censorship of particular words as a convenient guise for banning the expression of unpopular views. We have been able ... to discern little social benefit that might result from running the risk of opening the door to such grave results." *Cohen v. California.*

o. *Policy—Constitutional Tension Method, see p. 42* see p. 42

p. *Policy—Countervailing Private Rights, see p. 92* see p. 92

4. Symbolic Expression

a. *Summary*

This unit has offered our first introduction to *symbolic expression*—the use of symbolism that communicates a message without words, such as waving a flag, burning a flag, burning a cross, wearing a black armband, and wearing a uniform. See, respectively, *Stromberg v. California,* 283 U.S. 359 (1931); *Texas v. Johnson*; *Virginia v. Black* (p. 230) and *R.A.V. v. City of St. Paul* (p. 317); *Tinker v. Des Moines Indep. School Dist.* (1969) (p. 594); *Schacht v. United States,* 398 U.S. 58 (1970).

The notion that symbolic expression is constitutionally protected alongside verbal expression has deep roots in American law. The first Supreme Court case reversing a conviction on free speech grounds was a symbolic expression case (*Stromberg*), and the Court there seemed to think it obvious that the freedom of speech extended to waving a flag and not just to the use of words. And even in the late 1700s and early 1800s, American law treated symbolic and pictorial expression much the same way that it treated verbal expression. Eugene Volokh, *Symbolic Expression and the Original Meaning of the First Amendment*, 97 Geo. L.J. 1057 (2009).

Rule:

1. The First Amendment protections given to speech also apply to symbolic expression (also called expressive conduct), defined as conduct that satisfies these three conditions:

a. the expression "inten[ds] to convey a particularized message,"

b. "the likelihood [is] great that the message would be understood by those who viewed it." *Texas v. Johnson* (1989) (p. 363), and

c. the message is "created by the conduct itself," not "by [explanatory] speech that accompanies it." *Rumsfeld v. FAIR* (2006) (p. 220).

or that satisfies this one condition:

d. It is within a traditionally protected genre, such as painting (even if it's abstract, such as a Jackson Pollock), music (even if it's purely instrumental and atonal, such as an Arnold Schoenberg composition), poetry (even if it's nonsensical, such as Lewis Carroll's *Jabberwocky*), or a parade (even if it lacks "a narrow, succinctly articulable message," for instance as many St. Patrick's Day parades might). *Hurley v. Irish-American Gay, Lesbian & Bisexual Group* (1995) (p. 531).

2. But symbolic expression is no less restrictable as verbal expression,

a. for instance if it falls within an exception to free speech protection, such as fighting words or threats,

b. or if the restriction is applied to the symbolic expression for reasons unrelated to the communicative impact of the expression (see Part IV).

b. Texas v. Johnson, 491 U.S. 397 (1989)

[For the facts, see p. 188. For why the flag desecration ban is treated as content-based rather than content-neutral, see p. 363.—ed.]

Justice Brennan delivered the opinion of the Court....

The First Amendment literally forbids the abridgment only of "speech," but we have long recognized that its protection does not end at the spoken or written word. While we have rejected "the view that an apparently limitless variety of conduct can be labeled 'speech' whenever the person engaging in the conduct intends thereby to express an idea," we have acknowledged that conduct may be "sufficiently imbued with elements of communication to fall within the scope of the First and Fourteenth Amendments."

In deciding whether particular conduct possesses sufficient communicative elements to bring the First Amendment into play, we have asked whether "[a]n intent to convey a particularized message was present, and [whether] the likelihood was great that the message would be understood by those who viewed it." Hence, we have recognized the expressive nature of students' wearing of black armbands to protest American military involvement in Vietnam; of a sit-in by blacks in a "whites only" area to protest segregation; of the wearing of American military uniforms in a dramatic presentation criticizing American involvement in Vietnam; and of picketing about a wide variety of causes....

Attaching a peace sign to the flag[,] refusing to salute the flag[,] and displaying a red flag, we have held, all may find shelter under the First Amendment. That we have had little difficulty identifying an expressive element in conduct relating to flags should not be surprising. The very purpose of a national flag is to serve as a symbol of our country ....

Johnson burned an American flag as part—indeed, as the culmination—of a political demonstration that coincided with the convening of the Republican Party and its renomination of Ronald Reagan for President. The expressive, overtly political nature of this conduct was both intentional and overwhelmingly apparent.... In these circumstances, Johnson's burning of the flag was conduct "sufficiently imbued with elements of communication" to implicate the First Amendment.

[The dissenters did not disagree on this point.—ed.]

c. *Rumsfeld v. FAIR, 547 U.S. 47 (2006)*

[Because this case involves three separate arguments for First Amendment protection—freedom to engage in symbolic expression, freedom of association, and freedom from speech compulsions—this book breaks the case up into three separate excerpts; for the other two, see pp. 412 and 545.—ed.]

Chief Justice Roberts delivered the [unanimous] opinion of the Court....

[A.] Forum for Academic and Institutional Rights, Inc. (FAIR), is an association of law schools and law faculties.... FAIR members have adopted policies expressing their opposition to discrimination based on, among other factors, sexual orientation. They would like to restrict military recruiting on their campuses because they object to the policy Congress has adopted [generally barring homosexuals from] the military....

[However, a federal statute called t]he Solomon Amendment denies federal funding to an institution of higher education that "has a policy or practice ... that either prohibits, or in effect prevents" the military "from gaining access to campuses, or access to students ... on campuses, for purposes of military recruiting in a manner that is at least equal in quality and scope to the access to campuses and to students that is provided to any other employer." The statute provides an exception for an institution with "a longstanding policy of pacifism based on historical religious affiliation." The Government and FAIR agree on what this statute requires: In order for a law school and its university to receive federal funding, the law school must offer military recruiters the same access to its campus and students that it provides to the nonmilitary recruiter receiving the most favorable access....

This case does not require us to determine when a condition placed on university funding ... becomes an unconstitutional condition [see Part VI.D.3, p. 643—ed.]. It is clear that a funding condition cannot be unconstitutional if it could be constitutionally imposed directly. Because the First Amendment would not prevent Congress from directly imposing the Solomon Amendment's access requirement, the statute does not place an unconstitutional condition on the receipt of federal funds.

[**B.**] The Solomon Amendment neither limits what law schools may say nor requires them to say anything. Law schools remain free under the statute to express whatever views they may have on the military's congressionally mandated employment policy, all the while retaining eligibility for federal funds. See Tr. of Oral Arg. (Solicitor General acknowledging that law schools "could put signs on the bulletin board next to the door, they could engage in speech, they could help organize student protests"). As a general matter, the Solomon Amendment regulates conduct, not speech. It affects what law schools must *do*—afford equal access to military recruiters—not what they may or may not *say*....

In *United States v. O'Brien,* we recognized that some forms of "'symbolic speech'" were deserving of First Amendment protection. [*O'Brien* mandated some not very demanding scrutiny even of content-neutral restrictions on expressive conduct.—ed.]. But we rejected the view that "conduct can be labeled 'speech' whenever the person engaging in the conduct intends thereby to express an idea." Instead, we have extended First Amendment protection only to conduct that is inherently expressive....

Unlike[, for instance,] flag burning, the conduct regulated by the Solomon Amendment is not inherently expressive. Prior to the adoption of the Solomon Amendment's equal-access requirement, law schools "expressed" their disagreement with the military by treating military recruiters differently from other recruiters. But these actions were expressive only because the law schools accompanied their conduct with speech explaining it.

For example, the point of requiring military interviews to be conducted on the undergraduate campus is not "overwhelmingly apparent." An observer who sees military recruiters interviewing away from the law school has no way of knowing whether the law school is expressing its disapproval of the military, all the law school's interview rooms are full, or the military recruiters decided for reasons of their own that they would rather interview someplace else. The expressive component of a law school's actions is not created by the conduct itself but by the speech that accompanies it. The fact that such explanatory speech is necessary is strong evidence that the conduct at issue here is not so inherently expressive that it warrants protection under *O'Brien*.

If combining speech and conduct were enough to create expressive conduct, a regulated party could always transform conduct into "speech" simply by talking about it. For instance, if an individual announces that he intends to express his disapproval of the Internal Revenue Service by refusing to pay his income taxes, we would have to apply *O'Brien* to determine whether the Tax Code violates the First Amendment. Neither *O'Brien* nor its progeny supports such a result....

F. Exceptions from Protection—Threats

a. Summary

Rule #1: True threats of violence, of illegal firing, and likely of other criminal or tortious conduct are constitutionally unprotected. But:

1. Threats are not punishable if a reasonable person would understand them as obvious hyperbole. *Watts v. United States* (1969) (p. 224).

2. It's not clear whether the speech is unprotected

   a. only when the speaker had the *purpose* of putting people in fear;

   b. when the speaker *knew* he was substantially certain to put people in fear (or had the purpose of doing so);

   c. when the speaker was *reckless* about the possibility that he was putting people in fear, which is to say that the speaker knew there was a substantial and unjustifiable risk that they would be put in fear; or

   d. when the speaker was *negligent* about this possibility, which is to say that a reasonable speaker should have known that the speech would put people in fear.

   — *Virginia v. Black* (2003) (p. 244) seemed to suggest the First Amendment standard is *purpose*; that opinion defined unprotected threats as those "direct[ed] ... to a person or group of persons with the intent of placing the victim in fear of bodily harm or death."

   — Both before and after *Black*, though, many lower courts held that the First Amendment standard is negligence.

   — In *Elonis v. United States*, 135 S. Ct. 2001 (2015), the Supreme Court initially agreed to consider the matter, but ultimately decided the case on statutory grounds: The federal threats statute, the Court held, required a minimum *mens rea* of either recklessness or knowledge (the Court didn't decide which it was), not mere negligence. Elonis's conviction, which was based on jury instructions that only required negligence, thus had to be reversed without the need to decide what the First Amendment required. The split on the constitutional *mens rea* question—what is the minimum *mens rea* that the First Amendment requires for a threat conviction?—remains unresolved.

3. *NAACP v. Claiborne Hardware Co.* (1982) (p. 225) seems to hold that even speech which does intentionally put people in fear of violence (see p. 229) may still sometimes be protected. But the Court didn't say exactly when this is so; lawyers thus just have to use *Claiborne* as a benchmark against which they compare the facts of their case.

4. When speech by employers or unions is challenged as a threat of illegal

firing under labor law, courts pay more attention to the possible implications of the speech, considering "the economic dependence of the employees on their employers [and on unions], and the necessary tendency of the former, because of that relationship, to pick up intended implications of the latter that might be more readily dismissed by a more disinterested ear." *NLRB v. Gissel Packing Co.*, 395 U.S. 575 (1969).

Rule #2: Threats of social ostracism, lawful boycott, or future speech that would produce ostracism or boycott, are constitutionally protected. *Claiborne Hardware*; *Organization for a Better Austin v. Keefe* (1971) (p. 193).

— What about blackmail—threats such as, "Do what I tell you to do, or else I will reveal something embarrassing about you"? The Supreme Court has never considered this, but some lower courts have. The dominant view among them is that such threats are protected if they involve a "nexus to a claim of right": if the speaker is demanding something to which he can plausibly claim to be entitled, and is threatening to reveal the target's refusal to give the speaker that something.

Thus, for instance, a consumer "who threatens a vendor that unless he is given a refund for a defective product he will complain to the Better Business Bureau" is constitutionally protected. *See, e.g.*, *State v. Pauling*, 69 P.3d 331, 335-36 (Wash. 2003). Likewise, in a *Claiborne*-like case, "stop shopping at white-owned stores, or else we'll publicize the fact that you're shopping there" is constitutionally protected. But the law can criminalize threatening a vendor that, unless you are paid $10,000 (when the vendor hasn't wronged you personally at all), you will reveal the vendor's crimes.

Common error to watch out for: People sometimes discuss the threat analysis as being focused on the question "Are the statements punishable threats, or are they political speech?" This is a mistake, because the two options aren't antonyms: Statements may be both punishable threats and political speech (*e.g.*, "I am planning to bomb the Chief of Police's residence to protest police brutality"), or they may be neither punishable threats nor political speech (*e.g.*, an obviously jocular "I envy you so much I want to kill you" said between friends). Rather, the question is whether the statements are punishable threats or *protected* speech, protected because they are hyperbole (political or otherwise), threats of social ostracism, or whatever else.

Policy justifications for the exception:

1. Threats cause unjustified emotional distress to the threatened person.

2. Threats may wrongfully coerce the threatened person into doing things he otherwise wouldn't do; and even if the person refuses to go along, he will often have to take expensive protective measures (such as hiring security guards, or, in the case of threats against the President, having the Secret Service expend extra effort investigating the threat).

3. People who threaten to do something are likely (though not certain) to eventually do it, or do some other bad thing. Locking them up for the

threat may prevent them from implementing the threat.

Policy arguments inferable from the existence of the exception:

1. Some kinds of speech seem so closely related to illegal conduct that they are often seen as being closer to conduct than to other speech.

2. Even speech that causes tangible economic loss to particular people through intimidation (and not merely persuasion) may nonetheless be constitutionally protected.

b. *Problem: Anti-Abortion Campaign*

The Crusade to Protect the Unborn decides to stop abortion in Omaha, Nebraska. It buys billboards saying "God will punish murderers for their sins"; gets its several hundred Omaha members to wear T-shirts with this slogan and to paint the slogan on their cars; and stages press conferences where it says that its goal is to "stop the butchery of innocent babies."

Shortly after the start of the campaign, a doctor is killed by a militant abortion opponent at a local abortion clinic. The killer had no ties with the Crusade. The Crusade calls a press conference at which it says that it doesn't urge others to follow in the killer's footsteps, but that it cannot condemn him any more than it could condemn a man who killed concentration camp guards in Nazi Germany. They put more effort into their T-shirt and car campaigns, and insert the word "more" between "punish" and "murderers" in red paint on the billboards.

Plaintiffs, representing an abortion clinic, a class of women who plan to seek abortions, and a class of people who work at abortion clinics, want to stop the Crusade through legal channels. Can they do this? Should they be able to? If you think the Crusaders crossed over the line into punishable threats, what do you think they may say while still remaining on the right side of the line? See *Planned Parenthood v. American Coalition of Life Activists,* 290 F.3d 1058 (9th Cir. 2002) (6-5 decision).

c. *Watts v. United States, 394 U.S. 705 (1969)*

Per curiam.

[P]etitioner was convicted of violating a 1917 statute which prohibits any person from "knowingly and willfully ... [making] any threat to take the life of or to inflict bodily harm upon the President ...."

[D]uring a public rally on the Washington Monument grounds [in 1966, t]he crowd present broke up into small discussion groups and petitioner joined a gathering scheduled to discuss police brutality. Most of those in the group were quite young, either in their teens or early twenties. Petitioner, who himself was 18 years old, entered into the discussion after one member of the group suggested that the young people present should get more education before expressing their views.

[P]etitioner responded: "They always holler at us to get an education. And now I have already received my draft classification as 1-A and I have got to report for my physical this Monday coming. I am not going. If they ever make me carry a rifle the first man I want to get in my sights is L.B.J." "They are not going to make me kill my black brothers." On the basis of this statement, the jury found that petitioner had committed a felony by knowingly and willfully threatening the President....

Threat

Certainly the statute ... is constitutional on its face. The Nation undoubtedly has a valid, even an overwhelming, interest in protecting the safety of its Chief Executive and in allowing him to perform his duties without interference from threats of physical violence.

Nevertheless, a statute such as this one, which makes criminal a form of pure speech, must be interpreted with the commands of the First Amendment clearly in mind. What is a threat must be distinguished from what is constitutionally protected speech....

[T]he statute initially requires the Government to prove a true "threat." We do not believe that the kind of political hyperbole indulged in by petitioner fits within that statutory term. For we must interpret the language Congress chose "against the background of a profound national commitment to the principle that debate on public issues should be uninhibited, robust, and wide-open, and that it may well include vehement, caustic, and sometimes unpleasantly sharp attacks on government and public officials."

True Threat

The language of the political arena ... is often vituperative, abusive, and inexact. We agree with petitioner that his only offense here was "a kind of very crude offensive method of stating a political opposition to the President." Taken in context, and regarding the expressly conditional nature of the statement and the reaction of the listeners, we do not see how it could be interpreted otherwise....

d. NAACP v. Claiborne Hardware Co., 458 U.S. 886 (1982)

Justice Stevens delivered the opinion of the Court....

[A.] [In October 1969, several Claiborne County, Miss. merchants sued to recover losses caused by a boycott by local black citizens of white-owned businesses, and to enjoin the boycott from continuing. The Mississippi Supreme Court upheld the imposition of liability on the NAACP and others, based on a tort theory of interference with economic advantage, concluding that:—ed.]

> In carrying out the agreement and design, certain of the defendants, acting for all others, engaged in acts of physical force and violence against the persons and property of certain customers and prospective customers. Intimidation, threats, social ostracism, vilification, and traduction were some of the devices used by the defendants to achieve the desired results. Most effective, also, was the stationing of guards ('enforcers,' 'deacons,' or 'black hats') in the vicinity of white-owned businesses. Unquestionably, the evidence shows that the volition of many black persons was overcome out of sheer fear, and they were forced and compelled against their personal wills to withhold their trade and business intercourse from the complainants.

On the basis of this finding, the court concluded that the entire boycott was unlawful. "If any of these factors—force, violence, or threats—is present, then the boycott is illegal regardless of whether it is primary, secondary, economical, political, social or other." {[The court also concluded] that all petitioners are liable for all losses resulting from the boycott.} ...

[B.] [In March 1966, a group of black citizens, with the unanimous support of at least 500 attendees at a local NAACP meeting, presented a petition to public officials of Port Gibson, Miss. and Claiborne County] ... call[ing] for the desegregation of all public schools and public facilities, the hiring of black policemen, public improvements in black residential areas, selection of blacks for jury duty, integration of bus stations so that blacks could use all facilities, and an end to verbal abuse by law enforcement officers. It stated that "Negroes are not to be addressed by terms as 'boy,' 'girl,' 'shine,' 'uncle,' or any other offensive term, but as 'Mr.,' 'Mrs.,' or 'Miss,' as is the case with other citizens." ... [An addendum stated:—ed.] "All stores must employ Negro clerks and cashiers." ...

A favorable response was not received. On April 1, 1966, the Claiborne County NAACP conducted another meeting at the First Baptist Church. As described by the chancellor: "Several hundred black people attended the meeting, and the purpose was to decide what action should be taken relative to the ... demands. Speeches were made by Evers and others, and a vote was taken. It was the unanimous vote of those present ... to place a boycott on the white merchants of Port Gibson and Claiborne County." ... {Although Evers' speech on April 1, 1966, was not recorded, the chancellor found: "Evers told his audience that they would be watched and that blacks who traded with white merchants would be *answerable to him.* According to Sheriff Dan McKay, who was present during the speech, Evers told the assembled black people that any 'uncle toms' who broke the boycott would 'have their necks broken' by their own people. Evers' remarks were directed to all 8,000-plus black residents of Claiborne County, and not merely the relatively few members of the Claiborne NAACP."} ... [The boycott was briefly lifted and then reimposed a few times in the following three years.—ed.]

[During the boycott, o]n April 18, 1969, a young black man named Roosevelt Jackson was shot and killed during an encounter with two Port Gibson police officers. Large crowds immediately gathered, first at the hospital and later at the church.... The local police requested reinforcements from the State Highway Patrol and sporadic acts of violence ensued. The Mayor and Board of Aldermen placed a dawn-to-dusk curfew into effect.

On April 19[, 1969], Charles Evers spoke to a group assembled at the First Baptist Church and led a march to the courthouse where he demanded the discharge of the entire Port Gibson Police Force. When this demand was refused, the boycott was reimposed on all white merchants. One of Evers' speeches on this date was recorded by the police. In that speech [http://volokh.com/firstamendment/extra.pdf] ... Evers stated that boycott violators would be "disciplined" by their own people and warned that the Sheriff could not sleep with boycott violators at night....

On April 21[, 1969], Evers gave another speech to several hundred people, in which he again called for a discharge of the police force and for a total boycott of all white-owned businesses in Claiborne County. Although this speech was not recorded, the chancellor found that Evers stated: "If we catch any of you going in any of them racist stores, we're gonna break your damn neck." ...

[C.] [C]ertain practices generally used to encourage support for the boycott were uniformly peaceful and orderly. The few marches associated with the boycott were carefully controlled by black leaders. Pickets used to advertise the boycott were often small children. The police made no arrests— and no complaints are recorded—in connection with the picketing and occasional demonstrations supporting the boycott....

One form of "discipline" of black persons who violated the boycott appears to have been employed with some regularity. Individuals stood outside of boycotted stores and identified those who traded with the merchants. Some of these "store watchers" were members of a group known as the "Black Hats" or the "Deacons."

The names of persons who violated the boycott were read at meetings of the Claiborne County NAACP and published in a mimeographed paper entitled the "Black Times." As stated by the chancellor, those persons "were branded as traitors to the black cause, called demeaning names, and socially ostracized for merely trading with whites."

The chancellor also concluded that a quite different form of discipline had been used against certain violators of the boycott. He specifically identified 10 incidents that "strikingly" revealed the "atmosphere of fear that prevailed among blacks from 1966 until 1970."

The testimony concerning four incidents convincingly demonstrates that they occurred because the victims were ignoring the boycott. In two cases, shots were fired at a house; in a third, a brick was thrown through a windshield; in the fourth, a flower garden was damaged. None of these four victims, however, ceased trading with white merchants.

The evidence concerning four other incidents is less clear, but again it indicates that an unlawful form of discipline was applied to certain boycott violators. In April 1966, a black couple named Cox asked for a police escort to go into a white-owned dry cleaner and, a week later, shots were fired into their home. In another incident, an NAACP member took a bottle of whiskey from a black man who had purchased it in a white-owned store. The third incident involved a fight between a commercial fisherman who did not observe the boycott and four men who "grabbed me and beat me up and took a gun off me." {One of his assailants testified that the incident resulted from an automobile accident, rather than the boycott.} In a fourth incident, ... a group of young blacks apparently pulled down the overalls of an elderly brick mason known as "Preacher White" and spanked him for not observing the boycott.

Two other incidents discussed by the chancellor are of less certain significance. Jasper Coleman testified that ... all four tires of his pickup truck had been slashed with a knife. Coleman testified that he did not participate in the boycott but was never threatened for refusing to do so. Finally, Willie Myles testified that he and his wife received a threatening phone call and that a boy on a barge told him that he would be whipped for buying his gas at the wrong place.

Five of these incidents occurred in 1966. The other five are not dated. The chancellor thus did not find that any act of violence occurred after 1966. In particular, he made no reference to any act of violence or threat of violence—with the exception, of course, of Charles Evers' speeches—after the shootings of Martin Luther King, Jr., in 1968 or Roosevelt Jackson in 1969....

[D.] [The Court reaffirmed that demonstrations, meetings, and picketing were constitutionally protected.—ed.] In addition, names of boycott violators were read aloud at meetings at the First Baptist Church and published in a local black newspaper. Petitioners admittedly sought to persuade others to join the boycott through social pressure and the "threat" of social ostracism.

Speech does not lose its protected character, however, simply because it may embarrass others or coerce them into action.... "[The First Amendment] extends to more than abstract discussion, unrelated to action. [It] is a charter for government, not for an institution of learning. 'Free trade in ideas' means free trade in the opportunity to persuade to action, not merely to describe facts." ... "The claim that the expressions were intended to exercise a coercive impact ... does not remove them from the reach of the First Amendment. Petitioners plainly intended to influence [people's] conduct by their activities; this is not fundamentally different from the function of a newspaper...." *Organization for a Better Austin v. Keefe*.... Through speech, assembly, and petition—rather than through riot or revolution—petitioners sought to change a social order that had consistently treated them as second-class citizens....

[The Court recognized that some purely economic boycotts may properly be punished by labor law and antitrust law, but distinguished this case as follows:—ed.] This Court has recognized the strong governmental interest in certain forms of economic regulation, even though such regulation may have an incidental effect on rights of speech and association. See *Giboney v. Empire Storage & Ice Co.*.... [But i]t is not disputed that a major purpose of the boycott in this case was to influence governmental action....

[P]etitioners certainly foresaw—and directly intended—that the merchants would sustain economic injury as a result of their campaign. Unlike [in purely economically motivated boycotts], however, the purpose of petitioners' campaign was not to destroy legitimate competition. Petitioners sought to vindicate rights of equality and of freedom that lie at the heart of the Fourteenth Amendment itself. The right of the States to regulate economic activity could not justify a complete prohibition against a nonviolent, politically motivated boycott designed to force governmental and economic change and to effectuate rights guaranteed by the Constitution itself....

[E.] The First Amendment does not protect violence…. No federal rule of law restricts a State from imposing tort liability for business losses that are caused by violence and by threats of violence. When such conduct occurs in the context of constitutionally protected activity, however, "precision of regulation" is demanded…. While the State legitimately may impose damages for the consequences of violent conduct, it may not award compensation for the consequences of nonviolent, protected activity….

Respondents … argue that liability may be imposed on individuals who were either "store watchers" or members of the "Black Hats." There is nothing unlawful in standing outside a store and recording names. Similarly, there is nothing unlawful in wearing black hats, although such apparel may cause apprehension in others…. [M]ere association with either group—absent a specific intent to further an unlawful aim embraced by that group—is an insufficient predicate for liability. At the same time, [those individuals who committed acts of violence] … may be held responsible for the injuries that they caused; a judgment tailored to the consequences of their unlawful conduct may be sustained….

[F.] To the extent that [Charles] Evers caused respondents to suffer business losses through his organization of the boycott, his emotional and persuasive appeals for unity in the joint effort, or his "threats" of vilification or social ostracism, Evers' conduct is constitutionally protected and beyond the reach of a damages award. Respondents point to Evers' speeches, however, as justification for the chancellor's damages award. Since respondents would impose liability on the basis of a public address—which predominantly contained highly charged political rhetoric lying at the core of the First Amendment we approach this suggested basis of liability with extreme care….

While many of the comments in Evers' speeches might have contemplated "discipline" in the permissible form of social ostracism, it cannot be denied that references to the possibility that necks would be broken and to the fact that the Sheriff could not sleep with boycott violators at night implicitly conveyed a sterner message. In the passionate atmosphere in which the speeches were delivered, they might have been understood as inviting an unlawful form of discipline or, at least, as intending to create a fear of violence whether or not improper discipline was specifically intended….

[M]ere advocacy of the use of force or violence does not remove speech from the protection of the First Amendment. [*Brandenburg v. Ohio*]…. The emotionally charged rhetoric of Charles Evers' speeches did not transcend the bounds of protected speech set forth in *Brandenburg*. The lengthy addresses generally contained an impassioned plea for black citizens to unify, to support and respect each other, and to realize the political and economic power available to them. In the course of those pleas, strong language was used.

If that language had been followed by acts of violence, a substantial question would be presented whether Evers could be held liable for the consequences of that unlawful conduct. In this case, however—with the possible exception of the Cox incident—the acts of violence identified in 1966 occurred weeks or months after the April 1, 1966 speech; the chancellor made no finding of any violence after the challenged 1969 speech.

Strong and effective extemporaneous rhetoric cannot be nicely channeled in purely dulcet phrases. An advocate must be free to stimulate his audience with spontaneous and emotional appeals for unity and action in a common cause. When such appeals do not incite lawless action, they must be regarded as protected speech. To rule otherwise would ignore the "profound national commitment" that "debate on public issues should be uninhibited, robust, and wide-open." For these reasons, we conclude that Evers' addresses did not exceed the bounds of protected speech....

[G.] A massive and prolonged effort to change the social, political, and economic structure of a local environment cannot be characterized as a violent conspiracy simply by reference to the ephemeral consequences of relatively few violent acts. Such a characterization must be supported by findings that adequately disclose the evidentiary basis for concluding that specific parties agreed to use unlawful means, that carefully identify the impact of such unlawful conduct, and that recognize the importance of avoiding the imposition of punishment for constitutionally protected activity.

The burden of demonstrating that fear rather than protected conduct was the dominant force in the movement is heavy. A court must be wary of a claim that the true color of a forest is better revealed by reptiles hidden in the weeds than by the foliage of countless freestanding trees....

e.   *Virginia v. Black, 538 U.S. 343 (2003)*

Justice O'Connor ... delivered the opinion of the Court with respects to Part [A, B, and C], and an opinion with respect to [Part D], in which ... Chief Justice [Rehnquist], Justice Stevens, and Justice Breyer join....

[W]hile a State ... may ban cross burning carried out with the intent to intimidate, ... [it may not treat every instance of] cross burning as prima facie evidence of intent to intimidate ....

[A.] Respondents Barry Black, Richard Elliott, and Jonathan O'Mara were convicted separately of violating Virginia's cross-burning statute, Va. Code Ann. § 18.2-423 ...:

> It shall be [a felony] for any person or persons, with the intent of intimidating any person or group of persons, to burn, or cause to be burned, a cross on the property of another, a highway or other public place....
>
> Any such burning of a cross shall be prima facie evidence of an intent to intimidate a person or group of persons....

Barry Black led a Ku Klux Klan rally in Carroll County, Virginia. Twenty-five to thirty people attended this gathering, which occurred on private property with the permission of the owner, who was in attendance. The property was located on an open field just off [a road] .... [A]bout 40 to 50 cars passed the site [in an hour] .... Eight to ten houses were located in the vicinity of the rally. Rebecca Sechrist, who was related to the owner of the property where the rally took place, "sat and watched to see wha[t] [was] going on" from the lawn of her in-laws' house....

During the rally, Sechrist heard Klan members speak about "what they were" and "what they believed in." The speakers "talked real bad about the blacks and the Mexicans." One speaker told the assembled gathering that "he would love to take a .30/.30 and just random[ly] shoot the blacks." The speakers also talked about "President Clinton and Hillary Clinton," and about how their tax money "goes to ... the black people." Sechrist testified that this language made her "very ... scared."

At the conclusion of the rally, the crowd circled around a 25- to 30-foot cross. The cross was between 300 and 350 yards away from the road.... As the cross burned, the Klan played Amazing Grace over the loudspeakers. Sechrist stated that the cross burning made her feel "awful" ....

Black was charged with burning a cross with the intent of intimidating a person or group of persons, in violation of § 18.2-423. At his trial, the jury was instructed that "intent to intimidate means the motivation to intentionally put a person or a group of persons in fear of bodily harm. Such fear must arise from the willful conduct of the accused rather than from some mere temperamental timidity of the victim." The trial court also instructed the jury that "the burning of a cross by itself is sufficient evidence from which you may infer the required intent." ... The jury found Black guilty ....

[R]espondents Richard Elliott and Jonathan O'Mara ... attempted to burn a cross on the yard of James Jubilee. Jubilee, an African-American, was Elliott's next-door neighbor in Virginia Beach, Virginia. Four months prior to the incident, Jubilee and his family had moved from California to Virginia Beach. Before the cross burning, Jubilee spoke to Elliott's mother to inquire about shots being fired from behind the Elliott home. Elliott's mother explained to Jubilee that her son shot firearms as a hobby, and that he used the backyard as a firing range....

[Respondents'] apparent motive was to "get back" at Jubilee for complaining about the shooting in the backyard. Respondents were not affiliated with the Klan. The next morning, as Jubilee was pulling his car out of the driveway, he noticed the partially burned cross approximately 20 feet from his house. After seeing the cross, Jubilee was "very nervous" because he "didn't know what would be the next phase," and because "a cross burned in your yard ... tells you that it's just the first round."

Elliott and O'Mara were charged with attempted cross burning .... O'Mara pleaded guilty ..., reserving the right to challenge the constitutionality of the cross-burning statute....

At Elliott's trial, ... the court instructed the jury that the Commonwealth must prove that "the defendant intended to commit cross burning," that "the defendant did a direct act toward the commission of the cross burning," and that "the defendant had the intent of intimidating any person or group of persons." The court did not instruct the jury on the meaning of the word "intimidate," nor on the prima facie evidence provision of § 18.2-423. The jury found Elliott guilty ....

[B.] From [the early 1900s], cross burnings have been used to communicate both threats of violence and messages of shared ideology.... Often, the [Ku Klux] Klan used cross burnings as a tool of intimidation and a threat of impending violence. [The Court gave examples in which the Klan targeted mostly blacks but also civil rights supporters, Jews, and union members.—ed.] These cross burnings embodied threats to people whom the Klan deemed antithetical to its goals. And these threats had special force given the long history of Klan violence....

[C]ross burnings have also remained potent symbols of shared group identity and ideology. The burning cross became a symbol of the Klan itself and a central feature of Klan gatherings.... To this day, regardless of whether the message is a political one or whether the message is also meant to intimidate, the burning of a cross is a "symbol of hate."

And while cross burning sometimes carries no intimidating message, at other times the intimidating message is the *only* message conveyed. For example, when a cross burning is directed at a particular person not affiliated with the Klan, the burning cross often serves as a message of intimidation, designed to inspire in the victim a fear of bodily harm.

Moreover, the history of violence associated with the Klan shows that the possibility of injury or death is not just hypothetical. The person who burns a cross directed at a particular person often is making a serious threat, meant to coerce the victim to comply with the Klan's wishes unless the victim is willing to risk the wrath of the Klan. Indeed, as the cases of respondents Elliott and O'Mara indicate, individuals without Klan affiliation who wish to threaten or menace another person sometimes use cross burning because of this association between a burning cross and violence.

In sum, while a burning cross does not inevitably convey a message of intimidation, often the cross burner intends that the recipients of the message fear for their lives. And when a cross burning is used to intimidate, few if any messages are more powerful....

[C.] [T]he First Amendment ... permits a State to ban a "true threat." "True threats" encompass those statements where the speaker means to communicate a serious expression of an intent to commit an act of unlawful violence to a particular individual or group of individuals.

The speaker need not actually intend to carry out the threat. Rather, a prohibition on true threats "protect[s] individuals from the fear of violence" and "from the disruption that fear engenders," in addition to protecting people "from the possibility that the threatened violence will occur." Intimidation in the constitutionally proscribable sense of the word is a type of true threat, where a speaker directs a threat to a person or group of persons with the intent of placing the victim in fear of bodily harm or death.... [S]ome cross burnings fit within this meaning of intimidating speech ....

[D (joined only by Chief Justice Rehnquist and Justices Stevens and Breyer).] ... The court in Barry Black's case ... instructed the jury that the [prima facie evidence] provision means: "The burning of a cross, by itself, is sufficient evidence from which you may infer the required intent." ...

As construed by the jury instruction, the prima facie provision ["any such burning of a cross shall be prima facie evidence of an intent to intimidate a person or group of persons"] strips away the very reason why a State may ban cross burning with the intent to intimidate. The prima facie evidence provision permits a jury to convict in every cross-burning case in which defendants exercise their constitutional right not to put on a defense. And even where a defendant like Black presents a defense, the prima facie evidence provision makes it more likely that the jury will find an intent to intimidate regardless of the particular facts of the case. The provision permits the Commonwealth to arrest, prosecute, and convict a person based solely on the fact of cross burning itself.

It is apparent that the provision as so interpreted "would create an unacceptable risk of the suppression of ideas." ... As the history of cross burning indicates, a burning cross is not always intended to intimidate. Rather, sometimes the cross burning is a statement of ideology, a symbol of group solidarity. It is a ritual used at Klan gatherings, and it is used to represent the Klan itself. Thus, "[b]urning a cross at a political rally would almost certainly be protected expression."

Indeed, occasionally a person who burns a cross does not intend to express either a statement of ideology or intimidation. Cross burnings have appeared in movies such as Mississippi Burning, and in plays such as the stage adaptation of Sir Walter Scott's The Lady of the Lake.

The prima facie provision makes no effort to distinguish among these different types of cross burnings. It does not distinguish between a cross burning done with the purpose of creating anger or resentment and a cross burning done with the purpose of threatening or intimidating a victim. It does not distinguish between a cross burning at a public rally or a cross burning on a neighbor's lawn. It does not treat the cross burning directed at an individual differently from the cross burning directed at a group of like-minded believers.

It allows a jury to treat a cross burning on the property of another with the owner's acquiescence in the same manner as a cross burning on the property of another without the owner's permission. To this extent [we] agree with Justice Souter [see p. 326 below—ed.] that the prima facie evidence provision can "skew jury deliberations toward conviction in cases where the evidence of intent to intimidate is relatively weak and arguably consistent with a solely ideological reason for burning."

It may be true that a cross burning, even at a political rally, arouses a sense of anger or hatred among the vast majority of citizens who see a burning cross. But this sense of anger or hatred is not sufficient to ban all cross burnings.... The prima facie evidence provision in this case ignores all of the contextual factors that are necessary to decide whether a particular cross burning is intended to intimidate. The First Amendment does not permit such a shortcut.

For these reasons, the prima facie evidence provision, as interpreted through the jury instruction and as applied in Barry Black's case, is unconstitutional on its face.... [T]he provision makes the statute facially invalid at this point.... We ... leave open the possibility that the provision is severable, and if so, [that] Elliott and O'Mara could be retried under § 18.2-423 [without the prima facie evidence provision]....

Justice Scalia, concurring in part and dissenting in part. [Omitted.—ed.]

Justice Souter, with whom Justice Kennedy and Justice Ginsburg join, concurring in the judgment in part and dissent in part. [This opinion, excerpted at p. 325, focused on whether the law may single out cross-burning threats for special punishment.—ed.]

Justice Thomas, dissenting....

In our culture, cross burning has almost invariably meant lawlessness and understandably instills in its victims well-grounded fear of physical violence....

[A] series of cross burnings in Virginia took place between 1949 and 1952. Most of the crosses were burned on the lawns of black families, who either were business owners or lived in predominantly white neighborhoods. At least one of the cross burnings was accompanied by a shooting.... These incidents were, in the words of the time, "*terroristic [sic]* and un-American act[s], designed to *intimidate* Negroes from seeking their rights as citizens."

In February 1952, in light of this series of cross burnings and attendant reports that the Klan, "long considered dead in Virginia, is being revitalized in Richmond," Governor Battle announced that "Virginia 'might well consider passing legislation to restrict the activities of the Ku Klux Klan.'" As newspapers reported at the time, the bill was "to ban the burning of crosses and other similar evidences of *terrorism*" (emphasis added). The bill was presented to the House of Delegates by a former FBI agent and future two-term Governor, Delegate Mills E. Godwin, Jr. "Godwin said law and order in the State were impossible if organized groups could *create fear by intimidation*" (emphasis added)....

The ban on cross burning with intent to intimidate demonstrates that even segregationists [who controlled the Virginia Legislature in the 1950s] understood the difference between intimidating and terroristic conduct and racist expression. It is simply beyond belief that, in passing the statute now under review, the Virginia Legislature was concerned with anything but penalizing conduct it must have viewed as particularly vicious.

Accordingly, this statute prohibits only conduct, not expression. And, just as one cannot burn down someone's house to make a political point and then seek refuge in the First Amendment, those who hate cannot terrorize and intimidate to make their point....

f.   Policy—Countervailing Private Rights, see p. 92

G. Exceptions from Protection—Speech Owned by Others

a. Summary

Rule: Various "intellectual property" rights—especially copyright, trademark, and the right of publicity—are speech restrictions: They bar people from printing or broadcasting the words, images, or sounds that they want to communicate, if that communication is sufficiently similar to the protected intellectual property. The Court has held that:

1. Copyright law is a constitutionally permissible speech restriction. *Harper & Row v. Nation Enterprises* (1985) (p. 237).

2. A specific kind of right of publicity law, which gives a performer a right to stop broadcasts of his entire act, is a constitutionally permissible speech restriction. *Zacchini v. Scripps-Howard Broadcasting Co.* (1977) (p. 241). The Court noted that it didn't have to consider the more common right of publicity statutes that give people the exclusive right to commercial exploitation of their names, likenesses, and voices.

3. The Court has also upheld some rather broad trademark-like rules, but only as to commercial advertising, which is less protected than other speech (see Part II.H, p. 243).

The court has never articulated a rule for which intellectual property rights are constitutional and which aren't. For now, the arguments have to be made by comparing and contrasting with *Harper & Row* and *Zacchini*.

Policy explanations:

1. What are the possible arguments justifying intellectual property laws?

a. Using others' intellectual property *unfairly profits* from the hard work of others, unjustly enriching the copier.

b. Using others' intellectual property *unfairly competes* with the property owners, unjustly impoverishing them.

c. Using others' intellectual property *diminishes the incentive* to produce more such works, impoverishing all of us. Restrictions on infringing speech can thus actually enrich the speech marketplace: As *Harper & Row* puts it, "copyright itself [is] the engine of free expression."

d. Using others' intellectual property is *immoral regardless of the economics*, because authors have a basic moral right to control their creations or their names and likenesses.

2. What makes intellectual property law more tolerable than other speech restrictions aimed at avoiding even greater harms? *Harper & Row* stresses that people may still copy the underlying ideas or facts, and even copy some of the words under "fair use," so people still have ample channels for expressing themselves about the topic.

Policy arguments inferable from this:

1. Sometimes speech can be restricted even based on rather speculative

and indirect risk of harm—and not very great harm at that—where private rights of third parties are involved.

2. Sometimes, contrary to *Cohen v. California*, courts can distinguish between laws that suppress ideas and laws that only suppress particular expressions of those ideas.

b. Problem: Commercial Use of Name or Likeness

Consider five situations:

1. Gary Saderup makes and sells T-shirts and prints of charcoal drawings of the Three Stooges. *Comedy III Productions v. Gary Saderup, Inc.*, 21 P.3d 797 (Cal. 2001).

2. American Heritage Products makes and sells busts of Martin Luther King, Jr. *Martin Luther King, Jr. Center for Social Change v. American Heritage Prods., Inc.*, 250 Ga. 135 (1982).

3. NBC makes and shows an unauthorized biography of Elizabeth Taylor. *Taylor v. NBC*, 1994 WL 780690 (Cal. Super.).

4. Todd McFarlane draws and markets comic books in which one character, a Mafia don returned from the dead with the Devil's help, is named Tony Twist; McFarlane publicly says the name is borrowed from Tony Twist, the name of a St. Louis Blues hockey player known for his aggressive play. Compare *Doe v. TCI Cablevision*, 110 S.W.3d 363 (Mo. 2003), with *Winters v. D.C. Comics*, 69 P.3d 473 (Cal. 2003).

5. C.B.C. Distribution creates and markets a fantasy baseball online game, in which players can organize fantasy teams out of real players. The game uses the players' names and playing statistics. *C.B.C. Distribution & Marketing, Inc. v. Major League Baseball Advanced Media, L.P.*, 505 F.3d 818 (8th Cir. 2007).

The people whose names or likenesses are being used sue, under a state law "right of publicity" tort that makes actionable "us[ing] plaintiff's name [or likeness] ... without consent and with the intent to obtain a commercial advantage." How would (and should) the cases be decided?

c. Problem: Copyright Remedies

Your client, Arvin Tseng, publishes a book; Vicki Levin sues, claiming that parts of Arvin's book are substantially similar in their expression (though not literally identical) to Vicki's book. Arvin's defense—on which he has the burden of proof, since it's an affirmative defense—is that those parts of his book are a fair use of Vicki's book, since they parody her work.

The jury decides in Vicki's favor. Under the Copyright Act, a successful plaintiff can choose either actual damages or statutorily defined damages, which are set at $200 to $30,000 for innocent infringements, $750 to $30,000 for negligent infringements, and $750 to $150,000 for willful infringements. Vicki asks for statutory damages, since her actual damages are hard to prove. The jury finds Arvin was negligent, and awards Vicki $30,000 in statutory damages. Arvin hires you to challenge the verdict.

What arguments can you make, and what arguments should you expect the other side to make in response?

d. *Harper & Row v. Nation Enterprises, 471 U.S. 539 (1985)*

Justice O'Connor delivered the opinion of the Court....

[A.] [F]ormer President Gerald R. Ford contracted with ... Harper & Row ... to publish his as yet unwritten memoirs. The memoirs were to contain "significant hitherto unpublished material" concerning the Watergate crisis, Mr. Ford's pardon of former President Nixon and "Mr. Ford's reflections on this period of history, and the morality and personalities involved." ... [T]he agreement [also] gave petitioners the exclusive right to license prepublication excerpts, known in the trade as "first serial rights."

[In 1979], as the memoirs [titled "A Time to Heal"] were nearing completion, petitioners negotiated a prepublication licensing agreement with Time, a weekly news magazine. Time agreed to pay $25,000, $12,500 in advance and an additional $12,500 at publication, in exchange for the right to excerpt 7,500 words from Mr. Ford's account of the Nixon pardon. The issue featuring the excerpts was timed to appear approximately one week before shipment of the full length book version to bookstores. Exclusivity was an important consideration ....

Two to three weeks before the Time article's scheduled release, an unidentified person secretly brought a copy of the Ford manuscript to Victor Navasky, editor of The Nation, a political commentary magazine. Mr. Navasky knew that his possession of the manuscript was not authorized and that the manuscript must be returned quickly to his "source" to avoid discovery. He hastily put together what he believed was "a real hot news story" composed of quotes, paraphrases, and facts drawn exclusively from the manuscript. Mr. Navasky attempted no independent commentary, research or criticism, in part because of the need for speed if he was to "make news" by "publish[ing] in advance of publication of the Ford book." ... As a result of The Nation's [2,250-word] article, Time canceled its piece and refused to pay the remaining $12,500.

Petitioners brought suit ..., alleging ... violations of the Copyright Act.... The court awarded actual damages of $12,500....

[B.] Article I, § 8, of the Constitution provides: "The Congress shall have Power ... to Promote the Progress of Science and useful Arts, by securing for limited Times to Authors and Inventors the exclusive Right to their respective Writings and Discoveries." ... "[This] limited grant ... is intended to motivate the creative activity of authors and inventors by the provision of a special reward, and to allow the public access to the products of their genius after the limited period of exclusive control has expired." "The monopoly created by copyright thus rewards the individual author in order to benefit the public."

This principle applies equally to works of fiction and nonfiction. The book at issue here, for example, was two years in the making, and began with a contract giving the author's copyright to the publishers in exchange for their services in producing and marketing the work.... [T]he monopoly granted by copyright actively served its intended purpose of inducing the creation of new material of potential historical value....

Under the Copyright Act, [certain exclusive] rights—to publish, copy, and distribute the author's work—vest in the author ... [and are commonly sold] to publishers who offer royalties in exchange for their services in producing and marketing the author's work. The copyright owner's rights, however, are subject to certain statutory exceptions. Among these is § 107 which codifies the traditional privilege of other authors to make "fair use" of an earlier writer's work. In addition, no author may copyright facts or ideas. The copyright is limited to those aspects of the work—termed "expression"— that display the stamp of the author's originality....

The Nation ... lift[ed] verbatim quotes of the author's original language totaling between 300 and 400 words and constituting some 13% of The Nation article. In using generous verbatim excerpts of Mr. Ford's unpublished manuscript to lend authenticity to its account of the forthcoming memoirs, The Nation effectively arrogated to itself the right of first publication, an important marketable subsidiary right. For the reasons set forth below, we find that this use of the copyrighted manuscript, even stripped to the verbatim quotes conceded by The Nation to be copyrightable expression, was not a fair use within the meaning of the Copyright Act....

[C.] Respondents ... contend that First Amendment values require [that their speech be protected against liability].... Respondents explain their copying of Mr. Ford's expression as essential to reporting the news story it claims the book itself represents. In respondents' view, not only the facts contained in Mr. Ford's memoirs, but "the precise manner in which [he] expressed himself [were] as newsworthy as what he had to say." Respondents argue that the public's interest in learning this news as fast as possible outweighs the right of the author to control its first publication....

[C]opyright's idea/expression dichotomy "strike[s] a definitional balance between the First Amendment and the Copyright Act by permitting free communication of facts while still protecting an author's expression." No author may copyright his ideas or the facts he narrates.... But copyright assures those who write and publish factual narratives such as "A Time to Heal" that they may at least enjoy the right to market the original expression contained therein as just compensation for their investment.

{"[Respondent] possessed an unfettered right to use any factual information revealed in [the memoirs] for the purpose of enlightening its audience, but it can claim no need to 'bodily appropriate' [Mr. Ford's] 'expression' of that information by utilizing portions of the actual [manuscript]. The public interest in the free flow of information is assured by the law's refusal to recognize a valid copyright in facts." ...}

Respondents' theory, however, would ... effectively destroy any expectation of copyright protection in the work of a public figure. Absent such protection, there would be little incentive to create or profit in financing such memoirs, and the public would be denied an important source of significant historical information. The promise of copyright would be an empty one if it could be avoided merely by dubbing the infringement a fair use "news report" of the book....

In our haste to disseminate news, it should not be forgotten that the Framers intended copyright itself to be the engine of free expression. By establishing a marketable right to the use of one's expression, copyright supplies the economic incentive to create and disseminate ideas....

It is fundamentally at odds with the scheme of copyright to accord lesser rights in those works that are of greatest importance to the public. Such a notion ignores the major premise of copyright and injures author and public alike. "[T]o propose that fair use be imposed whenever the 'social value [of dissemination] ... outweighs any detriment to the artist,' would be to propose depriving copyright owners of their right in the property precisely when they encounter those users who could afford to pay for it." ... "If every volume that was in the public interest could be pirated away by a competing publisher, ... the public [soon] would have nothing worth reading."

Moreover, freedom of thought and expression "includes both the right to speak freely and the right to refrain from speaking at all." *Wooley v. Maynard*. We do not suggest this right not to speak would sanction abuse of the copyright owner's monopoly as an instrument to suppress facts. But ... "[t]he essential thrust of the First Amendment is to prohibit improper restraints on the *voluntary* public expression of ideas; it shields the man who wants to speak or publish when others wish him to be quiet. There is necessarily, and within suitably defined areas, a concomitant freedom not to speak publicly, one which serves the same ultimate end as freedom of speech in its affirmative aspect." ... [C]opyright, and the right of first publication in particular, serve this countervailing First Amendment value.

In view of the First Amendment protections already embodied in the Copyright Act's distinction between copyrightable expression and uncopyrightable facts and ideas, and the latitude for scholarship and comment traditionally afforded by fair use, we see no warrant for expanding the doctrine of fair use to create what amounts to a public figure exception to copyright. Whether verbatim copying from a public figure's manuscript in a given case is or is not fair must be judged according to the traditional equities of fair use....

[D.] [Under 17 U.S.C. § 107,]

{[T]he fair use of a copyrighted work ... for purposes such as criticism, comment, news reporting, teaching (including multiple copies for classroom use), scholarship, or research, is not an infringement of copyright. In determining whether the use made of a work in any particular case is a fair use the factors to be considered shall include—

(1) the purpose and character of the use, including whether such use is of a commercial nature or is for nonprofit educational purposes;

(2) the nature of the copyrighted work;

(3) the amount and substantiality of the portion used in relation to the copyrighted work as a whole; and

(4) the effect of the use upon the potential market for or value of the

copyrighted work.}

Purpose of the Use.... News reporting is one of the examples enumerated in § 107 to "give some idea of the sort of activities the courts might regard as fair use under the circumstances." ... [But] that an article arguably is "news" and therefore a productive use is simply one factor ....

[T]hat a {user stands to profit from exploitation of the copyrighted material without paying the customary price} as opposed to [being a nonprofit user] is a separate factor that tends to weigh against a finding of fair use.... [Moreover,] The Nation's use had not merely the incidental effect but the *intended purpose* of supplanting the copyright holder's commercially valuable right of first publication [by scooping the forthcoming abstracts]....

Nature of the Copyrighted Work.... The law generally recognizes a greater need to disseminate factual works than works of fiction or fantasy.... Some of the briefer quotes from the memoirs are arguably necessary adequately to convey the facts; for example, Mr. Ford's characterization of the White House tapes as the "smoking gun" is perhaps so integral to the idea expressed as to be inseparable from it. But The Nation did not stop at isolated phrases and instead excerpted subjective descriptions and portraits of public figures whose power lies in the author's individualized expression. Such use, focusing on the most expressive elements of the work, exceeds that necessary to disseminate the facts....

[T]hat a work is unpublished is a critical element of its "nature." ... While even substantial quotations might qualify as fair use in a review of a published work or a news account of a speech that had been delivered to the public or disseminated to the press, the author's right to control the first public appearance of his expression weighs against such use of the work before its release....

Amount and Substantiality of the Portion Used.... In absolute terms, the words actually quoted were an insubstantial portion of "A Time to Heal." The District Court, however, found that "[T]he Nation took what was essentially the heart of the book." ... A Time editor described the chapters on the pardon as "the most interesting and moving parts of the entire manuscript."

The portions actually quoted were selected by Mr. Navasky as among the most powerful passages in those chapters. He testified that he used verbatim excerpts because simply reciting the information could not adequately convey the "absolute certainty with which [Ford] expressed himself"; or show that "this comes from President Ford"; or carry the "definitive quality" of the original. In short, he quoted these passages precisely because they qualitatively embodied Ford's distinctive expression....

Effect on the Market [or Value of the Work].... This last factor is undoubtedly the single most important element of fair use. "Fair use, when properly applied, is limited to copying by others which does not materially impair the marketability of the work which is copied." The trial court found not merely a potential but an actual effect on the market. Time's cancellation of its projected serialization and its refusal to pay the $12,500 were the direct effect of the infringement....

Placed in a broader perspective, a fair use doctrine that permits extensive prepublication quotations from an unreleased manuscript without the copyright owner's consent poses substantial potential for damage to the marketability of first serialization rights in general. "Isolated instances of minor infringements, when multiplied many times, become in the aggregate a major inroad on copyright that must be prevented." [The Court concluded the use wasn't fair, and the Nation was thus liable.—ed.] ...

Justice Brennan, with whom Justice White and Justice Marshall join, dissenting....

Copyright[, by not protecting even laboriously uncovered facts,] does not protect that which is often of most value in a work of history, and courts must resist the tendency to reject the fair use defense on the basis of their feeling that an author of history has been deprived of the full value of his or her labor....

The urge to compensate for subsequent use of information and ideas is perhaps understandable. An inequity seems to lurk in the idea that much of the fruit of the historian's labor may be used without compensation.

This, however, is not some unforeseen byproduct of a statutory scheme intended primarily to ensure a return for works of the imagination.... [The distinction between copyright-protected expression and unprotected facts] is at the essence of copyright. The copyright laws serve as the "engine of free expression" only when the statutory monopoly does not choke off multifarious indirect uses and consequent broad dissemination of information and ideas. To ensure the progress of arts and sciences and the integrity of First Amendment values, ideas and information must not be freighted with claims of proprietary right.

{This congressional limitation on the scope of copyright does not threaten the production of history. That this limitation results in significant diminution of economic incentives is far from apparent. In any event noneconomic incentives motivate much historical research and writing. For example, former public officials often have great incentive to "tell their side of the story." And much history is the product of academic scholarship. Perhaps most importantly, the urge to preserve the past is as old as humankind.}

In my judgment, the Court's fair use analysis has fallen to the temptation to find copyright violation based on a minimal use of literary form in order to provide compensation for the appropriation of information from a work of history.... [The dissent's application of § 107 is omitted.—ed.] ...

e.   *Zacchini v. Scripps-Howard Broad. Co., 433 U.S. 562 (1977)*

Justice White delivered the opinion of the Court....

[A.] Hugo Zacchini ... performs a "human cannonball" act in which he is shot from a cannon into a net some 200 feet away. Each performance occupies some 15 seconds.... [P]etitioner was engaged to perform his act on a regular basis [in a fenced area] at the Geauga County Fair ....

[A] freelance reporter ... videotaped the entire act [over Zacchini's express objection]. This film clip, approximately 15 seconds in length, was shown on the 11 o'clock news program that night, together with favorable commentary. Petitioner then brought this action for damages ....

[B.] If ... respondent had merely reported that petitioner was performing at the fair and described or commented on his act, with or without showing his picture on television, we would have a very different case. But ... respondent filmed [Zacchini's] entire act and displayed that film on television for the public to see and enjoy....

The Ohio Supreme Court agreed that [under Ohio law] petitioner had "a right of publicity" that gave him "personal control over commercial display and exploitation of his personality and the exercise of his talents[,]" ... [but the court] held that the challenged invasion was [protected by the First Amendment] .... {[T]he case before us is more limited than the broad category of lawsuits that may arise under the heading of "appropriation." Petitioner does not merely assert that some general use, such as advertising, was made of his name or likeness; he relies on the much narrower claim that respondent televised an entire act that he ordinarily gets paid to perform.} ...

Wherever the line in particular situations is to be drawn between media reports that are protected and those that are not, we are quite sure that the First and Fourteenth Amendments do not immunize the media when they broadcast a performer's entire act without his consent. The Constitution no more prevents a State from requiring respondent to compensate petitioner for broadcasting his act on television than it would privilege respondent to film and broadcast a copyrighted dramatic work without liability to the copyright owner, or to film and broadcast a prize fight or a baseball game where the promoters or the participants had other plans for publicizing the event....

The broadcast of a film of petitioner's entire act poses a substantial threat to the economic value of that performance.... [T]his act is the product of petitioner's own talents and energy, the end result of much time, effort, and expense. Much of its economic value lies in the "right of exclusive control over the publicity given to his performance"; if the public can see the act free on television, it will be less willing to pay to see it at the fair. The effect of a public broadcast of the performance is similar to preventing petitioner from charging an admission fee. {It is possible, of course, that respondent's news broadcast increased the value of petitioner's performance by stimulating the public's interest in seeing the act live. In these circumstances, petitioner would not be able to prove damages and thus would not recover. But petitioner has alleged that the broadcast injured him to the extent of $25,000, and we think the State should be allowed to authorize compensation of this injury if proved.}

"The rationale for [protecting the right of publicity] is the straight-forward one of preventing unjust enrichment by the theft of good will. No social purpose is served by having the defendant get free some aspect of the plaintiff that would have market value and for which he would normally pay." Moreover, the broadcast of petitioner's entire performance, unlike the unauthorized use of another's name for purposes of trade or the incidental use of a name or picture by the press, goes to the heart of petitioner's ability to earn a living as an entertainer....

Ohio's decision to protect petitioner's right of publicity here ... [also] provides an economic incentive for him to make the investment required to produce a performance of interest to the public. This same consideration underlies the patent and copyright laws long enforced by this Court.... The Constitution does not prevent Ohio from making a similar choice here in deciding to protect the entertainer's incentive in order to encourage the production of this type of work....

[E]ntertainment, as well as news, enjoys First Amendment protection. It is also true that entertainment itself can be important news. But ... neither the public nor respondent will be deprived of the benefit of petitioner's performance as long as his commercial stake in his act is appropriately recognized. Petitioner does not seek to enjoin the broadcast of his performance; he simply wants to be paid for it....

Justice Powell, with whom Justice Brennan and Justice Marshall join, dissenting. [Omitted.—ed.]

[Justice Stevens dissented on procedural grounds.—ed.]

f. *Policy—Constitutional Tension Method, see p. 42*

g. *Policy—Countervailing Private Rights, see p. 178*

h. *Policy—Alternative Channels Available to Speakers, see p. 217*

H. DIMINISHED PROTECTION—COMMERCIAL ADVERTISING

1. THE BASIC TEST

a. *Summary*

Rule: "Commercial speech"—more properly called commercial *advertising*—is less protected than other kinds of speech:

Less protected

1. False commercial advertising can be punished (even if it's said without "actual malice" or even without negligence).

2. Misleading commercial advertising can be punished (misleading political speech generally cannot be).

a. Courts scrutinize with some care claims that a particular kind of speech is inherently misleading. See, *e.g.*, *Peel v. Attorney Reg. & Discip. Comm'n* (1990) (p. 261).

b. While "[actually or inherently m]isleading advertising may be prohibited entirely," the government "may not place an absolute prohibition on certain types of potentially misleading information ... if the information also may be presented in a way that is not deceptive." *Peel*; *In re R.M.J.*, 455 U.S. 191, 203 (1982).

c. The government may generally require disclosures aimed at keeping consumers from being misled, even if such disclosures couldn't be required for political speech. *Zauderer v. Office of Disciplinary Counsel*, 471 U.S. 626 (1985).

3. Commercial advertising concerning unlawful activities can be punished (even if the *Brandenburg v. Ohio* incitement criteria aren't met).

4. Other commercial advertising may be restricted if

a. the restriction is justified by a *substantial* government interest

— Preventing undue pressure on the customer is a substantial interest. *Ohralik v. Ohio State Bar Ass'n* (1978) (p. 256).

— So are promoting energy conservation and ensuring that utility rates are fair and efficient. *Central Hudson Gas & Elec. v. Public Serv. Comm'n* (1980) (p. 247).

— Preventing offense to readers and listeners is not a substantial interest. *Bolger v. Youngs Drug Products*, 463 U.S. 60 (1983).

b. [and] it *directly advances* this interest

— "[T]he regulation may not be sustained if it provides only ineffective or remote support for the government's purpose." *Central Hudson*.

— The government must persuade the court that the law will indeed significantly accomplish its goal. *44 Liquormart, Inc. v. Rhode Island*, 517 U.S. 484 (1996).

— Scientific evidence of this is not required—common-sense evidence may be enough. *Id.*

— Trying to advance the interest by shielding customers from information that might lead them to make unwise choices is impermissible:

> [T]he "state's own explanation of how" [the statute] "advances its interests cannot be said to be direct." ...[T]he "fear that people would make bad decisions if given truthful information" cannot justify content-based burdens on speech. "The First Amendment directs us to be especially skeptical of regulations that seek to keep people in the dark for what the government perceives to be their own good."

IMS Health v. Sorrell (2011) (p. 257); see also *Thompson v. Western States Medical Center*, 535 U.S. 357, 374 (2002). *Central Hudson*, where the Court suggested that it would be constitutional to ban ads for products that "would cause [a] net increase in total energy use," seems to take the opposite view, and it hasn't been formally overruled. Nonetheless, the block quote above seems to represent the emerging rule, which is also a revival of the *Virginia Pharmacy* rule (see the end of section B in the casebook excerpt of that case). That rule doesn't seem to fit neatly under any of the prongs, so one might think of it as a separate, extra prong that doesn't appear in *Central Hudson*.

c. *and it is not more extensive than is necessary* to serve that interest. *Central Hudson*.

    [margin note: Not more extensive than necessary]

— There must be a "reasonable fit" between the restriction and the interest. *Board of Trustees v. Fox*, 492 U.S. 469 (1989), quoted on p. 254. The government is allowed to restrict some speech that doesn't implicate the interest, but not too much speech. And the availability of less restrictive alternatives doesn't necessarily show the law is unconstitutional, but cuts against its validity.

— *Ohralik* holds that prophylactic rules that suppress some speech that may ultimately prove harmless are allowed when it's hard to define in advance which speech is harmful. *Central Hudson* says such rules are *not* allowed when the harmful speech is identifiable up front: "The State cannot regulate speech that poses no danger to the asserted state interest."

— Query whether the "reasonable fit" requirement imposes a limit on the *Ohralik* principle: One can argue that if, say, 90% of the prohibited speech would ultimately prove harmless, a ban on the speech has an "unreasonable fit" with the interest even though it's impossible to distinguish in advance the harmful speech from the harmless. The Court, though, has never made this clear.

— If each instance of commercial speech and noncommercial speech equally implicate the government interest, it seems that the government may not restrict the commercial speech just because it's supposedly less valuable, at least so long as the commercial speech is only a small part of the problem. *City of Cincinnati v. Discovery Network*, 507 U.S. 410 (1993). Compare *Martin v. City of Struthers*, 319 U.S. 141 (1943), with *Breard v. Alexandria*, 341 U.S. 622 (1951). This doesn't seem to fit neatly under any of the prongs.

d. This framework is structurally similar to (though in important details different from) strict scrutiny, which is discussed in the next section.

5. What is "commercial speech"?

a. Generally, *speech that proposes a commercial transaction, i.e.,* commercial advertising. *Bolger v. Youngs Drug Products*, 463 U.S. 60, 66 (1983).

b. Speech is not made commercial by being sold (cf. newspapers, books).

c. Speech is not made commercial by being labeled an "advertisement" (cf. the ad in *New York Times v. Sullivan*).

d. Speech is not made commercial by the speaker's economic motivation (cf. speech by union members advocating higher pay).

e. Speech that indirectly promotes the speaker's product may be "commercial speech" even if it doesn't specifically offer a product for sale. *Bolger v. Youngs Drug Products*. It's not clear exactly where the line is drawn; for instance, would a press release about a new product be commercial speech? A magazine article written by a company's employee that paints the company and its products in a good light?

6. The overbreadth doctrine doesn't apply when the law is only overbroad as to commercial advertising: Commercial advertising is viewed as so "hardy" that we needn't fear its being "chilled." *Fox*, 492 U.S. at 481. The question isn't whether the challenger's speech is commercial advertising; rather, it's whether the other speech, which the challenger argues is improperly prohibited, is commercial advertising.

— Example: Say you publish a misleading commercial ad, and you're prosecuted under a law that bans all "misleading statements." If you argue the law is overbroad, you might win: Though your speech is unprotected, the law also impermissibly restricts protected speech that's not commercial advertising (since misleading speech generally cannot be restricted unless it's commercial advertising).

— But say a law bans all "commercial advertisements for alcohol," and you're prosecuted under the law for publishing a false advertisement about alcohol. If you argue that the law is overbroad, you'll lose. Your speech is unprotected; though the law probably impermissibly restricts some other people's speech—many commercial ads for alcohol are protected—that restricted speech is commercial advertising.

Terminological note: People sometimes speak of the "four-prong" *Central Hudson* test. The first prong is what is listed above as points 1 through 3; the other prongs are points 4a, 4b, and 4c.

Policy explanations for the lower protection given to commercial advertising (for all of which there are the obvious counterarguments in favor of full protection):

1. Regulating commercial advertising to protect consumers is more necessary than is regulating other speech.

2. Commercial advertising is less important to debate on political or social issues than other speech.

3. Commercial advertising is less central to people's abilities to express themselves than other speech.

4. Regulations of commercial advertising are less likely to "chill" speech that's outside their literal terms because commercial speakers have an incentive to keep talking.

5. Politicians have less incentive to restrict commercial advertising in self-serving ways than they do for other speech.

Policy explanations for commercial advertising getting at least some protection:

1. Commercial advertising communicates important information.

2. Commercial advertising is often related to political or social issues.

3. Commercial advertising is speech and should thus be presumptively protected.

4. It's hard to draw a clear line between commercial speech and noncommercial speech.

Policy arguments inferable from the existence of this doctrine:

1. Some speech might deserve some protection but not full protection.

2. Courts should recognize "commonsense differences" in the importance of various kinds of speech.

b. *Problem: Cigarette Advertising*

California bans cigarette advertising in all print publications, except ads that contain only print with no pictures or graphics. Is this constitutional?

c. *Virginia State Bd. of Pharmacy v. Virginia Citizens Consumer Council, Inc., 425 U.S. 748 (1976)*

Justice Blackmun delivered the opinion of the Court.

The plaintiff-appellees in this case attack ... [a Virginia statute that] provides that a pharmacist licensed in Virginia is guilty of unprofessional conduct if he "... publishes, advertises or promotes ... any ... price ... for any drugs which may be dispensed only by prescription." ...

[A.] Freedom of speech presupposes a willing speaker. But where a speaker exists, as is the case here, the protection afforded is to the communication, to its source and to its recipients both.... If there is a right to advertise, there is a reciprocal right to receive the advertising, and it may be asserted by these appellees.

The appellants contend that the advertisement of prescription drug prices is outside the protection of the First Amendment because it is "commercial speech." ... [In *Valentine v. Chrestensen*, 316 U.S. 52 (1942), the Court had held that the First Amendment doesn't protect "purely commercial advertising," but here the Court reversed *Valentine*, reasoning:—ed.] ....

[S]peech does not lose its First Amendment protection because money is spent to project it, as in a paid advertisement of one form or another. Speech likewise is protected even though it is carried in a form that is "sold" for profit, and even though it may involve a solicitation to purchase or otherwise pay or contribute money....

[Nor is speech unprotected because it is] simply ... on a commercial subject. No one would contend that our pharmacist may be prevented from being heard on the subject of whether, in general, pharmaceutical prices should be regulated, or their advertisement forbidden. Nor can it be dispositive that a commercial advertisement is noneditorial, and merely reports a fact. Purely factual matter of public interest may claim protection....

[Likewise, that] the advertiser's interest is a purely economic one ... hardly disqualifies him from protection under the First Amendment. The interests of the contestants in a labor dispute are primarily economic, but it has long been settled that both the employee and the employer are protected by the First Amendment when they express themselves on the merits of the dispute in order to influence its outcome.... It was observed in *Thornhill v.*

Alabama, 310 U.S. 88 (1940) [a labor speech case], that "the practices in a single factory may have economic repercussions upon a whole region and affect widespread systems of marketing." Since the fate of such a "single factory" could as well turn on its ability to advertise its product as on the resolution of its labor difficulties, we see no satisfactory distinction between the two kinds of speech.

As to the particular consumer's interest in the free flow of commercial information, that interest may be as keen, if not keener by far, than his interest in the day's most urgent political debate.... [In this case, t]hose whom the suppression of prescription drug price information hits the hardest are the poor, the sick, and particularly the aged. A disproportionate amount of their income tends to be spent on prescription drugs; yet they are the least able to learn, by shopping from pharmacist to pharmacist, where their scarce dollars are best spent. When drug prices vary as strikingly as they do, information as to who is charging what becomes more than a convenience. It could mean the alleviation of physical pain or the enjoyment of basic necessities.

Generalizing, society also may have a strong interest in the free flow of commercial information. Even an individual advertisement, though entirely "commercial," may be of general public interest[, for instance] advertisements stating that referral services for legal abortions are available; that a manufacturer of artificial furs promotes his product as an alternative to the extinction by his competitors of fur-bearing mammals; and that a domestic producer advertises his product as an alternative to imports that tend to deprive American residents of their jobs.

Obviously, not all commercial messages contain the same or even a very great public interest element. There are few to which such an element, however, could not be added. Our pharmacist, for example, could cast himself as a commentator on store-to-store disparities in drug prices, giving his own and those of a competitor as proof. We see little point in requiring him to do so, and little difference if he does not.

Moreover, there is another consideration that suggests that no line between publicly "interesting" or "important" commercial advertising and the opposite kind could ever be drawn. Advertising, however tasteless and excessive it sometimes may seem, is nonetheless dissemination of information as to who is producing and selling what product, for what reason, and at what price. So long as we preserve a predominantly free enterprise economy, the allocation of our resources in large measure will be made through numerous private economic decisions. It is a matter of public interest that those decisions, in the aggregate, be intelligent and well informed. To this end, the free flow of commercial information is indispensable.

And if it is indispensable to the proper allocation of resources in a free enterprise system, it is also indispensable to the formation of intelligent opinions as to how that system ought to be regulated or altered. Therefore, even if the First Amendment were thought to be primarily an instrument to enlighten public decisionmaking in a democracy, we could not say that the free flow of information does not serve that goal.

[B.] Arrayed against these substantial individual and societal interests are a number of justifications for the advertising ban.... Price advertising, it is argued, will place in jeopardy the pharmacist's expertise and, with it, the customer's health. It is claimed that the aggressive price competition that will result from unlimited advertising will make it impossible for the pharmacist to supply professional services in the compounding, handling, and dispensing of prescription drugs. Such services are time consuming and expensive; if competitors who economize by eliminating them are permitted to advertise their resulting lower prices, the more painstaking and conscientious pharmacist will be forced either to follow suit or to go out of business.

It is also claimed that prices might not necessarily fall as a result of advertising. If one pharmacist advertises, others must, and the resulting expense will inflate the cost of drugs. It is further claimed that advertising will lead people to shop for their prescription drugs among the various pharmacists who offer the lowest prices, and the loss of stable pharmacist-customer relationships will make individual attention and certainly the practice of monitoring impossible.

Finally, it is argued that damage will be done to the professional image of the pharmacist. This image, that of a skilled and specialized craftsman, attracts talent to the profession and reinforces the better habits of those who are in it. Price advertising, it is said, will reduce the pharmacist's status to that of a mere retailer.

The strength of these proffered justifications is greatly undermined by the fact that high professional standards, to a substantial extent, are guaranteed by the close regulation to which pharmacists in Virginia are subject.... Surely, any pharmacist guilty of professional dereliction that actually endangers his customer will promptly lose his license....

[O]n close inspection it is seen that the State's protectiveness of its citizens rests in large measure on the advantages of their being kept in ignorance. The advertising ban does not directly affect professional standards one way or the other. It affects them only through the reactions it is assumed people will have to the free flow of drug price information.

There is no claim that the advertising ban in any way prevents the cutting of corners by the pharmacist who is so inclined. That pharmacist is likely to cut corners in any event. The only effect the advertising ban has on him is to insulate him from price competition and to open the way for him to make a substantial, and perhaps even excessive, profit in addition to providing an inferior service. The more painstaking pharmacist is also protected but, again, it is a protection based in large part on public ignorance.

It appears to be feared that if the pharmacist who wishes to provide low cost, and assertedly low quality, services is permitted to advertise, he will be taken up on his offer by too many unwitting customers. They will choose the low-cost, low-quality service and drive the "professional" pharmacist out of business. They will respond only to costly and excessive advertising, and end up paying the price. They will go from one pharmacist to another, following the discount, and destroy the pharmacist-customer relationship. They will lose respect for the profession because it advertises. All this is not in their best interests, and all this can be avoided if they are not permitted to know who is charging what.

There is, of course, an alternative to this highly paternalistic approach. That alternative is to assume that this information is not in itself harmful, that people will perceive their own best interests if only they are well enough informed, and that the best means to that end is to open the channels of communication rather than to close them. If they are truly open, nothing prevents the "professional" pharmacist from marketing his own assertedly superior product, and contrasting it with that of the low-cost, high-volume prescription drug retailer.

But the choice among these alternative approaches is not ours to make or the Virginia General Assembly's. It is precisely this kind of choice, between the dangers of suppressing information, and the dangers of its misuse if it is freely available, that the First Amendment makes for us. Virginia is free to require whatever professional standards it wishes of its pharmacists; it may subsidize them or protect them from competition in other ways. But it may not do so by keeping the public in ignorance of the entirely lawful terms that competing pharmacists are offering....

[C.] [We] do not hold that [commercial speech] can never be regulated .... Untruthful speech, commercial or otherwise, has never been protected for its own sake.... [Even] commercial speech [that] is not provably false, or even wholly false, but only deceptive or misleading [may be regulated]....

{There are commonsense differences between speech that does "no more than propose a commercial transaction," and other varieties. Even if the differences do not justify the conclusion that commercial speech is valueless, and thus subject to complete suppression by the State, they nonetheless suggest that a different degree of protection is necessary to insure that the flow of truthful and legitimate commercial information is unimpaired.

The truth of commercial speech, for example, may be more easily verifiable by its disseminator than, let us say, news reporting or political commentary, in that ordinarily the advertiser seeks to disseminate information about a specific product or service that he himself provides and presumably knows more about than anyone else. Also, commercial speech may be more durable than other kinds. Since advertising is the sine qua non of commercial profits, there is little likelihood of its being chilled by proper regulation and forgone entirely.

Attributes such as these, the greater objectivity and hardiness of commercial speech, may make it less necessary to tolerate inaccurate statements for fear of silencing the speaker. They may also make it appropriate to require that a commercial message appear in such a form, or include such additional information, warnings, and disclaimers, as are necessary to prevent its being deceptive. They may also make inapplicable the prohibition against prior restraints.}

The First Amendment ... does not prohibit the State from insuring that the stream of commercial information flow cleanly as well as freely.... [But] a State may [not] completely suppress the dissemination of concededly truthful information about entirely lawful activity, fearful of that information's effect upon its disseminators and its recipients....

Justice Rehnquist, dissenting....

Arguments for free flow of commercial information] should presumptively be the concern of the Virginia Legislature, which sits to balance these and other claims in the process of making laws .... [And] there is certainly nothing in the United States Constitution which requires the Virginia Legislature to hew to the teachings of Adam Smith in its legislative decisions regulating the pharmacy profession....

The Court insists that the rule it lays down is consistent even with the view that the First Amendment is "primarily an instrument to enlighten public decisionmaking in a democracy." I had understood this view to relate to public decisionmaking as to political, social, and other public issues, rather than the decision of a particular individual as to whether to purchase one or another kind of shampoo....

It is one thing to say that the line between strictly ideological and political commentaries and other kinds of commentary is difficult to draw, and that the mere fact that the former may have in it an element of commercialism does not strip it of First Amendment protection. But it is another thing to say that because that line is difficult to draw, we will stand at the other end of the spectrum ....

d. *Central Hudson Gas & Elec. v. Public Serv. Comm'n, 447 U.S. 557 (1980)*

Justice Powell delivered the opinion of the Court....

[A.] In December 1973, the Commission ... [ordered all electric utilities not to engage in] "... advertising intended to stimulate the purchase of utility services ..." ...

[B.] The Commission's order restricts only commercial speech, that is, expression related solely to the economic interests of the speaker and its audience. The First Amendment ... protects commercial speech from unwarranted governmental regulation. Commercial expression not only serves the economic interest of the speaker, but also assists consumers and furthers the societal interest in the fullest possible dissemination of information.

In applying the First Amendment to this area, we have rejected the "highly paternalistic" view that government has complete power to suppress or regulate commercial speech. "[P]eople will perceive their own best interests if only they are well enough informed, and ... the best means to that end is to open the channels of communication rather than to close them...." Even when advertising communicates only an incomplete version of the relevant facts, the First Amendment presumes that some accurate information is better than no information at all.

Nevertheless, our decisions have recognized "the 'commonsense' distinction between speech proposing a commercial transaction, which occurs in an area traditionally subject to government regulation, and other varieties of speech." The Constitution therefore accords a lesser protection to commercial speech than to other constitutionally guaranteed expression....

{[T]he concurring opinion of Justice Stevens ... [apparently] would accord full First Amendment protection to all promotional advertising that includes claims "relating to ... questions frequently discussed and debated by our political leaders." ... But many, if not most, products may be tied to public concerns with the environment, energy, economic policy, or individual health and safety....

[U]tilities enjoy the full panoply of First Amendment protections for their direct comments on public issues. There is no reason for providing similar constitutional protection when such statements are made only in the context of commercial transactions.... [Commercial] speech, although meriting some protection, is of less constitutional moment than other forms of speech.... [T]he failure to distinguish between commercial and noncommercial speech "could invite dilution, simply by a leveling process, of the force of the [First] Amendment's guarantee with respect to the latter kind of speech."}

[C.] The First Amendment's concern for commercial speech is based on the informational function of advertising. Consequently, there can be no constitutional objection to the suppression of commercial messages that do not accurately inform the public about lawful activity. The government may ban forms of communication more likely to deceive the public than to inform it, or commercial speech related to illegal activity.

{[C]ommercial speakers have extensive knowledge of both the market and their products. Thus, they are well situated to evaluate the accuracy of their messages and the lawfulness of the underlying activity. In addition, commercial speech, the offspring of economic self-interest, is a hardy breed of expression that is not "particularly susceptible to being crushed by overbroad regulation."}

[D.] If the communication is neither misleading nor related to unlawful activity, the government's power is more circumscribed. The State must assert a substantial interest to be achieved by restrictions on commercial speech.

Moreover, the regulatory technique must be in proportion to that interest.... First, the restriction must directly advance the state interest involved; the regulation may not be sustained if it provides only ineffective or remote support for the government's purpose.... [T]he Court has declined to uphold regulations that only indirectly advance the state interest involved[, for instance concluding] ... that an advertising ban could not be imposed to protect the ethical or performance standards of a profession. The Court noted in *Virginia Pharmacy Board v. Virginia Citizens Consumer Council* that "[t]he advertising ban does not directly affect professional standards one way or the other." In *Bates v. State Bar*, 433 U.S. 350 (1977), the Court overturned an advertising prohibition that was designed to protect the "quality" of a lawyer's work. "Restraints on advertising ... are an ineffective way of deterring shoddy work."

{Second, if the governmental interest could be served as well by a more limited restriction on commercial speech, the excessive restrictions cannot survive.} ... The regulatory technique may extend only as far as the interest it serves. The State cannot regulate speech that poses no danger to the asserted state interest, nor can it completely suppress information when narrower restrictions on expression would serve its interest as well. For example, in *Bates* the Court explicitly did not "foreclose the possibility that some limited supplementation, by way of warning or disclaimer or the like, might be required" in promotional materials. {We review with special care regulations that entirely suppress commercial speech in order to pursue a non-speech-related policy. In those circumstances, a ban on speech could screen from public view the underlying governmental policy.} ...

In commercial speech cases, then, a four-part analysis has developed.... For commercial speech to come within that provision, it at least must concern lawful activity and not be misleading. Next, we ask whether the asserted governmental interest is substantial. If both inquiries yield positive answers, we must determine whether the regulation directly advances the governmental interest asserted, and whether it is not more extensive than is necessary to serve that interest....

[1.] [In this case, t]he Commission does not claim that the expression at issue either is inaccurate or relates to unlawful activity ....

[2.] In view of our country's dependence on energy resources beyond our control, ... the state interest [in energy conservation] asserted is substantial. [The rather technical discussion of a different interest in keeping some consumers from cross-subsidizing others omitted.—ed.] ...

[3.] [T]he State's interest in energy conservation is directly advanced by the Commission order at issue here. There is an immediate connection between advertising and demand for electricity. Central Hudson would not contest the advertising ban unless it believed that promotion would increase its sales. Thus, we find a direct link between the state interest in conservation and the Commission's order.

[4.] We come finally to ... whether the Commission's complete suppression of speech ... is no more extensive than necessary to further the State's interest in energy conservation.... [T]he energy conservation rationale, as important as it is, cannot justify suppressing information about electric devices or services that would cause no net increase in total energy use. In addition, no showing has been made that a more limited restriction on the content of promotional advertising would not serve adequately the State's interests.

Appellant insists that but for the ban, it would advertise products and services that use energy efficiently. These include the "heat pump," which both parties acknowledge to be a major improvement in electric heating, and the use of electric heat as a "backup" to solar and other heat sources....

The Commission's order prevents appellant from promoting electric services that would reduce energy use by diverting demand from less efficient sources, or that would consume roughly the same amount of energy as do alternative sources. In neither situation would the utility's advertising endanger conservation .... To the extent that the Commission's order suppresses speech that in no way impairs the State's interest in energy conservation, the Commission's order violates the First [Amendment] ....

The Commission also has not demonstrated that its interest in conservation cannot be protected adequately by more limited regulation of appellant's commercial expression. To further its policy of conservation, the Commission could attempt to restrict the format and content of Central Hudson's advertising. It might, for example, require that the advertisements include information about the relative efficiency and expense of the offered service, both under current conditions and for the foreseeable future. In the absence of a showing that more limited speech regulation would be ineffective, we cannot approve the complete suppression of Central Hudson's advertising....

[**In a later case**, *Board of Trustees v. Fox*, 492 U.S. 469 (1989), the Court modified this prong significantly, saying, in relevant part:—ed.]

{[W]e have not gone so far as to impose upon [regulators] the burden of demonstrating that the distinguishment [between speech that jeopardizes the government interest and speech that doesn't] is 100% complete, or that the manner of restriction is absolutely the least severe that will achieve the desired end. What our decisions require is a "'fit' between the legislature's ends and the means chosen to accomplish those ends"—a fit that is not necessarily perfect, but reasonable; that represents not necessarily the single best disposition but one whose scope is "in proportion to the interest served"; that employs not necessarily the least restrictive means but ... a means narrowly tailored to achieve the desired objective....

[S]ince the State bears the burden of justifying its restrictions, it must affirmatively establish the reasonable fit we require. By declining to impose, in addition, a least-restrictive-means requirement, we take account of the difficulty of establishing with precision the point at which restrictions become more extensive than their objective requires, and provide the Legislative and Executive Branches needed leeway in a field (commercial speech) "traditionally subject to governmental regulation."}

Justice Blackmun, with whom Justice Brennan joins, concurring in the judgment....

I seriously doubt whether suppression of information concerning the availability and price of a legally offered product is ever a permissible way for the State to "dampen" demand for or use of the product.... [Such suppression] is a covert attempt by the State to manipulate the choices of its citizens, not by persuasion or direct regulation, but by depriving the public of the information needed to make a free choice.... [T]he State's policy choices are insulated from the visibility and scrutiny that direct regulation would entail and the conduct of citizens is molded by the information that government chooses to give them....

The differences [between commercial and noncommercial speech] justify a more permissive approach to regulation of the manner of commercial speech for the purpose of protecting consumers from deception or coercion, and these differences explain why doctrines designed to prevent "chilling" of protected speech are inapplicable to commercial speech. No differences between commercial speech and other protected speech justify suppression of commercial speech in order to influence public conduct through manipulation of the availability of information....

Justice Stevens, with whom Justice Brennan joins, concurring in the judgment....

[The New York] ban encompasses a great deal more than mere proposals to engage in certain kinds of commercial transactions.... It curtails expression by an informed and interested group of persons of their point of view on questions relating to the production and consumption of electrical energy—questions frequently discussed and debated by our political leaders.

For example, an electric company's advocacy of the use of electric heat for environmental reasons, as opposed to wood-burning stoves, would seem to fall squarely within New York's promotional advertising ban and also within the bounds of maximum First Amendment protection. The breadth of the ban thus exceeds the boundaries of the commercial speech concept, however that concept may be defined.

The justification for the regulation is nothing more than the expressed fear that ... truthful [and noncoercive] communication may persuade some citizens to consume more electricity than they otherwise would.... But if the perceived harm associated with greater electrical usage is not sufficiently serious to justify direct regulation [of electricity consumption], surely it does not constitute the kind of clear and present danger that can justify the suppression of speech....

Justice Rehnquist, dissenting....

The Court's decision ... returns to the bygone era of *Lochner v. New York*, 198 U.S. 45 (1905), in which it was common practice for this Court to strike down economic regulations adopted by a State based on the Court's own notions of the most appropriate means for the State to implement its considered policies.... [Given the rejection of *Lochner*,] the Public Service Commission [could have permissibly] chosen to raise the price of electricity, to condition its sale on specified terms, or to restrict its production. In terms of constitutional values, I think that such controls are virtually indistinguishable from the State's ban on promotional advertising....

While it is true that an important objective of the First Amendment is to foster the free flow of information, identification of speech that falls within its protection is not aided by the metaphorical reference to a "marketplace of ideas." There is no reason for believing that the marketplace of ideas is free from market imperfections any more than there is to believe that the invisible hand will always lead to optimum economic decisions in the commercial market.

{Although the Constitution attaches great importance to freedom of speech under the First Amendment so that individuals will be better informed and their thoughts and ideas will be uninhibited, it does not follow that "people will perceive their own best interests," or that if they do they will act to promote them. With respect to governmental policies that do not offer immediate tangible benefits and the success of which depends on incremental contributions by all members of society, such as would seem to be the case with energy conservation, a strong argument can be made that while a policy may be in the longrun interest of all members of society, some rational individuals will perceive it to their own shortrun advantage to not act in accordance with that policy. When the regulation of commercial speech is at issue, I think this is a consideration that the government may properly take into account.} ...

The notion that more speech is the remedy to expose falsehood and fallacies is wholly out of place in the commercial bazaar, where if applied logically the remedy of one who was defrauded would be merely a statement, available upon request, reciting the Latin maxim *"caveat emptor."* ... [I disagree with *Virginia State Bd. of Pharmacy*, f]or in a democracy, the economic is subordinate to the political ....

e.   Ohralik v. Ohio State Bar Ass'n, 436 U.S. 447 (1978)

Justice Powell delivered the opinion of the Court....

[A.] [T]he State ... constitutionally may discipline a lawyer for soliciting clients in person, for pecuniary gain, under circumstances likely to pose dangers that the State has a right to prevent.... [Ohralik had solicited two 18-year-old women in a hospital shortly after they were involved in an accident, and seemingly pressured them into retaining him.—ed.]

[B.] [Protection of the public from] those aspects of solicitation that involve fraud, undue influence, intimidation, overreaching, and other forms of "vexatious conduct" ... is a legitimate and important state interest....

[Appellant challenges the Rules as applied to him, and argues] that none of those evils was found to be present in his acts of solicitation.... [A]ppellant errs in assuming that the constitutional validity of [his punishment for violating the Rules] depends on proof that his conduct constituted actual overreaching or inflicted some specific injury on [his prospective clients].... The Rules prohibiting solicitation are prophylactic measures whose objective is the prevention of harm before it occurs.

The Rules were applied in this case to discipline a lawyer for soliciting employment for pecuniary gain under circumstances likely to result in the adverse consequences the State seeks to avert. In such a situation, which is inherently conducive to overreaching and other forms of misconduct, the State has a strong interest in adopting and enforcing rules of conduct designed to protect the public from harmful solicitation by lawyers whom it has licensed.

The State's perception of the potential for harm in circumstances such as those presented in this case is well founded. The detrimental aspects of face-to-face selling even of ordinary consumer products have been recognized and addressed by the Federal Trade Commission, and it hardly need be said that the potential for overreaching is significantly greater when a lawyer, a professional trained in the art of persuasion, personally solicits an unsophisticated, injured, or distressed lay person. Such an individual may place his trust in a lawyer, regardless of the latter's qualifications or the individual's actual need for legal representation, simply in response to persuasion under circumstances conducive to uninformed acquiescence.

{Most lay persons are unfamiliar with the law, with how legal services normally are procured, and with typical arrangements between lawyer and client. To be sure, the same might be said about the lay person who seeks out a lawyer for the first time. But the critical distinction is that in the latter situation the prospective client has made an initial choice of a lawyer at least for purposes of a consultation; has chosen the time to seek legal advice; has had a prior opportunity to confer with family, friends, or a public or private referral agency; and has chosen whether to consult with the lawyer alone or accompanied.}

[C.] Although it is argued that personal solicitation is valuable because it may apprise a victim of misfortune of his legal rights, the very plight of that person not only makes him more vulnerable to influence but also may make advice all the more intrusive. Thus, under these adverse conditions the overtures of an uninvited lawyer may distress the solicited individual simply because of their obtrusiveness and the invasion of the individual's privacy, even when no other harm materializes. Under such circumstances, it is not unreasonable for the State to presume that in-person solicitation by lawyers more often than not will be injurious to the person solicited.

[D.] The efficacy of the State's effort to prevent such harm to prospective clients would be substantially diminished if, having proved a solicitation in circumstances like those of this case, the State were required in addition to prove actual injury.... Often there is no witness other than the lawyer and the lay person whom he has solicited, rendering it difficult or impossible to obtain reliable proof of what actually took place.... If appellant's view were sustained, in-person solicitation would be virtually immune to effective oversight and regulation ....

[A] State [may therefore] respond with what in effect is a prophylactic rule.... Under our view of the State's interest in averting harm by prohibiting solicitation in circumstances where it is likely to occur, the absence of explicit proof or findings of harm or injury is immaterial....

f. Sorrell v. IMS Health Inc., 564 U.S. 552 (2011)

Justice Kennedy delivered the opinion of the Court....

[A.] Pharmaceutical manufacturers promote their drugs to doctors through a process called "detailing." This often involves a scheduled visit to a doctor's office to persuade the doctor to prescribe a particular pharmaceutical. Detailers bring drug samples as well as medical studies that explain the "details" and potential advantages of various prescription drugs. Interested physicians listen, ask questions, and receive followup data. Salespersons can be more effective when they know the background and purchasing preferences of their clientele, and pharmaceutical salespersons are no exception.

Knowledge of a physician's prescription practices—called "prescriber-identifying information"—enables a detailer better to ascertain which doctors are likely to be interested in a particular drug and how best to present a particular sales message. Detailing is an expensive undertaking, so pharmaceutical companies most often use it to promote high-profit brand-name drugs protected by patent. Once a brand-name drug's patent expires, less expensive bioequivalent generic alternatives are manufactured and sold.

Law →

[A Vermont law, § 4631(d), did several things, including barring pharmaceutical marketers from using prescriber-identifying information (bought from pharmacies) to market to prescribers. The case was complex, and involved other restrictions and a variety of interests; the material quoted below focuses on the marketing restriction, and the particular interests implicated by those restrictions. The case did not involve marketers receiving or using *patient*-identifying information.—ed.]

[B.] [Section 4631(d)] is designed to impose a specific, content-based burden on protected expression. It follows that heightened judicial scrutiny is warranted.... [T]he "distinction between laws burdening and laws banning speech is but a matter of degree" and [so] the "Government's content-based burdens must satisfy the same rigorous scrutiny as its content-based bans." ...

The First Amendment requires heightened scrutiny whenever the government creates "a regulation of speech because of disagreement with the message it conveys." ... Commercial speech is no exception. A "consumer's concern for the free flow of commercial speech often may be far keener than his concern for urgent political dialogue." That reality has great relevance in the fields of medicine and public health, where information can save lives....

Under a commercial speech inquiry, it is the State's burden to justify its content-based law as consistent with the First Amendment. To sustain the targeted, content-based burden § 4631(d) imposes on protected expression, the State must show at least that the statute directly advances a substantial governmental interest and that the measure is drawn to achieve that interest. See *Central Hudson Gas & Elec. Corp. v. Public Serv. Comm'n of N.Y.* There must be a "fit between the legislature's ends and the means chosen to accomplish those ends." As in other contexts, these standards ensure not only that the State's interests are proportional to the resulting burdens placed on speech but also that the law does not seek to suppress a disfavored message.

[C.] The State's asserted justifications for § 4631(d) come under two general headings. First, the State contends that its law is necessary to protect medical privacy, including ... avoidance of harassment [of physicians] and the integrity of the doctor-patient relationship. Second, the State argues that § 4631(d) is integral to the achievement of policy objectives—namely, improved public health and reduced healthcare costs. Neither justification withstands scrutiny....

[1.] The State ... contends that § 4631(d) protects doctors from "harassing sales behaviors." "Some doctors in Vermont are experiencing an undesired increase in the aggressiveness of pharmaceutical sales representatives," the Vermont Legislature found, "and a few have reported that they felt coerced and harassed." It is doubtful that concern for "a few" physicians who may have "felt coerced and harassed" by pharmaceutical marketers can sustain a broad content-based rule like§ 4631(d). Many are those who must endure speech they do not like, but that is a necessary cost of freedom. See *Cohen v. California.*

In any event the State offers no explanation why remedies other than content-based rules would be inadequate. Physicians can, and often do, simply decline to meet with detailers, including detailers who use prescriber-identifying information. Doctors who wish to forgo detailing altogether are free to give "No Solicitation" or "No Detailing" instructions to their office managers or to receptionists at their places of work. Personal privacy even in one's own home receives "ample protection" from the "resident's unquestioned right to refuse to engage in conversation with unwelcome visitors." A physician's office is no more private and is entitled to no greater protection.

[2.] Vermont argues that detailers' use of prescriber-identifying information undermines the doctor-patient relationship by allowing detailers to influence treatment decisions. According to the State, "unwanted pressure occurs" when doctors learn that their prescription decisions are being "monitored" by detailers. Some physicians accuse detailers of "spying" or of engaging in "underhanded" conduct in order to "subvert" prescription decisions. And Vermont claims that detailing makes people "anxious" about whether doctors have their patients' best interests at heart.

But ... this asserted interest is contrary to basic First Amendment principles.... If pharmaceutical marketing affects treatment decisions, it does so because doctors find it persuasive. Absent circumstances far from those presented here, the fear that speech might persuade provides no lawful basis for quieting it. *Brandenburg v. Ohio.*

[3.] The State contends that § 4631(d) advances important public policy goals by lowering the costs of medical services and promoting public health. If prescriber-identifying information were available for use by detailers, the State contends, then detailing would be effective in promoting brand-name drugs that are more expensive and less safe than generic alternatives....

While Vermont's stated policy goals may be proper, § 4631(d) does not advance them in a permissible way. As the Court of Appeals noted, the "state's own explanation of how" § 4631(d) "advances its interests cannot be said to be direct." The State seeks to achieve its policy objectives through the indirect means of restraining certain speech by certain speakers—that is, by diminishing detailers' ability to influence prescription decisions.... But the "fear that people would make bad decisions if given truthful information" cannot justify content-based burdens on speech. *Virginia Bd. of Pharmacy v. Virginia Citizens Consumer Council, Inc.* "The First Amendment directs us to be especially skeptical of regulations that seek to keep people in the dark for what the government perceives to be their own good." These precepts apply with full force when the audience, in this case prescribing physicians, consists of "sophisticated and experienced" consumers....

The defect in Vermont's law is made clear by the fact that many listeners find detailing instructive. Indeed the record demonstrates that some Vermont doctors view targeted detailing based on prescriber-identifying information as "very helpful" because it allows detailers to shape their messages to each doctor's practice.... There are divergent views regarding detailing and the prescription of brand-name drugs. Under the Constitution, resolution of that debate must result from free and uninhibited speech. As one Vermont physician put it: "We have a saying in medicine, information is power. And the more you know, or anyone knows, the better decisions can be made."

There are similar sayings in law, including that "information is not in itself harmful, that people will perceive their own best interests if only they are well enough informed, and that the best means to that end is to open the channels of communication rather than to close them." *Virginia Bd. of Pharmacy.* The choice "between the dangers of suppressing information, and the dangers of its misuse if it is freely available" is one that "the First Amendment makes for us." *Ibid....*

[D.] [T]he government's legitimate interest in protecting consumers from "commercial harms" explains "why commercial speech can be subject to greater governmental regulation than noncommercial speech." The Court has noted, for example, that "a State may choose to regulate price advertising in one industry but not in others, because the risk of fraud ... is in its view greater there." Here, however, Vermont has not shown that its law has a neutral justification....

Justice Breyer, with whom Justice Ginsburg and Justice Kagan join, dissenting....

The [Vermont] statute helps to focus sales discussions on an individual drug's safety, effectiveness, and cost, perhaps compared to other drugs (including generics). These drug-related facts have everything to do with general information that drug manufacturers likely possess. They have little, if anything, to do with the name or prior prescription practices of the particular doctor to whom a detailer is speaking.

Shaping a detailing message based on an individual doctor's prior prescription habits may help sell more of a particular manufacturer's particular drugs. But it does so by diverting attention from scientific research about a drug's safety and effectiveness, as well as its cost. This diversion comes at the expense of public health and the State's fiscal interests....

The majority ... says that doctors "can, and often do, simply decline to meet with detailers." This fact, while true, is beside the point. Closing the office door entirely has no similar tendency to lower costs (by focusing greater attention upon the comparative advantages and disadvantages of generic drug alternatives).... In any event, physicians are unlikely to turn detailers away at the door, for those detailers, whether delivering a balanced or imbalanced message, are nonetheless providers of much useful information. Forcing doctors to choose between targeted detailing and no detailing at all could therefore jeopardize the State's interest in promoting public health....

2. What Is "Misleading"?

a. Problem: Health Benefits of Alcohol

Medical evidence seems to pretty strongly suggest that drinking one alcoholic drink per day (for women) and two per day (for men) will, on average, improve a typical person's health; the American Heart Association has endorsed this view. (It's unclear whether the benefits are especially acute for red wine.) Such moderate consumption slightly increases the risk of cancer and cirrhosis of the liver, but since heart disease is a bigger killer than either cancer or cirrhosis, on balance moderate drinking seems to be good for your health. On the other hand, even one drink can in some measure affect one's mental faculties, among other things making one a less careful driver.

A winemaker wants to place on its bottles the label that I reproduce above. Is it constitutional for the Bureau of Alcohol, Tobacco, and Firearms to prohibit such labels? (The label was produced by the Competitive Enterprise Institute, a Washington, D.C. libertarian free-market think-tank.)

b. Peel v. Attorney Reg. & Discip. Comm'n, 496 U.S. 91 (1990)

Justice Stevens ... delivered an opinion, in which Justice Brennan, Justice Blackmun, and Justice Kennedy join.

[A.] ... [T]he National Board of Trial Advocacy (NBTA) ... has developed a set of standards and procedures for periodic certification of lawyers with experience and competence in trial work. Those standards, which have been approved by a board of judges, scholars, and practitioners, are objective and demanding. They require specified experience as lead counsel in both jury and nonjury trials, participation in approved programs of continuing legal education, a demonstration of writing skills, and the successful completion of a day-long examination. Certification expires in five years unless the lawyer again demonstrates his or her continuing qualification. [Details omitted.—ed.] ...

Petitioner ... has tried to verdict over 100 jury trials and over 300 nonjury trials, and has participated in hundreds of other litigated matters that were settled. NBTA issued petitioner a "Certificate in Civil Trial Advocacy" in 1981, renewed it in 1986, and listed him in its 1985 Directory of "Certified Specialists and Board Members."

Since 1983 petitioner's professional letterhead has contained a statement referring to his NBTA certification and to the three States in which he is licensed. It appears as follows:

Gary E. Peel
        Certified Civil Trial Specialist
        By the National Board of Trial Advocacy
Licensed: Illinois, Missouri, Arizona.

[The Attorney Registration and Disciplinary Commission of Illinois recommended censuring Peel for] ... publicly holding himself out as a certified legal specialist in violation of Rule 2-105(a)(3)[,] ... "... Except [patent, trademark, and admiralty lawyers], no lawyer may hold himself out as 'certified' or a 'specialist.'" ... [The state supreme court affirmed.—ed.] ...

[B.] In this case we must consider whether petitioner's statement was misleading and, even if it was not, whether the potentially misleading character of such statements creates a state interest sufficiently substantial to justify a categorical ban on their use.

The facts stated on petitioner's letterhead are true and verifiable.... There is no contention that any potential client or person was actually misled or deceived by petitioner's stationery. Neither the Commission nor the State Supreme Court made any factual finding of actual deception or misunderstanding, but rather concluded, as a matter of law, that petitioner's claims of being "certified" as a "specialist" were necessarily misleading absent an official state certification program....

In evaluating petitioner's claim of certification, the Illinois Supreme Court focused not on its facial accuracy, but on its implied claim "as to the quality of [petitioner's] legal services," and concluded that such a qualitative claim "might be so likely to mislead as to warrant restriction." This analysis confuses the distinction between statements of opinion or quality and statements of objective facts that may support an inference of quality....

Measures of trial experience and hours of continuing education, like information about what schools the lawyer attended or his or her bar activities, are facts about a lawyer's training and practice. A claim of certification is not an unverifiable opinion of the ultimate quality of a lawyer's work or a promise of success, but is simply a fact, albeit one with multiple predicates, from which a consumer may or may not draw an inference of the likely quality of an attorney's work in a given area of practice.

We must assume that some consumers will infer from petitioner's statement that his qualifications in the area of civil trial advocacy exceed the general qualifications for admission to a state bar. Thus if the certification had been issued by an organization that had made no inquiry into petitioner's fitness, or by one that issued certificates indiscriminately for a price, the statement, even if true, could be misleading.

In this case, there is no evidence that a claim of NBTA certification suggests any greater degree of professional qualification than reasonably may be inferred from an evaluation of its rigorous requirements. Much like a trademark, the strength of a certification is measured by the quality of the organization for which it stands....

Nor can we agree with the Illinois Supreme Court's somewhat contradictory fears that juxtaposition of the references to being "certified" as a "specialist" with the identification of the three States in which petitioner is "licensed" conveys, on the one hand, the impression that NBTA had the authority to grant those licenses and, on the other, that the NBTA certification was the product of official state action. The separate character of the two references is plain from their texts: one statement begins with the verb "[c]ertified" and identifies the source as the "*National* Board of Trial Advocacy," while the second statement begins with the verb "[l]icensed" and identifies *States* as the source of licensure.

The references are further distinguished by the fact that one is indented below petitioner's name while the other uses the same margin as his name. There has been no finding that any person has associated certification with governmental action—state or federal—and there is no basis for belief that petitioner's representation generally would be so construed.

We are satisfied that the consuming public understands that licenses—to drive cars, to operate radio stations, to sell liquor—are issued by governmental authorities and that a host of certificates—to commend job performance, to convey an educational degree, to commemorate a solo flight or a hole in one—are issued by private organizations. The dictionary definition of "certificate" ... comports with this common understanding ....

[Likewise], it seems unlikely that petitioner's statement about his certification as a "specialist" by an identified national organization necessarily would be confused with formal state recognition. The Federal Trade Commission, which has a long history of reviewing claims of deceptive advertising, fortifies this conclusion with its observation that "one can readily think of numerous other claims of specialty—from 'air conditioning specialist' in the realm of home repairs to 'foreign car specialist' in the realm of automotive repairs—that cast doubt on the notion that the public would automatically mistake a claim of specialization for a claim of formal recognition by the State." ... Given the complete absence of any evidence of deception in the present case, we must reject the contention that petitioner's letterhead is actually misleading.

[C.] Even if petitioner's letterhead is not actually misleading, the Commission defends Illinois' categorical prohibition against lawyers' claims of being "certified" or a "specialist" on the assertion that these statements are potentially misleading. In the Commission's view, the State's interest in avoiding any possibility of misleading some consumers with such communications is so substantial that it outweighs the cost of providing other consumers with relevant information about lawyers who are certified as specialists.

We may assume that statements of "certification" as a "specialist," even though truthful, may not be understood fully by some readers. However, such statements pose no greater potential of misleading consumers than advertising admission to "Practice before: The United States Supreme Court," *In re R.M.J.*, 455 U.S. 191 (1982), of exploiting the audience of a targeted letter, *Shapero v. Kentucky Bar Assn.*, 486 U.S. 466 (1988), or of confusing a reader with an accurate illustration, *Zauderer v. Office of Disciplinary Counsel*, 471 U.S. 626 (1985). In this case, as in those, we conclude that the particular state rule restricting lawyers' advertising is "'broader than reasonably necessary to prevent the' perceived evil." The need for a complete prophylactic against any claim of specialty is undermined by the fact that use of titles such as "Registered Patent Attorney" and "Proctor in Admiralty," which are permitted under Rule 2-105(a)'s exceptions, produces the same risk of deception....

We do not ignore the possibility that some unscrupulous attorneys may hold themselves out as certified specialists when there is no qualified organization to stand behind that certification. A lawyer's truthful statement that "XYZ Board" has "certified" him as a "specialist in admiralty law" would not necessarily be entitled to First Amendment protection if the certification were a sham. States can require an attorney who advertises "XYZ certification" to demonstrate that such certification is available to all lawyers who meet objective and consistently applied standards relevant to practice in a particular area of the law. There has been no showing—indeed no suggestion—that the burden of distinguishing between certifying boards that are bona fide and those that are bogus would be significant, or that bar associations and official disciplinary committees cannot police deceptive practices effectively.

"If the naivete of the public will cause advertising by attorneys to be misleading, then it is the bar's role to assure that the populace is sufficiently informed as to enable it to place advertising in its proper perspective." To the extent that potentially misleading statements of private certification or specialization could confuse consumers, a State might consider screening certifying organizations or requiring a disclaimer about the certifying organization or the standards of a specialty. {It is not necessary here ... to consider when a State might impose some disclosure requirements, rather than a total prohibition, in order to minimize the possibility that a reader will misunderstand the significance of a statement of fact that is protected by the First Amendment. We agree with Justice Marshall that a holding that a total ban is unconstitutional does not necessarily preclude less restrictive regulation of commercial speech.}

A State may not, however, completely ban statements that are not actually or inherently misleading, such as certification as a specialist by bona fide organizations such as NBTA. Information about certification and specialties facilitates the consumer's access to legal services and thus better serves the administration of justice. {A principal reason why consumers do not consult lawyers is because they do not know how to find a lawyer able to assist them with their particular problems. Justice O'Connor would extend this convenience to consumers who seek admiralty, patent, and trademark lawyers, but not to consumers who need a lawyer certified or specializing in more commonly needed areas of the law.} ...

Justice Marshall, with whom Justice Brennan joins, concurring in the judgment....

States may prohibit actually or inherently misleading commercial speech entirely. They may not, however, ban *potentially* misleading commercial speech [such as petitioner's letterhead] if narrower limitations could be crafted to ensure that the information is presented in a nonmisleading manner....

The name "National Board of Trial Advocacy" could create [to nonlawyers] the misimpression that the NBTA is an agency of the Federal Government.... Furthermore, the juxtaposition on petitioner's letterhead of the phrase "Certified Civil Trial Specialist By the National Board of Trial Advocacy" with "Licensed: Illinois, Missouri, Arizona" could lead even lawyers to believe that the NBTA, though not a governmental agency, is somehow sanctioned by the States listed on the letterhead.... For instance, many States prescribe requirements for, and "certify" public accountants as, "Certified Public Accountants." ...

In addition, the reference to petitioner's certification as a civil trial specialist may cause people to think that petitioner is necessarily a better trial lawyer than attorneys without the certification.... [And e]ven if, as the plurality suggests, NBTA-certified lawyers are *generally* more highly qualified for trial work than the average attorney, petitioner's statement is still potentially misleading because a person reasonably could draw a different inference from it. A person could think, for instance, that "Certified Civil Trial Specialist" means that petitioner has an unusually high success rate in civil trials. Alternatively, a person could think that all lawyers are considered by the NBTA for certification as a specialist, so that petitioner is *necessarily* a better trial lawyer than every lawyer not so certified.... The record contains no evidence ... that the NBTA['s] ... certification requirements are widely known....

Because a claim of certification by the NBTA as a civil trial specialist is potentially misleading, States may enact measures other than a total ban to prevent deception or confusion.... States may, for example, require "some limited supplementation, by way of warning or disclaimer or the like, ... so as to assure that the consumer is not misled."

The Court's decisions in *Shapero* and *Zauderer* provide helpful guidance in this area. In *Shapero*, the Court held ... that States could ... requir[e] that a personalized letter [from a lawyer to a] {potential client[] known to face particular legal problems} bear a label identifying it as an advertisement or a statement informing the recipient how to report an inaccurate or misleading letter. In *Zauderer*, ... the Court held that the State could require attorneys advertising contingent-fee services to disclose that clients would have to pay costs even if their lawsuits were unsuccessful ....

[A] State could require a lawyer claiming certification by the NBTA as a civil trial specialist to provide additional information in order to prevent that claim from being misleading. The State might, for example, require a disclaimer stating that the NBTA is a private organization not affiliated with, or sanctioned by, the State or Federal Government. The State also could require information about the NBTA's requirements for certification as a specialist so that any inferences drawn by consumers about the quality of services offered by an NBTA-certified attorney would be based on more complete knowledge of the meaning of NBTA certification.

{The precise amount of information necessary to avoid misunderstandings need not be decided here. The poles of the spectrum of disclosure requirements, however, are clear. A State may require an attorney to provide more than just the fact of his certification as a civil trial specialist by the NBTA. But a State may not require an attorney to include in his letterhead an exhaustive, detailed recounting of the NBTA's certification requirements because more limited disclosure would suffice to prevent the possibility that people would be misled.}

{Justice O'Connor suggests that any regulation short of a total ban on claims such as petitioner's would require "case-by-case review" of each certification claim and would be unduly burdensome on the State. On the contrary, a State could easily establish generally applicable regulations setting forth what types of information must accompany a claim of certification or specialty. The state agency in charge of enforcing those regulations could then investigate and adjudicate alleged violations of the regulations, just as such agencies do under existing disciplinary rules.... In any event, this Court's primary task in cases such as this is to determine whether a state law or regulation unduly burdens the speaker's exercise of First Amendment rights, not whether respect for those rights would be unduly burdensome for the State.} ...

Justice White, dissenting. [Omitted.—ed.]

Justice O'Connor, with whom ... Chief Justice [Rehnquist] and Justice Scalia join, dissenting....

[The dissent agreed with the concurrence's concerns about the possibly misleading nature of the NBTA certification claim, but concluded this made the statement "inherently misleading" and thus prohibitable. It added:— ed.]

Petitioner does not suggest a less burdensome means of regulating attorney claims of certification than case-by-case determination. Under petitioner's theory, the First Amendment requires States that would protect their consumers from misleading claims of certification to provide an individual hearing for each and every claim of certification, extending well beyond NBTA certification to any organization that may be used by a resourceful lawyer. In my view, the First Amendment does not require the State to establish such an onerous system and permits the State simply to prohibit such inherently misleading claims....

[Moreover, i]f the information cannot be presented in a way that is not deceptive, even statements that are merely potentially misleading may be regulated with an absolute prohibition. It is difficult to believe that a disclaimer could be fashioned, as the plurality suggests, that would make petitioner's claim of certification on his letterhead not potentially misleading. Such a disclaimer would have to communicate three separate pieces of information in a space that could reasonably fit on a letterhead ...: (1) that the claim to certification does not necessarily indicate that the attorney provides higher quality representation than those who are not certified; (2) that the certification is not state sanctioned; and (3) either the criteria for certification or a reasonable means by which the consumer could determine what those criteria are. Even if the State were to permit claims of certification along with disclaimers, in order to protect consumers adequately, the State would have to engage in case-by-case review to ensure that the misleading character of a particular claim to certification was cured by a particular disclaimer....

c. *Policy—Search for Truth, see p. 31*

d. *Policy—No-Value or Low-Value Speech, see p. 90*

e. *Policy—Self-Expression (as argument for speech restriction)*

Basic argument: "This speech may be restricted because it doesn't really represent the expression of a person's own beliefs, in the following way: _____."

1. "[Commercial speech ought not be protected because the presence of the profit motive] breaks the connection between speech and any vision, or attitude, or value of the individual or group engaged in advocacy. Thus the content and form of commercial speech cannot be attributed to individual value allegiances." C. Edwin Baker, *Commercial Advertising: A Problem in the Theory of Freedom,* 62 Iowa L. Rev. 1, 17 (1976).

"[T]he use of communication as a means of self-expression, self-realization, and self-fulfillment[] is not ... furthered by corporate speech.... [T]he communications of profitmaking corporations are not 'an integral part of the development of ideas, of mental exploration and of the affirmation of self.' They do not represent a manifestation of individual freedom or choice." *First Nat'l Bank of Boston v. Bellotti* (White, J., dissenting).

2. Response to 1: This speech *is* self-expression, because _____. For

instance, the fact that a speaker is motivated by profit doesn't make his statements any less expressive of his views; likewise, corporate speech is speech of particular people—the corporation's owners or managers—that just happens to be channeled through a corporate entity.

3. Response to 1: Even if this speech isn't the speaker's genuine self-expression, it does further the *listener's* interests, interests that deserve constitutional recognition, and it furthers *society's* interests in a rich public debate, by _____. (See the next policy argument section.)

"[First Amendment doctrine is] based not only on the role of the First Amendment in fostering individual self-expression but also on its role in affording the public access to discussion, debate, and the dissemination of information and ideas." *First Nat'l Bank of Boston* (concluding that corporate speech is constitutionally protected).

f.   *Policy—Listener Interests*

Basic argument: "Independently of the speaker's interest in making this statement, listeners have a constitutionally protected interest in hearing it, because _____, and hearing it is valuable to them because _____."

1. "These might be troublesome cases if the addressees predicated their claim for relief upon the First Amendment rights of the senders ...[, foreign entities sending] political propaganda prepared and printed abroad by or on behalf of a foreign government. [But] the addressees assert First Amendment claims in their own right: they contend that the Government is powerless to interfere with the delivery of the material because the First Amendment 'necessarily protects the right to receive it.'" *Lamont v. Postmaster General*, 381 U.S. 301, 307-08 (1965) (Brennan, J., concurring).

"[Where] a willing speaker ... exists, the protection afforded is to the communication, to its source and to its recipients both.... If there is a right to advertise, there is a reciprocal right to receive the advertising .... [A] consumer's interest in the free flow of commercial information ... may be as keen, if not keener by far, than his interest in the day's most urgent political debate." *Va. State Bd. of Pharmacy v. Va. Citizens Consumer Council* (1976) (p. 247).

"[First Amendment doctrine is] based not only on the role of the First Amendment in fostering individual self-expression but also on its role in affording the public access to discussion, debate, and the dissemination of information and ideas." *First Nat'l Bank of Boston v. Bellotti* (1978) (p. 479) (concluding that corporate speech is constitutionally protected).

2. Response to 1 and rejoinder to 3: The First Amendment protects the freedom of *speech,* not the freedom of *listening,* because _____. The government cannot simply say "It's illegal to listen to this kind of speech," because this would interfere with the rights of the speakers; but if the speakers have no rights of their own to say something, the listeners have no independent ground to challenge the restriction.

3. Rejoinder to 2: Protecting listener interests is important to protecting

some other free speech value, namely _____, because _____.

"It is true that the First Amendment contains no specific guarantee of access to publications. However, the protection of the Bill of Rights goes beyond the specific guarantees to protect ... those equally fundamental personal rights necessary to make the express guarantees fully meaningful.... The dissemination of ideas can accomplish nothing if otherwise willing addressees are not free to receive and consider them. It would be a barren marketplace of ideas that had only sellers and no buyers." *Lamont,* 381 U.S. at 308 (Brennan, J. concurring).

III. Strict Scrutiny

> Law, says the judge, as he looks down his nose,
> Speaking clearly and most severely.
> Law is as I've told you before,
> Law is as you know I suppose,
> Law is but let me explain it once more,
> Law is The Law.
> —W.H. Auden, *Law Like Love*

A. Content Discrimination When Speech Is Not Within an Exception

1. Outline of Strict Scrutiny of Content-Based Speech Restrictions

a. *Generally*

If a kind of speech does *not* fall into an "exceptions from protection" category or into a "diminished protection" category, there is a very strong presumption that the government may not suppress it. (We're still talking here only about the government acting as sovereign to suppress speech because of its communicative impact.) Such speech is often called "fully protected speech" or just "protected speech."

But these terms are a bit misleading, because the Court has left open the possibility that even this supposedly protected speech can be suppressed if the restriction passes "strict scrutiny": if it's "narrowly tailored" to a "compelling state interest." Thus, even the most important kinds of speech can (rarely) be restricted if the government has a really good reason for restricting them, and enacts a sufficiently narrow restriction.

Here's how the test works (for case cites, see Eugene Volokh, *Freedom of Speech, Permissible Tailoring, and Transcending Strict Scrutiny*, 144 U. Pa. L. Rev. 2417, 2418-24 (1996)):

b. *Compelling Governmental Interest*

The law must serve a compelling governmental interest. Think of this as a normative judgment about the ends rather than the means of the legislation—is the government concern at stake important enough to justify restricting speech?

1. The government can have no compelling interest in privileging subclasses of core protected speech—discussion about economic, social and political matters—over other subclasses. All such core protected speech "rest[s] on the highest rung of the hierarchy of First Amendment values." The mere interest in furthering a subset of this speech (for instance, labor picketing) "without more, cannot justify [a content-based] exemption" for such speech. *E.g.*, *Carey v. Brown* (1980) (p. 279).

2. Avoiding offense and restricting bad ideas are not compelling interests

by themselves: "[T]he government may not prohibit the expression of an idea simply because society finds the idea itself offensive or disagreeable." *E.g.*, *Texas v. Johnson* (1989) (p. 204).

3. A law's underinclusiveness—its failure to reach all speech that implicates the interest—may be evidence that an interest is not compelling. Such underinclusiveness suggests that the government itself doesn't see the interest as compelling enough to justify a broader restriction. *E.g.*, *Florida Star v. B.J.F.* (1989) (p. 286). It may also suggest that the government's true interest isn't really the one that the government is asserting. *E.g.*, *Carey v. Brown*.

4. An asserted interest might *itself* be impermissibly underinclusive, even if the law is narrowly fitted to the interest: The government (at least sometimes) may not claim a compelling interest in fighting one particular ill, but refuse to deal with other ills that seem very similar.

— Example: Say the government decides to ban only anti-abortion picketing, and claims that its interest is "preventing obstruction of sidewalks." *The law is underinclusive with respect to the interest*, because all picketing—whether anti-abortion picketing or not—risks obstructing sidewalks. The government's willingness to tolerate this risk for, say, labor picketing seems to suggest that the government doesn't think that keeping sidewalks clear is really that important.

— But say the government claims that the interest is "preventing obstruction of sidewalks by anti-abortion protesters." Here the law is not underinclusive relative to the interest—it covers precisely the speech that implicates the interest. But *the interest itself is underinclusive*, because the government can't explain why obstruction of sidewalks by labor protesters at the same clinic or animal rights protesters at a hospital is any less damaging than obstruction by anti-abortion protesters. *Simon & Schuster, Inc. v. Members of N.Y. State Crime Victims Bd.,* 502 U.S. 105, 1120-21(1991)

5. Outside these general areas, the Court has recognized several specific interests as compelling:

— "combating terrorism," *Holder v. Humanitarian Law Project* (p. 296);

— protecting the "psychological well-being of minors," including "shielding minors from the influence of literature that is not obscene by adult standards." *Sable Communications v. FCC*, 492 U.S. 115 (1989);

— protecting voters from confusion, undue influence, and intimidation (at least flowing from the physical presence of electioneers around polling places), *Burson v. Freeman,* 504 U.S. 191, 199 (1992) (plurality);

— preventing the sale of legislative votes, *McIntyre v. Ohio Elections Commission* (1995) (p. 441);

— "maintaining a stable political system," *Eu v. San Francisco County Democratic Cent. Comm.,* 489 U.S. 214, 226 (1989);

— "protecting the integrity of the judiciary," *Williams-Yulee v. Florida Bar* (2015) (p. 305);

— "maintaining the public's confidence in an impartial judiciary," *id.*;

— ensuring that "criminals do not profit from their crimes" and that victims are compensated by the criminals, *Simon & Schuster, Inc. v. Members of N.Y. State Crime Victims Bd.,* 502 U.S. 105, 118-19 (1991);

— protecting the right of "members of groups that have historically been subjected to discrimination ... to live in peace where they wish," *R.A.V. v. City of St. Paul* (1992) (p. 317).

6. On the other hand, the Court has held that the following interests are *not* compelling:

— "equalizing the relative ability of individuals and groups to influence the outcome of elections," *Buckley*;

— "reducing the allegedly skyrocketing costs of political campaigns," *id.*;

— "preserving party unity during a primary," *Eu*;

— protecting speakers who "are incapable of deciding for themselves the most effective way to exercise their First Amendment rights," *Riley v. National Fed'n for the Blind* (1988) (p. 518);

— producing elected officials who better represent the electorate, *California Democratic Party v. Jones* (2000) (p. 393);

— expanding candidate debate beyond the scope of partisan concerns, *id.*;

— "produc[ing] a society free of ... biases" against certain groups, *Hurley* (1995) (p. 531).

7. How do we know whether an interest is compelling or not? The Court has never explained. Lawyers have to:

— make common-sense arguments about why a particular interest is or is not very important;

— compare with the interests accepted or rejected by the cases; and

— argue by counterexample ("if this interest were compelling, then look at the restrictions that would be allowed; but these restrictions are clearly unconstitutional, so the interest cannot be compelling").

c. *Narrow Tailoring*

Most cases striking down speech restrictions rely primarily on the narrow tailoring prong. This is a mostly empirical inquiry into the means—as a factual matter, do the means satisfy all the following elements?

i. *Advancement of the Interest*

For a law to be narrowly tailored, the government must prove to the Court's satisfaction that the law actually materially advances the interest.

— The government needn't prove this scientifically, but may use common-sense argument, if persuasive enough. "The quantum of empirical evidence needed to satisfy heightened judicial scrutiny of legislative judgments will vary up or down with the novelty and plausibility of the justification raised." *Nixon v. Shrink Mo. Gov't PAC,* 528 U.S. 377 (2000).

ii. No Overinclusiveness

(2)

A law is __not__ narrowly tailored if it restricts a significant amount of speech that doesn't implicate the government interest. The theory here is that if the government can serve the interest while burdening less speech (without having to "draw ... unworkable" lines, *Williams-Yulee v. Florida Bar* (2015) (p. 305)), it should do so.

— There are two possible definitions of overinclusiveness: (1) a law is over-inclusive whenever it covers some speech that doesn't materially impli-cate the interest, and (2) a law is overinclusive __only__ if it covers speech that *can be practically identified* as not implicating the interest, and that can therefore be excluded from coverage.

— Consider a law that bans all large campaign contributions because of a concern that many large contributions will actually be hidden bribes. See *Buckley v. Valeo* (1976) (p. 466). Not all large contributions will *actually* jeopardize the interest, since not all large contributions are bribes; the trouble, though, is that there's no way of *conveniently identifying* which contributions jeopardize the interest. Under version (1) of overinclusiveness, the law is overinclusive because it bans contributions that aren't in fact bribes. But under version (2), the law isn't overinclu-sive because it's impossible to tell for sure which large contributions are bribes and which aren't, which means that all large contributions are *potentially* bribes and thus implicate the interest.

— Likewise, consider a law that bans all leafletting because of a concern that some people who get the leaflets will throw them on the ground. See *Schneider v. New Jersey* (1939) (p. 342), discussed in Part IV.A. Not all leaflets will *actually* jeopardize the interest, since not all leaflets will be thrown on the ground. But there's no way of *identifying* which leaflets are likely to be thus tossed away (since there won't always be a police-man there watching for litterers). Under version (1) of overinclusive-ness, the law is overinclusive because it bans some leafletting that doesn't in fact lead to littering. But under version (2), the law isn't over-inclusive because it's impossible to tell which leaflets will become litter, which means that all leafletting *potentially* leads to littering and thus implicates the interest.

— Generally, courts seem to adopt the second definition of overinclusive-ness (see, *e.g.*, *Williams-Yulee*), though *Schneider* may be an exception.

2nd def - not over-inclus it impossible to tell

(3)

iii. Least Restrictive Alternative

A law is __not__ narrowly tailored if there are less speech-restrictive means available that would serve the interest essentially as well as the speech re-striction would.

— Possible less restrictive alternatives: Restricting unprotected conduct rather than speech, or just limiting the speech rather than banning it.

Conduct

— The government need not, however, choose an alternative that "fall[s] short of serving [the] compelling interests." *Burson v. Freeman*, 504 U.S. 191 (1992) (plurality). The alternative must be the "least restrictive means among available, *effective* alternatives." *Ashcroft v. ACLU (II)* (p. 280). If you want to defeat a law by showing a less restrictive alternative, the alternative should be pretty much as effective as the restriction that's being challenged.

— It's not clear whether the proposed alternative has to be *exactly* as effective as the law that's being challenged: It seems that if it's *pretty close* (query how close that is) in effectiveness, that should be enough.

These first three items (*i* to *iii*) of narrowly tailoring are closely related, and all of them could be subsumed within the "least restrictive alternative" inquiry: If the law doesn't materially advance the interest, then not having the law at all would be a less restrictive but equally effective alternative. Likewise, if the law is overinclusive (at least under definition (2)), then a narrower law that exempted speech which doesn't implicate the interest would be less restrictive and equally effective. When the Court says that a law must be "necessary to serve a compelling state interest," it seems to be referring to these three components.

iv. No Underinclusiveness

A law is not narrowly tailored if it fails to restrict a significant amount of speech that harms the government interest to about the same degree as does the restricted speech.

— Underinclusiveness may suggest, as mentioned above, that the interest isn't very important.

— Underinclusiveness may also suggest that the government's real interest wasn't the stated one but was rather just a desire to favor one form of speech, or to suppress offensive or otherwise disfavored speech. *See, e.g., Williams-Yulee v. Florida Bar* (2015) (p. 305).

— Underinclusiveness, if sufficiently great, may "reveal that a law does not actually advance a compelling interest." *Williams-Yulee*; *Florida Star v. B.J.F.* (1989) (p. 286).

— Underinclusiveness may show the presence of content discrimination beyond that justified by the compelling interest. Because content discrimination presumptively violates the First Amendment, and is allowed only when justified by a compelling interest, the presence of this extra, unjustified distinction makes the law unconstitutional.

— Example: *Carey v. Brown* (p. 279), which held that a bar on nonlabor residential picketing was not narrowly tailored to the interest in preserving residential privacy because labor picketing and nonlabor picketing were equally intrusive.

— But see *Williams-Yulee*, which held that a law may permissibly target the speech "most likely to undermine" the government interest, and that the government "need not address all aspects of a problem in one fell swoop; policymakers may focus on their most pressing concerns."

v. Low Burden on Speech?

Some recent cases suggest that the degree to which the law burdens speech is important to the strict scrutiny inquiry: If the law restricts only a modest amount of speech, it might pass strict scrutiny; but if the law restricts a lot of speech, it might fail, even if that broad restriction is indeed the least restrictive means of serving that interest.

— Thus, *Holder v. Humanitarian Law Project* (2010) (p. 296) repeatedly stressed that the law banned only speech *coordinated* with a foreign terrorist organization, and left *independent advocacy* unpunished. The Court expressly noted that, in upholding the ban on coordinated speech, "we in no way suggest that a regulation of independent speech would pass constitutional muster, even if the Government were to show that such speech benefits foreign terrorist organizations."

  This suggests that, even if banning independent advocacy was seen as necessary to fighting terrorism—see Justice Breyer's dissent, which argues that independent advocacy can "legitima[te]" terrorist groups as much as coordinated advocacy does—such a broad ban might be too broad to be constitutional.

— Likewise, *Williams-Yulee v. Florida Bar* (2015) (p. 305) repeatedly stressed the narrowness of the restriction ("By any measure, Canon 7C(1) restricts a narrow slice of speech"), which suggested that a broader restriction—however necessary to preventing appearances of impropriety—might be unconstitutional.

vi. Permissible Tailoring

The Court has never expressly said so, but there's good reason to think that it would strike down some speech restrictions *even if* they are necessary to serve a compelling government interest and aren't underinclusive.

— For instance, bans on abstract advocacy of violence might well be the least restrictive means of serving the compelling interest in preventing violence: The alternative means—counterspeech and law enforcement—may be substantially less effective than a combination of counterspeech, law enforcement, and the advocacy ban. Still, presumably the Court would strike down such a restriction as an impermissible way of accomplishing the interest, effectively holding that such speech must be protected *even though* it does genuinely jeopardize a compelling government interest.

— Likewise, consider *Florida Star v. B.J.F.* (1989) (p. 286): The Court suggested that protecting rape victims' privacy and encouraging future victims to come forward may be compelling interests. But then the Court faulted the law for applying even when "the identity of the victim has ... become a reasonable subject of public concern—because, perhaps, questions have arisen whether the victim fabricated an assault by a particular person." (The Court also rejected the law on other grounds, which basically relate to overinclusiveness, less restrictive alternatives, and underinclusiveness.)

  Yet even if such questions about the victim's veracity have arisen, restricting publication of the victim's name is still necessary to serve the government interests. The questions might be unfounded, so the victim may still be entitled to her privacy. And future victims may be reluctant to come forward if they know they can be publicly named simply if questions arise about their veracity.

So if speech restrictions really are constitutional whenever they are necessary to serve a compelling interest, then a restriction on publishing rape victims' names should be upheld *even if it lacks a "reasonable subject of public concern" exception*. Yet the Court rejected this restriction—which suggests that some restrictions are unconstitutional *even when* they are necessary to a compelling government interest.

— One can argue that cases defining the boundaries of First Amendment exceptions (such as *Brandenburg* and *Miller*) themselves implicitly define some "permissible tailoring" rules by indicating what sorts of restrictions are permissible ways of avoiding certain kinds of harms: preventing incitement of violence, controlling the indirect harms flowing from exposure of willing adults to pornography, and the like. Thus, the argument would go, if a law serves an interest in "preventing violence," and the speech jeopardizes the interest by persuading people to act violently, then only those restrictions allowed by *Brandenburg* are "permissibly tailored"; *Brandenburg* has resolved the permissible tailoring question at least as to that particular kind of harm.

— This suggests that, in addition to asking whether a speech restriction is actually necessary to serving a compelling government interest (and isn't underinclusive with respect to that interest), the Court also implicitly asks whether the restriction is nonetheless somehow improper—too restrictive, or premised on a rationale that's inconsistent with the Court's view of the First Amendment. Some of the First Amendment policy arguments, such as the need to protect speech in order to protect the search for truth or democratic self-government, might come into play in performing this normative analysis.

— For more on this, see Volokh, 144 U. Pa. L. Rev. at 2418-24.

vii. Overinclusiveness vs. Overbreadth

"Overinclusiveness" in the strict scrutiny test (or in the intermediate scrutiny test applicable to content-neutral restrictions, see Part IV.A.a, p. 339) is *not* the same as "overbreadth" (p. 11).

Overbreadth defines when a statute can be challenged on its face. A person might argue: "Even if my speech fits within a First Amendment exception, and so could be banned under a narrow statute, this statute is overbroad—it bans a substantial amount of speech that can't constitutionally be restricted. The statute should thus be struck down as facially unconstitutional, since otherwise it will keep chilling all that protected speech." So, for instance, if there's a statute banning "all derogatory words said in public," and it has been interpreted as broadly as it's written, I can challenge it as overbroad even if I'm arrested under it for words that could have been punished under a narrower statute (*e.g.*, one limited to fighting words).

Overinclusiveness, on the other hand, is an aspect of the strict scrutiny and intermediate scrutiny inquiries, and comes into play only when such "means-ends" scrutiny is invoked. A statute is overinclusive with respect to a particular government interest if it prohibits speech that doesn't implicate that interest. Thus, for instance, in *Florida Star* the statute was likely overinclusive with respect to the interest in preventing the offender from killing or threatening to kill a victim-witness, partly because it applied even in situations where the victim's identity was already known to the offender (*e.g.,* because they were acquainted).

Of course, many laws that are overinclusive are also overbroad. Moreover, the overbreadth analysis asks whether the law covers a substantial amount of speech that can't constitutionally be restricted, and the question whether speech can constitutionally be restricted will often require asking whether the law passes strict scrutiny. Thus, the overbreadth and overinclusiveness analyses might often have to be conducted in the same case.

But they are conceptually different. Overbreadth is a doctrine related to when someone has standing to challenge a law on the grounds that it improperly chills third-party speakers. Overinclusiveness is an aspect of the strict scrutiny/intermediate scrutiny inquiry.

2. Problems

a. Problem: Drive-In Nudity

The city of Jacksonville bans showing films containing nudity in drive-in theaters when the theater's screen is visible from the street. Is this constitutional? Cf. *Erznoznik v. City of Jacksonville,* 422 U.S. 205 (1975).

b. Problem: Violence on Television

Your employer, Representative Dina Colosimo, asks you whether Congress may constitutionally prohibit violence on television (she doesn't give you any more specifics). What's your answer? Assume for purposes of this problem that television broadcasts are entitled to as much constitutional protection as any other medium of communication.

c. Problem: Candidate Speech During Wartime

The United States is fighting a slow, Vietnamesque war against Albania. Things seem to be going slowly in our favor, but the Albanians appear able to hold out until at least the next election. The current U.S. administration is offering the Albanians peace on harsh terms.

The U.S. presidential campaign is about to start, and Congress is concerned: What if a candidate announces that he would give the Albanians a more favorable offer? If this happens, the Albanians might refuse to come to terms until after the election, hoping the dovish candidate will win. And, of course, every month that peace is delayed could mean thousands of lost lives, both American and foreign.

Congress therefore bans all prospective presidential candidates from stating that they would offer peace terms that are more favorable than those the current administration is proposing. Would the ban be constitutional?

d. Problem: Treason

18 U.S.C. § 2381 provides:

> Whoever, owing allegiance to the United States, levies war against them or adheres to their enemies, giving them aid and comfort within the United States or elsewhere, is guilty of treason ....

"Owing allegiance" has generally been interpreted as covering all U.S. citizens and permanent residents. "Adher[ing] to [the United States'] enemies" has been interpreted as requiring intent to help the enemy, rather than just knowledge that one's actions help the enemy. Employment by the enemy isn't required, though; for instance, hiding an enemy saboteur with the intent of helping the enemy would qualify. "Giving ... aid and comfort" has been interpreted to cover even relatively slight aid.

Mildred Gillars, a U.S. citizen who worked for the Nazi propaganda service during World War II, is tried for recording the "Vision of Invasion" broadcast while working for the Nazis:

> This program was a radio play of an hour's length broadcast in the month before the Allied invasion of Europe. The scenes alternated between soldiers on a ship in the invasion and the home of an American soldier. The ship is sunk, the soldier is killed and he appears in a dream of his mother. The general theme is expressed in the following colloquy between the American mother and father:
>
> "Mother: But everyone says the invasion is suicide. The simplest person knows that. Between seventy and ninety percent of the boys will be killed or crippled for the rest of their lives.
>
> "Father: What can we do about it?
>
> "Mother: Bah. We could have done a lot about it. Have we got a government by the people or not? Roosevelt had no right to go to war."
>
> Witnesses who participated in the broadcast testified that the purpose was to prevent the invasion of Europe by telling the American people and soldiers that an attempted invasion would be risky with respect to the lives of the soldiers.

Gillars v. United States, 182 F.2d 962 (D.C. Cir. 1950).

Under modern First Amendment law, would Gillars be convicted? Should she be convicted? Consider also three alternative scenarios:

(1) Gillars broadcasts this from the U.S., paid by the Nazi government.

(2) Gillars broadcasts this from the U.S. for free, but discusses with Nazi agents what she should say.

(3) Gillars broadcasts this from the U.S. entirely on her own, but intending to help the Nazis win.

3. CASES: STRICT SCRUTINY NOT SATISFIED

a. *Carey v. Brown, 447 U.S. 455 (1980)*

Justice Brennan delivered the opinion of the Court.

[An Illinois] statute ... generally bars picketing of residences ..., but exempts ... "the peaceful picketing of a place of employment involved in a labor dispute." ... [S]everal of the appellees [were convicted under the statute for participating] in a peaceful demonstration on the public sidewalk in front of the home of ... [the] Mayor of Chicago, protesting his alleged failure to support the busing of schoolchildren to achieve racial integration....

[A.] [T]he Illinois statute discriminates between lawful and unlawful conduct based upon the content of the demonstrator's communication. On its face, the Act accords preferential treatment to the expression of views on one particular subject; information about labor disputes may be freely disseminated, but discussion of all other issues is restricted....

When government regulation discriminates among speech-related activities in a public forum, the Equal Protection Clause mandates that the legislation be finely tailored to serve substantial state interests, and the justifications offered for any distinctions it draws must be carefully scrutinized. [In later cases, the Court held that this test also applies under the Free Speech Clause, and concluded a *compelling* interest, not just a substantial one, is required.—ed.] [Appellant] argues that the state interests here are especially compelling and particularly well served by a statute that accords differential treatment to labor and nonlabor picketing....

[B.] We find it unnecessary ... to consider [the place of] the State's interest in residential privacy ... in the hierarchy of societal values. For even the most legitimate goal may not be advanced in a constitutionally impermissible manner. And though we might agree that certain state interests may be so compelling that where no adequate alternatives exist a content-based distinction—if narrowly drawn—would be a permissible way of furthering those objectives, this is not such a case.

First, the generalized classification which the statute draws suggests that Illinois itself has determined that residential privacy is not a transcendent objective: While broadly permitting all peaceful labor picketing notwithstanding the disturbances it would undoubtedly engender, the statute makes no attempt to distinguish among various sorts of nonlabor picketing on the basis of the harms they would inflict on the privacy interest. The apparent overinclusiveness and underinclusiveness of the statute's restriction would seem largely to undermine appellant's claim that the prohibition of all nonlabor picketing can be justified by reference to the State's interest in maintaining domestic tranquility.

More fundamentally, the exclusion for labor picketing cannot be upheld as a means of protecting residential privacy for the simple reason that nothing in the content-based labor-nonlabor distinction has any bearing whatsoever on privacy.... [N]othing inherent in the nature of peaceful labor picketing [makes] it any less disruptive of residential privacy than peaceful picketing on issues of broader social concern....

{[A]ppellant asserts that the exception for labor picketing does not contravene the State's interest in preserving residential tranquility because of the unique character of a residence that is a "place of employment." By "inviting" a worker into his home and converting that dwelling into a place of employment, the argument goes, the resident has diluted his entitlement to total privacy.... [H]e has "waived" his right to be free from picketing with respect to disputes arising out of the employment relationship, thereby justifying the statute's narrow labor exception ....

[But n]umerous types of peaceful picketing other than labor picketing would have but a negligible impact on privacy interests, and numerous other actions of a homeowner might constitute "nonresidential" uses of his property and would thus serve to vitiate the right to residential privacy. For example, the resident who prominently decorates his windows and front yard with posters promoting the qualifications of one candidate for political office might be said to "invite" a counter-demonstration for supporters of an opposing candidate.

Similarly, a county chairman who uses his home to meet with his district captains and to discuss some controversial issue might well expect that those who are deeply concerned about the decision the chairman will ultimately reach would want to make their views known by demonstrating outside his home during the meeting. And, with particular regard to the facts of the instant case, it borders on the frivolous to suggest that a resident who invites a repairman into his home to fix his television set has "waived" his right to privacy with respect to a dispute between the repairman and the local union, but that the official who has voluntarily chosen to enter the public arena has not likewise "waived" his right to privacy with respect to a challenge to his views on significant issues of social and economic policy.}

[C.] The second important objective advanced by appellant in support of the statute is the State's interest in providing special protection for labor protests.... [But we reject the view that] labor picketing is more deserving of First Amendment protection than are public protests over other issues, particularly the important economic, social....

Public-issue picketing, "an exercise of ... basic constitutional rights in their most pristine and classic form," has always rested on the highest rung of the hierarchy of First Amendment values .... While the State's motivation in protecting the First Amendment rights of employees involved in labor disputes is commendable, that factor, without more, cannot justify the labor picketing exemption....

Justice Rehnquist, with whom ... Chief Justice [Burger] and Justice Blackmun join, dissenting. [Omitted.—ed.]

b. *Ashcroft v. ACLU (II), 542 U.S. 656 (2004)*

Justice Kennedy delivered the opinion of the Court....

[A.] [The Child Online Protection Act] imposes criminal penalties of a $50,000 fine and six months in prison for the knowing posting, for "commercial purposes," of World Wide Web content that is "harmful to minors." Material that is "harmful to minors" is defined as:

any communication, picture, image, ... recording, writing, or other matter of any kind that is obscene or that—

(A) the average person, applying contemporary community standards, would find, taking the material as a whole and with respect to minors, is designed to appeal to, or is designed to pander to, the prurient interest;

(B) depicts, describes, or represents, in a manner patently offensive with respect to minors, an actual or simulated sexual act or sexual contact, an actual or simulated normal or perverted sexual act, or a lewd exhibition of the genitals or post-pubescent female breast; and

(C) taken as a whole, lacks serious literary, artistic, political, or scientific value for minors.

"Minors" are defined as "any person under 17 years of age." A person acts for "commercial purposes only if such person is engaged in the business of making such communications[]" ... "although it is not necessary ... that the making or offering to make such communications be the person's sole or principal business or source of income."

[T]he statute ... also provides an affirmative defense to those who [show that they have] ...

restricted access by minors to material that is harmful to minors—

(A) by requiring use of a credit card, debit account, adult access code, or adult personal identification number;

(B) by accepting a digital certificate that verifies age, or

(C) by any other reasonable measures that are feasible under available technology....

[The District Court preliminarily enjoined the enforcement of COPA, though the injunction didn't purport to prevent prosecution based on material that's obscene even for adults.—ed.]

[B.] A statute that "effectively suppresses a large amount of speech that adults have a constitutional right to receive and to address to one another ... is unacceptable if less restrictive alternatives would be at least as effective in achieving the legitimate purpose that the statute was enacted to serve." ... In considering this question, a court assumes that certain protected speech may be regulated, and then asks what is the least restrictive alternative that can be used to achieve that goal. The purpose of the test is not to consider whether the challenged restriction has some effect in achieving Congress' goal[, but] ... to ensure that speech is restricted no further than necessary to achieve the goal, for it is important to assure that legitimate speech is not chilled or punished.

For that reason, the test does not begin with the status quo of existing regulations, then ask whether the challenged restriction has some additional ability to achieve Congress' legitimate interest. Any restriction on speech could be justified under that analysis. Instead, the court should ask whether the challenged regulation is the least restrictive means among available, effective alternatives.

In deciding whether to grant a preliminary injunction ..., a district court must consider whether the plaintiffs have demonstrated that they are likely to prevail on the merits.... As the Government bears the burden of proof on the ultimate question of COPA's constitutionality, respondents must be deemed likely to prevail unless the Government has shown that respondents' proposed less restrictive alternatives are less effective than COPA.... [But] on this record there are a number of plausible, less restrictive alternatives to the statute.

The primary alternative considered by the District Court was blocking and filtering software.... Filters are less restrictive than COPA. They impose selective restrictions on speech at the receiving end, not universal restrictions at the source. Under a filtering regime, adults without children may gain access to speech they have a right to see without having to identify themselves or provide their credit card information. Even adults with children may obtain access to the same speech on the same terms simply by turning off the filter on their home computers.

Above all, promoting the use of filters does not condemn as criminal any category of speech, and so the potential chilling effect is eliminated, or at least much diminished. All of these things are true, moreover, regardless of how broadly or narrowly the definitions in COPA are construed.

Filters also may well be more effective than COPA. First, a filter can prevent minors from seeing all pornography, not just pornography posted to the Web from America. The District Court noted in its factfindings that one witness estimated that 40% of harmful-to-minors content comes from overseas. COPA does not prevent minors from having access to those foreign harmful materials. That alone makes it possible that filtering software might be more effective in serving Congress' goals. Effectiveness is likely to diminish even further if COPA is upheld, because the providers of the materials that would be covered by the statute simply can move their operations overseas.

It is not an answer to say that COPA reaches some amount of materials that are harmful to minors; the question is whether it would reach more of them than less restrictive alternatives. In addition, the District Court found that verification systems may be subject to evasion and circumvention, for example by minors who have their own credit cards. Finally, filters also may be more effective because they can be applied to all forms of Internet communication, including e-mail, not just communications available via the World Wide Web....

Filtering software, of course, is not a perfect solution to the problem of children gaining access to harmful-to-minors materials. It may block some materials that are not harmful to minors and fail to catch some that are.

Whatever the deficiencies of filters, however, the Government failed to introduce specific evidence proving that existing technologies are less effective than the restrictions in COPA. The District Court made a specific factfinding that "[n]o evidence was presented to the Court as to the percentage of time that blocking and filtering technology is over- or underinclusive." In the absence of a showing as to the relative effectiveness of COPA and the alternatives proposed by respondents, it was not an abuse of discretion for the District Court to grant the preliminary injunction....

[T]he argument that filtering software is not an available alternative because Congress may not require it to be used ... carries little weight, because Congress undoubtedly may act to encourage the use of filters. We have held that Congress can give strong incentives to schools and libraries to use them. It could also take steps to promote their development by industry, and their use by parents. It is incorrect, for that reason, to say that filters are part of the current regulatory status quo.

The need for parental cooperation does not automatically disqualify a proposed less restrictive alternative. In enacting COPA, Congress said its goal was to prevent the "widespread availability of the Internet" from providing "opportunities for minors to access materials ... in a manner that can frustrate parental supervision or control." COPA presumes that parents lack the ability, not the will, to monitor what their children see. By enacting programs to promote use of filtering software, Congress could give parents that ability without subjecting protected speech to severe penalties....

[C.] [T]here are substantial factual disputes remaining .... [T]here is a serious gap in the evidence as to the effectiveness of filtering software.... [Also], the factual record does not reflect current technological reality—a serious flaw in any case involving the Internet.... More and better filtering alternatives may exist than when the District Court entered its findings [in February 1999, over five years ago]....

Delay between the time that a district court makes factfindings and the time that a case reaches this Court is inevitable .... We do not mean, therefore, to set up an insuperable obstacle to fair review. Here, however, the usual gap has doubled because the case has been through the Court of Appeals twice.... By affirming the preliminary injunction and remanding for trial, we allow the parties to update and supplement the factual record to reflect current technological realities....

[Finally, s]ince the District Court made its factfindings, Congress has passed at least two further statutes that might qualify as less restrictive alternatives to COPA—a prohibition on misleading domain names, and a statute creating a minors-safe "Dot Kids" domain. Remanding for trial will allow the District Court to take into account those additional potential alternatives....

Justice Scalia, dissenting. [Omitted.—ed.]

Justice Breyer, with whom ... Chief Justice [Rehnquist] and Justice O'Connor join, dissenting....

[A.] [T]he Act, properly interpreted, imposes a burden on protected speech that is no more than modest. [T]he addition of the words "with respect to minors," and "for minors" ... to a definition that would otherwise cover only obscenity expands the statute's scope only slightly.

[M]aterial that appeals to the "prurient interest[s]" of some group of adolescents or postadolescents will almost inevitably appeal to the "prurient interest[s]" of some group of adults as well.... [And] one cannot easily imagine material that has serious literary, artistic, political, or scientific value for a significant group of adults, but lacks such value for any significant group of minors. Thus, the statute, read literally, insofar as it extends beyond the legally obscene, could reach only borderline cases....

Respondents fear prosecution for the Internet posting of[,] ... for example: an essay about a young man's experience with masturbation and sexual shame; "a serious discussion about birth control practices, homosexuality, ... or the consequences of prison rape"; an account by a 15-year-old, written for therapeutic purposes, of being raped when she was 13; a guide to self-examination for testicular cancer; a graphic illustration of how to use a condom; or any of the other postings of modern literary or artistic works or discussions of sexual identity, homosexuality, sexually transmitted diseases, sex education, or safe sex, [and] Aldous Huxley's Brave New World, J.D. Salinger's Catcher in the Rye, or, as the complaint would have it, "Ken Starr's report on the Clinton-Lewinsky scandal" [citing various parties' and amici's statements—ed.]. These materials are *not* both (1) "designed to appeal to ... the prurient interest" of significant groups of minors *and* (2) lacking in "serious literary, artistic, political, or scientific value" for significant groups of minors. Thus, they fall outside [the Act]....

[B.] The Act does not censor the material it covers. Rather, it requires providers of the "harmful to minors" material to restrict minors' access to it by verifying age. They can do so by inserting screens that verify age using a credit card, adult personal identification number, or other similar technology. In this way, the Act requires creation of an internet screen that minors, but not adults, will find difficult to bypass....

[T]he screening requirement imposes some burden on adults who seek access to the regulated material, as well as on its providers.... [A] Web site could store card numbers or passwords at between 15 and 20 cents per number. And verification services provide free verification to Web site operators, while charging users less than $20 per year.... In addition to the monetary cost, and despite strict requirements that identifying information be kept confidential, the identification requirements inherent in age-screening may lead some users to fear embarrassment. Both monetary costs and potential embarrassment can deter potential viewers and, in that sense, the statute's requirements may restrict access to a site. But ... restrictions of this kind do not automatically violate the Constitution....

[C.] [T]he relevant constitutional question [under strict scrutiny] is not the question the Court asks: Would it be less restrictive to do nothing? Of course it would be.

Rather, the relevant question posits a comparison of (a) a status quo that includes filtering software with (b) a change in that status quo that adds to it an age-verification screen requirement. Given the existence of filtering software, does the problem Congress identified remain significant?...

Does the Act, compared to the status quo, significantly advance the ball? (An affirmative answer to these questions will not justify "[a]ny restriction on speech," as the Court claims, for a final answer in respect to constitutionality must take account of burdens and alternatives as well.)

The answers to these intermediate questions are clear: Filtering software, as presently available, does not solve the "child protection" problem. It suffers from four serious inadequacies that prompted Congress to pass legislation instead of relying on its voluntary use.

First, its filtering is faulty, allowing some pornographic material to pass through without hindrance.... [T]he software alone cannot distinguish between the most obscene pictorial image and the Venus de Milo....

Second, filtering software costs money. Not every family has the $40 or so necessary to install it. By way of contrast, age screening costs less.

Third, filtering software depends upon parents willing to decide where their children will surf the Web and able to enforce that decision. As to millions of American families, that is not a reasonable possibility. More than 28 million school age children have both parents or their sole parent in the work force, at least 5 million children are left alone at home without supervision each week, and many of those children will spend afternoons and evenings with friends who may well have access to computers and more lenient parents.

Fourth, software blocking lacks precision, with the result that those who wish to use it to screen out pornography find that it blocks a great deal of material that is valuable.... Indeed, the [ACLU] ... told Congress that filtering software "block[s] out valuable and protected information, such as ... web sites including those of the American Association of University Women, the AIDS Quilt, the Town Hall Political Site (run by ... [various] conservative groups)." The software "is simply incapable of discerning between constitutionally protected and unprotected speech." It "inappropriately blocks valuable, protected speech, and does not effectively block the sites [it is] intended to block." ...

Thus, Congress could reasonably conclude that a system that relies entirely upon the use of [filtering] software is not an effective system. And a law that adds to that system an age-verification screen requirement significantly increases the system's efficacy. That is to say, at a modest additional cost to those adults who wish to obtain access to a screened program, that law will bring about better, more precise blocking, both inside and outside the home.

The Court's response—that 40% of all pornographic material may be of foreign origin—is beside the point. Even assuming (I believe unrealistically) that *all* foreign originators will refuse to use screening, the Act would make a difference in respect to 60% of the Internet's commercial pornography. I cannot call that difference insignificant....

[D.] The Court proposes two real alternatives, *i.e.*, two potentially less restrictive ways in which Congress might alter the status quo in order to achieve its "compelling" objective.

First, the Government might "act to encourage" the use of blocking and filtering software.... If one imagines enough government resources devoted to the problem and perhaps additional scientific advances, then, of course, the use of software might become as effective and less restrictive. Obviously, the Government could give all parents, schools, and Internet cafes free computers with filtering programs already installed, hire federal employees to train parents and teachers on their use, and devote millions of dollars to the development of better software. The result might be an alternative that is extremely effective.

But the Constitution does not, because it cannot, require the Government to disprove the existence of magic solutions, *i.e.*, solutions that, put in general terms [and without considering budgetary constraints], will solve any problem less restrictively but with equal effectiveness.... Perhaps that is why no party has argued seriously that additional expenditure of government funds to encourage the use of screening is a "less restrictive alternative."

Second, the majority suggests decriminalizing the statute, noting the "chilling effect" of criminalizing ... speech. To remove a major sanction, however, would make the statute less effective, virtually by definition....

c.   *Florida Star v. B.J.F., 491 U.S. 524 (1989)*

Justice Marshall delivered the opinion of the Court.

[A.] [A]ppellee B.J.F. reported to the Duval County, Florida, Sheriff's Department ... that she had been robbed and sexually assaulted by an unknown assailant. The Department prepared a report on the incident which identified B.J.F. by her full name. The Department then placed the report in its [publicly accessible] pressroom....

A Florida Star reporter ... prepared a one-paragraph article about the crime, derived entirely from [a] copy of the police report. The article included B.J.F.'s full name[, and read] ...:

> [B.J.F.] reported on Thursday, October 20, she was crossing Brentwood Park, which is in the 500 block of Golfair Boulevard, enroute to her bus stop, when an unknown black man ran up behind the lady and placed a knife to her neck and told her not to yell. The suspect then undressed the lady and had sexual intercourse with her before fleeing the scene with her 60 cents, Timex watch and gold necklace. Patrol efforts have been suspended concerning this incident because of a lack of evidence.

In printing B.J.F.'s full name, The Florida Star violated its internal policy of not publishing the names of sexual offense victims....

B.J.F. [sued] the Department and The Florida Star, alleging that these parties negligently violated § 794.03[, which makes it unlawful to "print, publish, or broadcast ... in any instrument of mass communication" the name of the victim of a sexual offense].... The jury awarded B.J.F. $75,000 in compensatory damages and $25,000 in punitive damages. Against the actual damages award, the judge set off B.J.F.'s settlement with the Department....

[B.] [We need not] accept appellant's invitation to hold broadly that truthful publication may never be punished consistent with the First Amendment. Our cases have carefully eschewed reaching this ultimate question, mindful that the future may bring scenarios which prudence counsels our not resolving anticipatorily....

[Instead, we analyze the case] with reference to [a more] limited First Amendment principle [set forth in *Smith v. Daily Mail Publishing Co.,* 443 U.S. 97 (1979)] ...: "[I]f a newspaper lawfully obtains truthful information about a matter of public significance then state officials may not constitutionally punish publication of the information, absent a need to further a state interest of the highest order." ... [T]hat principle is supported by at least three separate considerations, in addition to ... the overarching "public interest, secured by the Constitution, in the dissemination of truth."

First, because the *Daily Mail* formulation only protects the publication of information which a newspaper has "lawfully obtain[ed]," the government retains ample means of safeguarding significant interests upon which publication may impinge, including protecting a rape victim's anonymity. To the extent sensitive information rests in private hands, the government may under some circumstances forbid its nonconsensual acquisition, thereby bringing outside of the *Daily Mail* principle the publication of any information so acquired.

To the extent sensitive information is in the government's custody, it ... may classify certain information, establish and enforce procedures ensuring its redacted release, and extend a damages remedy against the government or its officials where the government's mishandling of sensitive information leads to its dissemination. Where information is entrusted to the government, a less drastic means than punishing truthful publication almost always exists for guarding against the dissemination of private facts. {[We have no occasion to decide here] whether, in cases where information has been acquired *unlawfully* by a newspaper or by a source, government may ever punish not only the unlawful acquisition, but the ensuing publication as well....}

[Second,] ... punishing the press for its dissemination of information which is already publicly available is relatively unlikely to advance the interests in the service of which the State seeks to act. It is not, of course, always the case that information lawfully acquired by the press is known, or accessible, to others. But where the government has made certain information publicly available, it is highly anomalous to sanction persons other than the source of its release.... "By placing the information in the public domain on official court records, the State must be presumed to have concluded that the public interest was thereby being served."

A third and final consideration is the "timidity and self-censorship" which may result from allowing the media to be punished for publishing certain truthful information.... A contrary rule, depriving protection to those who rely on the government's implied representations of the lawfulness of dissemination, would force upon the media the onerous obligation of sifting through government press releases, reports, and pronouncements to prune out material arguably unlawful for publication....

[A]ppellant lawfully obtained B.J.F.'s name.... [T]hat the Department apparently failed to fulfill its obligation under § 794.03 not to "cause or allow to be ... published" the name of a sexual offense victim [does not] make the newspaper's ensuing receipt of this information unlawful. Even assuming the Constitution permitted a State to proscribe *receipt* of information, Florida has not taken this step.

It is, clear, furthermore, that the news article concerned "a matter of public significance" in the sense in which the *Daily Mail* synthesis of prior cases used that term. That is, the article generally, as opposed to the specific identity contained within it, involved a matter of paramount public import: the commission, and investigation, of a violent crime which had been reported to authorities.

[C.] The second inquiry is whether imposing liability on appellant pursuant to § 794.03 serves "a need to further a state interest of the highest order." Appellee argues that a rule punishing publication furthers three closely related interests: [(a)] the privacy of victims of sexual offenses; [(b)] the physical safety of such victims, who may be targeted for retaliation if their names become known to their assailants; and [(c)] the goal of encouraging victims of such crimes to report these offenses without fear of exposure....

[T]hese are highly significant interests, a fact underscored by the Florida Legislature's explicit attempt to protect these interests by enacting a criminal statute prohibiting much dissemination of victim identities. We accordingly do not rule out the possibility that, in a proper case, imposing civil sanctions for publication of the name of a rape victim might be so overwhelmingly necessary to advance these interests as to satisfy the *Daily Mail* standard. For three independent reasons, however, imposing liability for publication under the circumstances of this case is too precipitous a means of advancing these interests to convince us that there is a "need" ... for Florida to take this extreme step.

[1.] First is the manner in which appellant obtained the identifying information in question. As we have noted, where the government itself provides information to the media, it is most appropriate to assume that the government had, but failed to utilize, far more limited means of guarding against dissemination than the extreme step of punishing truthful speech.

That assumption is richly borne out in this case. B.J.F.'s identity would never have come to light were it not for the erroneous, if inadvertent, inclusion by the Department of her full name in an incident report made available in a pressroom open to the public....

Where, as here, the government has failed to police itself in disseminating information, ... the imposition of damages against the press for its subsequent publication can hardly be said to be a narrowly tailored means of safeguarding anonymity. Once the government has placed such information in the public domain, "reliance must rest upon the judgment of those who decide what to publish or broadcast," and hopes for restitution must rest upon the willingness of the government to compensate victims for their loss of privacy and to protect them from the other consequences of its mishandling of the information which these victims provided in confidence.

That appellant gained access to the information in question through a government news release makes it especially likely that, if liability were to be imposed, self-censorship would result. Reliance on a news release is a paradigmatically "routine newspaper reporting techniqu[e]." The government's issuance of such a release, without qualification, can only convey to recipients that the government considered dissemination lawful, and indeed expected the recipients to disseminate the information further....

[2.] A second problem with Florida's imposition of liability for publication is the broad sweep of the negligence *per se* standard applied under the civil cause of action implied from § 794.03. Unlike claims based on the common law tort of invasion of privacy, civil actions based on § 794.03 require no case-by-case findings that the disclosure of a fact about a person's private life was one that a reasonable person would find highly offensive.

On the contrary, under the *per se* theory of negligence adopted by the courts below, liability follows automatically from publication. This is so regardless of whether the identity of the victim is already known throughout the community; whether the victim has voluntarily called public attention to the offense; or whether the identity of the victim has otherwise become a reasonable subject of public concern—because, perhaps, questions have arisen whether the victim fabricated an assault by a particular person.

Nor is there a scienter requirement of any kind under § 794.03, engendering the perverse result that truthful publications challenged [under § 794.03] are less protected by the First Amendment than even the least protected defamatory falsehoods: those involving purely private figures, where liability [requires] ... negligence.... More individualized adjudication is ... indispensable where the State, seeking to safeguard the anonymity of crime victims, sets its face against publication of their names.

[3.] Third, ... [the] underinclusiveness of § 794.03 raises serious doubts about whether Florida is, in fact, serving, with this statute, the significant interests which appellee invokes in support of affirmance. Section 794.03 prohibits the publication of identifying information only if this information appears in an "instrument of mass communication" .... An individual who maliciously spreads word of the identity of a rape victim is thus not covered, despite the fact that the communication of such information to persons who live near, or work with, the victim may have consequences as devastating as the exposure of her name to large numbers of strangers.

When a State attempts the extraordinary measure of punishing truthful publication in the name of privacy, it must demonstrate its commitment to advancing this interest by applying its prohibition evenhandedly, to the smalltime disseminator as well as the media giant. Where important First

Amendment interests are at stake, the mass scope of disclosure is not an acceptable surrogate for injury. A ban on disclosures effected by "instrument[s] of mass communication" simply cannot be defended on the ground that partial prohibitions may effect partial relief. Without more careful and inclusive precautions against alternative forms of dissemination, we cannot conclude that Florida's selective ban on publication by the mass media satisfactorily accomplishes its stated purpose....

Justice Scalia, concurring in part and ... in the judgment.

I think it sufficient ... to rely upon the third ground set forth in the Court's opinion: that a law cannot be regarded as protecting an interest "of the highest order," and thus as justifying a restriction upon truthful speech, when it leaves appreciable damage to that supposedly vital interest unprohibited.... I would anticipate that the rape victim's discomfort at the dissemination of news of her misfortune among friends and acquaintances would be at least as great as her discomfort at its publication by the media to people to whom she is only a name. Yet the law in question does not prohibit the former in either oral or written form. Nor is it at all clear, as I think it must be to validate this statute, that Florida's general privacy law would prohibit such gossip.

Nor ... is it credible that the interest meant to be served by the statute is the protection of the victim against a rapist still at large—an interest that arguably would extend only to mass publication. There would be little reason to limit a statute with that objective to rape alone; or to extend it to all rapes, whether or not the felon has been apprehended and confined....

This law has every appearance of a prohibition that society is prepared to impose upon the press but not upon itself. Such a prohibition does not protect an interest "of the highest order." ...

Justice White, with whom ... Chief Justice [Rehnquist] and Justice O'Connor join, dissenting....

For B.J.F., ... the violation she suffered at a rapist's knifepoint marked only the beginning of her ordeal.... [As a result of her name being published,] B.J.F. received harassing phone calls, required mental health counseling, was forced to move from her home, and was even threatened with being raped again. Yet today, the Court holds that a jury award of $75,000 to compensate B.J.F. for the harm she suffered due to the Star's negligence is at odds with the First Amendment....

[A.] "The government's issuance of [a press] release, without qualification, can only convey to recipients that the government considered dissemination lawful," the Court suggests.... [But h]ere, the "release" of information provided by the government was not, as the Court says, "without qualification." ... [T]he crime incident report that inadvertently included B.J.F.'s name was posted in a room that contained signs making it clear that the names of rape victims ... were not to be published[, and the Star's reporter understood this limitation]....

By amending its public records statute to exempt rape victims' names from disclosure, and forbidding its officials to release such information, the

State has taken virtually every step imaginable to prevent what happened here.... Unfortunately, as this case illustrates, mistakes happen .... [I]t is not too much to ask the press, in instances such as this, to respect simple standards of decency and refrain from publishing a victims' name ....

[B.] Second, ... [t]he Court says that negligence *per se* permits a plaintiff to hold a defendant liable without a showing that the disclosure was "of a fact about a person's private life ... that a reasonable person would find highly offensive." But ... the legislature—reflecting popular sentiment—has determined that disclosure of the fact that a person was raped is categorically a revelation that reasonable people find offensive.

And as for the Court's suggestion that the Florida courts' theory permits liability without regard for whether the victim's identity is already known, or whether she herself has made it known—these are facts that would surely enter into the calculation of damages in such a case. In any event, none of these mitigating factors was present [in this case] ....

[C.] Third, the Court faults the Florida criminal statute for being underinclusive: § 794.03 covers disclosure of rape victims' names in "instrument[s] of mass communication," but not other means of distribution, the Court observes.... [But the law] excludes neighborhood gossips, because presumably the Florida Legislature has determined that neighborhood gossips do not pose the danger and intrusion to rape victims that "instrument[s] of mass communication" do.... Florida wanted to prevent the widespread distribution of rape victims' names, and therefore enacted a statute tailored almost as precisely as possible to achieving that end.

Moreover, ... Florida does recognize a tort of publication of private facts. Thus, it is quite possible that the neighborhood gossip whom the Court so fears being left scot free to spread news of a rape victim's identity would be subjected to the same (or similar) liability regime under which appellant was taxed....

[D.] If the First Amendment prohibits wholly private persons (such as B.J.F.) from recovering for the publication of the fact that she was raped, I doubt that there remain any "private facts" which persons may assume will not be published in the newspapers or broadcast on television.... [Yet] "[f]airly defined areas of privacy must have the protection of law if the quality of life is to continue to be reasonably acceptable. The public's right to know is, then, subject to reasonable limitations so far as concerns the private facts of its individual members." ...

Today, we hit the bottom of the slippery slope.... I would find a place to draw the line higher on the hillside: a spot high enough to protect B.J.F.'s desire for privacy and peace-of-mind in the wake of a horrible personal tragedy. There is no public interest in publishing the names, addresses, and phone numbers of persons who are the victims of crime—and no public interest in immunizing the press from liability in the rare cases where a State's efforts to protect a victim's privacy have failed....

d.   Brown v. Entertainment Merchants Ass'n, 564 U.S. 786 (2011)

[As we saw in Part II.C.3.b, p. 150, the majority in this case concluded that violent video games—even distributed to children—are just as protected as other speech, such as books, movies, and the like. We turn now to the Court's discussion of whether this protection can still be overcome by a compelling government interest.—ed.]

Justice Scalia delivered the opinion of the Court....

[A.] Because the Act imposes a restriction on the content of protected speech, it is invalid unless California can demonstrate that it passes strict scrutiny—that is, unless it is justified by a compelling government interest and is narrowly drawn to serve that interest. The State must specifically identify an "actual problem" in need of solving, and the curtailment of free speech must be actually necessary to the solution. That is a demanding standard. "It is rare that a regulation restricting speech because of its content will ever be permissible." California cannot meet that standard....

[B.] California relies primarily on the research of Dr. Craig Anderson and a few other research psychologists whose studies purport to show a connection between exposure to violent video games and harmful effects on children. These studies have been rejected by every court to consider them, and with good reason: They do not prove that violent video games *cause* minors to *act* aggressively (which would at least be a beginning).

Instead, "[n]early all of the research is based on correlation, not evidence of causation, and most of the studies suffer from significant, admitted flaws in methodology." They show at best some correlation between exposure to violent entertainment and minuscule real-world effects, such as children's feeling more aggressive or making louder noises in the few minutes after playing a violent game than after playing a nonviolent game. {One study, for example, found that children who had just finished playing violent video games were more likely to fill in the blank letter in "explo_e" with a "d" (so that it reads "explode") than with an "r" ("explore"). The prevention of this phenomenon, which might have been anticipated with common sense, is not a compelling state interest.}

Even taking for granted Dr. Anderson's conclusions that violent video games produce some effect on children's feelings of aggression, those effects are both small and indistinguishable from effects produced by other media. In his testimony in a similar lawsuit, Dr. Anderson admitted that the "effect sizes" of children's exposure to violent video games are "about the same" as that produced by their exposure to violence on television. And he admits that the *same* effects have been found when children watch cartoons starring Bugs Bunny or the Road Runner, or when they play video games like Sonic the Hedgehog that are rated "E" (appropriate for all ages), or even when they "vie[w] a picture of a gun."

{Perhaps [violent video games] do present a [serious] problem, and perhaps none of us would allow our own children to play them. But there are all sorts of "problems"—some of them surely more serious than this one—that cannot be addressed by governmental restriction of free expression: for example, the problem of encouraging anti-Semitism (*National Socialist Party of America v. Skokie,* 432 U.S. 43 (1977)), the problem of spreading a political philosophy hostile to the Constitution (*Noto v. United States,* 367 U.S. 290 (1961)), or the problem of encouraging disrespect for the Nation's flag (*Texas v. Johnson*).} ...

[C.] Of course, California has (wisely) declined to restrict Saturday morning cartoons, the sale of games rated for young children, or the distribution of pictures of guns. The consequence is that its regulation is wildly underinclusive when judged against its asserted justification, which in our view is alone enough to defeat it. Underinclusiveness raises serious doubts about whether the government is in fact pursuing the interest it invokes, rather than disfavoring a particular speaker or viewpoint. Here, California has singled out the purveyors of video games for disfavored treatment—at least when compared to booksellers, cartoonists, and movie producers—and has given no persuasive reason why.

The Act is also seriously underinclusive in another respect—and a respect that renders irrelevant the contentions of the concurrence and the dissents that video games are qualitatively different from other portrayals of violence. The California Legislature is perfectly willing to leave this dangerous, mind-altering material in the hands of children so long as one parent (or even an aunt or uncle) says it's OK. And there are not even any requirements as to how this parental or avuncular relationship is to be verified; apparently the child's or putative parent's, aunt's, or uncle's say-so suffices. That is not how one addresses a serious social problem....

[D.] California claims that the Act is justified in aid of parental authority: By requiring that the purchase of violent video games can be made only by adults, the Act ensures that parents can decide what games are appropriate. At the outset, we note our doubts that punishing third parties for conveying protected speech to children just in case their parents disapprove of that speech is a proper governmental means of aiding parental authority. Accepting that position would largely vitiate the rule that "only in relatively narrow and well-defined circumstances may government bar public dissemination of protected materials to [minors]."

But leaving that aside, California cannot show that the Act's restrictions meet a substantial need of parents who wish to restrict their children's access to violent video games but cannot do so. The video-game industry has in place a voluntary rating system designed to inform consumers about the content of games. [Details omitted.—ed.]

{Justice Breyer concludes that [filling the gaps left by imperfect compliance with the rating system justifies the restriction] because, according to the FTC's report, some "20% of those under 17 are still able to buy M-rated games." But some gap in compliance is unavoidable.... Even if the sale of violent video games to minors could be deterred further by increasing regulation, the government does not have a compelling interest in each marginal percentage point by which its goals are advanced.}

And finally, the Act's purported aid to parental authority is vastly over-inclusive. Not all of the children who are forbidden to purchase violent video games on their own have parents who *care* whether they purchase violent video games. While some of the legislation's effect may indeed be in support of what some parents of the restricted children actually want, its entire effect is only in support of what the State thinks parents *ought* to want. This is not the narrow tailoring to "assisting parents" that restriction of First Amendment rights requires....

Justice Alito, with whom the Chief Justice joins, concurring in the judgment....

[Justice Alito thought that the statute was unconstitutionally vague, but argued that a clearer restriction should be constitutional, in part because of the government interest in helping parents control what their children play.—ed.]

[The video-game industry adopted its voluntary rating system] in response to the threat of federal regulation, a threat that the Court's opinion may now be seen as largely eliminating.... [C]ompliance with this system at the time of the enactment of the California law left much to be desired—[and] future enforcement may decline if the video-game industry perceives that any threat of government regulation has vanished. {A 2004 Federal Trade Commission Report showed that 69 percent of unaccompanied children ages 13 to 16 were able to buy M-rated games and that 56 percent of 13-year-olds were able to buy an M-rated game.} ... [And] many parents today are simply not able to monitor their children's use of computers and gaming devices.} ...

Justice Breyer, dissenting.

[Justice Breyer didn't think strict scrutiny was called for here, but he did think the potential dangerousness of the video games would be relevant to whether they could be restricted. Here is his analysis.—ed.]

[A.] [T]here is considerable evidence that California's statute significantly furthers [the] {compelling interest in protecting the physical and psychological well-being of minors}. That is, in part, because video games are excellent teaching tools. Learning a practical task often means developing habits, becoming accustomed to performing the task, and receiving positive reinforcement when performing that task well. Video games can help develop habits, accustom the player to performance of the task, and reward the player for performing that task well. Why else would the Armed Forces incorporate video games into its training?

When the military uses video games to help soldiers train for missions, it is using this medium for a beneficial purpose. But California argues that when the teaching features of video games are put to less desirable ends, harm can ensue. In particular, extremely violent games can harm children by rewarding them for being violently aggressive in play, and thereby often teaching them to be violently aggressive in life. And video games can cause more harm in this respect than can typically passive media, such as books or films or television programs.

There are many scientific studies that support California's views. Social scientists, for example, have found *causal* evidence that playing these games results in harm. Longitudinal studies, which measure changes over time, have found that increased exposure to violent video games causes an increase in aggression over the same period. Experimental studies in laboratories have found that subjects randomly assigned to play a violent video game subsequently displayed more characteristics of aggression than those who played nonviolent games.

Surveys of 8th and 9th grade students have found a correlation between playing violent video games and aggression. Cutting-edge neuroscience has shown that "virtual violence in video game playing results in those neural patterns that are considered characteristic for aggressive cognition and behavior." And "meta-analyses," *i.e.,* studies of all the studies, have concluded that exposure to violent video games "was positively associated with aggressive behavior, aggressive cognition, and aggressive affect," and that "playing violent video games is a *causal* risk factor for long-term harmful outcomes."

Some of these studies take care to explain in a commonsense way why video games are potentially more harmful than, say, films or books or television. In essence, they say that the closer a child's behavior comes, not to watching, but to *acting* out horrific violence, the greater the potential psychological harm. [V]ideo games stimulate more aggression because "[p]eople learn better when they are actively involved," players are "more likely to identify with violent characters," and "violent games directly reward violent behavior[."]

Experts debate the conclusions of all these studies. Like many, perhaps most, studies of human behavior, each study has its critics, and some of those critics have produced studies of their own in which they reach different conclusions.... I, like most judges, lack the social science expertise to say definitively who is right.

But associations of public health professionals who do possess that expertise have reviewed many of these studies and found a significant risk that violent video games, when compared with more passive media, are particularly likely to cause children harm[:] ... "[O]ver 1000 studies ... point overwhelmingly to a causal connection between media violence and aggressive behavior in some children ... [and] the impact of violent interactive entertainment (video games and other interactive media) on young people ... may be *significantly more severe* than that wrought by television, movies, or music." "... Recent longitudinal studies ... have revealed that in as little as 3 months, high exposure to violent video games increased physical aggression. Other recent longitudinal studies ... have revealed similar effects across 2 years." [Similar quotes omitted.—ed.] ...

I would find sufficient grounds in these studies and expert opinions for this Court to defer to an elected legislature's conclusion that the video games in question are particularly likely to harm children....

[B.] I can find no "less restrictive" alternative to California's law that would be "at least as effective." ... [The] voluntary [rating] system has serious enforcement gaps.... The industry also argues for an alternative technological solution, namely "filtering at the console level." But it takes only a quick search of the Internet to find guides explaining how to circumvent any such technological controls. YouTube viewers, for example, have watched one of those guides (called "How to bypass parental controls on the Xbox 360") more than 47,000 times....

[C.] [W]here [government] interests [in preventing harm to children and protecting parental control over minors] work in tandem, it is not fatally "underinclusive" for a State to advance its interests in protecting children against the special harms present in an interactive video game medium through a default rule that still allows parents to provide their children with what their parents wish.

4.   Cases: Strict Scrutiny Satisfied

a.   *Holder v. Humanitarian Law Project, 561 U.S. 1 (2010)*

Chief Justice Roberts delivered the opinion of the Court....

[A.] 18 U.S.C. §2339B ... makes it a federal crime to "knowingly provid[e] material support or resources to a foreign terrorist organization." ...

"[M]aterial support or resources" means any property, tangible or intangible, or *service*, {except medicine or religious materials,} including

[a] [money] or ... financial services, lodging, {safehouses, false documentation or identification, communications equipment, facilities, weapons, lethal substances, explosives}, [and] {transportation},

[b] *training*[, which] {means instruction or teaching designed to impart a specific skill, as opposed to general knowledge},

[c] *expert advice or assistance*[, which] {means advice or assistance derived from scientific, technical or other specialized knowledge}, [and]

[d] *personnel* (1 or more individuals who may be or include oneself)[,] {defined as [people who would] "... work under that terrorist organization's direction or control or to organize, manage, supervise, or otherwise direct the operation of that organization"}. [Emphasis added.—ed.]

{"[P]ersonnel" does not cover *independent* advocacy: "Individuals who act entirely independently of the foreign terrorist organization to advance its goals or objectives shall not be considered to be working under the foreign terrorist organization's direction and control." "[S]ervice" similarly refers to concerted activity [performed in coordination with, or at the direction of, a foreign terrorist organization], not independent advocacy.} ...

[The Secretary of State may] designate an entity a "foreign terrorist organization"... upon finding that it is foreign, engages in "terrorist activity" or "terrorism," and thereby "threatens the security of United States nationals or" ... "the national defense, foreign relations, or economic interests of the United States." An entity designated a foreign terrorist organization may seek review of that designation before the D.C. Circuit within 30 days of that designation.

In 1997, the Secretary of State designated 30 groups as foreign terrorist organizations. Two of those groups are the Kurdistan Workers' Party (also known as the Partiya Karkeran Kurdistan, or PKK) and the Liberation Tigers of Tamil Eelam (LTTE). The PKK ... [aims to establish] an independent Kurdish state in southeastern Turkey. The LTTE ... [aims to create] an independent Tamil state in Sri Lanka.

The District Court ... found that the PKK and the LTTE engage in political and humanitarian activities. The Government has presented evidence that both groups have also committed numerous terrorist attacks, some of which have harmed American citizens. The LTTE sought judicial review of its designation as a foreign terrorist organization; the D.C. Circuit upheld that designation. The PKK did not challenge its designation.

Plaintiffs ... are ... the Humanitarian Law Project ... (a human rights organization with consultative status to the United Nations) [and other citizens and groups] .... Plaintiffs [claim that] § 2339B's prohibition on four types of material support—"training," "expert advice or assistance," "service," and "personnel["—] ... is invalid to the extent it prohibits them from ...: (1) "train[ing] members of [the] PKK on how to use humanitarian and international law to peacefully resolve disputes"; (2) "engag[ing] in political advocacy on behalf of Kurds who live in Turkey"; ... (3) "teach[ing] PKK members how to petition various representative bodies such as the United Nations for relief["; and (4)] "engag[ing] in political advocacy on behalf of Tamils who live in Sri Lanka." ...

[B.] [T]he material-support statute ... is carefully drawn to cover only a narrow category of speech to, under the direction of, or in coordination with foreign groups that the speaker knows to be terrorist organizations. {The dissent ... analyzes the statute as if it prohibited "[p]eaceful political advocacy" or "pure speech and association," without more. Section 2339B does not do that, and we do not address the constitutionality of any such prohibitions.} {The Government briefly analogizes speech coordinated with foreign terrorist organizations to [entirely unprotected] speech effecting a crime, like the words that constitute a conspiracy. *See, e.g., Giboney v. Empire Storage & Ice Co.* We do not consider any such argument because the Government does not develop it ....} ....

[The Court concluded the statute was content-based, see p. 375, and then analyzed it this way:—ed.] Everyone agrees that the Government's interest in combating terrorism is an urgent objective of the highest order. Plaintiffs' complaint is that the ban on material support, applied to what they wish to do, is not "necessary to further that interest[,]" ... because their support will advance only the legitimate activities of the designated terrorist organizations, not their terrorism.

Whether foreign terrorist organizations meaningfully segregate support of their legitimate activities from support of terrorism is an empirical question.... Congress made specific findings ... explicitly reject[ing] plaintiffs' contention that their support would not further the terrorist activities of the PKK and LTTE: "[F]oreign organizations that engage in terrorist activity are so tainted by their criminal conduct that *any contribution to such an organization* facilitates that conduct." ... We are convinced that Congress was justified in [so finding].

The PKK and the LTTE are deadly groups. "The PKK's insurgency has claimed more than 22,000 lives." The LTTE has engaged in extensive suicide bombings and political assassinations, including killings of the Sri Lankan President, Security Minister, and Deputy Defense Minister. "On January 31, 1996, the LTTE exploded a truck bomb filled with an estimated 1,000 pounds of explosives at the Central Bank in Colombo, killing 100 people and injuring more than 1,400. This bombing was the most deadly terrorist incident in the world in 1996." {The PKK and the LTTE have committed terrorist acts against American citizens abroad ....} It is not difficult to conclude as Congress did that the "tain[t]" of such violent activities is so great that working in coordination with or at the command of the PKK and LTTE serves to legitimize and further their terrorist means.

Material support meant to "promot[e] peaceable, lawful conduct" can further terrorism by foreign groups in multiple ways.... Such support frees up other resources within the organization that may be put to violent ends. It also importantly helps lend legitimacy to foreign terrorist groups—legitimacy that makes it easier for those groups to persist, to recruit members, and to raise funds—all of which facilitate more terrorist attacks....

"... [T]errorist groups systematically conceal their activities behind charitable, social, and political fronts." "Indeed, some designated foreign terrorist organizations use social and political components to recruit personnel to carry out terrorist operations, and to provide support to criminal terrorists and their families in aid of such operations." [For instance,] "... Hamas is able to use its overt political and charitable organizations as a financial and logistical support network for its terrorist operations[."] ...

[Likewise,] "[f]unds raised ostensibly for charitable purposes have in the past been redirected by some terrorist groups to fund the purchase of arms and explosives." ... {Both common sense and the evidence submitted by the Government make clear that material support of a terrorist group's lawful activities[—including not just funds or goods but also the support plaintiffs seek to provide—]facilitates the group's ability to attract "funds," "financing," and "goods" that will further its terrorist acts.}

The dissent argues that there is "no natural stopping place" for the proposition that aiding a foreign terrorist organization's lawful activity promotes the terrorist organization as a whole. But Congress has settled on just such a natural stopping place: The statute reaches only material support coordinated with or under the direction of a designated foreign terrorist organization. Independent advocacy that might be viewed as promoting the group's legitimacy is not covered.

[C.] Providing foreign terrorist groups with material support in any form also furthers terrorism by straining the United States' relationships with its allies and undermining cooperative efforts between nations to prevent terrorist attacks.... For example, [NATO member] Turkey ... is defending itself against a violent insurgency waged by the PKK. That nation and our other allies would react sharply to Americans furnishing material support to foreign groups like the PKK, and would hardly be mollified by the explanation that the support was meant only to further those groups' "legitimate" activities....

[D.] In analyzing whether it is possible in practice to distinguish material support for a foreign terrorist group's violent activities and its nonviolent activities, ... [the] evaluation of the facts by the Executive [and Congress] ... is entitled to deference. This litigation implicates sensitive and weighty interests of national security and foreign affairs....

We are one with the dissent that the Government's "authority and expertise in these matters do not automatically trump the Court's own obligation to secure the protection that the Constitution grants to individuals." But when it comes to collecting evidence and drawing factual inferences in this area, "the lack of competence on the part of the courts is marked," and respect for the Government's conclusions is appropriate.

One reason for that respect is that national security and foreign policy concerns arise in connection with efforts to confront evolving threats in an area where information can be difficult to obtain and the impact of certain conduct difficult to assess. The dissent slights these real constraints in demanding hard proof—with "detail," "specific facts," and "specific evidence"—that plaintiffs' proposed activities will support terrorist attacks. That would be a dangerous requirement.

In this context, conclusions must often be based on informed judgment rather than concrete evidence, and that reality affects what we may reasonably insist on from the Government.... The Government, when seeking to prevent imminent harms in the context of international affairs and national security, is not required to conclusively link all the pieces in the puzzle before we grant weight to its empirical conclusions. "[B]ecause of the changeable and explosive nature of contemporary international relations, ... Congress ... must of necessity paint with a brush broader than that it customarily wields in domestic areas[."] ...

[E.] We also find it significant that Congress has been conscious of its own responsibility to consider how its actions may implicate constitutional concerns. First, §2339B only applies to designated foreign terrorist organizations. There is, and always has been, a limited number of those organizations designated by the Executive Branch, and any groups so designated may seek judicial review of the designation.

Second, in response to the lower courts' holdings in this litigation, Congress added clarity to the statute by providing narrowing definitions of the terms "training," "personnel," and "expert advice or assistance," as well as an explanation of the knowledge required to violate §2339B.

Third, in effectuating its stated intent not to abridge First Amendment rights, Congress has also displayed a careful balancing of interests in creating limited exceptions to the ban on material support ..., for example [for] medicine and religious materials. In this area perhaps more than any other, the Legislature's superior capacity for weighing competing interests means that "we must be particularly careful not to substitute our judgment of what is desirable for that of Congress."

Finally, and most importantly, Congress has avoided any restriction on independent advocacy, or indeed any activities not directed to, coordinated with, or controlled by foreign terrorist groups....

[F.] We turn to the particular speech plaintiffs propose to undertake. [Congress may constitutionally prohibit] "train[ing] members of [the] PKK on how to use humanitarian and international law to peacefully resolve disputes." ... It is wholly foreseeable that the PKK could use the "specific skill[s]" that plaintiffs propose to impart as part of a broader strategy to promote terrorism. The PKK could, for example, pursue peaceful negotiation as a means of buying time to recover from short-term setbacks, lulling opponents into complacency, and ultimately preparing for renewed attacks.... [(Consider] the PKK's suspension of armed struggle and subsequent return to violence[.)] A foreign terrorist organization introduced to the structures of the international legal system might use the information to threaten, manipulate, and disrupt. This possibility is real, not remote.

Second, plaintiffs propose to "teach PKK members how to petition various representative bodies such as the United Nations for relief." ... [Such speech] teaches the organization how to acquire "relief," which plaintiffs never define with any specificity, and which could readily include monetary aid. Indeed, earlier in this litigation, plaintiffs sought to teach the LTTE "to present claims for tsunami-related aid to mediators and international bodies," which naturally included monetary relief ... [that] could be redirected to funding the group's violent activities.

Finally, plaintiffs propose to "engage in political advocacy on behalf of Kurds [and Tamils] who live in Turkey [and Sri Lanka.]" ... [But] plaintiffs do not specify their expected level of coordination with the PKK or LTTE or suggest what exactly their "advocacy" would consist of. Plaintiffs' proposals are phrased at such a high level of generality that they cannot prevail in this preenforcement challenge....

{Plaintiffs [also] argue that ... [there are] difficult questions of exactly how much direction or coordination is necessary for [such political advocacy] to constitute a [statutorily prohibited] "service." ... "Would any communication with any member be sufficient? With a leader? Must the 'relationship' have any formal elements, such as an employment or contractual relationship? What about a relationship through an intermediary?" ...

The problem with these questions is that they are entirely hypothetical. Plaintiffs have not provided any specific articulation of the degree to which *they* seek to coordinate their advocacy with the PKK and the LTTE. They have instead described the form of their intended advocacy only in the most general terms[, *e.g.*,] ... "... offer[ing] their services to advocate on behalf of the rights of the Kurdish people and the PKK before the United Nations and the United States Congress" ... [and] "writ[ing] and distribut[ing] publications supportive of the PKK and the cause of Kurdish liberation" and "advocat[ing] for the freedom of political prisoners in Turkey" .... Deciding whether activities described at such a level of generality would constitute prohibited "service[s]" under the statute would require "sheer speculation"—which means that plaintiffs cannot prevail in their preenforcement challenge.}

[G.] The dissent seems unwilling to entertain the prospect that training and advising a designated foreign terrorist organization on how to take advantage of international entities might benefit that organization in a way that facilitates its terrorist activities. In the dissent's world, such training is all to the good.

Congress and the Executive, however, have concluded that we live in a different world: one in which the designated foreign terrorist organizations "are so tainted by their criminal conduct that any contribution to such an organization facilitates that conduct." One in which, for example, "the United Nations High Commissioner for Refugees was forced to close a Kurdish refugee camp in northern Iraq because the camp had come under the control of the PKK, and the PKK had failed to respect its 'neutral and humanitarian nature.'" Training and advice on how to work with the United Nations could readily have helped the PKK in its efforts to use the United Nations camp as a base for terrorist activities.

If only good can come from training our adversaries in international dispute resolution, presumably it would have been unconstitutional to prevent American citizens from training the Japanese Government on using international organizations and mechanisms to resolve disputes during World War II. It would, under the dissent's reasoning, have been contrary to our commitment to resolving disputes through "'deliberative forces'" for Congress to conclude that assisting Japan on that front might facilitate its war effort more generally. That view is not one the First Amendment requires us to embrace.

[H.] All this is not to say that any future applications of the material-support statute to speech or advocacy will survive First Amendment scrutiny. It is also not to say that any other statute relating to speech and terrorism would satisfy the First Amendment.

In particular, we in no way suggest that a regulation of independent speech would pass constitutional muster, even if the Government were to show that such speech benefits foreign terrorist organizations. We also do not suggest that Congress could extend the same prohibition on material support at issue here to domestic organizations.

We simply hold that, in prohibiting the particular forms of support that plaintiffs seek to provide to foreign terrorist groups, §2339B does not violate the freedom of speech....

Justice Breyer, with whom Justices Ginsburg and Sotomayor join, dissenting....

[A.] All the activities [in which plaintiffs want to engage] involve the communication and advocacy of political ideas and lawful means of achieving political ends. Even the subjects the plaintiffs wish to teach ... concern political speech[, including] ... advocacy in *this* country directed to *our* government and *its* policies. The plaintiffs, for example, wish to write and distribute publications and to speak before the United States Congress....

[B.] Although in the Court's view the statute applies only where the PKK helps to coordinate a defendant's activities, the simple fact of "coordination" alone cannot readily remove protection that the First Amendment would otherwise grant. That amendment, after all, also protects the freedom of association.... [T]he First Amendment protects advocacy even of *unlawful* action so long as that advocacy is not "directed to inciting or producing *imminent lawless action* and ... *likely to incite or produce* such action." *Brandenburg v. Ohio*. Here the plaintiffs seek to advocate peaceful, *lawful* action to secure *political* ends; and they seek to teach others how to do the same....

Moreover, ... a person who associates with a group that uses unlawful means to achieve its ends does not thereby necessarily forfeit the First Amendment's protection for freedom of association.... [Even] in respect to associating with a group advocating overthrow of the Government through force and violence[,]

> If the persons assembling have committed crimes elsewhere ..., they may be prosecuted for their ... violation of valid laws. But it is a different matter when the State, instead of prosecuting them for such offenses, seizes upon mere participation in a peaceable assembly and a lawful public discussion as the basis for a criminal charge.

De Jonge v. Oregon, 299 U.S. 353 (1937) (striking down conviction for attending and assisting at Communist Party meeting because "[n]otwithstanding [the party's] objectives, the defendant still enjoyed his personal right of free speech and to take part in peaceable assembly having a lawful purpose").

{[Moreover, c]onversations, discussions, or logistical arrangements might well prove necessary to carry out the speech-related activities here at issue (just as conversations and discussions are a necessary part of *membership* in any organization).} {[T]here is no practical way to organize classes for a group (say, wishing to learn about human rights law) without "*coordination*."} {I am not aware of any form of words that might be used to describe "coordination" that would not, at a minimum, seriously chill not only the kind of activities the plaintiffs raise before us, but also the "independent advocacy" the Government purports to permit.} ...

[C.] [I do not dispute the importance of the compelling] interest in protecting the security of the United States and its nationals from the threats that foreign terrorist organizations pose by denying those organizations financial and other fungible resources.... But ... precisely how does application of the statute to the protected activities before us *help achieve* that important security-related end? ...

First, the Government says that the plaintiffs' support for these organizations is "fungible" ... [in that it] could, for example, free up other resources, which the organization might put to terrorist ends.... [But t]here is no *obvious* way in which undertaking advocacy for political change through peaceful means or teaching the PKK and LTTE, say, how to petition the United Nations for political change is fungible with other resources that might be put to more sinister ends in the way that donations of money, food, or computer training are fungible.... [And t]he Government has provided us with no empirical information that might convincingly support this claim. Instead, the Government cites only to evidence that Congress was concerned about the "fungible" nature in general of resources, predominately money and material goods....

Second, the Government says that the plaintiffs' proposed activities will "bolste[r] a terrorist organization's efficacy and strength in a community" and "undermin[e] this nation's efforts to *delegitimize and weaken* those groups." ... The Court [likewise] suggests that, armed with ... greater "legitimacy," these organizations will more readily be able to obtain material support of the kinds Congress plainly intended to ban—money, arms, lodging, and the like.

Yet the Government does not claim that the statute forbids *any* speech "legitimating" a terrorist group. Rather, it reads the statute as permitting (1) membership in terrorist organizations, (2) "peaceably assembling with members of the PKK and LTTE for lawful discussion," or (3) "independent advocacy" on behalf of these organizations. The Court, too, emphasizes that activities not "*coordinated with*" the terrorist groups are not banned.... [But o]nce one accepts [that the "legitimating" effect of coordinated speech justifies a ban], there is no natural stopping place. The argument applies as strongly to "independent" as to "coordinated" advocacy. That fact is reflected in part in the Government's claim that the ban here, so supported, prohibits a lawyer hired by a designated group from filing on behalf of that group an *amicus* brief before the United Nations or even before this Court.

That fact is also reflected in the difficulty of drawing a line designed to accept the legitimacy argument in some instances but not in others. It is inordinately difficult to distinguish when speech activity will and when it will not initiate the chain of causation ... that leads from peaceful advocacy to "legitimacy" to increased support for the group to an increased supply of material goods that support its terrorist activities.

Even were we to find some such line of distinction, its application would seem so inherently uncertain that it would often, perhaps always, "chill" protected speech beyond its boundary. In short, the justification, put forward simply in abstract terms and without limitation, must *always*, or it will *never*, be sufficient. Given the nature of the plaintiffs' activities, "always" cannot possibly be the First Amendment's answer.

Regardless, the "legitimacy" justification itself is inconsistent with critically important First Amendment case law.... [For instance, the Court has] held that the First Amendment protected an American's right to belong to [the Communist] party—despite whatever "legitimating" effect membership might have had—as long as the person did not share the party's unlawful purposes. See, *e.g.*, *Scales v. United States*, 367 U.S. 203 (1961).... [T]hose cases draw further support from other cases permitting pure advocacy of even the most unlawful activity—as long as that advocacy is not "directed to inciting or producing imminent lawless action and ... likely to incite or produce such action," *Brandenburg*. The Government's "legitimating" theory would seem to apply to these cases with equal justifying force; and, if recognized, it would have led this Court to conclusions other than those it reached....

[Moreover,] *independent* advocacy ... is *more* likely, not *less* likely, to confer legitimacy than [*coordinated* advocacy]. Thus, other things being equal, the distinction "coordination" makes is arbitrary in respect to furthering the statute's purposes. And a rule of law that finds the "legitimacy" argument adequate in respect to the latter would have a hard time distinguishing a statute that sought to attack the former....

[D.] [T]he majority [justifies the criminalization of] ... "'train[ing] members of [the] PKK on how to use humanitarian and international law to peacefully resolve disputes[]'" ... in significant part on the ground that "peaceful negotiation[s]" might just "bu[y] time ..., lulling opponents into complacency." And the PKK might use its new information about "the structures of the international legal system ... to threaten, manipulate, and disrupt."

What is one to say about these arguments—arguments that would deny First Amendment protection to the peaceful teaching of international human rights law on the ground that a little knowledge about "the international legal system" is too dangerous a thing; that an opponent's subsequent willingness to negotiate might be faked, so let's not teach him how to try? What might be said of these claims by those who live, as we do, in a Nation committed to the resolution of disputes through "deliberative forces"? *Whitney v. California* (Brandeis, J., concurring)....

Moreover, the risk that those who are taught will put otherwise innocent speech or knowledge to bad use is omnipresent, at least where that risk rests on little more than (even informed) speculation. Hence to accept this kind of argument without more and to apply it to the teaching of a subject such as international human rights law is to adopt a rule of law that ... would automatically forbid the teaching of any subject in a case where national security interests conflict with the First Amendment. The Constitution does not allow all such conflicts to be decided in the Government's favor....

[The majority's only argument with respect to] the plaintiffs' proposal to "'teach PKK members how to petition various representative bodies such as the United Nations *for relief*[]'" ... is that the relief obtained "could readily include monetary aid," which the PKK might use to buy guns. The majority misunderstands the word "relief." In *this* context, as the record makes clear, the word "relief" does not refer to "money." It refers to recognition under the Geneva Conventions. [The dissent cites here the Humanitarian Law Project's statements during litigation.—ed.]

[E.] Throughout, the majority emphasizes that it would defer strongly to Congress' "informed judgment." But here, there is no evidence that Congress has made such a judgment regarding the specific activities at issue in these cases. In any event, "whenever the fundamental rights of free speech and assembly are alleged to have been invaded ...," ... a legislative declaration "does not preclude enquiry into the question whether, at the time and under the circumstances, the conditions existed which are essential to validity under the Federal Constitution." *Whitney* (Brandeis, J., concurring).

I concede that the Government's expertise in foreign affairs may warrant deference in respect to many matters, *e.g.*, our relations with Turkey. But it remains for this Court to decide whether the Government has shown that such an interest justifies criminalizing speech activity otherwise protected by the First Amendment. And the fact that other nations may like us less for granting that protection cannot in and of itself carry the day....

[F.] [Because there is] "a serious doubt" as to the statute's constitutionality ..., we must "ascertain whether a construction of the statute is fairly possible by which the question may be avoided." ... I would read the statute as criminalizing First-Amendment-protected pure speech and association only when the defendant knows or intends that those activities will assist the organization's unlawful terrorist actions [other than simply by helping to legitimate the organization] ... or willfully blinds himself to[] a significant likelihood that his or her conduct will materially support the organization's terrorist ends.... Where the activity fits into these categories ..., the act of providing material support to a known terrorist organization bears a close enough relation to terrorist acts that, in my view, it likely can be prohibited notwithstanding any First Amendment interest. *Cf. Brandenburg*.... [Statutory construction details omitted; the majority had concluded that the dissent's construction of the statute was implausible.—ed.]

b.   *Williams-Yulee v. Florida Bar, 135 S. Ct. 1656 (2015)*

Chief Justice Roberts delivered the opinion of the Court....

[A.] Canon 7C(1) [of the Florida Code of Judicial Conduct] governs fundraising in judicial elections ...[:]

> A candidate, including an incumbent judge, for a judicial office ...
> [1] shall not personally solicit campaign funds, or solicit attorneys for publicly stated support,
> [2] but may establish committees ... [that solicit and spend] funds for the candidate's campaign and ... obtain public statements of support ....

Lanell Williams-Yulee, who refers to herself as Yulee, ... decided to run for a seat on the county court for Hillsborough County, a jurisdiction of about 1.3 million people that includes the city of Tampa. Shortly after filing paperwork to enter the race, Yulee drafted a letter announcing her candidacy. The letter described her experience and desire to "bring fresh ideas and positive solutions to the Judicial bench." The letter then stated:

"An early contribution of $25, $50, $100, $250, or $500, made payable to 'Lanell Williams-Yulee Campaign for County Judge,' will help raise the initial funds needed to launch the campaign and get our message out to the public. I ask for your support [i]n meeting the primary election fund raiser goals. Thank you in advance for your support."

Yulee signed the letter and mailed it to local voters. She also posted the letter on her campaign Web site.... [Yulee] lost the primary to the incumbent judge. Then the Florida Bar filed a complaint against her.... [Yulee was found to have violated Canon 7C(1), and was] publicly reprimanded and ordered to pay the costs of the proceeding ($1,860)....

[B (joined by Chief Justice Roberts and Justices Breyer, Sotomayor, and Kagan).] We have [upheld] ... laws restricting the solicitation of contributions to charity ... only if they are narrowly tailored to serve a compelling interest. See *Riley v. National Federation of Blind of N.C., Inc.* As we have explained, noncommercial solicitation "is characteristically intertwined with informative and perhaps persuasive speech." ...

The principles underlying these charitable solicitation cases apply with even greater force here. Before asking for money in her fundraising letter, Yulee explained her fitness for the bench and expressed her vision for the judiciary.... [S]peech about public issues and the qualifications of candidates for elected office commands the highest level of First Amendment protection....

[We reject the Bar's contention] that we should subject the Canon to a more permissive standard [than strict scrutiny]: that it be "closely drawn" to match a "sufficiently important interest." *Buckley v. Valeo*.... The Court adopted that [standard] in *Buckley* to address a claim that campaign contribution limits violated a contributor's "freedom of political association." Here, Yulee does not claim that Canon 7C(1) violates her right to free association; she argues that it violates her right to free speech....

[Justice Ginsburg didn't join this part, explaining that she "would not apply exacting scrutiny to a State's endeavor sensibly to" distinguish campaigns for political office from campaigns for judicial office.—ed.]

[C.] "[I]t is the rare case" in which a State demonstrates that a speech restriction is narrowly tailored to serve a compelling interest. *Burson v. Freeman,* 504 U.S. 191 (1992) (plurality opinion). But those cases do arise. Here, Canon 7C(1) advances the State's compelling interest in preserving public confidence in the integrity of the judiciary, and it does so through means narrowly tailored to avoid unnecessarily abridging speech....

[1.] Canon 7C(1) ... promote[s] the State's interests in "protecting the integrity of the judiciary" and "maintaining the public's confidence in an impartial judiciary." ... Judges, charged with exercising strict neutrality and independence, cannot supplicate campaign donors without diminishing public confidence in judicial integrity....

[A] State's interest in preserving public confidence in the integrity of its judiciary extends beyond its interest in preventing the appearance of corruption in legislative and executive elections.... States may regulate judicial elections differently than they regulate political elections, because the role of judges differs from the role of politicians. Politicians are expected to be

Different interests w/ judges

appropriately responsive to the preferences of their supporters.... [But]n deciding cases, a judge is not to follow the preferences of his supporters, or provide any special consideration to his campaign donors....

"[E]ven if judges were able to refrain from favoring donors, the mere possibility that judges' decisions may be motivated by the desire to repay campaign contributions is likely to undermine the public's confidence in the judiciary." In the eyes of the public, a judge's personal solicitation could result (even unknowingly) in "a possible temptation ... which might lead him not to hold the balance nice, clear and true." That risk is especially pronounced because most donors are lawyers and litigants who may appear before the judge they are supporting.

The concept of public confidence in judicial integrity does not easily reduce to precise definition, nor does it lend itself to proof by documentary record. But no one denies that it is genuine and compelling.... Moreover, personal solicitation by a judicial candidate "inevitably places the solicited individuals in a position to fear retaliation if they fail to financially support that candidate." Potential litigants then fear that "the integrity of the judicial system has been compromised, forcing them to search for an attorney in part based upon the criteria of which attorneys have made the obligatory contributions." A State's decision to elect its judges does not require it to tolerate these risks....

[2.] [Yulee argues] that the Canon's failure to restrict other speech [such as solicitation by the judge's campaign committee] equally damaging to judicial integrity and its appearance undercuts the Bar's position....

It is always somewhat counterintuitive to argue that a law violates the First Amendment by abridging *too little* speech. We have recognized, however, that underinclusiveness can raise "doubts about whether the government is in fact pursuing the interest it invokes, rather than disfavoring a particular speaker or viewpoint." In a textbook illustration of that principle, we invalidated a city's ban on ritual animal sacrifices because the city failed to regulate vast swaths of conduct that similarly diminished its asserted interests in public health and animal welfare. *Church of Lukumi Babalu Aye, Inc. v. Hialeah*.

Underinclusiveness can also reveal that a law does not actually advance a compelling interest. For example, a State's decision to prohibit newspapers, but not electronic media, from releasing the names of juvenile defendants suggested that the law did not advance its stated purpose of protecting youth privacy.

Although a law's underinclusivity raises a red flag, the First Amendment imposes no freestanding "underinclusiveness limitation." *R.A.V. v. St. Paul*. A State need not address all aspects of a problem in one fell swoop; policymakers may focus on their most pressing concerns. We have accordingly upheld laws—even under strict scrutiny—that conceivably could have restricted even greater amounts of speech in service of their stated interests. *Burson*.

Viewed in light of these principles, Canon 7C(1) raises no fatal underinclusivity concerns. The solicitation ban aims squarely at the conduct most likely to undermine public confidence in the integrity of the judiciary: personal requests for money by judges and judicial candidates.... And unlike some laws that we have found impermissibly underinclusive, Canon 7C(1) is not riddled with exceptions....

Florida, along with most other States, has reasonably concluded that solicitation by the candidate personally creates a categorically different and more severe risk of undermining public confidence than does solicitation by a campaign committee. The identity of the solicitor matters, as anyone who has encountered a Girl Scout selling cookies outside a grocery store can attest. When the judicial candidate himself asks for money, the stakes are higher for all involved. The candidate has personally invested his time and effort in the fundraising appeal; he has placed his name and reputation behind the request.

The solicited individual knows that, and also knows that the solicitor might be in a position to singlehandedly make decisions of great weight: The same person who signed the fundraising letter might one day sign the judgment. This dynamic inevitably creates pressure for the recipient to comply, and it does so in a way that solicitation by a third party does not. Just as inevitably, the personal involvement of the candidate in the solicitation creates the public appearance that the candidate will remember who says yes, and who says no.... However similar the two solicitations may be in substance, a State may conclude that they present markedly different appearances to the public....

{Yulee also points out that Florida permits judicial candidates to write thank you notes to campaign donors ....} Yulee argues that permitting thank you notes heightens the likelihood of actual bias by ensuring that judicial candidates know who supported their campaigns, and ensuring that the supporter knows that the candidate knows. Maybe so. But the State's compelling interest is implicated most directly by the candidate's personal solicitation itself. A failure to ban thank you notes for contributions not solicited by the candidate does not undercut the Bar's rationale.

In addition, the State has a good reason for allowing candidates to write thank you notes and raise money through committees. These accommodations reflect Florida's effort to respect the First Amendment interests of candidates and their contributors—to resolve the "fundamental tension between the ideal character of the judicial office and the real world of electoral politics." ...

[3.] The principal dissent also suggests that Canon 7C(1) is underinclusive because Florida does not ban judicial candidates from asking individuals for personal gifts or loans. But Florida law treats a personal "gift" or "loan" as a campaign contribution if the donor makes it "for the purpose of influencing the results of an election," and Florida's Judicial Qualifications Commission has determined that a judicial candidate violates Canon 7C(1) by personally soliciting such a loan.

In any event, ... [u]nderinclusivity creates a First Amendment concern when the State regulates one aspect of a problem while declining to regulate a different aspect of the problem that affects its stated interest *in a comparable way*. See *Florida Star v. B.J.F.* The principal dissent offers no basis to conclude that judicial candidates are in the habit of soliciting personal loans, football tickets, or anything of the sort. Even under strict scrutiny, "[t]he First Amendment does not require States to regulate for problems that do not exist." *Burson* (State's regulation of political solicitation around a polling place, but not charitable or commercial solicitation, was not fatally underinclusive under strict scrutiny).

Taken to its logical conclusion, the position advanced by Yulee and the principal dissent is that Florida may ban the solicitation of funds by judicial candidates only if the State bans *all* solicitation of funds in judicial elections. The First Amendment does not put a State to that all-or-nothing choice. We will not punish Florida for leaving open more, rather than fewer, avenues of expression, especially when there is no indication that the selective restriction of speech reflects a pretextual motive....

[4.] Canon 7C(1) restricts a narrow slice of speech.... Canon 7C(1) leaves judicial candidates free to discuss any issue with any person at any time. Candidates can write letters, give speeches, and put up billboards. They can contact potential supporters in person, on the phone, or online. They can promote their campaigns on radio, television, or other media.

They cannot say, "Please give me money." They can, however, direct their campaign committees to do so. Whatever else may be said of the Canon, it is surely not a "wildly disproportionate restriction upon speech."

← Under Inclusiveness

[5.] Indeed, Yulee concedes—and the principal dissent seems to agree— that Canon 7C(1) is valid in numerous applications. Yulee acknowledges that Florida can prohibit judges from soliciting money from lawyers and litigants appearing before them. In addition, she says the State "might" be able to ban "direct one-to-one solicitation of lawyers and individuals or businesses that could reasonably appear in the court for which the individual is a candidate." She also suggests that the Bar could forbid "in person" solicitation by judicial candidates.

But Yulee argues that the Canon cannot constitutionally be applied to her chosen form of solicitation: a letter posted online and distributed via mass mailing. No one, she contends, will lose confidence in the integrity of the judiciary based on personal solicitation to such a broad audience.

This argument misperceives the breadth of the compelling interest that underlies Canon 7C(1). Florida has reasonably determined that personal appeals for money by a judicial candidate inherently create an appearance of impropriety that may cause the public to lose confidence in the integrity of the judiciary. That interest may be implicated to varying degrees in particular contexts, but the interest remains whenever the public perceives the judge personally asking for money.

Moreover, the lines Yulee asks us to draw are unworkable. Even under her theory of the case, a mass mailing would create an appearance of impropriety if addressed to a list of all lawyers and litigants with pending cases. So would a speech soliciting contributions from the 100 most frequently appearing attorneys in the jurisdiction.

Yulee says she might accept a ban on one-to-one solicitation, but is the public impression really any different if a judicial candidate tries to buttonhole not one prospective donor but two at a time? Ten? Yulee also agrees that in person solicitation creates a problem. But would the public's concern recede if the request for money came in a phone call or a text message?

We decline to wade into this swamp. The First Amendment requires that Canon 7C(1) be narrowly tailored, not that it be "perfectly tailored." The impossibility of perfect tailoring is especially apparent when the State's compelling interest is as intangible as public confidence in the integrity of the judiciary....

[M]ost problems arise in greater and lesser gradations, and the First Amendment does not confine a State to addressing evils in their most acute form. Here, Florida has concluded that all personal solicitations by judicial candidates create a public appearance that undermines confidence in the integrity of the judiciary; banning all personal solicitations by judicial candidates is narrowly tailored to address that concern.

[6.] In considering Yulee's tailoring arguments, we are mindful that most States with elected judges have determined that drawing a line between personal solicitation by candidates and solicitation by committees is necessary to preserve public confidence in the integrity of the judiciary. These considered judgments deserve our respect, especially because they reflect sensitive choices by States in an area central to their own governance—how to select those who "sit as their judges."

[7.] Finally, Yulee contends that Florida can accomplish its compelling interest through the less restrictive means of recusal rules and campaign contribution limits. We disagree. A rule requiring judges to recuse themselves from every case in which a lawyer or litigant made a campaign contribution would disable many jurisdictions. And a flood of postelection recusal motions could "erode public confidence in judicial impartiality" and thereby exacerbate the very appearance problem the State is trying to solve. Moreover, the rule that Yulee envisions could create a perverse incentive for litigants to make campaign contributions to judges solely as a means to trigger their later recusal—a form of peremptory strike against a judge that would enable transparent forum shopping.

As for campaign contribution limits, Florida already applies them to judicial elections. {Contributors may not donate more than $1,000 per election to a trial court candidate or more than $3,000 per retention election to a Supreme Court justice.} A State may decide that the threat to public confidence created by personal solicitation exists apart from the amount of money that a judge or judicial candidate seeks. Even if Florida decreased its contribution limit, the appearance that judges who personally solicit funds might improperly favor their campaign donors would remain....

[D.] Judicial candidates have a First Amendment right to speak in support of their campaigns. States have a compelling interest in preserving public confidence in their judiciaries. When the State adopts a narrowly tailored restriction like the one at issue here, those principles do not conflict. A State's decision to elect judges does not compel it to compromise public confidence in their integrity....

Justice Scalia, with whom Justice Thomas joins[, and whose views Justices Kennedy and Alito generally endorse] (dissenting...).

[A.] Neither the Court nor the State identifies the slightest evidence that banning requests for contributions will substantially improve public trust in judges. Nor does common sense make this happy forecast obvious.

The concept of judicial integrity "dates back at least eight centuries," and judicial elections in America date back more than two centuries—but rules against personal solicitations date back only to 1972. The peaceful coexistence of judicial elections and personal solicitations for most of our history calls into doubt any claim that allowing personal solicitations would imperil public faith in judges. Many States allow judicial candidates to ask for contributions even today, but nobody suggests that public confidence in judges fares worse in these jurisdictions than elsewhere.

And in any event, if candidates' appeals for money are "'characteristically intertwined'" with discussion of qualifications and views on public issues, how can the Court be so sure that the public will regard them as improprieties rather than as legitimate instances of campaigning? In the final analysis, Florida comes nowhere near making the convincing demonstration required by our cases that the speech restriction in this case substantially advances its objective....

[B.] [In any event,] Florida must show that the ban restricts no more speech than necessary to achieve the objective.... [But] Canon 7C(1) bans candidates from asking for contributions even in messages that do not target any listener in particular—mass-mailed letters, flyers posted on telephone poles, speeches to large gatherings, and Web sites addressed to the general public. Messages like these do not share the features that lead the Court to pronounce personal solicitations a menace to public confidence in the judiciary.

Consider online solicitations. They avoid "'the spectacle of lawyers or potential litigants directly handing over money to judicial candidates.'" People who come across online solicitations do not feel "pressure" to comply with the request. Nor does the candidate's signature on the online solicitation suggest "that the candidate will remember who says yes, and who says no." Yet Canon 7C(1) prohibits these and similar solicitations anyway....

[T]he Court argues that "the lines Yulee asks [it] to draw are unworkable." ... [But] the Court could have chosen from a whole spectrum of workable rules. It could have held that States may regulate no more than solicitation of participants in pending cases, or solicitation of people who are likely to appear in the candidate's court, or even solicitation of any lawyer or litigant. And it could have ruled that candidates have the right to make fundraising appeals that are not directed to any particular listener (like requests in mass-mailed letters), or at least fundraising appeals plainly directed to the general public (like requests placed online).

The Supreme Court of Florida has made similar accommodations in other settings. It allows sitting judges to solicit memberships in civic organizations if (among other things) the solicitee is not "likely ever to appear before the court on which the judge serves." And it allows sitting judges to accept gifts if (among other things) "the donor is not a party or other person ... whose interests have come or are likely to come before the judge." It is not too much to ask that the State show election speech similar consideration....

[C.] [Moreover, a]mong its other functions, the First Amendment is a kind of Equal Protection Clause for ideas. The state ordinarily may not regulate one message because it harms a government interest yet refuse to regulate other messages that impair the interest in a comparable way. [*E.g.,*] *Carey v. Brown*....

[Yet] although Canon 7C(1) prevents Yulee from asking a lawyer for a few dollars to help her buy campaign pamphlets, it does not prevent her asking the same lawyer for a personal loan, access to his law firm's luxury suite at the local football stadium, or even a donation to help her fight the Florida Bar's charges. What could possibly justify these distinctions? Surely the Court does not believe that requests for campaign favors erode public confidence in a way that requests for favors unrelated to elections do not. Could anyone say with a straight face that it looks *worse* for a candidate to say "please give my campaign $25" than to say "please give *me* $25"? ...

[T]he Court says that "the First Amendment imposes no freestanding 'underinclusiveness limitation.'" This analysis elides the distinction between selectivity on the basis of content and selectivity on other grounds. Because the First Amendment does not prohibit underinclusiveness as such, lawmakers may target a problem only at certain times or in certain places. Because the First Amendment *does* prohibit content discrimination as such, lawmakers may *not* target a problem only in certain messages....

This case involves selectivity on the basis of content. The Florida Supreme Court has decided to eliminate the appearances associated with "personal appeals for money," when the appeals seek money for a campaign but not when the appeals seek money for other purposes. That distinction violates the First Amendment.

Even on the Court's own terms, Canon 7C(1) cannot stand. The Court concedes that "underinclusiveness can raise 'doubts about whether the government is in fact pursuing the interest it invokes.'" Canon 7C(1)'s scope suggests that it has nothing to do with the appearances created by judges' asking for money, and everything to do with hostility toward judicial campaigning.

How else to explain the Florida Supreme Court's decision to ban *all* personal appeals for campaign funds (even when the solicitee could never appear before the candidate), but to tolerate appeals for other kinds of funds (even when the solicitee will surely appear before the candidate)? It should come as no surprise that the ABA, whose model rules the Florida Supreme Court followed when framing Canon 7C(1), opposes judicial elections—preferring instead a system in which (surprise!) a committee of lawyers proposes candidates from among whom the Governor must make his selection....

[D.] One cannot have judicial elections without judicial campaigns, and judicial campaigns without funds for campaigning, and funds for campaigning without asking for them. When a society decides that its judges should be elected, it necessarily decides that selection by the people is more important than the oracular sanctity of judges, their immunity from the (shudder!) indignity of begging for funds, and their exemption from those shadows of impropriety that fall over the proletarian public officials who must run for office....

[E.] [T]he preservation of public respect for the courts [is] a policy objective of the highest order ...—but so too are preventing animal torture, protecting the innocence of children, and honoring valiant soldiers. The Court did not relax the Constitution's guarantee of freedom of speech when legislatures pursued those goals; it should not relax the guarantee when the Supreme Court of Florida pursues this one....

Justice Kennedy, dissenting....

[Justice Kennedy argued that the Canon impermissibly disadvantages little-known candidates, who wouldn't draw donations unless they ask for them, relative to prominent candidates who are "well known to business and civic leaders." He then added:—ed.]

If there is concern about principled, decent, and thoughtful discourse in election campaigns, the First Amendment provides the answer. That answer is more speech. For example, candidates [or vote groups] might ... agree to appoint members of a panel charged with [public] periodic evaluation of campaign statements, candor, and fairness....

[And w]hether as a result of disclosure laws or a candidate's voluntary decision to make the campaign transparent, the Internet can reveal almost at once how a candidate sought funds; who the donors were; and what amounts they gave.... Based on disclosures the voters can decide, among other matters, whether the public is well served by an elected judiciary; how each candidate defines appropriate campaign conduct (which may speak volumes about his or her judicial demeanor); and what persons and groups support or oppose a particular candidate.... The speech the Court now holds foreclosed might itself have been instructive in this regard, and it could have been open to the electorate's scrutiny. Judicial elections, no less than other elections, presuppose faith in democracy....

Justice Alito, dissenting.

[T]his rule is about as narrowly tailored as a burlap bag. It applies to all solicitations made in the name of a candidate for judicial office—including, as was the case here, a mass mailing. It even applies to an ad in a newspaper.... If this rule can be characterized as narrowly tailored, then narrow tailoring has no meaning, and strict scrutiny, which is essential to the protection of free speech, is seriously impaired....

B. Content Discrimination Within the Exceptions to Protection

a. *Summary*

The above materials have generally distinguished "unprotected" speech —speech that falls within one of the exceptions to protection—from "fully protected" speech. This, though, is an oversimplification. As Part III showed, even "fully protected" speech might be restrictable if the restriction passes strict scrutiny. Likewise, even a restriction on "unprotected" speech, the Court has held, might sometimes be unconstitutional if it is improperly discriminatory.

Rule: A restriction on "unprotected" speech or commercial advertising must pass *strict scrutiny* if it includes a content discrimination *in addition to* the one that makes the speech unprotected, for instance if it restricts

— "obscenity which includes offensive *political* messages,"

— "only those threats against the President that mention his policy on aid to inner cities," or

— "only that commercial advertising that depicts men in a demeaning fashion."

(All quotes in this section for which sources aren't given are from *R.A.V. v. City of St. Paul* (1992) (p. 317).)

Exceptions:

1. Content discrimination within an unprotected category need not be justified under strict scrutiny "[w]hen the basis for the content discrimination consists *entirely of the very reason the entire class of speech at issue is proscribable.*"

— Examples: "A State might choose to prohibit only that obscenity which is the most patently offensive *in its prurience*—i.e., that which involves the most lascivious displays of sexual activity."

— "[T]he Federal Government can criminalize only those threats of violence that are directed against the President—since the reasons why threats of violence are outside the First Amendment (protecting individuals from the fear of violence, from the disruption that fear engenders, and from the possibility that the threatened violence will occur) have special force when applied to the person of the President."

— "[A] State may choose to regulate price advertising in one industry but not in others, because the risk of fraud (one of the characteristics of commercial speech that justifies depriving it of full First Amendment protection) is in its view greater there."

— Imposing special penalties for "cross burning with intent to intimidate" is permissible because "burning a cross is a particularly virulent form of intimidation": Its "long and pernicious history as a signal of impending violence" makes it especially threatening, and thus subject to special punishment. *Virginia v. Black* (2003) (p. 230).

— Example of something that the Court held doesn't qualify under this exception: The very discrimination at issue in *R.A.V.* "[T]he reason why fighting words are categorically excluded from the protection of the First Amendment is not that their content communicates any particular idea, but that their content embodies a particularly intolerable (and socially unnecessary) *mode* of expressing *whatever* idea the speaker wishes to convey. St. Paul has not singled out an especially offensive mode of expression—it has not, for example, selected for prohibition only those fighting words that communicate ideas in a threatening (as opposed to a merely obnoxious) manner."

2. Content discrimination within an unprotected category need not be justified under strict scrutiny when "the subclass happens to be associated with particular 'secondary effects' of the speech, so that the regulation is *'justified* without reference to the content of the ... speech.'" (For more on secondary effects, see Part IV.B, p. 359.)

— Example: "A State could, for example, permit all obscene live performances except those involving minors."

— The offensiveness and persuasiveness of speech, and effects that flow from them, are *not* secondary effects. "The emotive impact of speech on its audience is not a 'secondary effect.'" "[When] the 'chain of causation' ... *necessarily* 'run[s] through the persuasive effect of the expressive component' of the conduct, [the law] regulates on the basis of the 'primary' effect of the speech—*i.e.*, its persuasive (or repellant) force."

3. A generally applicable law that applies both to speech and conduct need not pass strict scrutiny when "a particular content-based subcategory of a proscribable class of speech can be swept up incidentally within the reach of a statute directed at conduct rather than speech."

— Example: "[S]exually derogatory 'fighting words,' among other words, may produce a violation of Title VII's general prohibition against sexual discrimination in employment practices."

4. More generally, content discrimination within an unprotected category need not be justified under strict scrutiny when "the nature of the content discrimination is such that there is no realistic possibility that official suppression of ideas is afoot."

— Example: "We cannot think of any First Amendment interest that would stand in the way of a State's prohibiting only those obscene motion pictures with blue-eyed actresses."

These exceptions are not models of clarity on their face, and have been elaborated only in one case since *R.A.V.*, *Virginia v. Black*. This doctrine is thus less well-defined than, say, the doctrines related to libel, obscenity, strict scrutiny, and the like, which have been made somewhat more precise by subsequent precedents.

Important distinction: *R.A.V.* deals only with restrictions on bigoted *speech*; it does not deal with heightened penalties for bias-motivated *conduct*. *Wisconsin v. Mitchell,* 508 U.S. 476 (1993), unanimously upheld a state law that raised the penalties for various crimes when the criminal "[i]ntentionally select[ed] the person against whom the crime ... is committed ... because of the race, religion, color, disability, sexual orientation, national origin or ancestry of that person." Such selection, the Court held, is not itself expression (unlike the speech in *R.A.V.*).

Moreover, while the defendant's speech during, before, or after the crime might be used as evidence of his intentions, the Court has consistently held that such use of speech as evidence of intent (or as evidence of some other element of the crime) is not itself a First Amendment violation. See, *e.g.,* *Haupt v. United States,* 330 U.S. 631, 642-43 (1947). Thus, for instance, in murder cases, a defendant's out-of-court statements about the victim might be used as evidence that his act was intentional; in robbery cases, a defendant's statements might be used as evidence that the defendant did indeed commit the robbery.

Though such use of a person's speech as evidence can deter people from saying certain things, the Court has concluded that this chilling effect is not enough to justify any special First Amendment restraints. The First Amendment comes into play only when speech is *part of what is being punished, and not just evidence of a person's mental state or conduct.*

b. Problem: Absolute Immunity in Libel Cases

Cal. Civil Code § 47(b) provides that statements—even false ones—made "[i]n any ... judicial proceeding, ... in any other official proceeding authorized by law, or ... in the initiation or course of any other proceeding authorized by law" are absolutely immune from libel liability.

There are two exceptions to this absolute immunity. § 47(b)(1) exempts statements "contained in any pleading or affidavit filed in an action for marital dissolution ... made of or concerning a person by or against whom no affirmative relief is prayed in the action ...." § 47.5 exempts

> a peace officer['s] ... action for defamation against an individual who has filed a complaint with that officer's employing agency alleging misconduct, criminal conduct, or incompetence, if that complaint is false, the complaint was made with knowledge [or recklessness] that it was false and that it was made with spite, hatred, or ill will....

(Assume § 47 would otherwise apply to complaints against police officers.)

Is § 47(b) constitutional? What about § 47(b)(1)? What about § 47.5? Compare *Loshonkohl v. Kinder,* 109 Cal. App. 4th 510 (2003), with *Eakins v. Nevada,* 219 F. Supp. 2d 1113 (D. Nev. 2002).

c.   *R.A.V. v. City of St. Paul, 505 U.S. 377 (1992)*

Justice Scalia delivered the opinion of the Court.

In the predawn hours of June 21, 1990, petitioner and several other teenagers ... allegedly burned [a] cross inside the fenced yard of a black family that lived across the street from the house where petitioner was staying. Although this conduct could have been punished under any of a number of laws [such as those punishing terroristic threats, arson, and property damage], ... St. Paul chose to charge petitioner (then a juvenile) [under] the St. Paul Bias-Motivated Crime Ordinance, which [outlaws]

> plac[ing] on public or private property a symbol [or] ... appellation[] ... including, but not limited to, a burning cross or Nazi swastika, which one knows or has reasonable grounds to know arouses anger, alarm or resentment in others on the basis of race, color, creed, religion or gender ....

{Petitioner has also been charged ... with ... racially motivated assault[]. Petitioner did not challenge this count.}

[A.] In construing the St. Paul ordinance, we are bound by the ... Minnesota Supreme Court's authoritative [construction] that the ordinance reaches only those expressions that constitute "fighting words" within the meaning of *Chaplinsky v. New Hampshire* ["those which by their very utterance inflict injury or tend to incite an immediate breach of the peace"— ed.]....

Content-based regulations [of speech and expressive conduct] are presumptively invalid. From 1791 to the present, however, our society ... has permitted restrictions upon the content of speech in a few limited areas, which are "of such slight social value as a step to truth that any benefit that may be derived from them is clearly outweighed by the social interest in order and morality." ... "[T]he freedom of speech" ... does not include a freedom to disregard these traditional limitations....

We have sometimes said that these categories of expression are "not within the area of constitutionally protected speech," or that the "protection of the First Amendment does not extend" to them.... [But, in context, these statements mean] that these areas of speech can, consistently with the First Amendment, be regulated *because of their constitutionally proscribable content* (obscenity, defamation, etc.)—not that they are categories of speech entirely invisible to the Constitution, so that they may be made the vehicles for content discrimination unrelated to their distinctively proscribable content. {It is not true that "fighting words" have at most a *"de minimis"* expressive content, or that their content is *in all respects* "worthless and undeserving of constitutional protection"; sometimes they are quite expressive indeed. We have not said that they constitute *"no* part of the expression of ideas," but only that they constitute "no *essential* part of any exposition of ideas."}

Thus, the government may proscribe libel; but it may not make the further content discrimination of proscribing *only* libel critical of the government.... [A] city council could [not] enact an ordinance prohibiting only those

legally obscene works that contain criticism of the city government or, indeed, that do not include endorsement of the city government. {Justice
White concedes that a city council cannot prohibit only those legally obscene
works that contain criticism of the city government, but asserts that to be
the consequence, not of the First Amendment, but of the Equal Protection
Clause. Such content-based discrimination would not, he asserts, "be rationally related to a legitimate government interest." But of course the only *reason* that government interest is not a "legitimate" one is that it violates the
First Amendment.} ...

[**B.**] The proposition that a particular instance of speech can be proscribable on the basis of one feature (*e.g.*, obscenity) but not on the basis of another (*e.g.*, opposition to the city government) is commonplace .... [For example,] nonverbal expressive activity can be banned because of the action it
entails, but not because of the ideas it expresses—so that burning a flag in
violation of an ordinance against outdoor fires could be punishable, whereas
burning a flag in violation of an ordinance against dishonoring the flag is
not.... [T]he power to proscribe particular speech on the basis of a noncon-
tent element (*e.g.*, noise) does not entail the power to proscribe the same
speech on the basis of a content element[. S]o also, the power to proscribe it
on the basis of *one* content element (*e.g.*, obscenity) does not entail the power
to proscribe it on the basis of *other* content elements.

In other words, the exclusion of "fighting words" from the scope of the
First Amendment simply means that, for purposes of that Amendment, the
unprotected features of the words are, despite their verbal character, essentially a "nonspeech" element of communication. Fighting words are thus
analogous to a noisy sound truck: Each is ... a "mode of speech"; both can be
used to convey an idea; but neither has, in and of itself, a claim upon the
First Amendment. As with the sound truck, however, so also with fighting
words: The government may not regulate use based on hostility—or favoritism—towards the underlying message expressed....

[T]he First Amendment imposes not an "underinclusiveness" limitation
but a "content discrimination" limitation upon a State's prohibition of proscribable speech. There is no problem whatever, for example, with a State's
prohibiting obscenity (and other forms of proscribable expression) only in
certain media or markets, for although that prohibition would be "underinclusive," it would not discriminate on the basis of content.

[**C.**] Even the prohibition against content discrimination that we assert
the First Amendment requires ... applies differently in the context of proscribable speech than in the area of fully protected speech. The rationale of
the general prohibition, after all, is that content discrimination "raises the
specter that the Government may effectively drive certain ideas or viewpoints from the marketplace." But content discrimination among various
instances of a class of proscribable speech often does not pose this threat.

[**1.**] When the basis for the content discrimination consists entirely of
the very reason the entire class of speech at issue is proscribable, no signif-

icant danger of idea or viewpoint discrimination exists. Such a reason, having been adjudged neutral enough to support exclusion of the entire class of speech from First Amendment protection, is also neutral enough to form the basis of distinction within the class....

A State might choose to prohibit only that obscenity which is the most patently offensive *in its prurience*—*i.e.*, that which involves the most lascivious displays of sexual activity. But it may not prohibit, for example, only that obscenity which includes offensive *political* messages....

[T]he Federal Government can criminalize only those threats of violence that are directed against the President—since the reasons why threats of violence are outside the First Amendment (protecting individuals from the fear of violence, from the disruption that fear engenders, and from the possibility that the threatened violence will occur) have special force when applied to the person of the President. But the Federal Government may not criminalize only those threats against the President that mention his policy on aid to inner cities....

[Likewise,] a State may choose to regulate price advertising in one industry but not in others, because the risk of fraud (one of the characteristics of commercial speech that justifies depriving it of full First Amendment protection) is in its view greater there. But a State may not prohibit only that commercial advertising that depicts men in a demeaning fashion.

[2.] Another valid basis for according differential treatment to even a content-defined subclass of proscribable speech is that the subclass happens to be associated with particular "secondary effects" of the speech, so that the regulation is *"justified* without reference to the content of the ... speech." A State could, for example, permit all obscene live performances except those involving minors.

[3.] Moreover, since words can in some circumstances violate laws directed not against speech but against conduct (a law against treason, for example, is violated by telling the enemy the Nation's defense secrets), a particular content-based subcategory of a proscribable class of speech can be swept up incidentally within the reach of a statute directed at conduct rather than speech. Thus, for example, sexually derogatory "fighting words," among other words, may produce a violation of Title VII's general prohibition against sexual discrimination in employment practices. Where the government does not target conduct on the basis of its expressive content, acts are not shielded from regulation merely because they express a discriminatory idea or philosophy.

[4.] These bases for distinction refute the proposition that the selectivity of the restriction is "even arguably 'conditioned upon the sovereign's agreement with what a speaker may intend to say.'" There may be other such bases as well.

Indeed, to validate such selectivity (where totally proscribable speech is at issue) it may not even be necessary to identify any particular "neutral" basis, so long as the nature of the content discrimination is such that there is no realistic possibility that official suppression of ideas is afoot. (We cannot think of any First Amendment interest that would stand in the way of a State's prohibiting only those obscene motion pictures with blue-eyed actresses.) Save for that limitation, the regulation of "fighting words," like the regulation of noisy speech, may address some offensive instances and leave other, equally offensive, instances alone....

[D.] [T]he [St. Paul] ordinance applies only to "fighting words" that insult, or provoke violence, "on the basis of race, color, creed, religion or gender." Displays containing abusive invective, no matter how vicious or severe, are permissible unless they are addressed to one of the specified disfavored topics. Those who wish to use "fighting words" in connection with other ideas—to express hostility, for example, on the basis of political affiliation, union membership, or homosexuality—are not covered. The First Amendment does not permit St. Paul to impose special prohibitions on those speakers who express views on disfavored subjects.

In its practical operation, moreover, the ordinance goes even beyond mere content discrimination, to actual viewpoint discrimination. Displays containing some words—odious racial epithets, for example—would be prohibited to proponents of all views. But "fighting words" that do not themselves invoke race, color, creed, religion, or gender—aspersions upon a person's mother, for example—would seemingly be usable *ad libitum* in the placards of those arguing *in favor* of racial, color, etc., tolerance and equality, but could not be used by those speakers' opponents.

One could hold up a sign saying, for example, that all "anti-Catholic bigots" are misbegotten; but not that all "papists" are, for that would insult and provoke violence "on the basis of religion." St. Paul has no such authority to license one side of a debate to fight freestyle, while requiring the other to follow Marquis of Queensberry rules. What we have here[] ... is not a prohibition of fighting words that are directed at certain persons or groups (which would be *facially* valid if it met the requirements of the Equal Protection Clause); but rather, a prohibition of fighting words that contain ... messages of "bias-motivated" hatred and in particular, as applied to this case, messages "based on virulent notions of racial supremacy." ...

St. Paul's brief asserts that a general "fighting words" law would not meet the city's needs because only a content-specific measure can communicate to minority groups that the "group hatred" aspect of such speech "is not condoned by the majority." The point of the First Amendment is that majority preferences must be expressed in some fashion other than silencing speech on the basis of its content....

[E.] [Nor can the ordinance be defended on the grounds that it is directed] to particular "injur[ies]" that are "qualitatively different" from other injuries.... What makes the anger, fear, sense of dishonor, etc., produced by violation of this ordinance distinct from the anger, fear, sense of dishonor, etc., produced by other fighting words is nothing other than the fact that it is caused by a distinctive idea, conveyed by a distinctive message. The First Amendment cannot be evaded that easily.

It is obvious that the symbols which will arouse "anger, alarm or resentment in others on the basis of race, color, creed, religion or gender" are those symbols that communicate a message of hostility based on one of these characteristics. St. Paul concedes in its brief that the ordinance applies only to "racial, religious, or gender-specific symbols" such as "a burning cross, Nazi swastika or other instrumentality of like import." Indeed, St. Paul argued in the Juvenile Court that "[t]he burning of a cross does express a message and it is, in fact, the content of that message which the St. Paul Ordinance attempts to legislate."

The content-based discrimination reflected in the St. Paul ordinance ... [thus] does not fall within the exception for content discrimination based on the very reasons why the particular class of speech at issue (here, fighting words) is proscribable. As explained earlier, the reason why fighting words are categorically excluded from the protection of the First Amendment is not that their content communicates any particular idea, but that their content embodies a particularly intolerable (and socially unnecessary) *mode* of expressing *whatever* idea the speaker wishes to convey. St. Paul has not singled out an especially offensive mode of expression—it has not, for example, selected for prohibition only those fighting words that communicate ideas in a threatening (as opposed to a merely obnoxious) manner. Rather, it has proscribed fighting words of whatever manner that communicate messages of racial, gender, or religious intolerance.

Selectivity of this sort creates the possibility that the city is seeking to handicap the expression of particular ideas. That possibility would alone be enough to render the ordinance presumptively invalid, but St. Paul's comments and concessions in this case elevate the possibility to a certainty.

[F.] St. Paul argues that the ordinance comes within another of the specific exceptions we mentioned, the one that allows content discrimination aimed only at the "secondary effects" of the speech. According to St. Paul, the ordinance is intended, "not to impact on [*sic*] the right of free expression of the accused," but rather to "protect against the victimization of a person or persons who are particularly vulnerable because of their membership in a group that historically has been discriminated against."

Even assuming that an ordinance that completely proscribes, rather than merely regulates, a specified category of speech can ever be considered to be directed only to the secondary effects of such speech, it is clear that the St. Paul ordinance is not directed to secondary effects .... "Listeners' reactions to speech are not ... [to be considered] 'secondary effects' ...." "The emotive impact of speech on its audience is not a 'secondary effect.'"

{[E]ven if one assumes (as appears unlikely)} {that the ordinance merely regulates that subclass of fighting words which is most likely to provoke a violent response ..., that would not justify selective regulation under a "secondary effects" theory. The only reason why such expressive conduct would be especially correlated with violence is that it conveys a particularly odious message; because the "chain of causation" thus *necessarily* "run[s] through the persuasive effect of the expressive component" of the conduct, it is clear that the St. Paul ordinance regulates on the basis of the "primary" effect of the speech—*i.e.*, its persuasive (or repellant) force.} ...

[Nor does] the ordinance ... fall within some more general exception permitting *all* selectivity that for any reason is beyond the suspicion of official suppression of ideas. The statements of St. Paul in this very case afford ample basis for, if not full confirmation of, that suspicion.

[G.] Finally, St. Paul [argues] ... that, even if the ordinance regulates expression based on hostility towards its protected ideological content, this discrimination is nonetheless justified because it is narrowly tailored to serve compelling state interests. Specifically, they assert that the ordinance helps to ensure the basic human rights of members of groups that have historically been subjected to discrimination, including the right of such group members to live in peace where they wish.

We do not doubt that these interests are compelling, and that the ordinance can be said to promote them. But the "danger of censorship" presented by a facially content-based statute requires that that weapon be employed only where it is "*necessary* to serve the asserted [compelling] interest." The existence of adequate content-neutral alternatives thus "undercut[s] significantly" any defense of such a statute, casting considerable doubt on the government's protestations that "the asserted justification is in fact an accurate description of the purpose and effect of the law."

The dispositive question in this case, therefore, is whether content discrimination is reasonably necessary to achieve St. Paul's compelling interests; it plainly is not. An ordinance not limited to the favored topics, for example, would have precisely the same beneficial effect.

In fact the only interest distinctively served by the content limitation is that of displaying the city council's special hostility towards the particular biases thus singled out. That is precisely what the First Amendment forbids. The politicians of St. Paul are entitled to express that hostility—but not through the means of imposing unique limitations upon speakers who (however benightedly) disagree.... [B]urning a cross in someone's front yard is reprehensible. But St. Paul has sufficient means at its disposal to prevent such behavior without adding the First Amendment to the fire....

Justice White, with whom Justice Blackmun and Justice O'Connor join, and with whom Justice Stevens joins except as to Part [A], concurring in the judgment....

[A.] It is inconsistent to hold that the government may proscribe an entire category of speech ..., but that the government may not treat a subset of that category differently without violating the First Amendment; the content of the subset is by definition worthless and undeserving of constitutional protection. The majority's observation that fighting words are "quite expressive indeed," is no answer. Fighting words are not a means of exchanging views, rallying supporters, or registering a protest; they are directed against individuals to provoke violence or to inflict injury. Therefore, a ban on all fighting words or on a subset of the fighting words category would restrict only the social evil of hate speech, without creating the danger of driving viewpoints from the marketplace....

Any contribution of this holding to First Amendment jurisprudence is surely a negative one, since it necessarily signals that expressions of violence, such as the message of intimidation and racial hatred conveyed by burning a cross on someone's lawn, are of sufficient value to outweigh the social interest in order and morality that has traditionally placed such fighting words outside the First Amendment. Indeed, by characterizing fighting words as a form of "debate," the majority legitimates hate speech as a form of public discussion....

[B.] [T]he ordinance ... [should also] survive under the strict scrutiny applicable [even to] protected expression.... {The majority ... argu[es] that the availability of content-neutral alternatives "undercut[s] significantly" a claim that content-based legislation is "*necessary* to serve the asserted [compelling] interest." ... But the Court's analysis today ... substitut[es] the majority's policy judgment that a *more* restrictive alternative could adequately serve the compelling need identified by St. Paul lawmakers. The result would be: (a) a statute that was not tailored to fit the need identified by the government; and (b) a greater restriction on fighting words, even though the Court clearly believes that fighting words have protected expressive content.}

The majority appears to believe that its [approach] is necessary to prevent our elected lawmakers from prohibiting libel against members of one political party but not another and from enacting similarly preposterous laws.... [But a]lthough the First Amendment does not apply to categories of unprotected speech, such as fighting words, the Equal Protection Clause requires that the regulation of unprotected speech be rationally related to a legitimate government interest. A defamation statute that drew distinctions on the basis of political affiliation or "an ordinance prohibiting only those legally obscene works that contain criticism of the city government," would unquestionably fail rational-basis review....

[C.] The Court has patched up its argument with an apparently nonexhaustive list of ad hoc exceptions .... For instance, ... [the majority argues that] the statute making it illegal to threaten the life of the President is constitutional, "since the reasons why threats of violence are outside the First Amendment (protecting individuals from the fear of violence, from the disruption that fear engenders, and from the possibility that the threatened violence will occur) have special force when applied to the person of the President."

The exception swallows the majority's rule. Certainly, it should apply to the St. Paul ordinance, since "the reasons why [fighting words] are outside the First Amendment ... have special force when applied to [groups that have historically been subjected to discrimination]." ... A prohibition on fighting words ... is a ban on a class of speech that conveys an overriding message of personal injury and imminent violence, a message that is at its ugliest when directed against groups that have long been the targets of discrimination. Accordingly, the ordinance falls within the first exception to the majority's theory....

[T]he majority [also] concocts a catchall exclusion to protect against unforeseen problems, ... [which] would apply in cases in which "there is no realistic possibility that official suppression of ideas is afoot." As I have demonstrated, this case does not concern the official suppression of ideas. The majority discards this notion out of hand....

[Justice White nonetheless concluded that the St. Paul ordinance is unconstitutional. He reasoned that the Minnesota Supreme Court had interpreted the ordinance as covering all words "which by their very utterance inflict injury or tend to incite an immediate breach of the peace," including those that don't risk starting a fight but only "by [their] very utterance" cause "anger, alarm or resentment." This, he said, made the ordinance overbroad, since speech that merely causes anger, alarm, or resentment is constitutionally protected.—ed.]

d. *Virginia v. Black, 538 U.S. 343 (2003)*

[For the facts of this case, see p. 230.—ed.]

Justice O'Connor ... delivered the opinion of the Court [as to the parts excerpted below—ed.]....

Respondents Barry Black, Richard Elliott, and Jonathan O'Mara were convicted ... of violating Virginia's cross-burning statute, § 18.2-423....:

> It shall be [a felony] for any person ..., with the intent of intimidating any person or group of persons, to burn, or cause to be burned, a cross on the property of another, a highway or other public place....
>
> Any such burning of a cross shall be prima facie evidence of an intent to intimidate a person or group of persons....

[In *R.A.V. v. City of St. Paul*, we held that,] "When the basis for the content discrimination [within a proscribable class of speech] consists entirely of the very reason the entire class of speech at issue is proscribable, no significant danger of idea or viewpoint discrimination exists. Such a reason, having been adjudged neutral enough to support exclusion of the entire class of speech from First Amendment protection, is also neutral enough to form the basis of distinction within the class." Indeed, we noted that it would be constitutional to ban only a particular type of threat: "[T]he Federal Government can criminalize only those threats of violence that are directed against the President ... since the reasons why threats of violence are outside the First Amendment ... have special force when applied to the person of the President." ...

Similarly, Virginia's statute does not run afoul of the First Amendment insofar as it bans cross burning with intent to intimidate[, which the Court concluded is a subcategory of proscribable threats—ed.]. Unlike the statute at issue in *R.A.V.*, the Virginia statute does not single out for opprobrium only that speech directed toward "one of the specified disfavored topics." It does not matter whether an individual burns a cross with intent to intimidate because of the victim's race, gender, or religion, or because of the victim's "political affiliation, union membership, or homosexuality." ... See, *e.g.,* [sources omitted] (noting the instances of cross burnings directed at union members ... [and] describing the case of a defendant who burned a cross in the yard of the lawyer who had previously represented him and who was currently prosecuting him). Indeed, in the case of Elliott and O'Mara, it is at least unclear whether the respondents burned a cross due to racial animus ... [or because] "... their neighbor had complained about the presence of a firearm shooting range in the Elliott's yard ...." ...

The First Amendment permits Virginia to outlaw cross burnings done with the intent to intimidate because burning a cross is a particularly virulent form of intimidation ... in light of cross burning's long and pernicious history as a signal of impending violence. Thus, just as a State may regulate only that obscenity which is the most obscene due to its prurient content, [*R.A.V.,*] so too may a State choose to prohibit only those forms of intimidation that are most likely to inspire fear of bodily harm....

Justice Souter, with whom Justice Kennedy and Justice Ginsburg join, ... dissenting in [relevant] part....

[A.] [T]hreats against the President are not generally identified by reference to the content of any message that may accompany the threat, let alone any viewpoint, and there is no obvious correlation in fact between victim and message. Millions of statements are made about the President every day on every subject and from every standpoint; threats of violence are not an integral feature of any one subject or viewpoint as distinct from others....

A content-based proscription of cross burning, on the other hand, may be a subtle effort to ban not only the intensity of the intimidation cross burning causes when done to threaten, but also the particular message of white supremacy that is broadcast even by nonthreatening cross burning. I ... read *R.A.V.*'s examples of the particular virulence exception as covering prohibitions that are not clearly associated with a particular viewpoint, and that are consequently different from the Virginia statute....

[I thus] read the majority opinion as treating *R.A.V.*'s virulence exception in a more flexible, pragmatic manner than the original illustrations [in *R.A.V.*] would suggest. Actually, another way of looking at today's decision would see it as a slight modification of *R.A.V.*'s ... exception [that] allows content-based discrimination within a proscribable category when its "nature" is such "that there is no realistic possibility that official suppression of ideas is afoot." The majority's approach could be taken as recognizing an exception to *R.A.V.* when circumstances show that the statute's ostensibly valid reason for punishing particularly serious proscribable expression probably is not a ruse for message suppression, even though the statute may have a greater (but not exclusive) impact on adherents of one ideology than on others....

[B.] Yet ... the prima facie evidence provision [*i.e.,* that burning a cross on the property of another or in a public place is "prima facie evidence of an intent to intimidate ..."] stands in the way of any finding of ... a high probability {that no "official suppression of ideas is afoot."} ...

[T]he symbolic act of burning a cross, without more, is consistent with both intent to intimidate and intent to make an ideological statement free of any aim to threaten. One can tell the intimidating instance from the wholly ideological one only by reference to some further circumstance.... Sometimes those circumstances will show an intent to intimidate, but sometimes they will be at least equivocal, as in cases where a white supremacist group burns a cross at an initiation ceremony or political rally visible to the public. In such a case, ... the provision will encourage a factfinder to err on the side of a finding of intent to intimidate when the evidence of circumstances fails to point with any clarity either to the criminal intent or to the permissible one.... The provision will thus tend to draw nonthreatening ideological expression within the ambit of the prohibition of intimidating expression ....

To the extent the prima facie evidence provision skews prosecutions, then, it skews the statute toward suppressing ideas.... It is difficult to conceive of an intimidation case that could be easier to prove than one with cross burning, assuming any circumstances suggesting intimidation are present. The provision, apparently so unnecessary to legitimate prosecution of intimidation, is therefore quite enough to raise the question whether Virginia's content-based statute seeks more than mere protection against a virulent form of intimidation.

It consequently bars any conclusion that an exception to the general rule of *R.A.V.* is warranted on the ground "that there is no realistic [or little realistic] possibility that official suppression of ideas is afoot." {The same conclusion also goes for the second *R.A.V.* exception relating to "secondary effects." Our "secondary effects" jurisprudence presupposes that the regulation at issue is "unrelated to the suppression of free expression."} Since no *R.A.V.* exception can save the statute as content based, it can only survive if narrowly tailored to serve a compelling state interest, a stringent test the statute cannot pass; a content-neutral statute banning intimidation would achieve the same object without singling out particular content....

Justice Thomas, dissenting....

[Justice Thomas chronicles the cross-burnings and accompanying violence that prompted the enactment of the Virginia statute, and the contemporaneous descriptions of the events as forms of terrorism (see p. 234 above), and goes on to say:—ed.] Strengthening ... my conclusion, that the legislature sought to criminalize terrorizing *conduct* is the fact that at the time the statute was enacted, racial segregation was not only the prevailing practice, but also the law in Virginia. And, just two years after the enactment of this statute, Virginia's General Assembly embarked on a campaign of "massive resistance" in response to *Brown v. Board of Ed..*

It strains credulity to suggest that a state legislature that adopted a litany of segregationist laws self-contradictorily intended to squelch the segregationist message. Even for segregationists, violent and terroristic conduct, the Siamese twin of cross burning, was intolerable. The ban on cross burning with intent to intimidate demonstrates that even segregationists understood the difference between intimidating and terroristic conduct and racist expression. It is simply beyond belief that, in passing the statute now under review, the Virginia legislature was concerned with anything but penalizing conduct it must have viewed as particularly vicious....

C. Some Unsolved Problems

There are some important kinds of restrictions that the Court has never squarely confronted. What can you say about them, by analogy to existing exceptions (Part II), by considering the strict scrutiny doctrine (Part III), and by applying First Amendment policy arguments?

1. Crime-Facilitating Speech

a. The Issue

Let's define "crime-facilitating" speech as speech that

(1) intentionally or not,

(2) communicates information to some listeners or readers

(3) which they can use to more easily or effectively

    (a) commit crimes or other harmful acts (such as torts, hostile acts of foreign nations, or possibly suicide), or

    (b) get away with committing crimes or harmful acts.

"[The Court's] cases have not yet considered whether, and if so to what extent, the First Amendment protects such instructional speech." *Stewart v. McCoy*, 537 U.S. 993 (2002) (Stevens, J., respecting the denial of certiorari). Incitement doctrine deals with when speech may be restricted because it may *persuade* people to commit crimes. But no doctrine explains when the law may restrict speech that *informs* people how to commit crimes, in situations where they already want to commit the crime but don't know exactly how to do it successfully.

[handwritten margin note: Incitement ~ persuade]

b. Problem: Designing a Rule

Consider the following scenarios:

    (a) A book describes how to commit contract murder and get away with it. It sells 13,000 copies.

    (b) A mystery novel accurately describes a little-known and nonobvious way of committing the perfect crime.

    (c) A chemistry textbook describes how people can make explosives.

    (d) A Web site aimed at anarchists describes how to build bombs.

    (e) A book describes how to evade taxes while minimizing the risk of being detected.

[handwritten margin note: 1. Incitement 2. Strict Scrutiny — content 3. Policy]

(f) A Web site explains how to decrypt encrypted copyrighted material. Such decryption has been outlawed.

(g) A Web site or a newspaper article publishes the address of a Web site that contains copyright-infringing material.

(h) When the speech in (a) through (g) is suppressed, a self-described anticensorship Web site provides a copy. The site operator doesn't intend to facilitate crime, but wants to protest and resist speech suppression, and wants to preserve the controversial materials for the benefit of people who are interested in the controversy.

(i) A newspaper article identifies a crime witness, thus making it easier for the criminal to intimidate or kill the witness.

(j) A leaflet or a Web site identifies abortion providers, strikebreakers, registered sex offenders, or people who aren't complying with a boycott, thus making it easier for others to retaliate against them.

(k) A Web site posts people's social security numbers and computer passwords.

(l) A newspaper publishes the sailing dates of troopships, secret military plans, or the names of undercover agents in enemy countries.

(m) A magazine describes in detail how one can build a nuclear bomb or a biological weapon.

(n) The government issues a secret subpoena to a library, bank, or service provider; a statute bars anyone who knows about the subpoena from revealing its existence. The recipient illegally tells a newspaper about the subpoena; the newspaper illegally publishes this information. The suspects learn they're being targeted, and flee.

(o) A master criminal advises a less experienced friend on how best to commit a crime, or on how a criminal gang should maintain power.

(p) A lookout, or a passerby who dislikes the police, warns a criminal that the police are coming.

What doctrine would you suggest for dealing with these cases? What results would your proposal reach in each case? Do you think these would be the right results? Cf. cases and statutes cited in Eugene Volokh, *Crime-Facilitating Speech*, 57 Stan. L. Rev. 1095, 1097-1102 (2005).

2. Professional-Client Speech

a. *The Issue*

Professional-client relationships—whether the professional is a lawyer, accountant, psychotherapist, or even a doctor—often consist mostly of speech. Sometimes, of course, they involve physical conduct (surgery) or the submission of statements to the government (a lawyer arguing in court). But often they consist solely of two people talking with each other, one explaining the problem and the other giving advice.

Yet this communication is often subject to speech restrictions and compulsions that would generally be forbidden in other contexts. For instance:

(a) Many professionals may not advise clients without a government license. This would be a prior restraint if applied to other speech.

(b) The government holds professionals liable for negligent advice, including not just false statements of fact but also negligent predictions, which would otherwise be protected opinions.

(c) Many professionals may not reveal client confidences. This isn't just an implied contract term (which might be defensible under *Cohen v. Cowles Media Co.* (1991) (p. 574)), because under some rules the obligation can't be disclaimed even if the professional expressly tells the client that he doesn't promise confidentiality.

(d) Some professionals, including lawyers and psychotherapists, are barred from having sexual relationships with their clients. Laws constraining the sexual choices of authors of advice books, or of trusted talk show hosts, would violate the First Amendment—and perhaps *Lawrence v. Texas*—because they burden people based on their speech. Yet the law constrains the sexual choices of professionals because of their speech (their advice to the clients).

Such restrictions may be constitutionally permissible: something in a professional-client relationship might justify such extra regulation. But the Court has never explained (1) exactly which relationships trigger such lower protection, and (2) what speech restrictions would be allowed in such relationships. The cases on the subject are scant, and reproduced in relevant part below; query what they amount to.

b. Problem: Counseling That Advocates Race-Based Decisions

A state has long required that all marriage and family counselors—defined as "any person who offers advice related to marriage and family matters in exchange for money"—be licensed and follow rules prescribed by the state's Marriage and Family Counseling Licensing Board.

The Board learns that some such counselors are advising clients not to enter into interracial marriages or adoptions. Some are even advising clients who are in interracial marriages that the interracial nature of the marriage may be a source of the problem, and are suggesting in some instances that divorce may therefore be the only solution.

The Board believes such advice is offensive, and harmful to patients. It therefore enacts this rule: "Any marriage and family counselor who uses a patient's race, or the race of a patient's spouse, children, or prospective adoptive children or stepchildren, as part of the basis for the counselor's recommendation, shall have his or her license suspended for six months."

Counselor Mary Moe has her license suspended for giving advice that violates this rule. Her former patients, Laura Loh (who is East Asian) and Richard Roe (who is white), who divorced each other partly on Moe's advice but have since reconciled, also sue Moe for emotional distress caused by her advice, which they claim constituted malpractice. The judge awards them $100,000 in a bench trial. One of the judge's findings of fact is that Moe's advice was unreasonable by the profession's standards; the sole evidence of those standards on which the judge relies is the Board's rule.

What should be the proper analysis under the First Amendment?

c. *Planned Parenthood v. Casey, 505 U.S. 833 (1992)*

[The Court upheld, among other things, a requirement that doctors give patients certain state-provided information before getting the patient's consent to an abortion.—ed.]

Justices O'Connor, Kennedy, and Souter announced the judgment of the Court....

[T]he physician's First Amendment rights not to speak are implicated, see *Wooley v. Maynard*, but only as part of the practice of medicine, subject to reasonable licensing and regulation by the State. We see no constitutional infirmity in the requirement that the physician provide the information mandated by the State here.

[But see *Planned Parenthood v. Rounds*, 2006 WL 2864454 (D.S.D.) (holding *Casey* covers only mandated factual disclosures and not requirements that the doctor "enunciate the State's viewpoint on an unsettled medical, philosophical, theological, and scientific issue, that is, whether a fetus is a human being"), *aff'd*, 467 F.3d 716 (8th Cir. 2006).—ed.]

[The other six Justices did not opine on this.—ed.]

d. *Lowe v. SEC, 472 U.S. 181 (1985)*

Justice White, joined by Chief Justice Burger and Justice Rehnquist), concurring....

[Justice White concluded that a federal statute requiring professional investment advisors to register with the government couldn't be applied to a newsletter containing investment advice:—ed.]

The power of government to regulate the professions is not lost whenever the practice of a profession entails speech. The underlying principle was expressed by the Court in *Giboney v. Empire Storage & Ice Co.*: "it has never been deemed an abridgment of freedom of speech or press to make a course of conduct illegal merely because the conduct was in part initiated, evidenced, or carried out by means of language ...." ...

One who takes the affairs of a client personally in hand and purports to exercise judgment on behalf of the client in the light of the client's individual needs and circumstances is properly viewed as engaging in the practice of a profession. Just as offer and acceptance are communications incidental to the regulable transaction called a contract, the professional's speech is incidental to the conduct of the profession. If the government enacts generally applicable licensing provisions limiting the class of persons who may practice the profession, it cannot be said to have enacted a limitation on freedom of speech or the press subject to First Amendment scrutiny.

[But w]here the personal nexus between professional and client does not exist, and a speaker does not purport to be exercising judgment on behalf of any particular individual with whose circumstances he is directly acquainted, government regulation ceases to function as legitimate regulation of professional practice with only incidental impact on speech; it becomes regulation of speaking or publishing as such, subject to the First Amendment ....

[The majority interpreted the statute in a way that made it unnecessary to resolve the First Amendment issue. See also *Thomas v. Collins*, 323 U.S. 516 (1945) (holding that union organizing couldn't be restricted on the grounds that such a restriction was just a regulation of the "profession" of union organizer).—ed.]

e. *Holder v. Humanitarian Law Project, 561 U.S. 1 (2010)*

[For the facts, which involved a lawyers' group that wanted to give legal advice to designated foreign terrorist organizations, see p. 296.—ed.]

Chief Justice Roberts delivered the opinion of the Court [which was unanimous on this point]...

[T]he Government ... [argues] that the only thing truly at issue in this litigation is conduct, not speech. Section 2339B is directed at the fact of plaintiffs' interaction with the [foreign terrorist groups], the Government contends, and only incidentally burdens their expression. The Government argues that the proper standard of review is therefore the one set out in *United States v. O'Brien*....

The Government is wrong that the only thing actually at issue in this litigation is conduct .... *O'Brien* does not provide the applicable standard for reviewing a content-based regulation of speech, and § 2339B regulates speech on the basis of its content. Plaintiffs want to speak to the [foreign groups], and whether they may do so under § 2339B depends on what they say. If plaintiffs' speech to those groups imparts a "specific skill" or communicates advice derived from "specialized knowledge"—for example, training on the use of international law or advice on petitioning the United Nations—then it is barred....

[The Court therefore held that the restriction on the Humanitarian Law Project's proposed advice to the foreign groups was subject to strict scrutiny. The majority then upheld the law under strict scrutiny, relying on the compelling government interest in fighting terrorism. For lower court cases applying *Holder* to regulation of professional-client speech, see *King v. Governor*, 767 F.3d 216 (3d Cir. 2014); *Wollschlaeger v. Governor*, 814 F.3d 1159 (11th Cir. 2015), *reh'g en banc pending*.—ed.]

3. DISCLOSURE OF PRIVATE FACTS ABOUT PEOPLE

a. *The Issue*

Many states have recognized the tort of "publicity given to private life" or "disclosure of private facts" (sometimes referred to as "the right to privacy," though that phrase also covers various other claims). Here's the formulation from Restatement (Second) of Torts § 652D:

> One who gives publicity to a matter concerning the private life of another is subject to liability ~~... if the~~ matter publicized is of a kind that
>   (a) would be highly offensive to a reasonable person, and
>   (b) is not of legitimate concern to the public.

Is the tort constitutional? The Supreme Court has never confronted that question. *Florida Star v. B.J.F.* (1989) (p. 286), which struck down a state statute that banned publishing rape victims' names, suggests that privacy-based speech restrictions may often be unconstitutional; but the Court pointedly refused "to hold broadly that truthful publication may never be punished consistent with the First Amendment."

Lower courts have generally upheld the tort, but have generally limited it severely—among other things, reading "legitimate concern to the public" quite broadly—to minimize First Amendment problems. Nonetheless, it's not clear that, even as limited, the tort is constitutional.

b.   Problem: Writing About People's Past Crimes

> "The Big Business of Hijacking," published by [*Reader's Digest*] 11 years after the hijacking [committed by the plaintiff], commences with a picture whose caption reads, "Today's highwaymen are looting trucks at a rate of more than $100 million a year. But the truckers have now declared all-out war." The article describes various truck thefts and the efforts being made to stop such thefts....
>
> One sentence in the article refers to plaintiff: "Typical of many beginners, Marvin Briscoe and [another man] stole a 'valuable-looking' truck in Danville, Ky., and then fought a gun battle with the local police, only to learn that they had hijacked four bowling-pin spotters." There is nothing in the article to indicate that the hijacking occurred in 1956.
>
> As the result of defendant's publication, plaintiff's 11-year-old daughter, as well as his friends, for the first time learned of this incident. They thereafter scorned and abandoned him.

So the California Supreme Court described the facts in *Briscoe v. Reader's Digest Ass'n*, 483 P.2d 34, 36 (Cal. 1971). The court held that Briscoe's lawsuit could go forward, and specified that at trial, "It is for the trier of fact to determine (1) whether plaintiff had become a rehabilitated member of society, (2) whether identifying him as a former criminal would be highly offensive and injurious to the reasonable man, (3) whether defendant published this information with a reckless disregard for its offensiveness, and (4) whether any independent justification for printing plaintiff's identity existed."

How would the case come out under current First Amendment law? What do you think the law ought to be here? See *Gates v. Discovery Communications, Inc.*, 34 Cal. 4th 679 (2004), *overruling Briscoe*.

c. Problem: Transsexual Student Government Official

Toni Diaz, the first woman student body president at College of Alameda, a California community college, was a transsexual. The *Oakland Tribune* published this fact. Diaz sued, and the court of appeals held that her lawsuit could go forward; if a jury found that Diaz's transsexuality wasn't newsworthy, she could prevail. See *Diaz v. Oakland Tribune*, 188 Cal. Rptr. 762 (Ct. App. 1983).

How would the case come out under current First Amendment law? What do you think the law ought to be here?

d. Problem: Videotapes of People Having Sex

A Web site operator gets and posts a videotape of a prominent actress having sex with her then-boyfriend. The video was made by the boyfriend, long before the actress became famous. The boyfriend had the actress's permission to make the video, but not to distribute the video further. Nonetheless, the video did end up getting out. (The now-ex-boyfriend claims it was stolen from his home, but that's not clear.)

The actress sues, seeking compensatory damages for emotional distress, punitive damages, and an injunction against further distribution of the video. What should the result be? Cf. *Michaels v. Internet Entertainment Group, Inc.*, 5 F. Supp. 2d 823 (C.D. Cal. 1998).

4. HOSTILE ENVIRONMENT HARASSMENT LAW

a. Hostile Work Environment Harassment Law

Over the past 30 years, courts have interpreted federal and state employment discrimination laws (such as Title VII of the Civil Rights Act of 1964) to prohibit employers from tolerating "hostile work environments." The general rule is that employers are liable for damages when the employer, its employees, or its patrons engage in conduct or speech that is

   (a) "severe or pervasive" enough

   (b) to create a "hostile, abusive, or offensive work environment"

   (c) based on race, religion, sex, national origin, age, disability, or in some situations veteran status,

   (d) for the plaintiff and

   (e) for a reasonable person.

If a state law or a city ordinance also prohibits discrimination based on other attributes—such as sexual orientation, marital status, citizenship, or political affiliation—then those attributes would be added in that state or city to item (c) above. (You can see other aspects of this issue in the vagueness problem on p. 157, the captive audiences problem on p. 192, and the injunction problem on p. 694.)

Courts have applied this both to speech said directly to the offended person and to speech (such as signs, e-mails, coworker conversations, and the like) seen or overheard by the person. Courts have generally said that the "severe or pervasive" requirement is usually not satisfied by a single instance of offensive speech, but can be satisfied by speech that happens several times over the span of several weeks or months.

Employers are liable when they know or have reason to know about the speech. As to speech by patrons, employers are liable when they have the power to control the speech (for instance, by ejecting offending patrons). "Hostile environment" harassment is different from "quid pro quo" harassment, in which a supervisor threatens to retaliate against an employee unless the employee has sex with the supervisor.

Many hostile environment harassment cases involve only offensive conduct and speech that falls within an exception to protection, such as threats or fighting words. But other cases involve otherwise protected speech, such as

(a) insults that do not qualify as fighting words;

(b) sexually themed material, including pornography, pinups of scantily clad women, and "legitimate" art;

(c) racially, religiously, or sexually offensive political statements;

(d) sexually themed humor; and

(e) religious proselytizing (whether it insults other religions or not),

so long as the speech is found to be "severe or pervasive" enough. See Kingsley R. Browne, *Title VII as Censorship*, 52 Ohio St. L.J. 481 (1991); Deborah Epstein, *Can a "Dumb Ass Woman" Achieve Equality in the Workplace?*, 84 Geo. L.J. 399 (1996); Cynthia Estlund, *Freedom of Expression in the Workplace and the Problem of Discriminatory Harassment*, 75 Tex. L. Rev. 687 (1997); Richard H. Fallon, Jr., *Sexual Harassment, Content Neutrality, and the First Amendment Dog That Didn't Bark*, 1994 Sup. Ct. Rev. 1; Eugene Volokh, Comment, *Freedom of Speech and Workplace Harassment*, 39 UCLA L. Rev. 1791 (1992), updated at http://www.law.ucla.edu/volokh/harass/substanc.htm; Eugene Volokh, *What Speech Does "Hostile Work Environment" Harassment Law Restrict?*, 85 Geo. L.J. 627 (1997), updated at http://www.law.ucla.edu/volokh/harass/breadth.htm.

The Supreme Court has never squarely considered hostile work environment harassment law (though *R.A.V. v. City of St. Paul* (p. 317) touches on it). Some lower courts have suggested that hostile work environment harassment law may violate the First Amendment in at least some situations; others have said it's categorically constitutional.

Such rules would almost certainly be constitutional if the government applied them to *its own* employees. Under the "government as employer" doctrine (Part VI.A), the government may restrict even speech on matters of public concern if the speech is disruptive enough, and speech that creates an offensive environment generally is disruptive. The question is whether the government as sovereign may require even *private* employers to restrict their employees' speech this way, on pain of legal liability.

b. Hostile Educational Environment Harassment Law

State and federal laws also prohibit discrimination in education, not just in employment. (The federal Title VI and Title IX apply only to federally-funded education, but many state antidiscrimination laws apply regardless of funding.) The theory of hostile work environment harassment law is that an employer's tolerating a hostile, abusive, or offensive environment is a form of discrimination, so employers have an obligation to restrict employee speech that creates such an environment. The same theory applies to educational institutions that tolerate speech which creates a hostile, abusive, or offensive environment for their students.

Thus, private and public universities and K-12 schools would also face damages liability unless they restrict conduct or speech—by classmates, teachers, staff, and visitors—that fits the "hostile work environment" definition (except with "educational" replacing "work" in prong (b)).

Here, though, lower courts have been more skeptical: Many such public university student speech codes (imposed by the government acting as university educator) have been struck down, even when they were defended as means of trying to prevent a hostile educational environment. See, *e.g.*, *McCauley v. Univ. of V.I.*, 618 F.3d 232 (3d Cir. 2010); *Dambrot v. Cent. Mich. Univ.*, 55 F.3d 1177 (6th Cir. 1995); *Iota Xi Chapter of Sigma Chi Fraternity v. George Mason Univ.*, 993 F.2d 386 (4th Cir. 1993). *cases*

Presumably courts would be even more ready to strike down government attempts to mandate such speech codes where the government is imposing liability on private universities, and thus acting as sovereign, rather than just limiting speech at its own universities. Cf. Eugene Volokh, *Freedom of Speech, Cyberspace, Harassment Law, and the Clinton Administration*, 63 L. & Contemp. Probs. 299, 313-17 (2000) (discussing the federal government's attempt to impose such a speech code under Title IX, as a condition of the school's getting federal education funds). But again the Supreme Court has not confronted this question.

c. Hostile Public Accommodations Environment Harassment Law

The "hostile environment" theory has also been applied under state and federal laws that ban discrimination in places of public accommodation, which might cover restaurants, bars, theaters, other businesses, or even Internet discussion groups. Again, the theory of hostile work environment harassment law is that an employer's tolerating an offensive environment is a form of discrimination, so employers have an obligation to restrict speech that creates such an environment. Likewise, the theory of hostile public accommodations environment law is that business owners are liable to their patrons for sufficiently offensive speech by fellow patrons (and by the business's own employees).

Thus, a bar might be liable to patrons for allowing a racially offensive display put up by a bar employee. A bus line might be liable when bus riders tell jokes that are offensive to disabled fellow riders. A private club might be liable for misogynistic comments said by club members.

There have been only a few such cases, and most of them have not confronted the First Amendment issues. *See* Eugene Volokh, *Freedom of Speech, Cyberspace, Harassment Law, and the Clinton Administration*, 63 L. & Contemp. Probs. 299, 318-26 (2000) (collecting cases and government agency statements); Daniel Koontz, *Hostile Public Accommodations Laws and the First Amendment*, 3 NYU J. L. & Lib. 197 (2008); see also *Noah v. AOL Time Warner, Inc.*, 261 F. Supp. 2d 532 (E.D. Va. 2003) (rejecting on statutory grounds a harassment claim brought against America Online based on anti-Muslim speech in an America Online chatroom).

d. Hostile Housing Environment Harassment Law

A few recent cases have applied hostile environment law to housing as well. Under this theory, landlords and condominium associations might be liable for tolerating speech by residents (and by the landlord's or association's employees) that creates an offensive environment for other residents. In principle, this might apply to statements made in hallways, overheard remarks in common areas, or material that people post on their own doors. It's not clear, though, how far hostile housing environment doctrine will go; it is still very much in its infancy.

e. Problem: Hostile Environment Harassment Law

Do you think hostile environment harassment law is constitutionally sound? Unsound, whether because it is too vague or too broad? Sound in some areas but not in others—and, if so, what's the basis for distinguishing the areas? Consider these test cases:

(1) Jane Doe is a Catholic woman who works for Western Widgets. Some of her coworkers display calendars that show women in swimsuits. Others often make sexually themed jokes that she overhears. Others sometimes say that women belong at home, and shouldn't be working in certain jobs. Others harshly condemn Catholicism. Still others tell jokes about Catholics. She believes this speech put together has created a sexually and religiously hostile environment, and she sues Western Widgets.

(2) Same speech, but Doe works for *Maxim* magazine, and the offending coworkers are writers who sometimes write stories about sex, women and the workplace, religious views on abortion and contraception, church sex scandals, and so on.

(3) Same speech, but Doe is a student at Coachella Community College, and the offending speech comes from classmates.

(4) Same speech, but Doe is a patron at Paul's Pub, and the offending speech is communicated partly by the pub owner (who has put pictures of women in swimsuits on pub walls) and partly by fellow patrons.

(5) Same speech, but Doe lives in Amalfi Apartments, and the offending speech is communicated by fellow tenants.

Should Doe's lawsuits succeed?

Say they do, and say someone representing another employer, university, place of public accommodation, or apartment building comes to you for advice. "I would rather not restrict people's speech any more than necessary," he says, "but I certainly want to avoid expensive litigation, and the risk of massive liability. What speech restrictions should I impose on my employees, students, patrons, or tenants to minimize my risk of being sued for their offensive speech?" How do you reply?

5. CHILD CUSTODY SPEECH RESTRICTIONS

a. The Issue

In child custody and visitation cases, courts are generally required by state law to decide based on "the best interests of the child." Thus, for instance, they may conclude that the mother should have custody because she has been the primary caregiver, but the father should have the right to have the children visit with him over the weekend. Or they may decide that because the mother has a drinking problem or has beaten the children, the father should have custody and the mother should have only short periods of supervised visitation.

Does the Free Speech Clause constrain courts' power (1) to consider a parent's likely future speech under the "best interests" test, or (2) to enjoin a parent from saying certain things to the child on the grounds that such speech would be against the child's best interests? Lower courts have considered whether the Religion Clauses limit consideration of parents' religious speech, but they've rarely considered whether the Free Speech Clause limits consideration of parents' speech, religious or not.

Note that from the 1930s to the present, courts have indeed at times considered parents' speech to their children—for instance, Communist, Nazi, atheist, fundamentalist, pro-polygamy, pro-adultery, pro-gay-rights, anti-gay-rights, or racist speech—as counting against the parent under the best interests test. See generally Eugene Volokh, *Parent-Child Speech and Child Custody Speech Restrictions*, 81 N.Y.U. L. Rev. 631 (2006).

b. Problem: Criticisms of the Other Parent

A married couple, Frank and Mary, have a son, Sid. When Sid is seven, Frank realizes that he's homosexual, and concludes that he can't be happy in a heterosexual relationship; the couple get divorced. Mary is unhappy about this, and also believes that homosexuality is immoral. Frank learns that Mary is likely to teach the child that homosexuality is immoral, and at the custody hearing asks the judge to order Mary not to "teach Sid, or expose Sid to, anything that can be considered homophobic."

The judge, Anne Turk, gives Mary custody, because she concludes this is in Sid's best interests, since Mary has been the primary caretaker. She gives Frank visitation rights on every other weekend. (The judge doesn't consider Frank's sexual orientation in the custody decision.)

You are Judge Turk's law clerk, and the judge asks you whether she should issue the order that Frank requests—whether the order would satisfy the "best interests" test, and whether it would be constitutional. What do you say? Cf. *In re E.L.M.C.*, 100 P.3d 546 (Colo. App. 2004)).

c. *Problem: Racist Speech*

An unmarried couple, Frank and Mary, have a son, Sid. When Sid is twelve, the couple breaks up. At the custody hearing, Mary introduces evidence that Frank has expressed racist views about blacks to Sid, and is likely to continue doing so. She argues that it would thus be in Sid's best interests to be raised by her, with Frank getting only limited visitation.

Were it not for Frank's racist teachings, the judge (Benjamin Pereira) would have been inclined to give Frank and Mary equal time with the child, and equal control over Sid's upbringing. But he's not sure to what extent he should consider the views that Frank is likely to teach Sid.

The Judge Pereira asks you (his law clerk) (1) what you think is in Sid's best interests, and (2) what constraints the Free Speech Clause imposes on his decisions. What do you say? Cf., *e.g.*, *Tipton v. Aaron*, 2004 WL 1344916 (Ark. Ct. App.).

d. *Problem: Jihadist Speech*

During their marriage, Daniel Powell and Allison Blumenthal followed a "quasi-Muslim philosophy." They also "amassed a large quantity of weapons," and Daniel was imprisoned for illegal weapons possession and for making threats. Allison testified that Daniel abused her and that she went along with his actions only because she was afraid of him. The couple divorced ten years ago, when Daniel was in prison. They are parents of Mujahid Daniel and Mujahid David, ages 13 and 11.

Daniel, now out on parole, wants to see his children. Allison objects, based on Daniel's "violent felony conviction record ... domestic violence ... extremist views regarding religion, including ... jihad; and the letters written to the children while he was incarcerated, lecturing about religion and reminding the children that their names are Mujahid." ("Mujahid" means a soldier fighting for Islam; "mujahedin" is the plural.)

A state court, applying the "best interests of the children" standard, holds that Daniel should be allowed supervised visitation after his parole expires, but orders that Daniel not discuss with the children "any issues pertaining to his religion." Cf. *Powell v. Blumenthal*, 35 A.D.3d 615 (N.Y. App. Div. 2006). The order is appealed.

You are Judge Samuel Pereira's law clerk, and you are reviewing the trial court's order under an abuse of discretion standard of review. The judge asks you (1) whether you think the order is in the boys' best interests, (2) whether you think the trial court judge abused his discretion in concluding the order was in the boys' best interests, and (3) what constraints the Free Speech Clause imposes on the decision. What do you say?

IV. CONTENT-NEUTRAL RESTRICTIONS

A. CONTENT-NEUTRAL RESTRICTIONS ON SPEECH AND EX-PRESSIVE CONDUCT

a. Summary

Parts II and III discussed restrictions on speech (and on symbolic expression) justified by the harms that supposedly flow from what the speech communicated—*e.g.*, when speech persuades people to do bad things, injures people's reputations, offends people by its content, and such.

But speech also has a noncommunicative component, which can cause harms independently of what it expresses. Loud speech in the middle of the night can wake people up. Leaflets can end up littered on the ground. A parade can tie up traffic.

And this is especially so with regard to symbolic expression, which often triggers generally applicable laws that don't even mention speech. Burning a draft card destroys a government document, and can interfere with the bureaucratic system that relies on the existence of those documents; and this effect is unrelated to whether the burning is expressive. Burning a flag could start a bigger fire, quite apart from whether the flag burning is expressive. Because of this, First Amendment law gives the government considerable—but not unlimited—authority to restrict speech and symbolic expression based on their noncommunicative impact.

Rule: Restrictions on the time, place, or manner of speech—as well as conduct restrictions applied to expressive conduct—are permissible if they:

1. Are justified without reference to the content of the regulated speech or the communicative impact of the symbolic expression (*i.e.*, are *content-neutral*) (see Part IV.B (p. 359)),

   a. focusing on the text and structure of the law, *not* the legislators' supposed motive, *United States v. O'Brien* (p. 351).

2. Serve a *substantial government interest*,

   a. such as preserving residential privacy, *Frisby v. Schultz* (1988) (p. 343), preventing excessive noise, preventing tie-ups either in car traffic or pedestrian traffic in crowded areas, and so on.

3. Are *narrowly tailored* to serve this interest, which

   a. is *not* the same narrow tailoring as required under strict scrutiny (see subitems (e) and (f) below);

   b. does require that the law advance the government interest, see *Turner Broadcasting Sys. v. FCC*, 512 U.S. 622, 664 (1994), in the sense that removing the restriction—or exempting the challenger's conduct and other conduct like it—would materially interfere with the government interest, *Clark v. CCNV* (1984) (p. 354);

339

c. does require that the law not burden a substantial amount of speech that doesn't implicate the government's interest (*i.e.*, in the parlance of the strict scrutiny inquiry, the law may not be overinclusive);

d. does require that the law not impose a burden on speech that's disproportionate to the degree to which the speech implicates the interest, see *Schneider v. New Jersey* (1939) (p. 342);

e. does *not* require that the law be the least restrictive means, *Ward v. Rock Against Racism,* 491 U.S. 781 (1989);

f. does *not* evaluate whether the law is underinclusive, *Members of the City Council v. Taxpayers for Vincent,* 466 U.S. 789 (1984).

4. And leave open *ample alternative channels* for communicating the information; a proposed alternative channel may be inadequate if it is:

a. too expensive (see, *e.g.*, *City of Ladue v. Gilleo* (1994) (p. 345), which pointed out that "[r]esidential signs are an unusually cheap and convenient form of communication"; "[e]specially for persons of modest means or limited mobility, a yard or window sign may have no practical substitute");

b. unlikely to reach pretty much the same audience (see *id.,* pointing out that signs can easily reach neighbors, "an audience that could not be reached nearly as well by other means"); or

c. likely to implicitly carry a significantly different message from the one that the speaker prefers (see *id.,* reasoning that "[d]isplaying a sign from one's own residence often carries a message quite distinct from placing the same sign someplace else").

— These are all questions of degree, and the Court has never provided any clear lines to explain how "ample" is ample enough. Most content-neutral restrictions, after all, interfere in *some* measure with the ease of reaching the target audience, in *some* measure change the implicit message of the speech, and often tend to make the speech *somewhat* more expensive—but *Frisby* and other cases have upheld such restrictions, concluding the alternative channels were "ample" enough.

— The "ample alternative channels" prong has never been officially extended to the test for restrictions on expressive conduct. Such a prong, however, may be implicit but almost always met, because there's almost always a good, if imperfect, alternative to expressive conduct—speech that communicates pretty much the same message. Cf. *O'Brien* (Harlan, J., concurring); *Clark* (stressing presence of alternatives).

5. To decide whether the challenger's behavior even qualifies as symbolic expression, see Part II.E.4 (p. 218).

6. Cases dealing with symbolic expression often arise in a somewhat different procedural posture from cases dealing with content-neutral speech restrictions. The symbolic expression claimants are often asking for an exemption from a generally applicable law. In *Clark*, for instance, the claimants were saying not that the government must entirely allow sleeping in public parks, but only that expressive sleeping—sleeping

that's part of trying to send a message—should be exempted from the general ban. Challengers of content-neutral speech restrictions generally challenge the law on its face. But despite this difference, the test for content-neutral speech restrictions and expressive conduct restrictions has ended up being pretty much the same.

Core theory behind the "ample alternative channels" prong:

a. So long as ample alternative channels are present, the restriction doesn't really ban speech, only reroutes it into other, pretty much as effective, forms of communication.

b. Consider the "undue burden" inquiry set forth in *Planned Parenthood v. Casey*, 505 U.S. 833 (1992):

— If the law substantially burdens the right to abortion, then it's invalid.

— If the law only modestly burdens the right, then it only needs to pass the rational basis test.

c. Likewise, consider the test for the right to marry set forth in *Zablocki v. Redhail*, 434 U.S. 374 (1978):

— If the law substantially burdens the right to marry, then it must pass a form of heightened scrutiny.

— If the law only modestly burdens the right, then it only needs to pass the rational basis test.

d. The time/place/manner test uses a similar framework, though the components are slightly different:

— If the law substantially burdens speech—by not leaving open ample alternative channels—then the time/place/manner analysis doesn't apply, and the law must pass strict scrutiny (under the framework discussed in Part III).

— If the law imposes a less-than-substantial burden—by closing only one channel but leaving open ample alternatives—then the law must pass a sort of intermediate scrutiny (must serve a substantial interest and must not restrict more speech than necessary).

See Alan Brownstein, *How Rights Are Infringed: The Role of Undue Burden Analysis in Constitutional Doctrine*, 45 Hastings L.J. 867 (1994).

b. Problem: Door-to-Door Solicitation

The City of Struthers, Ohio has an ordinance that prohibits "any person distributing handbills ... to ring the door bell ... or otherwise summon the ... inmates of any residence to the door for the purpose of receiving such handbills ...." Is the ordinance constitutional, when applied to noncommercial speech? Cf. *Martin v. City of Struthers*, 319 U.S. 141 (1943).

c. Problem: Publishing Intercepted Conversations

Federal law bars people from intercepting certain communications, including cellular phone calls. It also bars people from intentionally disclosing "the contents of any [covered] communication, knowing or having reason to know" that the communication was illegally intercepted, even if they weren't the ones who intercepted it. Violators may be sued by those whose conversations are revealed.

Radio talk show host Hugh Hewitt is sent a tape of a cellular phone call between Senator Harry Reid and one of his political consultants. Hewitt believes the conversation demonstrates the Senator's deviousness, and plays the conversation on his show. He is then sued by the consultant. Would allowing a verdict against Hewitt violate Hewitt's First Amendment rights? Compare *Peavy v. WFAA-TV, Inc.*, 221 F.3d 158 (5th Cir. 2000) and *Boehner v. McDermott,* 191 F.3d 463 (D.C. Cir. 1999) with *Bartnicki v. Vopper*, 532 U.S. 514 (2001).

d.   Problem: Marijuana Performance Art

The National Organization for the Reform of Marijuana Laws (NORML) decides to put on a work of performance art in San Rafael depicting the many valuable uses of hemp. It includes some performers dancing in hemp shoes (which are quite lawful), some people eating hemp cheese (which apparently does not contain any prohibited substances), and a woman smoking one joint of marijuana. State law makes it unlawful to possess or smoke marijuana. The smoker gets busted, and raises a First Amendment defense. What result?

e.   Problem: Wearing Police Uniforms

Phoenix City Code § 23-21 bars people from wearing the official insignia of the Phoenix Police Department—which includes police uniforms—without authorization. Is this statute constitutional? Cf. *Sult v. State*, 906 So.2d 1013 (Fla. 2005); *State v. McLamb,* 932 P.2d 266 (Ariz. App. 1996) .

f.   Schneider v. New Jersey, 308 U.S. 147 (1939)

Justice Roberts delivered the opinion of the Court....

Municipal authorities, as trustees for the public, have the duty to keep their communities' streets open and available for movement of people and property, the primary purpose to which the streets are dedicated. So long as legislation to this end does not abridge the constitutional liberty of one rightfully upon the street to impart information through speech or the distribution of literature, it may lawfully regulate the conduct of those using the streets.

For example, a person could not exercise this liberty by taking his stand in the middle of a crowded street, contrary to traffic regulations, and maintain his position to the stoppage of all traffic; a group of distributors could not insist upon a constitutional right to form a cordon across the street and to allow no pedestrian to pass who did not accept a tendered leaflet; nor does the guarantee of freedom of speech or of the press deprive a municipality of power to enact regulations against throwing literature broadcast in the streets. Prohibition of such conduct would not abridge the constitutional liberty since such activity bears no necessary relationship to the freedom to speak, write, print or distribute information or opinion....

[Three of the] ordinances under review ... absolutely prohibit [the distribution of literature to the public] in the streets .... The motive of the legislation ... is held by the courts below to be the prevention of littering of the streets and, although the alleged offenders were not charged with themselves scattering paper in the streets, their convictions were sustained upon the theory that distribution by them encouraged or resulted in such littering.... [But] the purpose to keep the streets clean and of good appearance is insufficient to justify an ordinance which prohibits a person rightfully on a public street from handing literature to one willing to receive it. Any burden imposed upon the city authorities in cleaning and caring for the streets as an indirect consequence of such distribution results from the constitutional protection of the freedom of speech and press.

This constitutional protection does not deprive a city of all power to prevent street littering. There are obvious methods of preventing littering. Amongst these is the punishment of those who actually throw papers on the streets....

[Speaking of another ordinance also challenged in this case—an ordinance that banned door-to-door distribution of literature without a permit from the police department, and was justified as a means of preventing fraud and trespass—the Court continued:] Frauds may be denounced as offenses and punished by law. Trespasses may similarly be forbidden. If it is said that these means are less efficient and convenient than bestowal of power on police authorities to decide what information may be disseminated from house to house, and who may impart the information, the answer is that considerations of this sort do not empower a municipality to abridge freedom of speech and press....

g. *Frisby v. Schultz, 487 U.S. 474 (1988)*

Justice O'Connor delivered the opinion of the Court....

[A.] The appellees ... express[ed] their views [opposed to abortion] by picketing on a public street outside the ... residence of a doctor who apparently performs abortions .... [They assembled] outside the doctor's home on at least six occasions [within one month], for periods ranging from one to one and a half hours. The size of the group varied from 11 to more than 40. The picketing was generally orderly and peaceful; the town never had occasion to invoke any of its various ordinances prohibiting obstruction of the streets, loud and unnecessary noises, or disorderly conduct.

Nonetheless, the picketing generated substantial controversy and numerous complaints. The Town Board therefore [enacted an ordinance providing that] ... "It is unlawful for any person to engage in picketing before or about the residence or dwelling of any individual ...." ...

[B.] The antipicketing ordinance operates at the core of the First Amendment by prohibiting appellees from engaging in picketing on an issue of public concern. Because of the importance of "uninhibited, robust, and wide-open" debate on public issues ... we have traditionally subjected restrictions on public issue picketing to careful scrutiny....

[T]he Brookfield ordinance is content neutral. Accordingly, we turn to consider whether the ordinance is "narrowly tailored to serve a significant government interest" and whether it "leave[s] open ample alternative channels of communication." ...

[1.] [T]he ordinance serves a significant government interest.... Our prior decisions have often remarked on the unique nature of the home, "the last citadel of the tired, the weary, and the sick," and have recognized that "[p]reserving the sanctity of the home, the one retreat to which men and women can repair to escape from the tribulations of their daily pursuits, is surely an important value."

One important aspect of residential privacy is protection of the unwilling listener. Although in many locations, we expect individuals simply to avoid speech they do not want to hear, cf. *Cohen v. California*, the home is different. "That we are often 'captives' outside the sanctuary of the home and subject to objectionable speech ... does not mean we must be captives everywhere." *Rowan v. U.S. Post Office Dep't*. Instead, a special benefit of the privacy all citizens enjoy within their own walls, which the State may legislate to protect, is an ability to avoid intrusions.... See, *e.g.*, *FCC v. Pacifica Foundation*. {Because the picketing prohibited by the Brookfield ordinance is speech directed primarily at those who are presumptively unwilling to receive it, the State has a substantial and justifiable interest in banning it.} ...

[2.] A statute is narrowly tailored if it targets and eliminates no more than the exact source of the "evil" it seeks to remedy. A complete ban can be narrowly tailored, but only if each activity within the proscription's scope is an appropriately targeted evil. {[T]he "evil" of targeted residential picketing, "the very presence of an unwelcome visitor at the homes" is "created by the medium of expression itself." Accordingly, the Brookfield ordinance's complete ban of that particular medium of expression is narrowly tailored.} ...

[With] more generally directed means of communication that may not be completely banned in residential areas[,] ... "the flow of information [is not] into ... household[s], but to the public." *Organization for a Better Austin v. Keefe*. Here, in contrast, the picketing is narrowly directed at the household, not the public. The type of picketers banned by the Brookfield ordinance generally do not seek to disseminate a message to the general public, but to intrude upon the targeted resident, and to do so in an especially offensive way.

Moreover, even if some such picketers have a broader communicative purpose, their activity nonetheless inherently and offensively intrudes on residential privacy. The devastating effect of targeted picketing on the quiet enjoyment of the home is beyond doubt: "To those inside ... the home becomes something less than a home when and while the picketing ... continue[s].... [The] tensions and pressures may be psychological, not physical, but they are not, for that reason, less inimical to family privacy and truly domestic tranquility." ... [T]he actual size of the group is irrelevant; even a solitary picket can invade residential privacy.... "[F]ew of us ... would feel comfortable knowing that a stranger lurks outside our home" ....

[**3.**] {[T]he limited nature of the prohibition makes it virtually self-evident that ample alternatives remain: "Protestors have not been barred from the residential neighborhoods. They may enter such neighborhoods, alone or in groups, even marching.... They may go door-to-door to proselytize their views. They may distribute literature in this manner ... or through the mails. They may contact residents by telephone, short of harassment."}

(4)

] Ex of Channels

Justice Brennan, with whom Justice Marshall joins, dissenting....

[T]he government could constitutionally regulate the number of residential picketers, the hours during which a residential picket may take place, or the noise level of such a picket.... [S]ubstantial regulation is permitted to neutralize the intrusive or unduly coercive aspects of picketing around the home.... [But o]nce size, time, volume, and the like have been controlled to ensure that the picket is no longer intrusive or coercive, only the speech itself remains, conveyed perhaps by a lone, silent individual, walking back and forth with a sign. Such speech ... no longer implicates the heightened governmental interest in residential privacy ....

Not narrowly tailored

{[T]he discomfort to which the Court must refer is merely that of knowing there is a person outside who disagrees with someone inside. This may indeed be uncomfortable, but it does not implicate the town's interest in residential privacy ....} Therefore, the ordinance[, which covers even such speech,] is not narrowly tailored....

[The Court's argument that the picketing is directed at the household and not at the public] is flawed.... While picketers' signs might be seen from the resident's house, they are also visible to passersby.... Even the site-specific aspect of the picket identifies to the public the object of the picketers' attention. Nor does the picketers' ultimate goal—to influence the resident's conduct—change the analysis; ... such a goal does not defeat First Amendment protection.

Visible to public

Justice Stevens, dissenting. [Omitted.—ed.]

h. City of Ladue v. Gilleo, 512 U.S. 43 (1994)

Justice Stevens delivered the opinion of the Court....

Margaret P. Gilleo ... placed an 8.5- by 11-inch sign in the second story window of her home stating, "For Peace in the Gulf." [A Ladue city] ordinance contains a general prohibition of "signs" [in residential areas]....

Speech
Law (1) CN

Ladue's sign ordinance is supported principally by the City's interest in minimizing the visual clutter associated with signs, an interest that is concededly valid but certainly [not especially] compelling....

(2) GI – not compell

Ladue has almost completely foreclosed a venerable means of communication that is both unique and important. It has totally foreclosed that medium to political, religious, or personal messages.

(3) Not NT

Signs that react to a local happening or express a view on a controversial issue both reflect and animate change in the life of a community. Often placed on lawns or in windows, residential signs play an important part in political campaigns, during which they are displayed to signal the resident's support for particular candidates, parties, or causes. They may not afford the same opportunities for conveying complex ideas as do other media, but residential signs have long been an important and distinct medium of expression.

Our prior decisions have voiced particular concern with laws that foreclose an entire medium of expression. Thus, we have held invalid ordinances that completely banned the distribution of pamphlets within the municipality, handbills on the public streets, the door-to-door distribution of literature, and live entertainment. Although prohibitions foreclosing entire media may be completely free of content or viewpoint discrimination, ... by eliminating a common means of speaking, such measures can suppress too much speech.

Ladue contends, however, that its ordinance is a mere regulation of the "time, place, or manner" of speech, because residents remain free to convey their desired messages by other means, such as *hand-held* signs, "letters, handbills, flyers, telephone calls, newspaper advertisements, bumper stickers, speeches, and neighborhood or community meetings." However, even regulations that do not foreclose an entire medium of expression, but merely shift the time, place, or manner of its use, must "leave open ample alternative channels for communication." ... [W]e are not persuaded that adequate substitutes exist for the important medium of speech that Ladue has closed off.

Displaying a sign from one's own residence often carries a message quite distinct from placing the same sign someplace else, or conveying the same text or picture by other means. Precisely because of their location, such signs provide information about the identity of the "speaker," ... [which] is an important component of many attempts to persuade. A sign advocating "Peace in the Gulf" in the front lawn of a retired general or decorated war veteran may provoke a [particular reaction] .... An espousal of socialism may carry different implications when displayed on the grounds of a stately mansion than when pasted on a factory wall or an ambulatory sandwich board.

Residential signs are an unusually cheap and convenient form of communication. Especially for persons of modest means or limited mobility, a yard or window sign may have no practical substitute. Even for the affluent, the added costs in money or time of taking out a newspaper advertisement, handing out leaflets on the street, or standing in front of one's house with a hand-held sign may make the difference between participating and not participating in some public debate. Furthermore, a person who puts up a sign at her residence often intends to reach *neighbors*, an audience that could not be reached nearly as well by other means....

Whereas the government's need to mediate among various competing uses, including expressive ones, for public streets and facilities is constant and unavoidable, its need to regulate temperate speech from the home is surely much less pressing. Our decision that Ladue's ban on almost all residential signs violates the First Amendment by no means leaves the City powerless to address the ills that may be associated with residential signs....

[Moreover,] individual residents themselves have strong incentives to keep their own property values up and to prevent "visual clutter" in their own yards and neighborhoods—incentives markedly different from those of persons who erect signs on others' land, in others' neighborhoods, or on public property. Residents' self-interest diminishes the danger of the "unlimited" proliferation of residential signs that concerns the City of Ladue. We are confident that more temperate measures could in large part satisfy Ladue's stated regulatory needs without harm to the First Amendment rights of its citizens....

i.   McCullen v. Coakley, 134 S. Ct. 2518 (2014)

Chief Justice Roberts delivered the opinion of the Court.

[A.] [The Massachusetts Reproductive Health Care Facilities Act] makes it a crime to knowingly stand on a "public way or sidewalk" within 35 feet of an entrance or driveway to any place, other than a hospital, where abortions are performed [with some exceptions that aren't relevant here—ed.] ...

[B.] [The Court concluded the law was content-neutral, for reasons excerpted below at p. 376, but still struck down the law:—ed.]

"[P]ublic way[s]" and "sidewalk[s]" ...—which we have labeled "traditional public fora"—"have immemorially been held in trust for the use of the public and, time out of mind, have been used for purposes of assembly, communicating thoughts between citizens, and discussing public questions." ... Even today, they remain one of the few places where a speaker can be confident that he is not simply preaching to the choir.

With respect to other means of communication, an individual confronted with an uncomfortable message can always turn the page, change the channel, or leave the Web site. Not so on public streets and sidewalks. There, a listener often encounters speech he might otherwise tune out. In light of the First Amendment's purpose "to preserve an uninhibited marketplace of ideas in which truth will ultimately prevail," this aspect of traditional public fora is a virtue, not a vice....

Even though the Act is content neutral, it still must be "narrowly tailored to serve a significant governmental interest[,]" ... [which here means that] it must not "burden substantially more speech than is necessary to further the government's legitimate interests." Such a regulation, unlike a content-based restriction of speech, "need not be the least restrictive or least intrusive means of" serving the government's interests. But the government still "may not regulate expression in such a manner that a substantial portion of the burden on speech does not serve to advance its goals." {[B]y demanding a close fit between ends and means, the tailoring requirement prevents the government from too readily "sacrific[ing] speech for efficiency."}

...

[1.] {Some of the individuals who stand outside Massachusetts abortion clinics are fairly described as protestors, who express their moral or religious opposition to abortion through signs and chants or, in some cases, more aggressive methods such as face-to-face confrontation. Petitioners take a different tack. They attempt to engage women approaching the clinics in what they call "sidewalk counseling," which involves offering information about alternatives to abortion and help pursuing those options. Petitioner Eleanor McCullen, for instance, will typically initiate a conversation this way: "Good morning, may I give you my literature? Is there anything I can do for you? I'm available if you have any questions." If the woman seems receptive, McCullen will provide additional information.

McCullen and the other petitioners consider it essential to maintain a caring demeanor, a calm tone of voice, and direct eye contact during these exchanges. Such interactions, petitioners believe, are a much more effective means of dissuading women from having abortions than confrontational methods such as shouting or brandishing signs, which in petitioners' view tend only to antagonize their intended audience.} {And for good reason: It is easier to ignore a strained voice or a waving hand than a direct greeting or an outstretched arm.}

In unrefuted testimony, petitioners say they have collectively persuaded hundreds of women to forgo abortions. The buffer zones have displaced petitioners from their previous positions outside the clinics....

[T]he buffer zones impose serious burdens on petitioners' speech.... At each of the ... clinics where petitioners attempt to counsel patients, the zones ... push[] petitioners well back from the clinics' entrances and driveways. The zones thereby compromise petitioners' ability to initiate the close, personal conversations that they view as essential to "sidewalk counseling."

For example, in uncontradicted testimony, McCullen explained that she often cannot distinguish patients from passersby outside the Boston clinic in time to initiate a conversation before they enter the buffer zone. And even when she does manage to begin a discussion outside the zone, she must stop abruptly at its painted border, which she believes causes her to appear "untrustworthy" or "suspicious." Given these limitations, McCullen is often reduced to raising her voice at patients from outside the zone—a mode of communication sharply at odds with the compassionate message she wishes to convey.... Although McCullen claims that she has persuaded about 80 women not to terminate their pregnancies since the 2007 amendment, she also says that she reaches "far fewer people" than she did before the amendment....

The buffer zones have also made it substantially more difficult for petitioners to distribute literature to arriving patients. As explained, because petitioners in Boston cannot readily identify patients before they enter the zone, they often cannot approach them in time to place literature near their hands—the most effective means of getting the patients to accept it.... In short, the Act operates to deprive petitioners of their two primary methods of communicating with patients....

[W]hile the First Amendment does not guarantee a speaker the right to any particular form of expression, some forms—such as normal conversation and leafletting on a public sidewalk—have historically been more closely associated with the transmission of ideas than others.... When the government makes it more difficult to engage in these modes of communication, it imposes an especially significant First Amendment burden....

Significant Burden to Speech

It is thus no answer to say that petitioners can still be "seen and heard" by women within the buffer zones. If all that the women can see and hear are vociferous opponents of abortion, then the buffer zones have effectively stifled petitioners' [more personal, conversational] message.... → *personal message*

[2.] The buffer zones burden substantially more speech than necessary to achieve the Commonwealth's asserted interests.... [T]he Act is truly exceptional: Respondents and their *amici* identify no other State with a law that creates fixed buffer zones around abortion clinics[, though they do identify five localities with similar laws]. That of course does not mean that the law is invalid. It does, however, raise concern that the Commonwealth has too readily forgone options that could serve its interests just as well, without substantially burdening the kind of speech in which petitioners wish to engage.

(3) NT not

☆

That is the case here. The Commonwealth's interests include ensuring public safety outside abortion clinics, preventing harassment and intimidation of patients and clinic staff, and combating deliberate obstruction of clinic entrances. The Act itself contains a separate provision ... that prohibits much of this conduct.... Massachusetts ... could [also] enact legislation similar to the federal Freedom of Access to Clinic Entrances Act of 1994, which subjects to both criminal and civil penalties anyone who "by force or threat of force or by physical obstruction, intentionally injures, intimidates or interferes with ... any person ... in order to intimidate [any] person ... from[] obtaining or providing reproductive health services." ...

Alt Options to Law.

[T]he Commonwealth ... could also consider an ordinance such as the one adopted in New York City that ... makes it a crime "to follow and harass another person within 15 feet of the premises of a reproductive health care facility." {Whether such a law would pass constitutional muster would depend on a number of other factors, such as whether the term "harassment" had been authoritatively construed to avoid vagueness and overbreadth problems ....} ... All of the foregoing measures are, of course, in addition to available generic criminal statutes forbidding assault, breach of the peace, trespass, vandalism, and the like....

We have [also] noted the First Amendment virtues of targeted injunctions as alternatives to broad, prophylactic measures. Such an injunction "regulates the activities, and perhaps the speech, of a group," but only "because of the group's past *actions* in ... a specific dispute between real parties." Moreover, ... courts can tailor [an injunction] to ensure that it restricts no more speech than necessary[, but] ... focuses on the precise individuals and the precise conduct causing a particular problem. The Act, by contrast, categorically excludes non-exempt individuals from the buffer zones, unnecessarily sweeping in innocent individuals and their speech....

[As to] preventing congestion, ... [s]ome localities, for example, have ordinances that require crowds blocking a clinic entrance to disperse when ordered to do so by the police, and that forbid the individuals to reassemble within a certain distance of the clinic for a certain period.... [Moreover, t]he portions of the record that respondents cite to support the anticongestion interest pertain mainly to one place at one time: the Boston Planned Parenthood clinic on Saturday mornings. [State officials] point us to no evidence that individuals regularly gather at other clinics, or at other times in Boston, in sufficiently large groups to obstruct access. For a problem shown to arise only once a week in one city at one clinic, creating 35-foot buffer zones at every clinic across the Commonwealth is hardly a narrowly tailored solution....

Respondents have but one reply: "We have tried other approaches, but they do not work." ... [But though state officials] claim that Massachusetts "tried other laws already on the books," they identify not a single prosecution brought under those laws within at least the last 17 years. And while they also claim that the Commonwealth "tried injunctions," the last injunctions they cite date to the 1990s. In short, the Commonwealth has not shown that it seriously undertook to address the problem with less intrusive tools readily available to it....

[State officials] contend that ..., given the "widespread" nature of the problem, it is simply not "practicable" to rely on individual prosecutions and injunctions. But far from being "widespread," the problem appears from the record to be limited principally to the Boston clinic on Saturday mornings. Moreover, by their own account, the police appear perfectly capable of singling out lawbreakers.

The legislative testimony preceding the 2007 Act revealed substantial police and video monitoring at the clinics, especially when large gatherings were anticipated.... Attorney General Coakley relied on video surveillance to show legislators conduct she thought was "clearly against the law." If Commonwealth officials can compile an extensive record of obstruction and harassment to support their preferred legislation, we do not see why they cannot do the same to support injunctions and prosecutions against those who might deliberately flout the law....

[3.] [State officials also argue that] a showing of intentional or deliberate obstruction, intimidation, or harassment [required by some laws] ... is often difficult to prove. As Captain Evans predicted in his legislative testimony, fixed buffer zones would "make our job so much easier."

Of course they would. But that is not enough to satisfy the First Amendment. To meet the requirement of narrow tailoring, the government must demonstrate that alternative measures that burden substantially less speech would fail to achieve the government's interests, not simply that the chosen route is easier. A painted line on the sidewalk is easy to enforce, but the prime objective of the First Amendment is not efficiency.

In any case, we do not think that showing intentional obstruction is nearly so difficult in this context as respondents suggest. To determine whether a protestor intends to block access to a clinic, a police officer need only order him to move. If he refuses, then there is no question that his continued conduct is knowing or intentional.

[4.] [In] *Burson* v. *Freeman*, 504 U.S. 191 (1992), ... we upheld [under the strict scrutiny applicable to content-based speech restrictions] a state statute that established 100-foot buffer zones outside polling places on election day within which no one could display or distribute campaign materials or solicit votes. We approved the buffer zones as a valid prophylactic measure, noting that existing "[i]ntimidation and interference laws fall short of serving a State's compelling interests because they 'deal with only the most blatant and specific attempts' to impede elections." Such laws were insufficient because "[v]oter intimidation and election fraud are ... difficult to detect." Obstruction of abortion clinics and harassment of patients, by contrast, are anything but subtle.

We also noted in *Burson* that under state law, "law enforcement officers generally are barred from the vicinity of the polls to avoid any appearance of coercion in the electoral process," with the result that "many acts of interference would go undetected." Not so here. Again, the police maintain a significant presence outside Massachusetts abortion clinics. The buffer zones in *Burson* were justified because less restrictive measures were inadequate. Respondents have not shown that to be the case here....

[C.] {Because we find that the Act is not narrowly tailored, we need not consider whether the Act leaves open ample alternative channels of communication.} ...

Justice Scalia, with whom Justice Kennedy and Justice Thomas join, concurring in the judgment. [Justice Scalia concluded that the restriction was content-based, and expressed no opinion on how it should be analyzed if viewed as content-neutral.—ed.]

Justice Alito, concurring in the judgment. [Justice Alito concluded that the restriction was content-based, but agreed with the majority that, even if viewed as content-neutral, it was unconstitutional.—ed.]

j. *United States v. O'Brien, 391 U.S. 367 (1968)*

[For the Court's rejection of the argument that the law should be seen as content-based, because of the Congress's supposed speech-restrictive motive, see p. 363 below.—ed.]

Chief Justice Warren delivered the opinion of the Court....

[A.] David Paul O'Brien ... burned [his] Selective Service registration certificate[] on the steps of the South Boston Courthouse ... to influence others to adopt his antiwar beliefs .... [O'Brien was tried for violating 50 U.S.C. § 462(b)(3) (amended 1965), which punished anyone] "who forges, alters, knowingly destroys, knowingly mutilates, or in any manner changes any such certificate...." ...

When a male reaches the age of 18, he is required ... to register with a local draft board. He is assigned a Selective Service number, and within five days he is issued a registration certificate.... [Shortly after that, he is issued a classification certificate.—ed.] Both the registration and classification certificates are small white cards, approximately 2 by 3 inches.

The registration certificate specifies the name of the registrant, the date of registration, and the number and address of the local board with which he is registered. Also inscribed upon it are the date and place of the registrant's birth, his residence at registration, his physical description, his signature, and his Selective Service number. The Selective Service number itself indicates his State of registration, his local board, his year of birth, and his chronological position in the local board's classification record.

The classification certificate shows the registrant's name, Selective Service number, signature, and eligibility classification.... It contains the address of his local board and the date the certificate was mailed.

Both the registration and classification certificates bear notices that the registrant must notify his local board in writing of every change in address, physical condition, and occupational, marital, family, dependency, and military status, and of any other fact which might change his classification. Both also contain a notice that the registrant's Selective Service number should appear on all communications to his local board.

Congress demonstrated its concern that certificates issued by the Selective Service System might be abused well before the 1965 Amendment here challenged.... Under ... the 1948 Act, it was unlawful [to fraudulently use a certificate, as well as to] forge, alter, "or in any manner" change a certificate .... [Regulations also] required registrants to keep both their registration and classification certificates in their personal possession .... By the 1965 Amendment, Congress added to ... the 1948 Act the provision here at issue, subjecting to criminal liability not only one who "forges, alters, or in any manner changes" but also one who "knowingly destroys [or] knowingly mutilates" a certificate....

[B.] [T]he 1965 Amendment ... on its face ... deals with conduct having no connection with speech. It prohibits the knowing destruction of certificates issued by the Selective Service System, and there is nothing necessarily expressive about such conduct. The Amendment does not distinguish between public and private destruction, and it does not punish only destruction engaged in for the purpose of expressing views....

[Yet] O'Brien ... argues that the 1965 Amendment is unconstitutional as applied to him because his act of burning his registration certificate was protected "symbolic speech" within the First Amendment.... We cannot accept the view that an apparently limitless variety of conduct can be labeled "speech" whenever the person engaging in the conduct intends thereby to express an idea. However, even on the assumption that the alleged communicative element in O'Brien's conduct is sufficient to bring into play the First Amendment, it does not necessarily follow that the destruction of a registration certificate is constitutionally protected activity....

[W]hen "speech" and "nonspeech" elements are combined in the same course of conduct, a sufficiently important governmental interest in regulating the nonspeech element can justify incidental limitations on First Amendment freedoms.... [A] government regulation is sufficiently justified ... if it furthers an important or substantial governmental interest; if the governmental interest is unrelated to the suppression of free expression; and if the incidental restriction on alleged First Amendment freedoms is no greater than is essential to the furtherance of that interest. We find that the 1965 Amendment... meets all of these requirements ....

— Holding

(2) GI

The issuance of certificates indicating the registration and eligibility classification of individuals is a legitimate and substantial administrative aid in the functioning of [the selective service system instituted pursuant to Congress's power to raise armies]. And legislation to insure the continuing availability of issued certificates serves a legitimate and substantial purpose in the system's administration.... Many of [the certificates' purposes] would be defeated by the certificates' destruction or mutilation....:

1.... Voluntarily displaying the two certificates is an easy and painless way for a young man to dispel a question as to whether he might be delinquent in his Selective Service obligations. Correspondingly, the availability of the certificates for such display relieves the Selective Service System of the administrative burden it would otherwise have in verifying the registration and classification of all suspected delinquents.

Further, since both certificates are in the nature of "receipts" attesting that the registrant has done what the law requires, it is in the interest of the just and efficient administration of the system that they be continually available, in the event, for example, of a mix-up in the registrant's file. Additionally, in a time of national crisis, reasonable availability to each registrant of the two small cards assures a rapid and uncomplicated means for determining his fitness for immediate induction, no matter how distant in our mobile society he may be from his local board.

2. The information supplied on the certificates facilitates communication between registrants and local boards, simplifying the system and benefiting all concerned.... [E]ach certificate bears the address of the registrant's local board, ... [and] the registrant's Selective Service number .... [And] a registrant's inquiry, particularly through a local board other than his own, concerning his eligibility status is frequently answerable simply on the basis of his classification certificate ....

3. Both certificates carry continual reminders that the registrant must notify his local board of any change of address, and other specified changes in his status.... [T]he destruction of certificates deprives the system of a potentially useful notice device.

4.... The destruction or mutilation of certificates obviously increases the difficulty of detecting and tracing [forgeries and deceptive misuses, and] a mutilated certificate might itself be used for deceptive purposes....

[T]he continuing availability to each registrant of his Selective Service certificates substantially furthers the ... vital interest in having a system for raising armies that functions with maximum efficiency ....

It is equally clear that the 1965 Amendment specifically protects this substantial governmental interest. We perceive no alternative means that would more precisely and narrowly assure the continuing availability of issued Selective Service certificates than a law which prohibits their wilful mutilation or destruction.... [B]oth the governmental interest and the operation of the 1965 Amendment are limited to the noncommunicative aspect of O'Brien's conduct. The governmental interest and the scope of the 1965 Amendment are limited to preventing harm to the smooth and efficient functioning of the Selective Service System. When O'Brien deliberately rendered unavailable his registration certificate, he wilfully frustrated this governmental interest.

[C.] For this noncommunicative impact of his conduct, and for nothing else, [O'Brien] was convicted. The case at bar is therefore unlike one where the alleged governmental interest in regulating conduct arises in some measure because the communication allegedly integral to the conduct is itself thought to be harmful. In *Stromberg v. California*, 283 U.S. 359 (1931), for example, this Court struck down a statutory phrase which punished people who expressed their "opposition to organized government" by displaying "any flag, badge, banner, or device." Since the statute there was aimed at suppressing communication it could not be sustained as a regulation of noncommunicative conduct.

Justice Harlan, concurring....

[The Court's opinion] does not foreclose consideration of First Amendment claims in those rare instances when an "incidental" restriction upon expression, imposed by a regulation which furthers an "important or substantial" governmental interest and satisfies the Court's other criteria, in practice has the effect of entirely preventing a "speaker" from reaching a significant audience with whom he could not otherwise lawfully communicate. This is not such a case, since O'Brien manifestly could have conveyed his message in many ways other than by burning his draft card.

Justice Douglas, dissenting [on grounds unrelated to the First Amendment].... [Omitted.—ed.]

k. *Clark v. Community for Creative Non-Violence, 468 U.S. 288 (1984)*

Justice White delivered the opinion of the Court.

[A.] The issue in this case is whether a National Park Service regulation prohibiting camping in certain parks violates the First Amendment when applied to prohibit demonstrators from sleeping in Lafayette Park and the Mall in connection with a demonstration intended to call attention to the plight of the homeless....

Lafayette Park is a roughly 7-acre square located across Pennsylvania Avenue from the White House, ... a "garden park with a ... formal landscaping of flowers and trees, with fountains, walks and benches." ... The Mall is a stretch of land running westward from the Capitol to the Lincoln Memorial some two miles away. It includes the Washington Monument, a series of reflecting pools, trees, lawns, and other greenery.... Both the Park and the Mall ... are visited by vast numbers of visitors ....

Under the regulations involved in this case, camping in National Parks is permitted only in campgrounds designated for that purpose. No such campgrounds have ever been designated in Lafayette Park or the Mall. Camping is defined as "the use of park land for living accommodation purposes such as sleeping activities ..." ...

In 1982, the Park Service issued a renewable permit to respondent Community for Creative Non-Violence (CCNV) to conduct a wintertime demonstration in Lafayette Park and the Mall for the purpose of demonstrating the plight of the homeless. The permit authorized the erection of two symbolic tent cities: 20 tents in Lafayette Park that would accommodate 50 people and 40 tents in the Mall with a capacity of up to 100. The Park Service, however, relying on the above regulations, specifically denied CCNV's request that demonstrators be permitted to sleep in the symbolic tents....

[B.] We [assume, but do not decide,] that overnight sleeping in connection with the demonstration is expressive conduct protected to some extent by the First Amendment.... Symbolic expression ... may be forbidden or regulated ... if the regulation is narrowly drawn to further a substantial governmental interest, and if the interest is unrelated to the suppression of free speech....

[C.] [T]he prohibition on camping, and on sleeping specifically, is content-neutral and is not being applied because of disagreement with the message presented....

[D.] [Even] without overnight sleeping[,] the plight of the homeless could ... be communicated in other ways. The regulation otherwise left the demonstration intact, with its symbolic city, signs, and the presence of those who were willing to take their turns in a day-and-night vigil. Respondents do not suggest that there was, or is, any barrier to delivering to the media, or to the public by other means, the intended message concerning the plight of the homeless....

[E.] [T]he regulation narrowly focuses on the Government's substantial interest in maintaining the parks in the heart of our Capital in an attractive and intact condition, readily available to the millions of people who wish to see and enjoy them by their presence. To permit camping—using these areas as living accommodations—would be totally inimical to these purposes ....

It is urged by respondents ... that if the symbolic city of tents was to be permitted ..., the incremental benefit to the parks could not justify the ban on sleeping, which was here an expressive activity said to enhance the message concerning the plight of the poor and homeless. We cannot agree. In the first place, we seriously doubt that the First Amendment requires the Park Service to permit a demonstration in Lafayette Park and the Mall involving a 24-hour vigil and the erection of tents to accommodate 150 people.

Furthermore, although we have assumed for present purposes that the sleeping banned in this case would have an expressive element, it is evident that its major value to this demonstration would be facilitative. Without a permit to sleep, it would be difficult to get the poor and homeless to participate or to be present at all. This much is apparent from the permit application filed by respondents: "Without the incentive of sleeping space or a hot meal, the homeless would not come to the site." The sleeping ban, if enforced, would thus effectively limit the nature, extent, and duration of the demonstration and to that extent ease the pressure on the parks.

[F.] Beyond this, however, it is evident from our cases that the validity of this regulation need not be judged solely by reference to the demonstration at hand. Absent the prohibition on sleeping, there would be other groups who would demand permission to deliver an asserted message by camping in Lafayette Park. Some of them would surely have as credible a claim in this regard as does CCNV, and the denial of permits to still others would present difficult problems for the Park Service. With the prohibition, however, as is evident in the case before us, at least some around-the-clock demonstrations lasting for days on end will not materialize, others will be limited in size and duration, and the purposes of the regulation will thus be materially served.

Perhaps these purposes would be more effectively and not so clumsily achieved by preventing tents and 24-hour vigils entirely in the core areas. But the Park Service's decision to permit nonsleeping demonstrations does not, in our view, impugn the camping prohibition as a valuable, but perhaps imperfect, protection to the parks.

If the Government has a legitimate interest in ensuring that the National Parks are adequately protected, which we think it has, and if the parks would be more exposed to harm without the sleeping prohibition than with it, the ban is safe from invalidation .... [T]he regulation "responds precisely to the substantive problems which legitimately concern the [Government]." ...

[G.] We are unmoved by the ... view that the challenged regulation is unnecessary, and hence invalid, because there are less speech-restrictive alternatives that could have satisfied the Government interest in preserving park lands. There is no gainsaying that preventing overnight sleeping will avoid a measure of actual or threatened damage to Lafayette Park and the Mall.

The Court of Appeals' suggestions that the Park Service minimize the possible injury by reducing the size, duration, or frequency of demonstrations would still curtail the total allowable expression in which demonstrators could engage, whether by sleeping or otherwise, and these suggestions represent no more than a disagreement with the Park Service over how much protection the core parks require or how an acceptable level of preservation is to be attained. We do not believe, however, that either *United States v. O'Brien* or the time, place, or manner decisions assign to the judiciary the authority to replace the Park Service as the manager of the Nation's parks or endow the judiciary with the competence to judge how much protection of park lands is wise and how that level of conservation is to be attained....

Justice Marshall, with whom Justice Brennan joins, dissenting....

[A.] The primary purpose for [and likely effect of] making *sleep* an integral part of the demonstration was "to re-enact the central reality of homelessness," and to impress upon public consciousness, in as dramatic a way as possible, that homelessness is a widespread problem, often ignored, that confronts its victims with life-threatening deprivations. As one of the homeless men seeking to demonstrate explained: "Sleeping in Lafayette Park or on the Mall, for me, is to show people that conditions are so poor for the homeless and poor in this city that we would actually sleep *outside* in the winter to get the point across." ...

The Government contends that a foreseeable difficulty of administration counsels against recognizing sleep as a mode of expression protected by the First Amendment. The predicament the Government envisions [is] ... the problem of distinguishing bona fide protesters from imposters whose requests for permission to sleep in Lafayette Park or the Mall on First Amendment grounds would mask ulterior designs—the simple desire, for example, to avoid the expense of hotel lodgings. The Government maintains that such distinctions cannot be made without inquiring into the sincerity of demonstrators and that such an inquiry would itself pose dangers to First Amendment values because it would necessarily be content-sensitive....

[But, f]irst, a variety of circumstances *already* require government agencies to engage in the delicate task of inquiring into the sincerity of claimants asserting First Amendment rights. See, *e.g., Wisconsin v. Yoder* (exception of members of religious group from compulsory education statute justified by group's adherence to deep religious conviction rather than subjective secular values); *Welsh v. United States* (eligibility for exemption from military service as conscientious objector status justified by sincere religious beliefs).... [S]crutiny of the asserted purpose of persons seeking a permit to display sleeping as a form of symbolic speech would [thus not] import something altogether new and disturbing into our First Amendment jurisprudence.

Second, the administrative difficulty the Government envisions is now nothing more than a vague apprehension. If permitting sleep to be used as a form of protected First Amendment activity actually created the administrative problems the Government now envisions, there would emerge a clear factual basis upon which to establish the necessity for the limitation the Government advocates....

[B.] Although sleep in the context of this case is symbolic speech protected by the First Amendment, it is nonetheless subject to reasonable time, place, and manner restrictions.... [T]he interest in "maintaining the parks in the heart of our capital in an attractive and intact condition, readily available to the millions of people who wish to see and enjoy them by their presence" ... is indeed significant.

However, neither the Government nor the majority adequately explains how prohibiting respondents' planned activity will substantially further that interest.... [The majority's arguments are not] supported by a factual showing that evinces a real, as opposed to a merely speculative, problem.

The majority fails to offer any evidence indicating that the absence of an absolute ban on sleeping would present administrative problems to the Park Service that are substantially more difficult than those it ordinarily confronts. A mere apprehension of difficulties should not be enough to overcome the right to free expression.... [Likewise, t]he majority cites no evidence indicating that sleeping engaged in as symbolic speech will cause *substantial* wear and tear on park property.

Furthermore, the Government's application of the sleeping ban in the circumstances of this case is strikingly underinclusive. The majority acknowledges that a proper time, place, and manner restriction must be "narrowly tailored." Here, however, the tailoring requirement is virtually forsaken inasmuch as the Government offers no justification for applying its absolute ban on sleeping yet is willing to allow respondents to engage in activities—such as feigned sleeping—that [are] no less burdensome....

[C.] [T]he Court has dramatically lowered its scrutiny of governmental regulations once it has determined that such regulations are content-neutral.... [Yet though t]he consistent imposition of silence upon all may fulfill the dictates of an even handed content-neutrality[,] ... it offends our "profound national commitment to the principle that debate on public issues should be uninhibited, robust, and wide-open."

{[And] a content-neutral regulation does not necessarily fall with random or equal force upon different groups or different points of view. A content-neutral regulation that restricts an inexpensive mode of communication will fall most heavily upon relatively poor speakers and the points of view that such speakers typically espouse[, as it does in this case].... [T]his case ... lends credence to the charge that judicial administration of the First Amendment, in conjunction with a social order marked by large disparities in wealth and other sources of power, tends systematically to discriminate against efforts by the relatively disadvantaged to convey their political ideas....} ...

[Finally,] public officials have strong incentives to overregulate even in the absence of an intent to censor particular views. This incentive stems from the fact that of the two groups whose interests officials must accommodate—on the one hand, the interests of the general public and, on the other, the interests of those who seek to use a particular forum for First Amendment activity—the political power of the former is likely to be far greater than that of the latter....

l. Policy—Government Controlling Noncommunicative Impact

Basic argument: "Regulation of the noncommunicative impact of speech—*e.g.*, noise, blocking traffic, littering—isn't quite regulation of speech as such, or is not as dangerous as regulation of the communicative impact, because _____."

1. "Prohibition of [blocking streets with a demonstration or littering with leaflets] would not abridge the [freedom of speech] since such activity bears no necessary relationship to the freedom to speak, write, print or distribute information or opinion." *Schneider v. New Jersey*.

"[W]hen 'speech' and 'nonspeech' elements are combined in the same course of conduct, a sufficiently important governmental interest in regulating the nonspeech element can justify incidental limitations on First Amendment freedoms.... The case at bar is therefore unlike one where the alleged governmental interest in regulating conduct arises in some measure because the communication allegedly integral to the conduct is itself thought to be harmful ... [and where the law is] aimed at suppressing communication ...." *United States v. O'Brien*.

"[C]ontent-based discriminations are subject to strict scrutiny because they place the weight of government behind the disparagement or suppression of some messages, whether or not with the effect of approving or promoting others.... [But] when a law addresses not the content of speech but the circumstances of its delivery[, t]he right to express unpopular views does not necessarily immunize a speaker from liability for resorting to otherwise impermissible behavior meant to shock members of the speaker's audience, or to guarantee their attention." *Hill v. Colorado*.

2. Regulating the noncommunicative effects of speech is necessary, because _____.

"Municipal authorities, as trustees for the public, have the duty to keep their communities' streets open and available for movement of people and property, the primary purpose to which the streets are dedicated." *Schneider*.

3. Response to 1 and 2: But the restrictions *do* interfere with the spread of ideas, because _____.

"[Though a restriction] may be completely free of content or viewpoint discrimination, the danger [it] pose[s] to the freedom of speech is readily apparent—by eliminating a common means of speaking, [it] can suppress too much speech." *City of Ladue v. Gilleo*.

B. When Is a Restriction Content-Neutral?

a. Summary: Generally

1. **Facial content discrimination:** A restriction is content-based if it

- "on its face" draws distinctions based on the "communicative content" of what a speaker conveys, *Reed v. Town of Gilbert* (2015) (p. 381), or
- "require[s] 'enforcement authorities' to 'examine the content of the message that is conveyed to determine whether' a violation has occurred." *McCullen v. Coakley* (2014) (p. 376).

This includes (but isn't limited to)

- restrictions based on "viewpoint," "subject matter," or the "function or purpose" of the speech, *Reed*,

- restrictions on words that are seen as vulgar, *Cohen v. California* (1971) (p. 207), and

- restrictions on the communication of particular facts, such as the names of rape victims, *Florida Star v. B.J.F.* (1989) (p. 300).

And a facially content-based law "is subject to strict scrutiny regardless of the government's benign motive, content-neutral justification, or lack of 'animus toward the ideas contained' in the regulated speech." *Reed*.

2. **Laws being applied to speech because of its content:** Some laws might be called *harm-based:* they bar any conduct (speech or not) that causes, is intended to cause, or is likely to cause a certain harm. Yet these laws are treated as content-based when a law is applied to a speaker "because of what his speech communicated." *Holder v. Humanitarian Law Project* (2010) (p. 381). Though *Cohen*, for instance, "involved a generally applicable regulation of conduct, barring breaches of the peace," "when Cohen was convicted for wearing a jacket bearing an epithet, ... we recognized that the generally applicable law was directed at Cohen because of what his speech communicated—he violated the breach of the peace statute because of the offensive content of his particular message." *Holder*.

The same can be said of the intentional infliction of emotional distress tort in *Snyder v. Phelps* and the interference with business relations tort in *NAACP v. Claiborne Hardware*: the laws punished all conduct that had certain effects, but they were applied to certain speech because *the effects flowed from what the speech communicated*. The Court held such application to be unconstitutional; and while the Court didn't expressly call the laws content-based, it viewed them with the skepticism usually reserved for content-based restrictions. *See* Eugene Volokh, *Speech as Conduct: Generally Applicable Laws, Illegal Courses of Conduct, "Situation-Altering Utterances," and the Uncharted Zones*, 90 Cornell L. Rev. 1277 (2005).

But had the effects flowed from the noncommunicative components of the speech, the results would likely have been different. Had Snyder sued Phelps for using loudspeakers outside his house in the middle of the night, had Claiborne Hardware sued the NAACP for physically blockading the store, or had Cohen been prosecuted for breaching the peace by shouting loudly in the courthouse, the court would probably have treated the law as content-neutral as applied.

3. **Laws justified with reference to content or motivated by disagreement with content:** *Reed* states that "facially content neutral" laws "will be considered content-based regulations of speech" if they "cannot be justified without reference to the content of the regulated speech'" or if they "were adopted by the government 'because of disagreement with the message [the speech] conveys.'" Classic examples:

- Laws that *restrict symbolic expression because of its communicative impact*. In this situation, the term "content" doesn't neatly fit: "the content of a flag burning" or "the content of a black armband" sounds odd. Symbolic expression cases, such as *Texas v. Johnson* (1989) (p. 364), thus focus on whether the laws are justified with reference to the message that the symbolic expression communicates.

- Restrictions *"impermissibly motivated by a desire to suppress a particular point of view,"* *Cornelius v. NAACP Legal Defense & Ed. Fund, Inc., 473* U.S. 788 (1985). This is also true even as to restrictions on speech in nonpublic fora (see Part V.E.1.a, p. 622), where only viewpoint discrimination (and not content discrimination) is forbidden. But at least where it comes to statutes rather than executive regulations (as in *Cornelius*), a facially neutral statute won't be invalidated as content-based simply because some legislatures said that they voted for the statute because of hostility to a particular sort of speech. *United States v. O'Brien* (1968) (p. 351).

On the other hand,

- A facially content-neutral law *remains content-neutral even if it disproportionately affects certain speech. McCullen v. Coakley* (2014) (p. 376).

- The Court has upheld some facially content-based restrictions on the grounds that they target only the "*secondary effects*" of speech (see below). These cases seem hard to reconcile with the "facially content-based laws are content-based" rule that *Reed* sets forth. But *Reed* does not purport to overrule them (and there's a fairly long line of them).

- *Hill v. Colorado* (2000) (p. 374) (controversially) treated as content-neutral a law imposing special restrictions on "oral protest, education, or counseling." This may be inconsistent with *Reed*, because whether speech falls in these categories turns on the "communicative content" of speech, at least as much as does the distinction between political speech, ideological speech, and speech about events. And *Hill* may be inconsistent with *McCullen*, because deciding whether speech is protest, education, or counseling "require[s] 'enforcement authorities' to 'examine the content of the message that is conveyed to determine whether' a violation has occurred." The *Reed* and *McCullen* majorities didn't favorably cite or distinguish *Hill*; indeed, the *Reed* majority favorably cited the *Hill* dissents twice. Yet *Reed* and *McCullen* didn't expressly overrule *Hill*, which presumably remains binding on lower courts.

Should be content!!

b. *Summary: "Secondary Effects"*

The "secondary effects" test treats as content-neutral some facially content-based restrictions, when the Court concludes that the government's real motivation was to target the "secondary effects" of speech. *City of Renton v. Playtime Theatres, Inc.* (1986) (p. 365). But which effects qualify as merely "secondary"?

Many speech restrictions are ultimately justified by the fear that the speech will cause noncommunicative effects—for instance, that advocacy of crime will cause crime, or that offensive speech will cause a fight. But most such restrictions are treated as content-based, because they are seen as focusing on the "primary" effects of the speech, rather than as content-neutral regulations of secondary effects. In particular:

1.   The tendency of speech to offend people is not treated as a secondary effect, and neither is the tendency of speech to cause harms that flow from such offense—for instance, potential fights, *R.A.V. v. City of St. Paul* (1992) (p. 317), policing costs needed to prevent fights, *Forsyth County v. Nationalist Movement*, 505 U.S. 123 (1992), and injury to foreign diplomats' dignity caused by protests outside their embassies, *Boos v. Barry*, 485 U.S. 312 (1988).

     Restrictions justified by such harms are thus seen as content-based. "'The emotive impact of speech on its audience is not a 'secondary effect' unrelated to the content of the expression itself." *Johnson*, quoting *Boos*; see also *R.A.V.* "Listeners' reaction to speech is not a content-neutral basis for regulation." *Nationalist Movement*; see also *R.A.V.*

2.   The tendency of speech to persuade people to do bad things, and the harms that flow from such persuasion, are likewise not treated as secondary effects. "[When] the 'chain of causation' ... *necessarily* 'run[s]' through the persuasive effect of the expressive component' of the conduct, [the law] regulates on the basis of the 'primary' effect of the speech—*i.e.*, its persuasive (or repellant) force." *R.A.V.*

3.   The tendency of speech to send bad messages to children is not seen as a secondary effect, and neither is its tendency to cause harms that flow from such messages—for instance, tobacco use, *Lorillard Tobacco Co. v. Reilly*, 533 U.S. 525 (2001), and the harms flowing from viewing pornography, *United States v. Playboy Entertainment Group*, 529 U.S. 803 (2000); *Reno v. ACLU*.

4.   Even if a restriction's core purpose is unrelated to content—*e.g.*, when a newsrack ordinance limits newsracks on sidewalks to eliminate physical and visual clutter—any *content-based distinctions within the restriction* make the restriction content-based, unless the content is closely related to the restriction's neutral purpose. Thus, in *City of Cincinnati v. Discovery Network*, 507 U.S. 410 (1993), the Court held that a ban on newsracks containing publications that consisted chiefly of advertising was content-based: "[T]here are no secondary effects attributable to [the advertising-only] newsracks that distinguish them from the newsracks Cincinnati permits to remain on its sidewalks."

5.   *Renton* concluded that the tendency of speech to physically attract people who may commit nonspeech crimes (*e.g.*, prostitution), and whose presence may in turn attract other undesirables, did involve a "secondary effect." Yet this tendency does flow from the "emotive impact of speech," which is what brings in the undesirable viewers.

c.   *Problem: Panhandling*

     A city, concerned about panhandling, enacts an ordinance that bans "solicitation and receipt of funds" "in a continuous or repetitive manner" on any sidewalk in the city center. The ordinance applies equally to panhandling, collecting money for charitable or ideological causes, and sale of goods. The ordinance has been interpreted as covering only "personal solicitations for immediate payment of money," as opposed to (for instance) speech urging people to donate to some cause (or buy some product) when they get home.

Is the ordinance content-neutral or content-based, under current law? Is it constitutional? Should it be? See *ISKCON v. Lee*, 505 U.S. 672, 704 (1992) (Kennedy, J., concurring in the judgment); *Norton v. City of Springfield*, 806 F.3d 411 (7th Cir. 2015).

d. *United States v. O'Brien, 391 U.S. 367 (1968)*

[For the facts, see p. 351 above.—ed.]

Chief Justice Warren delivered the opinion of the Court....

O'Brien ... argues that the 1965 Amendment is unconstitutional as enacted because what he calls the "purpose" of Congress was "to suppress freedom of speech." ... [T]his Court will not strike down an otherwise constitutional statute on the basis of an alleged illicit legislative motive....

When the issue is simply the interpretation of legislation, the Court will look to statements by legislators for guidance as to the purpose of the legislature, because the benefit to sound decision-making in this circumstance is thought sufficient to risk the possibility of misreading Congress' purpose. It is entirely a different matter when we are asked to void a statute that is, under well-settled criteria, constitutional on its face, on the basis of what fewer than a handful of Congressmen said about it.

What motivates one legislator to make a speech about a statute is not necessarily what motivates scores of others to enact it, and the stakes are sufficiently high for us to eschew guesswork. We decline to void[,] essentially on the ground that it is unwise[,] legislation which Congress had the undoubted power to enact and which could be reenacted in its exact form if the same or another legislator made a "wiser" speech about it....

[Moreover, t]here was little floor debate on this legislation in either House.... It is principally on the basis of the statements by ... [the] three Congressmen [who commented on the Amendment] that O'Brien makes his congressional-"purpose" argument.... [And while] the more authoritative reports of the Senate and House Armed Services Committees ... make clear a concern with the "defiant" destruction of so-called "draft cards" and with "open" encouragement to others to destroy their cards, both reports also indicate that this concern stemmed from an apprehension that unrestrained destruction of cards would disrupt the smooth functioning of the Selective Service System....

e. *Texas v. Johnson, 491 U.S. 397 (1989)*

[For the facts, see p. 188.—ed.]

Justice Brennan delivered the opinion of the Court....

[We must] decide whether the State's regulation is related to the suppression of free expression. If the State's regulation is not related to expression, then the less stringent standard we announced in *United States v. O'Brien* for regulations of noncommunicative conduct controls. If it is, then we are outside of *O'Brien*'s test, and we must ask whether this interest justifies Johnson's conviction under [strict scrutiny] ....

[A.] The [law] ... may not ... proscribe particular conduct *because* it has expressive elements. "[W]hat might be termed the more generalized guarantee of freedom of expression makes the communicative nature of conduct an inadequate *basis* for singling out that conduct for proscription. A law *directed at* the communicative nature of conduct must, like a law directed at speech itself, be justified by the substantial showing of need that the First Amendment requires." It is, in short, not simply the verbal or nonverbal nature of the expression, but the governmental interest at stake, that helps to determine whether a restriction on that expression is valid....

In order to decide whether *O'Brien*'s test applies here, therefore, we must decide whether Texas has asserted an interest in support of Johnson's conviction that is unrelated to the suppression of expression.... The State ... asserts an interest in preserving the flag as a symbol of nationhood and national unity.... We are ... persuaded that this interest is related to expression in the case of Johnson's burning of the flag.

The State, apparently, is concerned that such conduct will lead people to believe either that the flag does not stand for nationhood and national unity, but instead reflects other, less positive concepts, or that the concepts reflected in the flag do not in fact exist, that is, that we do not enjoy unity as a Nation. These concerns blossom only when a person's treatment of the flag communicates some message, and thus are related "to the suppression of free expression" within the meaning of *O'Brien*. We are thus outside of *O'Brien*'s test altogether....

{Texas claims that "Texas is not endorsing, protecting, avowing or prohibiting any particular philosophy." If Texas means to suggest that its asserted interest does not prefer Democrats over Socialists, or Republicans over Democrats, for example, then it is beside the point, for Johnson does not rely on such an argument. He argues instead that the State's desire to maintain the flag as a symbol of nationhood and national unity assumes that there is only one proper view of the flag. Thus, if Texas means to argue that its interest does not prefer *any* viewpoint over another, it is mistaken; surely one's attitude toward the flag and its referents is a viewpoint.}

Johnson was prosecuted because he knew that his politically charged expression would cause "serious offense." If he had burned the flag as a means of disposing of it because it was dirty or torn, he would not have been convicted of flag desecration under this Texas law: federal law designates burning as the preferred means of disposing of a flag "when it is in such condition that it is no longer a fitting emblem for display," and Texas has no quarrel with this means of disposal.

The Texas law is thus not aimed at protecting the physical integrity of the flag in all circumstances, but is designed instead to protect it only against impairments that would cause serious offense to others.... Whether Johnson's treatment of the flag violated Texas law thus depended on the likely communicative impact of his expressive conduct.

Communicative Impact

[Similarly,] in *Boos v. Barry*, 485 U.S. 312 (1988), ... we considered the constitutionality of a law prohibiting "the display of any sign within 500 feet of a foreign embassy if that sign tends to bring that foreign government into 'public odium' or 'public disrepute.'" Rejecting the argument that the law was content neutral because it was justified by "our international law obligation to shield diplomats from speech that offends their dignity," we held that "[t]he emotive impact of speech on its audience is not a 'secondary effect'" unrelated to the content of the expression itself. According to the principles announced in *Boos*, Johnson's political expression was restricted because of the content of the message he conveyed. We must therefore subject the State's asserted interest in preserving the special symbolic character of the flag to "the most exacting scrutiny."

[B.] {Our inquiry is, of course, bounded by the particular facts of this case and by the statute under which Johnson was convicted. There was no evidence that Johnson himself stole the flag he burned, nor did the prosecution or the arguments urged in support of it depend on the theory that the flag was stolen.... We also emphasize that Johnson was prosecuted *only* for flag desecration—not for trespass, disorderly conduct, or arson.}

[For why the law fails strict scrutiny, see the excerpt at p. 204.—ed.]

Justice Stevens, dissenting [on this point] .... [Omitted.—ed.]

f. City of Renton v. Playtime Theatres, Inc., 475 U.S. 41 (1986)

Justice Rehnquist delivered the opinion of the Court....

[Renton] Ordinance No. 3526 ... [prohibits] any "adult motion picture theater" from locating within 1,000 feet of any residential zone, single- or multiple-family dwelling, church, [school,] or park .... The term "adult motion picture theater" was defined as "[a]n enclosed building used for presenting motion picture films ... characteri[zed] by an emphasis on matter depicting ... 'specified sexual activities' or 'specified anatomical areas' ... for observation by patrons therein."

In early 1982, respondents acquired two existing theaters in downtown Renton, with the intention of using them to exhibit feature-length adult films. The theaters were located within the area proscribed by Ordinance No. 3526. At about the same time, respondents [sued] .... While the federal action was pending, the City Council amended the ordinance in several respects, [including by] adding a statement of reasons for its enactment ....

This Court has long held that regulations enacted for the purpose of restraining speech on the basis of its content presumptively violate the First Amendment. On the other hand, so-called "content-neutral" time, place, and manner regulations are acceptable so long as they are designed to serve a substantial governmental interest and do not unreasonably limit alternative avenues of communication.

At first glance, the Renton ordinance ... does not appear to fit neatly into either the "content-based" or the "content-neutral" category. To be sure, the ordinance treats theaters that specialize in adult films differently from other kinds of theaters. Nevertheless, as the District Court concluded, the Renton ordinance is aimed not at the *content* of the films shown at "adult motion picture theatres," but rather at the *secondary effects* of such theaters on the surrounding community. The District Court found that the City Council's "*predominate* concerns" were with the secondary effects of adult theaters, and not with the content of adult films themselves....

The District Court's finding as to "predominate" intent ... is more than adequate to establish that the city's pursuit of its zoning interests here was unrelated to the suppression of free expression. The ordinance by its terms is designed to prevent crime, protect the city's retail trade, maintain property values, and generally "protec[t] and preserv[e] the quality of [the city's] neighborhoods, commercial districts, and the quality of urban life," not to suppress the expression of unpopular views.... "[I]f [the city] had been concerned with restricting the message purveyed by adult theaters, it would have tried to close them or restrict their number rather than circumscribe their choice as to location."

In short, the Renton ordinance is completely consistent with our definition of "content-neutral" speech regulations as those that "are *justified* without reference to the content of the regulated speech." The ordinance does not contravene the fundamental principle that underlies our concern about "content-based" speech regulations: that "government may not grant the use of a forum to people whose views it finds acceptable, but deny use to those wishing to express less favored or more controversial views." ... "... We have here merely a decision by the city to treat certain movie theaters differently because they have markedly different effects upon their surroundings...."

The appropriate inquiry in this case, then, is whether the Renton ordinance is designed to serve a substantial governmental interest and allows for reasonable alternative avenues of communication. [Application of the test for content-neutral restrictions generally omitted; but in the course of applying the narrow tailoring prong, the Court said:—ed.]

Respondents contend that the Renton ordinance is "underinclusive," in that it fails to regulate other kinds of adult businesses that are likely to produce secondary effects similar to those produced by adult theaters. On this record the contention must fail. There is no evidence that, at the time the Renton ordinance was enacted, any other adult business was located in, or was contemplating moving into, Renton....

That Renton chose first to address the potential problems created by one particular kind of adult business in no way suggests that the city has "singled out" adult theaters for discriminatory treatment. We simply have no basis on this record for assuming that Renton will not, in the future, amend its ordinance to include other kinds of adult businesses that have been shown to produce the same kinds of secondary effects as adult theaters.

Justice Blackmun concurred in the judgment [without opinion—ed.].

Justice Brennan, with whom Justice Marshall joins, dissenting.

[B]oth the language of the ordinance and its dubious legislative history belie the Court's conclusion that "the city's pursuit of its zoning interests here was unrelated to the suppression of free expression." ...

The ordinance discriminates on its face against certain forms of speech based on content. Movie theaters specializing in "adult motion pictures" may not be located within 1,000 feet of any residential zone, single- or multiple-family dwelling, church, park, or school. Other motion picture theaters, and other forms of "adult entertainment," such as bars, massage parlors, and adult bookstores, are not subject to the same restrictions. This selective treatment strongly suggests that Renton was interested not in controlling the "secondary effects" associated with adult businesses, but in discriminating against adult theaters based on the content of the films they exhibit.

The Court ignores this discriminatory treatment, declaring that Renton is free "to address the potential problems created by one particular kind of adult business," and to amend the ordinance in the future to include other adult enterprises. However, because of the First Amendment interests at stake here, this one-step-at-a-time analysis is wholly inappropriate.... In this case, the city has not justified treating adult movie theaters differently from other adult entertainment businesses. The ordinance's underinclusiveness is cogent evidence that it was aimed at the *content* of the films shown in adult movie theaters.

{The Court also explains that "[t]here is no evidence that, at the time the Renton ordinance was enacted, any other adult business was located in, or was contemplating moving into, Renton." However, at the time the ordinance was enacted, there was no evidence that any adult movie theaters were located in, or considering moving to, Renton. Thus, there was no legitimate reason for the city to treat adult movie theaters differently from other adult businesses.} ...

The city points to [the amendments made after the lawsuit was filed] as evidence that the ordinance was designed to control the secondary effects associated with adult movie theaters, rather than to suppress the content of the films they exhibit. However, the "legislative history" of the ordinance strongly suggests otherwise.

Prior to the amendment, there was no indication that the ordinance was designed to address any "secondary effects" a single adult theater might create. In addition to the suspiciously coincidental timing of the amendment, many of the City Council's "findings" do not relate to legitimate land-use concerns.... "[M]any of the stated reasons for the ordinance were no more than expressions of dislike for the subject matter." { For example, "finding" number 2 states that "[l]ocation of adult entertainment land uses on the main commercial thoroughfares of the City gives an impression of legitimacy to, and causes a loss of sensitivity to the adverse effect of pornography upon children, established family relations, respect for marital relationship and for the sanctity of marriage relations of others, and the concept of non-aggressive, consensual sexual relations."

"Finding" number 6 states that "[l]ocation of adult land uses in close proximity to residential uses, churches, parks, and other public facilities, and schools, will cause a degradation of the community standard of morality. Pornographic material has a degrading effect upon the relationship between spouses."} That some residents may be offended by the *content* of the films shown at adult movie theaters cannot form the basis for state regulation of speech.

Some of the "findings" added by the City Council do relate to supposed "secondary effects" associated with adult movie theaters. {For example, "finding" number 12 states that "[l]ocation of adult entertainment land uses in proximity to residential uses, churches, parks and other public facilities, and schools, may lead to increased levels of criminal activities, including prostitution, rape, incest and assaults in the vicinity of such adult entertainment land uses."} However, the Court cannot, as it does, merely accept these *post hoc* statements at face value. "[T]he presumption of validity that traditionally attends a local government's exercise of its zoning powers carries little, if any, weight where the zoning regulation trenches on rights of expression protected under the First Amendment." ...

In sum, the circumstances here strongly suggest that the ordinance was designed to suppress expression, even that constitutionally protected, and thus was not to be analyzed as a content-neutral time, place, and manner restriction. {"[A]nyone with any knowledge of human nature should naturally assume that the decision to adopt almost any content-based restriction might have been affected by an antipathy on the part of at least some legislators to the ideas or information being suppressed. The logical assumption, in other words, is not that there is not improper motivation but, rather, because legislators are only human, that there is a substantial risk that an impermissible consideration has in fact colored the deliberative process."} ...

{The Court apparently finds comfort in the fact that the ordinance does not "deny use to those wishing to express less favored or more controversial views." However, content-based discrimination is not rendered "any less odious" because it distinguishes "among entire classes of ideas, rather than among points of view within a particular class." Moreover, the Court's conclusion that the restrictions imposed here were viewpoint neutral is patently flawed. "As a practical matter, the speech suppressed by restrictions such as those involved [here] will almost invariably carry an implicit, if not explicit, message in favor of more relaxed sexual mores. Such restrictions, in other words, have a potent viewpoint-differential impact...."}

Rather than speculate about Renton's motives for adopting such measures, our cases require the conclusion that the ordinance, like any other content-based restriction on speech, is constitutional "only if the [city] can show that [it] is a precisely drawn means of serving a compelling [governmental] interest." Only this strict approach can insure that cities will not use their zoning powers as a pretext for suppressing constitutionally protected expression. [Strict scrutiny analysis omitted.—ed.] Even assuming that the ordinance should be treated like a content-neutral time, place, and manner restriction, I would still find it unconstitutional.... [Analysis omitted.—ed.]

g. *Hill v. Colorado, 530 U.S. 703 (2000)*

Justice Stevens delivered the opinion of the Court....

[A.] [A Colorado statute] makes it unlawful within [100 feet of a health care facility] for any person to "knowingly approach" within eight feet of another person, without that person's consent, "for the purpose of passing a leaflet or handbill to, displaying a sign to, or engaging in oral protest, education, or counseling with such other person...." [The statute] does not require a standing speaker to move away from anyone passing by....

[Petitioners sued, claiming they wanted to engage] in ... "[s]idewalk counseling" [near abortion clinics] ... "... by means of verbal or written speech, including conversation and/or display of signs and/or distribution of literature." They ... allege[] that such activities frequently entail being within eight feet of other persons .... [The discussion of the legitimacy of protecting people from certain unwanted speech omitted; this excerpt focuses on the content discrimination question.—ed.] ...

[B.] [1.] As we explained in *Ward v. Rock Against Racism*, 491 U.S. 781 (1989): "The principal inquiry in determining content neutrality, in speech cases generally and in time, place, or manner cases in particular, is whether the government has adopted a regulation of speech because of disagreement with the message it conveys." The Colorado statute passes that test for three independent reasons.

First, it is not a "regulation of speech." Rather, it is a regulation of the places where some speech may occur.

Second, it was not adopted "because of disagreement with the message it conveys." This conclusion is supported not just by the Colorado courts' interpretation of legislative history, but more importantly by the State Supreme Court's unequivocal holding that the statute's "restrictions apply equally to all demonstrators, regardless of viewpoint, and the statutory language makes no reference to the content of the speech."

Third, the State's interests in protecting access and privacy, and providing the police with clear guidelines, are unrelated to the content of the demonstrators' speech. As we have repeatedly explained, government regulation of expressive activity is "content neutral" if it is justified without reference to the content of regulated speech....

[2.] With respect to persons who are neither leafletters nor sign carriers, ... the statute does not apply unless their approach is "for the purpose of ... engaging in oral protest, education, or counseling." Petitioners contend that an individual near a health care facility who knowingly approaches a pedestrian to say "good morning" or to randomly recite lines from a novel would not be subject to the statute's restrictions. Because the content of the oral statements made by an approaching speaker must sometimes be examined to determine whether the knowing approach is covered by the statute, petitioners argue that the law is "content-based" under our reasoning in *Carey v. Brown*....

It is common in the law to examine the content of a communication to determine the speaker's purpose. Whether a particular statement constitutes a threat, blackmail, an agreement to fix prices, a copyright violation, a public offering of securities, or an offer to sell goods often depends on the precise content of the statement....

With respect to the conduct that is the focus of the Colorado statute, it is unlikely that there would often be any need to know exactly what words were spoken in order to determine whether "sidewalk counselors" are engaging in "oral protest, education, or counseling" rather than pure social or random conversation. Theoretically, of course, cases may arise in which it is necessary to review the content of the statements made by a person approaching within eight feet of an unwilling listener to determine whether the approach is covered by the statute. But that review need be no more extensive than a determination of whether a general prohibition of "picketing" or "demonstrating" applies to innocuous speech.

The regulation of such expressive activities, by definition, does not cover social, random, or other everyday communications. See *Webster's Third New International Dictionary* (1993) (defining "demonstrate" as "to make a public display of sentiment for or against a person or cause" and "picket" as an effort "to persuade or otherwise influence"). Nevertheless, we have never suggested that the kind of cursory examination that might be required to exclude casual conversation from the coverage of a regulation of picketing would be problematic....

The Colorado statute's regulation of the location of protests, education, and counseling is easily distinguishable from *Carey*. It places no restrictions on—and clearly does not prohibit—either a particular viewpoint or any subject matter that may be discussed by a speaker. Rather, it simply establishes a minor place restriction on an extremely broad category of communications with unwilling listeners.

Instead of drawing distinctions based on the subject that the approaching speaker may wish to address, the statute applies equally to used car salesmen, animal rights activists, fundraisers, environmentalists, and missionaries. Each can attempt to educate unwilling listeners on any subject, but without consent may not approach within eight feet to do so....

[C.] As Justice Scalia points out, the vice of content-based legislation in this context is that "it lends itself" to being "used for invidious thought-control purposes." But a statute that restricts certain categories of speech only lends itself to invidious use if there is a significant number of communications, raising the same problem that the statute was enacted to solve, that fall outside the statute's scope, while others fall inside.

Here, the statute's restriction seeks to protect those who enter a health care facility from the harassment, the nuisance, the persistent importuning, the following, the dogging, and the implied threat of physical touching that can accompany an unwelcome approach within eight feet of a patient by a person wishing to argue vociferously face-to-face and perhaps thrust an undesired handbill upon her. The statutory phrases, "oral protest, education, or counseling," distinguish speech activities likely to have those consequences from speech activities (such as Justice Scalia's "happy speech") that are most unlikely to have those consequences.

The statute does not distinguish among speech instances that are similarly likely to raise the legitimate concerns to which it responds. Hence, the statute cannot be struck down for failure to maintain "content neutrality," or for "underbreadth."

[D.] Also flawed is Justice Kennedy's theory that a statute restricting speech becomes unconstitutionally content based because of its application "to the specific locations where [that] discourse occurs." A statute prohibiting solicitation in airports that was motivated by the aggressive approaches of Hare Krishnas does not become content based solely because its application is confined to airports—"the specific location where [that] discourse occurs." A statute making it a misdemeanor to sit at a lunch counter for an hour without ordering any food would also not be "content based" even if it were enacted by a racist legislature that hated civil rights protesters (although it might raise separate questions about the State's legitimate interest at issue).

Similarly, the contention that a statute is "viewpoint based" simply because its enactment was motivated by the conduct of the partisans on one side of a debate is without support. The antipicketing ordinance upheld [as content-neutral] in *Frisby v. Schultz*, a decision in which both of today's dissenters joined, was obviously enacted in response to the activities of antiabortion protesters who wanted to protest at the home of a particular doctor to persuade him and others that they viewed his practice of performing abortions to be murder....

Justice Souter, with whom Justice O'Connor, Justice Ginsburg, and Justice Breyer join, concurring....

[A] restriction is content based only if it is imposed because of the content of the speech, and not because of offensive behavior identified with its delivery.... [This statute] simply does not forbid the statement of any position on any subject.... What it forbids ... is approaching another person closer than eight feet (absent permission) to deliver the message....

[Of course,] enforcement of the approach restriction will have [some] effect on speech .... The effect of speech is a product of ideas and circumstances, and time, place, and manner are circumstances.

The question is simply whether the ostensible reason for regulating the circumstances is really something about the ideas. Here, the evidence indicates that the ostensible reason is the true reason. The fact that speech by a stationary speaker is untouched by this statute shows that the reason for its restriction on approaches goes to the approaches, not to the content of the speech of those approaching. What is prohibited is a close encounter when the person addressed does not want to get close....

Justice Scalia, with whom Justice Thomas joins, dissenting....

[A.] [Under the statute, a] speaker wishing to approach another for the purpose of communicating *any* message except one of protest, education, or counseling may do so without first securing the other's consent. Whether a speaker must obtain permission before approaching within eight feet—and whether he will be sent to prison for failing to do so—depends entirely on *what he intends to say* when he gets there.

I have no doubt that this regulation would be deemed content-based *in an instant* if the case before us involved antiwar protesters, or union members seeking to "educate" the public about the reasons for their strike. "[I]t is," we would say, "the content of the speech that determines whether it is within or without the statute's blunt prohibition." *Carey*. But the jurisprudence of this Court has a way of changing when abortion is involved.

[B.] The Court asserts that this statute is not content-based for purposes of our First Amendment analysis because it neither (1) discriminates among viewpoints nor (2) places restrictions on "any subject matter that may be discussed by a speaker." But we have never held that the universe of content-based regulations is limited to those two categories, and such a holding would be absurd.

Imagine, for instance, special place-and-manner restrictions on all speech except that which "conveys a sense of contentment or happiness." This "happy speech" limitation would not be "viewpoint-based"—citizens would be able to express their joy in equal measure at either the rise or fall of the NASDAQ, at either the success or the failure of the Republican Party—and would not discriminate on the basis of subject matter, since gratification could be expressed about anything at all. Or consider a law restricting the writing or recitation of poetry—neither viewpoint-based nor limited to any particular subject matter. Surely this Court would consider such regulations to be "content-based" ....

{The Court responds that statutes which restrict categories of speech—as opposed to subject matter or viewpoint—are constitutionally worrisome only if a "significant number of communications, raising the same problem that the statute was enacted to solve, ... fall outside the statute's scope, while others fall inside." I am not sure that is correct, but let us assume, for the sake of argument, that it is.

The Court then proceeds to assert that "[t]he statutory phrases, 'oral protest, education, or counseling,' distinguish speech activities likely to" present the problem of "harassment, ... nuisance, ... persistent importuning, ... following, ... dogging, and ... implied threat of physical touching," from "speech activities [such as my example of 'happy speech'] that are most unlikely to have those consequences." Well. That may work for "oral protest"; but it is beyond imagining why "education" and "counseling" are especially *likely*, rather than especially *unlikely*, to involve such conduct.... *Unless*, of course, "education" and "counseling" are code words for efforts to dissuade women from abortion—in which event the statute would not be viewpoint neutral, which the Court concedes makes it invalid.}

"The vice of content-based legislation—what renders it deserving of the high standard of strict scrutiny—is not that it is always used for invidious, thought-control purposes, but that it lends itself to use for those purposes." A restriction that operates only on speech that communicates a message of protest, education, or counseling presents exactly this risk. When applied, as it is here, at the entrance to medical facilities, it is a means of impeding speech against abortion.

The Court's confident assurance that the statute poses no special threat to First Amendment freedoms because it applies alike to "used car salesmen, animal rights activists, fundraisers, environmentalists, and missionaries," is a wonderful replication (except for its lack of sarcasm) of Anatole France's observation that "[t]he law, in its majestic equality, forbids the rich as well as the poor to sleep under bridges...." This Colorado law is no more targeted at used car salesmen, animal rights activists, fund raisers, environmentalists, and missionaries than French vagrancy law was targeted at the rich. We know what the Colorado legislators, by their careful selection of content ("protest, education, and counseling"), were taking aim at, for they set it forth in the statute itself: the "right to protest or counsel *against* certain medical procedures" on the sidewalks and streets surrounding health care facilities.

The Court is unpersuasive in its attempt to equate the present restriction with content-neutral regulation of demonstrations and picketing— as one may immediately suspect from the opinion's wildly expansive definitions of demonstrations as "public display[s] of sentiment for or against a person or cause," and of picketing as an effort "to persuade or otherwise influence." (On these terms, Nathan Hale was a demonstrator and Patrick Henry a picket.)

When the government regulates "picketing," or "demonstrating," it restricts a particular manner of expression that is ... "a mixture of conduct and communication." ... "Picketing by an organized group is more than free speech, since it involves patrol of a particular locality and since the very presence of a picket line may induce action of one kind or another, quite irrespective of the nature of the ideas which are being disseminated. Hence those aspects of picketing make it the subject of restrictive regulation." ...

[But t]here comes a point—and the Court's opinion today passes it—at which the regulation of action intimately and unavoidably connected with traditional speech is a regulation of speech itself. The strictures of the First Amendment cannot be avoided by regulating the act of moving one's lips; and they cannot be avoided by regulating the act of extending one's arm to deliver a handbill, or peacefully approaching in order to speak....

As for the Court's appeal to the fact that we often "examine the content of a communication" to determine whether it "constitutes a threat, blackmail, an agreement to fix prices, a copyright violation, a public offering of securities, or an offer to sell goods," the distinction is almost too obvious to bear mention: Speech of a certain content is constitutionally proscribable. The Court has not yet taken the step of consigning "protest, education, and counseling" to that category.

[C.] Finally, the Court is not correct in its assertion that the restriction here is content-neutral because it is "*justified* without reference to the content of regulated speech," in the sense that "the State's interests in protecting access and privacy, and providing the police with clear guidelines, are unrelated to the content of the demonstrators' speech." That is not an accurate statement of our law....

Even a law that has as its purpose something unrelated to the suppression of particular content cannot irrationally single out that content for its prohibition. An ordinance directed at the suppression of noise (and therefore "justified without reference to the content of regulated speech") cannot be applied only to sound trucks delivering messages of "protest." ... [T]he "justified by reference to content" language ... is a prohibition *in addition to*, rather than in place of, the prohibition of facially content-based restrictions....

[D.] But in any event, ... it is clear that the regulation is *both* based on content *and* justified by reference to content.... The purpose of [the statute] ... (according to the Court)[] is to protect "[t]he unwilling listener's interest in avoiding unwanted communication." On this analysis, Colorado has restricted certain categories of speech—protest, counseling, and education—out of an apparent belief that only speech with this content is sufficiently likely to be annoying or upsetting as to require consent before it may be engaged in at close range.

It is reasonable enough to conclude that even the most gentle and peaceful close approach by a so-called "sidewalk counselor"—who wishes to "educate" the woman entering an abortion clinic about the nature of the procedure, to "counsel" against it and in favor of other alternatives, and perhaps even (though less likely if the approach is to be successful) to "protest" her taking of a human life—will often, indeed usually, have what might be termed the "secondary effect" of annoying or deeply upsetting the woman who is planning the abortion. *But that is not an effect which occurs "without reference to the content" of the speech.* This singling out of presumptively "unwelcome" communications fits precisely the description of prohibited regulation set forth in *Boos v. Barry*, 485 U.S. 312, 321 (1988): It "targets the *direct impact* of a particular category of speech, not a secondary feature that happens to be associated with that type of speech."

{The Court's contention that the statute is content-neutral because it is not a "regulation of speech" but a "regulation of the places where some speech may occur" ... is both absurd and contradicted by innumerable cases. See, *e.g.*, *Carey*. [Moreover,] the fact that a restriction is framed as a "regulation of the places where some speech may occur" has nothing whatever to do with whether the restriction is content-neutral—which is why *Boos* held to be content-based the ban on displaying, within 500 feet of foreign embassies, banners designed to "bring into public odium any foreign government."}

In sum, it blinks reality to regard this statute, in its application to oral communications, as anything other than a content-based restriction upon speech in the public forum. As such, it must survive ... "strict scrutiny" ....

Justice Kennedy, dissenting....

"[O]ral protest, education, or counseling" outside the entrances to medical facilities concern a narrow range of topics—indeed, one topic in particular. By confining the law's application to the specific locations where the prohibited discourse occurs, the State has made a content-based determination.... [Justice Kennedy's opinion largely anticipates Justice Scalia's concurrence in the judgment, which Justice Kennedy joined, in *McCullen v. Coakley* (2014) (p. 376).—ed.]

h.   Holder v. Humanitarian Law Project, 561 U.S. 1 (2010)

[For more details on the case, see p. 296.—ed.]

Chief Justice Roberts delivered the opinion of the Court [on a point on which the Court was unanimous]....

[A federal statute,] 18 U.S.C. § 2339B[,] ... makes it a federal crime to "knowingly provid[e] material support or resources to a foreign terrorist organization[]" ... including ... "... instruction or teaching designed to impart a specific skill, as opposed to general knowledge[.]" ...

[T]he Government ... claim[s] that the only thing truly at issue in this litigation is conduct, not speech. Section 2339B is directed at the fact of plaintiffs' interaction with [two particular foreign terrorist organizations], the Government contends, and only incidentally burdens their expression. The Government argues that the proper standard of review is therefore the one set out in *United States v. O'Brien*....

[But] *O'Brien* does not provide the applicable standard for reviewing a content-based regulation of speech, and § 2339B regulates speech on the basis of its content.... If plaintiffs' speech ... imparts a "specific skill" or communicates advice derived from "specialized knowledge"—for example, training on the use of international law or advice on petitioning the United Nations—then it is barred. On the other hand, plaintiffs' speech is not barred if it imparts only general or unspecialized knowledge.

The Government argues that § 2339B should nonetheless receive intermediate scrutiny because it *generally* functions as a regulation of conduct. That argument runs headlong into a number of our precedents, most prominently *Cohen v. California. Cohen* also involved a generally applicable regulation of conduct, barring breaches of the peace. But when Cohen was convicted for wearing a jacket bearing an epithet, ... we recognized that the generally applicable law was directed at Cohen because of what his speech communicated—he violated the breach of the peace statute because of the offensive content of his particular message. We accordingly applied more rigorous scrutiny and reversed his conviction....

This suit falls into the same category.... [A]s applied to plaintiffs [in this case] the conduct triggering coverage under the statute consists of communicating a message. As we explained in *Texas v. Johnson*: "If the [Government's] regulation is not related to expression, then the less stringent standard we announced in *O'Brien* for regulations of noncommunicative conduct controls. If it is, then we are outside of *O'Brien*'s test, and we must [apply] a more demanding standard."

i.   *McCullen v. Coakley, 134 S. Ct. 2518 (2014)*

Chief Justice Roberts delivered the opinion of the Court.

[A.] [The Massachusetts Reproductive Health Care Facilities Act] makes it a crime to knowingly stand on a "public way or sidewalk" within 35 feet of an entrance or driveway to any place, other than a hospital, where abortions are performed ... [but] exempts ... (1) "persons entering or leaving such facility"; (2) "employees or agents of such facility acting within the scope of their employment"; (3) "... municipal agents acting within the scope of their employment"; and (4) "persons using the public [way or] sidewalk ... solely for ... reaching a destination other than such facility." ...

[B.] [T]he Act does not draw content-based distinctions on its face. The Act would be content based if it required "enforcement authorities" to "examine the content of the message that is conveyed to determine whether" a violation has occurred. {[And] the Act would not be content neutral if it were concerned with undesirable effects that arise from "the direct impact of speech on its audience" or "[l]isteners' reactions to speech." If, for example, the speech outside Massachusetts abortion clinics caused offense or made listeners uncomfortable, such offense or discomfort would not give the Commonwealth a content-neutral justification to restrict the speech.}

[C.] But ... [w]hether petitioners violate the Act "depends" not "on what they say," but simply on where they say it.... [B]y limiting the buffer zones to abortion clinics, the Act has the "inevitable effect" of restricting abortion-related speech more than speech on other subjects. But a facially neutral law does not become content based simply because it may disproportionately affect speech on certain topics. On the contrary, "[a] regulation that serves purposes unrelated to the content of expression is deemed neutral, even if it has an incidental effect on some speakers or messages but not others." The question in such a case is whether the law is ""justified without reference to the content of the regulated speech."

The Massachusetts Act is. Its stated purpose is to "increase forthwith public safety at reproductive health care facilities." Respondents have articulated similar purposes before this Court—namely, "public safety, patient access to healthcare, and the unobstructed use of public sidewalks and roadways." It is not the case [as Justice Scalia's concurrence argues] that "[e]very objective indication shows that the provision's primary purpose is to restrict speech that opposes abortion." ...

[T]he foregoing concerns [are] content neutral. Obstructed access and congested sidewalks are problems no matter what caused them. A group of individuals can obstruct clinic access and clog sidewalks just as much when they loiter as when they protest abortion or counsel patients.... [And a]ll of the problems identified by the Commonwealth here ... arise irrespective of any listener's reactions. Whether or not a single person reacts to abortion protestors' chants or petitioners' counseling, large crowds outside abortion clinics can still compromise public safety, impede access, and obstruct side-walks....

[D.] [We cannot infer that] the Massachusetts Legislature [acted from] a purpose to "single[] out for regulation speech about one particular topic: abortion." ... The Massachusetts Legislature [enacted this version of the Act] in response to a problem that was, in its experience, limited to abortion clinics. There was a record of crowding, obstruction, and even violence outside such clinics. There were apparently no similar recurring problems associated with other kinds of ... facilities ....

{"... The First Amendment does not require States to regulate for problems that do not exist."} In light of the limited nature of the problem, it was reasonable for the Massachusetts Legislature to enact a limited solution. When selecting among various options for combating a particular problem, legislatures should be encouraged to choose the one that restricts less speech, not more.

Justice Scalia objects that the statute does restrict more speech than necessary, because "only one [Massachusetts abortion clinic] is known to have been beset by the problems that the statute supposedly addresses." But there are no grounds for inferring content-based discrimination here simply because the legislature acted with respect to abortion facilities generally rather than proceeding on a facility-by-facility basis. On these facts, the poor fit noted by Justice Scalia goes to the question of narrow tailoring, which we consider [at p. 347] ....

[E.] "[A]n exemption from an otherwise permissible regulation of speech may represent a governmental 'attempt to give one side of a debatable public question an advantage in expressing its views to the people.'" At least on the record before us, however, the statutory exemption for clinic employees and agents acting within the scope of their employment [which covers not only clinic escorts but also employees such as workers shoveling snowy side-walks] does not appear to be such an attempt....

Given the need for an exemption for clinic employees, the "scope of their employment" qualification simply ensures that the exemption is limited to its purpose of allowing the employees to do their jobs.... Contrary to the suggestion of Justice Scalia, there is little reason to suppose that the Massachusetts Legislature intended to incorporate a common law doctrine developed for determining vicarious liability in tort when it used the phrase "scope of their employment" for the wholly different purpose of defining the scope of an exemption to a criminal statute.

The limitation instead makes clear—with respect to both clinic employees and municipal agents—that exempted individuals are allowed inside the zones only to perform those acts authorized by their employers. There is no suggestion in the record that any of the clinics authorize their employees to speak about abortion in the buffer zones. The "scope of their employment" limitation thus seems designed to protect against exactly the sort of conduct that petitioners and Justice Scalia fear....

[I]f it turned out that a clinic authorized escorts to speak about abortion inside the buffer zones ..., [t]he Act's exemption for clinic employees would then facilitate speech on only one side of the abortion debate—a clear form of viewpoint discrimination that would support an as-applied challenge to the buffer zone at that clinic. But the record before us contains insufficient evidence to show that the exemption operates in this way ..., perhaps because the clinics do not want to doom the Act by allowing their employees to speak about abortion within the buffer zones....

{[A] plaintiff generally cannot prevail on an *as-applied* challenge without showing that the law has in fact been (or is sufficiently likely to be) unconstitutionally *applied* to him. Specifically, when someone challenges a law as viewpoint discriminatory but it is not clear from the face of the law which speakers will be allowed to speak, he must show that he was prevented from speaking while someone espousing another viewpoint was permitted to do so.}

[F.] We thus conclude that the Act is neither content nor viewpoint based and therefore need not be analyzed under strict scrutiny.... [The Court nonetheless struck it down as overinclusive even under the test applicable to content-neutral restrictions, see p. 347.—ed.]

Justice Scalia, with whom Justice Kennedy and Justice Thomas join, concurring in the judgment....

[A.] It blinks reality to say ... that a blanket prohibition on the use of streets and sidewalks where speech on only one politically controversial topic is likely to occur—and where that speech can most effectively be communicated—is not content based. Would the Court exempt from strict scrutiny a law banning access to the streets and sidewalks surrounding the site of the Republican National Convention? Or those used annually to commemorate the 1965 Selma-to-Montgomery civil rights marches? Or those outside the Internal Revenue Service? Surely not....

[A] facially neutral speech restriction [does] escape[] strict scrutiny, even when it "may disproportionately affect speech on certain topics," so long as it is "justified without reference to the content of the regulated speech." ... [But e]very objective indication [other than the statute's stated purpose and the explanations offered by state officials] shows that the provision's primary purpose is to restrict speech that opposes abortion....

[1.] [T]he Act burdens only the public spaces outside abortion clinics.... [This cannot be justified] by arguing that those locations regularly face the safety and access problems that it says the Act was designed to solve.... [A]lthough the statute applies to all abortion clinics in Massachusetts, only one is known to have been beset by the problems that the statute supposedly addresses.... [This is] powerfully relevant ... to whether the law is really directed to safety and access concerns or rather to the suppression of a particular type of speech. Showing that a law that suppresses speech on a specific subject is so far-reaching that it applies even when the asserted non-speech-related problems are not present is persuasive evidence that the law is content based....

[2.] The structure of the Act also indicates that it rests on content-based concerns. The goals of "public safety, patient access to healthcare, and the unobstructed use of public sidewalks and roadways," are already achieved by an earlier-enacted subsection of the statute, which provides criminal penalties for "[a]ny person who knowingly obstructs, detains, hinders, impedes or blocks another person's entry to or exit from a reproductive health care facility." As the majority recognizes, that provision is easy to enforce. Thus, the speech-free zones ... add nothing to safety and access; what they achieve, and what they were obviously designed to achieve, is the suppression of speech opposing abortion....

[3.] [T]he Act ... [also] exempts "employees or agents" of an abortion clinic "acting within the scope of their employment." "[G]ranting waivers to favored speakers (or ... denying them to disfavored speakers) would of course be unconstitutional." ...

Is there any serious doubt that *abortion-clinic employees or agents* "acting within the scope of their employment" near clinic entrances may—indeed, often will—speak in favor of abortion ("You are doing the right thing")? Or speak in opposition to the message of abortion opponents—saying, for example, that "this is a safe facility" to rebut the statement that it is not? The Court's contrary assumption is simply incredible.

And the majority makes no attempt to establish the further necessary proposition that abortion-clinic employees and agents do not engage in non-speech activities directed to the suppression of antiabortion speech by hampering the efforts of counselors to speak to prospective clients. Are we to believe that a clinic employee sent out to "escort" prospective clients into the building would not seek to prevent a counselor like Eleanor McCullen from communicating with them? He could pull a woman away from an approaching counselor, cover her ears, or make loud noises to drown out the counselor's pleas....

The Court takes the peculiar view that, so long as the clinics have not specifically authorized their employees to speak in favor of abortion (or, presumably, to impede antiabortion speech), there is no viewpoint discrimination. But ... "scope of employment" is a well-known common-law concept that includes "[t]he range of reasonable and foreseeable activities that an employee engages in while carrying out the employer's business." The employer need not specifically direct or sanction each aspect of an employee's conduct for it to qualify.... Moreover, a statute that forbids one side but not the other to convey its message does not become viewpoint neutral simply because the favored side chooses voluntarily to abstain from activity that the statute permits....

[T]he assigned or foreseeable conduct of a clinic employee or agent can include both speaking in favor of abortion rights and countering the speech of people like petitioners.... The Web site for the Planned Parenthood

League of Massachusetts (which operates the three abortion facilities where petitioners attempt to counsel women), urges readers to "Become a Clinic Escort Volunteer" in order to "provide a safe space for patients by escorting them through protestors to the health center." The dangers that the Web site attributes to "protestors" are related entirely to speech, not to safety or access. "Protestors," it reports, "hold signs, try to speak to patients entering the building, and distribute literature that can be misleading." The "safe space" provided by escorts is protection from that speech.

Going from bad to worse, the majority's opinion contends that "the record before us contains insufficient evidence to show" that abortion-facility escorts have actually spoken in favor of abortion (or, presumably, hindered antiabortion speech) while acting within the scope of their employment. Here is a brave new First Amendment test: Speech restrictions favoring one viewpoint over another are not content based unless it can be shown that the favored viewpoint has actually been expressed. A city ordinance closing a park adjoining the Republican National Convention to all speakers except those whose remarks have been approved by the Republican National Committee is thus not subject to strict scrutiny unless it can be shown that someone has given committee-endorsed remarks. For this Court to suggest such a test is astonishing....

[B.] {It can be argued, and it should be argued in the next case, that by stating that "the Act would not be content neutral if it were concerned with undesirable effects that arise from ... '[l]isteners' reactions to speech,'" and then holding the Act unconstitutional for being insufficiently tailored to safety and access concerns, the Court itself has *sub silentio* (and perhaps inadvertently) overruled *Hill v. Colorado*. The unavoidable implication of that holding is that protection against unwelcome speech cannot justify restrictions on the use of public streets and sidewalks.}

Justice Alito, concurring in the judgment....

Consider this entirely realistic situation. A woman enters a buffer zone and heads haltingly toward the entrance. A sidewalk counselor, such as petitioners, enters the buffer zone, approaches the woman and says, "If you have doubts about an abortion, let me try to answer any questions you may have. The clinic will not give you good information." At the same time, a clinic employee, as instructed by the management, approaches the same woman and says, "Come inside and we will give you honest answers to all your questions." The sidewalk counselor and the clinic employee expressed opposing viewpoints, but only the first violated the statute.

Or suppose ... that there was a recent report of a botched abortion at the clinic. A nonemployee may not enter the buffer zone to warn about the clinic's health record, but an employee may enter and tell prospective clients that the clinic is safe....

Speech in favor of the clinic and its work by employees and agents is permitted; speech criticizing the clinic and its work is a crime. This is blatant viewpoint discrimination....

j.   *Reed v. Town of Gilbert, 135 S. Ct. 2218 (2015)*

Justice Thomas delivered the opinion of the Court.

[A.] The [Gilbert, Arizona] Sign Code prohibits the display of outdoor signs anywhere within the Town without a permit, but it then exempts 23 categories of signs from that requirement.... Three categories of exempt signs are particularly relevant here.

The first is "Ideological Sign[s]." This category includes any "sign communicating a message or ideas for noncommercial purposes that is not a Construction Sign, Directional Sign, Temporary Directional Sign Relating to a Qualifying Event, Political Sign, Garage Sale Sign, or a sign owned or required by a governmental agency." ... [T]he Code [allows] ideological signs ... to be up to 20 square feet in area and to be placed in all "zoning districts" without time limits.

The second category is "Political Sign[s]." This includes any "temporary sign ... designed to influence the outcome of an election ...." ... The Code allows the placement of political signs up to 16 square feet on residential property and up to 32 square feet on nonresidential property ... and "rights-of-way" [*e.g.,* publicly owned streets, landscaping, and sidewalks]. These signs may be displayed up to 60 days before a primary election and up to 15 days following a general election.

The third category is "Temporary Directional Signs Relating [*i.e.,* intended to direct passersby] to a Qualifying Event," ... defined as any "... activity ... promoted by a religious, charitable, community service, educational, or other similar non-profit organization." ... Temporary directional signs may be no larger than six square feet.... [N]o more than four signs may be placed on a single [private property or public right-of-way] at any time. And, they may be displayed no more than 12 hours before the "qualifying event" and no more than 1 hour afterward.

[B.] Petitioners Good News Community Church ... and its pastor, Clyde Reed, wish to advertise the time and location of their Sunday church services. The Church is a small, cash-strapped entity that owns no building, so it holds its services at elementary schools or other locations in or near the Town. In order to inform the public about its services, which are held in a variety of different locations, the Church began placing 15 to 20 temporary signs around the Town, frequently in the public right-of-way abutting the street.

The signs typically displayed the Church's name, along with the time and location of the upcoming service. Church members would post the signs early in the day on Saturday and then remove them around midday on Sunday. The display of these signs ... has proved to be an economical and effective way for the Church to let the community know where its services are being held each week. [The Church was cited for exceeding the time limits for displaying its temporary directional signs and for failing to include the event date on the signs. Reed and the Church sued.—ed.] ...

[C.] Under [the Free Speech] Clause, a government ... "has no power to restrict expression because of its message, its ideas, its subject matter, or its content." Content-based laws—those that target speech based on its communicative content—are presumptively unconstitutional and may be justified only if the government proves that they are narrowly tailored to serve compelling state interests.

Government regulation of speech is content based if a law applies to particular speech because of the topic discussed or the idea or message expressed. This commonsense meaning of the phrase "content based" requires a court to consider whether a regulation of speech "on its face" draws distinctions based on the message a speaker conveys.

Some facial distinctions based on a message are obvious, defining regulated speech by particular subject matter, and others are more subtle, defining regulated speech by its function or purpose. Both are distinctions drawn based on the message a speaker conveys, and, therefore, are subject to strict scrutiny.

{[[It does not matter that a restriction] "does not mention any idea or viewpoint, let alone single one out for differential treatment." ... "[T]he First Amendment's hostility to content-based regulation extends not only to restrictions on particular viewpoints, but also to prohibition of public discussion of an entire topic." Thus, a speech regulation targeted at specific subject matter is content based even if it does not discriminate among viewpoints within that subject matter. For example, a law banning the use of sound trucks for political speech—and only political speech—would be a content-based regulation, even if it imposed no limits on the political viewpoints that could be expressed.}

{[A] law that is content based on its face is subject to strict scrutiny regardless of the government's benign motive, content-neutral justification, or lack of "animus toward the ideas contained" in the regulated speech.... Although "a content-based purpose may be sufficient in certain circumstances to show that a regulation is content based, it is not necessary." ... [A]n innocuous justification cannot transform a facially content-based law into one that is content neutral....

Innocent motives do not eliminate the danger of censorship presented by a facially content-based statute, as future government officials may one day wield such statutes to suppress disfavored speech. That is why the First Amendment expressly targets the operation of the laws—*i.e.,* the "abridg[ement] of speech"—rather than merely the motives of those who enacted them. "'The vice of content-based legislation ... is not that it is always used for invidious, thought-control purposes, but that it lends itself to use for those purposes.'" *Hill v. Colorado* (Scalia, J., dissenting).} ...

[D.] [A] separate and additional category of laws ..., though facially content neutral, will be considered content-based regulations of speech: laws that cannot be "'justified without reference to the content of the regulated speech,'" or that were adopted by the government "because of disagreement with the message [the speech] conveys." Those laws, like those that are content based on their face, must also satisfy strict scrutiny.

[E.] The Town's Sign Code is content based on its face.... The restrictions in the Sign Code that apply to any given sign ... depend entirely on the communicative content of the sign. If a sign informs its reader of the time and place a book club will discuss John Locke's Two Treatises of Government, that sign will be treated differently from a sign expressing the view that one should vote for one of Locke's followers in an upcoming election, and both signs will be treated differently from a sign expressing an ideological view rooted in Locke's theory of government.

More to the point, the Church's signs inviting people to attend its worship services are treated differently from signs conveying other types of ideas.... The Town's Sign Code ... singles out specific subject matter for differential treatment, even if it does not target viewpoints within that subject matter. Ideological messages are given more favorable treatment than messages concerning a political candidate, which are themselves given more favorable treatment than messages announcing an assembly of likeminded individuals. That is a paradigmatic example of content-based discrimination.

{[And a] regulation that targets a sign because it conveys an idea about a specific event is no less content based than a regulation that targets a sign because it conveys some other idea. Here, the Code singles out signs bearing a particular message: the time and location of a specific event. This type of ordinance may seem like a perfectly rational way to regulate signs, but a clear and firm rule governing content neutrality is an essential means of protecting the freedom of speech, even if laws that might seem "entirely reasonable" will sometimes be "struck down because of their content-based nature."} ...-

[F.] [The Court then applied strict scrutiny, and concluded that the ordinance was not narrowly tailored to the interests in "preserving the Town's aesthetic appeal and traffic safety. Assuming for the sake of argument that those are compelling governmental interests, the Code's distinctions fail as hopelessly underinclusive."—ed.]

[G.] Our decision today will not prevent governments from enacting effective sign laws.... The Town has ample content-neutral options available to resolve problems with safety and aesthetics. For example, its current Code regulates many aspects of signs that have nothing to do with a sign's message: size, building materials, lighting, moving parts, and portability. And on public property, the Town may go a long way toward entirely forbidding the posting of signs, so long as it does so in an evenhanded, content-neutral manner....

[Moreover, a] sign ordinance narrowly tailored to the challenges of protecting the safety of pedestrians, drivers, and passengers—such as warning signs marking hazards on private property, signs directing traffic, or street numbers associated with private houses—well might survive strict scrutiny....

[The majority did not discuss the *City of Renton v. Playtime Theatres, Inc.* line of cases, nor did it cite the *Hill v. Colorado* majority, though it cited the *Hill* dissenting opinions.—ed.]

Justice Alito, with whom Justice Kennedy and Justice Sotomayor join, concurring....

I join the opinion of the Court but add a few words ....

[A.] "[C]ontent-based" laws must satisfy strict scrutiny .... because they present, albeit sometimes in a subtler form, the same dangers as laws that regulate speech based on viewpoint. Limiting speech based on its "topic" or "subject" favors those who do not want to disturb the status quo.... [The opinion cited an earlier case, which stated, "If the marketplace of ideas is to remain free and open, governments must not be allowed to choose 'which issues are worth discussing or debating ....' To allow a government the choice of permissible subjects for public debate would be to allow that government control over the search for political truth."—ed.] ...

[B.] [M]unicipalities are [not] powerless to enact and enforce reasonable sign regulations. I will not attempt to provide anything like a comprehensive list, but here are some rules that would not be content based:

Rules regulating the size of signs ... distinguish[ing] among signs based on any content-neutral criteria ....

Rules regulating the locations in which signs may be placed. These rules may distinguish between freestanding signs and those attached to buildings.

Rules distinguishing between lighted and unlighted signs.

Rules distinguishing between signs with fixed messages and electronic signs with messages that change.

Rules that distinguish between the placement of signs on private and public property.

Rules distinguishing between the placement of signs on commercial and residential property.

Rules distinguishing between on-premises and off-premises signs.

Rules restricting the total number of signs allowed per mile of roadway.

Rules imposing time restrictions on signs advertising a one-time event. Rules of this nature do not discriminate based on topic or subject and are akin to rules restricting the times within which oral speech or music is allowed....

[G]overnment entities may also erect their own signs consistent with the principles that allow governmental speech. They may put up all manner of signs to promote safety, as well as directional signs and signs pointing out historic sites and scenic spots....

Justice Breyer, concurring in the judgment....

[A.] To use content discrimination to trigger strict scrutiny sometimes makes perfect sense. There are cases in which the Court has found content discrimination an unconstitutional method for suppressing a viewpoint. And there are cases where the Court has found content discrimination to reveal that rules governing a traditional public forum are, in fact, not a neutral way of fairly managing the forum in the interest of all speakers.... [C]ontent discrimination ... can [also] sometimes reveal weaknesses in the government's rationale for a rule that limits speech. If, for example, a city looks to litter prevention as the rationale for a prohibition against placing newsracks dispensing free advertisements on public property, why does it exempt other newsracks causing similar litter?

I also concede that, whenever government disfavors one kind of speech, it places that speech at a disadvantage, potentially interfering with the free marketplace of ideas and with an individual's ability to express thoughts and ideas that can help that individual determine the kind of society in which he wishes to live, help shape that society, and help define his place within it. Nonetheless, in these latter instances to use the presence of content discrimination automatically to trigger strict scrutiny and thereby call into play a strong presumption against constitutionality goes too far.... Regulatory programs almost always require content discrimination....

Consider governmental regulation of securities, *e.g.*, 15 U.S.C. §78*l* (requirements for content that must be included in a registration statement); of energy conservation labeling-practices, *e.g.*, 42 U.S.C. §6294 (requirements for content that must be included on labels of certain consumer electronics); of prescription drugs, *e.g.*, 21 U.S.C. §353(b)(4)(A) (requiring a prescription drug label to bear the symbol "Rx only"); of doctor-patient confidentiality, *e.g.*, 38 U.S.C. §7332 (requiring confidentiality of certain medical records, but allowing a physician to disclose that the patient has HIV to the patient's spouse or sexual partner); of income tax statements, *e.g.*, 26 U.S.C. §6039F (requiring taxpayers to furnish information about foreign gifts received if the aggregate amount exceeds $10,000); of commercial airplane briefings, *e.g.*, 14 CFR §136.7 (2015) (requiring pilots to ensure that each passenger has been briefed on flight procedures, such as seatbelt fastening); of signs at petting zoos, *e.g.*, N.Y. Gen. Bus. Law Ann. §399-ff(3) (West Cum. Supp. 2015) (requiring petting zoos to post a sign at every exit "'strongly recommend[ing] that persons wash their hands upon exiting the petting zoo area'"); and so on.

{[T]o hold that such content discrimination triggers strict scrutiny is to write a recipe for judicial management of ordinary government regulatory activity.} Nor can the majority avoid the application of strict scrutiny to all sorts of justifiable governmental regulations by relying on this Court's many subcategories and exceptions to the rule [such as the commercial speech doctrine].... [M]any justifiable instances of "content-based" regulation are noncommercial.... [And] escap[ing] the problem by watering down the force of the presumption against constitutionality that "strict scrutiny" normally carries with it ... [would] weaken the First Amendment's protection in instances where "strict scrutiny" should apply in full force.

[B.] The better approach is to generally treat content discrimination as a strong reason weighing against the constitutionality of a rule where a traditional public forum, or where viewpoint discrimination, is threatened, but elsewhere treat it as a rule of thumb, finding it a helpful, but not determinative legal tool, in an appropriate case, to determine the strength of a justification.

I would use content discrimination as a supplement to a more basic analysis, which ... asks whether the regulation at issue works harm to First Amendment interests that is disproportionate in light of the relevant regulatory objectives. Answering this question requires examining the seriousness of the harm to speech, the importance of the countervailing objectives, the extent to which the law will achieve those objectives, and whether there are other, less restrictive ways of doing so.

Admittedly, this approach does not have the simplicity of a mechanical use of categories. But it does permit the government to regulate speech in numerous instances where the voters have authorized the government to regulate and where courts should hesitate to substitute judicial judgment for that of administrators....

Here, ... [t]here is no traditional public forum nor do I find any general effort to censor a particular viewpoint. Consequently, the specific regulation at issue does not warrant "strict scrutiny." ...

Justice Kagan, with whom Justice Ginsburg and Justice Breyer join, concurring in the judgment.

[A.] Countless ... towns across America have adopted ordinances regulating the posting of signs, while exempting certain categories of signs based on their subject matter[, *e.g.*,] signs that identify the address of a home or the name of its owner[,] ... safety signs such as "Blind Pedestrian Crossing" and "Hidden Driveway"[,] ... historic site markers[,] ... [or signs] direct[ing] travelers to "scenic and historical attractions" or advertis[ing] free coffee.... [M]any sign ordinances of that kind are now in jeopardy....

[A]lthough the majority holds out hope that some sign laws with subject-matter exemptions "might survive" [strict scrutiny], the likelihood is that most will be struck down.... [C]ourts would have to determine that a town has a compelling interest in informing passersby where George Washington slept. And likewise, courts would have to find that a town has no other way to prevent hidden-driveway mishaps than by specially treating hidden-driveway signs. (Well-placed speed bumps? Lower speed limits? Or how about just a ban on hidden driveways?) ... [C]ommunities ... will have to either repeal the exemptions that allow for helpful signs on streets and sidewalks, or else lift their sign restrictions altogether and resign themselves to the resulting clutter.

{According to Justice Alito, the majority does not subject to strict scrutiny regulations of "signs advertising a one-time event." But ... the precise reason the majority applies strict scrutiny here is that "the Code singles out signs bearing a particular message: the time and location of a specific event."} ...

[B.] We apply strict scrutiny to facially content-based regulations of speech ... when there is any "realistic possibility that official suppression of ideas is afoot." That is always the case when the regulation facially differentiates on the basis of viewpoint.

It is also the case ... when a law restricts "discussion of an entire topic" in public debate. We have stated that "[i]f the marketplace of ideas is to remain free and open, governments must not be allowed to choose 'which issues are worth discussing or debating.'" And we have recognized that such subject-matter restrictions, even though viewpoint-neutral on their face, may "suggest[] an attempt to give one side of a debatable public question an advantage in expressing its views to the people."

Subject-matter regulation, in other words, may have the intent or effect of favoring some ideas over others.... But when that is not realistically possible, we may do well to relax our guard so that "entirely reasonable" laws imperiled by strict scrutiny can survive.... Our concern with content-based regulation arises from the fear that the government will skew the public's debate of ideas—so when "that risk is inconsequential, ... strict scrutiny is unwarranted."

To do its intended work, of course, the category of content-based regulation triggering strict scrutiny must sweep more broadly than the actual harm; that category exists to create a buffer zone guaranteeing that the government cannot favor or disfavor certain viewpoints. But that buffer zone need not extend forever. We can administer our content-regulation doctrine with a dose of common sense, so as to leave standing laws that in no way implicate its intended function....

[C.] [Nonetheless,] the law's distinctions between directional signs and others ... [do] not pass strict scrutiny, or intermediate scrutiny, or even the laugh test. The Town, for example, ... offers no coherent justification for restricting the size of directional signs to 6 square feet while allowing other signs to reach 20 square feet....

V. Special Burdens on Free Speech

A. Generally

So far we have considered laws that directly restrict speech or symbolic expression. But the law may sometimes burden speakers, and interfere with their ability to effectively convey their messages, in other ways:

1. It can force expressive associations to accept certain people as members or speakers, which can affect the association's ability to express the views preferred by the current members or leaders.

2. It can require speakers, group members, or contributors to identify themselves, which can deter people from speaking, from joining groups, or from contributing to groups.

3. It can restrict the spending of money on speech, which can make it harder for people to speak effectively to a large audience.

4. It can compel people to say or write certain things, which (1) can itself be seen as an interference with the freedom of speech, in the sense of the freedom to choose what to speak, and (2) can restrict speakers' ability to create the particular speech products they want to create.

5. It can interfere with people's ability to gather information, which can make it impossible for them to then convey that information to others.

All these sorts of restrictions are therefore generally seen as potentially implicating the First Amendment.

B. Forced Association

a. Restrictions on Expressive Association Generally

> [T]he strength of the Pack is the Wolf, and
> The strength of the Wolf is the Pack.
> —Rudyard Kipling, *The Law of the Jungle*

To speak effectively, people generally need to organize into groups: political parties, advocacy groups (such as the ACLU, the NAACP, or the NRA), and the like. A restriction on expressive association can thus interfere with people's ability to effectively express their messages. And the Court has therefore interpreted the First Amendment as implicitly protecting people's right to associate with each other for expressive purposes.

This is often cast as a "right to expressive association," but the underlying right is the right to speak. Interference with expressive association is generally seen as unconstitutional because it interferes with free speech.

The right to expressive association is a different right from the right of *intimate association*—the right to associate for nonexpressive purposes. The intimate association right extends only to small groups, such as a family, a circle of friends, and probably roommates, *Fair Housing Council of San Fernando Valley v. Roommate.com LLC*, 666 F.3d 1216 (9th Cir. 2012), or a selective private club, see, *e.g.*, *Louisiana Debating & Literary Ass'n v. City of New Orleans*, 42 F.3d 1483 (5th Cir. 1995). The expressive association right extends to much larger groups, *but* only to the extent that interfering with the group's associational choices substantially burdens its ability to express itself. See *Roberts v. U.S. Jaycees* (1984) (p. 397); *Boy Scouts of America v. Dale* (2000) (p. 402).

Rule: Substantial burdens on expressive association are generally subject to strict scrutiny. Such burdens can come in many varieties, though this particular subsection will only discuss category 1 below:

1. Requirements that an expressive association accept unwanted members or voters, if the requirement substantially interferes with the organization's ability to convey its message. *Boy Scouts*; *California Democratic Party v. Jones* (2000) (p. 393).

a. Whether there is such a substantial burden is often hotly contested; to decide this in any particular case, you'd have to compare and contrast with *Roberts* and *Boy Scouts*.

b. *Rumsfeld v. FAIR* (2006) (p. 412) makes clear that, while this right may sometimes cover organizations' choice of members, it doesn't cover organizations' less important choices, such as the choice of which recruiters are allowed to use office space in the organization's building.

c. *Roberts* and *Boy Scouts* say such substantial burdens can be justified under strict scrutiny—but then *Boy Scouts* summarily dismisses the compelling interest argument, which suggests that the Court may be treating this sort of substantial burden on expressive association as per se invalid, rather than just subject to strict scrutiny. "[A] state requirement that the Boy Scouts retain Dale as an assistant scoutmaster would significantly burden the organization's right to oppose or disfavor homosexual conduct. The state interests embodied in New Jersey's public accommodations law do not justify such a severe intrusion on the Boy Scouts' rights to freedom of expressive association."

Boy Scouts also suggests that instead of the government interest trumping "the associational interest in freedom of expression," the two need to be set on opposite "side[s] of the scale" and presumably weighed; but the case doesn't tell us how this weighing would be done.

Likewise, even the dissent suggests that the freedom of expressive association may trump antidiscrimination law, though it would require a greater showing of burden on the expressive association right for that to happen: "Surely there are instances in which an organization that truly aims to foster a belief at odds with the purposes of a State's antidiscrimination laws will have a First Amendment right to association that precludes forced compliance with those laws."

2. Total prohibitions on expressive association with a particular kind of group, or liability for joining a group. Cf. *Dennis v. United States* (1951)

(p. 45). This is true even when other members of the group engage in illegal behavior, unless "the group itself possesse[s] unlawful goals and ... the individual [holds] a specific intent to further those illegal aims." *NAACP v. Claiborne Hardware* (1982) (p. 169). But these prohibitions can be upheld under strict scrutiny.

3. Limits on contributing money—or other valuable goods or services—to an expressive group. (These burdens are subject to something a bit less demanding than strict scrutiny.) See Part V.D.

4. Mandated disclosure of organizations' members and contributors. (These burdens are subject only to "exacting scrutiny," which seems a bit less demanding than strict scrutiny.) See Part V.C.

5. Forced contribution of money to a group (other than to the government itself via taxes, see *Keller v. State Bar* (1990) (p. 551)). See Part V.E.4.

b. *Problem: Newspaper Reporters*

California Labor Code § 1101 states:

No employer shall make ... or enforce any ... policy:
(a) Forbidding or preventing employees from engaging or participating in politics or from becoming candidates for public office.
(b) Controlling or directing, or tending to control or direct the political activities or affiliations of employees.

A *Los Angeles Times* policy bars reporters from participating in partisan politics. Fred Bernstein, who works for the *Times* as a political correspondent, volunteers to work in the campaign of a candidate for the Senate; the *Times* demands that he stop volunteering, and when he refuses to stop volunteering, he is fired. Fred sues under § 1101, but the *Times* claims that applying the statute to it would violate its First Amendment rights. What arguments can be made for Fred and for the *Times*? Cf. *Nelson v. McClatchy Newspapers, Inc.*, 936 P.2d 1123 (Wash. 1997).

c. *Problem: Blacks-Only Lecture*

"United African Movement is a private African-American membership organization that was formed to honor Marcus Garvey—an advocate for the creation of 'a separate Black nation.' ... Its 'nonassimilationist' doctrine is considered necessary 'to lift African people from the cycle of dependency on European largess and whims.' On Wednesday evenings, UAM holds forums designed to be a 'sanctuary' from racism where people of African descent can convene 'without any input from persons who harbor racial animus toward Africans.' In 1989 UAM members asserted their 'absolute refusal to allow Caucasians' to its Wednesday evening forums....

"Minoo Southgate is a Caucasian Jewish woman ... who has written articles focusing on 'the anti-Semitism that comes from a small number of militant Black nationalists' including UAM members and guest speakers.... [Southgate went to the theater that UAM had rented, but a man stopped her when she entered, and] asked if she was of African descent. When Complainant answered 'no,' he said, '[T]his place is only for African people. You are not allowed here.' ..." *Southgate v. United African Movement*, 1997 WL 1051933 (N.Y. Comm'n on Hum. Rts.).

The New York City Code bars any "provider of public accommodations because of the ... race ... of any person" from (1) "deny[ing] to such person any of the accommodations ... thereof" or (2) "mak[ing] any declaration ... that any of the accommodations ... shall be ... denied ... on account of race." The New York Commission on Human Rights held:

> [UAM] opened the Wednesday evening forums to the public by placing announcements in newspapers and on the radio. They also failed to have any screening process for patrons of the forums. Having made those "choices," the forums are subject to the provisions of the Code which prohibit race discrimination—regardless of the fact that they are organized by a "distinctly private" organization and held on private property and paid for by private funds....
>
> It is hereby ordered that ... [(1) UAM] either cease placing announcements for its forums in the media, or that the announcements specify that the forums are limited to members of UAM and their guests [and (2) UAM pay Southgate $2000 in damages and the City of New York $5000 in fines].

Is such an order constitutionally permissible?

d. Problem: Race-Matched Political Calls

The Parker Group (TPG) does "get out the vote" calling on behalf of political candidates. Part of its business is race-matched calling: callers who "sound black" (and who generally are indeed black) call voters in mostly black parts of town, and callers who "sound white" (and who generally are indeed white) call voters in mostly white parts of town.

TPG uses different scripts for voters based on their presumed race, and places black callers and white callers in separate rooms to make it easier to supervise callers who are using different scripts. There's no evidence that the black callers or the white callers are consistently placed in more or less comfortable rooms. When TPG isn't doing race-matched calling, it doesn't differentiate between black and white employees.

Shirley Ferrill, a black woman who was hired by TPG to call black voters, sued under 42 U.S.C. § 1981, which has been interpreted to bar race discrimination in assignment of job duties. Assume that § 1981 has been interpreted to treat discrimination based on perceived race—*i.e.*, based on a person's skin color, facial features, or voice, from which people are likely to infer a person's race—as race discrimination. Would TPG have a good First Amendment defense to the § 1981 claim? Should it? See *Ferrill v. Parker Group, Inc.*, 967 F. Supp. 472 (N.D. Ala. 1997).

e. Problem: The Boy Scouts v. Dale Dissent

Say that Justice Stevens's dissent in *Boy Scouts v. Dale* had prevailed, and the Boy Scouts had to admit Dale. The Boy Scouts then exclude another gay would-be scoutmaster, Kit Winter; when he sues, they argue: "During the *Dale* litigation, we repeatedly expressed the view that homosexuality is not 'clean' and 'morally straight.' The public now knows this is our official stance. We still prefer to talk more about what scouts should do, rather than what they shouldn't do, so we rarely expressly tell scouts that homosexuality is wrong. But our views are widely known.

"We are thus now entitled to an exemption—even if we weren't when *Dale* was decided—because Justice Stevens's opinion acknowledges that 'Surely there are instances in which an organization that truly aims to foster a belief at odds with the purposes of a State's antidiscrimination laws will have a First Amendment right to association that precludes forced compliance with those laws.' Our situation now is one such instance.

"Moreover, we think the Justices didn't pay enough attention to the following excerpt from the Boy Scout Handbook, pp. 527-28 (10th ed. 1990), which shows that we do indeed promote heterosexuality as the preferred way of living. The excerpt isn't fully quoted in any of the opinions, though Justice Stevens's opinion does quote a few sentences, see p. 407:"

SEXUAL RESPONSIBILITY

As you grow into manhood, your friendships will change. People around you are also changing. Girls you know are becoming young women. They are growing both physically and emotionally. Your relationships with them will become closer and more meaningful to you and to them.

You are maturing sexually, too. As a young man, you are capable of becoming a father. That is a profound responsibility with powerful consequences in your life and the lives of others. It is a responsibility that requires your very best judgment.

Sex is not the most important or most grown-up part of a relationship. Having sex is never a test of maturity. True manliness comes from accepting the responsibility for your actions ...:

- *Your responsibility to women....* You owe it to the women in your life to keep their best interests in mind. You can have a terrific time together enjoying life and growing emotionally. However, the difficulties created by a pregnancy can be enormous. Don't burden yourself and someone you care for with a child neither of you is ready to bear.

- *Your responsibility to children.* When you are fully grown and have become secure in yourself and in your relationship with another person, the two of you may decide to marry and have a child.... By waiting until you are thoroughly prepared to be parents, you can give your own child a close, loving family in which to grow.

- *Your responsibility to your beliefs.* For the followers of most religions, sex should take place only between married couples.... Abstinence until marriage is a very wise course of action....

If you have questions about growing up, about relationships, sex, or making good decisions, ask. Talk with your parents, religious leaders, teachers, or Scoutmaster.... Let them know your concerns.

Should the Scouts be free to exclude Winter, under Justice Stevens's opinion? If not, how much more must they say about homosexuality to satisfy Justice Stevens's requirements? See John C. O'Quinn, *"How Solemn Is the Duty of the Mighty Chief"*, 24 Harv. J.L. & Pub. Pol. 319 (2000).

f. California Democratic Party v. Jones, 530 U.S. 567 (2000)

Justice Scalia delivered the opinion of the Court.

[A.] This case presents the question whether the State of California may ... use a so-called "blanket" primary to determine a political party's nominee for the general election....

Until 1996, to determine the nominees of qualified parties California held what is known as a "closed" partisan primary, in which only persons who are members of the political party—*i.e.,* who have declared affiliation with that party when they register to vote—can vote on its nominee. In 1996 the citizens of California adopted by initiative Proposition 198. Promoted largely as a measure that would "weaken" party "hard-liners" and ease the way for "moderate problem-solvers" ([quoting the] ballot pamphlet distributed to voters), Proposition 198 changed California's partisan primary from a closed primary to a blanket primary.

Under the new system, "[a]ll persons entitled to vote, including those not affiliated with any political party, shall have the right to vote ... for any candidate regardless of the candidate's political affiliation." Whereas under the closed primary each voter received a ballot limited to candidates of his own party, as a result of Proposition 198 each voter's primary ballot now lists every candidate regardless of party affiliation and allows the voter to choose freely among them.... [T]he candidate of each party who wins the greatest number of votes "is the nominee of that party at the ensuing general election." ... [The California Democratic, Republican, Libertarian, and Peace and Freedom Parties allege] that California's blanket primary violated their First Amendment rights of association ....

[B.] States have a major role to play in structuring and monitoring the election process, including primaries.... [F]or example, ... a State may require parties to use the primary format for selecting their nominees, in order to assure that intraparty competition is resolved in a democratic fashion.

Similarly, in order to avoid burdening the general election ballot with frivolous candidacies, a State may require parties to demonstrate "a significant modicum of support" before allowing their candidates a place on that ballot.... [I]n order to prevent "party raiding"—a process in which dedicated members of one party formally switch to another party to alter the outcome of that party's primary—a State may require party registration a reasonable period of time before a primary election. {[And] when a State prescribes an election process that gives a special role to political parties, it "endorses, adopts and enforces the discrimination against Negroes" that the parties ... bring into the process—so that the parties' discriminatory action becomes state action under the Fifteenth Amendment.} ...

[But] the processes by which political parties select their nominees are [not] ... wholly public affairs that States may regulate freely. To the contrary, we have continually stressed that when States regulate parties' internal processes they must act within limits imposed by the Constitution.... [T]he First Amendment protects "the freedom to join together in furtherance of common political beliefs," which "necessarily presupposes the freedom to identify the people who constitute the association, and to limit the association to those people only." That is to say, a corollary of the right to associate is the right not to associate. "Freedom of association would prove an empty guarantee if associations could not limit control over their decisions to those who share the interests and persuasions that underlie the association's being.'"

In no area is the political association's right to exclude more important than in the process of selecting its nominee. That process often determines the party's positions on the most significant public policy issues of the day, and even when those positions are predetermined it is the nominee who becomes the party's ambassador to the general electorate in winning it over to the party's views. Some political parties—such as President Theodore Roosevelt's Bull Moose Party, the La Follette Progressives of 1924, the Henry Wallace Progressives of 1948, and the George Wallace American Independent Party of 1968—are virtually inseparable from their nominees (and tend not to outlast them)....

[Yet] Proposition 198 forces political parties to associate with—to have their nominees, and hence their positions, determined by—those who, at best, have refused to affiliate with the party, and, at worst, have expressly affiliated with a rival. In this respect, it is qualitatively different from a closed primary. Under that system, even when it is made quite easy for a voter to change his party affiliation the day of the primary, and thus, in some sense, to "cross over," at least he must formally *become a member of the party*; and once he does so, he is limited to voting for candidates of that party.

The evidence in this case demonstrates that under California's blanket primary system, the prospect of having a party's nominee determined by adherents of an opposing party is ... a clear and present danger. For example, in one 1997 survey of California voters 37 percent of Republicans said that they planned to vote in the 1998 Democratic gubernatorial primary, and 20 percent of Democrats said they planned to vote in the 1998 Republican United States Senate primary.... The impact of voting by nonparty members is much greater upon minor parties, such as the Libertarian Party and the Peace and Freedom Party. In the first primaries these parties conducted following California's implementation of Proposition 198, the total votes cast for party candidates in some races was more than *double* the total number of *registered party members*....

[And t]he 1997 survey of California voters revealed significantly different policy preferences between party members and primary voters who "crossed over" from another party. One expert went so far as to describe it as "inevitable [under Proposition 198] that parties will be forced in some circumstances to give their official designation to a candidate who's not preferred by a majority or even plurality of party members." ... [Even] a single election in which the party nominee is selected by nonparty members could be enough to destroy [or severely transform] the party....

In any event, the deleterious effects of Proposition 198 are not limited to altering the identity of the nominee. Even when the person favored by a majority of the party members prevails, he will have prevailed by taking somewhat different positions[to appeal to nonmembers]—and, should he be elected, will continue to take somewhat different positions in order to be *renominated*.... [T]he whole *purpose* of Proposition 198 was to favor nominees with "moderate" positions. It encourages candidates—and officeholders who hope to be renominated—to curry favor with persons whose views are more "centrist" than those of the party base....

[C.] [Because of this] heav[y] burden on a political party's associational freedom[,] Proposition 198 is ... unconstitutional unless it is narrowly tailored to serve a compelling state interest....

Respondents proffer seven state interests they claim are compelling. Two of them—producing elected officials who better represent the electorate and expanding candidate debate beyond the scope of partisan concerns—are simply circumlocution for producing nominees and nominee positions other than those the parties would choose if left to their own devices.... Respondents' third asserted compelling interest is that the blanket primary is the only way to ensure that {independents and members of the minority party in "safe" districts} persons enjoy the right ... to participate in what amounts to the determinative election—the majority party's primary .... But a "nonmember's desire to participate in the party's affairs is overborne by the countervailing and legitimate right of the party to determine its own membership qualifications." ...

[The asserted state interest in promoting fairness presumably addresses] the supposed inequity of not permitting nonparty members in "safe" districts to determine the party nominee. If that is unfair at all (rather than merely a consequence of the eminently democratic principle that—except where constitutional imperatives intervene—the majority rules), it seems to us less unfair than permitting nonparty members to hijack the party.

As for [the interest in] affording voters greater choice, it is obvious that the net effect of this scheme—indeed, its avowed purpose—is to *reduce* the scope of choice, by assuring a range of candidates who are all more "centrist." This may well be described as broadening the range of choices *favored by the majority*—but that is hardly a compelling state interest, if indeed it is even a legitimate one.

The interest in increasing voter participation is just a variation on the same theme (more choices favored by the majority will produce more voters), and suffers from the same defect.

[As to the asserted] privacy interest[,] ... [e]ven if (as seems unlikely) a scheme for administering a closed primary could not be devised in which the voter's declaration of party affiliation would not be public information, we do not think that the State's interest in assuring the privacy of this piece of information in all cases can conceivably be considered a "compelling" one....

Finally, ... even if all these state interests were compelling ones, Proposition 198 is not a narrowly tailored means of furthering them. Respondents could protect them all by resorting to a *nonpartisan* blanket primary. Generally speaking, under such a system, the State determines what qualifications it requires for a candidate to have a place on the primary ballot—which may include nomination by established parties and voter-petition requirements for independent candidates. Each voter, regardless of party affiliation, may then vote for any candidate, and the top two vote getters (or however many the State prescribes) then move on to the general election.

This system has all the characteristics of the partisan blanket primary, save the constitutionally crucial one: Primary voters are not choosing a party's nominee. Under a nonpartisan blanket primary, a State may ensure more choice, greater participation, increased "privacy," and a sense of "fairness"—all without severely burdening a political party's First Amendment right of association....

Justice Stevens, with whom Justice Ginsburg joins [in relevant part], dissenting....

[A.] A State's power to determine how its officials are to be elected is a quintessential attribute of sovereignty.... [But] the associational rights of political parties [as opposed to their rights to make endorsements or select a platform] are neither absolute nor as comprehensive as the rights enjoyed by wholly private associations.... [B]oth the general election and the primary are quintessential forms of state action.... The so-called "right not to associate" that the Court relies upon, then, is simply inapplicable to participation in a state election....

[Moreover], anyone can "join" a political party merely by asking for the appropriate ballot at the appropriate time or (at most) by registering within a state-defined reasonable period of time before an election; neither past voting history nor the voter's race, religion, or gender can provide a basis for the party's refusal to "associate" with an unwelcome new member. There is an obvious mismatch between a supposed constitutional right "not to associate" and a rule that turns on nothing more than the state-defined timing of the new associate's application for membership.... Assuming that a registered Democrat or independent who wants to vote in the Republican gubernatorial primary can do so merely by asking for a Republican ballot, the Republican Party's constitutional right "not to associate" is pretty feeble if the only cost it imposes on that Democrat or independent is a loss of his right to vote for non-Republican candidates for other offices....

It is not this Court's constitutional function to choose between the competing visions of what makes democracy work—party autonomy and discipline versus progressive inclusion of the entire electorate in the process of selecting their public officials—that are held by the litigants in this case. That choice belongs to the people.

[B.] Even if the "right not to associate" did authorize the Court to review the State's policy choice, its evaluation of the competing interests at stake is seriously flawed. For example, the Court's conclusion that a blanket primary severely burdens the parties' associational interests in selecting their standard-bearers does not appear to be borne out by experience with blanket primaries in Alaska and Washington.... [And] an empirically debatable assumption about the relative number and effect of likely crossover voters in a blanket primary, as opposed to an open primary or a nominally closed primary with only a brief preregistration requirement, is too thin a reed to support a credible First Amendment distinction.

On the other side of the balance, I would rank as "substantial, indeed compelling," just as the District Court did, California's interest in fostering democratic government by "[i]ncreasing the representativeness of elected officials, giving voters greater choice, and increasing voter turnout and participation in [electoral processes]." ... In an era of dramatically declining voter participation, States should be free to experiment with reforms designed to make the democratic process more robust by involving the entire electorate in the process of selecting those who will serve as government officials....

I would also give some weight to the First Amendment associational interests of nonmembers of a party seeking to participate in the primary process, to the fundamental right of such nonmembers to cast a meaningful vote for the candidate of their choice, and to the preference of almost 60% of California voters—including a majority of registered Democrats and Republicans—for a blanket primary. In my view, a State is unquestionably entitled to rely on this combination of interests in deciding who may vote in a primary election conducted by the State. It is indeed strange to find that the First Amendment forecloses this decision....

g. *Roberts v. U.S. Jaycees, 468 U.S. 609 (1984)*

Justice Brennan delivered the opinion of the Court....

[A.] The United States Jaycees ..., founded in 1920 as the Junior Chamber of Commerce, is a nonprofit membership corporation .... The objective of the Jaycees, as set out in its bylaws, is to pursue

> such educational and charitable purposes as will promote and foster the growth and development of young men's civic organizations in the United States, designed to inculcate in the individual membership of such organization a spirit of genuine Americanism and civic interest, and as a supplementary education institution to provide them with opportunity for personal development and achievement and an avenue for intelligent participation by young men in the affairs of their community, state and nation, and to develop true friendship and understanding among young men of all nations....

Regular membership is limited to young men between the ages of 18 and 35, while associate membership is available to individuals or groups ineligible for regular membership, principally women and older men. An associate member, whose dues are somewhat lower than those charged regular members, may not vote, hold local or national office, or participate in certain leadership training and awards programs.... At the time of trial in August 1981, the Jaycees had approximately 295,000 members in 7,400 local chapters .... There were at that time about 11,915 associate members [including about 6000 women]....

The national headquarters employs a staff to develop "program kits" for use by local chapters that are designed to enhance individual development, community development, and members' management skills. These materials include courses in public speaking and personal finances as well as community programs related to charity, sports, and public health.

The national office also makes available to members a range of personal products, including travel accessories, casual wear, pins, awards, and other gifts. The programs, products, and other activities of the organization are all regularly featured in publications made available to the membership, including a magazine entitled "Future." ...

[The] Minnesota Department of Human Rights ... [concluded] that the exclusion of women from full membership required by the national organization's bylaws violated the Minnesota Human Rights Act ..., which provides in part: "It is an unfair discriminatory practice ... [t]o deny any person the full and equal enjoyment of the goods, services, facilities, privileges, advantages, and accommodations of a place of public accommodation because of race, color, creed, religion, disability, national origin or sex." ....

[B.] Our decisions have referred to constitutionally protected "freedom of association" in two distinct senses[, intimate association and expressive association]....

[1.] [B]ecause the Bill of Rights is designed to secure individual liberty, it must afford the formation and preservation of certain kinds of highly personal relationships a substantial measure of sanctuary from unjustified interference by the State.... The personal affiliations that exemplify [this right] ..., and that therefore suggest some relevant limitations on the relationships that might be entitled to this sort of constitutional protection, are those that attend the creation and sustenance of a family—marriage; childbirth; the raising and education of children; and cohabitation with one's relatives. Family relationships, by their nature, involve deep attachments and commitments to the necessarily few other individuals with whom one shares not only a special community of thoughts, experiences, and beliefs but also distinctively personal aspects of one's life.

Among other things, therefore, they are distinguished by such attributes as relative smallness, a high degree of selectivity in decisions to begin and maintain the affiliation, and seclusion from others in critical aspects of the relationship. As a general matter, only relationships with these sorts of qualities are likely to reflect the considerations that have led to an understanding of freedom of association as an intrinsic element of personal liberty.... Accordingly, the Constitution undoubtedly imposes constraints on the State's power to control the selection of one's spouse that would not apply to regulations affecting the choice of one's fellow employees.... [The factors relevant to determining whether an intimate association claim exists] include size, purpose, policies, selectivity, congeniality, and other characteristics that in a particular case may be pertinent....

[T]he local chapters of the Jaycees are neither small nor selective. Moreover, much of the activity central to the formation and maintenance of the association involves the participation of strangers to that relationship. Accordingly, we conclude that the Jaycees chapters lack the distinctive characteristics that might afford constitutional [intimate association] protection to the decision of its members to exclude women....

[2.] An individual's freedom to speak, to worship, and to petition the government for the redress of grievances could not be vigorously protected from interference by the State unless a correlative freedom to engage in group effort toward those ends were not also guaranteed. According protection to collective effort on behalf of shared goals is especially important in preserving political and cultural diversity and in shielding dissident expression from suppression by the majority. Consequently, we have long understood as implicit in the right to engage in activities protected by the First Amendment a corresponding right to associate with others in pursuit of a wide variety of political, social, economic, educational, religious, and cultural ends.... [The Court labels this "expressive association."—ed.]

There can be no clearer example of an intrusion into the internal structure or affairs of an association than a regulation that forces the group to accept members it does not desire. Such a regulation may impair the ability of the original members to express only those views that brought them together. Freedom of association therefore plainly presupposes a freedom not to associate.

[C.] The right to associate for expressive purposes is not, however, absolute. Infringements on that right may be justified by regulations adopted to serve compelling state interests, unrelated to the suppression of ideas, that cannot be achieved through means significantly less restrictive of associational freedoms....

[The Minnesota] Act reflects the State's strong historical commitment to eliminating discrimination and assuring its citizens equal access to publicly available goods and services. That goal, which is unrelated to the suppression of expression, plainly serves compelling state interests of the highest order.... By prohibiting gender discrimination in places of public accommodation, the Minnesota Act protects the State's citizenry from a number of serious social and personal harms.

In the context of reviewing state actions under the Equal Protection Clause, this Court has frequently noted that discrimination based on archaic and overbroad assumptions about the relative needs and capacities of the sexes forces individuals to labor under stereotypical notions that often bear no relationship to their actual abilities. It thereby both deprives persons of their individual dignity and denies society the benefits of wide participation in political, economic, and cultural life....

Nor is the state interest in assuring equal access limited to the provision of purely tangible goods and services.... [T]he Minnesota court noted the various commercial programs and benefits offered to members and stated that "[l]eadership skills are 'goods,' [and] business contacts and employment promotions are 'privileges' and 'advantages'...." Assuring women equal access to such goods, privileges, and advantages clearly furthers compelling state interests.

Substantial Burden

[D.] In applying the Act to the Jaycees, the State has advanced those interests through the least restrictive means of achieving its ends. Indeed, the Jaycees has failed to demonstrate that the Act imposes any serious burdens on the male members' freedom of expressive association.

To be sure, ... a "not insubstantial part" of the Jaycees' activities constitutes protected expression on political, economic, cultural, and social affairs.... [T]he organization [has] taken public positions on a number of diverse issues, and members of the Jaycees regularly engage in a variety of civic, charitable, lobbying, fundraising, and other activities worthy of constitutional protection under the First Amendment.

There is, however, no basis in the record for concluding that admission of women as full voting members will impede the organization's ability to engage in these protected activities or to disseminate its preferred views. The Act requires no change in the Jaycees' creed of promoting the interests of young men, and it imposes no restrictions on the organization's ability to exclude individuals with ideologies or philosophies different from those of its existing members.

Moreover, the Jaycees already invites women to share the group's views and philosophy and to participate in much of its training and community activities. Accordingly, any claim that admission of women as full voting members will impair a symbolic message conveyed by the very fact that women are not permitted to vote is attenuated at best....

While acknowledging that "the specific content of most of the resolutions adopted over the years by the Jaycees has nothing to do with sex," the Court of Appeals nonetheless entertained the hypothesis that women members might have a different view or agenda with respect to these matters so that, if they are allowed to vote, "some change in the Jaycees' philosophical cast can reasonably be expected." It is similarly arguable that, insofar as the Jaycees is organized to promote the views of young men whatever those views happen to be, admission of women as voting members will change the message communicated by the group's speech because of the gender-based assumptions of the audience.

Generalizations

Neither supposition, however, is supported by the record. In claiming that women might have a different attitude about such issues as the federal budget, school prayer, voting rights, and foreign relations, or that the organization's public positions would have a different effect if the group were not "a purely young men's association," the Jaycees relies solely on unsupported generalizations about the relative interests and perspectives of men and women. Although such generalizations may or may not have a statistical basis in fact with respect to particular positions adopted by the Jaycees, we have repeatedly condemned legal decisionmaking that relies uncritically on such assumptions. In the absence of a showing far more substantial than that attempted by the Jaycees, we decline to indulge in the sexual stereotyping that underlies appellee's contention that, by allowing women to vote, application of the Minnesota Act will change the content or impact of the organization's speech.

[E.] In any event, even if enforcement of the Act causes some incidental abridgment of the Jaycees' protected speech, that effect is no greater than is necessary to accomplish the State's legitimate [and compelling] purposes.... In prohibiting [discriminatory] practices, the Minnesota Act therefore "responds precisely to the substantive problem which legitimately concerns" the State and abridges no more speech or associational freedom than is necessary to accomplish that purpose....

Justice O'Connor, [largely concurring as to intimate association] and concurring in the judgment [as to expressive association]....

[A.] The Court declares that the Jaycees' right of [expressive] association depends on the organization's making a "substantial" showing that the admission of unwelcome members "will change the message communicated by the group's speech." ... [But] would the Court's analysis of this case be different if, for example, the Jaycees membership had a steady history of opposing public issues thought (by the Court) to be favored by women? It might seem easy to conclude, in [such a] case, that the admission of women to the Jaycees' ranks would affect the content of the organization's message, but I do not believe that should change the outcome of this case. Whether an association is or is not constitutionally protected in the selection of its membership should not depend on what the association says or why its members say it....

[In my view], an association engaged exclusively in protected expression enjoys First Amendment protection of both the content of its message and the choice of its members.... Protection of the association's right to define its membership derives from the recognition that the formation of an expressive association is the creation of a voice, and the selection of members is the definition of that voice.... A ban on specific group voices on public affairs violates the most basic guarantee of the First Amendment—that citizens, not the government, control the content of public discussion.

Exclusively Exp. Assoc.

[B.] On the other hand, there is only minimal constitutional protection of the freedom of commercial association.... A shopkeeper has no constitutional right to deal only with persons of one sex....

[But] Comm. Org. ↳ Min Const. protec.

In my view, an association should be characterized as commercial, and therefore subject to rationally related state regulation of its membership and other associational activities, when, and only when, the association's activities are not predominantly of the type protected by the First Amendment. It is only when the association is predominantly engaged in protected expression that state regulation of its membership will necessarily affect, change, dilute, or silence one collective voice that would otherwise be heard.

An association must choose its market. Once it enters the marketplace of commerce in any substantial degree it loses the complete control over its membership that it would otherwise enjoy if it confined its affairs to the marketplace of ideas....

The purposes of an association, and the purposes of its members in adhering to it, are doubtless relevant in determining whether the association is primarily engaged in protected expression. Lawyering to advance social goals may be speech, but ordinary commercial law practice is not. A group boycott or refusal to deal for political purposes may be speech, *NAACP v. Claiborne Hardware Co.*, though a similar boycott for purposes of maintaining a cartel is not. Even the training of outdoor survival skills or participation in community service might become expressive when the activity is intended to develop good morals, reverence, patriotism, and a desire for self-improvement....

[C.] Notwithstanding its protected expressive activities, the Jaycees—otherwise known as the Junior Chamber of Commerce—is, first and foremost, an organization that, at both the national and local levels, promotes and practices the art of solicitation and management. The organization claims that the training it offers its members gives them an advantage in business, and business firms do indeed sometimes pay the dues of individual memberships for their employees.

Jaycees members hone their solicitation and management skills, under the direction and supervision of the organization, primarily through their active recruitment of new members. "One of the major activities of the Jaycees is the sale of memberships in the organization.... The Jaycees itself refers to its members as customers and membership as a product it is selling. More than 80 percent of the national officers' time is dedicated to recruitment, and more than half of the available achievement awards are in part conditioned on achievement in recruitment." ...

Recruitment and selling are commercial activities, even when conducted for training rather than for profit.... The State of Minnesota has a legitimate interest in ensuring nondiscriminatory access to the commercial opportunity presented by membership in the Jaycees. The members of the Jaycees may not claim constitutional immunity from Minnesota's antidiscrimination law by seeking to exercise their First Amendment rights through this commercial organization....

h. Boy Scouts of America v. Dale, 530 U.S. 640 (2000)

Chief Justice Rehnquist delivered the opinion of the Court....

[A.] James Dale entered Scouting in 1978 at the age of eight .... Dale became a Boy Scout in 1981 and remained a Scout until he turned 18. By all accounts, Dale was an exemplary Scout. In 1988, he achieved the rank of Eagle Scout, one of Scouting's highest honors. Dale applied for adult membership in the Boy Scouts in 1989. The Boy Scouts approved his application for the position of assistant scoutmaster of Troop 73.

Around the same time, Dale left home to attend Rutgers University. After arriving at Rutgers, Dale first acknowledged to himself and others that he is gay. He quickly became involved with, and eventually became the co-president of, the Rutgers University Lesbian/Gay Alliance. In 1990, Dale attended a seminar addressing the psychological and health needs of lesbian and gay teenagers.

A newspaper covering the event interviewed Dale about his advocacy of homosexual teenagers' need for gay role models.... [Shortly after] the newspaper published the interview[,] ... identifying him as the copresident of the Lesbian/Gay Alliance[,] ... [Dale's Boy Scouts membership was revoked on the grounds] that the Boy Scouts "specifically forbid membership to homosexuals." ...

[The New Jersey Supreme Court held that the Boy Scouts fit within the statutory definition of a place of public accommodation, and thus violated the New Jersey's statutory ban on discrimination on the basis of sexual orientation in places of public accommodation.—ed.]....

[B.] In *Roberts v. United States Jaycees,* we observed that "implicit in the right to engage in activities protected by the First Amendment" is "a corresponding right to associate with others in pursuit of a wide variety of political, social, economic, educational, religious, and cultural ends." This right is crucial in preventing the majority from imposing its views on groups that would rather express other, perhaps unpopular, ideas....

The forced inclusion of an unwanted person in a group infringes the group's freedom of expressive association if the presence of that person affects in a significant way the group's ability to advocate public or private viewpoints. But the freedom of expressive association, like many freedoms, is not absolute. We have held that the freedom could be overridden "by regulations adopted to serve compelling state interests, unrelated to the suppression of ideas, that cannot be achieved through means significantly less restrictive of associational freedoms." ...

Similar Test

[C.] The First Amendment's protection of expressive association is not reserved for advocacy groups. But to come within its ambit, a group must engage in some form of expression, whether it be public or private....

The Boy Scouts is a private, nonprofit organization. According to its mission statement:

> It is the mission of the Boy Scouts of America to serve others by helping to instill values in young people and, in other ways, to prepare them to make ethical choices over their lifetime in achieving their full potential.

The values we strive to instill are based on those found in the Scout Oath and Law:

Scout Oath

On my honor I will do my best
To do my duty to God and my country
and to obey the Scout Law;
To help other people at all times;
To keep myself physically strong,
mentally awake, and morally straight.

Scout Law

A Scout is:

Trustworthy	Obedient
Loyal	Cheerful
Helpful	Thrifty

Friendly	Brave
Courteous	Clean
Kind	Reverent.

Thus, the general mission of the Boy Scouts is clear: "[T]o instill values in young people." The Boy Scouts seeks to instill these values by having its adult leaders spend time with the youth members, instructing and engaging them in activities like camping, archery, and fishing. During the time spent with the youth members, the scoutmasters and assistant scoutmasters inculcate them with the Boy Scouts' values—both expressly and by example. It seems indisputable that an association that seeks to transmit such a system of values engages in expressive activity.

[D.] Given that the Boy Scouts engages in expressive activity, we must determine whether the forced inclusion of Dale as an assistant scoutmaster would significantly affect the Boy Scouts' ability to advocate public or private viewpoints. This inquiry necessarily requires us first to explore, to a limited extent, the nature of the Boy Scouts' view of homosexuality.

The values the Boy Scouts seeks to instill are "based on" those listed in the Scout Oath and Law. The Boy Scouts explains that the Scout Oath and Law provide "a positive moral code for living; they are a list of 'do's' rather than 'don'ts.'" The Boy Scouts asserts that homosexual conduct is inconsistent with the values embodied in the Scout Oath and Law, particularly with the values represented by the terms "morally straight" and "clean."

Obviously, the Scout Oath and Law do not expressly mention sexuality or sexual orientation. And the terms "morally straight" and "clean" are by no means self-defining. Different people would attribute to those terms very different meanings....

The New Jersey Supreme Court analyzed the Boy Scouts' beliefs and found that the "exclusion of members solely on the basis of their sexual orientation is inconsistent with Boy Scouts' commitment to a diverse and 'representative' membership ... [and] contradicts Boy Scouts' overarching objective to reach 'all eligible youth.'" The court concluded that the exclusion of members like Dale "appears antithetical to the organization's goals and philosophy." But ... it is not the role of the courts to reject a group's expressed values because they disagree with those values or find them internally inconsistent.... "[With] all expressions of First Amendment freedoms, the courts may not interfere on the ground that they view a particular expression as unwise or irrational."

The Boy Scouts asserts that it "teach[es] that homosexual conduct is not morally straight," and that it does "not want to promote homosexual conduct as a legitimate form of behavior." We accept the Boy Scouts' assertion. We need not inquire further to determine the nature of the Boy Scouts' expression with respect to homosexuality. But because the record before us contains written evidence of the Boy Scouts' viewpoint, we look to it as instructive, if only on the question of the sincerity of the professed beliefs.

A 1978 position statement to the Boy Scouts' Executive Committee, signed by ... the President of the Boy Scouts, and ... the Chief Scout Executive, expresses the Boy Scouts' "official position" with regard to "homosexuality and Scouting":

> Q. May an individual who openly declares himself to be a homosexual be a volunteer Scout leader?
>
> A. No. The Boy Scouts of America is a private, membership organization and leadership therein is a privilege and not a right. We do not believe that homosexuality and leadership in Scouting are appropriate. We will continue to select only those who in our judgment meet our standards and qualifications for leadership. ...

A position statement promulgated by the Boy Scouts in 1991 (after Dale's membership was revoked but before this litigation was filed) also supports its current view:

> We believe that homosexual conduct is inconsistent with the requirement in the Scout Oath that a Scout be morally straight and in the Scout Law that a Scout be clean in word and deed, and that homosexuals do not provide a desirable role model for Scouts.

This position statement was redrafted numerous times but its core message remained consistent.... [And t]he Boy Scouts publicly expressed its views with respect to homosexual conduct by its assertions in prior litigation. For example, throughout a California case with similar facts filed in the early 1980's, the Boy Scouts consistently asserted the same position with respect to homosexuality that it asserts today. We cannot doubt that the Boy Scouts sincerely holds this view.

[E.] We must then determine whether Dale's presence as an assistant scoutmaster would significantly burden the Boy Scouts' desire to not "promote homosexual conduct as a legitimate form of behavior." As we give deference to an association's assertions regarding the nature of its expression, we must also give deference to an association's view of what would impair its expression.

That is not to say that an expressive association can erect a shield against antidiscrimination laws simply by asserting that mere acceptance of a member from a particular group would impair its message. But here Dale, by his own admission, is one of a group of gay Scouts who have "become leaders in their community and are open and honest about their sexual orientation." Dale was the copresident of a gay and lesbian organization at college and remains a gay rights activist. Dale's presence in the Boy Scouts would, at the very least, force the organization to send a message, both to the youth members and the world, that the Boy Scouts accepts homosexual conduct as a legitimate form of behavior....

Here, we have found that the Boy Scouts believes that homosexual conduct is inconsistent with the values it seeks to instill in its youth members; it will not "promote homosexual conduct as a legitimate form of behavior." As the presence of GLIB in Boston's St. Patrick's Day parade [see *Hurley v. Irish-American Gay, Lesbian & Bisexual Group of Boston*] would have interfered with the parade organizers' choice not to propound a particular point of view, the presence of Dale as an assistant scoutmaster would just as surely interfere with the Boy Scouts' choice not to propound a point of view contrary to its beliefs.

The New Jersey Supreme Court determined that the Boy Scouts' ability to disseminate its message was not significantly affected by the forced inclusion of Dale as an assistant scoutmaster because of the following findings: "Boy Scout members do not associate for the purpose of disseminating the belief that homosexuality is immoral; Boy Scouts discourages its leaders from disseminating *any* views on sexual issues; and Boy Scouts includes sponsors and members who subscribe to different views in respect of homosexuality." We disagree with the New Jersey Supreme Court's conclusion drawn from these findings.

First, associations do not have to associate for the "purpose" of disseminating a certain message in order to be entitled to the protections of the First Amendment. An association must merely engage in expressive activity that could be impaired in order to be entitled to protection. For example, the purpose of the St. Patrick's Day parade in *Hurley* was not to espouse any views about sexual orientation, but we held that the parade organizers had a right to exclude certain participants nonetheless.

Second, even if the Boy Scouts discourages Scout leaders from disseminating views on sexual issues—a fact that the Boy Scouts disputes with contrary evidence—the First Amendment protects the Boy Scouts' method of expression. If the Boy Scouts wishes Scout leaders to avoid questions of sexuality and teach only by example, this fact does not negate the sincerity of its belief discussed above.

Third, the First Amendment simply does not require that every member of a group agree on every issue in order for the group's policy to be "expressive association." The Boy Scouts takes an official position with respect to homosexual conduct, and that is sufficient for First Amendment purposes.

In this same vein, Dale makes much of the claim that the Boy Scouts does not revoke the membership of heterosexual Scout leaders that openly disagree with the Boy Scouts' policy on sexual orientation. But if this is true, it is irrelevant. The presence of an avowed homosexual and gay rights activist in an assistant scoutmaster's uniform sends a distinctly different message from the presence of a heterosexual assistant scoutmaster who is on record as disagreeing with Boy Scouts policy. The Boy Scouts has a First Amendment right to choose to send one message but not the other. The fact that the organization does not trumpet its views from the housetops, or that it tolerates dissent within its ranks, does not mean that its views receive no First Amendment protection.

[F] We recognized in cases such as *Roberts* and *Board of Directors v. Rotary Club of Duarte*, 481 U.S. 537 (1987), that States have a compelling interest in eliminating discrimination against women in public accommodations. But in each of these cases we went on to conclude that the enforcement of these statutes would not materially interfere with the ideas that the organization sought to express.... [A]fter finding a compelling state interest, the Court went on to examine whether or not the application of the state law would impose any "serious burden" on the organization's rights of expressive association. So in these cases, the associational interest in freedom of expression has been set on one side of the scale, and the State's interest on the other.

Dale contends that we should apply the intermediate standard of review enunciated in *United States v. O'Brien* .... A law prohibiting the destruction of draft cards only incidentally affects the free speech rights of those who happen to use a violation of that law as a symbol of protest. But New Jersey's public accommodations law directly and immediately affects associational rights, in this case associational rights that enjoy First Amendment protection. Thus, *O'Brien* is inapplicable....

We have already concluded that a state requirement that the Boy Scouts retain Dale as an assistant scoutmaster would significantly burden the organization's right to oppose or disfavor homosexual conduct. The state interests embodied in New Jersey's public accommodations law do not justify such a severe intrusion on the Boy Scouts' rights to freedom of expressive association. That being the case, we hold that the First Amendment prohibits the State from imposing such a requirement through the application of its public accommodations law....

[G.] [H]omosexuality has gained greater societal acceptance [in recent years]. But this is scarcely an argument for denying First Amendment protection to those who refuse to accept these views.... [T]hat an idea may be embraced and advocated by increasing numbers of people is all the more reason to protect the First Amendment rights of those who wish to voice a different view....

[W]e must not be[] guided by our views of whether the Boy Scouts' teachings with respect to homosexual conduct are right or wrong; public or judicial disapproval of a tenet of an organization's expression does not justify the State's effort to compel the organization to accept members where such acceptance would derogate from the organization's expressive message. "While the law is free to promote all sorts of conduct in place of harmful behavior, it is not free to interfere with speech for no better reason than promoting an approved message or discouraging a disfavored one, however enlightened either purpose may strike the government." *Hurley*....

Justice Stevens, with whom Justice Souter, Justice Ginsburg and Justice Breyer join, dissenting....

[A.] [The New Jersey] law does not "impos[e] any serious burdens" on BSA's "collective effort on behalf of [its] shared goals," *Roberts*, nor does it force BSA to communicate any message that it does not wish to endorse. New Jersey's law, therefore, abridges no constitutional right of BSA....

[A] State's antidiscrimination law does not violate a group's right to associate simply because the law conflicts with that group's exclusionary membership policy. *Roberts*; *Rotary Club*.... Several principles are made perfectly clear by *Roberts* and *Rotary Club*.

First, to prevail on a claim of expressive association in the face of a

State's antidiscrimination law, it is not enough simply to engage in *some kind* of expressive activity. Both the Jaycees and the Rotary Club engaged in expressive activity protected by the First Amendment, yet that fact was not dispositive.

Second, it is not enough to adopt an openly avowed exclusionary membership policy. Both the Jaycees and the Rotary Club did that as well.

Third, it is not sufficient merely to articulate *some* connection between the group's expressive activities and its exclusionary policy. The Rotary Club, for example, justified its male-only membership policy by pointing to the "aspect of fellowship ... that is enjoyed by the [exclusively] male membership" and by claiming that only with an exclusively male membership could it "operate effectively" in foreign countries.

Rather, in *Jaycees,* we asked whether Minnesota's Human Rights Law requiring the admission of women "impose[d] any *serious burdens*" on the group's "collective effort on behalf of [its] *shared goals.*" Notwithstanding the group's obvious publicly stated exclusionary policy, we did not view the inclusion of women as a "serious burden" on the Jaycees' ability to engage in the protected speech of its choice. Similarly, in *Rotary Club,* we asked whether California's law would "affect in any *significant way* the existing members' ability" to engage in their protected speech, or whether the law would require the clubs "to abandon their *basic goals.*"

The relevant question is whether the mere inclusion of the person at issue would "impose any serious burden," "affect in any significant way," or be "a substantial restraint upon" the organization's "shared goals," "basic goals," or "collective effort to foster beliefs." Accordingly, it is necessary to examine what, exactly, are BSA's shared goals and the degree to which its expressive activities would be burdened, affected, or restrained by including homosexuals.

[B.] The evidence before this Court makes it exceptionally clear that BSA has, at most, simply adopted an exclusionary membership policy and has no shared goal of disapproving of homosexuality. BSA's mission statement and federal charter say nothing on the matter; its official membership policy is silent; its Scout Oath and Law—and accompanying definitions—are devoid of any view on the topic; its guidance for Scouts and Scoutmasters on sexuality declare that such matters are "not construed to be Scouting's proper area," but are the province of a Scout's parents and pastor; and BSA's posture respecting religion tolerates a wide variety of views on the issue of homosexuality.

Moreover, there is simply no evidence that BSA otherwise teaches anything in this area, or that it instructs Scouts on matters involving homosexuality in ways not conveyed in the Boy Scout or Scoutmaster Handbooks. In short, Boy Scouts of America is simply silent on homosexuality. There is no shared goal or collective effort to foster a belief about homosexuality at all—let alone one that is significantly burdened by admitting homosexuals. As in *Jaycees,* there is "no basis in the record for concluding that admission of [homosexuals] will impede the [Boy Scouts'] ability to engage in [its] protected activities or to disseminate its preferred views" and New Jersey's law "requires no change in [BSA's] creed." And like *Rotary Club,* New Jersey's law "does not require [BSA] to abandon or alter any of" its activities.

The evidence relied on by the Court is not to the contrary. The undisclosed 1978 policy certainly adds nothing to the actual views disseminated to the Scouts. It simply says that homosexuality is not "appropriate."

There is no reason to give that policy statement more weight than Rotary International's assertion that all-male membership fosters the group's "fellowship" and was the only way it could "operate effectively." As for BSA's postrevocation statements, at most they simply adopt a policy of discrimination, which is no more dispositive than the openly discriminatory policies held insufficient in *Jaycees* and *Rotary Club*; there is no evidence here that BSA's policy was necessary to—or even a part of—BSA's expressive activities or was every taught to Scouts.

Equally important is BSA's failure to adopt any clear position on homosexuality. BSA's temporary, though ultimately abandoned, view that homosexuality is incompatible with being "morally straight" and "clean" [(while the 1991 and 1992 statements tried to tie BSA's exclusionary policy to the meaning of the Scout Oath and Law, the 1993 statement abandoned that effort)] is a far cry from the clear, unequivocal statement necessary to prevail on its claim.

{It is plain as the light of day that neither one of these principles—"morally straight" and "clean"—says the slightest thing about homosexuality. Indeed, neither term in the Boy Scouts' Law and Oath expresses any position whatsoever on sexual matters.

BSA's published guidance on that topic underscores this point. Scouts, for example, are directed to receive their sex education at home or in school, but not from the organization: "Your parents or guardian or a sex education teacher should give you the facts about sex that you must know." Boy Scout Handbook (1992). To be sure, Scouts are not forbidden from asking their Scoutmaster about issues of a sexual nature, but Scoutmasters are, literally, the last person Scouts are encouraged to ask: "If you have questions about growing up, about relationships, sex, or making good decisions, ask. Talk with your parents, religious leaders, teachers, or Scoutmaster."}

Despite the solitary sentences in the 1991 and 1992 policies, the group continued to disclaim any single religious or moral position as a general matter and actively eschewed teaching any lesson on sexuality. It also continued to define "morally straight" and "clean" in the Boy Scout and Scoutmaster Handbooks without any reference to homosexuality....

[A] group [ought not] prevail on a right to expressive association if it, effectively, speaks out of both sides of its mouth. A State's antidiscrimination law does not impose a "serious burden" or a "substantial restraint" upon the group's "shared goals" if the group itself is unable to identify its own stance with any clarity.

[C.] The majority pretermits this entire analysis. It finds that BSA in fact "teach[es] that homosexual conduct is not morally straight." This conclusion, remarkably, rests entirely on statements in BSA's briefs.

Moreover, the majority insists that we must "give deference to an association's assertions regarding the nature of its expression" and "we must also give deference to an association's view of what would impair its expression." So long as the record "contains written evidence" to support a group's bare assertion, "[w]e need not inquire further." Once the organization "asserts" that it engages in particular expression, "[w]e cannot doubt" the truth of that assertion.

This is an astounding view of the law. I am unaware of any previous instance in which our analysis of the scope of a constitutional right was determined by looking at what a litigant asserts in his or her brief and inquiring no further....

An organization can adopt the message of its choice, and it is not this Court's place to disagree with it. But we must inquire whether the group is, in fact, expressing a message (whatever it may be) and whether that message (if one is expressed) is significantly affected by a State's antidiscrimination law. More critically, that inquiry requires our *independent* analysis, rather than deference to a group's litigating posture....

Surely there are instances in which an organization that truly aims to foster a belief at odds with the purposes of a State's antidiscrimination laws will have a First Amendment right to association that precludes forced compliance with those laws. But ... [t]o prevail in asserting a right of expressive association as a defense to a charge of violating an antidiscrimination law, the organization must at least show it has adopted and advocated an unequivocal position inconsistent with a position advocated or epitomized by the person whom the organization seeks to exclude.

If this Court were to defer to whatever position an organization is prepared to assert in its briefs, there would be no way to mark the proper boundary between genuine exercises of the right to associate, on the one hand, and sham claims that are simply attempts to insulate nonexpressive private discrimination, on the other hand. Shielding a litigant's claim from judicial scrutiny would, in turn, render civil rights legislation a nullity, and turn this important constitutional right into a farce....

There is, of course, a valid concern that a court's independent review may run the risk of paying too little heed to an organization's sincerely held views. But unless one is prepared to turn the right to associate into a free pass out of antidiscrimination laws, an independent inquiry is a necessity. Though the group must show that its expressive activities will be substantially burdened by the State's law, if that law truly has a significant effect on a group's speech, even the subtle speaker will be able to identify that impact. In this case, no such concern is warranted. It is entirely clear that BSA in fact expresses no clear, unequivocal message burdened by New Jersey's law.

[D.] Even if BSA's right to associate argument fails, it nonetheless might have a First Amendment right to refrain from including debate and dialogue about homosexuality as part of its mission to instill values in Scouts.... The majority ... contends that Dale's mere presence among the Boy Scouts will itself force the group to convey a message about homosexuality—even if Dale has no intention of doing so. The majority holds that "[t]he presence of an avowed homosexual and gay rights activist in an assistant scout-master's uniform sends a distinc[t] ... message," and, accordingly, BSA is entitled to exclude that message.... "Dale's presence in the Boy Scouts would, at the very least, force the organization to send a message, both to the youth members and the world, that the Boy Scouts accepts homosexual conduct as a legitimate form of behavior." ...

Though *Hurley*[, on which the majority heavily relies,] has a superficial similarity to the present case, a close inspection reveals a wide gulf between that case and the one before us today. First, it was critical to our analysis that GLIB was actually conveying a message by participating in the parade—otherwise, the parade organizers could hardly claim that they were being forced to include any unwanted message at all.... Second, we found it relevant that GLIB's message "would likely be perceived" as the parade organizers' own speech....

Dale's inclusion in the Boy Scouts is nothing like the case in *Hurley*. His participation sends no cognizable message to the Scouts or to the world. Unlike GLIB, Dale did not carry a banner or a sign; he did not distribute any fact sheet; and he expressed no intent to send any message....

The only apparent explanation for the majority's holding, then, is that homosexuals are simply so different from the rest of society that their presence alone—unlike any other individual's—should be singled out for special First Amendment treatment. Under the majority's reasoning, an openly gay male is irreversibly affixed with the label "homosexual." That label, even though unseen, communicates a message that permits his exclusion wherever he goes. His openness is the sole and sufficient justification for his ostracism.

Though unintended, reliance on such a justification is tantamount to a constitutionally prescribed symbol of inferiority. As counsel for the BSA remarked, Dale "put a banner around his neck when he ... got himself into the newspaper.... He created a reputation.... He can't take that banner off. He put it on himself and, indeed, he has continued to put it on himself." ...

[E.] Unfavorable opinions about homosexuals "have ancient roots." Like equally atavistic opinions about certain racial groups, those roots have been nourished by sectarian doctrine. Over the years, however, interaction with real people, rather than mere adherence to traditional ways of thinking about members of unfamiliar classes, have modified those opinions....

[S]uch prejudices are still prevalent and ... they have caused serious and tangible harm to countless members of the class New Jersey seeks to protect .... That harm can only be aggravated by the creation of a constitutional shield for a policy that is itself the product of a habitual way of thinking about strangers. As Justice Brandeis so wisely advised, "we must be ever on our guard, lest we erect our prejudices into legal principles." If we would guide by the light of reason, we must let our minds be bold....

i.   *Rumsfeld v. FAIR, 547 U.S. 47 (2006)*

[For the facts, see p. 220.—ed.]

Chief Justice Roberts delivered the [unanimous] opinion of the Court....

[A.] FAIR argues that the Solomon Amendment violates law schools' freedom of expressive association. According to FAIR, law schools' ability to express their message that discrimination on the basis of sexual orientation is wrong is significantly affected by the presence of military recruiters on campus and the schools' obligation to assist them....

To comply with the statute, law schools must allow military recruiters on campus and assist them in whatever way the school chooses to assist other employers. Law schools therefore "associate" with military recruiters in the sense that they interact with them.

But recruiters are not part of the law school. Recruiters are, by definition, outsiders who come onto campus for the limited purpose of trying to hire students—not to become members of the school's expressive association. This distinction is critical.

Unlike the public accommodations law in *Boy Scouts of Am. v. Dale*, the Solomon Amendment does not force a law school "'to accept members it does not desire.'" The law schools *say* that allowing military recruiters equal access impairs their own expression by requiring them to associate with the recruiters, but ... a speaker cannot "erect a shield" against laws requiring access "simply by asserting" that mere association "would impair its message." ...

[But t]he Solomon Amendment has no ... [such] effect on a law school's associational rights. Students and faculty are free to associate to voice their disapproval of the military's message; nothing about the statute affects the composition of the group by making group membership less desirable.... A military recruiter's mere presence on campus [therefore] does not violate a law school's right to associate, regardless of how repugnant the law school considers the recruiter's message.

[B.] [T]he freedom of expressive association ... [also prohibits laws that do not] directly interfere with an organization's composition, ... [but make] group membership less attractive, raising the same First Amendment concerns about affecting the group's ability to express its message. [T]he freedom of expressive association protects more than just a group's membership decisions. For example, we have held laws unconstitutional that require disclosure of membership lists for groups seeking anonymity, *Brown v. Socialist Workers '74 Campaign Comm.*, or impose penalties or withhold benefits based on membership in a disfavored group. Although these laws did not directly interfere with an organization's composition, they made group membership less attractive, raising the same First Amendment concerns about affecting the group's ability to express its message.

The Solomon Amendment has no similar effect on a law school's associational rights. Students and faculty are free to associate to voice their disapproval of the military's message; nothing about the statute affects the composition of the group by making group membership less desirable.

C. COERCED DISCLOSURE OF SPEAKERS' AND MEMBERS' IDENTITIES

1. SUMMARY

a. Policy Reasons _for_ Constitutional Restraints on _Forced_ Disclosure

Requiring that speakers, group members, or political contributors identify themselves does not itself ban the expression of any ideas. But it does affect speech in two ways.

First, requiring that the speakers' name be included in a statement—for instance, a requirement that all leaflets be signed—bans a particular form of statement: the anonymous leaflet. See, _e.g._, _McIntyre v. Ohio Elections Comm'n_ (1995) (p. 441); _Citizens United v. FEC_ (2010) (p. 446).

Second, even if the name must be disclosed somewhere other than on the statement (for instance, in a separate report that must be filed with the government), requiring such disclosure can deter people from speaking, joining groups, or contributing to causes. People might fear that, if they're identified, they'll face (a) violence, (b) governmental retaliation (say, by the police or by various administrative agencies), (c) retaliation by their employers or prospective business partners, (d) social ostracism, or (e) just a strain on their relationships with acquaintances, neighbors, fellow church members, classmates, colleagues, friends, or family members.

As a result, disclosure might make people less inclined to express themselves on controversial issues, unless they can be assured of confidentiality. And this can mean a substantial loss for discussion even if the potential consequences for the speaker are slight.

The development of the Internet exacerbates the risk of retaliation—and the possible deterrent effect on political activity—since formerly obscure records are now easily available. An employer Googling a prospective employee might see the employee's contribution records even if he hadn't been specifically looking for them. Political activists can also easily create maps pointing to the homes of all contributors to some cause, which happened as to the California anti-same-sex-marriage Proposition 8.

At the same time, learning speakers', group members', and political contributors' identities can be valuable. It can help the investigation of crimes or of civil wrongs; it can help deter bribery; it can help inform the public about who is supporting various candidates and ballot proposals; and more. The question in this unit is how First Amendment law reconciles all these concerns.

b.   The General Rule

Mandated disclosure of the identities of speakers, group members, or contributors generally violates the First Amendment, unless the regulation passes "exacting scrutiny." "Exacting scrutiny" "'requires a 'substantial relation' between the disclosure requirement and a 'sufficiently important' governmental interest.' To withstand this scrutiny, 'the strength of the governmental interest must reflect the seriousness of the actual burden on First Amendment rights.'" *Doe v. Reed* (2010) (p. 450); *Citizens United v. FEC* (2010) (p. 446). Exacting scrutiny seems to be something between intermediate scrutiny and strict scrutiny, though it's not clear how much such labels mean in this context. Rather, what this test means can be seen only by how it has been applied:

1. It is generally unconstitutional **to require that a statement include the author's or funder's name**, or that speakers identify themselves while speaking. *McIntyre v. Ohio Elections Comm'n* (1995) (p. 441) (ban on anonymous leaflets about ballot measures); *Talley v. California*, 362 U.S. 60 (1960) (ban on anonymous leaflets generally); *Buckley v. American Constitutional Law Foundation*, 525 U.S. 182 (1999) (requirement that initiative signature gatherers wear name tags).

   — Exception: It is constitutional to impose such a requirement limited to expensive paid-for speech (television ads) about political candidates. *Citizens United v. FEC* (2010) (p. 488).

2. It is generally unconstitutional **to require that a group disclose its members or contributors to the government**, or that a person likewise disclose which groups he belongs or contributes to. *NAACP v. Alabama ex rel. Patterson* (1958) (p. 417); *Shelton v. Tucker* (1960) (p. 420); *Gibson v. Florida Legis. Investig. Comm.*, 372 U.S. 539 (1963).

   — Exception: It is generally constitutional to require such disclosures of the identity of people who contribute money for election-related speech. This is true for contributions to candidates, to independent committees that advocate for or against candidates, or to committees that advocate for or against ballot measures. *Citizens United*; *Buckley v. Valeo* (1976) (p. 438); see also the discussion of *Buckley v. Valeo* in *McIntyre*; *Citizens Against Rent Control/Coalition for Fair Housing v. City of Berkeley*, 454 U.S. 290, 299-300 (1981).

3. It is generally constitutional for the government **to disclose the identity of people who have signed referendum petitions**, and presumably also initiative, recall, and candidate qualification petitions. *Doe v. Reed* (2010) (p. 450).

4. The government interests involved:

   — The Court has generally held that the interests in preventing and uncovering corruption, the appearance of corruption, fraud, and election officials' errors are "sufficiently important" to justify disclosure. *Buckley v. Valeo*; *Doe v. Reed*.

   — *McIntyre* held that the interest in providing more information to the public about who is backing a particular proposal is not "sufficiently important." But *Citizens United* held that this interest is indeed "sufficiently important," at least as to spending related to candidates.

5. Even when disclosure requirements are generally constitutional on their face, they may be challenged on an as-applied basis. The government must give exemptions from the requirements when challengers can show that their supporters (*e.g.*, contributors or petition signers) would face substantial retaliation for their speech, signature, or contribution. *Brown v. Socialist Workers '74 Campaign Comm.* (1982) (p. 458); *Doe v. Reed* (2010) (p. 460). But it's not clear just how much of a showing, and of how substantial a retaliation, is required.

c. **Exception:** *Forced Disclosure in Criminal or Civil Litigation*

In one area, the Court has been much more open to compelled disclosure of identity: when it happens through the normal criminal or civil justice process, for instance when (a) a grand jury orders a reporter to testify about the name of a source (*Branzburg v. Hayes* (1972) (p. 423)) or (b) an administrative agency investigates a discrimination complaint and seeks confidential evaluations that also contain the names of the evaluations' authors (*University of Pennsylvania v. EEOC* (1990) (p. 432)).

1. Here, the Court has expressly rejected strict scrutiny, and likely "exacting scrutiny" as well.

2. Many (but not all) lower courts have read Justice Powell's *Branzburg* concurrence as giving journalists a qualified privilege to refuse to testify about their confidential sources. Those courts have also generally concluded that this privilege can be overcome only if the journalists' testimony would be quite relevant (beyond just the lax standards of relevance required for normal subpoenas), and the information would not be reasonably available through other means. *See, e.g.*, *United States v. LaRouche Campaign*, 841 F.2d 1176 (1st Cir. 1988); *Silkwood v. Kerr-McGee Corp.*, 563 F.2d 433 (10th Cir. 1977); *but see, e.g.*, *In re Grand Jury Subpoena, Judith Miller*, 397 F.3d 964 (D.C. Cir. 2005) (reading *Branzburg* as rejecting such a privilege).

— This is odd, because Justice Powell joined the majority opinion, and that majority opinion—which generally rejects any special privilege for journalists—would normally be seen as controlling, without regard for any concurrences. Moreover, Justice Powell's concurrence specifically *refused* to adopt the dissent's proposed test, and the lower courts' test that I describe above is much like the dissent's test. (What test Justice Powell would adopt is not clear; read his opinion and decide for yourselves.) But in any event, many lower courts do cite Justice Powell's opinion as justifying the test described in the previous paragraph.

— Some state statutes and state constitutional provisions (see p. 432) do give the media special privileges, including in some instances a privilege not to testify.

— *Branzburg* and *University of Pennsylvania* involved anonymous speakers speaking in private (to the journalist or to members of the committees deciding whether to give a professor tenure). Nonetheless, their speech also helped influence the listeners' public speech—the journalist's news story and the university's teaching and scholarly output.

d. Discovery of Civil Defendants' Identities

In recent years, many lower court cases have dealt with plaintiffs issuing subpoenas to Internet Service Providers (ISPs) when trying to unmask anonymous online speakers whom the plaintiffs are suing. (The lawsuits are generally based on causes of action such as libel, breach of confidentiality agreement, and so on.)

Plaintiffs might legitimately need such subpoenas to vindicate their rights: You can't sue someone for libel—even if the statement is definitely libelous—if you don't know who the defendant is. But the subpoenas may also be used to retaliate against speakers whose speech is constitutionally protected: For instance, a plaintiff company might unmask a commenter who turns out to be a company employee, and then fire the employee even though the speech was not libelous or otherwise unprotected.

Courts have generally said that such subpoenas can be enforced when the complaint "set[s] forth a prima facie cause of action" that "can withstand a motion to dismiss for failure to state a claim upon which relief can be granted," and the plaintiff can provide "sufficient evidence supporting each element of its cause of action." See, *e.g.*, *Dendrite Int'l, Inc. v. Doe Number 3*, 775 A.2d 756 (N.J. Ct. App. 2001); *Mortgage Specialists, Inc. v. Implode-Explode Heavy Industries, Inc.*, 999 A.2d 184 (N.H. 2010).

Thus, for instance, say that a plaintiff is suing an anonymous online speaker for libel, and wants to use a subpoena to uncover the speaker's identity. The plaintiff must then show that the statements are factual assertions—rather than pure opinion—and introduce some evidence that they are false. If the plaintiff shows this, then the ISP can be ordered to comply with the subpoena, since otherwise the plaintiff would be unable to litigate a possibly meritorious case. But if the plaintiff can't show it, for instance because the speech is pure opinion, then the subpoena would not be enforced, and the ISP may keep the speaker's identity confidential. (The plaintiff need not show that the speaker was speaking with "actual malice" or "negligence," whichever test is required, since a plaintiff can't do that until the speaker is identified.)

2. Government Investigations

a. Problem: Discovery

The ACLU sues its building contractor over a dispute related to construction of its new building. The contractor is concerned that some of the ACLU's witnesses and some prospective jurors may be ACLU members, and thus biased in favor of the ACLU; the contractor's lawyer therefore demands that the ACLU turn over its membership lists, so he can check them as to each potential witness and prospective juror. In voir dire and at trial, he also asks all witnesses and prospective jurors whether they are or have been members of the ACLU. (Assume that under the rules of evidence a witness's organizational affiliations is admissible as evidence of bias, see, *e.g.*, Fed. R. Evid. 610 advisory committee's note. Assume also that jurors can be challenged peremptorily or perhaps even for cause based on their membership in an organization that is a party to the litigation.)

The ACLU refuses to turn over the membership list, and the witnesses and prospective jurors refuse to answer the questions, on freedom of association grounds. What arguments can be made for and against the freedom of association claim? Cf. *Britt v. Superior Court,* 574 P.2d 766 (Cal. 1978).

b. Problem: Employment

The University of California was sued for race discrimination by a black employee who claimed that his white manager refused to promote him because of the employee's race. At the trial, the employee introduced evidence that the white manager was a member of the National Association for the Advancement of White People, a group that reportedly harbors racist tendencies. The evidence was admitted, and the jury concluded that the manager did indeed discriminate based on race.

When the University's lawyers interviewed the jurors, many jurors said the manager's NAAWP membership played a big role in their decision, since discrimination cases are so focused on the decisionmaker's motivation. The University had to pay $1 million in damages, and suffered much adverse publicity.

Once bitten and thus twice shy, the University enacted a new policy of asking all new management employees and faculty members for the names of all the groups they belong to "that advocate the doctrine of the superiority or inferiority of any race, sex, ethnicity, religion, or sexual orientation." The University says it won't refuse to hire or promote anyone because of the information they reveal; but it hopes this information will let it more closely scrutinize managers' decisions, and perhaps take a second look at, say, NAAWP members' refusals to hire blacks. The University says it will, however, fire anyone who answers the group membership question falsely or incompletely. Is the University's policy constitutional?

c. NAACP v. Alabama ex rel. Patterson, 357 U.S. 449 (1958)

Justice Harlan delivered the opinion of the Court....

[A.] Alabama has a statute similar to those of many other States which requires [an out-of-state] corporation ... to qualify before doing business by filing its corporate charter with the Secretary of State and designating a place of business and an agent to receive service of process. The statute imposes a fine on a corporation transacting intrastate business before qualifying and provides for criminal prosecution of officers of such a corporation....

In 1956 the Attorney General of Alabama [sued] ... to enjoin the

[NAACP] from conducting further activities within ... the State. Among other things the [suit] alleged that the Association had[, without complying with the qualification statute,] opened a regional office and had organized various affiliates in Alabama; had recruited members and solicited contributions within the State; had given financial support and furnished legal assistance to Negro students seeking admission to the state university; and had supported a Negro boycott of the bus lines in Montgomery to compel the seating of passengers without regard to race....

Petitioner demurred[,] contend[ing] that its activities did not subject it to the qualification requirements of the statute .... [T]he State moved for the production of a large number of the Association's records and papers, including bank statements, leases, deeds, and records containing the names and addresses of all Alabama "members" and "agents" of the Association. It alleged that all such documents were necessary for adequate preparation for the hearing, in view of petitioner's denial of the conduct of intrastate business within the meaning of the qualification statute. Over petitioner's objections, the court ordered the production of a substantial part of the requested records, including the membership lists ....

[**B.**] Effective advocacy of both public and private points of view, particularly controversial ones, is undeniably enhanced by group association, as this Court has more than once recognized by remarking upon the close nexus between the freedoms of speech and assembly.... [F]reedom to engage in association for the advancement of beliefs and ideas is an inseparable aspect of the "liberty" assured by the Due Process Clause of the Fourteenth Amendment, which embraces freedom of speech.... [S]tate action which may have the effect of curtailing the freedom to associate is subject to the closest scrutiny.

The fact that Alabama, so far as is relevant to the validity of the contempt judgment presently under review, has taken no direct action to restrict the right of petitioner's members to associate freely, does not end inquiry into the effect of the production order.... [A]bridgement of [the rights of free speech, press, and association], even though unintended, may inevitably follow from varied forms of governmental action....

Inviolability of privacy in group association may in many circumstances be indispensable to preservation of freedom of association, particularly where a group espouses dissident beliefs.... [In this case, p]etitioner has made an uncontroverted showing that on past occasions revelation of the identity of its rank-and-file members has exposed these members to economic reprisal, loss of employment, threat of physical coercion, and other manifestations of public hostility.... [C]ompelled disclosure of petitioner's Alabama membership is likely to affect adversely the ability of petitioner and its members to pursue their collective effort to foster beliefs which they admittedly have the right to advocate, in that it may induce members to withdraw from the Association and dissuade others from joining it because of fear of exposure of their beliefs shown through their associations and of the consequences of this exposure.

It is not sufficient to answer, as the State does here, that whatever repressive effect compulsory disclosure of names of petitioner's members may have upon participation by Alabama citizens in petitioner's activities follows not from *state* action but from *private* community pressures. The crucial factor is the interplay of governmental and private action, for it is only after the initial exertion of state power represented by the production order that private action takes hold.

[C.] We turn to the final question whether Alabama has demonstrated [a compelling] interest in obtaining the disclosures it seeks from petitioner which is sufficient to justify the deterrent effect which we have concluded these disclosures may well have on the free exercise by petitioner's members of their constitutionally protected right of association....

[P]etitioner asserts no right to absolute immunity from state investigation, and no right to disregard Alabama's laws.... Petitioner has not objected to divulging the identity of its members who are employed by or hold official positions with it. It has urged the rights solely of its ordinary rank-and-file members. This is therefore not analogous to a case involving the interest of a State in protecting its citizens in their dealings with paid solicitors or agents of foreign corporations by requiring identifications.

Whether there was "justification" in this instance turns solely on the substantiality of Alabama's interest in obtaining the membership lists.... [T]he State's [avowed] reason for requesting the membership lists ... was to determine whether petitioner was conducting intrastate business in violation of the Alabama foreign corporation registration statute, and the membership lists were expected to help resolve this question....

[W]e are unable to perceive that the disclosure of the names of petitioner's rank-and-file members has a substantial bearing on ... [this]. As matters stand in the state court, petitioner (1) has admitted its presence and conduct of activities in Alabama since 1918; (2) has offered to comply in all respects with the state qualification statute, although preserving its contention that the statute does not apply to it; and (3) has apparently complied satisfactorily with the production order, except for the membership lists, by furnishing the Attorney General with varied business records, its charter and statement of purposes, the names of all of its directors and officers, and with the total number of its Alabama members and the amount of their dues. These last items would not on this record appear subject to constitutional challenge and have been furnished, but whatever interest the State may have in obtaining names of ordinary members has not been shown to be sufficient to overcome petitioner's constitutional objections to the production order....

New York ex rel. Bryant v. Zimmerman, 278 U.S. 63 (1928), cannot be relied on in support of the State's position, for that case involved markedly different considerations in terms of the interest of the State in obtaining disclosure. There, this Court upheld as applied to a member of a local chapter of the Ku Klux Klan, a ... statute requiring any unincorporated association which demanded an oath as a condition to membership to file with state officials copies of its "... constitution, by-laws, rules, regulations and oath of membership, together with a roster of its membership and a list of its officers for the current year." ...

The decision was based on the particular character of the Klan's activities, involving acts of unlawful intimidation and violence, which the Court assumed was before the state legislature when it enacted the statute, and of which the Court itself took judicial notice. Furthermore, the situation before us is significantly different from that in *Bryant*, because the organization there had made no effort to comply with any of the requirements of New York's statute but rather had refused to furnish the State with *any* information as to its local activities....

d. *Shelton v. Tucker, 364 U.S. 479 (1960)*

Justice Stewart delivered the opinion of the Court.

An Arkansas statute compels every teacher, as a condition of employment in a state-supported school or college, to file annually an affidavit listing without limitation every organization to which he has belonged or regularly contributed within the preceding five years.... B. T. Shelton, a teacher employed in the Little Rock Public School System, ... [sued, arguing that this requirement was unconstitutional] .... [Shelton had] declined to file the affidavit, and his contract for the ensuing school year [1959-60] was not renewed. At the trial the evidence showed that he was not a member of the Communist Party or of any organization advocating the overthrow of the Government by force, and that he was a member of the National Association for the Advancement of Colored People....

[A.] *First*. There can be no doubt of the right of a State to investigate the competence and fitness of those whom it hires to teach in its schools, as this Court before now has had occasion to recognize. "A teacher works in a sensitive area in a schoolroom. There he shapes the attitude of young minds towards the society in which they live. In this, the state has a vital concern." There is "no requirement in the Federal Constitution that a teacher's classroom conduct be the sole basis for determining his fitness. Fitness for teaching depends on a broad range of factors."

This controversy is thus not of a pattern with such cases as *NAACP v. Alabama* ...[, where] the Court held that there was no substantially relevant correlation between the governmental interest asserted and the State's effort to compel disclosure of the membership lists involved. Here, by contrast, there can be no question of the relevance of a State's inquiry into the fitness and competence of its teachers.

Second. It is not disputed that to compel a teacher to disclose his every associational tie is to impair that teacher's right of free association, a right closely allied to freedom of speech and a right which, like free speech, lies at the foundation of a free society. Such interference with personal freedom is conspicuously accented when the teacher serves at the absolute will of those to whom the disclosure must be made—those who any year can terminate the teacher's employment without bringing charges, without notice, without a hearing, without affording an opportunity to explain.

The statute does not provide that the information it requires be kept confidential. Each school board is left free to deal with the information as it wishes. The record contains evidence to indicate that fear of public disclosure is neither theoretical nor groundless.

Even if there were no disclosure to the general public, the pressure upon a teacher to avoid any ties which might displease those who control his professional destiny would be constant and heavy. Public exposure, bringing with it the possibility of public pressures upon school boards to discharge teachers who belong to unpopular or minority organizations, would simply operate to widen and aggravate the impairment of constitutional liberty.

The vigilant protection of constitutional freedoms is nowhere more vital than in the community of American schools.... "... [U]nwarranted inhibition upon the free spirit of teachers ... has an unmistakable tendency to chill that free play of the spirit which all teachers ought especially to cultivate and practice; it makes for caution and timidity in their associations by potential teachers." "Scholarship cannot flourish in an atmosphere of suspicion and distrust. Teachers and students must always remain free to inquire, to study and to evaluate...."

[B.] The question to be decided here is not whether the State of Arkansas can ask certain of its teachers about all their organizational relationships. It is not whether the State can ask all of its teachers about certain of their associational ties. It is not whether teachers can be asked how many organizations they belong to, or how much time they spend in organizational activity.

The question is whether the State can ask every one of its teachers to disclose every single organization with which he has been associated over a five-year period.... The statute requires a teacher to reveal the church to which he belongs, or to which he has given financial support. It requires him to disclose his political party, and every political organization to which he may have contributed over a five-year period. It requires him to list ... every conceivable kind of associational tie—social, professional, political, avocational, or religious. Many such relationships could have no possible bearing upon the teacher's occupational competence or fitness....

[E]ven though the governmental purpose be legitimate and substantial, that purpose cannot be pursued by means that broadly stifle fundamental personal liberties when the end can be more narrowly achieved. The breadth of legislative abridgment must be viewed in the light of less drastic means for achieving the same basic purpose.... The statute's comprehensive interference with associational freedom goes far beyond what might be justified in the exercise of the State's legitimate inquiry into the fitness and competency of its teachers....

Justice Harlan, whom Justice Frankfurter, Justice Clark and Justice Whittaker join, dissenting....

[I]nformation about a teacher's associations may be useful to school authorities in determining the moral, professional, and social qualifications of the teacher, as well as in determining the type of service for which he will be best suited in the educational system. Furthermore, I take the Court to acknowledge that ... the State may enquire into associations to the extent that the resulting information may be in aid of that legitimate purpose. [This case] therefore do[es] not present a situation such as we had in *NAACP v. Alabama*, ... where the required disclosure bears no substantial relevance to a legitimate state interest.

Despite these considerations this statute is stricken down because, in the Court's view, it is too broad, because it asks more than may be necessary to effectuate the State's legitimate interest.... [But it is] impossible to determine *a priori* the place where the line should be drawn between what would be permissible inquiry and overbroad inquiry in a situation like this. Certainly the Court does not point that place out. There can be little doubt that much of the associational information called for by the statute will be of little or no use whatever to the school authorities, but I do not understand how those authorities can be expected to fix in advance the terms of their enquiry so that it will yield only relevant information.

I do not mean to say that alternatives such as an enquiry limited to the names of organizations of whose character the State is presently aware, or to a class of organizations defined by their purposes, would not be more consonant with a decent respect for the privacy of the teacher, nor that such alternatives would be utterly unworkable. I do see, however, that these alternatives suffer from deficiencies so obvious where a State is bent upon discovering everything which would be relevant to its proper purposes, that I cannot say that it must ... adopt some such means instead of those which have been chosen here.

Finally, ... if it turns out that this statute is abused, either by an unwarranted publicizing of the required associational disclosures or otherwise, we would have a different kind of case than [that] presently before us. All that is now here is the validity of the statute on its face ....

e. Problem: Blog Lawsuit

I operate a blog, which gets about 30,000 visits per weekday. People often e-mail me material that I post, or that I use to do further research, and sometimes ask me to keep their identities secret. (Assume my blog is independent, as it was, rather than hosted by the *Washington Post*, as it is now.)

Gil Milbauer, who has e-mailed me in the past and whom I have found to be trustworthy, sends me this e-mail:

> Eugene: I saw that abortion clinic protest yesterday where, as this morning's paper says, Paul Protester was shot by Oliver Officer. The protester was trying to club the cop over the head with a heavy stick; I think the stick had been ripped off of one of the protesters' picket signs. No wonder the cop shot him—clear self-defense, if you ask me.
>
> Please don't use my name, though. I'm not involved with either the pro-life or the pro-choice people, and I'd like to stay out of that mess.
> Gil Milbauer

I then publish the message on my blog, but without Gil's name. It turns out there were several other known witnesses to the attack, but all except one were pro-life demonstrators, police officers, or clinic employees. The police witnesses and the clinic employees say Paul was swinging at Oliver with a stick; the demonstrators say he wasn't. The one seemingly impartial known witness agrees with the police witnesses.

The shooting spawns several cases. (A) Paul Protester is prosecuted by the district attorney's office for assaulting the officer. (B) Oliver Officer is prosecuted by the federal government for excessive use of force, on the theory that Paul had only punched Oliver, rather than trying to hit him with the stick. (C) Paul sues the police department under the same theory. (D) Paul sues me for libel, and (E) sues my source, naming him as a John Doe.

The D.A.'s office in (A), Oliver in (B), the police department in (C), and Paul in (D) and (E), all subpoena me, demanding my informant's name.

Should I be required to reveal Gil's name? Would I be, under

(1) the majority holding in *Branzburg v. Hayes*;

(2) the Powell concurrence;

(3) the dissent's opinion, if the dissent had prevailed; or

(4) the California, Florida, and Indiana rules quoted below?

What if this hadn't been a 30,000-visitor blog, but just one of the e-mail messages that I periodically send out to a few dozen of my friends?

f. Branzburg v. Hayes, 408 U.S. 665 (1972)

Opinion of the Court by Justice White ....

The issue in these cases is whether requiring newsmen to appear and testify before state or federal grand juries abridges the freedom of speech and press guaranteed by the First Amendment. We hold that it does not.... *H – no privilege to compel journalist testimony*

[A.] [T]he Courier-Journal carried a story under [Paul Branzburg]'s byline describing in detail his observations of two young residents of Jefferson County synthesizing hashish from marihuana, an activity which, they asserted, earned them about $5,000 in three weeks.... [Branzburg] was shortly subpoenaed by the Jefferson County grand jury; he appeared, but refused to identify the individuals he had seen possessing marihuana or the persons he had seen making hashish from marihuana. A state trial court judge ordered [Branzburg] to answer these questions ....

[The companion case] *United States v. Caldwell* arose from subpoenas issued by a federal grand jury ... [to] Earl Caldwell, a reporter for the New York Times assigned to cover the Black Panther Party and other black militant groups.... [Caldwell was subpoenaed] to appear before the grand jury to testify and to bring with him notes and tape recordings of interviews given him for publication by officers and spokesmen of the Black Panther Party concerning the aims, purposes, and activities of that organization.... [Caldwell] and his employer, the New York Times, moved to quash on the ground that the unlimited breadth of the subpoenas and the fact that Caldwell would have to appear in secret before the grand jury would destroy his working relationship with the Black Panther Party and "suppress vital First Amendment freedoms ... by driving a wedge of distrust and silence between the news media and the militants." ...

The Government filed [documents stating] ... that the grand jury was investigating ... possible violations of a number of criminal statutes, including 18 U.S.C. § 871 (threats against the President), 18 U.S.C. § 1751 (assassination, attempts to assassinate, conspiracy to assassinate the President), 18 U.S.C. § 231 (civil disorders), 18 U.S.C. § 2101 (interstate travel to incite a riot), and 18 U.S.C. § 1341 (mail frauds and swindles).

It was recited that on November 15, 1969, an officer of the Black Panther Party made a publicly televised speech in which he had declared that "[w]e will kill Richard Nixon" and that this threat had been repeated in three subsequent issues of the Party newspaper. Also referred to were various writings by Caldwell about the Black Panther Party, including an article published in the New York Times on December 14, 1969, stating that "[i]n their role as the vanguard in a revolutionary struggle the Panthers have picked up guns," and quoting the Chief of Staff of the Party as declaring: "We advocate the very direct overthrow of the Government by way of force and violence. By picking up guns and moving against it because we recognize it as being oppressive and in recognizing that we know that the only solution to it is armed struggle ...." ... [T]he Chief of Staff of the Party had [also] been indicted by the grand jury on December 3, 1969, for uttering threats against the life of the President ....

[B.] [The reporters argue] ... that to gather news it is often necessary to agree either not to identify the source of information published or to publish only part of the facts revealed ... [and] that if the reporter is nevertheless forced to reveal these confidences to a grand jury, ... confidential sources ... will be measurably deterred from furnishing publishable information, all to the detriment of the free flow of information protected by the First Amendment.

Although the newsmen in these cases do not claim an absolute privilege against official interrogation in all circumstances, they assert that the reporter should not be forced either to appear or to testify before a grand jury or at trial until and unless sufficient grounds are shown for believing [(1)] that the reporter possesses information relevant to a crime the grand jury is investigating, [(2)] that the information the reporter has is unavailable from other sources, and [(3)] that the need for the information is sufficiently compelling to override the claimed invasion of First Amendment interests occasioned by the disclosure.... The heart of the claim is that the burden on news gathering resulting from compelling reporters to disclose confidential information outweighs any public interest in obtaining the information....

[N]ews gathering does ... qualify for First Amendment protection; without some protection for seeking out the news, freedom of the press could be eviscerated. But these cases involve no ... restriction on what the press may publish .... The use of confidential sources ... is not forbidden ....

The sole issue before us is the obligation of reporters to respond to grand jury subpoenas as other citizens do and to answer questions relevant to an investigation into the commission of crime.... [T]he First Amendment does not invalidate every incidental burdening of the press that may result from the enforcement of civil or criminal statutes of general applicability.... [O]therwise valid laws serving substantial public interests may be enforced against the press as against others, despite the possible burden that may be imposed.... "[T]he publisher of a newspaper has no special immunity from the application of general laws...." [The Court cited labor, antitrust, and tax laws, restrictions on travel to Cuba, and the exclusion of the public from most government proceedings.—ed.] ...

Because its task is to inquire into the existence of possible criminal conduct and to return only well-founded indictments, [the grand jury's] investigative powers are necessarily broad.... Hence, the grand jury's authority to subpoena witnesses is not only historic, but essential to its task.... [T]he longstanding principle that "the public ... has a right to every man's evidence," except for those persons protected by a ... privilege, is particularly applicable to grand jury proceedings....

[Allowing subpoenas of reporters does not] threaten the vast bulk of confidential relationships between reporters and their sources.... Only where news sources themselves are implicated in crime or possess information relevant to the grand jury's task need they or the reporter be concerned about grand jury subpoenas. Nothing before us indicates that a large number or percentage of *all* confidential news sources falls into either category and would in any way be deterred by our holding that the Constitution does not, as it never has, exempt the newsman from performing the citizen's normal duty of appearing and furnishing information relevant to the grand jury's task.

[C.] The preference for anonymity of those confidential informants involved in actual criminal conduct is presumably a product of their desire to escape criminal prosecution, and this preference, while understandable, is hardly deserving of constitutional protection.... [T]he First Amendment ... [does not confer] a license on either the reporter or his news sources to violate valid criminal laws. Although stealing documents or private wiretapping could provide newsworthy information, neither reporter nor source is immune from conviction for such conduct, whatever the impact on the flow of news. Neither is immune, on First Amendment grounds, from testifying against the other, before the grand jury or at a criminal trial....

There remain those situations where a source is not engaged in criminal conduct but has information suggesting illegal conduct by others.... Such informants ... may fear that disclosure will threaten their job security or personal safety or that it will simply result in dishonor or embarrassment.... [B]ut the evidence fails to demonstrate that there would be a significant constriction of the flow of news to the public if [the Court holds that newsmen may be required to testify] .... [Among other things,] the relationship of many informants to the press is a symbiotic one which is unlikely to be greatly inhibited by the threat of subpoena: quite often, such informants are members of a minority political or cultural group that relies heavily on the media to propagate its views ... and magnify its exposure .... Moreover, grand juries characteristically conduct secret proceedings, and law enforcement officers are themselves experienced in dealing with informers, and have their own methods for protecting them without interference with the effective administration of justice....

Won't constrict news

[T]he common law recognized no such privilege, and the constitutional argument was not even asserted until 1958.... [Yet] the press has operated without constitutional protection for press informants, and the press has flourished ... [and has used] confidential news sources ....

No History

{Accepting the fact, however, that an undetermined number of informants not themselves implicated in crime will nevertheless, for whatever reason, refuse to talk to newsmen if they fear identification by a reporter in an official investigation, we cannot accept the argument that the public interest in possible future news about crime from undisclosed, unverified sources must take precedence over the public interest in pursuing and prosecuting those crimes reported to the press by informants and in thus deterring the commission of such crimes in the future.... Neither are we now convinced that a virtually impenetrable constitutional shield, beyond legislative or judicial control, should be forged to protect a private system of informers operated by the press to report on criminal conduct, a system that would be unaccountable to the public, would pose a threat to the citizen's justifiable expectations of privacy, and would equally protect well-intentioned informants and those who for pay or otherwise betray their trust to their employer or associates.}

[E.] We do not deal ... with a governmental institution that has abused its proper function, as a legislative committee does when it "expose[s] for the sake of exposure." Nothing in the record indicates that these grand juries were "prob[ing] at will and without relation to existing need." Nor did the grand juries attempt to invade protected First Amendment rights by forcing wholesale disclosure of names and organizational affiliations for a purpose that was not germane to the determination of whether crime has been committed, cf. *NAACP v. Alabama*, and the characteristic secrecy of grand jury proceedings is a further protection against the undue invasion of such rights....

The requirements of those cases which hold that a State's interest must be "compelling" or "paramount" to justify even an indirect burden on First Amendment rights are also met here.... [T]he investigation of crime by the grand jury implements a fundamental governmental role of securing the safety of the person and property of the citizen, and it appears to us that calling reporters to give testimony in the manner and for the reasons that other citizens are called "bears a reasonable relationship to the achievement of the governmental purpose asserted as its justification." ... [T]he State has

Compelling

the necessary interest in extirpating the traffic in illegal drugs, in forestalling assassination attempts on the President, and in preventing the community from being disrupted by violent disorders endangering both persons and property[.] ...

Similar considerations dispose of the reporters' claims that preliminary to requiring their grand jury appearance, the State must show that a crime has been committed and that they possess relevant information not available from other sources, for only the grand jury itself can make this determination.... "It is impossible to conceive that in such cases the examination of witnesses must be stopped until a basis is laid by an indictment formally preferred, when the very object of the examination is to ascertain who shall be indicted." ...

[**F.**] The privilege claimed here is conditional, not absolute; given the suggested preliminary showings and compelling need, the reporter would be required to testify. Presumably, such a rule would reduce the instances in which reporters could be required to appear, but predicting in advance when ... they could be compelled to do so would be difficult.... If newsmen's confidential sources are as sensitive as they are claimed to be, the prospect of being unmasked whenever a judge determines the situation justifies it is hardly a satisfactory solution to the problem. For them, it would appear that only an absolute privilege would suffice....

The administration of a constitutional newsman's privilege would [also] present practical and conceptual difficulties of a high order. Sooner or later, it would be necessary to define those categories of newsmen who qualified for the privilege, a questionable procedure in light of the traditional doctrine that liberty of the press is the right of the lonely pamphleteer ... just as much as of the large metropolitan publisher .... The informative function asserted by representatives of the organized press ... is also performed by lecturers, political pollsters, novelists, academic researchers, and dramatists. Almost any author may quite accurately assert that he is contributing to the flow of information to the public, that he relies on confidential sources of information, and that these sources will be silenced if he is forced to make disclosures before a grand jury.

{Such a privilege might [also] be claimed by groups that set up newspapers in order to engage in criminal activity and to therefore be insulated from grand jury inquiry, regardless of Fifth Amendment grants of immunity. It might appear that such "sham" newspapers would be easily distinguishable, yet the First Amendment ordinarily prohibits courts from inquiring into the content of expression ... and protects ... publications regardless of their motivation ....} ...

[And] by considering whether enforcement of a particular law served a "compelling" governmental interest, the courts would be inextricably involved in distinguishing between the value of enforcing different criminal laws. By requiring testimony from a reporter in investigations involving some crimes but not in others, they would be making a value judgment that a legislature had declined to make, since in each case the criminal law involved would represent a considered legislative judgment, not constitutionally suspect, of what conduct is liable to criminal prosecution. The task of judges, like other officials outside the legislative branch, is not to make the law but to uphold it in accordance with their oaths....

leave to states

[G.] [Congress and state legislatures have] freedom to determine whether a statutory newsman's privilege is necessary and desirable and to fashion standards and rules as narrow or broad as deemed necessary to deal with the evil discerned and, equally important, to refashion those rules as experience from time to time may dictate....

In addition, there is much force in the pragmatic view that the press has at its disposal powerful mechanisms of communication and is far from helpless to protect itself from harassment or substantial harm. Furthermore, if what the newsmen urged in these cases is true—that law enforcement cannot hope to gain and may suffer from subpoenaing newsmen before grand juries—prosecutors will be loath to risk so much for so little. Thus, at the federal level the Attorney General has already fashioned a set of rules for federal officials in connection with subpoenaing members of the press to testify before grand juries or at criminal trials....

Finally, as we have earlier indicated, news gathering is not without its First Amendment protections, and grand jury investigations if instituted or conducted other than in good faith, would pose wholly different issues for resolution under the First Amendment. Official harassment of the press undertaken not for purposes of law enforcement but to disrupt a reporter's relationship with his news sources would have no justification....

Justice Powell, concurring.

I add this brief statement to emphasize what seems to me to be the limited nature of the Court's holding. The Court does not hold that newsmen, subpoenaed to testify before a grand jury, are without constitutional rights with respect to the gathering of news or in safeguarding their sources.... [T]he Court states that no harassment of newsmen will be tolerated. If a newsman believes that the grand jury investigation is not being conducted in good faith he is not without remedy.

Balance of facts

Indeed, if the newsman is called upon to give information bearing only a remote and tenuous relationship to the subject of the investigation, or if he has some other reason to believe that his testimony implicates confidential source relationships without a legitimate need of law enforcement, he will have access to the court on a motion to quash and an appropriate protective order may be entered. The asserted claim to privilege should be judged on its facts by the striking of a proper balance between freedom of the press and the obligation of all citizens to give relevant testimony with respect to criminal conduct. The balance of these vital constitutional and societal interests on a case-by-case basis accords with the tried and traditional way of adjudicating such questions.

{[Under the Court's decision,] the court—when called upon to protect a newsman from improper or prejudicial questioning—would be free to balance the competing interests on their merits in the particular case. The new constitutional rule endorsed by that dissenting opinion would, as a practical matter, defeat such a fair balancing and the essential societal interest in the detection and prosecution of crime would be heavily subordinated.} ...

Justice Douglas, dissenting .... [Omitted for space reasons, but here is Justice Douglas's bottom line:—ed.] [T]here is no "compelling need" that can be shown which qualifies the reporter's immunity from appearing or testifying before a grand jury, unless the reporter himself is implicated in a crime. His immunity in my view is therefore quite complete, for, absent his involvement in a crime, the First Amendment protects him against an appearance before a grand jury and if he is involved in a crime, the Fifth Amendment stands as a barrier....

Justice Stewart, with whom Justice Brennan and Justice Marshall join, dissenting....

The Court ... invites state and federal authorities to undermine the historic independence of the press by attempting to annex the journalistic profession as an investigative arm of government. Not only will this decision impair performance of the press' constitutionally protected functions, but it will, I am convinced, in the long run harm rather than help the administration of justice....

[A.] The reporter's constitutional right to a confidential relationship with his source stems from the broad societal interest in a full and free flow of information to the public. It is this basic concern that underlies the Constitution's protection of a free press, because the guarantee is "not for the benefit of the press so much as for the benefit of all of us." ...

A corollary of the right to publish must be the right to gather news. The full flow of information to the public protected by the free-press guarantee would be severely curtailed if no protection whatever were afforded to the process by which news is assembled and disseminated.... As Madison wrote: "A popular Government, without popular information, or the means of acquiring it, is but a Prologue to a Farce or a Tragedy; or, perhaps both." ...

The right to gather news implies ... a right to a confidential relationship between a reporter and his source ...: (1) newsmen require informants to gather news; (2) confidentiality—the promise or understanding that names or certain aspects of communications will be kept off the record—is essential to the creation and maintenance of a news-gathering relationship with informants; and (3) an unbridled subpoena power—the absence of a constitutional right protecting, in *any* way, a confidential relationship from compulsory process—will either deter sources from divulging information or deter reporters from gathering and publishing information....

An officeholder may fear his superior; a member of the bureaucracy, his associates; a dissident, the scorn of majority opinion. All may have information valuable to the public discourse, yet each may be willing to relate that information only in confidence to a reporter whom he trusts, either because of excessive caution or because of a reasonable fear of reprisals or censure for unorthodox views.... [W]hen governmental officials possess an unchecked power to compel newsmen to disclose information received in confidence, sources will clearly be deterred from giving information, and reporters will clearly be deterred from publishing it, because uncertainty about exercise of the power will lead to "self-censorship." ...

After today's decision, the potential informant can never be sure that his identity or off-the-record communications will not subsequently be revealed through the compelled testimony of a newsman. A public-spirited person inside government, who is not implicated in any crime, will now be fearful of revealing corruption or other governmental wrongdoing, because he will now know he can subsequently be identified by use of compulsory process....

{The fact that *some* informants will not be deterred from giving information by the prospect of the unbridled exercise of the subpoena power only means that there will not *always* be a conflict between the grand jury's inquiry and the protection of First Amendment activities. But even if the percentage of such informants is relatively large compared to the total "universe" of potential informants, there will remain a large number of people in "absolute" terms who *will* be deterred ....} ...

The impairment of the flow of news cannot, of course, be proved with scientific precision, as the Court seems to demand.... [I]t is difficult to pinpoint precisely how many relationships do require a promise or understanding of nondisclosure. But we have never before demanded that First Amendment rights rest on elaborate empirical studies demonstrating beyond any conceivable doubt [the existence or size of] deterrent effects ....

Rather, on the basis of common sense and available information, we have asked, often implicitly, (1) whether there was a rational connection between the cause (the governmental action) and the effect (the deterrence or impairment of First Amendment activity), and (2) whether the effect would occur with some regularity, *i.e.*, would not be *de minimis*. And, in making this determination, we have [held that First Amendment rights] ... "... are protected not only against heavy-handed frontal attack, but also from being stifled by more subtle governmental interference." {Although ... we have held that the press is not free from the requirements of the National Labor Relations Act, the Fair Labor Standards Act, the antitrust laws, or nondiscriminatory taxation, these decisions were concerned "only with restraints on certain business or commercial practices" of the press. And due weight was given to First Amendment interests....} ...

To require any greater burden of proof is to shirk our duty to protect values securely embedded in the Constitution. We cannot await an unequivocal—and therefore unattainable—imprimatur from empirical studies. We can and must accept the evidence developed in the record, and elsewhere, that overwhelmingly supports the premise that deterrence will occur with regularity in important types of news-gathering relationships....

[B.] Posed against the First Amendment's protection of the newsman's confidential relationships in these cases is society's interest in the use of the grand jury to administer justice fairly and effectively.... Yet the longstanding rule making every person's evidence available to the grand jury is not absolute. The rule has been limited by the Fifth Amendment, the Fourth Amendment, and the evidentiary privileges of the common law.... [[T]he First Amendment protection of a confidential relationship that I have discussed above [surely qualifies as a similarly important interest] .... [T]his protection ... functions to insure nothing less than democratic decisionmaking through the free flow of information to the public ....

[W]hen a reporter is asked to appear before a grand jury and reveal confidences, I would hold that the government must (1) show that there is probable cause to believe that the newsman has information that is clearly relevant to a specific probable violation of law; (2) demonstrate that the information sought cannot be obtained by alternative means less destructive of First Amendment rights; and (3) demonstrate a compelling and overriding interest in the information....

{If [the probable cause] requirement is not met, then the government will basically be allowed to undertake a "fishing expedition" at the expense of the press. Such general, exploratory investigations will be most damaging to confidential news-gathering relationships, since they will create great uncertainty in both reporters and their sources....}

Similarly, a reporter may have information from a confidential source that is "related" to the commission of crime, but the government may be able to ... achieve its purposes by subpoenaing persons other than the reporter.... [W]hen government aims have been fully served, there can be no legitimate reason to disrupt a confidential relationship between a reporter and his source. To do so would not aid the administration of justice and would only impair the flow of information to the public....

{We need not, therefore, reach the question of whether government's interest in [such] cases is "overriding and compelling." I do not, however, believe, as the Court does, that *all* grand jury investigations automatically would override the newsman's testimonial privilege.}

No doubt the courts would be required to make some delicate judgments in working out this accommodation. But that, after all, is the function of courts of law. Better such judgments, however difficult, than the simplistic and stultifying absolutism adopted by the Court in denying any force to the First Amendment in these cases....

[C.] [I]n the name of advancing the administration of justice, the Court's decision, I think, will only impair the achievement of that goal. People entrusted with law enforcement responsibility, no less than private citizens, need general information relating to controversial social problems.

Obviously, press reports have great value to government, even when the newsman cannot be compelled to testify before a grand jury. The sad paradox of the Court's position is that when a grand jury may exercise an unbridled subpoena power, and sources involved in sensitive matters become fearful of disclosing information, the newsman will not only cease to be a useful grand jury witness; he will cease to investigate and publish information about issues of public import.... [I]n my view, the interests protected by the First Amendment are not antagonistic to the administration of justice. Rather, they can, in the long run, only be complementary, and for that reason must be given great "breathing space." ...

[D.] On the record before us [in *Caldwell*] the United States has not met the burden that I think the appropriate newsman's privilege should require.... [W]ith one exception, there has been no factual showing in this case of the probable commission of, or of attempts to commit, any crimes. The single exception relates to the allegation that a Black Panther Party leader, David Hilliard, violated 18 U.S.C. § 871 [(which prohibits threats against the president)] during the course of a speech in November 1969. But Caldwell was subpoenaed two months after an indictment was returned against Hilliard, and that charge could not, subsequent to the indictment, be investigated by a grand jury. Furthermore, the record before us does not show that Caldwell probably had any information about the violation of any other federal criminal laws, or that alternative means of obtaining the desired information were pursued....

[T]he Court of Appeals further found that Caldwell's confidential relationship with the leaders of the Black Panther Party would be impaired if he appeared before the grand jury at all to answer questions, even though not privileged.... [Such an impairment would happen] only in very rare circumstances .... But in this case, the reporter made out a prima facie case that the flow of news to the public would be curtailed. And he stated, without contradiction, that the only nonconfidential material about which he could testify was already printed in his newspaper articles.... [T]he appearance of Caldwell would [thus] ... be a "barren performance." But *this* aspect of the [decision, which is that Caldwell could refuse to appear before the grand jury at all,] I would confine to its own facts....

In ... *Branzburg v. Hayes* ..., I would ... remand ... for further proceedings not inconsistent with the views I have expressed in this opinion.

g.   *Reporter's Privilege: State Provisions*

Many states recognize reporter's privileges as a matter of state statute, explicit state constitutional provision, or state supreme court interpretation of generally worded state free speech provisions. A few samples:

i.   *California Constitution, art. I, § 2(b)*

[(i)] A ... person [now or once] connected with ... a newspaper, magazine, or other periodical publication ... [or a radio or television station] ...

[(ii)] shall not be adjudged in contempt ...

[(iiia)] for refusing to disclose the source of any information procured while so connected or employed for publication in a newspaper, magazine or other periodical publication [or for news or news commentary purposes on radio or television], or [(iiib)] for refusing to disclose any unpublished information obtained or prepared in gathering, receiving or processing of information for communication to the public....

ii. *Florida Statutes § 90.5015*

(1) ... (a) "Professional journalist" means a person

[(i)] regularly engaged in collecting, ... writing, editing, ... or publishing news,

[(ii)] for gain or livelihood,

[(iii)] who obtained the information sought while working as a salaried employee of, or independent contractor for,

[(iv)] a newspaper, news journal, ... [or] radio or television station ....

[(v)] Book authors and others who are not professional journalists, as defined in this paragraph, are not included ....

(b) "News" means information of public concern relating to local, statewide, national, or worldwide issues or events.

(2) ... A professional journalist has a qualified privilege ... not to disclose the information, including the identity of any source, that the professional journalist has obtained while actively gathering news.

This privilege applies only to information or eyewitness observations obtained within the normal scope of employment and does not apply to physical evidence, eyewitness observations, or visual or audio recording of crimes.

A party seeking to overcome this privilege must make a clear and specific showing that:

(a) The information is relevant and material to unresolved issues that have been raised in the proceeding for which the information is sought;

(b) The information cannot be obtained from alternative sources; and

(c) A compelling interest exists for requiring disclosure ....

iii. *Indiana Code §§ 34-46-4-1, -2*

[(i)] [A]ny [past or present] {owner, editorial or reportorial employee} ...

[(ii)] [of] a newspaper or other periodical issued at regular intervals and having a general circulation ... [or a radio or television station] ...

[(iii)] who receives or has received income from legitimate gathering, writing, editing[, interpreting, announcing, or broadcasting] of news ....

[(iv)] shall not be compelled to disclose ... the source of any information procured or obtained in the course of the person's employment or representation of a [media outlet] ....

h. *University of Pennsylvania v. EEOC, 493 U.S. 182 (1990)*

Justice Blackmun delivered the opinion of the [unanimous] Court.

[A.] In this case we are asked to decide whether a university enjoys a special privilege, grounded in either the common law or the First Amendment, against disclosure of peer review materials that are relevant to charges of racial or sexual discrimination in tenure decisions....

The University of Pennsylvania ... is a private institution. It currently operates 12 schools, including the Wharton School of Business .... In 1985, the University denied tenure to Rosalie Tung, an associate professor on the Wharton faculty. Tung then filed a sworn charge of [race, sex, and national origin] discrimination with respondent Equal Employment Opportunity Commission (EEOC or Commission)....

Tung stated that the department chairman had sexually harassed her and that, in her belief, after she insisted that their relationship remain professional, he had submitted a negative letter to the University's Personnel Committee which possessed ultimate responsibility for tenure decisions. She also alleged that her qualifications were "equal to or better than" those of five named male faculty members who had received more favorable treatment. Tung noted that the majority of the members of her department had recommended her for tenure, and stated that she had been given no reason for the decision against her, but had discovered of her own efforts that the Personnel Committee had attempted to justify its decision "on the ground that the Wharton School is not interested in China-related research." This explanation, Tung's charge alleged, was a pretext for discrimination: "simply their way of saying they do not want a Chinese-American, Oriental, woman in their school."

The Commission undertook an investigation into Tung's charge and requested a variety of relevant information from petitioner. When the University refused to provide certain of that information, the Commission's Acting District Director issued a subpoena seeking, among other things, Tung's tenure-review file and the tenure files of the five male faculty members identified in the charge.... [The University] applied to the Commission for modification of the subpoena to exclude what it termed "confidential peer review information," specifically, (1) confidential letters written by Tung's evaluators; (2) the department chairman's letter of evaluation; (3) documents reflecting the internal deliberations of faculty committees considering applications for tenure, including the Department Evaluation Report summarizing the deliberations relating to Tung's application for tenure; and (4) comparable portions of the tenure-review files of the five males. The University urged the Commission to "adopt a balancing approach reflecting the constitutional and societal interest inherent in the peer review process" and to resort to "all feasible methods to minimize the intrusive effects of its investigations."

The Commission denied the University's application. It concluded that the withheld documents were needed in order to determine the merit of Tung's charges.... The Commission also rejected petitioner's proposed balancing test, explaining that "such an approach in the instant case ... would impair the Commission's ability to fully investigate this charge of discrimination." ... The University continued to withhold the tenure-review materials. The Commission then applied to [a federal court] for enforcement of its subpoena....

[B.] [T]he University ... urges us to recognize a qualified common-law privilege against disclosure of confidential peer review materials. [Federal evidence law lets federal courts create such privileges.—ed.] [The University argues for] a requirement of a judicial finding of particularized necessity of access, beyond a showing of mere relevance, before peer review materials are disclosed to the Commission....

We readily agree with petitioner that universities and colleges play significant roles in American society. Nor need we question, at this point, petitioner's assertion that confidentiality is important to the proper functioning of the peer review process under which many academic institutions operate. The costs that ensue from disclosure, however, constitute only one side of the balance.

As Congress has recognized, the costs associated with racial and sexual discrimination in institutions of higher learning are very substantial. Few would deny that ferreting out this kind of invidious discrimination is a great, if not compelling, governmental interest. Often, ... disclosure of peer review materials will be necessary in order for the Commission to determine whether illegal discrimination has taken place. Indeed, if there is a "smoking gun" to be found that demonstrates discrimination in tenure decisions, it is likely to be tucked away in peer review files....

Moreover, we agree with the EEOC that the adoption of a requirement that the Commission demonstrate a "specific reason for disclosure" beyond a showing of relevance, would place a substantial litigation-producing obstacle in the way of the Commission's efforts to investigate and remedy alleged discrimination. Cf. *Branzburg* v. *Hayes*. A university faced with a disclosure request might well utilize the privilege in a way that frustrates the EEOC's mission. We are reluctant to "place a potent weapon in the hands of employers who have no interest in complying voluntarily with the Act, who wish instead to delay as long as possible investigations by the EEOC."

Acceptance of petitioner's claim would also lead to a wave of similar privilege claims by other employers who play significant roles in furthering speech and learning in society. What of writers, publishers, musicians, lawyers? It surely is not unreasonable to believe, for example, that confidential peer reviews play an important part in partnership determinations at some law firms. We perceive no limiting principle in petitioner's argument. Accordingly, we stand behind the breakwater Congress has established: unless specifically provided otherwise in the statute, the EEOC may obtain "relevant" evidence....

[C.] [The University similarly argues on First Amendment grounds for a requirement of a judicial finding of particularized necessity of access, beyond a showing of mere relevance, before peer review materials are disclosed to the Commission.] ... [The University] characterizes its First Amendment claim as one of "academic freedom." ... A tenure system, asserts petitioner, determines what the university will look like over time. "In making tenure decisions, therefore, a university is doing nothing less than shaping its own identity."

Petitioner next maintains that the peer review process is the most important element in the effective operation of a tenure system. A properly functioning tenure system requires the faculty to obtain candid and detailed written evaluations of the candidate's scholarship, both from the candidate's peers at the university and from scholars at other institutions. These evaluations, says petitioner, traditionally have been provided with express or implied assurances of confidentiality. It is confidentiality that ensures candor and enables an institution to make its tenure decisions on the basis of valid academic criteria.

Building from these premises, petitioner claims that requiring the disclosure of peer review evaluations on a finding of mere relevance will undermine the existing process of awarding tenure, and therefore will result in a significant infringement of petitioner's First Amendment right of academic freedom. As more and more peer evaluations are disclosed to the EEOC and become public, a "chilling effect" on candid evaluations and discussions of candidates will result. And as the quality of peer review evaluations declines, tenure committees will no longer be able to rely on them. "This will work to the detriment of universities, as less qualified persons achieve tenure causing the quality of instruction and scholarship to decline."

Compelling disclosure of materials "also will result in divisiveness and tension, placing strain on faculty relations and impairing the free interchange of ideas that is a hallmark of academic freedom." The prospect of these deleterious effects on American colleges and universities, concludes petitioner, compels recognition of a First Amendment privilege....

[W]e need not define today the precise contours of any academic-freedom right against governmental attempts to influence the content of academic speech through the selection of faculty or by other means, because petitioner does not allege that the Commission's subpoenas are intended to or will in fact direct the content of university discourse toward or away from particular subjects or points of view....

That the burden of which the University complains is neither content-based nor direct does not necessarily mean that petitioner has no valid First Amendment claim.... [But a]lthough we are sensitive to the effects that content-neutral government action may have on speech, and believe that burdens that are less than direct may sometimes pose First Amendment concerns, see, e. g., NAACP v. *Alabama ex rel. Patterson,* we think the First Amendment cannot be extended to embrace petitioner's claim.

First, by comparison with the cases in which we have found a cognizable First Amendment claim, the infringement the University complains of is extremely attenuated. To repeat, it argues that the First Amendment is infringed by disclosure of peer review materials because disclosure undermines the confidentiality which is central to the peer review process, and this in turn is central to the tenure process, which in turn is the means by which petitioner seeks to exercise its asserted academic-freedom right of choosing who will teach. To verbalize the claim is to recognize how distant the burden is from the asserted right.

Indeed, if the University's attenuated claim were accepted, many other generally applicable laws might also be said to infringe the First Amendment. In effect, petitioner says no more than that disclosure of peer review materials makes it more difficult to acquire information regarding the "academic grounds" on which petitioner wishes to base its tenure decisions.

But many laws make the exercise of First Amendment rights more difficult. For example, a university cannot claim a First Amendment violation simply because it may be subject to taxation or other government regulation, even though such regulation might deprive the university of revenue it needs to bid for professors who are contemplating working for other academic institutions or in industry. We doubt that the peer review process is any more essential in effectuating the right to determine "who may teach" than is the availability of money.

In addition to being remote and attenuated, the injury to academic freedom claimed by petitioner is also speculative. As the EEOC points out, confidentiality is not the norm in all peer review systems. Moreover, some disclosure of peer evaluations would take place even if petitioner's "special necessity" test were adopted. Thus, the "chilling effect" petitioner fears is at most only incrementally worsened by the absence of a privilege.

Finally, we are not so ready as petitioner seems to be to assume the worst about those in the academic community. Although it is possible that some evaluators may become less candid as the possibility of disclosure increases, others may simply ground their evaluations in specific examples and illustrations in order to deflect potential claims of bias or unfairness. Not all academics will hesitate to stand up and be counted when they evaluate their peers.

[D.] The case we decide today in many respects is similar to *Branzburg* v. *Hayes.* In *Branzburg,* the Court rejected the notion that under the First Amendment a reporter could not be required to appear or to testify as to information obtained in confidence without a special showing that the reporter's testimony was necessary. Petitioners there, like petitioner here, claimed that requiring disclosure of information collected in confidence would inhibit the free flow of information in contravention of First Amendment principles.

In the course of rejecting the First Amendment argument, this Court noted that "the First Amendment does not invalidate every incidental burdening of the press that may result from the enforcement of civil or criminal statutes of general applicability." We also indicated a reluctance to recognize a constitutional privilege where it was "unclear how often and to what extent informers are actually deterred from furnishing information when newsmen are forced to testify before a grand jury." We were unwilling then, as we are today, "to embark the judiciary on a long and difficult journey to ... an uncertain destination."

{In *Branzburg* we recognized that the bad-faith exercise of grand jury powers might raise First Amendment concerns. The same is true of EEOC subpoena powers. There is no allegation or indication of any such abuse by the Commission in this case.}

Because we conclude that the EEOC subpoena process does not infringe any First Amendment right enjoyed by petitioner, the EEOC need not demonstrate any special justification to sustain the constitutionality of Title VII as applied to tenure peer review materials in general or to the subpoena involved in this case. Accordingly, we need not address the Commission's alternative argument that any infringement of petitioner's First Amendment rights is permissible because of the substantial relation between the Commission's request and the overriding and compelling state interest in eradicating invidious discrimination....

3. ELECTION-RELATED SPEECH

a. *Problem: Contributions*

Visit http://www.opensecrets.org/indivs/index.asp and check your own contributions or contributions by someone you know. Can you imagine circumstances in which you would be deterred from contributing to a candidate by the knowledge that this information would be publicized? What exactly would be the source of the deterrence—the risk of lost employment opportunities, social opprobrium, violence, or something else?

If you really did want to donate to the candidate, and were willing to sue to establish your right to do so anonymously, do you think that—given your particular circumstances—you would win? Should you win?

b. *Problem: Antimask Laws*

A state statute bars any person from "wearing [in any public place] any mask, hood or device whereby any portion of the face is so covered as to conceal the identity of the wearer." The statute has exceptions for "traditional holiday costume[s]," masks worn for occupational safety, masquerade balls, civil defense drills, or "protection from the elements or while participating in a winter sport."

Members of the Ku Klux Klan organize a 20-person rally in front of City Hall in which they appear in full Klan regalia, which include a mask. When they are arrested for violating the mask law, they argue that the law violates the First Amendment. What arguments can be made for and against this defense? *Compare, e.g., Church of American Knights of the KKK v. Kerik*, 356 F.3d 197 (2d Cir. 2004) (holding such a statute constitutional) *and State v. Berrill*, 474 S.E.2d 508 (W. Va. 1996) (same) *with American Knights of the KKK v. City of Goshen*, 50 F. Supp. 2d 835 (N.D. Ind. 1999) (holding such a statute unconstitutional).

c. *Buckley v. Valeo, 424 U.S. 1 (1976)*

[You may want to skim the other parts of *Buckley,* which are reproduced on p. 466.—ed.]

Per curiam....

[A.] [Under the Federal Election Campaign Act, e]ach political committee is required ... to keep detailed records of both contributions [to the committee] and expenditures [by it]. These records must include the name and address of everyone making a contribution in excess of $10, along with the date and amount of the contribution. If a person's contributions aggregate more than $100, his occupation and principal place of business are also to be included. These files are subject to periodic audits ... by the Commission.

Each committee and each candidate also is required to file quarterly reports. The reports are to contain detailed financial information, including the full name, mailing address, occupation, and principal place of business of each person who has contributed over $100 in a calendar year, as well as the amount and date of the contributions. They are to be made available by the Commission "for public inspection and copying." ...

Every individual or group, other than a political committee or candidate, who makes "contributions" or "expenditures" of over $100 in a calendar year "other than by contribution to a political committee or candidate" is required to file a statement with the Commission....

[C]ompelled disclosure, in itself, can seriously infringe on privacy of association and belief guaranteed by the First Amendment.... Since *NAACP v. Alabama* we have required that the subordinating interests of the State must survive exacting scrutiny. We also have insisted that there be a "relevant correlation" or "substantial relation" between the governmental interest and the information required to be disclosed. This type of scrutiny is necessary even if any deterrent effect on the exercise of First Amendment rights arises, not through direct government action, but indirectly as an unintended but inevitable result of the government's conduct in requiring disclosure....

[G]roup association is protected because it enhances "[e]ffective advocacy." The right to join together "for the advancement of beliefs and ideas" is diluted if it does not include the right to pool money through contributions, for funds are often essential if "advocacy" is to be truly or optimally "effective." Moreover, the invasion of privacy of belief may be as great when the information sought concerns the giving and spending of money as when it concerns the joining of organizations, for "[f]inancial transactions can reveal much about a person's activities, associations, and beliefs." Our past decisions have not drawn fine lines between contributors and members but have treated them interchangeably....

[B.] But ... there are governmental interests sufficiently important to outweigh the possibility of infringement, particularly when the "free functioning of our national institutions" is involved....

First, disclosure provides the electorate with information "as to where political campaign money comes from and how it is spent by the candidate" in order to aid the voters in evaluating those who seek federal office. It allows voters to place each candidate in the political spectrum more precisely than is often possible solely on the basis of party labels and campaign speeches. The sources of a candidate's financial support also alert the voter to the interests to which a candidate is most likely to be responsive and thus facilitate predictions of future performance in office.

Second, disclosure requirements deter actual corruption and avoid the appearance of corruption by exposing large contributions and expenditures to the light of publicity. This exposure may discourage those who would use money for improper purposes either before or after the election. A public armed with information about a candidate's most generous supporters is better able to detect any post-election special favors that may be given in return....

Third, ... recordkeeping, reporting, and disclosure requirements are an essential means of gathering the data necessary to detect violations of the contribution limitations [imposed by federal law] [see p. 466—ed.].

[C.] The disclosure requirements, as a general matter, directly serve substantial governmental interests. In determining whether these interests are sufficient to justify the requirements we must look to the extent of the burden that they place on individual rights.

It is undoubtedly true that public disclosure of contributions to candidates and political parties will deter some individuals who otherwise might contribute. In some instances, disclosure may even expose contributors to harassment or retaliation. These are not insignificant burdens on individual rights, and they must be weighed carefully against the interests which Congress has sought to promote by this legislation.... [W]e note ... that disclosure requirements—certainly in most applications—appear to be the least restrictive means of curbing the evils of campaign ignorance and corruption that Congress found to exist....

[D.] [T]he damage done by disclosure to the associational interests of the minor parties and their members and to supporters of independents could be significant. These movements are less likely to have a sound financial base and thus are more vulnerable to falloffs in contributions. In some instances fears of reprisal may deter contributions to the point where the movement cannot survive. The public interest also suffers if that result comes to pass, for there is a consequent reduction in the free circulation of ideas both within and without the political arena.

There could well be a case, similar to [that] before the Court in *NAACP v. Alabama*, ... where the threat to the exercise of First Amendment rights is so serious and the state interest furthered by disclosure so insubstantial that the Act's requirements cannot be constitutionally applied. But no appellant in this case has tendered record evidence of the sort proffered in *NAACP v. Alabama*.

Instead, appellants primarily rely on "the clearly articulated fears of individuals, well experienced in the political process." At best they offer the testimony of several minor-party officials that one or two persons refused to make contributions because of the possibility of disclosure. On this record, the substantial public interest in disclosure identified by the legislative history of this Act outweighs the harm generally alleged.... [The rest of this section has been omitted, but *Brown v. Socialist Workers '74 Campaign Comm.* (p. 458) quotes it extensively.—ed.]

Chief Justice Burger, concurring in part and dissenting in part....

Serious dangers to the very processes of government justify disclosure of contributions of such dimensions reasonably thought likely to purchase special favors.... [But only the view that] disclosure [also] serves broad informational purposes, enabling the public to be fully informed on matters of acute public interest[,] ... [can justify] the otherwise irrationally low ceilings of $10 and $100 for anonymous contributions....

The public right to know ought not be absolute when its exercise reveals private political convictions.... [S]ecrecy and privacy as to political preferences and convictions are fundamental in a free society.

For example, one of the great political reforms was the advent of the secret ballot as a universal practice. Similarly, the enlightened labor legislation of our time has enshrined the secrecy of choice of a bargaining representative for workers. In other contexts, this Court has seen to it that governmental power cannot be used to force a citizen to disclose his private affiliations, even without a record reflecting any systematic harassment or retaliation, as in *Shelton v. Tucker*....

Congress gave little or no thought, one way or the other, to [the $10 and $100] limits, but rather lifted figures out of a 65-year-old statute.... Ten dollars in 1976 will ... purchase only what $1.68 would buy in 1910. To argue that a 1976 contribution of $10 or $100 entails a risk of corruption or its appearance is simply too extravagant to be maintained. No public right to know justifies the compelled disclosure of such contributions, at the risk of discouraging them....

d. McIntyre v. Ohio Elections Comm'n, 514 U.S. 334 (1995)

Justice Stevens delivered the opinion of the Court....

[A.] Margaret McIntyre distributed [unsigned] leaflets to persons attending a public meeting ... [at which] the superintendent of schools planned to discuss an imminent referendum on a proposed school tax levy. The leaflets expressed Mrs. McIntyre's opposition to the levy.... [The Ohio Elections Commission fined McIntyre $100 for violating an Ohio statute which provided that all written materials "designed to promote the nomination or election or defeat of a candidate, or to promote the adoption or defeat of any issue, or to influence the voters in any election" must include "the name and residence or business address" of their distributor.—ed.]

[B.] "Anonymous pamphlets, leaflets, brochures and even books have played an important role in the progress of mankind." Great works of literature have frequently been produced by authors writing under assumed names....

The decision in favor of anonymity may be motivated by fear of economic or official retaliation, by concern about social ostracism, or merely by a desire to preserve as much of one's privacy as possible.... Whatever the motivation may be, at least in the field of literary endeavor, the interest in having anonymous works enter the marketplace of ideas unquestionably outweighs any public interest in requiring disclosure as a condition of entry. Accordingly, an author's decision to remain anonymous, like other decisions concerning omissions or additions to the content of a publication, is ... protected by the First Amendment....

Anonymity ... provides a way for a writer who may be personally unpopular to ensure that readers will not prejudge her message simply because they do not like its proponent. Thus, even in the field of political rhetoric, where "the identity of the speaker is an important component of many attempts to persuade," the most effective advocates have sometimes opted for anonymity....

[C.] When a law burdens core political speech, ... we uphold the restriction only if it is narrowly tailored to serve an overriding state interest.... [T]he State argues that, even under the strictest standard of review, the disclosure requirement in [the statute] is justified by two important and legitimate state interests....

Insofar as the [first interest,] in informing the electorate[,] means nothing more than the provision of additional information that may either buttress or undermine the argument in a document, we think the identity of the speaker is no different from other components of the document's content that the author is free to include or exclude.... [T]he State may not compel a newspaper that prints editorials critical of a particular candidate to provide space for a reply by the candidate. *Miami Herald Pub. Co. v. Tornillo.* The simple interest in providing voters with additional relevant information does not justify a state requirement that a writer make statements or disclosures she would otherwise omit.

Moreover, in the case of a handbill written by a private citizen who is not known to the recipient, the name and address of the author adds little, if anything, to the reader's ability to evaluate the document's message. Thus, Ohio's informational interest is plainly insufficient to support the constitutionality of its disclosure requirement.

{[And while] "... the identity of the source is helpful in evaluating ideas [..,"] ... ["p]eople are intelligent enough to evaluate the source of an anonymous writing.... They can evaluate its anonymity along with its message, as long as they are permitted, as they must be, to read that message. And then, once they have done so, it is for them to decide what is 'responsible,' what is valuable, and what is truth."}

[D.] The ... [second] interest[,] in preventing fraud and libel[,] stands on a different footing. We agree ... that this interest carries special weight during election campaigns when false statements, if credited, may have serious adverse consequences for the public at large....

[But] Ohio's prohibition of anonymous leaflets plainly is not its principal weapon against fraud. Rather, it serves as an aid to enforcement of the specific [Ohio statutes that ban false statements during political campaigns] and as a deterrent to the making of false statements by unscrupulous prevaricators. Although these ancillary benefits are assuredly legitimate, we are not persuaded that they justify [the statute]'s extremely broad prohibition.

As this case demonstrates, the prohibition encompasses documents that are not even arguably false or misleading. It applies not only to the activities of candidates and their organized supporters, but also to individuals acting independently and using only their own modest resources. It applies not only to elections of public officers, but also to ballot issues that present neither a substantial risk of libel nor any potential appearance of corrupt advantage. It applies not only to leaflets distributed on the eve of an election, when the opportunity for reply is limited, but also to those distributed months in advance. It applies no matter what the character or strength of the author's interest in anonymity.

Moreover, as this case also demonstrates, the absence of the author's name on a document does not necessarily protect either that person or a distributor of a forbidden document from being held responsible for compliance with the Election Code. Nor has the State explained why it can more easily enforce the direct bans on disseminating false documents against anonymous authors and distributors than against wrongdoers who might use false names and addresses in an attempt to avoid detection. We recognize that a State's enforcement interest might justify a more limited identification requirement, but Ohio has shown scant cause for inhibiting the leafletting at issue here....

[E.] [I]n *Buckley v. Valeo,* ... we stressed the importance of providing "the electorate with information 'as to where political campaign money comes from and how it is spent by the candidate.'" We observed that the "sources of a candidate's financial support also alert the voter to the interests to which a candidate is most likely to be responsive and thus facilitate predictions of future performance in office."

Those comments concerned contributions to the candidate or expenditures authorized by the candidate .... They had no reference to the kind of independent activity pursued by Mrs. McIntyre. Required disclosures about the level of financial support a candidate has received from various sources are supported by an interest in avoiding the appearance of corruption that has no application to this case.

[F.] True, in another portion of the *Buckley* opinion we expressed approval of a requirement that even "independent expenditures" in excess of a threshold level be reported to the Federal Election Commission. But that requirement entailed nothing more than an identification to the Commission of the amount and use of money expended in support of a candidate. Though such mandatory reporting undeniably impedes protected First Amendment activity, the intrusion is a far cry from compelled self-identification on all election-related writings.

A written election-related document—particularly a leaflet—is often a personally crafted statement of a political viewpoint. Mrs. McIntyre's handbills surely fit that description. As such, identification of the author against her will is particularly intrusive; it reveals unmistakably the content of her thoughts on a controversial issue.

Disclosure of an expenditure and its use, without more, reveals far less information. It may be information that a person prefers to keep secret, and undoubtedly it often gives away something about the spender's political views. Nonetheless, even though money may "talk," its speech is less specific, less personal, and less provocative than a handbill—and as a result, when money supports an unpopular viewpoint it is less likely to precipitate retaliation.

[G.] Not only is the Ohio statute's infringement on speech more intrusive than the *Buckley* disclosure requirement, but it rests on different and less powerful state interests.... In candidate elections, the Government can identify a compelling state interest in avoiding the corruption that might result from campaign expenditures. Disclosure of expenditures lessens the risk that individuals will spend money to support a candidate as a *quid pro quo* for special treatment after the candidate is in office. Curriers of favor will be deterred by the knowledge that all expenditures will be scrutinized by the Federal Election Commission and by the public for just this sort of abuse.

Moreover, the federal Act contains numerous legitimate disclosure requirements for campaign organizations; the similar requirements for independent expenditures serve to ensure that a campaign organization will not seek to evade disclosure by routing its expenditures through individual supporters.... [A]lthough *Buckley* may permit a more narrowly drawn statute, it surely is not authority for upholding Ohio's open-ended provision....

Justice Thomas, concurring in the judgment.

I agree with the majority's conclusion that Ohio's election law is inconsistent with the First Amendment. I would apply, however, a different methodology to this case. Instead of asking whether "an honorable tradition" of anonymous speech has existed throughout American history, or what the "value" of anonymous speech might be, we should determine whether the phrase "freedom of speech, or of the press," as originally understood, protected anonymous political leafletting. I believe that it did.... [Historical discussion omitted.—ed.]

Justice Scalia, with whom ... Chief Justice [Rehnquist] joins, dissenting....

[Justice Scalia begins by disagreeing with Justice Thomas on the original meaning point, and by concluding that longstanding American legal traditions—which to him are the touchstone in such cases—point towards upholding the law. But he also says the following:—ed.]

[A.] The Court says that the State has not explained "why it can more easily enforce the direct bans on disseminating false documents against anonymous authors and distributors than against wrongdoers who might use false names and addresses in an attempt to avoid detection." I am not sure what this complicated comparison means. I am sure, however, that (1) a person who is required to put his name to a document is much less likely to lie than one who can lie anonymously, and (2) the distributor of a leaflet which is unlawful because it is anonymous runs much more risk of immediate detection and punishment than the distributor of a leaflet which is unlawful because it is false. Thus, people will be more likely to observe a signing requirement than a naked "no falsity" requirement; and, having observed that requirement, will then be significantly less likely to lie in what they have signed.

But the usefulness of a signing requirement lies not only in promoting observance of the law against campaign falsehoods (though that alone is enough to sustain it). It lies also in promoting a civil and dignified level of campaign debate—which the State has no power to command, but ample power to encourage by such undemanding measures as a signature requirement....

Not all [character assassination that harms the democratic process], in fact not much of it, consists of actionable untruth; most is innuendo, or demeaning characterization, or mere disclosure of items of personal life that have no bearing upon suitability for office. Imagine how much all of this would increase if it could be done anonymously. The principal impediment against it is the reluctance of most individuals and organizations to be publicly associated with uncharitable and uncivil expression.

Consider, moreover, the increased potential for "dirty tricks." It is not unheard-of for campaign operatives to circulate material over the name of their opponents or their opponents' supporters (a violation of election laws) in order to attract or alienate certain interest groups. How much easier—and sanction-free!—it would be to circulate anonymous material (for example, a *really* tasteless, though not actionably false, attack upon one's own candidate) with the hope and expectation that it will be attributed to, and held against, the other side.

[B.] The Court contends that demanding the disclosure of the pamphleteer's identity is no different from requiring the disclosure of any other information that may reduce the persuasiveness of the pamphlet's message. It cites *Tornillo,* which held it unconstitutional to require a newspaper that had published an editorial critical of a particular candidate to furnish space for that candidate to reply.

But it is not *usual* for a speaker to put forward the best arguments against himself, and it is a great imposition upon free speech to make him do so. Whereas it is quite usual—it is expected—for a speaker to *identify* himself, and requiring that is (at least when there are no special circumstances present) virtually no imposition at all....

[C.] The provision before us here serves the same informational interest [as the provisions upheld in *Buckley*], as well as more important interests, which I have discussed above.... Surely in many if not most cases, [the information required to be filed with the FEC] will readily permit identification of the particular message that the would-be-anonymous campaigner sponsored. Besides which the burden of complying with [the provision involved in *Buckley*], which includes the filing of quarterly reports, is infinitely more onerous than Ohio's simple requirement for signature of campaign literature....

[D.] I do not know where the Court derives its perception that "anonymous pamphleteering is ... an honorable tradition of advocacy and of dissent." I can imagine no reason why an anonymous leaflet is any more honorable, as a general matter, than an anonymous phone call or an anonymous letter. It facilitates wrong by eliminating accountability, which is ordinarily the very purpose of the anonymity.

There are of course exceptions, and where anonymity is needed to avoid "threats, harassment, or reprisals" the First Amendment will require an exemption from the Ohio law. Cf. *NAACP v. Alabama ex rel. Patterson.* But to strike down the Ohio law in its general application—and similar laws of 49 other States and the Federal Government—on the ground that all anonymous communication is in our society traditionally sacrosanct, seems to me a distortion of the past that will lead to a coarsening of the future....

e.   *Citizens United v. FEC, 558 U.S. 310 (2010)*

Justice Kennedy delivered the opinion of the Court [joined on this point by all the Justices except Justice Thomas]....

[A.] Citizens United ... challenges BCRA's [the Bipartisan Campaign Reform Act's] disclaimer and disclosure provisions as applied to [the pay-per-view television broadcast of] *Hillary* and the three advertisements [one 30-second and two 10-second] for the movie.

Under BCRA § 311, televised electioneering communications funded by anyone other than a candidate must include a disclaimer that "_____ is responsible for the content of this advertising.'" The required statement must be made in a "clearly spoken manner," and displayed on the screen in a "clearly readable manner" for at least four seconds. It must state that the communication "is not authorized by any candidate or candidate's committee"; it must also display the name and address (or Web site address) of the person or group that funded the advertisement.

Under BCRA § 201, any person who spends more than $10,000 on electioneering communications within a calendar year must file a disclosure statement with the FEC. That statement must identify the person making the expenditure, the amount of the expenditure, the election to which the communication was directed, and the names of certain contributors.

Disclaimer and disclosure requirements may burden the ability to speak, but they "impose no ceiling on campaign-related activities," and "do not prevent anyone from speaking." The Court has subjected these requirements to "exacting scrutiny," which requires a "substantial relation" between the disclosure requirement and a "sufficiently important" governmental interest....

[B.] The disclaimers required by § 311 "provid[e] the electorate with information," and "insure that the voters are fully informed" about the person or group who is speaking. At the very least, the disclaimers avoid confusion by making clear that the ads are not funded by a candidate or political party.

Citizens United argues that § 311 is underinclusive because it requires disclaimers for broadcast advertisements but not for print or Internet advertising. It asserts that § 311 decreases both the quantity and effectiveness of the group's speech by forcing it to devote four seconds of each advertisement to the spoken disclaimer. We rejected these arguments in *McConnell v. FEC*, 540 U.S. 93 (2003), [saying, "BCRA § 311's inclusion of electioneering communications in the ... disclosure regime bears a sufficient relationship to the important governmental interest of 'shed[ding] the light of publicity' on campaign financing."—ed.] And we now adhere to that decision as it pertains to the disclosure provisions....

[For similar reasons,] the ... interest [in providing voters with more information] is sufficient to justify application of § 201 to these ads .... {[P]rompt disclosure of expenditures can provide shareholders and citizens with the information needed to hold corporations and elected officials accountable for their positions and supporters. Shareholders can determine whether their corporation's political speech advances the corporation's interest in making profits, and citizens can see whether elected officials are "'in the pocket' of so-called moneyed interests." The First Amendment protects political speech; and disclosure permits citizens and shareholders to react to the speech of corporate entities in a proper way. This transparency enables the electorate to make informed decisions and give proper weight to different speakers and messages.}

Some *amici* point to recent events in which donors to certain causes were blacklisted, threatened, or otherwise targeted for retaliation.... [Section] 201 would be unconstitutional as applied to an organization if there were a reasonable probability that the group's members would face threats, harassment, or reprisals if their names were disclosed. The examples cited by *amici* are cause for concern.

Citizens United, however, has offered no evidence that its members may face similar threats or reprisals. To the contrary, Citizens United has been disclosing its donors for years and has identified no instance of harassment or retaliation....

For the same reasons we uphold the application of BCRA §§ 201 and 311 to the ads, we affirm their application to *Hillary*....

[C.] [The Court did not discuss why its § 311 holding is consistent with *McIntyre v. Ohio Elections Comm'n*, but **in *McConnell v. FEC* the Court said:**—ed.] "[P]reserving the integrity of the electoral process, preventing corruption, and 'sustain[ing] the active, alert responsibility of the individual citizen in a democracy for the wise conduct of the government' are interests of the highest importance." "Preservation of the individual citizen's confidence in government," ... "is equally important." BCRA's fidelity to those imperatives sets it apart ... from the Ohio statute banning the distribution of anonymous campaign literature, struck down in *McIntyre*.

Justice Thomas, ... dissenting in [relevant] part [back in *Citizens United*]....

[A.] Congress may not abridge the "right to anonymous speech" based on the "'simple interest in providing voters with additional relevant information'" (quoting *McIntyre*). In continuing to hold otherwise, the Court misapprehends the import of "recent events" that some *amici* describe "in which donors to certain causes were blacklisted, threatened, or otherwise targeted for retaliation." ...

Amici's examples relate principally to Proposition 8, a state ballot proposition that California voters narrowly passed in the 2008 general election. Proposition 8 amended California's constitution to provide that "[o]nly marriage between a man and a woman is valid or recognized in California." Any donor who gave more than $100 to any committee supporting or opposing Proposition 8 was required to disclose his full name, street address, occupation, employer's name (or business name, if self-employed), and the total amount of his contributions. [BCRA imposes similar disclosure requirements.]

Some opponents of Proposition 8 compiled this information and created Web sites with maps showing the locations of homes or businesses of Proposition 8 supporters. Many supporters (or their customers) suffered property damage, or threats of physical violence or death, as a result. They cited these incidents in a complaint they filed after the 2008 election, seeking to invalidate California's mandatory disclosure laws.

Supporters recounted being told: "Consider yourself lucky. If I had a gun I would have gunned you down along with each and every other supporter," or, "we have plans for you and your friends." Proposition 8 opponents also allegedly harassed the measure's supporters by defacing or damaging their property. Two religious organizations supporting Proposition 8 reportedly received through the mail envelopes containing a white powdery substance.

Those accounts are consistent with media reports describing Proposition 8-related retaliation. The director of the nonprofit California Musical Theater gave $1,000 to support the initiative; he was forced to resign after artists complained to his employer. The director of the Los Angeles Film Festival was forced to resign after giving $1,500 because opponents threatened to boycott and picket the next festival. And a woman who had managed her popular, family-owned restaurant for 26 years was forced to resign after she gave $100, because "throngs of [angry] protesters" repeatedly arrived at the restaurant and "shout[ed] 'shame on you' at customers." The police even had to "arriv[e] in riot gear one night to quell the angry mob" at the restaurant.

Some supporters of Proposition 8 engaged in similar tactics; one real estate businessman in San Diego who had donated to a group opposing Proposition 8 "received a letter from the Prop. 8 Executive Committee threatening to publish his company's name if he didn't also donate to the 'Yes on 8' campaign."

The success of such intimidation tactics has apparently spawned a cottage industry that uses forcibly disclosed donor information to *pre-empt* citizens' exercise of their First Amendment rights. Before the 2008 Presidential election, a "newly formed nonprofit group ... plann[ed] to confront donors to conservative groups, hoping to create a chilling effect that will dry up contributions." Its leader, "who described his effort as 'going for the jugular,'" detailed the group's plan to send a "warning letter ... alerting donors who might be considering giving to right-wing groups to a variety of potential dangers, including legal trouble, public exposure and watchdog groups digging through their lives."

[B.] These instances of retaliation sufficiently demonstrate why this Court should invalidate mandatory disclosure and reporting requirements. But *amici* present evidence of yet another reason to do so—the threat of retaliation from *elected officials*. As *amici's* submissions make clear, this threat extends far beyond a single ballot proposition in California.

For example, a candidate challenging an incumbent state attorney general reported that some members of the State's business community feared donating to his campaign because they did not want to cross the incumbent; in his words, "'I go to so many people and hear the same thing: 'I sure hope you beat [the incumbent], but I can't afford to have my name on your records. He might come after me next.'"" The incumbent won reelection in 2008.

My point is not to express any view on the merits of the political controversies I describe. Rather, it is to demonstrate—using real-world, recent examples—the fallacy in the Court's conclusion that "[d]isclaimer and disclosure requirements ... impose no ceiling on campaign-related activities, and do not prevent anyone from speaking." Of course they do. Disclaimer and disclosure requirements enable private citizens and elected officials to implement political strategies *specifically calculated* to curtail campaign-related activity and prevent the lawful, peaceful exercise of First Amendment rights.

[C.] The Court nevertheless insists that as-applied challenges to disclosure requirements will suffice to vindicate those speech rights, as long as potential plaintiffs can "show a reasonable probability that disclosure ... will subject them to threats, harassment, or reprisals from either Government officials or private parties." But the Court's opinion itself proves the irony in this compromise.

In correctly explaining why it must address the facial constitutionality of § 203 [the restriction on corporate and union speech—ed.], the Court recognizes that "[t]he First Amendment does not permit laws that force speakers to ... seek declaratory rulings before discussing the most salient political issues of our day"; that as-applied challenges to § 203 "would require substantial litigation over an extended time" and result in an "interpretive process [that] itself would create an inevitable, pervasive, and serious risk of chilling protected speech pending the drawing of fine distinctions that, in the end, would themselves be questionable"; ... and that avoiding a facial

challenge to § 203 "would prolong the substantial, nation-wide chilling effect" that § 203 causes. This logic, of course, applies equally to as-applied
challenges to §§ 201 and 311.

Irony aside, the Court's promise that as-applied challenges will adequately protect speech is a hollow assurance. Now more than ever, §§ 201
and 311 will chill protected speech because—as California voters can attest—"the advent of the Internet" enables "prompt disclosure of expenditures," which "provide[s]" political opponents "with the information needed"
to intimidate and retaliate against their foes. Thus, "disclosure permits citizens ... to react to the speech of [their political opponents] in a proper"—or
undeniably *improper*—"way" long before a plaintiff could prevail on an as-
applied challenge.

I cannot endorse a view of the First Amendment that subjects citizens
of this Nation to death threats, ruined careers, damaged or defaced property, or pre-emptive and threatening warning letters as the price for engaging in "core political speech, the 'primary object of First Amendment protection.'" Accordingly, I respectfully dissent from the Court's judgment upholding BCRA §§ 201 and 311.

f.   *Doe v. Reed, 561 U.S. 186 (2010)*

Chief Justice Roberts delivered the opinion of the Court.

[A.] The State of Washington allows its citizens to challenge state laws
by referendum. Roughly four percent of Washington voters must sign a petition to place such a referendum on the ballot. That petition, which by law
must include the names and addresses of the signers, is then submitted to
the government for verification and canvassing, to ensure that only lawful
signatures are counted. The Washington Public Records Act (PRA) authorizes private parties to obtain copies of government documents, and the State
construes the PRA to cover submitted referendum petitions.

This case arises out of a state law extending certain benefits to same-
sex couples, and a corresponding referendum petition [R–71] to put that law
to a popular vote. Respondent intervenors [Washington Coalition for Open
Government, a group that generally supports disclosure of public records,
and Washington Families Standing Together, a group that supports the
same-sex couple benefit law—ed.] invoked the PRA to obtain copies of the
petition, with the names and addresses of the signers. Certain petition signers and the petition sponsor objected, arguing that such public disclosure
would violate their rights under the First Amendment....

The issue at this stage of the case is not whether disclosure of this particular petition would violate the First Amendment, but whether disclosure
of referendum petitions in general would do so....

[B.] The compelled disclosure of signatory information on referendum
petitions is subject to review under the First Amendment. An individual
expresses a view on a political matter when he signs a petition under Washington's referendum procedure.... [T]he individual's signature will express
the view that the law subject to the petition should be overturned ... [or at

least] that the question should be considered "by the whole electorate." ... The State, having "cho[sen] to tap the energy and the legitimizing power of the democratic process, ... must accord the participants in that process the First Amendment rights that attach to their roles." ...

{Justice Scalia doubts whether petition signing is entitled to any First Amendment protection at all. His skepticism is based on the view that petition signing has "legal effects" in the legislative process, while other aspects of political participation ... do not. That line is not as sharp as Justice Scalia would have it; he himself recognizes "the existence of a First Amendment interest in voting," which of course also can have legal effect.

The distinction becomes even fuzzier given that only *some* petition signing has legal effect, and any such legal effect attaches only well after the expressive act of signing, if the secretary determines that the petition satisfies the requirements for inclusion on the ballot.} [And in any event] we do not see how adding such legal effect to an expressive activity somehow deprives that activity of its expressive component, taking it outside the scope of the First Amendment....

[C.] But ... the electoral context is [r]elevant to the nature of our First Amendment review. We allow States significant flexibility in implementing their own voting systems. To the extent a regulation concerns the legal effect of a particular activity in that process, the government will be afforded substantial latitude to enforce that regulation. Also pertinent to our analysis is the fact that the PRA is not a prohibition on speech, but instead a *disclosure* requirement. "[D]isclosure requirements may burden the ability to speak, but they ... do not prevent anyone from speaking." *Citizens United v. FEC....*

First Amendment challenges to disclosure requirements in the electoral context ... [are] reviewed ... under what has been termed "exacting scrutiny." See, *e.g.*, *Buckley v. Valeo*; *Citizens United*. That standard "requires a 'substantial relation' between the disclosure requirement and a 'sufficiently important' governmental interest." To withstand this scrutiny, "the strength of the governmental interest must reflect the seriousness of the actual burden on First Amendment rights." ...

[D.] The State's interest in preserving the integrity of the electoral process is undoubtedly important.... The State's interest is particularly strong with respect to efforts to root out fraud, which not only may produce fraudulent outcomes, but has a systemic effect as well: It "drives honest citizens out of the democratic process and breeds distrust of our government." The threat of fraud in this context is not merely hypothetical; respondents and their *amici* cite a number of cases of petition-related fraud across the country to support the point.

But the State's interest in preserving electoral integrity is not limited to combating fraud. That interest extends to efforts to ferret out invalid signatures caused not by fraud but by simple mistake, such as duplicate signatures or signatures of individuals who are not registered to vote in the State. That interest also extends more generally to promoting transparency and accountability in the electoral process, which the State argues is "essential to the proper functioning of a democracy."

Plaintiffs contend that the disclosure requirements of the PRA are not "sufficiently related" to the interest of protecting the integrity of the electoral process. They argue that disclosure is not necessary because the secretary of state is already charged with verifying and canvassing the names on a petition, advocates and opponents of a measure can observe that process, and any citizen can challenge the secretary's actions in court. They also stress that existing criminal penalties reduce the danger of fraud in the petition process.

But the secretary's verification and canvassing will not catch all invalid signatures: The job is large and difficult (the secretary ordinarily checks "only 3 to 5% of signatures"), and the secretary can make mistakes, too. Public disclosure can help cure the inadequacies of the verification and canvassing process.

Disclosure also helps prevent certain types of petition fraud otherwise difficult to detect, such as outright forgery and "bait and switch" fraud, in which an individual signs the petition based on a misrepresentation of the underlying issue. Cf. Brief for Massachusetts Gay and Lesbian Political Caucus et al. as *Amici Curiae* (detailing "bait and switch" fraud in a petition drive in Massachusetts). The signer is in the best position to detect these types of fraud, and public disclosure can bring the issue to the signer's attention.

Public disclosure thus helps ensure that the only signatures counted are those that should be, and that the only referenda placed on the ballot are those that garner enough valid signatures. Public disclosure also promotes transparency and accountability in the electoral process to an extent other measures cannot.... [P]ublic disclosure of referendum petitions in general is substantially related to the important interest of preserving the integrity of the electoral process. {Justice Thomas's contrary assessment ... is based on his determination that strict scrutiny applies, rather than the standard of review that we have concluded is appropriate.}

{Because we determine that the State's interest in preserving the integrity of the electoral process suffices to defeat the argument that the PRA is unconstitutional with respect to referendum petitions in general, we ... do not[] address the State's [interest in providing information to the electorate about who supports the petition].} ...

[E.] Plaintiffs' more significant objection is [their claim] that the objective of those seeking disclosure of the R–71 petition is not to prevent fraud, but to publicly identify those who had validly signed and to broadcast the signers' political views on the subject of the petition.... The question before us, however, is not whether PRA disclosure violates the First Amendment with respect to those who signed the R–71 petition, or other particularly controversial petitions.

The question instead is whether such disclosure in general violates the First Amendment rights of those who sign referendum petitions.... [T]ypical referendum petitions "concern tax policy, revenue, budget, or other state law issues." Voters care about such issues, some quite deeply—but there is no reason to assume that any burdens imposed by disclosure of typical referendum petitions would be remotely like the burdens plaintiffs fear in this case.... Several other petitions in the State "have been subject to release in recent years," ... but apparently that release has come without incident....

[Our] upholding the law against a broad-based challenge does not foreclose a litigant's success in a narrower [as-applied] one.... [P]laintiffs may press the [as-applied] challenge ... in ... the District Court....

Justice Sotomayor, with whom Justice Stevens and Justice Ginsburg join, concurring....

[T]he burden of public disclosure on speech and associational rights [is] minimal in this context.... "[D]isclosure requirements ... 'do not prevent anyone from speaking.'" ...

When it comes to initiatives and referenda, the impact of public disclosure on expressive interests is even more attenuated. While campaign-finance disclosure injects the government into what would otherwise have been private political activity, the process of legislating by referendum is inherently public.

To qualify a referendum for the ballot, citizens are required to sign a petition and supply identifying information to the State. The act of signing typically occurs in public, and the circulators who collect and submit signatures ordinarily owe signers no guarantee of confidentiality. For persons with the "civic courage" to participate in this process, the State's decision to make accessible what they voluntarily place in the public sphere should not deter them from engaging in the expressive act of petition signing....

Justice Stevens, with whom Justice Breyer joins, concurring in part and concurring in the judgment. [Justice Stevens largely agreed with Justice Sotomayor.—ed.]

Justice Scalia, concurring in the judgment....

[A.] I doubt whether signing a petition that has the effect of suspending a law fits within "the freedom of speech" at all. But even if ... it does, ... [o]ur Nation's longstanding traditions of legislating and voting in public refute the claim that the First Amendment accords a right to anonymity in the performance of an act with governmental effect....

When a Washington voter signs a referendum petition subject to the PRA, he is acting as a legislator. The Washington Constitution vests "[t]he legislative authority" of the State in the legislature, but "the people reserve to themselves the power ... to approve or reject at the polls any ... law passed by the legislature." ... The filing of a referendum petition that [contains enough signatures] has two legal effects: (1) It requires the secretary to place the measure referred to the people on the ballot at the next general election; and (2) it suspends operation of the measure, causing it only to have effect 30 days after it is approved during that election.

A voter who signs a referendum petition is therefore exercising legislative power because his signature, somewhat like a vote for or against a bill in the legislature, seeks to affect the legal force of the measure at issue. {[Even as to] petitions that ... lack the requisite number of signatures ..., the petition signer has exercised *his portion* of the legislative power when he signs the petition, much like a legislator who casts a losing vote.}

Plaintiffs ... identify [no] historical evidence demonstrating that "the freedom of speech" the First Amendment codified encompassed a right to legislate without public disclosure.... [T]he exercise of lawmaking power in the United States has traditionally been public. The public nature of federal lawmaking is constitutionally required.... State constitutions enacted around the time of the founding had similar provisions....

Moreover, even when the people *asked* Congress for legislative changes—by exercising their constitutional right to "to petition the Government for a redress of grievances"—they did so publicly. The petition was read aloud in Congress. The petitioner's name (when large groups were not involved), his request, and what action Congress had taken on the petition were consistently recorded in the House and Senate Journals. Even when the people exercised legislative power directly, they did so not anonymously, but openly in town hall meetings.

Petitioning the government and participating in the traditional town meeting were precursors of the modern initiative and referendum.... The most influential advocate of the initiative and referendum in the United States analogized the Swiss practice [on which the initiative and referendum were modeled] to the town meeting, because both "required open conduct of political affairs and free expression of opinions." Plaintiffs' argument implies that the public nature of these practices, so longstanding and unquestioned, violated the freedom of speech. There is no historical support for such a claim....

Voting was [also] public until 1888 .... We have acknowledged the existence of a First Amendment interest in voting, but we have never said that it includes the right to vote anonymously. The history of voting in the United States completely undermines that claim.

Initially, the Colonies mostly continued the English traditions of voting by a show of hands or by voice—*viva voce* voting. [Details omitted.—ed.] ... It was precisely discontent over the nonsecret nature of [earlier voting systems], and the abuses that produced, which led to the States' adoption of the Australian secret ballot [in 1888–96].... But I am aware of no contention that the Australian system was required by the First Amendment (or the state counterparts). That would have been utterly implausible, since the inhabitants of the Colonies, the States, and the United States had found public voting entirely compatible with "the freedom of speech" for several centuries....

As I said in *McIntyre*, "[w]here the meaning of a constitutional text (such as 'the freedom of speech') is unclear, the widespread and long-accepted practices of the American people are the best indication of what fundamental beliefs it was intended to enshrine." Just as the century-old practice of States' prohibiting anonymous electioneering was sufficient for me to reject the First Amendment claim to anonymity in *McIntyre*, the many-centuries-old practices of public legislating and voting are sufficient for me to reject plaintiffs' claim....

[B.] There are laws against threats and intimidation; and harsh criticism, short of unlawful action, is a price our people have traditionally been willing to pay for self-governance. Requiring people to stand up in public for their political acts fosters civic courage, without which democracy is doomed. For my part, I do not look forward to a society which, thanks to the Supreme Court, campaigns anonymously *(McIntyre)* and even exercises the direct democracy of initiative and referendum hidden from public scrutiny and protected from the accountability of criticism. This does not resemble the Home of the Brave.

Justice Thomas, dissenting.

[A.] Just as "[c]onfidence in the integrity of our electoral processes is essential to the functioning of our participatory democracy," so too is citizen *participation* in those processes .... In my view, compelled disclosure of signed referendum and initiative petitions under the Washington Public Records Act (PRA) severely burdens those rights and chills citizen participation in the referendum process....

[S]igning a referendum petition amounts to "'political association'" protected by the First Amendment.... "[T]he Constitution protects against the compelled disclosure of political associations and beliefs." ... [U]nlike the Court, I ... [would] require application of strict scrutiny to laws that compel disclosure of protected First Amendment association. Under that standard, a disclosure requirement passes constitutional muster only if it is narrowly tailored—*i.e.*, the least restrictive means—to serve a compelling state interest....

[B.] Washington first contends that it has a compelling interest in ... preserving the integrity of its election process, preventing corruption, deterring fraud, and correcting mistakes by the secretary of state or by petition signers....

[But] "[t]he risk of fraud or corruption, or the appearance thereof, is more remote at the petition stage of an initiative than at the time of balloting." Similarly, because "[r]eferenda are held on issues, not candidates for public office," the "risk of corruption perceived in cases involving candidate elections simply is not present in a popular vote on a public issue." *First Nat'l Bank of Boston v. Bellotti.* We should not abandon those principles merely because Washington and its *amici* can point to a mere eight instances of initiative-related fraud, among the 809 initiative measures placed on state ballots in this country between 1988 and 2008....

[And even assuming that] Washington's interest in protecting the integrity and reliability of its referendum process ... is compelling, on-demand disclosure of a referendum petition to any person under the PRA is "a blunderbuss approach" to furthering that interest, not the least restrictive means of doing so.... Washington ... could put the names and addresses of referendum signers into .... [an] electronic database that state employees could search *without* subjecting the name and address of each signer to wholesale public disclosure. The secretary could electronically cross-reference the referendum database against the "statewide voter registration list" contained in Washington's "statewide voter registration database," to ensure that each referendum signer meets Washington's residency and voter registration requirements. Doing so presumably would drastically reduce or eliminate possible errors or mistakes that Washington argues the secretary *might* make, since it would allow the secretary to verify virtually all of the signatures instead of the mere "3 to 5%" he "ordinarily checks."

An electronic referendum database would also enable the secretary to determine whether multiple entries correspond to a single registered voter, thereby detecting whether a voter had signed the petition more than once. In addition, the database would protect victims of "forgery" or "'bait and switch' fraud." In Washington, "a unique identifier is assigned to each legally registered voter in the state." Washington could create a Web site, linked to the electronic referendum database, where a voter concerned that his name had been fraudulently signed could conduct a search using his unique identifier to ensure that his name was absent from the database—without requiring disclosure of the names and addresses of all the voluntary, legitimate signers.... Implementing such a system would not place a heavy burden on Washington; "the Secretary of State's staff" already uses an "electronic voter registration database" in its "verification process."

Washington nevertheless contends that its citizens must "have access to public records ... to independently evaluate whether the Secretary properly determined to certify or not to certify a referendum to the ballot." ... [But under Washington law,] "the verification and canvass of signatures on the [referendum] petition may be observed by persons representing the advocates and opponents of the proposed measure so long as they make no record of the names, addresses, or other information on the petitions or related records except upon" court order....

Washington does not explain why this existing access, which petitioners do not challenge here, is insufficient to permit its citizens to oversee the verification process ..., or to decide intelligently whether to pursue a court challenge .... Moreover, if Washington had implemented the more narrowly tailored electronic referendum database discussed above, observers could see the secretary of state's employees examine the data using exactly the same techniques they would use if the data were released to them under the PRA....

It is readily apparent that Washington can vindicate its stated interest in "transparency and accountability" through a number of more narrowly tailored means than wholesale public disclosure. Accordingly, this interest cannot justify applying the PRA to a referendum petition.

[C.] Washington also contends that it has a compelling interest in "providing relevant information to Washington voters," and that on-demand disclosure to the public is a narrowly tailored means of furthering that interest.... [T]his Court has already rejected [this argument] in ... *McIntyre* .... People are intelligent enough to evaluate the merits of a referendum without knowing who supported it....

[D.] Significant practical problems will result from requiring as-applied challenges to protect referendum signers' constitutional rights. The Court's approach will "require substantial litigation over an extended time" before a potential signer of any referendum will learn whether, if he signs a referendum, his associational privacy right will remain intact....

[If] the sponsor [is allowed to] seek an injunction against disclosure through an as-applied challenge before filing the proposed measure, ... the sponsor will not be able to present any evidence specific to signers or potential signers of *that particular referendum* showing "a reasonable probability that the compelled disclosure [of personal information] will subject them to threats, harassment, or reprisals from either Government officials or private parties." Thus, to succeed at that stage of litigation, plaintiffs must point to (at least) one other instance of harassment arising from a similar referendum. The Court has never held that such evidence would be acceptable; but if it is, that necessarily means that some signers, at some point, will have suffered actual "threats, harassment, and reprisals" for engaging in protected First Amendment activity.

If the sponsor must wait at least until signature-gathering has started on *his* referendum to file an as-applied challenge, it is still unclear what sort of evidence of "threats, harassment, or reprisals" directed toward *his* supporters would satisfy the Court's standard. How many instances of "threats, harassment or reprisals" must a signer endure before a court may grant relief on an as-applied challenge? And how dispersed throughout the group of the necessary 120,000 signers, must these threats be?

More importantly, the Court's standard does not appear to require *actual* "threats, harassment, or reprisals," but merely a *"reasonable probability"* that disclosure of the signers' names and addresses will lead to such activity. What sort of evidence suffices to satisfy this apparently more relaxed, though perhaps more elusive, standard? Does one instance of actual harassment directed toward one signer mean that the "reasonable probability" requirement is met? And again, how widespread must this "reasonable probability" be? The Court does not answer any of these questions, leaving a vacuum to be filled on a case-by-case basis....

[E.] [Moreover, the availability of the Internet] creates at least *some* probability that signers of every referendum will be subjected to threats, harassment, or reprisals if their personal information is disclosed.... The Court apparently disagrees, asserting that "there is no reason to assume that any burdens imposed by disclosure of typical referendum petitions would be remotely like the burdens plaintiffs fear in this case." That conclusion rests on the premise that some referendum measures are so benign that the fact of public disclosure will not chill protected First Amendment activity. I am not convinced that this premise is correct....

[T]he referendum and initiative process first gained popularity as a means of "provid[ing] an occasional safety valve for interests that failed to get a fair hearing in the legislatures." Unsurprisingly, such interests tended to be controversial by nature. Early examples include "the single tax, prohibition, women's suffrage, prolabor legislation, and the graduated income tax." And proponents of initiative measures tended to include politically marginalized groups such as the "Farmer's Alliance" in rural states; "[t]housands of labor federations, notably the miners"; and "the Women's Suffrage Association," which "saw the initiative and referendum as a possible new means to overcome" repeated failed attempts in state legislatures to secure for women the right to vote....

"[D]isclosure requirements enable private citizens and elected officials to implement political strategies *specifically calculated* to curtail campaign-related activity and prevent the lawful, peaceful exercise of First Amendment rights." ... [T]he First Amendment does not require "case-by-case determinations" if "archetypical" First Amendment rights "would be chilled in the meantime." ... [In my view, signers of referendum petitions need not] resort to "substantial litigation over an extended time," to prevent Washington from trenching on their protected First Amendment rights by subjecting their referendum-petition signatures to on-demand public disclosure....

4.   ELECTION-RELATED SPEECH: AS-APPLIED CHALLENGES

a.   *Summary*

Even when disclosure requirements are generally constitutional on their face, they may be challenged as applied. The government must give exemptions from the requirements when challengers can show that their supporters (*e.g.*, contributors or petition signers) would face substantial retaliation for their speech, signature, or contribution. *Brown v. Socialist Workers '74 Campaign Comm.* (1982) (p. 458); *Doe v. Reed* (2010) (p. 460). But it's not clear just how much of a showing, and of how substantial a retaliation, is required.

b.   *Brown v. Socialist Workers '74 Campaign Comm., 459 U.S. 87 (1982)*

Justice Marshall delivered the opinion of the Court [which was unanimous on this point—ed.]....

[A.] The Socialist Workers Party is a small political party with approximately sixty members in the State of Ohio. The party states in its constitution that its aim is "the abolition of capitalism and the establishment of a workers' government to achieve socialism." As the District Court found, the SWP does not advocate the use of violence. It seeks instead to achieve social change through the political process ....

The SWP's candidates have had little success at the polls. In 1980, for example, the Ohio SWP's candidate for the United States Senate received fewer than 77,000 votes, less than 1.9% of the total vote. Campaign contributions and expenditures in Ohio have averaged about $15,000 annually since 1974.

In 1974 appellees [sued] ... challenging the constitutionality of the disclosure provisions of the Ohio Campaign Expense Reporting Law. The Ohio statute requires every candidate for political office to file a statement identifying each contributor .... The lists of names and addresses of contributors ... are open to public inspection ....

[**B.**] *Buckley v. Valeo* set forth the following test for determining when the First Amendment requires exempting minor parties from compelled disclosures: "The evidence offered need show only a reasonable probability that the compelled disclosure of a party's contributors' names will subject them to threats, harassment, or reprisals from either Government officials or private parties."

The Court acknowledged that "unduly strict requirements of proof could impose a heavy burden" on minor parties. Accordingly, the Court emphasized that "[m]inor parties must be allowed sufficient flexibility in the proof of injury." "The proof may include, for example, specific evidence of past or present harassment of members due to their associational ties, or of harassment directed against the organization itself. A pattern of threats or specific manifestations of public hostility may be sufficient. New parties that have no history upon which to draw may be able to offer evidence of reprisals and threats directed against individuals or organizations holding similar views."
...

[**C.**] Appellees introduced proof of specific incidents of private and government hostility toward the SWP and its members within the four years preceding the trial. These incidents, many of which occurred in Ohio and neighboring states, included threatening phone calls and hate mail, the burning of SWP literature, the destruction of SWP members' property, police harassment of a party candidate, and the firing of shots at an SWP office.

{Anti-SWP occurrences in places such as Chicago (SWP office vandalized) and Pittsburgh (shot fired at SWP building) are certainly relevant to the determination of the public's attitude toward the SWP in Ohio. In *Buckley* we stated that "[n]ew parties that have no history upon which to draw may ... offer evidence of reprisals and threats directed against individuals or organizations holding similar views." Surely the Ohio SWP may offer evidence of the experiences of other chapters espousing the same political philosophy.

Appellants point to the lack of direct evidence linking the Ohio statute's disclosure requirements to the harassment of campaign contributors .... [But we reject] such "unduly strict requirements of proof" in favor of "flexibility in the proof of injury." We thus rejected requiring a minor party to "come forward with witnesses who are too fearful to contribute but not too fearful to testify about their fears" or prove that "chill and harassment [are] directly attributable to the specific disclosures from which the exemption is sought."}

There was also evidence that in the 12-month period before trial 22 SWP members, including 4 in Ohio, were fired because of their party membership. Although appellants contend that two of the Ohio firings were not politically motivated, the evidence amply supports the District Court's conclusion that "private hostility and harassment toward SWP members make it difficult for them to maintain employment."

The District Court also found a past history of government harassment of the SWP. FBI surveillance of the SWP was "massive" and continued until at least 1976. The FBI also conducted a counterintelligence program against the SWP and the Young Socialist Alliance (YSA), the SWP's youth organization. One of the aims of the "SWP Disruption Program" was the dissemination of information designed to impair the ability of the SWP and YSA to function. This program included "disclosing to the press the criminal records of SWP candidates, and sending anonymous letters to SWP members, supporters, spouses, and employers."

Until at least 1976, the FBI employed various covert techniques to obtain information about the SWP, including information concerning the sources of its funds and the nature of its expenditures.... [T]he FBI had conducted surveillance of the Ohio SWP and had interfered with its activities within the State.... The United States Civil Service Commission also gathered information on the SWP, the YSA, and their supporters, and the FBI routinely distributed its reports to Army, Navy and Air Force Intelligence, the United States Secret Service, and the Immigration and Naturalization Service....

Appellants challenge the relevance of this evidence of Government harassment in light of recent efforts to curb official misconduct. Notwithstanding these efforts, the evidence suggests that hostility toward the SWP is ingrained and likely to continue.... In light of the substantial evidence of past and present hostility from private persons and government officials against the SWP, Ohio's campaign disclosure requirements cannot be constitutionally applied to the Ohio SWP.

c.   *Doe v. Reed, 561 U.S. 186 (2010)*

[For the facts, see p. 450.—ed.]

Chief Justice Roberts delivered the opinion of the Court....

[Our] upholding the law against a broad-based challenge does not foreclose a litigant's success in a narrower [as-applied] one.... [P]laintiffs may press the [as-applied] challenge ... in ... the District Court....

Justice Alito, concurring....

[A.] [P]laintiffs have provided no reason to think that disclosure of signatory information [for many kinds of referendum petitions] would significantly chill the willingness of voters to sign. Plaintiffs' facial challenge therefore must fail.

[B.] Nonetheless, ... [b]ecause compelled disclosure can "burden the ability to speak" and "seriously infringe on privacy of association and belief guaranteed by the First Amendment," the as-applied exemption plays a critical role in safeguarding First Amendment rights. [And t]he possibility of prevailing in an as-applied challenge provides adequate protection for First Amendment rights only if ... voters ... have some assurance *at the time when they are presented with the petition* that their names and identifying information will not be released to the public.

The only way a circulator can provide such assurance ... is if the circulator has sought and obtained an as-applied exemption from the disclosure requirement well before circulating the petition. Otherwise, the best the circulator could do would be to tell voters that an exemption might be obtained at some point in the future. Such speculation would often be insufficient to alleviate voters' concerns about the possibility of being subjected to threats, harassment, or reprisals.

Additionally, speakers must be able to obtain an as-applied exemption ... [just by showing] "... a *reasonable probability*" that disclosure will lead to threats, harassment, or reprisals.... [And] speakers [must be free] rely on a wide array of evidence to meet that standard, including "specific evidence of past or present harassment of [group] members," "harassment directed against the organization itself," or a "pattern of threats or specific manifestations of public hostility." Significantly, ... "[n]ew [groups] that have no history upon which to draw may be able to offer evidence of reprisals and threats directed against individuals or organizations holding similar views." ...

[T]he plaintiffs in this case [therefore] have a strong argument that the PRA violates the First Amendment as applied to the Referendum 71 petition. Consider first the burdens on plaintiffs' First Amendment rights. The widespread harassment and intimidation suffered by supporters of California's Proposition 8 provides strong support for an as-applied exemption in the present case.... See[, *e.g.*,] *Citizens United v. FEC* (opinion of Thomas, J.) [p. 448 above—ed.].... [I]f the evidence relating to Proposition 8 is not sufficient to obtain an as-applied exemption in this case, one may wonder whether that vehicle provides any meaningful protection for the First Amendment rights of persons who circulate and sign referendum and initiative petitions....

[Plaintiffs will also] have the opportunity to develop evidence of intimidation and harassment of Referendum 71 supporters—an opportunity that was pretermitted because of the District Court's decision to grant a preliminary injunction on [plaintiffs' facial challenge]. For example, plaintiffs allege that the campaign manager for one of the plaintiff groups received threatening e-mails and phone calls, and that the threats were so severe that the manager filed a complaint with the local sheriff and had his children sleep in an interior room of his home.

[C.] The inadequacy of the State's interests in compelling public disclosure of referendum signatory information further confirms that courts should be generous in granting as-applied relief in this context....

[1.] [R]espondents' asserted ... interest [in providing information to voters about who supports a referendum petition] will not in any case be sufficient to trump the First Amendment rights of signers and circulators who face a threat of harassment. Respondents maintain that publicly disclosing the names and addresses of referendum signatories provides the voting public with "insight into whether support for holding a vote comes predominantly from particular interest groups, political or religious organizations, or other group[s] of citizens," and thus allows voters to draw inferences about whether they should support or oppose the referendum. Additionally, respondents argue that disclosure "allows Washington voters to engage in discussion of referred measures with persons whose acts secured the election and suspension of state law."

The implications of accepting such an argument are breathtaking. Were we to accept respondents' asserted informational interest, the State would be free to require petition signers to disclose all kinds of demographic information, including the signer's race, religion, political affiliation, sexual orientation, ethnic background, and interest-group memberships[, in violation of the right to privacy of belief and association]....

Respondents' informational interest is no more legitimate when viewed as a means of providing the public with information needed to locate and contact supporters of a referendum. In the name of pursuing such an interest, the State would be free to require petition signers to disclose any information that would more easily enable members of the voting public to contact them and engage them in discussion, including telephone numbers, e-mail addresses, and Internet aliases[, in violation of the right to associational privacy]....

But more important, when speakers are faced with a reasonable probability of harassment or intimidation, the State no longer has *any* interest in enabling the public to locate and contact supporters of a particular measure—for in that instance, disclosure becomes a means of facilitating harassment that impermissibly chills the exercise of First Amendment rights. In this case, two groups proposed to place on the Internet the names and addresses of all those who signed Referendum 71, and it is alleged that their express aim was to encourage "uncomfortable conversation[s]." ... [A]nyone with access to a computer could [then] compile a wealth of information about all of those persons, including in many cases ... the names of their spouses and neighbors, their telephone numbers, directions to their homes, ... any information posted on a social networking site, and newspaper articles in which their names appeared (including such things as wedding announcements, obituaries, and articles in local papers about their children's school and athletic activities). The potential that such information could be used for harassment is vast....

[2.] I agree with the Court that preserving the integrity of the referendum process constitutes a sufficiently important state interest. But I harbor serious doubts as to whether public disclosure of signatory information serves that interest in a way that always "reflect[s] the seriousness of the actual burden on First Amendment rights."

First, the realities of Washington law undermine the State's argument that public disclosure is necessary to ensure the integrity of the referendum process.... Washington's laws pertaining to initiatives and referenda did not [in 1912, when the initiative was first authorized] and do not now authorize the public disclosure of signatory information. Instead, the public disclosure requirement stems from the PRA, which was enacted in 1972 and which requires the public disclosure of state documents generally, not referendum documents specifically.

Indeed, if anything, Washington's referenda and initiative laws suggest that signatory information should remain confidential: Outside observers are permitted to observe the secretary of state's verification and canvassing process only "so long as they make no record of [signer] names [or] addresses ...," and the State is required to destroy all those petitions that fail to qualify for the ballot.

Second, ... public disclosure of referendum signatory information is a relatively recent practice in Washington.... [I]t appears that the secretary [of state] did not release *any* initiative petitions until 2006.... That history substantially undermines the State's assertion that public disclosure is necessary to ensure the integrity of the referendum process. For nearly a century, Washington's referendum process operated—and apparently operated successfully—without the public disclosure of signatory information. The State has failed to explain how circumstances have changed so dramatically in recent years that public disclosure is now required.

Third, the experiences of other States demonstrates that publicly disclosing the names and identifying information of referendum signatories is not necessary to protect against fraud and mistake. To give but one example, California has had more initiatives on the ballot than any other State save Oregon. Nonetheless, California law explicitly protects the privacy of initiative and referendum signatories....

Finally, Washington could easily and cheaply employ alternative mechanisms for protecting against fraud and mistake that would be far more protective of circulators' and signers' First Amendment rights. For example, the Washington attorney general represented to us at oral argument that "the Secretary of State's first step after receiving submitted petitions is to take them to his archiving section and to have them digitized." With a digitized list, it should be relatively easy for the secretary to check for duplicate signatures on a referendum petition. And given that the secretary maintains a "centralized, uniform, interactive computerized statewide voter registration list that contains the name and registration information of every registered voter in the state," the secretary could use a computer program to cross-check the names and addresses on the petition with the names and addresses on the voter registration [rolls], thus ensuring the accuracy and legitimacy of each signature.

Additionally, using the digitized version of the referendum petition, the

State could set up a simple system for Washington citizens to check whether their names have been fraudulently signed to a petition. For example, on his Web site, the secretary maintains an interface that allows voters to confirm their voter registration information simply by inputting their name and date of birth. Presumably the secretary could set up a similar interface for referendum petitions. Indeed, the process would seem to be all the more simple given that Washington requires a "unique identifier [to] be assigned to each registered voter in the state." ...

Justice Sotomayor, with whom Justice Stevens and Justice Ginsburg join, concurring....

[A]ny party attempting to challenge particular applications of the State's regulations will bear a heavy burden. Even when a referendum involves a particularly controversial subject and some petition signers fear harassment from nonstate actors, a State's important interests in "protect[ing] the integrity and reliability of the initiative process" remain undiminished .... Likewise, because the expressive interests implicated by the act of petition signing are always modest, I find it difficult to see how any incremental disincentive to sign a petition would tip the constitutional balance.

Case-specific relief may be available [only] when a State selectively applies a facially neutral petition disclosure rule in a manner that discriminates based on the content of referenda or the viewpoint of petition signers, or in the rare circumstance in which disclosure poses a reasonable probability of serious and widespread harassment that the State is unwilling or unable to control. Cf. *NAACP v. Alabama ex rel. Patterson*.... [C]ourts presented with an as-applied challenge to a regulation authorizing the disclosure of referendum petitions should be deeply skeptical of any assertion that the Constitution, which embraces political transparency, compels States to conceal the identity of persons who seek to participate in lawmaking through a state-created referendum process....

Justice Stevens, with whom Justice Breyer joins, concurring in part and concurring in the judgment....

[Justice Stevens's opinion largely agreed with Justice Sotomayor's, but also mentioned the possibility of an as-applied challenge when "a State's disclosure would substantially limit a group's ability to 'garner the number of signatures necessary to place [a] matter on the ballot,' thereby 'limiting [its] ability to make the matter the focus of statewide discussion.'"—ed.]

D. Restrictions on Speech-Related Spending and Contributions

a. *Why Spending on Speech Is Constitutionally Protected*

Most effective speech—publishing a newspaper, buying a newspaper ad (as in *New York Times Co. v. Sullivan*), printing and distributing leaflets, and the like—requires spending money. Sometimes the speaker spends his own money. Sometimes many people pool their money by giving it to someone who can speak particularly effectively (which is one reason people contribute to the NAACP, NRA, ACLU, and the like).

Restrictions on spending money to speak thus diminish people's ability to speak effectively. And the Court has therefore held that such restrictions presumptively violate the First Amendment, though they might be upheld if they pass some sufficiently heightened level of scrutiny.

This issue has often been characterized as turning on whether money is speech. Supporters of restrictions on campaign contributions and independent expenditures sometimes argue that "money is not speech," and opponents of such restrictions sometimes argue that "money is speech."

This, however, is not a helpful framing of the issue, because it rests on metaphor, not reality. As Justice Breyer has pointed out, "a decision to contribute money to a campaign is a matter of First Amendment concern—not because money *is* speech (it is not); but because it *enables* speech." *Nixon v. Shrink Mo. Gov't PAC,* 528 U.S. 377 (2000) (Breyer, J., concurring). And the question is thus whether restricting people from speaking (or helping others speak) using money is a permissible speech restriction.

This can be made clear through two analogies:

1. A law restricting people from flying places to give speeches would be a speech restriction. Flying is not speech—but giving a speech is speech, and burdening such speech (by forbidding flying to speak) is a speech restriction. Likewise for restrictions on spending money for speech: They do restrict speech, and the question is whether they do so constitutionally.

2. A law restricting spending money to get an abortion, to hire a criminal lawyer, or to privately educate one's children would be treated as a restriction on the abortion right, the right to counsel, or parental rights. This is not because "money is an abortion," "money is a lawyer," or "money is an education." Rather, it is because such restrictions would substantially interfere with people's ability to exercise each right. Likewise, again, for restrictions on spending money for speech.

b. *Summary of the Rule*

1. Content-based restrictions on people's or groups' spending of money to speak (independently of candidates or political parties) are unconstitutional, unless they pass strict scrutiny. *Citizens United v. FEC* (2010) (p. 488); *First National Bank of Boston v. Bellotti* (1978) (p. 479).

a. This includes corporate and union speech as well as individual speech. *Citizens United; First National Bank of Boston.*

b. The Court has generally held that restrictions on independent expenditures fail strict scrutiny. See *Citizens United; Buckley.*

c. Even those Justices who think corporate and union speech about elections may generally be restricted would protect such speech by nonprofit ideological corporations (1) that are "formed for the express purpose of promoting political ideas, and cannot engage in business activities," (2) that have "no shareholders or other persons affiliated so as to have a claim on its assets or earnings," and (3) that were "not established by a business corporation or a labor union, and [have a] policy not to accept contributions from such entities." *FEC v. Massachusetts Citizens for Life*, 479 U.S. 238 (1986). These are often called "*MCFL* corporations."

2. Restrictions on contributions to candidates and parties are unconstitutional, unless they pass a heightened level of scrutiny that seems to be between intermediate and strict scrutiny. *Buckley v. Valeo* (1976) (p. 466); *Nixon v. Shrink Missouri Gov't PAC*, 528 U.S. 377, 387-88 (2000).

a. *Buckley* upheld $1000 limits on individual contributions to candidates, because the limits are narrowly tailored to the government interest in preventing corruption and the appearance of corruption.

b. *Randall v. Sorrell*, 548 U.S. 230 (2006), followed *Buckley*, but concluded that restrictions that are too low—such as a $400 limit on contributions to Vermont gubernatorial candidates—are unconstitutional:

> At some point the constitutional risks to the democratic electoral process [from contribution limits] become too great[,] ... because contribution limits that are too low can ... harm the electoral process by preventing challengers from mounting effective campaigns against incumbent officeholders, thereby reducing democratic accountability.... Thus, we see no alternative to the exercise of independent judicial judgment as a statute reaches those outer limits.

3. Restrictions on people's or groups' expenditures of money *in coordination with* candidates and parties are treated the same as restrictions on contributions, and are generally upheld. *Buckley*.

c. *Problem: Campaign Finance Amendment*

Senator Jeff Goldberg proposes a constitutional amendment:

Notwithstanding the First Amendment, it shall be unlawful for any person or entity to spend more than $1000 in support of or opposition to any candidate or ballot measure in any federal, state, or local election.

What arguments can you make for and against this proposal?

d. *Buckley v. Valeo, 424 U.S. 1 (1976)*

i. *"General Principles"*

Per curiam [later revealed to have been written by Justice Stewart, joined by Justices Brennan and Powell, joined in all the parts quoted here by Justice Rehnquist, and mostly joined by Justices Marshall and Blackmun; all parts got at least five votes—ed.].

These appeals present constitutional challenges to the key provisions of the Federal Election Campaign Act of 1971, ... as amended in 1974.... [T]he Act prohibit[s] individuals from contributing ... more than $1,000 to any single candidate for an election campaign and from spending more than $1,000 a year "relative to a clearly identified candidate." ... [The Act also limited a candidate's spending of personal or family money, and total spending by each campaign; and it required disclosure of contributions and expenditures, which is discussed in the Anonymous Speech and Association section, p. 438.—ed.]

[A.] ... In a republic where the people are sovereign, the ability of the citizenry to make informed choices among candidates for office is essential, for the identities of those who are elected will inevitably shape the course that we follow as a nation.... "[I]t can hardly be doubted that the [First Amendment] has its fullest and most urgent application precisely to the conduct of campaigns for political office."

The First Amendment protects political association as well as political expression.... "[E]ffective advocacy of both public and private points of view, particularly controversial ones, is undeniably enhanced by group association." ... [T]he First and Fourteenth Amendments guarantee "freedom to associate with others for the common advancement of political beliefs and ideas," a freedom that encompasses "[t]he right to associate with the political party of one's choice." ...

[B.] Appellees contend that what the Act regulates is conduct, and that its effect on speech and association is incidental at most.... [But] this Court has never suggested that the dependence of a communication on the expenditure of money operates itself to introduce a nonspeech element or to reduce the exacting scrutiny required by the First Amendment. [See, *e.g.*,] *New York Times Co. v. Sullivan*....

Even if the categorization of the expenditure of money as conduct were accepted, the limitations challenged here would not meet the *United States v. O'Brien* test [for content-neutral conduct restrictions], because the governmental interests advanced in support of the Act involve "suppressing communication." The interests served by the Act include restricting the voices of people and interest groups who have money to spend and reducing the overall scope of federal election campaigns. Although the Act does not focus on the ideas expressed by persons or groups subject to its regulations, it is aimed in part at equalizing the relative ability of all voters to affect electoral outcomes by placing a ceiling on expenditures for political expression by citizens and groups.... [T]he interest in regulating the alleged "conduct" of giving or spending money "arises in some measure because the communication allegedly integral to the conduct is itself thought to be harmful."
...

[C.] [T]he government may adopt reasonable time, place, and manner regulations, which do not discriminate among speakers or ideas, in order to further an important governmental interest unrelated to the restriction of communication.... [But that doctrine does not apply here, because the] Act's contribution and expenditure limitations impose direct quantity restrictions on political communication and association by persons, groups, candidates, and political parties in addition to any reasonable time, place, and manner regulations otherwise imposed.

A restriction on the amount of money a person or group can spend on political communication during a campaign necessarily reduces the quantity of expression by restricting the number of issues discussed, the depth of their exploration, and the size of the audience reached. This is because virtually every means of communicating ideas in today's mass society requires the expenditure of money.

The distribution of the humblest handbill or leaflet entails printing, paper, and circulation costs. Speeches and rallies generally necessitate hiring a hall and publicizing the event. The electorate's increasing dependence on television, radio, and other mass media for news and information has made these expensive modes of communication indispensable instruments of effective political speech.... The $1,000 ceiling on spending "relative to a clearly identified candidate" would appear to exclude all citizens and groups except candidates, political parties, and the institutional press from any significant use of the most effective modes of communication....

ii. Contributions

Per curiam....

[A.] {[Unlike an expenditure, a] contribution serves as a general expression of support for the candidate and his views, but does not communicate the underlying basis for the support.... A limitation on the amount of money a person may give to a candidate or campaign organization thus involves little direct restraint on his political communication, for it permits the symbolic expression of support evidenced by a contribution but does not in any way infringe the contributor's freedom to discuss candidates and issues. While contributions may result in political expression if spent by a candidate or an association to present views to the voters, the transformation of contributions into political debate involves speech by someone other than the contributor.

Given the important role of contributions in financing political campaigns, contribution restrictions could have a severe impact on political dialogue if the limitations prevented candidates and political committees from amassing the resources necessary for effective advocacy. There is no indication, however, that the contribution limitations imposed by the Act would have any dramatic adverse effect on the funding of campaigns and political associations....

[B.] The Act's contribution ... limitations also impinge on protected associational freedoms. Making a contribution, like joining a political party, serves to affiliate a person with a candidate. In addition, it enables like-minded persons to pool their resources in furtherance of common political goals.

The Act's contribution ceilings thus limit one important means of associating with a candidate or committee, but leave the contributor free to become a member of any political association and to assist personally in the association's efforts on behalf of candidates. And the Act's contribution limitations permit associations and candidates to aggregate large sums of money to promote effective advocacy.}

[G]overnmental "action which may have the effect of curtailing the freedom to associate is subject to the closest scrutiny." Yet ... "[n]either the right to associate nor the right to participate in political activities is absolute." Even a "'significant interference' with protected rights of political association" may be sustained if the State demonstrates a sufficiently important interest and employs means closely drawn to avoid unnecessary abridgment of associational freedoms.

Appellees argue that the Act's restrictions on large campaign contributions are justified by three governmental interests[:] ... [(1) The limits serve] the prevention of corruption and the appearance of corruption spawned by the real or imagined coercive influence of large financial contributions on candidates' positions and on their actions if elected to office.... [(2) T]he limits serve to mute the voices of affluent persons and groups in the election process and thereby to equalize the relative ability of all citizens to affect the outcome of elections.... [(3) T]he ceilings may to some extent act as a brake on the skyrocketing cost of political campaigns and thereby serve to open the political system more widely to candidates without access to sources of large amounts of money.

It is unnecessary to look beyond the Act's primary purpose to limit the actuality and appearance of corruption resulting from large individual financial contributions in order to find a constitutionally sufficient justification for the $1,000 contribution limitation. Under a system of private financing of elections, a candidate lacking immense personal or family wealth must depend on financial contributions from others to provide the resources necessary to conduct a successful campaign....

To the extent that large contributions are given to secure a political *quid pro quo* from current and potential office holders, the integrity of our system of representative democracy is undermined. Although the scope of such pernicious practices can never be reliably ascertained, the deeply disturbing examples surfacing after the 1972 election demonstrate that the problem is not an illusory one.

Of almost equal concern as the danger of actual *quid pro quo* arrangements is the impact of the appearance of corruption stemming from public awareness of the opportunities for abuse inherent in a regime of large individual financial contributions.... Congress could legitimately conclude that the avoidance of the appearance of improper influence "is also critical ... if confidence in the system of representative Government is not to be eroded to a disastrous extent."

[C.] Appellants contend that the contribution limitations must be invalidated because bribery laws and narrowly drawn disclosure requirements constitute a less restrictive means of dealing with "proven and suspected *quid pro quo* arrangements." But laws making criminal the giving and taking of bribes deal with only the most blatant and specific attempts of those with money to influence governmental action. And while disclosure requirements serve the many salutary purposes discussed elsewhere in this opinion, Congress was surely entitled to conclude that disclosure was only a partial measure, and that contribution ceilings were a necessary legislative concomitant to deal with the reality or appearance of corruption inherent in a system permitting unlimited financial contributions, even when the identities of the contributors and the amounts of their contributions are fully disclosed.

The Act's $1,000 contribution limitation focuses precisely on the problem of large campaign contributions—the narrow aspect of political association where the actuality and potential for corruption have been identified—while leaving persons free to engage in independent political expression, to associate actively through volunteering their services, and to assist to a limited but nonetheless substantial extent in supporting candidates and committees with financial resources. Significantly, the Act's contribution limitations in themselves do not undermine to any material degree the potential for robust and effective discussion of candidates and campaign issues by individual citizens, associations, the institutional press, candidates, and political parties....

[T]he weighty interests served by restricting the size of financial contributions to political candidates ... justify the limited effect upon First Amendment freedoms caused by the $1,000 contribution ceiling.

[D.] Appellants' first overbreadth challenge to the contribution ceilings rests on the proposition that most large contributors do not seek improper influence over a candidate's position or an officeholder's action.... [Yet n]ot only is it difficult to isolate suspect contributions, but, more importantly, Congress was justified in concluding that the interest in safeguarding against the appearance of impropriety requires that the opportunity for abuse inherent in the process of raising large monetary contributions be eliminated.

A second, related overbreadth claim is that the $1,000 restriction is unrealistically low because much more than that amount would still not be enough to enable an unscrupulous contributor to exercise improper influence over a candidate or officeholder, especially in campaigns for statewide or national office.... But "[if] ... some limit on contributions is necessary, a court has no scalpel to probe, whether, say, a $2,000 ceiling might not serve as well as $1,000." Such distinctions in degree become significant only when they can be said to amount to differences in kind....

Chief Justice Burger, concurring in part and dissenting [as to the Court's upholding contribution limits; Justice Blackmun largely agreed with this opinion] ....

[A.] [C]ontributions and expenditures are two sides of the same First Amendment coin.... Limiting contributions, as a practical matter, will limit expenditures and will put an effective ceiling on the amount of political activity and debate that the Government will permit to take place.... [P]eople—candidates and contributors—spend money on political activity because they wish to communicate ideas, and their constitutional interest in doing so is precisely the same whether they or someone else utters the words....

In striking down the limitations on campaign expenditures, the Court relies in part on its conclusion that other means—namely, disclosure and contribution ceilings—will adequately serve the statute's aim [of fighting the reality or appearance of corruption]. It is not clear why the same analysis is not also appropriate in weighing the need for contribution ceilings in addition to disclosure requirements. Congress may well be entitled to conclude that disclosure was a "partial measure," but ... Congress [may not] enact its conclusions in the First Amendment area into laws immune from the most searching review by this Court.

[B.] [I]n approving these limitations on contributions the Court must rest upon the proposition that "pooling" money is fundamentally different from other forms of associational or joint activity. I see only two possible ways in which money differs from volunteer work, endorsements, and the like. Money can be used to buy favors, because an unscrupulous politician can put it to personal use; second, giving money is a less visible form of associational activity.

With respect to the first problem, the Act does not attempt to do any more than the bribery laws to combat this sort of corruption. In fact, the Act does not reach at all, and certainly the contribution limits do not reach, forms of "association" that can be fully as corrupt as a contribution intended as a *quid pro quo*—such as the eleventh-hour endorsement by a former rival, obtained for the promise of a federal appointment. This underinclusiveness is not a constitutional flaw, but it demonstrates that the contribution limits do not clearly focus on this first distinction.

To the extent Congress thought that the second problem, the lesser visibility of contributions, required that money be treated differently from other forms of associational activity, disclosure laws are the simple and wholly efficacious answer ....

iii. Expenditures Independent of the Candidate

Per curiam....

The Act's expenditure ceilings impose direct and substantial restraints on the quantity of political speech.... {[They also] preclude[] most associations from effectively amplifying the voice of their adherents, the original basis for the recognition of First Amendment protection of the freedom of association. See *NAACP v. Alabama*.... [The] expenditure ceilings impose significantly more severe restrictions on protected freedoms of political expression and association than do its limitations on financial contributions.}

[A.] Section 608(e)(1) provides that "[n]o person may make any expenditure ... relative to a clearly identified candidate during a calendar year which, when added to all other expenditures made by such person during the year advocating the election or defeat of such candidate, exceeds $1,000." ... [This] prohibit[s] all individuals, who are neither candidates nor owners of institutional press facilities, and all groups, except political parties and campaign organizations, from voicing their views relative to a clearly identified candidate" through means that entail aggregate expenditures of more than $1,000 during a calendar year. The provision, for example, would make it a federal criminal offense for a person or association to place a single one-quarter page advertisement "relative to a clearly identified candidate" in a major metropolitan newspaper....

Close examination of [whether a law is unconstitutionally vague] is required where, as here, the legislation imposes criminal penalties in an area permeated by First Amendment interests. The test is whether the language of § 608(e)(1) affords the "[p]recision of regulation [that] must be the touchstone in an area so closely touching our most precious freedoms." ...

The use of so indefinite a phrase as "relative to" a candidate fails to clearly mark the boundary between permissible and impermissible speech .... [Even if the phrase is] read to mean "advocating the election or defeat of" a candidate ... the distinction between discussion of issues and candidates and advocacy of election or defeat of candidates may often dissolve in practical application. Candidates, especially incumbents, are intimately tied to public issues involving legislative proposals and governmental actions. Not only do candidates campaign on the basis of their positions on various public issues, but campaigns themselves generate issues of public interest....

[This difficulty] can be avoided only by reading § 608(e)(1) as limited to communications that include explicit words of advocacy of election or defeat of a candidate, much as the definition of "clearly identified" in § 608(e)(2) requires that an explicit and unambiguous reference to the candidate appear as part of the communication.... [I]n order to preserve the provision against invalidation on vagueness grounds, § 608(e)(1) must be construed to apply only to expenditures for communications that in express terms advocate the election or defeat of a clearly identified candidate for federal office.

How to deal with vagueness

[B.] We turn then to the basic First Amendment question whether § 608(e)(1), even as thus narrowly and explicitly construed, impermissibly burdens the constitutional right of free expression.... The discussion in [the "General Principles" section, starting at p. 466—ed.] explains why the Act's expenditure limitations impose far greater restraints on the freedom of speech and association than do its contribution limitations. The markedly greater burden on basic freedoms caused by § 608(e)(1) thus cannot be sustained simply by invoking the interest in maximizing the effectiveness of the less intrusive contribution limitations [by preventing circumvention of those limitations]....

We find that the governmental interest in preventing corruption and the appearance of corruption is inadequate to justify § 608(e)(1)'s ceiling on independent expenditures.

First, assuming, *arguendo*, that large independent expenditures pose the same dangers of actual or apparent *quid pro quo* arrangements as do large contributions, § 608(e)(1) does not provide an answer that sufficiently relates to the elimination of those dangers.... So long as persons and groups eschew expenditures that in express terms advocate the election or defeat of a clearly identified candidate, they are free to spend as much as they want to promote the candidate and his views. The exacting interpretation of the statutory language necessary to avoid unconstitutional vagueness thus undermines the limitation's effectiveness as a loophole-closing provision by facilitating circumvention by those seeking to exert improper influence upon a candidate or office-holder.

It would naively underestimate the ingenuity and resourcefulness of persons and groups desiring to buy influence to believe that they would have much difficulty devising expenditures that skirted the restriction on express advocacy of election or defeat but nevertheless benefited the candidate's campaign. Yet no substantial societal interest would be served by a loophole-closing provision designed to check corruption that permitted unscrupulous persons and organizations to expend unlimited sums of money in order to obtain improper influence over candidates for elective office.

Second, ... the independent advocacy restricted by the provision does not presently appear to pose dangers of real or apparent corruption comparable to those identified with large campaign contributions.... Unlike contributions, such independent expenditures may well provide little assistance to the candidate's campaign and indeed may prove counterproductive. The absence of prearrangement and coordination of an expenditure with the candidate or his agent not only undermines the value of the expenditure to the candidate, but also alleviates the danger that expenditures will be given as a *quid pro quo* for improper commitments from the candidate.... [The Court had earlier noted that "expenditures controlled by or coordinated with the candidate and his campaign ... are treated as contributions rather than expenditures under the Act," and are thus limited by "[§] 608(b)'s contribution ceilings rather than § 608(e)(1)'s independent expenditure limitation."—ed.]

While the independent expenditure ceiling thus fails to serve any substantial governmental interest in stemming the reality or appearance of corruption in the electoral process, it heavily burdens core First Amendment expression. For the First Amendment right to "speak one's mind ... on all public institutions" includes the right to engage in "'vigorous advocacy' no less than 'abstract discussion.'" Advocacy of the election or defeat of candidates for federal office is no less entitled to protection under the First Amendment than the discussion of political policy generally or advocacy of the passage or defeat of legislation.

[C.] It is argued, however, that the ancillary governmental interest in equalizing the relative ability of individuals and groups to influence the outcome of elections serves to justify the limitation on express advocacy of the election or defeat of candidates imposed by § 608(e)(1)'s expenditure ceiling. But the concept that government may restrict the speech of some elements of our society in order to enhance the relative voice of others is wholly foreign to the First Amendment, which was designed "to secure the widest possible dissemination of information from diverse and antagonistic sources," and "to assure unfettered interchange of ideas for the bringing about of political and social changes desired by the people." The First Amendment's protection against governmental abridgment of free expression cannot properly be made to depend on a person's financial ability to engage in public discussion....

Justice White, concurring in part and dissenting in part [as to the Court's striking down the expenditure limitations]....

[G]iving and spending money ... have First Amendment significance not because they are themselves communicative with respect to the qualifications of the candidate, but because money may be used to defray the expenses of ... communicating about the merits or demerits of federal candidates .... [G]iving money to political candidates, however, may have illegal or other undesirable consequences: it may be used to secure the express or tacit understanding that the giver will enjoy political favor if the candidate is elected....

Since the contribution and expenditure limitations are neutral as to the content of speech and are not motivated by fear of the consequences of ... political speech ..., this case depends on whether the nonspeech interests of the Federal Government in regulating the use of money in political campaigns are sufficiently urgent to justify the incidental effects that the limitations visit upon the First Amendment interests of candidates and their supporters....

The Court ... accepts the congressional judgment that the evils of unlimited contributions are sufficiently threatening to warrant restriction regardless of the impact of the limits on the contributor's [and the candidate's] opportunity for effective speech .... The congressional judgment, which I would also accept, was that other steps must be taken to counter the corrosive effects of money in federal election campaigns....

It would make little sense to me, and apparently made none to Congress, to limit the amounts an individual may give to a candidate or spend with his approval but fail to limit the amounts that could be spent on his behalf. Yet the Court permits the former while striking down the latter limitation.... I would take the word of those who know [the politicians who enacted the Act, and who are deeply involved in elective processes] that limiting independent expenditures is essential to prevent transparent and widespread evasion of the contribution limits....

iv. Total Expenditures by the Campaign Committee

Per curiam....

Section 608(c) places limitations on overall campaign expenditures by candidates seeking nomination for election and election to federal office. Presidential candidates may spend $10,000,000 in seeking nomination for office and an additional $20,000,000 in the general election campaign.... In senatorial primary elections, the limit is the greater of eight cents multiplied by the voting-age population or $100,000, and in the general election the limit is increased to 12 cents multiplied by the voting-age population or $150,000. [The limit is generally $70,000 for] both primary campaigns and general election campaigns for the House of Representatives .... These ceilings are to be adjusted [for inflation] ....

No governmental interest that has been suggested is sufficient to justify the restriction on the quantity of political expression imposed by § 608(c)'s campaign expenditure limitations. The major evil associated with rapidly increasing campaign expenditures is the danger of candidate dependence on large contributions. The interest in alleviating the corrupting influence of large contributions is served by the Act's contribution limitations and disclosure provisions rather than by § 608(c)'s campaign expenditure ceilings.

The ... assertion that the expenditure restrictions are necessary to reduce the incentive to circumvent direct contribution limits is not persuasive. There is no indication that the substantial criminal penalties for violating the contribution ceilings combined with the political repercussion of such violations will be insufficient to police the contribution provisions. Extensive reporting, auditing, and disclosure requirements applicable to both contributions and expenditures by political campaigns are designed to facilitate the detection of illegal contributions....

The interest in equalizing the financial resources of candidates competing for federal office is no more convincing a justification for restricting the scope of federal election campaigns. Given the limitation on the size of outside contributions, the financial resources available to a candidate's campaign, like the number of volunteers recruited, will normally vary with the size and intensity of the candidate's support.

There is nothing invidious, improper, or unhealthy in permitting such funds to be spent to carry the candidate's message to the electorate. Moreover, the equalization of permissible campaign expenditures might serve not to equalize the opportunities of all candidates, but to handicap a candidate who lacked substantial name recognition or exposure of his views before the start of the campaign....

[T]he mere growth in the cost of federal election campaigns in and of itself provides no basis for governmental restrictions on the quantity of campaign spending and the resulting limitation on the scope of federal campaigns. The First Amendment denies government the power to determine that spending to promote one's political views is wasteful, excessive, or unwise. In the free society ordained by our Constitution it is not the government, but the people—individually as citizens and candidates and collectively as associations and political committees—who must retain control over the quantity and range of debate on public issues in a political campaign....

Justice White, dissenting.

[A.] [T]he argument that money is speech and that limiting the flow of money to the speaker violates the First Amendment proves entirely too much.... [I]t has not been suggested, nor could it be successfully, that [laws such as labor laws, tax laws, antitrust laws, and occasional general price controls] are invalid because they siphon off or prevent the accumulation of large sums that would otherwise be available for communicative activities.

In any event, ... money is not always equivalent to or used for speech, even in the context of political campaigns. I accept the reality that communicating with potential voters is the heart of an election campaign and that widespread communication has become very expensive. There are, however, many expensive campaign activities that are not themselves communicative or remotely related to speech.

Furthermore, campaigns differ among themselves. Some seem to spend much less money than others and yet communicate as much as or more than those supported by enormous bureaucracies with unlimited financing. The record before us no more supports the conclusion that the communicative efforts of congressional and Presidential candidates will be crippled by the expenditure limitations than it supports the contrary. The judgment of Congress was that reasonably effective campaigns could be conducted within the limits established by the Act and that the communicative efforts of these campaigns would not seriously suffer.

[B.] In this posture of the case, there is no sound basis for invalidating the expenditure limitations, so long as the purposes they serve are legitimate and sufficiently substantial, which in my view they are. In the first place, expenditure ceilings reinforce the contribution limits and help eradicate the hazard of corruption.... [T]he expenditure limit imposed on candidates plays [a] role in lessening the chance that the contribution ceiling will be violated. Without limits on total expenditures, campaign costs will inevitably and endlessly escalate. Pressure to raise funds will constantly build and with it the temptation to resort in "emergencies" to those sources of large sums, who, history shows, are sufficiently confident of not being caught to risk flouting contribution limits.

Congress would save the candidate from this predicament by establishing a reasonable ceiling on all candidates.... [M]any successful candidates will also be saved from large, overhanging campaign debts which must be paid off with money raised while holding public office and at a time when they are already preparing or thinking about the next campaign....

[I]n addition[,] ... limiting the total that can be spent will ease the candidate's understandable obsession with fundraising, and so free him and his staff to communicate in more places and ways unconnected with the fundraising function. There is nothing objectionable—indeed it seems to me a weighty interest in favor of the provision—in the attempt to insulate the political expression of federal candidates from the influence inevitably exerted by the endless job of raising increasingly large sums of money....

It is also important to restore and maintain public confidence in federal elections. It is critical to obviate or dispel the impression that federal elections are purely and simply a function of money, that federal offices are bought and sold or that political races are reserved for those who have the facility—and the stomach—for doing whatever it takes to bring together those interests, groups, and individuals that can raise or contribute large fortunes in order to prevail at the polls.

The ceiling on candidate expenditures represents the considered judgment of Congress that elections are to be decided among candidates none of whom has overpowering advantage by reason of a huge campaign war chest. At least so long as the ceiling placed upon the candidates is not plainly too low, elections are not to turn on the difference in the amounts of money that candidates have to spend. This seems an acceptable purpose and the means chosen a common-sense way to achieve it....

[Justice Stevens, dissenting in *Randall v. Sorrell*, 548 U.S. 230 (2006)....]

[A.] ... [The time has come to overrule] *Buckley*'s holding on expenditure limits [by campaigns] .... [I]t is quite wrong to equate money and speech.... "The burden on actual speech imposed by limitations on the spending of money is minimal and indirect. All rights of direct political expression and advocacy are retained. Even under the campaign laws as originally enacted, everyone was free to spend as much as they chose to amplify their views on general political issues, just not specific candidates. The restrictions, to the extent they do affect speech, are viewpoint-neutral and indicate no hostility to the speech itself or its effects."

Accordingly, these limits on expenditures are far more akin to time, place, and manner restrictions than to restrictions on the content of speech. Like Justice White [in *Buckley*], I would uphold them "so long as the purposes they serve are legitimate and sufficiently substantial." ...

[B.] [P]rovided that [the campaign] budget is above a certain threshold, a candidate can exercise due care to ensure that her message reaches all voters.... [A] candidate need not flood the airways with ceaseless sound-bites of trivial information in order to provide voters with reasons to support her.

Indeed, the examples of effective speech in the political arena that did not depend on any significant expenditure by the campaigner are legion. It was the content of William Jennings Bryan's comments on the "Cross of Gold"—and William McKinley's responses delivered from his front porch in Canton, Ohio—rather than any expenditure of money that appealed to their cost-free audiences. Neither Abraham Lincoln nor John F. Kennedy paid for the opportunity to engage in the debates with Stephen Douglas and Richard Nixon that may well have determined the outcomes of Presidential elections.... [T]he seasoned campaigners who were Members of the Congress that endorsed the expenditure limits in the Federal Election Campaign Act Amendments of 1974 concluded that a modest budget would not preclude them from effectively communicating with the electorate ....

v. Expenditures by the Candidate and the Candidate's Family

Per curiam....

The Act also sets limits on expenditures by a candidate "from his personal funds, or the personal funds of his immediate family, in connection with his campaigns during any calendar year." § 608(a)(1). These ceilings vary from $50,000 for Presidential or Vice Presidential candidates to $35,000 for senatorial candidates, and $25,000 for most candidates for the House of Representatives....

The candidate, no less than any other person, has a First Amendment right to engage in the discussion of public issues and vigorously and tire-lessly to advocate his own election and the election of other candidates.... Section 608(a)'s ceiling on personal expenditures by a candidate in further-ance of his own candidacy thus clearly and directly interferes with constitu-tionally protected freedoms.

The primary governmental interest served by the Act—the prevention of actual and apparent corruption of the political process—does not support the limitation on the candidate's expenditure of his own personal funds.... Indeed, the use of personal funds reduces the candidate's dependence on outside contributions and thereby counteracts the coercive pressures and attendant risks of abuse to which the Act's contribution limitations are di-rected.

The ancillary interest in equalizing the relative financial resources of candidates competing for elective office, therefore, provides the sole relevant rationale for § 608(a)'s expenditure ceiling. That interest is clearly not suf-ficient to justify the provision's infringement of fundamental First Amend-ment rights.

First, the limitation may fail to promote financial equality among can-didates. A candidate who spends less of his personal resources on his cam-paign may nonetheless outspend his rival as a result of more successful fundraising efforts. Indeed, a candidate's personal wealth may impede his efforts to persuade others that he needs their financial contributions or vol-unteer efforts to conduct an effective campaign. Second, and more funda-mentally, the First Amendment simply cannot tolerate § 608(a)'s restriction upon the freedom of a candidate to speak without legislative limit on behalf of his own candidacy....

Justice Marshall, [dissenting in relevant part (though he other-wise agreed with the per curiam)—ed.].

[The limit on spending personal or family funds is supported by] the in-terest in promoting the reality and appearance of equal access to the politi-cal arena.... [T]he wealthy candidate's immediate access to a substantial personal fortune may give him an initial advantage that his less wealthy opponent can never overcome. And even if the advantage can be overcome, the perception that personal wealth wins elections may not only discourage potential candidates without significant personal wealth from entering the political arena, but also undermine public confidence in the integrity of the electoral process.

The concern that candidacy for public office not become, or appear to become, the exclusive province of the wealthy assumes heightened signifi-cance when one considers the impact of [the contribution limits], which the Court today upholds.... Large contributions are the less wealthy candidate's only hope of countering the wealthy candidate's immediate access to sub-stantial sums of money. With that option removed, the less wealthy candi-date is without the means to match the large initial expenditures of money of which the wealthy candidate is capable....

In view of § 608(b)'s limitations on contributions, then, § 608(a) emerges not simply as a device to reduce the natural advantage of the wealthy candidate, but as a provision providing some symmetry to a regulatory scheme that otherwise enhances the natural advantage of the wealthy. Regardless of whether the goal of equalizing access would justify a legislative limit on personal candidate expenditures standing by itself, I think it clear that that goal justifies § 608(a)'s limits when they are considered in conjunction with the remainder of the Act....

Justice White, dissenting.

[The limit on the use of personal wealth] helps to assure that only individuals with a modicum of support from others will be viable candidates. This in turn would tend to discourage any notion that the outcome of elections is primarily a function of money.

Similarly, [this limit] tends to equalize access to the political arena, encouraging the less wealthy, unable to bankroll their own campaigns, to run for political office. As with the campaign expenditure limits, Congress was entitled to determine that personal wealth ought to play a less important role in political campaigns than it has in the past....

e. *First Nat'l Bank of Boston v. Bellotti, 435 U.S. 765 (1978)*

   i. *Generally*

Justice Powell delivered the opinion of the Court....

[A.] Mass. Gen. Laws ch. 55, § 8, prohibits [corporations] from making contributions or expenditures "for the purpose of ... influencing or affecting the vote on any question submitted to the voters, other than one materially affecting any of the property, business or assets of the corporation." The statute further specifies that "[n]o question submitted to the voters solely concerning the taxation of the income, property or transactions of individuals shall be deemed materially to affect the property, business or assets of the corporation." ... [Appellants wanted to spend money to publicize their views about a ballot measure that would have authorized an individual income tax, and sued to invalidate the law.—ed.] ...

[B.] The inherent worth of the speech in terms of its capacity for informing the public does not depend upon the identity of its source, whether corporation, association, union, or individual.... [A]ppellee suggests that First Amendment rights generally have been afforded only to corporations engaged in the communications business or through which individuals express themselves .... But the press does not have a monopoly on either the First Amendment or the ability to enlighten.

{Certainly there are voters in Massachusetts, concerned with such economic issues as the tax rate, employment opportunities, and the ability to attract new business into the State and to prevent established businesses from leaving, who would be as interested in hearing appellants' views on a graduated tax as the views of media corporations that might be less knowledgeable on the subject.} ... In the realm of protected speech, the legislature is constitutionally disqualified from dictating the subjects about which persons may speak and the speakers who may address a public issue.

If a legislature may direct business corporations to "stick to business," it also may limit other corporations—religious, charitable, or civic—to their respective "business" when addressing the public. Such power in government to channel the expression of views is unacceptable under the First Amendment. Especially where, as here, the legislature's suppression of speech suggests an attempt to give one side of a debatable public question an advantage in expressing its views to the people, the First Amendment is plainly offended....

[C.] The constitutionality of § 8's prohibition of the "exposition of ideas" by corporations turns on whether it can survive the exacting scrutiny necessitated by a state-imposed restriction of freedom of speech.... "[T]he State may prevail only upon showing a subordinating interest which is compelling." ... Even then, the State must employ means "closely drawn to avoid unnecessary abridgment...." ...

Preserving the integrity of the electoral process, preventing corruption, and "sustain[ing] the active, alert responsibility of the individual citizen in a democracy for the wise conduct of government" are interests of the highest importance. Preservation of the individual citizen's confidence in government is equally important.

Appellee ... [argues that] corporate participation in discussion of a referendum issue ... would exert an undue influence on the outcome of a referendum vote, and—in the end—destroy the confidence of the people in the democratic process and the integrity of government. According to appellee, corporations are wealthy and powerful and their views may drown out other points of view.

If appellee's arguments were supported by record or legislative findings that corporate advocacy threatened imminently to undermine democratic processes, thereby denigrating rather than serving First Amendment interests, these arguments would merit our consideration. But there has been no showing that the relative voice of corporations has been overwhelming or even significant in influencing referenda in Massachusetts, or that there has been any threat to the confidence of the citizenry in government.

Nor are appellee's arguments inherently persuasive .... Referenda are held on issues, not candidates for public office. The risk of corruption perceived in cases involving candidate elections simply is not present in a popular vote on a public issue. {[O]ur consideration of a corporation's right to speak on issues of general public interest implies no comparable right in the quite different context of participation in a political campaign for election to public office. Congress might well be able to demonstrate the existence of a danger of real or apparent corruption in independent expenditures by corporations to influence candidate elections.} ...

[And] the fact that advocacy may persuade the electorate is hardly a reason to suppress it .... "[T]he concept that government may restrict the speech of some elements of our society in order to enhance the relative voice of others is wholly foreign to the First Amendment...."

{Justice White argues, without support in the record, that because corporations are given certain privileges by law they are able to "amass wealth" and then to "dominate" debate on an issue [and may thus have their speech restricted].... The potential impact of this argument, especially on the news media, is unsettling. One might argue with comparable logic that the State may control the volume of expression by the wealthier, more powerful corporate members of the press in order to "enhance the relative voices" of smaller and less influential members.}

Moreover, the people in our democracy are entrusted with the responsibility for judging and evaluating the relative merits of conflicting arguments. They may consider, in making their judgment, the source and credibility of the advocate. {Identification of the source of advertising may be required as a means of disclosure, so that the people will be able to evaluate the arguments to which they are being subjected.} But if there be any danger that the people cannot evaluate the information and arguments advanced by appellants, it is a danger contemplated by the Framers of the First Amendment....

Justice White, with whom Justice Brennan and Justice Marshall join, dissenting ....

[A.] [C]orporate expression ... is not fungible with communications emanating from individuals and is subject to restrictions which individual expression is not.

Indeed, what some have considered to be the principal function of the First Amendment, the use of communication as a means of self-expression, self-realization, and self-fulfillment, is not at all furthered by corporate speech.... {Ideas which are not a product of individual choice are entitled to less First Amendment protection.[a]}

Shareholders in [profitmaking corporations] do not share a common set of political or social views, and they certainly have not invested their money for the purpose of advancing political or social causes or in an enterprise engaged in the business of disseminating news and opinion. In fact, ... the government has a strong interest in assuring that investment decisions are not predicated upon agreement or disagreement with the activities of corporations in the political arena....

The self-expression of the communicator is not the only value encompassed by the First Amendment.... Any communication of ideas, and consequently any expenditure of funds which makes the communication of ideas possible, it can be argued, furthers the purposes of the First Amendment. This proposition does not establish, however, that the right of the general

---

[a] [Here's **the majority's** response:—ed.] The suggestion ... that the First Amendment affords less protection to ideas that are not the product of "individual choice" would seem to apply to newspaper editorials and every other form of speech created under the auspices of a corporate body....

public to receive communications financed by means of corporate expenditures is of the same dimension as that to hear other forms of expression....

[T]he restriction of corporate speech concerned with political matters impinges much less severely upon the availability of ideas to the general public than do restrictions upon individual speech. Even the complete curtailment of corporate communications concerning political or ideological questions not integral to day-to-day business functions would leave individuals, including corporate shareholders, employees, and customers, free to communicate their thoughts....

[B.] [Moreover, c]orporations are artificial entities created by law for the purpose of furthering certain economic goals. In order to facilitate the achievement of such ends, special rules relating to such matters as limited liability, perpetual life, and the accumulation, distribution, and taxation of assets are normally applied to them. States have provided corporations with such attributes in order to increase their economic viability and thus strengthen the economy generally.

It has long been recognized, however, that the special status of corporations has placed them in a position to control vast amounts of economic power which may, if not regulated, dominate not only the economy but also the very heart of our democracy, the electoral process.... [The state interest in restricting corporate political activity] is not one of equalizing the resources of opposing candidates or opposing positions, but rather of preventing institutions which have been permitted to amass wealth as a result of special advantages extended by the State for certain economic purposes from using that wealth to acquire an unfair advantage in the political process, especially where, as here, the issue involved has no material connection with the business of the corporation.

The State need not permit its own creation to consume it. Massachusetts could permissibly conclude that not to impose limits upon the political activities of corporations would have placed it in a position of departing from neutrality and indirectly assisting the propagation of corporate views because of the advantages its laws give to the corporate acquisition of funds to finance such activities. Such expenditures may be viewed as seriously threatening the role of the First Amendment as a guarantor of a free marketplace of ideas.

Ordinarily, the expenditure of funds to promote political causes may be assumed to bear some relation to the fervency with which they are held. Corporate political expression, however, is not only divorced from the convictions of individual corporate shareholders, but also, because of the ease with which corporations are permitted to accumulate capital, bears no relation to the conviction with which the ideas expressed are held by the communicator.

The Court ... assert[s] that "there has been no showing that the relative voice of corporations has been overwhelming or even significant in influencing referenda in Massachusetts," and ... suggest[s] that the statute ... represents an attempt to give an unfair advantage to those who hold views in opposition to positions which would otherwise be financed by corporations. It fails even to allude to the fact, however, that Massachusetts' most recent experience with unrestrained corporate expenditures in connection with ballot questions establishes precisely the contrary. In 1972, a proposed amendment to the Massachusetts Constitution which would have authorized the imposition of a graduated income tax on both individuals and corporations was put to the voters.... [A]n organized political committee[] raised and expended approximately $120,000 to oppose the proposed amendment, the bulk of it raised through large corporate contributions.... [T]he only political committee organized to support the 1972 amendment[] was able to raise and expend only approximately $7,000....ᵃ

[C.] {I need not decide whether newspapers have a First Amendment right to operate in a corporate form. It may be that for a State which generally permits businesses to operate as corporations to prohibit those engaged in the dissemination of information and opinion from taking advantage of the corporate form would constitute a departure from neutrality prohibited by the free press guarantee of the First Amendment. There can be no doubt, however, that the First Amendment does not immunize media corporations any more than other types of corporations from restrictions upon electoral contributions and expenditures.}

Justice Rehnquist, dissenting....

The appellants ... were created by the Commonwealth or were admitted into the Commonwealth only for the limited purposes described in their charters and regulated by state law.... [A corporation's] constitutional protections are [limited to those] "incidental to its very existence." ...

[W]hen a State creates a corporation with the power to acquire and utilize property, it necessarily and implicitly guarantees that the corporation will not be deprived of that property absent due process of law. Likewise, when a State charters a corporation for the purpose of publishing a newspaper, it necessarily assumes that the corporation is entitled to the liberty of the press essential to the conduct of its business.... [A] corporation's right of commercial speech ... might be considered necessarily incidental to the business of a commercial corporation.

It cannot be so readily concluded that the right of political expression is equally necessary to carry out the functions of a corporation organized for commercial purposes. A State grants to a business corporation the blessings

---

ᵃ [Here's **the majority's** response to this assertion:—ed.] ... [As to the 1972 election, t]he record shows only the extent of corporate and individual contributions to the two committees that were organized to support and oppose, respectively, the constitutional amendment.... [A]mounts of money expended independently of organized committees need not be reported under Massachusetts law, and therefore remain unknown.

Even if viewed as material, any inference that corporate contributions "dominated" the electoral process on this issue is refuted by the 1976 election. There the voters again rejected the proposed constitutional amendment even in the absence of any corporate spending, which had been forbidden by the decision below.

of potentially perpetual life and limited liability to enhance its efficiency as an economic entity. It might reasonably be concluded that those properties, so beneficial in the economic sphere, pose special dangers in the political sphere....

Indeed, the States might reasonably fear that the corporation would use its economic power to obtain further benefits beyond those already bestowed. I would think that any particular form of organization upon which the State confers special privileges or immunities different from those of natural persons would be subject to like regulation, whether the organization is a labor union, a partnership, a trade association, or a corporation....

ii. Shareholder Protection

Justice Powell delivered the opinion of the Court.

[A]ppellee argues that § 8 protects corporate shareholders ... by preventing the use of corporate resources in furtherance of views with which some shareholders may disagree. This purpose is belied, however, by the provisions of the statute, which are both underinclusive and overinclusive.

[A.] The underinclusiveness of the statute is self-evident. Corporate expenditures with respect to a referendum are prohibited, while corporate activity with respect to the passage or defeat of legislation is permitted, even though corporations may engage in lobbying more often than they take positions on ballot questions submitted to the voters. Nor does § 8 prohibit a corporation from expressing its views, by the expenditure of corporate funds, on any public issue until it becomes the subject of a referendum, though the displeasure of disapproving shareholders is unlikely to be any less.

The fact that a particular kind of ballot question has been singled out for special treatment undermines the likelihood of a genuine state interest in protecting shareholders. It suggests instead that the legislature may have been concerned with silencing corporations on a particular subject....

[Moreover,] § 8 is limited to banks and business corporations .... Excluded from its provisions and criminal sanctions are entities or organized groups in which numbers of persons may hold an interest or membership, and which often have resources comparable to those of large corporations.... Thus the exclusion of Massachusetts business trusts, real estate investment trusts, labor unions, and other associations undermines the plausibility of the State's purported concern for the persons who happen to be shareholders in the banks and corporations covered by § 8.

[**The majority in *Citizens United v. FEC***, which struck down a restriction on corporate speech about candidates within 30 or 60 days of an election (see p. 488), reasoned similarly in this paragraph:—ed.] [I]f Congress had been seeking to protect dissenting shareholders, it would not have banned corporate speech in only certain media within 30 or 60 days before an election. A dissenting shareholder's interests would be implicated by speech in any media at any time....

[B.] The overinclusiveness of the statute is demonstrated by the fact that § 8 would prohibit a corporation from supporting or opposing a referendum proposal even if its shareholders unanimously authorized the contribution or expenditure. Ultimately shareholders may decide, through the procedures of corporate democracy, whether their corporation should engage in debate on public issues. Acting through their power to elect the board of directors or to insist upon protective provisions in the corporation's charter, shareholders normally are presumed competent to protect their own interests...

{Appellee does not explain why the dissenting shareholder's wishes are entitled to such greater solicitude in this context than in many others where equally important and controversial corporate decisions are made by management or by a predetermined percentage of the shareholders.... [Cases involving the right of employees] not to be compelled, as a condition of employment, to support with financial contributions the political activities of other union members ... are irrelevant to the question presented in this case.... [N]o shareholder has been "compelled" to contribute anything. Apart from the fact, noted by the dissent, that compulsion by the State is wholly absent, the shareholder invests in a corporation of his own volition and is free to withdraw his investment at any time and for any reason.

A more relevant analogy, therefore, is to the situation where an employee voluntarily joins a union, or an individual voluntarily joins an association, and later finds himself in disagreement with its stance on a political issue... [Moreover,] it is by no means an automatic step from the remedy in [the union cases—the dissenter's right to a partial refund of his dues], which honored the interests of the minority without infringing the majority's rights, to the position adopted by the dissent which would completely silence the majority because a hypothetical minority might object.}

Assuming, *arguendo*, that protection of shareholders is a "compelling" interest under the circumstances of this case, we find "no substantially relevant correlation between the governmental interest asserted and the State's effort" to prohibit appellants from speaking....

[C.] [Another paragraph from **the *Citizens United* majority**:—ed.] [The asserted] interest in protecting dissenting shareholders from being compelled to fund corporate political speech ... would allow the Government to ban the political speech even of media corporations.... The First Amendment does not allow that .... There is, furthermore, little evidence of abuse that cannot be corrected by shareholders "through the procedures of corporate democracy." ...

Justice White, with whom Justice Brennan and Justice Marshall join, dissenting ....

[A]n additional overriding interest ... is [also] substantially advanced by Massachusetts' restrictions upon corporate contributions: assuring that shareholders are not compelled to support and financially further beliefs with which they disagree where, as is the case here, the issue involved does not materially affect the business, property, or other affairs of the corporation.... [This policy] protects the very freedoms that this Court has held to be guaranteed by the First Amendment.... [I]n *Abood v. Detroit Board of Ed.*, we ... held that a State may not, even indirectly, require an individual to contribute to the support of an ideological cause he may oppose as a condition of employment....

Presumably, unlike ... [in] *Abood*, the use of funds invested by shareholders with opposing views by Massachusetts corporations in connection with referenda or elections would not constitute state action and, consequently, would not violate the First Amendment. Until now, however, the States have always been free to adopt measures designed to further rights protected by the Constitution even when not compelled to do so....

In most contexts, of course, the views of the dissenting shareholder have little, if any, First Amendment significance. By purchasing interests in corporations shareholders accept the fact that corporations are going to make decisions concerning matters such as advertising integrally related to their business operations according to the procedures set forth in their charters and bylaws. Otherwise, corporations could not function.

First Amendment concerns of stockholders are directly implicated, however, when a corporation chooses to use its privileged status to finance ideological crusades which are unconnected with the corporate business or property and which some shareholders might not wish to support. Once again, we are provided no explanation whatsoever by the Court as to why the State's interest is of less constitutional weight than that of corporations to participate financially in the electoral process and as to why the balance between two First Amendment interests should be struck by this Court....

{The Court also asserts that Massachusetts' interest in protecting dissenting shareholders is "belied" by its failure to prohibit corporate activity with respect to the passage or defeat of legislation or to include business trusts, real estate investment trusts, and labor unions in its prohibition upon electoral expenditures.... [But] the state legislature could permissibly find on the basis of experience, which this Court lacks, that other activities and forms of association do not present problems of the same type or the same dimension....

The Court's further claim that "[t]he fact that a particular kind of ballot question has been singled out for special treatment undermines the likelihood of a genuine state interest in protecting shareholders [and] suggests instead that the legislature may have been concerned with silencing corporations on a particular subject" ignores the fact that ... the statutory provision stating that the personal income tax does not materially affect the business of corporations was enacted in response to prior judicial decisions construing the "materially affecting" requirement as not prohibiting corporate expenditures in connection with income tax referenda. To find evidence of hostility toward corporations on the basis of a decision of a legislature to clarify its intent following judicial rulings interpreting the scope of a statute is to elevate corporations to a level of deference which has not been seen at least since the days when substantive due process was regularly used to invalidate regulatory legislation thought to unfairly impinge upon established economic interests.} ...

Justice Stevens, joined by Justices Souter, Ginsburg, and Sotomayor[, dissenting in _Citizens United_].

[A.] The Court [argues] that abuses of shareholder money can be corrected "through the procedures of corporate democracy[]" .... [But in practice, the rights of shareholders to vote and to bring derivative suits for breach of fiduciary duty] "... are so limited as to be almost nonexistent," given the internal authority wielded by boards and managers and the expansive protections afforded by the business judgment rule....

[Also, m]ost American households that own stock do so through intermediaries such as mutual funds and pension plans, which makes it more difficult both to monitor and to alter particular holdings.... [And] if the corporation in question operates a PAC, an investor who sees the company's ads may not know whether they are being funded through the PAC or through the general treasury.

If and when shareholders learn that a corporation has been spending general treasury money on objectionable electioneering, they can divest. Even assuming that they reliably learn as much, however, this solution is only partial. The injury to the shareholders' expressive rights has already occurred; they might have preferred to keep that corporation's stock in their portfolio for any number of economic reasons; and they may incur a capital gains tax or other penalty from selling their shares, changing their pension plan, or the like.

The shareholder protection rationale has been criticized as underinclusive, in that corporations also spend money on lobbying and charitable contributions in ways that any particular shareholder might disapprove. But those expenditures do not implicate the selection of public officials, an area in which "the interests of unwilling ... corporate shareholders [in not being] forced to subsidize that speech" "are at their zenith." And in any event, the question is whether shareholder protection provides a basis for regulating expenditures in the weeks before an election, not whether additional types of corporate communications might similarly be conditioned on voluntariness....

[B.] {[W]ith a media corporation[, which is statutorily exempt from the statute challenged in _Citizens United_,] there is ... a lesser risk that investors will not understand, learn about, or support the advocacy messages that the corporation disseminates. Everyone knows and expects that media outlets may seek to influence elections in this way.}

[C.] {[Even after] today's decision[,] ... [l]egislatures remain free in their incorporation and tax laws to condition the types of activity in which corporations may engage, including electioneering activity, on specific disclosure requirements or on prior express approval by shareholders or members.}

f. *Citizens United v. FEC, 558 U.S. 310 (2010)*

[*Citizens United* struck down a restriction on corporate and union independent expenditures related to candidates. This overruled *Austin v. Michigan Chamber of Commerce*, 494 U.S. 652 (1990), and parts of *McConnell v. FEC*, 540 U.S. 93 (2003), which had upheld such a restriction. Because the decision is so long, it is divided here into several parts:

(1) The debate about whether speech by corporations should be less protected because of the speaker's corporate status as such.

(2) The related debate about how the most media outlets' status as corporations bears on item 1; that short excerpt begins at p. 115.

(3) The debate about whether restrictions on corporate speech about elections can be justified by the interest in protecting dissenting shareholders, which has been moved to the *First Nat'l Bank of Boston v. Bellotti* excerpt above (p. 484).

(4) The debate about whether corporate speech could be restricted because of the danger of corruption—a topic that also arises in *Buckley* as to speech by individuals and noncorporate advocacy groups.

(5) The debate about how the First Amendment was likely originally understood with regard to corporate speech.

(6) The debate (excerpted starting on p. 446) about the disclosure and reporting requirements related to corporate and union speech.

Note also that the restriction struck down in *Citizens United* applied equally to corporations and unions, and was held unconstitutional as to both, though nearly all the discussion in the case (and in media reports on the case) focused on corporate speech. Many commentators have assumed that the decision will help corporations more than unions (which means that the burden of the restriction fell disproportionately on corporate speech). But it's not clear whether this is actually so. Here is what detailed data I could find on this, though it is only suggestive and not dispositive, since there are limits to how generalizable it might be:

A. California is one of the 26 states that didn't restrict independent corporate and union expenditures even before *Citizens United*. California independent spending committees spent $88 million in 2001–06 California candidate races; $42.2 million was spent by the top 10 committees; and the $42.2 million broke down roughly thus:

1. Union spending: $16.6 million.

2. Indian tribe spending: $10.75 million.

3. Individual spending: $8 million (from a father and daughter advocating the election of a former business partner of the father's).

4. Corporate spending: $6.85 million.

See California Fair Political Practices Commission, *Independent Expenditures: The Giant Gorilla in Campaign Finance*.

B. From Jan. 21, 2010, when *Citizens United* was decided, to mid-2010,

"Unions have spent $9.7 million [on independent expenditures related to federal candidates], compared with $6.4 million ... spent by individuals and $3.4 million spent by corporations." T.W. Farnam, *Unions Outspending Corporations on Campaign Ads Despite Court Ruling*, Wash. Post, July 7, 2010. But this data reflects spending on primaries, and the results might be different in the general election; as of the time this textbook went to press, no comprehensive data on the 2010 election was available.—ed.]

i.   Corporate Speech Generally

Justice Kennedy delivered the opinion of the Court.

Federal law prohibits corporations and unions from using their general treasury funds to make independent expenditures for speech defined as an "electioneering communication" or for speech expressly advocating the election or defeat of a candidate. 2 U.S.C. § 441b....

[A.] Citizens United is a nonprofit corporation ... [with] an annual budget of about $12 million. Most of its funds are from donations by individuals; but, in addition, it accepts a small portion of its funds from for-profit corporations.

In January 2008, Citizens United released a film entitled *Hillary: The Movie....* It is a 90-minute documentary about then-Senator Hillary Clinton, who was a candidate in the Democratic Party's 2008 Presidential primary elections. *Hillary* ... depicts interviews with political commentators and other persons, most of them quite critical of Senator Clinton.

Hillary was released in theaters and on DVD, but Citizens United wanted to increase distribution by making it available through video-on-demand.... In December 2007, a cable company offered, for a payment of $1.2 million [but at no cost to viewers], to make *Hillary* available on a video-on-demand channel called "Elections '08." ... Citizens United was prepared to pay for the video-on-demand; and to promote the film {on broadcast and cable television}, it produced two 10-second ads and one 30-second ad for *Hillary*. Each ad includes a short (and, in our view, pejorative) statement about Senator Clinton, followed by the name of the movie and the movie's Website address.

[B.] Before the Bipartisan Campaign Reform Act of 2002 (BCRA), federal law prohibited—and still does prohibit—corporations and unions from using general treasury funds to make direct contributions to candidates or independent expenditures that expressly advocate the election or defeat of a candidate, through any form of media, in connection with certain qualified federal elections. BCRA § 203 amended § 441b to prohibit any "electioneering communication" as well. An electioneering communication is defined as "any broadcast, cable, or satellite communication" that "refers to a clearly identified candidate for Federal office" and is made within 30 days of a primary or 60 days of a general election....

Corporations and unions are barred from using their general treasury funds for express advocacy or electioneering communications. They may establish, however, a "separate segregated fund" (known as a political action committee, or PAC) for these purposes. The moneys received by the segregated fund are limited to donations from stockholders and employees of the corporation or, in the case of unions, members of the union.

Citizens United wanted to make *Hillary* available through video-on-demand within 30 days of the 2008 primary elections. It feared, however, that both the film and the ads would be covered by § 441b's ban on corporate-funded independent expenditures .... Citizens United sought declaratory and injunctive relief against the FEC....

[C.] Section 441b makes it a felony for all corporations—including nonprofit advocacy corporations—either to expressly advocate the election or defeat of candidates or to broadcast electioneering communications within 30 days of a primary election and 60 days of a general election. Thus, the following acts would all be felonies under § 441b: The Sierra Club runs an ad, within the crucial phase of 60 days before the general election, that exhorts the public to disapprove of a Congressman who favors logging in national forests; the National Rifle Association publishes a book urging the public to vote for the challenger because the incumbent U.S. Senator supports a handgun ban; and the American Civil Liberties Union creates a Web site telling the public to vote for a Presidential candidate in light of that candidate's defense of free speech. These prohibitions are classic examples of censorship.

Section 441b is a ban on corporate speech notwithstanding the fact that a PAC created by a corporation can still speak. A PAC is a separate association from the corporation. So the PAC exemption ... does not allow corporations to speak....

[Moreover,] PACs are burdensome alternatives; they are expensive to administer and subject to extensive regulations. For example, every PAC must appoint a treasurer, forward donations to the treasurer promptly, keep detailed records of the identities of the persons making donations, preserve receipts for three years, and file an organization statement and report changes to this information within 10 days. And that is just the beginning. [More details omitted.—ed.] ... This might explain why fewer than 2,000 of the millions of corporations in this country have PACs.... [And g]iven the onerous restrictions, a corporation may not be able to establish a PAC in time to make its views known regarding candidates and issues in a current campaign....

Section 441b's prohibition on corporate independent expenditures is thus a ban on speech. As a "restriction on the amount of money a person or group can spend on political communication during a campaign," that statute "necessarily reduces the quantity of expression by restricting the number of issues discussed, the depth of their exploration, and the size of the audience reached." *Buckley v. Valeo*.... If § 441b applied to individuals, no one would believe that it is merely a time, place, or manner restriction on speech. Its purpose and effect are to silence entities whose voices the Government deems to be suspect....

Laws that burden political speech are "subject to strict scrutiny," which requires the Government to prove that the restriction "furthers a compelling interest and is narrowly tailored to achieve that interest." ...

[D.] Premised on mistrust of governmental power, the First Amendment stands against attempts to disfavor certain subjects or viewpoints. Prohibited, too, are restrictions distinguishing among different speakers, allowing speech by some but not others. As instruments to censor, these categories are interrelated: Speech restrictions based on the identity of the speaker are all too often simply a means to control content.

Quite apart from the purpose or effect of regulating content, moreover, the Government may commit a constitutional wrong when by law it identifies certain preferred speakers. By taking the right to speak from some and giving it to others, the Government deprives the disadvantaged person or class of the right to use speech to strive to establish worth, standing, and respect for the speaker's voice. The Government may not by these means deprive the public of the right and privilege to determine for itself what speech and speakers are worthy of consideration. The First Amendment protects speech and speaker, and the ideas that flow from each.

The Court has upheld a narrow class of speech restrictions that operate to the disadvantage of certain persons, but these rulings were based on an interest in allowing governmental entities [such as schools, prisons, the military, and government employers] to perform their functions.... These precedents stand only for the proposition that there are certain governmental functions that cannot operate without some restrictions on particular kinds of speech. By contrast, it is inherent in the nature of the political process that voters must be free to obtain information from diverse sources in order to determine how to cast their votes....

[E.] The Court has recognized that First Amendment protection extends to corporations. [*E.g.,*] *New York Times Co. v. Sullivan*[;] ... *Grosjean v. American Press Co.,* 297 U.S. 233 (1936).... [P]olitical speech does not lose First Amendment protection "simply because its source is a corporation." *First Nat'l Bank of Boston v. Bellotti*.... [N]ot until 1947 did Congress first prohibit independent expenditures by corporations and labor unions ... [over] the veto of President Truman, who warned that the expenditure ban was a "dangerous intrusion on free speech." [History of the debate since then omitted.—ed.] ...

[F.] [The court now turns to the "antidistortion rationale" for restricting corporate speech about elections because of the alleged "corrosive and distorting effects of immense aggregations of wealth that are accumulated with the help of the corporate form and that have little or no correlation to the public's support for the corporation's political ideas."—ed.]

Buckley rejected the premise that the Government has an interest "in equalizing the relative ability of individuals and groups to influence the outcome of elections." ...

Leveling electoral opportunities means making and implementing judgments about which strengths [*i.e.,* wealth, celebrity status, or the benefit of a well-known family name] should be permitted to contribute to the outcome of an election. The Constitution, however, confers upon voters, not Congress, the power to choose the Members of the House of Representatives, and it is a dangerous business for Congress to use the election laws to influence the voters' choices[.]

The rule that political speech cannot be limited based on a speaker's wealth is a necessary consequence of the premise that the First Amendment generally prohibits the suppression of political speech based on the speaker's identity....

[Nor can laws prohibiting speech be justified by] distinguish[ing] wealthy individuals from corporations on the ground that "[s]tate law grants corporations special advantages—such as limited liability, perpetual life, and favorable treatment of the accumulation and distribution of assets." ... "... [T]he State cannot exact as the price of those special advantages the forfeiture of First Amendment rights."

It is irrelevant for purposes of the First Amendment that corporate funds may "have little or no correlation to the public's support for the corporation's political ideas." All speakers, including individuals and the media, use money amassed from the economic marketplace to fund their speech. The First Amendment protects the resulting speech, even if it was enabled by economic transactions with persons or entities who disagree with the speaker's ideas.... "Many persons can trace their funds to corporations, if not in the form of donations, then in the form of dividends, interest, or salary[."]

{If the antidistortion rationale were to be accepted, ... the Government could prohibit a corporation from expressing political views in media beyond those presented here, such as by printing books. The Government responds "that the FEC has never applied this statute to a book," and if it did, "there would be quite [a] good as-applied challenge." This troubling assertion of brooding governmental power cannot be reconciled with the confidence and stability in civic discourse that the First Amendment must secure.} ...

[G.] Most [corporations] are small corporations without large amounts of wealth. This fact belies the Government's argument that the statute is justified on the ground that it prevents the "distorting effects of immense aggregations of wealth." It is not even aimed at amassed wealth.

The censorship we now confront is vast in its reach. The Government has "muffle[d] the voices that best represent the most significant segments of the economy." And "the electorate [has been] deprived of information, knowledge and opinion vital to its function." By suppressing the speech of manifold corporations, both for-profit and nonprofit, the Government prevents their voices and viewpoints from reaching the public and advising voters on which persons or entities are hostile to their interests. Factions will necessarily form in our Republic, but the remedy of "destroying the liberty" of some factions is "worse than the disease." Factions should be checked by permitting them all to speak, and by entrusting the people to judge what is true and what is false.

The purpose and effect of this law is to prevent corporations, including small and nonprofit corporations, from presenting both facts and opinions to the public. This makes [the] antidistortion rationale all the more an aberration. "[T]he First Amendment protects the right of corporations to petition legislative and administrative bodies." Corporate executives and employees counsel Members of Congress and Presidential administrations on many issues, as a matter of routine and often in private....

When that phenomenon is coupled with § 441b, the result is that smaller or nonprofit corporations cannot raise a voice to object when other corporations, including those with vast wealth, are cooperating with the Government. That cooperation may sometimes be voluntary, or it may be at the demand of a Government official who uses his or her authority, influence, and power to threaten corporations to support the Government's policies. Those kinds of interactions are often unknown and unseen. The speech that § 441b forbids, though, is public, and all can judge its content and purpose. References to massive corporate treasuries should not mask the real operation of this law....

Even if § 441b's expenditure ban were constitutional, wealthy corporations could still lobby elected officials, although smaller corporations may not have the resources to do so. And wealthy individuals and unincorporated associations can spend unlimited amounts on independent expenditures. "In the 2004 election cycle, a mere 24 individuals contributed an astounding total of $142 million to [unincorporated 26 U.S.C. § 527 political advocacy organizations.]" Yet certain disfavored associations of citizens—those that have taken on the corporate form—are penalized for engaging in the same political speech.

When Government seeks to use its full power, including the criminal law, to command where a person may get his or her information or what distrusted source he or she may not hear, it uses censorship to control thought....

[H.] [M]ovies, television comedies, or skits on Youtube.com might portray public officials or public policies in unflattering ways. Yet if a covered transmission during the blackout period creates the background for candidate endorsement or opposition, a felony occurs solely because a corporation, other than an exempt media corporation, has made the "purchase, payment, distribution, loan, advance, deposit, or gift of money or anything of value" in order to engage in political speech. Speech would be suppressed in the realm where its necessity is most evident: in the public dialogue preceding a real election....

Some members of the public might consider *Hillary* to be insightful and instructive; some might find it to be neither high art nor a fair discussion on how to set the Nation's course; still others simply might suspend judgment on these points but decide to think more about issues and candidates. Those choices and assessments, however, are not for the Government to make....

Justice Stevens, with whom Justice Ginsburg, Justice Breyer, and Justice Sotomayor join, ... dissenting in [relevant] part.

[A.] [*The So-Called "Ban"*]

Pervading the Court's analysis is the ominous image of a "categorical ba[n]" on corporate speech.... [But BCRA does] "not impose an *absolute* ban on all forms of corporate political spending."

For starters, [it provides] exemptions for PACs, separate segregated funds established by a corporation for political purposes.... Under BCRA, any corporation's "stockholders and their families and its executive or administrative personnel and their families" can pool their resources to finance electioneering communications. A significant and growing number of corporations avail themselves of this option; during the most recent election cycle, corporate and union PACs raised nearly a billion dollars.

Administering a PAC entails some administrative burden, but so does complying with the disclaimer, disclosure, and reporting requirements that the Court today upholds, and no one has suggested that the burden is severe for a sophisticated for-profit corporation....

Like all other natural persons, every shareholder of every corporation remains entirely free ... to do however much electioneering she pleases outside of the corporate form. The owners of a "mom & pop" store can simply place ads in their own names, rather than the store's. If ideologically aligned individuals wish to make unlimited expenditures through the corporate form, they may utilize an *MCFL* organization [see p. 465 of the casebook—ed.] that has policies in place to avoid becoming a conduit for business or union interests.

[Restrictions on corporate independent expenditures] leave open many additional avenues for corporations' political speech.... [Section 203] has no application to genuine issue advertising—a category of corporate speech Congress found to be far more substantial than election-related advertising—or to Internet, telephone, and print advocacy. {[Section] 203 does not apply to printed material. And in light of the ordinary understanding of the terms "broadcast, cable, [and] satellite," coupled with Congress' clear aim of targeting "a virtual torrent of televised election-related ads," we highly doubt that § 203 could be interpreted to apply to a Web site or book that happens to be transmitted at some stage over airwaves or cable lines, or that the FEC would ever try to do so. If it should, the Government acknowledges "there would be quite [a] good as-applied challenge."}

Like numerous statutes, [§ 203] exempts media companies' news stories, commentaries, and editorials from its electioneering restrictions, in recognition of the unique role played by the institutional press in sustaining public debate. It also allows corporations to spend unlimited sums on political communications with their executives and shareholders, to fund additional PAC activity through trade associations, to distribute voting guides and voting records, to underwrite voter registration and voter turnout activities, to host fundraising events for candidates within certain limits, and to publicly endorse candidates through a press release and press conference....

In many ways, then, § 203 functions as a source restriction or a time, place, and manner restriction. It applies in a viewpoint-neutral fashion to a narrow subset of advocacy messages about clearly identified candidates for federal office, made during discrete time periods through discrete channels. In the case at hand, all Citizens United needed to do to broadcast *Hillary* right before the primary was to abjure business contributions or use the funds in its PAC, which by its own account is "one of the most active conservative PACs in America." ...

Laws such as § 203 ... burden political speech, and that is always a serious matter, demanding careful scrutiny. But the majority's incessant talk of a "ban" aims at a straw man.

[B.] *Identity-Based Distinctions*

The second pillar of the Court's opinion is its assertion that "the Government cannot restrict political speech based on the speaker's ... identity." ... [Yet t]he Government routinely places special restrictions on the speech rights of students, prisoners, members of the Armed Forces, foreigners, and its own employees. When such restrictions are justified by a legitimate governmental interest, they do not necessarily raise constitutional problems.

{The majority states that the cases just cited are "inapposite" because they "stand only for the proposition that there are certain governmental functions that cannot operate without some restrictions on particular kinds of speech." The majority's creative suggestion that these cases stand only for that one proposition is quite implausible. In any event the proposition lies at the heart of this case, as Congress and half the state legislatures have concluded, over many decades, that their core functions of administering elections and passing legislation cannot operate effectively without some narrow restrictions on corporate electioneering paid for by general treasury funds.} [T]he Government's interests may be more or less compelling with respect to different classes of speakers, and ... the constitutional rights of certain categories of speakers, in certain contexts, "'are not automatically coextensive with the rights'" that are normally accorded to members of our society, *Morse v. Frederick.*

The free speech guarantee thus does not render every other public interest an illegitimate basis for qualifying a speaker's autonomy; society could scarcely function if it did. It is fair to say that our First Amendment doctrine has "frowned on" certain identity-based distinctions, particularly those that may reflect invidious discrimination or preferential treatment of a politically powerful group. But ... we have [not] prohibited all legislative distinctions based on identity or content....

[For instance, a]lthough we have not reviewed them directly, we have never cast doubt on laws that place special restrictions on campaign spending by foreign nationals. And we have consistently approved laws that bar Government employees, but not others, from contributing to or participating in political activities.... [W]e have sustained them on the basis of longstanding practice and Congress' reasoned judgment that certain regulations which leave "untouched full participation ... in political decisions at the ballot box," help ensure that public officials are "sufficiently free from improper influences," and that "confidence in the system of representative Government is not ... eroded to a disastrous extent."

The same logic applies to this case with additional force because it is the identity of corporations, rather than individuals, that the Legislature has taken into account.... [L]egislatures are entitled to decide "that the special characteristics of the corporate structure require particularly careful regulation" in an electoral context.

Not only has the distinctive potential of corporations to corrupt the electoral process long been recognized, but within the area of campaign finance, corporate spending is also "furthest from the core of political expression, since corporations' First Amendment speech and association interests are derived largely from those of their members and of the public in receiving information." Campaign finance distinctions based on corporate identity tend to be less worrisome, in other words, because the "speakers" are not natural persons, much less members of our political community, and the governmental interests are of the highest order. Furthermore, when corporations, as a class, are distinguished from noncorporations, as a class, there is a lesser risk that regulatory distinctions will reflect invidious discrimination or political favoritism.

If taken seriously, our colleagues' assumption that the identity of a speaker has *no* relevance to the Government's ability to regulate political speech would lead to some remarkable conclusions. Such an assumption would have accorded the propaganda broadcasts to our troops by "Tokyo Rose" during World War II the same protection as speech by Allied commanders. More pertinently, it would appear to afford the same protection to multinational corporations controlled by foreigners as to individual Americans ....

{The Court all but confesses that a categorical approach to speaker identity is untenable when it acknowledges that Congress might be allowed to [restrict independent expenditures by foreigners, which U.S. campaign finance law had long done—ed.]. The notion that Congress might lack the authority to distinguish foreigners from citizens in the regulation of electioneering would certainly have surprised the Framers, whose "obsession with foreign influence derived from a fear that foreign powers and individuals had no basic investment in the well-being of the country." See also U.S. Const., Art. I, § 9, cl. 8 ("[N]o Person holding any Office of Profit or Trust ... shall, without the Consent of the Congress, accept of any present, Emolument, Office, or Title, of any kind whatever, from any King, Prince, or foreign State")…. [A] corporation might be analogized to a foreign power in this respect, "inasmuch as its legal loyalties necessarily exclude patriotism."}[a]

---

[a] [Here is the **majority's discussion** of foreigners' expenditures related to American political campaigns:—ed.] Section 441b is not limited to corporations or

Under the majority's view, I suppose it may be a First Amendment problem that corporations are not permitted to vote, given that voting is, among other things, a form of speech. {Of course, voting is not speech in a pure or formal sense, but then again neither is a campaign expenditure; both are nevertheless communicative acts aimed at influencing electoral outcomes.} ...

[C.] *Corporate Expenditures ...*

Unlike natural persons, corporations have "limited liability" for their owners and managers, "perpetual life," separation of ownership and control, "and favorable treatment of the accumulation and distribution of assets ... that enhance their ability to attract capital and to deploy their resources ...." Unlike voters in U.S. elections, corporations may be foreign controlled. {In state elections, even domestic corporations may be "foreign"-controlled in the sense that they are incorporated in another jurisdiction and primarily owned and operated by out-of-state residents.}

Unlike other interest groups, business corporations have been "effectively delegated responsibility for ensuring society's economic welfare"; they inescapably structure the life of every citizen. "[T]he resources in the treasury of a business corporation," furthermore, "are not an indication of popular support for the corporation's political ideas." "They reflect instead the economically motivated decisions of investors and customers...." ...

[C]orporations have no consciences, no beliefs, no feelings, no thoughts, no desires. Corporations help structure and facilitate the activities of human beings, to be sure, and their "personhood" often serves as a useful legal fiction. But they are not themselves members of "We the People" by whom and for whom our Constitution was established....

One fundamental concern of the First Amendment is to "protec[t] the individual's interest in self-expression." Freedom of speech helps "make men free to develop their faculties," it respects their "dignity and choice," and it facilitates the value of "individual self-realization."

Corporate speech, however, is derivative speech, speech by proxy. A regulation such as § 203 may affect the way in which individuals disseminate certain messages through the corporate form, but it does not prevent anyone from speaking in his or her own voice. "Within the realm of [campaign spending] generally," corporate spending is "furthest from the core of political expression."

It is an interesting question "who" is even speaking when a business corporation places an advertisement that endorses or attacks a particular candidate. Presumably it is not the customers or employees, who typically have no say in such matters. It cannot realistically be said to be the shareholders, who tend to be far removed from the day-to-day decisions of the

---

associations that were created in foreign countries or funded predominately by foreign shareholders. Section 441b therefore would be overbroad even if we assumed, *arguendo,* that the Government has a compelling interest in limiting foreign influence over our political process....

firm and whose political preferences may be opaque to management.

Perhaps the officers or directors of the corporation have the best claim to be the ones speaking, except their fiduciary duties generally prohibit them from using corporate funds for personal ends. Some individuals associated with the corporation must make the decision to place the ad, but the idea that these individuals are thereby fostering their self-expression or cultivating their critical faculties is fanciful. It is entirely possible that the corporation's electoral message will *conflict* with their personal convictions....

Corporate expenditures are distinguishable from individual expenditures in this respect.... Some ... individuals might feel that they need to spend large sums of money on behalf of a particular candidate to vindicate the intensity of their electoral preferences. This is obviously not the situation with business corporations, as their routine practice of giving "substantial sums to *both* major national parties" makes pellucidly clear. "[C]orporate participation" in elections ... "is more transactional than ideological."

In this transactional spirit, some corporations have affirmatively urged Congress to place limits on their electioneering communications. These corporations fear that officeholders will shake them down for supportive ads, that they will have to spend increasing sums on elections in an ever-escalating arms race with their competitors, and that public trust in business will be eroded. A system that effectively forces corporations to use their shareholders' money both to maintain access to, and to avoid retribution from, elected officials may ultimately prove more harmful than beneficial to many corporations. It can impose a kind of implicit tax.

In short, regulations such as § 203 ... impose only a limited burden on First Amendment freedoms not only because they target a narrow subset of expenditures and leave untouched the broader "public dialogue," but also because they leave untouched the speech of natural persons.

[D.] Recognizing the weakness of a speaker-based [argument], the Court places primary emphasis not on the corporation's right to electioneer, but rather on the listener's interest in hearing what every possible speaker may have to say. The Court's central argument is that laws such as § 203 have "deprived [the electorate] of information, knowledge and opinion vital to its function," and this, in turn, "interferes with the 'open marketplace' of ideas protected by the First Amendment."

There are many flaws in this argument. If the overriding concern depends on the interests of the audience, surely the public's perception of the value of corporate speech should be given important weight.... The distinctive threat to democratic integrity posed by corporate domination of politics was recognized at "the inception of the republic" and "has been a persistent theme in American political life" ever since....

[T]here are substantial reasons why a legislature might conclude that unregulated general treasury expenditures will give corporations "unfai[r] influence" in the electoral process, and distort public debate in ways that undermine rather than advance the interests of listeners. The legal structure of corporations allows them to amass and deploy financial resources on a scale few natural persons can match.

The structure of a business corporation, furthermore, draws a line between the corporation's economic interests and the political preferences of the individuals associated with the corporation; the corporation must engage the electoral process with the aim "to enhance the profitability of the company, no matter how persuasive the arguments for a broader or conflicting set of priorities." In a state election ..., the interests of nonresident corporations may be fundamentally adverse to the interests of local voters.

Consequently, when corporations grab up the prime broadcasting slots on the eve of an election, they can flood the market with advocacy that bears "little or no correlation" to the ideas of natural persons or to any broader notion of the public good. The opinions of real people may be marginalized. "The expenditure restrictions of ... § 441b are thus meant to ensure that competition among actors in the political arena is truly competition among ideas." ...

[E.] Corporate "domination" of electioneering can [also] generate the impression that corporations dominate our democracy.... [C]itizens ... may lose faith in their capacity, as citizens, to influence public policy. A Government captured by corporate interests, they may come to believe, will be neither responsive to their needs nor willing to give their views a fair hearing. The predictable result is cynicism and disenchantment: an increased perception that large spenders "call the tune" and a reduced "willingness of voters to take part in democratic governance."

To the extent that corporations are allowed to exert undue influence in electoral races, the speech of the eventual winners of those races may also be chilled. Politicians who fear that a certain corporation can make or break their reelection chances may be cowed into silence about that corporation.... At the least, ... a legislature is entitled to credit these concerns and to take tailored measures in response....

[C]orporations' "war chests" and their special "advantages" in the legal realm may [also] translate into special advantages in the market for legislation. When large numbers of citizens have a common stake in a measure that is under consideration, it may be very difficult for them to coordinate resources on behalf of their position.... [But c]orporations ... are uniquely equipped to seek laws that favor their owners, not simply because they have a lot of money but because of their legal and organizational structure....

The Court's facile depiction of corporate electioneering assumes away all of these complexities. Our colleagues ridicule the idea of regulating expenditures based on "nothing more" than a fear that corporations have a special "ability to persuade," as if corporations were our society's ablest debaters and viewpoint-neutral laws such as § 203 were created to suppress their best arguments.... [O]ur colleagues simply ignore the fundamental concerns of ... the legislatures that have passed laws like § 203: to safeguard the integrity, competitiveness, and democratic responsiveness of the electoral process. All of the majority's theoretical arguments turn on a proposition with undeniable surface appeal but little grounding in evidence or experience, "that there is no such thing as too much speech." {Of course, no presiding person in a courtroom, legislature, classroom, polling place, or family dinner would take this hyperbole literally.}

If individuals in our society had infinite free time to listen to and contemplate every last bit of speech uttered by anyone, anywhere; and if broadcast advertisements had no special ability to influence elections apart from the merits of their arguments (to the extent they make any); and if legislators always operated with nothing less than perfect virtue; then I suppose the majority's premise would be sound. In the real world, we have seen, corporate domination of the airwaves prior to an election may decrease the average listener's exposure to relevant viewpoints, and it may diminish citizens' willingness and capacity to participate in the democratic process....

[The] "concern about corporate domination of the political process" reflects more than a concern to protect governmental interests outside of the First Amendment. It also reflects a concern to *facilitate* First Amendment values by preserving some breathing room around the electoral "marketplace" of ideas, the marketplace in which the actual people of this Nation determine how they will govern themselves....

There are, to be sure, serious concerns with any effort to balance the First Amendment rights of speakers against the First Amendment rights of listeners. But when the speakers in question are not real people and when the appeal to "First Amendment principles" depends almost entirely on the listeners' perspective, it becomes necessary to consider how listeners will actually be affected....

[F.] At bottom, the Court's opinion is thus a rejection of the common sense of the American people, who have recognized a need to prevent corporations from undermining self-government since the founding, and who have fought against the distinctive corrupting potential of corporate electioneering since the days of Theodore Roosevelt....

ii. Corruption

Justice Kennedy delivered the opinion of the Court....

[The government argues] that corporate political speech can be banned in order to prevent corruption or its appearance.... [The majority responds using the arguments from *Buckley*, which held the anticorruption rationale to be an inadequate justification for restricting independent expenditures (as opposed to contributions), and it adds:—ed.]

Indeed, 26 States do not restrict independent expenditures by for-profit corporations. The Government does not claim that these expenditures have corrupted the political process in those States....

[Nor is it enough to argue that] there is a "sufficient" governmental interest in "ensur[ing] that substantial aggregations of wealth amassed" by corporations would not "be used to incur political debts from legislators who are aided by the contributions." ... When *Buckley* identified a sufficiently important governmental interest in preventing corruption or the appearance of corruption, that interest was limited to *quid pro quo* corruption. The fact that speakers may have influence over or access to elected officials does not mean that these officials are corrupt: "Favoritism and influence are not ... avoidable in representative politics. It is in the nature of an elected representative to favor certain policies, and, by necessary corollary, to favor the voters and contributors who support those policies. It is well understood that a substantial and legitimate reason, if not the only reason, to cast a vote for, or to make a contribution to, one candidate over another is that the candidate will respond by producing those political outcomes the supporter favors. Democracy is premised on responsiveness." Reliance on a "generic favoritism or influence theory ... is at odds with standard First Amendment analyses because it is unbounded and susceptible to no limiting principle."

The appearance of influence or access, furthermore, will not cause the electorate to lose faith in our democracy. By definition, an independent expenditure is political speech presented to the electorate that is not coordinated with a candidate. The fact that a corporation, or any other speaker, is willing to spend money to try to persuade voters presupposes that the people have the ultimate influence over elected officials. This is inconsistent with any suggestion that the electorate will refuse "'to take part in democratic governance'" because of additional political speech made by a corporation or any other speaker.

The *McConnell* record was "over 100,000 pages" long, yet it "does not have any direct examples of votes being exchanged for ... expenditures." This confirms *Buckley*'s reasoning that independent expenditures do not lead to, or create the appearance of, *quid pro quo* corruption. In fact, there is only scant evidence that independent expenditures even ingratiate. Ingratiation and access, in any event, are not corruption....

If elected officials succumb to improper influences from independent expenditures; if they surrender their best judgment; and if they put expediency before principle, then surely there is cause for concern. We must give weight to attempts by Congress to seek to dispel either the appearance or the reality of these influences. The remedies enacted by law, however, must comply with the First Amendment; and, it is our law and our tradition that more speech, not less, is the governing rule. An outright ban on corporate political speech during the critical preelection period is not a permissible remedy....

[Justice Scalia, in *McConnell v. FEC*, **540 U.S. 93 (2003)**, also made this argument, to which the *Citizens United* dissent responds in Part C below:—ed.]

[T]his legislation [challenged in *McConnell*] prohibits the criticism of Members of Congress by those entities most capable of giving such criticism loud voice: national political parties and corporations, both of the commercial and the not-for-profit sort. It forbids pre-election criticism of incumbents by corporations, even not-for-profit corporations, by use of their general funds; and forbids national-party use of "soft" money to fund "issue ads" that incumbents find so offensive.

To be sure, the legislation is evenhanded: It similarly prohibits criticism of the candidates who oppose Members of Congress in their reelection bids. But as everyone knows, this is an area in which evenhandedness is not fairness. If *all* electioneering were evenhandedly prohibited, incumbents would have an enormous advantage. Likewise, if incumbents and challengers are limited to the same quantity of electioneering, incumbents are favored. In other words, *any* restriction upon a type of campaign speech that is equally available to challengers and incumbents tends to favor incumbents.

Beyond that, however, the present legislation *targets* for prohibition certain categories of campaign speech that are particularly harmful to incumbents. Is it accidental, do you think, that incumbents raise about three times as much "hard money"—the sort of funding generally *not* restricted by this legislation—as do their challengers? Or that lobbyists (who seek the favor of incumbents) give 92 percent of their money in "hard" contributions?

Is it an oversight, do you suppose, that the so-called "millionaire provisions" raise the contribution limit for a candidate running against an individual who devotes to the campaign (as challengers often do) great personal wealth, but do not raise the limit for a candidate running against an individual who devotes to the campaign (as incumbents often do) a massive election "war chest"? And is it mere happenstance, do you estimate, that national-party funding, which is severely limited by the Act, is more likely to assist cash-strapped challengers than flush-with-hard-money incumbents? Was it unintended, by any chance, that incumbents are free personally to receive some soft money and even to solicit it for other organizations, while national parties are not? ...

Justice Stevens, with whom Justice Ginsburg, Justice Breyer, and Justice Sotomayor join, ... dissenting in [relevant] part....

[A.] *The Anticorruption Interest*

Undergirding the majority's approach to the merits is the claim that the only "sufficiently important governmental interest in preventing corruption or the appearance of corruption" is one that is "limited to *quid pro quo* corruption." ... [But] Congress[has a] legitimate interest in preventing the money that is spent on elections from exerting an "'undue influence on an officeholder's judgment'" and from creating "'the appearance of such influence,'" beyond the sphere of *quid pro quo* relationships.

Corruption can take many forms. Bribery may be the paradigm case. But the difference between selling a vote and selling access is a matter of degree, not kind. And selling access is not qualitatively different from giving special preference to those who spent money on one's behalf....

[In the words of Judge Kollar-Kotelly, a member of the three-judge court assigned to the initial BCRA litigation, summarizing the court's findings,] "... [C]orporations and labor unions routinely notify Members of Congress as soon as they air electioneering communications relevant to the Members' elections.... Members express appreciation to organizations for the airing of these election-related advertisements. Indeed, Members ... are particularly grateful when negative issue advertisements are run by these organizations, leaving the candidates free to run positive advertisements and be seen as 'above the fray.'

"Political consultants testify that campaigns are quite aware of who is running advertisements on the candidate's behalf, when they are being run, and where they are being run. Likewise, a prominent lobbyist testifies that these organizations use issue advocacy as a means to influence various Members ....

"... [Members also] seek to have corporations and unions run these advertisements on their behalf.... Members suggest that corporations or individuals make donations to interest groups with the understanding that the money contributed to these groups will assist the Member in a campaign. After the election, these organizations often seek credit for their support.... Finally, a large majority of Americans (80%) are of the view that corporations and other organizations that engage in electioneering communications, which benefit specific elected officials, receive special consideration from those officials when matters arise that affect these corporations and organizations."

Many of the relationships of dependency found by Judge Kollar-Kotelly seemed to have a *quid pro quo* basis, but other arrangements were more subtle. Her analysis shows the great difficulty in delimiting the precise scope of the *quid pro quo* category, as well as the adverse consequences that *all* such arrangements may have. There are threats of corruption that are far more destructive to a democratic society than the odd bribe. Yet the majority's understanding of corruption would leave lawmakers impotent to address all but the most discrete abuses.

Our "undue influence" cases have allowed the American people to cast a wider net through legislative experiments designed to ensure, to some minimal extent, "that officeholders will decide issues ... on the merits or the desires of their constituencies," and not "according to the wishes of those who have made large financial contributions"—or expenditures—"valued by the officeholder." When private interests are seen to exert outsized control over officeholders solely on account of the money spent on (or withheld from) their campaigns, the result can ... amount[] to a "subversion ... of the electoral process."

At stake in the legislative efforts to address this threat is therefore not only the legitimacy and quality of Government but also the public's faith therein, not only "the capacity of this democracy to represent its constituents [but also] the confidence of its citizens in their capacity to govern themselves." {The majority declares by fiat that the appearance of undue influence by high-spending corporations "will not cause the electorate to lose faith in our democracy." The electorate itself has consistently indicated otherwise, both in opinion polls, and in the laws its representatives have passed, and our colleagues have no basis for elevating their own optimism into a tenet of constitutional law.} ...

[B.] Quid Pro Quo *Corruption* ...

[But e]ven under the majority's "crabbed view of corruption," the Government should not lose this case.... Even in the cases that have construed the anticorruption interest most narrowly, we have never suggested that ... *quid pro quo* [political] debts must take the form of outright vote buying or bribes, which have long been distinct crimes. Rather, they encompass the myriad ways in which outside parties may induce an officeholder to confer a legislative benefit in direct response to, or anticipation of, some outlay of money the parties have made or will make on behalf of the officeholder....

The legislative and judicial proceedings relating to BCRA generated a substantial body of evidence suggesting that, as corporations grew more and more adept at crafting "issue ads" to help or harm a particular candidate, these nominally independent expenditures began to corrupt the political process in a very direct sense. The sponsors of these ads were routinely granted special access after the campaign was over; "candidates and officials knew who their friends were." Many corporate independent expenditures, it seemed, had become essentially interchangeable with direct contributions in their capacity to generate *quid pro quo* arrangements. In an age in which money and television ads are the coin of the campaign realm, it is hardly surprising that corporations deployed these ads to curry favor with, and to gain influence over, public officials.

The majority appears to think it decisive that the BCRA record does not contain "direct examples of votes being exchanged for ... expenditures." It would have been quite remarkable if Congress had created a record detailing such behavior by its own Members. Proving that a specific vote was exchanged for a specific expenditure has always been next to impossible: Elected officials have diverse motivations, and no one will acknowledge that he sold a vote.

Yet, even if "[i]ngratiation and access ... are not corruption" themselves, they are necessary prerequisites to it; they can create both the opportunity for, and the appearance of, *quid pro quo* arrangements. The influx of unlimited corporate money into the electoral realm also creates new opportunities for the mirror image of *quid pro quo* deals: threats, both explicit and implicit. Starting today, corporations with large war chests to deploy on electioneering may find democratically elected bodies becoming much more attuned to their interests....

In her analysis of the record, Judge Kollar-Kotelly documented the pervasiveness of this ingratiation and explained its significance under the majority's own touchstone for defining the scope of the anticorruption rationale, *Buckley*. Witnesses explained how political parties and candidates used corporate independent expenditures to circumvent [campaign finance law's] "hard-money" limitations. One former Senator candidly admitted to the District Court that "'[c]andidates whose campaigns benefit from [phony "issue ads"] greatly appreciate the help of these groups. In fact, Members will also be favorably disposed to those who finance these groups when they later seek access to discuss pending legislation.'"

One prominent lobbyist went so far as to state, in uncontroverted testimony, that "'unregulated expenditures—whether soft money donations to the parties or issue ad campaigns—can sometimes generate *far more* influence than direct campaign contributions.'" In sum, Judge Kollar-Kotelly found, "[t]he record powerfully demonstrates that electioneering communications paid for with the general treasury funds of labor unions and corporations endears those entities to elected officials in a way that could be perceived by the public as corrupting." ...

[C.] *Deference and Incumbent Self-Protection*

Rather than show any deference to a coordinate branch of Government, the majority thus rejects the anticorruption rationale without serious analysis. Today's opinion provides no clear rationale for being so dismissive of Congress, but the prior individual opinions on which it relies have offered one: the incentives of the legislators who passed BCRA. Section 203, our colleagues have suggested [in past cases], may be little more than "an incumbency protection plan," a disreputable attempt at legislative self-dealing rather than an earnest effort to facilitate First Amendment values and safeguard the legitimacy of our political system....

In my view, we should instead start by acknowledging that "Congress surely has both wisdom and experience in these matters that is far superior to ours." Many of our campaign finance precedents explicitly and forcefully affirm the propriety of such presumptive deference. Moreover, "[j]udicial deference is particularly warranted where, as here, we deal with a congressional judgment that has remained essentially unchanged throughout a century of careful legislative adjustment." In America, incumbent legislators pass the laws that govern campaign finance, just like all other laws. To apply a level of scrutiny that effectively bars them from regulating electioneering whenever there is the faintest whiff of self-interest, is to deprive them of the ability to regulate electioneering.

This is not to say that deference would be appropriate if there were a solid basis for believing that a legislative action was motivated by the desire to protect incumbents or that it will degrade the competitiveness of the electoral process. Along with our duty to balance competing constitutional concerns, we have a vital role to play in ensuring that elections remain at least minimally open, fair, and competitive. But it is the height of recklessness to dismiss Congress' years of bipartisan deliberation and its reasoned judgment on this basis, without first confirming that the statute in question was intended to be, or will function as, a restraint on electoral competition. "Absent record evidence of invidious discrimination against challengers as a class, a court should generally be hesitant to invalidate legislation which on its face imposes evenhanded restrictions."

We have no record evidence from which to conclude that § 203, or any of the dozens of state laws that the Court today calls into question, reflects or fosters such invidious discrimination. Our colleagues have opined that "*any* restriction upon a type of campaign speech that is equally available to challengers and incumbents tends to favor incumbents." This kind of airy speculation could easily be turned on its head. The electioneering prohibited by § 203 might well tend to favor incumbents, because incumbents have pre-existing relationships with corporations and unions, and groups that wish to procure legislative benefits may tend to support the candidate who, as a sitting officeholder, is already in a position to dispense benefits and is statistically likely to retain office. If a corporation's goal is to induce officeholders to do its bidding, the corporation would do well to cultivate stable, long-term relationships of dependency....

Nor does the legislative history give reason for concern. Congress devoted years of careful study to the issues underlying BCRA; "[f]ew legislative proposals in recent years have received as much sustained public commentary or news coverage"; "[p]olitical scientists and academic experts ... with no self-interest in incumbent protectio[n] were central figures in pressing the case for BCRA"; and the legislation commanded bipartisan support from the outset.

Finally, it is important to remember just how incumbent-friendly congressional races were prior to BCRA's passage...."[T]he evidence supports overwhelmingly that incumbents were able to get re-elected under the old system just fine." "It would be hard to develop a scheme that could be better for incumbents." ...

iii. Original Meaning

Justice Scalia, with whom [Justices Alito and Thomas join], concurring....

[T]he dissent purports to show that today's decision is not supported by the original understanding of the First Amendment. The dissent attempts this demonstration, however, in splendid isolation from the text of the First Amendment. It never shows why "the freedom of speech" that was the right of Englishmen did not include the freedom to speak in association with other individuals, including association in the corporate form. To be sure, in 1791 (as now) corporations could pursue only the objectives set forth in their charters; but the dissent provides no evidence that their speech in the pursuit of those objectives could be censored.

Instead of taking this straightforward approach to determining the Amendment's meaning, the dissent embarks on a detailed exploration of the Framers' views about the "role of corporations in society." The Framers didn't like corporations, the dissent concludes, and therefore it follows (as night the day) that corporations had no rights of free speech.

Of course the Framers' personal affection or disaffection for corporations is relevant only insofar as it can be thought to be reflected in the understood meaning of the text they enacted—not, as the dissent suggests, as a free-standing substitute for that text. But the dissent's distortion of proper analysis is even worse than that. Though faced with a constitutional text that makes no distinction between types of speakers, the dissent feels no necessity to provide even an isolated statement from the founding era to the effect that corporations are *not* covered, but places the burden on petitioners to bring forward statements showing that they *are* ("there is not a scintilla of evidence to support the notion that anyone believed [the First Amendment] would preclude regulatory distinctions based on the corporate form").

Despite the corporation-hating quotations the dissent has dredged up, it is far from clear that by the end of the 18th century corporations were despised. If so, how came there to be so many of them? ... There were approximately 335 charters issued to business corporations in the United States by the end of the 18th century. This was a "considerable extension of corporate enterprise in the field of business," and represented "unprecedented growth." Moreover, what seems like a small number by today's standards surely does not indicate the relative importance of corporations when the Nation was considerably smaller.... "[B]y the end of the eighteenth century the corporation was a familiar figure in American economic life."

Even if we thought it proper to apply the dissent's approach of excluding from First Amendment coverage what the Founders disliked, and even if we agreed that the Founders disliked founding-era corporations[,] modern corporations might not qualify for exclusion. Most of the Founders' resentment towards corporations was directed at the state-granted monopoly privileges that individually chartered corporations enjoyed. Modern corporations do not have such privileges, and would probably have been favored by most of our enterprising Founders—excluding, perhaps, Thomas Jefferson and others favoring perpetuation of an agrarian society. {"The chief cause for the changed popular attitude towards business corporations that marked the opening of the nineteenth century was the elimination of their inherent monopolistic character. This was accomplished primarily by an extension of the principle of free incorporation under general laws."}

Moreover, if the Founders' specific intent with respect to corporations is what matters, why does the dissent ignore the Founders' views about other legal entities that have more in common with modern business corporations than the founding-era corporations? At the time of the founding, religious, educational, and literary corporations were incorporated under general incorporation statutes, much as business corporations are today. {At times (though not always) the dissent seems to exclude such non-"business corporations" from its denial of free speech rights. Finding in a seemingly categorical text a distinction between the rights of business corporations and the rights of non-business corporations is even more imaginative than finding a distinction between the rights of all corporations and the rights of other associations.} There were also small unincorporated business associations, which some have argued were the "'true progenitors'" of today's business corporations. Were all of these silently excluded from the protections of the First Amendment?

The lack of a textual exception for speech by corporations cannot be explained on the ground that such organizations did not exist or did not speak. To the contrary, colleges, towns and cities, religious institutions, and guilds had long been organized as corporations at common law and under the King's charter, and as I have discussed, the practice of incorporation only expanded in the United States.

Both corporations and voluntary associations actively petitioned the Government and expressed their views in newspapers and pamphlets. For example: An antislavery Quaker corporation petitioned the First Congress, distributed pamphlets, and communicated through the press in 1790. The New York Sons of Liberty sent a circular to colonies farther south in 1766. And the Society for the Relief and Instruction of Poor Germans circulated a biweekly paper from 1755 to 1757. The dissent offers no evidence—none whatever—that the First Amendment's unqualified text was originally understood to exclude such associational speech from its protection.

{The best the dissent can come up with is that "[p]ostratification practice" supports its reading of the First Amendment. For this proposition, the dissent cites Justice White's statement (in dissent) that "[t]he common law was generally interpreted as prohibiting corporate political participation," *First Nat'l Bank of Boston v. Bellotti*. The sole authority Justice White cited for this proposition was a law-review note that made no such claim. To the contrary, it stated that the cases dealing with the propriety of corporate political expenditures were "few." More specifically, the note cites only two holdings to that effect, one by a Federal District Court, and one by the Supreme Court of Montana. Of course even if the common law was "generally interpreted" to prohibit corporate political expenditures as ultra vires, that would have nothing to do with whether political expenditures that were authorized by a corporation's charter could constitutionally be suppressed.}

Historical evidence relating to the textually similar clause "the freedom of ... the press" also provides no support for the proposition that the First Amendment excludes conduct of artificial legal entities from the scope of its protection. The freedom of "the press" was widely understood to protect the publishing activities of individual editors and printers. But these individuals often acted through newspapers, which (much like corporations) had their own names, outlived the individuals who had founded them, could be bought and sold, were sometimes owned by more than one person, and were operated for profit.

Their activities were not stripped of First Amendment protection simply because they were carried out under the banner of an artificial legal entity. And the notion which follows from the dissent's view, that modern newspapers, since they are incorporated, have free-speech rights only at the sufferance of Congress, boggles the mind.

In passing, the dissent also claims that the Court's conception of corruption is unhistorical. The Framers "would have been appalled," it says, by the evidence of corruption in the congressional findings supporting [BCRA]. For this proposition, the dissent cites a law review article arguing that "corruption" was originally understood to include "moral decay" and even actions taken by citizens in pursuit of private rather than public ends. It is hard to see how this has anything to do with what sort of corruption can be combated by restrictions on political speech. Moreover, if speech can be prohibited because, in the view of the Government, it leads to "moral decay" or does not serve "public ends," then there is no limit to the Government's censorship power.

The dissent says that when the Framers "constitutionalized the right to free speech in the First Amendment, it was the free speech of individual Americans that they had in mind." That is no doubt true. All the provisions of the Bill of Rights set forth the rights of individual men and women—not, for example, of trees or polar bears.

But the individual person's right to speak includes the right to speak *in association with other individual persons*. Surely the dissent does not believe that speech by the Republican Party or the Democratic Party can be censored because it is not the speech of "an individual American." It is the speech of many individual Americans, who have associated in a common cause, giving the leadership of the party the right to speak on their behalf. The association of individuals in a business corporation is no different-or at least it cannot be denied the right to speak on the simplistic ground that it is not "an individual American."

{The dissent says that "speech" refers to oral communications of human beings, and since corporations are not human beings they cannot speak. This is sophistry. The authorized spokesman of a corporation is a human being, who speaks on behalf of the human beings who have formed that association—just as the spokesman of an unincorporated association speaks on behalf of its members. The power to publish thoughts, no less than the power to speak thoughts, belongs only to human beings, but the dissent sees no problem with a corporation's enjoying the freedom of the press.

The same [portion of the dissent] asserts that "it has been 'claimed that the notion of institutional speech ... did not exist in post-revolutionary America.'" This is quoted from a law-review article ..., which offers as the sole support for its statement a treatise dealing with government speech. The cited pages of that treatise provide no support whatever for the statement—unless ... the "institutional speech" referred to was speech by the subject of the law-review article, governmental institutions. The other authority cited [by that portion of the dissent] ... contradicts the dissent, in that it would accord free-speech protection to associations.}

But to return to, and summarize, my principal point, which is the conformity of today's opinion with the original meaning of the First Amendment. The Amendment is written in terms of "speech," not speakers. Its text offers no foothold for excluding any category of speaker, from single individuals to partnerships of individuals, to unincorporated associations of individuals, to incorporated associations of individuals—and the dissent offers no evidence about the original meaning of the text to support any such exclusion....

Justice Stevens, with whom Justice Ginsburg, Justice Breyer, and Justice Sotomayor join, ... dissenting in [relevant] part....

[T]here is not a scintilla of [Framing-era] evidence to support the notion that anyone believed [the First Amendment] would preclude regulatory distinctions based on the corporate form. To the extent that the Framers' views are discernible and relevant to the disposition of this case, they would appear to cut strongly against the majority's position.

This is not only because the Framers and their contemporaries conceived of speech more narrowly than we now think of it, but also because they held very different views about the nature of the First Amendment right and the role of corporations in society. Those few corporations that existed at the founding were authorized by grant of a special legislative charter. Corporate sponsors would petition the legislature ... [for] a charter that specified the corporation's powers and purposes and "authoritatively fixed the scope and content of corporate organization," including "the internal structure of the corporation." {Scholars have found that only a handful of business corporations were issued charters during the colonial period, and only a few hundred during all of the 18th century.... Justice Scalia [argues] that it is improper to assess these figures by today's standards, [but] I believe he fails to substantiate his claim that "the corporation was a familiar figure in American economic life" by the century's end.}

Corporations were created, supervised, and conceptualized as quasi-public entities, "designed to serve a social function for the state." It was "assumed that [they] were legally privileged organizations that had to be closely scrutinized by the legislature because their purposes had to be made consistent with public welfare."

The individualized charter mode of incorporation reflected the "cloud of disfavor under which corporations labored" in the early years of this Nation.... "The word 'soulless' constantly recurs in debates over corporations .... Corporations, it was feared, could concentrate the worst urges of whole groups of men[."] Thomas Jefferson famously fretted that corporations would subvert the Republic. {See Letter from Thomas Jefferson to Tom Logan (Nov. 12, 1816) ("I hope we shall ... crush in [its] birth the aristocracy of our monied corporations which dare already to challenge our government to a trial of strength and bid defiance to the laws of our country").} General incorporation statutes, and widespread acceptance of business corporations as socially useful actors, did not emerge until the 1800's.

The Framers thus took it as a given that corporations could be comprehensively regulated in the service of the public welfare. Unlike our colleagues, they had little trouble distinguishing corporations from human beings, and when they constitutionalized the right to free speech in the First Amendment, it was the free speech of individual Americans that they had in mind. {In normal usage then, as now, the term "speech" referred to oral communications by individuals.

Indeed, it has been "claimed that the notion of institutional speech ... did not exist in post-revolutionary America." ... "In the intellectual heritage of the eighteenth century, the idea that free speech was individual and personal was deeply rooted and clearly manifest in the writings of Locke, Milton, and others on whom the framers of the Constitution and the Bill of Rights drew[."] Given that corporations were conceived of as artificial entities and do not have the technical capacity to "speak," the burden of establishing that the Framers and ratifiers understood "the freedom of speech" to encompass corporate speech is, I believe, far heavier than the majority acknowledges.} While individuals might join together to exercise their speech rights, business corporations, at least, were plainly not seen as facilitating such associational or expressive ends.

Even "the notion that business corporations could invoke the First Amendment would probably have been quite a novelty," given that "at the time, the legitimacy of every corporate activity was thought to rest entirely in a concession of the sovereign." Cf. *Trustees of Dartmouth College v. Woodward,* 4 Wheat. 518 (1819) (Marshall, C.J.) ("A corporation is an artificial being, invisible, intangible, and existing only in contemplation of law. Being the mere creature of law, it possesses only those properties which the charter of its creation confers upon it"). In light of these background practices and understandings, it seems to me implausible that the Framers believed "the freedom of speech" would extend equally to all corporate speakers, much less that it would preclude legislatures from taking limited measures to guard against corporate capture of elections....

As a matter of original expectations, then, it seems absurd to think that the First Amendment prohibits legislatures from taking into account the corporate identity of a sponsor of electoral advocacy. As a matter of original meaning, it likewise seems baseless—unless one evaluates the First Amendment's "principles" or its "purpose" at such a high level of generality that the historical understandings of the Amendment cease to be a meaningful constraint on the judicial task....

Justice Scalia criticizes the foregoing discussion for failing to adduce statements from the founding era showing that corporations were understood to be excluded from the First Amendment's free speech guarantee. Of course, Justice Scalia adduces no statements to suggest the contrary proposition, or even to suggest that the contrary proposition better reflects the kind of right that the drafters and ratifiers of the Free Speech Clause thought they were enshrining.

Although Justice Scalia makes a perfectly sensible argument that an individual's right to speak entails a right to speak with others for a common cause, he does not explain why those two rights must be precisely identical, or why that principle applies to electioneering by corporations that serve no "common cause." Nothing in his account dislodges my basic point that members of the founding generation held a cautious view of corporate power and a narrow view of corporate rights (not that they "despised" corporations), and that they conceptualized speech in individualistic terms.

If no prominent Framer bothered to articulate that corporate speech would have lesser status than individual speech, that may well be because the contrary proposition—if not also the very notion of "corporate speech"— was inconceivable. {Postratification practice bolsters the conclusion that the First Amendment, "as originally understood," did not give corporations political speech rights on a par with the rights of individuals. Well into the modern era of general incorporation statutes, "[t]he common law was generally interpreted as prohibiting corporate political participation," *First Nat'l Bank of Boston v. Bellotti* (White, J., dissenting) ....}

In any event, the text only leads us back to the questions who or what is guaranteed "the freedom of speech," and, just as critically, what that freedom consists of and under what circumstances it may be limited. Justice Scalia appears to believe that because corporations are created and utilized by individuals, it follows (as night the day) that their electioneering must be equally protected by the First Amendment and equally immunized from expenditure limits. That conclusion certainly does not follow as a logical matter, and Justice Scalia fails to explain why the original public meaning leads it to follow as a matter of interpretation.

The truth is we cannot be certain how a law such as BCRA § 203 meshes with the original meaning of the First Amendment.... [And] our campaign finance jurisprudence has never attended very closely to the views of the Framers, whose political universe differed profoundly from that of today. We have long since held that corporations are covered by the First Amendment .... But ... in light of the Court's effort to cast itself as guardian of ancient values, it pays to remember that nothing in our constitutional history dictates today's outcome. To the contrary, this history helps illuminate just how extraordinarily dissonant the decision is....

And whereas we have no evidence to support the notion that the Framers would have wanted corporations to have the same rights as natural persons in the electoral context, we have ample evidence to suggest that they would have been appalled by the evidence of corruption that Congress unearthed in developing BCRA.... "[T]he Framers were obsessed with corruption," which they understood to encompass the dependency of public office-holders on private interests. They discussed corruption "more often in the Constitutional Convention than factions, violence, or instability." When they brought our constitutional order into being, the Framers had their minds trained on a threat to republican self-government that this Court has lost sight of.

g. *Policy—Self-Expression (as argument for speech restriction), see p. 267*

h. *Policy—Self-Government, see p. 33.*

E. SPEECH COMPULSIONS

1. GENERALLY

a. Summary

i. Generally

Compelling people to say (or write or display or fund) things might lead to three different kinds of First Amendment objections.

1. A "complaining speaker's own message [can be] affected by the speech it was forced to accommodate," *Rumsfeld v. FAIR* (2006) (p. 545):

— Requiring a parade to include a float will change the parade's message. See *Hurley v. Irish-American Gay, Lesbian & Bisexual Group* (1995) (p.

531).

— Requiring a newspaper to include an <u>article</u> will <u>change</u> the content of the newspaper, because the newspaper (1) now includes an extra article, and (2) now excludes whatever had to be removed to make space for the article. See *Miami Herald Pub. Co. v. Tornillo* (1974) (p. 686).

— Requiring a newspaper to include a reply if it criticizes a candidate may <u>deter</u> the newspaper from publishing such criticism. *Id.*

2. Requiring someone to speak may interfere with the "freedom of speech" in the sense of <u>freedom</u> to choose <u>what to say</u>, even if it doesn't affect a speaker's own message.

— That's true, for instance, of requiring someone to say a <u>pledge</u> of allegiance. See *W. Va. State Bd. of Ed. Barnette* (1943) (p. 537)

— It could also be said of requiring someone to display a slogan on a car license plate, see *Wooley v. Maynard* (1977) (p. 540), though there is an argument there (rejected by the majority) that this isn't really requiring the car owner to speak.

3. Requiring someone to pay money to be used for speech may be seen as interfering with the person's <u>freedom of expressive association</u>, because it requires him to associate with the message in the sense of paying for it. See *Detroit Bd. of Ed.* (1977) (p. 547) (unions); *Keller v. State Bar* (1990) (p. 551) (bar association)

These three objections are often discussed under the rubric of "compelled speech" doctrine (or, in the case of item 3, "compelled association" doctrine), and some cases assert—without distinguishing objections 1 and 2—that the government is as constrained in mandating speech as it is in prohibiting speech. *E.g., Riley v. National Federation of the Blind* (p. 518). Query, though, whether that is indeed so.

ii. Summary: Speech Compulsions That Change the Content of Speech

When a speech compulsion interferes with the speaker's own <u>message</u>, it is presumptively unconstitutional. Such interference is found <u>when</u>:

a. The compulsion *is triggered by the content of speech the speaker has said in the past.* See, *e.g., Miami Herald.* Such a compulsion is a "content-based penalty," *Turner Broadcasting System v. FCC* (1994) (p. 529), similar to a content-based tax: If you say certain things, then a burden (the burden of having to carry others' speech) is placed on you. It's thus a *restriction* of the speech that triggers the compulsion, not just a compulsion of speech.

b. The compulsion interferes with *a speaker's ability to create its own coherent speech product* (something with "a common theme" or a common editorial voice rather than just "individual, unrelated segments that happen to be transmitted together for individual selection by members of the audience," *Hurley*). See, *e.g., Hurley; Tornillo; Riley;* possibly *Pacific Gas & Elec. Co. v. Public Util. Comm'n* (1986) (p. 524), as interpreted by *Rumsfeld.*

[handwritten margin note: 1. Content 2. Choice 3. Expressive Association]

Such a compulsion is likewise a speech *restriction* as well as a compulsion: The lower court decision in *Hurley*, for instance, barred a parade organizer from putting together the precise parade that he wanted. Likewise, the law in *Tornillo* barred an editor from printing a newspaper that contained precisely those articles that the editor chose. "Mandating speech that a speaker would not otherwise make necessarily alters the content of the speech." *Riley*.

c. The compulsion makes the burdened party *feel pressure to respond*, if only to disavow any connection with the message that it's compelled to carry. See, *e.g.*, the *Pacific Gas* plurality; some language in *Turner*; maybe the *PruneYard* concurrence. This, however, is less clear, because the Court hasn't squarely rested its majority holdings on this rationale, and because *Rumsfeld* seemed to largely ignore this possibility.

iii. "Pure" Speech Compulsions

When a speech compulsion does *not* pressure or require a speaker to change the content of its message, but purely compels speech, the matter is less clear.

a. A compulsion to say things orally, *Barnette*, or to display words on one's car, *Wooley*, is presumptively unconstitutional. See *Rumsfeld*.

b. But compulsion to allow people to speak on your business property is seemingly constitutional. See *PruneYard*; *Rumsfeld*. (Again, all the discussion within this "pure" speech compulsions item assumes that the compulsion doesn't deter you from expressing your own views.)

c. Speech compulsions "incidental to ... regulation of conduct"—including compulsions to actually distribute e-mails and the like—may also be constitutional. That's what *Rumsfeld* held about the requirement that law schools distribute administrative information about military recruiters, though the scope of this exception is not clear.

d. Requirements that you say certain things *to the government* (for instance, requirements that you file tax returns, that you report certain financial transactions, that you testify in court) might well be presumptively constitutional. They are routine, and the Supreme Court has never suggested that they're impermissible. There is, however, no Court holding on this score.

Consider, for instance, *State v. Grover*, 437 N.W.2d 60 (Minn. 1989), which rejected a compelled speech challenge to a state statute that obligated educators to report evidence of suspected child abuse. The court distinguished *Wooley* on the grounds that "[t]he statute does not compel the dissemination of an 'ideological point of view,' but only mandates the reporting of information—a requirement not altogether dissimilar from that imposed by the Internal Revenue Code." Is this consistent with *Riley*'s holding that both "compelled statements of opinion" and "compelled statements of 'fact'" "burden[] protected speech"?

e. The *Pacific Gas* plurality states that "The State, of course, has substan-

tial leeway in determining appropriate information disclosure requirements for business corporations. [T]he State is [not, however] equally
free to require corporations to carry the messages of third parties, where
the messages themselves are biased against or are expressly contrary to
the corporation's views."

f. *PruneYard* distinguished *Barnette* and *Maynard* on the grounds that in
    those cases a "specific message [was] dictated by the State to be dis-
    played on appellants' property," which created a "danger of governmen-
    tal discrimination for or against a particular message." This suggests
    that requirements that a speaker say or display *speech with particular
    government-specified content* would generally be subject to strict scru-
    tiny. Yet *Rumsfeld* held otherwise, because (i) the requirement to dis-
    tribute administrative information about military recruiters was inci-
    dental to a conduct requirement, and (ii) the requirement to allow mili-
    tary recruiters on the property was just a requirement to allow access,
    not a requirement to speak or to display speech.

iv. Forced Contributions of Money

Forced contributions of money don't restrict anyone's speech, and don't
even require anyone to say or publish anything himself, but the Court has
held that forced contribution of money to a group is generally presumptively
unconstitutional. There are three major exceptions:

a. When the requirement passes strict scrutiny: The Court has held that
    the interests in preventing strikes and in regulating lawyers can justify
    some forced contributions. *Abood*; *Keller*.

—   But *Abood* and *Keller* hold these interests only justify using the funds
    for speech "germane" to these interests (such as collective bargaining or
    attorney discipline), not for advocacy of broader political causes.

b. When the forced contribution is to a (i) *university-based* body such as a
    student government (ii) so long as the collected money will be spent in
    viewpoint-neutral ways. *Board of Regents v. Southworth* (2000) (p. 552).
    It's not clear how broadly this exception will ultimately extend.

c. When the forced contribution is to the government, via taxes that fund
    the government's own speech, see *Keller*; *Johanns v. Livestock Marketing
    Ass'n*, 544 U.S. 550 (2005) (discussed below).

—   Some government programs require all businesses in a certain field
    (usually agricultural producers) to contribute to commercial ads that ge-
    nerically promote some commodity, such as California plums. The the-
    ory, as with the union dues in *Abood* or the state bar dues in *Keller*, is
    that the funded speech helps the businesses generally, so it's fair to
    make all the businesses pay, even if they'd rather advertise their own
    branded products.

    Glickman v. Wileman Bros. & Elliott, Inc., 521 U.S. 457 (1997), said
    Abood doesn't apply to this, partly because the advertising was merely
    commercial, not political: "the assessments are not used to fund ideolog-
    ical activities." But *United States v. United Foods, Inc.*, 533 U.S. 405

(2001), held that *Abood* did apply, stressing "*Abood*'s statement that speech need not be characterized as political before it receives First Amendment protection."

The Court distinguished *Glickman* in *United Foods* on the basis that (1) in *Glickman* the funding compulsion was germane to a "broader regulatory system" in which producers (of California nectarines, plums, and peaches) were generally required to engage in cooperative price and sales quota setting, while (2) in *United Foods* the funding compulsion (for ads promoting mushrooms) was pretty much stand-alone. Many commentators, though, believe the reasoning of the two cases is not fully consistent; and all but two Justices—Stevens, who wrote *Glickman*, and Kennedy, who wrote *United Foods*—would have treated the two cases the same way.

Finally, in *Johanns*, the Court held that most such programs are constitutional after all, but on a different theory: "[C]ompelled funding of *government* speech does not alone raise First Amendment concerns" (emphasis added). So long as the government maintains ultimate control over the speech—in *Johanns*, "final approval authority over every word used in every promotional campaign"—*Abood* doesn't apply, even if the wording of the speech is chosen by some industry group selected by the government. *Abood*, *Keller*, and *United Foods* are thus applicable only when the speech is ultimately *not* controlled by the government, but is instead controlled by a private group (such as a union) or a specialized governmental organization such as the bar (see *Keller*).

   v. Level of Scrutiny

What does it mean that a restriction is presumptively unconstitutional? The government is (supposedly) as constrained in mandating speech as it is in prohibiting speech. *Riley v. National Federation of the Blind* (p. 518). Therefore,

a. Many speech compulsions must face strict scrutiny. See, *e.g.*, *Riley*.

b. But just as lower scrutiny is applicable to restrictions of *commercial advertising,* lower scrutiny is applicable to compulsions of speech in such advertising. In particular, disclosure requirements imposed to prevent the commercial advertising from being false or misleading are constitutional "as long as disclosure requirements are reasonably related to the [government's] interest in preventing deception of consumers." *Zauderer v. Office of Disciplinary Counsel*, 471 U.S. 626, 650-51 n.14 (1985); *Milavetz v. Gallop & Milavetz, P.A. v. United States*, 130 S. Ct. 1324, 1339-41 (2010).

c. Likewise, the rule is likely different when the government is acting *as employer/landlord/subsidizer/etc.* rather than as sovereign. See, *e.g.*, *Red Lion Broadcasting v. FCC* (1969) (p. 682) (government acting as regulator of the airwaves). But see *W. Va. State Bd. of Ed. v. Barnette* (1943) (p. 536), where the Court did not confront this possibility.

b. Policy—Compelled Speech

Basic argument: "Speech compulsions should be treated just like speech restrictions, because _____."

1. **Constitutional text:** "[T]he First Amendment guarantees 'freedom of speech,' a term necessarily comprising the decision of both what to say and what not to say." *Riley v. Nat'l Fed. of the Blind.*

What not to say

"'Since *all* speech inherently involves choices of what to say and what to leave unsaid,' one important manifestation of the principle of free speech is that one who chooses to speak may also decide 'what not to say.'" *Hurley v. Irish-American Gay, Lesbian and Bisexual Group.*

Self-expression: "[T]he right of freedom of thought protected by the First Amendment against state action includes both the right to speak freely and the right to refrain from speaking at all. A system which secures the right to proselytize religious, political, and ideological causes must also guarantee the concomitant right to decline to foster such concepts. The right to speak and the right to refrain from speaking are complementary components of the broader concept of 'individual freedom of mind.'" *Wooley v. Maynard.*

Freedom of Mind

Interference with speaker's thinking processes: "One may worry that compulsory, frequent repetition of the Pledge [of Allegiance] will have an influence on what and how one thinks, independent of one's direct deliberations on its subject matter. Routine recitation may make its message familiar. Through regularity, it may become a comfort and an internal source of authority for consultation. At a later point, one might instinctively, without further thought ..., characterize the polity as a republic, or as a place where there is freedom and justice, or ... be more likely assent to another's assertion to that effect....

Influence how one thinks

"[More generally,] what one regularly says may have an influence on what and how one thinks.... Commonly heard sentiments may become comfortable sentiments. Commonly voiced sentiments bear an even more intimate relation to the self. Isn't that a good part of why proponents advocate for the institution of such compelled speech rituals?" Seana Valentine Shiffrin, *What Is Really Wrong with Compelled Association?*, 99 Nw. U. L. Rev. 839, 854-55 (2005).

Speech compulsions are speech restrictions: "The Florida statute [requiring that newspapers publish replies] exacts a penalty on the basis of the content of a newspaper ... in printing and composing time and materials and in taking up space that could be devoted to other material the newspaper may have preferred to print.... Faced with the penalties that would accrue to any newspaper that published news or commentary arguably within the reach of the right-of-access statute, editors might well conclude that the safe course is to avoid controversy.... Government-enforced right of access [thus] inescapably 'dampens the vigor and limits the variety of public debate.'" *Miami Herald Co. v. Tornillo.*

Penalty

Deterrence

2. Response to 1: This sort of speech compulsion shouldn't be seen as a

burden on self-expression or as a speech restriction, because _____.

"Corporations generally have not played the historic role of newspapers as conveyers of individual ideas and opinion.... [C]orporate free speech rights do not arise because corporations, like individuals, have any interest in self-expression.... [S]uch rights are recognized as an instrumental means of furthering the First Amendment purpose of fostering a broad forum of information to facilitate self-government." *Pacific Gas & Elec. v. Public Util. Comm'n* (Rehnquist, J., dissenting).

"[A]ppellees could ... [display] a conspicuous bumper sticker explaining ... that they do not profess the motto 'Live Free or Die' .... Since any implication that they affirm the motto can be so easily displaced, I cannot agree that the state statutory system for motor vehicle identification and tourist promotion may be invalidated under the fiction that appellees are unconstitutionally forced to affirm, or profess belief in, the state motto." *Wooley v. Maynard* (Rehnquist, J., dissenting).

3. Response to 1: Speech compulsions generally add speech to public debate, rather than withdrawing it.

"The right of access here constitutes an effort to facilitate and enlarge public discussion; it therefore furthers rather than abridges First Amendment values." *Pacific Gas & Elec. Co. v. Public Util. Comm'n* (Rehnquist, J., dissenting).

2.   DIRECT INTERFERENCE WITH SPEAKER'S OTHER SPEECH

a.   Problem: Violence Ratings on TV Programs

Congress is considering enacting a statute requiring all TV programs to indicate how many murders or assaults with deadly weapons are depicted per hour of the program's running time. (This number would be displayed in the same manner that the voluntary ratings are displayed these days.) Your boss, Senator Margaret Garnett, is unsure whether such a compelled labeling requirement would be constitutional, and, knowing of your first-rate First Amendment training, asks you for your advice. What do you tell her?

b.   Problem: Web Page Response Law

As you know, adding an extra link to a Web page is easy and cheap, especially since Web pages can be pretty much any length, though it does make the page longer and may thus make it harder for readers to find other links listed on the page.

Say Congress enacts a law requiring all Web pages that contain allegations of criminal misconduct by named people to give those people a right of reply: If a person X complains to the Web page owner, the owner must include the text "For X's reply to the charges about him, see" followed by the link to X's own Web page (which X would create himself and maintain at his own expense). Would such a law be constitutional?

c. *Miami Herald Pub. Co. v. Tornillo, 418 U.S. 241 (1974)*

Chief Justice Burger delivered the opinion of the Court....

[A.] [A]ppellant printed editorials critical of appellee's candidacy [for the Florida House of Representatives].... Appellant declined to print the appellee's [proposed] replies and appellee brought suit ... [based] on Florida Statute § 104.38, a "right of reply" statute which provides that if a candidate for nomination or election is assailed regarding his personal character or official record by any newspaper, the candidate has the right to demand that the newspaper print, free of cost to the candidate, any reply the candidate may make to the newspaper's charges. The reply must appear in as conspicuous a place and in the same kind of type as the charges which prompted the reply, provided it does not take up more space than the charges. Failure to comply with the statute constitutes a first-degree misdemeanor [and may give rise to a civil suit—ed.]....

[B.] The appellee and supporting advocates of an enforceable right of access to the press vigorously argue that government has an obligation to ensure that a wide variety of views reach the public.... *← variety of news*

It is urged that at the time the First Amendment ... was ratified in 1791 ... the press was broadly representative of the people it was serving. While many of the newspapers were intensely partisan and narrow in their views, the press collectively presented a broad range of opinions to readers. Entry into publishing was inexpensive; pamphlets and books provided meaningful alternatives to the organized press for the expression of unpopular ideas and often treated events and expressed views not covered by conventional newspapers. A true marketplace of ideas existed in which there was relatively easy access to the channels of communication. *MOI*

Access advocates submit that ... the press of today is ... very different .... Newspapers have become big business and there are far fewer of them to serve a larger literate population. Chains of newspapers, national newspapers, national wire and news services, and one-newspaper towns, are the dominant features of a press that has become noncompetitive and enormously powerful and influential in its capacity to manipulate popular opinion and change the course of events....

The result of these vast changes has been to place in a few hands the power to inform the American people and shape public opinion. Much of the editorial opinion and commentary that is printed is that of syndicated columnists distributed nationwide and, as a result, we are told, on national and world issues there tends to be a homogeneity of editorial opinion, commentary, and interpretive analysis.

The abuses of bias and manipulative reportage are, likewise, said to be the result of the vast accumulations of unreviewable power in the modern media empires. In effect, it is claimed, the public has lost any ability to respond or to contribute in a meaningful way to the debate on issues. The monopoly of the means of communication allows for little or no critical analysis of the media except in professional journals of very limited readership.... [And] the same economic factors which have caused the disappearance of vast numbers of metropolitan newspapers, have made entry into the marketplace of ideas served by the print media almost impossible.

It is urged that the claim of newspapers to be "surrogates for the public" carries with it a concomitant fiduciary obligation to account for that stewardship ... [and] that the only effective way to insure fairness and accuracy and to provide for some accountability is for government to take affirmative action. The First Amendment interest of the public in being informed is said to be in peril because the "marketplace of ideas" is today a monopoly controlled by the owners of the market....

[C.] However much validity may be found in these arguments, [remedying the problem using] ... governmental coercion ... brings about a confrontation with the express provisions of the First Amendment and the judicial gloss on that Amendment developed over the years....

[1.] The Florida statute exacts a penalty on the basis of the content of a newspaper[,] ... exacted in terms of the cost in printing and composing time and materials and in taking up space that could be devoted to other material the newspaper may have preferred to print.... Faced with the penalties that would accrue to any newspaper that published news or commentary arguably within the reach of the right-of-access statute, editors might well conclude that the safe course is to avoid controversy. Therefore, under the operation of the Florida statute, political and electoral coverage would be blunted or reduced. Government-enforced right of access inescapably "dampens the vigor and limits the variety of public debate." ...

[2.] Even if a newspaper would face no additional costs to comply with a compulsory access law and would not be forced to forgo publication of news or opinion by the inclusion of a reply, the Florida statute fails to clear the barriers of the First Amendment because of its intrusion into the function of editors. A newspaper is more than a passive receptacle or conduit for news, comment, and advertising. The choice of material to go into a newspaper, and the decisions made as to limitations on the size and content of the paper, and treatment of public issues and public officials—whether fair or unfair—constitute the exercise of editorial control and judgment. It has yet to be demonstrated how governmental regulation of this crucial process can be exercised consistent with First Amendment guarantees of a free press as they have evolved to this time....

Justice White, concurring....

We have learned, and continue to learn, from what we view as the unhappy experiences of other nations where government has been allowed to meddle in the internal editorial affairs of newspapers. Regardless of how beneficent-sounding the purposes of controlling the press might be, we prefer "the power of reason as applied through public discussion" and remain intensely skeptical about those measures that would allow government to insinuate itself into the editorial rooms of this Nation's press....

Of course, the press is not always accurate, or even responsible, and may not present full and fair debate on important public issues. But the balance struck by the First Amendment with respect to the press is that society must take the risk that occasionally debate on vital matters will not be comprehensive and that all viewpoints may not be expressed.... [Any] system that would supplant private control of the press with the heavy hand of government intrusion[] would make the government the censor of what the people may read and know....

d. Riley v. National Federation of the Blind, 487 U.S. 781 (1988)

Justice Brennan delivered the opinion of the Court....

[A.] We [consider] the requirement that professional fundraisers disclose to potential donors, before an appeal for funds, the percentage of charitable contributions collected during the previous 12 months that were actually turned over to charity. Mandating speech that a speaker would not otherwise make necessarily alters the content of the speech. We therefore consider the Act as a content-based regulation of speech. See *Miami Herald Pub. Co. v. Tornillo* (statute compelling newspaper to print an editorial reply "exacts a penalty on the basis of the content of a newspaper").

The State argues that even if charitable solicitations generally are fully protected [by the First Amendment, which the Court had held in earlier cases—ed.], ... the Act regulates only commercial speech because it relates only to the professional fundraiser's profit from the solicited contribution.... [But] "solicitation is characteristically intertwined with informative and perhaps persuasive speech ..., [and] without solicitation the flow of such information and advocacy would likely cease." Thus, where, as here, the component parts of a single speech are inextricably intertwined, we cannot parcel out the speech, applying one test to one phrase and another test to another phrase. Such an endeavor would be both artificial and impractical. Therefore, we apply our test for fully protected expression.

{Of course, the dissent's analogy to the securities field entirely misses the point. Purely commercial speech is more susceptible to compelled disclosure requirements. See *Zauderer v. Office of Disciplinary Counsel,* 471 U.S. 626 (1985) [(a case holding that a lawyer may be required to include certain factual statements in his advertisements—ed.)].} ...

[B.] There is certainly some difference between compelled speech and compelled silence, but in the context of protected speech, the difference is without constitutional significance, for the First Amendment guarantees "freedom of speech," a term necessarily comprising the decision of both what to say and what *not* to say. [See, *e.g.*, *Miami Herald*; *Wooley v. Maynard.*] ...

These cases cannot be distinguished simply because they involved compelled statements of opinion while here we deal with compelled statements of "fact": either form of compulsion burdens protected speech. Thus, we would not immunize a law requiring a speaker favoring a particular government project to state at the outset of every address the average cost overruns in similar projects, or a law requiring a speaker favoring an incumbent candidate to state during every solicitation that candidate's recent travel budget. Although the foregoing factual information might be relevant to the listener, and, in the latter case, could encourage or discourage the listener from making a political donation, a law compelling its disclosure would clearly and substantially burden the protected speech.

[**C.**] We believe, therefore, that North Carolina's content-based regulation is subject to exacting First Amendment scrutiny. The State asserts as its interest the importance of informing donors how the money they contribute is spent in order to dispel the alleged misperception that the money they give to professional fundraisers goes in greater-than-actual proportion to benefit charity.... We conclude that this interest is not as weighty as the State asserts, and that the means chosen to accomplish it are unduly burdensome and not narrowly tailored.

Although we do not wish to denigrate the State's interest in full disclosure, the danger the State posits is not as great as might initially appear. First, the State presumes that the charity derives no benefit from funds collected but not turned over to it. Yet ... where the solicitation is combined with the advocacy and dissemination of information, the charity reaps a substantial benefit from the act of solicitation itself. Thus, a significant portion of the fundraiser's "fee" may well go toward achieving the charity's objectives even though it is not remitted to the charity in cash.

Second, an unchallenged portion of the disclosure law requires professional fundraisers to disclose their professional status to potential donors, thereby giving notice that at least a portion of the money contributed will be retained.[11] Donors are also undoubtedly aware that solicitations incur costs, to which part of their donation might apply. And, of course, a donor is free to inquire how much of the contribution will be turned over to the charity. Under another North Carolina statute, also unchallenged, fundraisers must disclose this information upon request. Even were that not so, if the solicitor refuses to give the requested information, the potential donor may (and probably would) refuse to donate.

Moreover, the compelled disclosure will almost certainly hamper the legitimate efforts of professional fundraisers to raise money for the charities they represent. First, this provision necessarily discriminates against small or unpopular charities, which must usually rely on professional fundraisers. Campaigns with high costs and expenses carried out by professional fundraisers must make unfavorable disclosures, with the predictable result that such solicitations will prove unsuccessful. Yet the identical solicitation with its high costs and expenses, if carried out by the employees of a charity or volunteers, results in no compelled disclosure, and therefore greater success.

Second, in the context of a verbal solicitation, if the potential donor is unhappy with the disclosed percentage, the fundraiser will not likely be given a chance to explain the figure; the disclosure will be the last words

---

[11] ... [S]uch a narrowly tailored requirement would withstand First Amendment scrutiny.

spoken as the donor closes the door or hangs up the phone. Again, the predictable result is that professional fundraisers will be encouraged to quit the State or refrain from engaging in solicitations that result in an unfavorable disclosure.

In contrast to the prophylactic, imprecise, and unduly burdensome rule the State has adopted to reduce its alleged donor misperception, more benign and narrowly tailored options are available. For example, as a general rule, the State may itself publish the detailed financial disclosure forms it requires professional fundraisers to file. This procedure would communicate the desired information to the public without burdening a speaker with unwanted speech during the course of a solicitation.

Alternatively, the State may vigorously enforce its antifraud laws to prohibit professional fundraisers from obtaining money on false pretenses or by making false statements. These more narrowly tailored rules are in keeping with the First Amendment directive that government not dictate the content of speech absent compelling necessity, and then, only by means precisely tailored....

Justice Scalia, concurring [except for footnote 11]....

I do not see how requiring the professional solicitor to disclose his professional status is narrowly tailored to prevent fraud. Where core First Amendment speech is at issue, the State can assess liability for specific instances of deliberate deception, but it cannot impose a prophylactic rule requiring disclosure even where misleading statements are not made. Since donors are assuredly aware that a portion of their donations may go to solicitation costs and other administrative expenses—whether the solicitor is a professional, an in-house employee, or even a volunteer—it is not misleading in the great mass of cases for a professional solicitor to request donations "for" a specific charity without announcing his professional status.

Compensatory employment is, I would judge, the natural order of things, and one would expect *volunteer* solicitors to announce that status as a selling point. The dictum in footnote 11 represents a departure from our traditional understanding, embodied in the First Amendment, that where the dissemination of ideas is concerned, it is safer to assume that the people are smart enough to get the information they need than to assume that the government is wise or impartial enough to make the judgment for them.

Chief Justice Rehnquist, with whom Justice O'Connor joins, dissenting....

This statute requires only that the professional solicitor disclose certain relevant and verifiable facts to the potential donor.... [This] is directly analogous to mandatory disclosure requirements that exist in other contexts, such as securities transactions.

In my view, the required disclosure of true facts in the course of what is at least in part a "commercial" transaction—the solicitation of money by a professional fundraiser—does not necessarily create such a burden on core protected speech as to require that strict scrutiny be applied.... [T]he disclosure required by the statute at issue here will have little, if any, effect on the [noncommercial] message itself, though it may have an effect on the potential donor's desire to contribute financially to the cause.

Of course, the percentage of previous collections turned over to charities is only a very rough surrogate for the percentage of collections which will be turned over by the fundraiser in the particular drive in question.... Nonetheless, because the statute is aimed at the commercial aspect of the solicitation, and because the State's interests in enacting the disclosure requirements are sufficiently strong, I cannot conclude that the First Amendment prevents the State from imposing the type of disclosure requirement involved here, at least in the absence of a showing that the effect of the disclosure is to dramatically limit contributions or impede a charity's ability to disseminate ideas or information....

e. *Pacific Gas & Elec. Co. v. Public Util. Comm'n, 475 U.S. 1 (1986)*

Justice Powell ... delivered an opinion, in which ... Chief Justice [Burger], Justice Brennan, and Justice O'Connor join....

[A.] [A]ppellant Pacific Gas and Electric Company ... distribute[s] a newsletter in its monthly billing envelope. Appellant's newsletter, called *Progress*, reaches over three million customers. It has included political editorials, feature stories on matters of public interest, tips on energy conservation, and straightforward information about utility services and bills.

In 1980, ... California's Public Utilities Commission ... decided that the envelope space that appellant had used to disseminate *Progress* is the property of the ratepayers.... In an effort to apportion this [space] between appellant and its customers, the Commission permitted [Toward Utility Rate Normalization (TURN), an advocacy group,] to use the [space] four times a year for the next two years.... The Commission placed no limitations on what TURN or appellant could say in the envelope, except that TURN is required to state that its messages are not those of appellant.

The Commission reserved the right to grant other groups access to the envelopes in the future. {The Commission has already *denied* access to at least one group based on the content of its speech. The Commission denied the application of a [pro-tax-reduction] group ... on the ground that that group neither wished to participate in Commission proceedings nor alleged that its use of the billing envelope space would improve consumer participation in those proceedings.} ...

[B.] Compelled access like that ordered in this case both penalizes the expression of particular points of view and forces speakers to alter their speech to conform with an agenda they do not set. These impermissible effects are not remedied by the Commission's definition of the relevant property rights....

Just as the State is not free to "tell a newspaper in advance what it can print and what it cannot," *Miami Herald Pub. Co. v. Tornillo*, the State is not free either to restrict appellant's speech to certain topics or views or to force appellant to respond to views that others may hold.... [A] forced access rule that would accomplish these purposes indirectly is similarly forbidden.

{Unlike the right-of-reply statute ... in *Tornillo*, the Commission's order does not require appellant to place TURN's message in appellant's newsletter [itself,] ... [but] appellant is still required to carry speech with which it disagreed, and might well feel compelled to reply or limit its own speech in response to TURN's.} ...

PruneYard Shopping Center v. Robins is not to the contrary. In *PruneYard,* ... [t]his Court held that [a] shopping center did not have a constitutionally protected right to exclude ... pamphleteers from the area open to the public .... Notably absent from *PruneYard* was any concern that access to [that area] might affect the shopping center owner's exercise of his own right to speak: the owner did not even allege that he objected to the content of the pamphlets; nor was the access right content based.... {In addition, the relevant forum in *PruneYard* ... was, almost by definition, peculiarly public in nature. There is no correspondingly public aspect to appellant's billing envelopes.}

The Commission's order ... does not simply award access to the public at large; rather, it discriminates on the basis of the viewpoints of the selected speakers. Two of the acknowledged purposes of the access order are to offer the public a greater variety of views in appellant's billing envelope, and to assist groups (such as TURN) that challenge appellant in the Commission's ratemaking proceedings in raising funds. Access to the envelopes thus ... is limited to persons or groups ... who disagree with appellant's views as expressed in *Progress* and who oppose appellant in Commission proceedings.

Such one-sidedness impermissibly burdens appellant's own expression.... [W]henever [appellant] speaks out on a given issue, it may be forced—at TURN's discretion—to help disseminate hostile views. Appellant "might well conclude" that, under these circumstances, "the safe course is to avoid controversy," thereby reducing the free flow of information and ideas that the First Amendment seeks to promote.

Appellant does not, of course, have the right to be free from vigorous debate. But it *does* have the right to be free from government restrictions that abridge its own rights in order to "enhance the relative voice" of its opponents. The Commission's order requires appellant to assist in disseminating TURN's views; it does not equally constrain both sides of the debate about utility regulation.... Unlike ... permissible government subsidies of speech, the Commission's order identifies a favored speaker "based on the identity of the interests that [the speaker] may represent," and forces the speaker's opponent—not the taxpaying public—to assist in disseminating the speaker's message. Such a requirement necessarily burdens the expression of the disfavored speaker.

The Commission's access order also impermissibly requires appellant to associate with speech with which appellant may disagree. The order on its face leaves TURN free to use the billing envelopes to discuss any issues it chooses. Should TURN choose, for example, to urge appellant's customers to vote for a particular slate of legislative candidates, or to argue in favor of legislation that could seriously affect the utility business, appellant may be forced either to appear to agree with TURN's views or to respond.

{The Commission's order is thus readily distinguishable from orders requiring appellant to carry various legal notices, such as notices of upcoming Commission proceedings or of changes in the way rates are calculated. The State, of course, has substantial leeway in determining appropriate information disclosure requirements for business corporations.... [But] the State is [not] equally free to require corporations to carry the messages of third parties, where the messages themselves are biased against or are expressly contrary to the corporation's views.} ... [And e]specially since TURN has been given access in part to create a multiplicity of views in the envelopes, there can be little doubt that appellant will feel compelled to respond to arguments and allegations made by TURN in its messages to appellant's customers.

[T]he choice to speak includes within it the choice of what not to say .... The danger that appellant will be required to alter its own message as a consequence of the government's coercive action is a proper object of First Amendment solicitude .... Where, as in this case, the danger ... arises from a content-based grant of access to private property, it is a danger that the government may not impose absent a compelling interest....

[C.] Notwithstanding that it burdens protected speech, the Commission's order could be valid if it were a narrowly tailored means of serving a compelling state interest....

First, ... [a]ppellees argue that the access order permits TURN to continue to help the Commission by assisting TURN in raising funds from the ratepayers whose interest TURN seeks to serve.... The State's interest in fair and effective utility regulation may be compelling[, and] ... [t]he State's interest may justify imposing on appellant the reasonable expenses of responsible groups that represent the public interest at ratemaking proceedings. But "we find 'no substantially relevant correlation between the governmental interest asserted and the State's effort'" to compel appellant to distribute TURN's speech in appellant's envelopes.

Second, appellees argue that the order furthers the State's interest in promoting speech by making a variety of views available to appellant's customers.... [T]his interest is not furthered by an order that is not content neutral. Moreover, the means chosen to advance variety tend to inhibit expression of appellant's views in order to promote TURN's.... [T]he State cannot advance some points of view by burdening the expression of others....

Justice Marshall, concurring in the judgment....

California has taken from appellant the right to deny access to its property—its billing envelope—to a group that wishes to use that envelope for expressive purposes. Two significant differences between the State's grant of access in this case and the grant of access in *PruneYard* lead me to find a constitutional barrier here that I did not find in the earlier case....

The first difference is the degree of intrusiveness of the permitted access.... The challenged rule [in *PruneYard*] did not permit a markedly greater intrusion onto the property than that which the owner had voluntarily encouraged .... In the present case, by contrast, appellant has never opened up its billing envelope to the use of the public. Appellant has not abandoned its right to exclude others from its property to the degree that the shopping center owner had done in *PruneYard*....

The second difference between this case and *PruneYard* is that the State has chosen to give TURN a right to speak at the expense of appellant's ability to use the property in question as a forum for the exercise of its own First Amendment rights.... By appropriating, four times a year, the space in appellant's envelope that appellant would otherwise use for its own speech, the State has necessarily curtailed appellant's use of its own forum. The regulation in this case, therefore, goes beyond a mere infringement of appellant's desire to remain silent.... While the interference with appellant's speech is, concededly, very slight, the State's justification—the subsidization of another speaker chosen by the State—is insufficient to sustain even that minor burden.

{The State seizes upon appellant's status as a regulated monopoly in order to argue that the inclusion of postage and other billing costs in the utility's rate base demonstrates that these items "belong" to the public, which has paid for them. However, a consumer who purchases food in a grocery store is "paying" for the store's rent, heat, electricity, wages, etc., but no one would seriously argue that the consumer thereby acquires a property interest in the store. That the utility passes on its overhead costs to ratepayers at a rate fixed by law rather than the market cannot affect the utility's ownership of its property, nor its right to use that property for expressive purposes.... Having chosen to keep utilities in private hands, ... the State may not arbitrarily appropriate property for the use of third parties by stating that the public has "paid" for the property by paying utility bills....}

Justice Blackmun [did not participate].

Justice Rehnquist, with whom Justice White and Justice Stevens join as to Part [A], dissenting....

[A.] [The] plurality does not adequately explain how the potential deterrent effect of the right of access here is sufficiently immediate and direct to warrant strict scrutiny....

Unlike the reply statute in *Tornillo*, which conditioned access upon discrete instances of certain expression, the right of access here bears no relationship to PG&E's future conduct. PG&E cannot prevent the access by remaining silent or avoiding discussion of controversial subjects.... [Groups given access, such as TURN,] will likely address ... controversial subjects in spite of PG&E's silence[, so] ... PG&E will have no incentive to adopt the conservative strategy {of avoiding certain topics in hopes that TURN will not think to address them on its own}....

[B.] The plurality argues, however, that ... if TURN has access to the envelopes, its speech will have the effect of *forcing* PG&E to address topics about which it would prefer to remain silent.... [But i]n *PruneYard*, this

Court held that the availability of an effective disclaimer was sufficient to eliminate any infringement upon negative free speech rights. [And i]f an alternative forum of communication [for TURN] exists, TURN or the other consumer groups will be able to *induce* PG&E to address the additional topics anyway. Finally, because PG&E retains complete editorial freedom over the content of its inserts, the effect of the right of access is likely to be qualitatively different from a direct prescription by the government of "what shall be orthodox in ... matters of opinion." ...

[C.] [N]atural persons enjoy negative free speech rights because of their interest in self-expression; an individual's right not to speak or to associate with the speech of others is a component of the broader constitutional interest of natural persons in freedom of conscience. [*West Va. Bd. of Ed. v. Barnette*; *Wooley v. Maynard*.] ... In *Tornillo*, the Court extended negative free speech rights to newspapers without much discussion....

Extension of the individual freedom of conscience decisions to business corporations strains the rationale of those cases beyond the breaking point. To ascribe to such artificial entities an "intellect" or "mind" for freedom of conscience purposes is to confuse metaphor with reality.

Corporations generally have not played the historic role of newspapers as conveyers of individual ideas and opinion.... [C]orporate free speech rights do not arise because corporations, like individuals, have any interest in self-expression.... [S]uch rights are recognized as an instrumental means of furthering the First Amendment purpose of fostering a broad forum of information to facilitate self-government.... [And t]he right of access here constitutes an effort to facilitate and enlarge public discussion; it therefore furthers rather than abridges First Amendment values....

Justice Stevens, dissenting....

[The Commission's] requirement differs little from regulations applied daily to a variety of commercial communications .... I assume that the plurality would not object to a utility commission rule dictating the format of the bill, even as to required warnings and the type size of various provisos and disclaimers. Such regulation is not too different from that applicable to credit card bills, loan forms, and media advertising. I assume also the plurality would permit the Commission to require the utility to disseminate legal notices of public hearings and ratemaking proceedings written by it. These compelled statements differ little from mandating disclosure of information in the bill itself, as the plurality recognizes.

Given that the Commission can require the utility to make certain statements and to carry the Commission's own messages to its customers, it seems but a small step to acknowledge that the Commission can also require the utility to act as the conduit for a public interest group's message that bears a close relationship to the purpose of the billing envelope. An analog to this requirement appears in securities law: the Securities and Exchange Commission requires the incumbent board of directors to transmit proposals of dissident shareholders which it opposes.... [The SEC requirement] performs the same function as the Commission's rule by making accessible the relevant audience, whether it be shareholders investing in the corporation or consumers served by the utility, to individuals or groups with demonstrable interests in reaching that audience for certain limited and approved purposes....

{This [SEC] regulation cannot be justified on the basis of the commercial character of the communication, because the Rule can and has been used to propagate purely political proposals. See, *e.g., Medical Committee for Human Rights v. SEC*, 432 F.2d 659 (D.C. Cir. 1970) (shareholder proposal to stop sale of napalm in part because of use in Vietnam).

Even if the SEC Rule were justified largely on the basis of the commercial character of the communication, that justification is not irrelevant in this case. The messages that the utility disseminates in its newsletter are unquestionably intended to advance the corporation's commercial interests, and its objections to the public interest group's messages are based on their potentially adverse impact on the utility's ability to obtain rate increases.

These commercial factors do not justify an abridgment of the utility's constitutionally protected right to communicate in *its* newsletter, but they do provide a legitimate and an adequate justification for the Commission's action in giving TURN access to the same audience that receives the utility's newsletter.}[a]

f.   *Turner Broadcasting Sys. v. FCC, 512 U.S. 622 (1994)*

Justice Kennedy ... delivered the opinion of the Court ....

[The] must-carry provisions [of the Cable Television Consumer Protection and Competition Act] ... require cable operators to carry the signals of a specified number of local broadcast television stations.... Cable systems ... are required to set aside up to one-third of their channels for commercial broadcast stations that request carriage [and approximately one-twelfth for local public broadcast television stations—ed.].... [If] there are more requesting broadcast stations than slots available, the cable operator is permitted to choose which of these stations it will carry....

Cable programmers and cable operators engage in and transmit speech,

---

[a] **[The plurality's response:]** Justice Stevens [errs in analogizing] this aspect of the Commission's order to Securities and Exchange Commission regulations that require management to transmit proposals of minority shareholders in shareholder mailings.... First, [the regulations] allocate shareholder property between management and certain groups of shareholders. Management has no interest in corporate property except such interest as derives from the shareholders; therefore, regulations that limit management's ability to exclude some shareholders' views from corporate communications do not infringe corporate First Amendment rights.

Second, the regulations govern speech by a corporation *to itself*.... [T]he Constitution protects corporations' right to speak to the public base`d on the informational value of corporate speech. Rules that define how corporations govern themselves do not limit the range of information that the corporation may contribute to the public debate. The Commission's order, by contrast, burdens appellant's right freely to speak to the public at large.

and they are entitled to the protection of the speech and press provisions of the First Amendment. Through "original programming or by exercising editorial discretion over which stations or programs to include in its repertoire," cable programmers and operators "see[k] to communicate messages on a wide variety of topics and in a wide variety of formats." ... [And] the rationale for applying a less rigorous standard of First Amendment scrutiny to broadcast regulation, whatever its validity in the cases elaborating it, does not apply in the context of cable regulation. [Explanation omitted.— ed.] ...

Appellants maintain that the must-carry provisions trigger strict scrutiny because they compel cable operators to transmit speech not of their choosing.... [But] unlike the access rules struck down in [*Miami Herald Co. v. Tornillo* and *Pacific Gas & Electric v. Pub. Util. Comm'n*], the must-carry rules are content neutral in application. They are not activated by any particular message spoken by cable operators and thus exact no content-based penalty. Cf. *Riley v. National Federation of Blind*. Likewise, they do not grant access to broadcasters on the ground that the content of broadcast programming will counterbalance the messages of cable operators.... Cf. *Pacific Gas & Elec. Co. v. Public Util. Comm'n*....

[N]or do we think ... that must-carry will force cable operators to alter their own messages to respond to the broadcast programming they are required to carry. Given cable's long history of serving as a conduit for broadcast signals, there appears little risk that cable viewers would assume that the broadcast stations carried on a cable system convey ideas or messages endorsed by the cable operator.... Cf. *PruneYard Shopping Center v. Robins*. Moreover, in contrast to the statute at issue in *Tornillo*, no aspect of the must-carry provisions would cause a cable operator or cable programmer to conclude that "the safe course is to avoid controversy," and by so doing diminish the free flow of information and ideas.

Finally, ... [a]lthough a daily newspaper and a cable operator both may enjoy monopoly status in a given locale, the cable operator exercises far greater control over access to the relevant medium. A daily newspaper, no matter how secure its local monopoly, does not possess the power to obstruct readers' access to other competing publications—whether they be weekly local newspapers, or daily newspapers published in other cities. Thus, when a newspaper asserts exclusive control over its own news copy, it does not thereby prevent other newspapers from being distributed to willing recipients in the same locale.

The same is not true of cable. When an individual subscribes to cable, the physical connection between the television set and the cable network gives the cable operator bottleneck, or gatekeeper, control over most (if not all) of the television programming that is channeled into the subscriber's home. Hence, simply by virtue of its ownership of the essential pathway for cable speech, a cable operator can prevent its subscribers from obtaining access to programming it chooses to exclude. A cable operator, unlike speakers in other media, can thus silence the voice of competing speakers with a mere flick of the switch....

The First Amendment's command that government not impede the freedom of speech does not disable the government from taking steps to ensure that private interests not restrict, through physical control of a critical pathway of communication, the free flow of information and ideas. We thus reject appellants' contention that *Tornillo* and *PG&E* require strict scrutiny of the access rules in question here....

Justice O'Connor, with whom Justice Scalia and Justice Ginsburg join, and with whom Justice Thomas joins [in part], concurring in part and dissenting in part. [This opinion, which primarily dealt with other matters, omitted.—ed.]

g. *Hurley v. Irish-American Gay, Lesbian & Bisexual Group, 515 U.S. 557 (1995)*

Justice Souter delivered the opinion of the Court....

[A.] Every year since [1947], the [South Boston Allied War Veterans] Council has applied for and received a permit for the [St. Patrick's Day Parade], which at times has included as many as 20,000 marchers and drawn up to 1 million watchers. No other applicant has ever applied for that permit....

In 1992, a number of gay, lesbian, and bisexual descendants of the Irish immigrants joined together with other supporters to form the respondent organization, GLIB, to march in the parade as a way to express pride in their Irish heritage as openly gay, lesbian, and bisexual individuals, to demonstrate that there are such men and women among those so descended, and to express their solidarity with like individuals who sought to march in New York's St. Patrick's Day Parade. Although the Council denied GLIB's application to take part in the 1992 parade, GLIB obtained a state-court order to include its contingent, which marched "uneventfully" among that year's 10,000 participants and 750,000 spectators.

In 1993, after the Council had again refused to admit GLIB to the upcoming parade, [GLIB] filed this suit against the Council, ... John J. "Wacko" Hurley [who selected parade participants on the Council's behalf—ed.], and the city of Boston, alleging violations of the State and Federal Constitutions and of the state public accommodations law, which prohibits "any distinction, discrimination or restriction on account of ... sexual orientation ... relative to the admission of any person to, or treatment in any place of public accommodation, resort or amusement." ...

[T]he state trial court ruled that the parade fell within the statutory definition of a public accommodation, which includes "any place ... which is open to ... the general public ... [including] (6) a boardwalk or other public highway [or] ... (8) a place of public amusement, recreation ... or entertainment." The court found that the Council had no written criteria and employed no particular procedures for admission, voted on new applications in batches, had occasionally admitted groups who simply showed up at the parade without having submitted an application, and did "not generally inquire into the specific messages or views of each applicant."

The court consequently rejected the Council's contention that the parade was "private" (in the sense of being exclusive), holding instead that "the lack of genuine selectivity in choosing participants and sponsors demonstrates that the Parade is a public event." It found the parade to be "eclectic," containing a wide variety of "patriotic, commercial, political, moral, artistic, religious, athletic, public service, trade union, and eleemosynary themes," as well as conflicting messages. While noting that the Council had indeed excluded the Ku Klux Klan and ROAR (an antibusing group), it attributed little significance to these facts, concluding ultimately that "[t]he only common theme among the participants and sponsors is their public involvement in the Parade."

The court rejected the Council's assertion that the exclusion of "groups with sexual themes merely formalized [the fact] that the Parade expresses traditional religious and social values," and found the Council's "final position [to be] that GLIB would be excluded because of its values and its message, *i.e.*, its members' sexual orientation." This position, in the court's view, was not only violative of the public accommodations law but "paradoxical" as well, since "a proper celebration of St. Patrick's and Evacuation Day requires diversity and inclusiveness." The court ... [rejected the Council's First Amendment claims on the grounds] that constitutional protection of any interest in expressive association would "requir[e] focus on a specific message, theme, or group" absent from the parade....

[B.] [The Court concluded that GLIB had abandoned its original claim that the Council's conduct was state action, and thus itself a violation of GLIB's First Amendment rights.—ed.] ...

[C.] "[P]arades are public dramas of social relations, and in them performers define who can be a social actor and what subjects and ideas are available for communication and consideration." Hence, we use the word "parade" to indicate marchers who are making some sort of collective point, not just to each other but to bystanders along the way.... Parades are thus a form of expression, ... and the inherent expressiveness of marching to make a point explains our cases involving protest marches....

The protected expression that inheres in a parade is not limited to its banners and songs, however, for the Constitution looks beyond written or spoken words as mediums of expression. Noting that "[s]ymbolism is a primitive but effective way of communicating ideas," our cases have recognized that the First Amendment shields such acts as saluting a flag (and refusing to do so), wearing an armband to protest a war, displaying a red flag, and even "[m]arching, walking or parading" in uniforms displaying the swastika. As some of these examples show, a narrow, succinctly articulable message is not a condition of constitutional protection, which if confined to expressions conveying a "particularized message," would never reach the unquestionably shielded painting of Jackson Pollock, music of Arnold Schoenberg, or Jabberwocky verse of Lewis Carroll.

Not many marches, then, are beyond the realm of expressive parades, and the South Boston celebration is not one of them. Spectators line the streets; people march in costumes and uniforms, carrying flags and banners with all sorts of messages (*e.g.*, "England get out of Ireland," "Say no to drugs"); marching bands and pipers play; floats are pulled along; and the whole show is broadcast over Boston television.

To be sure, we agree with the state courts that in spite of excluding some applicants, the Council is rather lenient in admitting participants. But a private speaker does not forfeit constitutional protection simply by combining multifarious voices, or by failing to edit their themes to isolate an exact message as the exclusive subject matter of the speech.

Nor ... does First Amendment protection require a speaker to generate, as an original matter, each item featured in the communication.... [T]he presentation of an edited compilation of speech generated by other persons is a staple of most newspapers' opinion pages, which, of course, fall squarely within the core of First Amendment security, *Miami Herald Pub. Co. v. Tornillo*, as does even the simple selection of a paid noncommercial advertisement for inclusion in a daily paper, see *New York Times v. Sullivan*. The selection of contingents to make a parade is entitled to similar protection....

[D.] Provisions like [the Massachusetts public accommodation law] ... do not, as a general matter, violate the First or Fourteenth Amendments. Nor [does this statute] ... target speech or discriminate on the basis of its content, the focal point of its prohibition being rather on the act of discriminating against individuals in the provision of publicly available goods, privileges, and services on the proscribed grounds.

In the case before us, however, the Massachusetts law has been applied in a peculiar way.... Petitioners disclaim any intent to exclude homosexuals as such, and no individual member of GLIB claims to have been excluded from parading as a member of any group that the Council has approved to march. Instead, the disagreement goes to the admission of GLIB as its own parade unit carrying its own banner. Since every participating unit affects the message conveyed by the private organizers, the state courts' application of the statute produced an order essentially requiring petitioners to alter the expressive content of their parade.

Altered Expressive Content

Although the state courts spoke of the parade as a place of public accommodation, ... the state courts' application of the statute had the effect of declaring the sponsors' speech itself to be the public accommodation. Under this approach any contingent of protected individuals with a message would have the right to participate in petitioners' speech, so that the communication produced by the private organizers would be shaped by all those protected by the law who wished to join in with some expressive demonstration of their own. But this use of the State's power violates the fundamental rule of protection under the First Amendment, that a speaker has the autonomy to choose the content of his own message.

"Since *all* speech inherently involves choices of what to say and what to leave unsaid," one important manifestation of the principle of free speech is that one who chooses to speak may also decide "what not to say." ... Rather like a composer, the Council selects the expressive units of the parade from potential participants, and though the score may not produce a particularized message, each contingent's expression in the Council's eyes comports with what merits celebration on that day. Even if this view gives the Council credit for a more considered judgment than it actively made, the Council clearly decided to exclude a message it did not like from the communication it chose to make, and that is enough to invoke its right as a private speaker to shape its expression by speaking on one subject while remaining silent on another.

The message it disfavored is not difficult to identify. Although GLIB's point (like the Council's) is not wholly articulate, a contingent marching behind the organization's banner would at least bear witness to the fact that some Irish are gay, lesbian, or bisexual, and the presence of the organized marchers would suggest their view that people of their sexual orientations have as much claim to unqualified social acceptance as heterosexuals and indeed as members of parade units organized around other identifying characteristics.

The parade's organizers may not believe these facts about Irish sexuality to be so, or they may object to unqualified social acceptance of gays and lesbians or have some other reason for wishing to keep GLIB's message out of the parade. But whatever the reason, it boils down to the choice of a speaker not to propound a particular point of view, and that choice is presumed to lie beyond the government's power to control.

[E.] Respondents argue that ... [as in *Turner Broadcasting Sys. v. FCC*,] admission of GLIB to the parade would not threaten the core principle of speaker's autonomy because the Council, like a cable operator, is merely "a conduit" for the speech of participants in the parade "rather than itself a speaker." But this metaphor is not apt here, because GLIB's participation would likely be perceived as having resulted from the Council's customary determination about a unit admitted to the parade, that its message was worthy of presentation and quite possibly of support as well. A newspaper, similarly, "is more than a passive receptacle or conduit for news, comment, and advertising," and we have held that "[t]he choice of material ...— whether fair or unfair—constitute[s] the exercise of editorial control and judgment" upon which the State can not intrude. *Tornillo*....

Unlike the programming offered on various channels by a cable network, the parade does not consist of individual, unrelated segments that happen to be transmitted together for individual selection by members of the audience. Although each parade unit generally identifies itself, each is understood to contribute something to a common theme, and accordingly there is no customary practice whereby private sponsors disavow "any identity of viewpoint" between themselves and the selected participants.

Practice follows practicability here, for such disclaimers would be quite curious in a moving parade. Without deciding on the precise significance of the likelihood of misattribution, it nonetheless becomes clear that in the context of an expressive parade, as with a protest march, the parade's overall message is distilled from the individual presentations along the way, and each unit's expression is perceived by spectators as part of the whole.

[F.] An additional distinction between *Turner Broadcasting* and this case points to the fundamental weakness of any attempt to justify the state-court order's limitation on the Council's autonomy as a speaker. A cable is not only a conduit for speech produced by others and selected by cable operators for transmission, but a franchised channel giving monopolistic opportunity to shut out some speakers.

This power gives rise to the Government's interest in limiting monopolistic autonomy in order to allow for the survival of broadcasters who might otherwise be silenced and consequently destroyed. The Government's interest in *Turner Broadcasting* was not the alteration of speech, but the survival of speakers. In thus identifying an interest going beyond abridgment of speech itself, the defenders of the law at issue in *Turner Broadcasting* addressed the threshold requirement of any review under the Speech Clause, whatever the ultimate level of scrutiny, that a challenged restriction on speech serve a compelling, or at least important, governmental object.

In this case, of course, there is no assertion comparable to the *Turner Broadcasting* claim that some speakers will be destroyed in the absence of the challenged law. True, the size and success of petitioners' parade makes it an enviable vehicle for the dissemination of GLIB's views, but that fact, without more, would fall far short of supporting a claim that petitioners enjoy an abiding monopoly of access to spectators.

Considering that GLIB presumably would have had a fair shot (under neutral criteria developed by the city) at obtaining a parade permit of its own, respondents have not shown that petitioners enjoy the capacity to "silence the voice of competing speakers," as cable operators do with respect to program providers who wish to reach subscribers. Nor has any other legitimate interest been identified in support of applying the Massachusetts statute in this way to expressive activity like the parade....

[G.] When the [public accommodations] law is applied to expressive activity in the way it was done here, its apparent object is simply to require speakers to modify the content of their expression to whatever extent beneficiaries of the law choose to alter it with messages of their own. But in the absence of some further, legitimate end, this object is merely to allow exactly what the general rule of speaker's autonomy forbids.

It might, of course, have been argued that a broader objective is apparent: that the ultimate point of forbidding acts of discrimination toward certain classes is to produce a society free of the corresponding biases. Requiring access to a speaker's message would thus be not an end in itself, but a means to produce speakers free of the biases, whose expressive conduct would be at least neutral toward the particular classes, obviating any future need for correction.

But if this indeed is the point of applying the state law to expressive conduct, it is a decidedly fatal objective.... The very idea that a noncommercial speech restriction be used to produce thoughts and statements acceptable to some groups or, indeed, all people, grates on the First Amendment,

Not a legitimate reason to compel

for it amounts to nothing less than a proposal to limit speech in the service of orthodox expression. The Speech Clause has no more certain antithesis....

3. No Direct Interference with Speaker's Other Speech

a. *Problem: Professional Responsibility Paper*

UCLA Law School changes its graduation requirements to require each student to write a graded 20-page paper on how the legal system can increase compliance with ethical rules. Does this violate the student's right to be free from compelled speech? Why or why not?

b. *Problem: Mandatory Job Reference Laws*

> [A] lady-lodger ... misses ... [a] lace-cuff[], and feels sure that the servant has taken it. There is not a particle of evidence to support this ...; but [the maid] being destitute, is consequently condemned without a trial, and dismissed without a character. She ... wanders off forlorn into a world that has no haven ... for her....
> —Wilkie Collins, *Laid up in Two Lodgings* (1856)

A statute requires certain employers in certain industries, when requested by a discharged employee, to write a letter stating the reason for the employee's discharge and to give this letter to the employee (who would then be able to show it to prospective employers). The Georgia, Carolina & Northern Railway Co., Wallace's former employer, refused to do this, and Wallace sued. The Georgia Supreme Court held for the Railway, saying:

> A statute which undertakes to make it the duty of incorporated railroad ... companies to engage in correspondence of this sort with their discharged agents and employés ... is violative of the general private right of silence enjoyed in this state by all persons, natural or artificial, from time immemorial .... Liberty of speech and of writing is secured by the constitution, and incident thereto is the correlative liberty of silence .... [C]ommunications, oral or written, wanted for private information, cannot be coerced by mere legislative mandate ....

Wallace v. Georgia, C. & N. Ry. Co., 94 Ga. 732 (1894). Wallace's petition for certiorari got lost, but over 100 years later the U.S. Supreme Court finds it and agrees to rehear the case. What result? Cf. *Atchison, T. & S.F. Ry. Co. v. Brown*, 80 Kan. 312 (1909) (taking the same view); *St. Louis Southwestern Ry. Co. v. Griffin*, 106 Tex. 477 (1914) (likewise); *Cheek v. Prudential Ins. Co.*, 192 S.W. 387 (Mo. 1916) (taking the opposite view).

c. *Problem: The Wedding Photographer*

Elane Huguenin is a professional photographer in New Mexico. Like most photographers and other service providers, she generally works for whoever pays her, unless she feels really strongly opposed to the activity she's asked to photograph. In particular, she refuses to photograph same-sex commitment ceremonies, because she finds same-sex relationships to be immoral, and also refuses to take photographs that she sees as positively portraying horror films, abortion, pornography, or nudity.

Because of her moral convictions, Huguenin refused to photograph Vanessa Willock's and Misti Collinsworth's same-sex commitment ceremony. Willock sued, claiming that this violated the New Mexico statutory ban on discrimination based on sexual orientation in a wide range of public accommodations. The New Mexico Human Rights Commission agreed with Willock, concluding that commercial photography services are a "public accommodation," and that discrimination against same-sex commitment ceremonies by someone who photographs opposite-sex weddings is prohibited discrimination. (Assume that this interpretation correctly reflects New Mexico law.) The Commission ordered Huguenin to pay over $6600 in attorney's fees and costs.

Does this violate the First Amendment? Assume that Elaine Huguenin works alone, rather than having many photographer employees to whom she could turn.

Would your answer be different if Huguenin had been a singer who often sings at weddings, or a portrait painter who often paints portraits of a couple to commemorate their wedding?

Would your answer be different if Huguenin had been asked to photograph an event organized by the Church of Scientology, and refused because she disapproved of that church? If Huguenin had been a freelance writer who was asked by the Scientologist to write press releases for the Church? Assume that state law bars discrimination against religious events and religious organizations to the same extent as it bars discrimination against same-sex commitment ceremonies.

See *Elane Photography, LLC. v. Willock*, 309 P.3d 53 (N.M. 2013).

d. *West Virginia State Bd. of Ed. v. Barnette, 319 U.S. 624 (1943)*

Justice Jackson delivered the opinion of the Court....

The Board of Education on January 9, 1942, adopted a resolution ... ordering that the salute to the flag become "a regular [and mandatory] part of the program of activities [for teachers and pupils] in the public schools" .... Failure to conform is "insubordination" dealt with by expulsion. Readmission is denied by statute until compliance. Meanwhile the expelled child is "unlawfully absent" and may be proceeded against as a delinquent. His parents or guardians are liable to prosecution, and if convicted are subject to fine not exceeding $50 and jail term not exceeding thirty days.

Appellees ... brought suit ... to restrain enforcement of these laws and regulations against Jehovah's Witnesses. The Witnesses are an unincorporated body teaching that the obligation imposed by law of God is superior to that of laws enacted by temporal government. Their religious beliefs include a literal version of Exodus, Chapter 20, verses 4 and 5, which says: "Thou shalt not make unto thee any graven image, or any likeness of anything that is in heaven above, or that is in the earth beneath, or that is in the water under the earth; thou shalt not bow down thyself to them nor serve them." They consider that the flag is an "image" within this command. For this reason they refuse to salute it....

[T]he compulsory flag salute and pledge requires affirmation of a belief and an attitude of mind. It is not clear whether the regulation contemplates that pupils forego any contrary convictions of their own and become unwilling converts to the prescribed ceremony or whether it will be acceptable if they simulate assent by words without belief and by a gesture barren of meaning....

[C]ensorship or suppression of expression of opinion is tolerated by our Constitution only when the expression presents a clear and present danger of action of a kind the State is empowered to prevent and punish. It would seem that involuntary affirmation could be commanded only on even more immediate and urgent grounds than silence. But here the power of compulsion is invoked without any allegation that remaining passive during a flag salute ritual creates a clear and present danger that would justify an effort even to muffle expression....

National unity as an end which officials may foster by persuasion and example is not in question. The problem is whether under our Constitution compulsion as here employed is a permissible means for its achievement.

Struggles to coerce uniformity of sentiment in support of some end thought essential to their time and country have been waged by many good as well as by evil men. Nationalism is a relatively recent phenomenon but at other times and places the ends have been racial or territorial security, support of a dynasty or regime, and particular plans for saving souls.

As first and moderate methods to attain unity have failed, those bent on its accomplishment must resort to an ever-increasing severity. As governmental pressure toward unity becomes greater, so strife becomes more bitter as to whose unity it shall be. Probably no deeper division of our people could proceed from any provocation than from finding it necessary to choose what doctrine and whose program public educational officials shall compel youth to unite in embracing.

Ultimate futility of such attempts to compel coherence is the lesson of every such effort from the Roman drive to stamp out Christianity as a disturber of its pagan unity, the Inquisition, as a means to religious and dynastic unity, the Siberian exiles as a means to Russian unity, down to the fast failing efforts of our present totalitarian enemies. Those who begin coercive elimination of dissent soon find themselves exterminating dissenters. Compulsory unification of opinion achieves only the unanimity of the graveyard....

[T]he First Amendment to our Constitution was designed to avoid these ends by avoiding these beginnings.... Authority here is to be controlled by public opinion, not public opinion by authority.

The case is made difficult not because the principles of its decision are obscure but because the flag involved is our own. Nevertheless, we apply the limitations of the Constitution with no fear that freedom to be intellectually and spiritually diverse or even contrary will disintegrate the social organization. To believe that patriotism will not flourish if patriotic ceremonies are voluntary and spontaneous instead of a compulsory routine is to make an unflattering estimate of the appeal of our institutions to free minds.

We can have intellectual individualism and the rich cultural diversities that we owe to exceptional minds only at the price of occasional eccentricity and abnormal attitudes.... [And] freedom to differ is not limited to things that do not matter much. That would be a mere shadow of freedom. The test of its substance is the right to differ as to things that touch the heart of the existing order.

If there is any fixed star in our constitutional constellation, it is that no official, high or petty, can prescribe what shall be orthodox in politics, nationalism, religion, or other matters of opinion or force citizens to confess by word or act their faith therein. If there are any circumstances which permit an exception, they do not now occur to us....

We think the action of the local authorities in compelling the flag salute and pledge transcends constitutional limitations on their power and invades the sphere of intellect and spirit which it is the purpose of the First Amendment to our Constitution to reserve from all official control....

Justice Frankfurter, dissenting...

[A.] [I]t is not for this Court to make psychological judgments as to the effectiveness of a particular symbol in inculcating concededly indispensable feelings, particularly if the state happens to see fit to utilize the symbol that represents our heritage and our hopes....

[B.] [O]nly flippancy could be responsible for the suggestion that constitutional validity of a requirement to salute our flag implies equal validity of a requirement to salute a dictator. The significance of a symbol lies in what it represents. To reject the swastika does not imply rejection of the Cross.... [I]t mocks reason and denies our whole history to find in the allowance of a requirement to salute our flag on fitting occasions the seeds of sanction for obeisance to a leader. To deny the power to employ educational symbols is to say that the state's educational system may not stimulate the imagination because this may lead to unwise stimulation.

The right of West Virginia to utilize the flag salute as part of its educational process is denied because, so it is argued, it cannot be justified as a means of meeting a "clear and present danger" to national unity.... [But t]o apply [a "clear and present danger"] test is for the Court to assume, however unwittingly, a legislative responsibility that does not belong to it. To talk about "clear and present danger" as the touchstone of allowable educational policy by the states whenever school curricula may impinge upon the boundaries of individual conscience, is to take a felicitous phrase out of the context of the particular situation where it arose and for which it was adapted....

[C.] Saluting the flag suppresses no belief nor curbs it. Children and their parents may believe what they please, avow their belief and practice it.... [T]he requirement for saluting the flag ... [leaves open] the fullest opportunity on the part both of the children and of their parents to disavow as publicly as they choose to do so the meaning that others attach to the gesture of salute. All channels of affirmative free expression are open to both children and parents....

Justice Roberts, joined by Justice Reed, dissenting. [We] adhere to the views expressed by the Court in *Minersville School District v. Gobitis,* 310 U.S. 586 (1940), and are of the opinion that the judgment below should be reversed.

[Note: *Barnette* represents a rare reversal of a case just three years after it was decided. *Gobitis* was an 8-1 decision upholding the Pledge requirement, but two members of the *Gobitis* majority (Chief Justice Hughes and Justice McReynolds) had retired, to be replaced by Justice Jackson and Rutledge, and three members (Justices Black, Douglas, and Murphy) changed their views.

Barnette did point to an important legal difference between the two cases: The *Gobitis* plaintiffs argued that their religious beliefs entitled them to a Free Exercise Clause exemption from the Pledge requirement, but the Court in *Barnette* held that all students—whatever their religious beliefs—had a Free Speech Clause right not to say the Pledge. But the *Gobitis* majority opinion (written by Justice Frankfurter) also more broadly defended government power to mandate the Pledge; on that point, *Barnette* expressly overruled *Gobitis.*—ed.]

e.   *Wooley v. Maynard, 430 U.S. 705 (1977)*

Chief Justice Burger delivered the opinion of the Court....

[A.] Since 1969 New Hampshire has required that noncommercial vehicles bear license plates embossed with the state motto, "Live Free or Die" [and prohibited covering up the motto] .... [George and Maxine Maynard, who are Jehovah's Witnesses,] consider the New Hampshire State motto to be repugnant to their moral, religious, and political beliefs, and therefore assert it objectionable to disseminate this message by displaying it on their automobiles.... [Mr. Maynard was fined and given a suspended six-month jail sentence for repeatedly covering up the motto.—ed.] ...

[T]he right of freedom of thought protected by the First Amendment against state action includes both the right to speak freely and the right to refrain from speaking at all. A system which secures the right to proselytize religious, political, and ideological causes must also guarantee the concomitant right to decline to foster such concepts. The right to speak and the right to refrain from speaking are complementary components of the broader concept of "individual freedom of mind." ...

Here, as in *W. Va. State Bd. of Ed. v. Barnette,* we are faced with a state measure which forces an individual, as part of his daily life—indeed constantly while his automobile is in public view—to be an instrument for fostering public adherence to an ideological point of view he finds unacceptable. In doing so, the State "invades the sphere of intellect and spirit which it is the purpose of the First Amendment to our Constitution to reserve from all official control."

New Hampshire's statute in effect requires that appellees use their private property as a "mobile billboard" for the State's ideological message—or suffer a penalty, as Maynard already has. As a condition to driving an automobile—a virtual necessity for most Americans—the Maynards must display "Live Free or Die" to hundreds of people each day. ...

[B.] Identifying the Maynards' interests as implicating First Amendment protections does not end our inquiry however. We must also determine whether the State's countervailing interest is sufficiently compelling to justify requiring appellees to display the state motto on their license plates. The two interests advanced by the State are that display of the motto (1) facilitates the identification of passenger vehicles, and (2) promotes appreciation of history, individualism, and state pride....

New Hampshire passenger license plates normally consist of a specific configuration of letters and numbers, which makes them readily distinguishable from other types of plates, even without reference to the state motto.... "[E]ven though the governmental purpose be legitimate and substantial, that purpose cannot be pursued by means that broadly stifle fundamental personal liberties when the end can be more narrowly achieved. The breadth of legislative abridgment must be viewed in the light of less drastic means for achieving the same basic purpose."

The State's second claimed interest is not ideologically neutral. The State is seeking to communicate to others an official view as to proper appreciation of history, state pride, and individualism. Of course, the State may legitimately pursue such interests in any number of ways. However, where the State's interest is to disseminate an ideology, no matter how acceptable to some, such interest cannot outweigh an individual's First Amendment right to avoid becoming the courier for such message.

[C.] {It has been suggested that today's holding will be read as sanctioning the obliteration of the national motto, "In God We Trust" from United States coins and currency. That question is not before us today but we note that currency, which is passed from hand to hand, differs in significant respects from an automobile, which is readily associated with its operator. Currency is generally carried in a purse or pocket and need not be displayed to the public. The bearer of currency is thus not required to publicly advertise the national motto.}

{Some States require that certain documents bear the seal of the State or some other official stamp for purposes of recordation. Such seal might contain, albeit obscurely, a symbol or motto having political or philosophical implications. The purpose of such seal, however, is not to advertise the message it bears but simply to authenticate the document by showing the authority of its origin.}

We conclude that the State of New Hampshire may not require appellees to display the state motto upon their vehicle license plates ....

Justice Rehnquist, with whom Justice Blackmun joins, dissenting....

The State has not forced appellees to "say" anything; and it has not forced them to communicate ideas with nonverbal actions reasonably likened to "speech," such as wearing a lapel button promoting a political candidate or waving a flag as a symbolic gesture.... Appellees have not been forced to affirm or reject [the State] motto; they are simply required by the State ... to carry a state auto license tag for identification and registration purposes....

The Court ... relies upon the "right to decline to foster [religious, political, and ideological] concepts," and treats the state law in this case as if it were forcing appellees to proselytize, or to advocate an ideological point of view. But this begs the question. The issue, unconfronted by the Court, is whether appellees, in displaying, as they are required to do, state license tags, the format of which is known to all as having been prescribed by the State, would be considered to be advocating political or ideological views....

The Court suggests that the test is whether the individual is forced "to be an instrument for fostering public adherence to an ideological point of view he finds unacceptable." But ... were New Hampshire to erect a multitude of billboards, each proclaiming "Live Free or Die," and tax all citizens for the cost of erection and maintenance, clearly the message would be "fostered" by the individual citizen-taxpayers and just as clearly those individuals would be "instruments" in that communication. Certainly, however, that case would not fall within the ambit of *Barnette*. In that case, as in this case, there is no *affirmation* of belief.

For First Amendment principles to be implicated, the State must place the citizen in the position of either apparently or actually "asserting as true" the message. This was the focus of *Barnette,* and clearly distinguishes this case from that one....

[A]ppellees could place on their bumper a conspicuous bumper sticker explaining in no uncertain terms that they do not profess the motto "Live Free or Die" and that they violently disagree with the connotations of that motto. Since any implication that they affirm the motto can be so easily displaced, I cannot agree that the state statutory system for motor vehicle identification and tourist promotion may be invalidated under the fiction that appellees are unconstitutionally forced to affirm, or profess belief in, the state motto....

I cannot imagine that the statutes proscribing defacement of United States currency [that contains the mottoes "In God We Trust" and "E Pluribus Unum"] impinge upon the First Amendment rights of an atheist. The fact that an atheist carries and uses United States currency does not, in any meaningful sense, convey any affirmation of belief on his part in the motto "In God We Trust." Similarly, there is no affirmation of belief involved in the display of state license tags upon the private automobiles involved here....

f. *PruneYard Shopping Center v. Robins, 447 U.S. 74 (1980)*

Justice Rehnquist delivered the opinion of the Court....

[A.] Appellant PruneYard is a privately owned shopping center in the city of Campbell, Cal[ifornia]. It covers approximately 21 acres—5 devoted to parking and 16 occupied by walkways, plazas, sidewalks, and buildings that contain more than 65 specialty shops, 10 restaurants, and a movie theater.

The PruneYard is open to the public for the purpose of encouraging the patronizing of its commercial establishments. It has a policy not to permit any visitor or tenant to engage in any publicly expressive activity, including the circulation of petitions, that is not directly related to its commercial purposes. This policy has been strictly enforced in a nondiscriminatory fashion. The PruneYard is owned by appellant Fred Sahadi.

Appellees are high school students who sought to solicit support for their opposition to a United Nations resolution against "Zionism." On a Saturday afternoon they set up a card table in a corner of PruneYard's central courtyard. They distributed pamphlets and asked passersby to sign petitions, which were to be sent to the President and Members of Congress. Their activity was peaceful and orderly and so far as the record indicates was not objected to by PruneYard's patrons.

Soon after appellees had begun soliciting signatures, a security guard informed them that they would have to leave because their activity violated PruneYard regulations.... [The students sued, and the California Supreme Court ultimately held in their favor, holding] that the California Constitution protects "speech and petitioning, reasonably exercised, in shopping centers even when the centers are privately owned." ...

[B.] [In *Wooley v. Maynard*,] the government itself prescribed the message [that had to be displayed], required it to be displayed openly on ... personal property that was used "as part of [the person's] daily life," and refused to permit him to take any measures to cover up the motto even though the Court found that the display of the motto served no important state interest. Here, by contrast, there are a number of distinguishing factors.

Most important, the shopping center by choice of its owner is not limited to the personal use of appellants. It is instead a business establishment that is open to the public to come and go as they please. The views expressed by members of the public in passing out pamphlets or seeking signatures for a petition thus will not likely be identified with those of the owner.

(1) No Attribution

Second, no specific message is dictated by the State to be displayed on appellants' property. There consequently is no danger of governmental discrimination for or against a particular message.

(2) No orthodoxy

Finally, as far as appears here appellants can expressly disavow any connection with the message by simply posting signs in the area where the speakers or handbillers stand. Such signs, for example, could disclaim any sponsorship of the message and could explain that the persons are communicating their own messages by virtue of state law....

(3) Disclaimers

W. Va. State Bd. of Ed v. Barnette is inapposite because it involved the compelled recitation of a message containing an affirmation of belief.... Appellants are not ... being compelled to affirm their belief in any governmentally prescribed position or view, and they are free to publicly dissociate themselves from the views of the speakers or handbillers....

[*Miami Herald Pub. Co. v. Tornillo*] rests on the principle that the State cannot tell a newspaper what it must print. The Florida statute contravened this principle in that it "exact[ed] a penalty on the basis of the content of a newspaper." There also was a danger in *Tornillo* that the statute would "dampe[n] the vigor and limi[t] the variety of public debate" by deterring editors from publishing controversial political statements that might trigger the application of the statute. Thus, the statute was found to be an "intrusion into the function of editors." These concerns obviously are not present here....

[A]ppellants' ... First Amendment rights have [not] been infringed by the California Supreme Court's decision recognizing a right of appellees to exercise state-protected rights of expression ... on appellants' property....

Justice Powell, with whom Justice White joins, concurring in part and in the judgment....

[A.] I do not believe that the result in *Wooley* would have changed had the State of New Hampshire directed its citizens to place the slogan "Live Free or Die" in their shop windows rather than on their automobiles.... And I can find no reason to exclude the owner whose property is "not limited to [his] personal use...." A person who has merely invited the public onto his property for commercial purposes cannot fairly be said to have relinquished his right to decline "to be an instrument for fostering public adherence to an ideological point of view he finds unacceptable," *Wooley* ...

[E]ven when no particular message is mandated by the State, ... a right of access is [often] no less intrusive than speech compelled by the State itself.... [See, *e.g.*,] *Miami Herald*.... [S]imilar speech interests [to those in *Miami Herald*] are affected when listeners are likely to identify opinions expressed by members of the public on commercial property as the views of the owner. If a state law mandated public access to the bulletin board[, entrance area, or lobby] of a freestanding store, hotel, office, or small shopping center, customers might well conclude that the messages reflect the view of the proprietor....

The property owner or proprietor would be faced with a choice: he either could permit his customers to receive a mistaken impression or he could disavow the messages. Should he take the first course, he effectively has been compelled to affirm someone else's belief. Should he choose the second, he had been forced to speak when he would prefer to remain silent. In short, he has lost control over his freedom to speak or not to speak on certain issues. The mere fact that he is free to dissociate himself from the views expressed on his property, cannot restore his "right to refrain from speaking at all."

A property owner also may be faced with speakers who wish to use his premises as a platform for views that he finds morally repugnant.... A minority-owned business confronted with leaflet distributers from the American Nazi Party or the Ku Klux Klan, a church-operated enterprise asked to host demonstrations in favor of abortion, or a union compelled to supply a forum to right-to-work advocates could be placed in an intolerable position if state law requires it to make its private property available to anyone who wishes to speak. The strong emotions evoked by speech in such situations may virtually compel the proprietor to respond.

The pressure to respond is particularly apparent when the owner has taken a position opposed to the view being expressed on his property. But an owner who strongly objects to some of the causes to which the state-imposed right of access would extend may oppose ideological activities "of *any* sort" that are not related to the purposes for which he has invited the public onto his property.

To require the owner to specify the particular ideas he finds objectionable enough to compel a response would force him to relinquish his "freedom to maintain his own beliefs without public disclosure." Thus, the right to control one's own speech may be burdened impermissibly even when listeners will not assume that the messages expressed on private property are those of the owner....

[B.] [Appellants, however, did not] introduce evidence that would support a holding in their favor under either of the legal theories outlined above. On the record before us, I cannot say that customers of this vast center would be likely to assume that appellees' limited speech activity expressed the views of the PruneYard or of its owner. The shopping center occupies several city blocks.... Persons solicited could not reasonably have believed that the petitions embodied the views of the shopping center merely because it owned the ground on which they stood.

Appellants have not alleged that they object to the ideas contained in the appellees' petitions. Nor do they assert that some groups who reasonably might be expected to speak at the PruneYard will express views that are so objectionable as to require a response even when listeners will not mistake their source.... [I therefore concur in the judgment, but] I do not interpret our decision today as a blanket approval for state efforts to transform privately owned commercial property into public forums....

g. *Rumsfeld v. FAIR, 547 U.S. 47 (2006)*

Chief Justice Roberts delivered the [unanimous] opinion of the Court....

[Reread Part A on p. 220.—ed.]

[A.] [R]ecruiting assistance provided by the schools often includes elements of speech. For example, schools may send e-mails or post notices on bulletin boards on an employer's behalf. Law schools offering such services to other recruiters must also send e-mails and post notices on behalf of the military to comply with the Solomon Amendment.... [T]hese compelled statements of fact ("The U.S. Army recruiter will meet interested students in Room 123 at 11 a.m."), like compelled statements of opinion, are subject to First Amendment scrutiny.... *Riley v. National Federation of Blind.*

This sort of recruiting assistance, however, is a far cry from the compelled speech in *West Virginia Bd. of Ed. v. Barnette* and *Wooley v. Maynard*. The Solomon Amendment, unlike the laws at issue in those cases, does not dictate the content of the speech at all, which is only "compelled" if, and to the extent, the school provides such speech for other recruiters. There is nothing in this case approaching a Government-mandated pledge or motto that the school must endorse.

The compelled speech to which the law schools point is plainly incidental to the Solomon Amendment's regulation of conduct, and "it has never been deemed an abridgment of freedom of speech or press to make a course of conduct illegal merely because the conduct was in part initiated, evidenced, or carried out by means of language, either spoken, written, or printed." *Giboney v. Empire Storage & Ice Co.*

Congress, for example, can prohibit employers from discriminating in hiring on the basis of race. The fact that this will require an employer to take down a sign reading "White Applicants Only" hardly means that the law should be analyzed as one regulating the employer's speech rather than conduct. See *R.A.V. v. St. Paul* ("[W]ords can in some circumstances violate laws directed not against speech but against conduct"). Compelling a law school that sends scheduling e-mails for other recruiters to send one for a military recruiter is simply not the same as forcing a student to pledge allegiance, or forcing a Jehovah's Witness to display the motto "Live Free or Die," and it trivializes the freedom protected in *Barnette* and *Wooley* to suggest that it is.

[B.] Our compelled-speech cases are not limited to the situation in which an individual must personally speak the government's message. We have also in a number of instances limited the government's ability to force one speaker to host or accommodate another speaker's message. See *Hurley v. Irish-American Gay, Lesbian and Bisexual Group of Boston* (state law cannot require a parade to include a group whose message the parade's organizer does not wish to send); *Pacific Gas & Elec. Co. v. Public Util. Comm'n* (state agency cannot require a utility company to include a third-party newsletter in its billing envelope); *Miami Herald Publishing Co. v. Tornillo* (right-of-reply statute violates editors' right to determine the content of their newspapers)....

The compelled-speech violation in each of our prior cases, however, resulted from the fact that the complaining speaker's own message was affected by the speech it was forced to accommodate.... [For instance, in *Pacific Gas*,] when the state agency ordered the utility to send a third-party newsletter four times a year, it interfered with the utility's ability to communicate its own message in its newsletter....

In this case, accommodating the military's message does not affect the law schools' speech, because the schools are not speaking when they host interviews and recruiting receptions. Unlike a parade organizer's choice of parade contingents, a law school's decision to allow recruiters on campus is not inherently expressive. Law schools facilitate recruiting to assist their students in obtaining jobs. A law school's recruiting services lack the expressive quality of a parade, a newsletter, or the editorial page of a newspaper; its accommodation of a military recruiter's message is not compelled speech because the accommodation does not sufficiently interfere with any message of the school.

The schools respond that if they treat military and nonmilitary recruiters alike in order to comply with the Solomon Amendment, they could be viewed as sending the message that they see nothing wrong with the military's policies, when they do. We rejected a similar argument in *PruneYard Shopping Center v. Robins.*... We explained that there was little likelihood that the views of those engaging in the expressive activities would be identified with the [mall] owner, who remained free to disassociate himself from those views and who was "not ... being compelled to affirm [a] belief in any governmentally prescribed position or view."

The same is true here. Nothing about recruiting suggests that law schools agree with any speech by recruiters, and nothing in the Solomon Amendment restricts what the law schools may say about the military's policies.... [Law] school students can appreciate the difference between speech a school sponsors and speech the school permits because legally required to do so, pursuant to an equal access policy.

4.   COMPELLED CONTRIBUTIONS OF MONEY

a.   *Problem: Public Art Assessment*

An ordinance in the City of Cucamonga requires that all developers of residential property pay 1% of the total building value to a local Citizens' Art Council, a volunteer-run nonprofit organization, which will then use it to buy public art and display it somewhere in the city. The City of Petaluma takes a different approach: It requires the developer to buy some art itself, at a cost equal to 1% of the total building value, and place the art somewhere in front of the building. Are the ordinances constitutional? Cf. *Ehrlich v. City of Culver City,* 12 Cal. 4th 854 (1996).

b.   *Abood v. Detroit Bd. of Ed., 431 U.S. 209 (1977)*

Justice Stewart delivered the opinion of the Court....

[A.] Among the ... provisions [of the collective-bargaining agreement between the Detroit Federation of Teachers (Union) and the Board of Education] was an "agency shop" clause, requiring every teacher who had not become a Union member within 60 days of hire ... to pay the Union a service charge equal to the regular dues required of Union members. A teacher who failed to meet this obligation was subject to discharge....

[Appellants, who are teachers, sued, alleging] that the Union "carries on various social activities for the benefit of its members which are not available to non-members as a matter of right," and that the Union is engaged "in ... activities and programs which are economic, political, professional, scientific and religious in nature of which Plaintiffs do not approve, and in which they will have no voice, and which are not and will not be collective bargaining activities, i.e., the negotiation and administration of contracts with Defendant Board, and that a substantial part of the sums required to be paid under said Agency Shop Clause are used and will continue to be used for the support of such activities and programs, and not solely for the purpose of defraying the cost of Defendant Federation of its activities as bargaining agent for teachers ...." ...

[B.] The principle of exclusive union representation, which underlies the National Labor Relations Act ..., is a central element in the congressional structuring of industrial relations. The designation of a single representative avoids the confusion that would result from attempting to enforce two or more agreements specifying different terms and conditions of employment. It prevents inter-union rivalries from creating dissension within the work force and eliminating the advantages to the employee of collectivization. It also frees the employer from the possibility of facing conflicting demands from different unions, and permits the employer and a single union to reach agreements and settlements that are not subject to attack from rival labor organizations.

The designation of a union as exclusive representative carries with it great responsibilities. The tasks of negotiating and administering a collective-bargaining agreement and representing the interests of employees in settling disputes and processing grievances are continuing and difficult ones. They often entail expenditure of much time and money. The services of lawyers, expert negotiators, economists, and a research staff, as well as general administrative personnel, may be required.

Moreover, in carrying out these duties, the union is obliged "fairly and equitably to represent all employees ..., union and nonunion," within the relevant unit. A union-shop arrangement has been thought to distribute fairly the cost of these activities among those who benefit, and it counteracts the incentive that employees might otherwise have to become "free riders"— to refuse to contribute to the union while obtaining benefits of union representation that necessarily accrue to all employees.

[C.] To compel employees financially to support their collective-bargaining representative has an impact upon their First Amendment interests. An employee may very well have ideological objections to a wide variety of activities undertaken by the union .... His moral or religious views about the desirability of abortion may not square with the union's policy in negotiating a medical benefits plan. One individual might disagree with a union policy of negotiating limits on the right to strike, believing that to be the road to serfdom for the working class, while another might have economic or political objections to unionism itself. An employee might object to the union's wage policy because it violates guidelines designed to limit inflation, or might object to the union's seeking a clause in the collective-bargaining agreement proscribing racial discrimination....

To be required to help finance the union as a collective-bargaining agent might well be thought, therefore, to interfere in some way with an employee's freedom to associate for the advancement of ideas, or to refrain from doing so, as he sees fit. But ... such interference as exists is constitutionally justified by the legislative assessment of the important contribution of the union shop to the system of labor relations established by Congress.... Thus, insofar as the service charge is used to finance expenditures by the Union for the purposes of collective bargaining, contract administration, and grievance adjustment, [the charge is permissible]....

[D.] [The union's use of agency fees for political purposes, however, is a different matter.] [A] government may not require an individual to relinquish rights guaranteed him by the First Amendment as a condition of public employment....

[C]ontributing to an organization for the purpose of spreading a political message is protected by the First Amendment. Because "[m]aking a contribution ... enables like-minded persons to pool their resources in furtherance of common political goals," ... limitations upon the freedom to contribute "implicate fundamental First Amendment interests." *Buckley v. Valeo*. The fact that the appellants are compelled to make, rather than prohibited from making, contributions for political purposes works no less an infringement of their constitutional rights. For at the heart of the First Amendment is the notion that an individual should be free to believe as he will, and that in a free society one's beliefs should be shaped by his mind and his conscience rather than coerced by the State....

These principles prohibit a State from compelling any individual to affirm his belief in God or to associate with a political party as a condition of retaining public employment. They are no less applicable to the case at bar, and they thus prohibit the appellees from requiring any of the appellants to contribute to the support of an ideological cause he may oppose as a condition of holding a job as a public school teacher.

We do not hold that a union cannot constitutionally spend funds for the expression of political views, on behalf of political candidates, or toward the advancement of other ideological causes not germane to its duties as collective-bargaining representative. Rather, the Constitution requires only that such expenditures be financed from charges, dues, or assessments paid by employees who do not object to advancing those ideas and who are not coerced into doing so against their will by the threat of loss of governmental employment.

[E.] There will, of course, be difficult problems in drawing lines between collective-bargaining activities, for which contributions may be compelled, and ideological activities unrelated to collective bargaining, for which such compulsion is prohibited.... [Collective bargaining] may require not merely concord at the bargaining table, but subsequent approval by other public authorities; related budgetary and appropriations decisions might be seen as an integral part of the bargaining process.

We have no occasion in this case, however, to try to define such a dividing line. The case comes to us after a judgment on the pleadings, and there is no evidentiary record of any kind.... [P]laintiffs are entitled to ... relief [for example, a refund of part of their agency fees] if they can prove the allegations contained in their complaints ....

Justice Powell, with whom ... Chief Justice [Burger] and Justice Blackmun join, concurring in the judgment....

[A.] [C]ompelling a government employee to give financial support to a union in the public sector—regardless of the uses to which the union puts the contribution—impinges seriously upon interests in free speech and association protected by the First Amendment. In *Buckley,* ... [w]e held that ... limitations on political contributions "impinge on protected associational freedoms": "Making a contribution, like joining a political party, serves to affiliate a person with a candidate. In addition, it enables like-minded persons to pool their resources in furtherance of common political goals...." ... [And a]n individual can no more be required to affiliate with a candidate by making a contribution than he can be prohibited from such affiliation....

[The same principle should apply to mandated contributions to unions.] The ultimate objective of a union in the public sector, like that of a political party, is to influence public decisionmaking in accordance with the views and perceived interests of its membership....

Nor is there any basis here for distinguishing "collective-bargaining activities" from "political activities" so far as the interests protected by the First Amendment are concerned. Collective bargaining in the public sector is "political" in any meaningful sense of the word.... Decisions reached through collective bargaining in the schools will affect not only the teachers and the quality of education, but also the taxpayers and the beneficiaries of other important public services.... Disassociation with a public-sector union and the expression of disagreement with its positions and objectives therefore lie at "the core of those activities protected by the First Amendment." ...

[B.] {Compelled support of a private association is fundamentally different from compelled support of government. Clearly, a local school board does not need to demonstrate a compelling state interest every time it spends a taxpayer's money in ways the taxpayer finds abhorrent. But the reason for permitting the government to compel the payment of taxes and to spend money on controversial projects is that the government is representative of the people. The same cannot be said of a union, which is representative only of one segment of the population, with certain common interests.}

[C.] "[T]he State has interests as an employer in regulating the speech of its employees that differ significantly from those it possesses in connection with regulation of the speech of the citizenry in general." Nevertheless, even in public employment, "a significant impairment of First Amendment rights must survive exacting scrutiny." ...

The justifications offered by the Detroit Board of Education must be tested under this settled [strict scrutiny] standard of review.... It may be that the Board of Education is in a position to demonstrate that [the government interests in preventing free-riding and preserving labor peace] are of paramount importance and that requiring public employees to pay certain union fees and dues as a condition of employment is necessary to serve those interests under an exclusive bargaining scheme. On the present record there is no assurance whatever that this is the case.

{[O]n some narrowly defined economic issues—teachers' salaries and pension benefits, for example—the case for requiring the teachers to speak through a single representative would be quite strong, while the concomitant limitation of First Amendment rights would be relatively insignificant. On such issues the case for requiring all teachers to contribute to the clearly identified costs of collective bargaining also would be strong, while the interest of the minority teacher, who is benefited directly, in withholding support would be comparatively weak. {The processing of individual grievances may [likewise] be an important union service for which a fee could be exacted with minimal intrusion on First Amendment interests.}

On other issues—including such questions as how best to educate the young—the strong First Amendment interests of dissenting employees might be expected to prevail.... [Similarly,] a strike against a public agency ... may be so controversial and of such general public concern that compelled financial support by all employees should not be permitted under the Constitution.} ...

I would ... require the State to come forward and demonstrate, as to each union expenditure for which it would exact support from minority employees, that the compelled contribution is necessary to serve overriding governmental objectives. This placement of the burden of litigation ... gives appropriate protection to First Amendment rights without sacrificing ends of government that may be deemed important.

c. *Keller v. State Bar, 496 U.S. 1 (1990)*

Chief Justice Rehnquist delivered the opinion of the [unanimous] Court.

[The Court held that objecting lawyers were entitled to a refund of that share of their compulsory Bar dues that was used "to finance political and ideological activities of the State Bar with which they disagree." But the Court also held that the Bar was entitled to use compulsory dues when "the challenged expenditures are necessarily or reasonably incurred for the purpose of regulating the legal profession or 'improving the quality of the legal service available to the people of the State.'" In the process, the Court said:—ed.]

[A.] The State Bar of California is a good deal different from most other entities that would be regarded in common parlance as "governmental agencies." Its principal funding comes, not from appropriations made to it by the legislature, but from dues levied on its members by the board of governors.... Respondent undoubtedly performs important and valuable services for the State by way of governance of the profession, but those services are essentially advisory in nature. The State Bar does not admit anyone to the practice of law, it does not finally disbar or suspend anyone, and it does not ultimately establish ethical codes of conduct. All of those functions are reserved by California law to the State Supreme Court....

[The] specialized characteristics of the State Bar ... serve[] to distinguish it from the role of the typical government official or agency. Government officials are expected as a part of the democratic process to represent and to espouse the views of a majority of their constituents.... If every citizen were to have a right to insist that no one paid by public funds express a view with which he disagreed, debate over issues of great concern to the public would be limited to those in the private sector, and the process of government as we know it radically transformed.

The State Bar of California was created, not to participate in the general government of the State, but to provide specialized professional advice to those with the ultimate responsibility of governing the legal profession. Its members and officers are such not because they are citizens or voters, but because they are lawyers.... [T]hese differences between the State Bar, on the one hand, and traditional government agencies and officials, on the other hand, render unavailing respondent's argument that it is not subject to the same constitutional rule with respect to the use of compulsory dues as are labor unions representing public and private employees....

[B.] Precisely where the line falls between those State Bar activities in which the officials and members of the Bar are acting essentially as professional advisers to those ultimately charged with the regulation of the legal profession [in California, the state Supreme Court], on the one hand, and those activities having political or ideological coloration which are not reasonably related to the advancement of such goals, on the other, will not always be easy to discern. But the extreme ends of the spectrum are clear: Compulsory dues may not be expended to endorse or advance a gun control or nuclear weapons freeze initiative; at the other end of the spectrum petitioners have no valid constitutional objection to their compulsory dues being spent for activities connected with disciplining members of the Bar or proposing ethical codes for the profession....

d. *Board of Regents v. Southworth, 529 U.S. 217 (2000)*

Justice Kennedy delivered the opinion of the Court....

[Λ.] By [Wisconsin] statute "[University of Wisconsin s]tudents in consultation with the chancellor and subject to the final confirmation of the board [of regents] shall have the responsibility for the disposition of those student fees which constitute substantial support for campus student activities." The students do so, in large measure, through their student government, called the Associated Students of Madison....

[T]he University ... require[s] full-time students ... to pay a nonrefundable activity fee ... [of] $331.50 per year. The fee is segregated from the University's tuition charge. Once collected, the activity fees are deposited by the University into the accounts of the State of Wisconsin.

The fees are drawn upon by the University to support various campus services and extracurricular student activities. In the University's view, the activity fees "enhance the educational experience" of its students by "promot[ing] extracurricular activities," "stimulating advocacy and debate on diverse points of view," enabling "participa[tion] in political activity," "promot[ing] student participa[tion] in campus administrative activity," and providing "opportunities to develop social skills," all consistent with the University's mission....

[Twenty percent] of the fee supports extracurricular endeavors pursued by the University's registered student organizations or RSO's. To qualify for RSO status students must organize as a not-for-profit group, limit membership primarily to students, and agree to undertake activities related to student life on campus.

During the 1995-1996 school year, 623 groups had RSO status on the Madison campus.... RSO's included the Future Financial Gurus of America; the International Socialist Organization; the College Democrats; the College Republicans; and the American Civil Liberties Union Campus Chapter. As one would expect, the expressive activities undertaken by RSO's are diverse in range and content, from displaying posters and circulating newsletters throughout the campus, to hosting campus debates and guest speakers, and to what can best be described as political lobbying.

RSO's may obtain a portion of the allocable fees [by seeking money from fee funds administered by the student government] .... [Funded RSO's] included a campus tutoring center, the student radio station, a student environmental group, a gay and bisexual student center, a community legal office, an AIDS support network, a campus women's center, and the Wisconsin Student Public Interest Research Group (WISPIRG).... [I]n addition to providing campus services (*e.g.*, tutoring and counseling), ... funded RSO's engage in political and ideological expression.... The parties have stipulated that, with respect to [such] funding, "[t]he process for reviewing and approving allocations for funding is administered in a viewpoint-neutral fashion" ....

A student referendum provides [another] means for an RSO to obtain funding.... [T]he student body can vote either to approve or to disapprove an assessment for a particular RSO. One referendum resulted in an allocation of $45,000 to WISPIRG during the 1995-1996 academic year.... [A] referendum could also operate to defund an RSO or to veto a funding decision of the [student government].... [The] stipulation regarding the program's viewpoint neutrality does not extend to the referendum process....

[Respondents, who are or were students, sued, contending] ... the University must grant them the choice not to fund those RSO's that engage in political and ideological expression offensive to their personal beliefs....

[B.] It is inevitable that government will adopt and pursue programs and policies within its constitutional powers but which nevertheless are contrary to the profound beliefs and sincere convictions of some of its citizens. The government, as a general rule, may support valid programs and policies by taxes or other exactions binding on protesting parties. Within this broader principle it seems inevitable that funds raised by the government will be spent for speech and other expression to advocate and defend its own policies. See, *e.g., Rust v. Sullivan*....

[But here t]he University's whole justification for fostering the challenged expression is that it springs from the initiative of the students, who alone give it purpose and content in the course of their extracurricular endeavors. The University having disclaimed that the speech is its own, we do not reach the question whether traditional political controls to ensure responsible government action would be sufficient to overcome First Amendment objections and to allow the challenged program under the principle that the government can speak for itself. If the challenged speech here were financed by tuition dollars and the University and its officials were responsible for its content, the case might be evaluated on the premise that the government itself is the speaker....

[C.] The University of Wisconsin exacts the fee at issue for the sole purpose of facilitating the free and open exchange of ideas by, and among, its students. We conclude the objecting students may insist upon certain safeguards with respect to the expressive activities which they are required to support.

Our public forum cases are instructive here by close analogy. This is true even though the student activities fund is not a public forum in the traditional sense of the term and despite the circumstance that those cases most often involve a demand for access, not a claim to be exempt from supporting speech. The standard of viewpoint neutrality found in the public forum cases provides the standard we find controlling. We decide that the viewpoint neutrality requirement of the University program is in general sufficient to protect the rights of the objecting students.

[D.] The student referendum aspect of the program for funding speech and expressive activities ... appears to be inconsistent with the viewpoint neutrality requirement. {It is unclear to us what protection, if any, there is for viewpoint neutrality in this part of the process. To the extent the referendum substitutes majority determinations for viewpoint neutrality it would undermine the constitutional protection the program requires.

The whole theory of viewpoint neutrality is that minority views are treated with the same respect as are majority views. Access to a public forum, for instance, does not depend upon majoritarian consent. That principle is controlling here. A remand is necessary and appropriate to resolve this point ....}

[E.] [As to nonreferendum funding, i]f the University conditions the opportunity to receive a college education, an opportunity comparable in importance to joining a labor union or bar association, on an agreement to support objectionable, extracurricular expression by other students, the rights acknowledged in *Abood v. Detroit Bd. of Ed.* and *Keller v. State Bar* become implicated. It infringes on the speech and beliefs of the individual to be required, by this mandatory student activity fee program, to pay subsidies for the objectionable speech of others without any recognition of the State's corresponding duty to him or her.

Yet recognition must be given as well to the important and substantial purposes of the University, which seeks to facilitate a wide range of speech. In *Abood* and *Keller* the constitutional rule took the form of limiting the required subsidy to speech germane to the purposes of the union or bar association. The standard of germane speech as applied to student speech at a university is unworkable, however ....

[I]t is difficult to define germane speech with ease or precision where a union or bar association is the party[. T]he standard becomes all the more unmanageable in the public university setting, particularly where the State undertakes to stimulate the whole universe of speech and ideas.

The speech the University seeks to encourage in the program before us is distinguished not by discernable limits but by its vast, unexplored bounds. To insist upon asking what speech is germane would be contrary to the very goal the University seeks to pursue. It is not for the Court to say what is or is not germane to the ideas to be pursued in an institution of higher learning....

If the standard of germane speech is inapplicable, then, it might be argued the remedy is to allow each student to list those causes which he or she will or will not support.... We decline to impose a system of that sort as a constitutional requirement, however. The restriction could be so disruptive and expensive that the program to support extracurricular speech would be ineffective. The First Amendment does not require the University to put the program at risk.

The University may determine that its mission is well served if students have the means to engage in dynamic discussions of philosophical, religious, scientific, social, and political subjects in their extracurricular campus life outside the lecture hall. If the University reaches this conclusion, it is entitled to impose a mandatory fee to sustain an open dialogue to these ends [so long as the program is viewpoint-neutral]....

Justice Souter, with whom Justice Stevens and Justice Breyer join, concurring in the judgment....

I agree that the University's scheme is permissible, but do not believe that the Court should take the occasion to impose a cast-iron viewpoint neutrality requirement [for the disbursement scheme]. {[T]he referendum issue was not adequately addressed in the [lower courts], and I would say nothing more on that subject.} ...

Indirectly transmitting a fraction of a student activity fee to an organization with an offensive message is in no sense equivalent to restricting or modifying the message a student wishes to express. Cf. *Hurley v. Irish-American Gay, Lesbian and Bisexual Group of Boston.* Nor does it require an individual to bear an offensive statement personally, as in *Wooley v. Maynard,* let alone to affirm a moral or political commitment, as in *W. Va. State Bd. of Ed. v. Barnette.* In each of these cases, the government was imposing far more directly and offensively on an objecting individual than collecting the fee that indirectly funds the jumble of other speakers' messages in this case....

[T]he *Abood* and *Keller* line of cases [also] does not control [here] .... First, the relationship between the fee payer and the ultimately objectionable expression is far more attenuated [than in those cases]. In the union and bar association cases, an individual was required to join or at least drop money in the coffers of the very organization promoting messages subject to objection. The connection between the forced contributor and the ultimate message was as direct as the unmediated contribution to the organization doing the speaking.

The student contributor, however, has to fund only a distributing agency having itself no social, political, or ideological character and itself engaging (as all parties agree) in no expression of any distinct message. Indeed, the disbursements, varying from year to year, are as likely as not to fund an organization that disputes the very message an individual student finds exceptionable. Thus, the clear connection between fee payer and offensive speech that loomed large in our decisions in the union and bar cases is simply not evident here.

Second, ... the challenged fees support a government program that aims to broaden public discourse.... [T]he university fee at issue is a tax. The state university compels it; it is paid into state accounts; and it is disbursed under the ultimate authority of the State.... [T]he government may properly use its tax revenue to promote general discourse....

Third, ... some educational value is derived from the activities supported by the fee, whereas there was no governmental interest in mandating union or bar association support beyond supporting the collective bargaining and professional regulatory functions of those organizations, see *Abood*. Nor was there any legitimate governmental interest in requiring the publication or affirmation of propositions with which the bearer or speaker did not agree. *Wooley*; *Barnette*.

Finally, ... [university] students are inevitably required to support the expression of personally offensive viewpoints .... No one disputes that some fraction of students' tuition payments may be used for course offerings that are ideologically offensive to some students, and for paying professors who say things in the university forum that are radically at odds with the politics of particular students.

Least of all does anyone claim that the University is somehow required to offer a spectrum of courses to satisfy a viewpoint neutrality requirement. The University need not provide junior years abroad in North Korea as well as France, instruct in the theory of plutocracy as well as democracy, or teach Nietzsche as well as St. Thomas. Since uses of tuition payments ... may fund offensive speech far more obviously than the student activity fee does, it is difficult to see how the activity fee could present a stronger argument for a refund....

F. Restrictions That Affect Newsgathering

1. Right of Access to Government Property and Operations

a. Summary

Limiting people's ability to gather information about certain subjects interferes with their ability to speak about those subjects, and interferes with listeners' ability to hear about those subjects. If no-one can attend a criminal trial, reporters will find it much harder to accurately report what happened at the trial.

At the same time, the Court has rejected the view that there is a First Amendment right to attend all government proceedings—*e.g.*, jury deliberations, executive agency meetings, and so on—or to access government documents. (The federal Freedom of Information Act and many state public records acts let the public access various documents, but those statutes stem from legislative decision, not constitutional command.) Instead, it has created a much narrower rule of constitutionally compelled access.

Rule:

1. The public and the media generally don't have a constitutional right to access government documents, government property (except traditional public fora, which consist of streets, sidewalks, and parks), or government-run proceedings.

2. But there is a right to access judicial proceedings, especially criminal trials (*Richmond Newspapers, Inc. v. Virginia* (1980) (p. 563)), jury selection in criminal trials (*Press-Enterprise Co. v. Superior Court (I)*, 464 U.S. 501 (1984)), certain preliminary hearings but not grand jury hearings (*Press-Enterprise Co. v. Superior Court (II)*, 478 U.S. 1 (1986)), and possibly also civil trials (*Richmond Newspapers*).

   a. To determine which proceedings qualify, the Court generally looks to whether "the place and process have historically been open to the press and general public" and "whether public access plays a significant positive role in the functioning of the particular process in question" (*Press-Enterprise (II)*).   *Ask*

   — The Court asks this about the type of proceeding generally (*e.g.*, a criminal trial) and not the specific subtype (*e.g.*, criminal trials involving minor sex victims). *Globe Newspaper Co. v. Superior Court* (1982) (p. 568) ("Whether the First Amendment right of access to criminal trials can be restricted in the context of any particular criminal trial ... depends not on the historical openness of that type of criminal trial but rather on the state interests assertedly supporting the restriction.").

   b. Even where this right to access is presumptively available, the government may still close the proceedings if the closure satisfies strict scrutiny (*Globe Newspaper*).   *Strict Scrutiny*

   — Under strict scrutiny, the court must "consider whether alternatives short of complete closure would have protected the interests of the accused." For instance, though "[p]ublicity concerning the proceedings at a pretrial hearing ... could influence public opinion against a defendant and inform potential jurors of inculpatory information wholly inadmissible at the actual trial," "this risk of prejudice does not automatically justify refusing public access to hearings on every motion to suppress. Through *voir dire*, cumbersome as it is in some circumstances, a court can identify those jurors whose prior knowledge of the case would disable them from rendering an impartial verdict.

"And even if closure were justified for the hearings on a motion to suppress, closure of an entire 41-day proceeding would rarely be warranted. The First Amendment right of access cannot be overcome by the conclusory assertion that publicity might deprive the defendant of [his fair trial] right. And any limitation must be 'narrowly tailored to serve that interest.'" *Press-Enterprise (II)*.

3. Discriminatory exclusion of the media from places that are generally open to others is probably unconstitutional (see *Houchins v. KQED* (1978) (p. 558), especially Justice Stewart's concurrence).

— It's possible—but not entirely clear—that this "equal access" requirement might sometimes let the media use special equipment, such as cameras, that lets them convey to viewers what individual visitors can see with their own eyes (see Justice Stewart in *Houchins*).

b. *Problem: University Disciplinary Hearings*

Assume that UCLA, a state-run university, has a policy of keeping student disciplinary hearings strictly confidential. This is applied even to hearings that may lead to a student's being expelled.

Alan Athlete, a prominent UCLA basketball player, is accused by an ex-girlfriend of trying to rape her. UCLA begins disciplinary proceedings against Alan. Also, the ex-girlfriend goes to a state court and asks for a restraining order against Alan, ordering him not to contact her and not to approach within 200 feet of her.

The UCLA student newspaper (*The Daily Bruin*) seeks access to the UCLA disciplinary hearing, but the administration refuses. The *Bruin* also seeks access to the restraining order hearing, which the judge has closed pursuant to a statute that allows such closures at the judge's discretion. The *Bruin* sues, claiming that it has a First Amendment right of access to both hearings. What should happen, given the Court's right of access jurisprudence? Is this a sound result?

c. *Houchins v. KQED, Inc., 438 U.S. 1 (1978)*

Chief Justice Burger ... delivered an opinion, in which Justice White and Justice Rehnquist joined.

The question presented is whether the news media have a constitutional right of access to a county jail, over and above that of other persons, to interview inmates and make sound recordings, films, and photographs for publication and broadcasting by newspapers, radio, and television.

[A.] Petitioner Houchins, as Sheriff of Alameda County, Cal., controls all access to the Alameda County Jail at Santa Rita.... On March 31, 1975, KQED [a local TV and radio station operator] reported the suicide of a prisoner in the Greystone portion of the Santa Rita jail. The report included a statement by a psychiatrist that the conditions at the Greystone facility were responsible for the illnesses of his patient-prisoners there, and a statement from petitioner denying that prison conditions were responsible for the prisoners' illnesses.

KQED requested permission to inspect and take pictures within the Greystone facility. After permission was refused, KQED [sued] ....

[Shortly after KQED's lawsuit, the Sheriff instituted a regular but limited public prison tour program] .... [R]espondents presented testimony and affidavits stating that other penal complexes had permitted media interviews of inmates and substantial media access without experiencing significant security or administrative problems. They contended that the monthly public tours at Santa Rita failed to provide adequate access to the jail for two reasons: (a) once the scheduled tours had been filled, media representatives who had not signed up for them had no access and were unable to cover newsworthy events at the jail; (b) the prohibition on photography and tape recordings, the exclusion of portions of the jail [the disciplinary cells and the portions of the jail known as "Little Greystone," the scene of alleged rapes, beatings, and adverse physical conditions,] from the tours, and the practice of keeping inmates generally removed from view substantially reduced the usefulness of the tours to the media....

[The Sheriff] did not claim that disruption had been caused by media access to other institutions. He asserted, however, that unregulated access by the media would infringe inmate privacy[.] {Inmates ... are not like animals in a zoo to be filmed and photographed at will by the public or by media reporters, however "educational" the process may be for others.} [He also asserted that unregulated access would] tend to create "jail celebrities," who in turn tend to generate internal problems and undermine jail security. He also contended that unscheduled media tours would disrupt jail operations....

[T]he District Court preliminarily enjoined petitioner from denying KQED news personnel and "responsible representatives" of the news media access to the Santa Rita facilities, including Greystone, "at reasonable times and hours" and "from preventing KQED news personnel and responsible representatives of the news media from utilizing photographic and sound equipment or from utilizing inmate interviews in providing full and accurate coverage of the Santa Rita facilities." ...

[B.] The public importance of conditions in penal facilities and the media's role of providing information afford no basis for reading into the Constitution a right of the public or the media to enter these institutions, with camera equipment, and take moving and still pictures of inmates for broadcast purposes.... [T]he Court [has been] concerned with the freedom of the media to *communicate* information once it is obtained; [but the Constitution does not compel] ... the government to provide the media with information or access to it on demand....

"[T]here are few restrictions on action which could not be clothed by ingenious argument in the garb of decreased data flow. For example, the prohibition of unauthorized entry into the White House diminishes the citizen's opportunities to gather information he might find relevant to his opinion of the way the country is being run, but that does not make entry into the White House a First Amendment right. *The right to speak and publish does not carry with it the unrestrained right to gather information.*"

The right to *receive* ideas and information is not the issue in this case. The issue is a claimed special privilege of access ..., a right which is not essential to guarantee the freedom to communicate or publish....

The respondents' argument ... invites the Court to involve itself in what is clearly a legislative task which the Constitution has left to the political processes. Whether the government should open penal institutions in the manner sought by respondents is a question of policy which a legislative body might appropriately resolve one way or the other....

Petitioner cannot prevent respondents from learning about jail conditions in a variety of ways, albeit not as conveniently as they might prefer. Respondents have a First Amendment right to receive letters from inmates criticizing jail officials and reporting on conditions. Respondents are free to interview those who render the legal assistance to which inmates are entitled. They are also free to seek out former inmates, visitors to the prison, public officials, and institutional personnel, as they sought out the complaining psychiatrist here.

Moreover, California statutes currently provide for a prison Board of Corrections that has the authority to inspect jails and prisons and *must* provide a public report at regular intervals. Health inspectors are required to inspect prisons and provide reports to a number of officials, including the State Attorney General and the Board of Corrections. Fire officials are also required to inspect prisons. Following the reports of the suicide at the jail involved here, the County Board of Supervisors called for a report from the County Administrator; held a public hearing on the report, which was open to the media; and called for further reports when the initial report failed to describe the conditions in the cells in the Greystone portion of the jail.... [U]ntil the political branches decree otherwise, as they are free to do, the media have no special right of access to the Alameda County Jail different from or greater than that accorded the public generally....

Justice Marshall and Justice Blackmun [did not participate].

Justice Stewart, concurring in the judgment....

[The First Amendment does not] guarantee the public a right of access to information generated or controlled by government, nor [does it] guarantee the press any basic right of access superior to that of the public generally. The Constitution does no more than assure the public and the press equal access once government has opened its doors....

[But whereas the Chief Justice] appears to view "equal access" as meaning access that is identical in all respects, I believe that the concept of equal access must be accorded more flexibility in order to accommodate the practical distinctions between the press and the general public.... That the First Amendment speaks separately of freedom of speech and freedom of the press is no constitutional accident, but an acknowledgment of the critical role played by the press in American society. The Constitution requires sensitivity to that role, and to the special needs of the press in performing it effectively.

A person touring Santa Rita jail can grasp its reality with his own eyes and ears. But if a television reporter is to convey the jail's sights and sounds to those who cannot personally visit the place, he must use cameras and sound equipment. In short, terms of access that are reasonably imposed on individual members of the public may, if they impede effective reporting without sufficient justification, be unreasonable as applied to journalists who are there to convey to the general public what the visitors see.... [The First Amendment] required the Sheriff to give members of the press *effective* access to the same areas [that the public was allowed to visit, and not] ... simply by allowing reporters to sign up for tours on the same terms as the public....

The District Court found that the press required access to the jail on a more flexible and frequent basis than scheduled monthly tours if it was to keep the public informed.... The District Court also found that the media required cameras and recording equipment for effective presentation to the viewing public of the conditions at the jail seen by individual visitors, and that their use could be kept consistent with institutional needs. These elements of the court's order were ... sanctioned by the Constitution ....

In two respects, however, the District Court's preliminary injunction was overbroad. It ordered the Sheriff to permit reporters into the Little Greystone facility and it required him to let them interview randomly encountered inmates. In both these respects, the injunction gave the press access to areas and sources of information from which persons on the public tours had been excluded, and thus enlarged the scope of what the Sheriff and Supervisors had opened to public view. The District Court erred in concluding that the First ... Amendment[] compelled this broader access for the press....

Justice Stevens, with whom Justice Brennan and Justice Powell join, dissenting....

The preservation of a full and free flow of information to the general public has long been recognized as a core objective of the First Amendment to the Constitution. It is for this reason that the First Amendment protects not only the dissemination but also the receipt of information and ideas....

Our system of self-government assumes the existence of an informed citizenry. As Madison wrote: "A popular Government, without popular information, or the means of acquiring it, is but a Prologue to a Farce or a Tragedy; or, perhaps both. Knowledge will forever govern ignorance: And a people who mean to be their own Governors, must arm themselves with the power which knowledge gives."

It is not sufficient, therefore, that the channels of communication be free of governmental restraints. Without some protection for the acquisition of information about the operation of public institutions such as prisons by the public at large, the process of self-governance contemplated by the Framers would be stripped of its substance. {"[T]he protection of the Bill of Rights goes beyond the specific guarantees to protect from ... abridgement those equally fundamental personal rights necessary to make the express guarantees fully meaningful...."} For that reason information gathering is entitled to some measure of constitutional protection....

{[T]he inmates' visitation and telephone privileges were [not] reasonable alternative means of informing the public at large about conditions within Santa Rita. Neither offered an opportunity to observe those conditions. Even if a member of the general public or a representative of the press were fortunate enough to obtain the name of an inmate to visit, access to the facility would not have included the inmate's place of confinement.... [And e]ven if a maximum-security inmate [who wants to complain about jail conditions] may make collect telephone calls, it is unlikely that a member of the general public or representative of the press would accept the charges, especially without prior knowledge of the call's communicative purpose.}

[T]he degree of public disclosure which should attend the operation of most governmental activity ... involve[s] questions of policy which generally must be resolved by the political branches of government. Moreover, there are unquestionably occasions when governmental activity may properly be carried on in complete secrecy. For example, the public and the press are commonly excluded from "grand jury proceedings, our own conferences, [and] the meetings of other official bodies gathered in executive session ...." In addition, some functions of government—essential to the protection of the public and indeed our country's vital interests—necessarily require a large measure of secrecy, subject to appropriate legislative oversight. In such situations the reasons for withholding information from the public are both apparent and legitimate....

[But prison] conditions are wholly without claim to confidentiality.... [T]here is no legitimate penological justification for concealing from citizens the conditions in which their fellow citizens are being confined.... Not only are [prisons] public institutions, financed with public funds and administered by public servants, they are an integral component of the criminal justice system.... [The] public interest [in the integrity of the trial, which is

Carries over

reflected in the Sixth Amendment's Public Trial Clause,] survives the judgment of conviction and appropriately carries over to an interest in how the convicted person is treated during his period of punishment and hoped-for rehabilitation.... [The convict] retains constitutional protections against cruel and unusual punishment, a protection which may derive more practical support from access to information about prisons by the public than by occasional litigation in a busy court.

Some inmates—in Santa Rita, a substantial number—are pretrial detainees. Though confined pending trial, they have not been convicted of an offense against society and are entitled to the presumption of innocence.... Society has a special interest in ensuring that unconvicted citizens are treated in accord with their status.

In this case, the [First Amendment claim does not depend] ... on any right of the press to special treatment beyond that accorded the public at large. Rather, the probable existence of a constitutional violation rest[s] upon the special importance of allowing a democratic community access to knowledge about how its servants were treating some of its members who have been committed to their custody....

d. *Richmond Newspapers, Inc. v. Virginia, 448 U.S. 555 (1980)*

Chief Justice Burger ... delivered an opinion, in which Justice White and Justice Stevens joined.

The narrow question presented in this case is whether the right of the public and press to attend criminal trials is guaranteed under the United States Constitution.

Crim trials

[A.] In March 1976, one Stevenson was indicted for the murder of a hotel manager .... Tried promptly in July 1976, Stevenson was convicted of second-degree murder .... The Virginia Supreme Court reversed the conviction in October 1977, holding that a bloodstained shirt purportedly belonging to Stevenson had been improperly admitted into evidence....

[Stevenson's] second trial ended in a mistrial on May 30, 1978, when a juror asked to be excused after trial had begun and no alternate was available. {A newspaper account published the next day reported the mistrial and went on to note that "[a] key piece of evidence in Stevenson's original conviction was a bloodstained shirt obtained from Stevenson's wife soon after the killing...."} A third trial, which began in the same court on June 6, 1978, also ended in a mistrial. It appears that the mistrial may have been declared because a prospective juror had read about Stevenson's previous trials in a newspaper and had told other prospective jurors about the case ....

Juror
Read article
└ told others

Stevenson was tried in the same court for a fourth time beginning on September 11, 1978.... Before the trial began, counsel for the defendant moved that it be closed to the public: "[T]here was this woman that was with the family of the deceased when we were here before. She had sat in the Courtroom. I would like to ask that everybody be excluded from the Courtroom because I don't want any information being shuffled back and forth when we have a recess as to what—who testified to what."

← Δ counsel (wanted closed trial)

[The prosecution had no objection.] ... The trial judge, who had presided over two of the three previous trials ... ordered "that the Courtroom be kept clear of all parties except the witnesses when they testify." {Virginia Code § 19.2-266 provides in part: "In the trial of all criminal cases, ... the court may ... exclude from the trial any persons whose presence would impair the conduct of a fair trial, provided that the right of the accused to a public trial shall not be violated."} ... [A]ppellants sought a hearing on a motion to vacate the closure order.... [C]ounsel for appellants observed that no evidentiary findings had been made by the court prior to the entry of its closure order and pointed out that the court had failed to consider any other, less drastic measures within its power to ensure a fair trial....

Counsel for defendant Stevenson pointed out that this was the fourth time he was standing trial. He also referred to "difficulty with information between the jurors," and stated that he "didn't want information to leak out," be published by the media, perhaps inaccurately, and then be seen by the jurors. Defense counsel argued that these things, plus the fact that "this is a small community," made this a proper case for closure.... The court ... ordered the trial to continue the following morning "with the press and public excluded." {At oral argument, it was represented to the Court that tapes of the trial were available to the public as soon as the trial terminated.} ...

[B.] [T]hroughout its [Anglo-American] evolution, the [criminal] trial has been open to all who cared to observe. [Long historical discussion omitted.—ed.] ... This [openness] is no quirk of history; rather, it has long been recognized as an indispensable attribute of an Anglo-American trial. Both Hale in the 17th century and Blackstone in the 18th saw the importance of openness to the proper functioning of a trial; it gave assurance that the proceedings were conducted fairly to all concerned, and it discouraged perjury, the misconduct of participants, and decisions based on secret bias or partiality. Jeremy Bentham not only recognized the therapeutic value of open justice but regarded it as the keystone:

"Without publicity, all other checks are insufficient: in comparison [to] publicity, all other checks are of small account. Recordation, appeal, whatever other institutions might present themselves in the character of checks, would be found to operate rather as cloaks than checks; as cloaks in reality, as checks only in appearance." ...

The early history of open trials in part reflects the widespread acknowledgment ... that public trials had significant community therapeutic value.... [E]specially in the administration of criminal justice, the means used to achieve justice must have the support derived from public acceptance of both the process and its results. When a shocking crime occurs, a community reaction of outrage and public protest often follows. Thereafter the open processes of justice serve an important prophylactic purpose, providing an outlet for community concern, hostility, and emotion.

Without an awareness that society's responses to criminal conduct are underway, natural human reactions of outrage and protest are frustrated and may manifest themselves in some form of vengeful "self-help" .... "The accusation and conviction or acquittal, as much perhaps as the execution of punishment, operat[e] to restore the imbalance which was created by the offense or public charge, to reaffirm the temporarily lost feeling of security and, perhaps, to satisfy that latent 'urge to punish.'" ... [But] no community catharsis can occur if justice is "done in a ... covert manner."

It is not enough to say that results alone will satiate the natural community desire for "satisfaction." ... [W]here the trial has been concealed from public view an unexpected outcome can cause a reaction that the system at best has failed and at worst has been corrupted.... [I]t is important that society's criminal process "satisfy the appearance of justice," and the appearance of justice can best be provided by allowing people to observe it....

People in an open society do not demand infallibility from their institutions, but it is difficult for them to accept what they are prohibited from observing. When a criminal trial is conducted in the open, there is at least an opportunity both for understanding the system in general and its workings in a particular case .... [And] people now acquire [information about trials] chiefly through the print and electronic media.... From this unbroken ... history, supported by reasons as valid today as in centuries past, we are bound to conclude that a presumption of openness inheres in the very nature of a criminal trial under our system of justice....

[C.] The Bill of Rights was enacted against the backdrop of the long history of trials being presumptively open. Public access to trials was then regarded as an important aspect of the process itself; the conduct of trials "before as many of the people as chuse to attend" was regarded as one of "the inestimable advantages of a free English constitution of government." In guaranteeing freedoms such as those of speech and press, the First Amendment can be read as protecting the right of everyone to attend trials so as to give meaning to those explicit guarantees.

"[T]he First Amendment goes beyond protection of the press and the self-expression of individuals to prohibit government from limiting the stock of information from which members of the public may draw." ... "In a variety of contexts this Court has referred to a First Amendment right to 'receive information and ideas.'" What this means in the context of trials is that the First Amendment guarantees of speech and press, standing alone, prohibit government from summarily closing courtroom doors which had long been open to the public at the time that Amendment was adopted....

"[W]ithout some protection for seeking out the news, freedom of the press could be eviscerated." The explicit, guaranteed rights to speak and to publish concerning what takes place at a trial would lose much meaning if access to observe the trial could, as it was here, be foreclosed arbitrarily.

[D.] The right of access to places traditionally open to the public, as criminal trials have long been, may be seen as assured by the amalgam of the First Amendment guarantees of speech and press; and their affinity to the right of assembly is not without relevance. From the outset, the right of assembly was regarded not only as an independent right but also as a catalyst to augment the free exercise of the other First Amendment rights with which it was deliberately linked by the draftsmen....

People assemble in public places not only to speak or to take action, but also to listen, observe, and learn; indeed, they may "assembl[e] for any lawful purpose." Subject to the traditional time, place, and manner restrictions, streets, sidewalks, and parks are places traditionally open, where First Amendment rights may be exercised; a trial courtroom also is a public place where the people generally—and representatives of the media—have a right to be present, and where their presence historically has been thought to enhance the integrity and quality of what takes place....

{[Prison access cases] ... were concerned with penal institutions which, by definition, are not "open" or public places. Penal institutions do not share the long tradition of openness ....}

[E.] Notwithstanding the appropriate caution against reading into the Constitution rights not explicitly defined, the Court has acknowledged that certain unarticulated rights ...[—f]or example, the rights of association and of privacy, the right to be presumed innocent, and the right to be judged by a standard of proof beyond a reasonable doubt in a criminal trial, as well as the right to travel[—are] indispensable to the enjoyment of rights explicitly defined. We hold that the right to attend criminal trials is implicit in the guarantees of the First Amendment; without the freedom to attend such trials, which people have exercised for centuries, important aspects of freedom of speech and "of the press could be eviscerated." {Whether the public has a right to attend trials of civil cases is a question not raised by this case, but we note that historically both civil and criminal trials have been presumptively open.} ...

[F.] [T]he trial judge made no findings to support closure; no inquiry was made as to whether alternative solutions would have met the need to ensure fairness .... There was no suggestion that any problems with witnesses could not have been dealt with by their exclusion from the courtroom or their sequestration during the trial. Nor is there anything to indicate that sequestration of the jurors would not have guarded against their being subjected to any improper information. All of the alternatives admittedly present difficulties for trial courts, but none of the factors relied on here was beyond the realm of the manageable. Absent an overriding interest articulated in findings, the trial of a criminal case must be open ....

{[O]ur holding today does not mean that the First Amendment rights of the public and representatives of the press are absolute. Just as a government may impose reasonable time, place, and manner restrictions upon the use of its streets in the interest of such objectives as the free flow of traffic, so may a trial judge, in the interest of the fair administration of justice, impose reasonable limitations on access to a trial.... [And i]t is far more important that trials be conducted in a quiet and orderly setting than it is to preserve that atmosphere on city streets. Moreover, since courtrooms have limited capacity, there may be occasions when not every person who wishes to attend can be accommodated. In such situations, reasonable restrictions on general access are traditionally imposed, including preferential seating for media representatives.}

Justice Powell [did not participate].

Justice Brennan, with whom Justice Marshall joins, concurring in the judgment....

[A.] While freedom of expression ..., with only rare and stringent exceptions, may not be suppressed, the First Amendment has not been viewed by the Court in all settings as providing an equally categorical assurance of the correlative freedom of access to information. ... [A]ny privilege of access to governmental information is subject to a degree of restraint dictated by the nature of the information and countervailing interests in security or confidentiality....

[B]ecause "the stretch of this protection [for a right to gather news] is theoretically endless," it must be invoked with discrimination and temperance.... "[T]here are few restrictions on action which could not be clothed by ingenious argument in the garb of decreased data flow." An assertion of the prerogative to gather information must accordingly be assayed by considering the information sought and the opposing interests invaded....

[A]t least two helpful principles may be sketched. First, the case for a right of access has special force when drawn from an enduring and vital tradition of public entree to particular proceedings or information. Such a tradition commands respect in part because the Constitution carries the gloss of history. More importantly, a tradition of accessibility implies the favorable judgment of experience.

Second, the value of access must be measured in specifics. Analysis is not advanced by rhetorical statements that all information bears upon public issues; what is crucial in individual cases is whether access to a particular government process is important in terms of that very process.... [The opinion goes on to discuss the traditional openness of the trial, and the value of open trials to the community, much as does the majority. It also goes on to note the following:—ed.] ...

[B.] [T]he trial ... plays a pivotal role in the entire judicial process, and, by extension, in our form of government. Under our system, judges are not mere umpires, but, in their own sphere, lawmakers—a coordinate branch of *government*. While individual cases turn upon the controversies between parties, or involve particular prosecutions, court rulings impose official and practical consequences upon members of society at large. Moreover, judges bear responsibility for the vitally important task of construing and securing constitutional rights. Thus, ... the conduct of the trial is pre-eminently a matter of public interest.

More importantly, ... "[t]he knowledge that every criminal trial is subject to contemporaneous review in the forum of public opinion is an effective restraint on possible abuse of judicial power"—an abuse that, in many cases, would have ramifications beyond the impact upon the parties before the court....

Finally, with some limitations, a trial aims at true and accurate fact-finding.... Facilitation of the trial factfinding process ... is of concern to the public as well as to the parties. Publicizing trial proceedings aids accurate factfinding. "Public trials come to the attention of key witnesses unknown to the parties." ... "[O]pen examination of witnesses ... is much more conducive to the clearing up of truth, than the private and secret examination ... where a witness may frequently depose that in private, which he will be ashamed to testify in a public and solemn tribunal." ...

Aids factfinding

Popular attendance at trials, in sum, substantially furthers the particular public purposes of that critical judicial proceeding. {In advancing these purposes, the availability of a trial transcript is no substitute for a public presence at the trial itself.... [T]he "cold" record is a very imperfect reproduction of events that transpire in the courtroom....} In that sense, public access is an indispensable element of the trial process itself....

{The presumption of public trials is, of course, not at all incompatible with reasonable restrictions imposed upon courtroom behavior in the interests of decorum. Thus, when engaging in interchanges at the bench, the trial judge is not required to allow public or press intrusion upon the huddle. Nor does this opinion intimate that judges are restricted in their ability to conduct conferences in chambers, inasmuch as such conferences are distinct from trial proceedings.}

What countervailing interests [such as national security concerns] might be sufficiently compelling to reverse [the] presumption of openness need not concern us now, for the statute at stake here authorizes trial closures at the unfettered discretion of the judge and parties....

Unconstitutional

[C.] {[No contention that] the media should enjoy greater access rights than the general public ... is at stake here. Since the media's right of access is at least equal to that of the general public, this case is resolved by a decision that the state statute unconstitutionally restricts public access to trials. As a practical matter, however, the institutional press is the likely, and fitting, chief beneficiary of a right of access because it serves as the "agent" of interested citizens ....}

Justice Stewart, concurring in the judgment. [Justice Stewart mostly agreed with the preceding two opinions.—ed.] ...

Justice Blackmun, concurring in the judgment.... [Justice Blackmun took the view that the Sixth Amendment's Public Trial Clause entitled not just the defendant, but the public, to a public trial; but he concluded that "as a secondary position, that the First Amendment must provide some measure of protection for public access to the trial."—ed.]

1A secondary measure

Justice Rehnquist, dissenting....

Being unable to find any ... prohibition [on trial closures] in the First, Sixth, Ninth, or any other Amendment ..., I dissent.

e.   *Globe Newspaper Co. v. Superior Court, 457 U.S. 596 (1982)*

Justice Brennan delivered the opinion of the Court.

[A.] Section 16A of Chapter 278 of the Massachusetts General Laws ... requires trial judges, at trials for specified sexual offenses involving a victim under the age of 18, to exclude the press and general public from the court-room during the testimony of that victim.... Globe Newspaper Co.[] unsuc-cessfully attempted to gain access to a ... [trial in which the defendant] had been charged with the forcible rape ... of three girls who were minors at the time of trial—two 16 years of age and one 17....

Although the right of access to criminal trials is of constitutional stat-ure, it is not absolute. But the circumstances under which the press and public can be barred from a criminal trial are limited; the State's justifica-tion in denying access must be a weighty one. Where ... the State attempts to deny the right of access in order to inhibit the disclosure of sensitive in-formation, it must be shown that the denial is necessitated by a compelling governmental interest, and is narrowly tailored to serve that interest. {Of course, limitations on the right of access that resemble "time, place, and manner" restrictions ... would not be subjected to such strict scrutiny.} ...

{Appellee argues that criminal trials have not always been open to the press and general public during the testimony of minor sex victims. Even if appellee is correct in this regard, the argument is unavailing.... *Richmond Newspapers v. Virginia* [was] ... based in part on a recognition that as a general matter criminal trials have long been presumptively open. Whether the First Amendment right of access to criminal trials can be restricted in the context of any particular criminal trial ... depends not on the historical openness of that type of criminal trial but rather on the state interests as-sertedly supporting the restriction.}

[B.] The state interests asserted to support § 16A ... are reducible to two; the protection of minor victims of sex crimes from further trauma and em-barrassment; and the encouragement of such victims to come forward and testify in a truthful and credible manner....

[T]he first interest—safeguarding the physical and psychological well-being of a minor [by avoiding] {the incremental injury suffered by testifying in the presence of the press and the general public}—is a compelling one. But ... [the interest] does not justify a *mandatory* closure rule, for it is clear that the circumstances of the particular case may affect the significance of the interest. A trial court can determine on a case-by-case basis whether closure is necessary to protect the welfare of a minor victim. Among the fac-tors to be weighed are the minor victim's age, psychological maturity and understanding, the nature of the crime, the desires of the victim, and the interests of parents and relatives.

Section 16A, in contrast, requires closure even if the victim does not seek the exclusion of the press and general public, and would not suffer injury by their presence. In the case before us, for example, the names of the minor victims were already in the public record, and the record indicates that the victims may have been willing to testify despite the presence of the press. If the trial court had been permitted to exercise its discretion, closure might well have been deemed unnecessary.

Not narrowly tailored

In short, § 16A cannot be viewed as a narrowly tailored means of accommodating the State's asserted interest: That interest could be served just as well by requiring the trial court to determine on a case-by-case basis whether the State's legitimate concern for the well-being of the minor victim necessitates closure. Such an approach ensures that the constitutional right of the press and public to gain access to criminal trials will not be restricted except where necessary to protect the State's interest.

2

[C.] Nor can § 16A be justified on the basis of the Commonwealth's second asserted interest—the encouragement of minor victims of sex crimes to come forward and provide accurate testimony. The Commonwealth has offered no empirical support for the claim that the rule of automatic closure contained in § 16A will lead to an increase in the number of minor sex victims coming forward and cooperating with state authorities....

Doesn't achieve "secrecy"
L Not advanced

[Moreover, such a claim] is also open to serious question as a matter of logic and common sense. Although the press is not denied access [by § 16A] to the transcript, court personnel, or any other possible source that could provide an account of the minor victim's testimony. Thus § 16A cannot prevent the press from publicizing the substance of a minor victim's testimony, as well as his or her identity. If the Commonwealth's interest in encouraging minor victims to come forward depends on keeping such matters secret, § 16A hardly advances that interest in an effective manner.

Alternatives

And even if § 16A effectively advanced the State's interest, it is doubtful that the interest would be sufficient to overcome the constitutional attack, for that same interest could be relied on to support an array of mandatory closure rules designed to encourage victims to come forward: Surely it cannot be suggested that minor victims of sex crimes are the *only* crime victims who, because of publicity attendant to criminal trials, are reluctant to come forward and testify. The State's argument based on this interest therefore proves too much) and runs contrary to the very foundation of the right of access recognized in *Richmond Newspapers*: namely, "that a presumption of openness inheres in the very nature of a criminal trial under our system of justice."

{To the extent that it is suggested that, quite apart from encouraging minor victims to testify, § 16A improves the quality and credibility of testimony, the suggestion also is speculative. And while closure may have such an effect in particular cases, the Court has recognized that, *as a general matter,* "[o]penness in court proceedings may *improve* the quality of testimony." In the absence of any showing that closure would improve the quality of testimony of *all* minor sex victims, the State's interest certainly cannot justify a *mandatory* closure rule.}

Narrow Holding

[D.] {[O]ur holding is a narrow one: that a rule of mandatory closure respecting the testimony of minor sex victims is constitutionally infirm. In individual cases, and under appropriate circumstances, the First Amendment does not necessarily stand as a bar to the exclusion from the courtroom of the press and general public during the testimony of minor sex-offense victims.} ...

Chief Justice Burger, with whom Justice Rehnquist joins, dissenting.

[A.] Historically our society has gone to great lengths to protect minors *charged* with crime, particularly by prohibiting the release of the names of offenders, barring the press and public from juvenile proceedings, and sealing the records of those proceedings. Yet today the Court holds unconstitutional a state statute designed to protect not the *accused*, but the minor *victims* of sex crimes....

In *Richmond Newspapers,* ... [t]he opinions of a majority of the Justices emphasized the historical tradition of open criminal trials.... Today Justice Brennan ignores the weight of historical practice. There is clearly a long history of exclusion of the public from trials involving sexual assaults, particularly those against minors.... {[And i]t is hard to find a limiting principle in the Court's analysis. The same reasoning might require a hearing before a trial judge could hold a bench conference or any *in camera* proceedings.}

[B.] [C]onsidering the minimal impact of the law on First Amendment rights and the overriding weight of the Commonwealth's interest in protecting child rape victims, ... the Massachusetts law is not unconstitutional.... [T]he press and the public have prompt and full access [via a transcript] to all of the victim's testimony. Their additional interest in actually being present during the testimony is minimal....

The law need not be precisely tailored so long as the state's interest overrides the law's impact on First Amendment rights and the restrictions imposed further that interest.... [T]his law, which excludes the press and public only during the actual testimony of the child victim of a sex crime, rationally serves the Commonwealth's overriding interest in protecting the child from ... severe—possibly permanent—psychological damage....

The law also seems a rational response to the undisputed problem of the underreporting of ... sexual offenses. The Court rejects the Commonwealth's argument that § 16A is justified by its interest in encouraging minors to report sex crimes, finding the claim "speculative in empirical terms ...." There is no basis whatever for this cavalier disregard of the reality of human experience. It makes no sense to criticize the Commonwealth for its failure to offer empirical data in support of its rule; only by allowing state experimentation may such empirical evidence be produced....

The Court apparently believes that the statute does not prevent any significant trauma, embarrassment, or humiliation on the part of the victim simply because the press is not prevented from discovering and publicizing both the identity of the victim and the substance of the victim's testimony. Section 16A is intended not to preserve confidentiality, but to prevent the risk of severe psychological damage caused by having to relate the details of the crime in front of a crowd which inevitably will include voyeuristic strangers. In most states, that crowd may be expanded to include a live television audience, with returns on the evening news. That ordeal could be difficult for an adult; to a child, the experience can ... leave permanent scars.

[C.] The Commonwealth's interests are clearly furthered by the mandatory nature of the closure statute.... The legislature did not act irrationally in deciding not to leave the closure determination to the idiosyncracies of individual judges subject to the pressures available to the media. The victim might very well experience considerable distress prior to the court appearance, wondering, in the absence of such statutory protection, whether public testimony will be required.

The mere possibility of public testimony may cause parents and children to decide not to report these heinous crimes.... [W]e cannot expect victims and their parents to be aware of all of the nuances of state law; a person who sees newspaper, or perhaps even television, reports of a minor victim's testimony may very well be deterred from reporting a crime on the belief that public testimony will be required. It is within the power of the state to provide for mandatory closure to alleviate such understandable fears and encourage the reporting of such crimes.

2. NEWSGATHERERS AND GENERALLY APPLICABLE LAWS

a. Summary

Rule: The media generally aren't constitutionally entitled to exemptions from laws that apply equally to everyone, media or not.

Possible exception: Many lower courts have read Justice Powell's concurrence in *Branzburg v. Hayes* (see the anonymous speech section, p. 423) as letting journalists have a qualified privilege to refuse to testify about their confidential sources. See the brief discussion of the lower courts' treatment of *Branzburg* on p. 415.

State statutory and state constitutional protections: Some state statutes and state constitutional provisions do give the media special privileges, including in some instances a privilege not to testify.

b. Problem: Undercover News Operations

"[P]roducers of ABC's *PrimeTime Live* program received a report alleging that Food Lion stores were engaging in unsanitary meat-handling practices.... [Two ABC reporters applied] for jobs with the grocery chain, submitting applications with false identities and references and fictitious local addresses ... [T]he applications failed to mention the reporters' concurrent employment with ABC and otherwise misrepresented their educational and employment experiences....

"[The reporters worked for Food Lion for only several days. They] used tiny cameras ... and microphones concealed on their bodies to secretly record Food Lion employees treating, wrapping and labeling meat, cleaning machinery, and discussing the practices of the meat department.... Some of the videotape was eventually used in a ... broadcast of *PrimeTime Live*. ABC contends the footage confirmed many of the allegations initially leveled against Food Lion.... The truth of the *PrimeTime Live* broadcast was not an issue in the litigation we now describe.

"Food Lion sued ABC and the *PrimeTime Live* producers and reporters ... [for] fraud ... [and] trespass, ... seeking millions in compensatory damages. Specifically, Food Lion sought to recover (1) administrative costs and wages paid in connection with the employment of [the reporters] and (2) broadcast (publication) damages for matters such as loss of good will, lost sales and profits, and diminished stock value. Punitive damages were also requested by Food Lion.... [T]he jury found all of the ABC defendants liable to Food Lion for fraud and two of them, [the reporters], additionally liable for ... trespass...." The jury awarded Food Lion $1402 in compensatory damages and over $5.5 million in punitive damages, which the trial court later reduced to $315,000. *Food Lion, Inc. v. Capital Cities/ABC, Inc.*, 194 F.3d 505 (4th Cir. 1999).

Assume the reporters' actions constituted fraud and trespass, under state tort law that barred (1) making knowingly false statements in commercial transactions, including on job applications, and (2) secretly videotaping on another's property, when one was only given consent to enter and not to videotape. Should the damages award against Food Lion be set aside (in whole or in part) on First Amendment grounds?

c. Problem: Audiotaping Without Permission

Mass. Gen. Laws Ann. ch. 272, § 99 makes it a felony for any person (except a law enforcement official acting within his duties) to "secretly record" any oral statement unless the person has been "given prior authority by all parties to such communication."

Cal. Penal Code §§ 632, 633.5, 637.2 make it a misdemeanor—and a tort—for any person (outside law enforcement) to record any "confidential communication" "without the consent of all parties to [the] communication," except "for the purpose of obtaining evidence reasonably believed to relate to the commission by another party to the communication of the crime of extortion, kidnapping, bribery, [or] any felony involving violence against the person." "Confidential communication" is defined to "include[]"

> any communication carried on in circumstances as may reasonably indicate that any party to the communication desires it to be confined to the parties ..., but exclud[ing] a communication made in a public gathering ... or in any other circumstance in which the parties ... may reasonably expect that the communication may be overheard or recorded....

Federal law, and the law of most states, only bans secret recording of confidential communications if *no party* consents. But several states, including California and Massachusetts, require consent of all parties.

1. Michael Hyde secretly records what police officers say to him when they stop him for speeding. When he complains about the officers' behavior during the stop, and produces the recording as evidence, he is prosecuted under the statutes quoted above. Is this constitutional? Compare *Commonwealth v. Hyde*, 750 N.E.2d 963 (Mass. 2001) with *ACLU v. Alvarez*, 679 F.3d 583 (7th Cir. 2012); *Glik v. Cunniffe*, 655 F.3d 78 (1st Cir. 2011).

2. An investigative journalist for a local TV station hears that a local

immigrant rights advocacy group is quietly instructing illegal immigrants about how they can better avoid getting caught, and about who is likely to illegally hire them. Group officials have denied this, but the journalist thinks they're lying. He therefore pretends to be an illegal immigrant, asks one of the officials for advice, and secretly tape records the conversation. When he plays the recording on his TV program, he is prosecuted for violating the statutes described above. Is such a prosecution constitutional?

d. Problem: Confidentiality Agreements

When Joe Schmoe went to work for Caduceus Pharmaceuticals, he signed a contract promising not to reveal any confidential information that he learned on the job. A year later, he learned Caduceus was secretly developing a more effective abortion pill. Caduceus was keeping this information secret because it didn't want to anger pro-life forces any earlier than necessary, and didn't want to tip off competitors about its plans.

Schmoe believes abortion is murder, and immediately quits his job. He then posts on his personal Web log (which gets 1000 readers a day) a note explaining Caduceus's plans. Newspapers pick up the story. Caduceus sues Schmoe for breach of contract.

Schmoe asks the state courts to follow the *Cohen v. Cowles Media* dissents in interpreting the state constitution's free speech clause, the text of which is similar to the federal Free Speech Clause. (Recall that state courts may interpret their state constitutions as they like, and need not go along with what they see as erroneous federal decisions.) Should the court adopt the majority's rule, the dissents' rule, or some other rule?

e.   Cohen v. Cowles Media Co., 501 U.S. 663 (1991)

Justice White delivered the opinion of the Court....

[A.] During the closing days of the 1982 Minnesota gubernatorial race, Dan Cohen, an active Republican associated with Wheelock Whitney's Independent-Republican gubernatorial campaign, approached reporters from the St. Paul Pioneer Press Dispatch ... and the Minneapolis Star and Tribune ... and offered to provide documents relating to a candidate in the upcoming election. Cohen made clear to the reporters that he would provide the information only if he was given a promise of confidentiality.

Reporters from both papers promised to keep Cohen's identity anonymous, and Cohen turned over copies of two public court records concerning Marlene Johnson, the Democratic-Farmer-Labor candidate for Lieutenant Governor. The first record indicated that Johnson had been charged in 1969 with three counts of unlawful assembly, and the second that she had been convicted in 1970 of petit theft. Both newspapers interviewed Johnson for her explanation ....

As it turned out, the unlawful assembly charges arose out of Johnson's participation in a protest of an alleged failure to hire minority workers on municipal construction projects, and the charges were eventually dismissed. The petit theft conviction was for leaving a store without paying for $6 worth of sewing materials. The incident apparently occurred at a time during which Johnson was emotionally distraught, and the conviction was later vacated.

After consultation and debate, the editorial staffs of the two newspapers independently decided to publish Cohen's name as part of their stories concerning Johnson. In their stories, both papers identified Cohen as the source of the court records, indicated his connection to the Whitney campaign, and included denials by Whitney campaign officials of any role in the matter. The same day the stories appeared, Cohen was fired [from his job as director of public relations for the advertising agency that was handling the advertising for the Whitney campaign].

Cohen sued respondents, the publishers of the Pioneer Press and Star Tribune, in Minnesota state court .... [The Minnesota Supreme Court rejected his breach-of-contract claim on state law grounds, and went on to decide] whether Cohen could establish a cause of action under Minnesota law on a promissory estoppel theory.... [T]he court concluded that "in this case enforcement of the promise of confidentiality under a promissory estoppel theory would violate defendants' First Amendment rights." ...

[B.] [G]enerally applicable laws do not offend the First Amendment simply because their enforcement against the press has incidental effects on its ability to gather and report the news.... The press may not with impunity break and enter an office or dwelling to gather news. Neither does the First Amendment relieve a newspaper reporter of the obligation shared by all citizens to respond to a grand jury subpoena and answer questions relevant to a criminal investigation, even though the reporter might be required to reveal a confidential source. *Branzburg v. Hayes.*

The press, like others interested in publishing, may not publish copyrighted material without obeying the copyright laws. *Zacchini v. Scripps-Howard Broadcasting Co.* Similarly, the media must obey the National Labor Relations Act and the Fair Labor Standards Act, may not restrain trade in violation of the antitrust laws; and must pay nondiscriminatory taxes.... "[T]he publisher of a newspaper has no special immunity from the application of general laws. He has no special privilege to invade the rights and liberties of others." ... {The dissenting opinions suggest that the press should not be subject to any law, including copyright law for example, which in any fashion or to any degree limits or restricts the press' right to report truthful information. The First Amendment does not grant the press such limitless protection.}

[T]he Minnesota doctrine of promissory estoppel is a law of general applicability. It does not target or single out the press.... [T]he doctrine is generally applicable to the daily transactions of all the citizens of Minnesota. The First Amendment does not forbid its application to the press.... *General law*

[C.] [In] cases like *Florida Star v. B.J.F.*[,] ... the State itself defined the content of publications that would trigger liability. Here, by contrast, Minnesota law simply requires those making promises to keep them. The parties themselves ... determine the scope of their legal obligations, and any *Unlike FL Star* restrictions which may be placed on the publication of truthful information are self-imposed. Also, ... [unlike] in *Florida Star*, where the rape victim's name was obtained through lawful access to a police report, respondents obtained Cohen's name only by making a promise which they did not honor....

Nor is Cohen attempting to use a promissory estoppel cause of action to avoid the strict requirements for establishing a libel ... claim.... Cohen is not seeking damages for injury to his reputation or his state of mind. He sought damages in excess of $50,000 for a breach of a promise that caused him to lose his job and lowered his earning capacity. Thus, this is not a case like *Hustler Magazine, Inc. v. Falwell*, 485 U.S. 46 (1988), where we held that the constitutional libel standards apply to a claim alleging that the publication of a parody was a state-law tort of intentional infliction of emotional distress....

Justice Blackmun, with whom Justice Marshall and Justice Souter join, dissenting....

I do not read the decision of the Supreme Court of Minnesota to create any exception to, or immunity from, the laws of that State for members of the press.... [T]he First Amendment protection afforded respondents would be equally available to nonmedia defendants. The majority's admonition that "[t]he publisher of a newspaper has no special immunity from the application of general laws," and its reliance on the cases that support that principle, are therefore misplaced....

[Moreover, the cases the majority cites as involving generally applicable laws] did *not* involve the imposition of liability based upon the content of speech. {[In t]he only arguable exception[,] *Zacchini*[,] ... [w]e made clear ... that our holding did not extend to the reporting of *information* about an event of public interest.} ... *Hustler* [is] precisely on point.... There was no doubt that Virginia's tort of intentional infliction of emotional distress was "a law of general applicability" unrelated to the suppression of speech. Nonetheless, a unanimous Court found that, when used to penalize the expression of opinion, the law was subject to the strictures of the First Amendment....

{The majority attempts to distinguish *Hustler* on the ground that there the plaintiff sought damages for injury to his state of mind whereas the petitioner here sought damages "for a breach of a promise that caused him to lose his job and lowered his earning capacity." I perceive no meaningful distinction between a statute that penalizes published speech in order to protect the individual's psychological well being or reputational interest and one that exacts the same penalty in order to compensate the loss of employment or earning potential ....}

As in *Hustler*, the operation of Minnesota's doctrine of promissory estoppel in this case cannot be said to have a merely "incidental" burden on speech; the publication of important political speech *is* the claimed violation. Thus, as in *Hustler*, the law may not be enforced to punish the expression of truthful information or opinion ... [unless the restriction is] in furtherance of a state interest "of the highest order." ...

Justice Souter, with whom Justice Marshall, Justice Blackmun and Justice O'Connor join, dissenting)...

[I cannot] accept the majority's position that we may dispense with balancing because the burden on publication is in a sense "self-imposed" by the newspaper's voluntary promise of confidentiality. This suggests both the possibility of waiver, the requirements for which have not been met here, as well as a conception of First Amendment rights as those of the speaker alone, with a value that may be measured without reference to the importance of the information to public discourse.

But freedom of the press is ultimately founded on the value of enhancing such discourse for the sake of a citizenry better informed and thus more prudently self-governed.... [T]he fact of Cohen's identity expanded the universe of information relevant to the choice faced by Minnesota voters in that State's 1982 gubernatorial election, the publication of which was thus of the sort quintessentially subject to strict First Amendment protection. The propriety of his leak to respondents could be taken to reflect on his character, which in turn could be taken to reflect on the character of the candidate who had retained him as an adviser. An election could turn on just such a factor; if it should, I am ready to assume that it would be to the greater public good, at least over the long run.

This is not to say that the breach of such a promise of confidentiality could never give rise to liability. One can conceive of situations in which the injured party is a private individual, whose identity is of less public concern than that of the petitioner; liability there might not be constitutionally prohibited. Nor do I mean to imply that the circumstances of acquisition are irrelevant to the balance, see, *e.g.*, *Florida Star*, although they may go only to what balances against, and not to diminish, the First Amendment value of any particular piece of information.

Because I believe the State's interest in enforcing a newspaper's promise of confidentiality insufficient to outweigh the interest in unfettered publication of the information revealed in this case, I respectfully dissent.

VI. Government Acting in Special Capacities

A. Government as Employer

a. Summary

i. Generally

Rule: The government may not fire, demote, or otherwise significantly discipline an employee based on the employee's speech if

1. the speech is on a matter of public concern, *and*

2. the speech is *not* said by the employee as part of the employee's job duties, *Garcetti v. Ceballos,* 547 U.S. 410 (2006), *and*

3. the damage caused by the speech to the efficiency of the government agency's operation does *not* outweigh the value of the speech to the employee and the public (the so-called *Pickering* balance). *Connick v. Myers* (1983) (p. 580).

— Thus, if (1) the speech is on a matter of private concern, or (2) the speech is said as part of the employee's duties, or (3) the government prevails on the *Pickering* balance, it can do what it pleases.

Related rule: The government generally may not discriminate in employment or contracting based on the employee's membership in an expressive association. *Elrod v. Burns,* 427 U.S. 347 (1976) (firing); *Branti v. Finkel,* 445 U.S. 507 (1980) (firing); *Rutan v. Republican Party,* 497 U.S. 62 (1990) (applying *Elrod* and *Branti* to hiring); *O'Hare Truck Serv., Inc. v. City of Northlake,* 518 U.S. 712 (1996) (applying the government employee cases to government contracting decisions).

— But the interest in employees' political loyalty may justify such discrimination when "party affiliation is an appropriate requirement for the effective performance of the public office involved." *Branti.*

ii. When Is Speech Treated as Being on a Matter of Public Concern?

a. This is supposed to be determined "by the content, form, and context of a given statement."

b. Even speech that refers to things that might interest the public—for instance, maladministration of a government office—may be found not to be "of public concern." *Connick.*

c. "The question of whether expression is of a kind that is of legitimate concern to the public is also the standard in ... a common-law action for invasion of privacy." *Connick;* see also *City of San Diego v. Roe,* 543 U.S. 77 (2004) (repeating this analogy). Query, though, whether this is right: If a local newspaper had simply published Myers' statements about her supervisors—statements the Court found to be not of public concern— and even if the statements revealed personal facts about the supervisors

578

[handwritten margin notes: "Limited Rule", "Expressive Association"]

(in the course of criticizing the supervisors' trustworthiness), could the newspaper have been liable for invasion of privacy?

d. Speech that has been held not to be on a matter of public concern: *NOT public*

— Speech aimed at gathering ammunition for controversy with superiors, *Connick.*

— "Employee grievance[s] concerning internal office policy," *id.*

— Pornographic videos sold on the Web by a police officer, at least when the videos and the Web site "[were] linked to [the employee's] official status as a police officer[] and [were] designed to exploit his employer's image." *City of San Diego v. Roe.* (The videos starred Roe wearing a generic police uniform, the site identified Roe as a police officer, and the site sold the San Diego police department's official uniforms.)

e. Speech that has been held to be on a matter of public concern: *YES public*

— Discussing with coworkers unlawful pressure to work in political campaigns, *id.*

— Complaining to one's boss about alleged discrimination by the employer, when this is "not tied to a personal employment dispute," *Givhan v. Western Line Consol. School Dist.,* 439 U.S. 410 (1979).

— Writing a letter to a newspaper about the allocation of government agency funds among various departments, *Pickering v. Board of Ed.,* 391 U.S. 563 (1968).

— Testifying before the legislature about whether a college should be elevated to four-year status, *Perry v. Sindermann,* 408 U.S. 593 (1972).

— Publicizing a principal's memorandum about teacher dress and appearance, *Mt. Healthy City Board of Ed. v. Doyle,* 429 U.S. 274 (1977).

— Saying to a coworker friend that one wishes the President had been assassinated, *Rankin v. McPherson* (1987) (p. 586).

f. *United States v. National Treasury Employees Union,* 513 U.S. 454, 466 (1995), suggests that speech said "to a public audience, ... outside the workplace, and involv[ing] content largely unrelated to [the speaker's] government employment" should generally be treated as being on a matter of public concern. *See also City of San Diego v. Roe* (reaffirming this, as to speech that is indeed unrelated to employment).

1. Public Audience 2. Outside Work 3. Largely unrelated to gov employment

g. Speech to the public at large is more likely to be seen as on matters of public concern than speech to one's coworkers would be. But speech even to one person might be protected if the content is of sufficiently public concern, *Givhan.*

To 1 person could be public

h. *Connick* suggested that the speaker's motive might be central to the public concern inquiry; consider its stress that Myers "did not seek to inform the public," and that "the focus of Myers' questions is not to evaluate the performance of the office but rather to gather ammunition for another round of controversy with her superiors." Some lower courts since *Connick* have at times focused largely on the speaker's motive, though others have not.

Motive's role

iii. How Are Courts to Perform the Pickering Balance?

a. A court may consider the degree to which speech

— interferes with close working relationships (*Connick*),

— disrupts the office (*id.*),

— takes up work time (*id.*),

— threatens the employer's authority (*id.*),

— or has *the potential* to do the above ("we do not see the necessity for an employer to allow events to unfold to the extent that the disruption of the office and the destruction of working relationships is manifest before taking action," *id.*),

— or violates an explicit work rule (*id.* at n.14).

[handwritten marginal note: Factors]

b. The more the speech is on a matter of public concern, the stronger the required showing of interference.

c. "Employee speech which transpires entirely on the employee's own time, and in non-work areas of the office ... might lead to a different conclusion" (*id.*).

b. Problem: Clinton Jokes

During the Bill Clinton Administration, John Doe, a secretary in the U.S. Attorney's office, forwarded by e-mail the following joke created by *top-five.com* (excerpted for brevity):

> The Top 16 Changes at the White House Now That the Clintons Have a Puppy
> 16) To avoid confusion, staff reverts back to referring to Madeleine Albright by name....
> 12) "Bitch" label now somewhat ambiguous.
> 11) Accusations of crotch-sniffing at the White House no longer automatically implicate the President.
> 10) New, unwelcome presents under the Christmas tree....
> 3) To the embarrassment of the trainers, dog still unable to tell Al Gore from a tree....

A female coworker, Mary Moe, found the use of the word "bitch" in item 12 offensive and complained to their manager, who fired John. Doe sued, claiming that the firing violated his First Amendment rights. What should the result have been?

c. Connick v. Myers, 461 U.S. 138 (1983)

Justice White delivered the opinion of the Court....

[A.] Sheila Myers was employed as an Assistant District Attorney in New Orleans for five and a half years. She served at the pleasure of petitioner Harry Connick, the District Attorney ....

In the early part of October 1980, Myers was informed that she would be transferred to prosecute cases in a different section of the criminal court. Myers was strongly opposed to the proposed transfer and expressed her view to several of her supervisors, including Connick [and Dennis Waldron]. {Myers' opposition was at least partially attributable to her concern that a conflict of interest would have been created by the transfer because of her participation in a counseling program for convicted defendants released on probation in the section of the criminal court to which she was to be assigned.} ... Myers later testified that, in response to Waldron's suggestion that her concerns were not shared by others in the office, she informed him that she would do some research on the matter....

Myers prepared [and distributed to 15 fellow Assistant DA's] a questionnaire soliciting the views of her fellow staff members concerning office transfer policy, office morale, the need for a grievance committee, the level of confidence in supervisors, and whether employees felt pressured to work in political campaigns.[a] ... [Connick fired Myers] because of her refusal to accept the transfer ... [and because] her distribution of the questionnaire was considered an act of insubordination. Connick particularly objected to the question which inquired whether employees "had confidence in and would rely on the word" of various superiors in the office, and to a question concerning pressure to work in political campaigns which he felt would be damaging if discovered by the press....

Questionnaire

[B.] [A] state cannot condition public employment on a basis that infringes the employee's constitutionally protected interest in freedom of expression. Our task, as we defined it in *Pickering v. Board of Ed.*, 391 U.S. 563 (1968), is to seek "a balance between the interests of the [employee], as a citizen, in commenting upon matters of public concern and the interest of the State, as an employer, in promoting the efficiency of the public services it performs through its employees." ...

The repeated emphasis in *Pickering* on the right of a public employee "as a citizen, in commenting upon matters of public concern," was not accidental.... The First Amendment "was fashioned to assure unfettered interchange of ideas for the bringing about of political and social changes desired

---

[a] [The questionnaire text, in relevant part, read:—ed.] ...
3. Were the transfers as they effected [sic] you discussed with you by any superior prior to the notice of them being posted?
4. Do you think as a matter of policy, they should have been?
5. ... [D]o you feel office procedure regarding transfers has been fair?
6. Do you believe there is a rumor mill active in the office?
7. If so, how do you think it effects [sic] overall working performance ...?
8. If so, how do you think it effects [sic] office morale? ...
10. Do you have confidence in and would you rely on the word of:
Bridget Bane   Fred Harper   Lindsay Larson   Joe Meyer   Dennis Waldron
11. Do you ever feel pressured to work in political campaigns on behalf of office supported candidates?
12. Do you feel a grievance committee would be a worthwhile addition to the office structure?
13. How would you rate office morale?
14. Please feel free to express any comments or feelings you have....

by the people." ... *Pickering* [and later cases] followed from this understanding of the First Amendment. In *Pickering* the Court held impermissible under the First Amendment the dismissal of a high school teacher for openly criticizing the Board of Education on its allocation of school funds between athletics and education and its methods of informing taxpayers about the need for additional revenue. Pickering's subject was "a matter of legitimate public concern" upon which "free and open debate is vital to informed decision-making by the electorate." [Discussion of similar cases omitted.—ed.]
...

[Thus,] if Myers' questionnaire cannot be fairly characterized as constituting speech on a matter of public concern, it is unnecessary for us to scrutinize the reasons for her discharge. When employee expression cannot be fairly considered as relating to any matter of political, social, or other concern to the community, government officials should enjoy wide latitude in managing their offices, without intrusive oversight by the judiciary in the name of the First Amendment. Perhaps the government employer's dismissal of the worker may not be fair, but ordinary dismissals from government service which violate no fixed tenure or applicable statute or regulation are not subject to judicial review even if the reasons for the dismissal are alleged to be mistaken or unreasonable.

We do not suggest, however, that Myers' speech, even if not touching upon a matter of public concern, is totally beyond the protection of the First Amendment. "The First Amendment does not protect speech and assembly only to the extent that it can be characterized as political...." We in no sense suggest that speech on private matters falls into one of the narrow and well-defined classes of expression which carries so little social value, such as obscenity, that the State can prohibit and punish such expression by all persons in its jurisdiction....

We hold only that when a public employee speaks not as a citizen upon matters of public concern, but instead as an employee upon matters only of personal interest, absent the most unusual circumstances, a federal court is not the appropriate forum in which to review the wisdom of a personnel decision taken by a public agency allegedly in reaction to the employee's behavior. Our responsibility is to ensure that citizens are not deprived of fundamental rights by virtue of working for the government; this does not require a grant of immunity for employee grievances not afforded by the First Amendment to those who do not work for the State.

[C.] Whether an employee's speech addresses a matter of public concern must be determined by the content, form, and context of a given statement, as revealed by the whole record. In this case, with but one exception, the questions posed by Myers to her coworkers do not fall under the rubric of matters of "public concern."

We view the questions pertaining to the confidence and trust that Myers' coworkers possess in various supervisors, the level of office morale, and the need for a grievance committee as mere extensions of Myers' dispute over her transfer .... [W]e do not believe these questions are of public import in evaluating the performance of the District Attorney as an elected official. Myers did not seek to inform the public that the District Attorney's office was not discharging its governmental responsibilities in the investigation and prosecution of criminal cases. Nor did Myers seek to bring to light actual or potential wrongdoing or breach of public trust on the part of Connick and others.

Indeed, the questionnaire, if released to the public, would convey no information at all other than the fact that a single employee is upset with the status quo. While discipline and morale in the workplace are related to an agency's efficient performance of its duties, the focus of Myers' questions is not to evaluate the performance of the office but rather to gather ammunition for another round of controversy with her superiors. These questions reflect one employee's dissatisfaction with a transfer and an attempt to turn that displeasure into a cause célèbre.

"Ammunition"

{[A] questionnaire not otherwise of public concern does not attain that status because its subject matter could, in different circumstances, have been the topic of a communication to the public that might be of general interest. The dissent's analysis of whether discussions of office morale and discipline could be matters of public concern is beside the point—it does not answer whether *this* questionnaire is such speech.}

To presume that all matters which transpire within a government office are of public concern would mean that virtually every remark—and certainly every criticism directed at a public official—would plant the seed of a constitutional case. While as a matter of good judgment, public officials should be receptive to constructive criticism offered by their employees, the First Amendment does not require a public office to be run as a roundtable for employee complaints over internal office affairs.

One question in Myers' questionnaire, however, does touch upon a matter of public concern. Question 11 inquires if assistant district attorneys "ever feel pressured to work in political campaigns on behalf of office supported candidates." ...

Exception (political campaign pressure)

[O]fficial pressure upon employees to work for political candidates not of the worker's own choice constitutes a coercion of belief in violation of fundamental constitutional rights. In addition, there is a demonstrated interest in this country that government service should depend upon meritorious performance rather than political service. Given this history, we believe it apparent that the issue of whether assistant district attorneys are pressured to work in political campaigns is a matter of interest to the community upon which it is essential that public employees be able to speak out freely without fear of retaliatory dismissal....

[D.] [The Court then applied the *Pickering* balance as to the one statement it found to be of public concern.—ed.]

Pickering Balance

The *Pickering* balance requires full consideration of the government's interest in the effective and efficient fulfillment of its responsibilities to the public.... "[I]t is important to the efficient and successful operation of the

District Attorney's office for Assistants to maintain close working relationships with their superiors." Connick's judgment, and apparently also that of his first assistant Dennis Waldron, who characterized Myers' actions as causing a "mini-insurrection," was that Myers' questionnaire was an act of insubordination which interfered with working relationships. {Waldron testified that from what he had learned of the events on October 7, Myers "was trying to stir up other people not to accept the changes [transfers] that had been made on the memorandum and that were to be implemented." In his view, the questionnaire was a "final act of defiance" and that, as a result of Myers' action, "there were going to be some severe problems about the changes."}

When close working relationships are essential to fulfilling public responsibilities, a wide degree of deference to the employer's judgment is appropriate. Furthermore, we do not see the necessity for an employer to allow events to unfold to the extent that the disruption of the office and the destruction of working relationships is manifest before taking action. We caution that a stronger showing may be necessary if the employee's speech more substantially involved matters of public concern....

Also relevant is the manner, time, and place in which the questionnaire was distributed.... Here the questionnaire was prepared, and distributed at the office; the manner of distribution required not only Myers to leave her work but for others to do the same in order that the questionnaire be completed. Although some latitude in when official work is performed is to be allowed when professional employees are involved, and Myers did not violate announced office policy, the fact that Myers, unlike Pickering, exercised her rights to speech at the office supports Connick's fears that the functioning of his office was endangered. {Employee speech which transpires entirely on the employee's own time, and in non-work areas of the office, bring different factors into the *Pickering* calculus, and might lead to a different conclusion.}

Finally, the context in which the dispute arose is also significant. This is not a case where an employee, out of purely academic interest, circulated a questionnaire so as to obtain useful research.... When employee speech concerning office policy arises from an employment dispute concerning the very application of that policy to the speaker, additional weight must be given to the supervisor's view that the employee has threatened the authority of the employer to run the office ....

Justice Brennan, with whom Justice Marshall, Justice Blackmun, and Justice Stevens join, dissenting....

The Court's decision today is flawed in three respects. First, the Court distorts the balancing analysis required under *Pickering* by suggesting that one factor, the context in which a statement is made, is to be weighed *twice*—first in determining whether an employee's speech addresses a matter of public concern and then in deciding whether the statement adversely affected the government's interest as an employer.

Second, in concluding that the effect of respondent's personnel policies on employee morale and the work performance of the District Attorney's Office is not a matter of public concern, the Court impermissibly narrows the class of subjects on which public employees may speak out without fear of retaliatory dismissal.

Third, the Court misapplies the *Pickering* balancing test in holding that Myers could constitutionally be dismissed for circulating a questionnaire addressed to at least one subject that *was* "a matter of interest to the community," in the absence of evidence that her conduct disrupted the efficient functioning of the District Attorney's Office....

[W]hether a particular statement by a public employee is addressed to a subject of public concern does not depend on where it was said or why. The First Amendment affords special protection to speech that may inform public debate about how our society is to be governed—regardless of whether it actually becomes the subject of a public controversy....

Myers' questionnaire addressed matters of public concern because it discussed subjects that could reasonably be expected to be of interest to persons seeking to develop informed opinions about the manner in which the Orleans Parish District Attorney, an elected official charged with managing a vital governmental agency, discharges his responsibilities. The questionnaire sought primarily to obtain information about the impact of the recent transfers on morale in the District Attorney's Office. It is beyond doubt that personnel decisions that adversely affect discipline and morale may ultimately impair an agency's efficient performance of its duties....

Obviously, not every remark directed at a public official by a public employee is protected by the First Amendment. But deciding whether a particular matter is of public concern is an inquiry that, by its very nature, is a sensitive one for judges charged with interpreting a constitutional provision intended to put "the decision as to what views shall be voiced largely into the hands of each of us...." ... [Yet, b]ased on its own narrow conception of which matters are of public concern, the Court implicitly determines that information concerning employee morale at an important government office will not inform public debate.

To the contrary, the First Amendment protects the dissemination of such information so that the people, not the courts, may evaluate its usefulness. The proper means to ensure that the courts are not swamped with routine employee grievances mischaracterized as First Amendment cases is not to restrict artificially the concept of "public concern," but to require that adequate weight be given to the public's important interests in the efficient performance of governmental functions and in preserving employee discipline and harmony sufficient to achieve that end....

[T]he Court [also] ... [wrongly holds] that a public employer's mere apprehension that speech will be disruptive justifies suppression of that speech when all the objective evidence suggests that those fears are essentially unfounded. *Pickering* recognized the difficulty of articulating "a general standard against which all ... statements may be judged"; it did, however, identify a number of factors that may affect the balance in particular cases.

Those relevant here are whether the statements are directed to persons with whom the speaker "would normally be in contact in the course of his daily work"; whether they had an adverse effect on "discipline by intermediate supervisors or harmony among coworkers"; whether the employment relationship in question is "the kind ... for which it can persuasively be claimed that personal loyalty and confidence are necessary to their proper functioning"; and whether the statements "have in any way impeded [the employee's] proper performance of his daily duties ... or ... interfered with the regular operations of the [office]." In addition, ... we [have] recognized that when the statements in question are made in private to an employee's immediate supervisor, "the employing agency's institutional efficiency may be threatened not only by the content of the ... message but also by the manner, time, and place in which it is delivered." ...

Dist. Ct. said no disruptive effect

In the face of the District Court's finding that the circulation of the questionnaire had no disruptive effect, the Court holds that respondent may be dismissed because petitioner "reasonably believed [the action] would disrupt the office, undermine his authority and destroy close working relationships." Even though the District Court found that the distribution of the questionnaire did not impair Myers' working relationship with her supervisors, the Court bows to petitioner's judgment because "[w]hen close working relationships are essential to fulfilling public responsibilities, a wide degree of deference to the employer's judgment is appropriate."

☆

Such extreme deference to the employer's judgment is not appropriate when public employees voice critical views concerning the operations of the agency for which they work. Although an employer's determination that an employee's statements have undermined essential working relationships must be carefully weighed in the *Pickering* balance, we must bear in mind that "the threat of dismissal from public employment is ... a potent means of inhibiting speech."

chill speech

If the employer's judgment is to be controlling, public employees will not speak out when what they have to say is critical of their supervisors. In order to protect public employees' First Amendment right to voice critical views on issues of public importance, the courts must make their own appraisal of the effects of the speech in question....

d. *Rankin v. McPherson, 483 U.S. 378 (1987)*

Justice Marshall delivered the opinion of the Court....

[A.] [Ardith McPherson was a probationary clerical employee in the office of the elected Constable of Harris County, Texas.] Her work station was a desk at which there was no telephone, in a room to which the public did not have ready access. Her job was to type data from court papers into a computer that maintained an automated record of the status of civil process in the county. {While the Constable's office is a law enforcement agency, Constable Rankin testified that other law enforcement departments were charged with the day-to-day enforcement of criminal laws in the county, and that more than 80% of the budget of his office was devoted to service of civil process, service of process in juvenile delinquency cases, and execution of mental health warrants. The involvement of his office in criminal cases, he testified, was in large part limited to warrants in bad check cases.} ...

On March 30, 1981, McPherson and some fellow employees heard on an office radio that there had been an attempt to assassinate [President Reagan].... Upon hearing that report, McPherson engaged a co-worker, Lawrence Jackson, who was apparently her boyfriend, in a brief conversation, which according to McPherson's uncontroverted testimony [included this statement]:

> ... Well, we were talking—it's a wonder why they did that. I felt like it would be a black person that did that, because I feel like most of my kind is on welfare and CETA [a job training program for the poor and unemployed—ed.], and they use medicaid, and at the time, I was thinking that's what it was.... But then after I said that, and then Lawrence said, yeah, he's cutting back medicaid and food stamps. And I said, yeah, welfare and CETA. I said, shoot, if they go for him again, I hope they get him.

McPherson's last remark was overheard by another [employee], who, unbeknownst to McPherson, was in the room at the time. The remark was reported to Constable Rankin, who summoned McPherson. McPherson readily admitted that she had made the statement, but testified that she told Rankin, upon being asked if she made the statement, "Yes, but I didn't mean anything by it." After their discussion, Rankin fired McPherson. McPherson [sued] ....

[B.] Considering the statement in context ... discloses that it plainly dealt with a matter of public concern. The statement was made in the course of ... addressing the policies of the President's administration. It came on the heels of a news bulletin regarding what is certainly a matter of heightened public attention: an attempt on the life of the President....

Plainly Public

McPherson's statement did not amount to [an unprotected threat] .... The inappropriate or controversial character of a statement is irrelevant to the question whether it deals with a matter of public concern. "[D]ebate on public issues should be uninhibited, robust, and wide-open, and ... may well include vehement, caustic, and sometimes unpleasantly sharp attacks on government and public officials."

Inappropriate character irrelevant

[C.] Because McPherson's statement addressed a matter of public concern, *Pickering* v. *Board of Ed.*, 391 U.S. 563 (1968), next requires that we balance McPherson's interest in making her statement against "the interest of the State, as an employer, in promoting the efficiency of the public services it performs through its employees." The State bears a burden of justifying the discharge on legitimate grounds. {We agree with Justice Powell that a purely private statement on a matter of public concern will rarely, if ever, justify discharge of a public employee. To the extent petitioners' claim that McPherson's speech rendered her an unsuitable employee for a law enforcement agency implicates a serious state interest and necessitates the application of the balancing element of the *Pickering* analysis, we proceed

Pickering Balance

to that task.}

In performing the balancing, the statement will not be considered in a vacuum; the manner, time, and place of the employee's expression are relevant, as is the context in which the dispute arose. We have previously recognized as pertinent considerations whether the statement impairs discipline by superiors or harmony among co-workers, has a detrimental impact on close working relationships for which personal loyalty and confidence are necessary, or impedes the performance of the speaker's duties or interferes with the regular operation of the enterprise....

While McPherson's statement was made at the workplace, there is no evidence that it interfered with the efficient functioning of the office. The Constable was evidently not afraid that McPherson had disturbed or interrupted other employees—he did not inquire to whom respondent had made the remark and testified that he "was not concerned who she had made it to." In fact, Constable Rankin testified that the possibility of interference with the functions of the Constable's office had *not* been a consideration in his discharge of respondent ....

Nor was there any danger that McPherson had discredited the office by making her statement in public. McPherson's speech took place in an area to which there was ordinarily no public access ....

Nor is there any evidence that employees other than Jackson who worked in the room even heard the remark. Not only was McPherson's discharge unrelated to the functioning of the office, it was not based on any assessment by the Constable that the remark demonstrated a character trait that made respondent unfit to perform her work.... [The Constable] fired McPherson based on the *content* of her speech. Evidently because McPherson had made the statement, and because the Constable believed that she "meant it," he decided that she was not a suitable employee to have in a law enforcement agency....

[I]n weighing the State's interest in discharging an employee based on any claim that the content of a statement made by the employee somehow undermines the mission of the public employer, some attention must be paid to the responsibilities of the employee within the agency.... Where, as here, an employee serves no confidential, policymaking, or public contact role, the danger to the agency's successful functioning from that employee's private speech is minimal.

We cannot believe that every employee in Constable Rankin's office, whether computer operator, electrician, or file clerk, is equally required, on pain of discharge, to avoid any statement susceptible of being interpreted by the Constable as an indication that the employee may be unworthy of employment in his law enforcement agency. At some point, such concerns are so removed from the effective functioning of the public employer that they cannot prevail over the free speech rights of the public employee. {This is not to say that clerical employees are insulated from discharge where their speech, taking the acknowledged factors into account, truly injures the public interest in the effective functioning of the public employer. Cf.

McMullen v. Carson, 754 F.2d 936 (11th Cir. 1985) (clerical employee in sheriff's office properly discharged for stating on television news that he was an employee for the sheriff's office and a recruiter for the Ku Klux Klan).} ...

McPherson's employment-related interaction with the Constable was apparently negligible. Her duties were purely clerical and were limited solely to the civil process function of the Constable's office. There is no indication that she would ever be in a position to further—or indeed to have any involvement with—the minimal law enforcement activity engaged in by the Constable's office. Given the function of the agency, McPherson's position in the office, and the nature of her statement, we are not persuaded that Rankin's interest in discharging her outweighed her rights under the First Amendment....

Justice Powell, concurring....

I think it is unnecessary to engage in the extensive analysis normally required by *Connick v. Myers* and *Pickering.* If a statement is on a matter of public concern, as it was here, it will be an unusual case where the employer's legitimate interests will be so great as to justify punishing an employee for this type of private speech that routinely takes place at all levels in the workplace. The risk that a single, offhand comment directed to only one other worker will lower morale, disrupt the work force, or otherwise undermine the mission of the office borders on the fanciful....

Justice Scalia, with whom ... Chief Justice [Rehnquist], Justice White, and Justice O'Connor join, dissenting....

[A.] [N]o law enforcement agency is required by the First Amendment to permit one of its employees to "ride with the cops and cheer for the robbers." ... As a law enforcement officer, the Constable obviously has a strong interest in preventing statements by any of his employees approving, or expressing a desire for, serious, violent crimes—regardless of whether the statements actually interfere with office operations at the time they are made or demonstrate character traits that make the speaker unsuitable for law enforcement work.... Statements like McPherson's obviously carry a ["clear potential for undermining office relations," *Connick,*] in an office devoted to law enforcement. Although that proposition is in my view evident on its face, we have actual evidence of it in the present record: The only reason McPherson's remark was brought to the Constable's attention was that one of his deputies, Captain Levrier, had overheard the remark and, according to the Constable, "was very upset because of [it]."

Statements by the Constable's employees to the effect that "if they go for the President again, I hope they get him" might also, to put it mildly, undermine public confidence in the Constable's office. A public employer has a strong interest in preserving its reputation with the public. We know—from undisputed testimony—that McPherson had or might have had some occasion to deal with the public while carrying out her duties.

The Court's sweeping assertion (and apparent holding) that where an employee "serves no confidential, policymaking, or public contact role, the danger to the agency's successful functioning from that employee's private speech is minimal," is simply contrary to reason and experience. Nonpolicy-making employees (the Assistant District Attorney in *Connick*, for example) can hurt working relationships and undermine public confidence in an organization every bit as much as policymaking employees.

Non-policy employees not shielded

I, for one, do not look forward to the new First Amendment world the Court creates, in which nonpolicymaking employees of the Equal Employment Opportunity Commission must be permitted to make remarks on the job approving of racial discrimination [and] nonpolicymaking employees of the Selective Service System to advocate noncompliance with the draft laws .... Constable Rankin's interest in maintaining both an esprit de corps and a public image consistent with his office's law enforcement duties outweighs any interest his employees may have in expressing on the job a desire that the President be killed ....

No NT req

[B.] The First Amendment contains no "narrow tailoring" requirement that speech the government is entitled to suppress must be suppressed by the mildest means possible. If Constable Rankin was entitled (as I think any reasonable person would say he was) to admonish McPherson for saying what she did on the job, within hearing of her co-workers, and to warn her that if she did it again a formal censure would be placed in her personnel file, then it follows that he is entitled to rule that particular speech out of bounds in that particular work environment ....

e. *Policy—Government Acting Differently as Manager*

Basic argument: "The government acting in its special capacity as *Manager* has more power to restrict speech than when it's acting as sovereign, because *achieve objectives*

1. "Within managerial domains [such as when the government is acting as employer], the state organizes its resources so as to achieve specified ends. The constitutional value of managerial domains is that of instrumental rationality, a value that conceptualizes persons as means to an end rather than as autonomous agents. Within managerial domains, therefore, ends may be imposed upon persons. Managerial domains are necessary so that a democratic state can actually achieve objectives that have been democratically agreed upon." Robert C. Post, *Subsidized Speech*, 106 Yale L.J. 151 (1996).

"[T]he government's role as employer [must give] it a freer hand in regulating the speech of its employees than it has in regulating the speech of the public at large.... [For instance, a] government employer may bar its employees from using Mr. Cohen's offensive utterance to members of the public, or to the people with whom they work. [Though] '[u]nder the First Amendment there is no such thing as a false idea' [and] the 'fitting remedy for evil counsels is good ones,' ... when an employee counsels her co-workers to do their job in a way with which the public employer disagrees, her managers may tell her to stop, rather than relying on counterspeech.... [T]hough a private person is perfectly free to uninhibitedly and robustly criticize a state governor's legislative program, we have never suggested that the Constitution bars the governor from firing a high-ranking deputy for doing the same thing." *Waters v. Churchill,* 511 U.S. 661, 672 (1994) (plurality).

2. Response to 1: Even when the government is acting as manager, speech restrictions can seriously burden speakers, specifically by _Chilling Speech_

"While criminal sanctions and damage awards have a somewhat different impact on the exercise of the right to freedom of speech from dismissal from employment, it is apparent that the threat of dismissal from public employment is nonetheless a potent means of inhibiting speech." *Pickering v. Board of Ed.,* 391 U.S. 563, 574 (1968).

3. Response to 1: Such inhibitions of speech can also hurt listeners and the marketplace of ideas by _fear of retaliation_

"[Because government employees have special knowledge about government inefficiencies or malfeasance,] it is essential that they be able to speak out freely on such questions without fear of retaliatory dismissal." *Id.* at 572.

f. *Policy—Surrender of Rights in Exchange for Benefit*

Basic argument: "If you want a certain government benefit, it's reasonable for the government to require you to surrender your right to say _____ as a condition of getting that benefit, because _____."

1. "[T]here is nothing in the constitution ... to prevent the city from attaching obedience to [a speech restriction] as a condition to the office of policeman, and making it part of the good conduct required. The petitioner may have a constitutional right to talk politics, but he has no constitutional right to be a policeman.... The [employee] cannot complain, as he takes the employment on the terms which are offered him...." *McAuliffe v. Mayor,* 155 Mass. 216 (1892) (Holmes, J.).

"[W]e are concerned solely and exclusively with the right ... to enjoy great privileges [the second-class mailing privilege] ... at the public expense, a right given to [certain mailers] by Congress upon condition of compliance with regulations deemed by that body incidental and necessary to the complete fruition of the public policy lying at the foundations of the privileges accorded." *Lewis Publishing Co. v. Morgan,* 229 U.S. 288 (1913).

2. Response to 1: The government isn't really providing a benefit from "its own" property; rather, the property itself belongs to us (including the speaker), and not just the government, because _____.

"[C]ongress has [no] right to impose such a condition upon any citizen of the United States. [Government jobs] do not belong to the Legislative Department to dispose of on any conditions it may choose to impose.... They belong to the United States, and not to Congress; and every citizen having the proper qualifications has the right to [be a government employee]. This is a fundamental right of which the legislature cannot deprive the citizen, nor clog its exercise with conditions that are repugnant to his other fundamental rights." *Ex parte Curtis,* 106 U.S. 371 (1882) (Bradley, J., dissenting) (arguing that Congress couldn't constitutionally bar federal employees from soliciting or giving political contributions).

"The United States may give up the Post Office when it sees fit, but while it carries it on the use of the mails is almost as much a part of free speech as the right to use our tongues ...." *United States ex rel. Milwaukee Social Democratic Pub. Co. v. Burleson,* 255 U.S. 407 (1921) (Holmes, J., dissenting).

3. Response to 1: This surrender of rights isn't actually voluntary, because _____. For instance, a child in a government-run school isn't really voluntarily there, and thus hasn't surrendered his free speech rights, because compulsory attendance law requires that he go to some school (and private schools may be too expensive).

4. Response to 1: Even if the *speaker* has surrendered his rights, this restriction distorts the marketplace of ideas and thus interferes with the rights of listeners by _____.

"The large-scale disincentive to Government employees' expression also imposes a significant burden on the public's right to read and hear what the employees would otherwise have written and said." *United States v. National Treasury Employees Union,* 513 U.S. 451 (1995).

5. Rejoinder to 2, 3, and 4: And yet there are the cases, mentioned in point 1 of "Government Acting Differently as Manager" (p. 590), where taking the government dollar must entail some voluntary surrender of free speech rights.

B. Government as Educator

a.   Summary

Rule for K-12 schools: The government acting as K-12 educator (*i.e.,* kindergarten through 12th grade) may restrict speech if

a.   The speech

   i.   "materially and substantially interfere[s] with the requirements of appropriate discipline in the operation of the school," *Tinker v. Des Moines School Dist.* (1969) (p. 594), or

   ii.   "inva[des] ... the rights of others," *id.* (query what rights these are—the Court has never discussed this, and the majority and Justice Alito's concurrence in *Morse v. Frederick* (2007) described *Tinker* by reciting only the disruption prong), or

   iii.   is "vulgar and offensive" because of its particular wording and not because of its viewpoint, *Bethel School Dist. No. 403 v. Fraser* (1986) (p. 600); see also *Morse* ("[*Fraser*] should not be read to encompass any speech that could fit under some definition of 'offensive.' After all, much political and religious speech might be perceived as offensive to some."), or

   iv.   "when that speech is reasonably viewed as promoting illegal drug use," at least when it does not "convey[] any sort of political or religious message," *Morse*; *see also id.* (Alito, J., concurring) (concluding that this exception applies only when the speech "can[not] plausibly be interpreted as commenting on any political or social issue, including speech on issues such as 'the wisdom of the war on drugs or of legalizing marijuana for medicinal use'").

b. Under *Tinker*, mere fear of interference isn't enough; there has to be some specific "reason to anticipate" interference.

— This is especially so if the restriction seems aimed at a particular viewpoint, though the Court has left open the possibility that even viewpoint-based restrictions would be allowed if certain viewpoints were particularly disruptive. *Tinker*.

c. *Fraser* seems to generally support the school's power to restrict vulgar speech by its students (consider the statement "[T]he First Amendment gives a high school student the classroom right to wear Tinker's armband, but not Cohen's jacket"). But one could also interpret *Fraser* as being limited to the speech of students who are participating in school-endorsed events, such as speaking to school assemblies. Justice Alito's *Morse* concurrence could be read as taking the latter view when it describes *Fraser* as covering "speech that is delivered in a lewd or vulgar manner as part of a middle school program."

Rule for colleges: The government acting as college educator is generally assumed by recent lower court cases to have no greater powers than the government acting as sovereign,

— at least when it comes to student speech outside class or class work. *Healey v. James*, 408 U.S. 169 (1972); *Papish v. Board of Curators*, 410 U.S. 667 (1973).

— Note, though, that a government-run college may have some power over on-campus speech because of its role as proprietor, see Part VI.D.

Rule for curriculum: In both public schools and colleges, the government has broad latitude over speech as part of class activities, speech on exams, and speech in school-run activities (such as high school newspapers).

— *Hazelwood School Dist. v. Kuhlmeier*, 484 U.S. 260 (1988), upheld a principal's exclusion of certain articles from a student-written school newspaper; but this generally reflects broad government-as-speaker law (see Part VI.D.3), and not special rules related to the government as K-12 educator. The government could, for instance, equally restrict what is published in government agency newsletters, though such newsletters' readers are employees and patrons, not students.

b. Problem: David Duke/Malcolm X T-Shirts

A high school prohibits its students from wearing T-shirts that refer to David Duke or Malcolm X. Is this constitutional? Cf. *High School Bans Ethnic Clothing*, UPI, Mar. 16, 1992; cf. *Castorina v. Madison County School Bd.*, 246 F.3d 536 (6th Cir. 2001), and *West v. Derby Unified School Dist.*,

206 F.3d 1358 (10th Cir. 2000), both dealing with confederate flags worn or drawn by K-12 students.

c. Problem: The Leonard Law

The Oregon legislature is considering a law based on Cal. Educ. Code § 48950 (the so-called Leonard Law, named after its author, state Senator Bill Leonard), which reads:

> School districts operating one or more high schools ... shall not make or enforce any rule subjecting any high school pupil to disciplinary sanctions solely on the basis of conduct that is speech or other communication that, when engaged in outside of the campus, is protected from governmental restriction by the First Amendment to the United States Constitution ....
>
> Nothing in this section prohibits the imposition of discipline for harassment, threats, or intimidation, unless constitutionally protected.
>
> The Legislature finds and declares that free speech rights are subject to reasonable time, place, and manner regulations.

Your boss, Senator Michael Greve, is trying to decide whether to vote for the proposal, and asks you to analyze the bill's pluses and minuses. What do you say?

d. Tinker v. Des Moines Indep. Comm. School Dist., 393 U.S. 503 (1969)

Justice Fortas delivered the opinion of the Court.

[A.] Petitioner John F. Tinker, 15 years old, and petitioner Christopher Eckhardt, 16 years old, attended high schools in Des Moines, Iowa. Petitioner Mary Beth Tinker, John's sister, was a 13-year-old student in junior high school.

In December 1965, a group of adults and students ... determined to publicize their objections to the hostilities in Vietnam ... by wearing black armbands during the holiday season .... On December 14, 1965, [the principals of the Des Moines schools] adopted a policy that any student wearing an armband to school would be asked to remove it, and if he refused he would be suspended until he returned without the armband. Petitioners were aware of the regulation that the school authorities adopted.

On December 16, Mary Beth and Christopher wore black armbands to their schools. John Tinker wore his armband the next day. They were all sent home and suspended from school until they would come back without their armbands. [They then sued, arguing that the suspensions violated the First Amendment.—ed.] ...

[B.] [N]either students [n]or teachers shed their constitutional rights to freedom of speech or expression at the schoolhouse gate.... "The [First Amendment] ... protects the citizen against the State itself and all of its creatures—Boards of Education not excepted.... That they are educating the young for citizenship is reason for scrupulous protection of Constitutional freedoms of the individual, if we are not to strangle the free mind at its source and teach youth to discount important principles of our government as mere platitudes." *W. Va. State Bd. of Ed. v. Barnette* [(striking down compulsory flag salute)].

{In our system, state-operated schools may not be enclaves of totalitarianism.... Students in school as well as out of school are "persons" under our Constitution. They are possessed of fundamental rights which the State must respect, just as they themselves must respect their obligations to the State.... [They] may not be regarded as closed-circuit recipients of only that which the State chooses to communicate. They may not be confined to the expression of those sentiments that are officially approved....

The principal use to which the schools are dedicated is to accommodate students during prescribed hours for the purpose of certain types of activities. Among those activities is personal intercommunication among the students. This is not only an inevitable part of the process of attending school; it is also an important part of the educational process....}

[B.] On the other hand, the Court has repeatedly emphasized the need for affirming the comprehensive authority of the States and of school officials, consistent with fundamental constitutional safeguards, to prescribe and control conduct in the schools.... {[A student] may express his opinions, even on controversial subjects ..., if he does so without "materially and substantially interfer[ing] with the requirements of appropriate discipline in the operation of the school" and without colliding with the rights of others. But conduct by the student, in class or out of it, which for any reason—whether it stems from time, place, or type of behavior—materially disrupts classwork or involves substantial disorder or invasion of the rights of others is, of course, not immunized by the constitutional guarantee of freedom of speech.} ...

The school officials banned and sought to punish petitioners for a silent, passive expression of opinion, unaccompanied by any disorder or disturbance on the part of petitioners. There is here no evidence whatever of petitioners' interference, actual or nascent, with the schools' work or of collision with the rights of other students to be secure and to be let alone. Accordingly, this case does not concern speech or action that intrudes upon the work of the schools or the rights of other students.

Only a few of the 18,000 students in the school system wore the black armbands. Only five students were suspended for wearing them. There is no indication that the work of the schools or any class was disrupted. Outside the classrooms, a few students made hostile remarks to the children wearing armbands, but there were no threats or acts of violence on school premises....

[U]ndifferentiated fear or apprehension of disturbance is not enough to overcome the right to freedom of expression. Any departure from absolute regimentation may cause trouble. Any variation from the majority's opinion may inspire fear. Any word spoken, in class, in the lunchroom, or on the campus, that deviates from the views of another person may start an argument or cause a disturbance. But our Constitution says we must take this risk, and our history says that it is this sort of hazardous freedom—this kind of openness—that is the basis of our national strength and of the independence and vigor of Americans who grow up and live in this relatively permissive, often disputatious, society.

In order for the State in the person of school officials to justify prohibition of a particular expression of opinion, it must be able to show that its action was caused by something more than a mere desire to avoid the discomfort and unpleasantness that always accompany an unpopular viewpoint. Certainly where [as here] there is no finding and no showing that engaging in the forbidden conduct would "materially and substantially interfere with the requirements of appropriate discipline in the operation of the school," the prohibition cannot be sustained....

On the contrary, the action of the school authorities appears to have been based upon an urgent wish to avoid the controversy which might result from the expression, even by the silent symbol of armbands, of opposition to this Nation's part in the conflagration in Vietnam. It is revealing, in this respect, that the meeting at which the school principals decided to issue the contested regulation was called in response to a student's statement to the journalism teacher in one of the schools that he wanted to write an article on Vietnam and have it published in the school paper. (The student was dissuaded.)

{The only suggestions of fear of disorder [justifying the restriction were] these: "A former student of one of our high schools was killed in Viet Nam. Some of his friends are still in school and it was felt that if any kind of a demonstration existed, it might evolve into something which would be difficult to control." "Students at one of the high schools were heard to say they would wear arm bands of other colors if the black bands prevailed."

Moreover, the testimony of school authorities at trial indicates that it was not fear of disruption that motivated the regulation prohibiting the armbands; the regulation was directed against "the principle of the demonstration" itself. School authorities simply felt that "the schools are no place for demonstrations," and if the students "didn't like the way our elected officials were handling things, it should be handled with the ballot box and not in the halls of our public schools."}

[C.] It is also relevant that the school authorities did not purport to prohibit the wearing of all symbols of political or controversial significance. The record shows that students in some of the schools wore buttons relating to national political campaigns, and some even wore the Iron Cross, traditionally a symbol of Nazism. The order prohibiting the wearing of armbands did not extend to these.

Instead, a particular symbol—black armbands worn to exhibit opposition to this Nation's involvement in Vietnam—was singled out for prohibition. Clearly, the prohibition of expression of one particular opinion, at least without evidence that it is necessary to avoid material and substantial interference with schoolwork or discipline, is not constitutionally permissible....

Justice Harlan, dissenting....

[P]ublic school authorities in the discharge of their responsibilities are not wholly exempt from the requirements of the Fourteenth Amendment respecting the freedoms of expression and association.... [Yet] school officials should be accorded the widest authority in maintaining discipline and good order in their institutions. To translate that proposition into a workable constitutional rule, I would, in cases like this, cast upon those complaining the burden of showing that a particular school measure was motivated by other than legitimate school concerns—for example, a desire to prohibit the expression of an unpopular point of view, while permitting expression of the dominant opinion. Finding nothing in this record which impugns the good faith of respondents in promulgating the armband regulation, I would affirm the judgment below.

Justice Black, dissenting....

[Some of the protesting students'] armbands caused comments, warnings by other students, the poking of fun at them, and a warning by an older football player that other, nonprotesting students had better let them alone. There is also evidence that a teacher of mathematics had his lesson period practically "wrecked" chiefly by disputes with Mary Beth Tinker, who wore her armband for her "demonstration." ...

[The] armband did divert students' minds from their regular lessons, and ... talk, comments, etc., made John Tinker "self-conscious" in attending school with his armband. While the absence of obscene remarks or boisterous and loud disorder perhaps justifies the Court's statement that the few armband students did not actually "disrupt" the classwork, ... the armbands did exactly what the elected school officials and principals foresaw they would, that is, took the students' minds off their classwork and diverted them to thoughts about the highly emotional subject of the Vietnam war....

[No] person has a constitutional right to say what he pleases, where he pleases, and when he pleases.... [C]ertainly a teacher is not paid to go into school and teach subjects the State does not hire him to teach as a part of its selected curriculum. Nor are public school students sent to the schools at public expense to broadcast political or any other views to educate and inform the public.

The original idea of schools, which I do not believe is yet abandoned as worthless or out of date, was that children had not yet reached the point of experience and wisdom which enabled them to teach all of their elders.... [T]he record amply shows that public protest in the school classes against the Vietnam war "distracted from that singleness of purpose which the state [here Iowa] desired to exist in its public educational institutions." ...

[D]isputes over ... the Vietnam war have disrupted and divided this country as few other issues ever have. Of course students, like other people, cannot concentrate on lesser issues when black armbands are being ostentatiously displayed in their presence to call attention to the wounded and dead of the war, some of the wounded and the dead being their friends and neighbors. It was, of course, to distract the attention of other students that some students insisted ... that they were determined to sit in school with their symbolic armbands....

The schools of this Nation have undoubtedly contributed to giving us tranquility and to making us a more law-abiding people. Uncontrolled and uncontrollable liberty is an enemy to domestic peace. We cannot close our eyes to the fact that some of the country's greatest problems are crimes committed by the youth, too many of school age.

School discipline, like parental discipline, is an integral and important part of training our children to be good citizens—to be better citizens. Here a very small number of students have crisply and summarily refused to obey a school order designed to give pupils who want to learn the opportunity to do so.... [A]fter the Court's holding today some students ... will be ready, able, and willing to defy their teachers on practically all orders....

e. *Morse v. Frederick, 551 U.S. 393 (2007): Should Speech in Public K-12 Schools Be Protected at All?*

[The chief debate in *Morse v. Frederick,* see p. 604, was about whether there should be an exception to protection for speech in K-12 schools that seems to advocate use of illegal drugs. But there was also an exchange about whether speech in public K-12 schools should be at all protected, with Justice Thomas reviving Justice Black's position, and elaborating on it.—ed.]

Justice Thomas, concurring ....

[A.] [T]he history of public education suggests that the First Amendment, as originally understood, does not protect student speech in public schools. Although colonial schools were exclusively private, ... [b]y the time the States ratified the Fourteenth Amendment, public schools had become relatively common. If students in public schools were originally understood as having free-speech rights, one would have expected 19th-century public schools to have respected those rights and courts to have enforced them [under state constitutions' speech clauses]. They did not.

During the colonial era, private schools ... managed classrooms with an iron hand.... Because public schools were initially created as substitutes for private schools, when States developed public education systems in the early 1800's, no one doubted the government's ability to educate and discipline children as private schools did.

Like their private counterparts, early public schools were not places for freewheeling debates or exploration of competing ideas. Rather, teachers instilled "a core of common values" in students and taught them self-control. A. Potter & G. Emerson, The School and the Schoolmaster: A Manual 125 (1843) ("By its discipline it contributes, insensibly, to generate a spirit of subordination to lawful authority, a power of self-control, and a habit of postponing present indulgence to a greater future good ...").

Teachers instilled these values not only by presenting ideas but also through strict discipline. Schools punished students for behavior the school considered disrespectful or wrong[, including] idleness, talking, profanity, and slovenliness[]. Rules of etiquette were enforced, and courteous behavior

was demanded. To meet their educational objectives, schools required absolute obedience. {Even at the college level, strict obedience was required of
students.}

[B.] Through the legal doctrine of *in loco parentis*, [19th-century] courts
upheld the right of [public as well as private] schools to discipline students,
to enforce rules, and to maintain order[,] [reasoning that] ... "One of the most
sacred duties of parents, is to train up and qualify their children, for becoming useful and virtuous members of society; this duty cannot be effectually
performed without the ability to command obedience, to control stubborn-
ness, to quicken diligence, and to reform bad habits .... The teacher is the
substitute of the parent; ... and in the exercise of these delegated duties, is
invested with his power." {My discussion is limited to elementary and secondary education. In these settings, courts have applied the doctrine of *in
loco parentis* regardless of the student's age. Therefore, the fact that Frederick was 18 and not a minor under Alaska law is inconsequential.}

In loco parentis

Applying *in loco parentis*, the judiciary was reluctant to interfere in the
routine business of school administration, allowing schools and teachers to
set and enforce rules and to maintain order. Thus, in the early years of public schooling, schools and teachers had considerable discretion in disciplinary matters[, including those related to speech] .... Courts routinely preserved the rights of teachers to punish speech that the school or teacher
thought was contrary to the interests of the school and its educational goals.
[Examples omitted.—ed.] The doctrine of *in loco parentis* limited the ability
of schools to set rules and control their classrooms in almost no way....

[C.] To be sure, our educational system faces administrative and pedagogical challenges different from those faced by 19th-century schools. And
the idea of treating children as though it were still the 19th century would
find little support today. But I see no constitutional imperative requiring
public schools to allow all student speech.

Parents decide whether to send their children to public schools. If parents do not like the rules imposed by those schools, they can seek redress in
school boards or legislatures; they can send their children to private schools
or home school them; or they can simply move. Whatever rules apply to student speech in public schools, those rules can be challenged by parents in
the political process.

Do they though?

In place of that democratic regime, *Tinker* substituted judicial oversight
of the day-to-day affairs of public schools.... [*Tinker*] imposed a new and malleable standard: Schools could not inhibit student speech unless it "substantially interfere[d] with the requirements of appropriate discipline in the operation of the school." Inherent in the application of that standard are judgment calls about what constitutes interference and what constitutes appropriate discipline. Historically, courts reasoned that only local school districts were entitled to make those calls. The *Tinker* Court usurped that traditional authority for the judiciary.

And because *Tinker* utterly ignored the history of public education,
courts ... routinely find it necessary to create ad hoc exceptions to its central

premise. This doctrine of exceptions creates confusion without fixing the underlying problem by returning to first principles....

Tinker has undermined the traditional authority of teachers to maintain order in public schools. "Once a society that generally respected the authority of teachers, deferred to their judgment, and trusted them to act in the best interest of school children, we now accept defiance, disrespect, and disorder as daily occurrences in many of our public schools."

We need look no further than this case for an example: Frederick asserts a constitutional right to utter at a school event what is either "[g]ibberish" or an open call to use illegal drugs. To elevate such impertinence to the status of constitutional protection would be farcical and would indeed be to "surrender control of the American public school system to public school students." *Tinker* (Black, J., dissenting) ...

Justice Alito, with whom Justice Kennedy joins, concurring [and responding to Justice Thomas] ....

It is a dangerous fiction to pretend that parents simply delegate their authority—including their authority to determine what their children may say and hear—to public school authorities. It is even more dangerous to assume that such a delegation of authority somehow strips public school authorities of their status as agents of the State.

Most parents, realistically, have no choice but to send their children to a public school and little ability to influence what occurs in the school. It is therefore wrong to treat public school officials, for purposes relevant to the First Amendment, as if they were private, nongovernmental actors standing *in loco parentis*....

f. *Bethel School Dist. No. 403 v. Fraser, 478 U.S. 675 (1986)*

Chief Justice Burger delivered the opinion of the Court....

[A.] Matthew N. Fraser, a student at Bethel High School in Pierce County, Washington, delivered a speech nominating a fellow student for student elective office[:]

{I know a man who is firm—he's firm in his pants, he's firm in his shirt, his character is firm—but most ... of all, his belief in you, the students of Bethel, is firm. Jeff Kuhlman is a man who takes his point and pounds it in. If necessary, he'll take an issue and nail it to the wall. He doesn't attack things in spurts—he drives hard, pushing and pushing until finally—he succeeds. Jeff is a man who will go to the very end—even the climax, for each and every one of you. So vote for Jeff for A.S.B. vice-president—he'll never come between you and the best our high school can be.}

Approximately 600 high school students, many of whom were 14-year-olds, attended the assembly.... The assembly was part of a school-sponsored educational program in self-government. Students who elected not to attend the assembly were required to report to study hall.

During the entire speech, Fraser referred to his candidate in terms of an elaborate, graphic, and explicit sexual metaphor. Two of Fraser's teachers, with whom he discussed the contents of his speech in advance, informed him that the speech was "inappropriate and that he probably should not deliver it," and that his delivery of the speech might have "severe consequences."

WARNED

During Fraser's delivery of the speech, a school counselor observed the reaction of students to the speech. Some students hooted and yelled; some by gestures graphically simulated the sexual activities pointedly alluded to in respondent's speech. Other students appeared to be bewildered and embarrassed by the speech. One teacher reported that on the day following the speech, she found it necessary to forgo a portion of the scheduled class lesson in order to discuss the speech with the class.

— Disrupt; talkin class

A Bethel High School disciplinary rule prohibiting the use of obscene language in the school provides: "Conduct which materially and substantially interferes with the educational process is prohibited, including the use of obscene, profane language or gestures." ... Fraser was ... suspended for three days [ultimately reduced to two days], and ... his name [was] removed from the list of candidates for graduation speaker[, though he was eventually permitted to speak at the graduation] ....

[B.] "[P]ublic education must prepare pupils for citizenship in the Republic.... It must inculcate the habits and manners of civility as values in themselves conducive to happiness and as indispensable to the practice of self-government in the community and the nation." ... These fundamental values of "habits and manners of civility" essential to a democratic society must, of course, include tolerance of divergent political and religious views, even when the views expressed may be unpopular. But these "fundamental values" must also take into account consideration of the sensibilities of others, and, in the case of a school, the sensibilities of fellow students.

"inculcate" prepare as citizens

The undoubted freedom to advocate unpopular and controversial views in schools and classrooms must be balanced against the society's countervailing interest in teaching students the boundaries of socially appropriate behavior. Even the most heated political discourse in a democratic society requires consideration for the personal sensibilities of the other participants and audiences.

Balance of Interests

In our Nation's legislative halls, where some of the most vigorous political debates in our society are carried on, there are rules prohibiting the use of expressions offensive to other participants in the debate. [Examples omitted.—ed.] Can it be that what is proscribed in the halls of Congress is beyond the reach of school officials to regulate?

Rules in legislatures

The First Amendment guarantees wide freedom in matters of adult public discourse.... It does not follow, however, that simply because the use of an offensive form of expression may not be prohibited to adults making what the speaker considers a political point, the same latitude must be permitted to children in a public school.... "[T]he First Amendment gives a high school student the classroom right to wear Tinker's armband, but not Cohen's jacket."

Same latitude not permitted to students

Surely it is a highly appropriate function of public school education to prohibit the use of vulgar and offensive terms in public discourse. Indeed, the "fundamental values necessary to the maintenance of a democratic political system" disfavor the use of terms of debate highly offensive or highly threatening to others. Nothing in the Constitution prohibits the states from insisting that certain modes of expression are inappropriate and subject to sanctions. The inculcation of these values is truly the "work of the schools." ...

The process of educating our youth for citizenship in public schools is not confined to books, the curriculum, and the civics class; schools must teach by example the shared values of a civilized social order. Consciously or otherwise, teachers—and indeed the older students—demonstrate the appropriate form of civil discourse and political expression by their conduct and deportment in and out of class.

Inescapably, like parents, they are role models. The schools, as instruments of the state, may determine that the essential lessons of civil, mature conduct cannot be conveyed in a school that tolerates lewd, indecent, or offensive speech and conduct such as that indulged in by this confused boy.

[C.] The pervasive sexual innuendo in Fraser's speech was plainly offensive to both teachers and students—indeed to any mature person. By glorifying male sexuality, and in its verbal content, the speech was acutely insulting to teenage girl students. The speech could well be seriously damaging to its less mature audience, many of whom were only 14 years old and on the threshold of awareness of human sexuality. Some students were reported as bewildered by the speech and the reaction of mimicry it provoked.

This Court's First Amendment jurisprudence has acknowledged limitations on the otherwise absolute interest of the speaker in reaching an unlimited audience where the speech is sexually explicit and the audience may include children. In *Ginsberg v. New York,* 390 U.S. 629 (1968), this Court upheld a New York statute banning the sale of sexually oriented material to minors, even though the material in question was entitled to First Amendment protection with respect to adults. And in addressing the question whether the First Amendment places any limit on the authority of public schools to remove books from a public school library, all Members of the Court ... acknowledged that the school board has the authority to remove books that are vulgar. *Board of Ed. v. Pico.*

These cases recognize the obvious concern on the part of parents, and school authorities acting *in loco parentis,* to protect children—especially in a captive audience—from exposure to sexually explicit, indecent, or lewd speech. We have also recognized an interest in protecting minors from exposure to vulgar and offensive spoken language. [See *FCC v. Pacifica Foundation.*] ...

Unlike the sanctions imposed on the students wearing armbands in *Tinker,* the penalties imposed in this case were unrelated to any political viewpoint. The First Amendment does not prevent the school officials from determining that to permit a vulgar and lewd speech such as respondent's would undermine the school's basic educational mission.

A high school assembly or classroom is no place for a sexually explicit monologue directed towards an unsuspecting audience of teenage students. Accordingly, it was perfectly appropriate for the school to disassociate itself to make the point to the pupils that vulgar speech and lewd conduct is wholly inconsistent with the "fundamental values" of public school education.... "... [T]he Federal Constitution [does not] compel the teachers, parents, and elected school officials to surrender control of the American public school system to public school students."

[D.] Respondent contends that the circumstances of his suspension violated due process because he had no way of knowing that the delivery of the speech in question would subject him to disciplinary sanctions.... [But g]iven the school's need to be able to impose disciplinary sanctions for a wide range of unanticipated conduct disruptive of the educational process, the school disciplinary rules need not be as detailed as a criminal code which imposes criminal sanctions. Two days' suspension from school does not rise to the level of a penal sanction calling for the full panoply of procedural due process protections applicable to a criminal prosecution. The school disciplinary rule proscribing "obscene" language and the prespeech admonitions of teachers gave adequate warning to Fraser that his lewd speech could subject him to sanctions....

Justice Blackmun concurs in the result.

Justice Brennan, concurring in the judgment....

[Justice Brennan reasoned that Fraser's speech wasn't very offensive, but held that school officials could punish it:—ed.] [T]he Court holds that under certain circumstances, high school students may properly be reprimanded for giving a speech at a high school assembly which school officials conclude disrupted the school's educational mission. Respondent's speech may well have been protected had he given it in school but under different circumstances, where the school's legitimate interests in teaching and maintaining civil public discourse were less weighty.

{The Court speculates that the speech was "insulting" to female students, and "seriously damaging" to 14-year-olds, so that school officials could legitimately suppress such expression in order to protect these groups. There is no evidence in the record that any students, male or female, found the speech "insulting." And while it was not unreasonable for school officials to conclude that respondent's remarks were inappropriate for a school-sponsored assembly, the language respondent used does not even approach the sexually explicit speech regulated in *Ginsberg v. New York,* or the indecent speech banned in *FCC v. Pacifica Foundation.*

Indeed, to my mind, respondent's speech was no more "obscene," "lewd," or "sexually explicit" than the bulk of programs currently appearing on prime time television or in the local cinema. Thus, I disagree with the Court's suggestion that school officials could punish respondent's speech out of a need to protect younger students.}

In the present case, school officials sought only to ensure that a high school assembly proceed in an orderly manner. There is no suggestion that school officials attempted to regulate respondent's speech because they disagreed with the views he sought to express.... Under the circumstances of this case, ... I believe that school officials did not violate the First Amendment in determining that respondent should be disciplined for the disruptive language he used while addressing a high school assembly....

Justice Marshall, dissenting....

[I]n my view the School District failed to demonstrate that respondent's remarks were indeed disruptive [under *Tinker*]....

Justice Stevens, dissenting....

[I]f a student is to be punished for using offensive speech, he is entitled to fair notice of the scope of the prohibition and the consequences of its violation. [Detailed discussion of why Justice Stevens thought that Fraser could not have reasonably expected his punishment omitted.—ed.]

g. *Morse v. Frederick, 551 U.S. 393 (2007)*

Chief Justice Roberts delivered the opinion of the Court....

[A.] On January 24, 2002, the Olympic Torch Relay passed through Juneau, Alaska, on its way to the winter games .... The torchbearers were to proceed along a street in front of Juneau-Douglas High School (JDHS) while school was in session. Petitioner Deborah Morse, the school principal, decided to permit staff and students to participate in the Torch Relay as an approved social event or class trip. Students were allowed to leave class to observe the relay from either side of the street. Teachers and administrative officials monitored the students' actions.

Respondent Joseph Frederick, a JDHS senior ... joined his friends (all but one of whom were JDHS students) across the street from the school to watch the event.... As the torchbearers and camera crews passed by, Frederick and his friends unfurled a 14-foot banner bearing the phrase: "BONG HiTS 4 JESUS." The large banner was easily readable by the students on the other side of the street....

Morse ... confiscated the banner and ... suspended [Frederick] for 10 days. Morse later explained that she told Frederick to take the banner down because she thought it encouraged illegal drug use, in violation of established school policy[, which] "... prohibits any ... public expression that ... advocates the use of substances that are illegal to minors ...." ...

[B.] [W]e reject Frederick's argument that this is not a school speech case .... The event occurred during normal school hours. It was sanctioned by Principal Morse "as an approved social event or class trip," and the school district's rules expressly provide that pupils in "approved social events and class trips are subject to district rules for student conduct."

Teachers and administrators were interspersed among the students and charged with supervising them. The high school band and cheerleaders performed. Frederick, standing among other JDHS students across the street from the school, directed his banner toward the school, making it plainly visible to most students.... There is some uncertainty at the outer boundaries as to when courts should apply school-speech precedents, but not on these facts....

[C.] Principal Morse thought the banner would be interpreted by those viewing it as promoting illegal drug use, and that interpretation is plainly a reasonable one.... First, the phrase could be interpreted as an imperative: "[Take] bong hits ..."—a message equivalent ... to "smoke marijuana" or "use an illegal drug." Alternatively, the phrase could be viewed as celebrating drug use—"bong hits [are a good thing]," or "[we take] bong hits"—and we discern no meaningful distinction between celebrating illegal drug use in the midst of fellow students and outright advocacy or promotion.

The pro-drug interpretation of the banner gains further plausibility given the paucity of alternative meanings the banner might bear.... Gibberish is surely a possible interpretation of the words on the banner, but it is not the only one, and dismissing the banner as meaningless ignores its undeniable reference to illegal drugs.... Frederick's "... explanation for the message—he just wanted to get on television" ... is a description of Frederick's *motive* for displaying the banner; it is not an interpretation of what the banner says. The way Frederick was going to fulfill his ambition of appearing on television was by unfurling a pro-drug banner at a school event, in the presence of teachers and fellow students....

[D.] [N]ot even Frederick argues that the banner conveys any sort of political or religious message.... [T]his is plainly not a case about political debate over the criminalization of drug use or possession....

[E.] [A] principal may, consistent with the First Amendment, restrict student speech at a school event, when that speech is reasonably viewed as promoting illegal drug use.... "[T]he constitutional rights of students in public school are not automatically coextensive with the rights of adults in other settings." ... [Moreover, as *Fraser* established,] *Tinker* is not the only basis for restricting student speech....

[D]eterring drug use by schoolchildren is an "important—indeed, perhaps compelling" interest. Drug abuse can cause severe and permanent damage to the health and well-being of young people. [Details omitted.—ed.] ... Nearly one in four 12th graders has used an illicit drug in the past month. Some 25% of high schoolers say that they have been offered, sold, or given an illegal drug on school property within the past year.

Congress has declared that part of a school's job is educating students about the dangers of illegal drug use. It has provided billions of dollars to support state and local drug-prevention programs, and required that schools receiving federal funds ... certify that their drug prevention programs "convey a clear and consistent message that ... the illegal use of drugs [is] wrong and harmful." ...

[P]eer pressure is perhaps "the single most important factor leading schoolchildren to take drugs," and ... students are more likely to use drugs when the norms in school appear to tolerate such behavior. Student speech celebrating illegal drug use at a school event, in the presence of school administrators and teachers, thus poses a particular challenge for school officials working to protect those entrusted to their care from the dangers of drug abuse.

The "special characteristics of the school environment," and the governmental interest in stopping student drug abuse ... allow schools to restrict student expression that they reasonably regard as promoting illegal drug use. *Tinker* warned that schools may not prohibit student speech because of "undifferentiated fear or apprehension of disturbance" or "a mere desire to avoid the discomfort and unpleasantness that always accompany an unpopular viewpoint." The danger here is far more serious and palpable. The particular concern to prevent student drug abuse at issue here, embodied in established school policy, extends well beyond an abstract desire to avoid controversy....

[F.] Petitioners urge us to adopt the broader rule that Frederick's speech is proscribable because it is plainly "offensive" as that term is used in Fraser. We think this stretches *Fraser* too far; that case should not be read to encompass any speech that could fit under some definition of "offensive." After all, much political and religious speech might be perceived as offensive to some. The concern here is not that Frederick's speech was offensive, but that it was reasonably viewed as promoting illegal drug use....

Justice Alito, with whom Justice Kennedy joins, concurring.

[A.] I join the opinion of the Court on the understanding that (a) it goes no further than to hold that a public school may restrict speech that a reasonable observer would interpret as advocating illegal drug use and (b) it provides no support for any restriction of speech that can plausibly be interpreted as commenting on any political or social issue, including speech on issues such as "the wisdom of the war on drugs or of legalizing marijuana for medicinal use." ...

I do not read the opinion to mean that there are necessarily any grounds for ... regulation [of speech by K-12 students] that are not already recognized in the holdings of this Court. In addition to *Tinker*, the decision in the present case allows the restriction of speech advocating illegal drug use; [and] *Fraser* permits the regulation of speech that is delivered in a lewd or vulgar manner as part of a middle school program ....

[B.] The opinion of the Court does not endorse the broad argument ... that the First Amendment permits public school officials to censor any student speech that interferes with a school's "educational mission." This argument can easily be manipulated in dangerous ways, and I would reject it before such abuse occurs....

During the *Tinker* era, a public school could have defined its educational mission to include solidarity with our soldiers and their families and thus could have attempted to outlaw the wearing of black armbands on the ground that they undermined this mission. Alternatively, a school could have defined its educational mission to include the promotion of world peace and could have sought to ban the wearing of buttons expressing support for the troops on the ground that the buttons signified approval of war. The "educational mission" argument would give public school authorities a license to suppress speech on political and social issues based on disagreement with the viewpoint expressed. The argument, therefore, strikes at the very heart of the First Amendment....

[C.] [A]ny argument for altering the usual free speech rules in the public schools ... [must] be based on some special characteristic of the school setting. The special characteristic that is relevant in this case is the threat to the physical safety of students.

School attendance can expose students to threats to their physical safety that they would not otherwise face.... During school hours, ... parents are not present to provide protection and guidance, and ... [s]tudents may be compelled on a daily basis to spend time at close quarters with other students who may do them harm....

In most settings, the First Amendment strongly limits the government's ability to suppress speech on the ground that it presents a threat of violence. See *Brandenburg v. Ohio*. But due to the special features of the school environment, school officials must have greater authority to intervene before speech leads to violence. And, in most cases, *Tinker*'s "substantial disruption" standard permits school officials to step in before actual violence erupts.

Speech advocating illegal drug use poses a threat to student safety that is just as serious, if not always as immediately obvious.... [I]llegal drug use presents a grave and in many ways unique threat to the physical safety of students. I therefore conclude that the public schools may ban speech advocating illegal drug use. But I regard such regulation as standing at the far reaches of what the First Amendment permits....

Justice Breyer, concurring in the judgment in part and dissenting in part. [Justice Breyer concluded that the issue in this case was difficult, and need not be reached for qualified immunity reasons that are not relevant here. But in the process he wrote:—ed.] ...

[A.] [The majority's holding could] authorize further viewpoint-based restrictions.... What about encouraging the [illegal] underage consumption of alcohol? .... What about a conversation during the lunch period where one student suggests that glaucoma sufferers should smoke marijuana to relieve the pain? What about deprecating commentary about an antidrug film shown in school? And what about drug messages mixed with other, more expressly political, content?

If, for example, Frederick's banner had read "LEGALIZE BONG HiTS," he might be thought to receive protection from the majority's rule, which goes to speech "encouraging illegal drug use." But speech advocating change in drug laws might also be perceived of as promoting the disregard of existing drug laws....

To say that illegal drug use is harmful to students, while surely true, does not itself constitute a satisfying explanation [of why drug use should be treated separately] because there are many such harms. During a real war, one less metaphorical than the war on drugs, the Court declined an opportunity to draw narrow subject-matter-based lines. Cf. *West Va. Bd. of Ed. v. Barnette* (holding students cannot be compelled to recite the Pledge of Allegiance during World War II). We should decline this opportunity today....

[B.] [The dissent, however,] would risk significant interference with reasonable school efforts to maintain discipline.... [W]hen a student unfurls a 14-foot banner (carrying an irrelevant or inappropriate message) during a school-related event in an effort to capture the attention of television cameras[,] ... a school official, knowing that adolescents often test the outer boundaries of acceptable behavior, may believe it is important (for the offending student and his classmates) to establish when a student has gone too far....

[C.] [A] decision on the underlying First Amendment issue is [thus] both difficult and unusually portentous. And that is a reason for us *not to decide* the issue unless we must. In some instances, it is appropriate to decide a constitutional issue in order to provide "guidance" for the future. But I cannot find much guidance in today's decision....

Nor ... is it easy to offer practically valuable guidance. Students will test the limits of acceptable behavior in myriad ways better known to schoolteachers than to judges; school officials need a degree of flexible authority to respond to disciplinary challenges; and the law has always considered the relationship between teachers and students special.

[Justice Breyer therefore concluded that the case should be decided on procedural grounds, which would let the Court decline to resolve the First Amendment issue.—ed.]

Justice Stevens, with whom Justice Souter and Justice Ginsburg join, dissenting....

[A.] [C]ensorship based on the content of speech, particularly censorship that depends on the viewpoint of the speaker, is subject to the most rigorous burden of justification .... [C]arving out pro-drug speech for uniquely harsh treatment finds no support in our case law and is inimical to the values protected by the First Amendment.

I will nevertheless assume for the sake of argument that the school's concededly powerful interest in protecting its students adequately supports its restriction on "any assembly or public expression that ... advocates the use of substances that are illegal to minors ...." Given that the relationship between schools and students "is custodial and tutelary, permitting a degree of supervision and control that could not be exercised over free adults," it might well be appropriate to tolerate some targeted viewpoint discrimination in this unique setting. And while conventional speech may be restricted only when likely to "incit[e] imminent lawless action," *Brandenburg*, it is possible that our rigid imminence requirement ought to be relaxed at schools.

[B.] But it is one thing to restrict speech that *advocates* drug use. It is another thing entirely to prohibit an obscure message with a drug theme that a third party subjectively—and not very reasonably—thinks is tantamount to express advocacy....

On occasion, the Court suggests it is deferring to the principal's "reasonable" judgment that Frederick's sign qualified as drug advocacy.... [But this] abdicates [the Court's] constitutional responsibility. The beliefs of third parties, reasonable or otherwise, have never dictated which messages amount to proscribable advocacy. Indeed, it would be a strange constitutional doctrine that would allow the prohibition of only the narrowest category of speech advocating unlawful conduct, yet would permit a listener's perceptions to determine which speech deserved constitutional protection. [Discussion of past cases omitted.—ed.] ...

[On the other hand, t]o the extent the Court independently finds that "BONG HiTS 4 JESUS" *objectively* amounts to the advocacy of illegal drug use—in other words, that it can *most* reasonably be interpreted as such—that conclusion practically refutes itself. This is a nonsense message, not advocacy. The Court's feeble effort to divine its hidden meaning is strong evidence of that. *Ante* (positing that the banner might mean, alternatively, "'[Take] bong hits,'" "'bong hits [are a good thing],'" or "'[we take] bong hits'"). Frederick's credible and uncontradicted explanation for the message—he just wanted to get on television—is also relevant because a speaker who does not intend to persuade his audience can hardly be said to be advocating anything....

[I]t takes real imagination to read a [cryptic] message ... with a slanting drug reference as an incitement to drug use.... The notion that the message on this banner would actually persuade either the average student or even the dumbest one to change his or her behavior is most implausible. That the Court believes such a silly message can be proscribed as advocacy underscores the novelty of its position, and suggests that the principle it articulates has no stopping point.

Even if advocacy could somehow be wedged into Frederick's obtuse reference to marijuana, that advocacy was at best subtle and ambiguous.... "[W]hen it comes to defining what speech qualifies as the functional equivalent of express advocacy ... we give the benefit of the doubt to speech, not censorship." ...

[C.] [The Court's] approach is deaf to the constitutional imperative to permit unfettered debate, even among high-school students, about the wisdom of the war on drugs or of legalizing marijuana for medicinal use. If Frederick's stupid reference to marijuana can in the Court's view justify censorship, then high school students everywhere could be forgiven for zipping their mouths about drugs [or alcohol] at school lest some "reasonable" observer ... punish them for promoting drugs [or alcohol]....

[But] it would be profoundly unwise to create special rules for speech about drug and alcohol use.... During [the] early stages [of the Vietnam War] "the dominant opinion" that Justice Harlan mentioned in his *Tinker* dissent regarded opposition to the war as unpatriotic, if not treason.... In 1965, when the Des Moines students wore their armbands, the school district's fear that they might "start an argument or cause a disturbance" was well founded.... [Yet a]s we now know, the then-dominant opinion about the Vietnam War was not etched in stone.

Reaching back still further, the current dominant opinion supporting the war on drugs in general, and our antimarijuana laws in particular, is reminiscent of the opinion that supported the nationwide ban on alcohol consumption when I was a student.... But just as prohibition ... was secretly questioned by thousands of otherwise law-abiding patrons of bootleggers and speakeasies, today the actions of literally millions of otherwise law-abiding users of marijuana, and of the majority of voters in each of the several States that tolerate medicinal uses of the product, lead me to wonder whether the fear of disapproval by those in the majority is silencing opponents of the war on drugs. Surely our national experience with alcohol should make us wary of dampening speech suggesting—however inarticulately—that it would be better to tax and regulate marijuana than to persevere in a futile effort to ban its use entirely.

Even in high school, a rule that permits only one point of view to be expressed is less likely to produce correct answers than the open discussion of countervailing views. In the national debate about a serious issue, it is the expression of the minority's viewpoint that most demands the protection of the First Amendment. Whatever the better policy may be, a full and frank discussion of the costs and benefits of the attempt to prohibit the use of marijuana is far wiser than suppression of speech because it is unpopular....

C. Government as Postmaster

Rule:

1. For content-based restrictions, same as government-as-sovereign.

— Until the mid-1900s, the government was seen as having almost unlimited authority over what it carried through its post office, especially when this involved special subsidies through the second class postage rate, *Milwaukee Social Dem. Pub. Co. v. Burleson,* 255 U.S. 407 (1921).

— In *Hannegan v. Esquire,* 327 U.S. 146 (1946), though, the Court signaled a retreat from this, and in *Lamont v. Postmaster General,* 381 U.S. 301 (1965), made it clear: The government has no extra authority to regulate the content of speech by virtue of its role as postmaster.

2. For content-neutral restrictions, the government probably has nearly unlimited authority to set rates, restrict package sizes, and so on.

D. Government as Landlord/Subsidizer/Speaker

1. Summary

a. *Summary: Property Used for Private Speech*

What happens when people try to speak (1) on government property (such as sidewalks, airport corridors, or rooms in a government building) or (2) using a government benefit program set up to promote private speech (such as funding for student newspapers or organizations)? The Court starts by classifying the program into one of the "forum" categories:

1. **The traditional public forum:** "government property that has traditionally been available for public expression"—sidewalks, parks, and the like (but not airports, *ISKCON v. Lee* (1992) (p. 616)).

— Here, the test is the same as when the government acts as sovereign. The government has no extra authority to restrict content stemming from its ownership of the property.

2. **The designated public forum:** "government property ... intentionally opened up for [the] purpose" of being a forum for the public at large to speak freely.

— Speech restrictions in such a forum "are subject to the same strict scrutiny as restrictions in a traditional public forum." *Christian Legal Society v. Martinez* (2010) (p. 633).

3. **The limited public forum:** government property "limited to use by certain groups or dedicated solely to the discussion of certain subjects."

— "[I]n such a forum, a governmental entity may impose restrictions on speech that are reasonable and viewpoint-neutral." *Christian Legal Society*. See item 4 for more details on this test; despite the separate labeling, limited public fora and nonpublic fora are treated similarly.

— Note: Some earlier cases, such as *ISKCON*, labeled this a type of designated public forum, and said that the test is the same as when the government acts as sovereign *except that* the government may limit the forum to the purposes for which it was created. But this in practice ended up being much the same as the reasonable-and-viewpoint-neutral test (since speaker and subject-matter limitations were permitted). And more recent cases, such as *Christian Legal Society*, have treated the limited public forum as a separate category, with the reasonable-and-viewpoint-neutral rule being the First Amendment test.

4. **Nonpublic forum:** all other government-owned property that's generally open to a defined group of people, but not for the purpose of promoting private speech (but instead just for the purpose of, say, flying from one city to another).

a. Restrictions on speech in a nonpublic forum must be *reasonable*,

— *i.e.*, "consistent with the [government's] legitimate interest in preserv[ing] the property" "for the use to which it is lawfully dedicated." *Perry*.

— The government need not show conclusive proof that the speech would interfere with the government's activities, but there must be some evidence of this. *Id.*

— This is somewhat more demanding than the rational basis test, see *ISKCON v. Lee* (O'Connor, J., for herself), though maybe not by much.

— A regulation is reasonable if the speech carried on by plaintiffs *as well as other similarly situated groups* would interfere in some measure with the state's interests. *ISKCON v. Lee.*

b. Restrictions on speech in a nonpublic forum must also be *viewpoint-neutral* (see the next subsection for more details on this).

c. In some government-owned places, such as military bases and prisons, the government's authority may be even broader. See *Brown v. Glines,* 444 U.S. 348 (1980); *Thornburgh v. Abbott,* 490 U.S. 401 (1989).

5. **Quality-based funding program:** Sometimes, the government creates a program to encourage private speech, but the program allocates scarce resources on the basis of some judgment of "quality," *e.g.*, the artistic excellence in *NEA v. Finley* (1997) (p. 626), rather than "indiscriminately" to an entire class of speakers (as in *Rosenberger*).

— "[I]nvidious viewpoint discrimination" may be impermissible here, but the government may "selectively fund a program to encourage certain activities it believes to be in the public interest."

— What "invidious viewpoint discrimination" means is not well-defined. For now, all we know is that a preference for "decency and respect" is not invidious viewpoint discrimination, but an attempt to "suppress[] ... dangerous ideas" probably would be.

6. **Not a forum at all—place for government speech:** Government property or a government funding program that the government uses to speak (through its employees or other agents)—for instance, a government-owned television channel, or perhaps an announcement board in a government building.

— Here, the government acting as speaker may decide what speech to allow, even based on viewpoint. *Rust v. Sullivan* (1991) (p. 643); *Walker v. Sons of Confederate Veterans* (2015) (p. 645); *Arkansas Ed. Television Comm'n v. Forbes*, 523 U.S. 666, 676-78 (1998).

Basic policy justification:

1. Traditional public fora may be government-owned, but they are held "in trust" for the public, *Hague v. CIO*, 307 U.S. 496 (1939), so members of the public should (generally) have as much right to speak there as they would on their own private property.

2. When the government opens a forum to the public, it shouldn't be able to skew public debate by then regulating speech there.

3. But on most government property, the government should be able to regulate speech in order to make its use of the property more efficient.

— Speech can interfere with efficiency by distracting people, interfering with traffic flow, and so on.

— It can also interfere with efficiency by making the government's "services [un]attractive to the marketplace" (*ISKCON v. Lee*).

b. *Summary: Viewpoint-Neutrality*

When the government restricts speech in its capacity as sovereign, or as proprietor of a traditional or designated public forum, the key question is often whether the restriction is *content-based*. But in limited public fora and nonpublic fora, the government has more power, except as to restrictions that are *viewpoint-based*. What's the difference?

Restrictions can be divided into three categories:

1. *Content-neutral* (which are therefore also viewpoint-neutral). Classic example: Noise restrictions; restrictions on the number of picketers.

2. *Content-based but viewpoint-neutral.* Classic example: Bans on profanity. More controversial example: Exclusion from a nonpublic forum of political (both candidate and issue) advertising, which a 4-Justice plurality held to be viewpoint-neutral in *Lehman v. Shaker Heights,* 418 U.S. 298 (1974).

3. *Viewpoint-based* (which are therefore also content-based). Classic examples: Restrictions on antiwar speech, racist speech, and the like. More controversial example: Exclusion of religious speech, held to be viewpoint-based in *Rosenberger v. Rector* (1995) (p. 623).

— A restriction isn't viewpoint-based simply because it is based on the legislators' viewpoint: All restrictions, even content-neutral ones, are based on legislators' viewpoints, for instance the viewpoint that noisy speech should be restricted.

— Nor is it viewpoint-based simply because the speech that it restricts expresses a viewpoint: Even content-neutral bans on residential picketing restrict speech that has some viewpoint.

— Nor is it viewpoint-based simply because it disproportionately affects some viewpoints: Bans on residential picketing in the 1980s, for example, probably disproportionately burdened anti-abortion picketers, since that movement was the one that most used such picketing then. See *Frisby v. Schultz* (1988) (p. 343).

— Rather, the question is whether the law inherently restricts some viewpoints while leaving others unrestricted.

c. Summary: Government Speech

Some government funding or benefit programs are treated as means for the government to express its own views. In those programs, the government may say whatever it wants to (setting aside possible Establishment Clause limits on pro- or anti-religious speech), even if this favors one viewpoint over another. These programs are sometimes labeled "government speech" and sometimes, as noted above, "not a forum at all."

The government is thus free to control—even based on viewpoint—what is said in its official publications (newspapers, broadcasts, and the like) or in material it officially endorses. And when the government spreads its message by paying private parties to convey the message, the government may require that the payment be used only for the speech it wants communicated. *Rust v. Sullivan* (1991) (p. 643).

How does one distinguish (A) such programs, which are "designed ... to promote a governmental message" (such as the "programmatic message recognized in *Rust*"), from (B) programs created "to encourage a diversity of views from private speakers," *Rosenberger v. Rector* (1995) (p. 623), in which viewpoint-neutrality is required? *Walker v. Sons of Confederate Veterans* (2015) (p. 645) tries to answer that question, but doesn't set forth a clear line. It holds that three factors are relevant:

1. Whether the *history* of the program shows that it has "long ... communicated messages from the [government]."

2. Whether the speech in the program is "*often closely identified in the public mind* with the [government]."

3. Whether the government "maintains *direct control* over the messages conveyed" in the program.

And *Walker* also reaffirms that three past cases involved nonpublic forums for private speech (where viewpoint-neutrality is required) and *not* government speech (where viewpoint discrimination is allowed):

1. *Perry Ed. Assn. v. Perry Local Educators' Assn.*, 460 U.S. 37 (1983), where "a school district's internal mail system" was "a nonpublic forum for private speech. There, ... a number of private organizations, including a teachers' union, had access to the mail system. It was therefore clear that private parties, and not only the government, used the system to communicate [without the speech being] ... formally approved by and stamped with the imprimatur of [the government]."

2. *Lehman v. City of Shaker Heights*, 418 U.S. 298 (1974), where "advertising space on city buses" was a nonpublic forum, because the "context (advertising space) [was] traditionally available for private speech" and "bore no indicia that the speech was owned or conveyed by the government."

3. *Cornelius v. NAACP Legal Defense & Ed. Fund, Inc.*, 473 U.S. 788 (1985), where "a charitable fundraising program directed at federal employees constituted a nonpublic forum" because it "had never been a medium for government speech," was not designed "to communicate messages from the government," and "did not appear on a government ID under the government's name." (This was so even though charitable organizations' pitches were placed in a government-printed pamphlet distributed by government employees in government workplaces.)

d. Summary: Government Subsidies Used to Control Other Speech

The government may not use conditions on government funding to control its recipients' privately funded speech. *Agency for Int'l Development v. Alliance for Open Society Int'l* (2013) (p. 655). The government

1. may impose "conditions that define the limits of the government spending program—those that specify the activities [the government] wants to subsidize"—but

2. may not "leverage funding to regulate speech outside the contours of the program itself."

e. Problem: Bruin Astrological Society

The UCLA College of Letters and Science decides to fund monthly student science newspapers. The Bruin Astrological Society applies for funds to print a newspaper devoted to astrology; the College refuses to pay up, and the BAS goes to court. What result?

f. Problem: City Web Site

The City of Cookeville sets up a Web site which contains, among other things, links to the Web pages of various local businesses. When the *Putnam Pit,* a local alternative newspaper, demands that the city include a link to its site, the city refuses. The *Putnam Pit* sues. What result? Cf. *Putnam Pit, Inc. v. City of Cookeville,* 221 F.3d 834 (6th Cir. 2000).

g. A Flowchart for Government as Subsidizer/Speaker

1. Is the government imposing conditions on how subsidy recipients *spend money they get from other sources*?

— If "yes," then

> apply the government-as-sovereign rules described in Parts II to V. *Agency for Int'l Dev. v. Alliance for Open Society Int'l,*

otherwise ask:

> 2. Is the government using the speakers to *express its own message,* or is it *trying to encourage a diversity of private views*?
>
> — If "express its own message," then
>
> > the program is constitutional, see *Rust v. Sullivan,*
>
> otherwise ask:
>
> > 3. Is the government trying to encourage a diversity of private views *using a quality judgment,* or *using an objective criterion*?
> >
> > — If "using a quality judgment," then
> >
> > > apply *NEA v. Finley*, which only prohibits "invidious viewpoint discrimination,"
> >
> > otherwise
> >
> > > apply forum analysis, which requires at least that the program be reasonable and viewpoint-neutral (*Rosenberger v. Rector*).

2. GOVERNMENT PROPERTY USED FOR PRIVATE SPEECH

a. Problem: "Hair"

Chattanooga, Tennessee owns a theater. Southeastern Promotions wants to put on a revival of the musical *Hair,* which contains some nudity. Chattanooga city policy is not to allow any plays involving nudity at its theater, so city officials refuse to let the musical be performed. Southeastern

Promotions sues, claiming a violation of the First Amendment. What result? Cf. *Southeastern Promotions, Ltd. v. Conrad,* 420 U.S. 546 (1975).

b. *ISKCON v. Lee, 505 U.S. 672 (1992), and Lee v. ISKCON, 505 U.S. 830 (1992)*

   i.   *Classifying the Forum*

Chief Justice Rehnquist delivered the opinion of the Court....

[A.] International Society for Krishna Consciousness, Inc. (ISKCON), is a not-for-profit religious corporation whose members perform a ritual known as *sankirtan.* The ritual consists of "going into public places, disseminating religious literature and soliciting funds to support the religion." The primary purpose of this ritual is raising funds for the movement....

Walter Lee ... was the police superintendent of the Port Authority of New York and New Jersey ...[, which] owns and operates ... John F. Kennedy ..., La Guardia ..., and Newark ... Airport[s].... The airports are funded by user fees and operated to make a regulated profit....

The terminals are generally accessible to the general public and contain various commercial establishments such as restaurants, snack stands, bars, newsstands, and stores of various types. Virtually all who visit the terminals do so for purposes related to air travel. These visitors principally include passengers, those meeting or seeing off passengers, flight crews, and terminal employees.

The Port Authority has adopted a regulation forbidding within the terminals [but not on the sidewalks outside the terminals] the repetitive solicitation of money or distribution of literature. The regulation states:

> ... The following conduct is prohibited within the interior areas of buildings or structures at an air terminal if conducted by a person to or with passersby in a continuous or repetitive manner:
> (a) The sale or distribution of any merchandise ....
> (b) The sale or distribution of flyers, brochures, pamphlets, books or any other printed or written material.
> (c) The solicitation and receipt of funds....

[B.] ... [Charitable solicitation] is a form of speech protected under the First Amendment [citing earlier cases—ed.].... [But w]here the government is acting as a proprietor, managing its internal operations, rather than acting as lawmaker with the power to regulate or license, its action will not be subjected to the heightened review to which its actions as a lawmaker may be subject.

Thus, we have upheld a ban on political advertisements in city-operated transit vehicles, even though the city permitted other types of advertising on those vehicles. *Lehman v. City of Shaker Heights,* 418 U.S. 298 (1974). Similarly, we have permitted a school district to limit access to an internal mail system used to communicate with teachers employed by the district. *Perry Ed. Assn. v. Perry Local Educators' Assn.,* 460 U.S. 37 (1983).

These cases reflect, either implicitly or explicitly, a "forum based" approach for assessing restrictions that the government seeks to place on the use of its property. Under this approach, regulation of speech on government property that has traditionally been available for public expression is subject to the highest scrutiny. Such regulations survive only if they are narrowly drawn to achieve a compelling state interest.

The second category of public property is the designated public forum, whether of a limited or unlimited character—property that the State has opened for expressive activity by part or all of the public. Regulation of such property is subject to the same limitations as that governing a traditional public forum.

Finally, there is all remaining public property. Limitations on expressive activity conducted on this last category of property ... need only be reasonable, as long as the regulation is not an effort to suppress the speaker's activity due to disagreement with the speaker's view....

The suggestion that the government has a high burden in justifying speech restrictions relating to traditional public fora made its first appearance in *Hague v. CIO,* 307 U.S. 496 (1939). Justice Roberts, concluding that individuals have a right to use "streets and parks for communication of views," reasoned that such a right flowed from the fact that "streets and parks ... have immemorially been held in trust for the use of the public and, time out of mind, have been used for purposes of assembly, communicating thoughts between citizens, and discussing public questions." ...

[A] traditional public forum is property that has as "a principal purpose ... the free exchange of ideas." Moreover, consistent with the notion that the government—like other property owners—"has power to preserve the property under its control for the use to which it is lawfully dedicated," the government does not create a public forum by inaction.

Nor is a public forum created "whenever members of the public are permitted freely to visit a place owned or operated by the Government." The decision to create a public forum must instead be made "by intentionally opening a nontraditional forum for public discourse." Finally, we have recognized that the location of property also has bearing because separation from acknowledged public areas may serve to indicate that the separated property is a special enclave, subject to greater restriction.

[C.] These precedents foreclose the conclusion that airport terminals are public fora. Reflecting the general growth of the air travel industry, airport terminals have only recently achieved their contemporary size and character. But given the lateness with which the modern air terminal has made its appearance, it hardly qualifies for the description of having "immemorially ... time out of mind" been held in the public trust and used for purposes of expressive activity.

Moreover, even within the rather short history of air transport, it is only "[i]n recent years [that] it has become a common practice for various religious and non-profit organizations to use commercial airports as a forum for the distribution of literature, the solicitation of funds, the proselytizing of new members, and other similar activities." Thus, the tradition of airport activity does not demonstrate that airports have historically been made available for speech activity.

Nor can we say that these particular terminals, or airport terminals generally, have been intentionally opened by their operators to such activity; the frequent and continuing litigation evidencing the operators' objections belies any such claim. In short, there can be no argument that society's time-tested judgment, expressed through acquiescence in a continuing practice, has resolved the issue in petitioners' favor.

Petitioners attempt to circumvent the history and practice governing airport activity by pointing our attention to the variety of speech activity that they claim historically occurred at various "transportation nodes" such as rail stations, bus stations, wharves, and Ellis Island. Even if we were inclined to accept petitioner's historical account describing speech activity at these locations, an account respondent contests, we think that such evidence is of little import for two reasons.

First, much of the evidence is irrelevant to *public* fora analysis, because sites such as bus and rail terminals traditionally have had *private* ownership. The development of privately owned parks that ban speech activity would not change the public fora status of publicly held parks. But the reverse is also true. The practices of privately held transportation centers do not bear on the government's regulatory authority over a publicly owned airport.

Second, the relevant unit for our inquiry is an airport, not "transportation nodes" generally. When new methods of transportation develop, new methods for accommodating that transportation are also likely to be needed. And with each new step, it therefore will be a new inquiry whether the transportation necessities are compatible with various kinds of expressive activity.

To make a category of "transportation nodes," therefore, would unjustifiably elide what may prove to be critical differences of which we should rightfully take account. The "security magnet," for example, is an airport commonplace that lacks a counterpart in bus terminals and train stations. And public access to air terminals is also not infrequently restricted—just last year the Federal Aviation Administration required airports for a 4-month period to limit access to areas normally publicly accessible. To blithely equate airports with other transportation centers, therefore, would be a mistake....

[A]irports are commercial establishments funded by user[] fees and designed to make a regulated profit, ... where nearly all who visit do so for some travel related purpose. As commercial enterprises, airports must provide services attractive to the marketplace. In light of this, it cannot fairly be said that an airport terminal has as a principal purpose promoting "the free exchange of ideas." ...

Justice Kennedy, [joined by] Justice Blackmun, Justice Stevens, and Justice Souter[, dissenting on this point] ....

[A.] The Court's approach is contrary to the underlying purposes of the public forum doctrine... Public places are of necessity the locus for discussion of public issues, as well as protest against arbitrary government action.... The recognition that certain government-owned property is a public forum provides open notice to citizens that their freedoms may be exercised there without fear of a censorial government, adding tangible reinforcement to the idea that we are a free people.

A fundamental tenet of our Constitution is that the government is subject to constraints which private persons are not. The public forum doctrine vindicates that principle by recognizing limits on the government's control over speech activities on property suitable for free expression....

[B.] The notion that traditional public forums are properties that have public discourse as their principal purpose is a most doubtful fiction. The types of property that we have recognized as the quintessential public forums are streets, parks, and sidewalks.... [But] the principal purpose of streets and sidewalks, like airports, is to facilitate transportation, not public discourse .... Similarly, the purpose for the creation of public parks may be as much for beauty and open space as for discourse. Thus under the Court's analysis, even the quintessential public forums would appear to lack the necessary elements of what the Court defines as a public forum....

In my view the policies underlying [public forum] doctrine cannot be given effect unless we recognize that open, public spaces and thoroughfares that are suitable for discourse may be public forums, whatever their historical pedigree and without concern for a precise classification of the property.... In a country where most citizens travel by automobile, and parks all too often become locales for crime rather than social intercourse, our failure to recognize the possibility that new types of government property may be appropriate forums for speech will lead to a serious curtailment of our expressive activity.

One of the places left in our mobile society that is suitable for discourse is a metropolitan airport.... [A]n airport is one of the few government-owned spaces where many persons have extensive contact with other members of the public. Given that private spaces of similar character are not subject to the dictates of the First Amendment, it is critical that we preserve these areas for protected speech.

In my view, our public forum doctrine must recognize this reality, and allow the creation of public forums that do not fit within the narrow tradition of streets, sidewalks, and parks.... If the objective, physical characteristics of the property at issue and the actual public access and uses that have been permitted by the government indicate that expressive activity would be appropriate and compatible with those uses, the property is a public forum. The most important considerations in this analysis are whether the property shares physical similarities with more traditional public forums, whether the government has permitted or acquiesced in broad public access to the property, and whether expressive activity would tend to interfere in a significant way with the uses to which the government has as a factual matter dedicated the property.

In conducting the last inquiry, courts must consider the consistency of those uses with expressive activities in general, rather than the specific sort of speech at issue in the case before it; otherwise the analysis would be one not of classification but rather of case-by-case balancing, and would provide little guidance to the State regarding its discretion to regulate speech. Courts must also consider the availability of reasonable time, place, and manner restrictions in undertaking this compatibility analysis. The possibility of some theoretical inconsistency between expressive activities and the property's uses should not bar a finding of a public forum, if those inconsistencies can be avoided through simple and permitted regulations....

[C.] Under this analysis, it is evident that the public spaces of the Port Authority's airports are public forums. First, ... the public spaces in the airports are[, like streets and sidewalks,] broad, public thoroughfares full of people and lined with stores and other commercial activities....

Second, the airport areas involved here are open to the public without restriction.... And while most people who come to the Port Authority's airports do so for a reason related to ... travel ... this does not distinguish an airport from streets or sidewalks ....

Third, ... when adequate time, place, and manner regulations are in place, expressive activity is quite compatible with the uses of major airports.... Inconvenience [cause by congestion] does not absolve the government of its obligation to tolerate speech.... [T]he logical consequence of the Port Authority's congestion argument is that the crowded streets and sidewalks of major cities cannot be public forums. These problems have been dealt with ... in other settings[] through proper time, place, and manner restrictions; and the Port Authority does not make any showing that similar regulations would not be effective in its airports....

ii. *Applying the Reasonableness Test: Solicitation*

[Once the majority concluded that the airport was a nonpublic forum, they had to decide whether the leafletting ban and the solicitation ban were reasonable. (The bans were clearly viewpoint-neutral.) The majority agreed that the solicitation ban was reasonable, but Justice O'Connor concluded that the leafletting ban was not reasonable; her vote, plus the votes of Justices Blackmun, Stevens, Kennedy, and Souter, led to the leafletting ban being struck down.—ed.]

Chief Justice Rehnquist [delivered the opinion of the Court upholding the solicitation ban]....

"Solicitation requires action by those who would respond: The individual solicited must decide whether or not to contribute (which itself might involve reading the solicitor's literature or hearing his pitch), and then, having decided to do so, reach for a wallet, search it for money, write a check, or produce a credit card." Passengers who wish to avoid the solicitor may have to alter their paths, slowing both themselves and those around them. The result is that the normal flow of traffic is impeded.

This is especially so in an airport, where "[a]ir travelers, who are often weighted down by cumbersome baggage ... may be hurrying to catch a plane or to arrange ground transportation." Delays may be particularly costly in this setting, as a flight missed by only a few minutes can result in hours worth of subsequent inconvenience.

In addition, face-to-face solicitation presents risks of duress that are an appropriate target of regulation. The skillful, and unprincipled, solicitor can target the most vulnerable, including those accompanying children or those suffering physical impairment and who cannot easily avoid the solicitation. The unsavory solicitor can also commit fraud through concealment of his affiliation or through deliberate efforts to shortchange those who agree to purchase.

Compounding this problem is the fact that, in an airport, the targets of such activity frequently are on tight schedules. This in turn makes such visitors unlikely to stop and formally complain to airport authorities. As a result, the airport faces considerable difficulty in achieving its legitimate interest in monitoring solicitation activity to assure that travelers are not interfered with unduly.

The Port Authority has concluded that its interest in monitoring the activities can best be accomplished by limiting solicitation and distribution to the sidewalk areas outside the terminals. This sidewalk area is frequented by an overwhelming percentage of airport users. Thus the resulting access of those who would solicit the general public is quite complete. In turn we think it would be odd to conclude that the Port Authority's terminal regulation is unreasonable despite the Port Authority having otherwise assured access to an area universally traveled.

The inconveniences to passengers and the burdens on Port Authority officials flowing from solicitation activity may seem small, but viewed against the fact that "pedestrian congestion is one of the greatest problems facing the three terminals," the Port Authority could reasonably worry that even such incremental effects would prove quite disruptive.

Moreover, "[t]he justification for the Rule should not be measured by the disorder that would result from granting an exemption solely to ISKCON." For if ISKCON is given access, so too must other groups. "Obviously, there would be a much larger threat to the State's interest in crowd control if all other religious, nonreligious, and noncommercial organizations could likewise move freely." As a result, we conclude that the solicitation ban is reasonable....

[Because Justices Blackmun, Stevens, Kennedy, and Souter thought the airport was a traditional public forum, they concluded that the solicitation ban should be evaluated under intermediate scrutiny; Justice Kennedy thought it passed intermediate scrutiny, and the other three Justices thought it failed. Those opinions are omitted, because they do not directly bear on the nonpublic forum rules we are considering here.—ed.]

iii. Applying the Reasonableness Test: Leafletting

Justice O'Connor, [concurring in the judgment striking down the leafletting ban—ed.]....

[R]estrictions on speech in nonpublic fora are valid only if they are "reasonable" and "not an effort to suppress expression merely because public officials oppose the speaker's view." ... "[R]easonableness ... must be assessed in light of the purpose of the forum and all the surrounding circumstances." ... [A] restriction on speech in a nonpublic forum is "reasonable" when it is "consistent with the [government's] legitimate interest in 'preserv[ing] the property ... for the use to which it is lawfully dedicated.'"

Ordinarily, this inquiry is relatively straightforward, because we have almost always been confronted with cases where the fora at issue were discrete, single-purpose facilities.... [But] the Port Authority is operating a shopping mall [with stores such as restaurants, cocktail lounges, banks, barber shops, and private clubs] as well as an airport. The reasonableness inquiry, therefore, is not whether the restrictions on speech are "consistent with ... preserving the property" for air travel, but whether they are reasonably related to maintaining the multipurpose environment that the Port Authority has deliberately created.

Applying that standard, [the solicitation ban is reasonable but the leafletting ban is not].... Although we do not "requir[e] that ... proof be present to justify the denial of access to a nonpublic forum on grounds that the proposed use may disrupt the property's intended function," we have required some explanation as to why certain speech is inconsistent with the intended use of the forum.... Because I cannot see how peaceful pamphleteering is incompatible with the multipurpose environment of the Port Authority airports, I cannot accept that a total ban on that activity is reasonable without an explanation as to why such a restriction "preserv[es] the property" for the several uses to which it has been put.

Justice Kennedy, with whom Justice Blackmun, Justice Stevens, and Justice Souter join [in relevant part], concurring in the judgment[as to leafletting—ed.]....

[Because these Justices concluded that the airport was a traditional public forum, they applied intermediate scrutiny, and held that the prohibition failed such scrutiny.—ed.]

Chief Justice Rehnquist, with whom Justice White, Justice Scalia, and Justice Thomas join, [dissenting as to the leafletting ban—ed.]....

Leafletting presents risks of congestion similar to those posed by solicitation ... [especially when considering] the cumulative impact that will result if all groups are permitted terminal access.... I [thus] conclude that the distribution ban, no less than the solicitation ban, is reasonable....

The weary, harried, or hurried traveler may have no less desire and need to avoid the delays generated by having literature foisted upon him than he does to avoid delays from a financial solicitation. And while a busy passenger perhaps may succeed in fending off a leafletter with minimal disruption to himself by agreeing simply to take the proffered material, this does not completely ameliorate the dangers of congestion flowing from such leafletting. Others may choose not simply to accept the material but also to stop and engage the leafletter in debate, obstructing those who follow. Moreover, those who accept material may often simply drop it on the floor once out of the leafletter's range, creating an eyesore, a safety hazard, and additional clean-up work for airport staff....

c.   *Rosenberger v. Rector, 515 U.S. 819 (1995)*

Justice Kennedy delivered the opinion of the Court.

[The University of Virginia had a policy of paying the printing bills of newspapers run by student groups, so long as the newspapers did not "primarily promot[e] or manifest[] a particular belie[f] in or about a deity or an ultimate reality" or engage in electioneering or lobbying. The students who published *Wide Awake,* a newspaper with a Christian editorial viewpoint, sued, claiming the policy violated the Free Speech Clause.—ed.] ...

Policy

[A.] [The State may not] exercise viewpoint discrimination, even [in a] limited public forum [that is] of its own creation.... The [funding program] is a forum more in a metaphysical than in a spatial or geographic sense, but the same principles are applicable....

Rule

[V]iewpoint discrimination is the proper way to interpret the University's objections to Wide Awake. By the very terms of the ... prohibition, the University does not exclude religion as a subject matter but selects for disfavored treatment those student journalistic efforts with religious editorial viewpoints. Religion may be a vast area of inquiry, but it also provides, as it did here, a specific premise, a perspective, a standpoint from which a variety of subjects may be discussed and considered. The prohibited perspective, not the general subject matter, resulted in the refusal to make third-party payments, for the subjects discussed were otherwise within the approved category of publications.

This is VP discr !!

Perspective

The dissent's assertion that no viewpoint discrimination occurs because the Guidelines discriminate against an entire class of viewpoints reflects an insupportable assumption that all debate is bipolar and that anti-religious speech is the only response to religious speech.... If the topic of debate is, for example, racism, then exclusion of several views on that problem is just as offensive to the First Amendment as exclusion of only one. It is as objectionable to exclude both a theistic and an atheistic perspective on the debate as it is to exclude one, the other, or yet another political, economic, or social viewpoint. The dissent's declaration that debate is not skewed so long as multiple voices are silenced is simply wrong; the debate is skewed in multiple ways....

Response to Dissent

[B.] [W]hen the State is the speaker, it may make content-based choices. When the University determines the content of the education it provides, it is the University speaking, and we have permitted the government to regulate the content of what is or is not expressed when it is the speaker or when it enlists private entities to convey its own message.

In the same vein, in *Rust v. Sullivan,* we upheld the government's prohibition on abortion-related advice applicable to recipients of federal funds
for family planning counseling. There, the government did not create a program to encourage private speech but instead used private speakers to
transmit specific information pertaining to its own program.... When the
government disburses public funds to private entities to convey a governmental message, it may take legitimate and appropriate steps to ensure that
its message is neither garbled nor distorted by the grantee.

It does not follow, however, ... that viewpoint-based restrictions are proper when the University does not itself speak or subsidize transmittal of a
message it favors but instead expends funds to encourage a diversity of
views from private speakers.... Although acknowledging that the Government is not required to subsidize the exercise of fundamental rights, we reaffirmed [in *Regan v. Taxation With Representation*] the requirement of
viewpoint neutrality in the Government's provision of financial benefits by
observing that "[t]he case would be different if Congress were to discriminate invidiously in its subsidies in such a way as to 'ai[m]' at the suppression
of dangerous ideas.'" ...

The distinction between the University's own favored message and the
private speech of students is evident .... [I]n the agreement each [eligible
group] must sign[, t]he University declares that the student groups eligible
for ... support are not the University's agents, are not subject to its control,
and are not its responsibility. Having offered to pay the third-party contractors on behalf of private speakers who convey their own messages, the University may not silence the expression of selected viewpoints.

The University urges that, from a constitutional standpoint, funding of
speech differs from provision of access to facilities because money is scarce
and physical facilities are not. Beyond the fact that in any given case this
proposition might not be true as an empirical matter, the underlying premise that the University could discriminate based on viewpoint if demand for
space exceeded its availability is wrong as well.... [In such a case, it would
be] incumbent on the State ... to ration or allocate the scarce resources on
some acceptable neutral principle ....

[C.] The prohibition on funding on behalf of publications that "primarily
promot[e] or manifes[t] a particular belie[f] in or about a deity or an ultimate
reality," in its ordinary and commonsense meaning, has a vast potential
reach. The term "promotes" as used here would comprehend any writing
advocating a philosophic position that rests upon a belief in a deity or ultimate reality. And the term "manifests" would bring within the scope of the
prohibition any writing that is explicable as resting upon a premise which
presupposes the existence of a deity or ultimate reality.

Were the prohibition applied with much vigor at all, it would bar funding of essays by hypothetical student contributors named Plato, Spinoza,
and Descartes. And if the regulation covers, as the University says it does,

those student journalistic efforts which primarily manifest or promote a belief that there is no deity and no ultimate reality, then undergraduates
named Karl Marx, Bertrand Russell, and Jean-Paul Sartre would likewise
have some of their major essays excluded from student publications....

[T]he regulation invoked to deny [funding] support, both in its terms and
in its application to these petitioners, is a denial of their right of free speech
guaranteed by the First Amendment. It remains to be considered whether
the violation following from the University's action is excused by the necessity of complying with the Constitution's prohibition against state establishment of religion.... [We conclude that there is no such necessity.] [See p. 910
for that discussion.—ed.]

**Justice Souter, with whom Justice Stevens, Justice Ginsburg,
and Justice Breyer join, dissenting....**

[W]hether a distinction is based on viewpoint does not turn simply on
whether a government regulation happens to be applied to a speaker who
seeks to advance a particular viewpoint; the issue, of course, turns on
whether the burden on speech is explained by reference to viewpoint....
"[T]he government's purpose is the controlling consideration." So, for example, a city that enforces its excessive noise ordinance by pulling the plug on
a rock band using a forbidden amplification system is not guilty of viewpoint
discrimination simply because the band wishes to use that equipment to
espouse antiracist views....

Accordingly, the prohibition on viewpoint discrimination serves that important purpose of the Free Speech Clause, which is to bar the government
from skewing public debate. Other things being equal, viewpoint discrimination occurs when government allows one message while prohibiting the
messages of those who can reasonably be expected to respond.

It is precisely this element of taking sides in a public debate that identifies viewpoint discrimination and makes it the most pernicious of all distinctions based on content. Thus, if government assists those espousing one
point of view, neutrality requires it to assist those espousing opposing points
of view, as well.... [But the university regulation] applies to Muslim and
Jewish and Buddhist advocacy as well as to Christian. And since it limits
funding to activities promoting or manifesting a particular belief not only
"in" but "about" a deity or ultimate reality, it applies to agnostics and atheists as well as it does to deists and theists.

The Guidelines, and their application to Wide Awake[, the manifest
function of which is to call students to repentance, to commitment to Jesus
Christ, and to particular moral action because of its Christian character],
thus do not skew debate by funding one position but not its competitors. As
understood by their application to Wide Awake, they simply deny funding
for hortatory speech that "primarily promotes or manifests" any view on the
merits of religion; they deny funding for the entire subject matter of religious apologetics.... [T]he regulation is being applied, not to deny funding
for those who discuss issues in general from a religious viewpoint, but to
those engaged in promoting or opposing religious conversion and religious

observances as such. If this amounts to viewpoint discrimination, the Court has all but eviscerated the line between viewpoint and content.

To put the point another way, the Court's decision equating a categorical exclusion of both sides of the religious debate with viewpoint discrimination suggests the Court has concluded that primarily religious and antireligious speech, grouped together, always provides an opposing (and not merely a related) viewpoint to any speech about any secular topic. Thus, the Court's reasoning requires a university that funds private publications about any primarily nonreligious topic also to fund publications primarily espousing adherence to or rejection of religion.

But a university's decision to fund a magazine about racism, and not to fund publications aimed at urging repentance before God does not skew the debate either about racism or the desirability of religious conversion. The Court's contrary holding amounts to a significant reformulation of our viewpoint discrimination precedents and will significantly expand access to limited-access forums.

d. Problem: NEA Grant Applications

Two artists, both technically excellent painters, apply for NEA grants. The first wants to create a mural depicting why America has been a force for evil in the world. The second wants to create a mural on the theme "the white race is superior to all others."

The advisory panel that's asked to consider the applications denies them. The panel's members reason that NEA funds are best spent to fund other projects, because (1) other projects are more likely than these two to show respect for America's diverse beliefs and values, (2) other projects are more likely to be artistically excellent than these two, because works that elevate the viewer are more likely to be artistically excellent than works that express contempt, and (3) the members anticipate little public interest in or appreciation of these two works. How would these denials be treated under the three opinions in this case? How should they be treated?

e. NEA v. Finley, 524 U.S. 569 (1998)

> In the Neolithic Age savage warfare did I wage
> For food and fame and woolly horses' pelt.
> I was singer to my clan in that dim, red Dawn of Man,
> And I sang of all we fought and feared and felt....
>> But a rival of Solutré told the tribe my style was outré—
>> 'Neath a tomahawk, of diorite, he fell.
>> And I left my views on Art, barbed and tanged, below the heart
>> Of a mammothistic etcher at Grenelle.
> Then I stripped them, scalp from skull, And my hunting-dogs fed full,
> And their teeth I threaded neatly on a thong;
> And I wiped my mouth and said, "It is well that they are dead,
> For I know my work is right and theirs was wrong."
> —Rudyard Kipling, *In the Neolithic Age*

Justice O'Connor delivered the opinion of the Court....

[A.] Applications for [National Endowment for the Arts] funding are initially reviewed by advisory panels composed of experts in the relevant field of the arts. Under the 1990 Amendments to the enabling statute, those panels must reflect "diverse artistic and cultural points of view" and include "wide geographic, ethnic, and minority representation," as well as "lay individuals who are knowledgeable about the arts." The panels report to the 26-member National Council on the Arts ..., which, in turn, advises the NEA Chairperson. The Chairperson has the ultimate authority to award grants but may not approve an application as to which the Council has made a negative recommendation....

Two provocative works ... prompted public controversy in 1989 .... The Institute of Contemporary Art at the University of Pennsylvania had used $30,000 of a visual arts grant it received from the NEA to fund a ... retrospective of photographer Robert Mapplethorpe's work. The exhibit, entitled The Perfect Moment, included homoerotic photographs that several Members of Congress condemned as pornographic. Members also denounced artist Andres Serrano's work Piss Christ, a photograph of a crucifix immersed in urine. Serrano had been awarded a $15,000 grant from the Southeast Center for Contemporary Art, an organization that received NEA support....

Ultimately, Congress adopted ... a bipartisan compromise between Members opposing any funding restrictions and those favoring some guidance to the agency ..., which directs the Chairperson, in establishing procedures to judge the artistic merit of grant applications, to "tak[e] into consideration general standards of decency and respect for the diverse beliefs and values of the American public." [20 U.S.C. § 954(d)(1).] The NEA has not promulgated any official interpretation of the provision, but in December 1990, the Council unanimously adopted a resolution to implement § 954(d)(1) merely by ensuring that the members of the advisory panels that conduct the initial review of grant applications represent geographic, ethnic, and aesthetic diversity[, and the Chairperson agreed] ....

Karen Finley, John Fleck, Holly Hughes, and Tim Miller[] are performance artists who applied for NEA grants before § 954(d)(1) was enacted. An advisory panel recommended approval of [the artists'] projects, both initially and after receiving [Chairperson John] Frohnmayer's request to reconsider three of the applications. A majority of the Council subsequently recommended disapproval, and [the artists were denied funding].... [The artists sued, claiming, among other things, that the provision was impermissibly viewpoint-based and vague.—ed.] ...

[B.] [T]he criteria in § 954(d)(1) inform the assessment of artistic merit, but Congress declined to disallow any particular viewpoints.... That § 954(d)(1) admonishes the NEA merely to take "decency and respect" into consideration and that the legislation was aimed at reforming procedures rather than precluding speech [legislative history omitted—ed.], undercut respondents' argument that the provision inevitably will be utilized as a tool for invidious viewpoint discrimination.... [T]he "decency and respect" criteria do not silence speakers by expressly "threaten[ing] censorship of ideas." Thus, we do not perceive a realistic danger that § 954(d)(1) will compromise

First Amendment values....

As respondents' own arguments demonstrate, the considerations that the provision introduces, by their nature, do not engender the kind of directed viewpoint discrimination that would prompt this Court to invalidate a statute on its face. Respondents assert, for example, that "[o]ne would be hard-pressed to find two people in the United States who could agree on what the 'diverse beliefs and values of the American public' are, much less on whether a particular work of art 'respects' them"; and they claim that "'[d]ecency' is likely to mean something very different to a sept[ua]genarian in Tuscaloosa and a teenager in Las Vegas."

The NEA likewise views the considerations enumerated in § 954(d)(1) as susceptible to multiple interpretations. Accordingly, the provision does not introduce considerations that, in practice, would effectively preclude or punish the expression of particular views....

[C.] Respondents' claim that the provision is facially unconstitutional may be reduced to the argument that the criteria in § 954(d)(1) are sufficiently subjective that the agency could utilize them to engage in viewpoint discrimination. Given the varied interpretations of the criteria and the vague exhortation to "take them into consideration," it seems unlikely that this provision will introduce any greater element of selectivity than the determination of "artistic excellence" itself....

The NEA's enabling statute contemplates a number of indisputably constitutional applications for both the "decency" prong of § 954(d)(1) and its reference to "respect for the diverse beliefs and values of the American public." Educational programs are central to the NEA's mission. And it is well established that "decency" is a permissible factor where "educational suitability" motivates its consideration.

Permissible applications of the mandate to consider "respect for the diverse beliefs and values of the American public" are also apparent. In setting forth the purposes of the NEA, Congress explained that "[i]t is vital to democracy to honor and preserve its multicultural artistic heritage." The agency expressly takes diversity into account, giving special consideration to "projects and productions ... that reach, or reflect the culture of, a minority, inner city, rural, or tribal community," as well as projects that generally emphasize "cultural diversity." Respondents do not contend that the criteria in § 954(d)(1) are impermissibly applied when they may be justified, as the statute contemplates, with respect to a project's intended audience ....

[R]eference to these permissible applications would not alone be sufficient to sustain the statute against respondents' First Amendment challenge. But neither are we persuaded that, in other applications, the language of § 954(d)(1) itself will give rise to the suppression of protected expression.

Any content-based considerations that may be taken into account in the grant-making process are a consequence of the nature of arts funding. The NEA has limited resources and it must deny the majority of the grant applications that it receives, including many that propose "artistically excellent" projects. The agency may decide to fund particular projects for a wide variety of reasons, "such as the technical proficiency of the artist, the creativity of the work, the anticipated public interest in or appreciation of the work, the work's contemporary relevance, its educational value, its suitability for or appeal to special audiences (such as children or the disabled), its service to a rural or isolated community, or even simply that the work could increase public knowledge of an art form." ...

Although the scarcity of NEA funding does not distinguish this case from *Rosenberger v. Rector*, the competitive process according to which the grants are allocated does. In the context of arts funding, in contrast to many other subsidies, the Government does not indiscriminately "encourage a diversity of views from private speakers," *Rosenberger*. The NEA's mandate is to make aesthetic judgments, and the inherently content-based "excellence" threshold for NEA support sets it apart from the subsidy at issue in *Rosenberger*—which was available to all student organizations that were "related to the educational purpose of the University"—and from comparably objective decisions on allocating public benefits, such as access to a school auditorium or a municipal theater, or the second class mailing privileges available to "all newspapers and other periodical publications."

[handwritten: Distinguishing Rosenberger]

[D.] Respondents do not allege discrimination in any particular funding decision.... Thus, we have no occasion here to address an as-applied challenge in a situation where the denial of a grant may be shown to be the product of invidious viewpoint discrimination. If the NEA were to leverage its power to award subsidies on the basis of subjective criteria into a penalty on disfavored viewpoints, then we would confront a different case.... [E]ven in the provision of subsidies, the Government may not "ai[m] at the suppression of dangerous ideas," and if a subsidy were "manipulated" to have a "coercive effect," then relief could be appropriate.

[handwritten: ← Limit]

In addition, ... a more pressing constitutional question would arise if government funding resulted in the imposition of a disproportionate burden calculated to drive "certain ideas or viewpoints from the marketplace." Unless and until § 954(d)(1) is applied in a manner that raises concern about the suppression of disfavored viewpoints, however, we uphold the constitutionality of the provision.

Finally, ... the Government may allocate competitive funding according to criteria that would be impermissible were direct regulation of speech or a criminal penalty at stake.... [A]s we held in *Rust v. Sullivan*, Congress may "selectively fund a program to encourage certain activities it believes to be in the public interest, without at the same time funding an alternative program which seeks to deal with the problem in another way." In doing so, "the Government has not discriminated on the basis of viewpoint; it has merely chosen to fund one activity to the exclusion of the other." ...

[E.] The terms of [§ 954(1)] are undeniably opaque, and if they appeared in a criminal statute or regulatory scheme, they could raise substantial vagueness concerns. It is unlikely, however, that speakers will be compelled to steer too far clear of any "forbidden area" in the context of grants of this nature. We recognize, as a practical matter, that artists may conform their speech to what they believe to be the decisionmaking criteria in order to acquire funding. But when the Government is acting as patron rather than as sovereign, the consequences of imprecision are not constitutionally severe.

In the context of selective subsidies, it is not always feasible for Congress to legislate with clarity. Indeed, if this statute is unconstitutionally vague, then so too are all Government programs awarding scholarships and grants on the basis of subjective criteria such as "excellence." ... Section 954(d)(1) merely adds some imprecise considerations to an already subjective selection process....

Justice Scalia, with whom Justice Thomas joins, concurring in the judgment....

[The concurrence argued that § 954(d)(1) did discriminate against viewpoints that "exhibit[] disrespect for the diverse beliefs and values of the American public or fail[] to comport with general standards of decency"—see Justice Souter's dissent for more on that—but concluded that this was nonetheless constitutional:—ed.]

[A.] "Congress shall make no law ... *abridging* the freedom of speech." To abridge is "to contract, to diminish; to deprive of" [citing a 1796 dictionary]. With the enactment of § 954(d)(1), Congress did not *abridge* the speech of those who disdain the beliefs and values of the American public, nor did it *abridge* indecent speech.

Those who wish to create indecent and disrespectful art are as unconstrained now as they were before the enactment of this statute. *Avant-garde artistes* such as respondents remain entirely free to *épater les bourgeois*;[2] they are merely deprived of the additional satisfaction of having the bourgeoisie taxed to pay for it.

It is preposterous to equate the denial of taxpayer subsidy with measures "aimed at the *suppression* of dangerous ideas." ... "... [S]uch a denial does not, as a general rule, have any significant coercive effect."

One might contend, I suppose, that a threat of rejection by the only available source of free money would constitute coercion and hence "abridgment" within the meaning of the First Amendment. I would not agree with such a contention, which would make the NEA the mandatory patron of all art too indecent, too disrespectful, or even too *kitsch* to attract private support. But even if one accepts the contention, it would have no application

---

[2] ["Shock the middle class."—ed.] Which they do quite well.... "[Karen] Finley visually recounts a sexual assault by stripping to the waist and smearing chocolate on her breasts and by using profanity to describe the assault.... John Fleck, in his stage performance 'Blessed Are All the Little Fishes,' ... appears dressed as a mermaid, urinates on the stage and creates an altar out of a toilet bowl by putting a photograph of Jesus Christ on the lid. Tim Miller ... uses vegetables in his performances to represent sexual symbols."

here. The NEA is far from the sole source of funding for art—even indecent, disrespectful, or just plain bad art. Accordingly, the Government may earmark NEA funds for projects it deems to be in the public interest without thereby abridging speech....

As we noted in *Rust,* when Congress chose to establish the National Endowment for Democracy it was not constitutionally required to fund programs encouraging competing philosophies of government—an example of funding discrimination that cuts much closer than this one to the core of *political* speech which is the primary concern of the First Amendment.... It is the very business of government to favor and disfavor points of view on (in modern times, at least) innumerable subjects—which is the main reason we have decided to elect those who run the government, rather than save money by making their posts hereditary.

And it makes not a bit of difference ... whether these officials further their (and, in a democracy, our) favored point of view by achieving it directly (having government-employed artists paint pictures, for example, or government-employed doctors perform abortions); or by advocating it officially (establishing an Office of Art Appreciation, for example, or an Office of Voluntary Population Control); or by giving money to others who achieve or advocate it (funding private art classes, for example, or Planned Parenthood). None of this has anything to do with abridging anyone's speech. *Rosenberger* ... found the viewpoint discrimination unconstitutional, not because funding of "private" speech was involved, but because the government had established a limited public forum—to which the NEA's granting of highly selective (if not highly discriminating) awards bears no resemblance.

[B.] {I suppose it would be unconstitutional for the government to give money to an organization devoted to the promotion of candidates nominated by the Republican Party—but it would be just as unconstitutional for the government itself to promote candidates nominated by the Republican Party, and I do not think that that unconstitutionality has anything to do with the First Amendment.} ...

Justice Souter, dissenting....

[A.] Because "the normal definition of 'indecent' ... refers to nonconformance with accepted standards of morality," restrictions turning on decency, especially those couched in terms of "general standards of decency," are quintessentially viewpoint based: they require discrimination on the basis of conformity with mainstream mores.... "In artistic ... settings, indecency may have strong communicative content, protesting conventional norms or giving an edge to a work by conveying otherwise inexpressible emotions.... Indecency often is inseparable from the ideas and viewpoints conveyed, or separable only with loss of truth or expressive power." ...

Just as self-evidently, a statute disfavoring speech that fails to respect America's "diverse beliefs and values" is the very model of viewpoint discrimination; it penalizes any view disrespectful to any belief or value espoused by someone in the American populace. Boiled down to its practical essence, the limitation obviously means that art that disrespects the ideology, opinions, or convictions of a significant segment of the American public is to be disfavored, whereas art that reinforces those values is not.

After all, the whole point of the proviso was to make sure that works like Serrano's ostensibly blasphemous portrayal of Jesus would not be funded, while a reverent treatment, conventionally respectful of Christian sensibilities, would not run afoul of the law. Nothing could be more viewpoint based than that. The fact that the statute disfavors art insufficiently respectful of America's "diverse" beliefs and values alters this conclusion not one whit: the First Amendment does not validate the ambition to disqualify many disrespectful viewpoints instead of merely one....

[B.] [In] the roles of government-as-speaker and government-as-buyer, ... the government is of course entitled to engage in viewpoint discrimination: if the Food and Drug Administration launches an advertising campaign on the subject of smoking, it may condemn the habit without also having to show a cowboy taking a puff on the opposite page; and if the Secretary of Defense wishes to buy a portrait to decorate the Pentagon, he is free to prefer George Washington over George the Third.

The Government freely admits, however, that it neither speaks through the expression subsidized by the NEA, nor buys anything for itself with its NEA grants. On the contrary, ... the Government acts as a patron, financially underwriting the production of art by private artists and impresarios for independent consumption....

[And the government-as-patron is much closer to government-as-regulator-of-private-speech than to the government-as-buyer-or-speaker.] ... The NEA, like the student activities fund in *Rosenberger* [and unlike the program in *Rust*], is a subsidy scheme created to encourage expression of a diversity of views from private speakers.... The NEA's purpose is to "support new ideas" and "to help create and sustain ... a climate encouraging freedom of thought, imagination, and inquiry." 20 U.S.C. § 951(7).... [Under *Rosenberger*, s]o long as Congress chooses to subsidize expressive endeavors at large, it has no business requiring the NEA to turn down funding applications of artists and exhibitors who devote their "freedom of thought, imagination, and inquiry" to defying our tastes, our beliefs, or our values. It may not use the NEA's purse to "suppres[s] ... dangerous ideas." *Regan v. Taxation with Representation.*

Rosenberger ... held ... that "[t]he government cannot justify viewpoint discrimination among private speakers on the economic fact of scarcity." {The Court's attempt to avoid *Rosenberger* by describing NEA funding in terms of competition, not scarcity, will not work. Competition implies scarcity, without which there is no exclusive prize to compete for; the Court's "competition" is merely a surrogate for "scarcity."}

Scarce money demands choices, of course, but choices "on some acceptable [viewpoint] neutral principle," like artistic excellence and artistic merit; "nothing in our decision[s] indicate[s] that scarcity would give the State the right to exercise viewpoint discrimination that is otherwise impermissible."

If the student activities fund at issue in *Rosenberger* had awarded competitive, merit-based grants to only 50%, or even 5%, of the applicants, on the basis of "journalistic merit taking into consideration the message of the newspaper," ... the Court would not have come out differently, leaving the University free to refuse funding after considering a publication's Christian perspective.

{Justice Scalia suggests that *Rosenberger* turned not on the distinction between government-as-speaker and government-as-facilitator-of-private-speech, but rather on the fact that "the government had established a limited public forum." ... [But l]ike this case, *Rosenberger* involved viewpoint discrimination, and we have made it clear that such discrimination is impermissible in all forums, even non-public ones, where, by definition, the government has not made public property generally available to facilitate private speech.} ...

[T]he overbreadth doctrine [applies] where the plaintiff mounts a facial challenge to a law investing the government with discretion to discriminate on viewpoint when it parcels out benefits in support of speech.... Since the decency and respect criteria may not be employed in the very many instances in which the art seeking a subsidy is neither aimed at children nor meant to celebrate a particular culture, the statute is facially overbroad....

[C.] {While criteria of "artistic excellence and artistic merit" may raise intractable issues about the identification of artistic worth, and could no doubt be used covertly to filter out unwanted ideas, there is nothing inherently viewpoint discriminatory about such merit-based criteria.... Decency and respect, on the other hand, are inherently and facially viewpoint based, and serve no legitimate and permissible end.... It is not to the point that the government necessarily makes choices among competing applications, or even that its judgments about artistic quality may be branded as subjective to some greater or lesser degree; the question here is whether the government may apply patently viewpoint-based criteria in making those choices.}

f. *Christian Legal Society v. Martinez, 561 U.S. 661 (2010)*

[The Justices in this case disagreed about the exact terms of the rule being challenged. This factual dispute is not that helpful to understanding the broader legal questions, so it has been generally edited out below.

Instead, two separate excerpts are given. In the first, the Justices debate the constitutionality of an "accept-all-comers" rule for registered student organizations. In the second, some Justices debate the constitutionality of a "non-discrimination" rule for such organizations. (The majority opinion does not discuss this second question, since it concludes the rule should be viewed as an "accept-all-comers" requirement.).—ed.]

i. *The Accept-All-Comers Policy: Reasonable and Viewpoint-Neutral?*

Justice Ginsburg delivered the opinion of the Court....

[A.] Hastings [a University of California public law school—ed.] encourages students to form extracurricular associations that "contribute to the

Hastings community and experience." These groups offer students "opportunities to pursue academic and social interests outside of the classroom [to] further their education" and to help them "develo[p] leadership skills."

Through its "Registered Student Organization" (RSO) program, Hastings extends official recognition to student groups.... RSOs are eligible to seek financial assistance from the Law School, which subsidizes their events using funds from a mandatory student-activity fee imposed on all students. RSOs may also ... place announcements in a weekly Office-of-Student-Services newsletter, advertise events on designated bulletin boards, send e-mails using a Hastings-organization address, and participate in an annual Student Organizations Fair designed to advance recruitment efforts. In addition, RSOs may apply for permission to use the Law School's facilities for meetings and office space. Finally, Hastings allows officially recognized groups to use its name and logo.

In exchange for these benefits, RSOs must abide by certain conditions. Only a "non-commercial organization whose membership is limited to Hastings students may become [an RSO]." ... [And] all RSOs must undertake to comply with Hastings' "Policies and Regulations ..." ... [which Hastings interprets] to mandate acceptance of all comers: School-approved groups must "allow any student to participate, become a member, or seek leadership positions in the organization, regardless of [her] status or beliefs[,"] {[though they may still impose] ... "... neutral and generally applicable membership requirements unrelated to 'status or beliefs.'" So long as all students have the opportunity to participate on equal terms, RSOs may require them, inter alia, to pay dues, maintain good attendance, refrain from gross misconduct, or pass a skill-based test, such as the writing competitions administered by law journals.} ...

In 2004, ... the leaders of a predecessor Christian organization ... formed CLS by affiliating with the national Christian Legal Society (CLS-National).... [CLS-National] chapters must adopt bylaws that, *inter alia*, require members and officers to sign a "Statement of Faith" and to conduct their lives in accord with prescribed principles. Among those tenets is the belief that sexual activity should not occur outside of marriage between a man and a woman; CLS thus interprets its bylaws to exclude from affiliation anyone who engages in "unrepentant homosexual conduct." CLS also excludes students who hold religious convictions different from those in the Statement of Faith....

[Hastings] rejected [CLS's] application ... because [the bylaws] barred students based on religion and sexual orientation.... If CLS instead chose to operate outside the RSO program, Hastings stated, the school "would be pleased to provide [CLS] the use of Hastings facilities for its meetings and activities."[a] CLS would also have access to chalkboards and generally available campus bulletin boards to announce its events....

---

[a] [**The dissent argued** that, despite this, Hastings in practice didn't respond to CLS's requests to use various facilities, and thus denied CLS access to them.—ed.]

Refusing to alter its bylaws, CLS did not obtain RSO status. It did, however, operate independently during the 2004-2005 academic year. CLS held weekly Bible-study meetings and invited Hastings students to Good Friday and Easter Sunday church services. It also hosted a beach barbeque, Thanksgiving dinner, campus lecture on the Christian faith and the legal practice, several fellowship dinners, an end-of-year banquet, and other informal social activities.... [CLS then sued, alleging] that Hastings' refusal to grant the organization RSO status violated CLS's ... rights to free speech, expressive association, and free exercise of religion....

[B.] [T]his Court has employed forum analysis to determine when a governmental entity, in regulating property in its charge, may place limitations on speech. {First, in traditional public forums, such as public streets and parks, "any restriction based on the content of ... speech must satisfy strict scrutiny ...." Second, governmental entities create designated public forums when "government property that has not traditionally been regarded as a public forum is intentionally opened up for that purpose"; speech restrictions in such a forum "are subject to the same strict scrutiny as restrictions in a traditional public forum."

Third, governmental entities establish limited public forums [like the RSO program here] by opening property "limited to use by certain groups or dedicated solely to the discussion of certain subjects." ... "[I]n such a forum, a governmental entity may impose restrictions on speech that are reasonable and viewpoint-neutral."} ...

"Freedom of association" ... "plainly presupposes a freedom not to associate." Insisting that an organization embrace unwelcome members ... "directly and immediately affects associational rights." ... [CLS's] expressive-association and free-speech arguments merge: *Who* speaks on its behalf, CLS reasons, colors *what* concept is conveyed.... [O]ur limited-public-forum precedents [thus] supply the appropriate framework for assessing both CLS's speech and association rights....

[One reason for applying the limited public forum framework to association claims is that] the strict scrutiny we have applied in some settings to laws that burden expressive association would, in practical effect, invalidate a defining characteristic of limited public forums—the State may "reserv[e] [them] for certain groups." ... "[A] speaker may be excluded from" a limited public forum "if he is not a member of the class of speakers for whose especial benefit the forum was created." ... [For example, s]chools, including Hastings, ordinarily, and without controversy, limit official student-group recognition to organizations comprising only students—even if those groups wish to associate with nonstudents.... [A] public university [may] "confin[e] a [speech] forum to the limited and legitimate purposes for which it was created." ...

[Moreover,] CLS, in seeking what is effectively a state subsidy, faces only indirect pressure to modify its membership policies; CLS may exclude any person for any reason if it forgoes the benefits of official recognition. The expressive-association precedents [such as *Boy Scouts* of America v. Dale

Compelled

① Reasonable

and *Roberts v. U.S. Jaycees*], in contrast, involved regulations that *compelled* a group to include unwanted members, with no choice to opt out.... Hastings, through its RSO program, is dangling the carrot of subsidy, not wielding the stick of prohibition....

[C.] "Once it has opened a limited [public] forum[]" ... "the State must respect the lawful boundaries it has itself set." ... "The State may not exclude speech where its distinction is not reasonable in light of the purpose served by the forum, ... nor may it discriminate against speech on the basis of ... viewpoint." ...

[D.] We first consider whether Hastings' policy is reasonable taking into account the RSO forum's function and "all the surrounding circumstances[]" ... [including] "... the special characteristics of the school environment." {A college's ... license to choose among pedagogical approaches ... is not confined to the classroom, for extracurricular programs are, today, essential parts of the educational process.} ...

[W]e owe no deference to universities when we consider that question. Cognizant that judges lack the on-the-ground expertise and experience of school administrators, however, we have cautioned courts in various contexts to resist "substitut[ing] their own notions of sound educational policy for those of the school authorities which they review." ... With appropriate regard for school administrators' judgment, we review the justifications Hastings offers in defense of its all-comers requirement.

First, the open-access policy "ensures that the leadership, educational, and social opportunities afforded by [RSOs] are available to all students." Just as "Hastings does not allow its professors to host classes open only to those students with a certain status or belief," so the Law School may decide, reasonably in our view, "that the ... educational experience is best promoted when all participants in the forum must provide equal access to all students." RSOs, we count it significant, are eligible for financial assistance drawn from mandatory student-activity fees; the all-comers policy ensures that no Hastings student is forced to fund a group that would reject her as a member.

Second, the all-comers requirement helps Hastings police the written terms of its Nondiscrimination Policy [which bans groups from discriminating based on race, religion, sex, sexual orientation, and the like—ed.] without inquiring into an RSO's motivation for membership restrictions....

Third, the Law School reasonably adheres to the view that an all-comers policy, to the extent it brings together individuals with diverse backgrounds and beliefs, "encourages tolerance, cooperation, and learning among students." {CLS's predecessor organization, the Hastings Christian Fellowship (HCF), experienced these benefits first-hand when it welcomed an openly gay student as a member during the 2003-2004 academic year. That student, testified another HCF member, "was a joy to have" in the group and brought a unique perspective to Bible-study discussions.} And if the policy sometimes produces discord, Hastings can rationally rank among RSO-program goals development of conflict-resolution skills, toleration, and readiness to find common ground.

Fourth, Hastings' policy, which incorporates ... state-law proscriptions on discrimination, conveys the Law School's decision "to decline to subsidize with public monies and benefits conduct of which the people of California disapprove." ... [S]o long as a public university does not contravene constitutional limits, its choice to advance state-law goals through the school's educational endeavors stands on firm footing.

In sum, [these justifications] are surely reasonable in light of the RSO forum's purposes.

[E.] The Law School's policy is all the more creditworthy in view of the "substantial alternative channels that remain open for [CLS-student] communication to take place[,]" ... [which is relevant w]hen access barriers are viewpoint neutral .... Hastings offered CLS access to school facilities to conduct meetings and the use of chalkboards and generally available bulletin boards to advertise events. Although CLS could not take advantage of RSO-specific methods of communication, the advent of electronic media and social-networking sites reduces the importance of those channels. Private groups, from fraternities and sororities to social clubs and secret societies, commonly maintain a presence at universities without official school affiliation.... [CLS likewise] hosted a variety of activities the year after Hastings denied it recognition, and the number of students attending those meetings and events doubled....

[F.] {CLS's concern, shared by the dissent, that an all-comers policy will squelch diversity has not been borne out by Hastings' experience. In the 2004-2005 academic year, approximately 60 student organizations, representing a variety of interests, [including Muslim, Jewish, and Christian groups,] registered with Hastings ....}

CLS also assails the reasonableness of the all-comers policy ... by forecasting that the policy will facilitate hostile takeovers ... [in which] saboteurs ... infiltrate groups to subvert their mission and message. This supposition strikes us as more hypothetical than real. CLS points to no history or prospect of RSO-hijackings at Hastings. Students tend to self-sort and presumably will not endeavor en masse to join—let alone seek leadership positions in—groups pursuing missions wholly at odds with their personal beliefs. And if a rogue student intent on sabotaging an organization's objectives nevertheless attempted a takeover, the members of that group would not likely elect her as an officer.

RSOs, moreover, ... may condition eligibility for membership and leadership on attendance, the payment of dues, or other neutral requirements designed to ensure that students join because of their commitment to a group's vitality, not its demise.... {[O]ther "checks [are also] in place" to prevent RSO-sabotage. "The [Law] School's student code of conduct applies to RSO activities and, inter alia, prohibits obstruction or disruption, disorderly conduct, and threats."}

Hastings, furthermore, could reasonably expect more from its law students than the disruptive behavior CLS hypothesizes—and to build this expectation into its educational approach. A reasonable policy need not anticipate and preemptively close off every opportunity for avoidance or manipulation. If students begin to exploit an all-comers policy by hijacking organizations to distort or destroy their missions, Hastings presumably would revisit and revise its policy.

Finally, CLS asserts ... that the Law School lacks any legitimate interest—let alone one reasonably related to the RSO forum's purposes—in urging "religious groups not to favor co-religionists for purposes of their religious activities." ... [But the CLS ignores] the interests of those it seeks to fence out .... Hastings, caught in the crossfire between a group's desire to exclude and students' demand for equal access, may reasonably draw a line in the sand permitting *all* organizations to express what they wish but *no* group to discriminate in membership....

[G.] Hastings' all-comers policy is viewpoint neutral.... It is ... hard to imagine a more viewpoint-neutral policy than one requiring *all* student groups to accept *all* comers. {The Law School's policy aims at the *act* of rejecting would-be group members without reference to the reasons motivating that behavior .... CLS's conduct—not its Christian perspective—is, from Hastings' vantage point, what stands between the group and RSO status.... "CLS is simply confusing its *own* viewpoint-based objections to ... nondiscrimination laws (which it is entitled to have and [to] voice) with viewpoint *discrimination.*"} ...

CLS attacks the regulation by pointing to its effect[,] ... [arguing that] "it systematically and predictably burdens most heavily those groups whose viewpoints are out of favor with the campus mainstream." ... [But] "[a] regulation that serves purposes unrelated to the content of expression is deemed neutral, even if it has an incidental effect on some speakers or messages but not others." ...

{CLS briefly argues that Hastings' all-comers condition violates the Free Exercise Clause. [But i]n *Employment Div. v. Smith,* the Court held that the Free Exercise Clause does not inhibit enforcement of otherwise valid regulations of general application that incidentally burden religious conduct.} ...

[H.] CLS contends that "[t]he peculiarity, incoherence, and suspect history of the all-comers policy all point to pretext." Neither the District Court nor the Ninth Circuit addressed an argument that Hastings selectively enforces its all-comers policy, and this Court is not the proper forum to air the issue in the first instance. On remand, the Ninth Circuit may consider CLS's pretext argument if ... it is preserved....

Justice Kennedy, concurring....

[Justice Kennedy's concurrence largely elaborates on the majority's arguments, but also notes:—ed.]

[A.] [T]he process of learning occurs both formally in a classroom setting and informally outside of it.... Extracurricular activities, such as those in the Hastings "Registered Student Organization" program, facilitate inter-actions between students, enabling them to explore new points of view, to develop interests and talents, and to nurture a growing sense of self. The [Hastings] program is designed to allow all students to interact with their colleagues across a broad, seemingly unlimited range of ideas, views, and activities.... [And a law] school quite properly may conclude that allowing an oath or belief-affirming requirement, or an outside conduct requirement, could be divisive for student relations and inconsistent with the basic con-cept that a view's validity should be tested through free and open discussion. The school's policy therefore represents a permissible effort to preserve the value of its forum....

[B.] [If] it could be demonstrated that a school has adopted or enforced its policy with the intent or purpose of discriminating or disadvantaging a group on account of its views, ... [or] if it were shown that the all-comers policy was either designed or used to infiltrate the group or challenge its leadership in order to stifle its views[, CLS] {would have a substantial case on the merits}. But that has not been shown to be so likely or self-evident ... that the Court can declare the school policy void without more facts ....

Justice Alito, with whom the Chief Justice, Justice Scalia, and Justice Thomas join, dissenting....

[A.] Once a state university opens a limited forum, it "must respect the lawful boundaries it has itself set." Hastings' regulations on the registration of student groups impose only two substantive limitations: A group seeking registration must have student members and must be non-commercial.... [T]he regulations plainly contemplate the creation of a forum within which Hastings students are free to form and obtain registration of essentially the same broad range of private groups that nonstudents may form off campus. That is precisely what the parties in this case stipulated: The RSO forum "seeks to promote a diversity of viewpoints *among* registered student organizations, including viewpoints on religion and human sexuality." ...

[B.] {Hastings' accept-all-comers policy is not reasonable in light of the stipulated purpose of the RSO forum: to promote a diversity of viewpoints "*among*"—not within—"registered student organizations."} The accept-all-comers policy is antithetical to the design of the RSO forum for the same reason that a state-imposed accept-all-comers policy would violate the First Amendment rights of private groups if applied off campus.[a]...

The Court ... says that the accept-all-comers policy is reasonable because it helps Hastings to ensure that "'leadership, educational, and social oppor-tunities'" are afforded to all students. The RSO forum, however, is designed

---

[a] [**The majority responds** to the dissent's argument this way:—ed.] ... [T]he dissent acknowledges that a university has the authority to set the boundaries of a limited public forum, ... [but] refuses to credit Hastings' all-comers policy as one of those boundaries[,] ... insisting that "Hastings' regulations ... impose only two sub-stantive limitations: A group ... must have student members and must be non-com-mercial." ... "[T]he design of the RSO forum," which the dissent discusses at length, is of its own tailoring....

to achieve these laudable ends in a very different way—by permitting groups of students, no matter how small, to form the groups they want. In this way, the forum multiplies the opportunity for students to serve in leadership positions; it allows students to decide which educational opportunities they wish to pursue through participation in extracurricular activities; and it permits them to create the "social opportunities" they desire by forming whatever groups they wish to create....

[T]he Court [also] argues that the accept-all-comers policy, by bringing together students with diverse views, encourages tolerance, cooperation, learning, and the development of conflict-resolution skills. These are obviously commendable goals, but they are not undermined by permitting a religious group to restrict membership to persons who share the group's faith.... Our country as a whole, no less than the Hastings College of Law, values tolerance, cooperation, learning, and the amicable resolution of conflicts. But we seek to achieve those goals through "[a] confident pluralism that conduces to civil peace and advances democratic consensus-building," not by abridging First Amendment rights....

[C.] In response to the argument that the accept-all-comers-policy would permit a small and unpopular group to be taken over by students who wish to silence its message, the Court states that the policy would permit a registered group to impose membership requirements "designed to ensure that students join because of their commitment to a group's vitality, not its demise." ... [But] the line between members who merely seek to change a group's message (who apparently must be admitted) and those who seek a group's "demise" (who may be kept out) is hopelessly vague.

Here is an example. Not all Christian denominations agree with CLS's views on sexual morality and other matters. During a recent year, CLS had seven members. Suppose that 10 students who are members of denominations that disagree with CLS decided that CLS was misrepresenting true Christian doctrine. Suppose that these students joined CLS, elected officers who shared their views, ended the group's affiliation with the national organization, and changed the group's message. The new leadership would likely proclaim that the group was "vital" but rectified, while CLS, I assume, would take the view that the old group had suffered its "demise." Whether a change represents reform or transformation may depend very much on the eye of the beholder.

Justice Kennedy takes a similarly mistaken tack. He contends that CLS "would have a substantial case on the merits if it were shown that the all-comers policy was ... used to infiltrate the group or challenge its leadership in order to stifle its views," but he does not explain on what ground such a claim could succeed. The Court holds that the accept-all-comers policy is viewpoint neutral and reasonable in light of the purposes of the RSO forum. How could those characteristics be altered by a change in the membership of one of the forum's registered groups? ...

[Likewise, r]ules requiring that members attend meetings, pay dues, and behave politely would not eliminate [the threat of a takeover].

The possibility of such takeovers, however, is by no means the most important effect of the Court's holding. There are religious groups that cannot in good conscience agree in their bylaws that they will admit persons who do not share their faith, and for these groups, the consequence of an accept-all-comers policy is marginalization....

[D.] {The Court is also wrong in holding that the accept-all-comers policy is viewpoint neutral....

Not VP Neutral

The adoption of a facially neutral policy for the purpose of suppressing the expression of a particular viewpoint is viewpoint discrimination. A simple example illustrates this obvious point. Suppose that a hated student group at a state university has never been able to attract more than 10 members. Suppose that the university administration, for the purpose of preventing that group from using the school grounds for meetings, adopts a new rule under which the use of its facilities is restricted to groups with more than 25 members. Although this rule would be neutral on its face, its adoption for a discriminatory reason would be illegal.

Here, CLS has made a strong showing that Hastings' sudden adoption and selective application of its accept-all-comers policy was a pretext for the law school's unlawful denial of CLS's registration application under the Nondiscrimination Policy. [Factual details omitted.—ed.]} ...

ii. The Nondiscrimination Policy: Reasonable and Viewpoint-Neutral?

Justice Stevens, concurring.

The Court ... correctly upholds the all-comers policy.... [But] the school's general Nondiscrimination Policy ... [is also] legitimate....

[A.] As written, the Nondiscrimination Policy is content and viewpoint neutral.... Indeed, it does not regulate expression or belief at all.... Those who hold religious beliefs are not "singled out"; those who engage in discriminatory *conduct* based on someone else's religious status and belief are singled out. Regardless of whether they are the product of secular or spiritual feeling, hateful or benign motives, all acts of religious discrimination are equally covered....

[T]he policy may end up having greater consequence for religious groups—whether and to what extent it will is far from clear *ex ante*—inasmuch as they are more likely than their secular counterparts to wish to exclude students of particular faiths. But ... disparate impact does not, in itself, constitute viewpoint discrimination....

[B.] What the policy does reflect is a judgment that discrimination by school officials or organizations on the basis of certain factors, such as race and religion, is less tolerable than discrimination on the basis of other factors. This approach may or may not be the wisest choice in the context of a Registered Student Organization (RSO) program. But it is at least a reasonable choice. Academic administrators routinely employ antidiscrimination rules to promote tolerance, understanding, and respect, and to safeguard students from invidious forms of discrimination, including sexual orientation discrimination. Applied to the RSO context, these values can, in turn, advance numerous pedagogical objectives....

In this case, petitioner excludes students who will not sign its Statement of Faith or who engage in "unrepentant homosexual conduct." The expressive association argument it presses, however, is hardly limited to these facts. Other groups may exclude or mistreat Jews, blacks, and women—or those who do not share their contempt for Jews, blacks, and women. A free society must tolerate such groups. It need not subsidize them, give them its official imprimatur, or grant them equal access to law school facilities.

Justice Alito, with whom the Chief Justice, Justice Scalia, and Justice Thomas join, dissenting....

[W]hen Hastings refused to register CLS, it claimed that the CLS by-laws impermissibly discriminated on the basis of religion and sexual orientation. As ... applied to CLS, both of these grounds constituted viewpoint discrimination.

Religion.... "[T]he forced inclusion of an unwanted person in a group infringes the group's freedom of expressive association if the presence of that person affects in a significant way the group's ability to advocate public or private viewpoints." *Dale*.... [T]he Nondiscrimination Policy [generally respected this freedom by] "permit[ting] political, social, and cultural student organizations to select officers and members who are dedicated to a particular set of ideals or beliefs."

But the policy singled out one category of expressive associations for disfavored treatment: groups formed to express a religious message. Only religious groups were required to admit students who did not share their views. An environmentalist group was not required to admit students who rejected global warming. An animal rights group was not obligated to accept students who supported the use of animals to test cosmetics. But CLS was required to admit avowed atheists.

This was patent viewpoint discrimination. "By the very terms of the [Nondiscrimination Policy], the University ... select[ed] for disfavored treatment those student [groups] with religious ... viewpoints." ...

Justice Stevens first argues that the Nondiscrimination Policy is viewpoint neutral because it "does not regulate expression or belief at all" but instead regulates conduct. This Court has held, however, that the particular conduct at issue here constitutes a form of expression that is protected by the First Amendment.... [T]he First Amendment shields the right of a group to engage in expressive association by limiting membership to persons whose admission does not significantly interfere with the group's ability to convey its views. See *Dale*; *Roberts*....

Justice Stevens also maintains that the Nondiscrimination Policy is viewpoint neutral because it prohibits all groups, both religious and secular, from engaging in religious speech.... In *Rosenberger,* the dissent, which Justice Stevens joined, made exactly this argument. The Court disagreed, holding that a policy that treated secular speech more favorably than religious speech discriminated on the basis of viewpoint....

Here, the Nondiscrimination Policy permitted membership requirements that expressed a secular viewpoint. (For example, the Hastings Democratic Caucus and the Hastings Republicans were allowed to exclude members who disagreed with their parties' platforms.) But religious groups were not permitted to express a religious viewpoint by limiting membership to students who shared their religious viewpoints.... [T]his was viewpoint discrimination....

Sexual orientation. The Hastings Nondiscrimination Policy, as interpreted by the law school, also discriminated on the basis of viewpoint regarding sexual morality. CLS has a particular viewpoint on this subject, namely, that sexual conduct outside marriage between a man and a woman is wrongful. Hastings would not allow CLS to express this viewpoint by limiting membership to persons willing to express a sincere agreement with CLS's views.

By contrast, nothing in the Nondiscrimination Policy prohibited a group from expressing a contrary viewpoint by limiting membership to persons willing to endorse that group's beliefs. A Free Love Club could require members to affirm that they reject the traditional view of sexual morality to which CLS adheres. It is hard to see how this can be viewed as anything other than viewpoint discrimination....

3. GOVERNMENT SPEECH: GENERALLY

a. Problem: Rust v. Sullivan

Do you think the rule announced and applied by *Rust v. Sullivan* is correct? If you think it's wrong, should the government ever be allowed to pay organizations money to spread one viewpoint (*e.g.*, advocacy of patriotism, democracy, abstinence from drugs, or racial tolerance) and not the contrary viewpoint? What should be the proper First Amendment rule for such cases?

b. Rust v. Sullivan, 500 U.S. 173 (1991)

Chief Justice Rehnquist delivered the opinion of the Court....

[For a brief summary of the facts of the case and its analysis, see *Agency for Int'l Development* above; but the following is also helpful for understanding the Court's reasoning in these cases:—ed.]

[A.] The Government [may] ... selectively fund a program to encourage certain activities it believes to be in the public interest, without at the same time funding an alternative program which seeks to deal with the problem in another way. In so doing, the Government has not discriminated on the basis of viewpoint; it has merely chosen to fund one activity to the exclusion of the other.

"[A] legislature's decision not to subsidize the exercise of a fundamental right does not infringe the right." ... "There is a basic difference between direct state interference with a protected activity and state encouragement of an alternative activity consonant with legislative policy." ...

The Title X program is designed not for prenatal care, but to encourage family planning. A doctor who wished to offer prenatal care to a project patient who became pregnant could properly be prohibited from doing so because such service is outside the scope of the federally funded program. The regulations prohibiting abortion counseling and referral are of the same ilk .... This is not a case of the Government "suppressing a dangerous idea," but of a prohibition on a project grantee or its employees from engaging in activities outside of the project's scope.

To hold that the Government unconstitutionally discriminates on the basis of viewpoint when it chooses to fund a program dedicated to advance certain permissible goals, because the program in advancing those goals necessarily discourages alternative goals, would render numerous Government programs constitutionally suspect. When Congress established a National Endowment for Democracy to encourage other countries to adopt democratic principles, it was not constitutionally required to fund a program to encourage competing lines of political philosophy such as communism and fascism....

[B.] This is not to suggest that funding by the Government, even when coupled with the freedom of the fund recipients to speak outside the scope of the Government-funded project, is invariably sufficient to justify Government control over the content of expression. For example, this Court has recognized that the existence of a Government "subsidy," in the form of Government-owned property, does not justify the restriction of speech in areas that have "been traditionally open to the public for expressive activity," or have been "expressly dedicated to speech activity." Similarly, we have recognized that the university is a traditional sphere of free expression so fundamental to the functioning of our society that the Government's ability to control speech within that sphere by means of conditions attached to the expenditure of Government funds is restricted by the vagueness and overbreadth doctrines of the First Amendment.

It could be argued by analogy that traditional relationships such as that between doctor and patient should enjoy protection under the First Amendment from Government regulation, even when subsidized by the Government. We need not resolve that question here, however, because the Title X program regulations do not significantly impinge upon the doctor-patient relationship. Nothing in them requires a doctor to represent as his own any opinion that he does not in fact hold.

Nor is the doctor-patient relationship established by the Title X program sufficiently all encompassing so as to justify an expectation on the part of the patient of comprehensive medical advice. The program does not provide post conception medical care, and therefore a doctor's silence with regard to abortion cannot reasonably be thought to mislead a client into thinking that the doctor does not consider abortion an appropriate option for her. The doctor is always free to make clear that advice regarding abortion is simply beyond the scope of the program. In these circumstances, the general rule that the Government may choose not to subsidize speech applies with full force....

Justice Blackmun, with whom Justice Marshall joins, [and] with whom Justice Stevens joins [in relevant part], dissenting....

[A.] "A regulation of speech that is motivated by nothing more than a desire to curtail expression of a particular point of view on controversial issues of general interest is the purest example of a law ... abridging the freedom of speech, or of the press." ... [T]he counseling and referral provisions at issue [here are] ... clearly viewpoint based. While suppressing speech favorable to abortion with one hand, the Secretary compels antiabortion speech with the other. For example, the Department of Health and Human Services' own description of the regulations makes plain that "Title X projects are *required* to facilitate access to prenatal care and social services, including adoption services, that might be needed by the pregnant client to promote her well-being and that of her child, while making it abundantly clear that the project is not permitted to promote abortion by facilitating access to abortion through the referral process." ...

Remarkably, the majority concludes that "the Government has not discriminated on the basis of viewpoint; it has merely chosen to fund one activity to the exclusion of the other." But the majority's claim that the regulations merely limit a Title X project's speech to preventive or preconceptional services rings hollow in light of the broad range of nonpreventive services that the regulations authorize Title X projects to provide [such as physical examinations, screening for breast cancer, treatment of gynecological problems, and treatment for sexually transmitted diseases]. By refusing to fund those family-planning projects that advocate abortion *because* they advocate abortion, the Government plainly has targeted a particular viewpoint.

The majority's reliance on the fact that the regulations pertain solely to funding decisions simply begs the question. Clearly, there are some bases upon which government may not rest its decision to fund or not to fund. For example, the Members of the majority surely would agree that government may not base its decision to support an activity upon considerations of race. As demonstrated above, our cases make clear that ideological viewpoint is a similarly repugnant ground upon which to base funding decisions....

[B.] [I]n addition to their impermissible focus upon the viewpoint of regulated speech, the provisions intrude upon a wide range of communicative conduct, including the very words spoken to a woman by her physician. By manipulating the content of the doctor-patient dialogue, the regulations upheld today force each of the petitioners "to be an instrument for fostering public adherence to an ideological point of view [he or she] finds unacceptable." *Wooley v. Maynard....*

Justice O'Connor, dissenting [on the grounds that the regulation was inconsistent with the statutes]. [Omitted.—ed.]

c.   Walker v. Texas Division, Sons of Confederate Veterans, Inc., 135 S. Ct. 2239 (2015)

[Texas allowed many groups to design specialty license plates that drivers could then buy through the Texas Department of Motor Vehicles Board.

Here are a few samples—Buffalo Soldiers, Choose Life, Re/Max (a real estate company), Mighty Fine Burgers (a fast food chain), University of Texas (Austin), and Louisiana State University:

The Sons of Confederate Veterans wanted a similar plate, which would have included the Confederate battle flag, and would have looked like this:

The Texas DMV Board rejected the plate, and the Sons of Confederate Veterans challenged the rejection. The case came down to whether the specialty plate program should be viewed as

LPF

   (1) a "limited public forum" or "nonpublic forum," where the state wouldn't be allowed to discriminate based on viewpoint, or as

GS

   (2) a "government speech" or "not a forum at all," in which case the government would be free to select which messages to allow.

Similar issues had arisen shortly before in other states when states wanted to allow "Choose Life" plates but not pro-abortion-rights plates, and when states wanted to forbid "Choose Life" plates. Here is how the Court analyzed the forum vs. government speech issue:—ed.]

Justice Breyer delivered the opinion of the Court....

[A.] When government speaks, it is not barred by the Free Speech Clause from determining the content of what it says.... [I]t is the democratic electoral process that first and foremost provides a check on government speech. Thus, government statements ... do not normally trigger the First Amendment rules designed to protect the marketplace of ideas. Instead, the Free Speech Clause helps produce informed opinions among members of the public, who are then able to influence the choices of a government that, through words and deeds, will reflect its electoral mandate.   *MPoI*

Were the Free Speech Clause interpreted otherwise, government would not work. How could a city government create a successful recycling program if officials, when writing householders asking them to recycle cans and bottles, had to include in the letter a long plea from the local trash disposal enterprise demanding the contrary? How could a state government effectively develop programs designed to encourage and provide vaccinations, if officials also had to voice the perspective of those who oppose this type of immunization? ... We have therefore refused "[t]o hold that the Government unconstitutionally discriminates on the basis of viewpoint when it chooses to fund a program dedicated to advance certain permissible goals, because the program in advancing those goals necessarily discourages alternative goals." *Rust v. Sullivan....*

[B.] In *Pleasant Grove City v. Summum,* 555 U.S. 460 (2009), we considered a religious organization's request to erect in a 2.5-acre city park a monument setting forth the organization's religious tenets. In the park were 15 other permanent displays. At least 11 of these—including a wishing well, a September 11 monument, a historic granary, the city's first fire station, and a Ten Commandments monument—had been donated to the city by private entities. The religious organization argued that the Free Speech Clause required the city to display the organization's proposed monument because, by accepting a broad range of permanent exhibitions at the park, the city had created a forum for private speech in the form of monuments....

We held[, though,] that the city had not "provid[ed] a forum for private speech" with respect to monuments. Rather, the city, even when "accepting a privately donated monument and placing it on city property," had "engage[d] in expressive conduct." The speech at issue, this Court decided, was "best viewed as a form of government speech" and "therefore [was] not subject to scrutiny under the Free Speech Clause."

We based our conclusion on several factors. First, history shows that   (1) *History* "[g]overnments have long used monuments to speak to the public." Thus, ... "[w]hen a government entity arranges for the construction of a monument, it does so because it wishes to convey some thought or instill some feeling in those who see the structure."

Second, ... it "is not common for property owners to open up their property for the installation of permanent monuments that convey a message   (2) *permanence* with which they do not wish to be associated." As a result, "persons who observe donated monuments routinely—and reasonably—interpret them as conveying some message on the property owner's behalf." And "observers" of such monuments, as a consequence, ordinarily "appreciate the identity of the speaker."

Third, we found relevant the fact that the city maintained control over the selection of monuments.... "... [T]hroughout our Nation's history, the general government practice with respect to donated monuments has been one of selective receptivity." ... [T]he city government in *Summum* "'effectively controlled' the messages sent by the monuments in the [p]ark by exercising 'final approval authority' over their selection." ...

[And] the involvement of private parties in designing the monuments was [not] sufficient to prevent the government from controlling which monuments it placed in its own public park. Cf. *Rust* (upholding a federal regulation limiting speech in a Government-funded program where the program was established and administered by private parties).

[C.] Our analysis in *Summum* leads us to the conclusion that here, too, government speech is at issue. First, the history of license plates shows that, insofar as license plates have conveyed more than state names and vehicle identification numbers, they long have communicated messages from the States. [The Court gave examples of images and slogans in other states since 1917.—ed.] Texas, too, has selected various messages to communicate through its license plate designs. [Until 1995, these were the Lone Star in 1919, "Centennial" in 1936, "Hemisfair 68," referring to a San Antonio event, in 1968, and a state silhouette in 1977.—ed.] ....

Second, Texas license plate designs "are often closely identified" in the public mind with the [State]." Each Texas license plate is a government article serving the governmental purposes of vehicle registration and identification.... The State places the name "TEXAS" in large letters at the top of every plate. Moreover, the State requires Texas vehicle owners to display license plates, and every Texas license plate is issued by the State. Texas also owns the designs on its license plates, including the designs that Texas adopts on the basis of proposals made by private individuals and organizations. And Texas dictates the manner in which drivers may dispose of unused plates[,] ... requiring that vehicle owners return unused specialty plates to the State ....

Texas license plates are, essentially, government IDs. And issuers of ID "typically do not permit" the placement on their IDs of "message[s] with which they do not wish to be associated." Consequently, "persons who observe" designs on IDs "routinely—and reasonably—interpret them as conveying some message on the [issuer's] behalf."

Indeed, a person who displays a message on a Texas license plate likely intends to convey to the public that the State has endorsed that message. If not, the individual could simply display the message in question in larger letters on a bumper sticker right next to the plate. But the individual prefers a license plate design to the purely private speech expressed through bumper stickers. That may well be because Texas's license plate designs convey government agreement with the message displayed.

Third, Texas maintains direct control over the messages conveyed on its specialty plates. Texas law provides that the State "has sole control over the design, typeface, color, and alphanumeric pattern for all license plates." The Board must approve every specialty plate design proposal before the design can appear on a Texas plate. And the Board and its predecessor have actively exercised this authority. Texas asserts, and SCV concedes, that the State has rejected at least a dozen proposed designs. Accordingly, like the city government in *Summum,* Texas "has 'effectively controlled' the messages [conveyed] by exercising 'final approval authority' over their selection."

This final approval authority allows Texas to choose how to present itself and its constituency. Thus, Texas offers plates celebrating the many educational institutions attended by its citizens. But it need not issue plates deriding schooling. Texas offers plates that pay tribute to the Texas citrus industry. But it need not issue plates praising Florida's oranges as far better. And Texas offers plates that say "Fight Terrorism." But it need not issue plates promoting al Qaeda....

{Texas's desire to communicate numerous messages does not mean that the messages conveyed are not Texas's own.} {[O]ur holding in *Summum* was not dependent on the precise number of monuments found within the park [the number was 15—ed.]. Indeed, we indicated that the [52] permanent displays in New York City's Central Park also constitute government speech.... Further, there may well be many more messages that Texas wishes to convey through its license plates than there were messages that the city in *Summum* wished to convey through its monuments.}

[Not] every element of our discussion in *Summum* is relevant here. For instance, in *Summum* ... [w]e believed that the speech at issue was government speech rather than private speech in part because we found it "hard to imagine how a public park could be opened up for the installation of permanent monuments by every person or group wishing to engage in that form of expression." Here, a State could theoretically offer a much larger number of license plate designs, and those designs need not be available for time immemorial.

But those characteristics of the speech at issue in *Summum* were particularly important because the government speech at issue occurred in public parks, which are traditional public forums for "the delivery of speeches and the holding of marches and demonstrations" by private citizens. By contrast, license plates are not traditional public forums for private speech....

[D.] Because the State is speaking on its own behalf, the First Amendment strictures that attend [restrictions on purely private speech in] the various types of government-established forums do not apply....

This case is not like *Perry Ed. Assn. v. Perry Local Educators' Assn.,* 460 U.S. 37 (1983), where we found a school district's internal mail system to be a nonpublic forum for private speech. There, ... a number of private organizations, including a teachers' union, had access to the mail system. It was therefore clear that private parties, and not only the government, used the system to communicate. Here, by contrast, each specialty license plate design is formally approved by and stamped with the imprimatur of Texas.

Nor is this case like *Lehman v. City of Shaker Heights*, 418 U.S. 298 (1974) (plurality opinion), where we found the advertising space on city buses to be a nonpublic forum. There, the messages were located in a context (advertising space) that is traditionally available for private speech. And the advertising space, in contrast to license plates, bore no indicia that the speech was owned or conveyed by the government.

Nor is this case like *Cornelius v. NAACP Legal Defense & Ed. Fund, Inc.*, 473 U.S. 788 (1985), where we determined that a charitable fundraising program directed at federal employees constituted a nonpublic forum. That forum lacked the kind of history present here. The fundraising drive had never been a medium for government speech. Instead, it was established "to bring order to [a] solicitation process" which had previously consisted of ad hoc solicitation by individual charitable organizations. The drive "was designed to minimize ... disruption to the [federal] workplace," not to communicate messages from the government. Further, the charitable solicitations did not appear on a government ID under the government's name. In contrast to the instant case, there was no reason for employees to "interpret [the solicitation] as conveying some message on the [government's] behalf."

{Additionally, the fact that Texas vehicle owners pay annual fees in order to display specialty license plates does not imply that the plate designs are merely a forum for private speech. While some nonpublic forums provide governments the opportunity to profit from speech, see, *e.g.*, *Lehman*, the existence of government profit alone is insufficient to trigger forum analysis. Thus, if the city in *Summum* had established a rule that organizations wishing to donate monuments must also pay fees to assist in park maintenance, we do not believe that the result in that case would have been any different.}
...

[E.] [L]icense plate designs ... do ... also implicate the free speech rights of private persons.... [D]rivers who display a State's selected license plate designs convey the messages communicated through those designs.... [T]he First Amendment stringently limits a State's authority to compel a private party to express a view with which the private party disagrees. *Wooley* v. *Maynard*. But here, compelled private speech is not at issue. And just as Texas cannot require SCV to convey "the State's ideological message," SCV cannot force Texas to include a Confederate battle flag on its specialty license plates....

Justice Alito, with whom the Chief Justice, Justice Scalia, and Justice Kennedy join, dissenting....

[A.] Suppose you sat by the side of a Texas highway and studied the license plates on the vehicles passing by. You would see, in addition to the standard Texas plates, an impressive array of specialty plates. (There are now more than 350 varieties.) You would likely observe plates that honor numerous colleges and universities. You might see plates bearing the name of a high school, a fraternity or sorority, the Masons, the Knights of Columbus, the Daughters of the American Revolution, a realty company, a favorite soft drink, a favorite burger restaurant, and a favorite NASCAR driver.

As you sat there watching these plates speed by, would you really think that the sentiments reflected in these specialty plates are the views of the State of Texas and not those of the owners of the cars? If a car with a plate that says "Rather Be Golfing" passed by at 8:30 am on a Monday morning, would you think: "This is the official policy of the State—better to golf than to work?"

Really 65?

If you did your viewing at the start of the college football season and you saw Texas plates with the names of the University of Texas's out-of-state competitors in upcoming games—Notre Dame, Oklahoma State, the University of Oklahoma, Kansas State, Iowa State—would you assume that the State of Texas was officially (and perhaps treasonously) rooting for the Longhorns' opponents? And when a car zipped by with a plate that reads "NASCAR—24 Jeff Gordon," would you think that Gordon (born in California, raised in Indiana, resides in North Carolina) is the official favorite of the State government?

The Court says that all of these messages are government speech. It is essential that government be able to express its own viewpoint, the Court reminds us, because otherwise, how would it promote its programs, like recycling and vaccinations? So when Texas issues a "Rather Be Golfing" plate, but not a "Rather Be Playing Tennis" or "Rather Be Bowling" plate, it is furthering a state policy to promote golf but not tennis or bowling. And when Texas allows motorists to obtain a Notre Dame license plate but not a University of Southern California plate, it is taking sides in that long-time rivalry.

[B.] This capacious understanding of government speech takes a large and painful bite out of the First Amendment.... [T]he State of Texas has converted ... [part of the space on] its specialty plates into little mobile billboards on which motorists can display their own messages. And what Texas did here was to reject one of the messages that members of a private group wanted to post on some of these little billboards because the State thought that many of its citizens would find the message offensive. That is blatant viewpoint discrimination.

Blatant VP discrimination!

If the State can do this with its little mobile billboards, could it do the same with big, stationary billboards? Suppose that a State erected electronic billboards along its highways. Suppose that the State posted some government messages on these billboards and then, to raise money, allowed private entities and individuals to purchase the right to post their own messages. And suppose that the State allowed only those messages that it liked or found not too controversial. Would that be constitutional?

What if a state college or university did the same thing with a similar billboard or a campus bulletin board or dorm list serve? What if it allowed private messages that are consistent with prevailing views on campus but banned those that disturbed some students or faculty? Can there be any doubt that these examples of viewpoint discrimination would violate the First Amendment? I hope not, but the future uses of today's precedent remain to be seen....

[C.] [The characteristics that] rendered public monuments government speech in *Summum*[] are not present in Texas's specialty plate program....

[1.] I begin with history. As we said in *Summum,* governments have used monuments since time immemorial to express important government messages, and there is no history of governments giving equal space to those wishing to express dissenting views.... [Likewise, up to the 1990's,] before the proliferation of specialty plates in Texas ..., the words on the Texas plates can be considered government speech. The messages were created by the State, and they plausibly promoted state programs.... [Likewise, similar plates in other States] were created by the States that issued them, and motorists generally had no choice but to accept them....

The words and symbols on plates of this sort were and are government speech, but plates that are essentially commissioned by private entities (at a cost that exceeds $8,000) and that express a message chosen by those entities are very different—and quite new. Unlike in *Summum,* history here does not suggest that the messages at issue are government speech.

[2.] The Texas specialty plate program also does not exhibit the "selective receptivity" present in *Summum*. To the contrary, Texas's program is *not* selective by design. The Board's chairman, who is charged with approving designs, explained that the program's purpose is "to encourage private plates" in order to "generate additional revenue for the state." And most of the time, the Board "base[s] [its] decisions on rules that primarily deal with reflectivity and readability." A Department brochure explains: "Q. Who provides the plate design? A. You do, though your design is subject to reflectivity, legibility, and design standards."

Pressed to come up with any evidence that the State has exercised "selective receptivity," Texas (and the Court) rely primarily on sketchy information not contained in the record, specifically that the Board's predecessor (might have) rejected a "pro-life" plate and perhaps others on the ground that they contained messages that were offensive. But even if this happened, it shows only that the present case may not be the only one in which the State has exercised viewpoint discrimination....

The Court believes that messages on privately created plates are government speech because motorists want a seal of state approval for their messages and therefore prefer plates over bumper stickers. This is dangerous reasoning. There is a big difference between government speech (that is, speech by the government in furtherance of its programs) and governmental blessing (or condemnation) of private speech. Many private speakers in a forum would welcome a sign of government approval. But in the realm of private speech, government regulation may not favor one viewpoint over another.

[3.] A final factor that was important in *Summum* was space. A park can accommodate only so many permanent monuments. Often large and made of stone, monuments can last for centuries and are difficult to move. License plates, on the other hand, are small, light, mobile, and designed to last for only a relatively brief time. The only absolute limit on the number of specialty plates that a State could issue is the number of registered vehicles. The variety of available plates is limitless, too....

[4.] [T]he Texas program [also] exhibits a very important characteristic that was missing in [*Summum*]: Individuals who want to display a Texas specialty plate, instead of the standard plate, must pay an increased annual registration fee. How many groups or individuals would clamor to pay $8,000 (the cost of the deposit required to create a new plate) in order to broadcast the government's message as opposed to their own?

4. Increased Fee

And if Texas really wants to speak out in support of, say, Iowa State University (but not the University of Iowa) or "Young Lawyers" (but not old ones), why must it be paid to say things that it really wants to say? The fees Texas collects pay for much more than merely the administration of the program.

States have not adopted specialty license plate programs like Texas's because they are now bursting with things they want to say on their license plates. Those programs were adopted because they bring in money.... [Texas's] program brings in many millions of dollars every year.

Texas has space available on millions of little mobile billboards. And Texas, in effect, sells that space to those who wish to use it to express a personal message—provided only that the message does not express a viewpoint that the State finds unacceptable. That is not government speech; it is the regulation of private speech [in a limited public forum]....

LPF

[D.] The Confederate battle flag is a controversial symbol. To the Texas Sons of Confederate Veterans, it is said to evoke the memory of their ancestors and other soldiers who fought for the South in the Civil War. To others, it symbolizes slavery, segregation, and hatred.

Whatever it means to motorists who display that symbol and to those who see it, the flag expresses a viewpoint. The Board rejected the plate design because it concluded that many Texans would find the flag symbol offensive. That was pure viewpoint discrimination.

pure VPD

If the Board's candid explanation of its reason for rejecting the SCV plate were not alone sufficient to establish this point, the Board's approval of the Buffalo Soldiers plate at the same meeting dispels any doubt. {[At the same meeting at which the Board rejected the Sons of Confederate Veterans plate,] the Board approved a Buffalo Soldiers plate design by a 5-to-3 vote. Proceeds from fees paid by motorists who select that plate benefit the Buffalo Soldier National Museum in Houston, which is "dedicated primarily to preserving the legacy and honor of the African American soldier." "Buffalo Soldiers" is a nickname that was originally given to black soldiers in the Army's 10th Cavalry Regiment, which was formed after the Civil War, and the name was later used to describe other black soldiers.

Buffalo Soldiers approved

The original Buffalo Soldiers fought with distinction in the Indian Wars, but the "Buffalo Soldiers" plate was opposed by some Native Americans. One leader commented that he felt "'the same way about the Buffalo Soldiers'" as African-Americans felt about the Confederate flag. "'When we see the U.S. Cavalry uniform,'" he explained, "'we are forced to relive an American holocaust.'"}

The proponents of both the SCV and Buffalo Soldiers plates saw them as honoring soldiers who served with bravery and honor in the past. To the opponents of both plates, the images on the plates evoked painful memories. The Board rejected one plate and approved the other.

Like these two plates, many other specialty plates have the potential to irritate and perhaps even infuriate those who see them. Texas allows a plate with the words "Choose Life," but the State of New York rejected such a plate because the message "'[is] so incredibly divisive,'" and the Second Circuit recently sustained that decision.... Allowing States to reject specialty plates based on their potential to offend is viewpoint discrimination....

d. Policy—Arguing by Counterexample

Basic argument: "This proposed test is wrong because, when applied to situation _____, it would yield results that are wrong because _____."

1. "To hold that the Government unconstitutionally discriminates on the basis of viewpoint when it chooses to fund a program dedicated to advance certain permissible goals, because the program in advancing those goals necessarily discourages alternative goals, would render numerous Government programs constitutionally suspect. When Congress established a National Endowment for Democracy to encourage other countries to adopt democratic principles, it was not constitutionally required to fund a program to encourage competing lines of political philosophy such as communism and fascism...." *Rust v. Sullivan.*

"[T]he government's role as employer [must] giv[e] it a freer hand in regulating the speech of its employees than it has in regulating the speech of the public at large.... [For instance, a] government employer may bar its employees from using Mr. Cohen's offensive utterance to members of the public, or to the people with whom they work. [Though] '[u]nder the First Amendment there is no such thing as a false idea' [and] the 'fitting remedy for evil counsels is good ones,' ... when an employee counsels her co-workers to do their job in a way with which the public employer disagrees, her managers may tell her to stop, rather than relying on counterspeech.... [T]hough a private person is perfectly free to uninhibitedly and robustly criticize a state governor's legislative program, we have never suggested that the Constitution bars the governor from firing a high-ranking deputy for doing the same thing." *Waters v. Churchill,* 511 U.S. 661, 672 (1994) (plurality).

2. Response to 1: The proposed test, if properly applied, wouldn't lead to the result you say it will, because _____

3. Response to 1: The actual test isn't really what you say it is; rather, it's something more nuanced, namely _____, that will not in fact lead to the incorrect result here.

4. Rejoinder to 3: The exception or modification that makes the proposed test "more nuanced" makes no sense, because _____.

For instance, a proposed constitutional test which says that "it is unconstitutional for the government to fund viewpoint A but not viewpoint B, except when viewpoint B encourages Communism or Fascism" might reach the right result in the example given in *Rust*—but it would do so only by incorporating a distinction that's unjustifiable under current First Amendment law, which insists that courts treat the advocacy of even the most evil ideas the same as the advocacy of good ones.

Likewise, a proposed test which says that "it is unconstitutional for the government to fund viewpoint A but not viewpoint B, so long as both viewpoints are consistent with American values" might be used by a court to reach the right result in the example given in *Rust,* but is too vague to be judicially manageable.

5. Response to 1: Though the result to which this test leads may seem clearly wrong, it's actually right, because _____.

6. Response to 1 (related to 5): We should expect that all tests will lead to some results that we don't like; this test will lead only to a few undesirable results, because _____, and this shouldn't lead us to abandon it, because _____.

4. **Government as Subsidizer Trying to Control Privately Funded Speech**

a. *Agency for Int'l Development v. Alliance for Open Society Int'l, 133 S. Ct. 2321 (2013)*

[Read this case carefully, both for its general analysis, and its summary of three important precedents—*Regan v. Taxation With Representation, FCC v. League of Women Voters*, and *Rust v. Sullivan.*—ed.]

Chief Justice Roberts delivered the opinion of the Court.

[A.] The United States Leadership Against HIV/AIDS, Tuberculosis, and Malaria Act of 2003 (Leadership Act) outlined a comprehensive strategy to combat the spread of HIV/AIDS around the world. As part of that strategy, Congress authorized the appropriation of billions of dollars to fund efforts by nongovernmental organizations to assist in the fight.

The Act imposes two related conditions on that funding: First, no funds made available by the Act "may be used to promote or advocate the legalization or practice of prostitution or sex trafficking." And second, no funds may be used by an organization "that does not have a policy explicitly opposing prostitution and sex trafficking." This case concerns the second of these conditions, referred to as the Policy Requirement. The question is whether that funding condition violates a recipient's First Amendment rights....

[B.] The Policy Requirement mandates that recipients of Leadership Act funds explicitly agree with the Government's policy to oppose prostitution and sex trafficking. It is, however, a basic First Amendment principle that "freedom of speech prohibits the government from telling people what they must say." ... [And] the Government "may not deny a benefit to a person on a basis that infringes his constitutionally protected ... freedom of speech even if he has no entitlement to that benefit." In some cases, a funding condition can result in an unconstitutional burden on First Amendment rights.

The dissent thinks that can only be true when the condition is not relevant to the objectives of the program (although it has its doubts about that), or when the condition is actually coercive, in the sense of an offer that cannot be refused. Our precedents, however, are not so limited.

In the present context, the relevant distinction that has emerged from our cases is between conditions that define the limits of the government spending program—those that specify the activities Congress wants to subsidize—and conditions that seek to leverage funding to regulate speech outside the contours of the program itself. The line is hardly clear, in part because the definition of a particular program can always be manipulated to subsume the challenged condition. We have held, however, that "Congress cannot recast a condition on funding as a mere definition of its program in every case, lest the First Amendment be reduced to a simple semantic exercise."

[1.] A comparison of two cases helps illustrate the distinction: In *Regan v. Taxation With Representation,* the Court upheld a requirement that nonprofit organizations seeking tax-exempt status under 26 U.S.C. § 501(c)(3) not engage in substantial efforts to influence legislation. The tax-exempt status, we explained, "ha[d] much the same effect as a cash grant to the organization." And by limiting § 501(c)(3) status to organizations that did not attempt to influence legislation, Congress had merely "chose[n] not to subsidize lobbying."

In rejecting the nonprofit's First Amendment claim, the Court highlighted ... the fact that the condition did not prohibit that organization from lobbying Congress altogether. By ... separately incorporating as a § 501(c)(3) organization and § 501(c)(4) organization ... the nonprofit could continue to claim § 501(c)(3) status for its nonlobbying activities, while attempting to influence legislation in its § 501(c)(4) capacity with separate funds. Maintaining such a structure, the Court noted, was not "unduly burdensome." The condition thus did not deny the organization a government benefit "on account of its intention to lobby."

[2.] In *FCC v. League of Women Voters*, 468 U.S. 364 (1984), by contrast, the Court struck down a condition on federal financial assistance to noncommercial broadcast television and radio stations that prohibited all editorializing, including with private funds. Even a station receiving only one percent of its overall budget from the Federal Government, the Court explained, was "barred absolutely from all editorializing."

Unlike the situation in *Regan,* the law provided no way for a station to limit its use of federal funds to noneditorializing activities, while using private funds "to make known its views on matters of public importance." The prohibition thus went beyond ensuring that federal funds not be used to subsidize "public broadcasting station editorials," and instead leveraged the federal funding to regulate the stations' speech outside the scope of the program.

[**3.**] Our decision in *Rust v. Sullivan* elaborated on the approach reflected in *Regan* and *League of Women Voters*. In *Rust*, we considered Title X of the Public Health Service Act, a ... program that issued grants to nonprofit health-care organizations "to assist in the establishment and operation of voluntary family planning projects [to] offer a broad range of acceptable and effective family planning methods and services." ...

[The regulations implementing the Act] barred Title X projects from advocating abortion as a method of family planning, and required grantees to ensure that their Title X projects were "physically and financially separate" from their other projects that engaged in the prohibited activities.... We explained that Congress can, without offending the Constitution, selectively fund certain programs to address an issue of public concern, without funding alternative ways of addressing the same problem.... The challenged regulations were simply "designed to ensure ..." ... "that public funds [are] spent for the purposes for which they were authorized."

In making this determination, the Court stressed that "Title X expressly distinguishes between a Title X *grantee* and a Title X *project.*" The regulations governed only the scope of the grantee's Title X projects, leaving it "unfettered in its other activities." "The Title X *grantee* can continue to ... engage in abortion advocacy; it simply is required to conduct those activities through programs that are separate and independent from the project that receives Title X funds." Because the regulations did not "prohibit[] the recipient from engaging in the protected conduct outside the scope of the federally funded program," they did not run afoul of the First Amendment....

[**C.**] By demanding that funding recipients adopt—as their own—the Government's view on an issue of public concern, the condition by its very nature affects "protected conduct outside the scope of the federally funded program." *Rust*. A recipient cannot avow the belief dictated by the Policy Requirement when spending Leadership Act funds, and then turn around and assert a contrary belief, or claim neutrality, when participating in activities on its own time and dime. By requiring recipients to profess a specific belief, the Policy Requirement goes beyond defining the limits of the federally funded program to defining the recipient.

The Government contends that the affiliate guidelines, established while this litigation was pending, save the program. Under those guidelines, funding recipients are permitted to work with affiliated organizations that do not abide by the condition, as long as the recipients retain "objective integrity and independence" from the unfettered affiliates. The Government suggests the guidelines alleviate any unconstitutional burden on the respondents' First Amendment rights by allowing them to either: (1) accept Leadership Act funding and comply with Policy Requirement, but establish affiliates to communicate contrary views on prostitution; or (2) decline funding themselves (thus remaining free to express their own views or remain neutral), while creating affiliates whose sole purpose is to receive and administer Leadership Act funds, thereby "cabin[ing] the effects" of the Policy Requirement within the scope of the federal program.

Neither approach is sufficient. When we have noted the importance of affiliates in this context, it has been because they allow an organization bound by a funding condition to exercise its First Amendment rights outside the scope of the federal program. Affiliates cannot serve that purpose when the condition is that a funding recipient espouse a specific belief as its own.

If the affiliate is distinct from the recipient, the arrangement does not afford a means for the *recipient* to express *its* beliefs. If the affiliate is more clearly identified with the recipient, the recipient can express those beliefs only at the price of evident hypocrisy....

[D.] The Government suggests that the Policy Requirement is necessary because, without it, the grant of federal funds could free a recipient's private funds "to be used to promote prostitution or sex trafficking." That argument assumes that federal funding will simply supplant private funding, rather than pay for new programs or expand existing ones. The Government offers no support for that assumption as a general matter, or any reason to believe it is true here. And if the Government's argument were correct, *League of Women Voters* would have come out differently, and much of the reasoning of *Regan* and *Rust* would have been beside the point....

[E.] {The dissent views the [Policy] Requirement as simply a selection criterion by which the Government identifies organizations "who believe in its ideas to carry them to fruition." As an initial matter, whatever purpose the Policy Requirement serves in selecting funding recipients, its effects go beyond selection. The Policy Requirement is an ongoing condition on recipients' speech and activities, a ground for terminating a grant after selection is complete.

In any event, as the Government acknowledges, it is not simply seeking organizations that oppose prostitution. Rather, it explains, "Congress has expressed its purpose 'to eradicate' prostitution and sex trafficking, and it wants recipients *to adopt* a similar stance" (emphasis added). This case is not about the Government's ability to enlist the assistance of those with whom it already agrees. It is about compelling a grant recipient to adopt a particular belief as a condition of funding.}

[F.] [T]he Policy Requirement goes beyond preventing recipients from using private funds in a way that would undermine the federal program. It requires them to pledge allegiance to the Government's policy of eradicating prostitution.... [But] "[i]f there is any fixed star in our constitutional constellation, it is that no official, high or petty, can prescribe what shall be orthodox in politics, nationalism, religion, or other matters of opinion or force citizens to confess by word or act their faith therein." *West Va. Bd. of Ed. v. Barnette.*

Justice Scalia, with whom Justice Thomas joins, dissenting....

[A.] [The] Policy Requirement is nothing more than a means of selecting suitable agents to implement the Government's chosen strategy to eradicate HIV/AIDS. That is perfectly permissible under the Constitution.

Just Selection

The First Amendment does not mandate a viewpoint-neutral government. Government must choose between rival ideas and adopt some as its own: competition over cartels, solar energy over coal, weapon development over disarmament, and so forth. Moreover, the government may enlist the assistance of those who believe in its ideas to carry them to fruition; and it need not enlist for that purpose those who oppose or do not support the ideas.

That seems to me a matter of the most common common sense. For example: One of the purposes of America's foreign-aid programs is the fostering of good will towards this country. If the organization Hamas—reputed to have an efficient system for delivering welfare—were excluded from a program for the distribution of U.S. food assistance, no one could reasonably object. And that would remain true if Hamas were an organization of United States citizens entitled to the protection of the Constitution. So long as the unfunded organization remains free to engage in its activities (including anti-American propaganda) "without federal assistance," refusing to make use of its assistance for an enterprise to which it is opposed does not abridge its speech.

And the same is true when the rejected organization is not affirmatively opposed to, but merely unsupportive of, the object of the federal program, which appears to be the case here. (Respondents do not promote prostitution, but neither do they wish to oppose it.) A federal program to encourage healthy eating habits need not be administered by the American Gourmet Society, which has nothing against healthy food but does not insist upon it.

The argument is that this commonsense principle will enable the government to discriminate against, and injure, points of view to which it is opposed. Of course the Constitution does not prohibit government spending that discriminates against, and injures, points of view to which the government is opposed; every government program which takes a position on a controversial issue does that. Anti-smoking programs injure cigar aficionados, programs encouraging sexual abstinence injure free-love advocates, etc.

The constitutional prohibition at issue here is not a prohibition against discriminating against or injuring opposing points of view, but the First Amendment's prohibition against the coercing of speech. I am frankly dubious that a condition for eligibility to participate in a minor federal program such as this one runs afoul of that prohibition even when the condition is irrelevant to the goals of the program. Not every disadvantage is a coercion.

[B.] But that is not the issue before us here. Here the views that the Government demands an applicant forswear—or that the Government insists an applicant favor—are relevant to the program in question. The program is valid only if the Government is entitled to disfavor the opposing view (here, advocacy of or toleration of prostitution). And if the program can disfavor it, so can the selection of those who are to administer the program.

There is no risk that this principle will enable the Government to discriminate arbitrarily against positions it disfavors. It would not, for example, permit the Government to exclude from bidding on defense contracts anyone who refuses to abjure prostitution. But here a central part of the Government's HIV/AIDS strategy is the suppression of prostitution, by which HIV is transmitted. It is entirely reasonable to admit to participation in the program only those who believe in that goal.

According to the Court, however, this transgresses a constitutional line between conditions that operate *inside* a spending program and those that control speech *outside* of it. I am at a loss to explain what this central pillar of the Court's opinion—this distinction that the Court itself admits is "hardly clear" …—has to do with the First Amendment.

The distinction was alluded to, to be sure, in *Rust v. Sullivan*, but not as (what the Court now makes it) an invariable requirement for First Amendment validity. That the pro-abortion speech prohibition was limited to "inside the program" speech was relevant in *Rust* because the program itself was not an anti-abortion program. The Government remained neutral on that controversial issue, but did not wish abortion to be promoted within its family-planning-services program. The statutory objective could not be impaired, in other words, by "outside the program" pro-abortion speech. The purpose of the limitation was to prevent Government funding from providing the *means* of pro-abortion propaganda, which the Government did not wish (and had no constitutional obligation) to provide.

The situation here is vastly different. Elimination of prostitution *is* an objective of the HIV/AIDS program, and *any* promotion of prostitution—whether made inside or outside the program—*does* harm the program.

Of course the most obvious manner in which the admission to a program of an ideological opponent can frustrate the purpose of the program is by freeing up the opponent's funds for use in its ideological opposition. To use the Hamas example again: Subsidizing that organization's provision of social services enables the money that it would otherwise use for that purpose to be used, instead, for anti-American propaganda.

Perhaps that problem does not exist in this case since the respondents do not affirmatively promote prostitution. But the Court's analysis categorically rejects that justification for ideological requirements in *all* cases, demanding "record indica[tion]" that "federal funding will simply supplant private funding, rather than pay for new programs."

This seems to me quite naive. Money is fungible. The economic reality is that when NGOs can conduct their AIDS work on the Government's dime, they can expend greater resources on policies that undercut the Leadership Act.

The Government need not establish by record evidence that this will happen. To make it a valid consideration in determining participation in federal programs, it suffices that this is a real and obvious risk.

None of the cases the Court cites for its holding provide support. I have already discussed *Rust*. As for *Taxation With Representation*, ... the fact that [certain] nonprofits were permitted to use a separate § 501(c)(4) affiliate for their lobbying ... was entirely nonessential to the Court's holding.... As for *League of Women Voters*, the ban on editorializing at issue there was disallowed precisely because it did not further a relevant, permissible policy of the Federal Communications Act—and indeed was simply incompatible with the Act's "affirmativ[e] encourage[ment]" of the "vigorous expression of controversial opinions" by licensed broadcasters....

[C.] Ideological-commitment requirements such as the one here are quite rare; but making the choice between competing applicants on relevant ideological grounds is undoubtedly quite common. See, *e.g., NEA v. Finley*. As far as the Constitution is concerned, it is quite impossible to distinguish between the two. If the government cannot demand a relevant ideological commitment as a condition of application, neither can it distinguish between applicants on a relevant ideological ground. And that is the real evil of today's opinion. One can expect, in the future, frequent challenges to the denial of government funding for relevant ideological reasons....

What Congress has done here—requiring an ideological commitment relevant to the Government task at hand—is approved by the Constitution itself. Americans need not support the Constitution; they may be Communists or anarchists. But "[t]he Senators and Representatives ..., and the Members of the several State Legislatures, and all executive and judicial Officers, both of the United States and of the several States, shall be bound by Oath or Affirmation, to support [the] Constitution." The Framers saw the wisdom of imposing affirmative ideological commitments prerequisite to assisting in the government's work. And so should we.

b.　*Regan v. Taxation With Representation, 461 U.S. 540 (1983)*

Justice Rehnquist delivered the opinion of the [unanimous] Court....

[For a brief summary of the facts of the case and its analysis, see *Agency for Int'l Development* above; but the following is also helpful for understanding the Court's reasoning in these cases:—ed.]

Both tax exemptions and tax deductibility are a form of subsidy that is administered through the tax system. A tax exemption has much the same effect as a cash grant to the organization of the amount of tax it would have to pay on its income. Deductible contributions are similar to cash grants of the amount of a portion of the individual's contributions.

The system Congress has enacted provides this kind of subsidy to nonprofit civic welfare organizations generally, and an additional subsidy to those charitable organizations that do not engage in substantial lobbying. In short, Congress chose not to subsidize lobbying as extensively as it chose to subsidize other activities that nonprofit organizations undertake to promote the public welfare....

[T]he government may not deny a benefit to a person because he exercises a constitutional right. But ... [t]he Code does not deny TWR the right to receive deductible contributions to support its nonlobbying activity, nor does it deny TWR any independent benefit on account of its intention to lobby. Congress has merely refused to pay for the lobbying out of public moneys. This Court has never held that Congress must grant a benefit such as TWR claims here to a person who wishes to exercise a constitutional right....

5. ACCESS TO MATERIAL IN LIBRARIES

a. *Problem: Public Library Filtering*

A public library that gets no federal funds installs a filter program on all its user-accessible computers. The program has a "block racist Web pages" option, which blocks those Web pages that the filter designers believe to be racist. The library turns on this option, and implements a policy that this option may *not* be turned off, even when an adult patron asks for a site to be unblocked. Is this constitutional? Should it be?

b. *Board of Ed. v. Pico, 457 U.S. 853 (1982)*

Justice Brennan ... delivered an opinion, in which Justice Marshall and Justice Stevens joined, and in which Justice Blackmun joined except for Part [B.1].

[A.] The ... question presented is whether the First Amendment imposes limitations upon the exercise by a local school board of its discretion to remove library books from high school and junior high school libraries....

In February 1976, ... the Board [of Education of Island Trees Union Free School District] gave an "unofficial direction" [to school officials] that [several] listed books[3] be removed from the library shelves and delivered to the Board's offices, so that Board members could read them.... [The Board later] characterized the removed books as "anti-American, anti-Christian, anti-Sem[i]tic, and just plain filthy," and concluded that "[i]t is our duty, our moral obligation, to protect the children in our schools from this moral danger as surely as from physical and medical dangers."

A short time later, the Board appointed a "Book Review Committee," consisting of four Island Trees parents and four members of the Island Trees schools staff, to read the listed books and to recommend to the Board whether the books should be retained, taking into account the books' "educational suitability," "good taste," "relevance," and "appropriateness to age and grade level." In July, the Committee made its final report to the Board,

---

[3] The nine books in the High School library were: Slaughter House Five, by Kurt Vonnegut, Jr.; The Naked Ape, by Desmond Morris; Down These Mean Streets, by Piri Thomas; Best Short Stories of Negro Writers, edited by Langston Hughes; Go Ask Alice, of anonymous authorship; Laughing Boy, by Oliver LaFarge; Black Boy, by Richard Wright; A Hero Ain't Nothin' But A Sandwich, by Alice Childress; and Soul On Ice, by Eldridge Cleaver. The book in the Junior High School library was A Reader for Writers, edited by Jerome Archer.... The Fixer, by Bernard Malamud, was found to be included in the curriculum of a twelfth-grade literature course.

recommending that five of the listed books be retained and that two others be removed .... As for the remaining four books, the Committee could not agree on two, took no position on one, and recommended that the last book be made available to students only with parental approval.

The Board substantially rejected the Committee's report later that month, deciding that only one book [Laughing Boy] should be returned to the High School library without restriction, that another [Black Boy] should be made available subject to parental approval [the Committee had recommended that both be retained—ed.], but that the remaining nine books should "be removed from [both] libraries and [from] use in the curriculum." ... [The Court of Appeals, in a fragmented decision, basically held that there was evidence that the removal was motivated by a desire to suppress ideas; that if this was indeed the motivation, the removal would be unconstitutional; and that a trial was therefore needed to determine the Board's actual motivation.—ed.] ...

[B.] Respondents do not seek in this Court to impose limitations upon their school Board's discretion to prescribe [class] curricula .... [T]he only books at issue in this case are *library* books, books that by their nature are optional rather than required reading....

Furthermore, even as to library books, the action before us does not involve the *acquisition* of books.... [T]he only action challenged in this case is the *removal* from school libraries of books originally placed there by the school authorities, or without objection from them....

[1.] [T]he First Amendment rights of students may be directly and sharply implicated by the removal of books from the shelves of a school library. Our precedents have focused "not only on the role of the First Amendment in fostering individual self-expression but also on its role in affording the public access to discussion, debate, and the dissemination of information and ideas." ... "[T]he State may not, consistently with the spirit of the First Amendment, contract the spectrum of available knowledge."

In keeping with this principle, we have held that in a variety of contexts "the Constitution protects the right to receive information and ideas." This right is an inherent corollary of the rights of free speech and press that are explicitly guaranteed by the Constitution, in two senses. First, the right to receive ideas follows ineluctably from the *sender's* First Amendment right to send them: ... "The dissemination of ideas can accomplish nothing if otherwise willing addressees are not free to receive and consider them...."

More importantly, the right to receive ideas is a necessary predicate to the *recipient's* meaningful exercise of his own rights of speech, press, and political freedom. Madison admonished us: "A popular Government, without popular information, or the means of acquiring it, is but a Prologue to a Farce or a Tragedy; or, perhaps both. Knowledge will forever govern ignorance: And a people who mean to be their own Governors, must arm themselves with the power which knowledge gives." ...

In sum, just as access to ideas makes it possible for citizens generally to exercise their rights of free speech and press in a meaningful manner, such access prepares students for active and effective participation in the pluralistic, often contentious society in which they will soon be adult members. Of course all First Amendment rights accorded to students must be construed "in light of the special characteristics of the school environment." But the special characteristics of the school *library* make that environment especially appropriate for the recognition of the First Amendment rights of students....

"[S]tudents must always remain free to inquire, to study and to evaluate, to gain new maturity and understanding." The school library is the principal locus of such freedom.... [I]n the school library "a student can ... discover areas of interest and thought not covered by the prescribed curriculum.... [The] student learns that a library is a place to test or expand upon ideas presented to him, in or out of the classroom."

Petitioners emphasize the inculcative function of secondary education, and argue that they must be allowed *unfettered* discretion to "transmit community values" through the Island Trees schools.... [T]he libraries afford [students] an opportunity at self-education and individual enrichment that is wholly optional. Petitioners might well defend their claim of absolute discretion in matters of *curriculum* by reliance upon their duty to inculcate community values. But we think that petitioners' reliance upon that duty is misplaced where, as here, they attempt to extend their claim of absolute discretion beyond the compulsory environment of the classroom, into the school library and the regime of voluntary inquiry that there holds sway....

[2.] Petitioners rightly possess significant discretion to determine the content of their school libraries. But that discretion may not be exercised in a narrowly partisan or political manner.

If a Democratic school board, motivated by party affiliation, ordered the removal of all books written by or in favor of Republicans, few would doubt that the order violated the constitutional rights of the students denied access to those books. The same conclusion would surely apply if an all-white school board, motivated by racial animus, decided to remove all books authored by blacks or advocating racial equality and integration. Our Constitution does not permit the official suppression of *ideas*.

Thus whether petitioners' removal of books from their school libraries denied respondents their First Amendment rights depends upon the motivation behind petitioners' actions. If petitioners *intended* by their removal decision to deny respondents access to ideas with which petitioners disagreed, and if this intent was the decisive factor in petitioners' decision, then petitioners have exercised their discretion in violation of the Constitution. To permit such intentions to control official actions would be to encourage the precise sort of officially prescribed orthodoxy unequivocally condemned in *W. Va. State Bd. of Ed. v. Barnette*.

On the other hand, ... an unconstitutional motivation would *not* be demonstrated if it were shown that petitioners had decided to remove the books at issue because those books were pervasively vulgar [or educationally unsuitable].... [S]uch motivations, if decisive of petitioners' actions, would not carry the danger of an official suppression of ideas, and thus would not violate respondents' First Amendment rights....

[C.] [The Court canvassed the evidence presented below and concluded:] The evidence plainly does not foreclose the possibility that petitioners' decision to remove the books rested decisively upon disagreement with constitutionally protected ideas in those books, or upon a desire on petitioners' part to impose upon ... students ... a political orthodoxy to which petitioners and their constituents adhered. [The Court held this sufficed to warrant a trial to determine the Board's motivation.—ed.] ...

Justice Blackmun, concurring in part [except for Part B.1] and concurring in the judgment....

In my view ... the principle involved here is both narrower and more basic than the "right to receive information" identified by the plurality.... [W]e strike a proper balance here by holding that school officials may not remove books for the *purpose* of restricting access to the political ideas or social perspectives discussed in them, when that action is motivated simply by the officials' disapproval of the ideas involved.

{I ... have some doubt that there is a theoretical distinction between removal of a book and failure to acquire a book. But ... there is a profound practical and evidentiary distinction between the two actions: "removal, more than failure to acquire, is likely to suggest that an impermissible political motivation may be present. There are many reasons why a book is not acquired, the most obvious being limited resources, but there are few legitimate reasons why a book, once acquired, should be removed from a library not filled to capacity."} ...

[S]tate action calculated to suppress novel ideas or concepts is fundamentally antithetical to the values of the First Amendment. At a minimum, allowing a school board to engage in such conduct hardly teaches children to respect the diversity of ideas that is fundamental to the American system. In this context, then, the school board must "be able to show that its action was caused by something more than a mere desire to avoid the discomfort and unpleasantness that always accompany an unpopular viewpoint," and that the board had something in mind in addition to the suppression of partisan or political views it did not share.... [Justice Blackmun then gives examples of *permissible* reasons for removal, including offensive language, psychological or intellectual inappropriateness for the age group, or possibly the book's ideas' being "manifestly inimical to the public welfare."—ed.]

It is not a sufficient answer ... that a State operates a school in its role as "educator," rather than its role as "sovereign," see *post* (Rehnquist, J., dissenting), for the First Amendment has application to all the State's activities. While the State may act as "property owner" when it prevents certain types of expressive activity from taking place on public lands, for example, few would suggest that the State may base such restrictions on the content of the speaker's message, or may take its action for the purpose of suppressing access to the ideas involved. And while it is not clear to me from Justice Rehnquist's discussion whether a State operates its public libraries in its "role as sovereign," surely difficult constitutional problems would arise if a State chose to exclude "anti-American" books from its public libraries ....

[S]chool officials must have the authority to make educationally appropriate choices in designing a curriculum .... {The school's finite resources—as well as the limited number of hours in the day—require that education officials make sensitive choices between subjects to be offered and competing areas of academic emphasis .... In any event, the Court has recognized that students' First Amendment rights in most cases must give way if they interfere "with the schools' work or [with] the rights of other students to be secure and to be let alone," and such interference will rise to intolerable levels if public participation in the management of the curriculum becomes commonplace.} Thus school officials may seek to instill certain values [such as patriotism] "by persuasion and example," or by choice of emphasis. That sort of positive educational action, however, is the converse of an intentional attempt to shield students from certain ideas that officials find politically distasteful....

Justice White, concurring in the judgment....

The unresolved factual issue, as I understand it, is the reason or reasons underlying the school board's removal of the books. I am not inclined to disagree with the Court of Appeals on such a fact-bound issue and hence concur in the judgment of affirmance. Presumably this will result in a trial and the making of a full record and findings on the critical issues....

[I see no need to decide now] the extent to which the First Amendment limits the discretion of the school board to remove books from the school library.... When findings of fact ... are made by the District Court, that may end the case. If, for example, the District Court concludes after a trial that the books were removed for their vulgarity, there may be no appeal.... [I]f there is an appeal, ... and if certiorari is sought and granted, there will be time enough to address the First Amendment issues ....

Chief Justice Burger, with whom Justice Powell, Justice Rehnquist, and Justice O'Connor join, dissenting....

[A.] [T]he "right to receive information and ideas" does not carry with it the ... right to have those ideas affirmatively provided at a particular place by the government....

If, as we have held, schools may legitimately be used as vehicles for "inculcating fundamental values necessary to the maintenance of a democratic political system," school authorities must have broad discretion to fulfill that obligation. Presumably all activity within a primary or secondary school involves the conveyance of information and at least an implied approval of the worth of that information. How are "fundamental values" to be inculcated except by having school boards make content-based decisions about the appropriateness of retaining materials in the school library and curriculum....

The plurality concludes that under the Constitution school boards cannot choose to retain or dispense with books if their discretion is exercised in a "narrowly partisan or political manner." The plurality concedes that permissible factors are whether the books are "pervasively vulgar" or educationally unsuitable. "Educational suitability," however, is a standardless phrase. This conclusion will undoubtedly be drawn in many—if not most—instances because of the decisionmaker's content-based judgment that the ideas contained in the book or the idea expressed from the author's method of communication are inappropriate for teenage pupils.

The plurality also tells us that a book may be removed from a school library if it is "pervasively vulgar." But why must the vulgarity be "pervasive" to be offensive? Vulgarity might be concentrated in a single poem or a single chapter or a single page, yet still be inappropriate.... A school board might also reasonably conclude that the school board's retention of such books gives those volumes an implicit endorsement.

Further, there is no guidance whatsoever as to what constitutes "political" factors.... [V]irtually all educational decisions necessarily involve "political" determinations.... Ultimately the federal courts will be the judge of whether the motivation for book removal was "valid" or "reasonable." Undoubtedly the validity of many book removals will ultimately turn on a judge's evaluation of the books. Discretion must be used, and the appropriate body to exercise that discretion is the local elected school board, not judges.

We can all agree that as a matter of *educational policy* students should have wide access to information and ideas. But the people elect school boards, who in turn select administrators, who select the teachers, and these are the individuals best able to determine the substance of that policy.... A school board reflects its constituency in a very real sense and thus could not long exercise unchecked discretion in its choice to acquire or remove books.... Finally, even if parents and students cannot convince the school board that book removal is inappropriate, they have alternative sources ... [such as] bookstores [and] public libraries ....

[B.] No amount of "limiting" language could rein in the sweeping "right" the plurality would create. The plurality distinguishes library books from textbooks because library books "by their nature are optional rather than required reading." It is not clear, however, why this distinction requires *greater* scrutiny before "optional" reading materials may be removed. It would appear that required reading and textbooks have a greater likelihood of imposing a "pall of orthodoxy" over the educational process than do optional reading. In essence, the plurality's view transforms the availability of this "optional" reading into a "right" to have this "optional" reading maintained at the demand of teenagers....

Justice Rehnquist, with whom ... Chief Justice [Burger] and Justice Powell join, dissenting....

[A.] I can cheerfully concede [that school boards may not remove all books written by or in favor of Republicans or all books authored by blacks or advocating racial equality and integration], but as in so many other cases the extreme examples are seldom the ones that arise in the real world of constitutional litigation. In *this case* the facts taken most favorably to respondents suggest that nothing of this sort happened. The nine books removed undoubtedly did contain "ideas," but ... eight of them contained demonstrable amounts of vulgarity and profanity, and the ninth contained nothing that could be considered partisan or political.... I would save for another day—feeling quite confident that that day will not arrive—the extreme examples posed in Justice Brennan's opinion.

[B.] [I]t is helpful to assess the role of government as educator, as compared with the role of government as sovereign. When it acts as an educator, at least at the elementary and secondary school level, the government is engaged in inculcating social values and knowledge in relatively impressionable young people. Obviously there are innumerable decisions to be made as to what courses should be taught, what books should be purchased, or what teachers should be employed. In every one of these areas the members of a school board will act on the basis of their own personal or moral values, will attempt to mirror those of the community, or will abdicate the making of such decisions to so-called "experts." ...

[I]t is "permissible and appropriate for local boards to make educational decisions based upon their personal social, political and moral views." ... [T]he mere decision to purchase some books will necessarily preclude the possibility of purchasing others. The decision to teach a particular subject may preclude the possibility of teaching another subject. A decision to replace a teacher because of ineffectiveness may by implication be seen as a disparagement of the subject matter taught.

In each of these instances, however, the book or the exposure to the subject matter may be acquired elsewhere. The managers of the school district are not proscribing it as to the citizenry in general, but are simply determining that it will not be included in the curriculum or school library. In short, actions by the government as educator do not raise the same First Amendment concerns as actions by the government as sovereign.

[C.] [1.] [A] right to receive information, in the junior high school and high school setting ... [is] inconsistent with the necessarily selective process of elementary and secondary education.... Nor does the right-to-receive doctrine recognized in our past decisions apply to schools by analogy.... [T]he denial of access to ideas inhibits one's own acquisition of knowledge only when that denial is relatively complete. If the denied ideas are readily available from the same source in other accessible locations, the benefits to be gained from exposure to those ideas have not been foreclosed by the State....

Public schools fulfill the vital role of teaching students the basic skills necessary to function in our society, and of "inculcating fundamental values necessary to the maintenance of a democratic political system." The idea that such students have a right of access, *in the school*, to information other than that thought by their educators to be necessary is contrary to the very nature of an inculcative education.

Education consists of the selective presentation and explanation of ideas. The effective acquisition of knowledge depends upon an orderly exposure to relevant information. Nowhere is this more true than in elementary and secondary schools, where, unlike the broad-ranging inquiry available to university students, the courses taught are those thought most relevant to the young students' individual development.... This winnowing process [of determining what to present and what not to present] necessarily leaves much information to be discovered by students at another time or in another place ....

Unlike university or public libraries, elementary and secondary school libraries are not designed for freewheeling inquiry; they are tailored, as the public school curriculum is tailored, to the teaching of basic skills and ideas.... [T]he First Amendment right to receive information simply has no application to the one public institution which, by its very nature, is a place for the selective conveyance of ideas....

[2.] Justice Brennan's own discomfort with the idea that students have a right to receive information from their elementary or secondary schools is demonstrated by the artificial limitations which he places upon the right—limitations ... which are inconsistent with the right itself. The attempt to confine the right to the library is one such limitation ....

As a second limitation, Justice Brennan distinguishes the act of removing a previously acquired book from the act of refusing to acquire the book in the first place .... If Justice Brennan truly has found a "right to receive ideas," however, this distinction between acquisition and removal makes little sense. The failure of a library to acquire a book denies access to its contents just as effectively as does the removal of the book ....

Presumably the distinction is based upon the greater visibility and the greater sense of conscious decision thought to be involved in the removal of a book, as opposed to that involved in the refusal to acquire a book. But if "suppression of ideas" is to be the talisman, one would think that a school board's public announcement of its refusal to acquire certain books would have every bit as much impact on public attention as would an equally publicized decision to remove the books....

The final limitation placed by Justice Brennan upon his newly discovered right is a motive requirement: the First Amendment is violated only "[i]f petitioners *intended* by their removal decision to deny respondents access to ideas with which petitioners disagreed." But bad motives and good motives alike deny access to the books removed. If Justice Brennan truly recognizes a constitutional right to receive information, it is difficult to see why the reason for the denial makes any difference....

It is [also] difficult to tell from Justice Brennan's opinion just what motives he would consider constitutionally impermissible. I had thought that the First Amendment proscribes content-based restrictions on the marketplace of ideas. Justice Brennan concludes, however, that a removal decision based solely upon the "educational suitability" of a book or upon its perceived vulgarity is "perfectly permissible." But such determinations are based as much on the content of the book as determinations that the book espouses pernicious political views.

Moreover, Justice Brennan's motive test is difficult to square with his distinction between acquisition and removal. If a school board's removal of books might be motivated by a desire to promote favored political or religious views, there is no reason that its acquisition policy might not also be so motivated. And yet the "pall of orthodoxy" cast by a carefully executed book-acquisition program apparently would not violate the First Amendment under Justice Brennan's view....

[An Appendix to one of the dissents included all the passages that the Board found troublesome; here are the first three items:—ed.]

1) *SOUL ON ICE* by Eldridge Cleaver
[pp.] 157-158 ' ... There are white men who will pay you to fuck their wives. They approach you and say, "How would you like to fuck a white woman?" "What is this?" you ask. "On the up-and-up," he assures you. "It's all right. She's my wife. She needs black rod, is all. She has to have it. It's like a medicine or drug to her. She has to have it. I'll pay you. It's all on the level, no trick involved. Interested?" ... There is a certain type who will leave you and his wife alone and tell you to pile her real good.... Then there are some who like to peep at you through a keyhole and watch you have his woman, or peep at you through a window, or lie under the bed and listen to the creaking of the bed as you work out. There is another type who likes to masturbate while he stands beside the bed and watches you pile her. There is the type who likes to eat his woman up after you get through piling her....'

2) *A HERO AIN'T NOTHING BUT A SANDWICH* by Alice Childress
[p.] 10 'Hell, no! *Fuck the society.*'
[pp.] 64-65 'The hell with the junkie, the wino, the capitalist, the welfare checks, the world ... yeah, and *fuck* you too!'
[pp.] 75-76 'They can have back the spread and curtains, I'm too old for them *fuckin* bunnies anyway.'

3) *THE FIXER* by Bernard Malamud
[p.] 52 'What do you think goes on in the wagon at night: Are the drivers on their knees *fucking their mothers?*'
[p.] 90 '*Fuck yourself*, said the blinker, etc.'
[p.] 92 'Who else would do anything like that but a *mother-fucking* Zhid?' ["Zhid" is a Russian pejorative for "Jew," similar to the English "kike."—ed.]
[p.] 146 'No more noise out of you or I'll shoot your *Jew cock off.*'
[p.] 189 'Also there's a lot of *fucking in the Old Testament*, so how is that religious?'
[p.] 192 'You better go *fuck yourself*, Bok, said Kogin, I'm onto your Jew tricks.'
[p.] 215 'Ding-dong giddyap. A *Jew's cock's* in the devil's hock.'
[p.] 216 'You *cocksucker* Zhid, I ought make you lick it up off the floor.' ...

c. *United States v. American Library Ass'n, 539 U.S. 194 (2003)*

Chief Justice Rehnquist ... delivered an opinion, in which Justice O'Connor, Justice Scalia, and Justice Thomas joined....

[A.] To help public libraries provide their patrons with Internet access, Congress offers two forms of federal assistance. First, the E-rate program ... entitles qualifying libraries to buy Internet access at a discount.... Second, pursuant to the Library Services and Technology Act (LSTA), [a federal agency] makes grants to state library administrative agencies [for computer infrastructure costs] .... [Combined, the programs are worth about $200 million per year to libraries.—ed.]

The accessibility of [pornography through the Internet] has created serious problems for libraries, which have found that patrons of all ages, including minors, regularly search for online pornography. Some patrons also expose others to pornographic images by leaving them displayed on Internet terminals or printed at library printers.... Congress became concerned that the E-rate and LSTA programs were facilitating access to illegal and harmful pornography....

Congress also learned that filtering software that blocks access to pornographic Web sites could provide a reasonably effective way to prevent such [access] .... By 2000, before Congress enacted [the Child Internet Protection Act], almost 17% of public libraries used such software on at least some of their Internet terminals, and 7% had filters on all of them. A library can set such software to block categories of material, such as "Pornography" or "Violence." When a patron tries to view a site that falls within such a category, a screen appears indicating that the site is blocked.

But a filter set to block pornography may sometimes block other sites that present neither obscene nor pornographic material, but that nevertheless trigger the filter. To minimize this problem, a library can set its software to prevent the blocking of material that falls into categories like "Education," "History," and "Medical." A library may also add or delete specific sites from a blocking category, and anyone can ask companies that furnish filtering software to unblock particular sites....

[CIPA] provides that a library may not receive E-rate or LSTA assistance unless it has "a policy of Internet safety for minors that includes the operation of a technology protection measure ... that protects against access" by all persons to "visual depictions" that constitute "obscen[ity]" or "child pornography," and that protects against access by minors to "visual depictions" that are "harmful to minors." The statute defines a "[t]echnology protection measure" as "a specific technology that blocks or filters Internet access to material covered by" CIPA. CIPA also permits the library to "disable" the filter "to enable access for bona fide research or other lawful purposes" ... "during use by an adult" [under the E-rate program or] ... during use by any person [under LSTA]. [A] group of libraries, library associations, library patrons, and Web site publishers ... sued ..., challenging the constitutionality of CIPA's filtering provisions....

[B.] Congress has wide latitude to attach conditions to the receipt of federal assistance in order to further its policy objectives. But Congress may not "induce" the recipient "to engage in activities that would themselves be unconstitutional." ...

To fulfill their traditional missions, public libraries must have broad discretion to decide what material to provide to their patrons. Although they seek to provide a wide array of information, their goal has never been to provide "universal coverage." Instead, public libraries seek to provide materials "that would be of the greatest direct benefit or interest to the community." To this end, libraries collect only those materials deemed to have "requisite and appropriate quality."

We have held in two analogous contexts that the government has broad discretion to make content-based judgments in deciding what private speech to make available to the public. In *Arkansas Ed. Television Comm'n v. Forbes*, 523 U.S. 666 (1998), we held that public forum principles do not generally apply to a public television station's editorial judgments regarding the private speech it presents to its viewers. "[B]road rights of access for outside speakers would be antithetical, as a general rule, to the discretion that stations and their editorial staff must exercise to fulfill their journalistic purpose and statutory obligations." ...

Similarly, in *NEA v. Finley*, we upheld an art funding program that required the National Endowment for the Arts (NEA) to use content-based criteria in making funding decisions. We explained that ... "[t]he very assumption of the NEA is that grants will be awarded according to the 'artistic worth of competing applicants,' and absolute neutrality is simply inconceivable." We expressly declined to apply forum analysis, reasoning that it would conflict with "NEA's mandate ... to make esthetic judgments, and the inherently content-based 'excellence' threshold for NEA support." ...

Just as forum analysis and heightened judicial scrutiny are incompatible with the role of public television stations and ... the NEA, they are also incompatible with the discretion that public libraries must have to fulfill their traditional missions. Public library staffs necessarily consider content in making collection decisions and enjoy broad discretion in making them....

Internet access in public libraries is neither a "traditional" nor a "designated" public forum.... The doctrines surrounding traditional public forums may not be extended to situations where [a longstanding history of use for public speech] is lacking [citing *ISKCON v. Lee*]. Nor does Internet access in a public library satisfy our definition of a "designated public forum" [as in cases such as *Rosenberger v. Rector*].... A public library does not acquire Internet terminals in order to create a public forum for Web publishers to express themselves, any more than it collects books in order to provide a public forum for the authors of books to speak.

It provides Internet access, not to "encourage a diversity of views from private speakers," but for the same reasons it offers other library resources: to facilitate research, learning, and recreational pursuits by furnishing materials of ... appropriate quality.... "[T]he Internet is simply another method for making information available in a school or library." It is "no more than a technological extension of the book stack." ...

[Though] a library reviews and affirmatively chooses to acquire every book in its collection, it does not review every Web site that it makes available.... [But a] library's failure to make quality-based judgments about all the material it furnishes from the Web does not somehow taint the judgments it does make.... Most libraries already exclude pornography from their print collections because they deem it inappropriate for inclusion. We do not subject these decisions to heightened scrutiny; it would make little sense to treat libraries' judgments to block online pornography any differently, when these judgments are made for just the same reason.

Moreover, because of the vast quantity of material on the Internet and the rapid pace at which it changes, libraries cannot possibly segregate, item by item, all the Internet material that is appropriate for inclusion from all that is not.... [I]t is [thus] entirely reasonable for public libraries to ... exclude certain categories of content, without making individualized judgments that everything they do make available has requisite and appropriate quality....

[C.] [T]he dissents fault the tendency of filtering software ... to erroneously block access to constitutionally protected speech that falls outside the categories that software users intend to block.... Assuming that such erroneous blocking presents constitutional difficulties, any such concerns are dispelled by the ease with which patrons may have the filtering software disabled.

When a patron encounters a blocked site, he need only ask a librarian to unblock it or (at least in the case of adults) disable the filter.... [T]he Solicitor General stated at oral argument that a "library may ... eliminate the filtering with respect to specific sites ... at the request of a patron."

With respect to adults, CIPA also expressly authorizes library officials to "disable" a filter altogether "to enable access for bona fide research or other lawful purposes." The Solicitor General ... explained that a patron would not "have to explain ... why he was asking a site to be unblocked or the filtering to be disabled."

The District Court viewed unblocking and disabling as inadequate because some patrons may be too embarrassed to request them. But the Constitution does not guarantee the right to acquire information at a public library without any risk of embarrassment....

[D.] Under [the unconstitutional conditions] doctrine, "the government 'may not deny a benefit to a person on a basis that infringes his constitutionally protected ... freedom of speech' even if he has no entitlement to that benefit." Appellees argue that CIPA imposes an unconstitutional condition on libraries ... by requiring them, as a condition on their receipt of federal funds, to surrender their First Amendment right to provide the public with access to constitutionally protected speech. The Government counters that ... Government entities do not have First Amendment rights.

We need not decide this question because, even assuming that appellees may assert an "unconstitutional conditions" claim, this claim would fail on the merits. Within broad limits, "when the Government appropriates public funds to establish a program it is entitled to define the limits of that program." *Rust v. Sullivan*.... The E-rate and LSTA programs were intended to help public libraries fulfill their traditional role of obtaining material of requisite and appropriate quality for educational and informational purposes. Congress may certainly insist that these "public funds be spent for the purposes for which they were authorized."

Especially because public libraries have traditionally excluded pornographic material from their other collections, Congress could reasonably impose a parallel limitation on its Internet assistance programs. As the use of filtering software helps to carry out these programs, it is a permissible condition under *Rust*.... [And t]o the extent that libraries wish to offer unfiltered access, they are free to do so without federal assistance....

Appellees mistakenly contend, in reliance on *Legal Services Corporation v. Velazquez*, that CIPA's filtering conditions "[d]istor[t] the [u]sual [f]unctioning of [p]ublic [l]ibraries." In *Velazquez*, the Court concluded that a Government program of furnishing legal aid to the indigent differed from the program in *Rust* "[i]n th[e] vital respect" that the role of lawyers who represent clients in welfare disputes is to advocate *against* the Government, and there was thus an assumption that counsel would be free of state control.... Public libraries, by contrast, have no comparable role that pits them against the Government, and there is no comparable assumption that they must be free of any conditions that their benefactors might attach to the use of donated funds ....

Velazquez held only that viewpoint-based restrictions are improper "when the [government] does not itself speak or subsidize transmittal of a message it favors *but instead expends funds to encourage a diversity of views from private speakers*." ... [P]ublic libraries do not install Internet terminals to provide a forum for Web publishers to express themselves, but rather to provide patrons with online material of requisite and appropriate quality.

Because public libraries' use of Internet filtering software does not violate their patrons' First Amendment rights, CIPA does not induce libraries to violate the Constitution, and is a valid exercise of Congress' spending power....

Justice Kennedy, concurring in the judgment.

If, on the request of an adult user, a librarian will unblock filtered material or disable the Internet software filter without significant delay, there is little to this case. The Government represents this is indeed the fact.... If some libraries do not have the capacity to unblock specific Web sites or to disable the filter or if it is shown that an adult user's election to view constitutionally protected Internet material is burdened in some other substantial way, that would be the subject for an as-applied challenge, not the facial challenge made in this case.... [Justices Breyer's and Souter's opinions also mentioned that as-applied challenges were possible.—ed.]

The interest in protecting young library users from material inappropriate for minors is legitimate, and even compelling .... Given this interest, and the failure to show that the ability of adult library users to have access to

the material is burdened in any significant degree, the statute is not unconstitutional on its face....

Justice Breyer, concurring in the judgment....

The Act ... restricts the public's receipt of information ... through limitations imposed by outside bodies (here Congress) upon two critically important sources of information—the Internet as accessed via public libraries.... [But t]o apply "strict scrutiny" to the "selection" of a library's collection (whether carried out by public libraries themselves or by other community bodies with a traditional legal right to engage in that function) would unreasonably interfere with the discretion necessary to create, maintain, or select a library's "collection" ....

Instead, I would examine the constitutionality of the Act's restrictions here as the Court has examined speech-related restrictions in other contexts where circumstances call for heightened, but not "strict," scrutiny—where, for example, complex, competing constitutional interests are potentially at issue or speech-related harm is potentially justified by unusually strong governmental interests.... In such cases the Court has asked whether the harm to speech-related interests is disproportionate in light of both the justifications and the potential alternatives. It has considered the legitimacy of the statute's objective, the extent to which the statute will tend to achieve that objective, whether there are other, less restrictive ways of achieving that objective, and ultimately whether the statute works speech-related harm that, in relation to that objective, is out of proportion.... Cf., e.g., *Central Hudson Gas & Elec. Corp. v. Public Serv. Comm'n*; *United States v. O'Brien*....

The Act seeks to restrict access to obscenity, child pornography, and, in respect to access by minors, material that is comparably harmful. These objectives are "legitimate," and indeed often "compelling." See, *e.g.*, *Miller v. California*; *Reno v. ACLU*; *New York v. Ferber*.... [S]oftware filters "provide a relatively cheap and effective" means of furthering these goals....

[F]ilters both "overblock," screening out some perfectly legitimate material, and "underblock," allowing some obscene material to escape detection .... But no one has presented any clearly superior or better fitting alternatives. At the same time, ... the Act allows libraries to permit any adult patron access to an "overblocked" Web site ....

The Act does impose upon the patron the burden of making this request. But it is difficult to see how that burden (or any delay associated with compliance) could prove more onerous than traditional library practices associated with segregating library materials in, say, closed stacks, or with interlibrary lending practices that require patrons to make requests that are not anonymous and to wait while the [library] obtains the desired materials .... Given the comparatively small burden that the Act imposes upon the library patron seeking legitimate Internet materials, I cannot say that any speech-related harm that the Act may cause is disproportionate when considered in relation to the Act's legitimate objectives....

Justice Stevens, dissenting.

"To fulfill their traditional missions, public libraries must have broad discretion to decide what material to provide their patrons." Accordingly, I agree ... that the 7% of public libraries that decided to use [filtering] software on *all* of their Internet terminals in 2000 did not act unlawfully.

Whether it is constitutional for the Congress of the United States to impose that requirement on the other 93%, however, raises a vastly different question. Rather than allowing local decisionmakers to tailor their responses to local problems, [CIPA] operates as a blunt nationwide restraint on adult access to "an enormous amount of valuable information" ....

[A.] Given the quantity and ever-changing character of Web sites offering free sexually explicit material, it is inevitable that a substantial amount of such material will never be blocked [by filters]. Because of this "underblocking," the statute will provide parents with a false sense of security without really solving the problem that motivated its enactment.

Conversely, the software's reliance on words to identify undesirable sites necessarily results in the blocking of thousands of pages that "contain content that is completely innocuous for both adults and minors ...." [A] statutory blunderbuss that mandates this vast amount of "overblocking" abridges the freedom of speech protected by the First Amendment.... Neither the interest in suppressing unlawful speech nor the interest in protecting children from access to harmful materials justifies this overly broad restriction on adult access to protected speech. "The Government may not suppress lawful speech as the means to suppress unlawful speech[," and] "[t]he State may not "reduce the adult population ... to reading only what is fit for children." *Ashcroft v. Free Speech Coalition.*[4] ...

[T]he District Court expressly found that ... "[l]ibraries may enforce Internet use policies that make clear to patrons that the library's Internet terminals may not be used to access illegal speech [as a less restrictive alternative to trying to filter out obscenity and child pornography]. Libraries may then impose penalties on patrons who violate these policies, ranging from a warning to notification of law enforcement ....

"Less restrictive alternatives to filtering that further libraries' interest in preventing minors from exposure to visual depictions that are harmful to minors include requiring parental consent to or presence during unfiltered access, or restricting minors' unfiltered access to terminals within view of library staff. Finally, optional filtering, privacy screens, recessed monitors, and placement of unfiltered Internet terminals outside of sight-lines [can]

---

4 **[The plurality responds:**—ed.] [The cases condemning restrictions that] "reduce the adult population ... to reading only what is fit for children[]" ... are inapposite because they addressed Congress' direct regulation of private conduct, not exercises of its Spending Power.... [A] public library does not have an obligation to add material to its collection simply because the material is constitutionally protected.

... prevent patrons from being unwillingly exposed to sexually explicit content on the Internet." Those findings are consistent with scholarly comment on the issue arguing that local decisions tailored to local circumstances are more appropriate than a mandate from Congress....[a]

[T]he Solicitor General's assurance that the statute permits individual librarians to disable filtering mechanisms whenever a patron so requests ... does not cure the constitutional infirmity in the statute. Until a blocked site ... is unblocked, a patron is unlikely to know what is being hidden and therefore whether there is any point in asking for the filter to be removed....

Inevitably, the interest of the authors of those works in reaching the widest possible audience would be abridged.... Unless we assume that the statute is a mere symbolic gesture, we must conclude that it will create a significant prior restraint on adult access to protected speech. A law that prohibits reading without official consent, like a law that prohibits speaking without consent, "constitutes a dramatic departure from our national heritage and constitutional tradition." ...

[B.] Given our Nation's deep commitment "to safeguarding academic freedom" and to the "robust exchange of ideas," a library's exercise of judgment [about what to include in and what to exclude from] its collection is entitled to First Amendment protection. A federal statute penalizing a library for failing to install filtering software on every one of its Internet-accessible computers would unquestionably violate that Amendment.

I think it equally clear that the First Amendment protects libraries from being denied funds for refusing to comply with an identical rule. An abridgment of speech by means of a threatened denial of benefits can be just as pernicious as an abridgment by means of a threatened penalty.... [For instance, n]either [employee] discharges, as in *Elrod v. Burns*, nor refusals to hire or promote, as in *Rutan v. Republican Party*, 497 U.S. 62 (1990), are immune from First Amendment scrutiny.[6] ...

[Likewise], we specifically held that when "the Government seeks to use an existing medium of expression and to control it, in a class of cases, in ways which distort its usual functioning," the distorting restriction must be

---

[a] **[The plurality responds**:—ed.] ... [W]e require ... least restrictive means only when the forum is a public one and strict scrutiny applies.... In any case, the suggested alternatives have their own drawbacks. Close monitoring of computer users would be far more intrusive than the use of filtering software, and would risk transforming the role of a librarian from a professional to whom patrons turn for assistance into a compliance officer whom many patrons might wish to avoid. Moving terminals to places where their displays cannot easily be seen by other patrons, or installing privacy screens or recessed monitors, would not address a library's interest in preventing patrons from deliberately using its computers to view online pornography....

[6] **[The plurality responds:**–ed.]... [Justice Stevens's] reliance on [the government employment cases] is misplaced. The invalidated state action in those cases involved true penalties, such as denial of a promotion or outright discharge from employment, not nonsubsidies.

struck down under the First Amendment. *Velazquez.* The question, then, is whether requiring the filtering software on all Internet-accessible computers distorts that medium. As I have discussed above, the over- and underblocking of the software does just that.

The plurality argues that the controversial decision in *Rust* requires rejection of appellees' unconstitutional conditions claim. But ... *Rust* ... only applies to ... governmental speech—that is, situations in which the government seeks to communicate a specific message.... [The] program[s] ... in this case do not subsidize any message favored by the Government....

Even if we were to construe the passage of CIPA as modifying the [subsidy] programs such that they now convey a governmental message that no "'visual depictions' that are 'obscene,' 'child pornography,' or in the case of minors, 'harmful to minors,'" should be expressed or viewed, the use of filtering software does not promote that message.... [Because of the frequency of over- and underblocking,] the message conveyed by the use of filtering software is not that all speech except that which is prohibited by CIPA is supported by the Government, but rather that all speech that gets through the software is supported by the Government.... [S]ince the message conveyed is far from the message the Government purports to promote—indeed, the material permitted past the filtering software does not seem to have any coherent message—*Rust* is inapposite.

The plurality's reliance on *Finley* is also misplaced.... Unlike [in] this case, the Federal Government was not seeking [in *Finley*] to impose restrictions on the administration of a nonfederal program.... [Nor did *Finley*] involve a challenge by the NEA to a governmental restriction on its ability to award grants. Instead, the respondents were performance artists who had applied for NEA grants but were denied funding. If this were a case in which library patrons had challenged a library's decision to install and use filtering software, it would be in the same posture as *Finley*. Because it is not, *Finley* does not control this case.

Also unlike [in] *Finley*, the Government does not merely seek to control a library's discretion with respect to computers purchased with Government funds or those computers with Government-discounted Internet access. CIPA requires libraries to install filtering software on *every* computer with Internet access if the library receives *any* [CIPA subsidy] .... [I]f a library attempts to provide Internet service for even *one* computer through an E-rate discount, that library must put filtering software on *all* of its computers with Internet access, not just the one computer with E-rate discount....

Justice Souter, with whom Justice Ginsburg joins, dissenting....

[A.] [I]f the only First Amendment interests raised here were those of children, I would uphold application of the Act.... [T]he governmental interest in "shielding" children from exposure to indecent material is "compelling," and I do not think that the awkwardness a child might feel on asking for an unblocked terminal is any such burden as to affect constitutionality.

Nor would I dissent if I agreed with the majority of my colleagues that an adult library patron could, consistently with the Act, obtain an unblocked terminal simply for the asking.... But the Federal Communications Commission, in its order implementing the Act, pointedly declined to set a federal policy on when unblocking by local libraries would be appropriate under the statute. Moreover, the District Court expressly found that "unblocking may take days, and may be unavailable, especially in branch libraries, which are often less well staffed ...." ...

[T]he unblocking provisions [of CIPA] simply cannot be construed ... to say that a library must unblock upon adult request, no conditions imposed and no questions asked. First, the statute says only that a library "may" unblock, not that it must. In addition, it allows unblocking only for a "bona fide research or other lawful purposes," and if the "lawful purposes" criterion means anything that would not ... render the "bona fide research" criterion superfluous, it must impose some limit on eligibility for unblocking. There is therefore necessarily some restriction, which is surely made more onerous by the uncertainty of its terms and the generosity of its discretion to library staffs ....

We therefore have to take the statute on the understanding that adults will be denied access to a substantial amount of nonobscene material harmful to children but lawful for adult examination, and a substantial quantity of text and pictures harmful to no one.... We likewise have to examine the statute on the understanding that the restrictions on adult Internet access have no justification in the object of protecting children....

The question for me, then, is whether a local library could itself constitutionally impose these restrictions on the content otherwise available to an adult patron through an Internet connection, at a library terminal provided for public use. The answer is no. [Such a policy] would be ... a content-based restriction on communication of material in the library's control that an adult could otherwise lawfully see. This would simply be censorship....

[B.] Public libraries are indeed selective in what they acquire to place in their stacks, as they must be. There is only so much money and so much shelf space, and the necessity to choose some material and reject the rest justifies the effort to be selective with an eye to demand, quality, and the object of maintaining the library as a place of civilized enquiry by widely different sorts of people.

Selectivity is thus necessary and complex, and these two characteristics explain why review of a library's selection decisions must be limited: the decisions are made all the time, and only in extreme cases could one expect particular choices to reveal ... reasons even the plurality would consider to be illegitimate[], like excluding books because their authors are Democrats or their critiques of organized Christianity are unsympathetic....

[But filtering] is not necessitated by scarcity of either money or space. ... [B]locking the Internet is merely blocking access purchased in its entirety .... The proper analogy therefore is not to passing up a book that might have been bought; it is either to buying a book and then keeping it from adults lacking an acceptable "purpose," or to buying an encyclopedia and then cutting out pages with anything thought to be unsuitable for all adults. {Of course, a library that allowed its patrons to use computers for any purposes might feel the need to purchase more computers to satisfy what would presumably be greater demand, but the answer to that problem would be to limit the number of unblocked terminals or the hours in which they could be used.}

The plurality claims to find support ... in the "traditional missio[n]" of the public library. The plurality thus argues, in effect, that the traditional responsibility of public libraries has called for denying adult access to certain books, or bowdlerizing the content of what the libraries let adults see.

But, in fact, the plurality's conception of a public library's mission has been rejected by the libraries themselves.... Institutional history of public libraries in America discloses an evolution toward a general rule, now firmly rooted, that any adult entitled to use the library has access to any of its holdings. [Detailed discussion of this history omitted.—ed.] ...

[Finally, a]fter a library has acquired material in the first place, ... the variety of possible reasons that might legitimately support an initial rejection are no longer in play.... Removal (and blocking) decisions being so often obviously correlated with content, they tend to show up for just what they are, and because such decisions tend to be few, courts can examine them without facing a deluge. The difference between choices to keep out and choices to throw out is thus enormous, a perception that underlay the good sense of the plurality's conclusion in *Board of Ed. v. Pico* ....

[C.] There is no good reason, then, to treat blocking of adult enquiry as anything different from the censorship it presumptively is. For this reason, I would hold in accordance with conventional strict scrutiny that a library's practice of blocking would violate an adult patron's First and Fourteenth Amendment right to be free of Internet censorship, when unjustified (as here) by any legitimate interest in screening children from harmful material....

E. Government as Regulator of the Airwaves

a. Summary

Rule: Regulations of speech on broadcast radio and television are permissible when they are

1. Narrowly tailored (same as in strict scrutiny)

2. to further a substantial government interest. *FCC v. League of Women Voters*, 468 U.S. 364 (1984).

a. Interests found to be substantial:

— "Ensuring adequate and balanced coverage of public issues," referring to *Red Lion Broadcasting v. FCC* (1969) (p. 677).

— Shielding listeners who may be offended by indecent language, referring to *FCC v. Pacifica Foundation* (1978) (p. 181).

— Shielding children from being "exposed to [indecent language] without parental supervision," *League of Women Voters* (referring to *Pacifica*).

— "[E]nsuring that the audiences of noncommercial stations will not be led to think that the broadcaster's editorials reflect the official view of the Government," *League of Women Voters*, though this interest may justify only disclaimers and not prohibition on editorializing.

b. Interests found not to be substantial:

— Shielding listeners from supposedly offensive ideas, *Pacifica*.

— (Probably) shielding listeners and children from expression (even offensive expression) "at the core of First Amendment protections" rather than "indecent expression," *League of Women Voters*.

3. This rule is applicable only to broadcasting over the airwaves,

— not to newspapers, *Miami Herald v. Tornillo* (1974) (p. 503),

— or the Internet, *Reno v. ACLU* (1997) (p. 140) (not included in the portion excerpted in these materials),

— or even to cable television, *Turner Broadcasting System v. FCC* (1994) (p. 514) (not included in the portion excerpted in these materials).

Policy justifications for this doctrine:

1. The government must pick and choose who can use the airwaves, so the government should have some power to attach conditions to broadcasting licenses, *Red Lion*, especially if the conditions are aimed at providing more access.

2. Broadcasting is uniquely intrusive into the home, *Pacifica*.

3. Broadcasting is uniquely accessible to young children, *id.*

Recent dissent from the rule: Justice Thomas in *FCC v. Fox Television Stations, Inc. (I)* (excerpted below) suggested that the lower protection offered to over-the-airwaves broadcasting was unsound, and so did Justice Ginsburg in *FCC v. Fox Television Stations, Inc. (II)*, 132 S. Ct. 2307 (2012). But the other Justices did not opine on the question, so *Pacifica* and *Red Lion* remain precedents.

FCC v. Fox (II) squarely raised the question whether *Pacifica* should be overruled; indeed, the Justices asked for briefing on "[w]hether the [FCC's] current indecency-enforcement regime violates the First ... Amendment ...." And more than five months elapsed from oral argument in the case to the handing down of the opinion, which suggests that the Justices were considering the broader First Amendment issue. Yet the Court's opinion was short, narrow, and unanimous (except for Justice Sotomayor, who was recused), concluding only that the sanctions imposed in the particular case violated the Due Process Clause, because they rested on the FCC's retroactive change to its indecency policy.

This suggests the Court may have been split 4–4, in light of Justice Sotomayor's recusal, perhaps with Chief Justice Roberts and Justices Scalia, Breyer, and Alito voting to uphold the policy on First Amendment grounds (a guess based on my view of their questions at oral argument and their general free speech opinions) and Justices Kennedy, Thomas, Ginsburg, and Kagan voting to strike it down. But this is just speculation.

b. Problem: Drug-Glorifying Songs on Radio

The FCC issues a notice to broadcasters stating that a broadcaster's playing songs "tending to promote or glorify the use of illegal drugs [such] as marijuana, LSD, 'speed,' etc." would "raise ... serious questions as to whether continued operation of the station is in the public interest" (the standard for license renewal). Despite this, KILO-FM has an "Everybody Must Get Stoned" weekend before their license comes up for renewal, during which it plays nothing but pro-drug songs.

The FCC concludes that this shows that KILO is not "operating in the public interest," and therefore declines to renew their license. Is the FCC's action constitutional? (The notice is real, see Licensee Responsibility to Review Records Before Their Broadcast, 28 F.C.C.2d 409 (1971), *quoted in* Thomas G. Krattenmaker & Lucas A. (Scot) Powe, Regulating Broadcast Programming 115-16 (1994); the KILO incident is fictional.)

c. Problem: Fairness Doctrine

Congress re-enacts the Fairness Doctrine—which required that whenever broadcasters comment on controversial issues on the air, or let their employees comment on controversial issues, they must provide equal time to people who want to present opposing views—and the Personal Attack Rule. The Court agrees to hear the case. What arguments would you make in defense of reaffirming *Red Lion*? In defense of overruling it?

d. Red Lion Broadcasting Co. v. FCC, 395 U.S. 367 (1969)

Justice White delivered the opinion of the Court.

[A.] The Federal Communications Commission has for many years imposed on radio and television broadcasters the requirement that discussion of public issues be presented on broadcast stations, and that each side of those issues must be given fair coverage. This is known as the fairness doctrine .... Two aspects of the fairness doctrine, relating to personal attacks in the context of controversial public issues and to political editorializing, were codified more precisely in the form of FCC regulations ....

On November 27, 1964, [a Red Lion radio station] carried a 15-minute broadcast by the Reverend Billy James Hargis as part of a "Christian Crusade" series. A book by Fred J. Cook entitled "Goldwater—Extremist on the Right" was discussed by Hargis, who said that Cook had been fired by a newspaper for making false charges against city officials; that Cook had then worked for a Communist-affiliated publication; that he had defended Alger Hiss and attacked J. Edgar Hoover and the Central Intelligence Agency; and that he had now written a "book to smear and destroy Barry Goldwater." When Cook heard of the broadcast he concluded that he had been personally attacked and demanded free reply time, which the station refused.... [The FCC ordered the station to provide reply time.—ed.]

[T]he [FCC] regulations read as follows: ...

(a) When, during the presentation of views on a controversial issue of public importance, an attack is made upon the honesty, character, integrity or like personal qualities of an identified person or group, the licensee shall ... transmit to the person or group attacked ... an offer of a reasonable opportunity to respond over the licensee's facilities.

(b) The provisions of paragraph (a) ... shall not be applicable

(1) to attacks on foreign groups or foreign public figures;

(2) to personal attacks which are made by legally qualified candidates ... or those associated with them in the campaign, on other such candidates ... or persons associated with the candidates in the campaign; and

(3) to bona fide newscasts, bona fide news interviews, and on-the-spot coverage of a bona fide news event ....

(c) Where a licensee, in an editorial, (i) endorses or (ii) opposes a legally qualified candidate ..., the licensee shall ... transmit to ... (i) the other qualified ... candidates ... or (ii) the candidate opposed in the editorial ... an offer of a reasonable opportunity ... to respond ....

[B.] [D]ifferences in the characteristics of new media justify differences in the First Amendment standards applied to them.... [B]ecause the frequencies reserved for public broadcasting were limited in number, it was essential for the Government to tell some applicants that they could not broadcast at all because there was room for only a few. Where there are substantially more individuals who want to broadcast than there are frequencies to allocate, it is idle to posit an unabridgeable First Amendment right to broadcast comparable to the right of every individual to speak, write, or publish.

If 100 persons want broadcast licenses but there are only 10 frequencies to allocate, all of them may have the same "right" to a license; but if there is to be any effective communication by radio, only a few can be licensed and the rest must be barred from the airwaves. It would be strange if the First Amendment, aimed at protecting and furthering communications, prevented the Government from making radio communication possible by requiring licenses to broadcast and by limiting the number of licenses so as not to overcrowd the spectrum....

Congress unquestionably has the power to grant and deny licenses and to eliminate existing stations. No one has a First Amendment right to a license or to monopolize a radio frequency; to deny a station license because "the public interest" requires it "is not a denial of free speech."

By the same token, as far as the First Amendment is concerned those who are licensed stand no better than those to whom licenses are refused. A license permits broadcasting, but the licensee has no constitutional right to be the one who holds the license or to monopolize a radio frequency to the exclusion of his fellow citizens. There is nothing in the First Amendment which prevents the Government from requiring a licensee to share his frequency with others and to conduct himself as a proxy or fiduciary with obligations to present those views and voices which are representative of his community and which would otherwise, by necessity, be barred from the airwaves.

This is not to say that the First Amendment is irrelevant to public broadcasting. On the contrary, it has a major role to play as the Congress itself recognized in § 326, which forbids FCC interference with "the right of free speech by means of radio communication." Because of the scarcity of radio frequencies, the Government is permitted to put restraints on licensees in favor of others whose views should be expressed on this unique medium. But the people as a whole retain their interest in free speech by radio and their collective right to have the medium function consistently with the ends and purposes of the First Amendment.

It is the right of the viewers and listeners, not the right of the broadcasters, which is paramount. It is the purpose of the First Amendment to preserve an uninhibited marketplace of ideas in which truth will ultimately prevail, rather than to countenance monopolization of that market, whether it be by the Government itself or a private licensee....

[We cannot] say that it is inconsistent with the First Amendment goal of producing an informed public capable of conducting its own affairs to require a broadcaster to permit answers to personal attacks occurring in the course of discussing controversial issues, or to require that the political opponents of those endorsed by the station be given a chance to communicate with the public. Otherwise, station owners and a few networks would have unfettered power to make time available only to the highest bidders, to communicate only their own views on public issues, people and candidates, and to permit on the air only those with whom they agreed.

There is no sanctuary in the First Amendment for unlimited private censorship operating in a medium not open to all. "Freedom of the press from governmental interference under the First Amendment does not sanction repression of that freedom by private interests."

[C.] It is strenuously argued, however, that if political editorials or personal attacks will trigger an obligation in broadcasters to afford the opportunity for expression to speakers who need not pay for time and whose views are unpalatable to the licensees, then broadcasters will be irresistibly forced to self-censorship and their coverage of controversial public issues will be eliminated or at least rendered wholly ineffective. Such a result would indeed be a serious matter, for should licensees actually eliminate their coverage of controversial issues, the purposes of the doctrine would be stifled....

At this point, however, ... that possibility is at best speculative. The communications industry, and in particular the networks, have taken pains to present controversial issues in the past, and even now they do not assert that they intend to abandon their efforts in this regard.... And if experience with the administration of those doctrines indicates that they have the net effect of reducing rather than enhancing the volume and quality of coverage, there will be time enough to reconsider the constitutional implications. The fairness doctrine in the past has had no such overall effect.

That this will occur now seems unlikely, however, since if present licensees should suddenly prove timorous, the Commission is not powerless to insist that they give adequate and fair attention to public issues. It does not violate the First Amendment to treat licensees given the privilege of using scarce radio frequencies as proxies for the entire community, obligated to give suitable time and attention to matters of great public concern.

To condition the granting or renewal of licenses on a willingness to present representative community views on controversial issues is consistent with the ends and purposes of those constitutional provisions forbidding the abridgment of freedom of speech and freedom of the press. Congress need not stand idly by and permit those with licenses to ignore the problems which beset the people or to exclude from the airways anything but their own views of fundamental questions....

e.   FCC v. Fox Television Stations, Inc., 556 U.S. 502 (2009)

[Justice Thomas was the only Justice opining on the First Amendment issue.—ed.]

Justice Thomas, concurring....

I write ... to note the questionable viability of ... *Red Lion Broadcasting Co. v. FCC* [and] *FCC v. Pacifica Foundation*. *Red Lion* and *Pacifica* were unconvincing when they were issued, and the passage of time has only increased doubt regarding their continued validity. "The text of the First Amendment makes no distinctions among print, broadcast, and cable media ...." ... [These cases'] deep intrusion into the First Amendment rights of broadcasters, which the Court has justified based only on the nature of the medium, is problematic on two levels.

First, ... the Court relied on a set of transitory facts, *e.g.*, the "scarcity of radio frequencies," to determine the applicable First Amendment standard. But the original meaning of the Constitution cannot turn on modern necessity: "Constitutional rights are enshrined with the scope they were understood to have when the people adopted them, whether or not future legislatures or (yes) even future judges think that scope too broad." In breaching this principle, *Red Lion* adopted, and *Pacifica* reaffirmed, a legal rule that lacks any textual basis in the Constitution. Indeed, the logical weakness of *Red Lion* and *Pacifica* has been apparent for some time: "It is certainly true that broadcast frequencies are scarce but it is unclear why that fact justifies content regulation of broadcasting in a way that would be intolerable if applied to the editorial process of the print media."

Highlighting the doctrinal incoherence of *Red Lion* and *Pacifica,* the Court has declined to apply the lesser standard of First Amendment scrutiny imposed on broadcast speech to federal regulation of telephone dial-in services, cable television programming, and the Internet. "There is no justification for this apparent dichotomy in First Amendment jurisprudence...." The justifications relied on by the Court in *Red Lion* and *Pacifica*—"spectrum scarcity, intrusiveness, and accessibility to children—neither distinguish broadcast from cable, nor explain the relaxed application of the principles of the First Amendment to broadcast." ... "It is ironic that streaming [Internet] video or audio content from a television or radio station would likely receive more constitutional protection than would the same exact content broadcast over-the-air[."]

Second, even if this Court's disfavored treatment of broadcasters under the First Amendment could have been justified at the time of *Red Lion* and *Pacifica,* dramatic technological advances have eviscerated the factual assumptions underlying those decisions. Broadcast spectrum is significantly less scarce than it was 40 years ago.... [T]he number of over-the-air broadcast stations grew from 7,411 in 1969, when *Red Lion* was issued, to 15,273 by the end of 2004....

Moreover, traditional broadcast television and radio are no longer the "uniquely pervasive" media forms they once were. For most consumers, traditional broadcast media programming is now bundled with cable or satellite services. Broadcast and other video programming is also widely available over the Internet. And like radio and television broadcasts, Internet access is now often freely available over the airwaves and can be accessed by portable computer, cell phones, and other wireless devices....

"If rules regulating broadcast content were ever a justifiable infringement of speech, it was because of the relative dominance of that medium in the communications marketplace of the past. As the Commission has long recognized, the facts underlying this justification are no longer true[."] {[And w]ith respect to reliance by *Pacifica* on the ease with which children could be exposed to indecent television programming, technology has provided innovative solutions to assist adults in screening their children from unsuitable programming—even when that programming appears on broadcast channels.} ...

f.   *Miami Herald Pub. Co. v. Tornillo, see p. 519*

g.   *FCC v. Pacifica Foundation, see p. 197*

F.   GOVERNMENT AS REGULATOR OF THE BAR

a.   Summary

Basic principle: The government has some extra power to regulate the speech of lawyers, partly because the lawyer is seen as an officer of the court—not a government employee as such, but something like that.

1.   The government may restrict lawyers' speech about the proceedings in which they're representing clients if there is a "substantial likelihood" that the speech will materially prejudice the trial by influencing jurors or potential jurors. *Gentile v. State Bar*, 501 U.S. 1030 (1991).

2.   More broadly, the Court suggests that lawyer speech will at least sometimes be subjected to a "balancing test": "When a state regulation implicates First Amendment rights, the Court must balance those interests against the State's legitimate interest in regulating the activity in ques-

tion." *Id.* It's not clear, though, when this test would be applied—for instance, whether it applies to lawyers generally or just to lawyers in pending cases—and how the "balancing" is to be performed.

3. On the other hand, lawyers continue to have substantial free speech rights. Even commercial advertising by lawyers is protected, see, *e.g.*, *Peel v. Attorney Reg. & Discip. Comm'n* (1990) (p. 261), though the Court has been somewhat more willing to credit claims that certain forms of lawyer-client speech tend to be more coercive than other kinds of promotional speech, compare *Ohralik v. Ohio State Bar Ass'n* (1978) (p. 256) (upholding restriction on face-to-face sales pitches by lawyer) with *Edenfield v. Fane*, 507 U.S. 761 (1993) (striking down a restriction on face-to-face sales pitches by accountants).

G. GOVERNMENT AS CONTROLLER OF THE MILITARY

a. *Summary*

Rule: The government has extremely broad authority to restrict the speech of members of the military, and even to use what would otherwise be unconstitutionally vague rules to do so. *Parker v. Levy*, 417 U.S. 733 (1974), doesn't specifically define the boundaries of this authority, but it suggests that the authority is indeed quite broad. And *Goldman v. Weinberger*, though a Free Exercise Clause case, likewise suggests that the First Amendment has little force in the military.

b. *Goldman v. Weinberger, 475 U.S. 503 (1986)*

Justice Rehnquist delivered the opinion of the Court....

Our review of military regulations challenged on First Amendment grounds is far more deferential than constitutional review of similar laws or regulations designed for civilian society. The military need not encourage debate or tolerate protest to the extent that such tolerance is required of the civilian state by the First Amendment; to accomplish its mission the military must foster instinctive obedience, unity, commitment, and esprit de corps. The essence of military service "is the subordination of the desires and interests of the individual to the needs of the service."

These aspects of military life do not, of course, render entirely nugatory in the military context the guarantees of the First Amendment. But "within the military community there is simply not the same [individual] autonomy as there is in the larger civilian community." ...

[And n]ot only are courts "ill-equipped to determine the impact upon discipline that any particular intrusion upon military authority might have," but the military authorities have been charged by the Executive and Legislative Branches with carrying out our Nation's military policy. "[J]udicial deference ... is at its apogee when legislative action under the congressional authority to raise and support armies and make rules and regulations for their governance is challenged." ...

H. Government as Prison Warden

a. *Summary*

Rule: Restrictions on prisoner speech are valid if they are "reasonably related to legitimate penological interests."

1. To determine this, courts consider four factors, *Thornburgh v. Abbott*, 490 U.S. 401 (1989):

a. "[W]hether the governmental objective underlying the regulations at issue is legitimate and neutral, and ... the regulations are rationally related to that objective." The "neutrality" doesn't require content neutrality, but simply that the restriction be justified by security concerns rather than mere disagreement with the speech.

b. "[W]hether there are alternative means of exercising the right that remain open to prison inmates." "The right" here seems to mean generally "the right to communicate," and not the right to say a particular thing or receive particular materials. A wide range of communication may be foreclosed, so long as inmates retain considerable rights to communicate about other matters or with other people.

c. "[T]he impact that accommodation of the asserted constitutional right will have on others (guards and inmates) in the prison."

d. "[T]he existence of obvious, easy alternatives {that fully accommodate[] the prisoner's rights at *de minimis* cost to valid penological interests} may be evidence that the regulation is not reasonable, but is an 'exaggerated response' to prison concerns."

— (a), (b), and (d) sound like elements of the normal time/place/manner restriction test (content neutrality, ample alternative channels to express one's message, and proportionality of burden, see p. 339); but they are interpreted in a much less government-constraining way than are the elements of the time/place/manner test.

b. Regulations on *outgoing* mail from prisoners to noninmates, however, still appear to be controlled by an earlier case, *Procunier v. Martinez*, 416 U.S. 396 (1974). The rule there is less pro-government:

i. "[T]he regulation or practice in question must further an important or substantial governmental interest unrelated to the suppression of expression"—an interest in "security, order, and rehabilitation"—and

ii. "the limitation of First Amendment freedoms must be no greater than is necessary or essential to the protection of the particular governmental interest involved[, rather than] unnecessarily broad."

— *Martinez* gave some examples of permissible restrictions on outgoing communications: bans on communicating "escape plans, plans relating to ongoing criminal activity, and threats of blackmail or extortion."

Related areas: Much the same rule applies to pretrial detainees, see generally *Bell v. Wolfish*, 441 U.S. 520 (1979), and likely probationers and parolees, see, *e.g.*, *Johnson v. State*, 659 N.E.2d 194 (Ind. App. 1995), though there the legitimate penological interests would focus on rehabilitation and protection of the public rather than on prison security.

I. GOVERNMENT AS REGULATOR OF IMMIGRATION

a. Summary

Rules:

1. **Criminal punishment and traditional civil liability:** The government may *not* criminally punish aliens—or, presumably, impose civil liability on them—based on speech that would be protected if said by a citizen. *Bridges v. Wixon*, 326 U.S. 135, 148 (1945).

2. **Entry:** The government may bar noncitizens from entering the United States based on their speech, even speech that would have been protected if said by a citizen. *Kleindienst v. Mandel*, 408 U.S. 753 (1972).

3. **Deportation:** The rule is unclear. The leading case, *Harisiades v. Shaughnessy*, 342 U.S. 580 (1952), speaks about nearly unlimited Congressional power over deportation, but that language is in the section dealing with the argument that the deportation of Harisiades violated the Due Process Clause. The First Amendment discussion rested on the conclusion that active membership in the Communist Party was substantively unprotected by the First Amendment—both for citizens and noncitizens—which was the law during that era (see *Dennis v. United States* (1951) (p. 45)).

Lower court cases are likewise mixed. For the view that *Harisiades* doesn't generally let the government act based on otherwise protected speech by aliens, see *American-Arab Anti-Discrim. Comm. v. Reno*, 70 F.3d 1045 (9th Cir. 1995), *rev'd on other grounds*, 525 U.S. 471 (1999); *Parcham v. INS*, 769 F.2d 1001 (4th Cir. 1985). For the view that *Harisiades* gives the government nearly unlimited immigration power over aliens, see *Price v. INS*, 941 F.2d 878 (9th Cir. 1991).

The Court has, however, squarely held that if the government tries to deport someone who has violated immigration law (for instance, by overstaying his visa, or working without authorization), the person may not challenge the deportation on the grounds that he was selectively prosecuted based on his otherwise protected speech. See *Reno v. American-Arab Anti-Discrim. Comm.*, 525 U.S. 471, 488-91 (1999). Outside the immigration context, such selective prosecution based on protected speech is generally unconstitutional. See *Wayte v. United States*, 470 U.S. 598 (1985).

4. **Citizenship:** It's unclear whether Congress can deny noncitizens citizenship based on speech that would be protected if said by a citizen. Cf. *Price* ("While a resident alien may not participate in the process of governing the country, naturalized citizens may. Naturalization decisions, therefore, deserve at least as much judicial deference as do decisions about initial admission.").

VII. PRIOR RESTRAINTS

A. SUMMARY

a. Generally

Whenever you see a licensing scheme ("you need a license to parade"), a prescreening scheme ("to display a work you must first clear it with this board"), or an injunction ("you may not say this, on pain of a contempt of court conviction"), there's a potential prior restraint issue involved.

But don't be too influenced by the characterization of a law as a "prior restraint." The prior restraint/subsequent punishment distinction was very important in the 1800s and early 1900s, when First Amendment doctrine was quite tolerant towards subsequent punishments. Now that subsequent punishments are mostly unconstitutional, there's little difference between how prior restraints and subsequent punishments are treated.

Rather, ask yourself exactly what sort of speech is being restricted, and how this restriction would be treated under the rules discussed in the preceding Parts. Then, use the following framework.

b. Content-Based Schemes

If a prior restraint is *justified by the communicative impact of the speech*, the analysis is like that for normal content-based restrictions.

1. **If the restrained speech can be criminally punished or can lead to civil liability**, the restriction is valid. Permanent injunctions of unprotected speech may thus be permissible. See, *e.g.*, *Kingsley Books, Inc. v. Brown* (1957) (p. 699) (obscenity); *Pittsburgh Press Co. v. Pittsburgh Comm'n on Human Relations,* 413 U.S. 376 (1973) (commercial advertising that promotes illegal transactions).

   — Likewise, for everyone except Douglas and Black, the *New York Times v. United States* (1971) (p. 706) injunction *could* have been permissible if the speech was shown to be harmful enough; but Brennan, Stewart, and White concluded that this level of harm hadn't been shown (Marshall concurred on non-First Amendment grounds). Thus, the Court seemed willing to uphold this sort of content-based ban if something like strict scrutiny were satisfied.

   — Possible exception: Some Justices have opined in favor of banning all or most injunctions even of unprotected speech. See, *e.g.*, Black & Douglas in *New York Times v. United States* (1971) (p. 706). Some state courts have read their state constitutions as imposing such a rule as to libel, and there's a long (though now a minority) tradition of not allowing any injunctions of libel. See, *e.g.*, *Brandreth v. Lance,* 8 Paige Ch. 24 (N.Y. 1839); *Willing v. Mazzocone,* 393 A.2d 1155 (Pa. 1978) .

2. **If the speech restrained cannot be punished or lead to liability,**

then the restriction is unconstitutional.

— Thus, the *Near v. Minnesota* (1931) (p. 695) ban is unconstitutional, because it restrains speech—including nonlibelous speech—for fear of its communicative impact.

— Likewise, the preliminary injunction in *Vance v. Universal Amusement Co.* (1980) (p. 711) was unconstitutional, because it "authorize[d] prior restraints of indefinite duration on the exhibition of motion pictures that have not been finally adjudicated to be obscene." It thus didn't just suppress material that had been determined to be within the obscenity exception. Rather, it also suppressed material that a court merely found to be "probable" obscenity, some of which might ultimately prove to be nonobscene and thus outside the exception. (*Kingsley Books*, on the other hand, chiefly involved permanent injunctions on material that had been found to be obscene, and any temporary injunctions before such a finding could last at most three days.)

3. **The cases that don't fit this framework** are *Times Film Corp. v. Chicago* (1961) (p. 702) and *Freedman v. Maryland* (1965) (p. 704). These cases allow a restraint on the showing of *any movie*—obscene or nonobscene—until the movie is screened for obscenity, if:

a. The screening procedure assures a prompt final judicial decision on whether the speech is in fact unprotected.

b. The censor promptly institutes the judicial proceedings.

c. The censor bears the burden of proving the speech is unprotected.

d. The judicial proceedings are adversarial, *i.e.*, the would-be speaker is represented.

— These prescreening rules are justified by the communicative impact of speech and apply to speech that's outside the exceptions—they delay the showing of many movies that ultimately prove to be nonobscene. Nonetheless, they are constitutional, if properly limited.

— The *Freedman* requirements might *not* apply to commercial speech. *Virginia State Bd. of Pharmacy v. Virginia Citizens Consumer Council, Inc.* (1976) (p. 247). The Supreme Court has not finally resolved this.

— Prescreening is also allowed for importation of books and pictures, *United States v. Thirty-Seven Photographs*, 402 U.S. 363 (1971).

— Courts probably wouldn't uphold schemes that screen newspapers for libel, incitement, or obscenity, because even a few days' delay would make a far bigger difference for the utility of newspapers than of movies; but the Court has never expressly decided this.

c. *Excessively Discretionary Schemes*

If a government actor has *unconstrained discretion* to deny or delay a permit, then the restriction is unconstitutional because of the danger of content-based denial or delay. See *Lovell v. Griffin* (1938) (p. 713); compare *Cox v. New Hampshire* (1941) (p. 713) (upholding a licensing scheme because it suitably constrained the licenser's discretion).

— This principle fits the theory of the cases that condemn content-based restrictions. Imagine two laws: Law 1 requires a permit for residential picketing that is to be granted "if the chief of police concludes the picketing will not be unduly offensive"; Law 2 bans all residential picketing "if the jury concludes that the picketing was unduly offensive."

Both laws—the prior restraint Law 1 and the subsequent punishment Law 2—would be practically content-based (like the law in *Carey v. Brown* and unlike the total ban in *Frisby v. Schulz*) because they would let police chiefs or juries treat some picketing better than other picketing based on its content.

— Note also the link to a policy argument supporting the void-for-vagueness doctrine: "A vague law impermissibly delegates basic policy matters to policemen, judges, and juries for resolution on an *ad hoc* and subjective basis, with the attendant dangers of arbitrary and discriminatory application." *Grayned v. City of Rockford* (1972) (p. 158).

d.   *Content-Neutral Schemes*

If a prior restraint is justified by the *noncommunicative impact of the speech*, and the scheme isn't unacceptably discretionary, then we have something similar to a content-neutral statute, and the law must be judged under the time, place, and manner standard.

— Thus, **content-neutral requirements of a license** for demonstrations—a requirement that officials must apply in a content-neutral way—are constitutional if they are narrowly tailored to the important interest in avoiding traffic tie-ups, and leave ample alternative channels (licensed demonstrations). *Cox v. New Hampshire* (1941) (p. 713).

— **Content-neutral injunctions** must "burden no more speech than necessary to serve a significant government interest." *Madsen v. Women's Health Center, Inc.*, 512 U.S. 753 (1994). This is only slightly more demanding than the content-neutral time/place/manner restrictions rule, which asks whether a statute "burden[s] substantially more speech than is necessary to further" the interest. *Ward v. Rock Against Racism,* 491 U.S. 781, 799 (1989). *Madsen* used this test to uphold an injunction banning picketing within 36 feet of abortion clinic entrances, issued against a group that had violated prior injunctions which merely banned trespass or obstruction of the entrance.

— **Content-neutral business licensing rules** applied to bookstores are likely governed just by the normal content-neutral restriction rules. *City of Littleton v. Z.J. Gifts D-4*, 541 U.S. 774 (2004).

e.   *What's New Beyond What We've Seen Outside Prior Restraints?*

1. The explanation of how to fit licensing/prescreening/injunctive restrictions into the standard framework for analyzing speech restrictions.

2. The rule that laws which give a government official discretion to decide

based on the content of speech (or to delay based on the content of speech) are treated like content-based rules.

3. The rule, established by *Times Film*, that the government may (sometimes) temporarily restrict even fully protected speech in the process of trying to screen out the unprotected.

4. The principles governing the speed required for prescreening systems (*Freedman*) justified by the potentially harmful content of speech.

5. The special rule governing content-neutral injunctions (*Madsen*).

f. Just What Is a Prior Restraint?

The Court has never given a clear definition, but it seems that:

1. A restriction justified by the communicative impact of speech is a prior restraint if it suppresses speech (through a preliminary injunction, a licensing requirement, or a prescreening system) "before an adequate determination that it is unprotected by the First Amendment," *Pittsburgh Press Co. v. Pittsburgh Comm'n on Human Relations*, 413 U.S. 376, 390 (1973). Under this definition, some prior restraints would be valid, see *Times Film Corp.*; "prior restraint" isn't the same as "unconstitutional prior restraint."

2. Content-neutral licensing and injunctive systems are not prior restraints, see *Cox*; *Madsen*.

Some say any system that restricts speech before it's *published* is a prior restraint; this would include permanent injunctions, even when they are entered following an adequate determination that the speech is unprotected by the First Amendment. The Court, though, has not accepted this.

[handwritten margin note: Prior restraint def.]

B. Injunctions and Prescreening Systems

a. Problem: Copyright Injunction *[handwritten star symbol]*

Courts routinely enter injunctions, both permanent and preliminary, in copyright infringement cases. Sara Rimensnyder believes that Craig Turk's forthcoming bestseller courtroom drama, *A Possibility of Reverter*, infringes her manuscript (titled *Fee Simple Determinable*).

Sara plans to ask for a permanent injunction, under which the court would enjoin Craig's distribution of his book if it finds that his work infringes Sara's. Before that, Sara plans to ask for a preliminary injunction, under which the court would temporarily enjoin the distribution of Craig's book—pending trial on the merits—so long as it thinks that Sara is likely to succeed on the merits. (This is an oversimplification of the preliminary injunction inquiry, but let's assume this is correct for now.)

What First Amendment defenses could Craig raise as to the permanent injunction? As to the preliminary injunction? Are these defenses likely to be winners? Cf. Mark Lemley & Eugene Volokh, *Freedom of Speech and Injunctions in Intellectual Property Cases,* 48 Duke L.J. 147 (1998).

b.   Problem: Internet Service Provider Blocking Obligations

Title 18 Pa. Stats. §§ 7621-7630 lets a court order an Internet service provider to "remove or disable access to child pornography items residing on or accessible through [the provider's] service" at a particular URL, if

(a) the Attorney General of Pennsylvania provides a "personal oath or affirmation" that

(b) "there is probable cause to believe that" items at that URL constitute child pornography.

Violations of the law may be punished with up to a $5000 fine for a first offense, up to a $20,000 fine for a second, or up to a $30,000 fine and seven years in prison for a third or later offense. Assume the law defines child pornography to track the child pornography exception discussed in Part II.D. Is the law constitutional? See *Center for Democracy & Tech. v. Pappert*, 337 F. Supp. 2d 606 (E.D. Pa. 2004).

c.   Problem: Injunction Against Ethnic Epithets

Several employees of Avis Rent-a-Car sued Avis for tolerating a hostile work environment, in violation of California antidiscrimination law. California law (like federal law and the law of most other states) holds employers legally liable when the employer, its employees, or its patrons engage in conduct or speech that is

(a) "severe or pervasive" enough

(b) to create a "hostile, abusive, or offensive work environment"

(c) based on race, religion, sex, national origin, disability, age, or (in California) medical condition, marital status, or sexual orientation

(d) for the plaintiff and

(e) for a reasonable person.

Courts have applied this both to speech said directly to the offended person and to speech—such as signs, e-mails, coworker conversations, and the like—seen or overheard by the person. Courts have generally said that the "severe or pervasive" requirement is usually not satisfied by a single instance of offensive speech, but can be satisfied by speech that happens several times over the span of several weeks or months. Employers are liable when they know or have reason to know about the speech. See Part III.C.4.a, p. 333 for more details.

Avis was held liable for damages at trial, partly because John Lawrence, an Avis Rent-a-Car employee, "routinely called only the Latino drivers 'motherfuckers' and other derogatory names, and continually demeaned them on the basis of their race, national origin and lack of English language skills." The court then issued the following injunction:

> Defendant John Lawrence shall cease ... using any derogatory racial or ethnic epithets directed at, or descriptive of, Hispanic/Latino employees of Avis Rent A Car System, Inc. ... as long as he is employed by Avis .... Defendant Avis ... shall cease ... allowing defendant John Lawrence to commit any of

the acts described in [the above quoted paragraph], under circumstances in which it knew or should have known of such acts ....

Is this injunction constitutional? Compare *Aguilar v. Avis Rent A Car System, Inc.*, 21 Cal. 4th 121 (1999) (4-3 decision) with *Avis Rent A Car System, Inc. v. Aguilar*, 529 U.S. 1138 (2000) (Thomas, J., dissenting from the denial of certiorari).

d. *Near v. Minnesota, 283 U.S. 697 (1931)*

Chief Justice Hughes delivered the opinion of the Court.

[A.] Chapter 285 of the [1925 Session Laws of Minnesota provides] ...:

... Any person who ... shall be engaged in the business of regularly or customarily producing [or] circulating ...

    (a) an obscene, lewd and lascivious newspaper, magazine, or other periodical, or

    (b) a malicious, scandalous and defamatory newspaper, magazine or other periodical,

is guilty of a nuisance, and ... may be enjoined ...

In actions brought under (b) above, there shall be available the defense that the truth was published with good motives and for justifiable ends and in such actions the plaintiff shall not have the right to ... [make its claim based on materials published] more than three months before the commencement of the action....

[T]he county attorney of Hennepin county brought this action to enjoin the publication of ... "The Saturday Press," published by the defendants [Near and some others] in the city of Minneapolis. The complaint alleged that the defendants, on [nine occasions] ... published and circulated editions of that periodical which were "largely devoted to malicious, scandalous and defamatory articles" concerning [various city officials, two newspapers, the Jewish Race, and others] ....

[T]he articles charged in substance that a Jewish gangster was in control of gambling, bootlegging and racketeering in Minneapolis, and that law enforcing officers and agencies were not energetically performing their duties.[1] Most of the charges were directed against the Chief of Police; he was

---

[1] The following articles appear in the last edition published, dated November 19, 1927 [excerpted to save space, and moved from the dissent—ed.]:

"FACTS NOT THEORIES.

"'I am a bosom friend of [the County Attorney],' snorted a gentleman of Yiddish blood, 'and I want to protest against your article,' and blah, blah, blah, ad infinitum, ad nauseam.

"I am not taking orders from men of [Mose Barnett's] faith .... There have been too many men in this city and especially those in official life, who HAVE been taking orders and suggestions from JEW GANGSTERS, therefore we HAVE Jew Gangsters, practically ruling Minneapolis. It was buzzards of the Barnett stripe who shot down my buddy. It was Barnett gunmen who staged the assault on Samuel Shapiro. It is Jew thugs who have 'pulled' practically every robbery in this city....

"I simply state a fact when I say that ninety per cent of the crimes committed

charged with gross neglect of duty, illicit relations with gangsters, and with participation in graft. The County Attorney was charged with knowing the existing conditions and with failure to take adequate measures to remedy them. The mayor was accused of inefficiency and dereliction. One member of the grand jury was stated to be in sympathy with the gangsters.... [T]he articles made serious accusations against the public officers named and others in connection with the prevalence of crimes and the failure to expose and punish them....

The District Court ... [found] that the editions in question were "chiefly devoted to malicious, scandalous and defamatory articles," concerning the individuals named. The court further found that the defendants through these publications "did engage in the business of regularly and customarily producing, publishing and circulating a malicious, scandalous and defamatory newspaper," and that "the said publication" "under said name of The Saturday Press, or any other name, constitutes a public nuisance under the laws of the State." ...

The [court] perpetually enjoined the defendants "from producing, editing, publishing, circulating, having in their possession, selling or giving away any publication whatsoever which is a malicious, scandalous or defamatory newspaper, as defined by law," and also "from further conducting said nuisance under the name and title of said The Saturday Press or any other name or title." ...

[B.] Liberty of speech, and of the press, is ... not an absolute right, and the State may punish its abuse. Liberty, in each of its phases, has its history and connotation, and, in the present instance, the inquiry is as to the historic conception of the liberty of the press and whether the statute under review violates the essential attributes of that liberty....

First. The statute is not aimed at the redress of individual or private wrongs. Remedies for libel remain available and unaffected. The statute, said the state court, "is not directed at threatened libel but at an existing business which, generally speaking, involves more than libel." It is aimed at the distribution of scandalous matter as "detrimental to public morals and to the general welfare," tending "to disturb the peace of the community" and "to provoke assaults and the commission of crime."

In order to obtain an injunction to suppress the future publication of the newspaper or periodical, it is not necessary to prove the falsity of the charges that have been made in the publication condemned. In the present action there was no allegation that the matter published was not true.

It is alleged, and the statute requires the allegation that the publication was "malicious." But, as in prosecutions for libel, there is no requirement of proof by the State of malice in fact as distinguished from malice inferred from the mere publication of the defamatory matter. The judgment in this case proceeded upon the mere proof of publication.

---

against society in this city are committed by Jew gangsters.... It is Jew, Jew, Jew, as long as one cares to comb over the records." ...

The statute permits the defense, not of the truth alone, but only that the truth was published with good motives and for justifiable ends. It is apparent that under the statute the publication is to be regarded as defamatory if it injures reputation, and that it is scandalous if it circulates charges of reprehensible conduct, whether criminal or otherwise, and the publication is thus deemed to invite public reprobation and to constitute a public scandal....

Second. The statute is directed not simply at the circulation of scandalous and defamatory statements with regard to private citizens, but at the continued publication by newspapers and periodicals of charges against public officers of corruption, malfeasance in office, or serious neglect of duty....

Third. The object of the statute is not punishment, in the ordinary sense, but suppression of the offending newspaper or periodical. The reason for the enactment, as the state court has said, is that prosecutions to enforce penal statutes for libel do not result in "efficient repression or suppression of the evils of scandal." ...

Under this statute, a publisher of a newspaper or periodical, undertaking to conduct a campaign to expose and to censure official derelictions, and devoting his publication principally to that purpose, must face not simply the possibility of a verdict against him in a suit or prosecution for libel, but a determination that his newspaper or periodical is a public nuisance to be abated, and that this abatement and suppression will follow unless he is prepared with legal evidence to prove the truth of the charges and also to satisfy the court that, in addition to being true, the matter was published with good motives and for justifiable ends....

Fourth. The statute not only operates to suppress the offending newspaper or periodical, but to put the publisher under an effective censorship.... [W]here a newspaper or periodical has been suppressed because of the circulation of charges against public officers of official misconduct, ... the renewal of the publication of such charges would constitute a contempt, and ... the judgment would lay a permanent restraint upon the publisher, to escape which he must satisfy the court as to the character of a new publication. Whether he would be permitted again to publish matter deemed to be derogatory to the same or other public officers would depend upon the court's ruling....

[C.] [I]t has been generally, if not universally, considered that it is the chief purpose of the guaranty to prevent previous restraints upon publication. The struggle in England, directed against the legislative power of the licenser, resulted in renunciation of the censorship of the press.

The liberty deemed to be established was thus described by Blackstone: "The liberty of the press is indeed essential to the nature of a free state; but this consists in laying no *previous* restraints upon publications, and not in freedom from censure for criminal matter when published. Every freeman has an undoubted right to lay what sentiments he pleases before the public; to forbid this, is to destroy the freedom of the press; but if he publishes what is improper, mischievous or illegal, he must take the consequence of his own temerity." ... In the present case, we have no occasion to inquire as to the permissible scope of subsequent punishment [or civil liability under libel law]....

[T]he protection even as to previous restraint is not absolutely unlimited. But the limitation has been recognized only in exceptional cases. "When a nation is at war many things that might be said in time of peace are such a hindrance to its effort that their utterance will not be endured so long as men fight and that no Court could regard them as protected by any constitutional right." *Schenck v. United States.* No one would question but that a government might prevent actual obstruction to its recruiting service or the publication of the sailing dates of transports or the number and location of troops.

On similar grounds, the primary requirements of decency may be enforced against obscene publications. The security of the community life may be protected against incitements to acts of violence and the overthrow by force of orderly government. The constitutional guaranty of free speech does not "protect a man from an injunction against uttering words that may have all the effect of force." These limitations are not applicable here. Nor are we now concerned with questions as to the extent of authority to prevent publications in order to protect private rights according to the principles governing the exercise of the jurisdiction of courts of equity....

Justice Butler[, joined by Justices Van Devanter, McReynolds, and Sutherland], dissenting....

[D]efendants' regular business was the publication of malicious, scandalous, and defamatory articles concerning the principal public officers, leading newspapers of the city, many private persons, and the Jewish race.... In every edition slanderous and defamatory matter predominates to the practical exclusion of all else....

The publications themselves disclose the need and propriety of the legislation.... [I]n 1916 Near [became a partner in a scandal sheet called the Twin City Reporter] ... and [later hired] Bevans. In 1919 Bevans acquired Near's interest, and has since ... continued the publication....

In a number of the editions [of the Saturday Press], defendants charge that, ever since Near sold his interest to Bevans in 1919, the Twin City Reporter has been used for blackmail, to dominate public gambling and other criminal activities, and as well to exert a kind of control over public officers and the government of the city. The articles in question also state that, when defendants announced their intention to publish the Saturday Press, they were threatened, and that soon after the first publication Guilford was waylaid and shot down before he could use the firearm which he had at hand for the purpose of defending himself against anticipated assaults. It also appears that Near apprehended violence and was not unprepared to repel it....

The long criminal career of the Twin City Reporter—if it is in fact as described by defendants—and the arming and shooting arising out of the publication of the Saturday Press, serve to illustrate the kind of conditions, in respect of the business of publishing malicious, scandalous, and defamatory periodicals, by which the state legislature presumably was moved to enact the law in question....

The Minnesota statute does not operate as a *previous* restraint on publication within the proper meaning of that phrase. It does not authorize administrative control in advance such as was formerly exercised by the licensers and censors, but prescribes a remedy to be enforced by a suit in equity. In this case there was previous publication made in the course of the business of regularly producing malicious, scandalous and defamatory periodicals. The business and publications unquestionably constitute an abuse of the right of free press.

The statute denounces the things done as a nuisance on the ground, as stated by the state supreme court, that they threaten morals, peace, and good order.... It is fanciful to suggest similarity between the granting or enforcement of the decree authorized by this statute to prevent *further* publication of malicious, scandalous, and defamatory articles and the *previous restraint* upon the press by licensers as referred to by Blackstone and described in the history of the times to which he alludes....

It is difficult to perceive any distinction, having any relation to constitutionality, between clause (a) [covering obscene periodicals] and clause (b) under which this action was brought. Both nuisances are offensive to morals, order and good government. As that resulting from lewd publications constitutionally may be enjoined it is hard to understand why the one resulting from a regular business of malicious defamation may not....

[E]xisting libel laws are inadequate effectively to suppress evils resulting from the kind of business and publications that are shown in this case. The [majority's reasoning] ... exposes the peace and good order of every community and the business and private affairs of every individual to the constant and protracted false and malicious assaults of any insolvent publisher who may have purpose and sufficient capacity to contrive and put into effect a scheme or program for oppression, blackmail or extortion....

e.   *Kingsley Books, Inc. v. Brown, 354 U.S. 436 (1957)*

Justice Frankfurter delivered the opinion of the Court....

[A.] [A]ppellants [were charged] with displaying for sale paper-covered obscene booklets ... under the general title of "Nights of Horror." The complaint prayed that appellants be enjoined from further distribution of the booklets, that they be required to surrender to the sheriff for destruction all copies in their possession, and, upon failure to do so, that the sheriff be commanded to seize and destroy those copies.

The same day the appellants were ordered to show cause within four days why they should not be enjoined *pendente lite* from distributing the booklets. {[The injunction was sought under N.Y. Code of Crim. Pro. § 22-a, which provided,] "The chief executive officer of any city ... in which a person ... distributes or is about to ... distribute ... any [publication] which is obscene, lewd, lascivious, filthy, indecent or disgusting ... may maintain an action for an injunction against such person ... to prevent the ... distribution ... of any [publication], herein described ...."} Appellants consented to the granting of an injunction *pendente lite* and did not bring the matter to issue promptly, as was their right under subdivision 2 of [§ 22-a], which provides that the persons sought to be enjoined "shall be entitled to a trial of the issues within one day after joinder of issue and a decision shall be rendered by the court within two days of the conclusion of the trial."

Clearly Obscene

After the case came to trial, the judge, sitting in equity, found that the booklets annexed to the complaint and introduced in evidence were clearly obscene—were "dirt for dirt's sake"; he enjoined their further distribution and ordered their destruction. He refused to enjoin "the sale and distribution of later issues" on the ground that "to rule against a volume not offered in evidence would ... impose an unreasonable prior restraint upon freedom of the press." ...

Authorization of an injunction *pendente lite*, as part of this scheme, during the period within which the issue of obscenity must be promptly tried and adjudicated in an adversary proceeding for which "[a]dequate notice, judicial hearing, [and] fair determination" are assured, is a safeguard against frustration of the public interest in effectuating judicial condemnation of obscene matter. It is a brake on the temptation to exploit a filthy business offered by the limited hazards of piecemeal prosecutions, sale by sale, of a publication already condemned as obscene....

[B.] The phrase "prior restraint" [cannot] ... serve as a talismanic test.... Wherein does § 22-a differ in its effective operation from ... [criminal obscenity statutes]? ... One would be bold to assert that the *in terrorem* effect of such statutes less restrains booksellers in the period before the law strikes than does § 22-a. Instead of requiring the bookseller to dread that the offer for sale of a book may, without prior warning, subject him to a criminal prosecution with the hazard of imprisonment, the civil procedure assures him that such consequences cannot follow unless he ignores a court order specifically directed to him for a prompt and carefully circumscribed determination of the issue of obscenity. Until then, he may keep the book for sale and sell it on his own judgment rather than steer "nervously among the treacherous shoals."

Put on notice

Criminal enforcement and the proceeding under § 22-a interfere with a book's solicitation of the public precisely at the same stage. In each situation the law moves after publication; the book need not in either case have yet passed into the hands of the public.... In each case the bookseller is put on notice by the complaint that sale of the publication charged with obscenity in the period before trial may subject him to penal consequences.

In the one case he may suffer fine and imprisonment for violation of the criminal statute, in the other, for disobedience of the temporary injunction. The bookseller may of course stand his ground and confidently believe that in any judicial proceeding the book could not be condemned as obscene, but both modes of procedure provide an effective deterrent against distribution prior to adjudication of the book's content—the threat of subsequent penalization. {This comparison of remedies takes note of the fact that we do not have before us a case where, although the issue of obscenity is ultimately decided in favor of the bookseller, the State nevertheless attempts to punish him for disobedience of the interim injunction. For all we know, New York may impliedly condition the temporary injunction so as not to subject the bookseller to a charge of contempt if he prevails on the issue of obscenity.}

The method devised by New York in § 22-a for determining whether a publication is obscene does not differ in essential procedural safeguards from that provided under many state statutes making the distribution of obscene publications a misdemeanor. For example, while the New York criminal provision brings the State's criminal procedure into operation, a defendant is not thereby entitled to a jury trial. [In 1957, the Sixth Amendment's Jury Trial Clause hadn't yet been applied to the states via the Fourteenth Amendment; even today, the Clause doesn't require jury trials for offenses punishable by six months or less in jail.—ed.] ...

Nor are the consequences of a judicial condemnation for obscenity under § 22-a more restrictive of freedom of expression than the result of conviction for a misdemeanor.... [A person jailed under a criminal obscenity ban would not only be] completely separated from society [while in jail] ... but [would also be] seriously restrained from trafficking in all obscene publications for a considerable time. Appellants, on the other hand, were enjoined from displaying for sale or distributing only the particular booklets theretofore published and adjudged to be obscene....

[T]he difference between *Near v. Minnesota* and this case is glaring .... Minnesota empowered its courts to enjoin the dissemination of future issues of a publication because its past issues had been found offensive.... This was enough to condemn the statute wholly apart from the fact that the proceeding in *Near* involved not obscenity but matters deemed to be derogatory to a public officer. Unlike *Near*, § 22-a is concerned solely with obscenity and, as authoritatively construed, it studiously withholds restraint upon matters not already published and not yet found to be offensive....

Chief Justice Warren, dissenting. [Dissent, which dealt with the substantive question of what constitutes obscenity, omitted.—ed.]

Justice Douglas, with whom Justice Black concurs, dissenting ....

[A.] [T]he provision for an injunction *pendente lite* gives the State the paralyzing power of a censor. A decree can issue *ex parte*—without a hearing and without any ruling or finding on the issue of obscenity.

This provision is defended on the ground that it is only a little encroachment, that a hearing must be promptly given and a finding of obscenity promptly made. But every publisher knows what awful effect a decree issued in secret can have.... [N]othing is more devastating to [First Amendment rights] than the power to restrain publication before even a hearing is held. This is prior restraint and censorship at its worst.

[B.] [T]he procedure for restraining by equity decree the distribution of all the condemned literature does violence to the First Amendment. The judge or jury which finds the publisher guilty in New York City acts on evidence that may be quite different from evidence before the judge or jury that finds the publisher not guilty in Rochester.

In New York City the publisher may have been selling his tracts to juveniles, while in Rochester he may have sold to professional people. The nature of the group among whom the tracts are distributed may have an important bearing on the issue of guilt in any obscenity prosecution. Yet the present statute makes one criminal conviction conclusive and authorizes a statewide decree that subjects the distributor to the contempt power. I think every publication is a separate offense which entitles the accused to a separate trial.

Juries or judges may differ in their opinions, community by community, case by case. The publisher is entitled to that leeway under our constitutional system. One is entitled to defend every utterance on its merits and not to suffer today for what he uttered yesterday.... The audience (in this case the judge or the jury) that hissed yesterday may applaud today, even for the same performance....

Justice Brennan, dissenting....

The jury represents a cross-section of the community and has a special aptitude for reflecting the view of the average person. Jury trial of obscenity therefore provides a peculiarly competent application of the standard for judging obscenity which, by its definition, calls for an appraisal of material according to the average person's application of contemporary community standards.

A statute which does not afford the defendant, of right, a jury determination of obscenity falls short, in my view, of giving proper effect to the standard fashioned as the necessary safeguard demanded by the freedoms of speech and press for material which is not obscene. Of course, as with jury questions generally, the trial judge must initially determine that there is a jury question, *i.e.*, that reasonable men may differ whether the material is obscene....

f. *Times Film Corp. v. Chicago, 365 U.S. 43 (1961)*

Justice Clark delivered the opinion of the Court.

Petitioner challenges on constitutional grounds the validity on its face of that portion of [a Chicago ordinance] which requires submission of all motion pictures for examination prior to their public exhibition....

Petitioner would have us hold that the public exhibition of motion pictures must be allowed under any circumstances. The State's sole remedy, it says, is the invocation of criminal process under the Illinois pornography statute, and then only after a transgression....

With this we cannot agree.... "[C]apacity for evil ... may be relevant in determining the permissible scope of community control," and ... motion pictures [are] not "necessarily subject to the precise rules governing any other particular method of expression. Each method ... tends to present its own peculiar problems." ...

[T]he State is [not] stripped of all constitutional power to prevent, in the most effective fashion, the utterance of [obscene] speech.... As to what may be decided when a concrete case involving a specific standard provided by this ordinance is presented, we intimate no opinion....

Chief Justice Warren, with whom Justice Black, Justice Douglas and Justice Brennan join, dissenting....

[This] decision presents a real danger of eventual censorship for every form of communication, be it newspapers, journals, books, magazines, television, radio or public speeches.... [N]o constitutional principle ... permits us to hold that the communication of ideas through one medium may be censored while other media are immune. Of course each medium presents its own peculiar problems, but they are not of the kind which would authorize the censorship of one form of communication and not others....

[The decision] gives official license to the censor, approving a grant of power to city officials to prevent the showing of any moving picture these officials deem unworthy of a license. It thus gives formal sanction to censorship in its purest and most far-reaching form, to a classical plan of licensing that, in our country, most closely approaches the English licensing laws of the seventeenth century which were commonly used to suppress dissent in the mother country and in the colonies....

One need not disagree with the Court that Chicago has chosen the most effective means of suppressing obscenity. Censorship has been so recognized for centuries. But, this is not to say that the Chicago plan, the old, abhorrent English system of censorship through licensing, is a permissible *form* of prohibiting unprotected speech....

A most distinguished antagonist of censorship, [John Milton,] in "a plea for unlicensed printing," has said: "If he [the censor] be of such worth as behoovs him, there cannot be a more tedious and unpleasing Journey-work, a greater loss of time levied upon his head, then to be made the perpetuall reader of unchosen books and pamphlets ...[.] [W]e may easily forsee what kind of licensers we are to expect hereafter, either ignorant, imperious, and remisse, or basely pecuniary."

There is no sign that Milton's fear of the censor would be dispelled in twentieth century America. The censor is beholden to those who sponsored the creation of his office, to those who are most radically preoccupied with the suppression of communication. The censor's function is to restrict and to restrain; his decisions are insulated from the pressures that might be brought to bear by public sentiment if the public were given an opportunity to see that which the censor has curbed.

The censor performs free from all of the procedural safeguards afforded litigants in a court of law. The likelihood of a fair and impartial trial disappears when the censor is both prosecutor and judge. There is a complete absence of rules of evidence; the fact is that there is usually no evidence at all as the system at bar vividly illustrates.... The inexistence of a jury to determine contemporary community standards is a vital flaw....

If the censor denies rights protected by the First and Fourteenth Amendments, the courts might be called upon to correct the abuse if the exhibitor decides to pursue judicial remedies. But, this is not a satisfactory answer as emphasized by this very case.... The instant litigation has now consumed almost three years. This is the delay occasioned by the censor; this is the injury done to the free communication of ideas.

This damage is not inflicted by the ordinary criminal penalties. The threat of these penalties, intelligently applied, will ordinarily be sufficient to deter the exhibition of obscenity. However, if the exhibitor believes that his film is constitutionally protected, he will show the film, and, if prosecuted under [a] criminal statute, will have ready that defense.

The perniciousness of a system of censorship is that the exhibitor's belief that his film is constitutionally protected is irrelevant. Once the censor has made his estimation that the film is "bad" and has refused to issue a permit, there is ordinarily no defense to a prosecution for showing the film without a license. Thus, the film is not shown, perhaps not for years and sometimes not ever....

g. *Freedman v. Maryland, 380 U.S. 51 (1965)*

Justice Brennan delivered the opinion of the Court.

Appellant ... challenge[s] the constitutionality of the Maryland motion picture censorship statute ....

The administration of a censorship system for motion pictures presents peculiar dangers to constitutionally protected speech. Unlike a prosecution for obscenity, a censorship proceeding puts the initial burden on the exhibitor or distributor. Because the censor's business is to censor, there inheres the danger that he may well be less responsive than a court—part of an independent branch of government—to the constitutionally protected interests in free expression. And if it is made unduly onerous, by reason of delay or otherwise, to seek judicial review, the censor's determination may in practice be final....

{The only question tendered for decision in [*Times Film Corp. v. City of Chicago*] was "whether a prior restraint was necessarily unconstitutional *under all circumstances*."} ... [We now] hold that a noncriminal process which requires the prior submission of a film to a censor avoids constitutional infirmity only if it takes place under procedural safeguards designed to obviate the dangers of a censorship system.

First, the burden of proving that the film is unprotected expression must rest on the censor.... "Where the transcendent value of speech is involved, due process certainly requires ... that the State bear the burden of persuasion to show that the appellants engaged in criminal speech."

Second, while the State may require advance submission of all films, in order to proceed effectively to bar all showings of unprotected films, the requirement cannot be administered in a manner which would lend an effect of finality to the censor's determination whether a film constitutes protected expression.... [B]ecause only a judicial determination in an adversary proceeding ensures the necessary sensitivity to freedom of expression, only a procedure requiring a judicial determination suffices to impose a valid final restraint.

To this end, the exhibitor must be assured, by statute or authoritative judicial construction, that the censor will, within a specified brief period, either issue a license or go to court to restrain showing the film. Any restraint imposed in advance of a final judicial determination on the merits must similarly be limited to preservation of the status quo for the shortest fixed period compatible with sound judicial resolution.

Moreover, ... even after expiration of a temporary restraint, an administrative refusal to license, signifying the censor's view that the film is unprotected, may have a discouraging effect on the exhibitor. Therefore, the procedure must also assure a prompt final judicial decision, to minimize the deterrent effect of an interim and possibly erroneous denial of a license.

Without these safeguards, it may prove too burdensome to seek review of the censor's determination. Particularly in the case of motion pictures, it may take very little to deter exhibition in a given locality. The exhibitor's stake in any one picture may be insufficient to warrant a protracted and onerous course of litigation. The distributor, on the other hand, may be equally unwilling to accept the burdens and delays of litigation in a particular area when, without such difficulties, he can freely exhibit his film in most of the rest of the country; for we are told that only four States and a handful of municipalities have active censorship laws....

[T]he Maryland procedural scheme does not satisfy these criteria.... ← *Doesn't Satisfy!*

The requirement of prior submission to a censor sustained in *Times Film* is consistent with our recognition that films differ from other forms of expression. Similarly, we think that the nature of the motion picture industry may suggest different time limits for a judicial determination.... [F]ilms are scheduled well before actual exhibition, and the requirement of advance submission in [the Maryland statute] recognizes this. One possible scheme would be to allow the exhibitor or distributor to submit his film early enough to ensure an orderly final disposition of the case before the scheduled exhibition date—far enough in advance so that the exhibitor could safely advertise the opening on a normal basis.

Failing such a scheme or sufficiently early submission under such a scheme, the statute would have to require adjudication considerably more prompt than has been the case under the Maryland statute. Otherwise, litigation might be unduly expensive and protracted, or the victorious exhibitor might find the most propitious opportunity for exhibition past. We do not mean to lay down rigid time limits or procedures, but to suggest considerations in drafting legislation to accord with local exhibition practices, and in doing so to avoid the potentially chilling effect of the Maryland statute on protected expression....

[The opinion was unanimous, though Justices Douglas and Black would have gone further and overruled *Times Film*. The three members of the *Times Film* majority still on the Court in 1965, Justices Clark, Harlan, and Stewart, joined Justice Brennan's opinion.—ed.]

h.   *New York Times Co. v. United States, 403 U.S. 713 (1971)*

Per curiam....

[T]he United States seeks to [preliminarily] enjoin the New York Times and the Washington Post from publishing the contents of a classified study entitled "History of U.S. Decision-Making Process on Viet Nam Policy." "Any system of prior restraints of expression comes to this Court bearing a heavy presumption against its constitutional validity." The Government "thus carries a heavy burden of showing justification for the imposition of such a restraint[,]" ... [which it has] not met ....

Justice Black, with whom Justice Douglas joins, concurring....

[The Bill of Rights was] offered to *curtail* and *restrict* the general powers granted to the Executive, Legislative, and Judicial Branches two years before in the original Constitution.... Yet the Solicitor General argues ... that the general powers of the Government adopted in the original Constitution should be interpreted to limit and restrict the specific and emphatic guarantees of the Bill of Rights adopted later. I can imagine no greater perversion of history....

In the First Amendment[,] ... [t]he Government's power to censor the press was abolished so that the press would remain forever free to censure the Government.... And paramount among the responsibilities of a free press is the duty to prevent any part of the government from deceiving the people and sending them off to distant lands to die of foreign fevers and foreign shot and shell. In my view, far from deserving condemnation for their courageous reporting, the New York Times, the Washington Post, and other newspapers should be commended for serving the purpose that the Founding Fathers saw so clearly....

The word "security" is a broad, vague generality whose contours should not be invoked to abrogate the fundamental law embodied in the First Amendment. The guarding of military and diplomatic secrets at the expense of informed representative government provides no real security for our Republic....

Justice Douglas, with whom Justice Black joins, concurring....

These disclosures may have a serious impact. But that is no basis for sanctioning a previous restraint on the press.... The dominant purpose of the First Amendment was to prohibit the widespread practice of governmental suppression of embarrassing information....

A debate of large proportions goes on in the Nation over our posture in Vietnam. That debate antedated the disclosure of the contents of the present documents. The latter are highly relevant to the debate in progress....

Justice Brennan, concurring....

[T]he Government's claim throughout these cases has been that publication of the material sought to be enjoined "could," or "might," or "may" prejudice the national interest in various ways. But the First Amendment tolerates absolutely no prior judicial restraints of the press predicated upon surmise or conjecture that untoward consequences may result. {*Freedman v. Maryland* and similar cases ... are not in point[, f]or those cases rest upon the proposition that "obscenity is not protected by the freedoms of speech and press." Here there is no question but that the material sought to be suppressed is within the protection of the First Amendment; the only question is whether, notwithstanding that fact, its publication may be enjoined for a time because of the presence of an overwhelming national interest. Similarly, copyright cases have no pertinence here: the Government is not asserting an interest in the particular form of words chosen in the documents, but is seeking to suppress the ideas expressed therein. And the copyright laws, of course, protect only the form of expression and not the ideas expressed.} ...

[O]nly governmental allegation and proof that publication must inevitably, directly, and immediately cause the occurrence of an event kindred to imperiling the safety of a transport already at sea [see *Near v. Minnesota*] can support even the issuance of an interim restraining order. In no event may mere conclusions be sufficient: for if the Executive Branch seeks judicial aid in preventing publication, it must inevitably submit the basis upon which that aid is sought to scrutiny by the judiciary. And therefore, every restraint issued in this case, whatever its form, has violated the First Amendment—and not less so because that restraint was justified as necessary to afford the courts an opportunity to examine the claim more thoroughly. Unless and until the Government has clearly made out its case, the First Amendment commands that no injunction may issue.

Justice Stewart, with whom Justice White joins, concurring....

[T]he only effective restraint upon executive policy and power in the areas of national defense and international affairs may lie in an enlightened citizenry—in an informed and critical public opinion which alone can here protect the values of democratic government.... [And] without an informed and free press there cannot be an enlightened people.

Yet ... the successful conduct of international diplomacy and the maintenance of an effective national defense require both confidentiality and secrecy. Other nations can hardly deal with this Nation in an atmosphere of mutual trust unless they can be assured that their confidences will be kept. And within our own executive departments, the development of considered and intelligent international policies would be impossible if those charged with their formulation could not communicate with each other freely, frankly, and in confidence. In the area of basic national defense the frequent need for absolute secrecy is, of course, self-evident.

I think there can be but one answer to this dilemma, if dilemma it be. The responsibility must be where the power is. If the Constitution gives the

Executive a large degree of unshared power in the conduct of foreign affairs and the maintenance of our national defense, then under the Constitution the Executive must have the largely unshared duty to determine and preserve the degree of internal security necessary to exercise that power successfully....

This is not to say that Congress and the courts have no role to play. Undoubtedly Congress has the power to enact specific and appropriate criminal laws to protect government property and preserve government secrets. Congress has passed such laws, and several of them are of very colorable relevance to the apparent circumstances of these cases. And if a criminal prosecution is instituted, it will be the responsibility of the courts to decide the applicability of the criminal law under which the charge is brought. Moreover, if Congress should pass a specific law authorizing civil proceedings in this field, the courts would likewise have the duty to decide the constitutionality of such a law as well as its applicability to the facts proved.

But in the cases before us we are asked neither to construe specific regulations nor to apply specific laws. We are asked, instead, to perform a function that the Constitution gave to the Executive, not the Judiciary. We are asked, quite simply, to prevent the publication by two newspapers of material that the Executive Branch insists should not, in the national interest, be published.

I am convinced that the Executive is correct with respect to some of the documents involved. But I cannot say that disclosure of any of them will surely result in direct, immediate, and irreparable damage to our Nation or its people. That being so, there can under the First Amendment be but one judicial resolution of the issues before us....

Justice White, with whom Justice Stewart joins, concurring....

I do not say that in no circumstances would the First Amendment permit an injunction against publishing information about government plans or operations. Nor, after examining the materials the Government characterizes as the most sensitive and destructive, can I deny that revelation of these documents will do substantial damage to public interests. Indeed, I am confident that their disclosure will have that result. But I nevertheless agree that the United States has not satisfied the very heavy burden that it must meet to warrant an injunction against publication in these cases, at least in the absence of express and appropriately limited congressional authorization for prior restraints in circumstances such as these....

It is not easy to reject the proposition urged by the United States and to deny relief on its good-faith claims in these cases that publication will work serious damage to the country. But that discomfiture is considerably dispelled by the infrequency of prior-restraint cases. Normally, publication will occur and the damage be done before the Government has either opportunity or grounds for suppression.

So here, publication has already begun and a substantial part of the threatened damage has already occurred. The fact of a massive breakdown in security is known, access to the documents by many unauthorized people is undeniable, and the efficacy of equitable relief against these or other newspapers to avert anticipated damage is doubtful at best.

What is more, terminating the ban on publication of the relatively few sensitive documents the Government now seeks to suppress does not mean that the law either requires or invites newspapers or others to publish them or that they will be immune from criminal action if they do. Prior restraints require an unusually heavy justification under the First Amendment; but failure by the Government to justify prior restraints does not measure its constitutional entitlement to a conviction for criminal publication. That the Government mistakenly chose to proceed by injunction does not mean that it could not successfully proceed in another way....

Congress has addressed itself [through various statutes imposing criminal penalties for publishing certain materials] to the problems of protecting the security of the country and the national defense from unauthorized disclosure of potentially damaging information. It has not, however, authorized the injunctive remedy against threatened publication. It has apparently been satisfied to rely on criminal sanctions and their deterrent effect on the responsible as well as the irresponsible press.

I am not, of course, saying that either of these newspapers has yet committed a crime or that either would commit a crime if it published all the material now in its possession. That matter must await resolution in the context of a criminal proceeding if one is instituted .... In that event, the issue of guilt or innocence would be determined by procedures and standards quite different from those that have purported to govern these injunctive proceedings.

Justice Marshall, concurring.... [Justice Marshall concurred on separation of powers grounds.—ed.]

Chief Justice Burger, dissenting.... [Chief Justice Burger dissented on grounds similar to those given by Justice Harlan.—ed.]

Justice Harlan, with whom ... Chief Justice [Burger] and Justice Blackmun join, dissenting....

[T]he Court has been almost irresponsibly feverish in dealing with these cases. Both the Court[s] of Appeals ... rendered judgment on June 23. The [parties' papers asking the Court to review the judgments were filed on] June 24 .... This Court's order setting a hearing before us on June 26 at 11 a.m. ... was issued less than 24 hours before.... The briefs of the parties were received less than two hours before argument on June 26.

This frenzied train of events took place in the name of the presumption against prior restraints created by the First Amendment. Due regard for the extraordinarily important and difficult questions involved in these litigations should have led the Court to shun such a precipitate timetable. In order to decide the merits of these cases properly, some or all of the following questions should have been faced: ...

2. Whether the First Amendment permits the federal courts to enjoin

publication of stories which would present a serious threat to national security. See *Near.*..

6. Whether the newspapers are entitled to retain and use the documents notwithstanding the seemingly uncontested facts that the documents, or the originals of which they are duplicates, were purloined from the Government's possession and that the newspapers received them with knowledge that they had been feloniously acquired....

These are difficult questions of fact, of law, and of judgment; the potential consequences of erroneous decision are enormous. The time which has been available to us, to the lower courts, and to the parties has been wholly inadequate for giving these cases the kind of consideration they deserve....

Forced as I am to reach the merits of these cases, I dissent from the opinion and judgments of the Court.... It is plain to me that the scope of the judicial function in passing upon the activities of the Executive Branch of the Government in the field of foreign affairs is very narrowly restricted. This view is, I think, dictated by the concept of separation of powers upon which our constitutional system rests.

In a speech on the floor of the House of Representatives, Chief Justice John Marshall, then a member of that body, stated: "The President is the sole organ of the nation in its external relations, and its sole representative with foreign nations." ... From this constitutional primacy in the field of foreign affairs, it seems to me that certain conclusions necessarily follow. Some of these were stated concisely by President Washington, declining the request of the House of Representatives for the papers leading up to the negotiation of the Jay Treaty: "The nature of foreign negotiations requires caution, and their success must often depend on secrecy; and even when brought to a conclusion a full disclosure of all the measures, demands, or eventual concessions which may have been proposed or contemplated would be extremely impolitic; for this might have a pernicious influence on future negotiations, or produce immediate inconveniences, perhaps danger and mischief, in relation to other powers." ...

[I]n my judgment the judiciary may not properly ... redetermine for itself the probable impact of disclosure on the national security. "[T]he very nature of executive decisions as to foreign policy is political, not judicial. Such decisions are wholly confided by our Constitution to the political departments of the government, Executive and Legislative. They are delicate, complex, and involve large elements of prophecy. They are and should be undertaken only by those directly responsible to the people whose welfare they advance or imperil. They are decisions of a kind for which the Judiciary has neither aptitude, facilities nor responsibility and have long been held to belong in the domain of political power not subject to judicial intrusion or inquiry." ...

Pending further hearings ... conducted under the appropriate ground rules [of deference to executive judgment], I would continue the restraints on publication. I cannot believe that the doctrine prohibiting prior restraints reaches to the point of preventing courts from maintaining the status quo long enough to act responsibly in matters of such national importance as those involved here.

Justice Blackmun, dissenting....

The First Amendment ... is only one part of an entire Constitution. Article II of the great document vests in the Executive Branch primary power over the conduct of foreign affairs and places in that branch the responsibility for the Nation's safety. Each provision of the Constitution is important, and I cannot subscribe to a doctrine of unlimited absolutism for the First Amendment at the cost of downgrading other provisions....

What is needed here is a weighing, upon properly developed standards, of the broad right of the press to print and of the very narrow right of the Government to prevent. Such standards are not yet developed.... I therefore would remand these cases to be developed expeditiously, of course, but on a schedule permitting the orderly presentation of evidence from both sides, with the use of discovery, if necessary, ... and with the preparation of briefs, oral argument, and court opinions of a quality better than has been seen to this point....

Judge Wilkey, dissenting in the District of Columbia case, after a review of only the affidavits before his court (the basic papers had not then been made available by either party), concluded that there were a number of examples of documents that, if in the possession of the Post, and if published, "could clearly result in great harm to the nation," and he defined "harm" to mean "the death of soldiers, the destruction of alliances, the greatly increased difficulty of negotiation with our enemies, the inability of our diplomats to negotiate...." ... [I] share his concern.... [If] damage has been done, and if, with the Court's action today, these newspapers proceed to publish the critical documents and there results therefrom "the death of soldiers, the destruction of alliances, the greatly increased difficulty of negotiation with our enemies, the inability of our diplomats to negotiate," ... prolongation of the war[,] and ... further delay in the freeing of United States prisoners, then the Nation's people will know where the responsibility for these sad consequences rests.

i.   Vance v. Universal Amusement Co., 445 U.S. 308 (1980)

Per curiam....

[Tex. Rev. Civ. Stat. Ann.] art. 4667(a) provides that certain habitual uses of premises shall constitute a public nuisance and shall be enjoined at the suit of either the State or any citizen. Among the prohibited uses is "the commercial manufacturing, commercial distribution, or commercial exhibition of obscene material." ... [O]rders temporarily restraining the exhibition of specific films [can] be entered [for up to ten days] *ex parte*. Moreover, such a temporary restraining order [can] be extended by a temporary injunction based on a showing of probable success on the merits and without a final determination of obscenity. {"... [Once t]he temporary injunction ... is obtained, there is no provision for treating the case any differently from any other civil case ... [and thus no] provision for a swift final adjudication on the obscenity question ...."} ...

The [Court of Appeals upheld the statute, reasoning:] ... "The statute authorizes an injunction against the commercial manufacture, distribution or exhibition of *obscene* material only. Because the injunction follows, rather than precedes, a judicial determination that obscene material has been shown or distributed or manufactured on the premises and because its prohibitions can apply only to further dealings with obscene and unprotected material, it does not constitute a prior restraint." ...

[T]he burden of supporting an injunction against a future exhibition is even heavier than the burden of justifying the imposition of a criminal sanction for a past communication. {[A] free society prefers to punish the few who abuse rights of speech *after* they break the law than to throttle them and all others beforehand. It is always difficult to know in advance what an individual will say, and the line between legitimate and illegitimate speech is often so finely drawn that the risks of freewheeling censorship are formidable.} ...

Art. 4667(a) ... authorizes prior restraints of indefinite duration on the exhibition of motion pictures that have not been finally adjudicated to be obscene. Presumably, an exhibitor would be required to obey such an order pending review of its merits and would be subject to contempt proceedings even if the film is ultimately found to be nonobscene. Such prior restraints would be more onerous and more objectionable than the threat of criminal sanctions after a film has been exhibited, since nonobscenity would be a defense to any criminal prosecution.

Nor does the fact that the temporary prior restraint is entered by a state trial judge rather than an administrative censor sufficiently distinguish this case from *Freedman v. Maryland*.... That a state trial judge might be thought more likely than an administrative censor to determine accurately that a work is obscene does not change the unconstitutional character of the restraint if erroneously entered.... [T]he absence of any special safeguards governing the entry and review of orders restraining the exhibition of named or unnamed motion pictures, without regard to the context in which they are displayed, precludes the enforcement of these nuisance statutes against motion picture exhibitors....

Justice White, with whom Justice Rehnquist joins, dissenting.... [The dissent would have interpreted art. 4667 more narrowly than the majority, and would have upheld it.—ed.]

Chief Justice Burger, with whom Justice Powell joins, dissenting [on procedural grounds]. [Omitted.—ed.]

C. LICENSING

a. *Problem: Billboard Licensing Ordinance*

A city enacts an ordinance that would require a permit before anyone erects a billboard; permits will only be issued if the billboard is found to be "not unduly distracting to motorists." Is the ordinance constitutional?

b. *Lovell v. Griffin, 303 U.S. 444 (1938)*

Chief Justice Hughes delivered the opinion of the Court....

Alma Lovell ... was sentenced to imprisonment for fifty days in default of the payment of a fine of fifty dollars [for violating an ordinance barring] "distributing ... literature of any kind ... within the limits of the City of Griffin, without first obtaining written permission from the City Manager ...." ... [Lovell] distribut[ed] without the required permission ... a pamphlet and magazine in the nature of religious tracts, setting forth the gospel of the "Kingdom of Jehovah." ...

The ordinance is not limited to "literature" that is obscene or offensive to public morals or that advocates unlawful conduct.... [The ordinance] is not limited to ways [of distribution] which might be regarded as inconsistent with the maintenance of public order, or as involving disorderly conduct, the molestation of the inhabitants, or the misuse or littering of the streets. The ordinance prohibits the distribution of literature of any kind at any time, at any place, and in any manner without a permit from the City Manager.

We think that the ordinance is invalid on its face.... The struggle for the freedom of the press was primarily directed against the power of the licensor. It was against that power that John Milton directed his assault by his "Appeal for the Liberty of Unlicensed Printing." And the liberty of the press became initially a right to publish "*without* a license what formerly could be published only *with* one." ... Legislation of the type of the ordinance in question would restore the system of license and censorship in its baldest form....

As the ordinance is void on its face, it was not necessary for appellant to seek a permit under it. She was entitled to contest its validity in answer to the charge against her....

c. *Cox v. New Hampshire, 312 U.S. 569 (1941)*

Chief Justice Hughes delivered the opinion of the Court....

The statutory prohibition is as follows: "... [N]o parade or procession upon any public street or way, and no open-air public meeting upon any ground abutting thereon, shall be permitted, unless a special license therefor shall first be obtained from the selectmen of the town ...." ...

The sixty-eight defendants and twenty other persons met at a hall in the City of Manchester on the evening of Saturday, July 8, 1939, "for the purpose of engaging in an information march." The company was divided into four or five groups, each with about fifteen to twenty persons. Each group then proceeded to a different part of the business district of the city and there "would line up in single-file formation and then proceed to march along the sidewalk, 'single-file,' that is, following one another."

Each of the defendants carried a small staff with a sign reading "Religion is a Snare and a Racket" and on the reverse "Serve God and Christ the

King." Some of the marchers carried placards bearing the statement "Fascism or Freedom. Hear Judge Rutherford and Face the Facts." The marchers also handed out printed leaflets announcing a meeting to be held at a later time in the hall from which they had started, where a talk on government would be given to the public free of charge....

The recital of facts which prefaced the opinion of the state court thus summarizes the effect of the march: "Manchester had a population of over 75,000 in 1930, and there was testimony that on Saturday nights in an hour's time 26,000 persons passed one of the intersections where the defendants marched. The marchers interfered with the normal sidewalk travel, but no technical breach of the peace occurred. The march was a prearranged affair, and no permit for it was sought, although the defendants understood that under the statute one was required." ... The sole charge against appellants was that they were "taking part in a parade or procession" on public streets without a permit as the statute required....

Civil liberties, as guaranteed by the Constitution, imply the existence of an organized society maintaining public order without which liberty itself would be lost in the excesses of unrestrained abuses. The authority of a municipality to impose regulations in order to assure the safety and convenience of the people in the use of public highways has never been regarded as inconsistent with civil liberties but rather as one of the means of safeguarding the good order upon which they ultimately depend.

The control of travel on the streets of cities is the most familiar illustration of this recognition of social need. Where a restriction of the use of highways in that relation is designed to promote the public convenience in the interest of all, it cannot be disregarded by the attempted exercise of some civil right which in other circumstances would be entitled to protection....

[T]he state court considered and defined the duty of the licensing authority and the rights of the appellants to a license for their parade, with regard only to considerations of time, place and manner so as to conserve the public convenience.... [T]he court held that the licensing board was not vested with arbitrary power or an unfettered discretion; that its discretion must be exercised with "uniformity of method of treatment upon the facts of each application, free from improper or inappropriate considerations and from unfair discrimination"; that a "systematic, consistent and just order of treatment, with reference to the convenience of public use of the highways, is the statutory mandate." The defendants, said the court, "had a right, under the Act, to a license to march when, where and as they did, if after a required investigation it was found that the convenience of the public in the use of the streets would not thereby be unduly disturbed, upon such conditions or changes in time, place and manner as would avoid disturbance."

If a municipality has authority to control the use of its public streets for parades or processions, as it undoubtedly has, it cannot be denied authority to give consideration, without unfair discrimination, to time, place and manner in relation to the other proper uses of the streets....

The decisions upon which appellants rely are not applicable. In *Lovell v.*

Griffin, the ordinance prohibited the distribution of literature of any kind at any time, at any place, and in any manner without a permit from the city manager, thus striking at the very foundation of the freedom of the press by subjecting it to license and censorship.

In *Hague v. CIO,* 307 U.S. 496 (1939), the ordinance dealt with the exercise of the right of assembly for the purpose of communicating views; it did not make comfort or convenience in the use of streets the standard of official action but enabled the local official absolutely to refuse a permit on his mere opinion that such refusal would prevent "riots, disturbances or disorderly assemblage." The ordinance thus created, as the record disclosed, an instrument of arbitrary suppression of opinions on public questions. The court said that "uncontrolled official suppression of the privilege cannot be made a substitute for the duty to maintain order in connection with the exercise of the right." ...

VIII. Nongovernmental Speech Restrictions

A. The Free Speech Clause Rule

1. Summary

The rule:

1. The Free Speech Clause only covers speech restrictions that are *imposed by the government* (whether by the legislature, a court, or an executive agency), or that the government coerces or pressures private entities to impose. Private shopping mall owners may thus eject speakers with no Free Speech Clause scrutiny, see, *e.g.*, *Hudgens v. NLRB*, 424 U.S. 507 (1976). Private employers may fire employees; private universities may expel students; private associations may expel members; private homeowners may kick out dinner guests.

2. Even if a private entity is heavily funded, regulated, or licensed by the government, restrictions that it imposes aren't covered by the Free Speech Clause unless the condition in item 1 is satisfied. See *Rendell-Baker v. Kohn*, 457 U.S. 830 (1982); *CBS v. DNC*, 412 U.S. 94 (1973).

3. Exception: The Court has held that when an entire town is privately owned, the Free Speech Clause applies to the owner's restricting speech on town sidewalks, see *Marsh v. Alabama*, 326 U.S. 501 (1946).

4. The main protections of speech against private restriction are:

a. *Market pressures*: Facebook, for instance, probably wouldn't ban antigovernment speech on its site, since that would lead many people to leave the site.

b. *Other economic constraints*: While in many states private employers are free to fire employees for (say) being Republicans, firing an employee leads to substantial hiring and retraining costs, a possible decline in coworkers' morale, and the like.

c. *Social norms*: A private university might think it's wrong to expel students because of the students' speech, and might worry that alumni, faculty at other universities, and the media would condemn the university for such actions.

d. *Contracts*: A private university may give a faculty member tenure, thus promising (among other things) not to fire him for his speech.

e. *Some federal statutes, state statutes, and state constitutional provisions*: More on that below.

716

B. STATUTORY AND STATE CONSTITUTIONAL RULES

1. PROPERTY OWNERS

a. Summary

A few courts have interpreted state constitutions to limit property owners' power to exclude speakers. The decisions are worth briefly summarizing, so we can consider which approach (if any) makes sense.

1. *California:* Large multi-store shopping malls must allow leafletters, signature gatherers, and other speakers (subject to reasonable content-neutral time, place, and manner restrictions). *Golden Gateway Center v. Golden Gateway Tenants Ass'n*, 29 P.3d 797 (Cal. 2001); *PruneYard Shopping Center v. Robins*, 592 P.2d 341 (Cal. 1979). The theory is that the property owner has voluntarily opened this property to the public for a wide range of purposes (including eating, seeing movies, socializing, and the like), and that the owner should therefore be required to also let the public speak there. Stand-alone stores, office buildings, and apartment buildings remain generally free to exclude private speakers, since their owners haven't voluntarily opened their property to the public for a wide range of purposes.

2. *Pennsylvania:* A California-like rule, but *only if* the property owner has deliberately opened the property *for public debate*, not just for business and social uses. Malls generally don't qualify, but private universities may. *Western Pa. Socialist Workers 1982 Campaign v. Connecticut General Life Ins. Co.*, 515 A.2d 1331 (Pa. 1986), discussing *Commonwealth v. Tate*, 432 A.2d 1382 (Pa. 1981).

3. *New Jersey:* A California-like rule, but also covers universities. *Green Party v. Hartz Mountain Industries, Inc.*, 752 A.2d 315 (N.J. 2000); *New Jersey Coalition Against War in the Middle East v. J.M.B.*, 650 A.2d 757 (N.J. 1994); *State v. Schmid*, 423 A.2d 615 (N.J. 1980).

4. *Colorado:* Private mall owners must allow speakers only if the private mall is somehow *specially intertwined with the government*, for instance if the government has substantially subsidized the mall (irrelevant under First Amendment law, see *Rendell-Baker v. Kohn*, 457 U.S. 830 (1982)) or if the government uses space in the mall for traditional government functions, such as a police substation. *Bock v. Westminster Mall Co.*, 819 P.2d 55 (Colo. 1991).

5. *Massachusetts:* Large shopping malls must let people *gather signatures to qualify a candidate or an initiative measure for the ballot. Batchelder v. Allied Stores Int'l, Inc.*, 445 N.E.2d 590 (Mass. 1983). This decision, though, was based on the state constitution's election provisions, not on the free speech provision. Massachusetts courts haven't decided whether other kinds of speech are protected under the state free speech clause.

Property owners may claim that requiring them to let speakers onto their property would compel them to carry others' speech, which would violate their own First Amendment rights. But the Supreme Court rejected this argument in *PruneYard Shopping Center v. Robins* (1980) (p. 542), and in a different context in *Rumsfeld v. FAIR* (2006) (p. 545).

b. Problem: Designing a Rule

You're a legislator, and you're asked to introduce a bill requiring private property owners to let speakers onto their property. Do you think such a law would be good? If so, what should its scope be? Consider how you think these test cases would and should come out under such a law:

(1) A pro-life group wants to hand out leaflets at a large shopping mall.

(2) A pro-life group wants to hand out leaflets in the pedestrian areas of an abortion clinic's private parking lot.

(3) A pro-life group and a pro-choice group both want to distribute their leaflets door to door inside an apartment building.

(4) The American Nazi Party wants to distribute their leaflets door to door inside an apartment building.

(5) A large shopping mall wants to institute a "no profanity or vulgarity" rule, under which people may be evicted from the mall for wearing clothes that contain profanity or sexually themed messages, or for loudly saying profanities or making sexually themed comments.

(6) A department store within the mall wants to institute the same policy.

(7) A stand-alone restaurant wants to institute the same policy.

c. Problem: Laws Letting Tenants Display American Flags

Florida Stats. Ann. § 83.67(4) provides:

> A landlord shall not prohibit a tenant from displaying one ... removable ... United States flag, not larger than 4 and 1/2 feet by 6 feet, in a respectful manner in or on the dwelling unit regardless of any provision in the rental agreement dealing with flags or decorations. The United States flag shall be displayed [without damaging any part of the landlord's property] .... Any United States flag may not infringe upon the space rented by any other tenant.

Other states have similar laws, either protecting tenants or letting homeowners and condominium owners fly flags even when the homeowners' association rules bar such displays.

Do you think this law is good? Do you think it's constitutional?

If you think it's unconstitutional because it's content-based, assume that the Massachusetts Constitution's free speech clause is interpreted as not entitling people to speak at private shopping malls. Massachusetts law would then protect the gathering of signatures to qualify candidates or initiatives for the ballot, but not other speech. Should that be constitutional?

2. Employers

a. *Summary*

Various statutes protect *specific kinds of speech* against retaliation by private employers:

1. The National Labor Relations Act generally bars employers from discriminating against employees based on their *union membership* or *speech that constitutes "concerted activities for the purpose of collective bargaining or other mutual aid or protection."* The Act also bars unions from retaliating against members who engage in such speech, or pressuring employers to so retaliate. 29 U.S.C. §§ 157, 158(a)(1), 158(a)(3), 158(b)(1)(A), 158(b)(2).

2. Federal and state antidiscrimination laws generally bar employers from discriminating against employees who *complain to management or to the government about alleged discrimination* (so long as the employee reasonably believed that the complaint was well-founded).

3. Some state statutes and tort law rules bar employers from discriminating against employees who *complain about violations of the law* (for instance, health and safety laws) to management, to government officials, and sometimes even to affected customers. See, *e.g.*, Fla. Stat. Ann. § 448.102; *Vermillion v. AAA Pro Moving & Storage*, 704 P.2d 1360 (Ariz. App. 1985); *Palmer v. Brown*, 752 P.2d 685 (Kan. 1988).

4. Title VII of the Civil Rights Act of 1964 and some similar state statutes protect *religiously motivated speech* (and other religiously motivated conduct) by private employees, when tolerating such speech wouldn't be an "undue hardship" on the employer. See Part XIV.A.b, p. 1072.

See generally Cynthia Estlund, *Free Speech and Due Process in the Workplace*, 71 Ind. L. J. 101 (1995) (discussing items 1, 2, and 3).

Also, about half the states have protected *speech generally, outside-the-workplace speech generally, political speech generally,* or *specific political activities* against employer retaliation (though many of them allow some restrictions when the speech seems especially harmful to the employer). *See* Eugene Volokh, *Private Employees' Speech and Political Activity: Statutory Protection Against Employer Retaliation*, 16 Tex. Rev. L. & Pol. 295 (2012). Some sample statutes are included below.

b. *Problem: Offensive Statements by a Baseball Player*

(1) Atlanta Braves pitcher John Rocker is interviewed by *Sports Illustrated*, and tells the interviewer the following (see Jeff Pearlman, *At Full Blast*, Sports Illustrated, Dec. 27, 1999):

—On ever playing for a New York team: "I would retire first. It's the most hectic, nerve-racking city. Imagine having to take the [Number] 7 train to the ballpark, looking like you're [riding through] Beirut next to some kid with purple hair next to some queer with AIDS right next to some dude who just got out of jail for the fourth time right next to some 20-year-old mom with four kids. It's depressing."

—On New York City itself: "The biggest thing I don't like about New York are the foreigners. I'm not a very big fan of foreigners. You can walk an entire block in Times Square and not hear anybody speaking English. Asians and Koreans and Vietnamese and Indians and Russians and Spanish people and everything up there. How the hell did they get in this country?"

Rocker's statements naturally offend many fans, and also some of Rocker's teammates (many of whom come from Spanish-speaking countries). Rocker's team wants to suspend him, both to pacify the fans and the teammates, and to deter him from making such statements again. How would this case come out under the state statutes given below?

(2) Assume Rocker instead published a blog where he one day posted an item calling Donald Trump a fascist; the Braves then fired him. Would the analysis be different than in (1)?

(3) What do you think should be the right rule in such cases?

c.   Conn. Gen. Stats. Ann. § 31-51q

Any employer ... who subjects any employee to discipline or discharge on account of the exercise by such employee of rights guaranteed by the [First Amendment] ..., provided such activity does not substantially or materially interfere with the employee's bona fide job performance or the working relationship between the employee and the employer, shall be liable to such employee for damages ..., including punitive damages, and for reasonable attorney's fees ....

d.   Colo. Rev. Stats. Ann. § 24-34-402.5

(1) [A]n employer [may not] terminate the employment of any employee due to that employee's engaging in any lawful activity off the premises of the employer during nonworking hours unless such a restriction:

(a) Relates to a bona fide occupational requirement or is reasonably and rationally related to the employment activities and responsibilities of a particular employee or a particular group of employees, rather than to all employees of the employer; or

(b) Is necessary to avoid a conflict of interest with any responsibilities to the employer or the appearance of such a conflict of interest.

(2) ... [T]he sole remedy [under this section shall be an award of] all wages and benefits which would have been due [the employee] up to ... the date of the judgment had the ... [termination] not occurred ....

e.   N.Y. Labor Law § 201-d

1.... "Political activities" shall mean (i) running for public office, (ii) campaigning for a candidate for public office, or (iii) participating in fund-raising activities for the benefit of a candidate, political party or political advocacy group ....

"Recreational activities" shall mean any lawful, leisure-time activity, for which the employee receives no compensation and which is generally engaged in for recreational purposes, including but not limited to sports, games, hobbies, exercise, reading and the viewing of television, movies and similar material ....

2.... [I]t shall be unlawful for any employer [to discriminate against an employee or prospective employee] because of ...

[(a)] an individual's [legal] political activities outside of working hours, off of the employer's premises and without use of the employer's equipment or other property [except when the employee is a professional journalist, or a government employee who is partly funded with federal money and thus covered by federal statutory bans on politicking by government employees] ... [or]

[(b)] an individual's legal recreational activities outside work hours, off of the employer's premises and without use of the employer's equipment or other property ....

3. [This section] ... shall not be deemed to protect activity which ... creates a material conflict of interest related to the employer's trade secrets, proprietary information or other proprietary or business interest ....

[Exceptions related to some government employment, and a minor exception related to private employment, omitted.—ed.]

f. Cal. Labor Code §§ 1101–1102

§ 1101: No employer shall make, adopt, or enforce any rule ... or policy:

(a) Forbidding or preventing employees from engaging or participating in politics or from becoming candidates for public office.

(b) Controlling or directing, or tending to control or direct the political activities or affiliations of employees.

§ 1102: No employer shall ... attempt to coerce or influence his employees ... by means of threat of ... loss of employment to ... follow or refrain from ... following any particular course ... of political action or political activity.

3. STUDENTS

a. Summary

California is the only state that broadly protects private college students and private high school students—except those at some religious institutions—from retaliation based on their speech.

b. Problem: Private School Civility Codes

The Judith Martin High School is a private high school in West Hollywood, California. One of its founding principles is the importance of good manners, both as an end in itself, and as a means towards more effective learning: Rudeness distracts kids, makes them feel bad, and (school administrators reason) makes it harder for them to learn. Moreover, rudeness to teachers undermines the teachers' authority, and makes kids more willing to violate school rules.

The school therefore wants to discipline students—with sanctions ranging from reprimands to suspension to expulsion—for swearing, insulting each other, insulting teachers or administrators, and even using intemperate rhetoric (for instance, calling an argument "idiotic" rather than "wrong" or "unsound"). May it do so, given Cal. Educ. Code § 48950? If the statute bars such discipline, may the school raise any constitutional defenses to the statute? Do you think the statute is a good idea?

c.   Cal. Educ. Code §§ 48950, 94367

[Because the sections related to private high schools (§ 48950) and colleges (§ 94367) are so similar, I've merged them.—ed.]

(a) ... [Private high schools and private postsecondary educational institutions] shall not make or enforce any rule subjecting any high school pupil [or college student] to disciplinary sanctions solely on the basis of conduct that is speech or other communication that, when engaged in outside of the campus, is protected from governmental restriction by the First Amendment to the United States Constitution ....

(c) This section does not apply to any [institution] that is controlled by a religious organization, to the extent that the application of this section would not be consistent with the religious tenets of the organization.

(d) Nothing in this section prohibits the imposition of discipline for harassment, threats, or intimidation, unless constitutionally protected....

[Applicable only to private high schools:—ed.] (f) The Legislature finds and declares that free speech rights are subject to reasonable time, place, and manner regulations.

IX.   RESERVED

X. THE RELIGION CLAUSE(S): OVERVIEW

A. SUMMARY

The First Amendment begins with the phrase "Congress shall make no law respecting an establishment of religion, or prohibiting the free exercise thereof." This can be thought of as containing two Religion Clauses—the Establishment Clause and the Free Exercise Clause—or as being a single Religion Clause. In fact, Establishment Clause and Free Exercise Clause protections often significantly overlap, as we'll see with the nondiscrimination principle and the no religious decisions principle, though they sometimes in some measure conflict, as we'll also see below.

Here's a brief summary of the following Parts, though more details are given at the start of each subsection:

XI. *The Requirements that the Government Disregard Religion.*

A. *The Non-Discrimination Principle* presumptively bars discrimination

1. against religious practices (*Lukumi, McDaniel*), though there is an exception for certain funding programs that exclude religious uses or organizations (*Locke v. Davey*),

2. among religions (*Larson*), and

3. against nonreligious people and nonreligious equivalents of religious practices (*Torcaso*), except as to some religious exemptions.

B.1. *The No Endorsement Principle* is an extension of non-discrimination reasoning: a general prohibition on government speaking in ways that endorse one religion or religion generally (though with several important exceptions).

B.2. *The No Primary Religious Purpose Principle* bars government actions that have a primary purpose of advancing religion.

C. *The No Coercion Principle* bars government actions that coerce people to engage in religious behavior.

D. *The No Religious Decisions Principle* bars government decisions about whether a religious doctrine

1. makes sense,

2. is internally consistent,

3. is true (*e.g.*, in a fraud prosecution for getting money based on false statements),

4. is central to a particular religion, or

5. is consistent with the orthodox tenets of a group's faith (more generally, the government cannot interpret religious doctrine).

The government may, however, decide whether a particular objector in fact sincerely believes what he claims to believe.

XII. *The Debate About Excluding Religion.*

A. *Facially Evenhanded Funding Programs and Religious Institutions.* May religious institutions participate in evenhanded funding programs, such as programs that help private schools (including religious ones), programs—like the GI Bill—that help students at various universities (including religious ones), or programs that fund a variety of student newspapers (including religious ones)?

This question has been hotly debated for many decades. Some answer it "no," because government funds generally may not flow to religious institutions. Others says "yes," because such programs should not (or even may not) discriminate against religious institutions and religious people; note the connection to the preceding section on nondiscrimination. The current rule is described in Part XII.A.1.

This, incidentally, is where the famous Establishment Clause *Lemon* test—more about it soon—was born.

B. *The No Delegation to Religious Institutions Principle.* The government may not delegate certain kinds of government power to religious institutions—may not, for instance, give churches the right to veto certain land uses by neighbors. This requirement might be interpretable as a nondiscrimination requirement, prohibiting only delegations that give preference to religion. But the leading case on the subject, *Larkin v. Grendel's Den*, didn't rely on nondiscrimination reasoning.

The Establishment Clause does not, however, bar politicians or voters from making policy choices that relate to secular topics (such as civil rights, abortion funding, polygamy, slavery, and the like) based on their personal religious views. Religious people are just as entitled to enact their policy preferences on these subjects into law as secular people are entitled to enact their own policy preferences.

XIII. *The Debate About Accommodating Religion.*

A. *Constitutionally Compelled Exemptions.* The Court has long debated whether the Free Exercise Clause generally requires the government to exempt religious objectors from generally applicable laws. From 1963 to 1990, the Court took the view that there was such a requirement, at least unless the generally applicable law passed strict scrutiny as applied to the objector; but since 1990, the Court has generally taken the opposite view.

B. *Legislatively Enacted Exemption Regimes.* The debate still rages, however, and the federal government and some states have now implemented a general exemption regime using statutes (the so-called Religious Freedom Restoration Acts, or RFRAs, plus the Religious Land Use and Institutionalized Persons Act, RLUIPA).

XIV. *Nongovernmental Actions and Religion.*

A. *Employer Actions.* Title VII of the Civil Rights Act of 1964, and similar state statutes—which apply both to government employers and private employers—generally (1) bar employers from discriminating against employees based on their religion, (2) require employers to exempt religious objectors from generally applicable work rules, if accommodating the objectors would be relatively cheap, and (3) require employers to prevent religiously hostile or offensive work environments, even when the environments are created by coworkers or patrons.

Note: Because the religion material is so interrelated, there will always be some forward references to cases or doctrines that haven't yet been covered, no matter what topical order the cases are arranged in (unless they're arranged chronologically, which would make them much harder to grasp conceptually). The materials are designed to say a bit about the doctrine that's being foreshadowed in such situations, and this bit ought to be enough; just be warned, and don't be frustrated if the big picture doesn't become completely clear until later in the course.

B. The Establishment Clause and the *Lemon* Test

The Supreme Court has announced an ostensible test to cover nearly all Establishment Clause cases: The so-called *Lemon* test, named after the case *Lemon v. Kurtzman*. Under this test, to be constitutional

1. a government action must have a secular legislative purpose;

2. the action's principal or primary effect must be one that neither advances nor inhibits religion;

3. the action must not foster an excessive government entanglement with religion.

The trouble is that the test is so abstract that it's rarely possible to tell, just from its terms, how it should apply in any particular situation. This abstractness need not always be a problem. Many abstract tests (say, the "duty" prong of the test for negligence in tort law, or for that matter strict scrutiny in free speech law) are vague on their face but are later clarified by the caselaw. Often, the caselaw turns the test into several more precise subtests that apply to several distinct kinds of laws. But the "test" itself should be seen more as a rule-generating device—as a set of factors courts should consider in defining the more precise rules—than as a rule itself.

In fact, the Court has used *Lemon* to create some specific rules, which are controversial and often vague but are at least clearer than the *Lemon* test. Thus, for instance (as we'll see in Part XI.B.1), the Court has concluded that trying to endorse religion is an impermissible *primary purpose*, and that endorsing religion is an impermissible *primary effect*. The most helpful way for phrasing the majority Establishment Clause test as to government speech is thus by saying "no endorsement" (with some exceptions) rather than by using the *Lemon* formulation directly.

Still, courts often do talk about the *Lemon* test as a general rule, and so do Bar Examiners. Here, then, is a summary of the *Lemon* test:

1. *A government action must have a primarily secular legislative purpose.* See generally The No Primary Religious Purpose Principle, Part XI.B.3, p. 844.

— Found to be permissible *secular* purposes:

   a. Educating children, even if religious schools are included in the program. *E.g., Lemon v. Kurtzman* (1971) (p. 897); *Zelman v. Simmons-Harris* (2002) (p. 924).

   b. Implementing secular conduct rules that coincide with or even flow from religious beliefs (for instance, no racial discrimination; no abortion funding; shops must close on Sundays, on the theory that Sundays are now conventional days off for most people, religious or not). See p. 845.

   c. Accommodating religious objectors by exempting them from generally applicable laws, at least so long as the government decisionmaker doesn't "abandon[] neutrality and act[] with the intent of promoting a particular point of view in religious matters." *Corporation of Presiding Bishop v. Amos* (1987) (p. 767).

   d. Protecting religious institutions from secular harms such as "the 'hurly-burly' associated with liquor outlets." *Larkin v. Grendel's Den* (1982) (p. 957).

— Found to be impermissible *religious* purposes:

   a. Endorsing religion. *County of Allegheny v. ACLU*, 492 U.S. 573 (1989); *Stone v. Graham,* 449 U.S. 39 (1980) (discussed in *Edwards v. Aguillard* (1987), p. 847); *Wallace v. Jaffree,* 472 U.S. 38 (1985) (noted at p. 844). See generally Part XI.B.1.

   b. Discrediting theories, such as evolution, that some see as antireligious. *Edwards*; *Epperson v. Arkansas,* 393 U.S. 97 (1968) (discussed in *Edwards*, p. 848).

   — "[T]he Court is normally deferential to a State's articulation of a secular purpose," but "it is required that the statement of such purpose be sincere and not a sham." *Edwards.*

2. *The action's principal or primary effect must be one that neither advances nor inhibits religion.*

— Found to be *permissible* primary effects:

   a. Money flowing to religious institutions under "a government aid program [that] is neutral with respect to religion, and provides assistance directly to a broad class of citizens who, in turn, direct government aid to [the religious institutions] wholly as a result of their own genuine and independent private choice." *Zelman.*

   b. Benefit flowing to religious speakers from their getting the same access to government property as is given to other speakers. *Capitol Square Review & Advisory Bd. v. Pinette* (1995) (p. 837); *Rosenberger v. Rector* (1995) (p. 910).

   c. Aid flowing under an evenhanded program to religious institutions

      i. other than via private choice as in *Witters* and *Zelman*, and

ii. other than in a limited public forum such as the one in *Rosen-berger*,

but only if the aid is not used for religious purposes. Mitchell v. Helms (2000) (p. 915) (plurality opinion coupled with Justice O'Connor's and Justice Breyer's concurrence in the judgment).

d. Religious institutions getting more freedom to advance religion by being exempted from generally applicable laws that may burden their religious practices. *Corporation of Presiding Bishop.*

— Found to be *impermissible* primary effects:

a. Endorsement of religion. *County of Allegheny v. ACLU*, 492 U.S. 573 (1989).

b. Aid flowing to religious institutions

i.   other than via private choice as in *Witters* and *Zelman*, and

ii. other than in a limited public forum such as the one in *Rosen-berger*,

if the aid ends up being used for religious purposes. Lemon, as modified by the cases culminating in Justice O'Connor's concurrence in the judgment in *Mitchell v. Helms.* (De minimis uses for religious purposes, caused by occasional violations of program rules, aren't enough to make the whole program unconstitutional, see p. 916.)

c. Preferential financial benefits for the spread of religious messages. *Texas Monthly v. Bullock* (1989) (p. 772) (three-judge lead opinion coupled with Justice O'Connor's and Justice Blackmun's concurrence in the judgment).

d. Mandating that private parties (*e.g.*, employers) accommodate people's religious observance, when the mandated accommodation involves "unyielding weighting in favor of [religious observers] over all other interests." *Estate of Thornton v. Caldor* (1985) (p. 764).

e. Delegating standardless government power (*e.g.*, the power to veto liquor licenses) to churches, when this creates an "appearance of a joint exercise of legislative authority by Church and State." *Larkin.* See generally The No Delegation to Religious Institutions Principle, Part XII.B, p. 956.

3. *The action must not foster an excessive government entanglement with religion.*

— Found *not to be* excessive entanglement:

a. Modest supervision of religious institutions to ensure compliance with various conditions attached to a government grant. *Agostini v. Felton*, 521 U.S. 203 (1997).

b. Action that reduces entanglement by reducing government regulation of religious institutions. *Corporation of Presiding Bishop.*

c. Some scrutiny of religious practices needed to implement an exemption for religious objectors. *Wisconsin v. Yoder* (1972) (p. 979) (Justice White's concurrence).

— Found *to be* excessive entanglement:

a. "[E]nmesh[ing] churches in the exercise of substantial governmental powers." *Larkin.*

b. Close supervision of religious institutions to ensure compliance with various conditions attached to a government grant. *Lemon*, though limited by *Agostini* (see above, and see the Note below).

c. Programs that require "public officials [to] determine whether some message or activity is consistent with 'the teaching of the faith.'" *Texas Monthly* (three-judge lead opinion only).

d. Programs that discriminate based on denomination. *Larson v. Valente*, 456 U.S. 228 (1982) (though this case was predominantly not decided under the *Lemon* test, see item 4 below).

e. Actions that "create[] the danger of '[p]olitical fragmentation and divisiveness along religious lines'" were once condemned on these grounds. *Larkin*; *Lemon*. More recently, though, the Court has generally rejected this inquiry. See *Corporation of Presiding Bishop* and *Zelman.*

— **Note:** For evenhanded aid programs, the entanglement prong has been folded into the effects prong, as one factor relevant to determining whether the program has the effect of advancing or inhibiting religion. *Mitchell*, p. 916, discussing *Agostini.*

4. The Court has *not* applied the *Lemon* test in some classes of Establishment Clause cases:

— If a program facially or intentionally *discriminates among religions*, it's judged under *Larson v. Valente*. See generally The No Discrimination Among Religions Principle, Part XI.A.2, p. 755.

— If a program coerces religious observance, it's invalid under *Lee v. Weisman* (1992) (p. 868). See generally The No Coercion Principle, Part XI.C, p. 864.

— Governmental *decisions about religious doctrine* are barred by The No Religious Decisions Principle cases, Part XI.D, p. 881.

— If a program is *approved by longstanding tradition*, it may be constitutional under *Marsh v. Chambers* (1983) (p. 791).

XI. COMPELLED DISREGARD OF RELIGION?

A. THE NON-DISCRIMINATION PRINCIPLE (FREE EXERCISE AND ESTABLISHMENT)

1. FREE EXERCISE CLAUSE: NO DISCRIMINATION AGAINST RELIGIOUS PRACTICES

a. Summary

Basic rules:

1. *No discrimination against religious believers.* The government generally may not prosecute someone or otherwise burden them (*e.g.*, tax them or fire them) for their religious *beliefs*. See, *e.g.*, *McDaniel v. Paty* (1978) (p. 732) (Free Exercise).

2. *No discrimination against religious conduct.* Any discrimination based on the religiosity of *conduct* must pass strict scrutiny. "[The] government ... cannot in a selective manner impose burdens only on conduct motivated by religious belief." *Church of the Lukumi Babalu Aye v. City of Hialeah* (1993) (p. 737) (Free Exercise). For example, even if the government may ban all killing of certain animals, with no exemption for religious conduct, it may not ban only religious sacrifice of animals.

— This applies both to facial discrimination and to intentional discrimination done using a facially neutral statute. *Lukumi.* It does not, however, apply to facially neutral laws that weren't intended to discriminate based on religion but that end up affecting one religious group more than others. *Employment Division v. Smith* (1990) (p. 992).

— The best evidence of intentional discrimination is the text of the statute; if the text singles out religion for special burden, intentional discrimination is clear. Courts can also find discrimination based on the statute's legislative history, or its dramatic over- and underinclusiveness with respect to any plausible nondiscriminatory interest, see *Lukumi,* though courts will generally do so only when the evidence is very clear.

— Exception: There is an exception to this where government funding programs are involved—the government is sometimes *required* to exclude religious institutions or uses from certain evenhanded funding programs, see Part XII.A, and is sometimes at least *allowed* to exclude such religious institutions or uses, see *Locke v. Davey* (2004) (p. 744).

3. *Strict scrutiny*: If the government discriminates against religious believers or against religious conduct (setting aside the *Locke* exception), courts apply strict scrutiny: They hold the government action unconstitutional unless it's "narrowly tailored to a compelling government interest."

This test also appears in the law of free speech (see Part III.A, p. 270), equal protection, substantive due process, and other fields. Though in one related field—religious accommodations—it was "strict in theory, feeble in fact" (at least from the 1960s to the 1980s), in most fields, including religious discrimination, it's "strict in theory, fatal in fact" (see p. 984). Here's a brief summary of what strict scrutiny means in religious discrimination cases:

1. To be constitutional, the law must serve a *compelling government interest*. Think of this as a normative judgment about the ends rather than the means of the legislation: Is the government concern at stake important enough to justify religious discrimination?

   a. A law's underinclusiveness—its failure to reach all conduct that implicates the interest—may be evidence that an interest is not compelling. Such underinclusiveness suggests that the government itself doesn't see the interest as compelling enough to justify a broader restriction. It may also suggest that the government's true interest isn't really the one that it's asserting.

   — "Where government restricts only conduct protected by the First Amendment and fails to enact feasible measures to restrict other conduct producing substantial harm or alleged harm of the same sort, the interest given in justification of the restriction is not compelling.... '[A] law cannot be regarded as protecting an interest 'of the highest order' ... when it leaves appreciable damage to that supposedly vital interest unprohibited.'" *Lukumi.*

   b. How can one decide whether an interest is compelling?

   — There are no precedents directly on point: All the religious discrimination cases in which the Court has applied strict scrutiny (*Lukumi*, *McDaniel v. Paty* (1978) (p. 732) (plurality), and *Larson v. Valente*, 456 U.S. 228 (1982)) struck down the law on narrow tailoring grounds, and thus didn't have to decide whether the interest would be compelling in the context of a more narrowly tailored law. Still, you can:

      i. argue by analogy to the compelling interest holdings in the free speech cases (see p. 271) and possibly in the religious accommodation cases (see p. 961), though recall that the religious accommodation cases have in practice applied a weaker form of strict scrutiny than the religious discrimination cases have;

      ii. make common-sense arguments about why a particular interest is or is not very important;

      iii. argue by counterexample ("if this interest were compelling, then look at the discrimination that would be allowed; but such discrimination would clearly be unconstitutional, so the interest can't be compelling").

2. The *narrow tailoring* prong is generally seen as a practical inquiry into whether the means satisfy all four of the following elements:

   a. *Advancement of the Interest*: The government must prove to the Court's satisfaction that the law *materially advances the interest*, which is to say that absence of the law would materially undermine the interest.

— Thus, for instance, the *McDaniel* plurality reasoned that, even if the "interest in preventing the establishment of a state religion" is compelling, "the American experience provides no persuasive support for the fear that clergymen in public office will be less careful of anti-establishment interests or less faithful to their oaths of civil office than their unordained counterparts." Letting clergy serve in the legislature thus wouldn't materially undermine the interest in preventing establishment of religion.

b. *No Overinclusiveness*: For a religiously discriminatory law to be narrowly tailored, the discriminatory law must be *limited to the behavior that actually threatens to undermine the government interest.*

— One reason *Lukumi* gave for striking the ordinances is that they "prohibit Santeria sacrifice even when it does not threaten the city's interest in the public health."

c. *Least Restrictive Alternative*: For a law to be narrowly tailored, the interest must *be unachievable "by narrower [laws] that burden[] religion to a far lesser degree." Lukumi.*

— Presumably those narrower laws (the "less restrictive alternatives") must be pretty much as effective at serving the government interest, or else they wouldn't count as a less restrictive alternative. See p. 273 for free speech cases discussing this point, and p. 968 for religious accommodation cases.

d. *No Underinclusiveness*: To be narrowly tailored, the law must *cover pretty much all the conduct that jeopardizes the interest.*

— *Lukumi*, for instance, condemned the ordinances because the government interest wasn't "pursued with respect to analogous nonreligious conduct."

— Likewise, *Larson* rejected the "fifty per cent rule" (which "provided that only those religious organizations that received more than half of their total contributions from members or affiliated organizations would remain exempt from [certain] registration and reporting requirements of the [charitable solicitation] Act") partly on underinclusiveness grounds: The Court believed that many of the groups that were *not* covered by the law posed as much of a risk of fraud as the religious groups that were covered.

— Underinclusiveness might suggest that the government interest isn't very important.

— Underinclusiveness may also suggest that the government's real interest wasn't the stated one but was rather a desire to burden a disfavored religion.

— Underinclusiveness also means that similar behaviors are treated differently, with no good reason—a violation of equality requirements.

b. *Problem: Religious Garb Statute*

A Pennsylvania statute, enacted in 1895, states that "no teacher in any public school shall wear in said school or while engaged in the performance of his duty as such teacher any dress, mark, emblem or insignia indicating the fact that such teacher is a member or adherent of any religious order, sect or denomination." The law otherwise lets teachers dress as they like.

Dan Klerman, a teacher who's an orthodox Jew, wears a Star of David and a *yarmulke* (a skullcap, pronounced "*yar*-mul-keh," with an accent on the first syllable) whenever he is awake. Jane Mikulski, a teacher who's a nun, always wears her order's habit outside her home. Does the law as applied to them violate the First Amendment? Cf. *United States v. Board of Ed.,* 911 F.2d 882 (3d Cir. 1990); *Cooper v. Eugene School Dist. No. 4J,* 301 Or. 358 (1986), *appeal dismissed without opinion,* 480 U.S. 942 (1987).

Assume the Establishment Clause bars the government from endorsing religion—*i.e.,* communicating that it favors a particular religion, or religions generally—or from coercing students into accepting a religion.

c.   *Problem: Mortmain Statutes*

Assume that D.C. Code § 18-302 provides that

> A devise or bequest of real or personal property to a minister, priest, rabbi, public teacher, or preacher of the gospel, as such, or to a religious sect, order or denomination, ... is not valid unless it is made at least 30 days before the death of the testator.

(This was in fact a D.C. statute in the 1970s.) Another statute, Fla. Stat. App. 2 § 731.19 provides:

> If a testator dies leaving [lineal descendants] ... or a spouse,
> [1] and if the will of such testator devises or bequeaths [property] ... to a benevolent, charitable, literary, scientific, religious or missionary institution, corporation, association or purpose [other than an institution of higher learning], ...
> [2] such devise or bequest shall be avoid[able] in its entirety ... by one or more of the above specified persons who would receive any interest in the devise or bequest so avoided, ...
> [3] unless said will was duly executed at least six months prior to the death of the testator....

On his deathbed, John Smith changed his will to leave some of his D.C. real estate and some of his Florida real estate to the Catholic Church. Smith's children ask that these gifts are to be set aside. Assume the disposition of real estate is decided according to the law of the place in which the real estate is located. What result? Cf. *Estate of French v. Doyle,* 365 A.2d 621 (D.C. Ct. App. 1976); *Shriners' Hospital for Crippled Children v. Hester,* 492 N.E.2d 153 (Ohio 1986).

d.   *McDaniel v. Paty, 435 U.S. 618 (1978)*

[This case was decided during the *Sherbert/Yoder* era, when the Free Exercise Clause was interpreted as requiring religious exemptions even from religion-neutral laws (see Part XIII.A.2), and not just as banning discrimination against religion. The plurality opinion thus rests partly on this "religious accommodation" rationale. Nonetheless, *McDaniel* has since been reinterpreted as a religious discrimination case, see *Church of the Lukumi Babalu Aye v. City of Hialeah* and *Employment Div. v. Smith,* and Justice Brennan's influential concurrence discusses it as a religious discrimination case.—ed.]

Chief Justice Burger ... delivered an opinion in which Justice Powell, Justice Rehnquist, and Justice Stevens joined....

[A.] [Since] its first Constitution, in 1796, Tennessee [has] disqualified ministers from serving as legislators.... The state legislature applied this provision to candidates for delegate to the State's 1977 limited constitutional convention .... 1976 Tenn. Pub Acts, ch. 848, § 4....

[Paul] McDaniel, an ordained minister of a Baptist Church in Chattanooga, ... filed as a candidate for delegate to the constitutional convention. An opposing candidate, appellee Selma Cash Paty, sued ... for a ... judgment striking [McDaniel's] name from the ballot. [The Tennessee courts eventually ruled against McDaniel.—ed.] ...

[B.] The disqualification of ministers from legislative office was a practice carried from England by seven of the original States; later six new States similarly excluded clergymen from some political offices.... The purpose of ... [this] disqualification was primarily to assure the success of a new political experiment, the separation of church and state. Prior to 1776, most of the 13 Colonies had some form of an established, or government-sponsored, church. Even after ratification of the First Amendment, which prohibited the Federal Government from following such a course, some States continued pro-establishment provisions. Massachusetts, the last State to accept disestablishment, did so in 1833.

In light of this history and a widespread awareness during that period of undue and often dominant clerical influence in public and political affairs here, in England, and on the Continent, it is not surprising that strong views were held by some that one way to assure disestablishment was to keep clergymen out of public office. Indeed, some of the foremost political philosophers and statesmen of that period held such views regarding the clergy. Earlier, John Locke argued for confining the authority of the English clergy "within the bounds of the church, nor can it in any manner be extended to civil affairs; because the church itself is a thing absolutely separate and distinct from the commonwealth."

Thomas Jefferson initially advocated such a position in his 1783 draft of a constitution for Virginia. James Madison, however, disagreed and vigorously urged the position which in our view accurately reflects the spirit and purpose of the Religion Clauses of the First Amendment. Madison's response to Jefferson's position was:

> Does not The exclusion of Ministers of the Gospel as such violate a fundamental principle of liberty by punishing a religious profession with the privation of a civil right? does it [not] violate another article of the plan itself which exempts religion from the cognizance of Civil power? does it not violate justice by at once taking away a right and prohibiting a compensation

for it? does it not in fine violate impartiality by shutting the door [against] the Ministers of one Religion and leaving it open for those of every other.

... As the value of the disestablishment experiment was perceived, 11 of the 13 States disqualifying the clergy from some types of public office gradually abandoned that limitation. New York, for example, took that step in 1846 after delegates to the State's constitutional convention argued that the exclusion of clergymen from the legislature was an "odious distinction." Only Maryland and Tennessee continued their clergy-disqualification provisions into this century ....

[C.] [A]t least during the early segment of our national life, [these] provisions enjoyed the support of responsible American statesmen and were accepted as having a rational basis. Against this background we do not lightly invalidate a statute enacted pursuant to a provision of a state constitution which has been sustained by its highest court....

However, the right to the free exercise of religion unquestionably encompasses the right to preach, proselyte, and perform other similar religious functions, or, in other words, to be a minister of the type McDaniel was found to be. Tennessee also acknowledges the right of its adult citizens generally to seek and hold office as legislators or delegates to the state constitutional convention. Yet under the clergy-disqualification provision, McDaniel cannot exercise both rights simultaneously because the State has conditioned the exercise of one on the surrender of the other....

[I]n James Madison's words, the State is "punishing a religious profession with the privation of a civil right." In so doing, Tennessee has encroached upon McDaniel's right to the free exercise of religion. "[T]o condition the availability of benefits [including access to the ballot] upon this appellant's willingness to violate a cardinal principle of [his] religious faith [by surrendering his religiously impelled ministry] effectively penalizes the free exercise of [his] constitutional liberties."

If the Tennessee disqualification provision were viewed as depriving the clergy of a civil right solely because of their religious beliefs, our inquiry would be at an end. The Free Exercise Clause categorically prohibits government from regulating, prohibiting, or rewarding religious beliefs as such.... [But] the Tennessee disqualification is directed primarily at status, acts, and conduct[,] ... [not] on *belief*.... [Therefore, the applicable rule here is that the restriction may be justified if it is supported by] "... interests of the highest order [that are] not otherwise served ..."

[D.] Tennessee asserts that its interest in preventing the establishment of a state religion is consistent with the Establishment Clause and thus of the highest order.... There is no occasion to inquire whether promoting such an interest is a permissible legislative goal, however, for Tennessee has failed to demonstrate that its views of the dangers of clergy participation in the political process have not lost whatever validity they may once have enjoyed.

The essence of the rationale underlying the Tennessee restriction on ministers is that if elected to public office they will necessarily exercise their powers and influence to promote the interests of one sect or thwart the interests of another, thus pitting one against the others, contrary to the anti-establishment principle with its command of neutrality. However widely that view may have been held in the 18th century by many, including enlightened statesmen of that day, the American experience provides no persuasive support for the fear that clergymen in public office will be less careful of anti-establishment interests or less faithful to their oaths of civil office than their unordained counterparts.... [The law thus] violates McDaniel's First Amendment right to the free exercise of his religion ....

Justice Blackmun [did not participate].

Justice Brennan, with whom Justice Marshall joins, concurring in the judgment....

[A.] [The Tennessee provision] establishes a religious classification—involvement in protected religious activity—governing the eligibility for office, which I believe is absolutely prohibited. The provision imposes a unique disability upon those who exhibit a defined level of intensity of involvement in protected religious activity....

A law which limits political participation to those who eschew prayer, public worship, or the ministry as much establishes a religious test as one which disqualifies Catholics, or Jews, or Protestants.... The purpose of the Tennessee provision is not to regulate activities associated with a ministry, such as dangerous snake handling or human sacrifice, which the State validly could prohibit, but to bar from political office persons regarded as deeply committed to religious participation because of that participation—participation itself not regarded as harmful by the State and which therefore must be conceded to be protected....

According to the plurality, McDaniel could not be and was not in fact barred for *his* belief in religion, but was barred because of his commitment to persuade or lead others to accept that belief. I simply cannot fathom why the Free Exercise Clause "categorically prohibits" hinging qualification for office on the *act* of declaring a belief in religion, but not on the act of discussing that belief with others.

{[Unlike when a generally applicable law incidentally burdens religion,] the determination of the validity of the statute involved here requires no balancing of interests. Since, "[b]y its terms, the Tennessee disqualification operates against McDaniel because of his *status* as a 'minister' or 'priest,'" it runs afoul of the Free Exercise Clause simply as establishing a religious classification as a basis for qualification for a political office....}

[B.] The State Supreme Court's justification of the prohibition, echoed here by the State, as intended to prevent those most intensely involved in religion from injecting sectarian goals and policies into the lawmaking process, and thus to avoid fomenting religious strife or the fusing of church with state affairs, itself raises the question whether the exclusion violates the Establishment Clause. As construed, the exclusion manifests patent hostility toward, not neutrality respecting, religion; forces or influences a minister or priest to abandon his ministry as the price of public office; and, in sum, has a primary effect which inhibits religion....

[T]he disqualification provisions contained in state constitutions contemporaneous with the United States Constitution and the Bill of Rights cannot furnish a guide concerning the understanding of the harmony of such provisions with the Establishment Clause[. This] is evident from the presence in state constitutions, side by side with disqualification clauses, of provisions which would have clearly contravened the First Amendment had it applied to the States, such as those creating an official church, and limiting political office to Protestants or theistic believers generally....

[T]he regime of religious liberty embodied in state constitutions was very different from that established by the Constitution of the United States. When, with the adoption of the Fourteenth Amendment, the strictures of the First Amendment became wholly applicable to the States, earlier conceptions of permissible state action with respect to religion—including those regarding clergy disqualification—were superseded....

Beyond [the] limited situations in which government may take cognizance of religion for purposes of accommodating our traditions of religious liberty, government may not use religion as a basis of classification for the imposition of duties, penalties, privileges or benefits. "State power is no more to be used so as to handicap religions, than it is to favor them." *Everson v. Board of Ed....* Fundamental to the conception of religious liberty protected by the Religion Clauses is the idea that religious beliefs are a matter of voluntary choice by individuals and their associations, and that each sect is entitled to "flourish according to the zeal of its adherents and the appeal of its dogma." Accordingly, religious ideas, no less than any other, may be the subject of debate which is "uninhibited, robust, and wide-open...." Government may not interfere with efforts to proselyte or worship in public places. It may not tax the dissemination of religious ideas. It may not seek to shield its citizens from those who would solicit them with their religious beliefs.

That public debate of religious ideas, like any other, may arouse emotion, may incite, may foment religious divisiveness and strife does not rob it of constitutional protection. The mere fact that a purpose of the Establishment Clause is to reduce or eliminate religious divisiveness or strife, does not place religious discussion, association, or political participation in a status less preferred than rights of discussion, association, and political participation generally. "Adherents of particular faiths and individual churches frequently take strong positions on public issues including ... vigorous advocacy of legal or constitutional positions. Of course, churches as much as secular bodies and private citizens have that right."

The State's goal of preventing sectarian bickering and strife may not be accomplished by regulating religious speech and political association. The Establishment Clause does not license government to treat religion and those who teach or practice it, simply by virtue of their status as such, as subversive of American ideals and therefore subject to unique disabilities. Government may not inquire into the religious beliefs and motivations of officeholders—it may not remove them from office merely for making public statements regarding religion, or question whether their legislative actions stem from religious conviction....

Religionists no less than members of any other group enjoy the full measure of protection afforded speech, association, and political activity generally. The Establishment Clause, properly understood, is a shield against any attempt by government to inhibit religion as it has done here. It may not be used as a sword to justify repression of religion or its adherents from any aspect of public life. {"... [C]hurch and religious groups in the United States have long exerted powerful political pressures on state and national legislatures, on subjects as diverse as slavery, war, gambling, drinking, prostitution, marriage, and education. To view such religious activity as suspect, or to regard its political results as automatically tainted, might be inconsistent with first amendment freedoms of religious and political expression—and might not even succeed in keeping religious controversy out of public life, given the 'political ruptures caused by the alienation of segments of the religious community.'" Laurence Tribe, *American Constitutional Law*.} ...

Justice Stewart, concurring in the judgment. [Justice Stewart largely agreed with Justice Brennan's Part A.—ed.]

Justice White, concurring in the judgment....

[McDaniel has] not felt compelled to abandon the ministry as a result of the challenged statute, nor has he been required to disavow any of his religious beliefs.... I am not persuaded that the Tennessee statute in any way interferes with McDaniel's ability to exercise his religion ....

[But o]ur cases have recognized the importance of the right of an individual to seek elective office and accordingly have afforded careful scrutiny to state regulations burdening that right.... Because I conclude that the State's justification for frustrating the desires of [the] voters [who wanted to vote for McDaniel] and for depriving McDaniel and all other ministers of the right to seek this position is insufficient, I would hold § 4 unconstitutional as a violation of the Equal Protection Clause.

e.   *Church of the Lukumi Babalu Aye, Inc. v. City of Hialeah, 508 U.S. 520 (1993)*

Justice Kennedy delivered the opinion of the Court, except as to Part [E]....

[A.] When ... members of the Yoruba people were brought as slaves from western Africa to Cuba, their traditional African religion absorbed significant elements of Roman Catholicism. The resulting syncretion, or fusion, is Santeria, "the way of the saints." ... [O]ne of the principal forms of [Santeria religious] devotion is an animal sacrifice ... [of] chickens, pigeons, doves, ducks, guinea pigs, goats, sheep, and turtles. The animals are killed by the cutting of the carotid arteries in the neck. The sacrificed animal is cooked and eaten, except after healing and death rituals....

In April 1987, the Church ... announced plans to establish a house of worship [in Hialeah, Florida,] as well as a school, cultural center, and museum.... The prospect of a Santeria church in their midst was distressing to many members of the Hialeah community, and the announcement of the plans to open a Santeria church in Hialeah prompted the city council to hold an emergency public session on June 9, 1987.

First, the city council adopted Resolution 87-66, which noted the "concern" expressed by residents of the city "that certain religions may propose to engage in practices which are inconsistent with public morals, peace or safety," and declared that "[t]he City reiterates its commitment to a prohibition against any and all acts of any and all religious groups which are inconsistent with public morals, peace or safety."

Next, the council approved an emergency ordinance, Ordinance 87-40, which incorporated in full, except as to penalty, Florida's animal cruelty laws. Among other things, the incorporated state law subjected to criminal punishment "[w]hoever ... unnecessarily or cruelly ... kills any animal." ...

In September 1987, the city council adopted three [more] ordinances .... Ordinance 87-52 defined "sacrifice" as "to unnecessarily kill, torment, torture, or mutilate an animal in a public or private ritual or ceremony not for the primary purpose of food consumption," and prohibited owning or possessing an animal "intending to use such animal for food purposes." It restricted application of this prohibition, however, to any individual or group that "kills, slaughters or sacrifices animals for any type of ritual, regardless of whether or not the flesh or blood of the animal is to be consumed." The ordinance contained an exemption for slaughtering by "licensed establishment[s]" of animals "specifically raised for food purposes."

Declaring, moreover, that the city council "has determined that the sacrificing of animals within the city limits is contrary to the public health, safety, welfare and morals of the community," the city council adopted Ordinance 87-71. That ordinance ... provided that "[i]t shall be unlawful for any person ... to sacrifice any animal [as defined in Ordinance 87-52] within ... the City of Hialeah, Florida."

The final Ordinance, 87-72, defined "slaughter" as "the killing of animals for food" and prohibited slaughter outside of areas zoned for slaughterhouse use. The ordinance provided an exemption, however, for the slaughter or processing for sale of "small numbers of hogs and/or cattle per week in accordance with an exemption provided by state law."

All ordinances and resolutions passed the city council by unanimous vote. Violations of each of the four ordinances were punishable by fines not exceeding $500 or imprisonment not exceeding 60 days, or both.... [T]he Church ... [sued the city] pursuant to 42 U.S.C. § 1983 ....

[B.] Although the practice of animal sacrifice may seem abhorrent to some, "religious beliefs need not be acceptable, logical, consistent, or comprehensible to others in order to merit First Amendment protection." Given the historical association between animal sacrifice and religious worship, petitioners' assertion that animal sacrifice is an integral part of their religion "cannot be deemed bizarre or incredible." Neither the city nor the courts below, moreover, have questioned the sincerity of petitioners' professed desire to conduct animal sacrifices for religious reasons. We must consider petitioners' First Amendment claim....

[C.] A law failing to satisfy [the interrelated] requirements [of neutrality and general applicability] must be justified by a compelling governmental interest and must be narrowly tailored to advance that interest....

[D.] We begin by discussing neutrality.... At a minimum, the protections of the Free Exercise Clause pertain if the law at issue discriminates against some or all religious beliefs or regulates or prohibits conduct because it is undertaken for religious reasons. Indeed, it was "historical instances of religious persecution and intolerance that gave concern to those who drafted the Free Exercise Clause." ... In *McDaniel v. Paty,* for example, we invalidated a State law that disqualified members of the clergy from holding certain public offices, because it "impose[d] special disabilities on the basis of ... religious status," *Employment Div. v. Smith.*... [I]f the object of a law is to infringe upon or restrict practices because of their religious motivation, the law is not neutral....

[1.] [T]he minimum requirement of neutrality is that a law not discriminate on its face. A law lacks facial neutrality if it refers to a religious practice without a secular meaning discernable from the language or context.... The words "sacrifice" and "ritual" have a religious origin, but current use admits also of secular meanings. The ordinances, furthermore, define "sacrifice" in secular terms, without referring to religious practices....

[But f]acial neutrality is not determinative.... Official action that targets religious conduct for distinctive treatment cannot be shielded by mere compliance with the requirement of facial neutrality.... [S]uppression of the central element of the Santeria worship service was the object of the ordinances.... [T]hough use of the words "sacrifice" and "ritual" does not compel a finding of improper targeting of the Santeria religion, the choice of these words is support for our conclusion.... [Furthermore,] Resolution 87-66 ... recited that "residents and citizens of the City of Hialeah have expressed their concern that certain religions may propose to engage in practices which are inconsistent with public morals, peace or safety," and "reiterate[d]" the city's commitment to prohibit "any and all [such] acts of any and all religious groups." ... [O]n this record it cannot be maintained[] that city officials had in mind a religion other than Santeria....

[2.] [T]he effect of a law in its real operation is strong evidence of its object. To be sure, adverse impact will not always lead to a finding of impermissible targeting. For example, a social harm may have been a legitimate concern of government for reasons quite apart from discrimination. The subject at hand does implicate, of course, multiple concerns unrelated to religious animosity, for example, the suffering or mistreatment visited upon the sacrificed animals and health hazards from improper disposal.

But the ordinances when considered together disclose an object remote from these legitimate concerns.... [A]lmost the only conduct subject to Ordinances 87-40, 87-52, and 87-71 is the religious exercise of Santeria church members....

Ordinance 87-71 ... [p]rohibits only "... unnecessarily kill[ing] ... an animal in a public or private ritual or ceremony not for the primary purpose of food consumption." The definition excludes almost all killings of animals except for religious sacrifice, and the primary purpose requirement narrows the proscribed category even further, in particular by exempting kosher slaughter [for food consumption]. We need not discuss whether this differential treatment of two religions is itself an independent constitutional violation. Cf. *Larson v. Valente*, 456 U.S. 228 (1982). It suffices to recite this feature of the law as support for our conclusion that Santeria alone was the exclusive legislative concern.... Indeed, careful drafting ensured that, although Santeria sacrifice is prohibited, killings that are no more necessary or humane in almost all other circumstances are unpunished....

Ordinance 87-52[similarly] prohibits the "possess[ion], sacrifice, or slaughter" of an animal with the "inten[t] to use such animal for food purposes[,]" ... if the animal is killed in "any type of ritual" .... The ordinance exempts, however, "any licensed [food] establishment" with regard to "any animals which are specifically raised for food purposes," if the activity is permitted by zoning and other laws. This exception, too, seems intended to cover kosher slaughter.

Again, the burden of the ordinance, in practical terms, falls on Santeria adherents but almost no others: If the killing is—unlike most Santeria sacrifices—unaccompanied by the intent to use the animal for food, then it is not prohibited by Ordinance 87-52; if the killing is specifically for food but does not occur during the course of "any type of ritual," it again falls outside the prohibition; and if the killing is for food and occurs during the course of a ritual, it is still exempted if it occurs in a properly zoned and licensed establishment and involves animals "specifically raised for food purposes."
...

Ordinance 87-40 incorporates the Florida animal cruelty statute. Its prohibition is broad on its face, punishing "[w]hoever ... unnecessarily ... kills any animal." ... The problem, however, is the interpretation given to the ordinance by [the city] and the Florida attorney general.... Killings for religious reasons are deemed unnecessary, whereas most other killings fall outside the prohibition. The city ... deems hunting, slaughter of animals for food, eradication of insects and pests, and euthanasia as necessary.... Indeed, one of the few reported Florida cases decided under [the animal cruelty statute] concludes that the use of live rabbits to train greyhounds is not unnecessary.

Further, because it requires an evaluation of the particular justification for the killing, this ordinance represents a system of "individualized governmental assessment of the reasons for the relevant conduct," *Smith*. As we noted in *Smith*, in [such] circumstances ..., the government "may not refuse to extend that system to cases of 'religious hardship' without compelling reason." Respondent's application of the ordinance's test of necessity devalues religious reasons for killing by judging them to be of lesser import than nonreligious reasons. Thus, religious practice is being singled out for discriminatory treatment.

[3.] We also find significant evidence of the ordinances' improper targeting of Santeria sacrifice in the fact that they proscribe more religious conduct than is necessary to achieve their stated ends. It is not unreasonable to infer, at least when there are no persuasive indications to the contrary, that a law which visits "gratuitous restrictions" on religious conduct seeks not to effectuate the stated governmental interests, but to suppress the conduct because of its religious motivation.

The legitimate governmental interests in protecting the public health and preventing cruelty to animals could be addressed by restrictions stopping far short of a flat prohibition of all Santeria sacrificial practice. If improper disposal, not the sacrifice itself, is the harm to be prevented, the city could have imposed a general regulation on the disposal of organic garbage. It did not do so.. Indeed, ... under the ordinances, Santeria sacrifices would be illegal even if they occurred in licensed, inspected, and zoned slaughterhouses. Thus, these broad ordinances prohibit Santeria sacrifice even when it does not threaten the city's interest in the public health.... The neutrality of a law is suspect if First Amendment freedoms are curtailed to prevent isolated collateral harms not themselves prohibited by direct regulation.... [N]arrower regulation would [also] achieve the city's interest in preventing [cruel keeping or killing of] animals....

[4.] Ordinance 87-72 ... does appear to apply to substantial nonreligious conduct and not to be overbroad.... [But it] was passed the same day as Ordinance 87-71 and was enacted, as were the three others, in direct response to the opening of the Church. It would be implausible to suggest that the three other ordinances, but not Ordinance 87-72, had as their object the suppression of religion. We need not decide whether the Ordinance 87-72 could survive constitutional scrutiny if it existed separately; it must be invalidated because it functions, with the rest of the enactments in question, to suppress Santeria religious worship.

[E (joined only by Justice Stevens).] In determining if the object of a law is a neutral one under the Free Exercise Clause, we can also find guidance in our equal protection cases.... Here, as in equal protection cases, we may determine the city council's object from both direct and circumstantial evidence. Relevant evidence includes, among other things, the historical background of the decision under challenge, the specific series of events leading to the enactment or official policy in question, and the legislative or administrative history, including contemporaneous statements made by members of the decisionmaking body....

That the ordinances were enacted "'because of,' not merely 'in spite of,'" their suppression of Santeria religious practice is revealed by the events preceding their enactment.... The minutes and taped excerpts of the June 9 session ... evidence significant hostility exhibited by residents, members of the city council, and other city officials toward the Santeria religion and its practice of animal sacrifice. [Details omitted.—ed.] ...

[F.] We turn next to a second requirement of the Free Exercise Clause, the rule that laws burdening religious practice must be of general applicability.... The Free Exercise Clause "protect[s] religious observers against unequal treatment," and inequality results when a legislature decides that the governmental interests it seeks to advance are worthy of being pursued only against conduct with a religious motivation.... [G]overnment, in pursuit of legitimate interests, cannot in a selective manner impose burdens only on conduct motivated by religious belief ....

Respondent claims that Ordinances 87-40, 87-52, and 87-71 advance two interests: protecting the public health and preventing cruelty to animals. The ordinances are underinclusive for those ends. They fail to prohibit nonreligious conduct that endangers these interests in a similar or greater degree than Santeria sacrifice does.

The underinclusion is substantial, not inconsequential. Despite the city's proffered interest in preventing cruelty to animals, the ordinances are drafted with care to forbid few killings but those occasioned by religious sacrifice. Many types of animal deaths or kills for nonreligious reasons are either not prohibited or approved by express provision. For example, fishing—which occurs in Hialeah—is legal. Extermination of mice and rats within a home is also permitted. Florida law incorporated by Ordinance 87-40 sanctions euthanasia of "stray, neglected, abandoned, or unwanted animals"; destruction of animals judicially removed from their owners "for humanitarian reasons" or when the animal "is of no commercial value"; the infliction of pain or suffering "in the interest of medical science"; the placing of poison in one's yard or enclosure; and the use of a live animal "to pursue or take wildlife or to participate in any hunting" and "to hunt wild hogs." ...

[The city argues] that animal sacrifice is "different" from the animal killings that are permitted by law. According to the city, it is "self-evident" that killing animals for food is "important"; the eradication of insects and pests is "obviously justified"; and the euthanasia of excess animals "makes sense." These *ipse dixits* do not explain why religion alone must bear the burden of the ordinances, when many of these secular killings fall within the city's interest in preventing the cruel treatment of animals.

The ordinances are also underinclusive with regard to the city's interest in public health, which is threatened by the disposal of animal carcasses in open public places and the consumption of uninspected meat... The health risks posed by the improper disposal of animal carcasses are the same whether Santeria sacrifice or some nonreligious killing preceded it. The city does not ... prohibit hunters from bringing their kill to their houses, nor does it regulate disposal after their activity. Despite substantial testimony at trial that the same public health hazards result from improper disposal of garbage by restaurants, restaurants are outside the scope of the ordinances. Improper disposal is a general problem that causes substantial health risks, but which respondent addresses only when it results from religious exercise.

The ordinances are underinclusive as well with regard to the health risk posed by consumption of uninspected meat. Under the city's ordinances, hunters may eat their kill and fishermen may eat their catch without undergoing governmental inspection. Likewise, [general state meat inspection] law ... exempts meat from animals raised for the use of the owner and "members of his household and nonpaying guests and employees." ...

Ordinance 87-72, which prohibits the slaughter of animals outside of areas zoned for slaughterhouses, is underinclusive on its face. The ordinance includes an exemption for "any person, group, or organization" that "slaughters or processes for sale, small numbers of hogs and/or cattle per week in accordance with an exemption provided by state law." Respondent has not explained why commercial operations that slaughter "small numbers" of hogs and cattle do not implicate its professed desire to prevent cruelty to animals and preserve the public health. Although the city has classified Santeria sacrifice as slaughter, subjecting it to this ordinance, it does not regulate other killings for food in like manner....

[E]ach of Hialeah's ordinances pursues the city's governmental interests only against conduct motivated by religious belief. The ordinances "ha[ve] every appearance of a prohibition that society is prepared to impose upon [Santeria worshippers] but not upon itself." *Florida Star v. B.J.F.* (Scalia, J., concurring in part and in the judgment). This precise evil is what the requirement of general applicability is designed to prevent.

[G.] A law burdening religious practice that is not neutral or not of general application must undergo the most rigorous of scrutiny ... [and] will survive [this] strict scrutiny only in rare cases....

[1.] [E]ven were the governmental interests compelling, the ordinances are not drawn in narrow terms to accomplish those interests. As we have discussed, all four ordinances are overbroad or underinclusive in substantial respects ... and [the] interests could be achieved by narrower ordinances that burdened religion to a far lesser degree....

[2.] [The city] has not demonstrated ... that, in the context of these ordinances, its governmental interests are compelling. Where government restricts only conduct protected by the First Amendment and fails to enact feasible measures to restrict other conduct producing substantial harm or alleged harm of the same sort, the interest given in justification of the restriction is not compelling.... "[A] law cannot be regarded as protecting an interest 'of the highest order' ... when it leaves appreciable damage to that supposedly vital interest unprohibited." ...

Justice Scalia, with whom ... Chief Justice [Rehnquist] joins, concurring in [all but Part E] and concurring in the judgment....

["Neutrality" and "general applicability"] ... substantially overlap.... [T]he defect of lack of neutrality applies primarily to those laws that *by their terms* impose disabilities on the basis of religion (*e.g.*, a law excluding members of a certain sect from public benefits, cf. *McDaniel v. Paty*); whereas the defect of lack of general applicability applies primarily to those laws which, though neutral in their terms, through their design, construction, or enforcement target the practices of a particular religion for discriminatory treatment. But certainly a law that is not of general applicability ... can be considered "nonneutral"; and certainly no law that is nonneutral ... can be thought to be of general applicability....

Justice Blackmun, with whom Justice O'Connor joins, concurring in the judgment....

When a law discriminates against religion as such, as do the ordinances in this case, it automatically will fail strict scrutiny .... This is true because a law that targets religious practice for disfavored treatment both burdens the free exercise of religion and, by definition, is not precisely tailored to a compelling governmental interest....

f.   Problem: Tax Exemptions for Secular Donations Only

Assume that Washington adopts a state income tax, with an exemption for donations to nonprofit institutions. But because of a concern about article I, § 11 of the Washington Constitution (see *Locke v. Davey* below), the legislature provides that the exemption will *not* be available for donations to nonprofit institutions that engage in religious proselytizing. A charitable donation to a private secular school or to an organization that tries to change people's political views would thus be deductible from the donor's income tax. A charitable donation to a private religious school or to an organization that tries to change people's religious views would not be.

The legislature's theory is that tax exemptions are economically equivalent to a matching grant, and that Washington law should therefore treated them as equivalent to such a grant. See *Texas Monthly v. Bullock* plurality (1989) (p. 772) ("Every tax exemption constitutes a subsidy that affects nonqualifying taxpayers, forcing them to become indirect and vicarious donors."); *Bob Jones Univ. v. United States* (1983) (p. 986) ("[T]he very fact of the exemption or deduction for the donor means that other taxpayers can be said to be indirect and vicarious 'donors.'"); *Regan v. Taxation With Representation* (1983) (p. 655) ("Both tax exemptions and tax deductibility are a form of subsidy ...."). If your income is $100,000, the tax rate is 5%, and the donation is $1000, your take-home would be $94,050, and the charity would get $1000. This has the same economic effect as would the government's offering (without a tax exemption) a roughly 5.25% ($50 for each $950) matching grant for each contribution, and your donating $950.

Assume the Washington Supreme Court agrees that the exclusion of such religious donations is required by art. I, § 11. Would such an exclusion violate the First Amendment?

g.   Locke v. Davey, 540 U.S. 712 (2004)

Chief Justice Rehnquist delivered the opinion of the Court....

[A.] In 1999, ... the [Washington] legislature created the Promise Scholarship Program, which provides a scholarship, renewable for one year, to eligible [academically gifted] students for postsecondary education expenses.... The scholarship was worth $1,542 for 2000-2001.

To be eligible for the scholarship, a student ... [must have sufficiently high grades or test scores, and a family income] less than 135% of the State's median. Finally, the student must enroll "at least half time in an eligible postsecondary institution in the state of Washington," [either public or accredited private,] and may not pursue a degree in theology at that institution while receiving the scholarship.... [This exception refers to theology] degrees that are "devotional in nature or designed to induce religious faith." ... The institution, rather than the State, determines whether the student's major is devotional....

Joshua Davey, [who] was awarded a Promise Scholarship, ... decided to pursue a double major in pastoral ministries and business management/administration. There is no dispute that the pastoral ministries degree is devotional and therefore excluded under the Promise Scholarship Program. [Davey sued, challenging this exclusion.—ed.] ...

[B.] [T]he Establishment Clause and the Free Exercise Clause[] are frequently in tension. Yet we have long said that "there is room for play in the joints" between them.... [T]here are some state actions permitted by the Establishment Clause but not required by the Free Exercise Clause....

Under our Establishment Clause precedent, the link between government funds and religious training is broken by the independent and private choice of recipients. See *Zelman v. Simmons-Harris*; *Witters v. Washington Dept. of Servs. for Blind*.... [T]he State could, consistent with the Federal Constitution, permit Promise Scholars to pursue a degree in devotional theology .... The question before us, however, is whether Washington, pursuant to its own constitution, which has been authoritatively interpreted [by Washington state courts] as prohibiting even indirectly funding religious instruction that will prepare students for the ministry, can deny them such funding without violating the Free Exercise Clause. {Washington Constitution, Art. I, § 11, states: "... No public money or property shall be appropriated for or applied to any religious worship, exercise or instruction, or the support of any religious establishment."}

Davey ... contends that under ... *Church of Lukumi Babalu Aye, Inc. v. Hialeah*, the program is presumptively unconstitutional because it is not facially neutral with respect to religion. ... [But here], the State's disfavor of religion (if it can be called that) is of a far milder kind [than in *Lukumi*]. It imposes neither criminal nor civil sanctions on any type of religious service or rite. It does not deny to ministers the right to participate in the political affairs of the community. See *McDaniel v. Paty*. And it does not require students to choose between their religious beliefs and receiving a government benefit. See[, *e.g.*,] *Sherbert v. Verner*. {Promise Scholars may still use their scholarship to pursue a secular degree at a different institution from where they are studying devotional theology.} The State has merely chosen not to fund a distinct category of instruction.

Justice Scalia argues, however, that generally available benefits are part of the "baseline against which burdens on religion are measured." Because the Promise Scholarship Program funds training for all secular professions, Justice Scalia contends the State must also fund training for religious professions. But training for religious professions and training for secular professions are not fungible. Training someone to lead a congregation is an essentially religious endeavor. Indeed, majoring in devotional theology is akin to a religious calling as well as an academic pursuit.

And the subject of religion is one in which both the United States and state constitutions embody distinct views—in favor of free exercise, but opposed to establishment—that find no counterpart with respect to other callings or professions. That a State would deal differently with religious education for the ministry than with education for other callings is a product of these views, not evidence of hostility toward religion.

Even though the differently worded Washington Constitution draws a more stringent line than that drawn by the United States Constitution, the interest it seeks to further is scarcely novel. In fact, we can think of few areas in which a State's antiestablishment interests come more into play. Since the founding of our country, there have been popular uprisings against procuring taxpayer funds to support church leaders, which was one of the hallmarks of an "established" religion. See J. Madison, Memorial and Remonstrance Against Religious Assessments ... (noting the dangers to civil liberties from supporting clergy with public funds). {Perhaps the most famous example of public backlash is the defeat of "A Bill Establishing A Provision for Teachers of the Christian Religion" in the Virginia Legislature. The bill sought to assess a tax for "Christian teachers," and was rejected after a public outcry. In its stead, the "Virginia Bill for Religious Liberty," which was originally written by Thomas Jefferson, was enacted. This bill guaranteed "that no man shall be compelled to frequent or support any religious worship, place, or ministry whatsoever."}

Most States that sought to avoid an establishment of religion around the time of the founding placed in their constitutions formal prohibitions against using tax funds to support the ministry. *E.g.*, Ga. Const., Art. IV, § 5 (1789) ("All persons shall have the free exercise of religion, without being obliged to contribute to the support of any religious profession but their own"); [and seven similar constitutions from 1776 to 1802—ed.]. The plain text of these constitutional provisions prohibited *any* tax dollars from supporting the clergy. We have found nothing to indicate, as Justice Scalia contends, that these provisions would not have applied so long as the State equally supported other professions or if the amount at stake was *de minimis*. That early state constitutions saw no problem in explicitly excluding *only* the ministry from receiving state dollars reinforces our conclusion that religious instruction is of a different ilk. {The *amici* contend that Washington's Constitution was born of religious bigotry because it contains a so-called "Blaine Amendment," which has been linked with anti-Catholicism.... Neither Davey nor *amici* have established a credible connection between the Blaine Amendment and Article I, §11 ....}

Far from evincing the hostility toward religion which was manifest in *Lukumi*, we believe that the entirety of the Promise Scholarship Program goes a long way toward including religion in its benefits. The program permits students to attend pervasively religious schools, so long as they are accredited.... And under the Promise Scholarship Program's current guide-lines, students are still eligible to take devotional theology courses....

{Washington has also been solicitous in ensuring that its constitution is not hostile towards religion, and at least in some respects, its constitution provides greater protection of religious liberties than the Free Exercise Clause, ... rejecting [the] standard in *Employment Div. v Smith* in favor of more protective rule[]. We have found nothing in Washington's overall ap-proach that indicates it "single[s] out" anyone "for special burdens on the basis of ... religious callings" as Justice Scalia contends.}

{Justice Scalia notes that the State's "philosophical preference" to pro-tect individual conscience is potentially without limit; however, the only in-terest at issue here is the State's interest in not funding the religious train-ing of clergy. Nothing in our opinion suggests that the State may justify any interest that its "philosophical preference" commands.}

[W]e find neither in the history or text of Article I, §11 of the Washington Constitution, nor in the operation of the Promise Scholarship Program, an-ything that suggests animus towards religion. Given the historic and sub-stantial state interest at issue, we therefore cannot conclude that the denial of funding for vocational religious instruction alone is inherently constitu-tionally suspect.... The State's interest in not funding the pursuit of devo-tional degrees is substantial and the exclusion of such funding places a rel-atively minor burden on Promise Scholars. If any room exists between the two Religion Clauses, it must be here....

[C.] {Davey, relying on *Rosenberger v. Rector*, contends that the Promise Scholarship Program is an unconstitutional viewpoint restriction on speech. But the Promise Scholarship Program is not a forum for speech. The pur-pose of the Promise Scholarship Program is to assist students from low- and middle-income families with the cost of postsecondary education, not to "'en-courage a diversity of views from private speakers.'" *United States v. Amer-ican Library Assn.* (quoting *Rosenberger*). Our cases dealing with speech fo-rums are simply inapplicable.

Davey also argues that the Equal Protection Clause protects against dis-crimination on the basis of religion. Because we hold that the program is not a violation of the Free Exercise Clause, however, we apply rational-basis scrutiny to his equal protection claims. For the reasons stated herein, the program passes such review.}

{[Finally, a]lthough we have sometimes characterized the Establish-ment Clause as prohibiting the State from "disapprov[ing]" of a particular religion or religion in general," for the reasons noted *supra*, the State has not impermissibly done so here.}

Justice Scalia, with whom Justice Thomas joins, dissenting.

In *Lukumi*, the majority opinion held that "[a] law burdening religious practice that is not neutral ... must undergo the most rigorous of scrutiny," and that "the minimum requirement of neutrality is that a law not discrim-inate on its face." The concurrence of two Justices [Blackmun and O'Connor] stated that "[w]hen a law discriminates against religion as such, ... it automatically will fail strict scrutiny." And the concurrence of a third Justice [Souter] endorsed the "noncontroversial principle" that "formal neutrality" is a "necessary conditio[n] for free-exercise constitutionality." These opinions are irreconcilable with today's decision, which sustains a public benefits program that facially discriminates against religion.

[A.] We articulated the principle that governs this case more than 50 years ago in *Everson v. Board of Ed.*: "New Jersey cannot hamper its citizens in the free exercise of their own religion. Consequently, it cannot exclude individual [people] ..., because of their faith, or lack of it, from receiving the benefits of public welfare legislation."

When the State makes a public benefit generally available, that benefit becomes part of the baseline against which burdens on religion are measured; and when the State withholds that benefit from some individuals solely on the basis of religion, it violates the Free Exercise Clause no less than if it had imposed a special tax. That is precisely what the State of Washington has done here. It has created a generally available public benefit ... [and] then carved out a solitary course of study for exclusion: theology. No field of study but religion is singled out for disfavor in this fashion. Davey is not asking for a special benefit to which others are not entitled. He seeks only *equal* treatment—the right to direct his scholarship to his chosen course of study, a right every other Promise Scholar enjoys.

The Court's reference to historical "popular uprisings against procuring taxpayer funds to support church leaders" is therefore quite misplaced. That history involved not the inclusion of religious ministers in public benefits programs like the one at issue here, but laws that singled them out for financial aid. For example, the Virginia bill at which Madison's Remonstrance was directed provided: "[F]or the support of Christian teachers ... [a tax] is hereby assessed ...." Laws supporting the clergy in other States operated in a similar fashion.

One can concede the Framers' hostility to funding the clergy *specifically*, but that says nothing about whether the clergy had to be excluded from benefits the State made available to all. No one would seriously contend, for example, that the Framers would have barred ministers from using public roads on their way to church.

{Equally misplaced is the Court's reliance on founding-era state constitutional provisions that prohibited the use of tax funds to support the ministry. There is no doubt what these provisions were directed against: measures ... singling out the clergy for public support. The Court offers no historical support for the proposition that they were meant to exclude clergymen from general benefits available to all citizens. In choosing to interpret them in that fashion, the Court needlessly gives them a meaning that not only is contrary to our Religion Clause jurisprudence, but has no logical stopping-point short of the absurd.

No State with such a constitutional provision has, so far as I know, ever prohibited the hiring of public employees who use their salary to conduct ministries, or excluded ministers from generally available disability or unemployment benefits. Since the Court cannot identify any instance in which these provisions were applied in such a discriminatory fashion, its appeal to their "plain text" adds nothing whatever to the "plain text" of Washington's own Constitution.}

[B.] The Court does not dispute that the Free Exercise Clause places some constraints on public benefits programs, but finds none here, based on a principle of "play in the joints." ... There is nothing anomalous about constitutional commands that abut. A municipality hiring public contractors may not discriminate *against* blacks or *in favor of* them; it cannot discriminate a little bit each way and then plead "play in the joints" ....

Even if "play in the joints" were a valid legal principle, surely it would apply only when it was a close call whether complying with one of the Religion Clauses would violate the other. But that is not the case here.... The establishment question *would not even be close*, as is evident from the fact that this Court's decision in *Witters* [p. 907—ed.] was unanimous....

In any case, the State already has all the play in the joints it needs. There are any number of ways it could respect both its unusually sensitive concern for the conscience of its taxpayers *and* the Federal Free Exercise Clause. It could make the scholarships redeemable only at public universities (where it sets the curriculum), or only for select courses of study. Either option would replace a program that facially discriminates against religion with one that just happens not to subsidize it.

The State could also simply abandon the scholarship program altogether. If that seems a dear price to pay for freedom of conscience, it is only because the State has defined that freedom so broadly that it would be offended by a program with such an incidental, indirect religious effect.

[C.] What is the nature of the State's asserted interest here? It cannot be protecting the pocketbooks of its citizens; given the tiny fraction of Promise Scholars who would pursue theology degrees, the amount of any citizen's tax bill at stake is *de minimis*. It cannot be preventing mistaken appearance of endorsement; where a State merely declines to penalize students for selecting a religious major, "[n]o reasonable observer is likely to draw ... an inference that the State itself is endorsing a religious practice or belief."

Nor can Washington's exclusion be defended as a means of assuring that the State will neither favor nor disfavor Davey in his religious calling. Davey will throughout his life contribute to the public fisc through sales taxes on personal purchases, property taxes on his home, and so on; and nothing in the Court's opinion turns on whether Davey winds up a net winner or loser in the State's tax-and-spend scheme....

[T]he interest to which the Court defers ... is a pure philosophical preference: the State's opinion that it would violate taxpayers' freedom of conscience *not* to discriminate against candidates for the ministry. This sort of protection of "freedom of conscience" has no logical limit and can justify the singling out of religion for exclusion from public programs in virtually any context. The Court never says whether it deems this interest compelling ...

but, self-evidently, it is not.

{The Court argues that those pursuing theology majors are not comparable to other Promise Scholars because "training for religious professions and training for secular professions are not fungible." That may well be, but all it proves is that the State has a *rational basis* for treating religion differently.... The question is not whether theology majors are different, but whether the differences are substantial enough to justify a discriminatory financial penalty that the State inflicts on no other major. Plainly they are not.

Equally unpersuasive is the Court's argument that the State may discriminate against theology majors in distributing public benefits because the Establishment Clause and its state counterparts are themselves discriminatory.... [T]he Establishment Clause [does] discriminate[] against religion by singling it out as the one thing a State may not establish. [But a]ll this proves is that a State has a compelling interest in not committing *actual* Establishment Clause violations. We have never inferred from this principle that a State has a constitutionally sufficient interest in discriminating against religion in whatever other context it pleases, so long as it claims some connection, however attenuated, to establishment concerns.}

[D.] The Court ... identifies two features thought to render its discrimination less offensive. The first is the lightness of Davey's burden.... The indignity of being singled out for special burdens on the basis of one's religious calling is so profound that the concrete harm produced can never be dismissed as insubstantial. The Court has not required proof of "substantial" concrete harm with other forms of discrimination, see, *e.g.*, *Brown v. Board of Ed.*, and it should not do so here.

Even if there were some threshold quantum-of-harm requirement, surely Davey has satisfied it. The First Amendment, after all, guarantees *free* exercise of religion, and when the State exacts a financial penalty of [about] $3,000 for religious exercise—whether by tax or by forfeiture of an otherwise available benefit—religious practice is anything *but* free.

The Court's only response is that "Promise Scholars may still use their scholarship to pursue a secular degree at a different institution from where they are studying devotional theology." But part of what makes a Promise Scholarship attractive is that the recipient can apply it to his *preferred* course of study at his *preferred* accredited institution. That is part of the "benefit" the State confers....

The other reason the Court thinks this particular facial discrimination less offensive is that the scholarship program was not motivated by animus toward religion. The Court does not explain why the legislature's motive matters, and I fail to see why it should. If a State deprives a citizen of trial by jury or passes an *ex post facto* law, we do not pause to investigate whether it was actually trying to accomplish the evil the Constitution prohibits. It is sufficient that the citizen's rights have been infringed....

[Likewise, i]n *McDaniel v. Paty*, we considered a Tennessee statute that disqualified clergy from participation in the state constitutional convention.... The State defended the statute as an attempt to be faithful to its constitutional separation of church and state, and we accepted that claimed benevolent purpose as bona fide. Nonetheless, ... [we held that] it did not justify facial discrimination against religion ....

This case is about discrimination against a religious minority. Most citizens of this country identify themselves as professing some religious belief, but the State's policy poses no obstacle to practitioners of only a tepid, civic version of faith. Those the statutory exclusion actually affects—those whose belief in their religion is so strong that they dedicate their study and their lives to its ministry—are a far narrower set. One need not delve too far into modern popular culture to perceive a trendy disdain for deep religious conviction. In an era when the Court is so quick to come to the aid of other disfavored groups, see, *e.g.*, *Romer v. Evans*, 517 U.S. 620 (1996), its indifference in this case, which involves a form of discrimination to which the Constitution actually speaks, is exceptional.

[E.] Today's holding is limited to training the clergy, but its logic is readily extendible, and there are plenty of directions to go. What next? Will we deny priests and nuns their prescription-drug benefits on the ground that taxpayers' freedom of conscience forbids medicating the clergy at public expense? This may seem fanciful, but recall that France has proposed banning religious attire from schools, invoking interests in secularism no less benign than those the Court embraces today.

When the public's freedom of conscience is invoked to justify denial of equal treatment, benevolent motives shade into indifference and ultimately into repression. Having accepted the justification in this case, the Court is less well equipped to fend it off in the future....

h. Policy—Equal Treatment

Basic argument: "This government action is unconstitutional, because it facially (or at least intentionally) discriminates based on religion by _____, and this is bad because _____."

"This government action is constitutional, because it treats everyone equally without regard to religion, and this makes it permissible because _____."

1. "[T]he exclusion [of clergy from public office] manifests patent hostility toward, not neutrality respecting, religion.... [G]overnment may not use religion as a basis of classification for the imposition of duties, penalties, privileges or benefits.... The Establishment Clause does not license government to treat religion and those who teach or practice it, simply by virtue of their status as such, as subversive of American ideals and therefore subject to unique disabilities.... Religionists no less than members of any other group enjoy the full measure of protection afforded speech, association, and political activity generally." *McDaniel v. Paty* (Brennan, J., concurring in the judgment).

"The viewpoint discrimination inherent in the University's [exclusion of religious student newspapers from a general student newspaper funding program] ... would risk fostering a pervasive bias or hostility to religion, which could undermine the very neutrality the Establishment Clause requires." *Rosenberger v. Rector.*

"Free exercise ... can be guaranteed only when legislators—and voters—are required to accord to their own religions the very same treatment given to small, new, or unpopular denominations.... '[T]here is no more effective practical guaranty against arbitrary and unreasonable government than to require that the principles of law which officials would impose upon a minority must be imposed generally.'" *Larson v. Valente*, 456 U.S. 228 (1982).

"The Establishment Clause ... prohibits government ... from 'making adherence to a religion relevant in any way to a person's standing in the political community' [by endorsing that person's or another person's religious beliefs]." *County of Allegheny v. ACLU*, 492 U.S. 573 (1989).

"If a program offers permissible aid to the religious (including the pervasively sectarian), the areligious, and the irreligious, it is a mystery which view of religion the government has established, and thus a mystery what the constitutional violation would be. The pervasively sectarian recipient has not received any special favor, and it is most bizarre [to] ... reserve special hostility for those who take their religion seriously, who think that their religion should affect the whole of their lives, or who make the mistake of being effective in transmitting their views to children." *Mitchell v. Helms* (plurality).

2. Response to 1: The important question isn't whether government action is facially discriminatory, but whether it has disparate effects on religions; and this facially discriminatory action has fewer such disparate effects than a facially neutral program would, because _____. See *Policy—Avoiding Disparate Effects Based on Religion*, p. 988.

"[In some cases, an exemption] comes closer to the proper sense of neutrality with respect to conscientious objection. People with a deeply held conscientious objection to a law are not similarly situated to people without such an objection. To insist on formally equal treatment of objectors and non-objectors is to pursue the same majestic equality that forbids the rich and the poor alike to sleep under bridges." Douglas Laycock, *Formal, Substantive, and Disaggregated Neutrality Toward Religion,* 39 DePaul L. Rev. 993, 1016 (1990).

3. Response to 1: Rejecting this sort of discrimination would itself be discriminatory or otherwise harmful, because _____.

"Rather than requiring government to avoid any action that acknowledges or aids religion, the Establishment Clause permits government some latitude in recognizing and accommodating the central role religion plays in our society. Any approach less sensitive to our heritage would border on latent hostility toward religion, as it would require government in all its multifaceted roles to acknowledge only the secular, to the exclusion and so to the detriment of the religious." *County of Allegheny v. ACLU* (Kennedy, J., dissenting).

"In holding [that Sabbatarians must be given a religion-specific accommodation], plainly we are not fostering the 'establishment' of the Seventh-day Adventist religion in South Carolina, for the extension of unemployment benefits to Sabbatarians in common with Sunday worshippers reflects nothing more than the governmental obligation of neutrality in the face of religious differences, and does not represent that involvement of religious with secular institutions which it is the object of the Establishment Clause to forestall." *Sherbert v. Verner.*

4a. Response to 1: The Constitution itself treats religion specially, and this justifies certain kinds of discrimination (namely, _____) in favor of it or against it.

"[T]he First Amendment itself contains a religious classification.... We should thus not labor to find a violation of the Establishment Clause when free exercise values prompt Congress to relieve religious believers from the burdens of the law at least in those instances where the law is not merely prohibitory but commands the performance of military duties that are forbidden by a man's religion." *Welsh v. United States* (White, J., dissenting).

"[T]he Establishment Clause uniquely privileges the right of conscientious objection to religious activity, speech, or expenditures by government ... [so that the] asymmetries that [some] describe as discrimination against religion [are] mandated by the Establishment Clause. In particular, the Establishment Clause will often require excluding religious organizations from public programs, or will necessitate religion-restrictive conditions on their participation." Kathleen M. Sullivan, *Religion and Liberal Democracy,* 59 U. Chi. L. Rev. 195, 211 (1992).

"[T]he purpose of accommodating religion can ... support action that might otherwise violate the Press Clause or the Speech Clause.... Such accommodation is unavoidably content based—because the Freedom of Religion Clause is content based. It is absurd to think that a State which chooses to prohibit booksellers from making stories about seduction available to children of tender years cannot make an exception for stories contained in sacred writings (*e.g.,* the story of Susanna and the Two Elders, Daniel 13:1-65)." *Texas Monthly v. Bullock* (Scalia, J., dissenting).

4b. Rebuttal to 4a: The Constitution's references to religion don't justify this form of discrimination in favor of or against religion; rather, the references only require equal treatment, because _____.

"[M]ention [of religion] in the text of the first amendment does not require constitutionally favored treatment other than protection against direct persecution. The press clause, also located in the first amendment, has been held not to confer a favored status on the media ... [but] only to protect the media from 'invidious discrimination.'" William P. Marshall, *The Case Against the Constitutionally Compelled Free Exercise Exemption,* 40 Case W. Res. L. Rev. 357, 375 (1990).

"Even if we imagined ... that the Religion Clauses ... should be read to privilege religion, we still would have to account for the subsequent impact of the Equal Protection Clause, which might have equalized (among other things) religion and nonreligion, and thereby deprived religion of any special constitutional respect it had enjoyed before Reconstruction." Christopher L. Eisgruber & Lawrence G. Sager, *The Vulnerability of Conscience: The Constitutional Basis for Protecting Religious Conduct*, 61 U. Chi. L. Rev. 1245, 1271-72 (1994).

5a. Response to 1: There's something special about religion, namely _____, and this justifies certain kinds of different treatment (favorable or unfavorable) of religion, because _____.

"[T]he government should not force people to violate moral duties if (in their system of belief) they will face transcendent consequences.... From a religious point of view, ... [t]he harm threatening the believer is more serious (loss of heavenly comforts, not domestic ones) and more lasting (eternal, not temporary). That is what justifies restricting this special kind of freedom to religious claimants alone." John H. Garvey, *An Anti-Liberal Argument for Religious Freedom,* 7 J. Contemp. Leg. Issues 275, 287 (1996).

"In general, religious beliefs and practices place demands on people that are more intense, less subject to reasons that regulate civil society, more likely to generate conflicts with the state if not accommodated, than do non-religious beliefs and practices." Kent Greenawalt, *Quo Vadis: The Status and Prospects of "Tests" Under the Religion Clauses,* 1995 Sup. Ct. Rev. 323, 340-41.

5b. Rebuttal to 5a: These differences between religion and parallel non-religious belief systems are overstated, because _____.

"The violation of deeply held moral or political principles may cause as much psychic harm to the believer as would a violation of a religious tenet, even if the latter is believed to have extra-temporal effect." William P. Marshall, *In Defense of Smith and Free Exercise Revisionism,* 58 U. Chi. L. Rev. 308, 321 (1991).

"[The argument] that conflicts over religious belief are particularly violent and disruptive of social order, and that giving religion special protection avoids this violence and disruption ... no longer works: There is nothing about religious belief and practice in contemporary America that is uniquely disruptive of the social order." Frederick Mark Gedicks, *An Unfirm Foundation: The Regrettable Indefensibility of Religious Exemptions,* 20 U. Ark. Little Rock L.J. 555, 563-64 (1998).

6a. Response to 1: This discrimination against (or in favor) of religion is permissible because it balances another kind of discrimination, namely _____, in favor of (or against) religion, and this balance is fair because _____.

"[T]hese two doctrinal rules, one providing religious institutions alone the special privilege of exemptions from general laws and the other prohibiting financial support to pervasively sectarian religious organizations ... are intrinsically connected and work effectively to justify each other.... Only the countervailing pressures of the two religion clauses may create the kind of check and balance of the power of religion and the state that the Constitution requires." Alan E. Brownstein, *Evaluating School Voucher Programs Through a Liberty, Equality, and Free Speech Matrix,* 31 Conn. L. Rev. 871, 899-900 (1999).

"[T]he Establishment Clause should be read to forbid enacting legislation for the express purpose of advancing the values believed to be commanded by religion.... [But i]f the Establishment Clause should be read to place a special burden on the role of religious values in politics, then those values should receive special treatment when they conflict with the values adopted by the legislature. Reading the Free Exercise Clause to require exemptions from law neither favors religion nor renders religious conscience 'a law unto itself.' Rather, these exemptions are merely the appropriate remedy for the damage that precluding religious values from grounding law causes religious people." Abner S. Greene, *The Political Balance of the Religion Clauses,* 102 Yale L.J. 1611, 1613 (1993).

6b. Rebuttal to 6a: Such an attempt to balance burdens and benefits is unsound because _____.

"First, [after *Employment Division v. Smith*] the special benefits that religion supposedly preferentially gets are actually pretty minor.... Second, ... the 'quid pro quo' argument gives us no way of deciding what amount of [compensatory] discrimination against religion is right and what amount ends up being too much.

"But, third, and most important, 'religion' isn't one person or entity that we can expect to pay for the benefits it gets.... Taking 'quid' from the Catholics [by denying them access to evenhanded school funding programs] to compensate for the 'quo' given the Amish [when they were given exemptions from compulsory schooling laws] isn't even rough justice; it's no justice at all." Eugene Volokh, *Equal Treatment Is Not Establishment,* 13 Notre Dame J.L., Ethics & Pub. Pol. 341, 357 (1999).

2. Establishment Clause: No Discrimination Among Religions

a. *Summary*

Basic rules:

1. *No discrimination based on religious affiliation*, unless it passes strict scrutiny (see p. 729). See *Larson v. Valente*, 456 U.S. 228 (1982).

2. *No discrimination against idiosyncratic religious beliefs.* The government generally may not treat people differently based on whether their religious beliefs are held by many or by only a few. Thus, courts must consider religious exemption requests without regard to whether the religious belief is shared by others of the claimant's denomination. See *Thomas v. Review Bd.* (1981) (p. 889). What matters is whether the claimant's religious beliefs are sincere, not whether they are widely held.

Likewise, statutory exemptions limited to people who are "member[s] of and adhere[] to established and traditional tenets ... of a bona fide religion, body, or sect which has historically held conscientious objections to [a certain practice]" are unconstitutional because they prefer members of certain denominations over people who have more idiosyncratic religious beliefs, see, *e.g.*, *Wilson v. NLRB*, 920 F.2d 1282, 1285-88 (6th Cir. 1990); *Pielech v. Massasoit Greyhound, Inc.*, 423 Mass. 534 (1996).

This only applies to discrimination among people based on the religious beliefs they possess. Laws that apply equally to people without regard to a person's religious beliefs, but are enacted because of the religious beliefs of the majority, are *not* subject to this rule; see the summary in Part XI.B.3.a, p. 844.

b. *Problem: Peyote Exemption*

Federal drug law bans the unprescribed distribution and possession of peyote, a hallucinogen, but exempts "the nondrug use of peyote in bona fide religious ceremonies of the Native American Church," 21 C.F.R. § 1307.31. Peyote is apparently quite important to the Church's ceremonies (*Employment Division v. Smith* says more about this). According to one case, "[t]he NAC was established in ... 1918 as the corporate form of a centuries-old Native American peyotist religion"; the NAC has about 250,000 Native American members, who "worship peyote as a deity and ingest the plant during traditional ritualized 'road meetings.'"

Immanuel Trujillo, an NAC member until 1966, founded the Peyote Way Church of God in 1979; Peyote Way has about 150 members, most of whom are not of Native American descent. Many of Peyote Way's tenets, including the divinity of peyote, are the same as the NAC's.

Peyote Way sues, claiming that the exemption for the Native American Church unconstitutionally discriminates against Peyote Way, and asking that the exemption be broadened. Analyze. Cf. *Peyote Way Church of God, Inc. v. Thornburgh*, 922 F.2d 1210 (5th Cir. 1991); *Kennedy v. Bureau of Narcotics & Dangerous Drugs*, 459 F.2d 415 (9th Cir. 1972).

3. ESTABLISHMENT CLAUSE/FREE EXERCISE CLAUSE: NO DISCRIMINATION AGAINST THE IRRELIGIOUS

a. *Summary*

Basic rule: Discrimination based on the absence of religiosity or the absence of belief in a deity is presumptively unconstitutional. See *Torcaso v. Watkins* (1961) (p. 759) (First Amendment generally).

There is an **exception**, though, for some religious exemptions from generally applicable laws:

1. When the Free Exercise Clause was read as requiring exemptions for religious believers, these exemptions were limited to religious believers. See *Wisconsin v. Yoder* (1972) (p. 979). Even after *Employment Div. v. Smith*, which held that religious exemptions are usually not constitutionally mandated, the few remaining zones of constitutionally compelled exemptions are likely limited to religious objectors.

2. As to religious exemptions provided by statute, the case law is mixed:

a. *Cutter v. Wilkinson* (2005) (p. 778) and *Corporation of Presiding Bishop v. Amos* (1987) (p. 767) upheld statutory exemptions that benefited only religious groups.

b. But *Texas Monthly v. Bullock* (1989) (p. 772) struck down a religion-specific exemption; so did *Estate of Thornton v. Caldor* (1985) (p. 764); and Justice Harlan's concurrence in the judgment in *Welsh v. United States* (1970) (p. 762) took the same view.

c. *Cutter* expressly holds that religion-only exemptions are constitutional if they (i) "alleviate[] exceptional government-created burdens on private religious exercise," (ii) require courts to "take adequate account of the burdens a requested accommodation may impose on nonbeneficiaries, and (iii) are "administered neutrally among different faiths." But *Cutter* doesn't resolve what happens if elements (i) and (ii) aren't satisfied. (If element (iii) isn't satisfied, the law is likely unconstitutional under *Larson v. Valente*, 456 U.S. 228 (1982).)

d. Part B of the three-Justice *Texas Monthly v. Bullock* lead opinion (p. 772) seems to say that religion-only exemptions are permissible if they

   i. "[do not] impose substantial burdens on nonbeneficiaries while allowing others to act according to their religious beliefs," *or*

   ii. are "designed to alleviate government intrusions that might significantly deter adherents of a particular faith from conduct protected by the Free Exercise Clause."

   But the second-to-last paragraph in Part A states the test with an effective "and" rather than an "or," so it's hard to tell what the lead opinion means. Moreover, this is not a majority opinion.

e. The one majority conclusion one can draw from *Texas Monthly* is that religion-only exemptions that (i) substantially burden nonbeneficiaries, (ii) aren't designed to alleviate substantial burdens on religious practice, *and* at the same time (iii) constitute "preference[s] for the dissemination of religious ideas" are unconstitutional. On this, the three-Justice lead opinion and the Justice O'Connor/Blackmun concurrence would agree.

3. The matter is still more complex when the issue involves preferences for religiously motivated speech, because such preferences might (or might not) violate the Free Speech Clause as well as the Establishment Clause. The concurrences in *Texas Monthly v. Bullock*, which rely at least partly on free speech principles, illustrate this problem.

b. *Problem: Clergy-Congregant Privilege*

Cal. Evid. Code §§ 1030-1034 provide, in relevant part:

1030. As used in this article, "member of the clergy" means a priest, minister, religious practitioner, or similar functionary of a church or of a religious denomination or religious organization.

1031. As used in this article, "penitent" means a person who has made a penitential communication to a member of the clergy.

1032. As used in this article, "penitential communication" means a communication made in confidence, in the presence of no third person so far as the penitent is aware, to a member of the clergy who, in the course of the discipline or practice of his church, denomination, or organization, is authorized or accustomed to hear those communications and, under the discipline or tenets of his or her church, denomination, or organization, has a duty to keep those communications secret.

1033.... [A] penitent ... has a privilege to refuse to disclose, and to prevent another from disclosing, a penitential communication ....

1034.... [A] member of the clergy ... has a privilege to refuse to disclose a penitential communication ....

This, of course, is the standard "priest-penitent" or "clergy-parishioner" privilege; it applies to the traditional Catholic confessional but also to confidential communications performed within other religious traditions.

Dan Bussel is admired by many of his friends and acquaintances for his wise judgment on moral, philosophical, and personal spiritual matters, which is why Adam Fraser came to him for moral advice related to a business dispute in which Adam was involved. Knowing that Adam had discussed the matter candidly with Dan, Gail Standish (the other party to the dispute) subpoenaed Dan to testify in his lawsuit against Adam.

Dan argues that he has a privilege to refuse to disclose his conversation with Adam. While Dan is not a clergyman—assume for the purposes of this problem that he isn't even a religious believer—he argues that he was acting as Adam's ethical and spiritual advisor, much as clergymen act as ethical and spiritual advisors to their penitents. He also claims that he has a deeply felt conscientious objection to revealing the things that Adam told him in confidence. Dan argues that denying him the privilege while allowing it to a "functionary of a church or of a religious denomination or religious organization" is unconstitutionally discriminatory. Analyze.

c. Problem: Exemption from Housing Discrimination Law

Assume state law bars landlords from discriminating based on marital status in the rental of housing. Your boss, State Senator Leslie Hakala, has been asked to introduce the following bill in the state legislature:

Any landlord who holds a sincere religious belief prohibiting renting to unmarried couples is exempt from the statutory ban on housing discrimination based on marital status.

The Senator would like to sponsor this bill, but asks you whether it is likely to raise constitutional problems. What do you tell her? Can you suggest possible amendments that would diminish the likelihood that the bill, if enacted, will be struck down?

d. Problem: Residential Picketing

Alice feels a religious compulsion to picket in front of an abortion provider's home. Such residential picketing is barred by a content-neutral city ordinance much like the one that was upheld in *Frisby v. Schultz* (p. 343), but Alice claims that her state's Religious Freedom Restoration Act (which is phrased like the federal RFRA, see p. 1016) entitles her to an exemption from the ordinance. Analyze. See *generally* Eugene Volokh, *Intermediate Questions of Religious Exemptions—A Research Agenda with Test Suites,* 21 Cardozo L. Rev. 595, 610-17 (1999).

e. *Torcaso v. Watkins, 367 U.S. 488 (1961)*

Justice Black delivered the opinion of the Court.

Article 37 of the Declaration of Rights of the Maryland Constitution provides: "[N]o religious test ought ever to be required as a qualification for any office of profit or trust in this State, other than a declaration of belief in the existence of God ...." ... [Torcaso sued because he] was refused a commission to serve [as Notary Public] because he would not declare his belief in God....

[T]he Maryland Declaration of Rights requirement ... sets up a religious test ... [that puts t]he power and authority of the State of Maryland ... on the side of one particular sort of believers—those who are willing to say they believe in "the existence of God." ...

[I]t was largely to escape religious test oaths and declarations that a great many of the early colonists left Europe and came here hoping to worship in their own way. It soon developed, however, that many of those who had fled to escape religious test oaths turned out to be perfectly willing ... to force dissenters from their faith to take test oaths in conformity with that faith. This brought on a host of laws in the New Colonies imposing burdens and disabilities ... upon varied beliefs depending largely upon what group happened to be politically strong enough to legislate in favor of its own beliefs. The effect of all this was the formal or practical "establishment" of particular religious faiths in most of the Colonies, with consequent burdens imposed on the free exercise of the faiths of nonfavored believers.

There were, however, wise and farseeing men in the Colonies ... who spoke out against test oaths and all the philosophy of intolerance behind them. {[For instance,] Oliver Ellsworth, a member of the Federal Constitutional Convention and later Chief Justice of this Court, included [in 1787] among his strong arguments against religious test oaths the following statement: "In short, test-laws are utterly ineffectual: they are no security at all; because men of loose principles will, by an external compliance, evade them. If they exclude any persons, it will be honest men, men of principle, who will rather suffer an injury, than act contrary to the dictates of their consciences...."} ...

When our Constitution was adopted, the desire to put the people "securely beyond the reach" of religious test oaths brought about the inclusion in Article VI of that document of a provision that "no religious Test shall ever be required as a Qualification to any Office or public Trust under the United States." {In discussing Article VI in the debate of the North Carolina Convention on the adoption of the Federal Constitution, James Iredell, later a Justice of this Court, said: "... [I]t is objected that the people of America may, perhaps, choose representatives who have no religion at all, and that pagans and Mahometans may be admitted into offices. But how is it possible to exclude any set of men, without taking away that principle of religious freedom which we ourselves so warmly contend for?" And another delegate pointed out that Article VI "leaves religion on the solid foundation of its own inherent validity, without any connection with temporal authority; and no kind of oppression can take place."} ...

Not satisfied, however, with Article VI ..., the First Congress proposed and the States very shortly thereafter adopted our Bill of Rights, including the First Amendment.... [Under the First Amendment, as incorporated against the States via the Fourteenth Amendment,] neither a State nor the Federal Government can constitutionally force a person "to profess a belief or disbelief in any religion." *Everson v. Board of Ed.* Neither can constitutionally pass laws or impose requirements which aid all religions as against non-believers, and neither can aid those religions based on a belief in the existence of God as against those religions founded on different beliefs. {Among religions in this country which do not teach what would generally be considered a belief in the existence of God are Buddhism, Taoism, Ethical Culture, Secular Humanism and others.}

In upholding the State's religious test for public office the highest court of Maryland said: "The petitioner is not compelled to believe or disbelieve, under threat of punishment or other compulsion. True, unless he makes the declaration of belief he cannot hold public office in Maryland, but he is not compelled to hold office." The fact, however, that a person is not compelled to hold public office cannot possibly be an excuse for barring him from office by state-imposed criteria forbidden by the Constitution.... This Maryland religious test for public office unconstitutionally invades the appellant's freedom of belief and religion and therefore cannot be enforced against him....

f.   Welsh v. United States, 398 U.S. 333 (1970)

Justice Black ... delivered an opinion in which Justice Douglas, Justice Brennan, and Justice Marshall join.

The petitioner ... was convicted ... of refusing to submit to induction into the Armed Forces [despite his claim of conscientious objector status] .... The controlling facts in this case are strikingly similar to those in *United States v. Seeger,* 380 U.S. 163 (1965).... [Seeger and Welsh] both made application to their local draft boards for conscientious objector exemptions from military service under § 6(j) of the Universal Military Training and Service Act ...:

> Nothing contained in this title shall be construed to require any person to be subject to combatant training and service in the armed forces of the United States who, by reason of religious training and belief, is conscientiously opposed to participation in war in any form. Religious training and belief in this connection means an individual's belief in a relation to a Supreme Being involving duties superior to those arising from any human relation, but does not include essentially political, sociological, or philosophical views or a merely personal moral code....

[B]oth Seeger and Welsh were unable to sign the statement that, as printed in the Selective Service form, stated "I am, by reason of my religious training and belief, conscientiously opposed to participation in war in any form." ... But both ... affirmed ... that they held deep conscientious scruples against taking part in wars where people were killed.... There was never any question about the sincerity and depth of Seeger's convictions as a conscientious objector, and the same is true of Welsh....

In *Seeger* the Court was confronted, first, with the problem that § 6(j) defined "religious training and belief" in terms of a "belief in a relation to a Supreme Being ...," a definition that arguably gave a preference to those who believed in a conventional God as opposed to those who did not.... [T]he Court construed the congressional intent as being in "keeping with its long-established policy of not picking and choosing among religious beliefs," and accordingly interpreted "the meaning of religious training and belief so as to embrace *all* religions...."

But, having decided that all religious conscientious objectors were entitled to the exemption, we faced the more serious problem of determining which beliefs were "religious" within the meaning of the statute.... [T]he Court stated that "[the] task is to decide whether the beliefs professed by a registrant are sincerely held and whether they are, *in his own scheme of things*, religious." ... [T]he central consideration in determining whether the registrant's beliefs are religious is whether these beliefs play the role of a religion and function as a religion in the registrant's life[—whether they are] ... "sincere and meaningful belief[s] which occup[y] in the life of [their] possessor a place parallel to that filled by the God of those admittedly qualifying for the exemption ...." ...

If an individual deeply and sincerely holds beliefs that are purely ethical or moral in source and content but that nevertheless impose upon him a duty of conscience to refrain from participating in any war at any time, those beliefs certainly occupy in the life of that individual "a place parallel to that filled by ... God" in traditionally religious persons. Because his beliefs function as a religion in his life, such an individual is as much entitled to a "religious" conscientious objector exemption under § 6(j) as is someone who derives his conscientious opposition to war from traditional religious convictions....

The Government ... [argues] that Welsh's views, unlike Seeger's, were "essentially political, sociological, or philosophical views or a merely personal moral code." ... The two groups of registrants that obviously do fall within these exclusions from the exemption are those whose beliefs are not deeply held and those whose objection to war does not rest at all upon moral, ethical, or religious principle but instead rests solely upon considerations of policy, pragmatism, or expediency....

In applying § 6(j)'s exclusion of those whose views are "essentially political, sociological, or philosophical" or of those who have a "merely personal moral code," it should be remembered that these exclusions are definitional and do not therefore restrict the category of persons who are conscientious objectors by "religious training and belief." Once the Selective Service System has taken the first step and determined under the standards set out here and in *Seeger* that the registrant is a "religious" conscientious objector, it follows that his views cannot be "essentially political, sociological, or philosophical." Nor can they be a "merely personal moral code."

Welsh stated that he "believe[d] the taking of life—anyone's life—to be morally wrong." ... On the basis of these beliefs and the conclusion of the Court of Appeals that he held them "with the strength of more traditional religious convictions," we think Welsh was clearly entitled to a conscientious objector exemption. Section 6(j) ... exempts from military service all those whose consciences, spurred by deeply held moral, ethical, or religious beliefs, would give them no rest or peace if they allowed themselves to become a part of an instrument of war....

Justice Harlan, concurring in the result....

[Justice Harlan concluded that the statute couldn't fairly be read as covering nonreligious conscientious objectors, but went on to conclude that such objectors were constitutionally entitled to equal treatment with the statutorily exempted religious objectors:—ed.]

[H]aving chosen to exempt [some objectors, Congress] cannot draw the line between theistic or nontheistic religious beliefs on the one hand and secular beliefs on the other. Any such distinctions are not, in my view, compatible with the Establishment Clause....

The implementation of the neutrality principle of [our precedents] requires, in my view, ... "an equal protection mode of analysis...." ... If the exemption is to be given application, it must encompass the class of individuals it purports to exclude, those whose beliefs emanate from a purely moral, ethical, or philosophical source. The common denominator must be the intensity of moral conviction with which a belief is held. Common experience teaches that among "religious" individuals some are weak and others strong adherents to tenets and this is no less true of individuals whose lives are guided by personal ethical considerations....

Justice White, with whom ... Chief Justice [Burger] and Justice Stewart join, dissenting....

[Justice White agreed with Justice Harlan that the statute couldn't fairly be read to cover nonreligious objectors, but concluded that this was constitutional:—ed.]

In exempting religious conscientious objectors, Congress was making one of two judgments, perhaps both. First, § 6(j) may represent a purely practical judgment that religious objectors ... would be of no more use in combat than many others unqualified for military service. Exemption was not extended to them to further religious belief or practice but to limit military service to those who were prepared to undertake the fighting that the armed services have to do. On this basis, the exemption has neither the primary purpose nor the effect of furthering religion....

Second, Congress may have granted the exemption because otherwise religious objectors would be forced into conduct that their religions forbid and because in the view of Congress to deny the exemption would violate the Free Exercise Clause or at least raise grave problems in this respect. True, this Court has ... stated its unwillingness to construe the First Amendment, standing alone, as requiring draft exemptions for religious believers. But this Court is not alone in being obliged to construe the Constitution in the course of its work; nor does it even approach having a monopoly on the wisdom and insight appropriate to the task. Legislative exemptions for those with religious convictions against war date from colonial days....

If there were no statutory exemption for religious objectors to war and failure to provide it was held by this Court to impair the free exercise of religion contrary to the First Amendment, an exemption reflecting this constitutional command would [not be] an establishment of religion .... [But even if an exemption is not constitutionally required, i]t is very likely that § 6 (j) is a recognition by Congress of free exercise values and its view of desirable or required policy in implementing the Free Exercise Clause. That judgment is entitled to respect....

[N]either support nor hostility, but neutrality, is the goal of the religion clauses of the First Amendment. "Neutrality," however, is not self-defining. If it is "favoritism" and not "neutrality" to exempt religious believers from the draft, is it "neutrality" and not "inhibition" of religion to compel religious believers to fight when they have special reasons for not doing so, reasons to which the Constitution gives particular recognition? ...

[T]he First Amendment itself contains a religious classification.... Although socially harmful acts may as a rule be banned despite the Free Exercise Clause even where religiously motivated, there is an area of conduct that cannot be forbidden to religious practitioners but that may be forbidden to others. We should thus not labor to find a violation of the Establishment Clause when free exercise values prompt Congress to relieve religious believers from the burdens of the law at least in those instances where the law is not merely prohibitory but commands the performance of military duties that are forbidden by a man's religion....

Justice Blackmun [did not participate].

g. *Wisconsin v. Yoder, 406 U.S. 205 (1972)*

[This case is excerpted in more detail in the section on constitutionally mandated exemption, see p. 979; but the brief summary is this: The Amish hold religious beliefs that require them to lead an agrarian and separatist lifestyle. They therefore sought a Free Exercise Clause exemption for their 14- and 15-year-old children from a generally applicable law requiring formal education (public or private) until age 16. The Court agreed that the law substantially burdened the religious practice of the Amish, and that requiring the extra two years of education from ages 14 to 16 was not necessary to serve any compelling government interest. In the process, the Court held that this sort of Free Exercise Clause exemption was available only to religious believers, see p. 987, and that such a religion-specific exemption wouldn't violate the Establishment Clause.—ed.]

Chief Justice Burger delivered the opinion of the Court....

[R]ecognizing an exemption for the Amish from the State's system of compulsory education [is not] an impermissible establishment of religion.... Accommodating the religious beliefs of the Amish can hardly be characterized as sponsorship or active involvement [in religious activity]. The purpose and effect of such an exemption are not to support, favor, advance, or assist the Amish, but to allow their centuries-old religious society ... to survive free from the heavy impediment compliance with the Wisconsin compulsory-education law would impose. Such an accommodation "reflects nothing more than the governmental obligation of neutrality in the face of religious differences, and does not represent that involvement of religious with secular institutions which it is the object of the Establishment Clause to forestall." *Sherbert v. Verner.*

Justice White, with whom Justice Brennan and Justice Stewart join, concurring....

Decision in cases such as this ... will inevitably involve the kind of close and perhaps repeated scrutiny of religious practices, as is exemplified in today's opinion, which the Court has heretofore been anxious to avoid. But such entanglement does not create a forbidden establishment of religion where it is essential to implement free exercise values threatened by an otherwise neutral program instituted to foster some permissible, nonreligious state objective....

h.   *Estate of Thornton v. Caldor, 472 U.S. 703 (1985)*

Chief Justice Burger delivered the opinion of the Court....

In early 1975, ... Donald E. Thornton began working for respondent Caldor, Inc., a chain of New England retail stores; he managed the men's and boys' clothing department in respondent's Waterbury, Connecticut, store. At that time, respondent's Connecticut stores were closed on Sundays pursuant to state law.

In 1977, following the state legislature's revision of the Sunday-closing laws, respondent opened its Connecticut stores for Sunday business. In order to handle the expanded store hours, respondent required its managerial employees to work every third or fourth Sunday. Thornton, a Presbyterian who observed Sunday as his Sabbath, initially complied ... [but eventually] informed respondent that he would no longer work on Sundays because he observed that day as his Sabbath; he invoked the protection of Conn. Gen. Stat. § 53-303e(b), which provides: "No person who states that a particular day of the week is observed as his Sabbath may be [dismissed] by his employer [for refusing] to work on such day." ...

Under the Religion Clauses, government must guard against activity that impinges on religious freedom, and must take pains not to compel people to act in the name of any religion.... [Here, t]he State has ... decreed that those who observe a Sabbath any day of the week as a matter of religious conviction must be relieved of the duty to work on that day, no matter what

burden or inconvenience this imposes on the employer or fellow workers....
[T]he Connecticut statute imposes on employers and employees an absolute
duty to conform their business practices to the particular religious practices
of the employee by enforcing observance of the Sabbath the employee unilaterally designates....

There is no exception under the statute for special circumstances, such
as the Friday Sabbath observer employed in an occupation with a Monday
through Friday schedule—a school teacher, for example; the statute provides for no special consideration if a high percentage of an employer's work
force asserts rights to the same Sabbath. Moreover, there is no exception
when honoring the dictates of Sabbath observers would cause the employer
substantial economic burdens or when the employer's compliance would require the imposition of significant burdens on other employees required to
work in place of the Sabbath observers. {Section 53-303e(b) gives Sabbath
observers the valuable right to designate a particular weekly day off—typically a weekend day, widely prized as a day off. Other employees who have
strong and legitimate, but non-religious, reasons for wanting a weekend day
off have no rights under the statute.

For example, those employees who have earned the privilege through
seniority to have weekend days off may be forced to surrender this privilege
to the Sabbath observer; years of service and payment of "dues" at the workplace simply cannot compete with the Sabbath observer's absolute right under the statute. Similarly, those employees who would like a weekend day
off, because that is the only day their spouses are also not working, must
take a back seat to the Sabbath observer.} Finally, the statute allows for no
consideration as to whether the employer has made reasonable accommodation proposals.

This unyielding weighting in favor of Sabbath observers over all other
interests contravenes a fundamental principle of the Religion Clauses ...:
"The First Amendment ... gives no one the right to insist that in pursuit of
their own interests others must conform their conduct to his own religious
necessities." As such, the statute goes beyond having an incidental or remote effect of advancing religion. The statute has a primary effect [under
Lemon v. Kurtzman] that impermissibly advances a particular religious
practice....

Justice Rehnquist dissents [without opinion].

**Justice O'Connor, with whom Justice Marshall joins, concur-
ring....**

In my view, the Connecticut Sabbath law has an impermissible [primary
effect that advances religion] because it conveys a message of endorsement
of the Sabbath observance. All employees ... would value ... the right to select
the day of the week in which to refrain from labor. Yet Connecticut requires
private employers to confer this valued and desirable benefit only on those
employees who adhere to a particular religious belief. The statute singles
out Sabbath observers for special and ... absolute protection without according similar accommodation to ethical and religious beliefs and practices of

other private employees.

There can be little doubt that an objective observer or the public at large would perceive this statutory scheme precisely as the Court does today. The message conveyed is one of endorsement of a particular religious belief, to the detriment of those who do not share it....

I do not read the Court's opinion as suggesting that the religious accommodation provisions of Title VII of the Civil Rights Act of 1964 are similarly invalid. These provisions preclude employment discrimination based on a person's religion and require private employers to reasonably accommodate the religious practices of employees unless to do so would cause undue hardship to the employer's business.

Like the Connecticut Sabbath law, Title VII attempts to lift a burden on religious practice that is imposed by *private* employers, and hence it is not the sort of accommodation statute specifically contemplated by the Free Exercise Clause.... [But s]ince Title VII calls for reasonable rather than absolute accommodation and extends that requirement to all religious beliefs and practices rather than protecting only the Sabbath observance, I believe an objective observer would perceive it as an anti-discrimination law rather than an endorsement of religion or a particular religious practice.

i.   *Hobbie v. Unemployment Appeals Comm'n, 480 U.S. 136 (1987)*

Justice Brennan delivered the opinion of the Court....

Appellant's employer discharged her when she refused to work certain scheduled hours because of sincerely held religious convictions [forbidding work from sundown Friday to sundown Saturday] adopted after beginning employment. The question ... is whether Florida's denial of unemployment compensation benefits to appellant violates the Free Exercise Clause ....

[The Court held, under *Sherbert v. Verner*—discussed in much more detail in Part XIII.A.2, starting at p. 964—that Hobbie was indeed entitled to such compensation; but this meant that Hobbie would be getting government funds, drawn from payments by employers, because of her religious beliefs. The state therefore objected on Establishment Clause grounds, and here is how the Court responded:—ed.]

This Court has long recognized that the government may (and sometimes must) accommodate religious practices and that it may do so without violating the Establishment Clause. *See, e. g., Wisconsin v. Yoder* (judicial exemption of Amish children from compulsory attendance at high school); *Walz v. Tax Comm'n*, 397 U.S. 664 (1970) (tax exemption for churches). As in *Sherbert*, the accommodation at issue here does not entangle the State in an unlawful fostering of religion:

> In holding as we do, plainly we are not fostering the 'establishment' of the Seventh-day Adventist religion in South Carolina, for the extension of unemployment benefits to Sabbatarians in common with Sunday worshipers reflects nothing more than the governmental obligation of neutrality in the face of religious differences, and does not represent the involvement of religious with secular institutions which it is the object of the Establishment

Clause to forestall.

{In *Estate of Thornton v. Caldor, Inc.*, we held that a Connecticut statute that provided employees with an absolute right not to work on their Sabbath violated the Establishment Clause.... The Court determined that the State's "unyielding weighting in favor of Sabbath observers over all other interests ... ha[d] a primary effect that impermissibly advance[d] a particular religious practice[.]" ... In contrast, Florida's provision of unemployment benefits to religious observers does not single out a particular class of such persons for favorable treatment and thereby have the effect of implicitly endorsing a particular religious belief. Rather, the provision of unemployment benefits generally available within the State to religious observers who must leave their employment due to an irreconcilable conflict between the demands of work and conscience neutrally accommodates religious beliefs and practices, without endorsement.} ...

Justice Stevens, concurring in the judgment. [Opinion omitted; Justice Stevens didn't opine on the Establishment Clause issue.—ed.]

j.   *Corporation of the Presiding Bishop v. Amos, 483 U.S. 327 (1987)*

Justice White delivered the opinion of the Court....

[A.] The Deseret Gymnasium ... in Salt Lake City, Utah, is a nonprofit facility, open to the public, run by the Corporation of the Presiding Bishop of The Church of Jesus Christ of Latter-day Saints (CPB) .... The CPB ... [is a] religious entit[y] associated with The Church of Jesus Christ of Latter-day Saints ..., sometimes called the Mormon or LDS Church.

Appellee Mayson worked at the Gymnasium for some 16 years as [a janitor] .... He was discharged in 1981 because he failed to qualify for a temple recommend, that is, a certificate that he is a member of the Church and eligible to attend its temples. {Temple recommends are issued only to individuals who observe the Church's standards in such matters as regular church attendance, tithing, and abstinence from coffee, tea, alcohol, and tobacco.}

Mayson and others [sued,] ... alleging ... discrimination on the basis of religion in violation of ... [Title VII of] the Civil Rights Act of 1964. The defendants moved to dismiss this claim on the ground that § 702 [of the Act, which exempts] {"a religious corporation, association, educational institution, or society with respect to the employment of individuals of a particular religion[,]"} shields them from liability. The plaintiffs contended that if construed to allow religious employers to discriminate on religious grounds in hiring for nonreligious jobs, § 702 violates the Establishment Clause....

[B.] "... [T]he government may (and sometimes must) accommodate religious practices and that it may do so without violating the Establishment Clause." ... "[T]he limits of permissible state accommodation to religion are by no means co-extensive with the noninterference mandated by the Free Exercise Clause." There is ample room under the Establishment Clause for "benevolent neutrality which will permit religious exercise to exist without sponsorship and without interference." At some point, accommodation may devolve into "an unlawful fostering of religion," but [not in this case] ....

[C.] *Lemon v. Kurtzman* requires first that the law at issue serve a "secular legislative purpose." This does not mean that the law's purpose must be unrelated to religion—that would amount to a requirement "that the government show a callous indifference to religious groups," and the Establishment Clause has never been so interpreted. Rather, *Lemon's* "purpose" requirement aims at preventing the [government] ... from abandoning neutrality and acting with the intent of promoting a particular point of view in religious matters. Under the *Lemon* analysis, it is a permissible legislative purpose to alleviate significant governmental interference with the ability of religious organizations to define and carry out their religious missions.

Appellees argue that there is no such purpose here because § 702 provided adequate protection for religious employers prior to the 1972 amendment, when it exempted only the religious activities of such employers from the statutory ban on religious discrimination. We may assume for the sake of argument that the pre-1972 exemption was adequate in the sense that the Free Exercise Clause required no more.

Nonetheless, it is a significant burden on a religious organization to require it, on pain of substantial liability, to predict which of its activities a secular court will consider religious. The line is hardly a bright one, and an organization might understandably be concerned that a judge would not understand its religious tenets and sense of mission. Fear of potential liability might affect the way an organization carried out what it understood to be its religious mission.

After a detailed examination of the legislative history of the 1972 amendment, the District Court concluded that Congress' purpose was to minimize governmental "interfer[ence] with the decision-making process in religions." ... [T]his purpose does not violate the Establishment Clause.

[D.] The second requirement under *Lemon* is that the law in question have "a principal or primary effect ... that neither advances nor inhibits religion." Undoubtedly, religious organizations are better able now to advance their purposes than they were prior to the 1972 amendment to § 702. But ... [a] law is not unconstitutional simply because it *allows* churches to advance religion, which is their very purpose. For a law to have forbidden "effects" under *Lemon*, it must be fair to say that the *government itself* has advanced religion through its own activities and influence....

The District Court appeared to fear that sustaining the exemption would permit churches with financial resources impermissibly to extend their influence and propagate their faith by entering the commercial, profit-making world. The cases before us, however, involve a nonprofit activity instituted over 75 years ago in the hope that "all who assemble here, and who come for the benefit of their health, and for physical blessings, [may] feel that they are in a house dedicated to the Lord." These cases therefore do not implicate the apparent concerns of the District Court.

Moreover, we find no persuasive evidence in the record before us that the Church's ability to propagate its religious doctrine through the Gymnasium is any greater now than it was prior to the passage of the Civil Rights Act in 1964. In such circumstances, we do not see how any advancement of religion achieved by the Gymnasium can be fairly attributed to the Government, as opposed to the Church. {Undoubtedly, Mayson's freedom of choice in religious matters was impinged upon, but it was the Church (through ... the CPB), and not the Government, who put him to the choice of changing his religious practices or losing his job.

This is a very different case than *Estate of Thornton v. Caldor, Inc.* In *Caldor,* ... Connecticut had given the force of law to the employee's designation of a Sabbath day and required accommodation by the employer regardless of the burden which that constituted for the employer or other employees. [Here], appellee Mayson was not legally obligated to take the steps necessary to qualify for a temple recommend, and his discharge was not required by statute. We find no merit in appellees' contention that § 702 "impermissibly delegates governmental power to religious [employers] and conveys a message of governmental endorsement of religious discrimination."}
...

[S]tatutes that give special consideration to religious groups are [not] *per se* invalid.... [T]here is ample room for accommodation of religion under the Establishment Clause. Where, as here, government acts with the proper purpose of lifting a regulation that burdens the exercise of religion, we see no reason to require that the exemption comes packaged with benefits to secular entities....

[E.] {The statute easily passes muster under the third part of the *Lemon* test.} It cannot be seriously contended that § 702 impermissibly entangles church and state; the statute effectuates a more complete separation of the two and avoids the kind of intrusive inquiry into religious belief that the District Court engaged in this case. {Appellees argue that § 702 creates danger of political divisiveness along [religious] lines.... "[T]his Court has not held that political divisiveness alone can serve to invalidate otherwise permissible conduct. And we decline to so hold today. This case does not involve a direct subsidy to ... religious institutions, and hence no inquiry into political divisiveness is even called for."}

[F.] {*Larson v. Valente* indicates that laws discriminating *among* religions are subject to strict scrutiny, [but] that laws "affording a uniform benefit to *all* religions" should be analyzed under *Lemon*. In cases such as these, where a statute is neutral on its face and motivated by a permissible purpose of limiting governmental interference with the exercise of religion, we see no justification for applying strict scrutiny to a statute that passes the *Lemon* test....}

Justice Brennan, with whom Justice Marshall joins, concurring in the judgment....

[A.] These cases present a confrontation between the rights of religious organizations and those of individuals.

Any exemption from Title VII's proscription on religious discrimination necessarily has the effect of burdening the religious liberty of prospective and current employees. An exemption says that a person may be put to the choice of either conforming to certain religious tenets or losing a job opportunity, a promotion, or, as in these cases, employment itself. {The fact that a religious organization is permitted, rather than required, to impose this burden is irrelevant; what is significant is that the burden is the effect of the exemption.} The potential for coercion created by such a provision is in serious tension with our commitment to individual freedom of conscience in matters of religious belief.

At the same time, religious organizations have an interest in autonomy in ordering their internal affairs, so that they may be free to: "select their own leaders, define their own doctrines, resolve their own disputes, and run their own institutions. Religion includes important communal elements for most believers. They exercise their religion through religious organizations, and these organizations must be protected by the [Free Exercise C]lause."

For many individuals, religious activity derives meaning in large measure from participation in a larger religious community. Such a community represents an ongoing tradition of shared beliefs, an organic entity not reducible to a mere aggregation of individuals. Determining that certain activities are in furtherance of an organization's religious mission, and that only those committed to that mission should conduct them, is thus a means by which a religious community defines itself.... [F]urtherance of the autonomy of religious organizations often furthers individual religious freedom as well.

The authority to engage in this process of self-definition inevitably involves what we normally regard as infringement on free exercise rights, since a religious organization is able to condition employment in certain activities on subscription to particular religious tenets. We are willing to countenance the imposition of such a condition because we deem it vital that, if certain activities constitute part of a religious community's practice, then a religious organization should be able to require that only members of its community perform those activities.

[B.] This rationale suggests that, ideally, religious organizations should be able to discriminate on the basis of religion *only* with respect to religious activities, so that a determination should be made in each case whether an activity is religious or secular. This is because the infringement on religious liberty that results from conditioning performance of *secular* activity upon religious belief cannot be defended as necessary for the community's self-definition.

Furthermore, the authorization of discrimination in such circumstances is not an accommodation that simply enables a church to gain members by the normal means of prescribing the terms of membership for those who seek to participate in furthering the mission of the community. Rather, it puts at the disposal of religion the added advantages of economic leverage in the secular realm. As a result, the authorization of religious discrimination with respect to nonreligious activities goes beyond reasonable accommodation, and has the effect of furthering religion in violation of the Establishment Clause.

What makes the application of a religious-secular distinction difficult is that the character of an activity is not self-evident. As a result, determining whether an activity is religious or secular requires a searching case-by-case analysis. This results in considerable ongoing government entanglement in religious affairs.

Furthermore, this prospect of government intrusion raises concern that a religious organization may be chilled in its free exercise activity. While a church may regard the conduct of certain functions as integral to its mission, a court may disagree. A religious organization therefore would have an incentive to characterize as religious only those activities about which there likely would be no dispute, even if it genuinely believed that religious commitment was important in performing other tasks as well.

As a result, the community's process of self-definition would be shaped in part by the prospects of litigation. A case-by-case analysis for all activities therefore would both produce excessive government entanglement with religion and create the danger of chilling religious activity.... Because of the nature of nonprofit activities [as opposed to for-profit activities, which are more likely to be secular], I believe that a categorical exemption for such enterprises appropriately balances these competing concerns....

Justice O'Connor, [with whom Justice Blackmun in substantial part agrees—ed.], concurring in the judgment....

[T]he Court seems to suggest that the "effects" prong of the *Lemon* test is not at all implicated as long as the government action can be characterized as "allowing" religious organizations to advance religion, in contrast to ... directly advancing religion.... [But a]lmost any government benefit to religion could be recharacterized as simply "allowing" a religion to better advance itself, unless perhaps it involved actual proselytization by government agents....

It is for this same reason that there is little significance to the Court's observation that it was the Church rather than the Government that penalized Mayson's refusal to adhere to Church doctrine. The Church had the power to put Mayson to a choice of qualifying for a temple recommend or losing his job because *the Government* had lifted from religious organizations the general regulatory burden imposed by § 702....

[T]o separate those benefits to religion that constitutionally accommodate the free exercise of religion from those that provide unjustifiable awards of assistance to religious organizations[,] ... the inquiry ... should be "whether government's purpose is to endorse religion and whether the statute actually conveys a message of endorsement." To ascertain whether the statute conveys a message of endorsement, the relevant issue is how it would be perceived by an objective observer, acquainted with the text, legislative history, and implementation of the statute.... [And] to perceive the government action as a permissible accommodation of religion, there must in fact be an identifiable burden *on the exercise of religion* that can be said to be lifted by the government action....

These cases involve a Government decision to lift from a nonprofit activity of a religious organization the burden of demonstrating that the particular nonprofit activity is religious as well as the burden of refraining from discriminating on the basis of religion. Because there is a probability that a nonprofit activity of a religious organization will itself be involved in the organization's religious mission, in my view the objective observer should perceive the Government action as an accommodation of the exercise of religion rather than as a Government endorsement of religion.

It is not clear, however, that activities conducted by religious organizations solely as profit-making enterprises will be as likely to be directly involved in the religious mission of the organization.... [T]he question of the constitutionality of the § 702 exemption as applied to for-profit activities of religious organizations remains open.

k.   Texas Monthly, Inc. v. Bullock, 489 U.S. 1 (1989)

Justice Brennan ... delivered an opinion, in which Justice Marshall and Justice Stevens join.

Texas exempts from its sales tax "[p]eriodicals that are published or distributed by a religious faith and that consist wholly of writings promulgating the teaching of the faith and books that consist wholly of writings sacred to a religious faith." [Texas Monthly, a nonexempt magazine, sued to challenge this.] ... We hold that, when confined exclusively to publications advancing the tenets of a religious faith, the exemption runs afoul of the Establishment Clause; accordingly, we need not reach the question whether it contravenes the Free Press Clause ....

[A.] The core notion animating the requirement that a statute possess "a secular legislative purpose" and that "its principal or primary effect ... be one that neither advances nor inhibits religion," *Lemon v. Kurtzman*, is not only that government may not be overtly hostile to religion but also that it may not place its prestige, coercive authority, or resources behind a single religious faith or behind religious belief in general, compelling nonadherents to support the practices or proselytizing of favored religious organizations and conveying the message that those who do not contribute gladly are less than full members of the community....

[We have not] required that legislative categories make no explicit reference to religion. Government need not resign itself to ineffectual diffidence because of exaggerated fears of contagion of or by religion, so long as neither intrudes unduly into the affairs of the other....

[But in our cases upholding tax exemptions for or indirect subsidies to religious groups,] we emphasized that the benefits derived by religious organizations flowed to a large number of nonreligious groups as well. Indeed, were those benefits confined to religious organizations, they could not have appeared other than as state sponsorship of religion; if that were so, we would not have hesitated to strike them down for lacking a secular purpose and effect. See, *e.g., Estate of Thornton v. Caldor, Inc.*

Texas' sales tax exemption for periodicals published or distributed by a religious faith and consisting wholly of writings promulgating the teaching of the faith lacks sufficient breadth to pass scrutiny under the Establishment Clause. {The fact that Texas grants other sales tax exemptions (*e.g.*, for sales of food, agricultural items, and property used in the manufacture of articles for ultimate sale) for *different* purposes does not rescue the exemption for religious periodicals from invalidation. What is crucial is that any subsidy afforded religious organizations be warranted by some overarching secular purpose that justifies like benefits for nonreligious groups. There is no evidence ... that the exemption for religious periodicals was grounded in some secular legislative policy that motivated similar tax breaks for nonreligious activities.}

Every tax exemption constitutes a subsidy that affects nonqualifying taxpayers, forcing them to become "indirect and vicarious 'donors.'" *Bob Jones Univ. v. United States*.... However, when government directs a subsidy exclusively to religious organizations that is not required by the Free Exercise Clause and that either burdens nonbeneficiaries markedly or cannot reasonably be seen as removing a significant state-imposed deterrent to the free exercise of religion, as Texas has done, it "provide[s] unjustifiable awards of assistance to religious organizations" and cannot but "conve[y] a message of endorsement" to slighted members of the community. *Corporation of Presiding Bishop v. Amos* (O'Connor, J., concurring in judgment).

This is particularly true where, as here, the subsidy is targeted at writings that *promulgate* the teachings of religious faiths. It is difficult to view Texas' narrow exemption as anything but state sponsorship of religious belief .... {The fact that such exemptions are of long standing cannot shield them from the strictures of the Establishment Clause.... "[N]o one acquires a vested or protected right in violation of the Constitution by long use, even when that span of time covers our entire national existence and indeed predates it."} ...

[B.] {[W]e in no way suggest that *all* benefits conferred exclusively upon religious groups or upon individuals on account of their religious beliefs are forbidden by the Establishment Clause unless they are mandated by the Free Exercise Clause. Our decisions in *Zorach v. Clauson,* 343 U.S. 306 (1952) [which upheld a program that let public school children leave school for one hour a week for "religious observance and education outside the school grounds"—ed.], and *Corporation of Presiding Bishop* offer two examples. Similarly, if the Air Force provided a sufficiently broad exemption from its dress requirements for servicemen whose religious faiths commanded them to wear certain headgear or other attire, that exemption presumably would not be invalid under the Establishment Clause even though this Court has not found it to be required by the Free Exercise Clause. See *Goldman v. Weinberger,* 475 U.S. 503 (1986).

All of these cases, however, involve legislative exemptions that [do not] impose substantial burdens on nonbeneficiaries while allowing others to act according to their religious beliefs, or that were designed to alleviate government intrusions that might significantly deter adherents of a particular faith from conduct protected by the Free Exercise Clause....

[The program in *Zorach*] was found not to coerce students who wished to remain behind to alter their religious beliefs, nor did it impose monetary costs on their parents or other taxpayers .... The hypothetical Air Force uniform exemption also would not place a monetary burden on those required to conform to the dress code or subject them to any appreciable privation. And the application of Title VII's exemption for religious organizations that we approved in *Corporation of Presiding Bishop,* though it had some adverse effect on those holding or seeking employment with those organizations (if not on taxpayers generally), prevented potentially serious encroachments on protected religious freedoms.

Texas' tax exemption, by contrast, does not remove a demonstrated and possibly grave imposition on religious activity sheltered by the Free Exercise Clause. Moreover, it burdens nonbeneficiaries by increasing their tax bills by whatever amount is needed to offset the benefit bestowed on subscribers to religious publications.}

[**C.**] Texas claims that [the exemption serves] a compelling interest in avoiding violations of the Free Exercise [Clause] .... [But] nothing in our decisions under the Free Exercise Clause prevents the State from eliminating altogether its exemption for religious publications.... [T]he State has adduced no evidence that the payment of a sales tax by subscribers to religious periodicals or purchasers of religious books would offend their religious beliefs or inhibit religious activity. The State therefore cannot claim persuasively that its tax exemption is compelled by the Free Exercise Clause in even a single instance, let alone in every case. No concrete need to accommodate religious activity has been shown.

Moreover, even if members of some religious group succeeded in demonstrating that payment of a sales tax ... would violate their religious tenets, it is by no means obvious that the State would be required by the Free Exercise Clause to make individualized exceptions for them. In *United States v. Lee,* we ruled unanimously that the Federal Government need not exempt an Amish employer from the payment of Social Security taxes, notwithstanding our recognition that compliance would offend his religious beliefs. We ... held that "[t]he state may justify a limitation on religious liberty by showing that it is essential to accomplish an overriding governmental interest." ... [A] State's interest in the uniform collection of a sales tax appears comparable to the Federal Government's interest in the uniform collection of Social Security taxes ....

[**D.**] Texas' further claim that the Establishment Clause mandates, or at least favors, its sales tax exemption for religious periodicals is equally unconvincing. Not only does the exemption seem a blatant endorsement of religion, but it appears, on its face, to produce greater state entanglement with religion than the denial of an exemption....

"[There exists an] overriding interest in keeping the government—

whether it be the legislature or the courts—out of the business of evaluating the relative merits of differing religious claims. The risk that governmental approval of some and disapproval of others will be perceived as favoring one religion over another is an important risk the Establishment Clause was designed to preclude." *United States v. Lee* (Stevens, J., concurring in the judgment). The prospect of inconsistent treatment and government embroilment in controversies over religious doctrine seems especially baleful where, as in the case of Texas' sales tax exemption, a statute requires that public officials determine whether some message or activity is consistent with "the teaching of the faith." See, *e.g., Presbyterian Church v. Mary Elizabeth Blue Hull Memorial Presbyterian Church.*

While ... compliance with government regulations by religious organizations and the monitoring of their compliance by government agencies would itself enmesh the operations of church and state to some degree, ... such compliance would generally not impede the evangelical activities of religious groups and ... the "routine and factual inquiries" commonly associated with the enforcement of tax laws "bear no resemblance to the kind of government surveillance the Court has previously held to pose an intolerable risk of government entanglement with religion." ...

Justice White, concurring in the judgment.

The Texas law at issue here discriminates on the basis of the content of publications .... This is plainly forbidden by the [Free] Press Clause ....

Justice Blackmun, with whom Justice O'Connor joins, concurring in the judgment....

It is possible for a State to write a tax-exemption statute consistent with both [Free Exercise Clause and Establishment Clause] values: for example, a state statute might exempt the sale not only of religious literature distributed by a religious organization but also of philosophical literature distributed by nonreligious organizations devoted to such matters of conscience as life and death, good and evil, being and nonbeing, right and wrong. Such a statute, moreover, should survive Press Clause scrutiny because its exemption would be narrowly tailored to meet the compelling interests that underlie both the Free Exercise and Establishment Clauses....

[But] by confining the tax exemption exclusively to the sale of religious publications, Texas engaged in preferential support for the communication of religious messages. Although some forms of accommodating religion are constitutionally permissible, see *Corporation of Presiding Bishop,* this one surely is not. A statutory preference for the dissemination of religious ideas offends our most basic understanding of what the Establishment Clause is all about ....

Justice Scalia, with whom ... Chief Justice [Rehnquist] and Justice Kennedy join, dissenting....

[A.] [T]he Court topples an exemption for religious publications of a sort that expressly appears in the laws of at least 15 of the 45 States that have sales and use taxes .... At least 45 States provide exemptions [from other taxes] for religious groups without analogous exemptions for other types of nonprofit institutions. For over half a century the federal Internal Revenue Code has allowed "minister[s] of the gospel" (a term interpreted broadly enough to include cantors and rabbis) to exclude from gross income the rental value of their parsonages. In short, religious tax exemptions of the type the Court invalidates today permeate the state and federal codes, and have done so for many years....

Today's opinions ... achieve a revolution in our Establishment Clause jurisprudence, effectively overruling ... cases that were based ... on the "accommodation of religion" rationale. According to Justice Brennan's opinion, no law is constitutional whose "benefits [are] confined to religious organizations"—except, of course, those laws that are unconstitutional *unless* they contain benefits confined to religious organizations.

Our jurisprudence affords no support for this unlikely proposition.... In such cases as *Sherbert v. Verner, Wisconsin v. Yoder, Thomas v. Review Bd.,* and *Hobbie v. Unemployment Appeals Comm'n,* 480 U.S. 136 (1987), we held that the Free Exercise Clause of the First Amendment *required* religious beliefs to be accommodated by granting religion-specific exemptions from otherwise applicable laws. We have often made clear, however, that "[t]he limits of permissible state accommodation to religion are by no means co-extensive with the noninterference mandated by the Free Exercise Clause." [See, *e.g., Zorach v. Clauson; Corporation of Presiding Bishop.*] ... It is not always easy to determine when accommodation slides over into promotion, and neutrality into favoritism, but the withholding of a tax upon the dissemination of religious materials is not even a close case....

Justice Brennan [repudiates] the accommodation principle .... By saying that what is not required cannot be allowed, Justice Brennan would completely block off the already narrow "channel between the Scylla [of what the Free Exercise Clause demands] and the Charybdis [of what the Establishment Clause forbids] through which any state or federal action must pass in order to survive constitutional scrutiny." ...

Justice Brennan's opinion ... [also finds] that § 151.312 has the impermissible "effect of sponsoring certain religious tenets or religious belief in general." ... [A] sales tax exemption aids religion, since it makes it less costly for religions to disseminate their beliefs. But that has never been enough to strike down an enactment under the Establishment Clause. "A law is not unconstitutional simply because it *allows* churches to advance religion, which is their very purpose." *Corporation of Presiding Bishop ....*

To be sure, we have set our face against the subsidizing of religion—and in other contexts we have suggested that tax exemptions and subsidies are equivalent. *E.g., Bob Jones University.* We have not treated them as equivalent, however, in the Establishment Clause context, and with good reason. "In the case of direct subsidy, the state forcibly diverts the income of both believers and nonbelievers to churches. In the case of an exemption, the state merely refrains from diverting to its own uses income independently generated by the churches through voluntary contributions." ... [T]he *primary* effect of a tax exemption [is] not to sponsor religious activity but to "restric[t] the fiscal relationship between church and state" and to "complement and reinforce the desired separation insulating each from the other."

[**B.**] Justice Brennan suggests that § 151.312 [constitutes] "excessive government entanglement" .... It is plain that the exemption does not foster the sort of "comprehensive, discriminating, and continuing state surveillance" necessary to [make entanglement excessive]. A State does not excessively involve itself in religious affairs merely by examining material to determine whether it is religious or secular in nature....

Moreover, ... elimination of the exemption will have the effect of *increasing* government's involvement with religion. The Court's invalidation of § 151.312 ensures that Texas churches selling publications that promulgate their religion will now be subject to numerous statutory and regulatory impositions, including audits, requirements for the filing of security, reporting requirements, writs of attachment without bond, tax liens, and the seizure and sale of property to satisfy tax delinquencies....

[**C.**] If the purpose of accommodating religion can support action that might otherwise violate the Establishment Clause, I see no reason why it does not also support action that might otherwise violate the Press Clause or the Speech Clause. To hold otherwise would be to narrow the accommodation principle enormously, leaving it applicable to only nonexpressive religious worship.

I do not think that is the law. Just as the Constitution sometimes *requires* accommodation of religious expression despite not only the Establishment Clause but also the Speech and Press Clauses, so also it sometimes *permits* accommodation despite all those Clauses. Such accommodation is unavoidably content based—because the Freedom of Religion Clause is content based. It is absurd to think that a State which chooses to prohibit booksellers from making stories about seduction available to children of tender years cannot make an exception for stories contained in sacred writings (*e.g.*, the story of Susanna and the Two Elders, Daniel 13:1-65).... And it is impossible to believe that the State is constitutionally prohibited from taxing Texas Monthly magazine more heavily than the Holy Bible....

l.   City of Boerne v. Flores, 521 U.S. 507 (1997)

[RFRA (see p. 1014) required federal, state, and local governments to accommodate religious objections from generally applicable laws, whenever the law substantially burdened religious practice and the burden wasn't narrowly tailored to a compelling government interest. The Court struck this down as to state and local governments on federalism grounds; but Justice Stevens would have struck down the law generally, on Establishment Clause grounds. The case arose when the Catholic Archbishop of San Antonio, P.F. Flores, challenged the application to a church of a generally applicable architectural preservation law.—ed.]

Justice Stevens, concurring.

In my opinion, the Religious Freedom Restoration Act of 1993 (RFRA) is a "law respecting an establishment of religion" that violates the First

Amendment to the Constitution.

If the historic landmark on the hill in Boerne happened to be a museum or an art gallery owned by an atheist, it would not be eligible for an exemption from the city ordinances that forbid an enlargement of the structure. Because the landmark is owned by the Catholic Church, it is claimed that RFRA gives its owner a federal statutory entitlement to an exemption from a generally applicable, neutral civil law. Whether the Church would actually prevail under the statute or not, the statute has provided the Church with a legal weapon that no atheist or agnostic can obtain. This governmental preference for religion, as opposed to irreligion, is forbidden by the First Amendment.

m. *Cutter v. Wilkinson, 544 U.S. 709 (2005)*

Justice Ginsburg delivered the opinion of the Court.

[A.] Section 3 of the Religious Land Use and Institutionalized Persons Act of 2000 (RLUIPA) provides in part: "No government shall impose a substantial burden on the religious exercise of a person residing in or confined to an institution," unless the burden furthers "a compelling governmental interest," and does so by "the least restrictive means."

[Petitioners] are current and former inmates of [Ohio prisons] and assert that they are adherents of "nonmainstream" religions: the Satanist, Wicca, and Asatru religions, and the Church of Jesus Christ Christian. They complain that Ohio prison officials (respondents here), in violation of RLUIPA, have failed to accommodate their religious exercise "in a variety of different ways, including ... denying them access to religious literature, ... [and] forbidding them to adhere to the dress and appearance mandates of their religions ...."

For purposes of this litigation at its current stage, respondents have stipulated that petitioners are members of bona fide religions and that they are sincere in their beliefs.... [R]espondents contend ... that the Act improperly advances religion in violation of the ... Establishment Clause....

[B.] RLUIPA is the latest of long-running congressional efforts to accord religious exercise heightened protection from government-imposed burdens, consistent with this Court's precedents. Ten years before RLUIPA's enactment, the Court held, in *Employment Div. v. Smith*, that the First Amendment's Free Exercise Clause does not inhibit enforcement of otherwise valid laws of general application that incidentally burden religious conduct.... The Court recognized, however, that the political branches could shield religious exercise through legislative accommodation, for example, by making an exception to proscriptive drug laws for sacramental peyote use.... [I]nvoking federal authority under the Spending and Commerce Clauses, [section 3 of] RLUIPA ... provides that "[n]o [state or local] government shall impose a substantial burden on the religious exercise of a person residing in or confined to an institution," unless the government shows that the burden furthers "a compelling governmental interest" and does so by "the least restrictive means."

The Act defines "religious exercise" to include "any exercise of religion, whether or not compelled by, or central to, a system of religious belief." Section 3 applies when "the substantial burden [on religious exercise] is imposed in a program or activity that receives Federal financial assistance," or "the substantial burden affects, or removal of that substantial burden would affect, commerce with foreign nations, among the several States, or with Indian tribes." ...

Before enacting § 3, Congress documented, in hearings spanning three years, that "frivolous or arbitrary" barriers impeded institutionalized persons' religious exercise. {"A state prison in Ohio refused to provide Moslems with Hallal food, even though it provided Kosher food." Across the country, Jewish inmates complained that prison officials refused to provide sack lunches, which would enable inmates to break their fasts after nightfall. The "Michigan Department of Corrections ... prohibit[ed] the lighting of Chanukah candles at all state prisons" even though "smoking" and "votive candles" were permitted.... [I]n Oklahoma[,] ... there "was [a] nearly yearly battle over the Catholic use of Sacramental Wine ... for the celebration of the Mass," and ... prisoners' religious possessions, "such as the Bible, the Koran, the Talmud or items needed by Native Americans[,] ... were frequently treated with contempt and were confiscated, damaged or discarded" by prison officials.}

To secure redress for inmates who encountered undue barriers to their religious observances, Congress [provided for] the "compelling governmental interest"/"least restrictive means" standard. Lawmakers anticipated, however, that courts entertaining complaints under § 3 would accord "due deference to the experience and expertise of prison and jail administrators." ...

[C.] Our decisions recognize that "there is room for play in the joints" between the Clauses, some space for legislative action neither compelled by the Free Exercise Clause nor prohibited by the Establishment Clause.... [Section 3, o]n its face, ... qualifies as a permissible legislative accommodation of religion that is not barred by the Establishment Clause.

Foremost, we find RLUIPA's institutionalized-persons provision compatible with the Establishment Clause because it alleviates exceptional government-created burdens on private religious exercise. See, *e.g.*, *Corporation of Presiding Bishop v. Amos* (O'Connor, J., concurring in judgment) (removal of government-imposed burdens on religious exercise is more likely to be perceived "as an accommodation of the exercise of religion rather than as a Government endorsement of religion"). Furthermore, the Act on its face does not founder on shoals our prior decisions have identified: Properly applying RLUIPA, courts must take adequate account of the burdens a requested accommodation may impose on nonbeneficiaries, see *Estate of Thornton v. Caldor, Inc.*; and they must be satisfied that the Act's prescriptions are and will be administered neutrally among different faiths, see *Board of Ed. of Kiryas Joel Village School Dist. v. Grumet*, 512 U.S. 687 (1994). {[And d]irected at obstructions institutional arrangements place on religious observances, RLUIPA does not require a State to pay for an inmate's devotional accessories.} ...

Section 3 covers state-run institutions—mental hospitals, prisons, and the like—in which the government exerts a degree of control unparalleled in civilian society and severely disabling to private religious exercise. RLUIPA thus protects institutionalized persons who are unable freely to attend to their religious needs and are therefore dependent on the government's permission and accommodation for exercise of their religion. {Respondents argue ... that RLUIPA goes beyond permissible reduction of impediments to free exercise. The Act, they project, advances religion by encouraging prisoners to "get religion," and thereby gain accommodations afforded under RLUIPA. While some accommodations of religious observance, notably the opportunity to assemble in worship services, might attract joiners seeking a break in their closely guarded day, we doubt that all accommodations would be perceived as "benefits." For example, congressional hearings on RLUIPA revealed that one state corrections system served as its kosher diet "a fruit, a vegetable, a granola bar, and a liquid nutritional supplement—each and every meal." The argument, in any event, founders on the fact that Ohio already facilitates religious services for mainstream faiths. The State provides chaplains, allows inmates to possess religious items, and permits assembly for worship.}

We note in this regard the Federal Government's accommodation of religious practice by members of the military. See, *e.g.*, 10 U.S.C. § 3073 (referring to Army chaplains). In *Goldman v. Weinberger*, 475 U.S. 503 (1986), we held that the Free Exercise Clause did not require the Air Force to exempt an Orthodox Jewish officer from uniform dress regulations so that he could wear a yarmulke indoors. In a military community, the Court observed, "there is simply not the same [individual] autonomy as there is in the larger civilian community." Congress responded to *Goldman* by prescribing that "a member of the armed forces may wear an item of religious apparel while wearing the uniform," unless "the wearing of the item would interfere with the performance [of] military duties [or] the item of apparel is not neat and conservative."

[D.] We do not read RLUIPA to elevate accommodation of religious observances over an institution's need to maintain order and safety. Our decisions indicate that an accommodation must be measured so that it does not override other significant interests. In *Caldor*, the Court struck down a Connecticut law that "arm[ed] Sabbath observers with an absolute and unqualified right not to work on whatever day they designate[d] as their Sabbath." We held the law invalid under the Establishment Clause because it "unyielding[ly] weigh[ted]" the interests of Sabbatarians "over all other interests."

We have no cause to believe that RLUIPA would not be applied in an appropriately balanced way, with particular sensitivity to security concerns. While the Act adopts a "compelling governmental interest" standard, "[c]ontext matters" in the application of that standard. Lawmakers supporting

RLUIPA were mindful of the urgency of discipline, order, safety, and security in penal institutions. They anticipated that courts would apply the Act's standard with "due deference to the experience and expertise of prison and jail administrators in establishing necessary regulations and procedures to maintain good order, security and discipline, consistent with consideration of costs and limited resources."

{The Sixth Circuit posited that an irreligious prisoner and member of the Aryan Nation who challenges prison officials' confiscation of his white supremacist literature as a violation of his free association and expression rights would have his claims evaluated under the deferential rational-relationship standard described in *Turner v. Safley*, 482 U.S. 78 (1987). A member of the Church of Jesus Christ Christian challenging a similar withholding, the Sixth Circuit assumed, would have a stronger prospect of success because a court would review his claim under RLUIPA's compelling-interest standard. Courts, however, may be expected to recognize the government's countervailing compelling interest in not facilitating inflammatory racist activity that could imperil prison security and order. Cf., *e.g.*, *Reimann v. Murphy*, 897 F. Supp. 398 (E.D. Wisc. 1995) (concluding, under [a similar statute], that excluding racist literature advocating violence was the least restrictive means of furthering the compelling state interest in preventing prison violence).} ...

[E.] The [Court of Appeals] misread our precedents to require invalidation of RLUIPA as "impermissibly advancing religion by giving greater protection to religious rights than to other constitutionally protected rights." Our decision in *Amos* counsels otherwise. There, we upheld against an Establishment Clause challenge a provision exempting "religious organizations from Title VII's prohibition against discrimination in employment on the basis of religion." ... Religious accommodations, we held, need not "come packaged with benefits to secular entities."

Were the Court of Appeals' view the correct reading of our decisions, all manner of religious accommodations would fall. Congressional permission for members of the military to wear religious apparel while in uniform would fail, as would accommodations Ohio itself makes ... [for] "traditionally recognized" religions: The State provides inmates with chaplains "but not with publicists or political consultants," and allows "prisoners to assemble for worship, but not for political rallies."

In upholding RLUIPA's institutionalized-persons provision, we emphasize that respondents "have raised a facial challenge to [the Act's] constitutionality, and have not contended that under the facts of any of [petitioners'] specific cases ... applying RLUIPA would produce unconstitutional results." ... Should inmate requests for religious accommodations become excessive, impose unjustified burdens on other institutionalized persons, or jeopardize the effective functioning of an institution, the facility would be free to resist the imposition. In that event, adjudication in as-applied challenges would be in order.

B. Non-Discrimination Extended (Establishment)

1. The No Endorsement Principle as to Government Speech

a. *Summary*

Basic principle: The government generally may not engage in *speech endorsing or disapproving of a particular faith, or of religion generally*. The theory is that such endorsement or disapproval violates the prohibition on "making adherence to a religion relevant in any way to a person's standing in the political community." See, *e.g.*, *County of Allegheny v. ACLU*, 492 U.S. 573, 594 (1989); *Engel v. Vitale* (1962) (p. 784).

1. Exception: This principle doesn't apply when the practice is nonsectarian and deeply ingrained in U.S. history—a circumstance that might be limited entirely to legislative prayer. See *Marsh v. Chambers* (1983) (p. 791) and *Allegheny*'s explanation of *Marsh*.

2. Twist: Under Justice Breyer's controlling concurrence in *Van Orden v. Perry* (2005) (p. 826), when the endorsement question is on the "borderline," the speech may be upheld if removing it seems likely to create more "religiously based divisiveness" than keeping it would.

3. Amplification: This principle doesn't bar the government from engaging in all facially religious speech, because some such speech—given its context and history—would not lead a reasonable observer to conclude that it actually endorses religion:

— For instance, menorahs or crèches that are part of a broader holiday display would be interpreted (the Court has held) as general celebrations of the season, not endorsements of religion. *Allegheny*.

— Likewise, "a typical museum setting, though not neutralizing the religious content of a religious painting, negates any message of endorsement of that content." *Allegheny* (in Justice O'Connor's solo opinion, but at least five Justices endorsed such a position).

— The same would almost certainly be true of facially religious geographical names, such as Santa Fe (sacred faith), Los Angeles (the full historical name of which translates as the City of Our Lady the Queen of the Angels, *i.e.*, the City of the Virgin Mary), and so on; they are no longer seen as communicating any religious message.

— The same may well be true of certain kinds of "ceremonial deism," even of relatively recent vintage, such as "In God We Trust" on currency or "one nation, under God" in the Pledge of Allegiance, because they no longer communicate a truly religious message. See *Allegheny* ("Our previous opinions have considered in dicta the motto and the pledge, characterizing them as consistent with the proposition that government may not communicate an endorsement of religious belief. We need not return to the subject of 'ceremonial deism,' because ... [h]owever history may affect the constitutionality of nonsectarian references to religion ..., history cannot legitimate practices that demonstrate the government's allegiance to a particular sect or creed.").

— Justice O'Connor (joined by Justices Souter and Breyer) has reasoned that the inquiry should focus on the views of a "reasonable observer" who is "deemed aware of the history and context of the community and forum in which the religious display appears," including "the general history of the place in which the cross is displayed." *Capitol Square Review Bd. v. Pinette* (1995) (p. 837).

4. Further amplification on private religious speech in public places:

— When the government gives private religious speech *preferential access* to public places, that violates the Establishment Clause. *Allegheny*; *Santa Fe Indep. School Dist. v. Doe,* 530 U.S. 290 (2000) (having high school students vote on whether to have a speaker lead a prayer is government action that prefers religion).

— But private speakers must generally be given *equal access* to public fora, or else the content-based discrimination would violate the Free Speech Clause. *Capitol Square.* The three concurring Justices in *Capitol Square*, however, would also require the government in such a situation to put up disclaimers or take other steps that make clear to the public that the government is not endorsing this speech.

5. Other significant endorsement cases:

— *Stone v. Graham,* 449 U.S. 39 (1980), struck down the posting of the Ten Commandments in a public K-12 school on the grounds that the posting had no secular purpose, but also expressed concern about endorsement.

— *Santa Fe Indep. School Dist. v. Doe,* which struck down government-sponsored prayers at football games, largely followed *Lee v. Weisman* but had more endorsement language (perhaps because by then there were five votes on the Court for the endorsement framework). *Lee* itself, which involved graduation prayers, was decided on coercion grounds (p. 868), but a three-Justice concurrence would have also struck down the prayer on endorsement grounds.

b. *Problem: Virginia Beach City Seal*

The seal of the City of Virginia Beach is shown below. Assume that the City's Web page describing the seal says (as it indeed once said) that:

The City Seal is reflective of our Nation's beginning, as well as landmarks and specialties for which [Virginia] Beach is recognized. Leaping marlins form its outer edge and represent sport fishing, boating and other water activities available in the City. Strawberry leaves combine to create an inner circle, representing the importance of agriculture to the City's economy. Prominent in the Seal's center is the Cape Henry Lighthouse and the cross marking the first landing of settlers on this Nation's soil. The Lighthouse and the cross symbolize the beginnings of [Virginia] Beach, as well as the United States. Bright sunshine and blue water join the sandy beach to indicate the importance of tourism and the pleasures of nature available to [Virginia] Beach residents and visitors.

The seal was chosen by a contest in December 1962; it was designed by a local commercial artist. The Cape Henry Lighthouse, erected in 1792, was the first lighthouse put up by the Federal Government. The Cape Henry Memorial Cross, erected in 1935, marks the approximate location of the 1607 Jamestown landing.

Assume the seal appears on city stationery, on city building walls, and on police cars and other city vehicles. Does the display of this seal violate the Establishment Clause? *Compare, e.g., Murray v. City of Austin,* 947 F.2d 147 (5th Cir. 1991), *with Friedman v. Board of County Comm'rs of Bernalillo,* 781 F.2d 777 (10th Cir. 1985), *and Harris v. City of Zion,* 927 F.2d 1401 (7th Cir. 1991); *see also ACLU v. Capitol Square Review & Advisory Bd.,* 243 F.3d 289 (6th Cir. 2001) (involving a state motto).

c. *Engel v. Vitale, 370 U.S. 421 (1962)*

Justice Black delivered the opinion of the Court....

[A.] [New York government agencies] directed the [New Hyde Park] School District's principal to cause the following prayer to be said aloud by each class in the presence of a teacher at the beginning of each school day: "Almighty God, we acknowledge our dependence upon Thee, and we beg Thy blessings upon us, our parents, our teachers and our Country." ... [T]he parents of ten pupils [sued] ....

[B]y using its public school system to encourage recitation of the Regents' prayer, the State of New York has adopted a practice wholly inconsistent with the Establishment Clause.... New York's program of daily classroom invocation of God's blessings as prescribed in the Regents' prayer is a religious activity. It is a solemn avowal of divine faith and supplication for the blessings of the Almighty....

[T]he constitutional prohibition against laws respecting an establishment of religion must at least mean that in this country it is no part of the business of government to compose official prayers for any group of the American people to recite as a part of a religious program carried on by government.... [T]his very practice of establishing governmentally composed prayers for religious services was one of the reasons which caused many of our early colonists to leave England and seek religious freedom in America.... The controversies over [such government-specified forms of prayer in the established, tax-supported Church of England] repeatedly threatened to disrupt the peace of that country as the accepted forms of prayer in the established church changed with the views of the particular ruler that happened to be in control at the time.... [Groups] lacking the necessary political power to influence the Government on the matter[] decided to leave England and its established church and seek freedom in America from England's governmentally ordained and supported religion.

It is an unfortunate fact of history that when some of the very groups which had most strenuously opposed the established Church of England found themselves sufficiently in control of colonial governments in this country to write their own prayers into law, they passed laws making their own religion the official religion of their respective colonies. Indeed, as late as the time of the Revolutionary War, there were established churches in at least eight of the thirteen former colonies and established religions in at least four of the other five.

But the successful Revolution against English political domination was shortly followed by intense opposition to the practice of establishing religion by law. This opposition crystallized rapidly into an effective political force in Virginia where the minority religious groups such as Presbyterians, Lutherans, Quakers and Baptists had gained such strength that the adherents to the established Episcopal Church were actually a minority themselves. In 1785-1786, those opposed to the established Church, led by James Madison and Thomas Jefferson, who, though themselves not members of any of these dissenting religious groups, opposed all religious establishments by law on grounds of principle, obtained the enactment of the famous "Virginia Bill for Religious Liberty" by which all religious groups were placed on an equal footing so far as the State was concerned. Similar though less far-reaching legislation was being considered and passed in other States.

By the time of the adoption of the Constitution, our history shows that there was a widespread awareness among many Americans of the dangers of a union of Church and State. These people knew, some of them from bitter personal experience, that one of the greatest dangers to the freedom of the individual to worship in his own way lay in the Government's placing its official stamp of approval upon one particular kind of prayer or one particular form of religious services. They knew the anguish, hardship and bitter strife that could come when zealous religious groups struggled with one another to obtain the Government's stamp of approval ....

The First Amendment was added to the Constitution to stand as a guarantee that neither the power nor the prestige of the Federal Government would be used to control, support or influence the kinds of prayer the American people can say—that the people's religions must not be subjected to the pressures of government for change each time a new political administration is elected to office. Under that Amendment's prohibition against governmental establishment of religion, as reinforced by the provisions of the Fourteenth Amendment, government in this country, be it state or federal, is without power to prescribe by law any particular form of prayer which is to be used as an official prayer in carrying on any program of governmentally sponsored religious activity....

[B.] Neither the fact that the prayer may be denominationally neutral nor the fact that its observance on the part of the students is voluntary [students are allowed to remain silent or be excused from the room] can serve to free it from the limitations of the Establishment Clause .... The Establishment Clause, unlike the Free Exercise Clause, does not depend upon any showing of direct governmental compulsion and is violated by the enactment of laws which establish an official religion whether those laws operate directly to coerce nonobserving individuals or not.

This is not to say, of course, that laws officially prescribing a particular form of religious worship do not involve coercion of such individuals. When the power, prestige and financial support of government is placed behind a particular religious belief, the indirect coercive pressure upon religious minorities to conform to the prevailing officially approved religion is plain. But the purposes underlying the Establishment Clause go much further than that.

Its first and most immediate purpose rested on the belief that a union of government and religion tends to destroy government and to degrade religion. The history of governmentally established religion, both in England and in this country, showed that whenever government had allied itself with one particular form of religion, the inevitable result had been that it had incurred the hatred, disrespect and even contempt of those who held contrary beliefs. That same history showed that many people had lost their respect for any religion that had relied upon the support for government to spread its faith. The Establishment Clause thus stands as an expression of principle on the part of the Founders of our Constitution that religion is too personal, too sacred, too holy, to permit its "unhallowed perversion" by a civil magistrate.

Another purpose of the Establishment Clause rested upon an awareness of the historical fact that governmentally established religions and religious persecutions go hand in hand. The Founders knew that only a few years after the Book of Common Prayer became the only accepted form of religious services in the established Church of England, an Act of Uniformity was passed to compel all Englishmen to attend those services and to make it a criminal offense to conduct or attend religious gatherings of any other kind—a law which was consistently flouted by dissenting religious groups in England and which contributed to widespread persecutions of people ... who persisted in holding "unlawful [religious] meetings ...." And they knew that similar persecutions had received the sanction of law in several of the colonies in this country soon after the establishment of official religions in those colonies....

[C.] It has been argued that to apply the Constitution in such a way as to prohibit state laws respecting an establishment of religious services in public schools is to indicate a hostility toward religion or toward prayer. Nothing, of course, could be more wrong. The history of man is inseparable from the history of religion.... It was doubtless largely due to men who believed [in the power of prayer] that there grew up a sentiment that caused men to leave the cross-currents of officially established state religions and religious persecution in Europe and come to this country filled with the hope that they could find a place in which they could pray when they pleased to the God of their faith in the language they chose.

And there were men of this same faith in the power of prayer who led the fight for adoption of our Constitution and also for our Bill of Rights with the very guarantees of religious freedom that forbid the sort of governmental activity which New York has attempted here. These men knew that the First Amendment, which tried to put an end to governmental control of religion and of prayer, was not written to destroy either.

They knew rather that it was written to quiet well-justified fears which nearly all of them felt arising out of an awareness that governments of the past had shackled men's tongues to make them speak only the religious thoughts that government wanted them to speak and to pray only to the God that government wanted them to pray to. It is neither sacrilegious nor antireligious to say that each separate government in this country should stay out of the business of writing or sanctioning official prayers and leave that purely religious function to the people themselves and to those the people choose to look to for religious guidance.

{There is of course nothing in the decision reached here that is inconsistent with the fact that school children and others are officially encouraged to express love for our country by reciting historical documents such as the Declaration of Independence which contain references to the Deity or by singing officially espoused anthems which include the composer's professions of faith in a Supreme Being, or with the fact that there are many manifestations in our public life of belief in God. Such patriotic or ceremonial occasions bear no true resemblance to the unquestioned religious exercise that the State of New York has sponsored in this instance.}

[D.] It is true that New York's establishment of its Regents' prayer as an officially approved religious doctrine of that State does not amount to a total establishment of one particular religious sect to the exclusion of all others—that, indeed, the governmental endorsement of that prayer seems relatively insignificant when compared to the governmental encroachments upon religion which were commonplace 200 years ago. To those who may subscribe to the view that because the Regents' official prayer is so brief and general there can be no danger to religious freedom in its governmental establishment, however, it may be appropriate to say in the words of James Madison, the author of the First Amendment:

> [I]t is proper to take alarm at the first experiment on our liberties.... Who does not see that the same authority which can establish Christianity, in exclusion of all other Religions, may establish with the same ease any particular sect of Christians, in exclusion of all other Sects? That the same authority which can force a citizen to contribute three pence only of his property for the support of any one establishment, may force him to conform to any other establishment in all cases whatsoever? ...

Justice Stewart, dissenting....

I cannot see how an "official religion" is established by letting those who want to say a prayer say it. On the contrary, I think that to deny the wish of these school children to join in reciting this prayer is to deny them the opportunity of sharing in the spiritual heritage of our Nation....

What is relevant to the issue here is not the history of an established church in sixteenth century England or in eighteenth century America, but the history of the religious traditions of our people, reflected in countless practices of the institutions and officials of our government. At the opening of each day's Session of this Court we stand, while one of our officials invokes the protection of God. Since the days of John Marshall our Crier has said, "God save the United States and this Honorable Court." Both the Senate and the House of Representatives open their daily Sessions with prayer. Each of our Presidents, from George Washington to John F. Kennedy, has upon assuming his Office asked the protection and help of God.

The Court today says that the state and federal governments are without constitutional power to prescribe any particular form of words to be recited by any group of the American people on any subject touching religion. One of the stanzas of "The Star-Spangled Banner," made our National Anthem by Act of Congress in 1931, contains these verses:

Blest with victory and peace, may the heav'n rescued land
Praise the Pow'r that hath made and preserved us a nation!
Then conquer we must, when our cause it is just,
And this be our motto "In God is our Trust."

In 1954 Congress added a phrase to the Pledge of Allegiance to the Flag so that it now contains the words "one Nation *under God*, indivisible, with liberty and justice for all." In 1952 Congress enacted legislation calling upon the President each year to proclaim a National Day of Prayer. Since 1865 the words "IN GOD WE TRUST" have been impressed on our coins. {I am at a loss to understand the Court's unsupported *ipse dixit* that these official expressions of religious faith in and reliance upon a Supreme Being "bear no true resemblance to the unquestioned religious exercise that the State of New York has sponsored in this instance." ... [I]s the Court suggesting that the Constitution permits judges and Congressmen and Presidents to join in prayer, but prohibits school children from doing so?} ...

I do not believe that this Court, or the Congress, or the President has by the actions and practices I have mentioned established an "official religion" in violation of the Constitution. And I do not believe the State of New York has done so in this case. What each has done has been to recognize and to follow the deeply entrenched and highly cherished spiritual traditions of our Nation—traditions which come down to us from those who almost two hundred years ago avowed their "firm Reliance on the Protection of divine Providence" when they proclaimed [in the Declaration of Independence] the freedom and independence of this brave new world....

[Justice Frankfurter and Justice White took no part in the decision of this case.]

d. Policy—Need To Avoid Religious Strife

Basic argument: "The First Amendment should be read to prohibit this sort of government action, because such action might otherwise lead to unacceptable levels of religious strife by _____."

1. "The [Framers] knew the anguish, hardship and bitter strife that could come when zealous religious groups struggled with one another to obtain the Government's stamp of approval .... The First Amendment was added to the Constitution to stand as a guarantee that neither the power nor the prestige of the Federal Government would be used to control, support or influence the kinds of prayer the American people can say ...." *Engel v. Vitale.*

"[The Bill Establishing a Provision for the Teachers of the Christian Religion] will destroy that moderation and harmony which the forbearance of our laws to intermeddle with Religion, has produced amongst its several sects. Torrents of blood have been spilt in the old world, by vain attempts of the secular arm to extinguish Religious discord, by proscribing all difference in Religious opinions." James Madison, *Memorial and Remonstrance Against Religious Assessments.*

"Partisans of parochial schools ... will inevitably champion this cause and promote political action to achieve their goals. Those who oppose state aid ... will inevitably respond and employ all of the usual political campaign techniques to prevail. Candidates will be forced to declare and voters to choose.... Ordinarily political debate and division ... are normal and healthy manifestations of our democratic system of government, but political division along religious lines was one of the principal evils against which the First Amendment was intended to protect." *Lemon v. Kurtzman.*

"[G]overnment establishment of religion is inextricably linked with conflict. In our own history, the turmoil thus produced has led to a rejection of the idea that government should subsidize religious education ...." *Mitchell v. Helms* (Souter, J., dissenting).

"The Framers and the citizens of their time intended ... to guard against the civic divisiveness that follows when the Government weighs in on one side of religious debate; nothing does a better job of roiling society, a point that needed no explanation to the descendants of English Puritans and Cavaliers (or Massachusetts Puritans and Baptists)." *McCreary County v. ACLU* (Souter, J., dissenting).

2. Response to 1: Such speculation is sheer guesswork; there's no reason to think that this particular government action does indeed cause divisiveness, because _____.

"[T]his Court has not held that political divisiveness alone can serve to invalidate otherwise permissible conduct.... The District Court stated that the inclusion of the crèche for the 40 years [that it has been erected] has been 'marked by no apparent dissension' and that the display has had a 'calm history.' Curiously, it went on to hold that the political divisiveness engendered by this lawsuit was evidence of excessive entanglement. A litigant cannot, by the very act of commencing a lawsuit, however, create the appearance of divisiveness and then exploit it as evidence of entanglement." *Lynch v. Donnelly,* 465 U.S. 668, 684 (1984); *see also Aguilar v. Felton,* 473 U.S. 402, 429 (1985) (O'Connor, J., dissenting) (arguing likewise as to a remedial education funding program).

"Professor Sullivan defends the parochial school aid cases on the ground that '[a]ll religions gain from the settlement of the war of all sects against all....' But nowhere does she explain why giving advantages to secular viewpoints over religious viewpoints is necessary to the achievement of civic peace. The 'war of all sects against all' is more plausibly averted by a universal principle of equal treatment, where none is permitted to gain an advantage through the force of government. To permit religious choices only at the cost of forfeiting an equal share in public goods is not freedom of religion." Michael W. McConnell, *Religious Freedom at a Crossroads,* 59 U. Chi. L. Rev. 115, 132-133 (1992).

3. Response to 1: Striking down this government action will cause more religious strife than the action itself would, because _____.

"The Founders of our Republic knew the fearsome potential of sectarian religious belief to generate civil dissension and civil strife. And they also knew that nothing, absolutely nothing, is so inclined to foster among religious believers of various faiths a toleration—no, an affection—for one another than voluntarily joining in prayer together, to the God whom they all worship and seek.... To deprive our society of that important unifying mechanism, in order to spare the nonbeliever what seems to me the minimal inconvenience of standing or even sitting in respectful nonparticipation, is as senseless in policy as it is unsupported in law." *Lee v. Weisman* (Scalia, J., dissenting).

"[C]hurch and religious groups in the United States have long exerted powerful political pressures ... on subjects as diverse as slavery, war, gambling, drinking, prostitution, marriage, and education. To view such religious activity as suspect ... might be inconsistent with first amendment freedoms of religious and political expression—and might not even succeed in keeping religious controversy out of public life, given the 'political ruptures caused by the alienation of segments of the religious community.'" Laurence Tribe, *American Constitutional Law* 866-67 (1st ed. 1978), quoted in *McDaniel v. Paty* (Brennan, J., concurring in the judgment).

"[The endorsement test] exacerbates religious division and discord by heightening the sense of grievance over symbolic injuries. When religious symbols are upheld, the judicial imprimatur adds to the injury (especially when the standard applied is that of the putative 'objective observer'—implying that the losers are not 'objective'). When religious symbols are driven from the public square, this alienates a different but equally sincere segment of the population. Does anyone believe that the annual outbreak of lawsuits over the symbols of the December holidays advances the cause of religious harmony or civic understanding? When a constitutional doctrine aggravates the very problem it is supposed to solve, without offering hope for resolution, it should be replaced." McConnell, *supra*, at 192-93.

4. Rebuttal to 3: The supposed hostility that striking down the government action would create is overstated, or shouldn't be considered in the Establishment Clause analysis, because _____.

"[T]o apply the Establishment Clause alienates those who wish to see a tighter bond between religion and state.... (I would vigorously deny, however, any claim that the Establishment Clause disfavors the much broader class of persons for whom religion is a necessary and important part of life.) But ... even this dissatisfaction is tempered by the knowledge that society is adhering to a fixed rule of neutrality rather than rejecting a particular expression of religious belief." *Marsh v. Chambers* (Brennan, J., dissenting).

5. Response to 1: Even the goal of preventing sectarian strife does not justify policies that discriminate against religion, because _____.

"The State's goal of preventing sectarian bickering and strife may not be accomplished by regulating religious speech and political association. The Establishment Clause does not license government to treat religion and those who teach or practice it, simply by virtue of their status as such, as subversive of American ideals and therefore subject to unique disabilities. Government may not ... remove [officeholders] from office merely for making public statements regarding religion, or question whether their legislative actions stem from religious conviction." *McDaniel v. Paty* (Brennan, J., concurring in the judgment).

"[T]he theory that the Court must strike down any supposed benefit to religion that generates political controversy ... was a particularly pernicious doctrine, because it armed opponents of religious interests with an invincible weapon: their mere opposition became a basis for a finding of unconstitutionality. Of course, the political victories of *either* side in such controversies could be divisive; but the doctrine did not—and could not—work both ways. In effect, the doctrine blamed the religious side of any controversy for the controversy." McConnell, *supra*, at 130.

e. *Marsh v. Chambers, 463 U.S. 783 (1983)*

Chief Justice Burger delivered the opinion of the Court....

[A.] The Nebraska Legislature begins each of its sessions with a prayer offered by a chaplain who is chosen biennially by the Executive Board of the Legislative Council and paid out of public funds. Robert E. Palmer, a Presbyterian minister, has served as chaplain since 1965 at a salary of $319.75 per month for each month the legislature is in session. Ernest Chambers is a member of the Nebraska Legislature [who served from 1970 until 2009—ed.] .... Claiming that the Nebraska Legislature's chaplaincy practice violates the Establishment Clause of the First Amendment, he ... [sought] to enjoin enforcement of the practice....

The opening of sessions of legislative and other deliberative public bodies with prayer is deeply embedded in the history and tradition of this country. From colonial times through the founding of the Republic and ever since, the practice of legislative prayer has coexisted with the principles of disestablishment and religious freedom. In the very courtrooms in which the United States District Judge and later three Circuit Judges heard and decided this case, the proceedings opened with an announcement that concluded, "God save the United States and this Honorable Court." The same invocation occurs at all sessions of this Court.

The tradition in many of the Colonies was, of course, linked to an established church, but the Continental Congress, beginning in 1774, adopted the traditional procedure of opening its sessions with a prayer offered by a paid chaplain. Although prayers were not offered during the Constitutional Convention, the First Congress, as one of its early items of business, adopted the policy of selecting a chaplain to open each session with prayer....

On Sept. 25, 1789, three days after Congress authorized the appointment of paid chaplains, final agreement was reached on the language of the Bill of Rights. {Interestingly, Sept. 25, 1789, was also the day that the House resolved to request the President to set aside a Thanksgiving Day to acknowledge "the many signal favors of Almighty God."} Clearly the men who wrote the First Amendment Religion Clause did not view paid legislative chaplains and opening prayers as a violation of that Amendment, for the practice of opening sessions with prayer has continued without interruption ever since that early session of Congress. It has also been followed consistently in most of the states, including Nebraska, where the institution of opening legislative sessions with prayer was adopted even before the State attained statehood.

Standing alone, historical patterns cannot justify contemporary violations of constitutional guarantees, but there is far more here than simply historical patterns. In this context, historical evidence sheds light not only on what the draftsmen intended the Establishment Clause to mean, but also on how they thought that Clause applied to the practice authorized by the First Congress—their actions reveal their intent. An act "passed by the first Congress assembled under the Constitution, many of whose members had taken part in framing that instrument, ... is contemporaneous and weighty evidence of its true meaning." ...

It can hardly be thought that in the same week Members of the First Congress voted to appoint and to pay a Chaplain for each House and also voted to approve the draft of the First Amendment for submission to the states, they intended the Establishment Clause of the Amendment to forbid what they had just declared acceptable.... This unique history leads us to accept the interpretation of the First Amendment draftsmen who saw no real threat to the Establishment Clause arising from a practice of prayer similar to that now challenged....

[B.] Respondent ... argues that we should not rely too heavily on "the advice of the Founding Fathers" because the messages of history often tend to be ambiguous and not relevant to a society far more heterogeneous than that of the Framers. Respondent also points out that John Jay and John Rutledge opposed the motion to begin the first session of the Continental Congress with prayer. {It also could be noted that objections to prayer were raised, apparently successfully, in Pennsylvania while ratification of the Constitution was debated, and that in the 1820s, Madison expressed doubts concerning the chaplaincy practice.}

We do not agree that evidence of opposition to a measure weakens the force of the historical argument; indeed it infuses it with power by demonstrating that the subject was considered carefully and the action not taken thoughtlessly, by force of long tradition and without regard to the problems posed by a pluralistic society. Jay and Rutledge specifically grounded their objection on the fact that the delegates to the Congress "were so divided in religious sentiments ... that [they] could not join in the same act of worship." Their objection was met by Samuel Adams, who stated that "he was no bigot, and could hear a prayer from a gentleman of piety and virtue, who was at the same time a friend to his country." This interchange emphasizes that the delegates did not consider opening prayers as a proselytizing activity or as symbolically placing the government's "official seal of approval on one religious view." ...

In light of the unambiguous and unbroken history of more than 200 years, there can be no doubt that the practice of opening legislative sessions with prayer has become part of the fabric of our society. To invoke Divine guidance on a public body entrusted with making the laws is not, in these circumstances, an "establishment" of religion or a step toward establishment; it is simply a tolerable acknowledgment of beliefs widely held among the people of this country. As Justice Douglas observed, "[w]e are a religious people whose institutions presuppose a Supreme Being." ...

[C.] [1.] Beyond the bare fact that a prayer is offered, ... [the challengers argue] that a clergyman of only one denomination—Presbyterian—has been selected for 16 years[.] {In comparison, the First Congress provided for the appointment of two chaplains of different denominations who would alternate between the two chambers on a weekly basis.} ...

We cannot, any more than Members of the Congresses of this century, perceive any suggestion that choosing a clergyman of one denomination advances the beliefs of a particular church. To the contrary, the evidence indicates that Palmer was reappointed because his performance and personal qualities were acceptable to the body appointing him.

Palmer was not the only clergyman heard by the Legislature; guest chaplains have officiated at the request of various legislators and as substitutes during Palmer's absences. Absent proof that the chaplain's reappointment stemmed from an impermissible motive, we conclude that his long tenure does not in itself conflict with the Establishment Clause.

[2.] Nor is the compensation of the chaplain from public funds a reason to invalidate the Nebraska Legislature's chaplaincy; remuneration is grounded in historic practice initiated, as we noted earlier, by the same Congress that adopted the Establishment Clause .... The Continental Congress paid its chaplain, as did some of the states....

[3.] {[The challengers also note that] the prayers are in the Judeo-Christian tradition.} {Although some of his earlier prayers were often explicitly Christian, Palmer removed all references to Christ after a 1980 complaint from a Jewish legislator.} Weighed against the historical background, these factors do not serve to invalidate Nebraska's practice....

The content of the prayer is not of concern to judges where, as here, there is no indication that the prayer opportunity has been exploited to proselytize or advance any one, or to disparage any other, faith or belief. That being so, it is not for us to embark on a sensitive evaluation or to parse the content of a particular prayer....

[The concern] that to have prayer in this context risks the beginning of the establishment the Founding Fathers feared ... is not well founded .... "It is of course true that great consequences can grow from small beginnings, but the measure of constitutional adjudication is the ability and willingness to distinguish between real threat and mere shadow." The unbroken practice for two centuries in the National Congress, for more than a century in Nebraska and in many other states, gives abundant assurance that there is no real threat "while this Court sits." ...

Justice Brennan, with whom Justice Marshall joins, dissenting....

[A.] [S]ome twenty years ago, in a concurring opinion in one of the cases striking down official prayer and ceremonial Bible reading in the public schools, I came very close to endorsing essentially the result reached by the Court today. Nevertheless, after much reflection, I have come to the conclusion that I was wrong then and that the Court is wrong today....

The principles of "separation" and "neutrality" implicit in the Establishment Clause serve many purposes. Four of these are particularly relevant here.

The first ... is to guarantee the individual right to conscience. The right to conscience ... [is] implicated when the government requires individuals to support the practices of a faith with which they do not agree....

The second purpose of separation and neutrality is to keep the state from interfering in the essential autonomy of religious life, either by taking upon itself the decision of religious issues, or by unduly involving itself in the supervision of religious institutions or officials.

The third purpose of separation and neutrality is to prevent the trivialization and degradation of religion by too close an attachment to the organs of government....

Finally, the principles of separation and neutrality help assure that essentially religious issues, precisely because of their importance and sensitivity, not become the occasion for battle in the political arena.... With regard to matters that are essentially religious, ... the Establishment Clause seeks that there should be no political battles, and that no American should at any point feel alienated from his government because that government has declared or acted upon some "official" or "authorized" point of view on a matter of religion. {It is [true that] the Establishment Clause alienates those who wish to see a tighter bond between religion and state.... But I would submit that even this dissatisfaction is tempered by the knowledge that society is adhering to a fixed rule of neutrality rather than rejecting a particular expression of religious belief.} ...

Even before the First Amendment was written, the Framers of the Constitution broke with the practice of the Articles of Confederation and many state constitutions, and did not invoke the name of God in the document. This "omission of a reference to the Deity was not inadvertent; nor did it remain unnoticed." Moreover, Thomas Jefferson and Andrew Jackson, during their respective terms as President, both refused on Establishment Clause grounds to declare national days of thanksgiving or fasting. {Jefferson expressed his views as follows:

> I consider the government of the United States as interdicted by the Constitution from intermeddling with religious institutions, their doctrines, discipline, or exercises.... I do not believe it is for the interest of religion to invite the civil magistrate to direct its exercises, its discipline, or its doctrine.... Every religious society has a right to determine for itself the times for [fasting and prayer], and the objects proper for them, according to their own particular tenets; and the right can never be safer than in their hands, where the Constitution has deposited it.}

And James Madison, writing subsequent to his own Presidency on essentially the very issue we face today, stated: ...

> ... The Constitution of the U.S. forbids everything like an establishment of a national religion. The law appointing Chaplains establishes a religious worship for the national representatives, to be performed by Ministers of religion, elected by a majority of them; and these are to be paid out of the national taxes. Does not this involve the principle of a national establishment, applicable to a provision for a religious worship for the Constituent as well as of the representative Body, approved by the majority, and conducted by Ministers of religion paid by the entire nation.

Legislative prayer clearly violates the principles of neutrality and separation that are embedded within the Establishment Clause.... It intrudes on the right to conscience by forcing some legislators either to participate in a "prayer opportunity," with which they are in basic disagreement, or to make their disagreement a matter of public comment by declining to participate. It forces all residents of the State to support a religious exercise that may be contrary to their own beliefs.

It requires the State to commit itself on fundamental theological issues. It has the potential for degrading religion by allowing a religious call to worship to be intermeshed with a secular call to order. And it injects religion into the political sphere by creating the potential that each and every selection of a chaplain, or consideration of a particular prayer, or even reconsideration of the practice itself, will provoke a political battle along religious lines and ultimately alienate some religiously identified group of citizens....

[B.] I agree that historical practice is "of considerable import in the interpretation of abstract constitutional language." This is a case, however, in which—absent the Court's invocation of history—there would be no question that the practice at issue was unconstitutional. And despite the surface appeal of the Court's argument, there are at least three reasons why specific historical practice should not in this case override that clear constitutional imperative. {Indeed, the sort of historical argument made by the Court should be advanced with some hesitation in light of certain other skeletons in the congressional closet. See, *e.g.,* An Act for the Punishment of certain Crimes against the United States, § 16, 1 Stat. 116 (1790) (enacted by the First Congress and requiring that persons convicted of certain theft offenses "be publicly whipped, not exceeding thirty-nine stripes"); Act of July 23, 1866, 14 Stat. 216 (reaffirming the racial segregation of the public schools in the District of Columbia; enacted exactly one week after Congress proposed Fourteenth Amendment to the States).}

First, it is significant that the Court's historical argument does not rely on the legislative history of the Establishment Clause itself. Indeed, that formal history is profoundly unilluminating on this and most other subjects. Rather, the Court assumes that the Framers of the Establishment Clause would not have themselves authorized a practice that they thought violated the guarantees contained in the Clause....

[But l]egislators, influenced by the passions and exigencies of the moment, the pressure of constituents and colleagues, and the press of business, do not always pass sober constitutional judgment on every piece of legislation they enact, and this must be assumed to be as true of the Members of the First Congress as any other. Indeed, ... James Madison, who voted for the bill authorizing the payment of the first congressional chaplains, later expressed the view that the practice was unconstitutional .... Madison's later views may not have represented so much a change of *mind* as a change of *role*, from a Member of Congress engaged in the hurley-burley of legislative activity to a detached observer engaged in unpressured reflection. Since the latter role is precisely the one with which this Court is charged, I am not at all sure that Madison's later writings should be any less influential in our deliberations than his earlier vote.

Second, the Court's analysis treats the First Amendment simply as an Act of Congress, as to whose meaning the intent of Congress is the single touchstone. Both the Constitution and its Amendments, however, became supreme law only by virtue of their ratification by the States, and the understanding of the States should be as relevant to our analysis as the understanding of Congress. ... [The] enactment [of the Bill of Rights] was forced upon Congress by a number of the States as a condition for their ratification of the original Constitution. To treat any practice authorized by the First Congress as presumptively consistent with the Bill of Rights is therefore somewhat akin to treating any action of a party to a contract as presumptively consistent with the terms of the contract....

{As a practical matter, "we know practically nothing about what went on in the state legislatures" during the process of ratifying the Bill of Rights.

Moreover, looking to state practices is, as the Court admits, of dubious relevance because the Establishment Clause did not originally apply to the States. Nevertheless, these difficulties give us no warrant to give controlling weight on the constitutionality of a specific practice to the collateral acts of the Members of Congress who proposed the Bill of Rights to the States.}

Finally, ... the Constitution is not a static document whose meaning on every detail is fixed for all time by the life experience of the Framers.... To be truly faithful to the Framers, "our use of the history of their time must limit itself to broad purposes, not specific practices." Our primary task must be to translate "the majestic generalities of the Bill of Rights, conceived as part of the pattern of liberal government in the eighteenth century, into concrete restraints on officials dealing with the problems of the twentieth century...."

The inherent adaptability of the Constitution and its amendments is particularly important with respect to the Establishment Clause. "[O]ur religious composition makes us a vastly more diverse people than were our forefathers.... In the face of such profound changes, practices which may have been objectionable to no one in the time of Jefferson and Madison may today be highly offensive to many persons, the deeply devout and the nonbelievers alike."

President John Adams issued during his Presidency a number of official proclamations calling on all Americans to engage in Christian prayer. Justice Story, in his treatise on the Constitution, contended that the "real object" of the First Amendment "was, not to countenance, much less to advance Mahometanism, Judaism, or infidelity, by prostrating Christianity; but to exclude all rivalry among Christian sects...." Whatever deference Adams' actions and Story's views might once have deserved in this Court, the Establishment Clause must now be read in a very different light....

[C.] [T]he Court [also] seems to regard legislative prayer as at most a *de minimis* violation, somehow unworthy of our attention.

I frankly do not know what should be the proper disposition of features of our public life such as "God save the United States and this Honorable Court," "In God We Trust," "One Nation Under God," and the like. I might well adhere to the view expressed in *Schempp* that such mottos are consistent with the Establishment Clause, not because their import is *de minimis*, but because they have lost any true religious significance....

[But] legislative prayer, unlike mottos with fixed wordings, can easily turn narrowly and obviously sectarian.... More fundamentally, ... *any* practice of legislative prayer, even if it might look "nonsectarian" to nine Justices of the Supreme Court, will inevitably and continuously involve the State in one or another religious debate. Prayer is serious business—serious theological business—and it is not a mere "acknowledgment of beliefs widely held among the people of this country" for the State to immerse itself in that business ....

[D.] The argument is made occasionally that a strict separation of religion and state robs the Nation of its spiritual identity. I believe quite the contrary.... [T]he judgment of the Establishment Clause is that neutrality by the organs of *government* on questions of religion is both possible and imperative.... Alexis de Tocqueville ... [observed in the 1830s that "t]he religious atmosphere of ... the United States" [stemmed from "]the complete separation of church and state."]... If the Court had struck down legislative prayer today, it would likely have stimulated a furious reaction. But it would also ... have invigorated both the "spirit of religion" and the "spirit of freedom." ...

Justice Stevens, dissenting.

In a democratically elected legislature, the religious beliefs of the chaplain tend to reflect the faith of the majority of the lawmakers' constituents.... Regardless of the motivation of the majority that exercises the power to appoint the chaplain, it seems plain to me that the designation of a member of one religious faith to serve as the sole official chaplain of a state legislature for a period of 16 years constitutes the preference of one faith over another in violation of the Establishment Clause ....

The Court declines to "embark on a sensitive evaluation or to parse the content of a particular prayer." Perhaps it does so because it would be unable to explain away the clearly sectarian content of some of the prayers given by Nebraska's chaplain. {On March 20, 1978, for example, Chaplain Palmer gave the following invocation: "Father in heaven, the suffering and death of your son brought life to the whole world moving our hearts to praise your glory. The power of the cross reveals your concern for the world and the wonder of Christ crucified. [Further details omitted.—ed.]...."} Or perhaps the Court is unwilling to acknowledge that the tenure of the chaplain must inevitably be conditioned on the acceptability of that content to the silent majority....

f. Policy—Original Meaning

Basic argument: "This government action is unconstitutional/constitutional, because _____ shows that the original meaning of the First Amendment is _____, which prohibits/authorizes such an action."

1. "An Act 'passed by the first Congress assembled under the Constitution, many of whose members had taken part in framing that instrument, ... is contemporaneous and weighty evidence of its true meaning.' ... It can hardly be thought that in the same week Members of the First Congress voted to appoint and to pay a chaplain for each House and also voted to approve the draft of the First Amendment for submission to the states, they intended the Establishment Clause of the Amendment to forbid what they had just declared acceptable...." *Marsh v. Chambers.*

"Our Founders were no more willing to let the content of their prayers and their privilege of praying whenever they pleased be influenced by the ballot box than they were to let these vital matters of personal conscience depend upon the succession of monarchs. The First Amendment was added to the Constitution to stand as a guarantee that neither the power nor the prestige of the Federal Government would be used to control, support or influence the kinds of prayer the American people can say ...." *Engel v. Vitale*.

"I continue to adhere to the view that to give concrete meaning to the Establishment Clause 'the line we must draw between the permissible and the impermissible is one which accords with history and faithfully reflects the understanding of the Founding Fathers' .... In sharp contrast to the 'undeviating acceptance given religious tax exemptions from our earliest days as a Nation,' subsidy of sectarian educational institutions became embroiled in bitter controversies very soon after the Nation was formed...." *Lemon v. Kurtzman* (Brennan, J., concurring).

"We have previously recognized the importance of interpreting the Religion Clauses in light of their history. The historical evidence casts doubt on the Court's current interpretation of the Free Exercise Clause." *City of Boerne v. Flores* (O'Connor, J., dissenting) (using "history" here in the sense of "original meaning").

2. Response to 1: The original meaning of the First Amendment is actually something quite different, namely _____, and this government action is permissible/prohibited under this meaning.

"Even assuming that the Virginia debate on the so-called 'Assessment Controversy' was indicative of the principles embodied in the Establishment Clause, this incident hardly compels the dissent's conclusion that government must actively discriminate against religion. The dissent's historical discussion glosses over the fundamental characteristic of the Virginia assessment bill that sparked the controversy: The assessment was to be imposed for the support of clergy in the performance of their function of teaching religion." *Rosenberger v. Rector* (Thomas, J., concurring).

"Had the understanding in the period surrounding the ratification of the Bill of Rights been that the various forms of accommodation discussed by the dissent were constitutionally required (either by State Constitutions or by the Federal Constitution), it would be surprising not to find a single state or federal case refusing to enforce a generally applicable statute because of its failure to make accommodation." *City of Boerne v. Flores* (Scalia, J., concurring).

3. Response to 1: It's a mistake to rely too heavily on this particular source in determining the original meaning, because _____.

"[T]he Court's historical argument does not rely on the legislative history of the Establishment Clause itself.... Rather, the Court assumes that the Framers of the Establishment Clause would not have themselves authorized a practice that they thought violated the guarantees contained in the clause.... [But l]egislators, influenced by the passions and exigencies of the moment, the pressure of constituents and colleagues, and the press of business, do not always pass sober constitutional judgment on every piece of legislation they enact, and this must be assumed to be as true of the members of the First Congress as any other." *Marsh* (Brennan, J., dissenting).

"[T]he Court's analysis treats the First Amendment simply as an Act of

Congress, as to whose meaning the intent of Congress is the single touchstone. Both the Constitution and its Amendments, however, became supreme law only by virtue of their ratification by the States, and the understanding of the States should be as relevant to our analysis as the understanding of Congress.... [There is] no warrant to give controlling weight on the constitutionality of a specific practice to the collateral acts of the Members of Congress who proposed the Bill of Rights to the States." *Id.*

"[T]he views of one man [Madison] do not establish the original understanding of the First Amendment." *Rosenberger* (Thomas, J., concurring).

4. Response to 1: The original meaning is unclear on this point, because _____, so we should look to other arguments (such as _____) rather than relying on original meaning.

5. Response to 1: Whatever the First Amendment might have meant in 1787, it may mean something different now, because _____ (*e.g.*, because we're now a more religiously diverse country, because the adoption of the Equal Protection Clause requires extra sensitivity to religious equality, or because government now affects people's lives much more).

"[T]he practices that were in place at the time any particular guarantee was enacted into the Constitution do not necessarily fix forever the meaning of that guarantee.... Our primary task must be to translate 'the majestic generalities of the Bill of Rights, conceived as part of the pattern of liberal government in the eighteenth century, into concrete restraints on officials dealing with the problems of the twentieth century....' '[O]ur religious composition makes us a vastly more diverse people than were our forefathers.... In the face of such profound changes, practices which may have been objectionable to no one in the time of Jefferson and Madison may today be highly offensive to many persons, the deeply devout and the nonbelievers alike.'" *Marsh v. Chambers* (Brennan, J. dissenting).

"I read ['religion'] to include newly emerged beliefs [such as atheistic or agnostic beliefs] that were not socially significant in the Founders' time but that fall easily into a category—beliefs about the nature of God—that we know the Founders meant to protect." Douglas Laycock, *Religious Liberty as Liberty,* 7 J. Contemp. Leg. Issues 313, 339 (1996).

"The overriding objective of the Religion Clauses was to render the new federal government irrelevant to the religious lives of the people. This objective has been vastly complicated by the emergence of the welfare-regulatory state. During the early days of the Republic, ... if the federal government simply took no actions directed at religion, the objectives of the Religion Clauses would [usually] be fulfilled. As the powers of the federal government expanded and the coverage of the First Amendment was extended to the states, however, this ceased to be true.

"The government now fosters a vast sector of publicly-supported, privately-administered social welfare programs, and the allocation of resources in this sector inevitably affects religion. The government also now regulates the non-profit sphere, and these regulations similarly affect religion. Where once the government could treat religious institutions with benign neglect, the welfare-regulatory state requires a substantive policy toward religion that will preserve the conditions of religious freedom without hobbling the activist state." Michael W. McConnell, *Religious Freedom at a Crossroads,* 59 U. Chi. L. Rev. 115, 136-37 (1992).

"[D]oes the word 'prohibit' in the First Amendment limit the Free Exercise Clause to ... direct prohibitions ... aimed at religion? I am not persuaded that a 1791 audience necessarily would have understood the term 'prohibitions' so narrowly; but even if it would have, we cannot fulfill the purposes of the Free Exercise Clause under modern conditions without adapting to the vastly expanded role that government now plays in our lives. Like every other constitutional protection, the Free Exercise Clause should be understood to be violated by unconstitutional conditions as well as by direct restraints." *Id.* at 171.

"The Court's analysis [in the neutral funding cases] failed to recognize the effect of the change in governmental roles [since the 1780s assessment controversy]. When the government provides no financial support to the nonprofit sector *except for churches* [as in the assessment controversy], it aids religion. But when the government provides financial support to the entire nonprofit sector, religious and nonreligious institutions alike, on the basis of objective criteria, it does *not* aid religion. It aids higher education, health care, or child care; it is neutral to religion. Indeed, to deny equal support to a college, hospital, or orphanage on the ground that it conveys religious ideas is to penalize it for being religious." *Id.* at 184.

g. *Policy—Propriety of Nonpreferential Support for Religion*

Basic argument: "The Establishment Clause ought to be read as barring only discrimination among religions or denominations, because _____; favoritism for religion in general is constitutional."

1. "[A]s reflected by [Madison's] actions on the floor of the House in 1789, [Madison] saw the Amendment as designed to prohibit the establishment of a national religion, and perhaps to prevent discrimination among sects. He did not see it as requiring neutrality on the part of government between religion and irreligion." *Wallace v. Jaffree,* 472 U.S. 38, 98 (1985) (Rehnquist, J., dissenting).

2. Response to 1: This is in unsound in principle, because _____.

"Nonpreferential establishment was rejected in the drafting of the Religion Clauses, and eventually in all the states. I think history is clearer on this than history usually is on most things." Douglas Laycock, *Religious Liberty as Liberty,* 7 J. Contemp. Leg. Issues 313, 341 (1996).

3. Response to 1: The proposed action in fact does prefer a particular religion or denomination, not just religion in general, by _____.

"[P]rayer is inescapably sectarian; there simply is no such thing as a 'nonsectarian prayer' that would prove equally acceptable to persons of all religious faiths and beliefs." Robert M. O'Neil, *Who Says You Can't Pray?,* 3 Va. J. Soc. Pol'y & L. 347, 367 (1996).

h. *Policy—Irrelevance of De Minimis Government Action*

Basic argument: "This government action is permissible, because any deviation from neutrality, any endorsement, or any other possible problem here is so small, given that _____."

1. "[The concern] that to have prayer in this context risks the beginning of the establishment the Founding Fathers feared ... is not well founded .... 'It is of course true that great consequences can grow from small beginnings, but the measure of constitutional adjudication is the ability and willingness to distinguish between real threat and mere shadow.'" *Marsh v. Chambers.*

"[O]f course nothing in the decision reached here ... is inconsistent with the fact that school children and others are officially encouraged to express love for our country by reciting historical documents such as the Declaration of Independence which contain references to the Deity or by singing officially espoused anthems which include the composer's professions of faith in a Supreme Being, or with the fact that there are many manifestations in our public life of belief in God. Such patriotic or ceremonial occasions bear no true resemblance to the unquestioned religious exercise that the State of New York has sponsored in this instance." *Engel v. Vitale.*

2. Response to 1: Actually, the deviation from proper constitutional norms is quite great, because _____.

"[L]egislative prayer, unlike mottos with fixed wordings, can easily turn narrowly and obviously sectarian.... More fundamentally, however, *any* practice of legislative prayer, even if it might look 'non-sectarian' to nine Justices of the Supreme Court, will inevitably and continuously involve the state in one or another religious debate. Prayer is serious business—serious theological business—and it is not a mere 'acknowledgment of beliefs widely held among the people of this country' for the State to immerse itself in that business." *Marsh* (Brennan, J., dissenting).

3. Response to 1: Even if the deviation here is small, this sets a bad precedent for the future, because _____.

"To those who may subscribe to the view that because the Regents' official prayer is so brief and general there can be no danger to religious freedom in its governmental establishment, however, it may be appropriate to say in the words of James Madison, ... '[I]t is proper to take alarm at the first experiment on our liberties....'" *Engel.*

See also Policy—Slippery Slope, p. 214.

4. Rebuttal to 3: Allowing litigation over such small matters ultimately does more harm than good, because _____.

"Courts should not encourage the proliferation of litigation by offering the false hope that perfect neutrality can be achieved through judicial fine-tuning. Judicial scrutiny should be reserved for cases in which a particular religious position is given such public prominence that the overall message becomes one of conformity ...." Michael W. McConnell, *Religious Freedom at a Crossroads,* 59 U. Chi. L. Rev. 115, 193 (1992).

i. The Ten Commandments Cases (McCreary County v. ACLU, 545 U.S. 844 (2005), and Van Orden v. Perry, 545 U.S. 677 (2005))

i. Summary

In 2005, the Court decided two cases involving Ten Commandments displays, *McCreary County v. ACLU* and *Van Orden v. Perry*.

McCreary involved a display that began (in 1999) as a standalone posting of the Ten Commandments in a courthouse, was replaced with the Ten Commandments joined by several American historical documents that had a religious tone, and was then replaced with the Ten Commandments joined by a broader range of historical documents. The Court struck this down by a 5-4 vote, chiefly on the grounds that the primary purpose of the displays was to endorse the Ten Commandments, rather than to show a wide array of historical legal sources that happened to include the Ten Commandments. (See p. 855 for more facts and the purpose analysis.)

Van Orden involved a park near the Texas state capitol in which many monuments were installed; one monument, donated to the state by the Fraternal Order of Eagles in 1961, displayed the Ten Commandments. (See p. 822 for more facts.) The Court upheld this, also by a 5-4 vote; Justice Breyer was the only Justice who was in the majority both times.

The decisions were nearly 40,000 words long, and quite fractured. To make them manageable, I've edited them down, and split them into sections, by topic. Here is a rough summary of the Justices' positions, coupled with references to the excerpts which discuss those positions:

Souter Stevens O'Connor Ginsburg	strike down both	(1) (a) The Framers understood the Establishment Clause as mandating government neutrality towards religion, and (b) the endorsement test properly implements that neutrality (even if the Framers might not have expected this). (2) The displays do endorse religion.	(1) Souter & Stevens in *Van Orden*, O'Connor in *McCreary* (p. 815). (2) Souter & Stevens in *Van Orden* (p. 806).
Rehnquist Scalia Kennedy Thomas	uphold both	This is a traditional practice and therefore constitutional, under a *Marsh v. Chambers*-like rationale.	Rehnquist in *Van Orden* (p. 822).
Breyer	uphold one, strike down other	(1) The Establishment Clause was aimed at preventing religious divisiveness (to which endorsement is relevant), so the risk of divisiveness should be the touchstone. (2) The *McCreary* display endorses religion but the *Van Orden* one doesn't.	(1) Breyer in *Van Orden* (p. 826). (2) Breyer in *Van Orden* (p. 804).
Scalia Rehnquist Thomas		The original meaning of the Establishment Clause lets government make religious statements that endorse monotheism.	Scalia in *McCreary* (p. 809).
Thomas		(1) The original meaning of the Fourteenth Amendment bars incorporating the Establishment Clause against the states. (2) The original meaning of the Establishment Clause is to ban coercion of religious practice.	(1) Thomas in *Newdow* (p. 836). (2) Thomas in *Van Orden* (p. 814).

Thus, Stevens, O'Connor, Souter, Ginsburg, and Breyer were in the majority in *McCreary*, and Rehnquist, Scalia, Kennedy, Thomas, and Breyer were in the majority in *Van Orden*; their opinions are split up in the book as follows:

(a) The application of the endorsement test, by the five Justices that applied it (Justices Stevens, O'Connor, Souter, and Ginsburg to reach one result, and Justice Breyer to reach another), p. 804.

(b) The discussions of the original meaning of the Establishment Clause, including whether the endorsement test captures that original meaning, p. 809.

(c) Chief Justice Rehnquist's *Marsh v. Chambers*-like tradition approach, p. 822.

(d) Justice Breyer's divisiveness approach, p. 826.

(e) The discussion of the role that government purpose (rather than just the action's effect) should play in the analysis, p. 855.

ii. Applying the Endorsement Test (Van Orden)

[Facts, from Chief Justice Rehnquist's plurality opinion:]

The 22 acres surrounding the Texas State Capitol contain 17 monuments and 21 historical markers commemorating the "people, ideals, and events that compose Texan identity." {The monuments are: Heroes of the Alamo, Hood's Brigade, Confederate Soldiers, Volunteer Fireman, Terry's Texas Rangers, Texas Cowboy, Spanish-American War, Texas National Guard, Ten Commandments, Tribute to Texas School Children, Texas Pioneer Woman, The Boy Scouts' Statue of Liberty Replica, Pearl Harbor Veterans, Korean War Veterans, Soldiers of World War I, Disabled Veterans, and Texas Peace Officers.} The monolith challenged here stands 6-feet high and 3½-feet wide. It is located to the north of the Capitol building, between the Capitol and the Supreme Court building. Its primary content is the text of the Ten Commandments. An eagle grasping the American flag, an eye inside of a pyramid, and two small tablets with what appears to be an ancient script are carved above the text of the Ten Commandments. Below the text are two Stars of David and the superimposed Greek letters Chi [X] and Rho [P], which represent Christ. The bottom of the monument bears the inscription "PRESENTED TO THE PEOPLE AND YOUTH OF TEXAS BY THE FRATERNAL ORDER OF EAGLES OF TEXAS 1961."

The legislative record surrounding the State's acceptance of the monument from the Eagles—a national social, civic, and patriotic organization—is limited to legislative journal entries. After the monument was accepted, the State selected a site for the monument based on the recommendation of the state organization responsible for maintaining the Capitol grounds. The Eagles paid the cost of erecting the monument, the dedication of which was presided over by two state legislators....

Justice Breyer, concurring in the judgment....

[Justice Breyer's opinion focused chiefly on whether government action is religiously divisive; but in the process Justice Breyer inquired into whether the action endorsed religion, since in his view such endorsement could be religiously divisive.—ed.]

The case before us is a borderline case.... [T]he Commandments' text undeniably has a religious message, invoking, indeed emphasizing, the [Deity]. On the other hand, focusing on the text of the Commandments alone cannot conclusively resolve this case. Rather, to determine the message that the text here conveys, we must examine how the text is *used*. And that inquiry requires us to consider the context of the display.

In certain contexts, a display of the tablets of the Ten Commandments can convey not simply a religious message but also a secular moral message (about proper standards of social conduct). And in certain contexts, a display of the tablets can also convey a historical message (about a historic relation between those standards and the law)—a fact that helps to explain the display of those tablets in dozens of courthouses throughout the Nation, including the Supreme Court of the United States.

Here the tablets have been used as part of a display that communicates not simply a religious message, but a secular message as well. The circumstances surrounding the display's placement on the capitol grounds and its physical setting suggest that the State itself intended the latter, nonreligious aspects of the tablets' message to predominate. And the monument's 40-year history on the Texas state grounds indicates that that has been its effect.

The group that donated the monument, the Fraternal Order of Eagles, a private civic (and primarily secular) organization, while interested in the religious aspect of the Ten Commandments, sought to highlight the Commandments' role in shaping civic morality as part of that organization's efforts to combat juvenile delinquency. The Eagles' consultation with a committee composed of members of several faiths in order to find a nonsectarian text underscores the group's ethics-based motives. The tablets, as displayed on the monument, prominently acknowledge that the Eagles donated the display, a factor which, though not sufficient, thereby further distances the State itself from the religious aspect of the Commandments' message.

The physical setting of the monument, moreover, suggests little or nothing of the sacred. The monument sits in a large park containing 17 monuments and 21 historical markers, all designed to illustrate the "ideals" of those who settled in Texas and of those who have lived there since that time.

The setting does not readily lend itself to meditation or any other religious activity. But it does provide a context of history and moral ideals. It (together with the display's inscription about its origin) communicates to visitors that the State sought to reflect moral principles, illustrating a relation between ethics and law that the State's citizens, historically speaking, have endorsed. That is to say, the context suggests that the State intended the display's moral message—an illustrative message reflecting the historical "ideals" of Texans—to predominate.

If these factors provide a strong, but not conclusive, indication that the

Commandments' text on this monument conveys a predominantly secular message, a further factor is determinative here. As far as I can tell, 40 years passed in which the presence of this monument, legally speaking, went unchallenged (until the single legal objection raised by petitioner). And I am not aware of any evidence suggesting that this was due to a climate of intimidation.

Hence, those 40 years suggest more strongly than can any set of formulaic tests that few individuals, whatever their system of beliefs, are likely to have understood the monument as amounting, in any significantly detrimental way, to a government effort to favor a particular religious sect, primarily to promote religion over nonreligion, to "engage in" any "religious practic[e]," to "compel" any "religious practic[e]," or to "work deterrence" of any "religious belief." Those 40 years suggest that the public visiting the capitol grounds has considered the religious aspect of the tablets' message as part of what is a broader moral and historical message reflective of a cultural heritage....

Justice Souter, with whom Justice Stevens and Justice Ginsburg join[, and with whom Justice O'Connor largely agreed], dissenting....

A governmental display of an obviously religious text cannot be squared with [the neutrality that the Establishment Clause generally requires], except in a setting that plausibly indicates that the statement is not placed in view with a predominant purpose on the part of government either to adopt the religious message or to urge its acceptance by others....

"... [T]he first part of the [Ten] Commandments concerns the religious duties of believers: worshipping the Lord God alone, avoiding idolatry, not using the Lord's name in vain, and observing the Sabbath Day." ... [T]he Ten Commandments constitute a religious statement, ... their message is inherently religious, and ... the purpose of singling them out in a display is clearly the same. {[T]he religious purpose was evident on the part of the donating organization.... [The Fraternal Order of Eagles stated] in a letter written to Kentucky when a [similar] monument was donated to that Commonwealth[,] "Most of today's younger generation either have not seen the Ten Commandments or have not been taught them. In our opinion the youth of today is in dire need of learning the simple laws of God ...[."] ....} ... To ensure that the religious nature of the monument is clear to even the most casual passerby, the word "Lord" appears in all capital letters (as does the word "am"), so that the most eye-catching segment of the quotation is the declaration "I AM the LORD thy God." ...

To drive the religious point home, and identify the message as religious to any viewer who failed to read the text, the engraved quotation is framed by religious symbols: two tablets with what appears to be ancient script on them, two Stars of David, and the superimposed Greek letters Chi and Rho as the familiar monogram of Christ.... {That the monument also surrounds the text of the Commandments with various American symbols (notably the U.S. flag and a bald eagle) only underscores the impermissibility of Texas's actions: by juxtaposing these patriotic symbols with the Commandments and other religious signs, the monument sends the message that being American means being religious ... [and] subscribing to the Commandments ....} ...

Texas seeks to take advantage of the recognition that visual symbol and written text can manifest a secular purpose in secular company, when it argues that its monument ... is not alone and ought to be viewed as only 1 among 17 placed on the 22 acres surrounding the state capitol. Texas, indeed, says that the Capitol grounds are like a museum for a collection of exhibits, the kind of setting that several Members of the Court have said can render the exhibition of religious artifacts permissible, even though in other circumstances their display would be seen as meant to convey a religious message forbidden to the State. So, for example, the Government of the United States does not violate the Establishment Clause by hanging Giotto's Madonna on the wall of the National Gallery.

But 17 monuments with no common appearance, history, or esthetic role scattered over 22 acres is not a museum, and anyone strolling around the lawn would surely take each memorial on its own terms without any dawning sense that some purpose held the miscellany together more coherently than fortuity and the edge of the grass....

The monument in this case sits on the grounds of the Texas State Capitol. There is something significant in the common term "statehouse" to refer to a state capitol building: it is the civic home of every one of the State's citizens. If neutrality in religion means something, any citizen should be able to visit that civic home without having to confront religious expressions clearly meant to convey an official religious position that may be at odds with his own religion, or with rejection of religion.

Finally, ... I do not see a persuasive argument for constitutionality in the plurality's observation that Van Orden's lawsuit comes "[f]orty years after the monument's erection ...[.]" ... Suing a State over religion puts nothing in a plaintiff's pocket and can take a great deal out, and even with volunteer litigators to supply time and energy, the risk of social ostracism can be powerfully deterrent. I doubt that a slow walk to the courthouse, even one that took 40 years, is much evidentiary help in applying the Establishment Clause.

Justice Stevens, with whom Justice Ginsburg joins, dissenting....

[D]espite the Eagles' best efforts to choose a benign nondenominational text, the Ten Commandments display projects not just a religious, but an inherently sectarian message. There are many distinctive versions of the Decalogue, ascribed to by different religions and even different denominations within a particular faith; to a pious and learned observer, these differences may be of enormous religious significance. {For example, in the Jewish version of the Sixth Commandment God commands: "You shall not murder"; whereas, the King James interpretation of the same command is: "Thou shalt not kill." ... Varying interpretations of this Commandment explain the actions of vegetarians who refuse to eat meat, pacifists who refuse to work for munitions makers, prison officials who refuse to administer lethal injections to death row inmates, and pharmacists who refuse to sell morning-after pills to women....}

{[Likewise, d]espite the Eagles' efforts, not all of the monuments they donated in fact conform to a "universally-accepted" text. Compare, *e.g.*, [the monument in this case] (including the command that "Thou shalt not make to thyself any graven images"), and [the monument in another case] (omitting that command altogether). The distinction represents a critical divide between the Protestant and Catholic faiths. During the Reformation, Protestants destroyed images of the Virgin Mary and of Jesus Christ that were venerated in Catholic churches. Even today there is a notable difference between the imagery in different churches, a difference that may in part be attributable to differing understandings of the meaning of what is the Second Commandment in the King James Bible translation and a portion of the First Commandment in the Catholic translation.}

In choosing to display this version of the Commandments, Texas tells the observer that the State supports this side of the doctrinal religious debate. The reasonable observer, after all, has no way of knowing that this text was the product of a compromise, or that there is a rationale of any kind for the text's selection.[17] The Establishment Clause, if nothing else, forbids government from "specifying details upon which men and women who believe in a benevolent, omnipotent Creator and Ruler of the world are known to differ." *Lee v. Weisman* (Scalia, J., dissenting).

Even if, however, the message of the monument, despite the inscribed text, fairly could be said to represent the belief system of all Judeo-Christians, it would still run afoul of the Establishment Clause by prescribing a compelled code of conduct from one God, namely a Judeo-Christian God, that is rejected by prominent polytheistic sects, such as Hinduism, as well as nontheistic religions, such as Buddhism. And, at the very least, the text of the Ten Commandments impermissibly commands a preference for religion over irreligion.

---

[17] [**Justice Scalia's response** in *McCreary* to Justice Stevens' argument:—ed.] Because there are interpretational differences between faiths and within faiths concerning the meaning and perhaps even the text of the Commandments, Justice Stevens maintains that any display of the text of the Ten Commandments is impermissible because it "invariably places the [government] at the center of a serious sectarian dispute." I think not. The sectarian dispute regarding text, if serious, is not widely known. I doubt that most religious adherents are even aware that there are competing versions with doctrinal consequences (I certainly was not). In any event, the context of the display here could not conceivably cause the viewer to believe that the government was taking sides in a doctrinal controversy.

[**Justice Stevens' rebuttal**:—ed.] Justice Scalia's willingness to dismiss the distinct textual versions adhered to by different faiths in the name of generic "monotheism" based on mere speculation regarding their significance ... serves to reinforce the concern that interjecting government into the religious sphere will offend "adherents who consider the particular advertisement disrespectful."

Any of those bases, in my judgment, would be sufficient to conclude that the message should not be proclaimed by the State of Texas on a permanent monument at the seat of its government.... [A]llowing the seat of government to serve as a stage for the propagation of an unmistakably Judeo-Christian message of piety would have the tendency to make nonmonotheists and nonbelievers "feel like [outsiders] in matters of faith, and [strangers] in the political community." "[D]isplays of this kind inevitably have a greater tendency to emphasize sincere and deeply felt differences among individuals than to achieve an ecumenical goal." {The fact that this particular display has stood unchallenged for over forty years does not suggest otherwise. One need look no further than the deluge of cases flooding lower courts to realize the discord these displays have engendered.} ...

iii. The Debate About Original Meaning

Justice Scalia, with whom ... Chief Justice [Rehnquist] and Justice Thomas join, ... dissenting [in *McCreary County v. ACLU*, voting to uphold the Ten Commandments display]....

[A.] On September 11, 2001 I was attending in Rome, Italy an international conference of judges and lawyers .... That night and the next morning virtually all of the participants watched, in their hotel rooms, the address to the Nation by the President of the United States concerning the murderous attacks upon the Twin Towers and the Pentagon, in which thousands of Americans had been killed. The address ended, as Presidential addresses often do, with the prayer "God bless America." The next afternoon I was approached by one of the judges from a European country, who, after extending his profound condolences for my country's loss, sadly observed "How I wish that the Head of State of my country, at a similar time of national tragedy and distress, could conclude his address 'God bless _____.' It is of course absolutely forbidden."

That is one model of the relationship between church and state—a model spread across Europe by the armies of Napoleon, and reflected in the Constitution of France, which begins "France is [a] ... secular ... Republic." Religion is to be strictly excluded from the public forum.

This is not, and never was, the model adopted by America. George Washington added to the form of Presidential oath prescribed by Art. II, §1, cl. 8, of the Constitution, the concluding words "so help me God." The Supreme Court under John Marshall opened its sessions with the prayer, "God save the United States and this Honorable Court."

The First Congress instituted the practice of beginning its legislative sessions with a prayer. The same week that Congress submitted the Establishment Clause as part of the Bill of Rights for ratification by the States, it enacted legislation providing for paid chaplains in the House and Senate. The day after the First Amendment was proposed, the same Congress that had proposed it requested the President to proclaim "a day of public thanksgiving and prayer, to be observed, by acknowledging, with grateful hearts, the many and signal favours of Almighty God."

President Washington offered the first Thanksgiving Proclamation shortly thereafter, devoting November 26, 1789 on behalf of the American people "to the service of that great and glorious Being who is the beneficent author of all the good that is, that was, or that will be," thus beginning a tradition of offering gratitude to God that continues today. The same Congress also reenacted the Northwest Territory Ordinance of 1787, Article III of which provided: "Religion, morality, and knowledge, being necessary to good government and the happiness of mankind, schools and the means of education shall forever be encouraged." And of course the First Amendment itself accords religion (and no other manner of belief) special constitutional protection.

These actions of our First President and Congress and the Marshall Court were not idiosyncratic; they reflected the beliefs of the period. Those who wrote the Constitution believed that morality was essential to the well-being of society and that encouragement of religion was the best way to foster morality. The "fact that the Founding Fathers believed devotedly that there was a God and that the unalienable rights of man were rooted in Him is clearly evidenced in their writings, from the Mayflower Compact to the Constitution itself."

President Washington opened his Presidency with a prayer, and reminded his fellow citizens at the conclusion of it that "reason and experience both forbid us to expect that National morality can prevail in exclusion of religious principle." President John Adams wrote to the Massachusetts Militia, "we have no government armed with power capable of contending with human passions unbridled by morality and religion.... Our Constitution was made only for a moral and religious people. It is wholly inadequate to the government of any other." Thomas Jefferson concluded his second inaugural address by inviting his audience to pray:

> I shall need, too, the favor of that Being in whose hands we are, who led our fathers, as Israel of old, from their native land and planted them in a country flowing with all the necessaries and comforts of life; who has covered our infancy with His providence and our riper years with His wisdom and power and to whose goodness I ask you to join in supplications with me that He will so enlighten the minds of your servants, guide their councils, and prosper their measures that whatsoever they do shall result in your good, and shall secure to you the peace, friendship, and approbation of all nations.

James Madison, in his first inaugural address, likewise placed his confidence "in the guardianship and guidance of that Almighty Being whose power regulates the destiny of nations, whose blessings have been so conspicuously dispensed to this rising Republic, and to whom we are bound to address our devout gratitude for the past, as well as our fervent supplications and best hopes for the future." {Justice Stevens finds that Presidential inaugural and farewell speeches (which are the only speeches upon which I have relied) do not violate the Establishment Clause only because everyone knows that they express the personal religious views of the speaker, and not government policy. This is a peculiar stance for one who has voted that a student-led invocation at a high school football game and a rabbi-led invocation at a high school graduation did constitute the sort of governmental endorsement of religion that the Establishment Clause forbids. See *Santa Fe Independent School Dist. v. Doe*, 530 U.S. 290 (2000); *Lee v. Weisman*.}

Nor have the views of our people on this matter significantly changed. Presidents continue to conclude the Presidential oath with the words "so help me God." Our legislatures, state and national, continue to open their sessions with prayer led by official chaplains. The sessions of this Court continue to open with the prayer "God save the United States and this Honorable Court." Invocation of the Almighty by our public figures, at all levels of government, remains commonplace. Our coinage bears the motto "IN GOD WE TRUST." And our Pledge of Allegiance contains the acknowledgment that we are a Nation "under God." As one of our Supreme Court opinions rightly observed, "We are a religious people whose institutions presuppose a Supreme Being." *Zorach v. Clauson*, 343 U.S. 306 (1952).

[B.] {[Justice Stevens argues that,} "[R]eliance on early religious proclamations and statements made by the Founders is ... problematic, ... because those views were not espoused at the Constitutional Convention in 1787 nor enshrined in the Constitution's text." But I have not relied upon (as he and the Court in this case do) mere "proclamations and statements" of the Founders. I have relied primarily upon official acts and official proclamations of the United States or of the component branches of its Government ... [or of federal officeholders who] .... spoke in at least a quasi-official capacity ....

The Court and Justice Stevens, by contrast, appeal to no official or even quasi-official action in support of their view of the Establishment Clause—only James Madison's Memorial and Remonstrance Against Religious Assessments, written before the federal Constitution had even been proposed, two letters written by Madison long after he was President, and the quasi-official *inaction* of Thomas Jefferson in refusing to issue a Thanksgiving Proclamation.

The Madison Memorial and Remonstrance, dealing as it does with enforced contribution to religion rather than public acknowledgment of God, is irrelevant; one of the letters is utterly ambiguous as to the point at issue here, and should not be read to contradict Madison's statements in his first inaugural address, quoted earlier; even the other letter does not disapprove public acknowledgment of God, unless one posits (what Madison's own actions as President would contradict) that reference to God contradicts "the equality of *all* religious sects." ... And ... the notoriously self-contradicting Jefferson did not choose to have his nonauthorship of a Thanksgiving Proclamation inscribed on his tombstone. What he did have inscribed was his authorship of the Virginia Statute for Religious Freedom, a governmental act which begins "Whereas Almighty God hath created the mind free ...."

It is no answer for Justice Stevens to say that the understanding that these official and quasi-official actions reflect was not "enshrined in the Constitution's text." The Establishment Clause, upon which Justice Stevens would rely, *was* enshrined in the Constitution's text, and these official actions show *what it meant*.... What is more probative of the meaning of the

Establishment Clause than the actions of the very Congress that proposed it, and of the first President charged with observing it?

[C.] With all of this reality (and much more) staring it in the face, how can the Court *possibly* assert that "the First Amendment mandates governmental neutrality between ... religion and nonreligion," and that "[m]anifesting a purpose to favor ... adherence to religion generally," is unconstitutional? Who says so?

Surely not the words of the Constitution. Surely not the history and traditions that reflect our society's constant understanding of those words. Surely not even the current sense of our society, recently reflected in an Act of Congress adopted *unanimously* by the Senate and with only 5 nays in the House of Representatives criticizing a Court of Appeals opinion that had held "under God" in the Pledge of Allegiance unconstitutional.

Nothing stands behind the Court's assertion that governmental affirmation of the society's belief in God is unconstitutional except the Court's own say-so ....

[D.] [T]he principle that the government cannot favor one religion over another ... is indeed a valid principle where public aid or assistance to religion is concerned, or where the free exercise of religion is at issue, but it necessarily applies in a more limited sense to public acknowledgment of the Creator. If religion in the public forum had to be entirely nondenominational, there could be no religion in the public forum at all. One cannot say the word "God," or "the Almighty," one cannot offer public supplication or thanksgiving, without contradicting the beliefs of some people that there are many gods, or that God or the gods pay no attention to human affairs.

With respect to public acknowledgment of religious belief, it is entirely clear from our Nation's historical practices that the Establishment Clause permits this disregard of polytheists and believers in unconcerned deities, just as it permits the disregard of devout atheists. The Thanksgiving Proclamation issued by George Washington at the instance of the First Congress was scrupulously nondenominational—but it was monotheistic.... [A]cknowledgment of a single Creator and the establishment of a religion ... is ... "a tolerable acknowledgment of beliefs widely held among the people of this country." The three most popular religions in the United States, Christianity, Judaism, and Islam—which combined account for 97.7% of all believers—are monotheistic. All of them, moreover (Islam included), believe that the Ten Commandments were given by God to Moses, and are divine prescriptions for a virtuous life.

Publicly honoring the Ten Commandments is thus indistinguishable, insofar as discriminating against other religions is concerned, from publicly honoring God. Both practices are recognized across such a broad and diverse range of the population—from Christians to Muslims—that they cannot be reasonably understood as a government endorsement of a particular religious viewpoint. {The Establishment Clause would prohibit ... governmental endorsement of a particular version of the Decalogue as authoritative. [But h]ere the display of the Ten Commandments alongside eight secular documents, and the plaque's explanation for their inclusion, make clear that they were not posted to take sides in a theological dispute.}

{The beliefs of [non-monotheists] are entirely protected by the Free Exercise Clause, and by those aspects of the Establishment Clause that do not relate to government acknowledgment of the Creator. Invocation of God despite their beliefs is permitted not because nonmonotheistic religions cease to be religions recognized by the religion clauses of the First Amendment, but because governmental invocation of God is not an establishment....

[I]n the context of public acknowledgments of God there are legitimate *competing* interests: On the one hand, the interest of that minority in not feeling "excluded"; but on the other, the interest of the overwhelming majority of religious believers in being able to give God thanks and supplication *as a people*, and with respect to our national endeavors. Our national tradition has resolved that conflict in favor of the majority. It is not for this Court to change a disposition that accounts, many Americans think, for the phenomenon remarked upon in a quotation attributed to various authors, ... but which I prefer to associate with Charles de Gaulle: "God watches over little children, drunkards, and the United States of America." ...}

{Justice Stevens also appeals to the undoubted fact that some in the founding generation thought that the Religion Clauses of the First Amendment should have a *narrower* meaning, protecting only the Christian religion or perhaps only Protestantism. I am at a loss to see how this helps his case .... (Since most thought the Clause permitted government invocation of monotheism, and some others thought it permitted government invocation of Christianity, he proposes that it be construed not to permit any government invocation of religion at all.)

At any rate, those narrower views of the Establishment Clause were as clearly rejected as the more expansive ones. Washington's First Thanksgiving Proclamation is merely an example. *All* of the actions of Washington and the First Congress upon which I have relied, virtually all Thanksgiving Proclamations throughout our history [except for a 1798 Adams proclamation and a 1972 Nixon proclamation], and *all* the other examples of our Government's favoring religion that I have cited, have invoked God, but not Jesus Christ.... [And] George Washington, ... in his famous Letter to the Hebrew Congregation of Newport, Rhode Island, wrote that,

> All possess alike liberty of conscience and immunities of citizenship. It is now no more that toleration is spoken of, as if it was by the indulgence of one class of people, that another enjoyed the exercise of their inherent natural rights.

The letter concluded, by the way, with an invocation of the one God: "May the father of all mercies scatter light and not darkness in our paths, and make us all in our several vocations useful here, and in his own due time and way everlastingly happy."}

[E.] Justice Stevens argues that original meaning should not be the touchstone anyway, but that we should rather "expoun[d] the meaning of constitutional provisions with one eye towards our Nation's history and the other fixed on its democratic aspirations." ... Even assuming, however, that the meaning of the Constitution ought to change according to "democratic aspirations," why are those aspirations to be found in Justices' notions of what the Establishment Clause ought to mean, rather than in the democratically adopted dispositions of our current society?

As I have observed above, numerous provisions of our laws and numerous continuing practices of our people demonstrate that the government's invocation of God (and hence the government's invocation of the Ten Commandments) is unobjectionable—including a statute enacted by Congress almost unanimously less than three years ago, stating that "under God" in the Pledge of Allegiance is constitutional. To ignore all this is not to give effect to "democratic aspirations" but to frustrate them....

Justice Thomas, concurring [in *Van Orden v. Perry*, voting to uphold the Ten Commandments display]....

[T]his Court's jurisprudence leaves courts, governments, and believers and nonbelievers alike confused ....

First, this Court's precedent permits even the slightest public recognition of religion to constitute an establishment of religion....

Second, in a seeming attempt to balance out its willingness to consider almost any acknowledgment of religion an establishment, in other cases Members of this Court have concluded that the term or symbol at issue has no religious meaning by virtue of its ubiquity or rote ceremonial invocation. See, *e.g., County of Allegheny v. ACLU*, 492 U.S. 573, 630-31 (1989) (O'Connor, J., concurring) [taking this view about "practices such as opening legislative sessions with legislative prayers or opening Court sessions with 'God save the United States and this honorable Court'" and about "the celebration of Thanksgiving as a public holiday"—ed.]. But words such as "God" have religious significance. For example, ... [t]elling either nonbelievers or believers that the words "under God" [in the Pledge of Allegiance] have no meaning contradicts what they know to be true....

[Moreover, f]or the nonadherent, who may well be more sensitive than the hypothetical "reasonable observer," or who may not know all the facts, [the "reasonable, well-informed observer" test] fails to capture completely the honest and deeply felt offense he takes from the government conduct. For the adherent, this analysis takes no account of the message sent by removal of the sign or display, which may well appear to him to be an act hostile to his religious faith....

Finally, the very "flexibility" of this Court's Establishment Clause precedent leaves it incapable of consistent application....

The unintelligibility of this Court's precedent raises the further concern that, either in appearance or in fact, adjudication of Establishment Clause challenges turns on judicial predilections. See, *e.g.*, Justice Breyer's opinion in this case [p. 827] ("I see no test-related substitute for the exercise of legal judgment"). The outcome of constitutional cases ought to rest on firmer grounds than the personal preferences of judges.

Much, if not all, of this would be avoided if the Court would return to the views of the Framers and adopt coercion as the touchstone for our Establishment Clause inquiry. {"... [E]stablishment at the founding involved, for example, mandatory observance or mandatory payment of taxes supporting ministers."} Every acknowledgment of religion would not give rise to an Establishment Clause claim. Courts would not act as theological commissions, judging the meaning of religious matters. Most important, our precedent would be capable of consistent and coherent application....

Justice Souter delivered the opinion of the Court [in *McCreary County v. ACLU*, striking down the Ten Commandments display]....

[A.] The Framers and the citizens of their time intended not only to protect the integrity of individual conscience in religious matters, but to guard against the civic divisiveness that follows when the Government weighs in on one side of religious debate; nothing does a better job of roiling society, a point that needed no explanation to the descendants of English Puritans and Cavaliers (or Massachusetts Puritans and Baptists). A sense of the past thus points to governmental neutrality as an objective of the Establishment Clause, and a sensible standard for applying it....

[B.] [S]ome of the Framers thought some endorsement of religion was compatible with the establishment ban .... But ... there is also evidence supporting the proposition that the Framers intended the Establishment Clause to require governmental neutrality in matters of religion, including neutrality in statements acknowledging religion. The very language of the Establishment Clause represented a significant departure from early drafts that merely prohibited a single national religion, and[] the final language instead "extended [the] prohibition to state support for 'religion' in general."

[Moreover, Thomas Jefferson] ... refused to issue Thanksgiving Proclamations because he believed that they violated the Constitution. And [James] Madison, whom [Justice Scalia] claims as supporting its thesis, criticized Virginia's general assessment tax not just because it required people to donate "three pence" to religion, but because "it is itself a signal of persecution. It degrades from the equal rank of Citizens all those whose opinions in Religion do not bend to those of the Legislative authority."

{[Justice Scalia] cites material suggesting that separationists like Jefferson and Madison were not absolutely consistent in abstaining from official religious acknowledgment. But, a record of inconsistent historical practice is too weak a lever to upset decades of precedent adhering to the neutrality principle. And it is worth noting that Jefferson thought his actions were consistent with non-endorsement of religion and Madison regretted any backsliding he may have done.}

The fair inference is that there was no common understanding about the limits of the establishment prohibition, and [Justice Scalia's] conclusion that its narrower view was the original understanding stretches the evidence beyond tensile capacity. What the evidence does show is a group of statesmen, like others before and after them, who proposed a guarantee with contours not wholly worked out, leaving the Establishment Clause with edges still to be determined. And none the worse for that. Indeterminate edges are the kind to have in a constitution meant to endure, and to meet "exigencies which, if foreseen at all, must have been seen dimly, and which can be best provided for as they occur." ...

[C.] [Justice Scalia] says that the deity the Framers had in mind was the God of monotheism, with the consequence that government may espouse a tenet of traditional monotheism.... [But] the religion of concern to the Framers was not that of the monotheistic faiths generally, but Christianity in particular, a fact that no member of this Court takes as a premise for construing the Religion Clauses. Justice Story probably reflected the thinking of the framing generation when he wrote in his Commentaries that the purpose of the Clause was "not to countenance, much less to advance, Mahometanism, or Judaism, or infidelity, by prostrating Christianity; but to exclude all rivalry among Christian sects."

The Framers would, therefore, almost certainly object to [Justice Scalia's] unstated reasoning that because Christianity was a monotheistic "religion," monotheism with Mosaic antecedents should be a touchstone of establishment interpretation. Even on originalist critiques of existing precedent there is, it seems, no escape from interpretative consequences that would surprise the Framers. Thus, it appears to be common ground in the interpretation of a Constitution "intended to endure for ages to come," that applications unanticipated by the Framers are inevitable....

[D.] We are centuries away from the St. Bartholomew's Day massacre and the treatment of heretics in early Massachusetts, but the divisiveness of religion in current public life is inescapable. This is no time to deny the prudence of understanding the Establishment Clause to require the Government to stay neutral on religious belief, which is reserved for the conscience of the individual....

Justice Stevens, joined by Justice Ginsburg, dissenting [in *Van Orden v. Perry*, voting to strike down a Ten Commandments display]....

[A.] [W]hen public officials deliver public speeches, we recognize that their words are not exclusively a transmission from *the* government because those oratories have embedded within them the inherently personal views of the speaker as an individual member of the polity. {It goes without saying that the analysis differs when a listener is coerced into listening to a prayer. *Santa Fe Independent School Dist. v. Doe*.} The permanent placement of a textual religious display on state property is different in kind; it amalgamates otherwise discordant individual views into a collective statement of government approval. Moreover, the message never ceases to transmit itself to objecting viewers whose only choices are to accept the message or to ignore the offense by averting their gaze. In this sense, although Thanksgiving Day proclamations and inaugural speeches undoubtedly seem official, in most circumstances they will not constitute the sort of governmental endorsement of religion at which the separation of church and state is aimed....

[B.] [T]o constrict narrowly the reach of the Establishment Clause to the views of the Founders ... would also leave us with an unincorporated constitutional provision—in other words, one that limits only the *federal* establishment of "a national religion." See *Elk Grove Unified School Dist. v. Newdow* (Thomas, J., concurring in judgment). Under this view, not only could a State constitutionally adorn all of its public spaces with crucifixes or passages from the New Testament, it would also have full authority to prescribe the teachings of Martin Luther or Joseph Smith as *the* official state religion. Only the Federal Government would be prohibited from taking sides[] (and only then as between Christian sects)....{32}

A reading of the First Amendment dependent on either [a historically grounded preference for Christianity or the nonincorporation approach] would eviscerate the heart of the Establishment Clause. It would replace Jefferson's "wall of separation" with a perverse wall of exclusion—Christians inside, non-Christians out. It would permit States to construct walls of their own choosing—Baptists inside, Mormons out; Jewish Orthodox inside, Jewish Reform out.

A Clause so understood might be faithful to the expectations of some of our Founders, but it is plainly not worthy of a society whose enviable hallmark over the course of two centuries has been the continuing expansion of religious pluralism and tolerance. Unless one is willing to renounce over 65 years of Establishment Clause jurisprudence and cross back over the incorporation bridge, appeals to the religiosity of the Framers ring hollow....

[C.] [Justice] Story's vision that States should not discriminate between Christian sects has as its foundation the principle that government must remain neutral between valid systems of belief. As religious pluralism has expanded, so has our acceptance of what constitutes valid belief systems. The evil of discriminating today against atheists, "polytheists[,] and believers in unconcerned deities" is in my view a direct descendent of the evil of

---

[32] **[Justice Scalia responds:]** {Justice Stevens says that if one is serious about following the original understanding of the Establishment Clause, he must repudiate its incorporation into the Fourteenth Amendment, and hold that it does not apply against the States.... [But] Justice Stevens did not feel that way last Term, when he joined an opinion insisting upon the original meaning of the Confrontation Clause, but nonetheless applying it against the State of Washington. See *Crawford v. Washington*, 541 U.S. 36 (2004). The notion that incorporation empties the incorporated provisions of their original meaning has no support in either reason or precedent.}

[Justice Stevens responds in turn:] Justice Scalia's answer—that incorporation does not empty "the incorporated provisions of their original meaning"—ignores the fact that the Establishment Clause has its own unique history. There is no evidence, for example, that incorporation of the Confrontation Clause ran contrary to the core of the Clause's original understanding. There is, however, some persuasive evidence to this effect regarding the Establishment Clause. See *Newdow* (Thomas, J., concurring in judgment) (arguing that the Clause was originally understood to be a "federalism provision" intended to prevent "Congress from interfering with state establishments"). It is this unique history, not incorporation writ large, that renders incoherent the postincorporation reliance on the Establishment Clause's original understanding....

discriminating among Christian sects. The Establishment Clause thus forbids it and, in turn, forbids Texas from displaying the Ten Commandments monument the plurality so casually affirms....

The plurality's reliance on early religious statements and proclamations made by the Founders is also problematic because those views were not espoused at the Constitutional Convention in 1787 nor enshrined in the Constitution's text.... [Also, n]otably absent from [the Chief Justice's and Justice Scalia's] historical snapshot is the fact that Thomas Jefferson refused to issue the Thanksgiving proclamations that Washington had so readily embraced based on the argument that to do so would violate the Establishment Clause.

The Chief Justice and Justice Scalia disregard the substantial debates that took place regarding the constitutionality of the early proclamations and acts they cite and paper over the fact that Madison more than once repudiated the views attributed to him by many, stating unequivocally that with respect to government's involvement with religion, the "tendency to a usurpation on one side, or the other, or to a corrupting coalition or alliance between them, will be best guarded against by an entire abstinence of the Government from interference, in any way whatever, beyond the necessity of preserving public order, & protecting each sect against trespasses on its legal rights by others." ... {Madison[also] ... argued that: "There has been another deviation from the strict principle in the Executive Proclamations of fasts & festivals, so far, at least, as they have spoken the language of *injunction*, or have lost sight of the equality of *all* religious sects in the eye of the Constitution...."}

{The contrary evidence cited by the Chief Justice and Justice Scalia only underscores the obvious fact that leaders who have drafted and voted for a text are eminently capable of violating their own rules. The first Congress was—just as the present Congress is—capable of passing unconstitutional legislation. Thus, it is no answer to say that the Founders' separationist impulses were "plainly rejected" simply because the first Congress enacted laws that acknowledged God. To adopt such an interpretive approach would misguidedly give authoritative weight to the fact that the Congress that passed the Fourteenth Amendment also enacted laws that tolerated segregation, and the fact that the Congress that passed the First Amendment also enacted laws, such as the Alien and Sedition Act[s], that indisputably violated our present understanding of the First Amendment.}

[D.] Many [early state constitutional religious freedom provisions] restricted "equal protection" and "free exercise" to Christians, and invocations of the divine were commonly understood to refer to Christ. That historical background likely informed the Framers' understanding of the First Amendment.

Accordingly, one influential thinker [Jasper Adams] wrote of the First Amendment that "[t]he meaning of the term 'establishment' in this amendment unquestionably is, the preference and establishment given by law to one sect of Christians over every other." ... [F]or nearly a century after the

Founding, many [including Chief Justice Marshall] accepted the idea that America was not just a *religious* nation, but "a Christian nation." ... The original understanding of the type of "religion" that qualified for constitutional protection under the Establishment Clause likely did not include those followers of Judaism and Islam who are among the preferred "monotheistic" religions Justice Scalia has embraced in his *McCreary County* opinion. The inclusion of Jews and Muslims inside the category of constitutionally favored religions surely would have shocked Chief Justice Marshall and Justice Story.

Indeed, Justice Scalia is unable to point to any persuasive historical evidence or entrenched traditions in support of his decision to give specially preferred constitutional status to all monotheistic religions. Perhaps this is because the history of the Establishment Clause's original meaning just as strongly supports a preference for Christianity as it does a preference for monotheism. Generic references to "God" hardly constitute evidence that those who spoke the word meant to be inclusive of all monotheistic believers [or] demonstrate that those who heard the word spoken understood it broadly to include all monotheistic faiths.

Justice Scalia's inclusion of Judaism and Islam is a laudable act of religious tolerance, but it is one that is unmoored from the Constitution's history and text, and moreover one that is patently arbitrary in its inclusion of some, but exclusion of other (*e.g.*, Buddhism), widely practiced non-Christian religions.... Given the original understanding of the men who championed our "Christian nation"—men who had no cause to view anti-Semitism or contempt for atheists as problems worthy of civic concern—one must ask whether Justice Scalia "has not had the courage (or the foolhardiness) to apply [his originalism] principle consistently."

{Besides marginalizing the belief systems of more than 7 million [non-Christian/Jewish/Muslim Americans by deeming them unworthy of the special protections he offers monotheists under the Establishment Clause, Justice Scalia's measure of analysis may be cause for concern even for the self-proclaimed "popular" religions of Islam and Judaism. The number of Buddhists alone is nearly equal to the number of Muslims in this country, and while those of the Islamic and Jewish faiths only account for 2.2% of all believers, Christianity accounts for 95.5%.}

[E.] {Justice Thomas contends that the Establishment Clause ... reaches only the governmental coercion of individual belief or disbelief. In my view, although actual religious coercion is undoubtedly forbidden by the Establishment Clause, that cannot be the full extent of the provision's reach. Jefferson's "wall" metaphor and his refusal to issue Thanksgiving proclamations would have been nonsensical if the Clause reached only direct coercion.

Further, under the "coercion" view, the Establishment Clause ... would not prohibit explicit state endorsements of religious orthodoxies of particular sects, actions that lie at the heart of what the Clause was meant to regulate. The government could, for example, take out television advertisements lauding Catholicism as the only pure religion. Under the reasoning endorsed by Justice Thomas, those programs would not be coercive because the viewer could simply turn off the television or ignore the ad.

[Moreover], the notion that the application of a "coercion" principle would somehow lead to a more consistent jurisprudence is dubious.... Coercion may seem obvious to some, while appearing nonexistent to others. Compare *Santa Fe Independent School Dist. v. Doe* with *Lee v. Weisman* (Scalia, J., dissenting).... "[R]easonable people could, and no doubt would, argue about whether coercion existed in a particular situation."}

[F.] It is our duty, therefore, to interpret the First Amendment's command that "Congress shall make no law respecting an establishment of religion" not by merely asking what those words meant to observers at the time of the founding, but instead by deriving from the Clause's text and history the broad principles that remain valid today....

In similar fashion, we have construed the Equal Protection Clause of the Fourteenth Amendment to prohibit segregated schools, even though those who drafted that Amendment evidently thought that separate was not unequal. We have held that the same Amendment prohibits discrimination against individuals on account of their gender, despite the fact that the contemporaries of the Amendment "doubt[ed] very much whether any action of a State not directed by way of discrimination against the negroes as a class, or on account of their race, will ever be held to come within the purview of this provision." And we have construed "evolving standards of decency" to make impermissible practices that were not considered "cruel and unusual" at the founding.

To reason from the broad principles contained in the Constitution does not, as Justice Scalia suggests, require us to abandon our heritage in favor of unprincipled expressions of personal preference. The task of applying the broad principles that the Framers wrote into the text of the First Amendment is, in any event, no more a matter of personal preference than is one's selection between two (or more) sides in a heated historical debate. We serve our constitutional mandate by expounding the meaning of constitutional provisions with one eye towards our Nation's history and the other fixed on its democratic aspirations. Constitutions, after all,

> are not ephemeral enactments, designed to meet passing occasions. They are, to use the words of Chief Justice Marshall, "designed to approach immortality as nearly as human institutions can approach it." The future is their care and provision for events of good and bad tendencies of which no prophecy can be made. In the application of a constitution, therefore, our contemplation cannot be only of what has been but of what may be. Under any other rule a constitution would indeed be as easy of application as it would be deficient in efficacy and power. Its general principles would have little value and be converted by precedent into impotent and lifeless formulas....

The principle that guides my analysis is neutrality. The basis for that principle is firmly rooted in our Nation's history and our Constitution's text.

I recognize that the requirement that government must remain neutral between religion and irreligion would have seemed foreign to some of the Framers; so too would a requirement of neutrality between Jews and Christians. Fortunately, we are not bound by the Framers' expectations—we are bound by the legal principles they enshrined in our Constitution.

Justice O'Connor, concurring [in *McCreary County v. ACLU*, voting to strike down a Ten Commandments display]....

[The Religion Clauses] were written by the descendents of people who had come to this land precisely so that they could practice their religion freely. Together with the other First Amendment guarantees ...[,] the Religion Clauses were designed to safeguard the freedom of conscience and belief that those immigrants had sought. They embody an idea that was once considered radical: Free people are entitled to free and diverse thoughts, which government ought neither to constrain nor to direct.... By enforcing the Clauses, we have kept religion a matter for the individual conscience, not for the prosecutor or bureaucrat.

At a time when we see around the world the violent consequences of the assumption of religious authority by government, Americans may count themselves fortunate: Our regard for constitutional boundaries has protected us from similar travails, while allowing private religious exercise to flourish. The well-known statement that "[w]e are a religious people" has proved true. Americans attend their places of worship more often than do citizens of other developed nations, and describe religion as playing an especially important role in their lives. Those who would renegotiate the boundaries between church and state must therefore answer a difficult question: Why would we trade a system that has served us so well for one that has served others so poorly?

Our guiding principle has been James Madison's—that "[t]he Religion ... of every man must be left to the conviction and conscience of every man." ... [And v]oluntary religious belief and expression may be as threatened when government takes the mantle of religion upon itself as when government directly interferes with private religious practices. When the government associates one set of religious beliefs with the state and identifies nonadherents as outsiders, it encroaches upon the individual's decision about whether and how to worship.

In the marketplace of ideas, the government has vast resources and special status. Government religious expression therefore risks crowding out private observance and distorting the natural interplay between competing beliefs. Allowing government to be a potential mouthpiece for competing religious ideas risks the sort of division that might easily spill over into suppression of rival beliefs. Tying secular and religious authority together poses risks to both....

It is true that the Framers lived at a time when our national religious diversity was neither as robust nor as well recognized as it is now.... But they did know that line-drawing between religions is an enterprise that, once begun, has no logical stopping point. They worried that "the same authority which can establish Christianity, in exclusion of all other Religions, may establish with the same ease any particular sect of Christians, in exclusion of all other Sects." The Religion Clauses, as a result, protect adherents of all religions, as well as those who believe in no religion at all....

iv. Chief Justice Rehnquist's Approach (Van Orden)

Chief Justice Rehnquist ... delivered an opinion, in which Justice Scalia, Justice Kennedy, and Justice Thomas join[, upholding a Ten Commandments display]....

[A.] Our cases, Januslike, point in two directions in applying the Establishment Clause. One face looks toward the strong role played by religion and religious traditions throughout our Nation's history.... The other face looks toward the principle that governmental intervention in religious matters can itself endanger religious freedom.... Our institutions presuppose a Supreme Being, yet these institutions must not press religious observances upon their citizens.... Reconciling these two faces requires that we neither abdicate our responsibility to maintain a division between church and state nor evince a hostility to religion by disabling the government from in some ways recognizing our religious heritage. {[W]e have not, and do not, adhere to the principle that the Establishment Clause bars any and all governmental preference for religion over irreligion. See, *e.g.*, Cutter v. Wilkinson; Corporation of Presiding Bishop v. Amos; Marsh v. Chambers..} ...

Whatever may be the fate of the *Lemon* test in the larger scheme of Establishment Clause jurisprudence, we think it not useful in dealing with the sort of passive monument that Texas has erected on its Capitol grounds. Instead, our analysis is driven both by the nature of the monument and by our Nation's history....

"There is an unbroken history of official acknowledgment by all three branches of government of the role of religion in American life from at least 1789." [Chief Justice Rehnquist points here to some of the historical evidence given in Justice Scalia's opinion, see p. 809.—ed.] ...

Recognition of the role of God in our Nation's heritage has also been reflected in our decisions. We have acknowledged, for example, that "religion has been closely identified with our history and government," *School Dist. of Abington Township v. Schempp*, 374 U.S. 203 (1963), and that "[t]he history of man is inseparable from the history of religion," *Engel v. Vitale*.

This recognition has led us to hold that the Establishment Clause permits a state legislature to open its daily sessions with a prayer by a chaplain paid by the State. *Marsh v. Chambers*. Such a practice, we thought, was "deeply embedded in the history and tradition of this country." As we observed there, "it would be incongruous to interpret [the Establishment Clause] as imposing more stringent First Amendment limits on the states than the draftsmen imposed on the Federal Government." {Indeed, we rejected the claim that an Establishment Clause violation was presented because the prayers had once been offered in the Judeo-Christian tradition: In

Marsh, the prayers were often explicitly Christian, but the chaplain removed all references to Christ the year after the suit was filed.} With similar reasoning, we have upheld laws, which originated from one of the Ten Commandments, that prohibited the sale of merchandise on Sunday....

[A]cknowledgments of the role played by the Ten Commandments in our Nation's heritage are common throughout America. We need only look within our own Courtroom. Since 1935, Moses has stood, holding two tablets that reveal portions of the Ten Commandments written in Hebrew, among other lawgivers in the south frieze. Representations of the Ten Commandments adorn the metal gates lining the north and south sides of the Courtroom as well as the doors leading into the Courtroom. Moses also sits on the exterior east facade of the building holding the Ten Commandments tablets.

Similar acknowledgments can be seen throughout a visitor's tour of our Nation's Capital. For example, a large statue of Moses holding the Ten Commandments, alongside a statue of the Apostle Paul, has overlooked the rotunda of the Library of Congress' Jefferson Building since 1897. And the Jefferson Building's Great Reading Room contains a sculpture of a woman beside the Ten Commandments with a quote above her from the Old Testament (Micah 6:8). A medallion with two tablets depicting the Ten Commandments decorates the floor of the National Archives.

Inside the Department of Justice, a statue entitled "The Spirit of Law" has two tablets representing the Ten Commandments lying at its feet. In front of the Ronald Reagan Building is another sculpture that includes a depiction of the Ten Commandments. So too a 24-foot-tall sculpture, depicting, among other things, the Ten Commandments and a cross, stands outside the federal courthouse that houses both the Court of Appeals and the District Court for the District of Columbia. Moses is also prominently featured in the Chamber of the United States House of Representatives.

{[Likewise, t]he apex of the Washington Monument is inscribed "Laus Deo," which is translated to mean "Praise be to God," and multiple memorial stones in the monument contain Biblical citations. The Jefferson Memorial is engraved with three quotes from Jefferson that make God a central theme. Inscribed on the wall of the Lincoln Memorial are two of Lincoln's most famous speeches, the Gettysburg Address and his Second Inaugural Address. Both inscriptions include those speeches' extensive acknowledgments of God.}

Our opinions, like our building, have recognized the role the Decalogue plays in America's heritage [citations omitted—ed.]. The Executive and Legislative Branches have also acknowledged the historical role of the Ten Commandments. These displays and recognitions of the Ten Commandments bespeak the rich American tradition of religious acknowledgments.

Of course, the Ten Commandments are religious—they were so viewed at their inception and so remain. The monument, therefore, has religious significance. According to Judeo-Christian belief, the Ten Commandments were given to Moses by God on Mt. Sinai. But Moses was a lawgiver as well as a religious leader. And the Ten Commandments have an undeniable historical meaning, as the foregoing examples demonstrate. Simply having religious content or promoting a message consistent with a religious doctrine does not run afoul of the Establishment Clause.

[B.] There are, of course, limits to the display of religious messages or symbols. For example, we held unconstitutional a Kentucky statute requiring the posting of the Ten Commandments in every public schoolroom. *Stone v. Graham*, 449 U.S. 39 (1980) (per curiam). In the classroom context, we found that the Kentucky statute had an improper and plainly religious purpose.... Neither *Stone* itself nor subsequent opinions have indicated that *Stone*'s holding would extend to a legislative chamber, see *Marsh v. Chambers*, or to capitol grounds. {Nor does anything suggest that Stone would extend to displays of the Ten Commandments that lack a "plainly religious," "pre-eminent purpose." Indeed, we need not decide in this case the extent to which a primarily religious purpose would affect our analysis because it is clear from the record that there is no evidence of such a purpose in this case.}

The placement of the Ten Commandments monument on the Texas State Capitol grounds is a far more passive use of those texts than was the case in *Stone*, where the text confronted elementary school students every day. Indeed, Van Orden, the petitioner here, apparently walked by the monument for a number of years before bringing this lawsuit. The monument is therefore also quite different from the prayers involved in *Schempp* and *Lee v. Weisman*.

Texas has treated her Capitol grounds monuments as representing the several strands in the State's political and legal history. The inclusion of the Ten Commandments monument in this group has a dual significance, partaking of both religion and government. We cannot say that Texas' display of this monument violates the Establishment Clause of the First Amendment....

Justice Souter, with whom Justice Stevens and Justice Ginsburg join[, and with whom Justice O'Connor largely agreed], dissenting[, voting to strike down the Ten Commandments display]....

[I include here excerpts, from the text and the footnotes, in which Justice Souter responds to specific factual assertions in the plurality opinion. Excerpts from Justice Souter's application of the endorsement test are at p. 806; excerpts from Justice Souter's argument for the endorsement test are at p. 815.—ed.]

[A.] The monument's presentation of the Commandments with religious text emphasized and enhanced stands in contrast to any number of perfectly constitutional depictions of them, the frieze of our own Courtroom providing a good example, where the figure of Moses stands among history's great lawgivers. While Moses holds the tablets of the Commandments showing some Hebrew text, no one looking at the lines of figures in marble relief is likely to see a religious purpose behind the assemblage or take away a religious message from it.

Only one other depiction represents a religious leader, and the historical personages are mixed with symbols of moral and intellectual abstractions like Equity and Authority. Since Moses enjoys no especial prominence on the frieze, viewers can readily take him to be there as a lawgiver in the company of other lawgivers; and the viewers may just as naturally see the tablets of the Commandments (showing the later ones, forbidding things like killing and theft, but without the divine preface) as background from which the concept of law emerged, ultimately having a secular influence in the history of the Nation.

Government may, of course, constitutionally call attention to this influence, and may post displays or erect monuments recounting this aspect of our history no less than any other, so long as there is a context and that context is historical. Hence, a display of the Commandments accompanied by an exposition of how they have influenced modern law would most likely be constitutionally unobjectionable. And the Decalogue could ... be integrated constitutionally into a course of study in public schools....

[B.] {For similar reasons, the other displays of the Commandments that the plurality mentions do not run afoul of the Establishment Clause. The statues of Moses and St. Paul in the Main Reading Room of the Library of Congress are 2 of 16 set in close proximity, statues that "represent men illustrious in the various forms of thought and activity ...." Moses and St. Paul represent religion, while the other 14 (a group that includes Beethoven, Shakespeare, Michelangelo, Columbus, and Plato) represent the nonreligious categories of philosophy, art, history, commerce, science, law, and poetry. Similarly, the sculpture of the woman beside the Decalogue in the Main Reading Room is one of 8 such figures "represent[ing] eight characteristic features of civilized life and thought," the same 8 features (7 of them nonreligious) that Moses, St. Paul, and the rest of the 16 statues represent.

The inlay on the floor of the National Archives Building is one of four such discs, the collective theme of which is not religious. Rather, the discs "symbolize the various types of Government records that were to come into the National Archive." (The four categories are war and defense, history, justice, and legislation. Each disc is paired with a winged figure; the disc containing the depiction of the Commandments, a depiction that, notably, omits the Commandments' text, is paired with a figure representing legislation.)

As for Moses's "prominen[t] featur[ing] in the Chamber of the United States House of Representatives," Moses is actually 1 of 23 portraits encircling the House Chamber, each approximately the same size, having no religious theme. The portraits depict "men noted in history for the part they played in the evolution of what has become American law." More importantly for purposes of this case, each portrait consists only of the subject's face; the Ten Commandments appear nowhere in Moses's portrait....}

[C.] [As to *Stone v. Graham*, p]lacing a monument on the ground is not more "passive" than hanging a sheet of paper on a wall when both contain the same text to be read by anyone who looks at it. The problem in *Stone* was simply that the State was putting the Commandments there to be seen, just as the monument's inscription is there for those who walk by it.

To be sure, Kentucky's compulsory-education law meant that the school-children were forced to see the display every day, whereas many see the monument by choice, and those who customarily walk the Capitol grounds can presumably avoid it if they choose. But in my judgment (and under our often inexact Establishment Clause jurisprudence, such matters often boil down to judgment), this distinction should make no difference.

The monument in this case sits on the grounds of the Texas State Capitol. There is something significant in the common term "statehouse" to refer to a state capitol building: it is the civic home of every one of the State's citizens. If neutrality in religion means something, any citizen should be able to visit that civic home without having to confront religious expressions clearly meant to convey an official religious position that may be at odds with his own religion, or with rejection of religion....

v. The Divisiveness Approach (Van Orden)

Justice Breyer, concurring in the judgment in [*Van Orden v. Perry*, voting to uphold the Ten Commandments display].

[A.] [The Religion Clauses] seek to "assure the fullest possible scope of religious liberty and tolerance for all." They seek to avoid that divisiveness based upon religion that promotes social conflict, sapping the strength of government and religion alike. They seek to maintain that "separation of church and state" that has long been critical to the "peaceful dominion that religion exercises in [this] country," where the "spirit of religion" and the "spirit of freedom" are productively "united," "reign[ing] together" but in separate spheres "on the same soil." They seek to further the basic principles set forth today by Justice O'Connor in her concurring opinion in *McCreary County v. ACLU* [see p. 821]....

[T]he realization of these goals means that government must "neither engage in nor compel religious practices," that it must "effect no favoritism among sects or between religion and nonreligion," and that it must "work deterrence of no religious belief." The government must avoid excessive interference with, or promotion of, religion.

But the Establishment Clause does not compel the government to purge from the public sphere all that in any way partakes of the religious. See, *e.g.*, *Marsh v. Chambers*. Such absolutism is not only inconsistent with our national traditions, but would also tend to promote the kind of social conflict the Establishment Clause seeks to avoid....

[B.] [T]he Court has found no single mechanical formula that can accurately draw the constitutional line in every case. Where the Establishment Clause is at issue, tests designed to measure "neutrality" alone are insufficient, both because it is sometimes difficult to determine when a legal rule is "neutral," and because "untutored devotion to the concept of neutrality can lead to invocation or approval of results which partake not simply of that noninterference and noninvolvement with the religious which the Constitution commands, but of a brooding and pervasive devotion to the secular and a passive, or even active, hostility to the religious."

Neither can this Court's other tests readily explain the Establishment Clause's tolerance, for example, of the prayers that open legislative meetings, see *Marsh*; certain references to, and invocations of, the Deity in the public words of public officials; the public references to God on coins, decrees, and buildings; or the attention paid to the religious objectives of certain holidays, including Thanksgiving.

If the relation between government and religion is one of separation, but not of mutual hostility and suspicion, one will inevitably find difficult borderline cases. And in such cases, I see no test-related substitute for the exercise of legal judgment. That judgment is not a personal judgment. Rather, as in all constitutional cases, it must reflect and remain faithful to the underlying purposes of the Clauses, and it must take account of context and consequences measured in light of those purposes....

[Justice Breyer went on to analyze the Ten Commandments posting in this case, and to conclude (see p. 804 for more details) that the facts "provide a strong, but not conclusive, indication that the Commandments' text on this monument conveys a predominantly secular message." He then concluded with this:—ed.]

[C.] This case ... is distinguishable from instances where the Court has found Ten Commandments displays impermissible. The display is not on the grounds of a public school, where, given the impressionability of the young, government must exercise particular care in separating church and state. See, *e.g.*, *Lee v. Weisman*; *Stone v. Graham*, 449 U.S. 39 (1980) (per curiam).

This case also differs from *McCreary County*, where the short (and stormy) history of the courthouse Commandments' displays demonstrates the substantially religious objectives of those who mounted them, and the effect of this readily apparent objective upon those who view them. That history there indicates a governmental effort substantially to promote religion, not simply an effort primarily to reflect, historically, the secular impact of a religiously inspired document. And, in today's world, in a Nation of so many different religious and comparable nonreligious fundamental beliefs, a more contemporary state effort to focus attention upon a religious text is certainly likely to prove divisive in a way that this longstanding, preexisting monument has not....

This display has stood apparently uncontested for nearly two generations. That experience helps us understand that as a practical matter of *degree* this display is unlikely to prove divisive. And this matter of degree is, I believe, critical in a borderline case such as this one.

At the same time, to reach a contrary conclusion here, based primarily upon on the religious nature of the tablets' text would, I fear, lead the law to exhibit a hostility toward religion that has no place in our Establishment Clause traditions. Such a holding might well encourage disputes concerning the removal of longstanding depictions of the Ten Commandments from public buildings across the Nation. And it could thereby create the very kind of religiously based divisiveness that the Establishment Clause seeks to avoid....

"[T]he First Amendment does not prohibit practices which by any realistic measure create none of the dangers which it is designed to prevent and which do not so directly or substantially involve the state in religious exercise or in the favoring of religion as to have meaningful and practical impact." That kind of practice is what we have here.

I recognize the danger of the slippery slope. Still, where the Establishment Clause is at issue, we must "distinguish between real threat and mere shadow." Here, we have only the shadow....

j.   *Town of Greece v. Galloway, 134 S. Ct. 1811 (2014)*

[The Court upheld the policy of having invocations before town council meetings, delivered by local clergy. The invocations were often specifically Christian, though this apparently happened because the selection method— picking clergy from the local phone book—uncovered only Christian clergy. (Some non-Christians—"a Jewish layman," "the chairman of the local Baha'i temple," and "[a] Wiccan priestess"— eventually did give invocations, after the controversy that led to the case began.)

Part of the disagreement between the majority and the dissent had to do with whether the town should have done more to invite other clergy. But, for space reasons, I focus below only on the legal guidelines that the majority announced, and those the dissent would have announced, to decide what sort of legislative prayer is permissible post-*Marsh*.—ed.]

Justice Kennedy delivered the opinion of the Court....

An insistence on nonsectarian or ecumenical prayer as a single, fixed standard is not consistent with the tradition of legislative prayer outlined in the Court's cases.... The relevant constraint [on such prayer] derives from its place at the opening of legislative sessions, where it is meant to lend gravity to the occasion and reflect values long part of the Nation's heritage. Prayer that is solemn and respectful in tone, that invites lawmakers to reflect upon shared ideals and common ends before they embark on the fractious business of governing, serves that legitimate function.

If the course and practice over time shows that the invocations denigrate nonbelievers or religious minorities, threaten damnation, or preach conversion, many present may consider the prayer to fall short of the desire to elevate the purpose of the occasion and to unite lawmakers in their common effort. That circumstance would present a different case than the one presently before the Court.

The tradition reflected in *Marsh v. Chambers* permits chaplains to ask their own God for blessings of peace, justice, and freedom that find appreciation among people of all faiths. That a prayer is given in the name of Jesus, Allah, or Jehovah, or that it makes passing reference to religious doctrines, does not remove it from that tradition. These religious themes provide particular means to universal ends....

Respondents point to [some] invocations that disparaged those who did not accept the town's prayer practice. One guest minister characterized objectors as a "minority" who are "ignorant of the history of our country," while another lamented that other towns did not have "God-fearing" leaders. Although these two remarks strayed from the rationale set out in *Marsh*, they do not despoil a practice that on the whole reflects and embraces our tradition. Absent a pattern of prayers that over time denigrate, proselytize, or betray an impermissible government purpose, a challenge based solely on the content of a prayer will not likely establish a constitutional violation....

Finally, ... the town of Greece [did not] contravene[] the Establishment Clause by inviting a predominantly Christian set of ministers to lead the prayer. The town made reasonable efforts to identify all of the congregations located within its borders and represented that it would welcome a prayer by any minister or layman who wished to give one. That nearly all of the congregations in town turned out to be Christian does not reflect an aversion or bias on the part of town leaders against minority faiths.

So long as the town maintains a policy of nondiscrimination, the Constitution does not require it to search beyond its borders for non-Christian prayer givers in an effort to achieve religious balancing. The quest to promote "a 'diversity' of religious views" would require the town "to make wholly inappropriate judgments about the number of religions [it] should sponsor and the relative frequency with which it should sponsor each," a form of government entanglement with religion that is far more troublesome than the current approach....

Justice Kagan, joined by Justices Ginsburg, Breyer, and Sotomayor, dissenting....

I agree with the Court's decision in *Marsh v. Chambers*, upholding the Nebraska Legislature's tradition of beginning each session with a chaplain's prayer. And I believe that pluralism and inclusion in a town hall can satisfy the constitutional requirement of neutrality; such a forum need not become a religion-free zone....

If the Town Board had let its chaplains know that they should speak in nonsectarian terms, common to diverse religious groups, then no one would have valid grounds for complaint. Priests and ministers, rabbis and imams give such invocations all the time; there is no great mystery to the project....

Or if the Board preferred, it might have invited clergy of many faiths to serve as chaplains, as ... Congress does. When one month a clergy member refers to Jesus, and the next to Allah or Jehovah—as the majority hopefully though counterfactually suggests happened here—the government does not identify itself with one religion or align itself with that faith's citizens, and the effect of even sectarian prayer is transformed....

{But ... the invocations given [at Greece's town meetings] ... were predominantly sectarian in content. Still more, Greece's Board did nothing to recognize religious diversity: In arranging for clergy members to open each meeting, the Town never sought (except briefly when this suit was filed) to involve, accommodate, or in any way reach out to adherents of non-Christian religions. So month in and month out for over a decade, prayers steeped in only one faith, addressed toward members of the public, commenced meetings to discuss local affairs and distribute government benefits. In my view, that practice does not square with the First Amendment's promise that every citizen, irrespective of her religion, owns an equal share in her government....}

k. Policy—No Endorsement of Religion

Basic argument: "The government may not act in ways that are reasonably perceived as endorsing (or disapproving of) religion, or that are intended to endorse (or disapprove of) religion, because _____; this action will indeed be so perceived or is so intended, because _____."

1. "[Government] may not place its prestige ... or resources behind a single religious faith or behind religious belief in general, ... conveying the message that those who do not contribute gladly are less than full members of the community.... [W]hen government directs a subsidy exclusively to religious organizations that is not required by the Free Exercise Clause and that either burdens nonbeneficiaries markedly or cannot reasonably be seen as removing a significant state-imposed deterrent to the free exercise of religion ... it 'provide[s] unjustifiable awards of assistance to religious organizations' and cannot but 'conve[y] a message of endorsement' to slighted members of the community." *Texas Monthly v. Bullock* (plurality).

"'When James H. Hammond, governor of South Carolina, announced a day of 'Thanksgiving, Humiliation, and Prayer' in 1844, he ... exhorted 'our citizens of all denominations to assemble at their respective places of worship, to offer up their devotions to God their Creator, and his Son Jesus Christ, the Redeemer of the world.' The Jews of Charleston protested, charging Hammond with 'such obvious *discrimination and preference* in the tenor of your proclamation, as amounted to an utter exclusion of a portion of the people of South Carolina.' ... [T]he Jews of Charleston succinctly captured the precise evil caused by such sectarian proclamations as Governor Hammond's: they demonstrate an official *preference* for Christianity and a corresponding official *discrimination* against all non-Christians, amounting to an exclusion of a portion of the political community. It is against this very evil that the Establishment Clause, in part, is directed." *County of Allegheny v. ACLU*, 492 U.S. 573, 590 n.39 (1989) (citing Borden, *Jews, Turks, and Infidels* (1984) (emphasis in original)).

"[T]he mere appearance of a joint exercise of legislative authority by Church and State [when a church is given the right to veto liquor licenses] provides a significant symbolic benefit to religion in the minds of some by reason of the power conferred[, thus] ... having a 'primary' and 'principal' effect of advancing religion." *Larkin v. Grendel's Den.*

"[When] a government program [provides] direct aid to religious schools based on the number of students attending each school ... [and] the religious school uses the aid to inculcate religion in its students, it is reasonable to say that the government has communicated a message of endorsement. Because the religious indoctrination is supported by government assistance, the reasonable observer would naturally perceive the aid program as *government* support for the advancement of religion." *Mitchell v. Helms* (O'Connor, J., concurring in the judgment).

2. Response to 1: There's nothing inherently wrong with the government endorsing religion, because _____.

"[W]hatever standard the Court applies to Establishment Clause claims, it must at least suggest results consistent with our precedents and the historical practices that, by tradition, have informed our First Amendment jurisprudence.... [But f]ew of our traditional practices recognizing the part religion plays in our society can withstand scrutiny under a faithful application of [the endorsement test]....

"Obsessive, implacable resistance to all but the most carefully scripted and secularized forms of accommodation requires this Court to act as a censor, issuing national decrees as to what is orthodox and what is not. What is orthodox, in this context, means what is secular; the only Christmas the State can acknowledge is one in which references to religion have been held to a minimum. The Court thus lends its assistance to an Orwellian rewriting of history as many understand it....

"[Under] the majority's approach, ... the Court also assumes the difficult and inappropriate task of saying what every religious symbol means.... This Court is ill equipped to sit as a national theology board, and I question both the wisdom and the constitutionality of its doing so." *County of Allegheny* (Kennedy, J., dissenting).

3. Response to 1: This action really doesn't endorse religion, because

_____.

"Our cases have ... equated 'endorsement' with 'promotion' or 'favoritism.' We find it peculiar to say that government 'promotes' or 'favors' a religious display by giving it the same access to a public forum that all other displays enjoy." *Capitol Square Review Bd. v. Pinette* (plurality).

"[W]hen government aid supports a school's religious mission only because of independent decisions made by numerous individuals to guide their secular aid to that school, '[n]o reasonable observer is likely to draw from the facts ... an inference that the State itself is endorsing a religious practice or belief.' Rather, endorsement of the religious message is reasonably attributed to the individuals who select the path of the aid." *Mitchell* (O'Connor, J., concurring in the judgment).

4. Response to 1: It's hard to tell whether something endorses religion, because _____, so the endorsement test is not a good constitutional rule.

"Whether a particular governmental action appears to endorse or disapprove religion depends on the presuppositions of the observer, and there is no 'neutral' position, outside the culture, from which to make this assessment. The bare concept of 'endorsement' therefore provides no guidance to legislatures or lower courts about what is an establishment of religion. It is nothing more than ... 'I know it when I see it.'

"Consider the following examples: (1) How would the parochial school aid cases fare under the endorsement test? ... A significant segment of the population believes that the use of government funds to assist religious education is tantamount to putting priests on the payroll. On the other hand, granting funds to secular schools but not to equally qualified religious schools creates at least the appearance of disapproval.... (2) Does tax-exempt status convey a message of endorsement of churches? The government grants tax exemptions on the theory that exempt organizations provide benefits to the public. Including churches on this list implies that they are wholesome and beneficial institutions.... But what message would be conveyed by excluding churches from the class of tax-exempt charities? ...

"(5) Does exemption of religious organizations or of religiously motivated individuals from a law of general applicability 'endorse' religion? Opponents of religious accommodations argue that '[s]pecial treatment for religion connotes sponsorship and endorsement'.... Justice O'Connor agrees that exemptions cause resentment, but holds that this resentment is 'entitled to little weight' because accommodations promote the 'values' of the Free Exercise Clause. Others, such as Professor Laycock, say that exemptions do not appear to endorse religion at all.

"I know all of these people to be reasonable observers, well schooled in the values underlying the First Amendment. That does not seem to help." Michael W. McConnell, *Religious Freedom at a Crossroads,* 59 U. Chi. L. Rev. 115, 150 (1992).

5. Response to 1: Barring this sort of action will itself send a message of disapproval of religion, because _____.

"Withholding access [to a generally available student newspaper funding program by a religious student newspaper] would leave an impermissible perception that religious activities are disfavored: '[T]he message [of evenhanded inclusion in the newspaper funding program] is one of neutrality rather than endorsement; if a State refused to let religious groups use facilities open to others, then it would demonstrate not neutrality but hostility toward religion.' 'The Religion Clauses prohibit the government from favoring religion, but they provide no warrant for discriminating *against* religion.'" *Rosenberger v. Rector* (O'Connor, J., concurring).

"[T]he Establishment Clause permits government some latitude in recognizing and accommodating the central role religion plays in our society. Any approach less sensitive to our heritage would border on latent hostility toward religion, as it would require government ... to acknowledge only the secular, to the exclusion and so to the detriment of the religious ... [thus] sending a clear message of disapproval." *County of Allegheny* (Kennedy, J., dissenting).

"If there be such a person as the 'reasonable observer,' ... he or she will take away a salient message from our holding [that a crèche display is unconstitutional but a Christmas-tree-and-menorah display is constitutional]: the Supreme Court of the United States has concluded that the First Amendment creates classes of religions based on the relative numbers of their adherents. Those religions enjoying the largest following must be consigned to the status of least-favored faiths so as to avoid any possible risk of offending members of minority religions." *Id.*

"[W]hen the government owns the street and parks, which are the principal sites for public communication and community celebrations, the schools, which are a principal means for transmitting ideas and values to future generations, and many of the principal institutions of culture, exclusion of religious ideas, symbols, and voices marginalizes religion in much the same way that the neglect of the contributions of African American and other minority citizens, or of the viewpoints and contributions of women, once marginalized those segments of the society. Silence about a subject can convey a powerful message. When the public sphere is open to ideas and symbols representing nonreligious viewpoints, cultures, and ideological commitments, to exclude all those whose basis is 'religious' would profoundly distort public culture." McConnell, *supra*, at 189.

6. Rebuttal to 5: No, barring this sort of action will not make people perceive that the law is hostile to religion (or at least any such perception would be far less than the perception of endorsement that would come from allowing this action), because _____.

"It is neither sacrilegious nor antireligious to say that each separate government in this country should stay out of the business of writing or sanctioning official prayers and leave that purely religious function to the people themselves and to those the people choose to look to for religious guidance." *Engel v. Vitale.*

"A view that 'private prayers' are most appropriate in private settings is neither novel nor disrespectful to religious speech." *Capitol Square Review Bd. v. Pinette* (Stevens, J, dissenting).

7. Friendly Amendment to 1: Even though it's right to inquire into whether the action endorses or disapproves religion, this inquiry must take into account _____.

"[T]he 'history and ubiquity' of a practice ... provides part of the context in which a reasonable observer evaluates whether a challenged governmental practice conveys a message of endorsement of religion. It is the combination of the longstanding existence of practices such as opening legislative sessions with legislative prayers or opening Court sessions with 'God save the United States and this honorable Court,' as well as their nonsectarian nature, that leads me to the conclusion that those particular practices, despite their religious roots, do not convey a message of endorsement of particular religious beliefs." *County of Allegheny* (O'Connor, J., concurring in the judgment).

"[T]he endorsement test should [not] focus on the actual perception of individual observers, who naturally have differing degrees of knowledge....

[T]he applicable observer is similar to the 'reasonable person' in tort law, who is ... '... a personification of a community ideal of reasonable behavior, determined by the [collective] social judgment.' ... [And] the reasonable observer in the endorsement inquiry must be deemed aware of the history and context of the community and forum in which the religious display appears." *Capitol Square* (O'Connor, J., concurring in the judgment).

"[The other Justices'] argument would assume an 'ultrareasonable observer' who understands the vagaries of this Court's First Amendment jurisprudence.... [But r]easonable people have differing degrees of knowledge; that does not ... make them unworthy of constitutional protection.... For a religious display to violate the Establishment Clause, I think it is enough that *some* reasonable observers would attribute a religious message to the State." *Id.* (Stevens, J., dissenting).

l.   Should the Establishment Clause Be Incorporated Against the States?

[The First Amendment expressly binds only "Congress"; but the Fourteenth Amendment says that "No State shall make or enforce any law which shall abridge the privileges or immunities of citizens of the United States; nor shall any State deprive any person of life, liberty, or property, without due process of law ...." From the 1890s to now, the Supreme Court gradually read the Due Process Clause as applying most of the Bill of Rights to the states (the exceptions being the Third Amendment's limits on quartering soldiers in people's homes, the Seventh Amendment's provision of jury trials in civil cases, the Grand Jury Presentment Clause, possibly the Excessive Fines Clause, and the unanimity requirement of the Criminal Jury Trial Clause). Many commentators argue that the incorporation should have been done via the Privileges or Immunities Clause rather than the Due Process Clause, but for historical reasons the Court has chosen the latter provision.

[In the 1920s, the Court generally asserted that the Free Speech Clause and the Free Exercise Clause were incorporated, and in *Everson v. Board of Ed.* (1947), the Court held the same about the Establishment Clause, without much discussion. Since then, however, some serious academic commentators—and one Supreme Court Justice, Clarence Thomas—have cast doubt on this conclusion. Here are the leading Supreme Court arguments on the question.—ed.]

Justice Brennan, concurring [in *School Dist. of Abington Township v. Schempp*, 374 U.S. 203 (1963)] ....

It has been suggested, with some support in history, that absorption of the First Amendment's ban against congressional legislation "respecting an establishment of religion" is conceptually impossible because the Framers meant the Establishment Clause also to foreclose any attempt by Congress to disestablish the existing official state churches. Whether or not such was the understanding of the Framers and whether such a purpose would have inhibited the absorption of the Establishment Clause at the threshold of the Nineteenth Century are questions not dispositive of our present inquiry. For it is clear on the record of history that the last of the formal state establishments was dissolved more than three decades before the Fourteenth Amendment was ratified, and thus the problem of protecting official state churches from federal encroachments could hardly have been any concern of those who framed the post-Civil War Amendments.

Any such objective of the First Amendment, having become historical anachronism by 1868, cannot be thought to have deterred the absorption of the Establishment Clause to any greater degree than it would, for example, have deterred the absorption of the Free Exercise Clause.... [T]he Fourteenth Amendment created a panoply of new federal rights for the protection of citizens of the various States. And among those rights was freedom from such state governmental involvement in the affairs of religion as the Establishment Clause had originally foreclosed on the part of Congress.

It has also been suggested that the "liberty" guaranteed by the Fourteenth Amendment logically cannot absorb the Establishment Clause because that clause is not one of the provisions of the Bill of Rights which in terms protects a "freedom" of the individual.... [But this] underestimates the role of the Establishment Clause as a co-guarantor, with the Free Exercise Clause, of religious liberty. The Framers did not entrust the liberty of religious beliefs to either clause alone....

Finally, it has been contended that absorption of the Establishment Clause is precluded by the absence of any intention on the part of the Framers of the Fourteenth Amendment to circumscribe the residual powers of the States to aid religious activities and institutions in ways which fell short of formal establishments. That argument relies in part upon the express terms of the abortive Blaine Amendment—proposed several years after the adoption of the Fourteenth Amendment—which would have added to the First Amendment a provision that "[n]o State shall make any law respecting an establishment of religion ...." Such a restriction would have been superfluous, it is said, if the Fourteenth Amendment had already made the Establishment Clause binding upon the States.

The argument proves too much, for the Fourteenth Amendment's protection of the free exercise of religion can hardly be questioned; yet the Blaine Amendment would also have added an explicit protection against state laws abridging that liberty. Even if we assume that the draftsmen of the Fourteenth Amendment saw no immediate connection between its protections against state action infringing personal liberty and the guarantees of the First Amendment, it is certainly too late in the day to suggest that their assumed inattention to the question dilutes the force of these constitutional guarantees in their application to the States. It is enough to conclude that the religious liberty embodied in the Fourteenth Amendment would not be viable if the Constitution were interpreted to forbid only establishments ordained by Congress.

{[Moreover], whatever "establishment" may have meant to the Framers of the First Amendment in 1791, the draftsmen of the Fourteenth Amendment three quarters of a century later understood the Establishment Clause to foreclose many incidental forms of governmental aid to religion which fell far short of the creation or support of an official church. The Report of a Senate Committee as early as 1853, for example, contained this view of the Establishment Clause:

> "If Congress has passed, or should pass, any law which, fairly construed, has in any degree introduced, or should attempt to introduce, in favor of any church, or ecclesiastical association, or system of religious faith, all or any one of these obnoxious particulars—endowment at the public expense, peculiar privileges to its members, or disadvantages or penalties upon those who should reject its doctrines or belong to other communions—such law would be a 'law respecting an establishment of religion,' and, therefore, in violation of the constitution."

Compare Thomas M. Cooley's exposition in the year in which the Fourteenth Amendment was ratified:

> "Those things which are not lawful under any of the American constitutions may be stated thus:—
> "1. Any law respecting an establishment of religion....
> "2. Compulsory support, by taxation or otherwise, of religious instruction. Not only is no one denomination to be favored at the expense of the rest, but all support of religious instruction must be entirely voluntary."} ...

Justice Thomas, concurring in the judgment [in *Elk Grove Unified School Dist. v. Newdow*, 542 U.S. 1 (2004)] ....

The text and history of the Establishment Clause strongly suggest that it is a federalism provision intended to prevent Congress from interfering with state establishments. Thus, unlike the Free Exercise Clause, which does protect an individual right, it makes little sense to incorporate the Establishment Clause....

The Establishment Clause provides that "Congress shall make no law respecting an establishment of religion." As a textual matter, this Clause probably prohibits Congress from establishing a national religion. Perhaps more importantly, the Clause made clear that Congress could not interfere with state establishments, notwithstanding any argument that could be made based on Congress' power under the Necessary and Proper Clause.

Nothing in the text of the Clause suggests that it reaches any further. The Establishment Clause does not purport to protect individual rights. By contrast, the Free Exercise Clause plainly protects individuals against congressional interference with the right to exercise their religion, and the remaining Clauses within the First Amendment expressly disable Congress from "abridging [particular] *freedom[s]*." (Emphasis added.) This textual analysis is consistent with the prevailing view that the Constitution left religion to the States. History also supports this understanding: At the founding, at least six States had established religions....

Quite simply, the Establishment Clause is best understood as a federalism provision—it protects state establishments from federal interference but does not protect any individual right. These two features independently make incorporation of the Clause difficult to understand.

The best argument in favor of incorporation would be that, by disabling Congress from establishing a national religion, the Clause protected an individual right, enforceable against the Federal Government, to be free from coercive federal establishments. Incorporation of this individual right, the argument goes, makes sense.... But even assuming that the Establishment Clause precludes the Federal Government from establishing a national religion, it does not follow that the Clause created or protects any individual right. For the reasons discussed above, it is more likely that States and only States were the direct beneficiaries.

Moreover, incorporation of this putative individual right leads to a peculiar outcome: It would prohibit precisely what the Establishment Clause was intended to protect—*state* establishments of religion. Nevertheless, the potential right against federal establishments is the only candidate for incorporation. I would welcome the opportunity to consider more fully the difficult questions whether and how the Establishment Clause applies against the States....

2. The Endorsement Test and Privately Selected Speech

a. Problem: Conflicts Among Rights

The Justices in *Capitol Square Review & Advisory Bd.* all seem to agree that "compliance with the Establishment Clause is a state interest sufficiently compelling to justify content-based restrictions on speech." The plurality and the concurrences simply reason that there's no real conflict here between the "no government endorsement" principle of the Establishment Clause and the "no content-based restrictions in traditional public fora" principle of the Free Speech Clause.

But say there was a conflict: How should the Court decide which Clause is to yield? Should it respond with the quote given above? Or should it say "compliance with the Free Speech Clause is a purpose sufficiently compelling to justify what would otherwise be seen as an impermissible endorsement of religion"?

b. Capitol Square Review & Advisory Bd. v. Pinette, 515 U.S. 753 (1995)

Justice Scalia ... delivered the opinion of the Court with respect to Parts [A and B], and an opinion with respect to [Parts C, D, and E], in which ... Chief Justice [Rehnquist], Justice Kennedy, and Justice Thomas join....

[A.] Capitol Square is a 10-acre, state-owned plaza surrounding the statehouse in Columbus, Ohio. For over a century the square has been used for public speeches, gatherings, and festivals advocating and celebrating a variety of causes, both secular and religious.

[Ohio law] makes the square available "for use by the public ... for free discussion of public questions, or for activities of a broad public purpose," and ... gives the Capitol Square Review and Advisory Board ... responsibility for regulating public access. To use the square, a group must simply fill out an official application form and meet several criteria, which concern primarily safety, sanitation, and non-interference with other uses of the square, and which are neutral as to the speech content of the proposed event.

It has been the Board's policy "to allow a broad range of speakers and other gatherings of people to conduct events on the Capitol Square." Such diverse groups as homosexual rights organizations, the Ku Klux Klan, and the United Way have held rallies. The Board has also permitted a variety of unattended displays on Capitol Square: a state-sponsored lighted tree during the Christmas season, a privately sponsored menorah during Chanukah, a display showing the progress of a United Way fundraising campaign, and booths and exhibits during an arts festival....

In November 1993, ... the Board authorized the State to put up its annual Christmas tree. On November 29, 1993, the Board granted a rabbi's application to erect a menorah. That same day, the Board received an application from ... an officer of the Ohio Ku Klux Klan, to place a cross on the square from December 8, 1993, to December 24, 1993. The Board denied that application on [the grounds of its obligation to comply with the Establishment Clause—ed.]. [The Klan sued.—ed.] ...

[B.] [P]rivate religious speech ... is as fully protected under the Free Speech Clause as secular private expression. Indeed, in Anglo-American history, at least, government suppression of speech has so commonly been directed *precisely* at religious speech that a free-speech clause without religion would be Hamlet without the prince....

[In a traditional public forum, such as Capitol Square, a state] ... may regulate expressive *content* only if such a restriction is necessary, and narrowly drawn, to serve a compelling state interest.... [C]ompliance with the Establishment Clause is a state interest sufficiently compelling to justify content-based restrictions on speech.... [But here t]he State did not sponsor respondents' expression, the expression was made on government property that had been opened to the public for speech, and permission was requested through the same application process and on the same terms required of other private groups. {[The government is] not directly sponsoring the [Cross display], and "any benefit to religion ... would have been no more than incidental." ... "[A]n open forum ... does not confer any imprimatur of state approval on religious sects or practices."} ...

[C (plurality only).] Petitioners argue that ... the forum's proximity to the seat of government ... may produce the perception that the cross bears the State's approval. They urge us to apply the so-called "endorsement test," and to find that, because an observer might mistake private expression for officially endorsed religious expression, the State's content-based restriction is constitutional....

"Endorsement" connotes an expression or demonstration of approval or support. Our cases have accordingly equated "endorsement" with "promotion" or "favoritism." We find it peculiar to say that government "promotes" or "favors" a religious display by giving it the same access to a public forum that all other displays enjoy....

Where we have tested for endorsement of religion, the subject of the test was either expression *by the government itself*, or else government action alleged to *discriminate in favor* of private religious expression or activity. The test petitioners propose, which would attribute to a neutrally behaving government *private* religious expression ... would better be called a "transferred endorsement" test....

"[T]here is a crucial difference between *government* speech endorsing religion, which the Establishment Clause forbids, and *private* speech endorsing religion, which the Free Speech and Free Exercise Clauses protect." Petitioners assert, in effect, that that distinction disappears when the private speech is conducted too close to the symbols of government. But that ... must be merely a subpart of a more general principle: that the distinction disappears whenever private speech can be mistaken for government speech. That proposition cannot be accepted, at least where, as here, the government has not fostered or encouraged the mistake.... Capitol Square is a genuinely public forum, is known to be a public forum, and has been widely used as a public forum for many, many years. Private religious speech cannot be subject to veto by those who see favoritism where there is none.

The contrary view ... exiles private religious speech to a realm of less-protected expression heretofore inhabited only by sexually explicit displays and commercial speech. It will be a sad day when this Court casts piety in with pornography, and finds the First Amendment more hospitable to private expletives, see *Cohen v. California,* than to private prayers....

Since petitioners' "transferred endorsement" principle cannot possibly be restricted to squares in front of state capitols, the Establishment Clause regime that it would usher in is most unappealing.... Petitioners' rule would require school districts adopting [policies allowing all groups, whether or not religious, to use school space for after-hours events] to guess whether some undetermined critical mass of the community might nonetheless perceive the district to be advocating a religious viewpoint.

Similarly, state universities would be forced to reassess our statement that "an open forum in a public university does not confer any imprimatur of state approval on religious sects or practices." Whether it does would henceforth depend upon immediate appearances. Policymakers would find themselves in a vise between the Establishment Clause on one side and the Free Speech and Free Exercise Clauses on the other [which generally require equal treatment for religious speakers, see, *e.g.*, *Rosenberger v. Rector*, p. 623—ed.].

Every proposed act of private, religious expression in a public forum would force officials to weigh a host of imponderables. How close to government is too close? What kind of building, and in what context, symbolizes state authority? If the State guessed wrong in one direction, it would be guilty of an Establishment Clause violation; if in the other, it would be liable for suppressing free exercise or free speech (a risk not run when the State restrains only its *own* expression)....

If Ohio is concerned about misperceptions, nothing prevents it from requiring all private displays in the Square to be identified as such. That would be a content-neutral "manner" restriction that is assuredly constitutional. But the State may not, on the claim of misperception of official endorsement, ban all private religious speech from the public square, or discriminate against it by requiring religious speech alone to disclaim public sponsorship.... Religious expression cannot violate the Establishment Clause where it (1) is purely private and (2) occurs in a traditional or designated public forum, publicly announced and open to all on equal terms....

[D (plurality only).] {[W]e do not inquire into the adequacy of the identification that was attached to the cross ultimately erected in this case. The difficulties posed by such an inquiry, however, are yet another reason to reject the principle of "transferred endorsement."

The only principled line for adequacy of identification would be identification that is legible at whatever distance the cross is visible. Otherwise, the uninformed viewer who does not have time or inclination to come closer to read the sign might be misled, just as (under current law) the uninformed viewer who does not have time or inclination to inquire whether speech in Capitol Square is publicly endorsed speech might be misled. Needless to say, such a rule would place considerable constraint upon religious speech .... But if one rejects that criterion, courts would have to decide (on what basis we cannot imagine) how large an identifying sign is large enough. Our Religion Clause jurisprudence is complex enough without the addition of this highly litigable feature.}

[E (plurality only).] {If ... [Justice O'Connor] would not "be likely to come to a different result from the plurality where truly private speech is allowed on equal terms in a vigorous public forum that the government has administered properly," then she is extending the "endorsement test" to private speech to cover an eventuality that is "not likely" to occur. Before doing that, it would seem desirable to explore the precise degree of the unlikelihood (is it perhaps 100%?)—for as we point out in text, the extension to private speech has considerable costs.

Contrary to what Justice O'Connor, Justice Souter, and Justice Stevens argue, the endorsement test does not supply an appropriate standard for the inquiry before us. It supplies no standard whatsoever.... [Consider] the debate between the concurrence and Justice Stevens' dissent as to whether the hypothetical beholder who will be the determinant of "endorsement" should be *any* beholder (no matter how unknowledgeable), or the *average* beholder, or (what Justice Stevens accuses the concurrence of favoring) the "ultra-reasonable" beholder. And, of course, even when one achieves agreement upon that question, it will be unrealistic to expect different judges (or should it be juries?) to reach consistent answers as to what any beholder, the average beholder, or the ultrareasonable beholder (as the case may be) would think. It is irresponsible to make the Nation's legislators walk this minefield.}

Justice Thomas, concurring....

Although the Klan might have sought to convey a message with some religious component, I think that the Klan had a primarily nonreligious purpose in erecting the cross. The Klan simply has appropriated one of the most sacred of religious symbols as a symbol of hate. In my mind, this suggests that this case may not have truly involved the Establishment Clause ....

Justice O'Connor, with whom Justice Souter and Justice Breyer join, concurring in [Parts A and B of the plurality opinion] and concurring in the judgment....

[A.] [A]n impermissible message of endorsement can be sent in a variety of contexts, not all of which involve direct government speech or outright favoritism.... [This is not] to suggest that I would be likely to come to a different result from the plurality where truly private speech is allowed on equal terms in a vigorous public forum that the government has administered properly. That the religious display at issue here was erected by a private group in a public square available "for use by the public ... for free discussion of public questions, or for activities of a broad public purpose," certainly informs the [endorsement inquiry] ....

To the plurality's consideration of the open nature of the forum and the private ownership of the display, however, I would add the presence of a sign disclaiming government sponsorship or endorsement on the Klan cross, which would make the State's role clear to the community.... [C]ertain aspects of the cross display in this case arguably intimate government approval of respondents' private religious message—particularly that the cross is an especially potent sectarian symbol which stood unattended in close proximity to official government buildings. In context, a disclaimer helps remove doubt about state approval of respondents' religious message....

[And] when the reasonable observer would view a government practice as endorsing religion, I believe that it is our *duty* to hold the practice invalid.... Where the government's operation of a public forum has the effect of endorsing religion, even if the governmental actor neither intends nor actively encourages that result, the Establishment Clause is violated. This is so not because of "transferred endorsement," or mistaken attribution of private speech to the State, but because the State's own actions (operating the forum in a particular manner and permitting the religious expression to take place therein) ... *actually convey* a message of endorsement.

At some point, for example, a private religious group may so dominate a public forum that a formal policy of equal access is transformed into a demonstration of approval. Other circumstances may produce the same effect—whether because of the fortuity of geography, the nature of the particular public space, or the character of the religious speech at issue, among others....

[B.] In my view, proper application of the endorsement test requires that the reasonable observer be deemed more informed than the casual passerby postulated by Justice Stevens.... [T]he applicable observer is similar to the "reasonable person" in tort law, who ... is "... a personification of a community ideal of reasonable behavior, determined by the [collective] social judgment." Thus, "we do not ask whether there is *any* person who could find an endorsement of religion, whether *some* people may be offended by the display, or whether *some* reasonable person *might* think [the State] endorses religion." ... There is always *someone* who, with a particular quantum of knowledge, reasonably might perceive a particular action as an endorsement of religion. A State has not made religion relevant to standing in the political community simply because a particular viewer of a display might feel uncomfortable.

It is for this reason that the reasonable observer in the endorsement inquiry must be deemed aware of the history and context of the community and forum in which the religious display appears ... [including] the general history of the place in which the cross is displayed ... [such as] that Capitol Square is a public park that has been used over time by private speakers of various types .... Moreover, this observer would certainly be able to read and understand an adequate disclaimer, which the Klan had informed the State it would include in the display at the time it applied for the permit, and the content of which the Board could have defined as it deemed necessary ....

Justice Souter, with whom Justice O'Connor and Justice Breyer join, concurring in [Parts A and B of the plurality opinion] and concurring in the judgment....

By allowing government to encourage what it cannot do on its own, the [plurality's] proposed *per se* rule would tempt a public body to contract out its establishment of religion, by encouraging the private enterprise of the religious to exhibit what the government could not display itself....

[Nonetheless,] a flat denial of the Klan's application was not the Board's only option to protect against an appearance of endorsement, and the Board was required to find its most "narrowly drawn" alternative.... The Board ... could have granted the application subject to the condition that the Klan attach a disclaimer sufficiently large and clear to preclude any reasonable inference that the cross was there to "demonstrat[e] the government's allegiance to, or endorsement of, the Christian faith." In the alternative, the Board could have instituted a policy of restricting all private, unattended displays to one area of the square, with a permanent sign marking the area as a forum for private speech carrying no endorsement from the State....

Justice Stevens, dissenting....

[A.] The Establishment Clause, "at the very least, prohibits government from appearing to take a position on questions of religious belief or from 'making adherence to a religion relevant in any way to a person's standing in the political community.'" At least when religious symbols are involved, the question whether the State is "appearing to take a position" is best judged from the standpoint of a "reasonable observer."

It is especially important to take account of the perspective of a reasonable observer who may not share the particular religious belief it expresses. A paramount purpose of the Establishment Clause is to protect such a person from being made to feel like an outsider in matters of faith, and a stranger in the political community. If a reasonable person could perceive a government endorsement of religion from a private display, then the State may not allow its property to be used as a forum for that display....

[B.] The "reasonable observer" of any symbol placed unattended in front of any capitol in the world will normally assume that the sovereign ... has sponsored and facilitated its message. {Even if the disclaimer at the foot of the cross [in this case] (which stated that the cross was placed there by a private organization) were legible, that inference would remain, because a property owner's decision to allow a third party to place a sign on her property conveys the same message of endorsement as if she had erected it herself.} {Indeed, I do not think *any* disclaimer could dispel the message of endorsement in this case. Capitol Square's location in downtown Columbus ... makes it inevitable that countless motorists and pedestrians would immediately perceive the proximity of the cross to the capitol without necessarily noticing any disclaimer of public sponsorship.} ...

{The plurality incorrectly assumes that a decision to exclude a category of speech from an inappropriate forum must rest on a judgment about the value of that speech. Yet, we have upheld the exclusion of all political signs from public vehicles, *Lehman v. Shaker Heights,* 418 U.S. 298 (1974), though political expression is at the heart of the protection afforded by the First Amendment. A view that "private prayers" are most appropriate in private settings is neither novel nor disrespectful to religious speech.} ...

[C.] The existence of a "public forum" in itself cannot dispel the message of endorsement. A contrary argument would assume an "ultrareasonable observer" who understands the vagaries of this Court's First Amendment jurisprudence. I think it presumptuous to consider such knowledge a precondition of Establishment Clause protection. Many (probably most) reasonable people do not know the difference between a "public forum," a "limited public forum," and a "non-public forum." They *do* know the difference between a state capitol and a church.... For a religious display to violate the Establishment Clause, I think it is enough that *some* reasonable observers would attribute a religious message to the State.

The plurality appears to rely on the history of this particular public forum—specifically, it emphasizes that Ohio has in the past allowed three other private unattended displays. Even if the State could not reasonably have been understood to endorse the prior displays, I would not find this argument convincing, because it assumes that all reasonable viewers know all about the history of Capitol Square—a highly unlikely supposition.

{Justice O'Connor apparently would not extend Establishment Clause protection to passers-by who are unaware of Capitol Square's history.... But passers-by ... are members of the body politic, and they are equally entitled to be free from government endorsement of religion.}

[D.] [T]he plurality's argument [also] fails on its own terms, because each of the three previous displays conveyed the same message of approval and endorsement that this one does. [Details omitted.—ed.] ...

Justice Ginsburg, dissenting....

[Near the] large Latin cross that stood alone and unattended in close proximity to Ohio's Statehouse ... were the government's flags and the government's statues. No human speaker was present to disassociate the religious symbol from the State. No other private display was in sight. No plainly visible sign informed the public that the cross belonged to the Klan and that Ohio's government did not endorse the display's message. If the aim of the Establishment Clause is genuinely to uncouple government from church, a State may not permit, and a court may not order, a display of this character....

3.   The No Primary Religious Purpose Principle

a.   Summary

Rule: The government may not do things for which the "pre-eminent purpose" is religious. *Stone v. Graham,* 449 U.S. 39 (1980). (This is the first *Lemon* prong.) The Court has found such a religious purpose in:

— A ban on the teaching of evolution in public schools, *Epperson v. Arkansas,* 393 U.S. 97 (1968), and a requirement that they teach creation science alongside evolution, *Edwards v. Aguillard* (1987) (p. 847).

— A requirement that the Ten Commandments be posted in public schools, *Stone v. Graham,* or in a courthouse, *McCreary County v. ACLU* (2005) (p. 855).

— The authorization of a moment of silence in public schools, where the legislative history suggested that the purpose of the moment of silence

was specifically to promote prayer, and not just whatever silent meditation the students might prefer. *Wallace v. Jaffree,* 472 U.S. 38 (1985).

— A high school's authorization of student-led prayer at football games,
Santa Fe Indep. School Dist. v. Doe, 530 U.S. 290 (2000).

Limitations on this rule:

1. The desire to implement into law the majority's moral views related to
secular topics—such as civil rights, abortion funding, polygamy, slavery,
and the like—is not seen as a religious purpose, even when the moral
views are derived from religion. *McGowan v. Maryland* (1961) (p. 846);
see also *Bob Jones Univ. v. United States* (1983) (p. 986) (upholding denial of tax exemption to university that has racially discriminatory policies); *Harris v. McRae,* 448 U.S. 297, 319-20 (1980) (upholding ban on
government funding of abortion).

2. Accommodating religious objectors by exempting them from generally
applicable laws is a permissible purpose, see *Corporation of Presiding
Bishop v. Amos* (1987) (p. 767), at least so long as the government decisionmaker does not "abandon[] neutrality and act[] with the intent of
promoting a particular point of view in religious matters."

b. *Problem: Evolution Disclaimer*

In April 1994, the Tangipahoa Parish, Louisiana, Board of Education
passed the following resolution:

> Whenever, in classes of elementary or high school, the scientific theory
> of evolution is to be presented, ... the following statement shall be quoted
> immediately before the unit of study begins as a disclaimer from endorse-
> ment of such theory[:]
> "It is hereby recognized by the Tangipahoa Board of Education, that the
> lesson to be presented, regarding the origin of life and matter, is known as
> the Scientific Theory of Evolution and should be presented to inform stu-
> dents of the scientific concept and not intended to influence or dissuade the
> Biblical version of Creation or any other concept.
> "It is further recognized by the Board of Education that it is the basic
> right and privilege of each student to form his/her own opinion or maintain
> beliefs taught by parents on this very important matter of the origin of life
> and matter. Students are urged to exercise critical thinking and gather all
> information possible and closely examine each alternative toward forming
> an opinion."

Is reading this disclaimer in class constitutional? *Compare Freiler v. Tangi-
pahoa Parish Bd. of Ed.,* 185 F.3d 337 (5th Cir. 1999), *and Selman v. Cobb
County School Dist.,* 2005 WL 83829 (N.D. Ga.), *with Freiler v. Tangipahoa
Parish Bd. of Ed.,* 201 F.3d 602 (5th Cir. 2000) (Barksdale, J., dissenting
from denial of rehearing en banc), *and Tangipahoa Parish Bd. of Ed. v.
Freiler,* 530 U.S. 1251 (2000) (Scalia, J., dissenting from denial of certiorari).

c. *Problem: Teaching That Human Life Is Precious*

Imagine that Massachusetts, in trying to broaden its students' moral education, requires that junior high school civics classes teach "elementary principles of right and wrong," such as the impropriety of violence, racism, and so on. The law also provides that all such classes "shall teach that all innocent human life is precious and valuable," and that no such class shall teach the moral propriety of abortion, infanticide, or euthanasia.

Some of the representatives who supported the law pointed out in debates that Massachusetts has a large Catholic population; that many Massachusetts voters and taxpayers believe abortion, infanticide, and euthanasia are wrong; that allowing the teaching of contrary views would lead even more parents to switch their children from public schools to private schools; and that if such contrary views are taught, even many of those parents who keep their parents in public schools would grow distrustful of the public schools, and would be much more reluctant to support them both by volunteering and by politically supporting higher school spending.

The law is challenged on First Amendment grounds. Analyze.

d. *McGowan v. Maryland, 366 U.S. 420 (1961)*

Chief Justice Warren delivered the opinion of the Court....

[The Court upheld a law mandating that most businesses close on Sundays; the majority concluded that such laws, though initially enacted for religious reasons, were now serving a secular goal:—ed.]

[T]he "Establishment" Clause does not ban ... regulation of conduct whose reason or effect merely happens to coincide or harmonize with the tenets of some or all religions. In many instances, ... legislatures conclude that the general welfare of society, wholly apart from any religious considerations, demands such regulation.

Thus, for temporal purposes, murder is illegal. And the fact that this agrees with the dictates of the Judaeo-Christian religions while it may disagree with others does not invalidate the regulation. So too with the questions of adultery and polygamy. The same could be said of theft, fraud, etc., because those offenses were also proscribed in the Decalogue....

[In this case,] the State seeks to set one day apart from all others as a day of rest, repose, recreation and tranquility—a day which all members of the family and community have the opportunity to spend and enjoy together, a day on which there exists relative quiet and disassociation from the everyday intensity of commercial activities, a day on which people may visit friends and relatives who are not available during working days.... It would seem unrealistic for enforcement purposes and perhaps detrimental to the general welfare to require a State to choose a common day of rest other than that which most persons would select of their own accord. For these reasons, we hold that the Maryland statutes are not laws respecting an establishment of religion....

Justice Frankfurter, joined by Justice Harlan, concurring in the judgment. [Omitted.—ed.]

Justice Douglas, dissenting. [Omitted.—ed.]

e.   Edwards v. Aguillard, 482 U.S. 578 (1987)

Justice Brennan delivered the opinion of the Court....

[A.] Louisiana's "Balanced Treatment for Creation-Science and Evolu-tion-Science in Public School Instruction" Act ... forbids the teaching of the theory of evolution in public schools unless accompanied by instruction in "creation science." ... If either [evolution or creation science] is taught, ... the other must also be taught. The theories of evolution and creation science are statutorily defined as "the scientific evidences for [creation or evolution] and inferences from those scientific evidences." ...

[B.] The Court has been particularly vigilant in monitoring compliance with the Establishment Clause in elementary and secondary schools. Fam-ilies entrust public schools with the education of their children, but condi-tion their trust on the understanding that the classroom will not purposely be used to advance religious views that may conflict with the private beliefs of the student and his or her family.

Students in such institutions are impressionable and their attendance is involuntary. The State exerts great authority and coercive power through mandatory attendance requirements, and because of the students' emula-tion of teachers as role models and the children's susceptibility to peer pres-sure. {The potential for undue influence is far less significant with regard to college students who voluntarily enroll in courses.... Thus, for instance, the Court has not questioned the authority of state colleges and universities to offer courses on religion or theology.} Furthermore, "[t]he public school is at once the symbol of our democracy and the most pervasive means for promot-ing our common destiny. In no activity of the State is it more vital to keep out divisive forces than in its schools...." ...

[C.] "... [W]hether government's actual purpose is to endorse or disap-prove of religion" ... may be evidenced by promotion of religion in general, or by advancement of a particular religious belief.... In this case, appellants have identified no clear secular purpose for the Louisiana Act.

True, the Act's stated purpose is to protect academic freedom. This phrase might, in common parlance, be understood as referring to enhancing the freedom of teachers to teach what they will...,. [But] the Act was not de-signed to further that goal. {[In] Louisiana, courses in public schools are prescribed by the State Board of Education and teachers are not free, absent permission, to teach courses different from what is required.... The Act ac-tually serves to diminish academic freedom by removing the flexibility to teach evolution without also teaching creation science, even if teachers de-termine that such curriculum results in less effective and comprehensive science instruction.} ...

Even if "academic freedom" is read to mean "teaching all of the evidence" with respect to the origin of human beings, the Act does not further this purpose. The goal of providing a more comprehensive science curriculum is not furthered either by outlawing the teaching of evolution or by requiring the teaching of creation science.

[D.] While the Court is normally deferential to a State's articulation of a secular purpose, it is required that the statement of such purpose be sincere and not a sham.... "It is not a trivial matter ... to require that the legislature manifest a secular purpose and omit all sectarian endorsements from its laws. That requirement is precisely tailored to the Establishment Clause's purpose of assuring that Government not intentionally endorse religion or a religious practice."

It is clear from the legislative history that the purpose of the legislative sponsor, Senator Bill Keith, was to narrow the science curriculum. During the legislative hearings, Senator Keith stated: "My preference would be that neither [creationism nor evolution] be taught." Such a ban on teaching does not promote—indeed, it undermines—the provision of a comprehensive scientific education.

It is equally clear that requiring schools to teach creation science with evolution does not advance academic freedom. The Act does not grant teachers a flexibility that they did not already possess to supplant the present science curriculum with the presentation of theories, besides evolution, about the origin of life. Indeed, the Court of Appeals found that no law prohibited Louisiana public school teachers from teaching any scientific theory.... The Act provides Louisiana school teachers with no new authority. Thus the stated purpose is not furthered by it....

Furthermore, the goal of basic "fairness" is hardly furthered by the Act's discriminatory preference for the teaching of creation science and against the teaching of evolution. {[None of the] other [statutory] provisions prescribing the courses of study in Louisiana's public schools ... nominally mandates "equal time" for opposing opinions ....} [And w]hile requiring that curriculum guides be developed for creation science, the Act says nothing of comparable guides for evolution.

Similarly, resource services are supplied for creation science but not for evolution. Only "creation scientists" can serve on the panel that supplies the resource services. The Act forbids school boards to discriminate against anyone who "chooses to be a creation-scientist" or to teach "creationism," but fails to protect those who choose to teach evolution or any other non-creation science theory, or who refuse to teach creation science.

If the Louisiana Legislature's purpose was solely to maximize the comprehensiveness and effectiveness of science instruction, it would have encouraged the teaching of all scientific theories about the origins of humankind. But under the Act's requirements, teachers who were once free to teach any and all facets of this subject are now unable to do so.

Moreover, the Act fails even to ensure that creation science will be taught, but instead requires the teaching of this theory only when the theory of evolution is taught.... [T]he Act [thus] does not serve to protect academic freedom, but has the distinctly different purpose of discrediting "evolution by counterbalancing its teaching at every turn with the teaching of creationism...."

[E.] [W]e need not be blind in this case to the legislature's preeminent religious purpose in enacting this statute. There is a historic and contemporaneous link between the teachings of certain religious denominations and the teaching of evolution.

It was this link that concerned the Court in *Epperson v. Arkansas,* 393 U.S. 97 (1968), which also involved a facial challenge to a statute regulating the teaching of evolution.... Although the Arkansas antievolution law did not explicitly state its predominant religious purpose, the Court could not ignore that "[t]he statute was a product of the upsurge of 'fundamentalist' religious fervor" that has long viewed this particular scientific theory as contradicting the literal interpretation of the Bible.... The Court found that there be no legitimate state interest in protecting particular religions from scientific views "distasteful to them," and concluded "that the First Amendment does not permit the State to require that teaching and learning must be tailored to the principles or prohibitions of any religious sect or dogma."

These same historic and contemporaneous antagonisms between the teachings of certain religious denominations and the teaching of evolution are present in this case. The preeminent purpose of the Louisiana Legislature was clearly to advance the religious viewpoint that a supernatural being created humankind.... Senator Keith's leading expert on creation science, Edward Boudreaux, testified at the legislative hearings that the theory of creation science included belief in the existence of a supernatural creator. Senator Keith also cited testimony from other experts to support the creation-science view that "a creator [was] responsible for the universe and everything in it." ...

Senator Keith[] explained during the legislative hearings that his disdain for the theory of evolution resulted from the support that evolution supplied to views contrary to his own religious beliefs. According to Senator Keith, the theory of evolution was consonant with the "cardinal principle[s] of religious humanism, secular humanism, theological liberalism, aetheistism *[sic]*." The state senator repeatedly stated that scientific evidence supporting his religious views should be included in the public school curriculum to redress the fact that the theory of evolution incidentally coincided with what he characterized as religious beliefs antithetical to his own. The legislation therefore sought to alter the science curriculum to reflect endorsement of a religious view that is antagonistic to the theory of evolution....

[T]he ... Act is designed *either* to promote the theory of creation science which embodies a particular religious tenet by requiring that creation science be taught whenever evolution is taught *or* to prohibit the teaching of a scientific theory disfavored by certain religious sects by forbidding the teaching of evolution when creation science is not also taught. The Establishment Clause, however, "forbids *alike* the preference of a religious doctrine *or* the prohibition of theory which is deemed antagonistic to a particular dogma." ...

We do not imply that a legislature could never require that scientific critiques of prevailing scientific theories be taught.... [T]eaching a variety of scientific theories about the origins of humankind to schoolchildren might be validly done with the clear secular intent of enhancing the effectiveness of science instruction. But because the primary purpose of the ... Act is to endorse a particular religious doctrine, the Act furthers religion in violation of the Establishment Clause....

Justice Scalia, with whom ... Chief Justice [Rehnquist] joins, dissenting....

[A.] [Under our Establishment Clause cases, "legislative purpose"] means the "actual" motives of those responsible for the challenged action.... Thus, if those legislators who supported the Balanced Treatment Act *in fact* acted with a "sincere" secular purpose [as at least one of their purposes], the Act survives the [purpose] test, regardless of whether that purpose is likely to be achieved by the provisions they enacted....

[Moreover,] we do not presume that the sole purpose of a law is to advance religion merely because it was supported strongly by organized religions or by adherents of particular faiths. To do so would deprive religious men and women of their right to participate in the political process. Today's religious activism may give us the Balanced Treatment Act, but yesterday's resulted in the abolition of slavery, and tomorrow's may bring relief for famine victims.

Similarly, we will not presume that a law's purpose is to advance religion merely because it "happens to coincide or harmonize with the tenets of some or all religions" .... We have, for example, turned back Establishment Clause challenges to restrictions on abortion funding and to Sunday closing laws, despite the fact that both "agre[e] with the dictates of [some] Judaeo-Christian religions." ...

Finally, our cases indicate that even certain kinds of governmental actions undertaken with the specific intention of improving the position of religion do not "advance religion" as that term is used in *Lemon*....

First, since we have consistently described the Establishment Clause as forbidding not only state action motivated by the desire to *advance* religion, but also that intended to "disapprove," "inhibit," or evince "hostility" toward religion[,] ... a State which discovers that its employees are inhibiting religion must take steps to prevent them from doing so, even though its purpose would clearly be to advance religion. Thus, if the Louisiana Legislature sincerely believed that the State's science teachers were being hostile to religion, our cases indicate that it could act to eliminate that hostility without running afoul of *Lemon*'s purpose test.

Second, we have held that intentional governmental advancement of religion [by granting religious exemptions from generally applicable laws] is sometimes required by the Free Exercise Clause ....

[Third,] in some circumstances government may act to accommodate religion, even if that action is not required by the First Amendment.... Title VII of the Civil Rights Act of 1964, which ... requires [private employers] reasonably to accommodate the religious practices of their employees, [does not violate] the Establishment Clause, even though its "purpose" is, of course, to advance religion .... {Since the existence of secular purpose is so entirely clear [for reasons discussed below], and thus dispositive, I will not [discuss these three exceptions further, except to say that the sponsor of the Act repeatedly urged his colleagues to pass his bill to remedy what he saw as the unconstitutional establishment of Secular Humanism, see item B(5) below].}

[B.] [T]here is ample evidence that the majority is wrong in holding that the Balanced Treatment Act is without secular purpose.... [The] Act did not fly through the Louisiana Legislature on wings of fundamentalist religious fervor—which would be unlikely, in any event, since only a small minority of the State's citizens belong to fundamentalist religious denominations. [History of the Act's year-long legislative path omitted.—ed.] ...

The legislators specifically designated the protection of "academic freedom" as the purpose of the Act. We cannot accurately assess whether this purpose is a "sham," until we first examine the evidence presented to the legislature far more carefully than the Court has done.... I by no means intend to endorse [the] accuracy [of] {the testimony of Senator Keith and his supporters}.... Our task[, though,] is not to judge the debate about teaching the origins of life, but to ascertain what the members of the Louisiana Legislature believed. The vast majority of them voted to approve a bill which explicitly stated a secular purpose; what is crucial is not their *wisdom* in believing that purpose would be achieved by the bill, but their *sincerity* in believing it would be....

Senator Keith and his witnesses testified essentially [thus] ...:

(1) There are two and only two scientific explanations for the beginning of life—evolution and creation science. Both are bona fide "sciences." Both posit a theory of the origin of life and subject that theory to empirical testing. Evolution posits that life arose out of inanimate chemical compounds and has gradually evolved over millions of years. Creation science posits that all life forms now on earth appeared suddenly and relatively recently and have changed little.

Since there are only two possible explanations of the origin of life, any evidence that tends to disprove the theory of evolution necessarily tends to prove the theory of creation science, and vice versa. For example, the abrupt appearance in the fossil record of complex life, and the extreme rarity of transitional life forms in that record, are evidence for creation science.

(2) ... The evidence for evolution is far less compelling than we have been led to believe....

(3) Creation science is educationally valuable. Students exposed to it better understand the current state of scientific evidence about the origin of life. Those students even have a better understanding of evolution....

(4) Although creation science is educationally valuable and strictly scientific, it is now being censored from or misrepresented in the public schools. Evolution, in turn, is misrepresented as an absolute truth. Teachers have

been brainwashed by an entrenched scientific establishment composed almost exclusively of scientists to whom evolution is like a "religion." These scientists discriminate against creation scientists so as to prevent evolution's weaknesses from being exposed.

(5) The censorship of creation science has at least two harmful effects. First, it deprives students of knowledge of one of the two scientific explanations for the origin of life and leads them to believe that evolution is proven fact .... Second, it violates the Establishment Clause. The United States Supreme Court has held that secular humanism is a religion [see *Torcaso v. Watkins*]. Belief in evolution is a central tenet of that religion. Thus, by censoring creation science and instructing students that evolution is fact, public school teachers are *now* advancing religion in violation of the Establishment Clause....

We have no way of knowing, of course, how many legislators believed the testimony of Senator Keith and his witnesses. But in the absence of evidence to the contrary, we have to assume that many of them did. Given that assumption, the Court today plainly errs in holding that the Louisiana Legislature passed the Balanced Treatment Act for exclusively religious purposes....

[C.] The Louisiana Legislature [also] explicitly set forth its secular purpose ("protecting academic freedom") in the very text of the Act.... [To the Legislature,] "academic freedom" meant[] *students'* freedom from *indoctrination*. The legislature wanted to ensure that students would be free to decide for themselves how life began, based upon a fair and balanced presentation of the scientific evidence—that is, to protect "the right of each [student] voluntarily to determine what to believe (and what not to believe) free of any coercive pressures from the State." ...[a] ...

[T]he Act pursues [this] purpose plainly and consistently. It requires that, whenever the subject of origins is covered, evolution be "taught as a theory, rather than as proven scientific fact" and that scientific evidence inconsistent with the theory of evolution (viz., "creation science") be taught as well.... [And] it treats the teaching of creation the same way. It does *not* mandate instruction in creation science; *forbids* teachers to present creation science "as proven scientific fact"; and *bans* the teaching of creation science unless the theory is (to use the Court's terminology) "discredit[ed] '... at every turn'" with the teaching of evolution....

The Act's reference to "creation" is not convincing evidence of religious purpose. The Act defines creation science as "*scientific evidenc[e],*" and Senator Keith and his witnesses repeatedly stressed that the subject can and should be presented without religious content.

---

[a] [**The majority's view on this:**—ed.] The dissent concludes that the Act's purpose was to protect the academic freedom of students, and not that of teachers. Such a view is not at odds with our conclusion that if the Act's purpose was to provide comprehensive scientific education (a concern shared by students and teachers ...), that purpose was not advanced by the statute's provisions....

We have no basis on the record to conclude that creation science need be anything other than a collection of scientific data supporting the theory that life abruptly appeared on earth. Creation science, its proponents insist, no more must explain *whence* life came than evolution must explain whence came the inanimate materials from which it says life evolved. But even if that were not so, to posit a past creator is not to posit the eternal and personal God who is the object of religious veneration....

The Court cites three provisions of the Act which, it argues, demonstrate a "discriminatory preference for the teaching of creation science" and no interest in "academic freedom." First, the Act prohibits discrimination only against creation scientists and those who teach creation science. Second, the Act requires local school boards to develop and provide to science teachers "a curriculum guide on presentation of creation-science." Finally, the Act requires the Governor to designate seven creation scientists who shall, upon request, assist local school boards in developing the curriculum guides. But none of these provisions casts doubt upon the sincerity of the legislators' articulated purpose of "academic freedom" ....

The Louisiana legislators had been told repeatedly that creation scientists were scorned by most educators and scientists, who themselves had an almost religious faith in evolution. It is hardly surprising, then, that in seeking to achieve a balanced, "nonindoctrinating" curriculum, the legislators protected from discrimination only those teachers whom they thought were *suffering* from discrimination. (Also, the legislators ... could quite reasonably have concluded that discrimination against evolutionists was already prohibited [by *Epperson*].) ... [Likewise, w]itnesses had informed the legislators that, because of the hostility of most scientists and educators to creation science, the topic had been censored from or badly misrepresented in elementary and secondary school texts.... [I]t was [thus] entirely reasonable for the legislature to conclude that science teachers attempting to implement the Act would need a curriculum guide on creation science, but not on evolution, and that those charged with developing the guide would need an easily accessible group of creation scientists....

The legislative history gives ample evidence of the sincerity of the Balanced Treatment Act's articulated purpose. Witness after witness urged the legislators to support the Act so that students would not be "indoctrinated" but would instead be free to decide for themselves, based upon a fair presentation of the scientific evidence, about the origin of life. [Examples omitted.—ed.] Senator Keith expressed similar views. Legislators other than Senator Keith made only a few statements providing insight into their motives, but those statements cast no doubt upon the sincerity of the Act's articulated purpose....

[D.] [W]hat prompted the legislature to direct its attention to the misrepresentation of evolution in the schools (rather than the inaccurate presentation of other topics) was its awareness of the tension between evolution and the religious beliefs of many children. But even appellees concede that a valid secular purpose is not rendered impermissible simply because its pursuit is prompted by concern for religious sensitivities. If a history teacher falsely told her students that the bones of Jesus Christ had been discovered, or a physics teacher that the Shroud of Turin had been conclusively established to be inexplicable on the basis of natural causes, ... legislators ... would [not] be constitutionally prohibited from taking corrective action, simply because that action was prompted by concern for the religious beliefs of the misinstructed students....

I am astonished by the Court's unprecedented readiness to [conclude that the asserted secular purpose is a sham], which I can only attribute to ... an instinctive reaction that any governmentally imposed requirements bearing upon the teaching of evolution must be a manifestation of Christian fundamentalist repression. In this case, however, it seems to me the Court's position is the repressive one. The people of Louisiana, including those who are Christian fundamentalists, are quite entitled, as a secular matter, to have whatever scientific evidence there may be against evolution presented in their schools, just as Mr. Scopes was entitled to present whatever scientific evidence there was for it....

[E.] [W]hile it is possible to discern the objective "purpose" of a statute (*i.e.*, the public good at which its provisions appear to be directed), ... discerning the subjective motivation of those enacting the statute is, to be honest, almost always an impossible task....

[1.] In the present case, for example, a particular legislator need not have voted for the Act either because he wanted to foster religion or because he wanted to improve education. He [(1)] may have thought the bill would provide jobs for his district, or [(2)] may have wanted to make amends with a faction of his party he had alienated on another vote, or he [(3)] may have been a close friend of the bill's sponsor,... or he [(4)] may have been pressured to vote for a bill he disliked by a wealthy contributor or by a flood of constituent mail, or he [(5)] may have been seeking favorable publicity, or he [(6)] may have been reluctant to hurt the feelings of a loyal staff member who worked on the bill, ... or, of course, he [(7)] ... very likely [had] a combination of some of the above and many other motivations. To look for *the sole purpose* of even a single legislator is probably to look for something that does not exist.

[2.] Putting that problem aside, however, where ought we to look for the individual legislator's purpose? We cannot of course assume that every member present ... agreed with the motivation expressed in a particular legislator's pre-enactment floor or committee statement.... Can we assume, then, that they all agree with the motivation expressed in the staff-prepared committee reports they might have read—even though we are unwilling to assume that they agreed with the motivation expressed in the very statute that they voted for? Should we consider postenactment floor statements? Or postenactment testimony from legislators, obtained expressly for the lawsuit? Should we consider media reports on the realities of the legislative bargaining?

All of these sources, of course, are eminently manipulable. Legislative histories can be contrived and sanitized, favorable media coverage orchestrated, and postenactment recollections conveniently distorted. Perhaps most valuable of all would be more objective indications—for example, evidence regarding the individual legislators' religious affiliations. And if that, why not evidence regarding the fervor or tepidity of their beliefs?

[3.] Having achieved, through these simple means, an assessment of what individual legislators intended, we must still confront the question (yet to be addressed in any of our cases) how *many* of them must have the invalidating intent. If a state senate approves a bill by vote of 26 to 25, and only one of the 26 intended solely to advance religion, is the law unconstitutional? What if 13 of the 26 had that intent? ... Or is it possible that the intent of the bill's sponsor is alone enough to invalidate it ...?

Because there are no good answers to these questions, this Court has recognized ... that determining the subjective intent of legislators is a perilous enterprise. It is perilous ... not just for the judges who will very likely reach the wrong result, but also for the legislators who find that they must assess the validity of proposed legislation ... not on the basis of what the legislation contains, nor even on the basis of what they themselves intend, but on the basis of what *others* have in mind. Given the many hazards involved in assessing the subjective intent of governmental decisionmakers, the [secular purpose requirement] is defensible, I think, only if the text of the Establishment Clause demands it. That is surely not the case....

In the past we have attempted to justify our embarrassing Establishment Clause jurisprudence on the ground that it "sacrifices clarity and predictability for flexibility." ... [T]his [is] "a euphemism ... for ... the absence of any principled rationale." I think it time that we sacrifice some "flexibility" for "clarity and predictability." Abandoning [the] purpose test—a test which exacerbates the tension between the Free Exercise and Establishment Clauses, has no basis in the language or history of the Amendment, and, as today's decision shows, has wonderfully flexible consequences—would be a good place to start.

f. *McCreary County v. ACLU, 545 U.S. 844 (2005)*

[In 1999, McCreary and Pulaski Counties in Kentucky put up large copies of the Ten Commandments in their courthouses. The ACLU sued.

Within a month, the counties put up a second display of the Ten Commandments, describing them as being "the precedent legal code upon which the civil and criminal codes of ... Kentucky are founded." The display also included several other documents referring to religion:

the "endowed by their Creator" passage from the Declaration of Independence; the Preamble to the Constitution of Kentucky; the national motto, "In God We Trust"; a page from the Congressional Record of February 2, 1983, proclaiming the Year of the Bible and including a statement of the Ten Commandments; a proclamation by President Abraham Lincoln designating April 30, 1863, a National Day of Prayer and Humiliation; an excerpt from President Lincoln's "Reply to Loyal Colored People of Baltimore upon Presentation of a Bible," reading that "[t]he Bible is the best gift God has ever given to man"; a proclamation by President Reagan marking 1983 the Year of the Bible; and the Mayflower Compact....

The district court enjoined this second display, so the counties put up a third display, containing a Ten Commandments that had more detailed text for each Commandment than the first display contained, plus

> framed copies of the Magna Carta, the Declaration of Independence, the Bill of Rights, the lyrics of the Star Spangled Banner, the Mayflower Compact, the National Motto, the Preamble to the Kentucky Constitution, and a picture of Lady Justice. The collection is entitled "The Foundations of American Law and Government Display" and each document comes with a statement about its historical and legal significance. The comment on the Ten Commandments reads:
>
>> The Ten Commandments have profoundly influenced the formation of Western legal thought and the formation of our country. That influence is clearly seen in the Declaration of Independence, which declared that 'We hold these truths to be self-evident, that all men are created equal, that they are endowed by their Creator with certain unalienable Rights, that among these are Life, Liberty, and the pursuit of Happiness.' The Ten Commandments provide the moral background of the Declaration of Independence and the foundation of our legal tradition.

The case before the Court involved a challenge to the third display.—ed.]

Justice Souter delivered the opinion of the Court.

[A.] [1.] When the government acts with the ostensible and predominant purpose of advancing religion, it violates th[e] central Establishment Clause value of official religious neutrality, there being no neutrality when the government's ostensible object is to take sides. Manifesting a purpose to favor one faith over another, or adherence to religion generally, clashes with the "understanding, reached ... after decades of religious war, that liberty and social stability demand a religious tolerance that respects the religious views of all citizens ...." By showing a purpose to favor religion, the government "sends the ... message to ... nonadherents 'that they are outsiders, not full members of the political community, and an accompanying message to adherents that they are insiders, favored members ....'"

Indeed, the purpose apparent from government action can have an impact more significant than the result expressly decreed: when the government maintains Sunday closing laws, it advances religion only minimally because many working people would take the day as one of rest regardless, but if the government justified its decision with a stated desire for all Americans to honor Christ, the divisive thrust of the official action would be inescapable.... *McGowan v. Maryland* ...

{[And if there is a religious motive that is hidden so well that it cannot be seen], then without something more the government does not make a divisive announcement that in itself amounts to taking religious sides. A secret motive stirs up no strife and does nothing to make outsiders of nonadherents, and it suffices to wait and see whether such government action turns out to have (as it may even be likely to have) the illegitimate effect of advancing religion....}

[2.] Examination of purpose is a staple of statutory interpretation that makes up the daily fare of every appellate court in the country, and governmental purpose is a key element of a good deal of constitutional doctrine, [citing cases applying the Equal Protection Clause, the dormant Commerce Clause, and the Free Exercise Clause].... [And] scrutinizing purpose does make practical sense ... where an understanding of official objective emerges from readily discoverable fact, without any judicial psychoanalysis of a drafter's heart of hearts. The eyes that look to purpose belong to an "objective observer," one who takes account of the traditional external signs that show up in the "text, legislative history, and implementation of the statute," or comparable official act....

[3.] [A]lthough a legislature's stated reasons will generally get deference, the secular purpose required has to be genuine, not a sham, and not merely secondary to a religious objective.... [Discussions of cases applying the purpose test omitted.—ed.] [T]he Court often does accept governmental statements of purpose, in keeping with the respect owed in the first instance to such official claims. But in those unusual cases where the claim was an apparent sham, or the secular purpose secondary, the unsurprising results have been findings of no adequate secular object, as against a predominantly religious one.

{The dissent nonetheless maintains that the purpose test is satisfied so long as any secular purpose for the government action is apparent.... [This] would leave the purpose test with no real bite, given the ease of finding some secular purpose for almost any government action.} ...

[The Counties also] argue that purpose in a case like this one should be inferred, if at all, only from the latest news about the last in a series of governmental actions, however close they may all be in time and subject. But the world is not made brand new every morning, and the Counties are simply asking us to ignore perfectly probative evidence; they want an absentminded objective observer, not one presumed to be familiar with the history of the government's actions and competent to learn what history has to show. The Counties' position just bucks common sense: reasonable observers have reasonable memories, and our precedents sensibly forbid an observer "to turn a blind eye to the context in which [the] policy arose."

{One consequence of taking account of the purpose underlying past actions is that the same government action may be constitutional if taken in the first instance and unconstitutional if it has a sectarian heritage. This presents no incongruity, however, because purpose matters.... [I]t will matter to objective observers whether posting the Commandments follows on the heels of displays motivated by sectarianism, or whether it lacks a history demonstrating that purpose.... [W]here one display has a history manifesting sectarian purpose that the other lacks, it is appropriate that they be treated differently, for the one display will be properly understood as demonstrating a preference for one group of religious believers as against another.} ...

[B.] [The Court went on to try to determine "what viewers may fairly understand to be the purpose of the display," based on "the progression leading up to the third display of the Commandments."—ed.] ...

[1.] [The first display] set out a text of the Commandments as distinct from any traditionally symbolic representation, and ... stood alone, not part of an arguably secular display.... [T]he Commandments [are] a central point of reference in the religious and moral history of Jews and Christians. They proclaim the existence of a monotheistic god (no other gods). They regulate details of religious obligation (no graven images, no sabbath breaking, no vain oath swearing). And they unmistakably rest even the universally accepted prohibitions (as against murder, theft, and the like) on the sanction of the divinity proclaimed at the beginning of the text.

Displaying that text is thus different from a symbolic depiction, like tablets with 10 roman numerals, which could be seen as alluding to a general notion of law, not a sectarian conception of faith....

What is more, at the ceremony for posting the framed Commandments in Pulaski County, the county executive was accompanied by his pastor, who testified to the certainty of the existence of God. The reasonable observer could only think that the Counties meant to emphasize and celebrate the Commandments' religious message....

[2.] Once the Counties were sued, they modified the exhibits and invited additional insight into their purpose in a display that hung for about six months. This new one was the product of forthright and nearly identical Pulaski and McCreary County resolutions listing a series of American historical documents with theistic and Christian references, which were to be posted in order to furnish a setting for displaying the Ten Commandments and any "other Kentucky and American historical documen[t]" without raising concern about "any Christian or religious references" in them.... The display's unstinting focus was on religious passages, showing that the Counties were posting the Commandments precisely because of their sectarian content.... Together, the display and resolution presented an indisputable, and undisputed, showing of an impermissible purpose....

[3.] In trying to persuade the District Court to lift the preliminary injunction, the Counties cited several new purposes for the third version, including a desire "to educate the citizens of the county regarding some of the documents that played a significant role in the foundation of our system of law and government[]"[;] ... {"to erect a display containing the Ten Commandments that is constitutional; ... to demonstrate that the Ten Commandments were part of the foundation of American Law and Government; ... [and to include the Ten Commandments] as part of the display for their significance in providing 'the moral background of the Declaration of Independence and the foundation of our legal tradition.'"} ....

[But t]hese new statements of purpose were presented only as a litigating position, there being no further authorizing action by the Counties' governing boards. And although repeal of the earlier county authorizations would not have erased them from the record of evidence bearing on current purpose, the extraordinary resolutions for the second display passed just months earlier were not repealed or otherwise repudiated. Indeed, the sectarian spirit of the common resolution found enhanced expression in the third display, which quoted more of the purely religious language of the Commandments than the first two displays had done....

Nor did the selection of posted material suggest a clear theme that might prevail over evidence of the continuing religious object. In a collection of documents said to be "foundational" to American government, it is at least odd to include a patriotic anthem, but to omit the Fourteenth Amendment, the most significant structural provision adopted since the original Framing. And it is no less baffling to leave out the original Constitution of 1787 while quoting the 1215 Magna Carta even to the point of its declaration that "fish-weirs shall be removed from the Thames."

{The Counties argue that the objective observer would not continue to believe that the resolution was in effect after the third display went up because the resolution authorized only the second display. But the resolution on its face is not limited to any particular display. On the contrary, it encourages the creation of a display with the Ten Commandments that also includes [other documents] .... The third display contains all of these documents, suggesting that it fell within the resolutions as well.}

If an observer found these choices and omissions perplexing in isolation, he would be puzzled for a different reason when he read the Declaration of Independence seeking confirmation for the Counties' posted explanation that the "Ten Commandments' ... influence is clearly seen in the Declaration"; in fact the observer would find that the Commandments are sanctioned as divine imperatives, while the Declaration of Independence holds that the authority of government to enforce the law derives "from the consent of the governed." If the observer had not thrown up his hands, he would probably suspect that the Counties were simply reaching for any way to keep a religious document on the walls of courthouses constitutionally required to embody religious neutrality....

[C.] [W]e do not decide that the Counties' past actions forever taint any effort on their part to deal with the subject matter. We hold only that purpose needs to be taken seriously under the Establishment Clause and needs to be understood in light of context; an implausible claim that governmental purpose has changed should not carry the day in a court of law any more than in a head with common sense....

Nor do we have occasion here to hold that a sacred text can never be integrated constitutionally into a governmental display on the subject of law, or American history.... [O]ur own courtroom frieze was deliberately designed in the exercise of governmental authority so as to include the figure of Moses holding tablets exhibiting a portion of the Hebrew text of the later, secularly phrased Commandments; in the company of 17 other lawgivers, most of them secular figures, there is no risk that Moses would strike an observer as evidence that the National Government was violating neutrality in religion....

Justice Scalia, with whom ... Chief Justice [Rehnquist] and Justice Thomas join, and with whom Justice Kennedy joins [in relevant part], dissenting....

[A.] [Justice Scalia criticized the secular purpose requirement, for reasons similar to those he gave in *Edwards v. Aguillard* (p. 850), and went on:—ed.] Today's opinion ... modifies [the secular purpose requirement] to ratchet up the Court's hostility to religion.

First, the Court justifies inquiry into legislative purpose, not as an end itself, but as a means to ascertain the appearance of the government action to an "objective observer." ... Under this approach, even if a government could show that its actual purpose was not to advance religion, it would presumably violate the Constitution as long as the Court's objective observer would think otherwise.... [T]he legitimacy of a government action with a wholly secular effect would [thus] turn on the *misperception* of an imaginary observer that the government officials behind the action had the intent to advance religion.

Second, the Court replaces [the] requirement that the government have "*a* secular ... purpose" with the heightened requirement that the secular purpose "predominate" over any purpose to advance religion.... I have urged that [the secular purpose test] be abandoned, because (as I have discussed [earlier] [see p. 809]) even an *exclusive* purpose to foster or assist religious practice is not necessarily invalidating. But today's extension makes things even worse. By shifting the focus ... from the search for a genuine, secular motivation to the hunt for a predominantly religious purpose, the Court converts what has in the past been a fairly limited inquiry into a rigorous review of the full record. Those responsible for the adoption of the Religion Clauses would surely regard it as a bitter irony that the religious values they designed those Clauses to *protect* have now become so distasteful to this Court that if they constitute anything more than a subordinate motive for government action they will invalidate it.

[B.] Even accepting the Court's ... premises, the displays at issue here were constitutional.

To any [casual visitor] ..., the displays must have seemed unremarkable—if indeed they were noticed at all. The walls of both courthouses were already lined with historical documents and other assorted portraits; each Foundations Display [*i.e.*, cach part of the third display—ed.] was exhibited in the same format as these other displays and nothing in the record suggests that either County took steps to give it greater prominence....

Posted with the documents was a plaque, identifying the display, and explaining that it "contains documents that played a significant role in the foundation of our system of law and government." The explanation related to the Ten Commandments was third in the list of nine and did not serve to distinguish it from the other documents. It stated:

> The Ten Commandments have profoundly influenced the formation of Western legal thought and the formation of our country. That influence is clearly seen in the Declaration of Independence, which declared that, 'We hold

these truths to be self-evident, that all men are created equal, that they are endowed by their Creator with certain unalienable Rights, that among these are Life, Liberty, and the pursuit of Happiness.' The Ten Commandments provide the moral background of the Declaration of Independence and the foundation of our legal tradition.

On its face, the Foundations Displays manifested the purely secular purpose that the Counties asserted before the District Court: "to display documents that played a significant role in the foundation of our system of law and government." ... [W]hen the Ten Commandments appear alongside other documents of secular significance in a display devoted to the foundations of American law and government, the context communicates that the Ten Commandments are included, not to teach their binding nature as a religious text, but to show their unique contribution to the development of the legal system. This is doubly true when the display is introduced by a document that informs passersby that it "contains documents that played a significant role in the foundation of our system of law and government." ...

Acknowledgment of the contribution that religion has made to our Nation's legal and governmental heritage partakes of a centuries-old tradition.... [R]eligious belief pervaded the National Government during the founding era. Display of the Ten Commandments is well within the mainstream of this practice of acknowledgment. Federal, State, and local governments across the Nation have engaged in such display.

The Supreme Court Building itself includes depictions of Moses with the Ten Commandments in the Courtroom ..., and symbols of the Ten Commandments "adorn the metal gates lining the north and south sides of the Courtroom as well as the doors leading into the Courtroom." Similar depictions of the Decalogue appear on public buildings and monuments throughout our Nation's Capital. The frequency of these displays testifies to the popular understanding that the Ten Commandments are a foundation of the rule of law, and a symbol of the role that religion played, and continues to play, in our system of government.

Perhaps in recognition of the centrality of the Ten Commandments as a widely recognized symbol of religion in public life, the Court is at pains to dispel the impression that its decision will require governments across the country to sandblast the Ten Commandments from the public square. The constitutional problem, the Court says, is with the Counties' *purpose* in erecting the Foundations Displays, not the displays themselves.

The Court adds ...: "One consequence of taking account of the purpose underlying past actions is that the same government action may be constitutional if taken in the first instance and unconstitutional if it has a sectarian heritage." This inconsistency may be explicable in theory, but I suspect that the "objective observer" with whom the Court is so concerned will recognize its absurdity in practice. By virtue of details familiar only to the parties to litigation and their lawyers, McCreary and Pulaski Counties, Kentucky ... have been ordered to remove the same display that appears in courthouses from Mercer County, Kentucky to Elkhart County, Indiana. Displays erected in silence (and under the direction of good legal advice) are permissible, while those hung after discussion and debate are deemed unconstitutional. Reduction of the Establishment Clause to such minutiae trivializes the Clause's protection against religious establishment; indeed, it may inflame religious passions by making the passing comments of every government official the subject of endless litigation.

[C.] In any event, the Court's conclusion that the Counties exhibited the Foundations Displays with the purpose of promoting religion is doubtful.... If, as discussed above, the Commandments have a proper place in our civic history, even placing them by themselves can be civically motivated—especially when they are placed, not in a school ..., but in a courthouse. And the fact that at the posting of the exhibit a clergyman was present is unremarkable (clergymen taking particular pride in the role of the Ten Commandments in our civic history); and even more unremarkable the fact that the clergyman "testified to the certainty of the existence of God." ...

Nor is it the case that a solo display of the Ten Commandments advances any one faith. They are assuredly a religious symbol, but they are not so closely associated with a single religious belief that their display can reasonably be understood as preferring one religious sect over another. The Ten Commandments are recognized by Judaism, Christianity, and Islam alike as divinely given.

The Court also points to the Counties' second displays, ... [arguing that] "[t]he [second] display's unstinting focus ... on religious passages, show[s] that the Counties were posting the Commandments precisely because of their sectarian content." No, all it necessarily shows is that the exhibit was meant to focus upon the historic role of religious belief in our national life—which is entirely permissible. And the same can be said of the resolution. To forbid any government focus upon this aspect of our history is to ... commit the Court (and the Nation) to a revisionist agenda of secularization.

Turning at last to the displays actually at issue in this case, the Court faults the Counties for not *repealing* the resolution expressing what the Court believes to be an impermissible intent. Under these circumstances, the Court says, "no reasonable observer could swallow the claim that the Counties had cast off the objective so unmistakable in the earlier displays." ... [But] it is unlikely that a reasonable observer *would even have been aware* of the resolutions .... The Court implies that the Counties may have been able to remedy the "taint" from the old resolutions by enacting a new one. But that action would have been wholly unnecessary in light of the explanation that the Counties included *with the displays themselves*: A plaque next to the documents informed all who passed by that each display "contains documents that played a significant role in the foundation of our system of law and government."

Additionally, there was no reason for the Counties to repeal or repudiate the resolutions adopted with the hanging of the second displays, since they related *only to the second displays*. After complying with the District Court's order to remove the second displays "immediately," and erecting new displays that in content and by express assertion reflected a *different* purpose from that identified in the resolutions, the Counties had no reason to believe that their previous resolutions would be deemed to be the basis for their actions. {Contrary to the Court's suggestion, it is clear that the resolutions were closely tied to the second displays, but not to the third.... Each of the documents included in the second displays was authorized by the resolutions .... The third displays, in contrast, included documents not mentioned in the resolutions ....} ...

In sum: The first displays did not necessarily evidence an intent to further religious practice; nor did the second displays, or the resolutions authorizing them; and there is in any event no basis for attributing whatever intent motivated the first and second displays to the third. Given the presumption of regularity that always accompanies our review of official action, the Court has identified no evidence of a purpose to advance religion in a way that is inconsistent with our cases. The Court may well be correct in identifying the third displays as the fruit of a desire to display the Ten Commandments, but neither our cases nor our history support its assertion that such a desire renders the fruit poisonous.

g. *Policy—Primary Purpose Must Not Be Advancement or Inhibition of Religion*

Basic argument: This government action is unconstitutional because its primary purpose is advancing or inhibiting religion, since _____.

1. "The preeminent purpose of the Louisiana Legislature was clearly to advance the religious viewpoint that a supernatural being created humankind.... Because the primary purpose of the Creationism Act is to advance a particular religious belief, the Act endorses religion in violation of the First Amendment." *Edwards v. Aguillard.*

"The pre-eminent purpose for posting the Ten Commandments on schoolroom walls is plainly religious in nature.... [T]he first part of the Commandments concerns the religious duties of believers: worshipping the Lord God alone, avoiding idolatry, not using the Lord's name in vain, and observing the Sabbath Day.... If the posted copies of the Ten Commandments are to have any effect at all, it will be to induce the schoolchildren to read, meditate upon, perhaps to venerate and obey, the Commandments.... [This] is not a permissible state objective under the Establishment Clause." *Stone v. Graham,* 449 U.S. 39, 41-42 (1980).

2. Response to 1: Actually the government action does have a secular purpose, whether or not a wise purpose, and that purpose is _____.

"Our task is not to judge the debate about teaching the origins of life, but to ascertain what the members of the Louisiana Legislature believed. The vast majority of them voted to approve a bill which explicitly stated a secular purpose; what is crucial is not their *wisdom* in believing that purpose would be achieved by the bill, but their *sincerity* in believing it would be.... The legislature wanted to ensure that students would be free to decide for themselves how life began, based upon a fair and balanced presentation of the scientific evidence ....'" *Edwards* (Scalia, J., dissenting).

3. Rebuttal to 2: The asserted secular purpose is just a sham, because _____; the true purpose was religious, namely _____.

"While the Court is normally deferential to a State's articulation of a secular purpose, it is required that the statement of such purpose be sincere and not a sham.... [R]equiring schools to teach creation science with evolution does not advance [the stated secular purpose of preserving] academic freedom.... [W]e need not be blind in this case to the legislature's preeminent religious purpose in enacting this statute." *Edwards*.

4. Response to 1: The assertedly religious purpose is actually legitimate, even though it has something to do with religion, because it aims at legitimately accommodating religion or preventing hostility to religion by _____, and this is permissible because _____.

"[E]ven if the Louisiana Legislature's purpose were exclusively to advance religion, some of the well-established exceptions to the impermissibility of that purpose might be applicable—the validating intent to eliminate a perceived discrimination against a particular religion, to facilitate its free exercise, or to accommodate it.... [Senator Keith] repeatedly urged his colleagues to pass his bill to *remedy* [an] Establishment Clause violation by ensuring state neutrality in religious matters, surely a permissible purpose under *Lemon*. Senator Keith's argument may be questionable, but nothing in the statute or its legislative history gives us reason to doubt his sincerity or that of his supporters." *Edwards* (Scalia, J., dissenting).

"[T]he District Court concluded that Congress' purpose was to minimize governmental 'interfer[ence] with the decision-making process in religions.' We agree with the District Court that this purpose does not violate the Establishment Clause." *Corporation of Presiding Bishop v. Amos*.

5. Response to 1: The entire inquiry into legislative purpose is misguided, because _____.

See *Edwards* (Scalia, J., dissenting) for the classic argument.

C. THE NO COERCION PRINCIPLE (ESTABLISHMENT)

a. Summary

Basic rule: The government may not coerce people to participate in religious activities.

1. What constitutes *coercion*?

a. Even psychological or social pressure, at least of the sort involved in the pressure to attend a graduation ceremony and stand and remain silent while a prayer takes place, is sufficient. *Lee v. Weisman*.

b. The same goes for the pressure to attend a football game at which public, government-sponsored prayers take place. *Santa Fe Indep. School Dist. v. Doe*, 530 U.S. 290 (2000).

c. A prayer at a city council meeting (where most of the audience consists of adults) is not coercive, at least so long as the prayer is seen as addressed primarily to the councilmembers, and the public is free to come after the prayer or leave briefly during the prayer. But "direct[ing] the public to participate in the prayers, singl[ing] out dissidents for opprobrium, or indicat[ing] that [government] decisions might be influenced by a person's acquiescence in the prayer opportunity" might make the prayer coercive. *Town of Greece v. Galloway* (2014) (p. 876).

2. What constitutes *participation in religious activities*?

a. "[S]tanding or remaining silent" during a graduation prayer, qualifies as "an expression of participation in the ... prayer," *Lee.*

3. The *Lee* dissent agreed that coercing people to participate in religious activities is unconstitutional, but disagreed both with the majority's definition of coercion and its definition of participation.

4. For Justices who believe the Establishment Clause bars any preferences for or endorsement of religion, this rule might not add much, since most coercion involves some such preference or endorsement.

b. Problem: University Graduation Prayer

Starting in 1840, Indiana University has included a religious invocation as part of its graduation programs. Leslie Pereira, a law student, challenges the inclusion of the invocation at her law school graduation, on the ground that it violates the Establishment Clause. Analyze. See *Tanford v. Brand,* 104 F.3d 982 (7th Cir. 1997).

c. Problem: Alcoholics Anonymous

A prison system wants convicts who committed their crimes while under the influence of alcohol to participate in Alcoholics Anonymous; to encourage them to participate, it offers participants expanded family visitation privileges. AA has seemingly proved to be effective in helping people stop abusing alcohol; it does this largely by relying on the "Twelve Steps," around which its programs are organized. The prison does not subsidize AA, or run the meetings, though it lets AA groups meet in prison facilities.

The AA Twelve Steps are:

1. We admitted we were powerless over alcohol—that our lives had become unmanageable.

2. Came to believe that a Power greater than ourselves could restore us to sanity.

3. Made a decision to turn our will and our lives over to the care of God as we understood Him.

4. Made a searching and fearless moral inventory of ourselves.

5. Admitted to God, to ourselves, and to another human being the exact nature of our wrongs.

6. Were entirely ready to have God remove all these defects of character.

7. Humbly asked Him to remove our shortcomings.

8. Made a list of all persons we had harmed, and became willing to make amends to them all.

9. Made direct amends to such people wherever possible, except when to do so would injure them or others.

10. Continued to take personal inventory and when we were wrong promptly admitted it.

11. Sought through prayer and meditation to improve our conscious contact with God as we understood Him, praying only for knowledge of His will for us and the power to carry that out.

12. Having had a spiritual awakening as the result of these steps, we tried to carry this message to alcoholics, and to practice these principles in all our affairs.

A prisoner sues, claiming the prison's actions violate the Establishment Clause. Analyze. Cf., *e.g.*, *Griffin v. Coughlin,* 88 N.Y.2d 674 (1996).

d. Problem: Get

Under Jewish law, as understood by many Jews, a civil divorce decree isn't enough to terminate the marriage from a religious standpoint—the wife may not remarry unless the husband gives the wife a bill of divorce, called a Get (pronounced just like the word "get"). If she civilly remarries before receiving a Get, her sexual relations with her new husband are seen as adulterous, notwithstanding her civil divorce; also, any children born of such a civil remarriage are treated as illegitimate, and may not marry freely within the Jewish community. A recalcitrant wife may cause similar problems for the divorcing husband if she refuses to accept the Get.

Of course, all these impairments are purely a matter of Jewish law; American secular law doesn't enforce them. Nonetheless, they are taken seriously by many observant Jews, and women who have been refused Gets and the smaller group of men whose ex-wives have refused to accept Gets are put in a difficult position. The ability to impose this position can also give a spouse substantial leverage to try to negotiate a more favorable settlement as a condition of giving (or receiving) the Get.

New York Domestic Relations Law § 253 was enacted to prevent this problem. The law, provides, in relevant part:

3. No final judgment of ... divorce shall thereafter be entered unless the plaintiff shall have filed and served a sworn statement:

(i) that, to the best of his or her knowledge, he or she has, prior to the entry of such final judgment, taken all steps solely within his or her power to remove all barriers to the defendant's remarriage following the ... divorce; or

(ii) that the defendant has waived in writing the requirements of this subdivision....

6.... "[B]arrier to remarriage" includes ... any religious or conscientious restraint ..., of which the party required to make the verified statement is aware, that is imposed on a party to a marriage, under the principles held by the clergyman ... who has solemnized the marriage, by reason of the other party's commission or withholding of any voluntary act....

7. No final judgment of ... divorce shall be entered, notwithstanding the filing of the plaintiff's sworn statement prescribed by this section, if the clergyman ... who has solemnized the marriage certifies, in a sworn statement,

that he or she has solemnized the marriage and that, to his or her knowledge, the plaintiff has failed to take all steps solely within his or her power to remove all barriers to the defendant's remarriage following the ... divorce, provided that the said clergyman ... is alive and available ... to testify at the time when final judgment would be entered....

9. Nothing in this section shall be construed to authorize any court to inquire into or determine any ecclesiastical or religious issue....

Simon Berkowitz, who was married to Leah Berkowitz in a ceremony solemnized by an orthodox rabbi, petitions for divorce, but refuses to give his wife a Get. The court refuses to finalize the divorce until Simon gives the Get. Does the court's action violate the First Amendment? Cf. *Megibow v. Megibow,* 612 N.Y.S.2d 758 (1994); *Aflalo v. Aflalo,* 295 N.J. Super. 527 (1996). See *generally* Lisa Zornberg, *Beyond the Constitution: Is the New York Get Legislation Good Law?,* 15 Pace L. Rev. 703 (1995). [Note: This is a simplified account both of New York law and of Jewish law.]

e. Problem: Pledge of Allegiance

Every morning, in public school classrooms throughout the country, teachers lead students in the Pledge of Allegiance, which reads:

I Pledge Allegiance to the flag of the United States of America and to the Republic for which it stands, one Nation under God, indivisible, with liberty and justice for all.

This text is prescribed by Congress, but the requirement that teachers lead students in the Pledge is generally set forth by state or local rules. Under *W. Va. State Bd. of Ed. v. Barnette* (1943) (p. 536), no student can be required to participate in the Pledge. The Pledge was originally written in 1892 without "under God," and was officially adopted by Congress in 1942. The words "under God" were added by Congress in 1954.

Michael Newdow, whose daughter goes to a California public school, challenges on Establishment Clause grounds the school district's practice of conducting the Pledge. Should he win? See *Newdow v. U.S. Congress,* 328 F.3d 466 (9th Cir. 2003), *rev'd on other grounds sub nom. Elk Grove Unified School Dist. v. Newdow,* 542 U.S. 1 (2004).

Should school music teachers be allowed to lead nonobjecting students in singing *The Star Spangled-Banner,* which includes the lines, "Then conquer we must, when our cause it is just, / And this be our motto: 'In God is our trust!'"? Or *My Country 'Tis of Thee,* which closes with:

Our father's God, to Thee
Author of liberty,
To Thee we sing.
Long may our land be bright
With freedom's holy light;
Protect us by Thy might,
Great God, our King!

What about *God Bless America?* What about recitations of the Declaration of Independence, which contains the following at the start and at the end:

> When in the Course of human events, it becomes necessary for one people ... to assume among the powers of the earth, the separate and equal station to which the Laws of Nature and of Nature's God entitle them, a decent respect to the opinions of mankind requires that they should declare the causes which impel them to the separation.
>
> We hold these truths to be self-evident, that all men are created equal, that they are endowed by their Creator with certain unalienable Rights, that among these are Life, Liberty and the pursuit of Happiness....
>
> We, therefore, the Representatives of the United States of America, ... appealing to the Supreme Judge of the world for the rectitude of our intentions, do ... solemnly publish and declare, That these United Colonies are, and of Right ought to be Free and Independent States .... And for the support of this Declaration, with a firm reliance on the protection of divine Providence, we mutually pledge to each other our Lives, our Fortunes and our sacred Honor.

What are the constitutionally relevant similarities between these works and the Pledge? What are the constitutionally relevant differences?

f.   Lee v. Weisman, 505 U.S. 577 (1992)

Justice Kennedy delivered the opinion of the Court....

[A.] Deborah Weisman graduated from Nathan Bishop Middle School, a public school in Providence, at a formal ceremony in June 1989. She was about 14 years old. For many years it has been the policy of the Providence School Committee and the Superintendent of Schools to permit principals to invite members of the clergy to give invocations and benedictions at middle school and high school graduations. Many, but not all, of the principals elected to include prayers as part of the graduation ceremonies.

Acting for himself and his daughter, Deborah's father, Daniel Weisman, objected to any prayers at Deborah's middle school graduation, but to no avail. The school principal, petitioner Robert E. Lee, invited a rabbi to deliver prayers at the graduation exercises for Deborah's class. Rabbi Leslie Gutterman, of the Temple Beth El in Providence, accepted.

It has been the custom of Providence school officials to provide invited clergy with a pamphlet entitled "Guidelines for Civic Occasions," prepared by the National Conference of Christians and Jews. The Guidelines recommend that public prayers at nonsectarian civic ceremonies be composed with "inclusiveness and sensitivity," though they acknowledge that "[p]rayer of any kind may be inappropriate on some civic occasions." The principal gave Rabbi Gutterman the pamphlet before the graduation and advised him the invocation and benediction should be nonsectarian.

Rabbi Gutterman's prayers were as follows:

INVOCATION

God of the Free, Hope of the Brave:

For the legacy of America where diversity is celebrated and the rights of minorities are protected, we thank You. May these young men and women grow up to enrich it.

For the liberty of America, we thank You. May these new graduates grow up to guard it.

For the political process of America in which all its citizens may participate, for its court system where all may seek justice we thank You. May those we honor this morning always turn to it in trust.

For the destiny of America we thank You. May the graduates of Nathan Bishop Middle School so live that they might help to share it.

May our aspirations for our country and for these young people, who are our hope for the future, be richly fulfilled.

AMEN

BENEDICTION

O God, we are grateful to You for having endowed us with the capacity for learning which we have celebrated on this joyous commencement.

Happy families give thanks for seeing their children achieve an important milestone. Send Your blessings upon the teachers and administrators who helped prepare them.

The graduates now need strength and guidance for the future, help them to understand that we are not complete with academic knowledge alone. We must each strive to fulfill what You require of us all: To do justly, to love mercy, to walk humbly.

We give thanks to You, Lord, for keeping us alive, sustaining us and allowing us to reach this special, happy occasion.

AMEN ...

[T]he students stood for the Pledge of Allegiance and remained standing during the rabbi's prayers.... [T]he rabbi's two presentations must not have extended much beyond a minute each, if that....

In July, 1989, Daniel Weisman ... [sought] a permanent injunction barring petitioners, various officials of the Providence public schools, from inviting the clergy to deliver invocations and benedictions at future graduations.... Deborah Weisman is enrolled as a student at Classical High School in Providence and ... it appears likely ... that an invocation and benediction will be conducted at her high school graduation....

[B.] Even for those students who object to the religious exercise [at graduation], their attendance and participation in the state-sponsored religious activity are in a fair and real sense obligatory, though the school district does not require attendance as a condition for receipt of the diploma.... [T]he Constitution guarantees that government may not coerce anyone to support or participate in religion or its exercise, or otherwise act in a way which "establishes a [state] religion or religious faith, or tends to do so." The State's involvement in the school prayers challenged today violates these central principles....

The degree of school involvement here made it clear that the graduation prayers bore the imprint of the State and thus put school-age children who objected in an untenable position.... [P]rayer exercises in public schools carry a particular risk of indirect coercion. The concern may not be limited to the context of schools, but it is most pronounced there. What to most believers may seem nothing more than a reasonable request that the nonbeliever respect their religious practices, in a school context may appear to the nonbeliever or dissenter to be an attempt to employ the machinery of the

State to enforce a religious orthodoxy.

We need not look beyond the circumstances of this case to see the phenomenon at work.... [T]he school district's supervision and control of a high school graduation ceremony places public pressure, as well as peer pressure, on attending students to stand as a group or, at least, maintain respectful silence during the invocation and benediction. This pressure, though subtle and indirect, can be as real as any overt compulsion....

There can be no doubt that for many, if not most, of the students at the graduation, the act of standing or remaining silent was an expression of participation in the rabbi's prayer. That was the very point of the religious exercise. It is of little comfort to a dissenter, then, to be told that for her the act of standing or remaining in silence signifies mere respect, rather than participation. What matters is that, given our social conventions, a reasonable dissenter in this milieu could believe that the group exercise signified her own participation or approval of it.

Finding no violation under these circumstances would place objectors in the dilemma of participating, with all that implies, or protesting. We do not address whether that choice is acceptable if the affected citizens are mature adults, but we think the State may not, consistent with the Establishment Clause, place primary and secondary school children in this position. Research in psychology supports the common assumption that adolescents are often susceptible to pressure from their peers towards conformity, and that the influence is strongest in matters of social convention.... [T]he government may no more use social pressure to enforce orthodoxy than it may use more direct means....

[T]he State, in a school setting, [has] in effect required participation in a religious exercise. It is, we concede, a brief exercise during which the individual can concentrate on joining its message, meditate on her own religion, or let her mind wander. But the embarrassment and the intrusion of the religious exercise cannot be refuted by arguing that these prayers, and similar ones to be said in the future, are of a *de minimis* character. To do so would be an affront to the rabbi who offered them and to all those for whom the prayers were an essential and profound recognition of divine authority.

And for the same reason, we think that the intrusion is greater than the two minutes or so of time consumed for prayers like these.... That the intrusion was in the course of promulgating religion that sought to be civic or nonsectarian rather than pertaining to one sect does not lessen the offense or isolation to the objectors. At best it narrows their number, at worst increases their sense of isolation and affront....

[C.] [T]he option of not attending the graduation [does not] excuse[] any inducement or coercion in the ceremony itself.... Law reaches past formalism. And to say a teenage student has a real choice not to attend her high school graduation is formalistic in the extreme.... Everyone knows that in our society and in our culture high school graduation is one of life's most significant occasions....

Attendance may not be required by official decree, yet it is apparent that a student is not free to absent herself from the graduation exercise in any real sense of the term "voluntary," for absence would require forfeiture of those intangible benefits which have motivated the student through youth and all her high school years. Graduation is a time for family and those closest to the student to celebrate success and express mutual wishes of gratitude and respect, all to the end of impressing upon the young person the role that it is his or her right and duty to assume in the community and all of its diverse parts....

[The school district's] contention, one of considerable force were it not for the constitutional constraints applied to state action, is that the prayers are an essential part of these ceremonies because for many persons an occasion of this significance lacks meaning if there is no recognition, however brief, that human achievements cannot be understood apart from their spiritual essence.... [But] what for many of Deborah's classmates and their parents was a spiritual imperative was for Daniel and Deborah Weisman religious conformance compelled by the State.... The Constitution forbids the State to exact religious conformity from a student as the price of attending her own high school graduation....

To say that a student must remain apart from the ceremony at the opening invocation and closing benediction is to risk compelling conformity in an environment analogous to the classroom setting, where we have said [in cases such as *Engel v. Vitale* that] the risk of compulsion is especially high....

Inherent differences between the public school system and a session of a state legislature distinguish this case from *Marsh v. Chambers*.... The atmosphere at the opening of a session of a state legislature where adults are free to enter and leave with little comment and for any number of reasons cannot compare with the constraining potential of the one school event most important for the student to attend. The influence and force of a formal exercise in a school graduation are far greater than the prayer exercise we condoned in *Marsh*.... Our Establishment Clause jurisprudence remains a delicate and fact-sensitive one, and we cannot accept the parallel relied upon by petitioners and the United States between the facts of *Marsh* and the case now before us....

[D.] We do not hold that every state action implicating religion is invalid if one or a few citizens find it offensive. People may take offense at all manner of religious as well as nonreligious messages, but offense alone does not in every case show a violation. We know too that sometimes to endure social isolation or even anger may be the price of conscience or nonconformity. But ... the conformity required of the student in this case was too high an exaction to withstand the test of the Establishment Clause....

Our society would be less than true to its heritage if it lacked abiding concern for the values of its young people, and we acknowledge the profound belief of adherents to many faiths that there must be a place in the student's life for precepts of a morality higher even than the law we today enforce. We express no hostility to those aspirations, nor would our oath permit us to do so. A relentless and all-pervasive attempt to exclude religion from every aspect of public life could itself become inconsistent with the Constitution. We recognize that, at graduation time and throughout the course of the educational process, there will be instances when religious values, religious practices, and religious persons will have some interaction with the public schools and their students.

But these matters, often questions of accommodation of religion, are not before us. The sole question presented is whether a religious exercise may be conducted at a graduation ceremony in circumstances where, as we have found, young graduates who object are induced to conform. No holding by this Court suggests that a school can persuade or compel a student to participate in a religious exercise. That is being done here, and it is forbidden by the Establishment Clause ....

Justice Souter, with whom Justice Stevens and Justice O'Connor join, concurring....

When public school officials, armed with the State's authority, convey an endorsement of religion to their students, they strike near the core of the Establishment Clause. However "ceremonial" their messages may be, they are flatly unconstitutional.

Justice Scalia, with whom ... Chief Justice [Rehnquist], Justice White, and Justice Thomas join, dissenting....

[A.] In holding that the Establishment Clause prohibits invocations and benedictions at public-school graduation ceremonies, the Court—with nary a mention that it is doing so—lays waste a tradition that is as old as public-school graduation ceremonies themselves, and that is a component of an even more longstanding American tradition of nonsectarian prayer to God at public celebrations generally.

As its instrument of destruction, the bulldozer of its social engineering, the Court invents a boundless, and boundlessly manipulable, test of psychological coercion .... Today's opinion shows more forcefully than volumes of argumentation why our Nation's protection, that fortress which is our Constitution, cannot possibly rest upon the changeable philosophical predilections of the Justices of this Court, but must have deep foundations in the historic practices of our people.

Justice Holmes' aphorism that "a page of history is worth a volume of logic" applies with particular force to our Establishment Clause jurisprudence. As we have recognized, our interpretation of the Establishment Clause should "compor[t] with what history reveals was the contemporaneous understanding of its guarantees" [citing one Court decision and then quoting another, plus two concurrences by Justice Brennan—ed.]....

The history and tradition of our Nation are replete with public ceremonies featuring prayers of thanksgiving and petition. [The opinion gives examples, including the Declaration of Independence, Washington's, Jefferson's, and Madison's inaugural addresses, legislative chaplains, and the Court's invocation of "God save the United States and this Honorable Court," used since the days of Chief Justice Marshall.—ed.]

In addition to this general tradition of prayer at public ceremonies, there exists a more specific tradition of invocations and benedictions at public school graduation exercises. By one account, the first public high school graduation ceremony took place in Connecticut in July 1868—the very month, as it happens, that the Fourteenth Amendment (the vehicle by which the Establishment Clause has been applied against the States) was ratified—when "15 seniors from the Norwich Free Academy marched in their best Sunday suits and dresses into a church hall and waited through majestic music and long prayers." ... [T]he invocation and benediction have long been recognized to be "as traditional as any other parts of the [school] graduation program and are widely established."

[B.] The Court presumably would separate graduation invocations and benedictions from other instances of public "preservation and transmission of religious beliefs" on the ground that they involve "psychological coercion." I find it a sufficient embarrassment that our Establishment Clause jurisprudence regarding holiday displays, has come to "requir[e] scrutiny more commonly associated with interior decorators than with the judiciary." [This refers to *County of Allegheny v. ACLU*, 492 U.S. 573 (1989), in which the Court controversially struck down a Christmas crèche display but upheld a holiday display that included a Christmas tree, a menorah, and a sign saluting liberty.—ed.]

But interior decorating is a rock-hard science compared to psychology practiced by amateurs.... [T]he Court has gone beyond the realm where judges know what they are doing. The Court's argument that state officials have "coerced" students to take part in the invocation and benediction at graduation ceremonies is, not to put too fine a point on it, incoherent....

According to the Court, students at graduation who want "to avoid the fact or appearance of participation," in the invocation and benediction are *psychologically* obligated by "public pressure, as well as peer pressure, ... to stand as a group or, at least, maintain respectful silence" during those prayers. This assertion—*the very linchpin of the Court's opinion*—is almost as intriguing for what it does not say as for what it says. It does not say, for example, that students are psychologically coerced to bow their heads, place their hands in a Dürer-like prayer position, pay attention to the prayers, utter "Amen," or in fact pray....

It claims only that students are psychologically coerced "to stand ... *or*, at least, maintain respectful silence." ... The Court's notion that a student who simply *sits* in "respectful silence" during the invocation and benediction (when all others are standing) has somehow joined—or would somehow be perceived as having joined—in the prayers is nothing short of ludicrous.... [S]urely "our social conventions" have not coarsened to the point that anyone who does not stand on his chair and shout obscenities can reasonably be deemed to have assented to everything said in his presence.

Since the Court does not dispute that students exposed to prayer at graduation ceremonies retain (despite "subtle coercive pressures") the free will to sit, there is absolutely no basis for the Court's decision. It is fanciful enough to say that "a reasonable dissenter," standing head erect in a class of bowed heads, "could believe that the group exercise signified her own participation or approval of it." It is beyond the absurd to say that she could entertain such a belief while pointedly declining to rise.

But let us assume the very worst, that the nonparticipating graduate is "subtly coerced" ... to stand! Even that half of the disjunctive does not remotely establish a "participation" (or an "appearance of participation") in a religious exercise. The Court acknowledges that "in our culture standing ... can signify adherence to a view or simple respect for the views of others." (Much more often the latter than the former, I think ....)

But if it is a permissible inference that one who is standing is doing so simply out of respect for the prayers of others that are in progress, then how can it possibly be said that a "reasonable dissenter ... could believe that the group exercise signified her own participation or approval"? Quite obviously, it cannot. I may add, moreover, that maintaining respect for the religious observances of others is a fundamental civic virtue that government (including the public schools) can and should cultivate—so that even if it were the case that the displaying of such respect might be mistaken for taking part in the prayer, I would deny that the dissenter's interest in avoiding *even the false appearance of participation* constitutionally trumps the government's interest in fostering respect for religion generally.

The opinion manifests that the Court itself has not given careful consideration to its test of psychological coercion. For if it had, how could it observe, with no hint of concern or disapproval, that students stood for the Pledge of Allegiance, which immediately preceded Rabbi Gutterman's invocation? The government can, of course, no more coerce political orthodoxy than religious orthodoxy. *W. Va. State Bd. of Ed. v. Barnette*. Moreover, since the Pledge of Allegiance has been revised since *Barnette* to include the phrase "under God," recital of the Pledge would appear to raise the same Establishment Clause issue as the invocation and benediction.

If students were psychologically coerced to remain standing during the invocation, they must also have been psychologically coerced, moments before, to stand for (and thereby, in the Court's view, take part in or appear to take part in) the Pledge. Must the Pledge therefore be barred from the public schools (both from graduation ceremonies and from the classroom)? In *Barnette* we held that a public school student could not be compelled to *recite* the Pledge; we did not even hint that she could not be compelled to observe respectful silence—indeed, even to *stand* in respectful silence—when those who wished to recite it did so. Logically, that ought to be the next project for the Court's bulldozer.

I also find it odd that the Court concludes that high school graduates may not be subjected to this supposed psychological coercion, yet refrains from addressing whether "mature adults" may. I had thought that the reason graduation from high school is regarded as so significant an event is that it is generally associated with transition from adolescence to young adulthood. Many graduating seniors, of course, are old enough to vote. Why, then, does the Court treat them as though they were first-graders? ...

[W]hile I have no quarrel with the Court's general proposition that the Establishment Clause "guarantees that government may not coerce anyone to support or participate in religion or its exercise," I see no warrant for expanding the concept of coercion beyond acts backed by threat of penalty—a brand of coercion that, happily, is readily discernible to those of us who have made a career of reading the disciples of Blackstone rather than of Freud. The Framers were indeed opposed to coercion of religious worship by the National Government; but, as their own sponsorship of nonsectarian prayer in public events demonstrates, they understood that "[s]peech is not coercive; the listener may do as he likes." ...

The Court relies on our "school prayer" cases, ... [b]ut whatever the merit of those cases, they do not support, much less compel, the Court's psycho-journey. In the first place, [the cases] do not constitute an exception to the rule, distilled from historical practice, that public ceremonies may include prayer; rather, they simply do not fall within the scope of the rule (for the obvious reason that school instruction is not a public ceremony). Second, we have made clear our understanding that school prayer occurs within a framework in which legal coercion to attend school (*i.e.*, coercion under threat of penalty) provides the ultimate backdrop....

And finally, our school prayer cases turn in part on the fact that the classroom is inherently an instructional setting, and daily prayer there—where parents are not present to counter "the students' emulation of teachers as role models and the children's susceptibility to peer pressure"—might be thought to raise special concerns regarding state interference with the liberty of parents to direct the religious upbringing of their children: "Families entrust public schools with the education of their children, but condition their trust on the understanding that the classroom will not purposely be used to advance religious views that may conflict with the private beliefs of the student and his or her family." Voluntary prayer at graduation—a one-time ceremony at which parents, friends, and relatives are present—can hardly be thought to raise the same concerns....

[C.] The reader has been told much in this case about the personal interest of Mr. Weisman and his daughter, and very little about the personal interests on the other side. They are not inconsequential.

Church and state would not be such a difficult subject if religion were, as the Court apparently thinks it to be, some purely personal avocation that can be indulged entirely in secret, like pornography, in the privacy of one's room. For most believers it is *not* that, and has never been.

Religious men and women of almost all denominations have felt it necessary to acknowledge and beseech the blessing of God as a people, and not just as individuals, because they believe in the "protection of divine Providence," as the Declaration of Independence put it, not just for individuals but for societies; because they believe God to be, as Washington's first Thanksgiving Proclamation put it, the "Great Lord and Ruler of Nations."

One can believe in the effectiveness of such public worship, or one can deprecate and deride it. But the longstanding American tradition of prayer at official ceremonies displays with unmistakable clarity that the Establishment Clause does not forbid the government to accommodate it.

The narrow context of the present case involves a community's celebration of one of the milestones in its young citizens' lives, and it is a bold step for this Court to seek to banish from that occasion, and from thousands of similar celebrations throughout this land, the expression of gratitude to God that a majority of the community wishes to make. The issue before us today is not the abstract philosophical question whether the alternative of frustrating this desire of a religious majority is to be preferred over the alternative of imposing "psychological coercion," or a feeling of exclusion, upon nonbelievers. Rather, the question is *whether a mandatory choice in favor of the former has been imposed by the United States Constitution*. As the age-old practices of our people show, the answer to that question is not at all in doubt.

I must add one final observation: The Founders of our Republic knew the fearsome potential of sectarian religious belief to generate civil dissension and civil strife. And they also knew that nothing, absolutely nothing, is so inclined to foster among religious believers of various faiths a toleration— no, an affection—for one another than voluntarily joining in prayer together, to the God whom they all worship and seek.

Needless to say, no one should be compelled to do that, but it is a shame to deprive our public culture of the opportunity, and indeed the encouragement, for people to do it voluntarily. The Baptist or Catholic who heard and joined in the simple and inspiring prayers of Rabbi Gutterman on this official and patriotic occasion was inoculated from religious bigotry and prejudice in a manner that cannot be replicated. To deprive our society of that important unifying mechanism, in order to spare the nonbeliever what seems to me the minimal inconvenience of standing or even sitting in respectful nonparticipation, is as senseless in policy as it is unsupported in law....

g. *Town of Greece v. Galloway, 134 S. Ct. 1811 (2014)*

Justice Kennedy[, joined in relevant part by Chief Justice Roberts and Justice Alito]....

[A.] Respondents ... contend that prayer conducted in the intimate setting of a town board meeting differs in fundamental ways from the invocations delivered in Congress and state legislatures, where the public remains segregated from legislative activity and may not address the body except by occasional invitation. Citizens attend town meetings, on the other hand, to accept awards; speak on matters of local importance; and petition the board for action that may affect their economic interests, such as the granting of permits, business licenses, and zoning variances.

Respondents argue that the public may feel subtle pressure to participate in prayers that violate their beliefs in order to please the board members from whom they are about to seek a favorable ruling. In their view the fact that board members in small towns know many of their constituents by name only increases the pressure to conform....

[G]overnment may not coerce its citizens "to support or participate in any religion or its exercise." On the record in this case the Court is not persuaded that the town of Greece, through the act of offering a brief, solemn, and respectful prayer to open its monthly meetings, compelled its citizens to engage in a religious observance. The inquiry remains a fact-sensitive one that considers both the setting in which the prayer arises and the audience to whom it is directed.

The prayer opportunity in this case must be evaluated against the backdrop of historical practice.... [L]egislative prayer has become part of our heritage and tradition, ... similar to the Pledge of Allegiance, inaugural prayer, or the recitation of "God save the United States and this honorable Court" at the opening of this Court's sessions. It is presumed that the reasonable observer is acquainted with this tradition and understands that its purposes are to lend gravity to public proceedings and to acknowledge the place religion holds in the lives of many private citizens, not to afford government an opportunity to proselytize or force truant constituents into the pews....

The principal audience for these invocations is not, indeed, the public but lawmakers themselves, who may find that a moment of prayer or quiet reflection sets the mind to a higher purpose and thereby eases the task of governing.... [See, e.g.,] Madison's Detached Memoranda 558 (characterizing prayer in Congress as "religious worship for national representatives"). To be sure, many members of the public find these prayers meaningful and wish to join them. But their purpose is largely to accommodate the spiritual needs of lawmakers and connect them to a tradition dating to the time of the Framers.

For members of town boards and commissions, who often serve part-time and as volunteers, ceremonial prayer may also reflect the values they hold as private citizens. The prayer is an opportunity for them to show who and what they are without denying the right to dissent by those who disagree.

[B.] The analysis would be different if town board members directed the public to participate in the prayers, singled out dissidents for opprobrium, or indicated that their decisions might be influenced by a person's acquiescence in the prayer opportunity. No such thing occurred in the town of Greece. Although board members themselves stood, bowed their heads, or made the sign of the cross during the prayer, they at no point solicited similar gestures by the public.

Respondents point to several occasions where audience members were asked to rise for the prayer. These requests, however, came not from town leaders but from the guest ministers, who presumably are accustomed to directing their congregations in this way and might have done so thinking the action was inclusive, not coercive. See[, e.g.,] App. 69a ("Would you bow your heads with me as we invite the Lord's presence here tonight?") ....

Respondents suggest that constituents might feel pressure to join the prayers to avoid irritating the officials who would be ruling on their petitions, but this argument has no evidentiary support. Nothing in the record indicates that town leaders allocated benefits and burdens based on participation in the prayer, or that citizens were received differently depending on whether they joined the invocation or quietly declined. In no instance did town leaders signal disfavor toward nonparticipants or suggest that their stature in the community was in any way diminished....

[In] *Lee v. Weisman*[, ...] the Court found that, in the context of a graduation where school authorities maintained close supervision over the conduct of the students and the substance of the ceremony, a religious invocation was coercive as to an objecting student.... [T]he circumstances the Court confronted [in *Lee*] are not present in this case .... Nothing in the record suggests that members of the public are dissuaded from leaving the meeting room during the prayer, arriving late, or even, as happened here, making a later protest.

In this case, as in *Marsh v. Chambers,* board members and constituents are "free to enter and leave with little comment and for any number of reasons." Should nonbelievers choose to exit the room during a prayer they find distasteful, their absence will not stand out as disrespectful or even noteworthy. And should they remain, their quiet acquiescence will not, in light of our traditions, be interpreted as an agreement with the words or ideas expressed. Neither choice represents an unconstitutional imposition as to mature adults, who "presumably" are "not readily susceptible to religious indoctrination or peer pressure." *Marsh.*

[C.] {[R]espondents state[] that the prayers gave them offense and made them feel excluded and disrespected. Offense, however, does not equate to coercion. Adults often encounter speech they find disagreeable; and an Establishment Clause violation is not made out any time a person experiences a sense of affront from the expression of contrary religious views in a legislative forum, especially where, as here, any member of the public is welcome in turn to offer an invocation reflecting his or her own convictions.}

[D.] In the town of Greece, the prayer is delivered during the ceremonial portion of the town's meeting. Board members are not engaged in policymaking at this time, but in more general functions, such as swearing in new police officers, inducting high school athletes into the town hall of fame, and presenting proclamations to volunteers, civic groups, and senior citizens. It is a moment for town leaders to recognize the achievements of their constituents and the aspects of community life that are worth celebrating.

By inviting ministers to serve as chaplain for the month, and welcoming them to the front of the room alongside civic leaders, the town is acknowledging the central place that religion, and religious institutions, hold in the lives of those present. Indeed, some congregations are not simply spiritual homes for town residents but also the provider of social services for citizens regardless of their beliefs. See[, *e.g.*,] App. 31a (thanking a pastor for his "community involvement") .... The inclusion of a brief, ceremonial prayer as part of a larger exercise in civic recognition suggests that its purpose and effect are to acknowledge religious leaders and the institutions they represent rather than to exclude or coerce nonbelievers.

Ceremonial prayer is but a recognition that, since this Nation was founded and until the present day, many Americans deem that their own existence must be understood by precepts far beyond the authority of government to alter or define and that willing participation in civic affairs can be consistent with a brief acknowledgment of their belief in a higher power, always with due respect for those who adhere to other beliefs. The prayer in this case has a permissible ceremonial purpose. It is not an unconstitutional establishment of religion.

Justice Thomas, with whom Justice Scalia joins [in relevant part]....

"The coercion that was a hallmark of historical establishments of religion was coercion of religious orthodoxy and of financial support *by force of law and threat of penalty.*" *Lee* (Scalia, J., dissenting). In a typical case, attendance at the established church was mandatory, and taxes were levied to generate church revenue. Dissenting ministers were barred from preaching, and political participation was limited to members of the established church....

[E]ven assuming that the framers of the Fourteenth Amendment reconceived the nature of the Establishment Clause as a constraint on the States, nothing in the history of the intervening period suggests a fundamental transformation in their understanding of *what constituted an establishment....* [T]here is no support for the proposition that the framers of the Fourteenth Amendment embraced wholly modern notions that the Establishment Clause is violated whenever the "reasonable observer" feels "subtle pressure" or perceives governmental "endors[ement]."

For example, of the 37 States in existence when the Fourteenth Amendment was ratified, 27 State Constitutions "contained an explicit reference to God in their preambles." In addition to the preamble references, 30 State Constitutions contained other references to the divine, using such phrases as "'Almighty God,'" "'[O]ur Creator,'" and "'Sovereign Ruler of the Universe.'" Moreover, the state constitutional provisions that prohibited religious "comp[ulsion]" made clear that the relevant sort of compulsion was legal in nature, of the same type that had characterized founding-era establishments. These provisions strongly suggest that, whatever nonestablishment principles existed in 1868, they included no concern for the finer sensibilities of the "reasonable observer." ...

Thus, to the extent coercion is relevant to the Establishment Clause analysis, it is actual legal coercion that counts—not the "subtle coercive pressures" allegedly felt by respondents in this case.... "[P]eer pressure, unpleasant as it may be, is not coercion[.]" ...

Justice Kagan, joined by Justices Ginsburg, Breyer, and Sotomayor, dissenting. [The dissent primarily argued that the prayers impermissibly endorsed religion, and didn't fit within the *Marsh* exception. But this passage could be relevant to the coercion issue:—ed.]

Let's say that a Muslim citizen of Greece goes before the Board to share her views on policy or request some permit.... But just before she gets to say her piece, a minister deputized by the Town asks her to pray "in the name of God's only son Jesus Christ."

She must think—it is hardly paranoia, but only the truth—that Christian worship has become entwined with local governance. And now she faces a choice—to pray alongside the majority as one of that group or somehow to register her deeply felt difference.

She is a strong person, but that is no easy call—especially given that the room is small and her every action (or inaction) will be noticed. She does not wish to be rude to her neighbors, nor does she wish to aggravate the Board members whom she will soon be trying to persuade. And yet she does not want to acknowledge Christ's divinity, any more than many of her neighbors would want to deny that tenet.

So assume she declines to participate with the others in the first act of the meeting—or even, as the majority proposes, that she stands up and leaves the room altogether. At the least, she becomes a different kind of citizen, one who will not join in the religious practice that the Town Board has chosen as reflecting its own and the community's most cherished beliefs. And she thus stands at a remove, based solely on religion, from her fellow citizens and her elected representatives.

Everything about that situation, I think, infringes the First Amendment.... That the Town Board selects, month after month and year after year, prayergivers who will reliably speak in the voice of Christianity, and so places itself behind a single creed. That in offering those sectarian prayers, the Board's chosen clergy members repeatedly call on individuals, prior to participating in local governance, to join in a form of worship that may be at odds with their own beliefs.

That the clergy thus put some residents to the unenviable choice of either pretending to pray like the majority or declining to join its communal activity, at the very moment of petitioning their elected leaders. That the practice thus divides the citizenry, creating one class that shares the Board's own evident religious beliefs and another (far smaller) class that does not. And that the practice also alters a dissenting citizen's relationship with her government, making her religious difference salient when she seeks only to engage her elected representatives as would any other citizen....

h. Policy—No Coercion

Basic argument: "This government action is impermissible because it coerces religious activity by _____, and that's bad because _____."

1. "[T]he Constitution guarantees that government may not coerce anyone to support or participate in religion or its exercise.... [T]he school district's supervision and control of a high school graduation ceremony [pressures] ... attending students to stand ... or, at least, maintain respectful silence during the invocation and benediction. This pressure, though subtle

and indirect, can be as real as any overt compulsion." *Lee v. Weisman.*

2. Response to 1: This government action is in fact not coercive in any meaningful sense, because _____.

"[T]he Court's notion that a student who simply *sits* in 'respectful silence' during the invocation and benediction (when all others are standing) has somehow joined—or would somehow be perceived as having joined—in the prayers is nothing short of ludicrous.... [And even if we] assume the very worst, that the nonparticipating graduate is 'subtly coerced' ... to stand ... [this] does not remotely establish a 'participation' (or an 'appearance of participation') in a religious exercise....

"[Moreover,] while I have no quarrel with the Court's general proposition that the Establishment Clause 'guarantees that government may not coerce anyone to support or participate in religion or its exercise,' I see no warrant for expanding the concept of coercion beyond acts backed by threat of penalty.... [As the Framers'] own sponsorship of nonsectarian prayer in public events demonstrates, they understood that '[s]peech is not coercive; the listener may do as he likes.'" *Id.* (Scalia, J., dissenting).

D. THE NO RELIGIOUS DECISIONS PRINCIPLE (FREE EXERCISE AND ESTABLISHMENT)

a. Summary

Basic rules:

1. Government officials, including judges and juries, may not decide whether religious beliefs *make sense* or are *internally consistent*. "[R]eligious beliefs need not be acceptable, logical, consistent, or comprehensible to others in order to merit First Amendment protection." *Thomas v. Review Bd.* (1981) (p. 889).

2. Government officials may not decide whether religious beliefs are *true*. *United States v. Ballard* (1944) (p. 883).

3. Government officials may not decide which beliefs are *central* or otherwise important to a belief system. *Employment Division v. Smith* (1990) (p. 992); *Hernandez v. Commissioner,* 490 U.S. 680, 699 (1989).

4. Government officials may not decide whether beliefs are *consistent with the teachings* of a particular religion, or *interpret religious doctrine* in other ways. *Presbyterian Church v. Mary Elizabeth Blue Hull Memorial Presbyterian Church* (1969) (p. 886); *Hernandez.*

— Example: Courts may not administer a provision in a will that leaves property to a church "so long as the church maintains fidelity to [certain religious principles]."

— But courts may interpret the secular terms of wills and other grants using neutral principles of law, and they can neutrally defer to the decision of the chief decisionmaking body of a hierarchical religion, so long as they don't inquire whether this decision is a departure from religious doctrine, or is somehow otherwise irrational or unfair.

— It's not clear whether there might be some room for the court to inquire into whether there was "'fraud' or 'collusion' when church tribunals act in bad faith for secular purposes." But even if there is, this would be a very narrow sort of review, and must be done without making any decisions about religious doctrine. See *Serbian Eastern Orthodox Diocese v. Milivojevich,* 426 U.S. 696, 713 (1976).

5. Government officials may, however, decide whether a particular person (for instance, someone who's claiming a religious exemption) *sincerely* holds a particular religious belief. *United States v. Ballard.*

b.   Problem: Kosher Enforcement

Orthodox Judaism includes a large body of dietary laws, called the "kosher" laws (pronounced in English as "*koe*-sher," accenting the first syllable). These relate to what animals may be eaten (pork and shellfish are forbidden), to animal slaughter, to food preparation (*e.g.,* blood must be fully drained from meat), to food mixing (*e.g.,* meat products may not be mixed with milk products), and to the making of wine.

Whether something is kosher often can't be directly determined by consumers. Jews who keep kosher naturally feel grievously defrauded when they learn they have been led to unwittingly consume unkosher food. Moreover, if one later learns that food one has eaten at home is unkosher, one must purify the plates and flatware used to eat it. Some material, such as expensive china, usually can't be purified and so must be thrown out.

Assume you are an aide to Joe Malchow, a state legislator whose constituents have complained about such fraud. Malchow asks you: Could a constitutionally valid law be drafted to prohibit such behavior? Could a generally applicable law that bars "intentional misrepresentation of product characteristics to consumers" be used by the state consumer affairs body to punish people who call meat "kosher" when it is not? Are there other laws that could constitutionally be used to prevent this sort of fraud? Cf. *Ran-Dav's County Kosher, Inc. v. State,* 129 N.J. 141 (1992) (4-3 decision); *Barghout v. Bureau of Kosher Meat & Food Control,* 66 F.3d 1337 (4th Cir. 1995); *Commack Self-Service Kosher Meats, Inc. v. Rubin,* 106 F. Supp. 2d 445 (E.D.N.Y. 2000).

c.   Problem: Negligent Hiring

Jane Doe, a married Episcopalian woman, goes to her priest, Richard Roe, for spiritual counseling, including guidance on her troubled marriage. They become sexually involved, though Episcopalian beliefs forbid that. The sexual relationship would also be malpractice if committed by a state-licensed secular marital counselor, but Roe does not hold himself out to be state-licensed or a secular marital counselor.

After the relationship ends, Doe suffers serious emotional distress. She then (1) sues Roe for clergy malpractice and (2) sues Roe's employer, the Diocese, for negligent hiring and negligent supervision. She claims that, had

Roe's employer paid reasonable attention to Roe's behavior and past history, it would have learned of his misconduct (or at least his propensity to such misconduct) and should have fired him.

Assume that state law generally recognizes causes of action for negligent hiring and negligent supervision, under which an employer is liable if (a) it unreasonably failed to exercise proper care, given all the circumstances, in deciding whether to hire a person, or in deciding to what extent to supervise the person, and (b) this failure causes harm to the plaintiff.

Would imposing liability on Roe and the Diocese be constitutional? Compare, *e.g., Swanson v. Roman Catholic Bishop,* 692 A.2d 441 (Me. 1997) and *L.L.N. v. Clauder,* 563 N.W.2d 434 (Wis. 1997) with *Moses v. Diocese of Colorado,* 863 P.2d 310 (Colo. 1993) and *Kenneth R. v. Roman Catholic Diocese,* 654 N.Y.S.2d 791 (App. Div. 1997).

d. *United States v. Ballard, 322 U.S. 78 (1944)*

Justice Douglas delivered the opinion of the Court.

[A.] Respondents were ... convicted for using ... the mails to defraud ... by organizing and promoting the I Am movement through the use of the mails. The charge was that ... literature [was] distributed and sold, funds solicited, and memberships in the I Am movement sought "by means of false and fraudulent representations, pretenses and promises." The false representations charged ... covered respondents' alleged religious doctrines or beliefs[, *e.g.,*] ...:

> that Guy W. Ballard, now deceased, alias Saint Germain, Jesus, [and] George Washington, ... had been selected ... as a divine messenger; and that ... the words of the alleged divine entity, Saint Germain, would be transmitted to mankind through the medium of ... Guy W. Ballard;
>
> that Guy W. Ballard ... and Edna W. Ballard, and Donald Ballard, by reason of their alleged high spiritual attainments and righteous conduct, had been selected as divine messengers through which the words of ... Saint Germain[] would be communicated to mankind under the teachings commonly known as the "I Am" movement;
>
> that Guy W. Ballard ... and Edna W. Ballard and Donald Ballard had, by reason of supernatural attainments, the power to heal persons of ... [incurable] diseases ..., ... and ... had in fact cured ... hundreds of persons ....

[T]he indictment ... alleged: "... the defendants ... knew that [the] representations were false ... and were made with the intention ... to obtain [money] from persons intended to be defrauded by the defendants ...." ...

[Defendants asserted] that the indictment attacked the religious beliefs of respondents and sought to restrict the free exercise of their religion ...[, but the District Court disagreed].... [The court, however,] confined the issues [at trial] ... to the question of the good faith of respondents. At the request of counsel for both sides the court advised the jury ...:

> ... [T]he defendants in this case made certain representations of belief in a divinity and in a supernatural power. Some of the teachings of the defendants, representations ... [such as] the appearance of Jesus to dictate

some of the works ..., ... or shaking hands with Jesus, to some people that might seem highly improbable....

Whether that is true or not is not [your] concern .... The issue is: Did these defendants honestly and in good faith believe those things? If they did, they should be acquitted.... If these defendants did not believe those things, ... but used the mail for the purpose of getting money, [you] should find them guilty. Therefore, gentlemen, religion cannot come into this case.

... [C]ounsel for the defense acquiesced in this treatment of the matter .... [Defendants were convicted, but the] Court of Appeals reversed .... In its view the restriction of the issue in question to that of good faith was error. Its reason was that the scheme to defraud alleged in the indictment was that respondents made the eighteen alleged false representations; and that to prove that defendants devised the scheme described in the indictment "it was necessary to prove ... that some, at least, of the representations which they schemed to make were false." ...

[B.] Freedom of thought, which includes freedom of religious belief, ... embraces the right to maintain theories of life and of death and of the hereafter which are rank heresy to followers of the orthodox faiths. Heresy trials are foreign to our Constitution. Men may believe what they cannot prove. They may not be put to the proof of their religious doctrines or beliefs. Religious experiences which are as real as life to some may be incomprehensible to others. Yet the fact that they may be beyond the ken of mortals does not mean that they can be made suspect before the law.

Many take their gospel from the New Testament. But it would hardly be supposed that they could be tried before a jury charged with the duty of determining whether those teachings contained false representations. The miracles of the New Testament, the Divinity of Christ, life after death, the power of prayer are deep in the religious convictions of many. If one could be sent to jail because a jury in a hostile environment found those teachings false, little indeed would be left of religious freedom....

The religious views espoused by respondents might seem incredible, if not preposterous, to most people. But if those doctrines are subject to trial before a jury charged with finding their truth or falsity, then the same can be done with the religious beliefs of any sect. When the triers of fact undertake that task, they enter a forbidden domain. The First Amendment does not select any one group or any one type of religion for preferred treatment. It puts them all in that position.... [T]he District Court [thus] ruled properly when it withheld from the jury all questions concerning the truth or falsity of the religious beliefs or doctrines of respondents....

Chief Justice Stone, dissenting[, joined by Justice Roberts and Justice Frankfurter]. [Omitted.—ed.]

Justice Jackson, dissenting[.]

I should say the defendants have done just that for which they are indicted. If I might agree to their conviction without creating a precedent, I cheerfully would do so. I can see in their teachings nothing but humbug, untainted by any trace of truth. But that does not dispose of the constitutional question whether misrepresentation of religious experience or belief is prosecutable; it rather emphasizes the danger of such prosecutions....

In the first place, as a matter of either practice or philosophy I do not see how we can separate an issue as to what is believed from considerations as to what is believable. The most convincing proof that one believes his statements is to show that they have been true in his experience. Likewise, that one knowingly falsified is best proved by showing that what he said happened never did happen.

How can the Government prove these persons knew something to be false which it cannot prove to be false? If we try religious sincerity severed from religious verity, we isolate the dispute from the very considerations which in common experience provide its most reliable answer.

In the second place, any inquiry into intellectual honesty in religion raises profound psychological problems.... [I]t is not theology and ceremonies which keep religion going. Its vitality is in the religious experiences of many people ...[·] ",.. conversations with the unseen, voices and visions, responses to prayer, changes of heart, deliverances from fear, inflowings of help, assurances of support, whenever certain persons set their own internal attitude in certain appropriate ways."

If religious liberty includes, as it must, the right to communicate such experiences to others, it seems to me an impossible task for juries to separate fancied ones from real ones, dreams from happenings, and hallucinations from true clairvoyance. Such experiences, like some tones and colors, have existence for one, but none at all for another. They cannot be verified to the minds of those whose field of consciousness does not include religious insight. When one comes to trial which turns on any aspect of religious belief or representation, unbelievers among his judges are likely not to understand and are almost certain not to believe him.

And then I do not know what degree of skepticism or disbelief in a religious representation amounts to actionable fraud.... Belief in what one may demonstrate to the senses is not faith. All schools of religious thought make enormous assumptions, generally on the basis of revelations authenticated by some sign or miracle. The appeal in such matters is to a very different plane of credulity than is invoked by representations of secular fact in commerce.

Some who profess belief in the Bible read literally what others read as allegory or metaphor, as they read Aesop's fables. Religious symbolism is even used by some with the same mental reservations one has in teaching of Santa Claus or Uncle Sam or Easter bunnies or dispassionate judges. It is hard in matters so mystical to say how literally one is bound to believe the doctrine he teaches and even more difficult to say how far it is reliance upon a teacher's literal belief which induces followers to give him money....

If the members of the ["I Am"] sect get comfort from the celestial guidance of their "Saint Germain," however doubtful it seems to me, it is hard to say that they do not get what they pay for. Scores of sects flourish in this country by teaching what to me are queer notions. It is plain that there is wide variety in American religious taste. The Ballards are not alone in catering to it with a pretty dubious product.

The chief wrong which false prophets do to their following is not financial. The collections aggregate a tempting total, but individual payments are not ruinous. I doubt if the vigilance of the law is equal to making money stick by over-credulous people.

But the real harm is on the mental and spiritual plane. There are those who hunger and thirst after higher values which they feel wanting in their humdrum lives. They live in mental confusion or moral anarchy and seek vaguely for truth and beauty and moral support. When they are deluded and then disillusioned, cynicism and confusion follow.

The wrong of these things, as I see it, is not in the money the victims part with half so much as in the mental and spiritual poison they get. But that is precisely the thing the Constitution put beyond the reach of the prosecutor, for the price of freedom of religion or of speech or of the press is that we must put up with, and even pay for, a good deal of rubbish....

I do not doubt that religious leaders may be convicted of fraud for making false representations on matters other than faith or experience, as for example if one represents that funds are being used to construct a church when in fact they are being used for personal purposes. But that is not this case, which reaches into wholly dangerous ground.

When does less than full belief in a professed credo become actionable fraud if one is soliciting gifts or legacies? Such inquiries may discomfort orthodox as well as unconventional religious teachers, for even the most regular of them are sometimes accused of taking their orthodoxy with a grain of salt. I would dismiss the indictment and have done with this business of judicially examining other people's faiths.

e. *Presbyterian Church in the United States v. Mary Elizabeth Blue Hull Memorial Presbyterian Church, 393 U.S. 440 (1969)*

Justice Brennan delivered the opinion of the Court....

[A.] Presbyterian Church in the United States[] is an association of local Presbyterian churches governed by a hierarchical structure of tribunals which consists of, in ascending order, (1) the Church Session, composed of the elders of the local church; (2) the Presbytery, composed of several churches in a geographical area; (3) the Synod, generally composed of all Presbyteries within a State; and (4) the General Assembly, the highest governing body.

A dispute arose between [Presbyterian Church] and two local churches in Savannah, Georgia—the respondents, Hull Memorial Presbyterian Church and Eastern Heights Presbyterian Church—over control of the properties used until then by the local churches. In 1966, the membership of the local churches, in the belief that certain actions and pronouncements of the general church were violations of that organization's constitution and departures from the doctrine and practice in force at the time of affiliation, voted to withdraw from the general church and to reconstitute the local churches as an autonomous Presbyterian organization. {[T]he claimed ... departures from petitioner's original tenets of faith and practice ... [included]: "ordaining of women as ministers and ruling elders, making pronouncements and recommendations concerning civil, economic, social and political matters [such as the Vietnam conflict], giving support to the removal of Bible reading and prayers by children in the public schools, ... and teaching neo-orthodoxy alien to the Confession of Faith ..."} ....

The ministers of the two churches renounced the general church's jurisdiction and authority over them, as did all but two of the ruling elders. In response, the general church, through the Presbytery of Savannah, established an Administrative Commission to seek a conciliation. The dissident local churchmen remained steadfast; consequently, the Commission acknowledged the withdrawal of the local leadership and proceeded to take over the local churches' property on behalf of the general church until new local leadership could be appointed.

The local churchmen made no effort to appeal the Commission's action to higher church tribunals—the Synod of Georgia or the General Assembly. Instead, the churches filed ... suits in the Superior Court of Chatham County to enjoin the general church from trespassing on the disputed property, title to which was in the local churches....

[B.] [T]he case was submitted to the jury on the theory that Georgia law implies a trust of local church property for the benefit of the general church on the sole condition that the general church adhere to its tenets of faith and practice existing at the time of affiliation by the local churches. Thus, the jury was instructed to determine whether the actions of the general church "amount to a fundamental or substantial abandonment of the original tenets and doctrines of the [general church], so that the new tenets and doctrines are utterly variant from the purposes for which the [general church] was founded." The jury returned a verdict for the local churches, and the trial judge thereupon declared that the implied trust had terminated and enjoined the general church from interfering with the use of the property in question....

It is of course true that the State has a legitimate interest in resolving property disputes, and that a civil court is a proper forum for that resolution. Special problems arise, however, when these disputes implicate controversies over church doctrine and practice.

The approach of this Court in such cases was originally developed in *Watson v. Jones,* 80 U.S. 679 (1872), a pre-*Erie R. Co. v. Tompkins* diversity decision decided before the application of the First Amendment to the States but nonetheless informed by First Amendment considerations. There, as here, civil courts were asked to resolve a property dispute between a national Presbyterian organization and local churches of that organization. There, as here, the disputes arose out of a controversy over church doctrine. There, as here, the Court was asked to decree the termination of an implied trust because of departures from doctrine by the national organization.

The *Watson* Court refused, pointing out that it was wholly inconsistent with the American concept of the relationship between church and state to permit civil courts to determine ecclesiastical questions. In language which has a clear constitutional ring, the Court said

> In this country the full and free right to entertain any religious belief, to practice any religious principle, and to teach any religious doctrine which does not violate the laws of morality and property, and which does not infringe personal rights, is conceded to all. The law knows no heresy, and is committed to the support of no dogma, the establishment of no sect....
>
> All who unite themselves to ... [the general church] do so with an implied consent to [its] government, and are bound to submit to it. But it would be a vain consent and would lead to the total subversion of such religious bodies, if any one aggrieved by one of their decisions could appeal to the secular courts and have [the decision] reversed. It is of the essence of these religious unions, and of their right to establish tribunals for the decision of questions arising among themselves, that those decisions should be binding in all cases of ecclesiastical cognizance, subject only to such appeals as the organism itself provides for.

The logic of this language leaves the civil courts *no* role in determining ecclesiastical questions in the process of resolving property disputes....

[N]eutral principles of law, developed for use in all property disputes, ... can be applied without "establishing" churches to which property is awarded. But First Amendment values are plainly jeopardized when church property litigation is made to turn on the resolution by civil courts of controversies over religious doctrine and practice. If civil courts undertake to resolve such controversies in order to adjudicate the property dispute, the hazards are ever present of inhibiting the free development of religious doctrine and of implicating secular interests in matters of purely ecclesiastical concern.

Because of these hazards, the First Amendment enjoins the employment of organs of government for essentially religious purposes; the Amendment therefore commands civil courts to decide church property disputes without resolving underlying controversies over religious doctrine. Hence, States, religious organizations, and individuals must structure relationships involving church property so as not to require the civil courts to resolve ecclesiastical questions....

[C.] The departure-from-doctrine element of the [Georgia] implied trust theory ... requires the civil judiciary to determine whether actions of the general church constitute such a "substantial departure" from the tenets of faith and practice existing at the time of the local churches affiliation that the trust in favor of the general church must be declared to have terminated.... [This] requires the civil court to determine matters at the very core of a religion—the interpretation of particular church doctrines and the importance of those doctrines to the religion. Plainly, the First Amendment forbids civil courts from playing such a role....

The departure-from-doctrine approach is not susceptible of the marginal judicial involvement contemplated in *Gonzalez v. Archbishop,* 280 U.S. 1 (1929). Gonzalez' rights under a will turned on a church decision, the Archbishop's, as to church law, the qualifications for the chaplaincy. It was the archbishopric, not the civil courts, which had the task of analyzing and interpreting church law in order to determine the validity of Gonzalez' claim to a chaplaincy.

Thus, the civil courts could adjudicate the rights under the will without interpreting or weighing church doctrine but simply by engaging in the narrowest kind of review of a specific church decision—*i.e.,* whether that decision resulted from fraud, collusion, or arbitrariness. Such review does not inject the civil courts into substantive ecclesiastical matters. [*Serbian Eastern Orthodox Diocese v. Milivojevich,* 426 U.S. 696 (1976), later held that "no 'arbitrariness' exception in the sense of an inquiry whether the decisions of the highest ecclesiastical tribunal of a hierarchical church complied with church laws and regulations is [permissible]."—ed.]

In contrast, under Georgia's departure-from-doctrine approach, it is not possible for the civil courts to play so limited a role. Under this approach, property rights do not turn on a church decision as to church doctrine. The standard of departure-from-doctrine, though it calls for resolution of ecclesiastical questions, is a creation of state, not church, law.... [To reach] the questions posed by the state standard ... would require the civil courts to engage in the forbidden process of interpreting and weighing church doctrine....

f. *Thomas v. Review Bd., 450 U.S. 707 (1981)*

[This case involved a claim for unemployment compensation that was like the claim in *Sherbert v. Verner* (p. 973). But it also spoke more broadly about how courts should deal with different sorts of religious beliefs.—ed.]

Chief Justice Burger delivered the opinion of the Court....

[Eddie C. Thomas, a Jehovah's Witness,] terminated his employment in the Blaw-Knox Foundry & Machinery Co. when he was transferred from the roll foundry to a department that produced turrets for military tanks. He claimed his religious beliefs prevented him from participating in the production of war materials....

[T]he resolution of [what is a "religious" belief or practice] is not to turn upon a judicial perception of the particular belief or practice in question; religious beliefs need not be acceptable, logical, consistent, or comprehensible to others in order to merit First Amendment protection.

In support of his claim for benefits, Thomas testified [that] "when ... I'm daily faced with the knowledge that these are tanks ... I really could not, you know, conscientiously continue to work with armaments. It would be against all of the ... religious principles that ... I have come to learn...." Based upon this and other testimony, the referee held that Thomas "quit due to his religious convictions." ...

The Indiana Supreme Court ... [concluded that Thomas "had made a merely 'personal philosophical choice rather than a religious choice,'" partly because] Thomas was "struggling" with his beliefs and that he was not able to "articulate" his belief precisely. It noted, for example, that Thomas admitted before the referee that he would not object to [work] "... produc[ing] the raw product necessary for the production of any kind of tank ... [because I] would not be a direct party to whoever they shipped it to [and] would not be ... chargeable in ... conscience...." The court found this position inconsistent with Thomas' stated opposition to participation in the production of armaments.

But Thomas' statements reveal no more than that he found work in the roll foundry sufficiently insulated from producing weapons of war.... Thomas drew a line, and it is not for us to say that the line he drew was an unreasonable one. Courts should not undertake to dissect religious beliefs because the believer admits that he is "struggling" with his position or because his beliefs are not articulated with the clarity and precision that a more sophisticated person might employ.

The Indiana court also appears to have given significant weight to the fact that another Jehovah's Witness had no scruples about working on tank turrets; for that other Witness, at least, such work was "scripturally" acceptable. Intrafaith differences of that kind are not uncommon among followers of a particular creed, and the judicial process is singularly ill equipped to resolve such differences in relation to the Religion Clauses.

One can, of course, imagine an asserted claim so bizarre, so clearly nonreligious in motivation, as not to be entitled to protection under the Free Exercise Clause; but that is not the case here, and the guarantee of free exercise is not limited to beliefs which are shared by all of the members of a religious sect. Particularly in this sensitive area, it is not within the judicial function and judicial competence to inquire whether the petitioner or his fellow worker more correctly perceived the commands of their common faith. Courts are not arbiters of scriptural interpretation....

On this record, it is clear that Thomas terminated his employment for religious reasons.

XII. COMPELLED EXCLUSION OF RELIGION?

A. FACIALLY EVENHANDED FUNDING PROGRAMS AND RELIGIOUS INSTITUTIONS

1. DOCTRINE

a. Summary: The Issue, and Historical Background

People often argue that the Establishment Clause means the government may not subsidize, even indirectly, religious institutions. When the subsidy goes to religious institutions and religious institutions alone, this argument fits well with the no discrimination principle. Such preferential benefits are now unconstitutional, though some disagree (see the dissent in *Texas Monthly v. Bullock* (1989) (p. 775)).

The controversy arises when religious institutions get government funds as part of an evenhanded funding program, such as a program that gives benefits to all K-12 schools, whether government-run, private secular, or private religious, or a program that gives scholarship vouchers to parents of children who go to all these schools. Here, money is going to religious institutions, but there isn't any facial violation of the no discrimination principle. In fact, excluding religious institutions would *itself* presumptively violate the no discrimination principle (cf. *McDaniel v. Paty* (1978) (p. 732); *Lukumi Babalu Aye* (1993) (p. 737)), though perhaps that presumption might be rebutted, see, *e.g.*, *Locke v. Davey* (2004) (p. 744).

During the 1970s, the Court's view was generally that religious organizations may *not* participate in many generally available aid programs. At the same time, the Court did uphold some programs that provided certain kinds of aid (such as secular textbooks), and it was broadly assumed that at least some such programs—such as the GI Bill, which funded college educations, even at religious institutions—were constitutional. In the 1980s, the Court began to shift towards allowing religious institutions to participate in evenhanded programs. In the 1990s, the Court generally upheld most programs in which religious institutions could equally participate, and reversed several earlier precedents that had barred many such programs. And in the early 2000s, the Court set forth a new rule.

b. Summary: The Current Rule

1. Evenhanded "private choice" funding programs—in which funds are routed by private individuals to institutions of their choice—are generally permissible *even when these funds end up being used for religious purposes*. See *Zelman v. Simmons-Harris* (2002) (p. 924).

2. Evenhanded "direct aid" programs—in which benefits are given directly to religious institutions—are

a. Permissible if and only if there's some assurance that the funds *will not be used for religious purposes.*

— Thus, a program that funds new buildings in all universities, and lets the universities use those buildings for religious purposes, is forbidden. *Tilton v. Richardson,* 403 U.S. 672 (1971).

— The program in *Mitchell v. Helms* (2000) (p. 915), or a program that gives schools secular equipment, such as secular books, *Board of Ed. v. Allen,* 392 U.S. 236 (1968), is permitted.

— This is the result of *Mitchell,* in which Justices O'Connor and Breyer took this view. Four other Justices (Rehnquist, Scalia, Kennedy, and Thomas) took the view that there is no Establishment Clause problem with religious institutions participating in any evenhanded benefit programs, so long as the benefits are not themselves religious (*i.e.,* so long as the benefits are money or secular books or supplies).

b. Justice O'Connor also voted to uphold the program in *Rosenberger,* even though it was not a "private choice" program—religious newspapers were directly subsidized, rather than getting funds through the private choices of individual students—and even though the funds were certain to be used for religious purposes. Query how this can be reconciled with Justice O'Connor's position in *Mitchell.*

A note about the *Lemon* test: The Justices have generally fit all this into the Lemon analysis by reasoning that (1) the programs have a secular *purpose* (providing children with an education), but debating (2) whether the routing of funds to a religious use is an impermissible *primary effect* (or whether the primary effect of such programs is education and educational choice) and (3) whether any safeguards set up to prevent such routing are excessively *entangling* (or whether any safeguards, if needed, can be implemented without undue entanglement).

c. *Problem: GI Bill*

The 1944 GI Bill of Rights provided that the government would pay for the education of any World War II veteran "at any approved educational ... institution at which he chooses to enroll." The government would pay for the "customary cost" of tuition, books, and supplies, up to "$500 for an ordinary school year," which at the time covered expenses at most top universities. (The veteran would also get $600 per year in living expenses, or $900 per year if he had dependents.) See 58 Stat. 284, 288-89 (1944).

Is this constitutional, as applied to veterans who want to study at religiously affiliated universities? Should it be? *Compare Committee for Public Ed. & Religious Liberty v. Nyquist,* 413 U.S. 756, 782 (1973) (dictum) *with Engel v. Vitale,* 370 U.S. 421, 437 n.1 (1962) (Douglas, J., concurring).

d. *Everson v. Board of Ed., 330 U.S. 1 (1947)*

Justice Black delivered the opinion of the Court.

[A.] A New Jersey statute authorizes its local school districts to make rules and contracts for the transportation of children to and from schools. The appellee ... acting pursuant to this statute authorized reimbursement to parents of money expended by them for the bus transportation of their children on regular busses operated by the public transportation system. Part of this money was for the payment of transportation of some children in the community to Catholic parochial schools....

[B.] [Justice Black made various historical arguments, from which he concluded—ed.:] The "establishment of religion" clause of the First Amendment means at least this: Neither a state nor the Federal Government can set up a church. Neither can pass laws which aid one religion, aid all religions, or prefer one religion over another. Neither can force nor influence a person to go to or to remain away from church against his will or force him to profess a belief or disbelief in any religion. No person can be punished for entertaining or professing religious beliefs or disbeliefs, for church attendance or non-attendance.

No tax in any amount, large or small, can be levied to support any religious activities or institutions, whatever they may be called, or whatever form they may adopt to teach or practice religion. Neither a state nor the Federal Government can, openly or secretly, participate in the affairs of any religious organizations or groups and *vice versa*. In the words of Jefferson, the clause against establishment of religion by law was intended to erect "a wall of separation between church and State." ... New Jersey cannot consistently with the "establishment of religion" clause of the First Amendment contribute tax-raised funds to the support of an institution which teaches the tenets and faith of any church.

On the other hand, ... New Jersey cannot hamper its citizens in the free exercise of their own religion. Consequently, it cannot exclude individual Catholics, Lutherans, Mohammedans, Baptists, Jews, Methodists, Non-believers, Presbyterians, or the members of any other faith, *because of their faith, or lack of it*, from receiving the benefits of public welfare legislation. While ... a state could ... provide transportation only to children attending public schools, we must be careful ... not [to] inadvertently prohibit New Jersey from extending its general state law benefits to all its citizens without regard to their religious belief.

[C.] Measured by these standards, we cannot say that the First Amendment prohibits New Jersey from spending tax-raised funds to pay the bus fares of parochial school pupils as a part of a general program under which it pays the fares of pupils attending public and other schools.

It is undoubtedly true that children are helped to get to church schools. There is even a possibility that some of the children might not be sent to the church schools if the parents were compelled to pay their children's bus fares out of their own pockets when transportation to a public school would have been paid for by the State. The same possibility exists where the state requires a local transit company to provide reduced fares to school children including those attending parochial schools, or where a municipally owned transportation system undertakes to carry all school children free of charge.

Moreover, state-paid policemen, detailed to protect children going to and from church schools from the very real hazards of traffic, would serve much the same purpose and accomplish much the same result as state provisions intended to guarantee free transportation of a kind which the state deems to be best for the school children's welfare. And parents might refuse to risk their children to the serious danger of traffic accidents going to and from parochial schools, the approaches to which were not protected by policemen. Similarly, parents might be reluctant to permit their children to attend schools which the state had cut off from such general government services as ordinary police and fire protection, connections for sewage disposal, public highways and sidewalks.

Of course, cutting off church schools from these services, so separate and so indisputably marked off from the religious function, would make it far more difficult for the schools to operate. But such is obviously not the purpose of the First Amendment. That Amendment requires the state to be a neutral in its relations with groups of religious believers and non-believers; it does not require the state to be their adversary. State power is no more to be used so as to handicap religions, than it is to favor them....

The State contributes no money to the [parochial] schools. It does not support them. Its legislation, as applied, does no more than provide a general program to help parents get their children, regardless of their religion, safely and expeditiously to and from accredited schools.

The First Amendment has erected a wall between church and state. That wall must be kept high and impregnable. We could not approve the slightest breach. New Jersey has not breached it here....

Justice Rutledge, with whom Justice Frankfurter, Justice Jackson and Justice Burton agree, dissenting....

[M]oney taken by taxation from one is not to be used or given to support another's religious training or belief, or indeed one's own.... [T]he furnishing of "contributions of money for the propagation of opinions which he disbelieves" is the forbidden exaction; and the prohibition is absolute for whatever measure brings that consequence and whatever amount may be sought or given to that end....

Here parents pay money to send their children to parochial schools and funds raised by taxation are used to reimburse them.... [T]he Catholic taxpayer to the extent of his proportionate share pays for the transportation of Lutheran, Jewish and otherwise religiously affiliated children to receive their non-Catholic religious instruction. Their parents likewise pay proportionately for the transportation of Catholic children to receive Catholic instruction. Each thus contributes to "the propagation of opinions which he disbelieves" in so far as their religions differ, as do others who accept no creed without regard to those differences. Each thus pays taxes also to support the teaching of his own religion, an exaction equally forbidden since it denies "the comfortable liberty" of giving one's contribution to the particular agency of instruction he approves....

[T]he cost of transportation is ... part of the cost of education or of the religious instruction given. That it is a substantial and a necessary element is shown most plainly by the continuing and increasing demand for the state to assume it.

Nor is there pretense that it relates only to the secular instruction given in religious schools or that any attempt is or could be made toward allocating proportional shares as between the secular and the religious instruction. It is precisely because the instruction is religious and relates to a particular faith ... that parents send their children to religious schools .... And the very purpose of the state's contribution is to defray the cost of conveying the pupil to the place where he will receive not simply secular, but also and primarily religious, teaching and guidance. {It is a matter not frequently recalled that President Grant opposed tax exemption of religious property as leading to a violation of the principle of separation of church and state.} ...

Nor is the case comparable to one of furnishing fire or police protection, or access to public highways. These things are matters of common right, part of the general need for safety. {The protections are of a nature which does not require appropriations specially made from the public treasury and earmarked, as is New Jersey's here, particularly for religious institutions or uses. The First Amendment does not exclude religious property or activities from protection against disorder or the ordinary accidental incidents of community life. It forbids support, not protection from interference or destruction.} Certainly the fire department must not stand idly by while the church burns. Nor is this reason why the state should pay the expense of transportation or other items of the cost of religious education....

e. Policy—No Taxpayer Money Going to Religious Uses

Basic argument: "This government action is unconstitutional because it funnels taxpayers' money to religious uses with which some taxpayers will disagree, by _____, and that is bad because _____."

1. "[T]o compel a man to furnish contributions of money for the propagation of opinions which he disbelieves, is sinful and tyrannical; ... even ... forcing him to support this or that teacher of his own religious persuasion, is depriving him of the comfortable liberty of giving his contributions to the particular pastor, whose morals he would make his pattern...." Thomas Jefferson, *Virginia Bill for Establishing Religious Freedom* (1785).

"When [tax money] is used to pay for transportation to religious schools, [each taxpayer] ... contributes to 'the propagation of opinions which he disbelieves' .... Each thus pays taxes also to support the teaching of his own religion, an exaction equally forbidden since it denies 'the comfortable liberty' of giving one's contribution to the particular agency of instruction he approves." *Everson v. Board of Ed.* (Rutledge, J., dissenting).

"[L]iberty of personal conviction requires freedom from coercion to support religion, and this means that the government can compel no aid to fund it." *Mitchell v. Helms* (Souter, J., dissenting).

2. Response to 1: There's nothing wrong with having taxpayers' money go to religious uses, so long as it goes as part of a program that satisfies the

condition that _____, because _____.

"[W]here a government aid program is neutral with respect to religion, and provides assistance directly to a broad class of citizens who, in turn, direct government aid to religious schools wholly as a result of their own genuine and independent private choice, the program is not readily subject to challenge under the Establishment Clause.... The incidental advancement of a religious mission ... is reasonably attributable to the individual recipient, not to the government ...." *Zelman v. Simmons-Harris.*

3. Response to 1: If we take the no-money-flow argument seriously, then the government can't provide *any* benefits, including _____ [give examples], which must be wrong, because _____. And this should lead us to conclude that there's nothing inherently improper with government aid going, under evenhanded programs, to entities that happen to be religious, so long as it doesn't go to them *because* they are religious.

"If the expenditure of governmental funds is prohibited whenever those funds pay for a service that is, pursuant to a religion-neutral program, used by a group for sectarian purposes, then [precedents requiring equal access for religious and secular speakers to government-owned limited public fora] would have to be overruled.... There is no difference in logic or principle ... between a school using its funds to operate a facility to which students have access, and a school paying a third-party contractor to operate the facility on its behalf.... Any benefit to religion is incidental to the government's provision of secular services for secular purposes on a religion-neutral basis." *Rosenberger v. Rector.*

"A student uses [GI Bill funds, Pell grants, and vocational education funds] for pervasively religious [college] education.... [A government] employee or welfare recipient contributes some of [his income] to a church or synagogue.... The government exempts charitable contributions from the income tax, thus in effect subsidizing charitable spending, whether religious or not.... A parent takes [a school voucher] and uses it for the pervasively religious education of his children. All four examples are structurally identical .... If the 'no money flow' theory is right, then all these examples are unconstitutional.... But surely this can't be so." Eugene Volokh, *Equal Treatment Is Not Establishment,* 13 Notre Dame J.L., Ethics & Pub. Pol. 341, 342-43 (1999).

4. Response to 3: It's possible to draw a line, namely _____, between the benefits that can flow to religion and those that can't.

"There may be no aid supporting a sectarian school's religious exercise or the discharge of its religious mission, while aid of a secular character with no discernible benefit to such a sectarian objective is allowable.... We have asked whether the government is acting neutrally in distributing its money, and about the form of the aid itself, its path from government to religious institution, its divertibility to religious nurture, its potential for reducing traditional expenditures of religious institutions, and its relative importance to the recipient, among other things." *Mitchell* (Souter, J., dissenting).

5. Response to 1: Excluding religious entities from such programs would itself be unconstitutional, because this would be discrimination against religion, and that's bad because _____.

"The viewpoint discrimination inherent in the University's regulation required public officials to scan and interpret student publications to discern their underlying philosophic assumptions respecting religious theory and belief. That course of action was a denial of the right of free speech and would risk fostering a pervasive bias or hostility to religion, which could undermine the very neutrality the Establishment Clause requires. There is no Establishment Clause violation in the University's honoring its duties under the Free Speech Clause." *Rosenberger.*

"... Establishment Clause case law has often required governmental discrimination against religion, discrimination both offensive to deep ideas of equality and wholly unsupported by the document." Akhil R. Amar, *Foreword: The Document and the Doctrine,* 114 Harv. L. Rev. 26 (2000).

6. Rebuttal to 5: The Establishment Clause requires certain kinds of discrimination against religion, because _____.

"[T]he Establishment Clause uniquely privileges the right of conscientious objection to religious activity, speech, or expenditures by government. The key legal consequence is that I view asymmetries that [others] would describe as discrimination against religion as mandated by the Establishment Clause.... [T]he Establishment Clause will often require excluding religious organizations from public programs, or will necessitate religion-restrictive conditions on their participation." Kathleen M. Sullivan, *Religion and Liberal Democracy,* 59 U. Chi. L. Rev. 195, 211 (1992).

f. Lemon v. Kurtzman, 403 U.S. 602 (1971)

Chief Justice Burger delivered the opinion of the Court....

[A.] The Rhode Island Salary Supplement Act was enacted in 1969. It rests on the legislative finding that the quality of education available in nonpublic elementary schools has been jeopardized by the rapidly rising salaries needed to attract competent and dedicated teachers. The Act authorizes state officials to supplement the salaries of teachers of secular subjects in nonpublic elementary schools by paying directly to a teacher an amount not in excess of 15% of his current annual salary. As supplemented, however, a nonpublic school teacher's salary cannot exceed the maximum paid to teachers in the State's public schools, and the recipient must be certified by the state board of education in substantially the same manner as public school teachers.

In order to be eligible for the Rhode Island salary supplement, the recipient must teach in a nonpublic school at which the average per-pupil expenditure on secular education is less than the average in the State's public schools during a specified period. Appellant State Commissioner of Education also requires eligible schools to submit financial data. If this information indicates a per-pupil expenditure in excess of the statutory limitation, the records of the school in question must be examined in order to assess how much of the expenditure is attributable to secular education and how much to religious activity. {The District Court found only one instance in which this breakdown between religious and secular expenses was necessary. The school in question was not affiliated with the Catholic church. The court found it unlikely that such determinations would be necessary with respect to Catholic schools because their heavy reliance on nuns kept their wage costs substantially below those of the public schools.}

The Act also requires that teachers eligible for salary supplements must teach only those subjects that are offered in the State's public schools ... [using] "only teaching materials which are used in the public schools." Finally, any teacher applying for a salary supplement must first agree in writing "not to teach a course in religion for so long as or during such time as he or she receives any salary supplements" under the Act.... [The case also involved a similar Pennsylvania statute. Taxpayers sued challenging both statutes under the Establishment Clause.—ed.]

Rhode Island's nonpublic elementary schools accommodate[] approximately 25% of the State's pupils. About 95% of these pupils attended schools affiliated with the Roman Catholic church. To date some 250 teachers have applied for benefits under the Act. All of them are employed by Roman Catholic schools.... Although ... concern for religious values does not necessarily affect the content of secular subjects, ... the parochial school system [is] "an integral part of the religious mission of the Catholic Church." ...

[B.] The language of the Religion Clauses of the First Amendment is at best opaque .... Its authors did not simply prohibit the establishment of a state church or a state religion, an area history shows they regarded as very important and fraught with great dangers. Instead they commanded that there should be "no law *respecting* an establishment of religion." A law may be one "respecting" the forbidden objective while falling short of its total realization.... A given law might not *establish* a state religion but nevertheless be one "respecting" that end in the sense of being a step that could lead to such establishment and hence offend the First Amendment. In the absence of precisely stated constitutional prohibitions, we must draw lines with reference to the three main evils against which the Establishment Clause was intended to afford protection: "sponsorship, financial support, and active involvement of the sovereign in religious activity." ...

Three ... tests may be gleaned from our cases. First, the statute must have a secular legislative purpose; second, its principal or primary effect must be one that neither advances nor inhibits religion; finally, the statute must not foster "an excessive government entanglement with religion." ...

[T]he statutes ... clearly state that they are intended to enhance the quality of the secular education in all schools covered by the compulsory attendance laws. There is no reason to believe the legislatures meant anything else. A State always has a legitimate concern for maintaining minimum standards in all schools it allows to operate.... [W]e find nothing here that undermines the stated legislative intent; it must therefore be accorded appropriate deference.

In *Board of Ed. v. Allen,* 392 U.S. 236 (1968), the Court acknowledged that secular and religious teachings were not necessarily so intertwined that secular textbooks furnished to students by the State were in fact instrumental in the teaching of religion. [The *Allen* Court thus upheld the textbook program.—ed.] The legislatures of Rhode Island and Pennsylvania have concluded that secular and religious education are identifiable and separable. In the abstract we have no quarrel with this conclusion.

The two legislatures, however, have also recognized that church-related elementary and secondary schools have a significant religious mission and that a substantial portion of their activities is religiously oriented. They have therefore sought to create statutory restrictions designed to guarantee the separation between secular and religious educational functions and to ensure that State financial aid supports only the former.

All these provisions are precautions taken in candid recognition that these programs approached, even if they did not intrude upon, the forbidden areas under the Religion Clauses. We need not decide whether these legislative precautions restrict the principal or primary effect of the programs to the point where they do not offend the Religion Clauses, for we conclude that the cumulative impact of the entire relationship arising under the statutes in each State involves excessive entanglement between government and religion.

[C.] In *Walz v. Tax Comm'n,* 397 U.S. 664 (1970), the Court upheld state tax exemptions for real property owned by religious organizations and used for religious worship. That holding, however, tended to confine rather than enlarge the area of permissible state involvement with religious institutions by calling for close scrutiny of the degree of entanglement involved in the relationship. The objective is to prevent, as far as possible, the intrusion of either into the precincts of the other....

[P]arochial schools involve substantial religious activity and purpose. The substantial religious character of these church-related schools gives rise to entangling church-state relationships of the kind the Religion Clauses sought to avoid....

The dangers and corresponding entanglements are enhanced by the particular form of aid that the Rhode Island Act provides. Our decisions from *Everson* to *Allen* have permitted the States to provide church-related schools with secular, neutral, or nonideological services, facilities, or materials. Bus transportation, school lunches, public health services, and secular textbooks supplied in common to all students were not thought to offend the Establishment Clause....

[T]eachers have a substantially different ideological character from books. In terms of potential for involving some aspect of faith or morals in secular subjects, a textbook's content is ascertainable, but a teacher's handling of a subject is not. We cannot ignore the danger that a teacher under religious control and discipline poses to the separation of the religious from the purely secular aspects of pre-college education....

We need not and do not assume that teachers in parochial schools will be guilty of bad faith or any conscious design to evade the limitations imposed by the statute and the First Amendment. We simply recognize that a dedicated religious person, teaching in a school affiliated with his or her faith and operated to inculcate its tenets, will inevitably experience great difficulty in remaining religiously neutral....

[D.] The Rhode Island Legislature has not, and could not, provide state aid on the basis of a mere assumption that secular teachers under religious discipline can avoid conflicts. The State must be certain, given the Religion Clauses, that subsidized teachers do not inculcate religion—indeed the State here has undertaken to do so....

A comprehensive, discriminating, and continuing state surveillance will inevitably be required to ensure that these restrictions are obeyed and the First Amendment otherwise respected. Unlike a book, a teacher cannot be inspected once so as to determine the extent and intent of his or her personal beliefs and subjective acceptance of the limitations imposed by the First Amendment. These prophylactic contacts will involve excessive and enduring entanglement between state and church....

[Moreover, if] the ... expenditures of an otherwise eligible school exceed [the comparable figures for public schools], the program requires the government to examine the school's records in order to determine how much of the total expenditures is attributable to secular education and how much to religious activity. This kind of state inspection and evaluation of the religious content of a religious organization is fraught with the sort of entanglement that the Constitution forbids. It is a relationship pregnant with dangers of excessive government direction of church schools and hence of churches.... [W]e cannot ignore here the danger that pervasive modern governmental power will ultimately intrude on religion and thus conflict with the Religion Clauses....

[E.] A broader base of entanglement of yet a different character is presented by the divisive political potential of these state programs. In a community where such a large number of pupils are served by church-related schools, it can be assumed that state assistance will entail considerable political activity.

Partisans of parochial schools, understandably concerned with rising costs and sincerely dedicated to both the religious and secular educational missions of their schools, will inevitably champion this cause and promote political action to achieve their goals. Those who oppose state aid, whether for constitutional, religious, or fiscal reasons, will inevitably respond and employ all of the usual political campaign techniques to prevail. Candidates will be forced to declare and voters to choose. It would be unrealistic to ignore the fact that many people confronted with issues of this kind will find their votes aligned with their faith.

Ordinarily political debate and division, however vigorous or even partisan, are normal and healthy manifestations of our democratic system of government, but political division along religious lines was one of the principal evils against which the First Amendment was intended to protect. The potential divisiveness of such conflict is a threat to the normal political process. To have States or communities divide on the issues presented by state aid to parochial schools would tend to confuse and obscure other issues of great urgency....

The highways of church and state relationships are not likely to be one-way streets, and the Constitution's authors sought to protect religious worship from the pervasive power of government. The history of many countries attests to the hazards of religion's intruding into the political arena or of political power intruding into the legitimate and free exercise of religious belief.

Of course, as the Court noted in *Walz*, "[a]dherents of particular faiths and individual churches frequently take strong positions on public issues." We could not expect otherwise, for religious values pervade the fabric of our national life. But in *Walz* we dealt with a status under state tax laws for the benefit of all religious groups. Here we are confronted with successive and very likely permanent annual appropriations that benefit relatively few religious groups. Political fragmentation and divisiveness on religious lines are thus likely to be intensified[, especially because of] ... the need for continuing annual appropriations and the likelihood of larger and larger demands as costs and populations grow....

[F.] In *Walz* it was argued that a tax exemption for places of religious worship would prove to be the first step in an inevitable progression leading to the establishment of state churches and state religion. That claim could not stand up against more than 200 years of virtually universal practice imbedded in our colonial experience and continuing into the present.

The progression argument, however, is more persuasive here. We have no long history of state aid to church-related educational institutions comparable to 200 years of tax exemption for churches.... [M]odern governmental programs have self-perpetuating and self-expanding propensities. These internal pressures are only enhanced when the schemes involve institutions whose legitimate needs are growing and whose interests have substantial political support....

[I]n constitutional adjudication some steps, which when taken were thought to approach "the verge," have become the platform for yet further steps. A certain momentum develops in constitutional theory and it can be a "downhill thrust" easily set in motion but difficult to retard or stop. Development by momentum is not invariably bad; indeed, it is the way the common law has grown, but it is a force to be recognized and reckoned with. The dangers are increased by the difficulty of perceiving in advance exactly where the "verge" of the precipice lies. As well as constituting an independent evil against which the Religion Clauses were intended to protect, involvement or entanglement between government and religion serves as a warning signal....

Justice Brennan, concurring....

[A.] [T]o give concrete meaning to the Establishment Clause "the line we must draw between the permissible and the impermissible is one which accords with history and faithfully reflects the understanding of the Founding Fathers.... [T]he Framers meant to foreclose ... those involvements of religious with secular institutions which (a) serve the essentially religious activities of religious institutions; (b) employ the organs of government for essentially religious purposes; or (c) use essentially religious means to serve governmental ends, where secular means would suffice." ... {[The Rhode Island Act violates principle (c).]} ...

In sharp contrast to the "undeviating acceptance given religious tax exemptions from our earliest days as a Nation," subsidy of sectarian educational institutions became embroiled in bitter controversies very soon after the Nation was formed.... Although the controversy over religious exercises in the public schools continued into this century, the opponents of subsidy to sectarian schools had largely won their fight by 1900.... [Details omitted.—ed.].... [T]he consensus, enforced by legislatures and courts ..., has been that public subsidy of sectarian schools constitutes an impermissible involvement of secular with religious institutions....

[B.] [The governmental involvement here threatens] "dangers—as much to church as to state—which the Framers feared would subvert religious liberty and the strength of a system of secular government." "[G]overnment and religion have discrete interests which are mutually best served when each avoids too close a proximity to the other. It is not only the nonbeliever who fears the injection of sectarian doctrines and controversies into the civil polity, but in as high degree it is the devout believer who fears the secularization of a creed which becomes too deeply involved with and dependent upon the government." ...

The Rhode Island statute requires Roman Catholic teachers to surrender their right to teach religion courses and to promise not to "inject" religious teaching into their secular courses. This has led at least one teacher to stop praying with his classes, a concrete testimonial to the self-censorship that inevitably accompanies state regulation of delicate First Amendment freedoms. Both ... statutes prescribe extensive standardization of the content of secular courses, and of the teaching materials and textbooks to be used in teaching the courses. And the regulations to implement those requirements necessarily require policing of instruction in the schools. The picture of state inspectors prowling the halls of parochial schools and auditing classroom instruction surely raises more than an imagined specter of governmental "secularization of a creed." ...

[C.] In any event, I do not believe that elimination of these aspects of "too close a proximity" would save these ... statutes. "[G]eneral subsidies of religious activities ... constitute impermissible state involvement with religion." I do not think the subsidies under these statutes fall outside "[g]eneral subsidies of religious activities" merely because they are restricted to support of the teaching of secular subjects....

"Though both [tax exemptions, such as in *Walz*, and general subsidies] provide economic assistance, ... '[i]n the case of direct subsidy, the state forcibly diverts the income of both believers and nonbelievers to churches,' while '[i]n the case of an exemption, the state merely refrains from diverting to its own uses income independently generated by the churches through voluntary contributions.' Thus, 'the symbolism of tax exemption is significant as a manifestation that organized religion is not expected to support the state; by the same token the state is not expected to support the church.'"
...

Justice White, dissenting....

[P]arochial schools in American society ... perform both religious and secular functions.... It is enough for me that the ... [government is] financing a separable secular function of overriding importance in order to sustain the legislation here challenged....

The Establishment Clause ... coexists in the First Amendment with the Free Exercise Clause and the latter is surely relevant in cases such as these. Where a state program seeks to ensure the proper education of its young, in private as well as public schools, free exercise considerations at least counsel against refusing support for students attending parochial schools simply because in that setting they are also being instructed in the tenets of the faith they are constitutionally free to practice....

No fault is found [by the Court] with the secular purpose of the program .... Nor does the Court find that the primary effect of the program is to aid religion rather than to implement secular goals. {The Court points to nothing in this record indicating that any participating teacher had inserted religion into his secular teaching or had had any difficulty in avoiding doing so. The testimony of the teachers [and the District Court's findings were] quite the contrary.} ...

The Court nevertheless finds that impermissible "entanglement" will result from administration of the program.... The Court ... creates an insoluble paradox for the State and the parochial schools. The State cannot finance secular instruction if it permits religion to be taught in the same classroom; but if it exacts a promise that religion not be so taught—a promise the school and its teachers are quite willing and on this record able to give—and enforces it, it is then entangled in the "no entanglement" aspect of the Court's Establishment Clause jurisprudence....

g. *Policy—Primary Effect Must Not Be Advancement or Inhibition of Religion*

Basic argument: "This government action is unconstitutional because it has a primary effect of advancing or inhibiting religion, namely _____, and that is bad because _____."

1. "The 'maintenance and repair' provisions of [the law] authorize direct payments to nonpublic schools, virtually all of which are Roman Catholic schools .... Nothing ... bars a qualifying school from paying out of state funds

the salaries of employees who maintain the school chapel, or the cost of renovating classrooms in which religion is taught, or the cost of heating and lighting those same facilities. Absent appropriate restrictions on expenditures for [such] purposes, ... this section has a primary effect that advances religion in that it subsidizes directly the religious activities of sectarian elementary and secondary schools." *Committee for Public Ed. & Religious Liberty v. Nyquist,* 413 U.S. 756, 774 (1973).

"[The] unyielding weighting in favor of Sabbath observers over all other interests [inherent in a statute that requires all employers to give Sabbath-observing employees their Sabbath as a day off] ... goes beyond having an incidental or remote effect of advancing religion. The statute has a primary effect that impermissibly advances a particular religious practice." *Estate of Thornton v. Caldor.*

"[T]he exclusion [of clergy from the legislature] manifests patent hostility toward, not neutrality respecting, religion; forces or influences a minister or priest to abandon his ministry as the price of public office; and, in sum, has a primary effect which inhibits religion." *McDaniel v. Paty* (Brennan, J., concurring in the judgment).

2. Response to 1: Actually, the primary effect is more properly seen as being _____, and any consequent advancement or inhibition of religion is just an indirect effect, because _____.

"Insofar as [a tax exemption] is conferred upon a wide array of nonsectarian groups as well as religious organizations in pursuit of some legitimate secular end, the fact that religious groups benefit incidentally does not deprive the subsidy of the secular ... primary effect mandated by the Establishment Clause." *Texas Monthly v. Bullock* (plurality).

"The University has opened its facilities for use by student groups, and the question is whether it can now exclude groups because of the content of their speech. In this context we are unpersuaded that the primary effect of the public forum, open to all forms of discourse, would be to advance religion." *Widmar v. Vincent,* 454 U.S. 263, 273 (1981).

"[S]tate programs that are wholly neutral in offering educational assistance to a class defined without reference to religion do not violate the ['primary effect' prong] of the *Lemon v. Kurtzman* test, because any aid to religion results from the private choices of individual beneficiaries." *Witters v. Wash. Dep't of Servs. for the Blind* (Powell, J., concurring).

"A law is not unconstitutional simply because it *allows* churches to advance religion, which is their very purpose. For a law to have forbidden 'effects' under *Lemon,* it must be fair to say that the *government itself* has advanced religion through its own activities and influence." *Corporation of Presiding Bishop v. Amos.*

"The Court's analysis [in the cases that struck down evenhanded funding schemes] failed to recognize the effect of the change in governmental roles [since the 1780s assessment controversy]. When the government provides no financial support to the nonprofit sector *except for churches* [as in the assessment controversy], it aids religion. But when the government provides financial support to the entire nonprofit sector, religious and nonreligious institutions alike, on the basis of objective criteria, it does *not* aid religion. It aids higher education, health care, or child care; it is neutral to religion. Indeed, to deny equal support to a college, hospital, or orphanage on the ground that it conveys religious ideas is to penalize it for being religious." Michael W. McConnell, *Religious Freedom at a Crossroads,* 59 U. Chi. L. Rev. 115, 184 (1992).

h. Policy—No Excessive Entanglement

Basic argument: "This government action is unconstitutional, because it excessively entangles the government with religion by _____, and this is bad because _____."

"This government action is constitutional, because it decreases the entanglement between government and religion by _____, and this is good because _____."

1. "A comprehensive, discriminating, and continuing state surveillance will inevitably be required to ensure that these restrictions are obeyed and the First Amendment otherwise respected.... These prophylactic contacts will involve excessive and enduring entanglement between state and church.... [And] the program [sometimes] requires the government to examine the school's records in order to determine how much of the total expenditures is attributable to secular education and how much to religious activity. This kind of state inspection and evaluation of the religious content of a religious organization is fraught with the sort of entanglement that the Constitution forbids. It is a relationship pregnant with dangers of excessive government direction of church schools and hence of churches." *Lemon v. Kurtzman.*

"[T]ermination of religious tax exemptions would [not] ... lessen the extent of state involvement with religion.... '[A]s a practical matter, the public welfare activities and the sectarian activities of religious institutions are so intertwined that they cannot be separated for the purpose of determining eligibility for tax exemptions.' If not impossible, the separation would certainly involve extensive state investigation into church operations and finances. Moreover, the termination of exemptions would give rise, as the Court says, to the necessity for 'tax valuation of church property, tax liens, tax foreclosures, and the direct confrontations and conflicts that follow in the train of those legal processes.'" *Walz v. Tax Comm'n,* 397 U.S. 664, 691 (1970) (Brennan, J., concurring) (arguing in favor of the constitutionality of tax exemptions for church property).

2. Response to 1: The entanglement that would be created (or avoided) is actually relatively minor, because _____.

"While Texas is correct in pointing out that compliance with government regulations by religious organizations and the monitoring of their compliance by government agencies would itself enmesh the operations of church and state to some degree, ... such compliance would generally not impede the evangelical activities of religious groups .... [T]he 'routine and factual inquiries' commonly associated with the enforcement of tax laws 'bear no resemblance to the kind of government surveillance the Court has previously held to pose an intolerable risk of government entanglement with religion.'" *Texas Monthly v. Bullock* (plurality).

"Interaction between church and state is inevitable, and we have always tolerated some level of involvement between the two. Entanglement must be 'excessive' before it runs afoul of the Establishment Clause.... [That a] program require[s] 'administrative cooperation' between the [government] and parochial schools ... [and that it] might increase the dangers of 'political divisiveness[]' ... are insufficient by themselves to create an 'excessive' entanglement." *Agostini v. Felton*, 521 U.S. 203 (1997).

3. Response to 1: The entanglement that would be created (or avoided) is justifiable because _____.

"Decision in cases such as this and the administration of an exemption for Old Order Amish from the State's compulsory school-attendance laws will inevitably involve the kind of close and perhaps repeated scrutiny of religious practices, as is exemplified in today's opinion, which the Court has heretofore been anxious to avoid. But such entanglement does not create a forbidden establishment of religion where it is essential to implement free exercise values threatened by an otherwise neutral program instituted to foster some permissible, nonreligious state objective." *Wisconsin v. Yoder* (White, J., concurring in the judgment).

4. Response to 1: The problematic entanglement exists only as a result of the Court's own unsound doctrine; if the doctrine were fixed by _____, then there wouldn't be any entanglement problem.

"The Court ... creates an insoluble paradox for the State and the parochial schools. The State cannot finance secular instruction if it permits religion to be taught in the same classroom; but if it exacts a promise that religion not be so taught—a promise the school and its teachers are quite willing and on this record able to give—and enforces it, it is then entangled in the 'no entanglement' aspect of the Court's Establishment Clause jurisprudence." *Lemon* (White, J., dissenting).

i. Problem: Income Tax Exemption for Charitable Contributions

Income tax laws let people deduct charitable contributions from their taxable income. This includes contributions to social service organizations, to educational institutions, to ideological organizations that don't engage in lobbying or overt electioneering, and to religious institutions, such as churches and synagogues. About 60% to 75% of all such contributions go to religious institutions. Does allowing tax exemptions for contributions to religious institutions violate the Establishment Clause?

Compare Texas Monthly, Inc. v. Bullock (Brennan, J., joined by Marshall and Stevens, JJ.) ("Every tax exemption constitutes a subsidy that affects nonqualifying taxpayers, forcing them to become indirect and vicarious donors.") *and Bob Jones Univ. v. United States* (Burger, C.J., joined by Brennan, J., among others) (saying, in the Free Exercise Clause context, that "When the Government grants exemptions or allows deductions all taxpayers are affected; the very fact of the exemption or deduction for the donor means that other taxpayers can be said to be indirect and vicarious 'donors.'") *with Walz v. Tax Comm'n of New York City,* 397 U.S. 664 (1970) (Brennan, J., concurring) ("Tax exemptions and general subsidies, however, are qualitatively different. Though both provide economic assistance, ... '[i]n the case of direct subsidy, the state forcibly diverts the income of both believers and nonbelievers to churches,' while '[i]n the case of an exemption, the state merely refrains from diverting to its own uses income independently generated by the churches through voluntary contributions.' Thus, 'the symbolism of tax exemption is significant as a manifestation that organized religion is not expected to support the state; by the same token the state is not expected to support the church.'").

Which of the views in these quotes do you find most persuasive?

j   Problem: Disaster Recovery Funds

According to Laura Vozzella, *Aftermath Gives New Confidence to Oklahomans,* Journal-Rec. (Oklahoma City), Apr. 19, 1996,

> [The] First United Methodist Church ..., one of at least four [churches] damaged in the [Oklahoma City Federal Building] bombing ... [sought] $12,000 from the Federal Emergency Management Agency to cover uninsured damages caused after the blast, when rescuers placed bloody bodies on the carpeted church floor and pitched tents in its newly resurfaced parking lot. FEMA refused by saying the aid would violate the constitutional separation of church and state. The agency later came around under some pressure from Oklahoma's congressional delegation.

(1) Assume FEMA generally compensates property owners for uninsured damages caused by terrorism and terrorism-related rescue efforts (up to some dollar amount). Would FEMA's ultimate decision to compensate the church violate the First Amendment?

(2) Assume FEMA adopted a regulation prohibiting "the use of any emergency funds for the repair or construction of churches or other buildings that are substantially used for the fostering of religion." Would such a regulation violate the First Amendment?

k.   Witters v. Wash. Dep't of Servs. for the Blind, 474 U.S. 481 (1986)

Justice Marshall delivered the opinion of the Court....

Wash. Rev. Code § 74.16.181 authorized the [Washington Commission for the Blind] ... to "[p]rovide for special education and/or training in the professions, business or trades" so as to "assist visually handicapped persons to overcome vocational handicaps and to obtain the maximum degree of self-support and self-care." Petitioner, suffering from a progressive eye condition, was eligible for vocational rehabilitation assistance under the terms of the statute. He was at the time attending Inland Empire School of the Bible, a private Christian college in Spokane, Washington, and studying the Bible, ethics, speech, and church administration in order to equip himself for a career as a pastor, missionary, or youth director. The Commission denied petitioner aid[, and Witters sued.—ed.]....

[A]ll parties concede the unmistakably secular purpose of the Washington program. That program was designed to promote the well-being of the visually handicapped through the provision of vocational rehabilitation services, and no more than a minuscule amount of the aid awarded under the program is likely to flow to religious education. No party suggests that the State's "actual purpose" in creating the program was to endorse religion, or that the secular purpose articulated by the legislature is merely "sham."

The answer to the question posed by the [effects] prong of the *Lemon* test is more difficult.... [T]he Establishment Clause is not violated every time money previously in the possession of a State is conveyed to a religious institution. For example, a State may issue a paycheck to one of its employees, who may then donate all or part of that paycheck to a religious institution, all without constitutional barrier; and the State may do so even knowing that the employee so intends to dispose of his salary....

[O]n the other hand, ... the State may not grant aid to a religious school, whether cash or in kind, where the effect of the aid is "that of a direct subsidy to the religious school" from the State. Aid may have that effect even though it takes the form of aid to students or parents. The question presented is whether ... extension of aid to petitioner and the use of that aid by petitioner to support his religious education is a permissible transfer similar to the hypothetical salary donation described above, or is an impermissible "direct subsidy."

Certain aspects of Washington's program are central to our inquiry. As far as the record shows, vocational assistance provided under the Washington program is paid directly to the student, who transmits it to the educational institution of his or her choice. Any aid provided under Washington's program that ultimately flows to religious institutions does so only as a result of the genuinely independent and private choices of aid recipients. {This is not the case described in *Grand Rapids School District v. Ball,* 473 U.S. 373 (1985) ("Where ... no meaningful distinction can be made between aid to the student and aid to the school, 'the concept of a loan to individuals is a transparent fiction'").} Washington's program is "made available generally without regard to the sectarian-nonsectarian, or public-nonpublic nature of the institution benefited," and is in no way skewed towards religion.

It is not one of "the ingenious plans for channeling state aid to sectarian schools that periodically reach this Court." It creates no financial incentive for students to undertake sectarian education. It does not tend to provide greater or broader benefits for recipients who apply their aid to religious education, nor are the full benefits of the program limited, in large part or in whole, to students at sectarian institutions.

On the contrary, aid recipients have full opportunity to expend vocational rehabilitation aid on wholly secular education, and as a practical matter have rather greater prospects to do so. Aid recipients' choices are made among a huge variety of possible careers, of which only a small handful are sectarian. In this case, the fact that aid goes to individuals means that the decision to support religious education is made by the individual, not by the State.

Further, and importantly, nothing in the record indicates that, if petitioner succeeds, any significant portion of the aid expended under the Washington program as a whole will end up flowing to religious education. The function of the Washington program is hardly "to provide desired financial support for nonpublic, sectarian institutions." The program, providing vocational assistance to the visually handicapped, does not seem well suited to serve as the vehicle for such a subsidy. No evidence has been presented indicating that any other person has ever sought to finance religious education or activity pursuant to the State's program. The combination of these factors, we think, makes the link between the State and the school petitioner wishes to attend a highly attenuated one.

On the facts we have set out, it does not seem appropriate to view any aid ultimately flowing to the Inland Empire School of the Bible as resulting from a *state* action sponsoring or subsidizing religion. Nor does the mere circumstance that petitioner has chosen to use neutrally available state aid to help pay for his religious education confer any message of state endorsement of religion.

Thus, while ... aid to a religious institution unrestricted in its potential uses, if properly attributable to the State, is "clearly prohibited under the Establishment Clause," because it may subsidize the religious functions of that institution, that observation is not apposite to this case. On the facts present here, we think the Washington program works no state support of religion prohibited by the Establishment Clause.

{We decline to address the "entanglement" issue at this time[, because it was not considered below].} ...

Justice Powell, with whom ... Chief Justice [Burger] and Justice Rehnquist join [and with whom Justice White generally agrees, in a separate concurring statement], concurring.... [This opinion basically made the private choice argument ultimately adopted in *Zelman v. Simmons-Harris* (2002) (p. 924).—ed.]

Justice O'Connor, concurring in part and concurring in the judgment.... [Justice O'Connor endorsed Justice Powell's argument, but also argued that the program didn't endorse religion, as she later did in her concurrence in *Zelman.*—ed.]

l. Problem: NEA and Religious and Antireligious Art

The National Endowment for the Arts, as you may recall from reading *NEA v. Finley,* administers an arts funding program. Artists submit grant applications, and NEA panels decide whether to fund the proposed projects, based primarily on the fairly vague criterion of "artistic excellence."

Noted artist Lenny da Vinci wants to get an NEA grant to paint a painting on the Christian theme of the Last Supper, inspired by his Christian faith. An NEA panel has concluded that his work is likely to be artistically excellent, but Donna Wells, the Chairwoman of the NEA, wants to make sure that giving the grant wouldn't violate the Constitution. She asks you, her legal advisor, your opinion.

1. How would you answer under the *Rosenberger* majority opinion?

2. How would the case come out before a judge who is inclined to follow Justice O'Connor's concurrence?

3. How would it have come out if Justice Souter had prevailed?

4. Which of these results do you think makes the most sense, and why?

m. Rosenberger v. Rector, 515 U.S. 819 (1995)

[See p. 623 for the facts. This case followed three unanimous or 8-to-1 precedents holding that public schools and universities could (under the Establishment Clause) and must (under the Free Speech Clause) give student religious groups the same access to meeting rooms as is given to nonreligious groups. *Widmar v. Vincent*, 454 U.S. 263 (1981); *Westside Community Bd. of Ed. v. Mergens*, 496 U.S. 226 (1990); *Lamb's Chapel v. Center Moriches Union Free School Dist.*, 508 U.S. 384 (1993).—ed.]

Justice Kennedy delivered the opinion of the Court....

The Court of Appeals ruled that withholding SAF [student activities fund] support from Wide Awake contravened the [Free] Speech Clause ..., but proceeded to hold that the University's action was justified by the necessity of avoiding a violation of the Establishment Clause, an interest it found compelling....

[A.] The governmental program here is neutral toward religion. There is no suggestion that the University created it to advance religion or adopted some ingenious device with the purpose of aiding a religious cause. The object of the SAF is to open a forum for speech and to support various student enterprises, including the publication of newspapers, in recognition of the diversity and creativity of student life.... The category of support here is for "student news, information, opinion, entertainment, or academic communications media groups," of which Wide Awake was 1 of 15 in the 1990 school year. WAP did not seek a subsidy because of its Christian editorial viewpoint; it sought funding as a student journal, which it was.

The neutrality of the program distinguishes the student fees from a tax levied for the direct support of a church or group of churches. A tax of that sort, of course, would run contrary to Establishment Clause concerns dating from the earliest days of the Republic. The apprehensions of our predecessors involved the levying of taxes upon the public for the sole and exclusive purpose of establishing and supporting specific sects.

The exaction here, by contrast, is a student activity fee designed to reflect the reality that student life in its many dimensions includes the necessity of wide-ranging speech and inquiry and that student expression is an integral part of the University's educational mission.... [T]he disbursements from the fund go to private contractors for the cost of printing [protected speech] .... This is a far cry from a general public assessment designed and effected to provide financial support for a church.

Government neutrality is apparent in the State's overall scheme in a further meaningful respect. The program respects the critical difference "between *government* speech endorsing religion, which the Establishment Clause forbids, and *private* speech endorsing religion, which the Free Speech and Free Exercise Clauses protect." ... "[T]he government has not fostered or encouraged" any mistaken impression that the student newspapers speak for the University. The University has taken pains to disassociate itself from the private speech involved in this case....

[B.] [Under the meeting room cases, i]t does not violate the Establishment Clause for a public university to grant access to its facilities on a religion-neutral basis to a wide spectrum of student groups, including groups that use meeting rooms for sectarian activities, accompanied by some devotional exercises. This is so even where the upkeep, maintenance, and repair of the facilities attributed to those uses are paid from a student activities fund to which students are required to contribute....

[It therefore] follows that a public university may maintain its own computer facility and give student groups access to that facility, including the use of the printers, on a religion neutral, say first-come-first-served, basis.... [And t]here is ... no difference of constitutional significance[] between a school using its funds to operate a facility to which students have access, and a school paying a third-party contractor to operate the facility on its behalf.... Any benefit to religion is incidental to the government's provision of secular services for secular purposes on a religion-neutral basis. Printing is a routine, secular, and recurring attribute of student life....

It is, of course, true that if the State pays a church's bills it is subsidizing it, and we must guard against this abuse. That is not a danger here, based on the considerations we have advanced and for the additional reason that the student publication is not a religious institution, at least in the usual sense of that term as used in our case law, and it is not a religious organization as used in the University's own regulations. It is instead a publication involved in a pure forum for the expression of ideas, ideas that would be both incomplete and chilled were the Constitution to be interpreted to require that state officials and courts scan the publication to ferret out views that principally manifest a belief in a divine being.

Were the dissent's view to become law, it would require the University, in order to avoid a constitutional violation, to scrutinize the content of student speech, lest the expression in question—speech otherwise protected by the Constitution—contain too great a religious content. The dissent, in fact, anticipates such censorship as "crucial" in distinguishing between "works characterized by the evangelism of Wide Awake and writing that merely happens to express views that a given religion might approve." ...

[But to impose a] standard of secular orthodoxy ... on student speech at a university is to imperil the very sources of free speech and expression.... [O]fficial censorship would be far more inconsistent with the Establishment Clause's dictates than would governmental provision of secular printing services on a religion-blind basis.... [It would deny] the right of free speech and would risk fostering a pervasive bias or hostility to religion, which could undermine the very neutrality the Establishment Clause requires. There is no Establishment Clause violation in the University's honoring its duties under the Free Speech Clause....

Justice O'Connor, concurring....

This case lies at the intersection of the principle of government neutrality and the prohibition on state funding of religious activities.... When two bedrock principles so conflict, understandably neither can provide the definitive answer. Reliance on categorical platitudes is unavailing. Resolution instead depends on the hard task of judging—sifting through the details and determining whether the challenged program offends the Establishment Clause. Such judgment requires courts to draw lines, sometimes quite fine, based on the particular facts of each case....

The nature of the dispute does not admit of categorical answers, nor should any be inferred from the Court's decision today. Instead, certain considerations specific to the program at issue lead me to conclude that by providing the same assistance to Wide Awake that it does to other publications, the University would not be endorsing the magazine's religious perspective.

First, the student organizations, at the University's insistence, remain strictly independent of the University [and must include a disclaimer so stating in their publications] .... Any reader of Wide Awake would be on notice of the publication's independence from the University.

Second, financial assistance is distributed in a manner that ensures its use only for permissible purposes. A student organization seeking assistance must submit disbursement requests; if approved, the funds are paid directly to the third-party vendor and do not pass through the organization's coffers.... This ... ensures that the funds are used only to further the University's purpose in maintaining a free and robust marketplace of ideas, from whatever perspective. This feature also makes this case analogous to a school providing equal access to a generally available printing press (or other physical facilities), and unlike a block grant to religious organizations.

Third, assistance is provided to the religious publication in a context that makes improbable any perception of government endorsement of the religious message. Wide Awake ... competes with 15 other magazines and newspapers {including ... a humor magazine that has targeted Christianity as a subject of satire, and [an Islamic publication]} for advertising and readership. The widely divergent viewpoints of these many purveyors of opinion, all supported on an equal basis by the University, significantly diminishes the danger that the message of any one publication is perceived as endorsed by the University.... This is not the harder case where religious speech threatens to dominate the forum. Cf. *Capitol Square Review and Advisory*

Bd. v. Pinette (O'Connor, J., concurring in part and concurring in judgment)....

Justice Souter, with whom Justice Stevens, Justice Ginsburg, and Justice Breyer join, dissenting....

[A.] The character of [Wide Awake] is candidly disclosed on the opening page of the first issue, where the editor-in-chief announces Wide Awake's mission in a letter to the readership signed, "Love in Christ": it is "to challenge Christians to live, in word and deed, according to the faith they proclaim and to encourage students to consider what a personal relationship with Jesus Christ means." [Further examples omitted.—ed.] ... These are not the words of "student news, information, opinion, entertainment, or academic communicatio[n] ..." (in the language of the University's funding criterion) .... The subject is not the discourse of the scholar's study or the seminar room, but of the evangelist's mission station and the pulpit. It is nothing other than the preaching of the word ....

[B.] The University exercises the power of the State to compel a student to pay [the student activity fee], and the use of any part of it for the direct support of religious activity thus strikes at what we have repeatedly held to be the heart of the prohibition on establishment.... [W]henever affirmative government aid ultimately benefits religion, the Establishment Clause requires some justification beyond evenhandedness on the government's part .... [D]irect public funding of core sectarian activities, even if accomplished pursuant to an evenhanded program, would be entirely inconsistent with the Establishment Clause and would strike at the very heart of the Clause's protection....

[T]he relationship between the prohibition on direct aid and the requirement of evenhandedness when affirmative government aid does result in some benefit to religion reflects the relationship between basic rule and marginal criterion. At the heart of the Establishment Clause stands the prohibition against direct public funding, but that prohibition does not answer the questions that occur at the margins of the Clause's application. Is any government activity that provides any incidental benefit to religion likewise unconstitutional? Would it be wrong to put out fires in burning churches, wrong to pay the bus fares of students on the way to parochial schools, wrong to allow a grantee of special education funds to spend them at a religious college? These are the questions that call for drawing lines, and it is in drawing them that evenhandedness becomes important....

In the doubtful cases (those not involving direct public funding), where there is initially room for argument about a law's effect, evenhandedness serves to weed out those laws that impermissibly advance religion by channelling aid to it exclusively. Evenhandedness is therefore a prerequisite to further enquiry into the constitutionality of a doubtful law, but evenhandedness goes no further. It does not guarantee success under Establishment Clause scrutiny....

Critical to our decisions [in cases such as *Witters v. Washington Dept. of Servs. for Blind*] was the fact that the aid was indirect; it reached religious institutions "only as a result of the genuinely independent and private choices of aid recipients." In noting and relying on this particular feature of each of the programs at issue, we in fact reaffirmed the core prohibition on direct funding of religious activities.

Thus, our holdings in these cases were little more than extensions of the unremarkable proposition that "a State may issue a paycheck to one of its employees, who may then donate all or part of that paycheck to a religious institution, all without constitutional barrier...." Such "attenuated financial benefit[s], ultimately controlled by the private choices of individual[s]," we have found, are simply not within the contemplation of the Establishment Clause's broad prohibition....

[C.] Since conformity with the marginal or limiting principle of even-handedness is insufficient of itself to demonstrate the constitutionality of providing a government benefit that reaches religion, the Court must identify some further element in the funding scheme that does demonstrate its permissibility.... [T]he Court's chosen element appears to be the fact that under the University's Guidelines, funds are sent to the printer chosen by Wide Awake, rather than to Wide Awake itself.

If the Court's suggestion is that this feature of the funding program brings this case into line with *Witters* [and similar cases], the Court has misread those cases, which turned on the fact that the choice to benefit religion was made by a nonreligious third party standing between the government and a religious institution. Here there is no third party standing between the government and the ultimate religious beneficiary to break the circuit by its independent discretion to put state money to religious use. The printer ... has no option to take the money and use it to print a secular journal instead of Wide Awake. It only gets the money because of its contract to print a message of religious evangelism at the direction of Wide Awake, and it will receive payment only for doing precisely that.

The formalism of distinguishing between payment to Wide Awake so it can pay an approved bill and payment of the approved bill itself cannot be the basis of a decision of constitutional law. If this indeed were a critical distinction, the Constitution would permit a State to pay all the bills of any religious institution ....

[D.] The common factual thread running through [the meeting room cases] is that a governmental institution created a limited forum ..., but sought to exclude speakers with religious messages.... While [the cases] do indeed allow a limited benefit to religious speakers, they rest on the recognition that all speakers are entitled to use the street corner (even though the State paves the roads and provides police protection to everyone on the street) and on the analogy between the public street corner and open class-room space....

The analogy breaks down entirely, however, if the cases are read more broadly than the Court wrote them, to cover more than forums for literal speaking. There is no traditional street corner printing provided by the government on equal terms to all comers, and the forum cases cannot be lifted to a higher plane of generalization without admitting that new economic benefits are being extended directly to religion in clear violation of the principle barring direct aid....

n. *Policy—Equal Treatment, see p. 751*

o. *Problem: Designing a Rule*

You've been appointed to the Supreme Court, and you're the swing vote on setting up a new Establishment Clause rule for cases involving evenhanded government benefits flowing to religion. You think the precedent is a mess, and you don't feel bound by it. What rule would you suggest? What arguments would you make for it, and anticipate against it?

Test your proposal against the following hypotheticals:

1. The government exempts all charitable contributions from the income tax. Cf. Problem XI.A.1.f (p. 744).

2. New Jersey gives salaries to its employees, and welfare payments to welfare recipients, with no conditions attached. Some of the employees and welfare recipients spend part of their income on a religious education for their children, or donate it to their house of worship.

3. New Jersey gives all students who are in the top 10% of their high school graduating classes scholarships that let them study at any university of their choice, whether government-run, private secular, or private religious. The scholarship amount is equal to the total per-pupil cost of education at Rutgers, the State University of New Jersey. Cf. Problem XII.A.1.c (p. 892) (discussing the GI Bill).

4. New Jersey gives parents of all K-12 students vouchers that let them send their children to any school of their choice, whether government-run, private secular, or private religious. The scholarship amount is equal to the total per-pupil cost of education in New Jersey public schools (over $11,000 per year). Cf. *Zelman v. Simmons-Harris* (2002) (p. 924).

5. The Federal Emergency Management Agency decides to give rebuilding funds to the owners of all buildings damaged in a major domestic terrorist attack; some of these funds go to rebuilding a church damaged in the attack. Cf. Problem XII.A.1.j (p. 907).

6. Rhode Island enacts a Salary Supplement Act, which "supplement[s] the salaries of teachers of secular subjects in nonpublic elementary schools by paying directly to a teacher an amount not in excess of 15% of his current annual salary," so long as the supplemented salary does not "exceed the maximum paid to teachers in the State's public schools." Cf. *Lemon v. Kurtzman* (1971) (p. 897).

p. *Mitchell v. Helms, 530 U.S. 793 (2000)*

Justice Thomas ... delivered an opinion, in which ... Chief Justice [Rehnquist], Justice Scalia, and Justice Kennedy join....

[A.] Chapter 2 of the Education Consolidation and Improvement Act of

1981 ... channels federal [education aid] funds to local educational agencies (LEA's), which are usually public school districts, via state educational agencies (SEA's) .... Among other things, Chapter 2 provides aid "for the acquisition and use of instructional and educational materials, including library services and materials (including media materials), assessments, reference materials, computer software and hardware for instructional use, and other curricular materials."

LEA's and SEA's must offer assistance to both public and [nonprofit] private schools .... Participating private schools receive Chapter 2 aid based on the number of children enrolled in each school, and allocations of Chapter 2 funds for those schools must generally be "equal (consistent with the number of children to be served) to expenditures ... for children enrolled in the public schools of the [LEA]." ... Further, Chapter 2 funds may only "supplement and, to the extent practical, increase the level of funds that would ... be made available from non-Federal sources." LEA's and SEA's may not operate their programs "so as to supplant funds from non-Federal sources." ...

[T]he "services, materials, and equipment" provided to private schools must be "secular, neutral, and nonideological." ... A private school ... submit[s] to the LEA an application detailing which items the school seeks and how it will use them; the LEA, if it approves the application, purchases those items from the school's allocation of funds, and then lends them to that school.

In Jefferson Parish (the Louisiana governmental unit at issue in this case), ... private schools have primarily used their allocations for ... library books, computers, ... computer software, ... slide and movie projectors, overhead projectors, television sets, tape recorders, VCR's, projection screens, laboratory equipment, maps, globes, filmstrips, slides, and cassette recordings.... [I]n an average year, about 30% of Chapter 2 funds spent in Jefferson Parish are allocated for private schools.... [Of the 46 private schools participating in 1986-87], 34 were Roman Catholic; 7 were otherwise religiously affiliated; and 5 were not religiously affiliated....

[B.] [The plurality generally argued that evenhanded aid programs, which treat religious and secular schools alike, are constitutional, for much the same reasons as those later given by the majority in *Zelman v. Simmons-Harris* below.—ed.]

Justice O'Connor, with whom Justice Breyer joins, concurring in the judgment....

[The concurrence reasoned that, with "direct aid" programs such as the one here—as opposed to "private choice" programs such as in *Witters*, "actual diversion of government aid to religious indoctrination" violates the Establishment Clause, but mere "divertibility" of the aid is not enough, so long as there are safeguards in place to prevent the diversion. The concurrence concluded that such safeguards were present here, and that any unprevented instances of actual diversion were rare enough to be *de minimis*.

Here is the concurrence's explanation of why the use of such "direct aid" (but not "private choice"-based funding) for religious teaching would be unconstitutional, even pursuant to an evenhanded aid program:—ed.]

First, when the government provides aid directly to the student beneficiary, that student can attend a religious school and yet retain control over whether the secular government aid will be applied toward the religious education. The fact that aid flows to the religious school and is used for the advancement of religion is therefore *wholly* dependent on the student's private decision....

Second, I believe the distinction between a per-capita school-aid program and a true private-choice program is significant for purposes of endorsement.... [If a] religious school uses [direct] aid to inculcate religion in its students, it is reasonable to say that the government has communicated a message of endorsement. Because the religious indoctrination is supported by government assistance, the reasonable observer would naturally perceive the aid program as *government* support for the advancement of religion.

That the amount of aid received by the school is based on the school's enrollment does not separate the government from the endorsement of the religious message. The aid formula does not—and could not—indicate to a reasonable observer that the inculcation of religion is endorsed only by the individuals attending the religious school, who each affirmatively choose to direct the secular government aid to the school and its religious mission. No such choices have been made.

In contrast, when government aid supports a school's religious mission only because of independent decisions made by numerous individuals to guide their secular aid to that school, "[n]o reasonable observer is likely to draw from the facts ... an inference that the State itself is endorsing a religious practice or belief." Rather, endorsement of the religious message is reasonably attributed to the individuals who select the path of the aid.

Finally, ... [i]f, as the plurality contends, a per-capita-aid program is identical in relevant constitutional respects to a true private-choice program, then there is no reason that, under the plurality's reasoning, the government should be precluded from providing direct money payments to religious organizations (including churches) based on the number of persons belonging to each organization. And, because actual diversion is permissible under the plurality's holding, the participating religious organizations (including churches) could use that aid to support religious indoctrination....

Justice Souter, with whom Justice Stevens and Justice Ginsburg join, dissenting....

[A.] At least three concerns have been expressed since the founding and run throughout our First Amendment jurisprudence. First, compelling an individual to support religion violates the fundamental principle of freedom of conscience... Madison's and Jefferson's now familiar words establish clearly that liberty of personal conviction requires freedom from coercion to support religion, and this means that the government can compel no aid to fund it. Madison put it simply: "[T]he same authority which can force a citizen to contribute three pence only of his property for the support of any one establishment, may force him to conform to any other establishment." ... {Jefferson's Virginia Bill for Establishing Religious Freedom provided "[t]hat no man shall be compelled to frequent or support any religious worship, place, or ministry whatsoever...." ... "... [T]he provisions of the First Amendment, in the drafting and adoption of which Madison and Jefferson played such leading roles, had the same objective and were intended to provide the same protection against governmental intrusion on religious liberty as the Virginia statute."}

Second, government aid corrupts religion. Madison argued that establishment of religion weakened the beliefs of adherents so favored, strengthened their opponents, and generated "pride and indolence in the Clergy; ignorance and servility in the laity; [and] in both, superstition, bigotry and persecution." "[E]xperience witnesseth that ecclesiastical establishments, instead of maintaining the purity and efficacy of Religion, have had a contrary operation."

In a variant of Madison's concern, we have repeatedly noted that a government's favor to a particular religion or sect threatens to taint it with "corrosive secularism." "[G]overnment and religion have discrete interests which are mutually best served when each avoids too close a proximity to the other. It is not only the nonbeliever who fears the injection of sectarian doctrines and controversies into the civil polity, but in as high degree it is the devout believer who fears the secularization of a creed which becomes too deeply involved with and dependent upon the government."

Third, government establishment of religion is inextricably linked with conflict. In our own history, the turmoil thus produced has led to a rejection of the idea that government should subsidize religious education, a position that illustrates the Court's understanding that any implicit endorsement of religion is unconstitutional.

[B.] These concerns are reflected in ... *Everson v. Board of Ed.*, [the Court's] first opinion directly addressing standards governing aid to religious schools[, which stated that] ... no government "can pass laws which aid one religion [or] all religions.... No tax in any amount ... can be levied to support any religious activities or institutions ... whatever form they may adopt to teach ... religion." Thus, the principle of "no aid," with which no one in *Everson* disagreed.

Immediately, however, there was the difficulty over what might amount to "aid" or "support." The problem for the *Everson* Court was not merely the imprecision of the words, but the "other language of the [First Amendment that] commands that [government] cannot hamper its citizens in the free exercise of their own religion," with the consequence that government must "be a neutral in its relations with groups of religious believers and non-believers." Since withholding some public benefits from religious groups could be said to "hamper" religious exercise indirectly, and extending other benefits said to aid it, an argument-proof formulation of the no-aid principle was impossible, and the Court wisely chose not to attempt any such thing.

Instead it gave definitive examples of public benefits provided pervasively throughout society that would be of some value to organized religion but not in a way or to a degree that could sensibly be described as giving it aid or violating the neutrality requirement: there was no Establishment Clause concern with "such general government services as ordinary police and fire protection, connections for sewage disposal, public highways and sidewalks." These "benefits of public welfare legislation," extended in modern times to virtually every member of the population and valuable to every person and association, were the paradigms of advantages that religious organizations could enjoy consistently with the prohibition against aid, and that governments could extend without deserting their required position of neutrality.

But paradigms are not perfect fits very often, and government spending resists easy classification as between universal general service or subsidy of favoritism.... The Court's [school aid] decisions demonstrate its repeated attempts to isolate considerations relevant in classifying particular benefits as between those that do not discernibly support or threaten support of a school's religious mission, and those that cross or threaten to cross the line into support for religion....

[C.] The insufficiency of [neutrality in the sense of evenhandedness as between religious and secular institutions] as a stand-alone criterion of constitutional intent or effect has been clear from the beginning of our interpretative efforts, for an obvious reason. Evenhandedness in distributing a benefit approaches ... constitutionality in this area only when the term refers to such universality of distribution that it makes no sense to think of the benefit as going to any discrete group. Conversely, when evenhandedness refers to distribution to limited groups within society, like groups of schools or schoolchildren, it does make sense to regard the benefit as aid to the recipients.

Hence, if we looked no further than evenhandedness, and failed to ask what activities the aid might support, or in fact did support, religious schools could be blessed with government funding as massive as expenditures made for the benefit of their public school counterparts, and religious missions would thrive on public money. This is why the consideration of less than universal neutrality has never been recognized as dispositive and has always been teamed with attention to other facts bearing on the substantive prohibition of support for a school's religious objective.

At least three main lines of enquiry addressed particularly to school aid have emerged to complement evenhandedness neutrality. First, we have noted that two types of aid recipients heighten Establishment Clause concern: pervasively religious schools and primary and secondary religious schools. Second, we have identified two important characteristics of the method of distributing aid: directness or indirectness of distribution and distribution by genuinely independent choice. Third, we have found relevance in at least five characteristics of the aid itself: its religious content;

its cash form; its divertibility or actually diversion to religious support; its supplantation of traditional items of religious school expense; and its substantiality.

[1.] Two types of school aid recipients have raised special concern. First, we have recognized the fact that the overriding religious mission of certain schools, those sometimes called "pervasively sectarian," is not confined to a discrete element of the curriculum, but permeates their teaching. {In fact, religious education in Roman Catholic schools is defined as part of required religious practice; aiding it is thus akin to aiding a church service.} ... As religious teaching cannot be separated from secular education in such schools or by such teachers, we have concluded that direct government subsidies to such schools are prohibited because they will inevitably and impermissibly support religious indoctrination.

Second, we have expressed special concern about aid to primary and secondary religious schools. On the one hand, we have understood how the youth of the students in such schools makes them highly susceptible to religious indoctrination. On the other, we have recognized that the religious element in the education offered in most sectarian primary and secondary schools is far more intertwined with the secular than in university teaching, where the natural and academic skepticism of most older students may separate the two. Thus, government benefits accruing to these pervasively religious primary and secondary schools raise special dangers of diversion into support for the religious indoctrination of children and the involvement of government in religious training and practice.

[2.] We have also ... asked whether aid is direct or indirect, observing distinctions between government schemes with individual beneficiaries and those whose beneficiaries in the first instance might be religious schools. Direct aid obviously raises greater risks, although recent cases have discounted this risk factor, looking to other features of the distribution mechanism.

[Furthermore,] we have distinguished between indirect aid that reaches religious schools only incidentally as a result of numerous individual choices and aid that is in reality directed to religious schools by the government or in practical terms selected by religious schools themselves. In these cases, we have declared the constitutionality of programs providing aid directly to parents or students as tax deductions or scholarship money, where such aid may pay for education at some sectarian institutions, but only as the result of "genuinely independent and private choices of aid recipients." We distinguished [in these cases] [other past cases, in which we had held that] "[w]here ... no meaningful distinction can be made between aid to the student and aid to the school, the concept of a loan to individuals is a transparent fiction." ...

[3.] [We have also considered] features of the aid itself .... First, we have barred aid with actual religious content, which would obviously run afoul of the ban on the government's participation in religion....

Second, we have long held government aid invalid when circumstances would allow its diversion to religious education. The risk of diversion is obviously high when aid in the form of government funds makes its way into the coffers of religious organizations, and so from the start we have understood the Constitution to bar outright money grants of aid to religion....

Third, our cases have recognized the distinction ... between aid that merely supplements and aid that supplants expenditures for offerings at religious schools, the latter being barred. Although we have never adopted the position that any benefit that flows to a religious school is impermissible because it frees up resources for the school to engage in religious indoctrination, ... we have repeatedly explained the unconstitutionality of aid that supplants an item of the school's traditional expense....

Finally, we have [held] ... "substantial" amounts of aid to be unconstitutional whether or not a plaintiff can show that it supplants a specific item of expense a religious school would have borne....

The object of all enquiries into such matters is the same whatever the particular circumstances: is the benefit intended to aid in providing the religious element of the education and is it likely to do so? ...

[E.] [T]he plurality's proposal would replace the principle of no aid with a formula for generous religious support. First, the plurality treats an external observer's attribution of religious support to the government as the sole impermissible effect of a government aid scheme. While perceived state endorsement of religion is undoubtedly a relevant concern under the Establishment Clause, it is certainly not the only one.... State aid not attributed to the government would still violate a taxpayer's liberty of conscience, threaten to corrupt religion, and generate disputes over aid....

{Adopting the plurality's rule would permit practically any government aid to religion so long as it could be supplied on terms ostensibly comparable to the terms under which aid was provided to nonreligious recipients. As a principle of constitutional sufficiency, the manipulability of this rule is breathtaking. A legislature would merely need to state a secular objective in order to legalize massive aid to all religions, one religion, or even one sect, to which its largess could be directed through the easy exercise of crafting facially neutral terms under which to offer aid favoring that religious group. Short of formally replacing the Establishment Clause, a more dependable key to the public fisc or a cleaner break with prior law would be difficult to imagine.}

Second, the plurality apparently assumes as a fact that equal amounts of aid to religious and nonreligious schools will have exclusively secular and equal effects, on both external perception and on incentives to attend different schools. But there is no reason to believe that this will be the case; the effects of same-terms aid may not be confined to the secular sphere at all. This is the reason that we have long recognized that unrestricted aid to religious schools will support religious teaching in addition to secular education, a fact that would be true no matter what the supposedly secular purpose of the law might be.

Third, the plurality assumes that per capita distribution rules safeguard the same principles as independent, private choices. But that is clearly not so. We approved university scholarships in *Witters* because we found them close to giving a government employee a paycheck and allowing him to spend it as he chose, but a per capita aid program is a far cry from awarding scholarships to individuals, one of whom makes an independent private choice. Not the least of the significant differences between per capita aid and aid individually determined and directed is the right and genuine opportunity of the recipient to choose not to give the aid. To hold otherwise would be to license the government to donate funds to churches based on the number of their members, on the patent fiction of independent private choice....

[F.] The facts most obviously relevant to the Chapter 2 scheme in Jefferson Parish are those showing divertibility and actual diversion in the circumstance of pervasively sectarian religious schools.... The aid that the government provided was highly susceptible to unconstitutional use. Much of the equipment provided under Chapter 2 was not of the type provided for individual students, but included "slide projectors, movie projectors, overhead projectors, television sets, tape recorders, projection screens, maps, globes, filmstrips, cassettes, computers," and computer software and peripherals, as well as library books and materials.

The videocassette players, overhead projectors, and other instructional aids were of the sort that we have found can easily be used by religious teachers for religious purposes. The same was true of the computers .... Although library books, like textbooks, have fixed content, religious teachers can assign secular library books for religious critique, and books for libraries may be religious, as any divinity school library would demonstrate. The sheer number and variety of books that could be and were ordered gave ample opportunity for such diversion. [Justice Souter goes on to give other reasons why the aid was easily divertible.—ed.] ...

Providing such governmental aid without effective safeguards against future diversion itself offends the Establishment Clause, and even without evidence of actual diversion, our cases have repeatedly held that a "substantial risk" of it suffices to invalidate a government aid program on establishment grounds. A substantial risk of diversion in this case was more than clear, as the plurality has conceded....

But the record here goes beyond risk, to instances of actual diversion.... Indeed, the plurality readily recognizes that the aid in question here was divertible and that substantial evidence of actual diversion exists. Although Justice O'Connor attributes limited significance to the evidence of divertibility and actual diversion, she also recognizes that it exists. The Court has no choice but to hold that the program as applied violated the Establishment Clause....

[G.] {Since the divertibility and diversion require a finding of unconstitutionality, I will not explore other grounds, beyond noting the likelihood that unconstitutional supplantation occurred as well. The record demonstrates that Chapter 2 aid impermissibly relieved religious schools of some costs that they otherwise would have borne, and so unconstitutionally supplanted support in some budgetary categories.... Chapter 2 aid was significant in the development of teaching curriculums, the introduction of new programs, and the support of old ones.

The evidence shows that the concept of supplementing instead of supplanting was poorly understood by the sole government official administering the program, who apparently believed that the bar on supplanting was nothing more than a prohibition on paying for replacements of equipment that religious schools had previously purchased. Government officials admitted that there was no way to determine whether payments for materials, equipment, books, or other assistance provided under the program reduced the amount of money budgeted for library and educational equipment, and the 1985 Monitoring Report shows that the officials of at least one religious school admitted that the government aid was used to create the library, with the school's regular funds, when occasionally available, used merely to supplement the government money.

The use records for audiovisual materials at one religious high school revealed that Chapter 2 funds were essential to the school's educational process, and a different school ... used a Chapter 2 computer to support its computer network when its own computers failed. The record is sparse, but these incidents suggest that the constitutional and statutory prohibition on supplanting expenses may have been largely aspirational.}

q. *Problem: School Choice*

Assume that California enacts the following school choice program:

1. School districts must offer resident families vouchers (one per school-age child) that could be redeemed at any willing private or public schools, inside or outside the district, that meet certain basic criteria.

2. The voucher must be worth 75% of the district's per-pupil expenditure for the relevant grade in its public schools.

a. If the school charges less than the voucher amount, the parents can just give the voucher to the school, and the school will be able to redeem the voucher for the cost of tuition, but no more.

b. If the school charges more than the voucher amount, the parents would give the school the voucher (which the school may redeem for its face value) plus however much extra the school charges.

c. Neither private schools nor public schools in other districts are required to accept voucher-bearing students.

In some rural areas, there are currently no private schools within an hour's driving distance, though backers of the program argue that the availability of vouchers will lead people to open more private schools, both religious and secular. In some places, the few nearby private schools are religious. In some places, the few nearby private schools are secular. In many urban areas, there are dozens of both private secular schools and religious schools nearby. Statewide, say that 85% of private schools are affiliated with various religious denominations; but the percentage varies from place to place, and may change once the voucher program starts.

Different public school districts also operate differently. Some open each public schools only to students who live in the neighborhood. Others let parents choose any school in the district that isn't full. Some let students go to various magnet schools (such as a math and science magnet); others don't have magnets. Some contain many charter schools, which are like the "community schools" in *Zelman v. Simmons-Harris*; others don't. Some accept vouchers from other districts and others don't.

Would this be program constitutional, under current law? Should the Establishment Clause allow such programs?

r.   *Problem: Conditions on School Choice Participation*

The Cleveland school choice program discussed in *Zelman* bars schools from participating unless they agree "not to discriminate on the basis of race, religion, or ethnic background" and "[not] to 'advocate or foster unlawful behavior or teach hatred of any person or group on the basis of race, ethnicity, national origin, or religion.'" This condition wasn't challenged in *Zelman*, and the Court expressed no opinion about it.

The Little Red Schoolhouse Leninist Education Commune applies to participate in the program, but is rejected because:

(1) It hires only nonreligious teachers, because it teaches that religion is the opiate of the masses, and believes that having religious teachers will compromise its message, since even if the teachers don't express their religious views in the classroom, students may learn of the teachers' religiosity in other ways. (Assume such discrimination isn't illegal under laws that ban religious discrimination, because the laws exempt religious organizations, and organizations that teach atheism qualify for this exemption as much as those that teach theism.)

(2) It teaches that unlawful behavior—such as revolution against capitalist oppressors, or for that matter sit-ins at segregated lunch counters or refusal to register for the draft—is sometimes morally imperative.

(3) It teaches that the clergy—especially Christian clergy—should be hated, because they delude the proletariat with their false dogma. The entrance to the school bears a quote attributed to the 18th-century French anti-clericalist Denis Diderot: "Man will never be free until the last king is strangled with the entrails of the last priest."

The Commune sues, claiming the program's conditions are unconstitutional. Are the conditions permissible? Should they be?

s.   *Zelman v. Simmons-Harris, 536 U.S. 639 (2002)*

Chief Justice Rehnquist delivered the opinion of the Court....

[A.] [1.] There are more than 75,000 children enrolled in the Cleveland City School District. The majority of these children are from low-income and minority families. Few of these families enjoy the means to send their children to any school other than an inner-city public school. For more than a generation, however, Cleveland's public schools have been among the worst performing public schools in the Nation....

It is against this backdrop that Ohio enacted, among other initiatives, its Pilot Project Scholarship Program. The program provides financial assistance to families in any Ohio school district that is or has been "under federal court order requiring supervision and operational management of the district by the state superintendent." Cleveland is the only Ohio school district to fall within that category....

[2.] [T]he program provides tuition aid for students in kindergarten through third grade, expanding each year through eighth grade, to attend a participating public or private school of their parent's choosing.... Any private school, whether religious or nonreligious, may ... accept program students so long as the school is located within the boundaries of a covered district and meets statewide educational standards. Participating private schools must agree not to discriminate on the basis of race, religion, or ethnic background, or to "advocate or foster unlawful behavior or teach hatred of any person or group on the basis of race, ethnicity, national origin, or religion."

Any public school located in a school district adjacent to the covered district may also participate in the program. Adjacent public schools are eligible to receive a $2,250 tuition grant for each program student accepted in addition to the full amount of per-pupil state funding attributable to each additional student. All participating schools, whether public or private, are required to accept students in accordance with rules and procedures established by the state superintendent.

Tuition aid is distributed to parents according to financial need. Families with incomes below 200% of the poverty line are given priority and are eligible to receive 90% of private school tuition up to $2,250. For these lowest-income families, participating private schools may not charge a parental co-payment greater than $250. For all other families, the program pays 75% of tuition costs, up to $1,875, with no co-payment cap. These families receive tuition aid only if the number of available scholarships exceeds the number of low-income children who choose to participate. {The number of available scholarships per covered district is determined annually by the Ohio Superintendent for Public Instruction.}

Where tuition aid is spent depends solely upon where parents who receive tuition aid choose to enroll their child. If parents choose a private school, checks are made payable to the parents who then endorse the checks over to the chosen school.

[T]he program [also] provides tutorial assistance through grants to any student in a covered district who chooses to remain in public school. Parents arrange for registered tutors to provide assistance to their children and then submit bills for those services to the State for payment. Students from low-income families receive 90% of the amount charged for such assistance up to $360. All other students receive 75% of that amount. The number of tu-torial assistance grants offered to students in a covered district must equal the number of tuition aid scholarships provided to students enrolled at par-ticipating private or adjacent public schools.

The program has been in operation within the Cleveland City School District since the 1996-1997 school year. In the 1999-2000 school year, 56 private schools participated in the program, 46 (or 82%) of which had a re-ligious affiliation. None of the public schools in districts adjacent to Cleve-land have elected to participate. More than 3,700 students participated in the scholarship program, most of whom (96%) enrolled in religiously affili-ated schools. Sixty percent of these students were from families at or below the poverty line. In the 1998-1999 school year, approximately 1,400 Cleve-land public school students received tutorial aid. This number was expected to double during the 1999-2000 school year.

[3.] The program is part of a broader undertaking by the State to en-hance the educational options of Cleveland's schoolchildren .... That under-taking includes programs governing community and magnet schools.

Community schools are funded under state law but are run by their own school boards, not by local school districts. These schools enjoy academic independence to hire their own teachers and to determine their own curric-ulum. They can have no religious affiliation and are required to accept stu-dents by lottery. During the 1999-2000 school year, there were 10 start-up community schools in the Cleveland City School District with more than 1,900 students enrolled. For each child enrolled in a community school, the school receives state funding of $4,518, twice the funding a participating program school may receive.

Magnet schools are public schools operated by a local school board that emphasize a particular subject area, teaching method, or service to stu-dents. For each student enrolled in a magnet school, the school district re-ceives $7,746, including state funding of $4,167, the same amount received per student enrolled at a traditional public school. As of 1999, parents in Cleveland were able to choose from among 23 magnet schools, which to-gether enrolled more than 13,000 students in kindergarten through eighth grade. These schools provide specialized teaching methods, such as Montes-sori, or a particularized curriculum focus, such as foreign language, comput-ers, or the arts....

[B.] The Establishment Clause ... prevents a State from enacting laws that have the "purpose" or "effect" of advancing or inhibiting religion. There is no dispute that the program challenged here was enacted for the valid secular purpose of providing educational assistance to poor children in a demonstrably failing public school system. Thus, the question presented is whether the Ohio program nonetheless has the forbidden "effect" of advanc-ing or inhibiting religion.

To answer that question, our decisions have drawn a consistent distinc-tion between government programs that provide aid directly to religious schools, *e.g.*, *Mitchell v. Helms*, and programs of true private choice, in which government aid reaches religious schools only as a result of the genuine and independent choices of private individuals, *e.g.*, *Witters v. Washington Dept. of Servs. for Blind*....

[W]here a government aid program is neutral with respect to religion, and provides assistance directly to a broad class of citizens who, in turn, direct government aid to religious schools wholly as a result of their own genuine and independent private choice, the program is not readily subject to challenge under the Establishment Clause. A program that shares these features permits government aid to reach religious institutions only by way of the deliberate choices of numerous individual recipients.

The incidental advancement of a religious mission, or the perceived endorsement of a religious message, is reasonably attributable to the individual recipient, not to the government, whose role ends with the disbursement of benefits.... "[I]f numerous private choices, rather than the single choice of a government, determine the distribution of aid, pursuant to neutral eligibility criteria, then a government cannot, or at least cannot easily, grant special favors that might lead to a religious establishment." ...

[T]he program challenged here is a program of true private choice ... and thus constitutional.... [T]he Ohio program is neutral in all respects toward religion. It is part of a general and multifaceted undertaking by the State of Ohio to provide educational opportunities to the children of a failed school district. It confers educational assistance directly to a broad class of individuals defined without reference to religion, *i.e.*, any parent of a school-age child who resides in the Cleveland City School District.

The program permits the participation of *all* schools within the district, religious or nonreligious. Adjacent public schools also may participate and have a financial incentive to do so. Program benefits are available to participating families on neutral terms, with no reference to religion....

There are no "financial incentive[s]" that "ske[w]" the program toward religious schools. Such incentives "[are] not present ... where the aid is allocated on the basis of neutral, secular criteria that neither favor nor disfavor religion, and is made available to both religious and secular beneficiaries on a nondiscriminatory basis." The program here in fact creates financial *dis*incentives for religious schools, with private schools receiving only half the government assistance given to community schools and one-third the assistance given to magnet schools. Adjacent public schools, should any choose to accept program students, are also eligible to receive two to three times the state funding of a private religious school.

Families too have a financial disincentive to choose a private religious school over other schools. Parents that choose to participate in the scholarship program and then to enroll their children in a private school (religious or nonreligious) must copay a portion of the school's tuition. Families that choose a community school, magnet school, or traditional public school pay nothing. Although such features of the program are not necessary to its constitutionality, they clearly dispel the claim that the program "creates ... financial incentive[s] for parents to choose a sectarian school." ...

[Moreover,] no reasonable observer would think a neutral program of private choice, where state aid reaches religious schools solely as a result of the numerous independent decisions of private individuals, carries with it the *imprimatur* of government endorsement.... [This is particularly so] since "the reasonable observer in the endorsement inquiry must be deemed aware" of the "history and context" underlying a challenged program. Any objective observer familiar with the full history and context of the Ohio program would reasonably view it as one aspect of a broader undertaking to assist poor children in failed schools, not as an endorsement of religious schooling in general.

There also is no evidence that the program fails to provide genuine opportunities for Cleveland parents to select secular educational options for their school-age children. Cleveland schoolchildren enjoy a range of educational choices: They may remain in public school as before, remain in public school with publicly funded tutoring aid, obtain a scholarship and choose a religious school, obtain a scholarship and choose a nonreligious private school, enroll in a community school, or enroll in a magnet school.

{Justice Souter ... claim[s] that community schools and magnet schools are separate and distinct from program schools, simply because the program itself does not include community and magnet school options. But none of the dissenting opinions explain how there is any perceptible difference between scholarship schools, community schools, or magnet schools from the perspective of Cleveland parents looking to choose the best educational option .... Parents who choose a program school in fact receive from the State precisely what parents who choose a community or magnet school receive—the opportunity to send their children largely at state expense to schools they prefer to their local public school.}

{Justice Souter suggests the program is not "neutral" because program students cannot spend scholarship vouchers at traditional public schools. This objection is mistaken: Public schools in Cleveland already receive $7,097 in public funding per pupil—$4,167 of which is attributable to the State. Program students who receive tutoring aid and remain enrolled in traditional public schools therefore direct almost twice as much state funding to their chosen school as do program students who receive a scholarship and attend a private school.}

[C.] That 46 of the 56 private schools now participating in the program are religious schools does not condemn it as a violation of the Establishment Clause. The Establishment Clause question is whether Ohio is coercing parents into sending their children to religious schools, and that question must be answered by evaluating *all* options Ohio provides Cleveland schoolchildren, only one of which is to obtain a program scholarship and then choose a religious school....

Cleveland's preponderance of religiously affiliated private schools certainly did not arise as a result of the program; it is a phenomenon common to many American cities. Indeed, by all accounts the program has captured a remarkable cross-section of private schools, religious and nonreligious.

It is true that 82% of Cleveland's participating private schools are religious schools, but it is also true that 81% of private schools in Ohio are religious schools. To attribute constitutional significance to this figure, moreover, would lead to the absurd result that a neutral school-choice program might be permissible in some parts of Ohio, such as Columbus, where a lower percentage of private schools are religious schools, but not in inner-city Cleveland, where Ohio has deemed such programs most sorely needed, but where the preponderance of religious schools happens to be greater. Likewise, an identical private choice program might be constitutional in some States, such as Maine or Utah, where less than 45% of private schools are religious schools, but not in other States, such as Nebraska or Kansas, where over 90% of private schools are religious schools.

{Justice Souter ... [assumes] that capping the amount of tuition charged to low-income students (at $2,500) favors participation by religious schools. But elsewhere he claims that the program spends *too much* money on private schools .... [And h]is assumption also finds no support in the record, which shows that nonreligious private schools operating in Cleveland also seek and receive substantial third-party contributions.

Indeed, the actual operation of the program refutes Justice Souter's argument that few but religious schools can afford to participate: Ten secular private schools operated within the Cleveland City School district when the program was adopted. All 10 chose to participate in the program and have continued to participate to this day. And while no religious schools have been created in response to the program, several *nonreligious* schools have been created, in spite of the fact that a principal barrier to entry of new private schools is the uncertainty caused by protracted litigation which has plagued the program since its inception.

Similarly mistaken is Justice Souter's reliance on the low enrollment of scholarship students in nonreligious schools during the 1999-2000 school year. These figures ignore the fact that the number of program students enrolled in nonreligious schools has widely varied from year to year, underscoring why the constitutionality of a neutral choice program does not turn on annual tallies of private decisions made in any given year by thousands of individual aid recipients.}

Respondents and Justice Souter claim that even if we do not focus on the number of participating schools that are religious schools, we should attach constitutional significance to the fact that 96% of scholarship recipients have enrolled in religious schools. They claim that this alone proves parents lack genuine choice, even if no parent has ever said so....

[But as we have held earlier, t]he constitutionality of a neutral educational aid program simply does not turn on whether and why, in a particular area, at a particular time, most private schools are run by religious organizations, or most recipients choose to use the aid at a religious school.... "[S]uch an approach would scarcely provide the certainty that this field stands in need of, nor can we perceive principled standards by which such statistical evidence might be evaluated."

This point is aptly illustrated here. The 96% figure upon which respondents and Justice Souter rely discounts entirely (1) the more than 1,900 Cleveland children enrolled in alternative community schools, (2) the more than 13,000 children enrolled in alternative magnet schools, and (3) the more than 1,400 children enrolled in traditional public schools with tutorial assistance. Including some or all of these children in the denominator of children enrolled in nontraditional schools during the 1999-2000 school year drops the percentage enrolled in religious schools from 96% to under 20%.

The 96% figure also represents but a snapshot of one particular school year. In the 1997-1998 school year, by contrast, only 78% of scholarship recipients attended religious schools. The difference was attributable to two private nonreligious schools that had accepted 15% of all scholarship students electing instead to register as community schools, in light of larger per-pupil funding for community schools and the uncertain future of the scholarship program generated by this litigation. Many of the students enrolled in these schools as scholarship students remained enrolled as community school students, thus demonstrating the arbitrariness of counting one type of school but not the other to assess primary effect....

[D.] {Justice Breyer would raise the invisible specters of "divisiveness" and "religious strife" to find the program unconstitutional. It is unclear exactly what sort of principle Justice Breyer has in mind, considering that the program has ignited no "divisiveness" or "strife" other than this litigation. Nor is it clear where Justice Breyer would locate this presumed authority to deprive Cleveland residents of a program that they have chosen but that we subjectively find "divisive." We quite rightly have rejected the claim that some speculative potential for divisiveness bears on the constitutionality of educational aid programs.}

[E.] [T]he Ohio program is entirely neutral with respect to religion. It provides benefits directly to a wide spectrum of individuals, defined only by financial need and residence in a particular school district. It permits such individuals to exercise genuine choice among options public and private, secular and religious. The program is therefore a program of true private choice [and thus] ... does not offend the Establishment Clause....

Justice O'Connor, concurring....

[A.] [A]t most $8.2 million of public funds flowed to religious schools under the voucher program in 1999-2000.... [At the same time, the federal] tax deduction for charitable contributions reduces federal tax revenues by nearly $25 billion annually, and it is reported that over 60 percent of household charitable contributions go to religious charities.... [This has] "much the same effect as [a grant] ... of the amount of tax [avoided]." ...

Federal dollars also reach religiously affiliated organizations through public health programs such as Medicare and Medicaid, through educational programs such as the Pell Grant program and the G.I. Bill of Rights, and through child care programs such as the Child Care and Development Block Grant Program.... A significant portion of the [hundreds of billions of dollars] appropriated for these programs reach religiously affiliated institutions, typically without restrictions on its subsequent use....

Against this background, the support that the Cleveland voucher program provides religious institutions is neither substantial nor atypical of existing government programs. While this observation is not intended to justify the Cleveland voucher program under the Establishment Clause, it places in broader perspective alarmist claims about implications of the Cleveland program and the Court's decision in these cases....

[B.] {[T]he goal of the Court's Establishment Clause jurisprudence is to determine whether, after the Cleveland voucher program was enacted, parents were free to direct state educational aid in either a nonreligious or religious direction. That inquiry requires an evaluation of all reasonable educational options Ohio provides the Cleveland school system, regardless of whether they are formally made available in the same section of the Ohio Code as the voucher program. Based on the reasoning in the Court's opinion, ... I am persuaded that the Cleveland voucher program affords parents of eligible children genuine nonreligious options and is consistent with the Establishment Clause.}

For nonreligious schools to qualify as genuine options for parents, they need not be superior to religious schools in every respect. They need only be adequate substitutes for religious schools in the eyes of parents.

The District Court record demonstrates that nonreligious schools were able to compete effectively with Catholic and other religious schools in the Cleveland voucher program. The best evidence of this is that many parents with vouchers selected nonreligious private schools over religious alternatives and an even larger number of parents send their children to community and magnet schools rather than seeking vouchers at all.... Justice Souter's theory that the Cleveland voucher program's cap on the tuition encourages low-income students to attend religious schools ignores that these students receive nearly double the amount of tuition assistance under the community schools program than under the voucher program and that none of the community schools is religious....

Likewise, the mere fact that some parents enrolled their children in religious schools associated with a different faith than their own says little about whether these parents had reasonable nonreligious options. Indeed, no voucher student has been known to be turned away from a nonreligious private school participating in the voucher program. This is impressive given evidence in the record that the present litigation has discouraged the entry of some nonreligious private schools into the voucher program....

Justice Thomas, concurring....

[Justice Thomas begins by questioning whether the Establishment Clause should be seen as incorporated by the Fourteenth Amendment against the states, an issue that has produced some academic debate over the last couple of decades; for more on this, see his *Newdow* opinion at p. 836. He then goes on to argue the following:—ed.]

The wisdom of allowing States greater latitude in dealing with matters of religion and education can be easily appreciated in this context. Respondents advocate using the Fourteenth Amendment to handcuff the State's ability to experiment with education. But without education one can hardly exercise the civic, political, and personal freedoms conferred by the Fourteenth Amendment.

Faced with a severe educational crisis, ... [Ohio] gives parents a greater choice as to where and in what manner to educate their children. This is a choice that those with greater means have routinely exercised.... [T]he State has a constitutional right to experiment with a variety of different programs to promote educational opportunity....

At the time of Reconstruction, blacks considered public education "a matter of personal liberation and a necessary function of a free society." Today, however, the promise of public school education has failed poor inner-city blacks.... Just as blacks supported public education during Reconstruction, many blacks and other minorities now support school choice programs because they provide the greatest educational opportunities for their children in struggling communities. {Nearly three-fourths of all public school parents with an annual income less than $20,000 support vouchers, compared to 57 percent of public school parents with an annual income of over $60,000. In addition, 75 percent of black public school parents support vouchers, as do 71 percent of Hispanic public school parents.}

Opponents of the program raise formalistic concerns about the Establishment Clause but ignore the core purposes of the Fourteenth Amendment.... The failure to provide education to poor urban children perpetuates a vicious cycle of poverty, dependence, criminality, and alienation that continues for the remainder of their lives. If society cannot end racial discrimination, at least it can arm minorities with the education to defend themselves from some of discrimination's effects....

Justice Souter, with whom Justice Stevens, Justice Ginsburg, and Justice Breyer join, dissenting....

[A.] [Even] the majority's twin standards of neutrality and free choice [which Justice Souter in any event rejects, for reasons given in Part D—ed.] ... cannot convincingly legitimize the Ohio scheme.

Consider first the criterion of neutrality.... In order to apply the neutrality test, ... it makes sense to focus on a category of aid that may be directed to religious as well as secular schools, and ask whether the scheme favors a religious direction. Here, one would ask whether the voucher provisions, allowing for as much as $2,250 toward private school tuition (or a grant to a public school in an adjacent district), were written in a way that skewed the scheme toward benefiting religious schools.

This, however, is not what the majority asks. The majority looks not to the provisions for tuition vouchers, but to every provision for educational opportunity: "The program permits the participation of *all* schools within the district, [as well as public schools in adjacent districts], religious or non-religious." The majority then finds confirmation that "participation of *all* schools" satisfies neutrality by noting that the better part of total state educational expenditure goes to public schools, thus showing there is no favor of religion.

The illogic is patent. If regular, public schools (which can get no voucher payments) "participate" in a voucher scheme with schools that can, and public expenditure is still predominantly on public schools, then the majority's reasoning would find neutrality in a scheme of vouchers available for private tuition in districts with no secular private schools at all. "Neutrality" as the majority employs the term is, literally, verbal and nothing more. This, indeed, is the only way the majority can gloss over the very nonneutral feature of the total scheme covering "*all* schools": public tutors may receive from the State no more than $324 per child to support extra tutoring (that is, the State's 90% of a total amount of $360), whereas the tuition voucher schools (which turn out to be mostly religious) can receive up to $2,250....

[**B.**] The majority's view that all educational choices are comparable for purposes of choice ... ignores the whole point of the choice test: it is a criterion for deciding whether indirect aid to a religious school is legitimate because it passes through private hands that can spend or use the aid in a secular school. The question is whether the private hand is genuinely free to send the money in either a secular direction or a religious one.

The majority now has transformed this question about private choice in channeling aid into a question about selecting from examples of state spending (on education) including direct spending on magnet and community public schools that goes through no private hands and could never reach a religious school under any circumstance. When the choice test is transformed from where to spend the money to where to go to school, it is cut loose from its very purpose.

Defining choice as choice in spending the money or channeling the aid is, moreover, necessary if the choice criterion is to function as a limiting principle at all. If "choice" is present whenever there is any educational alternative to the religious school to which vouchers can be endorsed, then there will always be a choice and the voucher can always be constitutional, even in a system in which there is not a single private secular school as an alternative to the religious school....

That is, in fact, just the kind of rhetorical argument that the majority accepts in these cases. In addition to secular private schools (129 students), the majority considers public schools with tuition assistance (roughly 1,400 students), magnet schools (13,000 students), and community schools (1,900 students), and concludes that fewer than 20% of pupils receive state vouchers to attend religious schools.... [This shows] how results may shift when a judge can pick and choose the alternatives to use in the comparisons, and [it] also show[s] what dependably comfortable results the choice criterion will yield if the identification of relevant choices is wide open....

Confining the relevant choices to spending choices, on the other hand, is not vulnerable to comparable criticism.... [L]imiting the choices to spending choices will not guarantee a negative result in every case. There may, after all, be cases in which a voucher recipient will have a real choice, with enough secular private school desks in relation to the number of religious ones, and a voucher amount high enough to meet secular private school tuition levels....

{[C]ommunity schools do exhibit some features of private schools: they are autonomously managed without any interference from the school district or State and two have prior histories as private schools. It may be, then, that community schools might arguably count as choices because they are not like other public schools run by the State or municipality, but in substance merely private schools with state funding outside the voucher program. But once any public school is deemed a relevant object of choice, there is no stopping this progression.} ...

[C.] If, contrary to the majority, we ask the right question about genuine choice to use the vouchers, the answer shows that something is influencing choices in a way that aims the money in a religious direction: of 56 private schools in the district participating in the voucher program (only 53 of which accepted voucher students in 1999-2000), 46 of them are religious; 96.6% of all voucher recipients go to religious schools, only 3.4% to nonreligious ones. Unfortunately for the majority position, there is no explanation for this that suggests the religious direction results simply from free choices by parents.

One answer to these statistics, for example, which would be consistent with the genuine choice claimed to be operating, might be that 96.6% of families choosing to avail themselves of vouchers choose to educate their children in schools of their own religion. This would not, in my view, render the scheme constitutional, but it would speak to the majority's choice criterion.

Evidence shows, however, that almost two out of three families using vouchers to send their children to religious schools did not embrace the religion of those schools. The families made it clear they had not chosen the schools because they wished their children to be proselytized in a religion not their own, or in any religion, but because of educational opportunity. {When asked specifically in one study to identify the most important factor in selecting among participating private schools, ... only 15% [of parents] mentioned the religious affiliation of the school as even a consideration.}

Even so, the fact that some 2,270 students chose to apply their vouchers to schools of other religions might be consistent with true choice if the students "chose" their religious schools over a wide array of private nonreligious options, or if it could be shown generally that Ohio's program had no effect on educational choices and thus no impermissible effect of advancing religious education. But both possibilities are contrary to fact.

First, even if all existing nonreligious private schools in Cleveland were willing to accept large numbers of voucher students, only a few more than the 129 currently enrolled in such schools would be able to attend, as the total enrollment at all nonreligious private schools in Cleveland for kindergarten through eighth grade is only 510 children, and there is no indication that these schools have many open seats. {Justice O'Connor points out that "there is no record evidence that any voucher-eligible student was turned away from a nonreligious private school in the voucher program." But there is equally no evidence to support her assertion that "many parents with vouchers selected nonreligious private schools over religious alternatives," and in fact the evidence is to the contrary, as only 129 students used vouchers at private nonreligious schools.}

Second, the $2,500 cap that the program places on tuition for participating low-income pupils has the effect of curtailing the participation of nonreligious schools: "nonreligious schools with higher tuition (about $4,000) stated that they could afford to accommodate just a few voucher students." By comparison, the average tuition at participating Catholic schools in Cleveland in 1999-2000 was $1,592, almost $1,000 below the cap.

Of course, the obvious fix would be to increase the value of vouchers so that existing nonreligious private and non-Catholic religious schools would be able to enroll more voucher students, and to provide incentives for educators to create new such schools given that few presently exist. Private choice, if as robust as that available to the seminarian in *Witters*, would then be "true private choice" under the majority's criterion.

But it is simply unrealistic to presume that parents of elementary and middle schoolchildren in Cleveland will have a range of secular and religious choices even arguably comparable to the statewide program for vocational and higher education in *Witters*. And to get to that hypothetical point would require that such massive financial support be made available to religion as to disserve every objective of the Establishment Clause even more than the present scheme does.

{The majority notes that I argue both that the Ohio program is unconstitutional because the voucher amount is too low to create real private choice and that any greater expenditure would be unconstitutional as well.... [But] there is no inconsistency here: any voucher program that satisfied the majority's requirement of "true private choice" would be even more egregiously unconstitutional than the current scheme due to the substantial amount of aid to religious teaching that would be required.}

There is, in any case, no way to interpret the 96.6% of current voucher money going to religious schools as reflecting a free and genuine choice by the families that apply for vouchers. The 96.6% reflects, instead, the fact that too few nonreligious school desks are available and few but religious schools can afford to accept more than a handful of voucher students.

And contrary to the majority's assertion, public schools in adjacent districts hardly have a financial incentive to participate in the Ohio voucher program, and none has. {[A]n out-of-district public school that participates will receive a $2,250 voucher for each Cleveland student on top of its normal state funding. The basic state funding, though, is a drop in the bucket as compared to the cost of educating that student, as much of the cost (at least in relatively affluent areas with presumptively better academic standards) is paid by local income and property taxes.} For the overwhelming number of children in the voucher scheme, the only alternative to the public schools is religious....

[D.] [E]ven if I assumed *arguendo* that the majority's formal criteria were satisfied on the facts, today's conclusion would be profoundly at odds with the Constitution. Proof of this is clear on two levels. The first is circumstantial, in the now discarded symptom of violation, the substantial dimension of the aid. The second is direct, in the defiance of every objective supposed to be served by the bar against establishment.

The scale of the aid to religious schools approved today is unprecedented, both in the number of dollars and in the proportion of systemic school expenditure supported.... The Cleveland voucher program has cost Ohio taxpayers $33 million since its implementation in 1996 ($28 million in voucher payments, $5 million in administrative costs), and its cost was expected to exceed $8 million in the 2001-2002 school year.... [T]he majority makes no pretense that substantial amounts of tax money are not systematically underwriting religious practice and indoctrination....

{[I find] irrelevant ... Justice O'Connor's argument that the $8.2 million in tax-raised funds distributed under the Ohio program to religious schools is permissible under the Establishment Clause because it "pales in comparison to the amount of funds that federal, state, and local governments already provide religious institutions." Our cases have consistently held that state benefits at some level can go to religious institutions when the recipients are not pervasively sectarian; when the benefit comes in the form of tax exemption or deduction; or when the aid can plausibly be said to go to individual university students. The fact that those cases often allow for large amounts of aid says nothing about direct aid to pervasively sectarian schools for religious teaching. This "greater justifies the lesser" argument not only ignores the aforementioned cases, it would completely swallow up our aid-to-school cases from *Everson* onward: if $8.2 million in vouchers is acceptable, for example, why is there any requirement against greater than *de minimis* diversion to religious uses?}

[The first objective of the Establishment Clause is] respect for freedom of conscience. Jefferson described it as the idea that no one "shall be compelled to ... support any religious worship, place, or ministry whatsoever," even a "teacher of his own religious persuasion," and Madison thought it violated by any "authority which can force a citizen to contribute three pence ... of his property for the support of any ... establishment." ...

As for the second objective, to save religion from its own corruption, Madison wrote of the "experience ... that ecclesiastical establishments, instead of maintaining the purity and efficacy of Religion, have had a contrary operation." ... [Today, the risk to religion] is one of "corrosive secularism" to religious schools, and the specific threat is to the primacy of the schools' mission to educate the children of the faithful according to the unaltered precepts of their faith. Even "[t]he favored religion may be compromised as political figures reshape the religion's beliefs for their own purposes; it may be reformed as government largesse brings government regulation."

The risk is already being realized. In Ohio, for example, a condition of receiving government money under the program is that participating religious schools may not "discriminate on the basis of ... religion," which means the school may not give admission preferences to children who are members of the patron faith; children of a parish are generally consigned to the same admission lotteries as nonbelievers....

[Likewise,] by its terms, a participating religious school may well be forbidden to choose a member of its own clergy to serve as teacher or principal over a layperson of a different religion claiming equal qualification for the job. Indeed, a separate condition that "[t]he school ... not ... teach hatred of any person or group on the basis of ... religion" could be understood (or subsequently broadened) to prohibit religions from teaching traditionally legitimate articles of faith as to the error, sinfulness, or ignorance of others, if they want government money for their schools....

When government aid goes up, so does reliance on it; the only thing likely to go down is independence.... A day will come when religious schools will learn what political leverage can do, just as Ohio's politicians are now getting a lesson in the leverage exercised by religion.

[The third objective Justice Souter mentions is prevention of religiously-based social conflict; he agrees with Justice Breyer's dissent.—ed.] ...

Justice Breyer, with whom Justice Stevens and Justice Souter join, dissenting....

[A.] The [Religion] Clauses reflect the Framers' vision of an American Nation free of the religious strife that had long plagued the nations of Europe.... [The Framers] undeniably intended an interpretation of the Religion Clauses that would implement this basic ... objective.... [We should aim at] the development of constitutional doctrine that reads the Establishment Clause as avoiding religious strife, *not* by providing every religion with an *equal opportunity* (say, to secure state funding or to pray in the public schools), but by drawing fairly clear lines of *separation* between church and state—at least where the heartland of religious belief, such as primary religious education, is at issue....

School voucher programs finance the religious education of the young. And, if widely adopted, they may well provide billions of dollars that will do so. Why will different religions not become concerned about, and seek to influence, the criteria used to channel this money to religious schools? Why will they not want to examine the implementation of the programs that provide this money—to determine, for example, whether implementation has biased a program toward or against particular sects, or whether recipient religious schools are adequately fulfilling a program's criteria? If so, just how is the State to resolve the resulting controversies without provoking legitimate fears of the kinds of religious favoritism that, in so religiously diverse a Nation, threaten social dissension?

Consider the voucher program here at issue. That program insists that the religious school accept students of all religions. Does that criterion treat fairly groups whose religion forbids them to do so?

The program also insists that no participating school "advocate or foster unlawful behavior or teach hatred of any person or group on the basis of race, ethnicity, national origin, or religion." And it requires the State to "revoke the registration of any school if, after a hearing, the superintendent determines that the school is in violation" of the program's rules. As one *amicus* argues, "it is difficult to imagine a more divisive activity" than the appointment of state officials as referees to determine whether a particular religious doctrine "teaches hatred or advocates lawlessness."

How are state officials to adjudicate claims that one religion or another is advocating, for example, civil disobedience in response to unjust laws, the use of illegal drugs in a religious ceremony, or resort to force to call attention to what it views as an immoral social practice? What kind of public hearing will there be in response to claims that one religion or another is continuing to teach a view of history that casts members of other religions in the worst possible light? How will the public react to government funding for schools that take controversial religious positions on topics that are of current popular interest—say, the conflict in the Middle East or the war on terrorism?

Yet any major funding program for primary religious education will require criteria. And the selection of those criteria, as well as their application, inevitably pose problems that are divisive. Efforts to respond to these problems not only will seriously entangle church and state, but also will promote division among religious groups, as one group or another fears (often legitimately) that it will receive unfair treatment ....

[B.] I concede that the Establishment Clause currently permits States to channel various forms of assistance to religious schools, for example, transportation costs for students, computers, and secular texts. States now certify the nonsectarian educational content of religious school education. Yet the consequence has not been great turmoil.

School voucher programs differ, however, in both *kind* and *degree* from aid programs upheld in the past. They differ in kind because they direct financing to a core function of the church: the teaching of religious truths to young children.... [Government funding] of this kind of religious endeavor is far more contentious than providing funding for secular textbooks, computers, vocational training, or even funding for adults who wish to obtain a college education at a religious university.

Contrary to Justice O'Connor's opinion, history also shows that government involvement in religious primary education is far more divisive than state property tax exemptions for religious institutions or tax deductions for charitable contributions, both of which come far closer to exemplifying the neutrality that distinguishes, for example, fire protection on the one hand from direct monetary assistance on the other. Federal aid to religiously based hospitals is even further removed from education, which lies at the heartland of religious belief.

Vouchers also differ in *degree*.... [Unlike with past aid programs,] the majority's analysis here appears to permit a considerable shift of taxpayer dollars from public secular schools to private religious schools. That fact, combined with the use to which these dollars will be put, exacerbates the conflict problem....

[C.] I do not believe that the "parental choice" aspect of the voucher program sufficiently offsets the concerns I have mentioned.... It will not satisfy religious minorities unable to participate because they are too few in number to support the creation of their own private schools. It will not satisfy groups whose religious beliefs preclude them from participating in a government-sponsored program, and who may well feel ignored as government funds primarily support the education of children in the doctrines of the dominant religions. And it does little to ameliorate the entanglement problems or the related problems of social division that [I have described]....

t. Policy—Protecting Religion from Harmful Effects of Government Aid

Basic argument: "The First Amendment should be read to prohibit this sort of government action, because even though the action might at first look like it benefits religion, it will in fact hurt religion by _____."

1. "Nor should I think that those who have done so well without this aid would want to see this separation between Church and State broken down. If the state may aid these religious schools, it may therefore regulate them." *Board of Ed. v. Everson* (Jackson, J., dissenting).

"The third purpose of separation and neutrality is to prevent the trivialization and degradation of religion by too close an attachment to the organs of government. The Establishment Clause 'stands as an expression of principle on the part of the Founders of our Constitution that religion is too personal, too sacred, too holy to permit its 'unhallowed perversion' by a civil magistrate.'" *Marsh v. Chambers* (Brennan, J., dissenting).

"[The Bill Establishing a Provision for the Teachers of the Christian Religion would] weaken in those who profess this Religion a pious confidence in its innate excellence, and the patronage of its Author; and to foster in those who still reject it, a suspicion that its friends are too conscious of its fallacies, to trust it to its own merits.... [And] experience witnesseth that ecclesiastical establishments, instead of maintaining the purity and efficacy of Religion, have had a contrary operation..... What have been [the fruits of legal establishment of Christianity through history]? ... [P]ride and indolence in the Clergy; ignorance and servility in the laity; in both, superstition, bigotry and persecution. Enquire of the Teachers of Christianity for the ages in which it appeared in its greatest lustre; those of every sect, point to the ages prior to its incorporation with Civil policy." James Madison, *Memorial and Remonstrance Against Religious Assessments*.

2. Response to 1: The action is in fact unlikely to hurt religion in the ways that are being claimed, because _____.

3. Response to 1: Using this argument as a justification for striking down this program would justify striking down others, such as _____, because _____, and that shows that such a justification is unsound.

"[The argument that aid would come with conditions] is equally applicable to all neutral programs, not just ones involving K-12 schools. If you take it seriously, you'd have to say that the GI Bill and the charitable tax deduction are also unconstitutional, because they could also come with strings that pressure recipients to compromise their religious beliefs. Exhibit A here would be *Bob Jones University v. United States*, in which the government [threatened to deny a tax exemption to] successfully pressure[] Goldsboro Christian Schools into abandoning its religiously motivated racially discriminatory admissions policy." Eugene Volokh, *Equal Treatment Is Not Establishment,* 13 Notre Dame J.L., Ethics & Pub. Pol. 341, 363-64 (1999).

4. Response to 1: Even if the aid might hurt religion, it hurts it less than the status quo does, because _____.

"The argument [is] that school choice is unconstitutional because it might hurt religious schools by bringing government oversight and regulation and thus destroying religious schools' independence. True, the argument runs, schools *could* just avoid the strings by rejecting the money; but when put to the choice of (1) taking the government subsidy and compromising their religious objections to the strings or (2) sticking by their beliefs but losing the subsidy, they may feel pressure to choose option two.

"[But this] ignores the greater pressure exerted by the status quo.... [J]ust as religious schools might conceivably object on religious grounds to some strings that come with school choice funds, so today many religious parents object on religious grounds to many aspects of the curriculum and environment in government-run public schools. The offer of a free education in a government-run school puts these parents to the choice of (1) taking this government subsidy and compromising their religious objections to the curriculum or environment or (2) sticking by their beliefs but losing the subsidy—and of course many of these parents feel pressure to choose option two.... [T]he supposed constitutional defect—here, the risk of government pressure that leads some to abandon their religious obligations—is as present under the existing system as under a school choice system." *Id.*

2.   THE DEBATE ABOUT ORIGINAL MEANING

> Each side [those who view religion as a good thing to be prompted, and those who view it as a dangerous force to be contained] claims that it won the late twentieth century culture wars and took over the government—two hundred years ago.
> —Douglas Laycock, *Religious Liberty as Liberty*, 7 J. Contemp. Leg. Issues 313 (1996)

a. *Bill Establishing a Provision for Teachers of the Christian Religion (Virginia, 1784)*

Whereas the general diffusion of Christian knowledge hath a natural tendency to correct the morals of men, restrain their vices, and preserve the peace of society; which cannot be effected without a competent provision for learned teachers, who may be thereby enabled to devote their time and attention to the duty of instructing such citizens, as from their circumstances and want of education, cannot otherwise attain such knowledge; and it is judged that such provision may be made by the Legislature, without counteracting the liberal principle heretofore adopted and intended to be preserved by abolishing all distinctions of pre-eminence amongst the different societies or communities of Christians;

Be it therefore enacted by the General Assembly, That for the support of Christian teachers, ... _____ in the pound on the sum payable for tax on the property within this Commonwealth, is hereby assessed ....

And be it enacted, That for every sum so paid, the Sheriff or Collector shall give a receipt, expressing therein to what society of Christians the person from whom he may receive the same shall direct the money to be paid, keeping a distinct account thereof in his books....

And be it further enacted, That the money to be raised by virtue of this Act, shall be by the Vestries, Elders, or Directors of each religious society, appropriated to a provision for a Minister or Teacher of the Gospel of their denomination, or the providing places of divine worship, and to none other use whatsoever; except in the denominations of Quakers and Menonists, who may receive what is collected from their members, and place it in their general fund, to be disposed of in a manner which they shall think best calculated to promote their particular mode of worship.

And be it enacted, That all sums which at the time of payment ... may not be appropriated by the person paying the same, shall be accounted for with the Court ...; and after deducting for his collection, the Sheriff shall pay the amount thereof ... into the public Treasury, to be disposed of under the direction of the General Assembly, for the encouragement of seminaries of learning within the Counties whence such sums shall arise, and to no other use or purpose whatsoever....

b. *Madison's Memorial and Remonstrance Against Religious Assessments (1785)*

TO ... THE GENERAL ASSEMBLY OF THE COMMONWEALTH OF VIRGINIA[,] A MEMORIAL AND REMONSTRANCE.

We, the subscribers, citizens of the said Commonwealth, having taken into serious consideration, ... "A Bill establishing a provision for teachers of the Christian Religion," and conceiving that the same ... will be a dangerous abuse of power, are bound as faithful members of a free State, to remonstrate against it, and to declare the reasons by which we are determined. We remonstrate against the said Bill,

1. Because we hold it for a fundamental and undeniable truth, "that Religion, or the duty which we owe to our Creator, and the Manner of discharging it, can be directed only by reason and conviction, not by force or violence" [citing Virginia Declaration of Rights]. The Religion then of every man must be left to the conviction and conscience of every man; and it is the right of every man to exercise it as these may dictate.

This right is in its nature an unalienable right. It is unalienable; because the opinions of men, depending only on the evidence contemplated by their own minds, cannot follow the dictates of other men: It is unalienable also; because what is here a right towards men, is a duty towards the Creator. It is the duty of every man to render to the Creator such homage, and such only, as he believes to be acceptable to him.

This duty is precedent both in order of time and degree of obligation, to the claims of Civil Society. Before any man can be considered as a member of Civil Society, he must be considered as a subject of the Governor of the Universe: And if a member of Civil Society, who enters into any subordinate Association, must always do it with a reservation of his duty to the general authority; much more must every man who becomes a member of any particular Civil Society, do it with a saving of his allegiance to the Universal Sovereign.

We maintain therefore that in matters of Religion, no man's right is abridged by the institution of Civil Society, and that Religion is wholly exempt from its cognizance. True it is, that no other rule exists, by which any question which may divide a Society, can be ultimately determined, but the will of the majority; but it is also true, that the majority may trespass on the rights of the minority....

3. Because, it is proper to take alarm at the first experiment on our liberties. We hold this prudent jealousy to be the first duty of citizens, and one of [the] noblest characteristics of the late Revolution. The freemen of America did not wait till usurped power had strengthened itself by exercise, and entangled the question in precedents. They saw all the consequences in the principle, and they avoided the consequences by denying the principle. We revere this lesson too much, soon to forget it.

Who does not see that the same authority which can establish Christianity, in exclusion of all other Religions, may establish with the same ease any particular sect of Christians, in exclusion of all other Sects? That the same authority which can force a citizen to contribute three pence only of his property for the support of any one establishment, may force him to conform to any other establishment in all cases whatsoever?

4. Because, the bill violates that equality which ought to be the basis of every law, and which is more indispensable, in proportion as the validity or expediency of any law is more liable to be impeached.... Whilst we assert for ourselves a freedom to embrace, to profess and to observe the Religion which we believe to be of divine origin, we cannot deny an equal freedom to those whose minds have not yet yielded to the evidence which has convinced us. If this freedom be abused, it is an offence against God, not against man: To God, therefore, not to men, must an account of it be rendered.

As the Bill violates equality by subjecting some to peculiar burdens; so it violates the same principle, by granting to others peculiar exemptions. Are the Quakers and Menonists the only sects who think a compulsive support of their religions unnecessary and unwarrantable? Can their piety alone be intrusted with the care of public worship? Ought their Religions to

be endowed above all others, with extraordinary privileges, by which prose-
lytes may be enticed from all others? ...

5. Because the bill implies either that the Civil Magistrate is a competent Judge of Religious truth; or that he may employ Religion as an engine
of Civil policy. The first is an arrogant pretension falsified by the contradictory opinions of Rulers in all ages, and throughout the world: The second an
unhallowed perversion of the means of salvation.

6. Because the establishment proposed by the Bill is not requisite for the
support of the Christian Religion. To say that it is, is a contradiction to the
Christian Religion itself; for every page of it disavows a dependence on the
powers of this world: it is a contradiction to fact; for it is known that this
Religion both existed and flourished, not only without the support of human
laws, but in spite of every opposition from them; and not only during the
period of miraculous aid, but long after it had been left to its own evidence,
and the ordinary care of Providence: Nay, it is a contradiction in terms; for
a Religion not invented by human policy, must have pre-existed and been
supported, before it was established by human policy.

It is moreover to weaken in those who profess this Religion a pious confidence in its innate excellence, and the patronage of its Author; and to foster in those who still reject it, a suspicion that its friends are too conscious
of its fallacies, to trust it to its own merits.

7. Because experience witnesseth that ecclesiastical establishments, instead of maintaining the purity and efficacy of Religion, have had a contrary
operation. During almost fifteen centuries, has the legal establishment of
Christianity been on trial. What have been its fruits? More or less in all
places, pride and indolence in the Clergy; ignorance and servility in the laity; in both, superstition, bigotry and persecution.

Enquire of the Teachers of Christianity for the ages in which it appeared
in its greatest lustre; those of every sect, point to the ages prior to its incorporation with Civil policy. Propose a restoration of this primitive state in
which its Teachers depended on the voluntary rewards of their flocks; many
of them predict its downfall. On which side ought their testimony to have
greatest weight, when for or when against their interest?

8. Because the establishment in question is not necessary for the support of Civil Government. If it be urged as necessary for the support of Civil
Government only as it is a means of supporting Religion, and it be not necessary for the latter purpose, it cannot be necessary for the former.

If Religion be not within [the] cognizance of Civil Government, how can
its legal establishment be said to be necessary to Civil Government? What
influence in fact have ecclesiastical establishments had on Civil Society? In
some instances they have been seen to erect a spiritual tyranny on the ruins
of Civil authority; in many instances they have been seen upholding the
thrones of political tyranny; in no instance have they been seen the guardians of the liberties of the people.

Rulers who wished to subvert the public liberties, may have found an established clergy convenient auxiliaries. A just government, instituted to secure & perpetuate it, needs them not. Such a government will be best supported by protecting every citizen in the enjoyment of his Religion with the same equal hand which protects his person and his property; by neither invading the equal rights of any Sect, nor suffering any Sect to invade those of another.

9. Because the proposed establishment is a departure from that generous policy, which, offering an asylum to the persecuted and oppressed of every Nation and Religion, promised a lustre to our country, and an accession to the number of its citizens....

10. Because, it will have a like tendency to banish our Citizens. The allurements presented by other situations are every day thinning their number. To superadd a fresh motive to emigration, by revoking the liberty which they now enjoy, would be the same species of folly which has dishonoured and depopulated flourishing kingdoms.

11. Because, it will destroy that moderation and harmony which the forbearance of our laws to intermeddle with Religion, has produced amongst its several sects. Torrents of blood have been spilt in the old world, by vain attempts of the secular arm to extinguish Religious discord, by proscribing all difference in Religious opinions. Time has at length revealed the true remedy. Every relaxation of narrow and rigorous policy, wherever it has been tried, has been found to assuage the disease.

The American Theatre has exhibited proofs, that equal and complete liberty, if it does not wholly eradicate it, sufficiently destroys its malignant influence on the health and prosperity of the State.... The very appearance of the Bill has transformed that "Christian forbearance, love and charity," which of late mutually prevailed, into animosities and jealousies, which may not soon be appeased. What mischiefs may not be dreaded should this enemy to the public quiet be armed with the force of a law?

12. Because, the policy of the bill is adverse to the diffusion of the light of Christianity. The first wish of those who enjoy this precious gift, ought to be that it may be imparted to the whole race of mankind. Compare the number of those who have as yet received it with the number still remaining under the dominion of false Religions; and how small is the former!

Does the policy of the Bill tend to lessen the disproportion? No; it at once discourages those who are strangers to the light of [revelation] from coming into the Region of it; and countenances, by example the nations who continue in darkness, in shutting out those who might convey it to them....

13. Because attempts to enforce by legal sanctions, acts obnoxious to so great a proportion of Citizens, tend to enervate the laws in general, and to slacken the bands of Society. If it be difficult to execute any law which is not generally deemed necessary or salutary, what must be the case where it is deemed invalid and dangerous? and what may be the effect of so striking an example of impotency in the Government, on its general authority....

15. Because, finally, "the equal right of every citizen to the free exercise

of his Religion according to the dictates of conscience" is held by the same tenure with all our other rights. If we recur to its origin, it is equally the gift of nature; if we weigh its importance, it cannot be less dear to us; if we consult the Declaration of those rights which pertain to the good people of Virginia, as the "basis and foundation of Government," it is enumerated with equal solemnity, or rather studied emphasis.

Either then, we must say, that the will of the Legislature is the only measure of their authority; and that in the plentitude of this authority, they may sweep away all our fundamental rights; or, that they are bound to leave this particular right untouched and sacred: Either we must say, that they may controul the freedom of the press, may abolish the trial by jury, may swallow up the Executive and Judiciary Powers of the State; nay that they may despoil us of our very right of suffrage, and erect themselves into an independent and hereditary assembly: or we must say, that they have no authority to enact into law the Bill under consideration.

We the subscribers say, that the General Assembly of this Commonwealth have no such authority: And that no effort may be omitted on our part against so dangerous an usurpation, we oppose to it, this remonstrance; earnestly praying, as we are in duty bound, that the Supreme Lawgiver of the Universe, by illuminating those to whom it is addressed, may on the one hand, turn their councils from every act which would affront his holy prerogative, or violate the trust committed to them: and on the other, guide them into every measure which may be worthy of his [blessing, may re]dound to their own praise, and may establish more firmly the liberties, the prosperity, and the Happiness of the Commonwealth.

c. *Virginia Statute for Religious Freedom (1786) (drafted by Thomas Jefferson)*

Whereas Almighty God hath created the mind free;

that all attempts to influence it by temporal punishments or burthens, or by civil incapacitations, tend only to beget habits of hypocrisy and meanness, and are a departure from the plan of the Holy author of our religion, who being Lord both of body and mind, yet chose not to propagate it by coercions on either, as it was in his Almighty power to do;

that the impious presumption of legislators and rulers, civil as well as ecclesiastical, who being themselves but fallible and uninspired men, have assumed dominion over the faith of others, setting up their own opinions and modes of thinking as the only true and infallible, and as such endeavouring to impose them on others, hath established and maintained false religions over the greatest part of the world, and through all time;

that to compel a man to furnish contributions of money for the propagation of opinions which he disbelieves, is sinful and tyrannical;

that even the forcing him to support this or that teacher of his own religious persuasion, is depriving him of the comfortable liberty of giving his contributions to the particular pastor, whose morals he would make his pattern, and whose powers he feels most persuasive to righteousness, and is withdrawing from the ministry those temporary rewards, which proceeding from an approbation of their personal conduct, are an additional incitement to earnest and unremitting labours for the instruction of mankind; that our civil rights have no dependence on our religious opinions, any more than our opinions in physics or geometry;

that therefore the proscribing any citizen as unworthy the public confidence by laying upon him an incapacity of being called to offices of trust and emolument, unless he profess or renounce this or that religious opinion, is depriving him injuriously of those privileges and advantages to which in common with his fellow-citizens he has a natural right;

that it tends only to corrupt the principles of that religion it is meant to encourage, by bribing with a monopoly of worldly honours and emoluments, those who will externally profess and conform to it;

that though indeed these are criminal who do not withstand such temptation, yet neither are those innocent who lay the bait in their way;

that to suffer the civil magistrate to intrude his powers into the field of opinion, and to restrain the profession or propagation of principles on supposition of their ill tendency, is a dangerous fallacy, which at once destroys all religious liberty, because he being of course judge of that tendency will make his opinions the rule of judgment, and approve or condemn the sentiments of others only as they shall square with or differ from his own;

that it is time enough for the rightful purposes of civil government, for its officers to interfere when principles break out into overt acts against peace and good order;

and finally, that truth is great and will prevail if left to herself, that she is the proper and sufficient antagonist to error, and has nothing to fear from the conflict, unless by human interposition disarmed of her natural weapons, free argument and debate, errors ceasing to be dangerous when it is permitted freely to contradict them:

Be it enacted by the General Assembly, That no man shall be compelled to frequent or support any religious worship, place, or ministry whatsoever, nor shall be enforced, restrained, molested, or burthened in his body or goods, nor shall otherwise suffer on account of his religious opinions or belief; but that all men shall be free to profess, and by argument to maintain, their opinion in matters of religion, and that the same shall in no wise diminish enlarge, or affect their civil capacities....

And though we well know that this assembly elected by the people for the ordinary purposes of legislation only, have no power to restrain the acts of succeeding assemblies, constituted with powers equal to our own, and that therefore to declare this act to be irrevocable would be of no effect in law; yet we are free to declare, and do declare, that the rights hereby asserted are of the natural rights of mankind, and that if any act shall be hereafter passed to repeal the present, or to narrow its operation, such act shall be an infringement of natural right.

d. *Does the Establishment Clause Require Exclusion of Religious Institutions from Evenhanded Funded Programs?*

Justice Thomas, concurring [in *Rosenberger v. Rector*]....

[A.] Even assuming that the Virginia debate on the so-called "Assessment Controversy" was indicative of the principles embodied in the Establishment Clause, this incident hardly compels the dissent's conclusion that government must actively discriminate against religion.

The dissent's historical discussion glosses over the fundamental characteristic of the Virginia assessment bill that sparked the controversy: The assessment was to be imposed for the support of clergy in the performance of their function of teaching religion. Thus, the "Bill Establishing a Provision for Teachers of the Christian Religion" provided for the collection of a specific tax, the proceeds of which were to be appropriated "by the Vestries, Elders, or Directors of each religious society ... to a provision for a Minister or Teacher of the Gospel of their denomination, or the providing places of divine worship, and to none other use whatsoever."

James Madison's *Memorial and Remonstrance Against Religious Assessments* ... must be understood in this context.... Madison's objection to the assessment bill did not rest on the premise that religious entities may never participate on equal terms in neutral government programs. Nor did Madison embrace the argument ... that monetary subsidies are constitutionally different from other neutral benefits programs.

Instead, Madison's comments are more consistent with the neutrality principle .... According to Madison, the Virginia assessment was flawed because it "violate[d] that equality which ought to be the basis of every law." Madison's *Remonstrance* ¶ 4. The assessment violated the "equality" principle not because it allowed religious groups to participate in a generally available government program, but because the bill singled out religious entities for special benefits. See *id.* (arguing that the assessment violated the equality principle "by subjecting some to peculiar burdens" and "by granting to others peculiar exemptions")....

[T]here is no indication that at the time of the framing [Madison] took the dissent's extreme view that the government must discriminate against religious adherents by excluding them from more generally available financial subsidies. {To the contrary, Madison's *Remonstrance* decried the fact that the assessment bill would require civil society to take "cognizance" of religion. Respondents' exclusion of religious activities from [Student Activities Fund] funding creates this very problem. It requires University officials to classify publications as "religious activities," and to discriminate against the publications that fall into that category. Such a policy also contravenes the principles expressed in Madison's *Remonstrance* by encouraging religious adherents to cleanse their speech of religious overtones, thus "degrad[ing] from the equal rank of Citizens all those whose opinions in Religion do not bend to those of the Legislative authority."}

In fact, Madison's own early legislative proposals cut against the dissent's suggestion. In 1776, when Virginia's Revolutionary Convention was drafting its Declaration of Rights, Madison prepared an amendment that would have disestablished the Anglican Church.

This amendment (which went too far for the Convention and was not adopted) is not nearly as sweeping as the dissent's version of disestablishment; Madison merely wanted the Convention to declare that "no man or class of men ought, on account of religion[,] to be invested with *peculiar* emoluments or privileges...." Likewise, Madison's *Remonstrance* ¶ 8 stressed that "just government" is "best supported by protecting every citizen in the enjoyment of his Religion with the same equal hand which protects his person and his property; by neither invading the equal rights of any Sect, nor suffering any Sect to invade those of another." ...

[B.] The dissent suggests that the [Virginia] assessment bill would have created a "generally available subsidy program" comparable to respondents' Student Activities Fund .... The dissent's characterization of the bill, however, is squarely at odds with the bill's clear purpose and effect to provide "for the support of Christian teachers."

Moreover, the section of the bill cited by the dissent simply indicated that funds would be "disposed of under the direction of the General Assembly, for the encouragement of seminaries of learning within the Counties whence such sums shall arise." This provision disposing of undesignated funds hardly transformed the "Bill Establishing a Provision for Teachers of the Christian Religion" into a truly neutral program that would benefit religious adherents as part of a large class of beneficiaries defined without reference to religion. Indeed, the only appropriation of money made by the bill would have been to promote "the general diffusion of Christian knowledge"; any possible appropriation for "seminaries of learning" depended entirely on future legislative action.

Even assuming that future legislators would adhere to the bill's directive in appropriating the undesignated tax revenues, nothing in the bill would prevent use of those funds solely for sectarian educational institutions. To the contrary, most schools at the time of the founding were affiliated with some religious organization, and in fact there was no system of public education in Virginia until several decades after the assessment bill was proposed.

Further, the clearly religious tenor of the Virginia assessment would seem to point toward appropriation of residual funds to sectarian "seminaries of learning." Finally, although modern historians have focused on the opt-out provision, the dissent provides no indication that Madison viewed the Virginia assessment as an evenhanded program; in fact, several of the objections expressed in Madison's *Remonstrance* focus clearly on the bill's violation of the principle of "equality," or evenhandedness.

[C.] The dissent purports to locate the prohibition against "direct public funding" at the "heart" of the Establishment Clause, but this conclusion fails to confront historical examples of funding that date back to the time of the founding. To take but one famous example, both Houses of the First Congress elected chaplains, and that Congress enacted legislation providing for an annual salary of $500 to be paid out of the Treasury. Madison himself was a member of the committee that recommended the chaplain system in the House. This same system of "direct public funding" of congressional chaplains has "continued without interruption ever since that early session of Congress." *Marsh v. Chambers.*

The historical evidence of government support for religious entities through property tax exemptions is also overwhelming.... A tax exemption in many cases is economically and functionally indistinguishable from a direct monetary subsidy.[5] In one instance, the government relieves religious entities (along with others) of a generally applicable tax; in the other, it relieves religious entities (along with others) of some or all of the burden of that tax by returning it in the form of a cash subsidy. Whether the benefit is provided at the front or back end of the taxation process, the financial aid to religious groups is undeniable. The analysis under the Establishment Clause must also be the same: "Few concepts are more deeply embedded in the fabric of our national life, beginning with pre-Revolutionary colonial times, than for the government to exercise at the very least this kind of benevolent neutrality toward churches and religious exercise...." ...

Our Nation's tradition of allowing religious adherents to participate in evenhanded government programs is hardly limited to the class of "essential public benefits" identified by the dissent. A broader tradition can be traced at least as far back as the First Congress, which ratified the Northwest Ordinance of 1787. Article III of that famous enactment of the Confederation Congress had provided: "Religion, morality, and knowledge ... being necessary to good government and the happiness of mankind, schools and the means of education shall forever be encouraged."

Congress subsequently set aside federal lands in the Northwest Territory and other territories for the use of schools. Many of the schools that enjoyed the benefits of these land grants undoubtedly were church-affiliated

---

[5] "... For example, a government with a general income tax, wanting to add $7,000 to the spendable income of a preacher whose top tax rate is 30%, ... can send the preacher a check for $10,000 and tax him on all of his income, or it can authorize him to reduce his taxable income by $23,333.33 [resulting in a tax saving of $7,000].... [T]he preacher would receive the same benefit from the tax deduction as he would from the direct payment." ... [Notwithstanding Professor Bittker's position,] "... the large body of literature about tax expenditures accepts the basic concept that special exemptions from tax function as subsidies...."

[**Justice Souter's response, in his *Rosenberger* dissent:** Justice Thomas's assertion that "[a] tax exemption in many cases is economically and functionally indistinguishable from a direct monetary subsidy" assumes that the "natural" or "correct" tax base is so self-evident that any provision excusing a person or institution from taxes to which others are subjected must be a departure from the natural tax base rather than part of the definition of the tax base itself. The equivalence (asserted by Justice Thomas) between a direct money subsidy and the tax liability avoided by an institution (because it is part of the class of institutions that defines the relevant tax base by its exclusion) was tested and dispatched long ago by Professor Bittker in *Churches, Taxes and the Constitution,* 78 Yale L.J. 1285 (1969).]

sectarian institutions as there was no requirement that the schools be "public." Nevertheless, early Congresses found no problem with the provision of such neutral benefits.

Numerous other government benefits traditionally have been available to religious adherents on neutral terms. Several examples may be found in the work of early Congresses, including copyright protection for "the author and authors of any map, chart, book or books," and a privilege allowing "every printer of newspapers [to] send one paper to each and every other printer of newspapers within the United States, free of postage." Neither of these laws made any exclusion for the numerous authors or printers who manifested a belief in or about a deity.... The dissent identifies no evidence that the Framers intended to disable religious entities from participating on neutral terms in evenhanded government programs. The evidence that does exist points in the opposite direction and provides ample support for today's decision.

Justice Souter, [joined by Justices Stevens, Ginsburg, and Breyer], dissenting [in *Rosenberger v. Rector*]....

Using public funds for the direct subsidization of preaching the word is categorically forbidden under the Establishment Clause, and if the Clause was meant to accomplish nothing else, it was meant to bar this use of public money. Evidence on the subject antedates even the Bill of Rights itself, as may be seen in the writings of Madison, whose authority on questions about the meaning of the Establishment Clause is well settled.

Four years before the First Congress proposed the First Amendment, Madison gave his opinion on the legitimacy of using public funds for religious purposes, in the *Memorial and Remonstrance Against Religious Assessments*, which played the central role in ensuring the defeat of the Virginia tax assessment bill in 1786 and framed the debate upon which the Religion Clauses stand: "Who does not see that ... the same authority which can force a citizen to contribute three pence only of his property for the support of any one establishment, may force him to conform to any other establishment in all cases whatsoever?"

Madison wrote against a background in which nearly every Colony had exacted a tax for church support, the practice having become "so commonplace as to shock the freedom-loving colonials into a feeling of abhorrence." Madison's *Remonstrance* captured the colonists' "conviction that individual religious liberty could be achieved best under a government which was stripped of all power to tax, to support, or otherwise to assist any or all religions, or to interfere with the beliefs of any religious individual or group."

Their sentiment, as expressed by Madison in Virginia, led not only to the defeat of Virginia's tax assessment bill, but also directly to passage of the Virginia Bill for Establishing Religious Freedom, written by Thomas Jefferson. That bill's preamble declared that "to compel a man to furnish contributions of money for the propagation of opinions which he disbelieves, is sinful and tyrannical," and its text provided "[t]hat no man shall be compelled to frequent or support any religious worship, place, or ministry what-soever...." We have "previously recognized that the provisions of the First Amendment, in the drafting and adoption of which Madison and Jefferson played such leading roles, had the same objective and were intended to provide the same protection against governmental intrusion on religious liberty as the Virginia statute."

{Justice Thomas attempts to cast doubt on this accepted version of Establishment Clause history by reference to historical facts that are largely inapposite. As I have said elsewhere, individual Acts of Congress, especially when they are few and far between, scarcely serve as an authoritative guide to the meaning of the Religion Clauses, for "like other politicians, [members of the early Congresses] could raise constitutional ideals one day and turn their backs on them the next. [For example,] ... [t]en years after proposing the First Amendment, Congress passed the Alien and Sedition Acts, measures patently unconstitutional by modern standards. If the early Congress's political actions were determinative, and not merely relevant, evidence of constitutional meaning, we would have to gut our current First Amendment doctrine to make room for political censorship." The legislation cited by Justice Thomas, including the Northwest Ordinance, is no more dispositive than the Alien and Sedition Acts in interpreting the First Amendment....

Justice Thomas's references to Madison's actions as a legislator also provide little support for his cause. Justice Thomas seeks to draw a significant lesson out of the fact that, in seeking to disestablish the Anglican Church in Virginia in 1776, Madison did not inveigh against state funding of religious activities. That was not the task at hand, however. Madison was acting with the specific goal of eliminating the special privileges enjoyed by Virginia Anglicans, and he made no effort to lay out the broader views of church and state that came to bear in his drafting of the First Amendment some 13 years later. That Madison did not speak in more expansive terms than necessary in 1776 was hardly surprising for, as it was, his proposal was defeated by the Virginia Convention as having gone too far.

Similarly, the invocation of Madison's tenure on the congressional committee that approved funding for legislative chaplains provides no support for more general principles that run counter to settled Establishment Clause jurisprudence.... Madison, upon retirement, "insisted that 'it was not with my approbation, that the deviation from [the immunity of religion from civil jurisdiction] took place in Congs., when they appointed Chaplains, to be paid from the Natl. Treasury.'"

And when we turned our attention to deciding whether funding of legislative chaplains posed an establishment problem, we did not address the practice as one instance of a larger class of permissible government funding of religious activities. Instead, *Marsh* explicitly relied on the singular, 200-year pedigree of legislative chaplains, noting that "[t]his unique history" justified carving out an exception for the specific practice in question. Given that the decision upholding this practice was expressly limited to its facts, then, it would stand the Establishment Clause on its head to extract from it a broad rule permitting the funding of religious activities.}

{Justice Thomas suggests that Madison would have approved of the assessment bill if only it had satisfied the principle of evenhandedness. Nowhere in the *Remonstrance*, however, did Madison advance the view that Virginia should be able to provide financial support for religion as part of a generally available subsidy program.

Indeed, while Justice Thomas claims that the "funding provided by the Virginia assessment was to be extended only to Christian sects," it is clear that the bill was more general in scope than this. While the bill ... provided that each taxpayer could designate a religious society to which he wanted his levy paid, it would also have allowed a taxpayer to refuse to appropriate his levy to any religious society, in which case the legislature was to use these unappropriated sums to fund "seminaries of learning." ([C]ontrary to Justice Thomas's unsupported assertion, this portion of the bill was no less obligatory than any other[.])

While some of these seminaries undoubtedly would have been religious in character, others would not have been, as a seminary was generally understood at the time to be "any school, academy, college or university, in which young persons are instructed in the several branches of learning which may qualify them for their future employments." Not surprisingly, then, scholars have generally agreed that the bill would have provided funding for nonreligious schools [citations omitted—ed.].

It is beside the point that "there was no system of public education in Virginia until several decades after the assessment bill was proposed"; because the bill was never passed, the funds that it would have made available for secular, public schools never materialized. The fact that the bill, if passed, would have funded secular as well as religious instruction did nothing to soften Madison's opposition to it.

Nor is it fair to argue that Madison opposed the bill only because it treated religious groups unequally. In various paragraphs of the *Remonstrance*, Madison did complain about the bill's peculiar burdens and exemptions, but to identify this factor as the sole point of Madison's opposition to the bill is unfaithful to the *Remonstrance*'s text. Madison strongly inveighed against the proposed aid for religion for a host of reasons (the *Remonstrance* numbers 15 paragraphs, each containing at least one point in opposition), and crucial here is the fact that many of those reasons would have applied whether or not the state aid was being distributed equally among sects, and whether or not the aid was going to those sects in the context of an evenhanded government program. See, *e.g.,* Madison's *Remonstrance* ¶ 1 ("[I]n matters of Religion, no man's right is abridged by the institution of Civil Society, and ... Religion is wholly exempt from its cognizance"); ¶ 6 (arguing that state support of religion "is a contradiction to the Christian Religion itself; for every page of it disavows a dependence on the powers of this world"); ¶ 7 ("[E]xperience witnesseth that ecclesiastical establishments, instead of maintaining the purity and efficacy of Religion, have had a contrary operation").

Madison's objections were supplemented by numerous other petitions in opposition to the bill that likewise do not suggest that the lack of evenhandedness was its dispositive flaw. For example, the petition that received the largest number of signatories was motivated by the view that religion should only be supported voluntarily. Indeed, Madison's *Remonstrance* did not argue for a bill distributing aid to all sects and religions on an equal basis, and the outgrowth of the *Remonstrance* and the defeat of the Virginia assessment was not such a bill; rather, it was the Virginia Bill for Establishing Religious Freedom, which ... proscribed the use of tax dollars for religious purposes....}

e. *Does the Establishment Clause Allow Preferences for Religious Institutions or People Over Others?*

Justice Thomas, concurring [in *Rosenberger v. Rector*]....

Legal commentators have disagreed about the historical lesson to take from the Assessment Controversy. For some, the experience in Virginia is consistent with the view that the Framers saw the Establishment Clause simply as a prohibition on governmental preferences for some religious faiths over others. Other commentators have rejected this view, concluding that the Establishment Clause forbids not only government preferences for some religious sects over others, but also government preferences for religion over irreligion.

I find much to commend the former view. Madison's focus on the preferential nature of the assessment was not restricted to the fourth paragraph of the *Remonstrance* discussed above. The funding provided by the Virginia assessment was to be extended only to Christian sects, and the *Remonstrance* seized on this defect: "Who does not see that the same authority which can establish Christianity, in exclusion of all other Religions, may establish with the same ease any particular sect of Christians, in exclusion of all other Sects." Madison's *Remonstrance* ¶ 3.

In addition to the third and fourth paragraphs of the *Remonstrance*, "Madison's seventh, ninth, eleventh, and twelfth arguments all speak, in some way, to the same intolerance, bigotry, unenlightenment, and persecution that had generally resulted from previous exclusive religious establishments." The conclusion that Madison saw the principle of nonestablishment as barring governmental preferences for *particular* religious faiths seems especially clear in light of statements he made in the more relevant context of the House debates on the First Amendment. See *Wallace v. Jaffree,* 472 U.S. 38 (1985) (Rehnquist, J., dissenting) (Madison's views "as reflected by actions on the floor of the House in 1789, [indicate] that he saw the [First] Amendment as designed to prohibit the establishment of a national religion, and perhaps to prevent discrimination among sects," but not "as requiring neutrality on the part of government between religion and irreligion").

Moreover, even if more extreme notions of the separation of church and state can be attributed to Madison, many of them clearly stem from "arguments reflecting the concepts of natural law, natural rights, and the social contract between government and a civil society," rather than the principle of nonestablishment in the Constitution. In any event, the views of one man do not establish the original understanding of the First Amendment.

But resolution of this debate is not necessary to decide this case. Under any understanding of the Assessment Controversy, the history cited by the dissent cannot support the conclusion that the Establishment Clause "categorically condemn[s] state programs directly aiding religious activity" when that aid is part of a neutral program available to a wide array of beneficiaries....

Justice Souter, concurring in *Lee v. Weisman*....

When James Madison arrived at the First Congress with a series of proposals to amend the National Constitution, one of the provisions read that "[t]he civil rights of none shall be abridged on account of religious belief or worship, nor shall any national religion be established, nor shall the full and equal rights of conscience be in any manner, or on any pretext, infringed."

Madison's language did not last long. It was sent to a Select Committee of the House, which, without explanation, changed it to read that "no religion shall be established by law, nor shall the equal rights of conscience be infringed." Thence the proposal went to the Committee of the Whole, which was in turn dissatisfied with the Select Committee's language and adopted an alternative proposed by Samuel Livermore of New Hampshire: "Congress shall make no laws touching religion, or infringing the rights of conscience." Livermore's proposal would have forbidden laws having anything to do with religion and was thus not only far broader than Madison's version, but broader even than the scope of the Establishment Clause as we now understand it.

The House rewrote the amendment once more before sending it to the Senate, this time adopting, without recorded debate, language derived from a proposal by Fisher Ames of Massachusetts: "Congress shall make no law establishing Religion, or prohibiting the free exercise thereof, nor shall the rights of conscience be infringed." Perhaps, on further reflection, the Representatives had thought Livermore's proposal too expansive, or perhaps ... they had simply worried that his language would not "satisfy the demands of those who wanted something said specifically against establishments of religion." We do not know; what we do know is that the House rejected the Select Committee's version, which arguably ensured only that "no religion" enjoyed an official preference over others, and deliberately chose instead a prohibition extending to laws establishing "religion" in general.

The sequence of the Senate's treatment of this House proposal, and the House's response to the Senate, confirm that the Framers meant the Establishment Clause's prohibition to encompass nonpreferential aid to religion. In September 1789, the Senate considered a number of provisions that would have permitted such aid, and ultimately it adopted one of them.

First, it briefly entertained this language: "Congress shall make no law establishing One Religious Sect or Society in preference to others, nor shall the rights of conscience be infringed." After rejecting two minor amendments to that proposal, the Senate dropped it altogether and chose a provision identical to the House's proposal, but without the clause protecting the "rights of conscience." With no record of the Senate debates, we cannot know what prompted these changes, but the record does tell us that, six days later, the Senate went half circle and adopted its narrowest language yet: "Congress shall make no law establishing articles of faith or a mode of worship, or prohibiting the free exercise of religion." The Senate sent this proposal to the House along with its versions of the other constitutional amendments proposed.

Though it accepted much of the Senate's work on the Bill of Rights, the House rejected the Senate's version of the Establishment Clause and called for a joint conference committee, to which the Senate agreed. The House conferees ultimately won out, persuading the Senate to accept this as the final text of the Religion Clauses: "Congress shall make no law respecting an establishment of religion, or prohibiting the free exercise thereof." What is remarkable is that, unlike the earliest House drafts or the final Senate proposal, the prevailing language is not limited to laws respecting an establishment of "a religion," "a national religion," "one religious sect," or specific "articles of faith." The Framers repeatedly considered and deliberately rejected such narrow language and instead extended their prohibition to state support for "religion" in general.

Implicit in their choice is the distinction between preferential and nonpreferential establishments, which the weight of evidence suggests the Framers appreciated. Of particular note, the Framers were vividly familiar with efforts in the Colonies and, later, the States to impose general, nondenominational assessments and other incidents of ostensibly ecumenical establishments.

{Some commentators have suggested that by targeting laws respecting "an" establishment of religion, the Framers adopted the very nonpreferentialist position whose much clearer articulation they repeatedly rejected. Yet the indefinite article before the word "establishment" is better seen as evidence that the Clause forbids any kind of establishment, including a nonpreferential one. If the Framers had wished, for some reason, to use the indefinite term to achieve a narrow meaning for the Clause, they could far more aptly have placed it before the word "religion."}

The Virginia statute for religious freedom, written by Jefferson and sponsored by Madison, captured the separationist response to such measures. Condemning all establishments, however nonpreferentialist, the statute broadly guaranteed that "no man shall be compelled to frequent or support any religious worship, place, or ministry whatsoever," including his own. Forcing a citizen to support even his own church would, among other things, deny "the ministry those temporary rewards, which proceeding from an approbation of their personal conduct, are an additional incitement to earnest and unremitting labours for the instruction of mankind." In general, Madison later added, "religion & Govt. will both exist in greater purity, the less they are mixed together."

What we thus know of the Framers' experience underscores the observation of one prominent commentator, that confining the Establishment Clause to a prohibition on preferential aid "requires a premise that the Framers were extraordinarily bad drafters—that they believed one thing but adopted language that said something substantially different, and that they did so after repeatedly attending to the choice of language." We must presume, since there is no conclusive evidence to the contrary, that the Framers embraced the significance of their textual judgment. Thus, on balance, history neither contradicts nor warrants reconsideration of the settled principle that the Establishment Clause forbids support for religion in general no less than support for one religion or some.

{In his dissent in *Wallace v. Jaffree*, 472 U.S. 38 (1985), the Chief Justice rested his nonpreferentialist interpretation partly on the post-ratification actions of the early National Government. Aside from the willingness of some (but not all) early Presidents to issue ceremonial religious proclamations, which were at worst trivial breaches of the Establishment Clause, he cited such seemingly preferential aid as a treaty provision, signed by Jefferson, authorizing federal subsidization of a Roman Catholic priest and church for the Kaskaskia Indians. But this proves too much, for if the Establishment Clause permits a special appropriation of tax money for the religious activities of a particular sect, it forbids virtually nothing. Although evidence of historical practice can indeed furnish valuable aid in the interpretation of contemporary language, acts like the one in question prove only that public officials, no matter when they serve, can turn a blind eye to constitutional principle.}

f.   Policy—Original Meaning, see p. 798

B. THE NO DELEGATION TO RELIGIOUS INSTITUTIONS PRINCIPLE

a.   Summary

Rule: The government may not delegate certain kinds of government power to religious institutions. *Larkin v. Grendel's Den* (1982) (p. 957).

— It's not clear what kinds of government power this covers.

— It's not clear whether this would apply to laws granting power equally to nonreligious and religious decisionmakers. Say, for instance, that any school—public, private secular, or religious—could veto a neighbor's liquor license application. Would schools run by religious entities have to be denied this ability? Cf. *Board of Ed. of Kiryas Joel Village School Dist. v. Grumet,* 512 U.S. 687, 699 (1994) (plurality) ("the difference lies in the distinction between a government's purposeful delegation on the basis of religion and a delegation on principles neutral to religion"). *Compare Myers v. State,* 714 N.E.2d 276 (Ind. App. 1999) (finding no violation when state law let private colleges, including religious ones, set up their own police departments, though relying on various factors besides the law's religious neutrality) *with State v. Pendleton,* 339 N.C. 379 (1994) (4-3 vote) (reaching the opposite conclusion).

— This principle bars the exercise of government power by religious *entities,* not by people who happen to be religious or by political communities who happen to be dominated by members of a particular religious denomination. Politicians and voters are entitled to enact their own religiously based beliefs into law, so long as the beliefs relate to secular topics (such as civil rights, abortion funding, polygamy, slavery, and the like) rather than to purely religious topics (such as prayer or idol worship). See Part XI.B.3.a (p. 845).

b. Problem: Copyright Protection

Under the Copyright Act, the owner of a copyrighted work has the right to stop others from making copies of the work (with exceptions that we can assume are inapplicable here). Copyright owners may refuse permission for any reason: A copyright is property, and it's up to the property owner to decide who will be allowed to use the property and who won't be.

The Worldwide Church of God owns the copyright in *Mystery of the Ages,* written by the WCG's founder, Herbert Armstrong. The WCG inherited the copyright from Armstrong, but after his death the WCG decided that the work no longer represented the church's views, and stopped publishing it. A splinter group, the Philadelphia Church of God, then decided to republish the book itself, and distribute it for free. WCG sues PCG for copyright infringement, asking for damages and for an injunction blocking future copying and publication.

Would allowing the lawsuit by WCG violates the *Larkin v. Grendel's Den* principle? Cf. *Worldwide Church of God v. Philadelphia Church of God,* 227 F.3d 1110 (9th Cir. 2000).

c. Larkin v. Grendel's Den, Inc., 459 U.S. 116 (1982)

Chief Justice Burger delivered the opinion of the Court....

[A.] Appellee operates a restaurant located in the Harvard Square area of Cambridge, Mass. The Holy Cross Armenian Catholic Parish is located adjacent to the restaurant; the back walls of the two buildings are ten feet apart. In 1977, appellee applied to the Cambridge License Commission for approval of an alcoholic beverages license for the restaurant.

Section 16C of Chapter 138 of the Massachusetts General Laws provides: "Premises ... located within a radius of five hundred feet of a church or [elementary or secondary school, public or private,] shall not be licensed for the sale of alcoholic beverages if the governing body of such church or school files written objection thereto." Holy Cross Church objected to appellee's application, expressing concern over "having so many licenses *so* near." {[T]here were [25] liquor licensees [at the time] in Harvard Square and within a 500-foot radius of Holy Cross Church ....} The License Commission voted to deny the application, citing only the objection of Holy Cross Church ....

[B.] Appellants contend that the State may ... enforce what it describes as a "zoning" law in order to shield schools and places of divine worship from the presence nearby of liquor-dispensing establishments [and] ... that a zone of protection around churches and schools is essential to protect diverse centers of spiritual, educational, and cultural enrichment....

However, § 16C is not simply a legislative exercise of zoning power.... § 16C delegates to private, nongovernmental entities power to veto certain liquor license applications. This is a power ordinarily vested in agencies of government.... We need not decide whether, or upon what conditions, such power may ever be delegated to nongovernmental entities; here, of two classes of institutions to which the legislature has delegated this important decisionmaking power, one is secular, but one is religious. Under these circumstances, the deference normally due a legislative zoning judgment is not merited....

[C.] The purpose of § 16C ... is to "protec[t] spiritual, cultural, and educational centers from the 'hurly-burly' associated with liquor outlets." There can be little doubt that this embraces valid secular legislative purposes. However, these valid secular objectives can be readily accomplished by other means—either through an absolute legislative ban on liquor outlets within reasonable prescribed distances from churches, schools, hospitals and like institutions, or by ensuring a hearing for the views of affected institutions at licensing proceedings where, without question, such views would be entitled to substantial weight.

Appellants argue that § 16C has only a remote and incidental effect on the advancement of religion.... [But §] 16C gives churches the right to determine whether a particular applicant will be granted a liquor license, or even which one of several competing applicants will receive a license.

The churches' power under the statute is standardless, calling for no reasons, findings, or reasoned conclusions. That power may therefore be used by churches to promote goals beyond insulating the church from undesirable neighbors; it could be employed for explicitly religious goals, for example, favoring liquor licenses for members of that congregation or adherents of that faith. We can assume that churches would act in good faith in their exercise of the statutory power, yet § 16C does not by its terms require that churches' power be used in a religiously neutral way. "[T]he potential for conflict inheres in the situation," and appellants have not suggested any "effective means of guaranteeing" that the delegated power "will be used exclusively for secular, neutral, and nonideological purposes."

In addition, the mere appearance of a joint exercise of legislative authority by Church and State provides a significant symbolic benefit to religion in the minds of some by reason of the power conferred. It does not strain our prior holdings to say that the statute can be seen as having a "primary" and "principal" effect of advancing religion.

Turning to the third phase of the inquiry called for by *Lemon v. Kurtz-man,* ... [t]his statute enmeshes churches in the exercise of substantial governmental powers contrary to our consistent interpretation of the Establishment Clause.... [T]he core rationale underlying the Establishment Clause is preventing "a fusion of governmental and religious functions." {At the time of the Revolution, Americans feared not only a denial of religious freedom, but the danger of political oppression through a union of civil and ecclesiastical control. In 18th-century England, such a union of civil and ecclesiastical power was reflected in legal arrangements granting church officials substantial control over various occupations, including the liquor trade.} The Framers did not set up a system of government in which important, discretionary governmental powers would be delegated to or shared with religious institutions.

Section 16C substitutes the unilateral and absolute power of a church for the reasoned decisionmaking of a public legislative body acting on evidence and guided by standards, on issues with significant economic and political implications. The challenged statute thus enmeshes churches in the processes of government and creates the danger of "[p]olitical fragmentation and divisiveness along religious lines," *Lemon*. Ordinary human experience and a long line of cases teach that few entanglements could be more offensive to the spirit of the Constitution....

Justice Rehnquist, dissenting....

In its original form, § 16C imposed a flat ban on the grant of an alcoholic beverages license to any establishment located within 500 feet of a church or a school[, which the majority concedes would be valid].... Over time, the legislature found that it could meet its goal of protecting people engaged in religious activities from liquor-related disruption with a less absolute prohibition. Rather than set out elaborate formulae ..., the legislature settled on the simple expedient of asking churches to object if a proposed liquor outlet would disturb them.... Nothing in the Court's opinion persuades me why the more rigid prohibition would be constitutional, but the more flexible not....

Section 16C does not sponsor or subsidize any religious group or activity. It does not encourage, much less compel, anyone to participate in religious activities or to support religious institutions. To say that it "advances" religion is to strain at the meaning of that word.

The Court states that § 16C "advances" religion because there is no guarantee that objections will be made "in a religiously neutral way." ... [But t]he concededly legitimate purpose of the statute is to protect citizens engaging in religious and educational activities from the incompatible activities of liquor outlets and their patrons. The only way to decide whether these activities are incompatible with one another in the case of a church is to ask whether the activities of liquor outlets and their patrons may interfere with religious activity; this question cannot, in any meaningful sense, be "religiously neutral."

In this sense, the flat ban of the original § 16C is no different from the present version. Whether the ban is unconditional or may be invoked only at the behest of a particular church, it is not "religiously neutral" so long as it enables a church to defeat the issuance of a liquor license when a similarly situated bank could not do the same. The State does not, in my opinion, "advance" religion by making provision for those who wish to engage in religious activities, as well as those who wish to engage in educational activities, to be unmolested by activities at a neighboring bar or tavern that have historically been thought incompatible.

The Court is apparently concerned for fear that churches might object to the issuance of a license for "explicitly religious" reasons, such as "favoring liquor licenses for members of that congregation or adherents of that faith." If a church were to seek to advance the interests of its members [through the liquor license denial process], there would be an occasion to determine whether it had violated any right of an unsuccessful applicant for a liquor license. But our ability to discern a risk of such abuse does not render § 16C violative of the Establishment Clause. The State can constitutionally protect churches from liquor for the same reasons it can protect them from fire, noise, and other harm....

XIII. COMPELLED ACCOMMODATION OF RELIGION?

A. COMPELLED EXEMPTIONS FOR RELIGIOUS OBSERVERS

1. GENERALLY

a. The Main Approaches

When should religious objectors get exemptions from generally applicable laws? Should a landlady who has religious objections to renting to unmarried couples be exempted from antidiscrimination law? Should Native American Church members, whose religion views peyote use as a sacrament, be exempted from drug laws? Should Rastafarians, who think the same as to marijuana? Should a mother who feels a religious duty not to testify against her daughter be exempted from the legal duty to testify?

Equally importantly, who should decide these matters? The debate for over a century has been between two primary models:

1. The *Statutory Exemption Model*, under which the legislature decides. For instance, Congress has long exempted some conscientious objectors from the military draft. Congress and many states have exempted some peyote worshippers from drug laws. During Prohibition, Congress exempted sacramental wine users from the alcohol ban.

On the other hand, legislatures have generally refused to accommodate other exemption requests, such as requests for religious exemptions from marijuana laws, from certain kinds of antidiscrimination laws, and the like. Legislatures make these decisions based on their own moral and pragmatic judgments about the importance of the law and about the degree to which the exemption undermines the law.

2. The *Constitutional Exemption Model*, under which the courts may grant, as a matter of constitutional law, certain exemptions even when the legislature has declined to do so. Thus, a court might say to a legislature "Even if you choose not to give religious objectors an exemption (for instance, from a requirement that they send their 14-year-old children to school), the Free Exercise Clause requires you to provide such an exemption." This is also known as the "compelled exemption" model, because it takes the view that the Constitution compels such exemptions rather than leaving them to the legislature's discretion.

Of course, courts wouldn't grant *all* such religious exemption requests. Involuntary human sacrifices, for instance, wouldn't be exempted from murder law. Courts would have to craft a test—generally strict scrutiny—to determine whether an exemption should indeed be granted, and use their own moral and pragmatic judgment in applying this test.

b. A Timetable of How the Debate Has Generally Progressed

1879: The U.S. Supreme Court adopted the statutory exemption regime by holding that the Free Exercise Clause doesn't entitle people to religious exemptions from generally applicable laws, for instance from polygamy laws applied against Mormons. *Reynolds v. U.S.* (1879) (p. 999). State courts also generally took this view, before and after 1879, as to their state constitutions' religious freedom provisions.

1940: The Court began to hint that the Free Exercise Clause might require religious exemptions (see *Cantwell v. Connecticut*, 310 U.S. 296 (1940); *Prince v. Massachusetts* (1944) (p. 969)), but sometimes denied this, *e.g.*, *Chaplinsky v. New Hampshire*, 315 U.S. 568 (1942). From 1940 to 1963, the Court generally rejected religious exemption requests except in religious speech cases (which also relied on the Free Speech Clause).

1963: In *Sherbert v. Verner* (p. 973), the Court adopted the constitutional exemption model, under which government actions that burden people's religious exercise must pass strict scrutiny.

1963-90: The Court applied the constitutional exemption model, but rejected most exemption requests that came before it; lower courts did likewise. Strict scrutiny here proved far weaker than the strict scrutiny applied to content-based speech restrictions or race classifications.

1990: In *Employment Division v. Smith* (p. 992), the Court generally rejected the constitutional exemption model and generally returned to the statutory exemption model.

1993: Congress enacted the Religious Freedom Restoration Act (RFRA) (p. 1016), which purported to restore the constitutional exemption model.

1997: In *City of Boerne v. Flores* (p. 1048), the Court held that RFRA as applied to *state and local* governments exceeded Congress's power.

1998-now: Many states enacted state-level RFRAs, thus requiring courts to give exemptions from state and local government action as a matter of state law. (Two of these statutes were enacted in 1993, but the others all followed *City of Boerne*.) Some state courts also interpreted their state constitutions as following the constitutional exemption model (as in *Sherbert* and *Yoder*). The Supreme Court has applied the federal RFRA quite forcefully, apparently more so than the Free Exercise Clause was applied in 1963-90; decisions under state RFRAs has been rare.

2000: Congress enacted the Religious Land Use and Institutionalized Persons Act (p. 1018), which generally applies RFRA-like standards to state and local decisions involving land use (chiefly resting on Congress's Commerce Clause power) and inmates in institutions that get federal funds (resting on Congress's Spending Clause power).

c. The Current Rules

1. The Free Exercise Clause doesn't compel exemptions, except in the few kinds of situations discussed below.

2. The federal RFRA compels federal government officials to give religious exemptions from federal government action, unless the government action passes strict scrutiny.

3. State and local land use decisions and decisions involving inmates in institutions that get federal funds are subject to RLUIPA, as well as any possible state RFRAs and state constitutional exemption regimes.

4. The law in other states varies, depending on (a) whether there's a state RFRA, and on (b) whether the state courts have interpreted the state constitution as requiring strict scrutiny of exemption claims, as requiring intermediate scrutiny, or as requiring no scrutiny (and not all state courts have rendered definitive decisions on that).

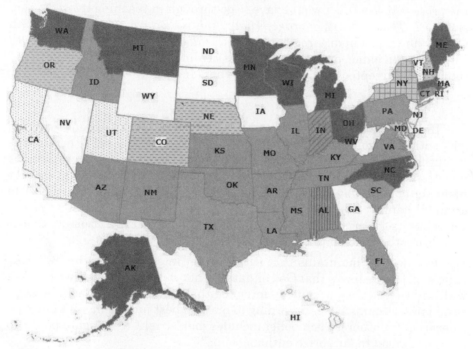

■ Strict scrutiny under state const. (AK, MA, ME, MI, MN, MT, NC, OH, WA, WI)

▨ Strict scrutiny under state RFRA (AR, AZ, CT, FL, ID, IL, KS, KY, LA, MO, MS, NM, OK, PA, RI, SC, TN, TX, VA)

▨ Strict scrutiny under both state const. and state RFRA (IN)

▥ Strict scrutiny under express state RFRA const. amendment (AL)

□ No decision on state const.; no RFRA (DE, GA, IA, ND, NJ, NV, SD, WV, WY)

▦ Courts noted uncertainty under state const.; no RFRA (CA, HI, UT, VT)

▦ Weak intermediate scrutiny under state const.; no RFRA (NY)

▦ No exemptions under state const.; no state RFRA (CO, MD, NE, NH, OR)

2. THE CONSTITUTIONALLY COMPELLED EXEMPTIONS REGIME

a. *Problem: Marital Status Discrimination in Housing*

Joyce Baker, an Anchorage landlady, believes it is sinful to rent apartments to unmarried couples. Premarital intercourse, she reasons, is fornication, and by renting to such couples (who she thinks are quite likely, even if not certain, to be engaging in premarital intercourse), she would be aiding such fornication and thus sinning herself. But state law bars marital status discrimination in housing, so she is fined for engaging in such discrimination and enjoined from engaging in it in the future.

What should the result be under *Sherbert/Yoder*? Does this result—and the process that a court would have to go through in reaching it—seem sensible? Cf. *Thomas v. Anchorage Equal Rights Comm'n*, 165 F.3d 692 (9th Cir. 1999) (2-1 opinion), *rev'd on procedural grounds*, 220 F.3d 1134 (9th Cir. 2000) (en banc), one of several cases dealing with such objections; some courts have accepted such claims and others have not.

b. *Problem: Assisted Suicide*

"[Robert] Sanderson is over eighty years old, and wishes to provide his wife with a durable medical power of attorney authorizing her to end his life by euthanasia, provided that two physicians agree his medical condition is hopeless. He filed this action seeking a declaratory judgment that neither his wife, nor the physician administering euthanasia, would be subject to criminal liability ... under [a Colorado] statute [that] provides that: 'A person commits the crime of manslaughter if: Such person intentionally causes or aids another person to commit suicide.' ...

"[Sanderson] maintains that [the statute] interferes with his religious beliefs .... [He] believes that God or nature endowed human kind with a 'free will' and that ... God, or nature, intended that the free will of man be exercised in all circumstances according to his own best judgment with due consideration for others. Such belief includes man's right to delegate power to another person to authorize euthanasia ...."

Sanderson v. People, 12 P.3d 851 (Colo. App. 2000); see also, *e.g.*, Winthrop Drake Thies, *Shall the Dying Be Denied Their Religious Freedom?*, Newark Star-Ledger, Feb. 6, 1997, at 26 (making such an argument); Amicus Brief of 36 Religious Organizations, Leaders, and Scholars, *Washington v. Glucksberg*, 521 U.S. 702 (1997) (likewise).

What should the result be under *Sherbert/Yoder*? What if Sanderson's wife claimed she felt a religious obligation to be the merciful Good Samaritan and ease Sanderson's suffering by assisting his suicide, if Sanderson asked for this help? Do these results—and the processes that a court would have to go through in reaching them—seem sensible?

Note that the Court in *Washington v. Glucksberg* held that bans on assisted suicide are subject only to rational basis scrutiny under substantive due process law, and pass this rational basis scrutiny.

c. Problem: Compelled Testimony in Civil Case

Jennifer Rothman is a CEO and the major shareholder of a company; her father, Eric Liebeler, is an occasional business consultant for the company. After a bad quarter, some disgruntled shareholders sue the company and Jennifer personally, claiming various acts of mismanagement and fraud; and the SEC begins a similar investigation which might lead to criminal charges. Eric is subpoenaed in the civil lawsuit and in the SEC investigation, but refuses to testify on the grounds that his religion—orthodox Judaism, as he sincerely understands it—prohibits parents from testifying against their children.

What should the result be under *Sherbert/Yoder*? Does this result—and the process that a court would have to go through in reaching it—seem sensible? Compare *In re The Grand Jury Empaneling of the Special Grand Jury*, 171 F.3d 826 (3d Cir. 1999), and *In re Doe*, 842 F.2d 244 (10th Cir. 1988) with *In re Greenberg*, 11 Fed. R. Evid. Serv. 579 (D. Conn. 1982), and *In re The Grand Jury Empaneling*, 171 F.3d at 837 (McKee, J., dissenting); cf. *Grossberg's Parents Ask to Keep Talks Confidential*, Newark Star-Ledger, Nov. 26, 1997, at 43:

> The parents of Amy Grossberg, the college student accused of killing her newborn in Delaware ... argued in court papers that talks with their daughter should be kept secret and that it is a violation of their right to the free exercise of religion [for prosecutors] to force them to divulge information. Rabbi Joel Roth, a legal expert at the Jewish Theological Seminary in New York City, confirmed yesterday he wrote an affidavit for the Grossbergs, stating that "under Jewish law, a mother and/or a father are not allowed to give testimony against their child in any legal proceeding."

d. Strict Scrutiny

Under the *Sherbert/Yoder* regime, the government had to grant exemptions to religious objectors who were substantially burdened by a generally applicable law, unless denying the exemption was (1) the "least restrictive means" (2) of serving "a compelling government interest." This strict scrutiny test remains under state RFRAs, the federal RFRA as applied to federal laws, RLUIPA (p. 1018), and the "hybrid rights" and "individualized exemption" exceptions to *Smith* (p. 992).

Strict scrutiny also appears in religious discrimination law (see Part XI.A.1.a, p. 729), free speech law (see Part III.A, p. 270), equal protection law, substantive due process law, and some other fields. In many fields, such strict scrutiny has been "strict in theory, fatal in fact." During the *Sherbert/Yoder* era, it was said to be "strict in theory, feeble in fact" (see p. 984), but the Supreme Court's RFRA cases (*O Centro*, *Hobby Lobby*, and *Holt*) seem to have read strict scrutiny fairly strictly. Here's a brief summary of what strict scrutiny has meant in accommodation cases:

i. Compelling Interest

The government must have a compelling interest justifying denying the exemption. Think of this as a normative judgment about the ends rather than the means of the legislation: Is the government concern at stake important enough that the exemption should be denied?

a. The Court has held that the government has a compelling interest in:

   i.   "maintaining a fair system for determining 'who [is compelled to serve in the military] when not all serve,'" *Gillette v. United States* (1971) (p. 976);

   ii. "maintaining a sound tax system," free of "myriad exceptions flowing from a wide variety of religious beliefs," *United States v. Lee* (1982) (p. 984); *Hernandez v. Commissioner*, 490 U.S. 680, 699-700 (1989) (applying this to income taxes);

   iii. "eradicating racial discrimination in education," *Bob Jones Univ. v. United States* (1983) (p. 986), though the Court also described this as the narrower interest in "denying *public support* to racial discrimination in education," *id.* (emphasis added);

   iv. "providing an equal opportunity to participate in the workforce without regard to race," *Burwell v. Hobby Lobby Stores, Inc.* (2014) (p. 1035).

   iv. protecting children from "crippling effects of child employment," *Prince v. Massachusetts* (1944) (p. 969) (*Prince* was decided before the strict scrutiny framework was established, but later cases, such as *Bob Jones*, have fit *Prince* into that framework);

   vi. "preventing fraud and abuse in the welfare system," *Bowen v. Roy*, 476 U.S. 693 (1986) (O'Connor, J., concurring, joined by Brennan and Marshall, JJ.);

   vii. preserving prison security, for instance "staunching the flow of contraband into and within" prisons and assuring "quick and reliable identification of prisoners," *Holt v. Hobbs* (2015) (p. 1044).

b. The Court has held that there's no compelling interest in

   i.   requiring children to have two years of high school education from age 14 to 16, *Wisconsin v. Yoder* (1972) (p. 979).

c. One can also:

   i.   argue by analogy to the compelling interest holdings in religious discrimination cases (see p. 729) and in free speech cases (see p. 271), though it's not clear whether such arguments will prevail;

   ii. make common-sense arguments about why a particular interest is or is not very important;

   iii. argue by counterexample ("if this interest were compelling, then look at the religious exemptions that would be denied; but these exemptions must be granted, so the interest can't be compelling").

d. "In applying RFRA 'courts must take adequate account of the burdens a requested accommodation may impose on nonbeneficiaries.' That consideration will often inform the analysis of the Government's compelling interest and the availability of a less restrictive means of advancing that interest." *Hobby Lobby*.

— But the interest in "requir[ing] the religious adherent to confer a benefit on third parties" is not always compelling. *Id.*

ii. Least Restrictive Means

The least restrictive means prong is essentially an empirical inquiry into *whether denying the exemption is necessary to serve the interest.* If there's some way of granting an exemption and yet accomplishing the government's goal, then there's no real need to interfere with the religious practice, so the exemption must be granted. *Hobby Lobby* (2014) (p. 1035) has described this as an "exceptionally demanding" standard.

a. Thus, if granting the exemption *wouldn't materially undermine the interest*, the denial wouldn't be the least restrictive means of serving the interest—enforcing the law against others but exempting the religious objectors would be less restrictive.

— For instance, *Sherbert v. Verner* (1963) (p. 973) reasoned that "[T]here is no proof whatever" "that the filing of fraudulent claims by unscrupulous claimants feigning religious objections to Saturday work" will "dilute the unemployment compensation fund" and "hinder the scheduling by employers of necessary Saturday work." Granting the exemption wouldn't undermine the government interests.

— Similarly, *Yoder* reasoned that granting the Amish an exemption from the requirements of "compulsory education for a year or two beyond the eighth grade" wouldn't undermine the true "goal of education," which should be "viewed as the preparation of the child for life in the separated agrarian community that is the keystone of the Amish faith." Granting an exemption also wouldn't undermine the goal of equipping children who may eventually leave the Amish religion for life outside the Amish community: "[W]e are unwilling to assume that persons possessing [the] valuable vocational skills and habits [taught by the Amish] are doomed to become burdens on society should they determine to leave the Amish faith, nor is there any basis in the record to warrant a finding that an additional one or two years of formal school education beyond the eighth grade would serve to eliminate any such problem that might exist."

— Likewise, Justices Brennan, White, Marshall, Blackmun, and O'Connor in *Bowen v. Roy* concluded that the government had to exempt objecting welfare and food stamp applicants from having to provide a social security number. "[V]ague allegations of administrative inconvenience and harm to the public fisc that are wholly unsubstantiated by the record"— "unanchored anxieties of the welfare bureaucracy"—weren't enough to show that the exemption would undermine the government interest in preventing fraud.

— If most jurisdictions allow religious exemptions, that is a strong reason to suspect that granting an exemption wouldn't materially undermine the government interest. *Holt v. Hobbs*.

b. Similarly, if there are *less restrictive alternatives* through which the government may largely or entirely grant the exemption but still serve the interest, the denial wouldn't be the least restrictive means of serving the interest:

— "[E]ven if the possibility of spurious claims did threaten to dilute the fund and disrupt the scheduling of work [*i.e.*, did jeopardize the compelling interest], it would plainly be incumbent upon the appellees to demonstrate that no alternative forms of regulation would combat such abuses without infringing First Amendment rights." *Sherbert v. Verner.*

— Likewise, in *Burwell v. Hobby Lobby Stores*, the Court concluded that, when the government could have assured that all employees had access to certain contraceptives by either (i) paying for those contraceptives itself, or (ii) ordering insurance companies to pay for the contraceptives.

c. Yet if the only alternatives are too likely to lead to erroneous decisions, to be otherwise ineffective in serving the government interest, or to jeopardize other compelling government interests, then those alternatives might not count. Denying the exemption would be seen as the least restrictive means *of serving the interest*, and thus constitutional, because the alternatives wouldn't adequately serve the interest:

— "To view the problem of fairness and evenhanded decisionmaking, in the present context, as merely a commonplace chore of weeding out 'spurious claims,' is to minimize substantial difficulties of real concern to a responsible legislative body.... [W]e must also recognize that 'sincerity' is a concept that can bear only so much adjudicative weight." *Gillette.*

— "[E]xemption of objectors to particular wars would weaken the resolve of those who otherwise would feel themselves bound to serve despite personal cost, uneasiness at the prospect of violence, or even serious moral reservations or policy objections concerning the particular conflict." *Id.*

— "[I]t would be difficult to accommodate the comprehensive social security system with myriad exceptions flowing from a wide variety of religious beliefs.... There is no principled way ..., for purposes of this case, to distinguish between general taxes and those imposed under the Social Security Act. If, for example, a religious adherent believes war is a sin, and if a certain percentage of the federal budget can be identified as devoted to war-related activities, such individuals would have a similarly valid claim to be exempt from paying that percentage of the income tax. The tax system could not function if denominations were allowed to challenge the tax system because tax payments were spent in a manner that violates their religious belief." *Lee.*

— "The interests asserted by petitioners cannot be accommodated with [the] compelling governmental interest [of eradicating race discrimination in education]; and no 'less restrictive means' are available to achieve the governmental interest." *Bob Jones.*

iii. No Underinclusiveness

In other strict scrutiny contexts, the Court has held that laws fail strict scrutiny when they're "underinclusive," which is to say when they fail to cover pretty much all the conduct that jeopardizes the interest. See pp. 274 (free speech) and 731 (religious discrimination).

— The Court's *Sherbert/Yoder*-era religious accommodation cases have not engaged in this inquiry, even though many of the laws involved—draft laws, tax laws, even race discrimination bans—were underinclusive with respect to the government interests.

— But *Holt v. Hobbs* did consider the law's underinclusiveness, at least to the extent it undermines the government's argument that an exemption would interfere too much with the government interest. "[T]he Department failed to establish why the risk that a prisoner will shave a ½-inch beard to disguise himself is so great that ½-inch beards cannot be allowed, even though prisoners are allowed to grow mustaches, head hair, or ¼-inch beards for medical reasons. All of these could also be shaved off at a moment's notice, but the Department apparently does not think that this possibility raises a serious security concern."

— And *Holt* also suggested that a law's underinclusiveness is an independent reason to grant religious exemptions from the law, even apart from the least restrictive analysis; at least this is so when the religious activity that is forbidden and the secular activity that is allowed endanger the government interest to a similar degree: "[T]he Department has [also] not adequately demonstrated why its grooming policy is substantially underinclusive in at least two respects. Although the Department denied petitioner's request to grow a ½-inch beard, it permits prisoners with a dermatological condition to grow ¼-inch beards. The Department does this even though both beards pose similar risks." "[T]he Department has failed to establish ... that a ¼-inch difference in beard length poses a meaningful increase in security risk."

iv. No Overinclusiveness.

In free speech and religious discrimination strict scrutiny cases, the Court often talks about whether the law is overinclusive, which is to say, whether the law applies to a substantial amount of conduct that doesn't implicate the government interest. But in religious accommodation cases, the overinclusiveness analysis is identical to the advancement-of-the-interest analysis, so it isn't discussed separately here.

e. *Prince v. Massachusetts, 321 U.S. 158 (1944)*

[*Prince* was a pre-*Sherbert* case, and thus didn't use the strict scrutiny framework; but it was cited favorably during the *Sherbert* era, with the strong suggestion that the *Prince* Court reached the right result.—ed.]

Justice Rutledge delivered the opinion of the Court....

[A.] Sarah Prince appeals from convictions for violating Massachusetts' child labor law ["No boy under twelve and no girl under eighteen shall ...

offer for sale any ... articles of merchandise of any description, or exercise ... any ... trade, in any street or public place."], by acts said to be a rightful exercise of her religious convictions. When the offenses were committed she was the aunt and custodian of Betty M. Simmons, a girl nine years of age.... Mrs. Prince ... is [also] the mother of two young sons [whose conduct was not the basis of this prosecution—ed.].... [The sons, Betty, and Mrs. Prince] are Jehovah's Witnesses and both Mrs. Prince and Betty testified they were ordained ministers.

[Mrs. Prince] was accustomed to go each week on the streets of Brockton to distribute "Watchtower" and "Consolation," according to the usual plan. {A common feature is that specified small sums are generally asked and received but the publications may be had without the payment if so desired.} She had permitted the children to engage in this activity previously .... [On the evening of December 18, 1941], as Mrs. Prince was preparing to leave her home, the children asked to go. She at first refused. Childlike, they resorted to tears and, motherlike, she yielded.

Arriving downtown, Mrs. Prince permitted the children "to engage in the preaching work with her upon the sidewalks." ... [Betty] and Mrs. Prince took positions about twenty feet apart near a street intersection. Betty held up in her hand, for passers-by to see, copies of "Watch Tower" and "Consolation." From her shoulder hung the usual canvas magazine bag, on which was printed: "Watchtower and Consolation 5¢ per copy."

No one accepted a copy from Betty that evening and she received no money. Nor did her aunt. But on other occasions, Betty had received funds and given out copies.... Betty believed it was her religious duty to perform this work and failure would bring condemnation "to everlasting destruction at Armageddon." ...

[B.] Appellant does not stand on freedom of the press ... [but] rests squarely on [her and Betty's] freedom of religion ... [and] a claim of parental right as secured by the due process clause .... Cf. *Meyer v. Nebraska,* 262 U.S. 390 (1923).... Thus, two claimed liberties are at stake. One is the parent's, to bring up the child in the way he should go, which for appellant means to teach him the tenets and the practices of their faith. The other freedom is the child's, to observe these; and among them is "to preach the gospel ... by public distribution" of "Watchtower" and "Consolation," in conformity with the scripture: "A little child shall lead them." ...

The rights of children to exercise their religion, and of parents to give them religious training and to encourage them in the practice of religious belief, ... have had recognition here .... It is cardinal with us that the custody, care and nurture of the child reside first in the parents, whose primary function and freedom include preparation for obligations the state can neither supply nor hinder....

But the family itself is not beyond regulation in the public interest, as against a claim of religious liberty. And neither rights of religion nor rights of parenthood are beyond limitation. Acting to guard the general interest in youth's well being, the state as *parens patriae* may restrict the parent's control by requiring school attendance, regulating or prohibiting the child's labor, and in many other ways.

Its authority is not nullified merely because the parent grounds his claim to control the child's course of conduct on religion or conscience. Thus, he cannot claim freedom from compulsory vaccination for the child more than for himself on religious grounds. The right to practice religion freely does not include liberty to expose the community or the child to communicable disease or the latter to ill health or death.... [T]he state has a wide range of power for limiting parental freedom and authority in things affecting the child's welfare; and ... this includes, to some extent, matters of conscience and religious conviction.

[C.] But it is said the state cannot do so here ... because when state action impinges upon a claimed religious freedom, it must fall unless shown to be necessary for or conducive to the child's protection against some clear and present danger, cf. *Schenck v. United States* .... The child's presence on the street, with her guardian, distributing or offering to distribute the magazines, it is urged, was in no way harmful to her, nor in any event more so than the presence of many other children at the same time and place, engaged in shopping and other activities not prohibited....

Concededly a statute or ordinance identical in terms with [the law in this case], except that it is applicable to adults or all persons generally, would be invalid [citing mostly free speech cases]. But the mere fact a state could not wholly prohibit this form of adult activity, whether characterized locally as a "sale" or otherwise, does not mean it cannot do so for children....

The state's authority over children's activities is broader than over like actions of adults. This is peculiarly true of public activities and in matters of employment. A democratic society rests, for its continuance, upon the healthy, well-rounded growth of young people into full maturity as citizens, with all that implies. It may secure this against impeding restraints and dangers within a broad range of selection. Among evils most appropriate for such action are the crippling effects of child employment, more especially in public places, and the possible harms arising from other activities subject to all the diverse influences of the street....

[T]he presence of the child's guardian ... may lessen the likelihood that some evils the legislation seeks to avert will occur. But it cannot forestall all of them. The zealous though lawful exercise of the right to engage in propagandizing the community, whether in religious, political or other matters, may and at times does create situations difficult enough for adults to cope with and wholly inappropriate for children, especially of tender years, to face. Other harmful possibilities could be stated, of emotional excitement and psychological or physical injury.

Parents may be free to become martyrs themselves. But it does not follow they are free, in identical circumstances, to make martyrs of their children before they have reached the age of full and legal discretion when they can make that choice for themselves.

Massachusetts has determined that an absolute prohibition, though one limited to streets and public places and to the incidental uses proscribed, is necessary to accomplish its legitimate objectives. Its power to attain them is broad enough to reach these peripheral instances in which the parent's supervision may reduce but cannot eliminate entirely the ill effects of the prohibited conduct....

Justice Murphy, dissenting....

The burden [in First Amendment cases is] on the state ... to prove the reasonableness and necessity of prohibiting children from engaging in religious activity of the type involved in this case. The burden in this instance, however, is not met by vague references to the reasonableness underlying child labor legislation in general. The great interest of the state in shielding minors from the evil vicissitudes of early life does not warrant every limitation on their religious training and activities. The reasonableness that justifies the prohibition of the ordinary distribution of literature in the public streets by children is not necessarily the reasonableness that justifies such a drastic restriction when the distribution is part of their religious faith.

If the right of a child to practice its religion in that manner is to be forbidden by constitutional means, there must be convincing proof that such a practice constitutes a grave and immediate danger to the state or to the health, morals or welfare of the child. The vital freedom of religion, which is "of the very essence of a scheme of ordered liberty," cannot be erased by slender references to the state's power to restrict the more secular activities of children....

[To the extent that] "the crippling effects of child employment, more especially in public places, and the possible harms arising from other activities subject to all the diverse influences of the street" ... flow from participation in ordinary commercial activities, these harms are irrelevant to this case. And the bare possibility that such harms might emanate from distribution of religious literature is not, standing alone, sufficient justification for restricting freedom of conscience and religion.

Nor can parents or guardians be subjected to criminal liability because of vague possibilities that their religious teachings might cause injury to the child. The evils must be grave, immediate, substantial. Yet there is not the slightest indication in this record, or in sources subject to judicial notice, that children engaged in distributing literature pursuant to their religious beliefs have been or are likely to be subject to any of the harmful "diverse influences of the street."

Indeed, if probabilities are to be indulged in, the likelihood is that children engaged in serious religious endeavor are immune from such influences. Gambling, truancy, irregular eating and sleeping habits, and the more serious vices are not consistent with the high moral character ordinarily displayed by children fulfilling religious obligations.

Moreover, Jehovah's Witness children invariably make their distributions in groups subject at all times to adult or parental control, as was done in this case. The dangers are thus exceedingly remote, to say the least. And the fact that the zealous exercise of the right to propagandize the community may result in violent or disorderly situations difficult for children to face is no excuse for prohibiting the exercise of that right....

f. Problem: Unemployment Compensation and Care for Child

Jane Braeburn belongs to a religion that teaches that mothers should—absent extraordinary financial necessity—stay home until their children are adults. Braeburn shares this view, and when her child is born, she tells her employer that she can no longer come to work. The employer then discharges her; though the Family Medical and Leave Act, 29 U.S.C. § 2612, requires employers to give employees 12 weeks of unpaid leave to care for a newborn child, it doesn't require anything more.

Braeburn then asks the state for unemployment compensation. State law provides that a claimant is ineligible for benefits "[i]f ... he has failed, without good cause ... to accept available suitable work when offered him by the employment office or the employer...." Braeburn, however, argues that she's entitled to a religious exemption from this requirement. The employer argues that if Braeburn wins, the employer would have to pay a higher unemployment compensation tax (the tax is determined by the past claims history of the employer's ex-employees, see, e.g., Conn. Gen. Stat. Ann. § 31-225a), which would improperly require the employer to subsidize Braeburn's religious beliefs.

Analyze Braeburn's claim under *Sherbert*.

g. Sherbert v. Verner, 374 U.S. 398 (1963)

Justice Brennan delivered the opinion of the Court.

[A.] Appellant, a member of the Seventh-day Adventist Church, was discharged by her South Carolina employer because she would not work on Saturday, the Sabbath Day of her faith. When she was unable to obtain other employment because from conscientious scruples she would not take Saturday work, she filed a claim for unemployment compensation benefits under the South Carolina Unemployment Compensation Act. {After her discharge, appellant sought employment with three other mills in the Spartanburg area, but found no suitable five-day work available at any of the mills.... [S]he expressed a willingness to accept employment at other mills, or even in another industry, so long as Saturday work was not required.... [O]f the 150 or more Seventh-day Adventists in the Spartanburg area, only appellant and one other have been unable to find suitable non-Saturday employment.}

That law provides that, to be eligible for benefits, a claimant must be "able to work and ... [be] available for work"; and, further, that a claimant is ineligible for benefits "[i]f ... he has failed, without good cause ... to accept available suitable work when offered him by the employment office or the employer...." The appellee Employment Security Commission ... found that appellant's restriction upon her availability for Saturday work brought her within the provision disqualifying for benefits insured workers who fail, without good cause, to accept "suitable work when offered ...." ...

[B.] [T]he disqualification for benefits imposes [a] burden on the free exercise of appellant's religion.... [T]he pressure upon [appellant] to forego [the practice of her religion] is unmistakable. The ruling forces her to choose between following the precepts of her religion and forfeiting benefits, on the one hand, and abandoning one of the precepts of her religion in order to accept work, on the other hand. Governmental imposition of such a choice puts the same kind of burden upon the free exercise of religion as would a fine imposed against appellant for her Saturday worship.

Nor may the South Carolina [scheme be defended] ... on the ground that unemployment compensation benefits are not appellant's "right" but merely a "privilege." ... [T]he liberties of religion and expression may be infringed by the denial of or placing of conditions upon a benefit or privilege....

Significantly South Carolina expressly saves the Sunday worshipper from having to make the kind of choice which we here hold infringes the Sabbatarian's religious liberty. When in times of "national emergency" the textile plants are authorized by the State Commissioner of Labor to operate on Sunday, "no employee shall be required to work on Sunday [or discriminated against for failure to do so] ... who is conscientiously opposed to Sunday work ...." ... The unconstitutionality of the disqualification of the Sabbatarian is thus compounded by the religious discrimination which South Carolina's general statutory scheme necessarily effects.

[C.] We must next consider whether some compelling state interest enforced in the eligibility provisions of the South Carolina statute justifies the substantial infringement of appellant's First Amendment right. It is basic that no showing merely of a rational relationship to some colorable state interest would suffice; in this highly sensitive constitutional area, "[o]nly the gravest abuses, endangering paramount interests, give occasion for permissible limitation." ...

The appellees suggest no more than a possibility that the filing of fraudulent claims by unscrupulous claimants feigning religious objections to Saturday work might not only dilute the unemployment compensation fund but also hinder the scheduling by employers of necessary Saturday work. But ... there is no proof whatever to warrant such fears of malingering or deceit as those which the respondents now advance.

Even if consideration of such evidence is not foreclosed by the prohibition against judicial inquiry into the truth or falsity of religious beliefs—a question as to which we intimate no view since it is not before us—it is highly doubtful whether such evidence would be sufficient to warrant a substantial infringement of religious liberties. For even if the possibility of spurious claims did threaten to dilute the fund and disrupt the scheduling of work, it would plainly be incumbent upon the appellees to demonstrate that no alternative forms of regulation would combat such abuses without infringing First Amendment rights....

[D.] In holding as we do, plainly we are not fostering the "establishment" of the Seventh-day Adventist religion in South Carolina, for the extension of unemployment benefits to Sabbatarians in common with Sunday worshippers reflects nothing more than the governmental obligation of neutrality in the face of religious differences, and does not represent that involvement of religious with secular institutions which it is the object of the Establishment Clause to forestall. Nor does the recognition of the appellant's right to unemployment benefits under the state statute serve to abridge any other person's religious liberties.

Nor do we, by our decision today, declare the existence of a constitutional right to unemployment benefits on the part of all persons whose religious convictions are the cause of their unemployment. This is not a case in which an employee's religious convictions serve to make him a nonproductive member of society....

South Carolina may not constitutionally apply the eligibility provisions so as to constrain a worker to abandon his religious convictions respecting the day of rest. This holding but reaffirms ... that no State may "exclude [people] *because of their faith, or lack of it*, from receiving the benefits of public welfare legislation." ...

Justice Stewart, concurring in the result....

If the appellant's refusal to work on Saturdays were based on indolence, ... South Carolina could ... hold that she was not "available for work" within the meaning of its statute. That being so, the Establishment Clause as construed by this Court not only *permits* but affirmatively *requires* South Carolina equally to deny the appellant's claim for unemployment compensation when her refusal to work on Saturdays is based upon her religious creed.

For, as said in *Everson v. Board of Ed.,* the Establishment Clause bespeaks "a government ... stripped of all power ... to support, or otherwise to assist any or all religions ...," and no State "can pass laws which aid one religion ...." ... In the words of the Court in *Engel v. Vitale,* ... the Establishment Clause forbids the "financial support of government" to be "placed behind a particular religious belief."

To require South Carolina ... to pay public money to the appellant under the circumstances of this case is thus clearly to require the State to violate the Establishment Clause as construed by this Court. This poses no problem for me, because I think the Court's mechanistic concept of the ... Clause is historically unsound and constitutionally wrong.... And I think that the guarantee of religious liberty embodied in the Free Exercise Clause affirmatively requires government to create an atmosphere of hospitality and accommodation to individual belief or disbelief....

Justice Harlan, whom Justice White joins, dissenting....

[T]he Court is holding ... that ... [the State] must *single out* for financial assistance those whose behavior is religiously motivated, even though it denies such assistance to others whose identical behavior (in this case, inability to work on Saturdays) is not religiously motivated .... I cannot subscribe to the conclusion that the State is constitutionally *compelled* to carve out an exception to its general rule of eligibility in the present case. Those situations in which the Constitution may require special treatment on account of religion are, in my view, few and far between .... Such compulsion in the present case is particularly inappropriate in light of the indirect, remote, and insubstantial effect of the decision below on the exercise of appellant's religion and in light of the direct financial assistance to religion that today's decision requires....

{The Court does suggest, in a rather startling disclaimer, that its holding is limited in applicability to those whose religious convictions do not make them "nonproductive" members of society, noting that most of the Seventh-day Adventists in the Spartanburg area are employed. But surely this disclaimer cannot be taken seriously, for the Court cannot mean that the case would have come out differently if none of the Seventh-day Adventists in Spartanburg had been gainfully employed, or if the appellant's religion had prevented her from working on Tuesdays instead of Saturdays.

Nor can the Court be suggesting that it will make a value judgment in each case as to whether a particular individual's religious convictions prevent him from being "productive." I can think of no more inappropriate function for this Court to perform.}

h. *Gillette v. United States, 401 U.S. 437 (1971)*

Justice Marshall delivered the opinion of the Court....

[A.] [Guy] Gillette was convicted of wilful failure to report for induction into the armed forces.... In support of his unsuccessful request for classification as a conscientious objector, [Gillette] had stated his willingness to participate in a war of national defense or a war sponsored by the United Nations as a peace-keeping measure, but declared his opposition to American military operations in Vietnam, which he characterized as "unjust." ... In affirming [Gillette's] conviction, the Court of Appeals concluded that Gillette's conscientious beliefs "were specifically directed against the war in Vietnam," while the relevant exemption provision of the Military Selective Service Act of 1967 requires opposition "to participation in war in any form." [Gillette's beliefs stemmed from deep secular conscientious principles, but another petitioner, Louis Negre, lodged similar objections based on his Catholic beliefs; these were likewise rejected.—ed.] ...

[B.] [In the course of rejecting Gillette's claim that the distinction between objections to all wars and objections to a particular war violated the Establishment Clause, the Court defended a lack of exemption for selective conscientious objectors this way:—ed.] ...

Apart from the Government's need for manpower, perhaps the central interest involved in the administration of conscription laws is the interest in maintaining a fair system for determining "who serves when not all serve." When the Government exacts so much, the importance of fair, even-handed, and uniform decisionmaking is obviously intensified.

The Government argues that the interest in fairness would be jeopardized by expansion of § 6(j) to include conscientious objection to a particular war. The contention is that the claim to relief on account of such objection is intrinsically a claim of uncertain dimensions, and that granting the claim in theory would involve a real danger of erratic or even discriminatory decisionmaking in administrative practice.

A virtually limitless variety of beliefs are subsumable under the rubric, "objection to a particular war." All the factors that might go into nonconscientious dissent from policy, also might appear as the concrete basis of an objection that has roots as well in conscience and religion. Indeed, over the realm of possible situations, opposition to a particular war may more likely be political and nonconscientious, than otherwise. The difficulties of sorting the two, with a sure hand, are considerable.

Moreover, the belief that a particular war at a particular time is unjust is by its nature changeable and subject to nullification by changing events. Since objection may fasten on any of an enormous number of variables, the claim is ultimately subjective, depending on the claimant's view of the facts in relation to his judgment that a given factor or congeries of factors colors the character of the war as a whole. In short, it is not at all obvious in theory what sorts of objections should be deemed sufficient to excuse an objector, and there is considerable force in the Government's contention that a program of excusing objectors to particular wars may be "impossible to conduct with any hope of reaching fair and consistent results...." ...

To view the problem of fairness and evenhanded decisionmaking, in the present context, as merely a commonplace chore of weeding out "spurious claims," is to minimize substantial difficulties of real concern to a responsible legislative body. For example, under the petitioners' unarticulated scheme for exemption, an objector's claim to exemption might be based on some feature of a current conflict that most would regard as incidental, or might be predicated on a view of the facts that most would regard as mistaken.

The particular complaint about the war may itself be "sincere," but it is difficult to know how to judge the "sincerity" of the objector's conclusion that the war *in toto* is unjust and that any personal involvement would contravene conscience and religion. To be sure we have ruled, in connection with § 6(j), that "the 'truth' of a belief is not open to question"; rather, the question is whether the objector's beliefs are "truly held." But we must also recognize that "sincerity" is a concept that can bear only so much adjudicative weight.

Ours is a Nation of enormous heterogeneity in respect of political views, moral codes, and religious persuasions. It does not bespeak an establishing of religion for Congress to forgo the enterprise of distinguishing those whose dissent has some conscientious basis from those who simply dissent. There is a danger that as between two would-be objectors, both having the same complaint against a war, that objector would succeed who is more articulate, better educated, or better counseled.

There is even a danger of unintended religious discrimination—a danger that a claim's chances of success would be greater the more familiar or salient the claim's connection with conventional religiosity could be made to appear. At any rate, it is true that "the more discriminating and complicated the basis of classification for an exemption—even a neutral one—the greater the potential for state involvement" in determining the character of persons' beliefs and affiliations, thus "entangl[ing] government in difficult classifications of what is or is not religious," or what is or is not conscientious. While the danger of erratic decisionmaking unfortunately exists in any system of conscription that takes individual differences into account, no doubt the dangers would be enhanced if a conscientious objection of indeterminate scope were honored in theory....

[C.] Further, it is not unreasonable to suppose that some persons who are *not* prepared to assert a conscientious objection, and instead accept the hardships and risks of military service, may well agree at all points with the objector, yet conclude, as a matter of conscience, that they are personally bound by the decision of the democratic process. The fear of the National Advisory Commission on Selective Service, apparently, is that exemption of objectors to particular wars would weaken the resolve of those who otherwise would feel themselves bound to serve despite personal cost, uneasiness at the prospect of violence, or even serious moral reservations or policy objections concerning the particular conflict....

As is shown by the long history of the very provision under discussion, it is not inconsistent with orderly democratic government for individuals to be exempted by law, on account of special characteristics, from general duties of a burdensome nature. But real dangers—dangers of the kind feared by the Commission—might arise if an exemption were made available that in its nature could not be administered fairly and uniformly over the run of relevant fact situations.

Should it be thought that those who go to war are chosen unfairly or capriciously, then a mood of bitterness and cynicism might corrode the spirit of public service and the values of willing performance of a citizen's duties that are the very heart of free government.... [I]t is supportable for Congress to have decided that the objector to all war—to all killing in war—has a claim that is distinct enough and intense enough to justify special status, while the objector to a particular war does not....

[D.] [The Court then rejected the free exercise claim by referring to the above discussion:—ed.] ... [True,] even as to neutral prohibitory or regulatory laws having secular aims, the Free Exercise Clause may condemn certain applications clashing with imperatives of religion and conscience, when the burden on First Amendment values is not justifiable in terms of the Government's valid aims. However, ... [t]he incidental burdens felt by persons in petitioners' position are strictly justified by substantial governmental interests that relate directly to the very impacts questioned. And more broadly, of course, there is the Government's interest in procuring the manpower necessary for military purposes, pursuant to the constitutional grant of power to Congress to raise and support armies....

Justice Douglas, dissenting. [Omitted.—ed.]

i.   *Problem: The Bad Amish*

Imagine that, inspired by the experience of the Amish, the Agrarian

Church (founded in 1975) decided to likewise retreat to a simple, pre-technological lifestyle. Like the Amish, it refuses to send its children to any school (public or private) past age 14, though the state generally requires children to be educated until age 16. The Agrarian Church's theology is nearly identical to that of the Amish.

Quite a few members of the Church, however—especially teenage boys and young men—have been arrested for a variety of crimes ranging from larceny to rape, and quite a few move away from the dozen or so Agrarian communities into the big city, where their lack of education often leads them to be unemployed and to go on public assistance. The majority of the Church's 3,000 members are entirely law-abiding, but the crime rate among Church members is nonetheless substantially higher than average.

The state of Wisconsin, where some Agrarians have settled, seeks to apply its compulsory education law to the Agrarians' children; the Agrarians object, citing *Wisconsin v. Yoder*. Analyze.

j. *Wisconsin v. Yoder, 406 U.S. 205 (1972)*

[The respondents belonged to the Old Order Amish, who believed in a separatist, agrarian lifestyle, removed from the secular world and from much modern technology. Because of that, respondents sincerely believed "that their children's attendance at high school [past eighth grade], public or private, was contrary to the Amish religion and way of life"; any education past that would unduly expose them to the secular world, and distract them from being integrated into the Amish religious community. But Wisconsin law required children to attend school until age 16, so the respondents were convicted of violating the law, and fined $5 each.]

Chief Justice Burger delivered the opinion of the Court....

[A.] [T]he traditional way of life of the Amish is not merely a matter of personal preference, but one of deep religious conviction, shared by an organized group, and intimately related to daily living. That the Old Order Amish daily life and religious practice stem from their faith is shown by the fact that it is in response to their literal interpretation of the Biblical injunction from the Epistle of Paul to the Romans, "be not conformed to this world...." This command is fundamental to the Amish faith....

[S]econdary schooling, by exposing Amish children to worldly influences in terms of attitudes, goals, and values contrary to beliefs, and by substantially interfering with the religious development of the Amish child and his integration into the way of life of the Amish faith community at the crucial adolescent stage of development, contravenes the basic religious tenets and practice of the Amish faith, both as to the parent and the child. The impact of the compulsory-attendance law on respondents' practice of the Amish religion is not only severe, but inescapable, for the Wisconsin law affirmatively compels them, under threat of criminal sanction, to perform acts undeniably at odds with fundamental tenets of their religious beliefs....

[The law also poses] precisely the kind of objective danger to the free exercise of religion that the First Amendment was designed to prevent. As the record shows, compulsory school attendance to age 16 for Amish children carries with it a very real threat of undermining the Amish community and religious practice as they exist today; they must either abandon belief and be assimilated into society at large, or be forced to migrate to some other and more tolerant region....

[B.] [The state contends] that its interest in its system of compulsory education is so compelling that even the established religious practices of the Amish must give way. Where fundamental claims of religious freedom are at stake, however, we cannot accept such a sweeping claim; despite its admitted validity in the generality of cases, we must searchingly examine the interests that the State seeks to promote by its requirement for compulsory education to age 16, and the impediment to those objectives that would flow from recognizing the claimed Amish exemption.... {[O]nly those interests [that are] of the highest order and ... [are] not otherwise served can overbalance legitimate claims to the free exercise of religion.}

{[A] State, having a high responsibility for education of its citizens, [may] impose reasonable regulations for the control and duration of basic education..... Yet even this paramount responsibility was, in *Pierce v. Society of Sisters,* 268 U.S. 510 (1925)[, which struck down a law mandating *public* education—ed.], made to yield to the right of parents to provide an equivalent education in a privately operated system.}

[We accept] that some degree of education is necessary to prepare citizens to participate effectively and intelligently in our open political system if we are to preserve freedom and independence. Further, education prepares individuals to be self-reliant and self-sufficient participants in society.... However, the evidence adduced by the Amish in this case is persuasively to the effect that an additional one or two years of formal high school for Amish children in place of their long-established program of informal vocational education would do little to serve those interests.

Respondents' experts testified at trial, without challenge, that the value of all education must be assessed in terms of its capacity to prepare the child for life. It is one thing to say that compulsory education for a year or two beyond the eighth grade may be necessary when its goal is the preparation of the child for life in modern society as the majority live, but it is quite another if the goal of education be viewed as the preparation of the child for life in the separated agrarian community that is the keystone of the Amish faith.

The State attacks respondents' position as one fostering "ignorance" from which the child must be protected by the State. No one can question the State's duty to protect children from ignorance but this argument does not square with the facts disclosed in the record.

Whatever their idiosyncrasies as seen by the majority, this record strongly shows that the Amish community has been a highly successful social unit within our society, even if apart from the conventional "mainstream." Its members are productive and very law-abiding members of society; they reject public welfare in any of its usual modern forms. The Congress itself recognized their self-sufficiency by authorizing exemption of such groups as the Amish from the obligation to pay social security taxes. {[T]he Green County Amish had never been known to commit crimes, ... none had been known to receive public assistance, and ... none were unemployed.} ...

[T]he Amish are opposed [not] to education beyond the eighth grade[, but] ... to conventional formal education of the type provided by a certified high school because it comes at the child's crucial adolescent period of religious development. Dr. Donald Erickson, for example, testified that their system of learning-by-doing was an "ideal system" of education in terms of preparing Amish children for life as adults in the Amish community, and that "I would be inclined to say they do a better job in this than most of the rest of us do." As he put it, "These people aren't purporting to be learned people, and it seems to me the self-sufficiency of the community is the best evidence I can point to—whatever is being done seems to function well." ...

The State [points to] ... the possibility that some such children will choose to leave the Amish community, and that if this occurs they will be ill-equipped for life.... However, on this record, that argument is highly speculative. There is no specific evidence of the loss of Amish adherents by attrition, nor is there any showing that upon leaving the Amish community Amish children, with their practical agricultural training and habits of industry and self-reliance, would become burdens on society because of educational shortcomings.... [The Amish] provide what has been characterized by the undisputed testimony of expert educators as an "ideal" vocational education for their children in the adolescent years.

There is nothing in this record to suggest that the Amish qualities of reliability, self-reliance, and dedication to work would fail to find ready markets in today's society. Absent some contrary evidence supporting the State's position, we are unwilling to assume that persons possessing such valuable vocational skills and habits are doomed to become burdens on society should they determine to leave the Amish faith, nor is there any basis in the record to warrant a finding that an additional one or two years of formal school education beyond the eighth grade would serve to eliminate any such problem that might exist.

Insofar as the State's claim rests on the view that a brief additional period of formal education is imperative to enable the Amish to participate effectively and intelligently in our democratic process, it must fall. The Amish alternative to formal secondary school education has enabled them to function effectively in their day-to-day life ..., and to survive and prosper in contemporary society as a separate, sharply identifiable and highly self-sufficient community for more than 200 years in this country. In itself this is strong evidence that they are capable of fulfilling the social and political responsibilities of citizenship without compelled attendance beyond the eighth grade at the price of jeopardizing their free exercise of religious belief.

{Aided by a history of three centuries as an identifiable religious sect and a long history as a successful and self-sufficient segment of American society, the Amish in this case have convincingly demonstrated the sincerity of their religious beliefs, the interrelationship of belief with their mode of life, the vital role that belief and daily conduct play in the continued survival of Old Order Amish communities and their religious organization, and the hazards presented by the State's enforcement of a statute generally valid as to others. Beyond this, they have carried the even more difficult burden of demonstrating the adequacy of their alternative mode of continuing informal vocational education in terms of precisely those overall interests that the State advances in support of its program of compulsory high school education.

In light of this convincing showing, one that probably few other religious groups or sects could make, and weighing the minimal difference between what the State would require and what the Amish already accept, it was incumbent on the State to show with more particularity how its admittedly strong interest in compulsory education would be adversely affected by granting an exemption to the Amish.} ...

[C.] [T]he State, on authority of *Prince v. Massachusetts,* argues that a decision exempting Amish children from the State's requirement fails to recognize the substantive right of the Amish child to a secondary education .... However, ... [the *Prince* decision relied on] the Court's severe characterization of the evils that it thought the legislature could legitimately associate with child labor, even when performed in the company of an adult.... This case, of course, is not one in which any harm to the physical or mental health of the child or to the public safety, peace, order, or welfare has been demonstrated or may be properly inferred....

The dissent argues that a child who expresses a desire to attend public high school in conflict with the wishes of his parents should not be prevented from doing so.... [But this] is not an issue in the case.... The State's position from the outset has been that it is empowered to apply its compulsory-attendance law ... without regard to the wishes of the child. That is the claim we reject today....

The State's argument ... appears to rest on the potential that exemption of Amish parents from the requirements of the compulsory-education law might allow some parents to act contrary to the best interests of their children by foreclosing their opportunity to make an intelligent choice between the Amish way of life and that of the outside world. The same argument could, of course, be made with respect to all church schools short of college.... [N]on-Amish parents generally [do not] consult with children of ages 14–16 if they are placed in a church school of the parents' faith.

Indeed ... if the State is empowered ... to "save" a child from himself or his Amish parents by requiring an additional two years of compulsory formal high school education, the State will in large measure influence, if not determine, the religious future of the child.... The history and culture of Western civilization reflect a strong tradition of parental concern for the nurture and upbringing of their children. This primary role of the parents in the upbringing of their children is now established ... as an enduring American tradition....

> The fundamental theory of liberty upon which all governments in this Union repose excludes any general power of the State to standardize its children by forcing them to accept instruction from public teachers only. The child is not the mere creature of the State; those who nurture him and direct his destiny have the right, coupled with the high duty, to recognize and prepare him for additional obligations. *Pierce v. Society of Sisters*....

Justice White, with whom Justice Brennan and Justice Stewart join, concurring....

[T]he State is ... attempting to nurture and develop the human potential of its children, whether Amish or non-Amish: to expand their knowledge, broaden their sensibilities, kindle their imagination, foster a spirit of free inquiry, and increase their human understanding and tolerance.... [Some Amish children] may wish to become nuclear physicists, ballet dancers, computer programmers, or historians, and for these occupations, formal training will be necessary.

There is evidence in the record that many children desert the Amish faith when they come of age.... A State has a legitimate interest not only in seeking to develop the latent talents of its children but also in seeking to prepare them for the life style that they may later choose, or at least to provide them with an option other than the life they have led in the past.

In the circumstances of this case, although the question is close, I am unable to say that the State has demonstrated that Amish children who leave school in the eighth grade will be intellectually stultified or unable to acquire new academic skills later. The statutory minimum school attendance age set by the State is, after all, only 16.... I join the Court because the sincerity of the Amish religious policy here is uncontested, because the potentially adverse impact of the state requirement is great, and because the State's valid interest in education has already been largely satisfied by the eight years the children have already spent in school.

Justice Douglas, dissenting in part [as to those parents whose children had not testified that their own religious beliefs match their parents'—ed.]....

[A.] [T]he inevitable effect [of this decision] is to impose the parents' notions of religious duty upon their children. Where the child is mature enough to express potentially conflicting desires, it would be an invasion of the child's rights to permit such an imposition without canvassing his views.... [I]f an Amish child desires to attend high school, and is mature enough to have that desire respected, the State may well be able to override the parents' religiously motivated objections....

While the parents, absent dissent, normally speak for the entire family, the education of the child is a matter on which the child will often have decided views.... If a parent keeps his child out of school beyond the grade school, then the child will be forever barred from entry into the new and amazing world of diversity that we have today. The child may decide that that is the preferred course, or he may rebel. It is the student's judgment, not his parents', that is essential ....

[B.] I think the emphasis of the Court on the "law and order" record of this Amish group of people is quite irrelevant. A religion is a religion irrespective of what the misdemeanor or felony records of its members might be. I am not at all sure how the Catholics, Episcopalians, the Baptists, Jehovah's Witnesses, the Unitarians, and my own Presbyterians would make out if subjected to such a test....

k.   *United States v. Lee, 455 U.S. 252 (1982)*

Chief Justice Burger delivered the opinion of the Court....

[A.] Appellee, a member of the Old Order Amish, is a farmer and carpenter. From 1970 to 1977, appellee employed several other Amish to work on his farm and in his carpentry shop [but did not withhold or pay social security taxes for them].... In 1978, the Internal Revenue Service assessed appellee in excess of $27,000 for unpaid [social security] taxes; he ... sued ..., claiming that imposition of the social security taxes violated his First Amendment free exercise rights and those of his Amish employees....

[B.] The preliminary inquiry in determining the existence of a constitutionally required exemption is whether the payment of social security taxes and the receipt of benefits interferes with the free exercise rights of the Amish. The Amish believe that there is a religiously based obligation to provide for their fellow members the kind of assistance contemplated by the social security system. {Appellee indicates that his scriptural basis for this belief was: "But if any provide not ... for those of his own house, he hath denied the faith, and is worse than an infidel." (I Timothy 5:8.)} Although the Government does not challenge the sincerity of this belief, the Government does contend that payment of social security taxes will not threaten the integrity of the Amish religious belief or observance.

It is not within "the judicial function and judicial competence," however, to determine whether appellee or the Government has the proper interpretation of the Amish faith; "[c]ourts are not arbiters of scriptural interpretation." {This is not an instance in which the asserted claim is "so bizarre, so clearly nonreligious in motivation, as not to be entitled to protection under the Free Exercise Clause." ...} We therefore accept appellee's contention that both payment and receipt of social security benefits is forbidden by the Amish faith. Because the payment of the taxes or receipt of benefits violates Amish religious beliefs, compulsory participation in the social security system interferes with their free exercise rights....

[C.] [But n]ot all burdens on religion are unconstitutional. The state may justify a limitation on religious liberty by showing that it is essential to accomplish an overriding governmental interest....

The social security system in the United States serves the public interest by providing a comprehensive insurance system with a variety of benefits available to all participants, with costs shared by employers and employees.... The design of the system requires support by mandatory contributions from covered employers and employees. This mandatory participation is indispensable to the fiscal vitality of the social security system. "[W]idespread individual voluntary coverage under social security ... would undermine the soundness of the social security program."

Moreover, a comprehensive national social security system providing for voluntary participation would be almost a contradiction in terms and difficult, if not impossible, to administer. Thus, the Government's interest in assuring mandatory and continuous participation in and contribution to the social security system is very high.

[D.] The remaining inquiry is whether accommodating the Amish belief will unduly interfere with fulfillment of the governmental interest.... To maintain an organized society that guarantees religious freedom to a great variety of faiths requires that some religious practices yield to the common good. Religious beliefs can be accommodated, but there is a point at which accommodation would "radically restrict the operating latitude of the legislature."

Unlike the situation presented in *Wisconsin v. Yoder*, it would be difficult to accommodate the comprehensive social security system with myriad exceptions flowing from a wide variety of religious beliefs.... There is no principled way ..., for purposes of this case, to distinguish between general taxes and those imposed under the Social Security Act.

If, for example, a religious adherent believes war is a sin, and if a certain percentage of the federal budget can be identified as devoted to war-related activities, such individuals would have a similarly valid claim to be exempt from paying that percentage of the income tax. The tax system could not function if denominations were allowed to challenge the tax system because tax payments were spent in a manner that violates their religious belief. Because the broad public interest in maintaining a sound tax system is of such a high order, religious belief in conflict with the payment of taxes affords no basis for resisting the tax.

[E.] Congress has accommodated, to the extent compatible with a comprehensive national program, the practices of those who believe it a violation of their faith to participate in the social security system. In 26 U.S.C. § 1402(g) Congress granted an exemption, on religious grounds, to self-employed Amish and others. Confining the § 1402(g) exemption to the self-employed provided for a narrow category which was readily identifiable. Self-employed persons in a religious community having its own "welfare" system are distinguishable from the generality of wage earners employed by others.

Congress and the courts have been sensitive to the needs flowing from the Free Exercise Clause, but every person cannot be shielded from all the burdens incident to exercising every aspect of the right to practice religious beliefs. When followers of a particular sect enter into commercial activity as a matter of choice, the limits they accept on their own conduct as a matter of conscience and faith are not to be superimposed on the statutory schemes which are binding on others in that activity.

Granting an exemption from social security taxes to an employer operates to impose the employer's religious faith on the employees. Congress drew a line in § 1402(g), exempting the self-employed Amish but not all persons working for an Amish employer. The tax imposed on employers to support the social security system must be uniformly applicable to all, except as Congress provides explicitly otherwise....

Justice Stevens, concurring in the judgment....

Congress already has granted the Amish a limited exemption from social security taxes. As a matter of administration, it would be a relatively simple matter to extend the exemption to the taxes involved in this case. As a matter of fiscal policy, an enlarged exemption probably would benefit the social security system because the nonpayment of these taxes by the Amish would be more than offset by the elimination of their right to collect benefits. In view of the fact that the Amish have demonstrated their capacity to care for their own, the social cost of eliminating this relatively small group of dedicated believers would be minimal. Thus, if we confine the analysis to the Government's interest in rejecting the particular claim to an exemption at stake in this case, the constitutional standard as formulated by the Court has not been met.

The Court rejects the particular claim of this appellee, not because it presents any special problems, but rather because of the risk that a myriad of other claims would be too difficult to process. The Court overstates the magnitude of this risk because the Amish claim applies only to a small religious community with an established welfare system of its own. {[And t]he Amish claim is readily distinguishable from the typical claim to an exemption from general tax obligations on the ground that the taxpayer objects to the government's use of his money; in the typical case the taxpayer is not in any position to supply the government with an equivalent substitute for the objectionable use of his money.}

Nevertheless, I agree with the Court's conclusion .... [Justice Stevens went on to explain, see p. 1001, that he thought the proper rule was similar to the one adopted later in *Employment Div. v. Smith*.—ed.]

l.   Bob Jones Univ. v. United States, 461 U.S. 574 (1983)

Chief Justice Burger delivered the opinion of the Court....

Until 1970, the Internal Revenue Service granted tax-exempt status to private schools, without regard to their racial admissions policies, under § 501(c)(3) of the Internal Revenue Code, and granted charitable deductions for contributions to such schools under § 170 of the Code. [In 1970, the IRS changed its views.] ...

Bob Jones University [in South Carolina] ... is dedicated to the teaching and propagation of its fundamentalist Christian religious beliefs.... Its teachers are required to be devout Christians, and all courses at the University are taught according to the Bible. Entering students are screened as to their religious beliefs, and their public and private conduct is strictly regulated by standards promulgated by University authorities.

The sponsors of the University genuinely believe that the Bible forbids interracial dating and marriage. To effectuate these views, Negroes were completely excluded until 1971. From 1971 to May 1975, the University accepted no applications from unmarried Negroes, but did accept applications from Negroes married within their race.

Following [a court decision] prohibiting racial exclusion from private schools, the University revised its policy. Since May 29, 1975, the University has permitted unmarried Negroes to enroll; but a disciplinary rule prohibits interracial dating and marriage.... {Although a ban on intermarriage or interracial dating applies to all races, decisions of this Court firmly establish that discrimination on the basis of racial affiliation and association is a form of racial discrimination....}

Petitioners contend that [the IRS rule barring tax exemptions for racially discriminatory institutions] ... cannot constitutionally be applied to schools that engage in racial discrimination on the basis of sincerely held religious beliefs.... [T]he Government has a fundamental, overriding interest in eradicating racial discrimination in education—discrimination that prevailed, with official approval, for the first 165 years of this Nation's constitutional history. {We deal here only with religious *schools*—not with churches or other purely religious institutions; here, the governmental interest is in denying public support to racial discrimination in education.... [R]acially discriminatory schools "exer[t] a pervasive influence on the entire educational process," outweighing any public benefit that they might otherwise provide.} That governmental interest substantially outweighs whatever burden denial of tax benefits places on petitioners' exercise of their religious beliefs. The interests asserted by petitioners cannot be accommodated with that compelling governmental interest; and no "less restrictive means" are available to achieve the governmental interest.

{Bob Jones University also contends that denial of tax exemption violates the Establishment Clause by preferring religions whose tenets do not require racial discrimination over those which believe racial intermixing is forbidden.... [A] regulation does not violate the Establishment Clause merely because it "happens to coincide or harmonize with the tenets of some or all religions." The IRS policy at issue here is founded on a "neutral, secular basis," and does not violate the Establishment Clause.} ...

m. *Should Constitutionally Compelled Exemptions Be Limited to Religious Observers?*

i. *Wisconsin v. Yoder, 406 U.S. 205 (1972)*

Chief Justice Burger delivered the opinion of the Court....

A way of life, however virtuous and admirable, may not be interposed as a barrier to reasonable state regulation of education if it is based on purely secular considerations; to have the protection of the Religion Clauses, the claims must be rooted in religious belief. Although a determination of what is a "religious" belief or practice entitled to constitutional protection may present a most delicate question, the very concept of ordered liberty precludes allowing every person to make his own standards on matters of conduct in which society as a whole has important interests.

Thus, if the Amish asserted their claims because of their subjective evaluation and rejection of the contemporary secular values accepted by the majority, much as Thoreau rejected the social values of his time and isolated himself at Walden Pond, their claims would not rest on a religious basis. Thoreau's choice was philosophical and personal rather than religious, and such belief does not rise to the demands of the Religion Clauses....

Justice Douglas[, dissenting in part] ....

[The Court is mistaken when it says Thoreau's] "choice was philosophical and personal rather than religious, and such belief does not rise to the demands of the Religion Clauses." That is contrary to what we held in *United States v. Seeger,* 380 U.S. 163 (1965), where we were concerned with the meaning of the words "religious training and belief" in the Selective Service Act, which were the basis of many conscientious objector claims....: "Within that phrase would come all sincere religious beliefs which are based upon a power or being, or upon a faith, to which all else is subordinate or upon which all else is ultimately dependent ... [—a]sincere and meaningful belief which occupies in the life of its possessor a place parallel to that filled by the God of those admittedly qualifying for the exemption comes within the statutory definition...."

Welsh v. United States was in the same vein .... I adhere to these exalted views of "religion" and see no acceptable alternative to them now that we have become a Nation of many religions and sects, representing all of the diversities of the human race.

ii. *Frazee v. Illinois Dep't of Emp. Sec., 489 U.S. 829 (1989)*

[This case accepted a Sabbatarian's religious exemption claim, which was much like the one in *Sherbert,* and in the process reaffirmed *Yoder*'s view of the limited scope of the Free Exercise Clause.—ed.]

Justice White delivered the opinion of [a unanimous] Court...

There is no doubt that "[o]nly beliefs rooted in religion are protected by the Free Exercise Clause." Purely secular views do not suffice....

n. *Policy—Avoiding Disparate Effects Based on Religion*

Basic argument: "The First Amendment should be read as prohibiting this government action because, while it's facially neutral, it disproportionately benefits or burdens certain religious groups (or religious groups generally) by _____."

"The First Amendment should be read as allowing this government action because, while it's facially discriminatory, it in fact eliminates what would otherwise be a disproportionate benefit to or burden on certain religious groups (or religious groups generally), namely _____."

1. "In holding [that Sherbert is entitled to an exemption], plainly we are not fostering the 'establishment' of the Seventh-day Adventist religion in South Carolina, for the extension of unemployment benefits to Sabbatarians in common with Sunday worshippers reflects nothing more than the governmental obligation of neutrality in the face of religious differences...." *Sherbert v. Verner.*

"[T]he bulk of the tax benefits afforded by the Minnesota [tax deduction for school tuition and supplies] are enjoyed by parents of parochial school children .... Of the total number of [eligible] taxpayers ..., approximately 96% send their children to religious schools.... [T]he deduction permitted for tuition expenses primarily benefits those who send their children to religious schools.... Because Minnesota, like every other State, is committed to providing free public education, tax assistance for tuition payments inevitably redounds to the benefit of nonpublic, sectarian schools and parents who send their children to those schools." *Mueller v. Allen,* 463 U.S. 388, 409-11 (1983) (Marshall, J., dissenting).

"[In cases like *Sherbert,*] Sabbath observers are not 'favored' over co-workers, any more than injured workers are 'favored' when given disability leave. The law simply alleviates for them a conflict of loyalties not faced by their secular co-workers." Michael W. McConnell, *Religious Freedom at a Crossroads,* 59 U. Chi. L. Rev. 115 (1992).

"[As *Employment Div. v. Smith*] acknowledges, its interpretation will place 'those religious practices that are not widely engaged in' at a 'relative disadvantage.' ... [Mainstream religions'] practices rarely, if ever, will conflict with an 'otherwise valid law,' because, in a democracy, the laws will reflect the beliefs and preferences of the median groups. Religious groups whose practices and beliefs are outside the mainstream are most likely to need [and often not get] exceptions and accommodations.... *Smith* thus not only increases the power of the state over religion, it introduces a bias in favor of mainstream over nonmainstream religions." *Id.*

"[In some cases, a constitutionally compelled exemption] comes closer to the proper sense of neutrality with respect to conscientious objection. People with a deeply held conscientious objection to a law are not similarly situated to people without such an objection. To insist on formally equal treatment of objectors and non-objectors is to pursue the same majestic equality that forbids the rich and the poor alike to sleep under bridges." Douglas Laycock, *Formal, Substantive, and Disaggregated Neutrality Toward Religion,* 39 DePaul L. Rev. 993 (1990).

"[S]ubstantive neutrality[, defined in terms of reducing government incentives to change religious behavior,] is sometimes achieved by special treatment for religion and sometimes by identical treatment.... Restrictions on private religious speech discourage religion.... Equal access [is thus] substantively neutral; censoring speech is not.

"The same analysis applies to funding.... [T]he neutral course is to fund whoever will provide the service and to not interfere with the religious environment in which some providers deliver the service.

"With respect to self-interested exemptions [under the Free Exercise Clause], the analysis is the same.... If religious objectors to paying taxes do not have to pay, there is an incentive to adopt the faith that gives rise to the objection.... But with respect to most exemptions, exemptions minimize the incentive effects [and should thus be constitutionally required]...." Douglas Laycock, *Religious Liberty as Liberty,* 7 J. Contemp. Leg. Issues 313 (1996).

2. Response to 1: If one compares the disparate effects created by this new government policy against the disparate effects that exist under the status quo, one sees that the new policy will actually diminish (or at least not increase) these disparate effects, because _____.

"[O]nly 9% of American K-12 students go to religious schools. The claim that 'most school choice funds will end up flowing to religious schools' is plausible only if one puts on blinders that exclude the number one beneficiary of school spending: government-run schools, which teach 89% out of the remaining 91%.... Right now, all standard K-12 spending goes to secular education; this itself is a powerful 'disparate impact' favoring secular uses and disfavoring religious uses. School choice will *diminish* this disparate impact." Eugene Volokh, *Equal Treatment Is Not Establishment,* 13 Notre Dame J.L., Ethics & Pub. Pol. 341, 349-350 (1999).

"[The] disparate impact [of school choice programs on different faiths] is even more present under the current system. People of various religious groups have beliefs that keep them from taking advantage of the government-run schools, either because of the schools' teachings or because of the schools' general policies on student behavior, modesty, and so on. Just as some secular parents might feel unable to send their children to a school which teaches a pervasively Christian curriculum, so some Christian parents might feel unable to send their children to a school which teaches a pervasively secular curriculum.

"Many religious groups, especially majority groups, can tolerate government-run schools; under the current system, they are the big winners. A few other religious groups, such as Catholics, are big enough and prosperous enough that they can set up their own schools; under the current system, they make do. But smaller groups whose religious beliefs keep them from using the government-run schools—including groups that are big enough that they could set up a school of their own if they could participate in a school choice program, but are too small or poor to set it up without such a program—are the losers.... School choice will lessen this disparate impact, because it will broaden the choices available to everyone.... True, some poor parents will still be unable to find a school that fits their particular religious beliefs—but under the current system, many more parents are in this boat." *Id.* at 349-50.

3. Response to 1: Courts shouldn't look to disparate effects, but should focus on facial equality or discriminatory purpose, because trying to mitigate disparate effects by a facially discriminatory rule would do more harm than good by _____.

"The interest in uniformity [of clothing in the military] ... is the interest in uniform treatment for the members of all religious faiths. The very strength of Captain Goldman's claim [to wear a yarmulke, caused in part by the familiarity of the yarmulke,] creates the danger that a similar claim on behalf of a Sikh or a Rastafarian might readily be dismissed as 'so extreme, so unusual, or so faddish an image that public confidence in his ability to perform his duties will be destroyed' [quoting the dissent's test].

"If exceptions from dress code regulations are to be granted on the basis of a multifactored test such as that proposed by Justice Brennan, inevitably the decisionmaker's evaluation of the character and the sincerity of the requester's faith—as well as the probable reaction of the majority to the favored treatment of a member of that faith—will play a critical part in the decision.... [T]he rule that is challenged in this case is based on a neutral, completely objective standard—visibility.... An exception for yarmulkes would represent a fundamental departure from the true principle of uniformity that supports that rule." *Goldman v. Weinberger,* 475 U.S. 503, 512-13 (1986) (Stevens, J., concurring).

"[T]he principal reason for adopting a strong presumption against [religious exemption] claims is not a matter of administrative convenience. It is the overriding interest in keeping the government— whether it be the legislature or the courts—out of the business of evaluating the relative merits of differing religious claims. The risk that governmental approval of some and disapproval of others will be perceived as favoring one religion over another is an important risk the Establishment Clause was designed to preclude." *United States v. Lee* (Stevens, J., concurring in the judgment).

3. The Current Doctrine

a. Summary

Rule: The Free Exercise Clause does not require the government to grant religious exemptions from neutral, generally applicable laws, except:

1. The Clause does require exemptions where "the State has in place a system of individual exemptions," as in the unemployment cases such as *Sherbert.* See also *Church of the Lukumi Babalu Aye, Inc. v. City of Hialeah* (1993) (p. 737).

2. The Clause may require exemptions in "hybrid situation[s]" where a claim is made based both on the Free Exercise Clause and some other right, such as free speech, parental rights, or freedom of association. Lower courts are split on whether this requires a winning claim under the other right (in which case the Free Exercise Clause is irrelevant), or just a colorable claim that isn't enough to win on its own but enough to seriously implicate the right (whatever that means).

— Many academic observers believe that these two kinds of exemptions are not consistent with the logic of *Smith,* but were included only so the Court could avoid overruling *Sherbert* and *Wisconsin v. Yoder.* Nonetheless, these rules are formally part of the doctrine.

3. Churches have the right to select their clergy and likely other employees

who play important roles in spreading church doctrine, without regard to antidiscrimination law. *Hosanna-Tabor Evangelical Lutheran Church v. EEOC* (2012) (p. 1005).

— Most antidiscrimination laws statutorily exempt some discriminatory hiring decisions by churches: Title VII, for instance, generally lets churches discriminate based on religion (see *Corporation of Presiding Bishop v. Amos*), and states that sex, religion, and national origin may sometimes constitute "bona fide occupational qualifications." When those exceptions apply, there's no need for a constitutional exemption. But Title VII has no exceptions to its race discrimination ban, and some state antidiscrimination laws are even more restrictive. So the constitutional principle described here is important in many cases.

b. Problem: Applying Smith

Consider those problems from XIII.A.2.a-XIII.A.2.c (on p. 964) that you did for that section. How would they come out under *Employment Div. v. Smith*? What are the advantages of the *Smith* approach over the *Sherbert/Yoder* approach? What are the disadvantages?

c. Employment Division v. Smith, 494 U.S. 872 (1990)

Justice Scalia delivered the opinion of the Court....

[A.] Oregon law prohibits the knowing or intentional possession of a "controlled substance" [including peyote] unless the substance has been prescribed by a medical practitioner.... Respondents Alfred Smith and Galen Black ... were fired from their jobs with a private drug rehabilitation organization because they ingested peyote for sacramental purposes at a ceremony of the Native American Church, of which both are members. When respondents applied to petitioner Employment Division ... for unemployment compensation, they were determined to be ineligible for benefits because they had been discharged for work-related "misconduct." ... [The Oregon Supreme Court eventually concluded that under the Free Exercise Clause religious use of peyote could not be criminalized.] The court therefore reaffirmed its previous ruling that the State could not deny unemployment benefits to respondents for having engaged in that practice....

[B.] The free exercise of religion means, first and foremost, the right to believe and profess whatever religious doctrine one desires. Thus, the First Amendment obviously excludes all "governmental regulation of religious *beliefs* as such." The government may not compel affirmation of religious belief, see *Torcaso v. Watkins,* punish the expression of religious doctrines it believes to be false, see *United States v. Ballard,* impose special disabilities on the basis of religious views or religious status, see *McDaniel v. Paty,* or lend its power to one or the other side in controversies over religious authority or dogma, see *Presbyterian Church v. Mary Elizabeth Blue Hull Memorial Presbyterian Church.*

But the "exercise of religion" often involves not only belief and profession but the performance of (or abstention from) physical acts: assembling with others for a worship service, participating in sacramental use of bread and wine, proselytizing, abstaining from certain foods or certain modes of transportation.... [A] State would be "prohibiting the free exercise [of religion]" if it sought to ban such acts or abstentions only when they are engaged in for religious reasons, or only because of the religious belief that they display. It would doubtless be unconstitutional, for example, to ban the casting of "statues that are to be used for worship purposes," or to prohibit bowing down before a golden calf.

Respondents in the present case, however, seek to carry the meaning of "prohibiting the free exercise [of religion]" one large step further. They contend that their religious motivation for using peyote places them beyond the reach of a criminal law that is not specifically directed at their religious practice, and that is concededly constitutional as applied to those who use the drug for other reasons. They assert, in other words, that "prohibiting the free exercise [of religion]" includes requiring any individual to observe a generally applicable law that requires (or forbids) the performance of an act that his religious belief forbids (or requires).

As a textual matter, we do not think the words must be given that meaning. It is no more necessary to regard the collection of a general tax, for example, as "prohibiting the free exercise [of religion]" by those citizens who believe support of organized government to be sinful, than it is to regard the same tax as "abridging the freedom ... of the press" of those publishing companies that must pay the tax as a condition of staying in business. It is a permissible reading of the text, in the one case as in the other, to say that if prohibiting the exercise of religion (or burdening the activity of printing) is not the object of the tax but merely the incidental effect of a generally applicable and otherwise valid provision, the First Amendment has not been offended.

Our decisions reveal that the latter reading is the correct one. We have never held that an individual's religious beliefs excuse him from compliance with an otherwise valid law prohibiting conduct that the State is free to regulate. On the contrary, the record of more than a century of our free exercise jurisprudence contradicts that proposition....

We first had occasion to assert that principle in *Reynolds v. U.S.,* where we rejected the claim that criminal laws against polygamy could not be constitutionally applied to those whose religion commanded the practice.... Subsequent decisions have consistently held that the right of free exercise does not relieve an individual of the obligation to comply with a "valid and neutral law of general applicability on the ground that the law proscribes (or prescribes) conduct that his religion prescribes (or proscribes)." In *Prince v. Massachusetts,* we held that a mother could be prosecuted under the child labor laws for using her children to dispense literature in the streets, her religious motivation notwithstanding.... In *Gillette v. United States,* we sustained the military Selective Service System against the claim that it violated free exercise by conscripting persons who opposed a particular war on religious grounds.

Our most recent decision involving a neutral, generally applicable regulatory law that compelled activity forbidden by an individual's religion was *United States v. Lee*. There, an Amish employer, on behalf of himself and his employees, sought exemption from collection and payment of Social Security taxes on the ground that the Amish faith prohibited participation in governmental support programs. We rejected the claim that an exemption was constitutionally required....

[C.] The only decisions in which we have held that the First Amendment bars application of a neutral, generally applicable law to religiously motivated action have involved not the Free Exercise Clause alone, but the Free Exercise Clause in conjunction with other constitutional protections, such as freedom of speech and of the press, see[, *e.g.*,] *Cantwell v. Connecticut,* 310 U.S. 296 (1940), or the right of parents ... to direct the education of their children, see *Wisconsin v. Yoder*.... And it is easy to envision a case in which a challenge on freedom of association grounds would likewise be reinforced by Free Exercise Clause concerns. Cf. *Roberts v. U.S. Jaycees*. The present case does not present such a hybrid situation ....

[D.] Respondents argue that even though exemption from generally applicable criminal laws need not automatically be extended to religiously motivated actors, at least the claim for a religious exemption must be evaluated under the balancing test set forth in *Sherbert v. Verner*.... Applying that test we have ... invalidated state unemployment compensation rules that conditioned the availability of benefits upon an applicant's willingness to work under conditions forbidden by his religion....

Even if we were inclined to breathe into *Sherbert* some life beyond the unemployment compensation field, we would not apply it to require exemptions from a generally applicable criminal law. The *Sherbert* test, it must be recalled, was developed in a context that lent itself to individualized governmental assessment of the reasons for the relevant conduct[, *i.e.*,] ... the particular circumstances behind an applicant's unemployment .... As the plurality pointed out in *Bowen v. Roy,* 476 U.S. 693 (1986), our decisions in the unemployment cases stand for the proposition that where the State has in place a system of individual exemptions, it may not refuse to extend that system to cases of "religious hardship" without compelling reason. [*Roy* supported the distinction this way: "If a state creates [a mechanism for individualized exemptions], its refusal to extend an exemption to an instance of religious hardship suggests a discriminatory intent. Thus, ... to consider a religiously motivated resignation to be 'without good cause' tends to exhibit hostility, not neutrality, towards religion."—ed.]

Whether or not the decisions are that limited, they at least have nothing to do with an across-the-board criminal prohibition on a particular form of conduct. Although ... we have sometimes used the *Sherbert* test to analyze free exercise challenges to such laws, see *Lee; Gillette*, we have never applied the test to invalidate one. We conclude today that the sounder approach, and the approach in accord with the vast majority of our precedents, is to hold the test inapplicable to such challenges.

[E.] The government's ability to enforce generally applicable prohibitions of socially harmful conduct, like its ability to carry out other aspects of public policy, "cannot depend on measuring the effects of a governmental action on a religious objector's spiritual development." To make an individual's obligation to obey such a law contingent upon the law's coincidence with his religious beliefs, except where the State's interest is "compelling"— permitting him, by virtue of his beliefs, "to become a law unto himself"— contradicts both constitutional tradition and common sense.

The "compelling government interest" requirement seems benign, because it is familiar from other fields [such as race classifications and content-based speech restrictions].... [But w]hat it produces in those other fields—equality of treatment and an unrestricted flow of contending speech—are constitutional norms; what it would produce here—a private right to ignore generally applicable laws—is a constitutional anomaly.

{[A] comparison with other fields [such as freedom from race discrimination and freedom of speech] supports ... the conclusion we draw today. Just as we subject to the most exacting scrutiny laws that make classifications based on race, or on the content of speech, so too we strictly scrutinize governmental classifications based on religion, see *McDaniel v. Paty*.

But we have held that race-neutral laws that have the *effect* of disproportionately disadvantaging a particular racial group do not thereby become subject to compelling-interest analysis under the Equal Protection Clause, and we have held that generally applicable laws unconcerned with regulating speech that have the *effect* of interfering with speech do not thereby become subject to compelling-interest analysis under the First Amendment.}

Nor is it possible to limit the impact of respondents' proposal by requiring a "compelling state interest" only when the conduct prohibited is "central" to the individual's religion. It is no more appropriate for judges to determine the "centrality" of religious beliefs before applying a "compelling interest" test in the free exercise field, than it would be for them to determine the "importance" of ideas before applying the "compelling interest" test in the free speech field.

What principle of law or logic can be brought to bear to contradict a believer's assertion that a particular act is "central" to his personal faith? Judging the centrality of different religious practices is akin to the unacceptable "business of evaluating the relative merits of differing religious claims" [or] ... "... the validity of particular litigants' interpretations of those creeds." ... [C]ourts must not presume to determine the place of a particular belief in a religion or the plausibility of a religious claim. [Justice O'Connor agreed on this particular point.—ed.]

{[Yet] dispensing with a "centrality" inquiry [while maintaining a constitutional exemption regime] is utterly unworkable. It would require, for example, the same degree of "compelling state interest" to impede the practice of throwing rice at church weddings as to impede the practice of getting married in church....

Nor is this difficulty avoided by Justice Blackmun's assertion that "although ... courts should refrain from delving into questions whether, as a matter of religious doctrine, a particular practice is 'central' to the religion, ... I do not think this means that the courts must turn a blind eye to the severe impact of a State's restrictions on the adherents of a minority religion." As Justice Blackmun's opinion proceeds to make clear, inquiry into "severe impact" is no different from inquiry into centrality. He has merely substituted for the question "How important is X to the religious adherent?" the question "How great will be the harm to the religious adherent if X is taken away?" There is no material difference.}

If the "compelling interest" test is to be applied at all, then, it must be applied across the board, to all actions thought to be religiously commanded. Moreover, if "compelling interest" really means what it says (and watering it down here would subvert its rigor in the other fields where it is applied), many laws will not meet the test. Any society adopting such a system would be courting anarchy, but that danger increases in direct proportion to the society's diversity of religious beliefs, and its determination to coerce or suppress none of them.

Precisely because "we are a cosmopolitan nation made up of people of almost every conceivable religious preference," and precisely because we value and protect that religious divergence, we cannot afford the luxury of deeming *presumptively invalid*, as applied to the religious objector, every regulation of conduct that does not protect an interest of the highest order. The rule respondents favor would open the prospect of constitutionally required religious exemptions from civic obligations of almost every conceivable kind—ranging from compulsory military service, to the payment of taxes; to health and safety regulation such as manslaughter and child neglect laws, compulsory vaccination laws, drug laws, and traffic laws; to social welfare legislation such as minimum wage laws, child labor laws, animal cruelty laws, environmental protection laws, and laws providing for equality of opportunity for the races [citing cases involving claimed exemptions from each of these laws—ed.]. The First Amendment's protection of religious liberty does not require this.

{Justice O'Connor contends that [this] "parade of horribles" ... only "demonstrates ... that courts have been quite capable of ... strik[ing] sensible balances between religious liberty and competing state interests." But the cases we cite have struck "sensible balances" only because they have all applied the general laws, despite the claims for religious exemption.

In any event, ... the purpose of our parade ... is not to suggest that courts would necessarily permit harmful exemptions from these laws (though they might), but to suggest that courts would constantly be in the business of determining whether the "severe impact" of various laws on religious practice (to use Justice Blackmun's terminology) or the "constitutiona[l] significan[ce]" of the "burden on the specific plaintiffs" (to use Justice O'Connor's terminology) suffices to permit us to confer an exemption. It is a parade of horribles because it is horrible to contemplate that federal judges will regularly balance against the importance of general laws the significance of religious practice.}

[F.] Values that are protected against government interference through enshrinement in the Bill of Rights are not thereby banished from the political process.... [A] society that believes in the negative protection accorded to religious belief can be expected to be solicitous of that value in its legislation .... It is therefore not surprising that a number of States have made an exception to their drug laws for sacramental peyote use.

But to say that a nondiscriminatory religious-practice exemption is permitted, or even ... desirable, is not to say that it is constitutionally required, and that the appropriate occasions for its creation can be discerned by the courts. It may fairly be said that leaving accommodation to the political process will place at a relative disadvantage those religious practices that are not widely engaged in; but that unavoidable consequence of democratic government must be preferred to a system in which each conscience is a law unto itself or in which judges weigh the social importance of all laws against the centrality of all religious beliefs....

Justice O'Connor[, concurring in the judgment, joined in relevant part by] Justice Brennan, Justice Marshall, and Justice Blackmun....

[T]he "free *exercise*" of religion often, if not invariably, requires the performance of (or abstention from) certain acts. Cf. *A New English Dictionary on Historical Principles* (1897) (defining "exercise" to include "[t]he practice and performance of rites and ceremonies, worship, etc.; the right or permission to celebrate the observances (of a religion)" and religious observances such as acts of public and private worship, preaching, and prophesying).... Because the First Amendment does not distinguish between religious belief and religious conduct, conduct motivated by sincere religious belief, like the belief itself, must be at least presumptively protected by the Free Exercise Clause....

A person who is barred from engaging in religiously motivated conduct is barred from freely exercising his religion [and coerced to violate his religious conscience] ... regardless of whether the law prohibits the conduct only when engaged in for religious reasons, only by members of that religion, or by all persons.... If the First Amendment is to have any vitality, it ought not be construed to cover only the extreme and hypothetical situation in which a State directly targets a religious practice....

[T]he freedom to act, unlike the freedom to believe, cannot be absolute.... [But] the approach more consistent with our role as judges to decide each case on its individual merits[] is to apply [the strict scrutiny] test in each case to determine whether the burden on the specific plaintiffs before us is constitutionally significant and whether the particular criminal interest asserted by the State before us is compelling. Even if, as an empirical matter, a government's criminal laws might usually serve a compelling interest in health, safety, or public order, the First Amendment at least requires a case-by-case determination of the question, sensitive to the facts of each particular claim....

Although the Court suggests that the compelling interest test, as applied to generally applicable laws, would result in a "constitutional anomaly," the First Amendment unequivocally makes freedom of religion, like freedom from race discrimination and freedom of speech, a "constitutional nor[m]," not an "anomaly." Nor would application of our established free exercise doctrine to this case necessarily be incompatible with our equal protection cases, cf. *Rogers v. Lodge,* 458 U.S. 613 (1982) (race-neutral law that "bears more heavily on one race than another" may violate equal protection); *Castaneda v. Partida,* 430 U.S. 482 (1977) (grand jury selection), [though w]e have in any event recognized that the Free Exercise Clause protects values distinct from those protected by the Equal Protection Clause.... Our free speech cases similarly recognize that neutral regulations that affect free speech values are subject to a balancing, rather than categorical, approach. See, *e.g., United States v. O'Brien....*

Finally, the Court today suggests that the disfavoring of minority religions is an "unavoidable consequence" under our system of government and that accommodation of such religions must be left to the political process. In my view, however, the First Amendment was enacted precisely to protect the rights of those whose religious practices are not shared by the majority and may be viewed with hostility.... The compelling interest test reflects the First Amendment's mandate of preserving religious liberty to the fullest extent possible in a pluralistic society. For the Court to deem this command a "luxury," is to denigrate "[t]he very purpose of a Bill of Rights."

{The Court endeavors to escape from [cases such as *Cantwell* and *Yoder*]... by labeling them "hybrid" decisions, but there is no denying that both cases expressly relied on the Free Exercise Clause, and that we have consistently regarded those cases as part of the mainstream of our free exercise jurisprudence. Moreover, in each of the other cases cited by the Court to support its categorical rule, we rejected the particular constitutional claims before us only after carefully weighing the competing interests.... The Court's parade of horribles not only fails as a reason for discarding the compelling interest test, it instead demonstrates just the opposite: that courts have been quite capable of applying our free exercise jurisprudence to strike sensible balances between religious liberty and competing state interests.}

[Justice O'Connor—but not Justices Blackmun, Brennan, and Marshall—nonetheless concurred in the judgment, because she thought denying the exemption from peyote law was necessary to serve a compelling government in preventing drug abuse: "Because the health effects caused by the use of controlled substances exist regardless of the motivation of the user, the use of such substances, even for religious purposes, violates the very purpose of the laws that prohibit them. Moreover, in view of the societal interest in preventing trafficking in controlled substances, uniform application of the criminal prohibition at issue is essential to the effectiveness of Oregon's stated interest in preventing any possession of peyote."—ed.]

Justice Blackmun, with whom Justice Brennan and Justice Marshall join, dissenting....

[Justice Blackmun argued that granting the religious exemption from peyote law wouldn't sufficiently undermine the government interest, partly because "The carefully circumscribed ritual context in which respondents used peyote is far removed from the irresponsible and unrestricted recreational use of unlawful drugs. The Native American Church's internal restrictions on, and supervision of, its members' use of peyote substantially obviate the State's health and safety concerns." But he also added some arguments that responded to the majority's broader argument:—ed.]

[A.] "Behind every free exercise claim is a spectral march; grant this one, a voice whispers to each judge, and you will be confronted with an endless chain of exemption demands from religious deviants of every stripe." ... [But t]he State's apprehension of a flood of other religious claims is purely speculative. Almost half the States, and the Federal Government, have maintained an exemption for religious peyote use for many years, and apparently have not found themselves overwhelmed by claims to other religious exemptions. {Over the years, various sects have raised free exercise claims regarding drug use [mostly involving marijuana, but also heroin, LSD, and hashish—ed.]. In no reported case, except those involving claims of religious peyote use, has the claimant prevailed.}

Allowing an exemption for religious peyote use would not necessarily oblige the State to grant a similar exemption to other religious groups. The unusual circumstances that make the religious use of peyote compatible with the State's interests in health and safety [the Native American Church's using peyote only in a limited ceremonial context] and in preventing drug trafficking [the absence of a substantial black market in peyote] would not apply to other religious claims....

Though the State must treat all religions equally, and not favor one over another, this obligation is fulfilled by the uniform application of the "compelling interest" *test* to all free exercise claims, not by reaching uniform *results* as to all claims. A showing that religious peyote use does not unduly interfere with the State's interests is "one that probably few other religious groups or sects could make"; this does not mean that an exemption limited to peyote use is tantamount to an establishment of religion.

[B.] Finally, although I agree ... that courts should refrain from delving into questions whether, as a matter of religious doctrine, a particular practice is "central" to the religion, I do not think this means that the courts must turn a blind eye to the severe impact of a State's restrictions on the adherents of a minority religion. Respondents believe, and their sincerity has *never* been at issue, that the peyote plant embodies their deity, and eating it is an act of worship and communion. Without peyote, they could not enact the essential ritual of their religion....

d. Reynolds v. United States, 98 U.S. 145 (1879)

This is an indictment ... in ... the Territory of Utah, charging George

Reynolds with [violating the bigamy statute:] ... "Every person having a husband or wife living, who marries another ... in a Territory[,] ... is guilty of bigamy, and shall be punished by a fine of not more than $500, and by imprisonment for ... not more than five years." ...

Chief Justice Waite delivered the opinion of the court....

[T]he question ... is, whether those who make polygamy a part of their religion are excepted from the operation of the statute.... This would be introducing a new element into criminal law. Laws are made for the government of actions, and while they cannot interfere with mere religious belief and opinions, they may with practices.

Suppose one believed that human sacrifices were a necessary part of religious worship, would it be seriously contended that the civil government under which he lived could not interfere to prevent a sacrifice? Or if a wife religiously believed it was her duty to burn herself upon the funeral pile of her dead husband, would it be beyond the power of the civil government to prevent her carrying her belief into practice?

So here, ... it is provided that plural marriages shall not be allowed. Can a man excuse his practices to the contrary because of his religious belief? To permit this would be to make the professed doctrines of religious belief superior to the law of the land, and in effect to permit every citizen to become a law unto himself. Government could exist only in name under such circumstances....

e.   *Thomas v. Review Bd., 450 U.S. 707 (1981) (Rehnquist, J., dissenting)*

[Then-Associate Justice Rehnquist was an early supporter of what came to be the *Smith* rule; he wrote this in a case that basically applied *Sherbert v. Verner* to a similar unemployment compensation claim:—ed.]

{[T]oday's decision ... reads the Free Exercise Clause too broadly and it fails to squarely acknowledge that such a reading conflicts with many of our Establishment Clause cases.} ...

Although today's decision requires a State to provide direct financial assistance to persons solely on the basis of their religious beliefs, the Court nonetheless blandly assures us, just as it did in *Sherbert*, that its decision "plainly" does not foster the "establishment" of religion. I would agree that the Establishment Clause, properly interpreted, would not be violated if Indiana voluntarily chose to grant unemployment benefits to those persons who left their jobs for religious reasons. But I also believe that the decision below is inconsistent with many of our prior Establishment Clause cases....

If Indiana were to legislate what the Court today requires—an unemployment compensation law which permitted benefits to be granted to those persons who quit their jobs for religious reasons—the statute would "plainly" violate the Establishment Clause as interpreted in such cases as *Lemon* .... First, although the unemployment statute as a whole would be enacted to serve a secular legislative purpose, the proviso would clearly serve only a religious purpose. It would grant financial benefits for the sole purpose of accommodating religious beliefs. Second, there can be little doubt that the primary effect of the proviso would be to "advance" religion by facilitating the exercise of religious belief.

Third, any statute including such a proviso would surely "entangle" the State in religion far more than the mere grant of tax exemptions ... or the award of tuition grants and tax credits .... By granting financial benefits to persons solely on the basis of their religious beliefs, the State must necessarily inquire whether the claimant's belief is "religious" and whether it is sincerely held....

{To the extent *Sherbert* was correctly decided, it might be argued that cases such as [*Engel v. Vitale*, *Lemon v. Kurtzman*, and others] were wrongly decided. The "aid" rendered to religion in these latter cases may not be significantly different, in kind or degree, than the "aid" afforded Mrs. Sherbert or Thomas.

For example, if the State in *Sherbert* could not deny compensation to one refusing work for religious reasons, it might be argued that a State may not deny reimbursement to students who choose for religious reasons to attend parochial schools. The argument would be that although a State need not allocate any funds to education, once it has done so, it may not require any person to sacrifice his religious beliefs in order to obtain an equal education. There can be little doubt that to the extent secular education provides answers to important moral questions without reference to religion or teaches that there are no answers, a person in one sense sacrifices his religious belief by attending secular schools. And even if such "aid" were not constitutionally compelled by the Free Exercise Clause, Justice Harlan may well have been right in *Sherbert* when he found sufficient flexibility in the Establishment Clause to permit the States to voluntarily choose to grant such benefits to individuals.} ...

f. United States v. Lee, 455 U.S. 252 (1982) (Stevens, J., concurring in the judgment)

[Justice Stevens was also an early supporter of the *Smith* rule; he wrote this in a case where the Court applied strict scrutiny to a claim by the Amish that they were entitled to a religious exemption from the obligation to pay social security taxes.—ed.]

... [T]he principal reason for adopting a strong presumption against [claims to tax exemption on religious grounds] ... is the overriding interest in keeping the government—whether it be the legislature or the courts—out of the business of evaluating the relative merits of differing religious claims. The risk that governmental approval of some and disapproval of others will be perceived as favoring one religion over another is an important risk the Establishment Clause was designed to preclude....

g. Policy—Value of Bright-Line Rules

Basic argument: "The best way to interpret the First Amendment is as requiring _____, because the alternatives will lead to too much subjectivity, judicial discretion, discrimination, or entanglement of the government in religious disputes, which is bad because _____. And under this bright-line reading this particular government action is constitutional/unconstitutional, because _____."

1. "There is no principled way, ... for purposes of this case, to distinguish between general taxes and those imposed under the Social Security Act. If, for example, a religious adherent believes war is a sin, and if a certain percentage of the federal budget can be identified as devoted to war-related activities, such individuals would have a similarly valid claim to be exempt from paying that percentage of the income tax. The tax system could not function if denominations were allowed to challenge the tax system because tax payments were spent in a manner that violates their religious belief." *United States v. Lee.*

"Nor is it possible to limit the impact of respondents' proposal by requiring a 'compelling state interest' only when the conduct prohibited is 'central' to the individual's religion. It is no more appropriate for judges to determine the 'centrality' of religious beliefs before applying a 'compelling interest' test in the free exercise field, than it would be for them to determine the 'importance' of ideas before applying the 'compelling interest' test in the free speech field." *Employment Div. v. Smith.*

"Justice O'Connor contends that the 'parade of horribles' in the text only 'demonstrates ... that courts have been quite capable of ... strik[ing] sensible balances between religious liberty and competing state interests.' But the cases we cite have struck 'sensible balances' only because they have all applied the general laws, despite the claims for religious exemption. In any event, ... the purpose of our parade ... is not to suggest that courts would necessarily permit harmful exemptions from these laws (though they might), but to suggest that courts would constantly be in the business of determining whether the 'severe impact' of various laws on religious practice ... or the 'constitutiona[l] significan[ce]' of the 'burden on the specific plaintiffs' ... suffices to permit us to confer an exemption. It is a parade of horribles because it is horrible to contemplate that federal judges will regularly balance against the importance of general laws the significance of religious practice." *Id.*

"[B]alancing tests ... are susceptible to overt and, even more important, unconscious manipulation. Those administering them, not excluding the Justices of the Supreme Court, may sincerely believe that they are giving appropriate weight to the individual's claims and the government's interest, but may in fact be assigning erroneous weights.... [P]recisely because [the facial neutrality] analysis calls for the invocation of a rigid and easily applied test—'Does the regulation at issue utilize a religious classification?'— it is preferable as doctrine to the competitors; unlike them, it is unlikely to produce distorted outcomes because of the judges' unconscious predilections." Mark Tushnet, *"Of Church and State and the Supreme Court": Kurland Revisited,* 1989 Sup. Ct. Rev. 373, 382, 400.

See also the quotes under item 3 on p. 964.

2. Response to 1: In fact, the alternative to the bright-line rule, namely _____, will work just fine, because _____.

"The Court's parade of horribles not only fails as a reason for discarding the compelling interest test, it instead demonstrates just the opposite: that courts have been quite capable of applying our free exercise jurisprudence to strike sensible balances between religious liberty and competing state interests." *Smith* (O'Connor, J., concurring in the judgment).

"The State's apprehension of a flood of other religious claims is purely speculative. Almost half the States, and the Federal Government, have maintained an exemption for religious peyote use for many years, and apparently have not found themselves overwhelmed by claims to other religious exemptions. Allowing an exemption for religious peyote use would not necessarily oblige the State to grant a similar exemption to other religious groups. The unusual circumstances that make the religious use of peyote compatible with the State's interests in health and safety and in preventing drug trafficking would not apply to other religious claims." *Id.* (Blackmun, J., dissenting).

"Though the State must treat all religions equally, and not favor one over another, this obligation is fulfilled by the uniform application of the 'compelling interest' *test* to all free exercise claims, not by reaching uniform *results* as to all claims. A showing that religious peyote use does not unduly interfere with the State's interests is 'one that probably few other religious groups or sects could make'; this does not mean that an exemption limited to peyote use is tantamount to an establishment of religion." *Id.* (Blackmun, J., dissenting).

"In most areas of constitutional law, ... the Court does not hesitate to weigh the social importance of laws against their impact on constitutional rights. There is no particular reason to believe that judgments under the Free Exercise Clause are any more discretionary or prone to judicial abuse than judgments under the Commerce Clause, the Due Process Clause, or the Free Speech Clause ...." Michael W. McConnell, *Free Exercise Revisionism and the Smith Decision,* 57 U. Chi. L. Rev. 1109, 1144 (1990).

h. Policy—Text

Basic argument: "[T]he constitutional text must be interpreted as meaning _____, because _____, and applied here this means that this government action is constitutional/unconstitutional."

1. "As a textual matter, we do not think the words must be given [a] meaning [compelling the granting of exemptions]. It is no more necessary to regard the collection of a general tax, for example, as 'prohibiting the free exercise [of religion]' by those citizens who believe support of organized government to be sinful, than it is to regard the same tax as 'abridging the freedom ... of the press' of those publishing companies that must pay the tax as a condition of staying in business. It is a permissible reading of the text,

in the one case as in the other, to say that if prohibiting the exercise of religion (or burdening the activity of printing) is not the object of the tax but merely the incidental effect of a generally applicable and otherwise valid provision, the First Amendment has not been offended." *Employment Div. v. Smith.*

"The establishment clause actually adopted is one of the broadest versions considered by either House. It forbids not only establishments, but also any law respecting or relating to an establishment. Most important, it forbids any law respecting an establishment of 'religion.' It does not say 'a religion,' 'a national religion,' 'one sect or society,' or 'any particular denomination of religion.' It is religion generically that may not be established." Douglas Laycock, *"Nonpreferential" Aid to Religion: A False Claim About Original Intent,* 27 Wm. & Mary L. Rev. 875, 881 (1985/86).

"[T]he final draft [of the Establishment Clause] contains the word 'respecting.' Like 'touching,' 'respecting' means concerning, or with reference to. But it also means with respect—that is, 'reverence,' 'goodwill,' 'regard'—to. Taking into account this richer meaning, the Establishment Clause, in banning laws that concern religion, especially prohibits those that pay homage to religion." *County of Allegheny v. ACLU,* 492 U.S. 573, 649 (1989) (Stevens, J., concurring in part and dissenting in part).

"[The First Amendment's] authors did not simply prohibit the establishment of a state church or a state religion .... Instead they commanded that there should be 'no law *respecting* an establishment of religion.' A law may be one 'respecting' the forbidden objective while falling short of its total realization.... A given law might not *establish* a state religion but nevertheless be one 'respecting' that end in the sense of being a step that could lead to such establishment and hence offend the First Amendment." *Lemon v. Kurtzman.*

2. Response to 1: No, the text means something else, namely _____.

"[T]he 'free *exercise*' of religion often, if not invariably, requires the performance of (or abstention from) certain acts [citing a dictionary definition].... [A] law that prohibits certain conduct—conduct that happens to be an act of worship for someone—manifestly does prohibit that person's free exercise of his religion. A person who is barred from engaging in religiously motivated conduct is barred from freely exercising his religion[,] ... regardless of whether the law prohibits the conduct only when engaged in for religious reasons, only by members of that religion, or by all persons." *Smith* (O'Connor, J., concurring in the judgment).

"Congress could not enact legislation operable at the *state* level on certain matters pertaining to ('respecting') religion. {The word 'respecting' in the Establishment Clause is synonymous with 'pertaining to' or 'concerning.' Chief Justice Burger was mistaken when, without any authority, he remarked that 'respecting' meant 'a step that could lead to' an establishment.} ... [T]he new central government was without competence to abolish state religious establishments. Likewise, the national government was without power to undo state laws that had earlier disestablished a church....

Congress [also] had no authority to set up a national church, or even to support financially the full spectrum of American religions on a nonpreferential basis." Carl H. Esbeck, *The Establishment Clause as a Structural Restraint on Government Power,* 84 Iowa L. Rev. 1, 14, 18 & n.52 (1998).

i.   *Hosanna-Tabor Evangelical Lutheran Church v. EEOC, 132 S. Ct. 694 (2012)*

  i.   *Should There Be a Ministerial Exemption?*

Chief Justice Roberts delivered the opinion [for the unanimous] Court....

[A.] Hosanna-Tabor operated a small school in Redford, Michigan, offering a "Christ-centered education" to students in kindergarten through eighth grade. [Cheryl Perich was a kindergarten and fourth-grade teacher at the school since 1999.] ...

Perich became ill in June 2004 with what was eventually diagnosed as narcolepsy. Symptoms included sudden and deep sleeps from which she could not be roused. Because of her illness, Perich began the 2004–2005 school year on disability leave. On January 27, 2005, however, Perich notified the school principal, Stacey Hoeft, that she would be able to report to work the following month. Hoeft responded that the school had already contracted with a lay teacher to fill Perich's position for the remainder of the school year. Hoeft also expressed concern that Perich was not yet ready to return to the classroom.

On January 30, Hosanna-Tabor held a meeting of its congregation at which school administrators stated that Perich was unlikely to be physically capable of returning to work that school year or the next. The congregation voted to offer Perich a "peaceful release" from her call, whereby the congregation would pay a portion of her health insurance premiums in exchange for her resignation as a called teacher. Perich refused to resign and produced a note from her doctor stating that she would be able to return to work on February 22. The school board urged Perich to reconsider, informing her that the school no longer had a position for her, but Perich stood by her decision not to resign.

On the morning of February 22—the first day she was medically cleared to return to work—Perich presented herself at the school. Hoeft asked her to leave but she would not do so until she obtained written documentation that she had reported to work. Later that afternoon, Hoeft called Perich at home and told her that she would likely be fired. Perich responded that she had spoken with an attorney and intended to assert her legal rights.

Following a school board meeting that evening, board chairman Scott Salo ... advis[ed] Perich that the congregation would consider whether to rescind her call[, citing] ... Perich's "insubordination and disruptive behavior" on February 22, as well as the damage she had done to her "working relationship" with the school by "threatening to take legal action." The congregation voted to rescind Perich's call on April 10, and Hosanna-Tabor sent her a letter of termination the next day....

[T]he Americans with Disabilities Act ... prohibits an employer from discriminating against a qualified individual on the basis of disability. It also prohibits an employer from retaliating "against any individual because such individual has opposed any act or practice made unlawful by [the ADA] ...." The [Equal Employment Opportunity Commission and Perich] brought suit against Hosanna-Tabor, alleging that Perich had been fired in retaliation for threatening to file an ADA lawsuit ... [and seeking] Perich's reinstatement to her former position (or frontpay in lieu thereof), along with backpay, compensatory and punitive damages, attorney's fees, and other injunctive relief....

[B.] Both Religion Clauses bar the government from interfering with the decision of a religious group to fire one of its ministers.... It was against [the] background [of English government control over church selection of ministers] that the First Amendment was adopted. Familiar with life under the established Church of England, the founding generation sought to foreclose the possibility of a national church. By forbidding the "establishment of religion" and guaranteeing the "free exercise thereof," the Religion Clauses ensured that the new Federal Government—unlike the English Crown—would have no role in filling ecclesiastical offices. The Establishment Clause prevents the Government from appointing ministers, and the Free Exercise Clause prevents it from interfering with the freedom of religious groups to select their own.

This understanding of the Religion Clauses was reflected in two events involving James Madison, "the leading architect of the religion clauses of the First Amendment." The first occurred in 1806, when John Carroll, the first Catholic bishop in the United States, solicited the Executive's opinion on who should be appointed to direct the affairs of the Catholic Church in the territory newly acquired by the Louisiana Purchase. After consulting with President Jefferson, then-Secretary of State Madison responded that the selection of church "functionaries" was an "entirely ecclesiastical" matter left to the Church's own judgment. The "scrupulous policy of the Constitution in guarding against a political interference with religious affairs," Madison explained, prevented the Government from rendering an opinion on the "selection of ecclesiastical individuals."

The second episode occurred in 1811, when Madison was President. Congress had passed a bill incorporating the Protestant Episcopal Church in the town of Alexandria in what was then the District of Columbia. Madison vetoed the bill, on the ground that it "exceeds the rightful authority to which Governments are limited, by the essential distinction between civil and religious functions, and violates, in particular, the article of the Constitution of the United States, which declares, that 'Congress shall make no law respecting a religious establishment.'" Madison explained:

> The bill enacts into, and establishes by law, sundry rules and proceedings relative purely to the organization and polity of the church incorporated, and comprehending even the election and removal of the Minister of the same; so that no change could be made therein by the particular society, or

by the general church of which it is a member, and whose authority it recognises....

[C.] [T]he Courts of Appeals have uniformly recognized the existence of a "ministerial exception," grounded in the First Amendment, that precludes application of [antidiscrimination laws] to claims concerning the employment relationship between a religious institution and its ministers.

We agree that there is such a ministerial exception. The members of a religious group put their faith in the hands of their ministers. Requiring a church to accept or retain an unwanted minister, or punishing a church for failing to do so, intrudes upon more than a mere employment decision. Such action interferes with the internal governance of the church, depriving the church of control over the selection of those who will personify its beliefs. By imposing an unwanted minister, the state infringes the Free Exercise Clause, which protects a religious group's right to shape its own faith and mission through its appointments. According the state the power to determine which individuals will minister to the faithful also violates the Establishment Clause, which prohibits government involvement in such ecclesiastical decisions.

{[Even awards of] frontpay in lieu of reinstatement, backpay, compensatory and punitive damages, and attorney's fees ... would operate as a penalty on the Church for terminating an unwanted minister, and would be no less prohibited by the First Amendment than an order overturning the termination. Such relief would depend on a determination that [a religious group] was wrong to have relieved [a minister] of her position, and it is precisely such a ruling that is barred by the ministerial exception.}

The EEOC and Perich ... grant ... that it would violate the First Amendment for courts to apply [employment discrimination] laws to compel the ordination of women by the Catholic Church or by an Orthodox Jewish seminary. According to the EEOC and Perich, religious organizations could successfully defend against employment discrimination claims in those circumstances by invoking the constitutional right to freedom of association—a right "implicit" in the First Amendment. *Roberts v. United States Jaycees.* The EEOC and Perich thus see no need—and no basis—for a special rule for ministers grounded in the Religion Clauses themselves.

We find this position untenable. The right to freedom of association is a right enjoyed by religious and secular groups alike. It follows under the EEOC's and Perich's view that the First Amendment analysis should be the same, whether the association in question is the Lutheran Church, a labor union, or a social club. That result is hard to square with the text of the First Amendment itself, which gives special solicitude to the rights of religious organizations. We cannot accept the remarkable view that the Religion Clauses have nothing to say about a religious organization's freedom to select its own ministers....

The EEOC and Perich also contend that our decision in *Employment Div. v. Smith* precludes recognition of a ministerial exception.... [But] *Smith* involved government regulation of only outward physical acts. The present case, in contrast, concerns government interference with an internal church decision that affects the faith and mission of the church itself. See *Smith* (distinguishing the government's regulation of "physical acts" from its "lend[ing] its power to one or the other side in controversies over religious authority or dogma")....

{The interest of society in the enforcement of employment discrimination statutes is undoubtedly important. But so too is the interest of religious groups in choosing who will preach their beliefs, teach their faith, and carry out their mission. When a minister who has been fired sues her church alleging that her termination was discriminatory, the First Amendment has struck the balance for us. The church must be free to choose those who will guide it on its way.} ...

[D.] The EEOC ... foresee[s] a parade of horribles that will follow our recognition of a ministerial exception to employment discrimination suits. According to the EEOC ..., such an exception could protect religious organizations from liability for retaliating against employees for reporting criminal misconduct or for testifying before a grand jury or in a criminal trial. What is more, the EEOC contends, the logic of the exception would confer on religious employers "unfettered discretion" to violate employment laws by, for example, hiring children or aliens not authorized to work in the United States.

Hosanna-Tabor responds that the ministerial exception would not in any way bar criminal prosecutions for interfering with law enforcement investigations or other proceedings. Nor, according to the Church, would the exception bar government enforcement of general laws restricting eligibility for employment, because the exception applies only to suits by or on behalf of ministers themselves. Hosanna-Tabor also notes that the ministerial exception has been around in the lower courts for 40 years, and has not given rise to the dire consequences predicted by the EEOC ....

The case before us is an employment discrimination suit brought on behalf of a minister, challenging her church's decision to fire her. Today we hold only that the ministerial exception bars such a suit. We express no view on whether the exception bars other types of suits, including actions by employees alleging breach of contract or tortious conduct by their religious employers. There will be time enough to address the applicability of the exception to other circumstances if and when they arise....

Justice Alito, with whom Justice Kagan joins, concurring....

Throughout our Nation's history, religious bodies have been the preeminent example of private associations that have "act[ed] as critical buffers between the individual and the power of the State." *Roberts*. In a case like the one now before us—where the goal of the civil law in question, the elimination of discrimination against persons with disabilities, is so worthy—it is easy to forget that the autonomy of religious groups, both here in the United States and abroad, has often served as a shield against oppressive civil laws.

To safeguard this crucial autonomy, we have long recognized that the

Religion Clauses ... guarantee[] religious bodies "independence from secular control or manipulation—in short, power to decide for themselves, free from state interference, matters of church government as well as those of faith and doctrine." Religious autonomy means that religious authorities must be free to determine who is qualified to serve in positions of substantial religious importance....

Applying the protection of the First Amendment to roles of religious leadership, worship, ritual, and expression focuses on the objective functions that are important for the autonomy of any religious group, regardless of its beliefs.... "[F]orcing a group to accept certain members may impair [its ability] to express those views, and only those views, that it intends to express." *Boy Scouts of America v. Dale.* That principle applies with special force with respect to religious groups, whose very existence is dedicated to the collective expression and propagation of shared religious ideals. See *Smith* (noting that the constitutional interest in freedom of association may be "reinforced by Free Exercise Clause concerns").

As the Court notes, the First Amendment "gives special solicitude to the rights of religious organizations," but our expressive-association cases are nevertheless useful in pointing out what those essential rights are. Religious groups are the archetype of associations formed for expressive purposes, and their fundamental rights surely include the freedom to choose who is qualified to serve as a voice for their faith.

When it comes to the expression and inculcation of religious doctrine, there can be no doubt that the messenger matters.... A religion cannot depend on someone to be an effective advocate for its religious vision if that person's conduct fails to live up to the religious precepts that he or she espouses. For this reason, a religious body's right to self-governance must include the ability to select, and to be selective about, those who will serve as the very "embodiment of its message" and "its voice to the faithful." ... A religious body's control over such "employees" is an essential component of its freedom to speak in its own voice, both to its own members and to the outside world....

ii. *Who Should Be Covered by the Ministerial Exemption?*

Chief Justice Roberts delivered the opinion [for the unanimous] Court....

We are reluctant ... to adopt a rigid formula for deciding when an employee qualifies as a minister. It is enough for us to conclude, in this our first case involving the ministerial exception, that the exception covers Perich, given all the circumstances of her employment.

[A.] To begin with, Hosanna-Tabor held Perich out as a minister, with a role distinct from that of most of its members. {The Synod classifies teachers into two categories: "called" and "lay." "Called" teachers are regarded as having been called to their vocation by God through a congregation. To be eligible to receive a call from a congregation, a teacher must satisfy certain academic requirements.... "Lay" or "contract" teachers, by contrast, are not required to be [religiously trained] or even to be Lutheran.... Although teachers at the school generally performed the same duties regardless of whether they were lay or called, lay teachers were hired only when called teachers were unavailable.}

When Hosanna-Tabor extended [Perich] a call, it issued her a "diploma of vocation" according her the title "Minister of Religion, Commissioned." She was tasked with performing that office "according to the Word of God and the confessional standards of the Evangelical Lutheran Church as drawn from the Sacred Scriptures." The congregation prayed that God "bless [her] ministrations to the glory of His holy name, [and] the building of His church." In a supplement to the diploma, the congregation undertook to periodically review Perich's "skills of ministry" and "ministerial responsibilities," and to provide for her "continuing education as a professional person in the ministry of the Gospel."

Perich's title as a minister reflected a significant degree of religious training followed by a formal process of commissioning. To be eligible to become a commissioned minister, Perich had to complete eight college-level courses in subjects including biblical interpretation, church doctrine, and the ministry of the Lutheran teacher. She also had to obtain the endorsement of her local Synod district by submitting a petition that contained her academic transcripts, letters of recommendation, personal statement, and written answers to various ministry-related questions. Finally, she had to pass an oral examination by a faculty committee at a Lutheran college.

It took Perich six years to fulfill these requirements. And when she eventually did, she was commissioned as a minister only upon election by the congregation, which recognized God's call to her to teach. At that point, her call could be rescinded only upon a supermajority vote of the congregation—a protection designed to allow her to "preach the Word of God boldly."

Perich held herself out as a minister of the Church by accepting the formal call to religious service, according to its terms.... [She also] claimed a special housing allowance on her taxes that was available only to employees earning their compensation "'in the exercise of the ministry.'" In a form she submitted to the Synod following her termination, Perich again indicated that she regarded herself as a minister at Hosanna-Tabor, stating: "I feel that God is leading me to serve in the teaching ministry.... I am anxious to be in the teaching ministry again soon."

{Although [the title "commissioned minister"], by itself, does not automatically ensure coverage, the fact that an employee has been ordained or commissioned as a minister is surely relevant, as is the fact that significant religious training and a recognized religious mission underlie the description of the employee's position.}

[B.] Perich's job duties reflected a role in conveying the Church's message and carrying out its mission. Hosanna-Tabor expressly charged her with "lead[ing] others toward Christian maturity" and "teach[ing] faithfully the Word of God, the Sacred Scriptures, in its truth and purity and as set forth in all the symbolical books of the Evangelical Lutheran Church." In fulfilling these responsibilities, Perich taught her students religion four days a week, and led them in prayer three times a day. Once a week, she took her students to a school-wide chapel service, and—about twice a year—she took her turn leading it, choosing the liturgy, selecting the hymns, and delivering a short message based on verses from the Bible. During her last year of teaching, Perich also led her fourth graders in a brief devotional exercise each morning.

As a source of religious instruction, Perich performed an important role in transmitting the Lutheran faith to the next generation. {[Though it is relevant that] lay teachers at the school performed the same religious duties as Perich ... it cannot be dispositive ...[,] particularly when, as here, they did so only because commissioned ministers were unavailable.}

{It is true that [Perich's] religious duties consumed only 45 minutes of each workday, and that the rest of her day was devoted to teaching secular subjects.... The EEOC regards that as conclusive, contending that any ministerial exception "should be limited to those employees who perform exclusively religious functions." We cannot accept that view. Indeed, we are unsure whether any such employees exist. The heads of congregations themselves often have a mix of duties, including secular ones such as helping to manage the congregation's finances, supervising purely secular personnel, and overseeing the upkeep of facilities....

[Nor can we] regard the relative amount of time Perich spent performing religious functions as [not conclusive but] largely determinative.... The issue before us ... is not one that can be resolved by a stopwatch. The amount of time an employee spends on particular activities is relevant in assessing that employee's status, but that factor cannot be considered in isolation, without regard to the nature of the religious functions performed and the other considerations discussed above.}

In light of these considerations—the formal title given Perich by the Church, the substance reflected in that title, her own use of that title, and the important religious functions she performed for the Church—we conclude that Perich was a minister covered by the ministerial exception.

Justice Thomas, concurring....

A religious organization's right to choose its ministers would be hollow ... if secular courts could second-guess the organization's sincere determination that a given employee is a "minister" under the organization's theological tenets. {[T]hat Hosanna-Tabor sincerely considered Perich a minister ... would be sufficient for me to conclude that Perich's suit is properly barred by the ministerial exception.}

Our country's religious landscape includes organizations with different leadership structures and doctrines that influence their conceptions of ministerial status. The question whether an employee is a minister is itself religious in nature, and the answer will vary widely. Judicial attempts to fashion a civil definition of "minister" through a bright-line test or multi-factor analysis risk disadvantaging those religious groups whose beliefs, practices, and membership are outside of the "mainstream" or unpalatable to some.

Moreover, uncertainty about whether its ministerial designation will be rejected, and a corresponding fear of liability, may cause a religious group to conform its beliefs and practices regarding "ministers" to the prevailing secular understanding. See *Corporation of Presiding Bishop v. Amos* ("[I]t is a significant burden on a religious organization to require it, on pain of substantial liability, to predict which of its activities a secular court will consider religious. The line is hardly a bright one, and an organization might understandably be concerned that a judge would not understand its religious tenets and sense of mission. Fear of potential liability might affect the way an organization carried out what it understood to be its religious mission"). These are certainly dangers that the First Amendment was designed to guard against....

Justice Alito, with whom Justice Kagan joins, concurring....

{[W]hile a ministerial title is undoubtedly relevant in applying the First Amendment rule at issue, such a title is neither necessary nor sufficient.} The term "minister" is commonly used by many Protestant denominations to refer to members of their clergy, but the term is rarely if ever used in this way by Catholics, Jews, Muslims, Hindus, or Buddhists. In addition, the concept of ordination as understood by most Christian churches and by Judaism has no clear counterpart in some Christian denominations and some other religions. {In Islam, for example, "every Muslim can perform the religious rites, so there is no class or profession of ordained clergy. Yet there are religious leaders who are recognized for their learning and their ability to lead communities of Muslims in prayer, study, and living according to the teaching of the Qur'an and Muslim law."} {And ... some faiths [*e.g.*, Jehovah's Witnesses] consider the ministry to consist of all or a very large percentage of their members.} ...

Instead, courts should focus on the function performed by persons who work for religious bodies. The First Amendment protects the freedom of religious groups to engage in certain key religious activities, including the conducting of worship services and other religious ceremonies and rituals, as well as the critical process of communicating the faith. Accordingly, religious groups must be free to choose the personnel who are essential to the performance of these functions.

The "ministerial" exception should be tailored to this purpose. It should apply to any "employee" who leads a religious organization, conducts worship services or important religious ceremonies or rituals, or serves as a messenger or teacher of its faith. If a religious group believes that the ability of such an employee to perform these key functions has been compromised, then the constitutional guarantee of religious freedom protects the group's right to remove the employee from his or her position.

{The ministerial exception applies to respondent because, as the Court notes, she played a substantial role in "conveying the Church's message and carrying out its mission."} ...

iii. Is a "Sincerely Felt Religious Command" Required?

[In a typical religious exemption case, whether under a *Sherbert/Yoder* constitutional exemption regime or under RFRA, claimants can get exemptions only if they can show that the government action *substantially burdens* their religious practice. *See, e.g.*, RFRA (p. 1048); *United States v. Lee* (p. 1021); Part XIII.A.6.a (p. 1068). This usually means that the claimants must sincerely believe that following the law would violate their religious obligations. *See* Part XIII.A.6.a. One question in *Hosanna-Tabor* was whether (a) this substantial burden requirement should apply in ministerial exemption cases, or whether instead (b) courts should avoid inquiring into an institution's true motivation in rejecting a minister, but should instead leave institutions with a categorical right to reject the minister on any grounds.

In some cases, such as the Catholic Church's refusal to employ women as priests, the result would be the same under either approach, because the Catholic Church sincerely believes women shouldn't be priests. But in other cases, the (a) vs. (b) choice would matter: Say, for instance, that a would-be priest claims that the Catholic Church discriminated against him based on race, something the Church does *not* believe is religiously compelled; and say the Church says instead that it rejected him because it thought he wasn't spiritually prepared to be a priest. Should it be up to the jury to decide what the Church's true reason was (as would be the case under alternative (a))? Or should the Church be free from even the inquiry into its supposed true motivations (as would be the case under alternative (b))? The excerpt below discusses this.—ed.]

Chief Justice Roberts delivered the opinion [for the unanimous] Court....

The EEOC and Perich suggest that Hosanna-Tabor's asserted religious reason for firing Perich—that she violated the Synod's commitment to internal dispute resolution—was pretextual. That suggestion misses the point of the ministerial exception. The purpose of the exception is not to safeguard a church's decision to fire a minister only when it is made for a religious reason. The exception instead ensures that the authority to select and control who will minister to the faithful—a matter "strictly ecclesiastical"—is the church's alone....

Justice Alito, with whom Justice Kagan joins, concurring....

Hosanna-Tabor discharged respondent because she threatened to file suit against the church in a civil court. This threat contravened the Lutheran doctrine that disputes among Christians should be resolved internally without resort to the civil court system and all the legal wrangling it entails. {See The Lutheran Church–Missouri Synod, Commission on Theology and Church Relations, 1 Corinthians 6:1–11: An Exegetical Study, p. 10 (Apr. 1991) (stating that instead of suing each other, Christians should seek "an amicable settlement of differences by means of a decision by fellow Christians"). See also 1 Corinthians 6:1–7 ("If any of you has a dispute with another, dare he take it before the ungodly for judgment instead of before the saints?").} In Hosanna-Tabor's view, respondent's disregard for this doctrine compromised her religious function, disqualifying her from serving effectively as a voice for the church's faith.

Respondent ... argues that this was a mere pretext for her firing, which was really done for nonreligious reasons. [But f]or civil courts to engage in [a] pretext inquiry ... would dangerously undermine ... religious autonomy .... In order to probe the real reason for respondent's firing, a civil court—and perhaps a jury—would be required to make a judgment about church doctrine.

The credibility of Hosanna-Tabor's asserted reason for terminating respondent's employment could not be assessed without taking into account both the importance that the Lutheran Church attaches to the doctrine of internal dispute resolution and the degree to which that tenet compromised respondent's religious function. If it could be shown that this belief is an obscure and minor part of Lutheran doctrine, it would be much more plausible for respondent to argue that this doctrine was not the real reason for her firing. If, on the other hand, the doctrine is a central and universally known tenet of Lutheranism, then the church's asserted reason for her discharge would seem much more likely to be nonpretextual.

But whatever the truth of the matter might be, the mere adjudication of such questions would pose grave problems for religious autonomy: It would require calling witnesses to testify about the importance and priority of the religious doctrine in question, with a civil factfinder sitting in ultimate judgment of what the accused church really believes, and how important that belief is to the church's overall mission....

Hosanna-Tabor believes that the religious function that respondent performed made it essential that she abide by the doctrine of internal dispute resolution; and the civil courts are in no position to second-guess that assessment. This conclusion rests not on respondent's ordination status or her formal title, but rather on her functional status as the type of employee that a church must be free to appoint or dismiss in order to exercise the religious liberty that the First Amendment guarantees.

4. THE RELIGIOUS FREEDOM RESTORATION ACT (RFRA) REGIME

a. *Summary*

As Part XIII.A.1.b explained, the federal RFRA (1993) was enacted in response to the *Smith* decision, and purported to restore the strict scrutiny requirement as a statutory measure. In *City of Boerne v. Flores* (1997) (p. 1048), the U.S. Supreme Court held that RFRA exceeded Congress's power as applied to the states. But the logic of the opinion strongly suggests that RFRA is still applicable to federal laws and other federal government actions; moreover, since 1990, over a dozen states have enacted state RFRAs, which cover state and local laws and government actions.

The debate over the state RFRAs has operated on the assumption that a state RFRA regime reinstates the constitutional exemption framework—that, as under *Sherbert*, a religious exemption is judicially guaranteed whenever a law substantially burdens religious practice and can't pass muster under strict scrutiny. And indeed the state RFRAs, though statutes, don't fit the traditional statutory exemption model. Under the statutory model, the legislature decides when a particular exemption should be granted; under state RFRAs, with their relatively vague standards of "compelling government interest" and "least restrictive alternative," the decision is made by a court.

But state RFRAs, being state statutes, can be modified by the legislatures that enacted them. Say a court concludes that a ban on marital-status discrimination in housing fails strict scrutiny, and a legislature disagrees, perhaps because it believes that tenants have a right to be free from such discrimination. The legislature can then simply enact a new statute: "Whereas we conclude that marital status housing discrimination violates what we see as tenants' rights, the statute banning marital status discrimination in housing shall be applied without regard to [the state RFRA]."

Thus, under these state RFRAs (or under the federal RFRA as applied to federal law), the answer to the question "When should religious exemptions be granted, and who should decide when they should be granted?" is "When the courts think such an exemption doesn't unduly jeopardize compelling state interests *and the legislature hasn't specifically overridden this judgment.*" This represents a significant change from the constitutional exemption model, under which courts had the final say.

The state RFRA can be called a *common-law exemption model* because it embodies two aspects of common-law decision making—(1) initial judicial decisionmaking, and (2) room for potential legislative revision. Unlike the statutory exemption model, and like the constitutional exemption model, state RFRAs delegate the initial decision to judicial discretion: Both the state RFRAs' text and the existing free exercise strict scrutiny case law are so vague that they rarely bind courts to any particular results. But unlike the constitutional exemption model and like the statutory exemption model, state RFRAs leave to legislatures the discretion to make the *final* decision as to whether to maintain or repeal a judicially created exemption.

Eventually, then, a state's religious exemption law may end up being mostly a creation of the courts, but with legislative modifications. When the legislature concludes that a court was too stingy with exemptions from some law, it will enact an explicit religious exemption. When the legislature concludes that a court was too generous, it will specifically provide that the law has no exemption, or a narrower exemption. The result may be much like the tort law, contract law, and property law of many states—a basic body of judge-made law, with alterations imposed by legislators when they disagree with the judges.

Thus, the defenses and criticisms of RFRAs must in some ways differ from the defenses and criticisms of the *Sherbert/Yoder* regime. On the one hand, RFRAs can't be defended as very strong protections of the minority from the majority, since they can be overridden by the legislature (though of course they do provide some important protection in the first instance). On the other hand, judicial decisions using a RFRA to grant religious exemptions can't be criticized as unwarranted judicial trumping of a democratically enacted statute—the grant of an exemption is itself the *implementation* of a democratically enacted statute (the RFRA).

Nor is it as apt to criticize judges who carve out exemptions under state RFRAs for exercising the moral and pragmatic judgment that is necessarily involved whenever strict scrutiny is applied under the *Sherbert/Yoder* model. When judges use their own moral and pragmatic judgment to permanently override the legislative will on a wide range of religiously neutral statutes, this poses problems in a democracy, where the final calls on most moral and pragmatic questions are generally supposed to be in the hands of the legislature. But in the making of the common law, judges have long been expected to exercise moral and pragmatic judgment, in part precisely because the legislature can override the common law decision by statute. See generally Eugene Volokh, *A Common-Law Model for Religious Exemptions*, 46 UCLA L. Rev. 1465 (1999).

b. *Problem: RFRA vs. Sherbert/Yoder*

Think back on problems (a) through (c) on pp. 964-965, and assume they arose in a state which has a RFRA. How would you, as attorney for the claimant, argue that the judge should be *more* willing to rule for you than he would be under the *Sherbert/Yoder*-era cases? How would you, as attorney for the other side, argue that the judge should be *less* willing to rule for the claimant than under the *Sherbert/Yoder*-era cases?

c. *Religious Freedom Restoration Act (RFRA), 42 U.S.C. §§ 2000bb to 2000bb-4 (enacted 1993)*

[State RFRAs are generally quite similar to this federal RFRA.—ed.]

§ 2000bb. Congressional Findings And Declaration Of Purposes

(a) ... The Congress finds that—

(1) the framers of the Constitution, recognizing free exercise of religion as an unalienable right, secured its protection in the First Amendment to the Constitution;

(2) laws "neutral" toward religion may burden religious exercise as surely as laws intended to interfere with religious exercise;

(3) governments should not substantially burden religious exercise without compelling justification;

(4) in Employment Division v. Smith, 494 U.S. 872 (1990) the Supreme Court virtually eliminated the requirement that the government justify burdens on religious exercise imposed by laws neutral toward religion; and

(5) the compelling interest test as set forth in prior Federal court rulings is a workable test for striking sensible balances between religious liberty and competing prior governmental interests.

(b) ... The purposes of this chapter are—

(1) to restore the compelling interest test as set forth in Sherbert v. Verner, 374 U.S. 398 (1963) and Wisconsin v. Yoder, 406 U.S. 205 (1972) and to guarantee its application in all cases where free exercise of religion is substantially burdened; and

(2) to provide a claim or defense to persons whose religious exercise is substantially burdened by government.

§ 2000bb-1. Free exercise of religion protected

(a) ... Government shall not substantially burden a person's exercise of religion even if the burden results from a rule of general applicability, except as provided in subsection (b) of this section.

(b) ... Government may substantially burden a person's exercise of religion only if it demonstrates that application of the burden to the person—

(1) is in furtherance of a compelling governmental interest; and

(2) is the least restrictive means of furthering that compelling governmental interest....

§ 2000bb-2. Definitions

As used in this chapter—

(1) the term "government" includes a branch, department, agency, instrumentality, and official (or other person acting under color of law) of the United States ...; ...

(3) the term "demonstrates" means meets the burdens of going forward with the evidence and of persuasion; and

(4) the term "exercise of religion" [includes any exercise of religion, whether or not compelled by, or central to, a system of religious belief].

[RFRA originally applied to state and local governments and laws as well as to the federal government and federal laws, but this aspect of RFRA was held unconstitutional in *City of Boerne v. Flores*.—ed.]

§ 2000bb-3. Applicability

(a) ... This chapter applies to all Federal law, and the implementation of that law, whether statutory or otherwise, and whether adopted before or after November 16, 1993.

(b) ... Federal statutory law adopted after November 16, 1993 is subject to this chapter unless such law explicitly excludes such application by reference to this chapter....

d. *Problem: RLUIPA*

Jerusalem, Ohio has a population of 10,000. Of its land, 90% is zoned to allow only single-family residential uses (together with public schools). The remaining 10% is zoned commercial, a category that allows nonprofits, including religious institutions, as well as ordinary businesses. The typical residential lot is about half an acre (about 150 feet by 150 feet).

Orthodox Jews have a religious obligation to go to synagogue at least on Friday evenings and Saturdays, and not to drive from Friday sundown to

Saturday sundown. They therefore need a synagogue within walking distance; unfortunately, for many houses in Jerusalem, the business district is more than two miles away.

Forty Orthodox families have bought a large centrally-located house, no more than a mile away from their houses, and they want to use it as a synagogue. They ask the city for a zoning variance—an exception from the zoning rules. The city council has the legal power to grant such a variance, and it has considered variance requests in the past, though it has never granted an exemption from the single-family residential use requirement.

Neighbors, however, object: They don't want to have over a hundred people converging on a neighboring house twice a week. Moreover, synagogues often hold services and other functions during the week, when Orthodox Jews are allowed to drive. Neighbors thus also worry that the synagogue will bring with it more traffic, traffic noise, and parking headaches, though obviously not on Friday nights and Saturdays.

The city council asks you for advice on whether RLUIPA requires the council to grant the variance. What do you say? (Note that the town of Jerusalem is real, but all the other facts are made up for this problem.)

e. *Religious Land Use and Institutionalized Persons Act (RLUIPA), 42 U.S.C. §§ 2000cc to 2000cc-5 (enacted 2000)*

[This statute—enacted after *City of Boerne v. Flores*—is mostly limited to federally funded programs, regulations affecting commerce, and individualized exemption schemes that remain subject to Free Exercise Clause challenge, see p. 991. In *Cutter v. Wilkinson*, the Court held that the institutionalized-persons part of the law was within Congress's power.—ed.]

§ 2000cc. Protection of land use as religious exercise

(a) ... (1) ... No government shall impose or implement a land use regulation in a manner that imposes a substantial burden on the religious exercise of a person, including a religious assembly or institution, unless the government demonstrates that imposition of the burden on that person, assembly, or institution—

(A) is in furtherance of a compelling governmental interest; and

(B) is the least restrictive means of furthering that compelling governmental interest.

(2) ... This subsection applies in any case in which—

(A) the substantial burden is imposed in a program or activity that receives Federal financial assistance, even if the burden results from a rule of general applicability;

(B) the substantial burden affects, or removal of that substantial burden would affect, commerce with foreign nations, among the several States, or with Indian tribes, even if the burden results from a rule of general applicability; or

(C) the substantial burden is imposed in the implementation of a land use regulation or system of land use regulations, under which a government makes, or has in place formal or informal procedures or practices that permit the government to make, individualized assessments of the proposed uses for the property involved....

(b) ... (3) ... No government shall impose or implement a land use regulation that—

(A) totally excludes religious assemblies from a jurisdiction; or

(B) unreasonably limits religious assemblies, institutions, or structures within a jurisdiction.

§ 2000cc-1. Protection of religious exercise of institutionalized persons

(a) ... No government shall impose a substantial burden on the religious exercise of a person residing in or confined to [a prison, a jail, or an institution for the ill or disabled] even if the burden results from a rule of general applicability, unless the government demonstrates that imposition of the burden on that person—

(1) is in furtherance of a compelling governmental interest; and

(2) is the least restrictive means of furthering that compelling governmental interest.

(b) ... This section applies in any case in which—

(1) the substantial burden is imposed in a program or activity that receives Federal financial assistance; or

(2) the substantial burden affects, or removal of that substantial burden would affect, commerce with foreign nations, among the several States, or with Indian tribes.

§ 2000cc-3. Rules of construction ...

(c) ... Nothing in this chapter shall create or preclude a right of any religious organization to receive funding or other assistance from a government, or of any person to receive government funding for a religious activity, but this chapter may require a government to incur expenses in its own operations to avoid imposing a substantial burden on religious exercise.

§ 2000cc-5. Definitions ...

(1) ... The term "claimant" means a person raising a claim or defense under this chapter.

(2) ... The term "demonstrates" means meets the burdens of going forward with the evidence and of persuasion....

(4) ... The term "government" [means any state or local government entity, or any person] acting under color of State law ....

(5) ... The term "land use regulation" means a zoning or landmarking law, or the application of such a law, that limits or restricts a claimant's use or development of land (including a structure affixed to land) ....

(7) ... The term "religious exercise" includes any exercise of religion,

whether or not compelled by, or central to, a system of religious belief.... The use, building, or conversion of real property for the purpose of religious exercise shall be considered to be religious exercise of the person or entity that uses or intends to use the property for that purpose.

f.   *Gonzales v. O Centro Espírita Beneficente União do Vegetal, 546 U.S. 418 (2006)*

Chief Justice Roberts delivered the opinion of the [unanimous] Court....

[A.] The Controlled Substances Act, 21 U.S.C. § 801 *et seq.*, regulates the importation, manufacture, distribution, and use of psychotropic substances.... Substances listed in Schedule I of the Act are subject to ... an outright ban on all importation and use, except pursuant to strictly regulated research projects. The Act authorizes the imposition of a criminal sentence for simple possession of Schedule I substances, and mandates the imposition of a criminal sentence for possession "with intent to manufacture, distribute, or dispense" such substances.

O Centro Espírita Beneficente União do Vegetal (UDV) is a Christian Spiritist sect based in Brazil, with an American branch of approximately 130 individuals. Central to the UDV's faith is receiving communion through *hoasca* (pronounced "wass-ca"), a sacramental tea made from two plants unique to the Amazon region.... [D]imethyltryptamine (DMT), a hallucinogen [contained in the plants] ..., as well as "any material, compound, mixture, or preparation, which contains any quantity of [DMT]," is listed in Schedule I ....

In 1999, United States Customs inspectors intercepted a shipment to the American UDV containing three drums of *hoasca*. A subsequent investigation revealed that the UDV had received 14 prior shipments of *hoasca*. The inspectors seized the intercepted shipment and threatened the UDV with prosecution.... [UDV challenged this under RFRA.—ed.]

[B.] The Government contends that the [Controlled Substances] Act's description of Schedule I substances as having "a high potential for abuse," "no currently accepted medical use in treatment in the United States," and "a lack of accepted safety for use ... under medical supervision," 21 U.S.C. § 812(b)(1), by itself precludes any consideration of individualized exceptions such as that sought by the UDV. The Government goes on to argue that the ... [Act's prohibition on] all use of controlled substances except as authorized by the Act itself—"cannot function with its necessary rigor and comprehensiveness if subjected to judicial exemptions."

According to the Government, there would be no way to cabin religious exceptions once recognized, and "the public will misread" such exceptions as signaling that the substance at issue is not harmful after all. Under the Government's view, there is no need to assess the particulars of the UDV's use or weigh the impact of an exemption for that specific use, because the Controlled Substances Act serves a compelling purpose and simply admits of no exceptions.

[C.] RFRA, and the strict scrutiny test it adopted, contemplate an inquiry more focused than the Government's categorical approach. RFRA requires the Government to demonstrate that the compelling interest test is satisfied through application of the challenged law "to the person"—the particular claimant whose sincere exercise of religion is being substantially burdened.

RFRA expressly adopted the compelling interest test "as set forth in Sherbert v. Verner, 374 U.S. 398 (1963) and Wisconsin v. Yoder, 406 U.S. 205 (1972)." In each of those cases, this Court looked beyond broadly formulated interests justifying the general applicability of government mandates and scrutinized the asserted harm of granting specific exemptions to particular religious claimants....

Under the more focused inquiry required by RFRA and the compelling interest test, the Government's mere invocation of the general characteristics of Schedule I substances, as set forth in the Controlled Substances Act, cannot carry the day. It is true, of course, that Schedule I substances such as DMT are exceptionally dangerous. Nevertheless, there is no indication that Congress, in classifying DMT, considered the harms posed by the particular use at issue here—the circumscribed, sacramental use of *hoasca* by the UDV.... Congress' determination that DMT should be listed under Schedule I simply does not provide a categorical answer that relieves the Government of the obligation to shoulder its burden under RFRA.

This conclusion is reinforced by the Controlled Substances Act itself. The Act contains a provision authorizing the Attorney General to "waive the requirement for registration of certain manufacturers, distributors, or dispensers if he finds it consistent with the public health and safety." The fact that the Act itself contemplates that exempting certain people from its requirements would be "consistent with the public health and safety" indicates that congressional findings with respect to Schedule I substances should not carry the determinative weight, for RFRA purposes, that the Government would ascribe to them.

And in fact an exception has been made to the Schedule I ban for religious use. For the past 35 years, there has been a regulatory exemption for use of peyote—a Schedule I substance—by the Native American Church. In 1994, Congress extended that exemption to all members of every recognized Indian Tribe. Everything the Government says about the DMT in *hoasca*— that, as a Schedule I substance, Congress has determined that it "has a high potential for abuse," "has no currently accepted medical use," and has "a lack of accepted safety for use ... under medical supervision"—applies in equal measure to the mescaline in peyote, yet both the Executive and Congress itself have decreed an exception from the Controlled Substances Act for Native American religious use of peyote.

If such use is permitted in the face of the congressional findings in § 812(b)(1) for hundreds of thousands of Native Americans practicing their faith, it is difficult to see how those same findings alone can preclude any consideration of a similar exception for the 130 or so American members of the UDV who want to practice theirs. See *Church of Lukumi Babalu Aye, Inc. v. Hialeah* ("It is established in our strict scrutiny jurisprudence that 'a law cannot be regarded as protecting an interest 'of the highest order' ... when it leaves appreciable damage to that supposedly vital interest unprohibited'").

The Government responds that there is a "unique relationship" between the United States and the Tribes, but never explains what about that "unique" relationship justifies overriding the same congressional findings on which the Government relies in resisting any exception for the UDV's religious use of *hoasca*.... Nothing about the unique political status of the Tribes makes their members immune from the health risks the Government asserts accompany any use of a Schedule I substance, nor insulates the Schedule I substance the Tribes use in religious exercise from the alleged risk of diversion.

The Government argues that the existence of a *congressional* exemption for peyote does not indicate that the Controlled Substances Act is amenable to *judicially crafted* exceptions. RFRA, however, plainly contemplates that *courts* would recognize exceptions .... Congress' role in the peyote exemption—and the Executive's—confirms that the findings in the Controlled Substances Act do not preclude exceptions altogether; RFRA makes clear that it is the obligation of the courts to consider whether exceptions are required under the [RFRA] test set forth by Congress.

[D.] The well-established peyote exception also fatally undermines the Government's broader contention that the Controlled Substances Act establishes a closed regulatory system that admits of no exceptions under RFRA. The Government argues that the effectiveness of the Controlled Substances Act will be "necessarily ... undercut" if the Act is not uniformly applied, without regard to burdens on religious exercise. The peyote exception, however, has been in place since the outset of the Controlled Substances Act, and there is no evidence that it has "undercut" the Government's ability to enforce the ban on peyote use by non-Indians.

The Government points to some pre-*Employment Div. v. Smith* cases relying on a need for uniformity in rejecting claims for religious exemptions under the Free Exercise Clause, but those cases strike us as quite different from the present one. Those cases did not embrace the notion that a general interest in uniformity justified a substantial burden on religious exercise; they instead scrutinized the asserted need and explained why the denied exemptions could not be accommodated.

In *United States v. Lee*, for example, the Court rejected a claimed exception to the obligation to pay Social Security taxes, noting that "mandatory participation is indispensable to the fiscal vitality of the social security system" and that the "tax system could not function if denominations were allowed to challenge the tax system because tax payments were spent in a manner that violates their religious belief." In *Braunfeld v. Brown*, 366 U.S. 599 (1961) (plurality opinion), the Court denied a claimed exception to Sunday closing laws, in part because allowing such exceptions "might well provide [the claimants] with an economic advantage over their competitors who must remain closed on that day." The whole point of a "uniform day of rest for all workers" would have been defeated by exceptions. These cases show that the Government can demonstrate a compelling interest in uniform application of a particular program by offering evidence that granting the requested religious accommodations would seriously compromise its ability to administer the program.

Here the Government's argument for uniformity is different; it rests not so much on the particular statutory program at issue as on slippery-slope concerns that could be invoked in response to any RFRA claim for an exception to a generally applicable law. The Government's argument echoes the classic rejoinder of bureaucrats throughout history: If I make an exception for you, I'll have to make one for everybody, so no exceptions.

But RFRA operates by mandating consideration, under the compelling interest test, of exceptions to "rule[s] of general applicability." Congress determined that the legislated test "is a workable test for striking sensible balances between religious liberty and competing prior governmental interests." This determination finds support in our cases; in *Sherbert*, for example, we rejected a slippery-slope argument similar to the one offered in this case, dismissing as "no more than a possibility" the State's speculation "that the filing of fraudulent claims by unscrupulous claimants feigning religious objections to Saturday work" would drain the unemployment benefits fund....

We do not doubt that there may be instances in which a need for uniformity precludes the recognition of exceptions to generally applicable laws under RFRA. But it would have been surprising to find that this was such a case, given the longstanding exemption from the Controlled Substances Act for religious use of peyote, and the fact that the very reason Congress enacted RFRA was to respond to a decision denying a claimed right to sacramental use of a controlled substance.

And in fact the Government has not offered evidence demonstrating that granting the UDV an exemption would cause the kind of administrative harm recognized as a compelling interest in *Lee* ... and *Braunfeld*. The Government failed to convince the District Court ... that health or diversion concerns provide a compelling interest in banning the UDV's sacramental use of *hoasca*. It cannot compensate for that failure now with the bold argument that there can be no RFRA exceptions at all to the Controlled Substances Act.

[E.] The Government argues that it has a compelling interest in meeting its international obligations by complying with {the 1971 United Nations Convention on Psychotropic Substances[,] ... which calls on signatories [including the U.S.] to prohibit the use of hallucinogens, including DMT}.... [T]hat *hoasca* is covered by the Convention, however, does not automatically mean that the Government has demonstrated a compelling interest in applying the Controlled Substances Act, which implements the Convention, to the UDV's sacramental use of the tea....

[T]he Government did not even *submit* evidence addressing the international consequences of granting an exemption for the UDV. The Government simply submitted two affidavits by State Department officials attesting to the general importance of honoring international obligations and of maintaining the leadership position of the United States in the international war on drugs. We do not doubt the validity of these interests, any more than we doubt the general interest in promoting public health and safety by enforcing the Controlled Substances Act, but under RFRA invocation of such general interests, standing alone, is not enough.

[F.] The Government repeatedly invokes Congress' findings and purposes underlying the Controlled Substances Act, but Congress had a reason for enacting RFRA, too. Congress recognized that "laws 'neutral' toward religion may burden religious exercise as surely as laws intended to interfere with religious exercise," and legislated "the compelling interest test" as the means for the courts to "strik[e] sensible balances between religious liberty and competing prior governmental interests."

We have no cause to pretend that the task assigned by Congress to the courts under RFRA is an easy one. Indeed, the very sort of difficulties highlighted by the Government here were cited by this Court in deciding that the approach later mandated by Congress under RFRA was not required as a matter of constitutional law under the Free Exercise Clause.

But Congress has determined that courts should strike sensible balances, pursuant to a compelling interest test that requires the Government to address the particular practice at issue. Applying that test, we conclude that the courts below did not err in determining that the Government failed to demonstrate, at the preliminary injunction stage, a compelling interest in barring the UDV's sacramental use of *hoasca*....

g. *Burwell v. Hobby Lobby Stores, Inc.*, 134 S. Ct. 2751 (2014)

i. *Background*

Justice Alito delivered the opinion of the Court....

[A.] At issue in these cases are HHS [United States Department of Health and Human Services] regulations promulgated under the Patient Protection and Affordable Care Act of 2010 (ACA). ACA generally requires employers with 50 or more full-time employees to offer "a group health plan or group health insurance coverage" that provides "minimum essential coverage." ...

[I]f a covered employer provides group health insurance but its plan fails to comply with ACA's group-health plan requirements, the employer may be required to pay $100 per day for each affected "individual." And if the employer decides to stop providing health insurance altogether and at least one full-time employee enrolls in a health plan and qualifies for a subsidy on one of the government-run ACA exchanges, the employer must pay $2,000 per year for each of its fulltime employees.

Unless an exception applies, ACA requires an employer's group health plan or group-health-insurance coverage to furnish "preventive care and screenings" for women without "any cost sharing requirements." Congress itself, however, did not specify what types of preventive care must be covered. Instead, Congress authorized the Health Resources and Services Administration (HRSA), a component of HHS, to make that important and sensitive decision.... In August 2011, ... the HRSA promulgated ... Guidelines [under which] nonexempt employers are generally required to provide "coverage, without cost sharing" for "[a]ll Food and Drug Administration [(FDA)] approved contraceptive methods, sterilization procedures, and patient education and counseling." Although many of the required, FDA-approved methods of contraception work by preventing the fertilization of an egg, four of those methods (those specifically at issue in these cases) may have the effect of preventing an already fertilized egg from developing any further by inhibiting its attachment to the uterus [citing the HHS brief that so stated—ed.].

HHS also authorized the HRSA to establish exemptions from the contraceptive mandate for "religious employers." That category encompasses "churches, their integrated auxiliaries, and conventions or associations of churches," as well as "the exclusively religious activities of any religious order." In its Guidelines, HRSA exempted these organizations from the requirement to cover contraceptive services.

In addition, HHS has effectively exempted certain religious nonprofit organizations, described under HHS regulations as "eligible organizations," from the contraceptive mandate. An "eligible organization" means a nonprofit organization that "holds itself out as a religious organization" and "opposes providing coverage for some or all of any contraceptive services required to be covered ... on account of religious objections." ...

When a group-health-insurance issuer receives notice that one of its clients has invoked this provision, the issuer must then exclude contraceptive coverage from the employer's plan and provide separate payments for contraceptive services for plan participants without imposing any cost-sharing requirements on the eligible organization, its insurance plan, or its employee beneficiaries. Although this procedure requires the issuer to bear the cost of these services, HHS has determined that this obligation will not impose any net expense on issuers because its cost will be less than or equal to the cost savings resulting from the services.

{In the case of self-insured religious organizations entitled to the accommodation, the third-party administrator of the organization must "provide or arrange payments for contraceptive services" for the organization's employees without imposing any cost-sharing requirements on the eligible organization, its insurance plan, or its employee beneficiaries. The regulations establish a mechanism for these third-party administrators to be compensated for their expenses by obtaining a reduction in the fee paid by insurers to participate in the federally facilitated exchanges. HHS believes that these fee reductions will not materially affect funding of the exchanges because "payments for contraceptive services will represent only a small portion of total [exchange] user fees."}

In addition to these exemptions for religious organizations, ACA exempts a great many employers from most of its coverage requirements. {[T]he contraceptive mandate "presently does not apply to tens of millions of people."} Employers providing "grandfathered health plans"—those that existed prior to March 23, 2010, and that have not made specified changes after that date—need not comply with many of the Act's requirements, including the contraceptive mandate. {Over one-third of the 149 million non-elderly people in America with employer-sponsored health plans were enrolled in grandfathered plans in 2013.} {While the Government predicts that this number will decline over time, the total number of ... [exempted employees] is still substantial, and there is no legal requirement that grandfathered plans ever be phased out.} And employers with fewer than 50 employees are not required to provide health insurance at all.... [Such smaller employers employ] 34 million workers....

[B.] Fifty years ago, Norman Hahn started a wood-working business in his garage, and since then, this company, Conestoga Wood Specialties, has grown and now has 950 employees.... The Hahns exercise sole ownership [and control] of the closely held [corporation] ....

The Hahns believe that they are required to run their business "in accordance with their [Mennonite Christian] religious beliefs and moral principles." To that end, the company's mission, as they see it, is to "operate in a professional environment founded upon the highest ethical, moral, and Christian principles." The company's "Vision and Values Statements" affirms that Conestoga endeavors to "ensur[e] a reasonable profit in [a] manner that reflects [the Hahns'] Christian heritage."

As explained in Conestoga's board-adopted "Statement on the Sanctity of Human Life," the Hahns [alongside other Mennonites] believe that "human life begins at conception." It is therefore "against [their] moral conviction to be involved in the termination of human life" after conception, which they believe is a "sin against God to which they are held accountable." The Hahns have accordingly excluded from the group-health-insurance plan they offer to their employees certain contraceptive methods that they consider to be abortifacients.

The Hahns and Conestoga sued HHS and other federal officials and agencies under RFRA ..., seeking to enjoin application of ACA's contraceptive mandate insofar as it requires them to provide health-insurance coverage for four FDA-approved contraceptives that may operate after the fertilization of an egg. These include two forms of emergency contraception commonly called "morning after" pills and two types of intrauterine devices. In opposing the requirement to provide coverage for the contraceptives to which they object, the Hahns argued that "it is immoral and sinful for [them] to intentionally participate in, pay for, facilitate, or otherwise support these drugs." ...

David and Barbara Green and their three children are Christians who own and operate two family businesses. Forty-five years ago, David Green started an arts-and-crafts store that has grown into a nationwide chain called Hobby Lobby. There are now 500 Hobby Lobby stores, and the company has more than 13,000 employees....

One of David's sons started an affiliated business, Mardel, which operates 35 Christian bookstores and employs close to 400 people.... [The] two businesses ... remain closely held [corporations], and David, Barbara, and their children retain exclusive control of both companies.... Hobby Lobby's statement of purpose commits the Greens to "[h]onoring the Lord in all [they] do by operating the company in a manner consistent with Biblical principles." Each family member has signed a pledge to run the businesses in accordance with the family's religious beliefs and to use the family assets to support Christian ministries.

In accordance with those commitments, Hobby Lobby and Mardel stores close on Sundays, even though the Greens calculate that they lose millions in sales annually by doing so. The businesses refuse to engage in profitable transactions that facilitate or promote alcohol use; they contribute profits to Christian missionaries and ministries; and they buy hundreds of full-page newspaper ads inviting people to "know Jesus as Lord and Savior." [The Hanhs' beliefs about abortifacients are very similar to the Greens'.—ed.] ... The Greens, Hobby Lobby, and Mardel sued HHS and other federal agencies and officials to challenge the contraceptive mandate under RFRA ....

ii. Does RFRA Apply to Corporations?

Justice Alito delivered the opinion of the Court....

[A.] RFRA prohibits the "Government [from] substantially burden[ing] *a person's* exercise of religion even if the burden results from a rule of general applicability" .... The first question that we must address is whether this provision applies to regulations that govern the activities of for-profit corporations like Hobby Lobby, Conestoga, and Mardel....

[I]n *Braunfeld v. Brown*, 366 U.S. 599 (1961) ..., five Orthodox Jewish merchants who ran small retail businesses in Philadelphia challenged a Pennsylvania Sunday closing law as a violation of the Free Exercise Clause. Because of their faith, these merchants closed their shops on Saturday, and they argued that requiring them to remain shut on Sunday threatened them with financial ruin.

The Court entertained their claim (although it ruled against them on the merits), and if a similar claim were raised today under RFRA ..., the merchants would be entitled to be heard. According to HHS, however, if these merchants chose to incorporate their businesses—without in any way changing the size or nature of their businesses—they would forfeit all RFRA (and free-exercise) rights.

HHS would put these merchants to a difficult choice: either give up the right to seek judicial protection of their religious liberty or forgo the benefits, available to their competitors, of operating as corporations.... Is there any reason to think that the Congress that enacted [the] sweeping protection [provided by RFRA] put small-business owners to the choice that HHS suggests? ...

[B.] Congress provided protection for people like the Hahns and Greens by employing a familiar legal fiction: It included corporations within RFRA's definition of "persons." But ... [a] corporation is simply a form of organization used by human beings to achieve desired ends. An established body of law specifies the rights and obligations of the *people* (including shareholders, officers, and employees) who are associated with a corporation in one way or another.

When rights, whether constitutional or statutory, are extended to corporations, the purpose is to protect the rights of these people. For example, extending Fourth Amendment protection to corporations protects the privacy interests of employees and others associated with the company. Protecting corporations from government seizure of their property without just compensation protects all those who have a stake in the corporations' financial well-being. And protecting the free-exercise rights of corporations like Hobby Lobby, Conestoga, and Mardel protects the religious liberty of the humans who own and control those companies....

[C.] [We must consult] the Dictionary Act, 1 U.S.C. § 1, ... "[i]n determining the meaning of any Act of Congress, unless the context indicates otherwise." Under the Dictionary Act, "the wor[d] 'person' ... include[s] corporations, companies, associations, firms, partnerships, societies, and joint stock companies, as well as individuals." ... We see nothing in RFRA that suggests a congressional intent to depart from the Dictionary Act definition .... We have entertained RFRA and free-exercise claims brought by nonprofit corporations, see *Gonzales v. O Centro Espírita Beneficente União do Vegetal* (RFRA); *Hosanna-Tabor Evangelical Lutheran Church and School v. EEOC* (Free Exercise); *Church of the Lukumi Babalu Aye, Inc. v. Hialeah* (Free Exercise), and [the government] concedes that a nonprofit corporation can be a "person" within the meaning of RFRA.

This concession effectively dispatches any argument that the term "person" as used in RFRA does not reach the closely held corporations involved in these cases.... The term "person" sometimes encompasses artificial persons (as the Dictionary Act instructs), and it sometimes is limited to natural persons. But no conceivable definition of the term includes natural persons and nonprofit corporations, but not for-profit corporations....

According to HHS and the dissent, [for-profit] corporations are not protected by RFRA because they cannot exercise religion.... [Yet t]he corporate form alone cannot [justify this conclusion] because, as we have pointed out, HHS concedes that nonprofit corporations can be protected by RFRA. The dissent suggests that nonprofit corporations are special because furthering their religious "autonomy ... often furthers individual religious freedom as well." But this principle applies equally to for-profit corporations: Furthering their religious freedom also "furthers individual religious freedom." In these cases, for example, allowing Hobby Lobby, Conestoga, and Mardel to assert RFRA claims protects the religious liberty of the Greens and the

Hahns. {Although the principal dissent seems to think that Justice Brennan's statement in *Amos* provides a ground for holding that for-profit corporations may not assert free-exercise claims, that was not Justice Brennan's view. See *Gallagher v. Crown Kosher Super Market of Mass., Inc.*, 366 U.S. 617 (1961) (dissenting opinion) [discussed below—ed.].}

If the corporate form is not enough, what about the profit-making objective? In *Braunfeld*, we entertained the free-exercise claims of individuals who were attempting to make a profit as retail merchants, and the Court never even hinted that this objective precluded their claims.... Business practices that are compelled or limited by the tenets of a religious doctrine fall comfortably within [exercise of religion]. Thus, a law that "operates so as to make the practice of ... religious beliefs more expensive" in the context of business activities imposes a burden on the exercise of religion. *Braunfeld*; see *United States v. Lee* (recognizing that "compulsory participation in the social security system interferes with [Amish employers'] free exercise rights")....

[Moreover,] ... modern corporate law does not require for-profit corporations to pursue profit at the expense of everything else, and many do not do so. For-profit corporations, with ownership approval, support a wide variety of charitable causes, and it is not at all uncommon for such corporations to further humanitarian and other altruistic objectives....

[A] for-profit corporation may take costly pollution-control and energy-conservation measures that go beyond what the law requires. A for-profit corporation that operates facilities in other countries may exceed the requirements of local law regarding working conditions and benefits. If for-profit corporations may pursue such worthy objectives, there is no apparent reason why they may not further religious objectives as well.

{The principal dissent ... stat[es] that "[f]or-profit corporations are different from religious nonprofits in that they use labor to make a profit, rather than to perpetuate the religious values shared by a community of believers." ... [But] some for-profit corporations do seek "to perpetuate the religious values shared" ... by their owners [citing as examples Conestoga and Hobby Lobby, see p. 1026 above—ed.].

The dissent also believes that history is not on our side because even Blackstone recognized the distinction between "ecclesiastical and lay" corporations.... [But] Blackstone recognized that even what he termed "lay" corporations might serve "the promotion of piety." And whatever may have been the case at the time of Blackstone, modern corporate law ... allows for-profit corporations to "perpetuat[e] religious values."} ...

[Moreover,] not all corporations that decline to organize as nonprofits do so in order to maximize profit. For example, organizations with religious and charitable aims might organize as for-profit corporations because of the potential advantages of that corporate form [as opposed to organization as nonprofit corporations], such as the freedom to participate in lobbying for legislation or campaigning for political candidates who promote their religious or charitable goals....

[D.] HHS [also] argues that RFRA did no more than codify this Court's pre-*Smith* Free Exercise Clause precedents, and because none of those cases squarely held that a for-profit corporation has free-exercise rights, RFRA does not confer such protection. This argument has many flaws.

First, … [w]hen first enacted, RFRA defined the "exercise of religion" to mean "the exercise of religion under the First Amendment"—not the exercise of religion as recognized only by then-existing Supreme Court precedents.…

Second, … the amendment of RFRA through RLUIPA … deleted the prior reference to the First Amendment, and neither HHS nor the principal dissent can explain why Congress did this if it wanted to tie RFRA coverage tightly to the specific holdings of our pre-*Smith* free-exercise cases. Moreover, … the amendment went further, providing that the exercise of religion "shall be construed in favor of a broad protection of religious exercise, to the maximum extent permitted by the terms of this chapter and the Constitution." 42 U.S.C. § 2000cc-3(g). It is simply not possible to read these provisions as restricting the concept of the "exercise of religion" to those practices specifically addressed in our pre-*Smith* decisions.

Third, the one pre-*Smith* case involving the free-exercise rights of a for-profit corporation suggests, if anything, that for-profit corporations possess such rights. In *Gallagher*, the Massachusetts Sunday closing law was challenged by a kosher market that was organized as a for-profit corporation, by customers of the market, and by a rabbi. The Commonwealth argued that the corporation lacked "standing" to assert a free-exercise claim, but not one member of the Court expressed agreement with that argument.…

Finally, the results would be absurd if RFRA merely restored this Court's pre-*Smith* decisions in ossified form and did not allow a plaintiff to raise a RFRA claim unless that plaintiff fell within a category of plaintiffs one of whom had brought a free-exercise claim that this Court entertained in the years before *Smith*. For example, we are not aware of any pre-*Smith* case in which this Court entertained a free-exercise claim brought by a resident noncitizen. Are such persons also beyond RFRA's protective reach simply because the Court never addressed their rights before *Smith*? …

[E.] These cases … do not involve publicly traded corporations, and it seems unlikely that … corporate giants … will often assert RFRA claims.… [T]hat unrelated shareholders—including institutional investors with their own set of stakeholders—would agree to run a corporation under the same religious beliefs seems improbable. In any event, we have no occasion in these cases to consider RFRA's applicability to such companies. The companies in the cases before us are closely held corporations, each owned and controlled by members of a single family, and no one has disputed the sincerity of their religious beliefs.…

[F.] [T]he scope of RLUIPA shows that Congress was confident of the ability of the federal courts to weed out insincere claims. RLUIPA applies to "institutionalized persons," a category that consists primarily of prisoners, and by the time of RLUIPA's enactment, the propensity of some prisoners to assert claims of dubious sincerity was well documented. Nevertheless, ... Congress enacted RLUIPA to preserve the right of prisoners to raise religious liberty claims. If Congress thought that the federal courts were up to the job of dealing with insincere prisoner claims, there is no reason to believe that Congress limited RFRA's reach out of concern for the seemingly less difficult task of doing the same in corporate cases....

[G.] [T]he possibility of disputes among the owners of corporations ... is not a problem that arises because of RFRA or that is unique to this context. The owners of closely held corporations may—and sometimes do—disagree about the conduct of business.... State corporate law provides a ready means for resolving any conflicts by, for example, dictating how a corporation can establish its governing structure. Courts will turn to that structure and the underlying state law in resolving disputes....

Justice Ginsburg, [joined in relevant part by Justice Sotomayor,] dissenting....

[A.] The Dictionary Act's definition [of "person"] controls only where "context" does not "indicat[e] otherwise." Here, context does so indicate. RFRA speaks of "a person's *exercise of religion*." Whether a corporation qualifies as a "person" capable of exercising religion is an inquiry one cannot answer without reference to the "full body" of pre-*Smith* "free-exercise caselaw." There is in that case law no support for the notion that free exercise rights pertain to for-profit corporations.

Until this litigation, no decision of this Court recognized a for-profit corporation's qualification for a religious exemption from a generally applicable law, whether under the Free Exercise Clause or RFRA. The absence of such precedent is just what one would expect, for the exercise of religion is characteristic of natural persons, not artificial legal entities. As Chief Justice Marshall observed nearly two centuries ago, a corporation is "an artificial being, invisible, intangible, and existing only in contemplation of law." Corporations, Justice Stevens more recently reminded, "have no consciences, no beliefs, no feelings, no thoughts, no desires."

{The Court regards *Gallagher* as "suggest[ing] ... that for-profit corporations possess [free-exercise] rights." The suggestion is barely there. True, one of the five challengers to the Sunday closing law assailed in *Gallagher* was a corporation owned by four Orthodox Jews. The other challengers were human individuals, not artificial, law-created entities, so there was no need to determine whether the corporation could institute the litigation. Accordingly, the plurality stated it could pretermit the question "whether appellees ha[d] standing" because *Braunfeld*, which upheld a similar closing law, was fatal to their claim on the merits.}

The First Amendment's free exercise protections, the Court has indeed recognized, shelter churches and other nonprofit religion-based organizations. "For many individuals, religious activity derives meaning in large measure from participation in a larger religious community," and "furtherance of the autonomy of religious organizations often furthers individual religious freedom as well." ... [But] until today, religious exemptions had never been extended to any entity operating in "the commercial, profit-making world." ... Had Congress intended RFRA to initiate a change so huge, a clarion statement to that effect likely would have been made in the legislation. The text of RFRA makes no such statement and the legislative history does not so much as mention for-profit corporations.

{That is not to say that a category of plaintiffs, such as resident aliens, may bring RFRA claims only if this Court expressly "addressed their [free-exercise] rights before *Smith*." Continuing with the Court's example, resident aliens, unlike corporations, are flesh-and-blood individuals who plainly count as persons sheltered by the First Amendment [and] ... RFRA.}

{Religious organizations exist to foster the interests of persons subscribing to the same religious faith. Not so of for-profit corporations. [Their workers] commonly are not drawn from one religious community. Indeed, by law, no religion-based criterion can restrict the work force of for-profit corporations.}

[T]hat for-profit corporations may support charitable causes and use their funds for religious ends [is not enough to undermine] the distinction between such corporations and religious nonprofit organizations.... [And r]ecognition of the discrete characters of "ecclesiastical and lay" corporations dates back to Blackstone .... "[F]or-profit corporations are different from religious nonprofits in that they use labor to make a profit, rather than to perpetuate [the] religious value[s] [shared by a community of believers]" [citing a recent Court of Appeals case] ...

[E]ven accepting, *arguendo*, the premise that unincorporated business enterprises may gain religious accommodations under the Free Exercise Clause, ... [i]n a sole proprietorship, the business and its owner are one and the same. By incorporating a business, however, an individual separates herself from the entity and escapes personal responsibility for the entity's obligations. One might ask why the separation should hold only when it serves the interest of those who control the corporation....

[B.] Although the Court attempts to cabin its language to closely held corporations, its logic extends to corporations of any size, public or private. Little doubt that RFRA claims will proliferate, for the Court's expansive notion of corporate personhood—combined with its other errors in construing RFRA—invites for-profit entities to seek religion-based exemptions from regulations they deem offensive to their faith....

Justice Breyer and Justice Kagan, dissenting....

We agree with Justice Ginsburg that the plaintiffs' challenge to the contraceptive coverage requirement fails on the merits. We need not and do not decide whether either for-profit corporations or their owners may bring claims under [RFRA] ....

iii. Substantial Burden

Justice Alito delivered the opinion of the Court....

[A.] [T]he HHS contraceptive mandate "substantially burden[s]" the exercise of religion.... [T]he Hahns and Greens have a sincere religious belief that life begins at conception. They therefore object on religious grounds to providing health insurance that covers methods of birth control that, as HHS acknowledges, may result in the destruction of an embryo. By requiring the Hahns and Greens and their companies to arrange for such coverage, the HHS mandate demands that they engage in conduct that seriously violates their religious beliefs.

If the Hahns and Greens and their companies do not yield to this demand, the economic consequences will be severe.... For Hobby Lobby, the [$100-per-employee-per-day tax] bill could amount to ... about $475 million per year; for Conestoga, the assessment could be ... $33 million per year; and for Mardel, it could be ... about $15 million per year. These sums are surely substantial.... [If] plaintiffs ... avoid these assessments by dropping insurance coverage altogether and thus forc[e] their employees to obtain health insurance on one of the exchanges established under ACA, ... [the $2,000-per-employee penalty] would amount to roughly $26 million for Hobby Lobby, $1.8 million for Conestoga, and $800,000 for Mardel....

[**B.**] [The main argument that] the HHS mandate does not impose a substantial burden on the exercise of religion ... is basically that the connection between what the objecting parties must do (provide health-insurance coverage for four methods of contraception that may operate after the fertilization of an egg) and the end that they find to be morally wrong (destruction of an embryo) is simply too attenuated. HHS and the dissent note that providing the coverage would not itself result in the destruction of an embryo; that would occur only if an employee chose to take advantage of the coverage and to use one of the four methods at issue.

{This argument is not easy to square with the position taken by HHS in providing exemptions from the contraceptive mandate for religious employers, such as churches, that have the very same religious objections as the Hahns and Greens and their companies.} This argument [also] dodges the question that RFRA presents (whether the HHS mandate imposes a substantial burden on the ability of the objecting parties to conduct business in accordance with *their religious beliefs*) and instead addresses a very different question that the federal courts have no business addressing (whether the religious belief asserted in a RFRA case is reasonable).

The Hahns and Greens believe that providing the coverage demanded by the HHS regulations is connected to the destruction of an embryo in a way that is sufficient to make it immoral for them to provide the coverage. This belief implicates a difficult and important question of religion and moral philosophy, namely, the circumstances under which it is wrong for a person to perform an act that is innocent in itself but that has the effect of enabling or facilitating the commission of an immoral act by another....

"... [C]ourts must not presume to determine ... the plausibility of a religious claim[.]" ... [I]n *Thomas v. Review Bd.*, we considered and rejected an argument that is nearly identical to the one now urged by HHS and the dissent. In *Thomas*, a Jehovah's Witness was initially employed making sheet steel for a variety of industrial uses, but he was later transferred to a job making turrets for tanks. Because he objected on religious grounds to participating in the manufacture of weapons, he lost his job and sought unemployment compensation.

Ruling against the employee, the state court had difficulty with the line that the employee drew between work that he found to be consistent with his religious beliefs (helping to manufacture steel that was used in making weapons) and work that he found morally objectionable (helping to make the weapons themselves). This Court, however, held that "it is not for us to say that the line he drew was an unreasonable one."

Similarly, in these cases, the Hahns and Greens and their companies sincerely believe that providing the insurance coverage demanded by the HHS regulations lies on the forbidden side of the line, and it is not for us to say that their religious beliefs are mistaken or insubstantial.... [O]ur "narrow function ... in this context is to determine" whether the line drawn reflects "an honest conviction," and there is no dispute that it does....

Justice Ginsburg, joined by Justice Sotomayor, [and joined in relevant part by Justices Breyer and Kagan], dissenting....

[A.] Congress no doubt meant the modifier "substantially" [in "substantially burdens"] to carry weight. In the original draft of RFRA, the word "burden" appeared unmodified. The word "substantially" was inserted pursuant to a clarifying amendment offered by Senators Kennedy and Hatch. In proposing the amendment, Senator Kennedy stated that RFRA, in accord with the Court's pre-*Smith* case law, "does not require the Government to justify every action that has some effect on religious exercise." ...

[T]he Green and Hahn families' [sincere] religious convictions regarding contraception ..., however deeply held, do not suffice to sustain a RFRA claim.... RFRA ... distinguishes between "factual allegations that [plaintiffs'] beliefs are sincere and of a religious nature," which a court must accept as true, and the "legal conclusion ... that [plaintiffs'] religious exercise is substantially burdened," an inquiry the court must undertake. That distinction is a facet of the pre-*Smith* jurisprudence RFRA incorporates.

Bowen v. Roy, 476 U.S. 693 (1986), is instructive. There, the Court rejected a free exercise challenge to the Government's use of a Native American child's Social Security number for purposes of administering benefit programs. Without questioning the sincerity of the father's religious belief that "use of [his daughter's Social Security] number may harm [her] spirit," the Court concluded that the Government's internal uses of that number "place[d] [no] restriction on what [the father] may believe or what he may do." Recognizing that the father's "religious views may not accept" the position that the challenged uses concerned only the Government's internal affairs, the Court explained that "for the adjudication of a constitutional claim, the Constitution, rather than an individual's religion, must supply the frame of reference." ...

[B.] [T]he connection between the families' religious objections and the contraceptive coverage requirement is too attenuated to rank as substantial. The requirement carries no command that Hobby Lobby or Conestoga purchase or provide the contraceptives they find objectionable. Instead, it calls on the companies covered by the requirement to direct money into undifferentiated funds that finance a wide variety of benefits under comprehensive health plans....

Importantly, the decisions whether to claim benefits under the plans are made not by Hobby Lobby or Conestoga, but by the covered employees and dependents, in consultation with their health care providers.... "[N]o individual decision by an employee and her physician—be it to use contraception, treat an infection, or have a hip replaced—is in any meaningful sense [her employer's] decision or action."

It is doubtful that Congress, when it specified that burdens must be "substantia[l]," had in mind a linkage thus interrupted by independent decisionmakers (the woman and her health counselor) standing between the challenged government action and the religious exercise claimed to be infringed. Any decision to use contraceptives made by a woman covered under Hobby Lobby's or Conestoga's plan will not be propelled by the Government, it will be the woman's autonomous choice, informed by the physician she consults.

iv. Strict Scrutiny

Justice Alito delivered the opinion of the Court....

[A.] Since the HHS contraceptive mandate imposes a substantial burden on the exercise of religion, we must move on and decide whether HHS has shown that the mandate both "(1) is in furtherance of a compelling governmental interest; and (2) is the least restrictive means of furthering that compelling governmental interest."

HHS asserts that the contraceptive mandate serves a variety of important interests, but many of these are couched in very broad terms, such as promoting "public health" and "gender equality." RFRA, however, contemplates a "more focused" inquiry: It "requires the Government to demonstrate that the compelling interest test is satisfied through application of the challenged law 'to the person'—the particular claimant whose sincere exercise of religion is being substantially burdened." This requires us to "loo[k] beyond broadly formulated interests" and to "scrutiniz[e] the asserted harm of granting specific exemptions to particular religious claimants"—in other words, to look to the marginal interest in enforcing the contraceptive mandate in these cases.

In addition to asserting these very broadly framed interests, HHS maintains that the mandate serves a compelling interest in ensuring that all women have access to all FDA-approved contraceptives without cost sharing. Under our cases, women (and men) have a constitutional right to obtain contraceptives, and HHS tells us that "[s]tudies have demonstrated that even moderate copayments for preventive services can deter patients from receiving those services."

[B.] The objecting parties contend that HHS has not shown that the mandate serves a compelling government interest, and it is arguable that there are features of ACA that support that view. As we have noted, many employees—those covered by grandfathered plans and those who work for employers with fewer than 50 employees—may have no contraceptive coverage without cost sharing at all.

HHS responds that many legal requirements have exceptions and the existence of exceptions does not in itself indicate that the principal interest served by a law is not compelling. Even a compelling interest may be outweighed in some circumstances by another even weightier consideration.

In these cases, however, the interest served by one of the biggest exceptions, the exception for grandfathered plans, is simply the interest of employers in avoiding the inconvenience of amending an existing plan. Grandfathered plans are required "to comply with a subset of the Affordable Care Act's health reform provisions" that provide what HHS has described as "particularly significant protections." But the contraceptive mandate is expressly excluded from this subset.

We find it unnecessary[, though,] to adjudicate this issue.

[C.] We will assume that the interest in guaranteeing cost-free access to the four challenged contraceptive methods is compelling within the meaning of RFRA, and we will proceed to consider ... whether HHS has shown that the contraceptive mandate is "the least restrictive means of furthering that compelling governmental interest." ...

The least-restrictive-means standard is exceptionally demanding, and it is not satisfied here. HHS has not shown that it lacks other means of achieving its desired goal without imposing a substantial burden on the exercise of religion by the objecting parties in these cases.

[1.] The most straightforward way of doing this would be for the Government to assume the cost of providing the four contraceptives at issue to any women who are unable to obtain them under their health-insurance policies due to their employers' religious objections. This would certainly be less restrictive of the plaintiffs' religious liberty, and HHS has not shown that this is not a viable alternative.

HHS has not provided any estimate of the average cost per employee of providing access to these contraceptives, two of which, according to the FDA, are designed primarily for emergency use. Nor has HHS provided any statistics regarding the number of employees who might be affected because they work for corporations like Hobby Lobby, Conestoga, and Mardel. Nor has HHS told us that it is unable to provide such statistics.

It seems likely, however, that the cost of providing the forms of contraceptives at issue in these cases (if not all FDA-approved contraceptives) would be minor when compared with the overall cost of ACA.... ACA's insurance coverage provisions [is expected to] cost the Federal Government more than $1.3 trillion through the next decade. If, as HHS tells us, providing all women with cost-free access to all FDA-approved methods of contraception is a Government interest of the highest order, it is hard to understand HHS's argument that it cannot be required under RFRA to pay anything in order to achieve this important goal.

HHS contends that RFRA does not permit us to take this option into account because "RFRA cannot be used to require creation of entirely new programs." But we see nothing in RFRA that supports this argument, and drawing the line between the "creation of an entirely new program" and the modification of an existing program (which RFRA surely allows) would be fraught with problems.

We do not doubt that cost may be an important factor in the least-restrictive-means analysis, but both RFRA and its sister statute, RLUIPA, may in some circumstances require the Government to expend additional funds to accommodate citizens' religious beliefs. Cf. §2000cc–3(c) (RLUIPA: "[T]his chapter may require a government to incur expenses in its own operations to avoid imposing a substantial burden on religious exercise."). HHS's view that RFRA can never require the Government to spend even a small amount reflects a judgment about the importance of religious liberty that was not shared by the Congress that enacted that law.

[2.] In the end, however, we need not rely on the option of a new, government-funded program in order to conclude that the HHS regulations fail the least-restrictive-means test. HHS itself has demonstrated that it has at its disposal an approach that is less restrictive than requiring employers to fund contraceptive methods that violate their religious beliefs. As we explained above, HHS has already established an accommodation for nonprofit organizations with religious objections.

Under that accommodation, the organization can self-certify that it opposes providing coverage for particular contraceptive services. If the organization makes such a certification, the organization's insurance issuer or third-party administrator must "[e]xpressly exclude contraceptive coverage from the group health insurance coverage provided in connection with the group health plan" and "[p]rovide separate payments for any contraceptive services required to be covered" without imposing "any cost-sharing requirements ... on the eligible organization, the group health plan, or plan participants or beneficiaries." {HHS has concluded that ... [this accommodation imposes no cost on insurers] and ... will not have a material effect on the funding of the exchanges [for reasons discussed at p. 1025—ed.].}

We do not decide today whether an approach of this type complies with RFRA for purposes of all religious claims. At a minimum, however, it does not impinge on the plaintiffs' religious belief that providing insurance coverage for the contraceptives at issue here violates their religion, and it serves HHS's stated interests equally well.

The principal dissent identifies no reason why this accommodation would fail to protect the asserted needs of women as effectively as the contraceptive mandate, and there is none. {In the principal dissent's view, the Government has not had a fair opportunity to address this accommodation, but the Government itself apparently believes that when it "provides an exception to a general rule for secular reasons (or for only certain religious reasons), [it] must explain why extending a comparable exception to a specific plaintiff for religious reasons would undermine its compelling interests." Brief for the United States as Amicus Curiae in *Holt v. Hobbs*, No. 13–6827, p. 10, now pending before the Court.}

Under the accommodation, the plaintiffs' female employees would continue to receive contraceptive coverage without cost sharing for all FDA-approved contraceptives, and they would continue to "face minimal logistical and administrative obstacles," because their employers' insurers would be responsible for providing information and coverage. Ironically, it is the dissent's approach that would "[i]mped[e] women's receipt of benefits by 'requiring them to take steps to learn about, and to sign up for, a new government funded and administered health benefit,'" because the dissent would effectively compel religious employers to drop health-insurance coverage altogether, leaving their employees to find individual plans on government-run exchanges or elsewhere....

[D.] {In a related argument, HHS appears to maintain that a plaintiff cannot prevail on a RFRA claim that seeks an exemption from a legal obligation requiring the plaintiff to confer benefits on third parties. Nothing in the text of RFRA or its basic purposes supports giving the Government an entirely free hand to impose burdens on religious exercise so long as those burdens confer a benefit on other individuals.

It is certainly true that in applying RFRA "courts must take adequate account of the burdens a requested accommodation may impose on nonbeneficiaries." *Cutter v. Wilkinson* (applying RLUIPA). That consideration will often inform the analysis of the Government's compelling interest and the availability of a less restrictive means of advancing that interest.

But it could not reasonably be maintained that any burden on religious exercise, no matter how onerous and no matter how readily the government interest could be achieved through alternative means, is permissible under RFRA so long as the relevant legal obligation requires the religious adherent to confer a benefit on third parties. Otherwise, for example, the Government could decide that all supermarkets must sell alcohol for the convenience of customers (and thereby exclude Muslims with religious objections from owning supermarkets), or it could decide that all restaurants must remain open on Saturdays to give employees an opportunity to earn tips (and thereby exclude Jews with religious objections from owning restaurants).

By framing any Government regulation as benefiting a third party, the Government could turn all regulations into entitlements to which nobody could object on religious grounds, rendering RFRA meaningless. In any event, our decision in these cases need not result in any detrimental effect on any third party. As we explain, the Government can readily arrange for other methods of providing contraceptives, without cost sharing, to employees who are unable to obtain them under their health-insurance plans due to their employers' religious objections.}

[E.] HHS and the principal dissent argue that a ruling in favor of the objecting parties in these cases will lead to a flood of religious objections regarding a wide variety of medical procedures and drugs, such as vaccinations and blood transfusions, but HHS has made no effort to substantiate this prediction. HHS points to no evidence that insurance plans in existence prior to the enactment of ACA excluded coverage for such items. Nor has HHS provided evidence that any significant number of employers sought exemption, on religious grounds, from any of ACA's coverage requirements other than the contraceptive mandate.

It is HHS's apparent belief that no insurance-coverage mandate would violate RFRA—no matter how significantly it impinges on the religious liberties of employers—that would lead to intolerable consequences. Under HHS's view, RFRA would permit the Government to require all employers to provide coverage for any medical procedure allowed by law in the jurisdiction in question—for instance, third-trimester abortions or assisted suicide. The owners of many closely held corporations could not in good conscience provide such coverage, and thus HHS would effectively exclude these people from full participation in the economic life of the Nation. RFRA was enacted to prevent such an outcome.

In any event, our decision in these cases is concerned solely with the contraceptive mandate. Our decision should not be understood to hold that an insurance-coverage mandate must necessarily fall if it conflicts with an employer's religious beliefs. Other coverage requirements, such as immunizations, may be supported by different interests (for example, the need to combat the spread of infectious diseases) and may involve different arguments about the least restrictive means of providing them....

[As to] discrimination in hiring, ... [t]he government has a compelling interest in providing an equal opportunity to participate in the workforce without regard to race, and prohibitions on racial discrimination are precisely tailored to achieve that critical goal....

[F.] HHS analogizes the contraceptive mandate to the requirement to pay Social Security taxes, which we upheld in *United States v. Lee* despite the religious objection of an employer, but these cases are quite different.

Our holding in *Lee* turned primarily on the special problems associated with a national system of taxation.... [W]e explained that ... "[t]he tax system could not function if denominations were allowed to challenge the tax system because tax payments were spent in a manner that violates their religious belief." ... [T]here simply is no less restrictive alternative to the categorical requirement to pay taxes. Because of the enormous variety of government expenditures funded by tax dollars, allowing taxpayers to withhold a portion of their tax obligations on religious grounds would lead to chaos.

Recognizing exemptions from the contraceptive mandate is very different. ACA does not create a large national pool of tax revenue for use in purchasing healthcare coverage. Rather, individual employers like the plaintiffs purchase insurance for their own employees. And contrary to the principal dissent's characterization, the employers' contributions do not necessarily funnel into "undifferentiated funds." The accommodation established by HHS requires issuers to have a mechanism by which to "segregate premium revenue collected from the eligible organization from the monies used to provide payments for contraceptive services." Recognizing a religious accommodation under RFRA for particular coverage requirements, therefore, does not threaten the viability of ACA's comprehensive scheme in the way that recognizing religious objections to particular expenditures from general tax revenues would.

{... HHS notes the statement [in *Lee*] that "[w]hen followers of a particular sect enter into commercial activity as a matter of choice, the limits they accept on their own conduct as a matter of conscience and faith are not to be superimposed on the statutory schemes which are binding on others in that activity." *Lee* was a free exercise, not a RFRA, case, and the statement to which HHS points, if taken at face value, is squarely inconsistent with the plain meaning of RFRA. Under RFRA, when followers of a particular religion choose to enter into commercial activity, the Government does not have a free hand in imposing obligations that substantially burden their exercise of religion. Rather, the Government can impose such a burden only if the strict RFRA test is met.} ...

[G.] The dissent worries about forcing the federal courts to apply RFRA to a host of claims made by litigants seeking a religious exemption from generally applicable laws, and the dissent expresses a desire to keep the courts out of this business. In making this plea, the dissent reiterates a point made forcefully by the Court in *Smith*[, which argued that] ... applying the *Sherbert* test to all free-exercise claims "would open the prospect of constitutionally required religious exemptions from civic obligations of almost every conceivable kind[.]" ...

But Congress, in enacting RFRA, took the position that "the compelling interest test as set forth in prior Federal court rulings is a workable test for striking sensible balances between religious liberty and competing prior governmental interests." The wisdom of Congress's judgment on this matter is not our concern. Our responsibility is to enforce RFRA as written, and under the standard that RFRA prescribes, the HHS contraceptive mandate is unlawful....

Justice Kennedy, concurring....

Among the reasons the United States is so open, so tolerant, and so free is that no person may be restricted or demeaned by government in exercising his or her religion. Yet neither may that same exercise unduly restrict other persons, such as employees, in protecting their own interests, interests the law deems compelling.

In these cases the means to reconcile those two priorities are at hand in the existing accommodation the Government has designed, identified, and used for circumstances closely parallel to those presented here. RFRA requires the Government to use this less restrictive means. As the Court explains, this existing model, designed precisely for this problem, might well suffice to distinguish the instant cases from many others in which it is more

difficult and expensive to accommodate a governmental program to countless religious claims based on an alleged statutory right of free exercise....

Justice Ginsburg, joined by Justice Sotomayor, [and joined in relevant part by Justices Breyer and Kagan], dissenting....

[A.] [T]he contraceptive coverage for which the ACA provides furthers compelling interests in public health and women's well being.... [T]he man-dated contraception coverage enables women to avoid the health problems unintended pregnancies may visit on them and their children. The coverage helps safeguard the health of women for whom pregnancy may be hazard-ous, even life threatening. And the mandate secures benefits wholly unre-lated to pregnancy, preventing certain cancers, menstrual disorders, and pelvic pain.

That Hobby Lobby and Conestoga resist coverage for only 4 of the 20 FDA-approved contraceptives does not lessen these compelling interests. Notably, the corporations exclude intrauterine devices (IUDs), devices sig-nificantly more effective, and significantly more expensive than other con-traceptive methods. The cost of an IUD is nearly equivalent to a month's full-time pay for workers earning the minimum wage; ... almost one-third of women would change their contraceptive method if costs were not a factor; and ... only one-fourth of women who request an IUD actually have one in-serted after finding out how expensive it would be. {Moreover, the Court's reasoning appears to permit commercial enterprises like Hobby Lobby and Conestoga to exclude from their group health plans all forms of contracep-tives.} ...

[B.] Stepping back from its assumption that compelling interests sup-port the contraceptive coverage requirement, the Court notes that small em-ployers and grandfathered plans are not subject to the requirement. If there is a compelling interest in contraceptive coverage, the Court suggests, Con-gress would not have created these exclusions.

Federal statutes often include exemptions for small employers, and such provisions have never been held to undermine the interests served by these statutes. The ACA's grandfathering provision, allows a phasing-in period for compliance with a number of the Act's requirements (not just the contra-ceptive coverage or other preventive services provisions). Once specified changes are made, grandfathered status ceases.... The percentage of em-ployees in grandfathered plans is steadily declining, having dropped from 56% in 2011 to 48% in 2012 to 36% in 2013. In short, far from ranking as a categorical exemption, the grandfathering provision is "temporary, intended to be a means for gradually transitioning employers into mandatory cover-age."

The Court ultimately acknowledges a critical point: RFRA's application "must take adequate account of the burdens a requested accommodation may impose on nonbeneficiaries." No tradition, and no prior decision under RFRA, allows a religion-based exemption when the accommodation would be harmful to others—here, the very persons the contraceptive coverage re-quirement was designed to protect. {As the Court made clear in *Cutter*, the government's license to grant religion-based exemptions from generally applicable laws is constrained by the Establishment Clause.} ...

[C.] [T]he Government has shown that there is no less restrictive, equally effective means that would both (1) satisfy the challengers' religious objections to providing insurance coverage for certain contraceptives (which they believe cause abortions); and (2) carry out the objective of the ACA's contraceptive coverage requirement, to ensure that women employees receive, at no cost to them, the preventive care needed to safeguard their health and well being. A "least restrictive means" cannot require employees to relinquish benefits accorded them by federal law in order to ensure that their commercial employers can adhere unreservedly to their religious tenets.

Then let the government pay (rather than the employees who do not share their employer's faith), the Court suggests. "The most straightforward [alternative]," the Court asserts, "would be for the Government to assume the cost of providing ... contraceptives ... to any women who are unable to obtain them under their health-insurance policies due to their employers' religious objections."

The ACA, however, requires coverage of preventive services through the existing employer-based system of health insurance "so that [employees] face minimal logistical and administrative obstacles." Impeding women's receipt of benefits "by requiring them to take steps to learn about, and to sign up for, a new [government funded and administered] health benefit" was scarcely what Congress contemplated.

Moreover, Title X of the Public Health Service Act, "is the nation's only dedicated source of federal funding for safety net family planning services." "Safety net programs like Title X are not designed to absorb the unmet needs of ... insured individuals." Note, too, that Congress declined to write into law the preferential treatment Hobby Lobby and Conestoga describe as a less restrictive alternative.

And where is the stopping point to the "let the government pay" alternative? Suppose an employer's sincerely held religious belief is offended by health coverage of vaccines, or paying the minimum wage, or according women equal pay for substantially similar work? Does it rank as a less restrictive alternative to require the government to provide the money or benefit to which the employer has a religion-based objection?

Because the Court cannot easily answer that question, it proposes something else: Extension to commercial enterprises of the accommodation already afforded to nonprofit religion-based organizations. "At a minimum," according to the Court, such an approach would not "impinge on [Hobby Lobby's and Conestoga's] religious belief." ... [But] the "special solicitude" generally accorded nonprofit religion-based organizations that exist to serve a community of believers ... [has] never before [been] accorded to commercial enterprises comprising employees of diverse faiths....

In sum, in view of what Congress sought to accomplish, *i.e.*, comprehensive preventive care for women furnished through employer-based health plans, none of the proffered alternatives would satisfactorily serve the compelling interests to which Congress responded....

[D.] *United States v. Lee* made two key points one cannot confine to tax cases. "When followers of a particular sect enter into commercial activity as a matter of choice," the Court observed, "the limits they accept on their own conduct as a matter of conscience and faith are not to be superimposed on statutory schemes which are binding on others in that activity." The statutory scheme of employer-based comprehensive health coverage involved in these cases is surely binding on others engaged in the same trade or business as the corporate challengers here, Hobby Lobby and Conestoga.

Further, the Court recognized in *Lee* that allowing a religion-based exemption to a commercial employer would "operat[e] to impose the employer's religious faith on the employees." No doubt the Greens and Hahns and all who share their beliefs may decline to acquire for themselves the contraceptives in question. But that choice may not be imposed on employees who hold other beliefs. Working for Hobby Lobby or Conestoga, in other words, should not deprive employees of the preventive care available to workers at the shop next door, at least in the absence of directions from the Legislature or Administration to do so....

Why should decisions of this order be made by Congress or the regulatory authority, and not this Court? Hobby Lobby and Conestoga surely do not stand alone as commercial enterprises seeking exemptions from generally applicable laws on the basis of their religious beliefs. Would RFRA require exemptions in cases of [claimed exemptions from bans on race, marital status discrimination, sex, and sexual orientation discrimination]? And if not, how does the Court divine which religious beliefs are worthy of accommodation, and which are not? Isn't the Court disarmed from making such a judgment given its recognition that "courts must not presume to determine ... the plausibility of a religious claim"?

Would the exemption the Court holds RFRA demands for employers with religiously grounded objections to the use of certain contraceptives extend to employers with religiously grounded objections to blood transfusions (Jehovah's Witnesses); antidepressants (Scientologists); medications derived from pigs, including anesthesia, intravenous fluids, and pills coated with gelatin (certain Muslims, Jews, and Hindus); and vaccinations (Christian Scientists, among others)? According to counsel for Hobby Lobby, "each one of these cases ... would have to be evaluated on its own ... apply[ing] the compelling interest-least restrictive alternative test." Not much help there for the lower courts bound by today's decision....

[E.] There is an overriding interest, I believe, in keeping the courts "out of the business of evaluating the relative merits of differing religious claims," *Lee* (Stevens, J., concurring in judgment), or the sincerity with which an asserted religious belief is held. Indeed, approving some religious claims while deeming others unworthy of accommodation could be "perceived as favoring one religion over another," the very "risk the Establishment Clause was designed to preclude."

The Court, I fear, has ventured into a minefield, by its immoderate reading of RFRA. I would confine religious exemptions under that Act to organizations formed "for a religious purpose," "engage[d] primarily in carrying out that religious purpose," and not "engaged ... substantially in the exchange of goods or services for money beyond nominal amounts." ...

h.   Holt v. Hobbs, 135 S. Ct. 853 (2015)

Justice Alito delivered the opinion of the Court....

[A.] [Petitioner Gregory Holt, a Muslim,] is in the custody of the Arkansas Department of Correction and he objects on religious grounds to the Department's [no-beards policy] .... Petitioner sought permission to grow a beard and, although he believes that his faith requires him not to trim his beard at all, he proposed a "compromise" under which he would grow only a ½-inch beard. Prison officials denied his request [and petitioner sued under RLUIPA] ....

[B.] [Petitioner believes] growing ... a beard ... is a dictate of his religious faith, and the Department does not dispute the sincerity of petitioner's belief.... The Department's grooming policy requires petitioner to shave his beard and thus to "engage in conduct that seriously violates [his] religious beliefs." If petitioner contravenes that policy and grows his beard, he will face serious disciplinary action. Because the grooming policy puts petitioner to this choice, it substantially burdens his religious exercise....

[T]he District Court ... [erred] in suggesting that the burden on petitioner's religious exercise was slight because, according to petitioner's testimony, his religion would "credit" him for attempting to follow his religious beliefs, even if that attempt proved to be unsuccessful. RLUIPA ... applies to an exercise of religion regardless of whether it is "compelled." § 2000cc-5(7)(A)....

[T]he District Court [also] went astray when it relied on petitioner's testimony that not all Muslims believe that men must grow beards. Petitioner's belief is by no means idiosyncratic. But even if it were, the protection of RLUIPA, no less than the guarantee of the Free Exercise Clause, is "not limited to beliefs which are shared by all of the members of a religious sect." *Thomas v. Review Bd.*

[C.] Since petitioner met his burden of showing that the Department's grooming policy substantially burdened his exercise of religion, the burden shifted to the Department to show that its refusal to allow petitioner to grow a ½-inch beard "(1) [was] in furtherance of a compelling governmental interest; and (2) [was] the least restrictive means of furthering that compelling governmental interest." § 2000cc-1(a).

The Department argues that its grooming policy represents the least restrictive means of furthering ... the Department's compelling interest in prison safety and security. But ... RLUIPA requires us to "'scrutiniz[e] the asserted harm of granting specific exemptions to particular religious claimants'" and "to look to the marginal interest in enforcing" the challenged government action in that particular context. In this case, that means the enforcement of the Department's policy to prevent petitioner from growing a ½-inch beard....

[1.] The Department ... claims that the no-beard policy prevents prisoners from hiding contraband ..., including razors, needles, drugs, and cellular phone subscriber identity module (SIM) cards.

We readily agree that the Department has a compelling interest in staunching the flow of contraband into and within its facilities, but the argument that this interest would be seriously compromised by allowing an inmate to grow a ½-inch beard is hard to take seriously.... An item of contraband would have to be very small indeed to be concealed by a ½-inch beard, and a prisoner seeking to hide an item in such a short beard would have to find a way to prevent the item from falling out. Since the Department does not demand that inmates have shaved heads or short crew cuts, it is hard to see why an inmate would seek to hide contraband in a ½-inch beard rather than in the longer hair on his head....

[The lower courts] thought that they were bound to defer to the Department's assertion that allowing petitioner to grow such a beard would undermine its interest in suppressing contraband.... Prison officials are experts in running prisons and evaluating the likely effects of altering prison rules, and courts should respect that expertise.

But that respect does not justify the abdication of the responsibility, conferred by Congress, to apply RLUIPA's rigorous standard. And without a degree of deference that is tantamount to unquestioning acceptance, it is hard to swallow the argument that denying petitioner a ½-inch beard actually furthers the Department's interest in rooting out contraband.

Even if the Department could make that showing, its contraband argument would still fail because the Department cannot show that forbidding very short beards is the least restrictive means of preventing the concealment of contraband. "The least-restrictive-means standard is exceptionally demanding," and it requires the government to "sho[w] that it lacks other means of achieving its desired goal without imposing a substantial burden on the exercise of religion by the objecting part[y]." ...

The Department failed to establish that it could not satisfy its security concerns by simply searching petitioner's beard. The Department already searches prisoners' hair and clothing, and it presumably examines the ¼-inch beards of inmates with dermatological conditions[, which are exempted from the no-beards policy]. It has offered no sound reason why hair, clothing, and ¼-inch beards can be searched but ½-inch beards cannot....

[2.] The Department contends that its grooming policy is necessary to further an additional compelling interest, *i.e.,* preventing prisoners from disguising their identities. The Department tells us that the no-beard policy allows security officers to identify prisoners quickly and accurately. It claims that bearded inmates could shave their beards and change their appearance in order to enter restricted areas within the prison, to escape, and to evade apprehension after escaping.

We agree that prisons have a compelling interest in the quick and reliable identification of prisoners .... But as petitioner has argued, the Department could largely solve this problem by requiring that all inmates be photographed without beards when first admitted to the facility and, if necessary, periodically thereafter. Once that is done, an inmate like petitioner could be allowed to grow a short beard and could be photographed again when the beard reached the ½-inch limit. Prison guards would then have a bearded and clean-shaven photo to use in making identifications. In fact, the Department (like many other States) already has a policy of photographing a prisoner both when he enters an institution and when his "appearance changes at any time during [his] incarceration."

The Department argues that the dual-photo method is inadequate because, even if it might help authorities apprehend a bearded prisoner who escapes and then shaves his beard once outside the prison, this method is unlikely to assist guards when an inmate quickly shaves his beard in order to alter his appearance within the prison. The Department contends that the identification concern is particularly acute at petitioner's prison, where inmates live in barracks and work in fields. Counsel for the Department suggested at oral argument that a prisoner could gain entry to a restricted area by shaving his beard and swapping identification cards with another inmate while out in the fields.

We are unpersuaded by these arguments for at least two reasons. First, the Department failed to show, in the face of petitioner's evidence, that its prison system is so different from the many institutions that allow facial hair that the dual-photo method cannot be employed at its institutions.

Second, the Department failed to establish why the risk that a prisoner will shave a ½-inch beard to disguise himself is so great that ½-inch beards cannot be allowed, even though prisoners are allowed to grow mustaches, head hair, or ¼-inch beards for medical reasons. All of these could also be shaved off at a moment's notice, but the Department apparently does not think that this possibility raises a serious security concern....

[3.] [T]he Department has [also] not adequately demonstrated why its grooming policy is substantially underinclusive in at least two respects. Although the Department denied petitioner's request to grow a ½-inch beard, it permits prisoners with a dermatological condition to grow ¼-inch beards. The Department does this even though both beards pose similar risks. {[T]he Department has failed to establish ... that a ¼-inch difference in beard length poses a meaningful increase in security risk.}

{The Department ... asserts that few inmates require beards for medical reasons while many may request beards for religious reasons. But the Department has not argued that denying petitioner an exemption is necessary to further a compelling interest in cost control or program administration. At bottom, this argument is but another formulation of the "classic rejoinder of bureaucrats throughout history: If I make an exception for you, I'll have to make one for everybody, so no exceptions." *Gonzales v. O Centro*. We have rejected a similar argument in analogous contexts, see *ibid.*; *Sherbert v. Verner*, and we reject it again today.}

And the Department permits inmates to grow more than a ½-inch of hair on their heads. With respect to hair length, the grooming policy provides only that hair must be worn "above the ear" and "no longer in the back than the middle of the nape of the neck." Hair on the head is a more plausible place to hide contraband than a ½-inch beard—and the same is true of an inmate's clothing and shoes.

Nevertheless, the Department does not require inmates to go about bald, barefoot, or naked. Although the Department's proclaimed objectives are to stop the flow of contraband and to facilitate prisoner identification, "[t]he proffered objectives are not pursued with respect to analogous nonreligious conduct," which suggests that "those interests could be achieved by narrower ordinances that burdened religion to a far lesser degree." *Church of Lukumi Babalu Aye, Inc. v. Hialeah.*...

[4.] [T]he Department [also] failed to show ... why the vast majority of States and the Federal Government permit inmates to grow ½-inch beards, either for any reason or for religious reasons, but it cannot.... That so many other prisons allow inmates to grow beards while ensuring prison safety and security suggests that the Department could satisfy its security concerns through a means less restrictive than denying petitioner the exemption he seeks.

We do not suggest that RLUIPA requires a prison to grant a particular religious exemption as soon as a few other jurisdictions do so. But when so many prisons offer an accommodation, a prison must, at a minimum, offer persuasive reasons why it believes that it must take a different course, and the Department failed to make that showing here.

Despite this, the courts below deferred to these prison officials' mere say-so that they could not accommodate petitioner's request. RLUIPA, however, demands much more. Courts must hold prisons to their statutory burden, and they must not "assume a plausible, less restrictive alternative would be ineffective." ...

[5.] RLUIPA ... affords prison officials ample ability to maintain security.... First, in applying RLUIPA's statutory standard, courts should not blind themselves to the fact that the analysis is conducted in the prison setting. Second, if an institution suspects that an inmate is using religious activity to cloak illicit conduct, "prison officials may appropriately question whether a prisoner's religiosity, asserted as the basis for a requested accommodation, is authentic." Third, even if a claimant's religious belief is sincere, an institution might be entitled to withdraw an accommodation if the claimant abuses the exemption in a manner that undermines the prison's compelling interests....

Justice Ginsburg, with whom Justice Sotomayor joins, concurring.

Unlike the exemption this Court approved in *Burwell v. Hobby Lobby*

Stores, Inc., accommodating petitioner's religious belief in this case would not detrimentally affect others who do not share petitioner's belief....

5.   The Debate About Original Meaning

a.   *City of Boerne v. Flores, 521 U.S. 507 (1997)*

[The issue in *Boerne* (pronounced like the name "Bernie") was whether Congress, in enacting the federal RFRA, had the enumerated power to mandate that states exempt religious objectors from generally applicable state laws under the *Sherbert/Yoder* standard. The Court held that Congress lacked such power: Congress could enact laws enforcing the Free Exercise Clause, but given *Smith*, the Clause did not mandate exemptions and thus RFRA wasn't really enforcing the Clause's commands.

Of course, if a Justice thought that *Smith* was wrongly decided, then the Justice would have to conclude that Congress *did* have the power to enact RFRA, because RFRA would then just be pretty much restating what the Free Exercise Clause already commanded. This created an occasion for Justices Scalia and O'Connor to debate a subject that they hadn't focused on in *Smith*: the original meaning of the Clause.—ed.]

Justice Scalia, with whom Justice Stevens joins, concurring in part....

[**A.**] {[T]he protections afforded by} various statutory and constitutional protections of religion enacted by Colonies, States, and Territories in the period leading up to the ratification of the Bill of Rights ... are in fact more consistent with *Employment Div. v. Smith*'s interpretation of free exercise than with the dissent's understanding of it....

[T]he early "free exercise" enactments cited by the dissent protect only against action that is taken "for" or "in respect of" religion (Maryland Act Concerning Religion of 1649, Rhode Island Charter of 1663, and New Hampshire Constitution); or action taken "on account of" religion (Maryland Declaration of Rights of 1776 and Northwest Ordinance of 1787); or "discriminat[ory]" action (New York Constitution); or, finally (and unhelpfully for purposes of interpreting "free exercise" in the Federal Constitution), action that interferes with the "free exercise" of religion (Maryland Act Concerning Religion of 1649 and Georgia Constitution). It is eminently arguable that application of neutral, generally applicable laws of the sort the dissent refers to ... would not constitute action taken "for," "in respect of," or "on account of" one's religion, or "discriminatory" action.

Assuming, however, that the affirmative protection of religion accorded by the early "free exercise" enactments sweeps as broadly as the dissent's theory would require, those enactments do not support the dissent's view, since they contain "provisos" that significantly qualify the affirmative protection they grant.... In fact, the most plausible reading of the "free exercise" enactments (if their affirmative provisions are read broadly, as the dissent's view requires) is a virtual restatement of *Smith*: Religious exercise shall be permitted *so long as it does not violate general laws governing conduct.*

The "provisos" in the enactments negate a license to act in a manner "unfaithfull to the Lord Proprietary" (Maryland Act Concerning Religion of 1649), or "behav[e]" in other than a "peaceabl[e] and quie[t]" manner (Rhode Island Charter of 1663), or "disturb the public peace" (New Hampshire Constitution), or interfere with the "peace [and] safety of th[e] State" (New York, Maryland, and Georgia Constitutions), or "demea[n]" oneself in other than a "peaceable and orderly manner" (Northwest Ordinance of 1787). At the time these provisos were enacted, keeping "peace" and "order" seems to have meant, precisely, obeying the laws. "[E]very breach of a law is against the peace." *Queen v. Lane,* 87 Eng. Rep. 884 (Q.B. 1704).

Even as late as 1828, when Noah Webster published his *American Dictionary of the English Language,* he gave as one of the meanings of "peace": "8. Public tranquility; that quiet, order and security which is guaranteed by the laws; as, to keep the *peace*; to break the *peace*." {The word "licentious," used in several of the early enactments, likewise meant "[e]xceeding the limits of law."} This limitation upon the scope of religious exercise would have been in accord with the background political philosophy of the age (associated most prominently with John Locke), which regarded freedom as the right "to do only what was not lawfully prohibited." "Thus, the disturb-the-peace caveats apparently permitted government to deny religious freedom, not merely in the event of violence or force, but, more generally, upon the occurrence of illegal actions." Hamburger, *A Constitutional Right of Religious Exemption: An Historical Perspective,* 60 Geo. Wash. Law Rev. 915 (1992).

{The same explanation applies, of course, to George Mason's initial draft of Virginia's religious liberty clause. When it said "unless, under colour of religion, any man disturb the peace ... of society," it probably meant "unless under color of religion any man break the law." Thus, it is not the case that "*both* Mason's and [James] Madison's formulations envisioned that, when there was a conflict [between religious exercise and generally applicable laws], a person's interest in freely practicing his religion was to be balanced against state interests," at least insofar as regulation of *conduct* was concerned.}

And while, under this interpretation, these early "free exercise" enactments support the Court's judgment in *Smith,* I see no sensible interpretation that could cause them to support what I understand to be the position of Justice O'Connor, or any of *Smith*'s other critics. No one in that camp, to my knowledge, contends that their favored "compelling state interest" test conforms to any possible interpretation of "breach of peace and order"—*i.e.,* that *only* violence or force, or any other category of action (more limited than "violation of law") which can possibly be conveyed by the phrase "peace and order," justifies state prohibition of religiously motivated conduct.

[B.] [T]hat legislatures sometimes (though not always) found it "appropriate" to accommodate religious practices does not establish that accommodation was understood to be constitutionally *mandated* by the Free Exercise Clause.... [Likewise, t]here is no reason to think [that Framers' statements about proposed legislative enactments] were meant to describe what was constitutionally required (and judicially enforceable), as opposed to what was thought to be legislatively or even morally desirable.

Thus, for example, the pamphlet written by James Madison opposing Virginia's proposed general assessment for support of religion does not argue that the assessment would violate the "free exercise" provision in the Virginia Declaration of Rights, although that provision had been enacted into law only eight years earlier; rather the pamphlet argues that the assessment wrongly placed civil society ahead of personal religious belief and, thus, should not be approved by the legislators. Likewise, the letter from George Washington to the Quakers by its own terms refers to Washington's "wish and desire" that religion be accommodated, not his belief that existing constitutional provisions required accommodation....

The one exception is the statement by Thomas Jefferson that he considered "the government of the United States as interdicted by the Constitution from intermeddling with religious institutions, their doctrines, discipline, or exercises"; but it is quite clear that Jefferson did not in fact espouse the broad principle of affirmative accommodation advocated by the dissent, see McConnell, *The Origins and Historical Understanding of Free Exercise of Religion,* 103 Harv. L. Rev. 1409, 1415 (1990) [("Jefferson's understanding of the scope and rationale of free exercise rights, however, was more limited even than Locke's. Like Locke, he based his advocacy of freedom of religion on the judgment that religion, properly confined, can do no harm: 'The legitimate powers of government extend to such acts only as are injurious to others. But it does me no injury for my neighbour to say there are twenty gods, or no god. It neither picks my pocket nor breaks my leg.'")]....

[C.] Had the understanding in the period surrounding the ratification of the Bill of Rights been that the various forms of accommodation discussed by the dissent were constitutionally required (either by State Constitutions or by the Federal Constitution), it would be surprising not to find a single state or federal case refusing to enforce a generally applicable statute because of its failure to make accommodation. Yet the dissent cites none—and to my knowledge, and to the knowledge of the academic defenders of the dissent's position, none exists.

The closest one can come in the period prior to 1850 is the decision of a New York City municipal court in 1813, holding that the New York Constitution of 1777 required acknowledgment of a priest-penitent privilege, to protect a Catholic priest from being compelled to testify as to the contents of a confession. *People v. Phillips* (N.Y. Ct. Gen. Sess. 1813). Even this lone case is weak authority, not only because it comes from a minor court [conducted by the Mayor, who had never been a jurist], but also because it did not involve a statute, and the same result might possibly have been achieved (without invoking constitutional entitlement) by the court's simply modifying the common-law rules of evidence to recognize such a privilege.

On the other side of the ledger, moreover, there are two cases, from the Supreme Court of Pennsylvania, flatly rejecting the dissent's view. In *Philips v. Gratz,* 2 Pen. & W. 412 (Pa. 1831), the court held that a litigant was not entitled to a continuance of trial on the ground that appearing on his Sabbath would violate his religious principles. And in *Stansbury v. Marks*, 2 Dall. 213 (Pa. 1793), decided just two years after the ratification of the Bill of Rights, the court imposed a fine on a witness who "refused to be sworn, because it was his Sabbath." {Indeed, the author of *Philips* could well have written *Smith*: "[C]onsiderations of policy address themselves with propriety to the legislature, and not to a magistrate whose course is prescribed not by discretion, but rules already established."} ...

[D.] The historical evidence marshalled by the dissent ... is more supportive of [*Smith*] than destructive of it. And ... that evidence is not compatible with any theory I am familiar with that has been proposed as an alternative to *Smith*....

Justice O'Connor, with whom Justice Breyer joins [as to the excerpted material], dissenting....

[A.] Although the Framers may not have asked precisely the questions about religious liberty that we do today, the historical record indicates that they believed that the Constitution affirmatively protects religious free exercise and that it limits the government's ability to intrude on religious practice....

[I]n 1649, the Maryland Assembly enacted the first free exercise clause by passing the Act Concerning Religion: "[N]o person ... professing to believe in Jesus Christ, shall from henceforth be any ways troubled, molested or discountenanced for or in respect of his or her religion nor in the free exercise thereof ... nor any way [be] compelled to the belief or exercise of any other Religion against his or her consent, so as they be not unfaithful to the Lord Proprietary, or molest or conspire against the civil Government." [Archaic spelling updated here and in the next paragraph.—ed.]

Rhode Island's Charter of 1663 used the analogous term "liberty of conscience." It protected residents from being in any ways "molested, punished, disquieted, or called in question, for any differences in opinion, in matters of religion, and do not actually disturb the civil peace of our said colony." The Charter further provided that residents may "freely, and fully have and enjoy his and their own judgments, and conscience in matters of religious concernments ...; they behaving themselves peaceably and quietly and not using this liberty to licentiousness and profaneness; nor to the civil injury, or outward disturbance of others." Various agreements between prospective settlers and the proprietors of Carolina, New York, and New Jersey similarly guaranteed religious freedom, using language that paralleled that of the Rhode Island Charter of 1663.

These documents suggest that, early in our country's history, several Colonies acknowledged that freedom to pursue one's chosen religious beliefs was an essential liberty. Moreover, these Colonies appeared to recognize that government should interfere in religious matters only when necessary to protect the civil peace or to prevent "licentiousness."

In other words, when religious beliefs conflicted with civil law, religion prevailed unless important state interests militated otherwise....

[B.] The principles expounded in these early charters re-emerged over a century later in state constitutions that were adopted in the flurry of constitution drafting that followed the American Revolution. By 1789, every State but Connecticut had incorporated some version of a free exercise clause into its constitution.

These state provisions, which were typically longer and more detailed than the Federal Free Exercise Clause, are perhaps the best evidence of the original understanding of the Constitution's protection of religious liberty. After all, it is reasonable to think that the States that ratified the First Amendment assumed that the meaning of the federal free exercise provision corresponded to that of their existing state clauses.

The precise language of these state precursors to the Free Exercise Clause varied, but most guaranteed free exercise of religion or liberty of conscience, limited by particular, defined state interests. For example, the New York Constitution of 1777 provided: "[T]he free exercise and enjoyment of religious profession and worship, without discrimination or preference, shall forever hereafter be allowed, within this State, to all mankind: *Provided*, That the liberty of conscience, hereby granted, *shall not be so construed as to excuse acts of licentiousness, or justify practices inconsistent with the peace or safety of this State.*"

Similarly, the New Hampshire Constitution of 1784 declared: "Every individual has a natural and unalienable right to worship GOD according to the dictates of his own conscience, and reason; and no subject shall be hurt, molested, or restrained in his person, liberty or estate for worshipping GOD, in the manner and season most agreeable to the dictates of his own conscience, ... *provided he doth not disturb the public peace, or disturb others*, in their religious worship."

The Maryland Declaration of Rights of 1776 read: "[N]o person ought by any law to be molested in his person or estate on account of his religious persuasion or profession, or for his religious practice; unless, under colour of religion, *any man shall disturb the good order, peace or safety of the State, or shall infringe the laws of morality, or injure others*, in their natural, civil, or religious rights."

The religious liberty clause of the Georgia Constitution of 1777 stated: "All persons whatever shall have the free exercise of their religion; provided *it be not repugnant to the peace and safety of the State.*"

In addition to these state provisions, the Northwest Ordinance of 1787—which was enacted contemporaneously with the drafting of the Constitution and reenacted by the First Congress—established a bill of rights for a territory that included what is now Ohio, Indiana, Michigan, Wisconsin, and part of Minnesota. Article I of the Ordinance declared: "No person, *demeaning himself in a peaceable and orderly manner*, shall ever be molested on account of his mode of worship or religious sentiments, in the said territory."

[This language] strongly suggests that, around the time of the drafting of the Bill of Rights, it was generally accepted that the right to "free exercise" required, where possible, accommodation of religious practice. If not—

and if the Court was correct in *Smith* that generally applicable laws are enforceable regardless of religious conscience—there would have been no need for these documents to specify, as the New York Constitution did, that rights of conscience should not be "construed as to excuse acts of licentiousness, or justify practices inconsistent with the peace or safety of [the] State." Such a proviso would have been superfluous. Instead, these documents make sense only if the right to free exercise was viewed as generally superior to ordinary legislation, to be overridden only when necessary to secure important government purposes.

The Virginia Legislature may have debated the issue most fully. In May 1776, the Virginia Constitutional Convention wrote a constitution containing a Declaration of Rights with a clause on religious liberty. The initial drafter of the clause, George Mason, proposed the following: "That religion, or the duty which we owe to our CREATOR, and the manner of discharging it, can be (directed) only by reason and conviction, not by force or violence; and therefore, *that all men should enjoy the fullest toleration in the exercise of religion*, according to the dictates of conscience, unpunished and unrestrained by the magistrate, *unless, under colour of religion, any man disturb the peace, the happiness, or safety of society*. And that it is the mutual duty of all to practice Christian forbearance, love, and charity towards each other."

Mason's proposal did not go far enough for a 26-year-old James Madison, who had recently completed his studies at the Presbyterian College of Princeton. He objected first to Mason's use of the term "toleration," contending that the word implied that the right to practice one's religion was a governmental favor, rather than an inalienable liberty.

Second, Madison thought Mason's proposal countenanced too much state interference in religious matters, since the "exercise of religion" would have yielded whenever it was deemed inimical to "the peace, happiness, or safety of society." Madison suggested the provision read instead: "That religion, or the duty we owe our Creator, and the manner of discharging it, being under the direction of reason and conviction only, not of violence or compulsion, *all men are equally entitled to the full and free exercise of it, according to the dictates of conscience*; and therefore that no man or class of men ought on account of religion to be invested with peculiar emoluments or privileges, nor subjected to any penalties or disabilities, *unless under color of religion the preservation of equal liberty, and the existence of the State be manifestly endangered*."

Thus, Madison wished to shift Mason's language of "toleration" to the language of rights. Additionally, under Madison's proposal, the State could interfere in a believer's religious exercise only if the State would otherwise "be manifestly endangered." In the end, neither Mason's nor Madison's language regarding the extent to which state interests could limit religious exercise made it into the Virginia Constitution's religious liberty clause. Like the Federal Free Exercise Clause, the Virginia religious liberty clause was simply silent on the subject, providing only that "all men are equally entitled to the free exercise of religion, according to the dictates of conscience."

For our purposes, however, it is telling that *both* Mason's and Madison's formulations envisioned that, when there was a conflict, a person's interest in freely practicing his religion was to be balanced against state interests. Although Madison endorsed a more limited state interest exception than did Mason, the debate would have been irrelevant if either had thought the right to free exercise did not include a right to be exempt from certain generally applicable laws. Presumably, the Virginia Legislature intended the scope of its free exercise provision to strike some middle ground between Mason's narrower and Madison's broader notions of the right to religious freedom.

[C.] The practice of the Colonies and early States bears out the conclusion that, at the time the Bill of Rights was ratified, it was accepted that government should, when possible, accommodate religious practice....

For example, Quakers and certain other Protestant sects refused on Biblical grounds to subscribe to oaths or "swear" allegiance to civil authority. Without accommodation, their beliefs would have prevented them from participating in civic activities involving oaths, including testifying in court. Colonial governments created alternatives to the oath requirement for these individuals. In early decisions, for example, the Carolina proprietors applied the religious liberty provision of the Carolina Charter of 1665 to permit Quakers to enter pledges in a book. Similarly, in 1691, New York enacted a law allowing Quakers to testify by affirmation, and in 1734, it permitted Quakers to qualify to vote by affirmation. By 1789, virtually all of the States had enacted oath exemptions.

Early conflicts between religious beliefs and generally applicable laws also occurred because of military conscription requirements. Quakers and Mennonites, as well as a few smaller denominations, refused on religious grounds to carry arms. Members of these denominations asserted that liberty of conscience should exempt them from military conscription.

Obviously, excusing such objectors from military service had a high public cost, given the importance of the military to the defense of society. Nevertheless, Rhode Island, North Carolina, and Maryland exempted Quakers from military service in the late 1600's. New York, Massachusetts, Virginia, and New Hampshire followed suit in the mid-1700's. The Continental Congress likewise granted exemption from conscription:

> As there are some people, who, from religious principles, cannot bear arms in any case, this Congress intend no violence to their consciences, but earnestly recommend it to them, to contribute liberally in this time of universal calamity, to the relief of their distressed brethren in the several colonies, and to do all other services to their oppressed Country, which they can consistently with their religious principles....

States and Colonies with established churches encountered a further religious accommodation problem. Typically, these governments required citizens to pay tithes to support either the government-established church or the church to which the tithepayer belonged. But Baptists and Quakers, as well as others, opposed all government-compelled tithes on religious grounds. Massachusetts, Connecticut, New Hampshire, and Virginia responded by exempting such objectors from religious assessments....

[Likewise, b]oth North Carolina and Maryland excused Quakers from the requirement of removing their hats in court; Rhode Island exempted Jews from the requirements of the state marriage laws [that barred uncle-niece marriages, which Jewish law accepted—ed.]; and Georgia allowed groups of European immigrants to organize whole towns according to their own faith.

To be sure, legislatures, not courts, granted these early accommodations. But these were the days before there *was* a Constitution to protect civil liberties—judicial review did not yet exist. These legislatures apparently believed that the appropriate response to conflicts between civil law and religious scruples was, where possible, accommodation of religious conduct. It is reasonable to presume that the drafters and ratifiers of the First Amendment—many of whom served in state legislatures—assumed courts would apply the Free Exercise Clause similarly, so that religious liberty was safeguarded.

[D.] The writings of the early leaders who helped to shape our Nation provide a final source of insight into the original understanding of the Free Exercise Clause. The thoughts of James Madison—one of the principal architects of the Bill of Rights—as revealed by the controversy surrounding Virginia's General Assessment Bill of 1784, are particularly illuminating....

"A Bill Establishing a Provision for the Teachers of the Christian Religion," which proposed that citizens be taxed in order to support the Christian denomination of their choice, with those taxes not designated for any specific denomination to go to a public fund to aid seminaries. Madison ... took the case against religious assessment to the people of Virginia in his now-famous "Memorial and Remonstrance Against Religious Assessments." ... The bill eventually died in committee, and Virginia instead enacted a Bill for Establishing Religious Freedom, which Thomas Jefferson had drafted in 1779.

The "Memorial and Remonstrance" begins with the recognition that "[t]he Religion ... of every man must be left to the conviction and conscience of every man; and it is the right of every man to exercise it as these may dictate." By its very nature, Madison wrote, the right to free exercise is "unalienable," both because a person's opinion "cannot follow the dictates of other[s]," and because it entails "a duty towards the Creator." Madison continued:

> This duty [owed the Creator] is precedent both in order of time and degree of obligation, to the claims of Civil Society.... [E]very man who becomes a member of any particular Civil Society, [must] do it with a saving of his allegiance to the Universal Sovereign. We maintain therefore that in matters of Religion, no man's right is abridged by the institution of Civil Society, and that Religion is wholly exempt from its cognizance.

To Madison, then, duties to God were superior to duties to civil authorities—the ultimate loyalty was owed to God above all. Madison did not say that duties to the Creator are precedent only to those laws specifically directed at religion, nor did he strive simply to prevent deliberate acts of persecution or discrimination. The idea that civil obligations are subordinate to religious duty is consonant with the notion that government must accommodate, where possible, those religious practices that conflict with civil law.

Other early leaders expressed similar views regarding religious liberty. Thomas Jefferson, the drafter of Virginia's Bill for Establishing Religious Freedom, wrote in that document that civil government could interfere in religious exercise only "when principles break out into overt acts against peace and good order." In 1808, he indicated that he considered "the government of the United States as interdicted by the Constitution from intermeddling with religious institutions, their doctrines, discipline, or exercises." Moreover, Jefferson believed that "[e]very religious society has a right to determine for itself the time of these exercises, and the objects proper for them, according to their own particular tenets; and this right can never be safer than in their own hands, where the Constitution has deposited it."

George Washington expressly stated that he believed that government should do its utmost to accommodate religious scruples, writing in a letter to a group of Quakers: "[I]n my opinion the conscientious scruples of all men should be treated with great delicacy and tenderness; and it is my wish and desire, that the laws may always be as extensively accommodated to them, as a due regard to the protection and essential interests of the nation may justify and permit." Oliver Ellsworth, a Framer of the First Amendment and later Chief Justice of the United States, expressed the similar view that government could interfere in religious matters only when necessary "to prohibit and punish gross immoralities and impieties; because the open practice of these is of evil example and detriment." Isaac Backus, a Baptist minister who was a delegate to the Massachusetts ratifying convention of 1788, declared that "every person has an unalienable right to act in all religious affairs according to the full persuasion of his own mind, where others are not injured thereby." ...

[T]hese early leaders [thus] accorded religious exercise a special constitutional status. The right to free exercise was a substantive guarantee of individual liberty, no less important than the right to free speech or the right to just compensation for the taking of property. As Madison put it in the concluding argument of his "Memorial and Remonstrance": "'[T]he equal right of every citizen to the free exercise of his Religion according to the dictates of [his] conscience' is held by the same tenure with all our other rights.... [I]t is equally the gift of nature; ... it cannot be less dear to us; ... it is enumerated with equal solemnity, or rather studied emphasis."

[Moreover], all agreed that government interference in religious practice was not to be lightly countenanced. Finally, all shared the conviction that "true religion and good morals are the only solid foundation of public liberty and happiness." To give meaning to these ideas—particularly in a society characterized by religious pluralism and pervasive regulation—there will be times when the Constitution requires government to accommodate the needs of those citizens whose religious practices conflict with generally applicable law....

b. *Policy—Original Meaning, see p. 798*

6. THE BURDEN THRESHOLD

a. *Summary*

Rule: Under both the constitutional exemption regime (*Sherbert/Yoder*) and the RFRA regime, a claimant is entitled to a religious exemption only if the government action *substantially burdens* the claimant's religious practice. If there is no substantial burden, the court wouldn't reach strict scrutiny; no exemption would be available.

What constitutes a substantial burden?

1. The government's compelling someone to do something that violates his religious beliefs, or prohibiting someone from doing something that is mandated by his religious beliefs. *Wisconsin v. Yoder* (1972) (p. 979); *Prince v. Massachusetts* (1944) (p. 969); *Gillette v. United States* (1971) (p. 976); *United States v. Lee* (1982) (p. 984).

2. The government's denying someone a tax exemption or unemployment compensation unless he does something that violates his religious beliefs, or refrains from something that is mandated by his religious beliefs. *Bob Jones Univ. v. United States* (1983) (p. 986); *Sherbert v. Verner* (1963) (p. 973). (Query whether this applies to all benefit programs; cf. *Rust v. Sullivan* (1991) (p. 643) as to free speech.)

3. As to state and federal constitutional regimes, it's not clear whether the above also applies when the objector's conduct is merely motivated and not actually mandated by his religious beliefs (*e.g.*, the objector thinks it's religiously valuable for him to stay home on the Sabbath, but not a religious commandment). Cf. *Mack v. O'Leary*, 80 F.3d 1175, 1178 (7th Cir. 1996) (Posner, J.); Douglas Laycock, *The Remnants of Free Exercise*, 1990 Sup. Ct. Rev. 1, 24-27. The federal RFRA, many state RFRAs, and RLUIPA expressly apply to "any exercise of religion, whether or not compelled by ... a system of religious belief."

4. The beliefs need not be longstanding; they need only be sincere. *Hobbie v. Unemployment Appeals Comm'n*, 480 U.S. 136 (1987).

5. The beliefs need not be central to the claimant's religious beliefs; they need only be sincere. *Employment Division v. Smith* (1990) (p. 992); *Hernandez v. Commissioner*, 490 U.S. 680 (1989); RFRA; RLUIPA.

What doesn't constitute a substantial burden?

1. Requirements that the objectors can obey without going against their sincere religious beliefs; for instance, if someone has a religious objection to getting paid for his work, a minimum wage law doesn't burden his beliefs, because he can just return the wages to the employer. *Tony & Susan Alamo Found. v. Secretary of Labor*, 471 U.S. 290 (1985). Of

course, much turns on exactly what the sincere belief is—if the objector can sincerely say "I object not just to getting paid, but even to receiving the paycheck and then returning it," then there is a substantial burden; and courts must accept the objector's own formulation of the objection, if the objector is sincere, see, *e.g., United States v. Lee.*

2. The government's applying a generally applicable tax to activity that happens to be religious, unless "the mere act of paying the tax, by itself, violates [the objector's] sincere religious beliefs." *Jimmy Swaggart Ministries v. Board of Equalization*, 493 U.S. 378 (1990).

3. The government's organizing its own operations or managing its own property in a way that the objector believes frustrates his exercise of his religion or does him spiritual harm. *Lyng v. Northwest Indian Cemetery Protective Ass'n* (1988) (p. 1059); *Bowen v. Roy*, 476 U.S. 693 (1986) (described in *Lyng*).

— Note that if the government in *Lyng* had *excluded* everyone from certain government property which the Indians felt a religious obligation to visit (rather than just altering the property in a way that the Indians believed frustrated their religious practices), this would have been a burden, since it would have actually prohibited the Indians from doing something that they felt a religious obligation to do. It might, however, have been subject to lower scrutiny, on the theory that the government was acting as proprietor, see Part XIII.A.7 (p. 1068).

4. (Probably) the government's imposing a requirement that indirectly makes certain religious practices more expensive.

— Laws that require stores to close on Sundays probably wouldn't be seen as creating a substantial burden even though businesspeople who feel a religious obligation to close on Saturdays thus end up being closed both weekend days. See *Braunfeld v. Brown,* 366 U.S. 599, 605-06 (1961) (plurality); *Bowen v. Roy,* 476 U.S. 693, 704 n.14 (1986) (so characterizing *Braunfeld*). There is language in *Braunfeld* that suggests such laws might in fact impose a substantial burden, 366 U.S. at 607, yet are justifiable in any event because they are needed to serve the government interest. But since it's hard to see how Sunday closing laws serve a *compelling* government interest, the favorable cites to *Braunfeld* throughout the *Sherbert/Yoder* era suggest that courts must have seen such laws as not imposing a substantial burden.

— Nondiscriminatory taxes that deplete a person's income (for instance, to pay for public schools) aren't a substantial burden even when they leave the person without the money needed to engage in religiously mandated conduct, such as sending his child to a religious school.

b. Problem: The Secluded Shrines

The Church of the New Prophet was founded in 1965 by Prophet Josh Bornstein, who taught a mix of Christianity and Eastern religions with a focus on meditation and contemplation. Church members consider (1) the hill on which Bornstein first experienced his revelation, (2) Bornstein's home at the time, and (3) Bornstein's grave in a local cemetery—all located in a small Nevada town—to be holy places. Church members view going on pilgrimages to those places, and meditating there on the Prophet's life and teaching, as a sacrament; most members try to go on such pilgrimages at least every three years. To preserve the proper frame for meditation, members are expected to park some distance away from the shrines, and walk to them rather than disturbing others by driving.

The Church owns the home. The hill is federal government property. The cemetery is privately owned (by a corporation that is unrelated to the Church) but open to the public, as most cemeteries are. When Bornstein founded the Church, the three holy places were quite secluded, but the population of the area has since grown. The federal government, which owns the hill and owns property next to the house and to the cemetery, plans to sell the hill and the other property to developers.

Church members fear that this sale will prevent them from going to the hill, and will dramatically decrease the spiritual value of the pilgrimages because it will interfere with the peace and the seclusion of the house and the cemetery. They sue to block the sale on Free Exercise Clause grounds. How would the case come out under *Lyng*? How would it have come out if the *Lyng* dissent were law?

Cf. Carrie A. Moore, *Historic Palmyra,* Deseret News, Oct. 8, 2000 (describing pilgrimages by members of the Church of Jesus Christ of Latter-Day Saints—also known as the Mormon church—to Palmyra, New York, and in particular to a hill on which Joseph Smith, the founder of the Church, is said to have been visited by an angel who gave him gold plates containing the Book of Mormon).

c. *Lyng v. Northwest Indian Cemetery Protective Ass'n, 485 U.S. 439 (1988)*

Justice O'Connor delivered the opinion of the Court....

[A.] As part of a project to create a paved 75-mile road linking two California towns, Gasquet and Orleans, the United States Forest Service has upgraded 49 miles of previously unpaved roads on federal land. In order to complete this project (the G-O road), the Forest Service must build a 6-mile paved segment through the Chimney Rock section of the Six Rivers National Forest. That section of the forest is situated between two other portions of the road that are already complete....

[T]he Forest Service commissioned a study of American Indian cultural and religious sites in the area.... [T]he Chimney Rock area has historically been used for religious purposes by Yurok, Karok, and Tolowa Indians. The commissioned study, ... completed in 1979, found that the entire area "is significant as an integral and indispensable part of Indian religious conceptualization and practice." Specific sites are used for certain rituals, and "successful use of the [area] is dependent upon and facilitated by certain qualities of the physical environment, the most important of which are privacy, silence, and an undisturbed natural setting."

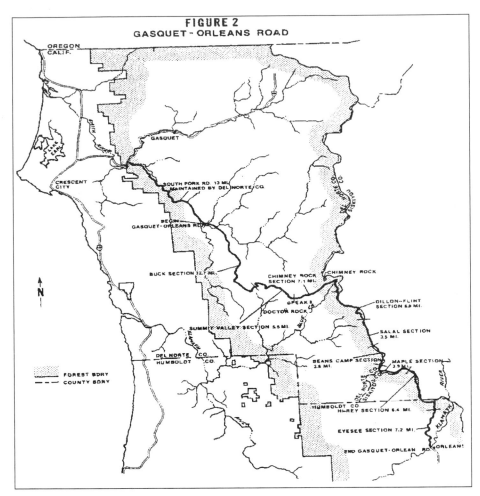

FIGURE 2
GASQUET - ORLEANS ROAD

The study concluded that constructing a road along any of the available routes "would cause serious and irreparable damage to the sacred areas which are an integral and necessary part of the belief systems and lifeway of Northwest California Indian peoples." Accordingly, the report recommended that the G-O road not be completed.

In 1982, the Forest Service decided not to adopt this recommendation .... The Regional Forester selected a route that avoided archeological sites and was removed as far as possible from the sites used by contemporary Indians for specific spiritual activities. Alternative routes that would have avoided the Chimney Rock area altogether were rejected because they would have required the acquisition of private land, had serious soil stability problems, and would in any event have traversed areas having ritualistic value to American Indians.

At about the same time, the Forest Service adopted a management plan allowing for the harvesting of significant amounts of timber in this area of the forest. The management plan provided for one-half mile protective zones around all the religious sites identified in the [study] .... [Respondents, including an Indian organization and individual Indians challenged] ... the road-building and timber-harvesting decisions [in court] ....

[B.] It is undisputed that the Indian respondents' beliefs are sincere and that the Government's proposed actions will have severe adverse effects on the practice of their religion. Those respondents contend that the burden on their religious practices is heavy enough to violate the Free Exercise Clause unless the Government can demonstrate a compelling need to complete the G-O road or to engage in timber harvesting in the Chimney Rock area. We disagree.

In *Bowen v. Roy,* 476 U.S. 693 (1986), we considered a challenge to a federal statute that required the States to use Social Security numbers in administering certain welfare programs. Two applicants for benefits under these programs contended that their religious beliefs prevented them from acceding to the use of a Social Security number for their 2-year-old daughter because the use of a numerical identifier would "'rob the spirit' of [their] daughter and prevent her from attaining greater spiritual power."

Similarly, in this case, it is said that disruption of the natural environment caused by the G-O road will diminish the sacredness of the area in question and create distractions that will interfere with "training and ongoing religious experience of individuals using [sites within] the area for personal medicine and growth ... and as integrated parts of a system of religious belief and practice which correlates ascending degrees of personal power with a geographic hierarchy of power." The Court rejected this kind of challenge in *Roy*:

> The Free Exercise Clause simply cannot be understood to require the Government to conduct its own internal affairs in ways that comport with the religious beliefs of particular citizens. Just as the Government may not insist that [the Roys] engage in any set form of religious observance, so [they] may not demand that the Government join in their chosen religious practices by refraining from using a number to identify their daughter.... The Free Exercise Clause affords an individual protection from certain forms of governmental compulsion; it does not afford an individual a right to dictate the conduct of the Government's internal procedures.

The building of a road or the harvesting of timber on publicly owned land cannot meaningfully be distinguished from the use of a Social Security number in *Roy*. In both cases, the challenged Government action would interfere significantly with private persons' ability to pursue spiritual fulfillment according to their own religious beliefs. In neither case, however, would the affected individuals be coerced by the Government's action into violating their religious beliefs; nor would either governmental action penalize religious activity by denying any person an equal share of the rights, benefits, and privileges enjoyed by other citizens.

We are asked to distinguish this case from *Roy* on the ground that the infringement on religious liberty here is "significantly greater," or on the ground that the Government practice in *Roy* was "purely mechanical" whereas this case involves "a case-by-case substantive determination as to how a particular unit of land will be managed." Similarly, we are told that this case can be distinguished from *Roy* because "the government action is not at some physically removed location where it places no restriction on what a practitioner may do." ...

[One respondent argues] that the Social Security number in *Roy* "could be characterized as interfering with Roy's religious tenets from a subjective point of view, where the government's conduct of 'its own internal affairs' was known to him only secondhand and did not interfere with his ability to practice his religion." In this case, however, it is said that the proposed road will "physically destro[y] the environmental conditions and the privacy without which the [religious] practices cannot be conducted." ...

[But t]his Court cannot determine the truth of the underlying beliefs that led to the religious objections here or in *Roy*, and accordingly cannot weigh the adverse effects on the appellees in *Roy* and compare them with the adverse effects on the Indian respondents. Without the ability to make such comparisons, we cannot say that the one form of incidental interference with an individual's spiritual activities should be subjected to a different constitutional analysis than the other. {[And r]obbing the spirit of a child, and preventing her from attaining greater spiritual power, is both a "substantial external effect" and one that is remarkably similar to the injury claimed by respondents in the case before us today.}

[C.] Respondents insist, nonetheless, that the courts below properly relied on a factual inquiry into the degree to which the Indians' spiritual practices would become ineffectual if the G-O road were built.... [I]ndirect coercion or penalties on the free exercise of religion, not just outright prohibitions, are subject to scrutiny under the First Amendment [as in *Sherbert v. Verner*]....

[But t]his does not and cannot imply that incidental effects of government programs, which may make it more difficult to practice certain religions but which have no tendency to coerce individuals into acting contrary to their religious beliefs, require government to bring forward a compelling justification for its otherwise lawful actions. The crucial word in the constitutional text is "prohibit": "For the Free Exercise Clause is written in terms of what the government cannot do to the individual, not in terms of what the individual can exact from the government." Whatever may be the exact line between unconstitutional prohibitions on the free exercise of religion and the legitimate conduct by government of its own affairs, the location of the line cannot depend on measuring the effects of a governmental action on a religious objector's spiritual development....

Even if we assume that we should accept the Ninth Circuit's prediction, according to which the G-O road will "virtually destroy the ... Indians' ability to practice their religion," the Constitution simply does not provide a principle that could justify upholding respondents' legal claims. However much we might wish that it were otherwise, government simply could not operate if it were required to satisfy every citizen's religious needs and desires.

A broad range of government activities—from social welfare programs to foreign aid to conservation projects—will always be considered essential to the spiritual well-being of some citizens, often on the basis of sincerely held religious beliefs. Others will find the very same activities deeply offensive, and perhaps incompatible with their own search for spiritual fulfillment and with the tenets of their religion.

The First Amendment must apply to all citizens alike, and it can give to none of them a veto over public programs that do not prohibit the free exercise of religion. The Constitution does not, and courts cannot, offer to reconcile the various competing demands on government, many of them rooted in sincere religious belief, that inevitably arise in so diverse a society as ours. That task, to the extent that it is feasible, is for the legislatures and other institutions....

[D.] Respondents attempt to stress the limits of the religious servitude that they are now seeking to impose on the Chimney Rock area of the Six Rivers National Forest. While defending an injunction against logging operations and the construction of a road, they apparently do not *at present* object to the area's being used by recreational visitors, other Indians, or forest rangers. Nothing in the principle for which they contend, however, would distinguish this case from another lawsuit in which they (or similarly situated religious objectors) might seek to exclude all human activity but their own from sacred areas of the public lands. The Indian respondents insist that "*[p]rivacy* during the power quests is required for the practitioners to maintain the purity needed for a successful journey." ...

[S]uch beliefs could easily require *de facto* beneficial ownership of some rather spacious tracts of public property. Even without anticipating future cases, the diminution of the Government's property rights, and the concomitant subsidy of the Indian religion, would in this case be far from trivial: the District Court's order [which accepted the petitioners' claim] permanently forbade commercial timber harvesting, or the construction of a two-lane road, anywhere within an area covering a full 27 [square-mile] sections (*i.e.* more than 17,000 acres) of public land....

The Constitution does not permit government to discriminate against religions that treat particular physical sites as sacred, and a law prohibiting the Indian respondents from visiting the Chimney Rock area would raise a different set of constitutional questions. Whatever rights the Indians may have to the use of the area, however, those rights do not divest the Government of its right to use what is, after all, *its* land....

Nothing in our opinion should be read to encourage governmental insensitivity to the religious needs of any citizen.... It is worth emphasizing, therefore, that the Government has taken numerous steps in this very case to minimize the impact that construction of the G-O road will have on the Indians' religious activities.... [Details omitted.—ed.] Except for abandoning its project entirely, and thereby leaving the two existing segments of road to dead-end in the middle of a National Forest, it is difficult to see how the Government could have been more solicitous....

[E.] [T]he dissent proposes a legal test under which it would decide which public lands are "central" or "indispensable" to which religions .... Unless a "showing of 'centrality'" is nothing but an assertion of centrality, the dissent thus offers us the prospect of this Court's holding that some sincerely held religious beliefs and practices are not "central" to certain religions, despite protestations to the contrary from the religious objectors who brought the lawsuit. In other words, the dissent's approach would require us to rule that some religious adherents misunderstand their own religious beliefs. We think such an approach cannot be squared with the Constitution or with our precedents, and that it would cast the Judiciary in a role that we were never intended to play....

Justice Brennan, with whom Justice Marshall and Justice Blackmun join, dissenting....

[A.] The Court does not for a moment suggest that the interests served by the G-O road are in any way compelling, or that they outweigh the destructive effect construction of the road will have on respondents' religious practices. Instead, the Court embraces the Government's contention that its prerogative as landowner should always take precedence over a claim that a particular use of federal property infringes religious practices....

Attempting to justify this rule, the Court argues that the First Amendment bars only outright prohibitions, indirect coercion, and penalties on the free exercise of religion.... [But t]he land-use decision challenged here will restrain respondents from practicing their religion as surely and as completely as any of the governmental actions we have struck down in the past, and the Court's efforts simply to define away respondents' injury as nonconstitutional are both unjustified and ultimately unpersuasive....

[B.] [We have] nowhere suggested that ... coercive compulsion exhausted the range of religious burdens recognized under the Free Exercise Clause. Indeed, in *Wisconsin v. Yoder*, we struck down a state compulsory school attendance law on free exercise grounds not so much because of the affirmative coercion the law exerted on individual religious practitioners, but because of "the *impact* that compulsory high school attendance could have on the continued survival of Amish communities." ...

[T]he parents in *Yoder* did not argue that their religion expressly proscribed public education beyond the eighth grade; rather, they objected to the law because "the *values* ... of the modern secondary school are in sharp conflict with the fundamental *mode of life* mandated by the Amish religion." By exposing Amish children "to a 'worldly' influence in conflict with their beliefs," and by removing those children "from their community, physically and emotionally, during the crucial and formative adolescent period of life" when Amish beliefs are inculcated, the compulsory school law posed "a very real threat of undermining the Amish community and religious practice." Admittedly, this threat arose from the compulsory nature of the law at issue, but it was the "impact" on religious practice itself, not the source of that impact, that led us to invalidate the law.[a] ... [Likewise,] construction of the G-O road will completely frustrate the practice of [respondents'] religion, for as the lower courts found, the proposed logging and construction activities will virtually destroy respondents' religion, and will therefore necessarily force them into abandoning those practices altogether.

Indeed, the Government's proposed activities will restrain religious practice to a far greater degree here than in any of the cases cited by the Court today. None of the religious adherents in [the *Sherbert* line of unemployment compensation cases], for example, claimed or could have claimed that the denial of unemployment benefits rendered the practice of their religions impossible; at most, the challenged laws made those practices more expensive.

Here, in stark contrast, respondents have claimed—and proved—that the desecration of the [particular area involved] will prevent religious leaders from attaining the religious power or medicine indispensable to the success of virtually all their rituals and ceremonies.... [R]espondents here do not even have the option, however unattractive it might be, of migrating to more hospitable locales; the site-specific nature of their belief system renders it nontransportable....

Ultimately, the Court's coercion test turns on a distinction between governmental actions that compel affirmative conduct inconsistent with religious belief, and those governmental actions that prevent conduct consistent with religious belief.... [But t]he crucial word in the constitutional text, as the Court itself acknowledges, is "prohibit," a comprehensive term that in no way suggests that the intended protection is aimed only at governmental actions that coerce affirmative conduct. {The Court is apparently of the view that the term "prohibit" in the Free Exercise Clause somehow limits the constitutional protection such that it cannot possibly be understood to reach "*any* form of government action that frustrates or inhibits religious practice." Although the dictionary is hardly the final word on the meaning of constitutional language, it is noteworthy that Webster's includes, as one of the two accepted definitions of "prohibit," "to prevent from doing something." Government action that frustrates or inhibits religious practice fits far more comfortably within this definition than does the Court's affirmative compulsion test.}

Nor does the Court's distinction comport with the principles animating the constitutional guarantee: religious freedom is threatened no less by governmental action that makes the practice of one's chosen faith impossible than by governmental programs that pressure one to engage in conduct inconsistent with religious beliefs.

---

[a] [Here's **the majority's response** on this:—ed.] The statute ... in [*Yoder*] prohibited the Amish parents, on pain of criminal prosecution, from providing their children with the kind of education required by the Amish religion.... [T]here is nothing whatsoever in the *Yoder* opinion to support the proposition that the "impact" on the Amish religion would have been constitutionally problematic if the statute at issue had not been coercive in nature.

The Court attempts to explain the line it draws by arguing that the protections of the Free Exercise Clause "cannot depend on measuring the effects of a governmental action on a religious objector's spiritual development," for in a society as diverse as ours, the Government cannot help but offend the "religious needs and desires" of some citizens. While I agree that governmental action that simply offends religious sensibilities may not be challenged under the Clause, we have recognized that laws that affect spiritual development by impeding the integration of children into the religious community or by increasing the expense of adherence to religious principles—in short, laws that frustrate or inhibit religious *practice*—trigger the protections of the constitutional guarantee....

[C.] [T]he Court professes an inability to differentiate *Roy* from the present case, suggesting that "[t]he building of a road or the harvesting of timber on publicly owned land cannot meaningfully be distinguished from the use of a Social Security number." ... [But i]n *Roy*, we repeatedly stressed the "internal" nature of the Government practice at issue: noting that *Roy* objected to "the widespread use of the social security number by the federal or state governments *in their computer systems*," we likened the use of such recordkeeping numbers to decisions concerning the purchase of office equipment. When the Government processes information, of course, it acts in a purely internal manner, and any free exercise challenge to such internal recordkeeping in effect seeks to dictate how the Government conducts its own affairs.

Federal land-use decisions, by contrast, are likely to have substantial external effects that government decisions concerning office furniture and information storage obviously will not, and they are correspondingly subject to public scrutiny and public challenge in a host of ways that office equipment purchases are not.... Ultimately, in *Roy* we concluded that, however much the Government's recordkeeping system may have offended Roy's sincere religious sensibilities, he could not challenge that system under the Free Exercise Clause because the Government's practice did not "in any degree impair Roy's 'freedom to believe, express, and *exercise*' his religion." That determination distinguishes the injury at issue here, which the Court finds so "remarkably similar" to Roy's, for respondents have made an uncontroverted showing that the proposed construction and logging activities will impair their freedom to exercise their religion in the greatest degree imaginable, and Congress has "accurately identifie[d]" such injuries as falling within the scope of the Free Exercise Clause....

[D.] [T]he Court's refusal to recognize the constitutional dimension of respondents' injuries stems from its concern that acceptance of respondents' claim could potentially strip the Government of its ability to manage and use vast tracts of federal property. In addition, the nature of respondents' site-specific religious practices raises the specter of future suits in which Native Americans seek to exclude all human activity from such areas.

These concededly legitimate concerns lie at the very heart of this case, which represents yet another stress point in the longstanding conflict between two disparate cultures—the dominant Western culture, which views land in terms of ownership and use, and that of Native Americans, in which concepts of private property are not only alien, but contrary to a belief system that holds land sacred. Rather than address this conflict in any meaningful fashion, however, the Court disclaims all responsibility for balancing these competing and potentially irreconcilable interests, choosing instead to turn this difficult task over to [Congress].

Such an abdication is more than merely indefensible as an institutional matter: by defining respondents' injury as "nonconstitutional," the Court has effectively bestowed on one party to this conflict the unilateral authority to resolve all future disputes in its favor, subject only to the Court's toothless exhortation to be "sensitive" to affected religions. In my view, however, Native Americans deserve—and the Constitution demands—more than this.

[E.] Prior to today's decision, several Courts of Appeals ... required Native Americans to demonstrate that any land-use decisions they challenged involved lands that were "central" or "indispensable" to their religious practices. Although this requirement limits the potential number of free exercise claims that might be brought to federal land management decisions, ... it has been criticized as inherently ethnocentric, for it incorrectly assumes that Native American belief systems ascribe religious significance to land in a traditionally Western hierarchical manner.

It is frequently the case in constitutional litigation, however, that courts are called upon to balance interests that are not readily translated into rough equivalents. At their most absolute, the competing claims that both the Government and Native Americans assert in federal land are fundamentally incompatible, and unless they are tempered by compromise, mutual accommodation will remain impossible.

I believe it appropriate, therefore, to require some showing of "centrality" before the Government can be required either to come forward with a compelling justification for its proposed use of federal land or to forego that use altogether.... [W]hile Native Americans need not demonstrate, as respondents did here, that the Government's land-use decision will assuredly eradicate their faith, I do not think it is enough to allege simply that the land in question is held sacred. Rather, adherents challenging a proposed use of federal land should be required to show that the decision poses a substantial and realistic threat of frustrating their religious practices. Once such a showing is made, the burden should shift to the Government to come forward with a compelling state interest sufficient to justify the infringement of those practices.

The Court today suggests that such an approach would place courts in the untenable position of deciding which practices and beliefs are "central" to a given faith and which are not, and invites the prospect of judges advising some religious adherents that they "misunderstand their own religious beliefs." In fact, however, courts need not undertake any such inquiries: like all other religious adherents, Native Americans would be the arbiters of which practices are central to their faith, subject only to the normal requirement that their claims be genuine and sincere.

The question for the courts, then, is not whether the Native American claimants understand their own religion, but rather whether they have discharged their burden of demonstrating, as the Amish did with respect to the compulsory school law in *Yoder*, that the land-use decision poses a substantial and realistic threat of undermining or frustrating their religious practices. Ironically, the Court's apparent solicitude for the integrity of religious belief and its desire to forestall the possibility that courts might second-guess the claims of religious adherents leads to far greater inequities than those the Court postulates: today's ruling sacrifices a religion at least as old as the Nation itself, along with the spiritual well-being of its approximately 5,000 adherents, so that the Forest Service can build a 6-mile segment of road that two lower courts found had only the most marginal and speculative utility, both to the Government itself and to the private lumber interests that might conceivably use it.

Similarly, the Court's concern that the claims of Native Americans will place "religious servitudes" upon vast tracts of federal property cannot justify its refusal to recognize the constitutional injury respondents will suffer here.... Should respondents or any other group seek to force the Government to protect their religious practices from the interference of private parties, such a demand would implicate not only the concerns of the Free Exercise Clause, but also those of the Establishment Clause as well. That case, however, is most assuredly not before us today, and in any event cannot justify the Court's refusal to acknowledge that the injuries respondents will suffer as a result of the Government's proposed activities are sufficient to state a constitutional cause of action....

[Historical note: Following the Court's decision in this case, Congress barred the Forest Service from building the road.—ed.]

7. Constitutional/RFRA Exemptions and the Government Acting in Special Roles

a. Summary

Constitutional exemption model (*Sherbert/Yoder*): During the constitutional exemption era, the Court never had the occasion to develop special rules for the government acting as employer, K-12 educator, landlord, and the like (much as it had for the Free Speech Clause). It did, however, hold that the Clause leaves the government great latitude in the special contexts of the government controlling the military, see *Goldman v. Weinberger,* 475 U.S. 503 (1986), and prisons, see *O'Lone v. Estate of Shabazz,* 482 U.S. 342 (1987); and many of the arguments for relaxed free speech scrutiny in the government-as-employer/educator/landlord contexts apply to religious exemptions, too. Some lower courts in fact did apply lower levels of scrutiny in such situations.

Statutory exemption model (*Smith*): Under *Smith*, this problem is less important, but still remains when government action fits within the "individualized exemption" and "hybrid rights" exceptions (see p. 991).

Congress has indeed created an exemption provision for religious objections by employees (both government and private), in Title VII of the Civil Rights Act of 1964 (see Part XIV.A, p. 1071). But this provides a rather weak "reasonable accommodation" standard rather than strict scrutiny, and it's a Congressional choice, not a constitutional command.

Common-law exemption model (RFRAs): The enactment of RFRAs makes the matter more complex:

— RFRAs were meant to restore the *Sherbert/Yoder* regime, presumably including its openness to special rules for the government acting in special capacities.

— On the other hand, the language of the RFRAs explicitly commands strict scrutiny, with no allowance for lower standards in particular situations. The lower courts have not yet resolved this uncertainty.

b. *Problem: Government as Employer*

Police officer Angelo Rodriguez and county hospital nurse Elaine Tramm believe it would be sinful for them to in any way assist in abortions, directly or indirectly; they think such action would violate the commandment "Thou shalt not kill." Rodriguez asks to be excused from helping to guard abortion clinics. Tramm asks to be excused from participating in abortions, cleaning and preparing instruments used in performing abortions, and handling fetal tissue after abortion procedures.

Their requests are denied, and they sue, claiming this denial violates their state constitution's Free Exercise Clause—which the state Supreme Court has interpreted to follow the *Sherbert/Yoder* constitutional exemption model rather than the *Smith* statutory exemption model—and their state's RFRA, which generally tracks the language of the federal RFRA. Analyze the cases under both theories.

Cf. *Rodriguez v. City of Chicago,* 975 F. Supp. 1055 (N.D. Ill. 1997), *aff'd,* 156 F.3d 771 (7th Cir. 1998); *Tramm v. Porter Mem'l Hosp.,* 128 F.R.D. 666 (N.D. Ind. 1989). (The problem is based on these cases, but some facts have been changed to make the problem more interesting.)

c. *Problem: Sikhs and Knives in Schools*

A public elementary school bars students from bringing any knives to school. Rajinder Cheema, age 10, is a Sikh boy, which means that he is religiously obligated to wear a dagger, also known as a "kirpan" (generally pronounced in English as "*ker*-pahn," with the accent on the first syllable). Some Sikhs interpret this commandment as requiring them to wear a sharp, fairly long knife, but Cheema and his family believe that the commandment can be satisfied by wearing a knife with a 3½-inch long blade that is blunted and sewn into its sheath.

Cheema sues, claiming the rule violates the state constitution's Free Exercise Clause—which the state Supreme Court has interpreted to follow the

Sherbert/Yoder constitutional exemption model rather than the *Smith* statutory exemption model—and the state's RFRA, which generally tracks the language of the federal RFRA. Analyze the case under both theories.

(Sikhism originated in Punjab in northern India about 500 years ago; it has about 20 million followers worldwide, and 500,000 in the U.S.)

d. Problem: Religious Objections to School Curriculum

Vicki Frost and Bob Mozert are parents of children who go to sixth grade in a public school. Both have a religious belief that their children ought not be exposed to some of the material in the standard textbooks (the Holt readers) used in the school's English classes:

> Mrs. Frost testified that she ... had found numerous passages [in the Holt series] that offended her religious beliefs. She stated that the offending materials fell into seventeen categories ... [including] evolution[,] .... "secular humanism[,]" ... "futuristic supernaturalism," pacifism, magic and false views of death.... Illustrative is her first category, futuristic supernaturalism, which she defined as teaching "Man As God." Passages that she found offensive described Leonardo da Vinci as the human with a creative mind that "came closest to the divine touch." Similarly, she felt that a passage entitled "Seeing Beneath the Surface" related to an occult theme, by describing the use of imagination as a vehicle for seeing things not discernible through our physical eyes....

> [Likewise, d]escribing evolution as a teaching that there is no God, she identified 24 passages that she considered to have evolution as a theme.... [Mr. Mozert] ... also found objectionable passages in the readers that dealt with magic, role reversal or role elimination, particularly biographical material about women who have been recognized for achievements outside their homes, and emphasis on one world or a planetary society. Both witnesses testified under cross-examination that the plaintiff parents objected to passages that expose their children to other forms of religion and to the feelings, attitudes and values of other students that contradict the plaintiffs" religious views without a statement that the other views are incorrect and that the plaintiffs" views are the correct ones.

Frost and Mozert want their children exempted from having to read the offending passages in the readers, and to instead get substitute assignments. When the school refuses, they sue, claiming they are entitled to an exemption under the state constitution's Free Exercise Clause—which the state Supreme Court has interpreted to follow the *Sherbert/Yoder* constitutional exemption model rather than the *Smith* statutory exemption model—and the state's RFRA, which generally tracks the language of the federal RFRA. Analyze the case under both theories. See *Mozert v. Hawkins County Board of Ed.*, 827 F.2d 1058 (6th Cir. 1987).

XIV. Nongovernmental Actions and Religion

A. Actions by Employers

a. Summary

Federal antidiscrimination law provides three sets of religion-related rights to employees, public or private, when the employer has 15 or more employees. Similar state laws generally provide similar rights. (I set aside disparate impact claims unrelated to religious accommodation, and religious affirmative action programs; these come up very rarely.)

1. *The right to be free from religious discrimination:* Employers generally may not treat employees differently because of their religion (or lack of religion). 42 U.S.C. § 2000e-2(a).

2. *The right to reasonable religious accommodation:* An employer must give religious employees special exemptions from generally applicable job requirements if the requirements interfere with an employee's sincerely felt religious obligations *and* such an exemption doesn't impose "undue hardship on the conduct of the employer's business." 42 U.S.C. § 2000e(j); *TWA v. Hardison* (1977) (p. 1074). The EEOC and most lower courts have agreed that this applies not just to religious objectors but also to people who have "moral or ethical beliefs as to what is right and wrong which are sincerely held with the strength of traditional religious views," 29 C.F.R. § 1605.1 (adapting the *Welsh v. United States* standard). See, *e.g.*, *Protos v. Volkswagen of Am., Inc.*, 797 F.2d 129 (3d Cir. 1986).

3. *The right to not be exposed to a religiously hostile environment:* Employers are liable for damages when the employer, its employees, or its patrons engage in conduct or speech that is

(a) "severe or pervasive" enough

(b) to create a "hostile, abusive, or offensive work environment"

(c) based on religion

(d) for the plaintiff and

(e) for a reasonable person.

The theory is that tolerating behavior that creates a hostile environment constitutes discrimination in the "terms [and] conditions ... of employment," 42 U.S.C. § 2000e-2(a). Courts have applied hostile environment law both to speech said directly to the offended person and to speech (signs, e-mails, coworker conversations, and the like) seen or overheard by the person. Courts have generally said that the "severe or pervasive" requirement is usually not satisfied by a single instance of offensive speech, but can be satisfied by several incidents over the span of weeks or months.

Employers are generally liable when they know or have reason to know about the speech. As to speech by patrons, employers are liable only when

1071

they have the power to control the speech (for instance, by instructing employees to eject offending patrons). Religious harassment cases may involve religious insults or even noninsulting religious proselytizing, if a jury concludes that the speech meets the five criteria laid out above.

An employer can also have three possible defenses to religious discrimination claims, defenses that may possibly apply to the other two kinds of claims as well:

1. Religious employers are free to discriminate based on religion. 42 U.S.C. §§ 2000e-1(a), 2000e-2(e)(2).

2. All employers may discriminate based on religion when religion is a bona fide occupational qualification (BFOQ) reasonably necessary to the employer's operation. 42 U.S.C. § 2000e-2(e)(1); see *Pime v. Loyola Univ. of Chicago*, 803 F.2d 351 (7th Cir. 1986) (religion may sometimes be BFOQ when hiring teachers at a university that has a religious tradition, even when the university isn't pervasively religious enough to qualify as a "religious educational institution" under § 2000e-1(a)); *Kern v. Dynalectron Corp.*, 577 F. Supp. 1196 (N.D. Tex. 1983) (converting to Islam is BFOQ for pilots who fly to Mecca, when under Saudi law non-Muslims who go to Mecca are to be executed), *aff'd without op.*, 746 F.2d 810 (5th Cir. 1984).

This, though, is a narrow exception. For instance, "[t]he refusal to hire an individual because of the preferences of coworkers, the employer, clients or customers" is generally not justifiable as a BFOQ in sex discrimination cases, 29 C.F.R. § 1604.2(a)(1)(iii), and the same likely applies in religion cases (setting aside extreme situations such as *Kern*).

3. Courts have also generally held that churches have a constitutional right to discriminate based on any criteria they wish—not just religion, but also race, sex, and other criteria—in hiring ministers or employees who have at least some minister-like duties. See, *e.g.*, *EEOC v. Catholic Univ. of Am.*, 83 F.3d 455 (D.C. Cir. 1996); *Rayburn v. General Conference of Seventh-Day Adventists*, 772 F.2d 1164 (4th Cir. 1985). The church need not claim that it has a religious duty to discriminate on such grounds; it can simply assert an unconditional right to choose its ministers in any way it likes. But this particular defense is limited to churches (unlike the BFOQ defense), and to ministerial employees, not janitors, secretaries, or even teachers of secular subjects (unlike the 42 U.S.C. § 2000e-1 defense).

b.   *Title VII of the Civil Rights Act of 1964, as amended*

42 U.S.C. § 2000e-2(a): It shall be ... unlawful ... for an employer ... to ... discriminate against any individual with respect to ... [hiring, discharge,] compensation, terms, conditions, or privileges of employment, because of such individual's race, color, religion, sex, or national origin.

§ 2000e(j): The term "religion" includes all aspects of religious observance and practice, as well as belief, unless an employer demonstrates that he is unable to reasonably accommodate to an employee's or prospective employee's religious observance or practice without undue hardship on the conduct of the employer's business.

§ 2000e-2(e)(1): [I]t shall not be ... unlawful ... for an employer to ... employ employees ... on the basis of [their] religion, sex, or national origin in those certain instances where religion, sex, or national origin is a bona fide occupational qualification reasonably necessary to the normal operation of that particular business or enterprise ....

§ 2000e-2(e)(2): [I]t shall not be ... unlawful ... for ... [an] educational institution ... to ... employ employees of a particular religion if such [institution] ... is ... owned, supported, controlled, or managed by a particular ... religious ... association ..., or if the curriculum of such [institution] ... is directed toward the propagation of a particular religion.

§ 2000e-1(a): [Title VII] shall not apply to ... a religious ... association[or] educational institution ... with respect to the employment of individuals of a particular religion to perform work connected with the carrying on by such ... [employer] of its activities.

c. Problem: Religious Symbols

Alice, Bob, Carl, Diane, Eric, and Fanny are waiters in a restaurant. Alice is a Jew who wears a Star of David. Bob is a Wiccan who wears a pentagram, which some see as a Satanic symbol (though Bob stresses he isn't a Satanist). Carl is a Hindu who wears a swastika, which is a Hindu religious symbol.

Diane is a Falun Gong practitioner who wears the Falun Gong emblem, which also contains a swastika; at least some Falun Gong documents say that Falun Gong is not a religion, though the emblem is adopted from Buddhism. Eric is a member of the Aryan Nations Church, a religious group that believes in white Gentile separatism from Jews and nonwhites; the Church also uses a swastika as a symbol. Fanny is a Christian who has taken a religious vow to wear a pin with a picture of an aborted fetus, as a statement of her religious conviction that abortion is murder.

Different patrons complain about each of these items. The restaurant's manager demands that each employee hide the item under clothing (or stop wearing it). Is the restaurant's action legal? Should it be legal? If you don't like the way the current Title VII rules play out here, which would you suggest in their place? See Eugene Volokh, *Intermediate Questions of Religious Exemptions—A Research Agenda with Test Suites*, 21 Cardozo L. Rev. 595, 644-48 (1999), for citations to such controversies.

d. Problem: Religious Objection to Posted Material

Victor Lambert works for Condor Manufacturing. Lambert's coworkers have posted pictures of nude women in the workplace; Lambert has a religious objection to working around such pictures (presumably because he thinks that he must keep his mind pure of the evil thoughts that the pictures induce). He demands that Condor order the employees to take down the pictures. Condor refuses; has it violated the law? See *Lambert v. Condor Mfg., Inc.*, 768 F. Supp. 600 (E.D. Mich. 1991) (taking the view that an employer may indeed have such an obligation).

Assume also that Lambert's coworkers often say "Damn," "Hell," "God," and "Jesus," and Lambert has a religious objection to working in a place where he would hear blasphemy. He demands that Condor order the employees to stop saying such things around him. Condor refuses; has it violated either religious accommodation law or religious harassment law?

Should employers have a legal obligation to restrict employee speech when coworkers feel a religious duty not to hear such speech? See Testimony of Prof. Douglas Laycock, 103rd Cong. 22-99 (1994) (stating that when "[a] nonreligious supervisor often uses the expressions 'Jesus Christ!' and 'God [damn]' when angry or frustrated," this is probably not religious harassment under existing law, but "the First Amendment [does not stand] in the way if the [Equal Employment Opportunity] Commission chooses to call it religious harassment"). If you don't like the way the current Title VII rules play out here, which would you suggest in their place?

e. Problem: Religious Objection to Assisting with Abortions

Angelo Rodriguez, a police officer, and Elaine Tramm, a nurse in a county hospital, believe it would be sinful for them to in any way assist in abortions, directly or indirectly; they think such action would violate the commandment "Thou shalt not kill." Rodriguez asks to be excused from helping to guard abortion clinics. Tramm asks to be excused from participating in abortions, cleaning and preparing instruments used in performing abortions, and handling fetal tissue after abortion procedures.

May their employers nonetheless insist that Rodriguez and Tramm perform such tasks? Should they be allowed to so insist? If you don't like the way the current Title VII rules play out here, what other rules would you suggest in their place? The problem tracks problem XIII.A.7.b on p. 1069, but asks you to apply Title VII rather than a RFRA.

f. TWA v. Hardison, 432 U.S. 63 (1977)

Justice White delivered the opinion of the Court....

[A.] Larry G. Hardison was hired by [Trans World Airlines] to work as a clerk in the Stores Department at its [large Kansas City maintenance and overhaul] base. Because of its essential role in the Kansas City operation, the Stores Department must operate 24 hours per day, 365 days per year, and whenever an employee's job in that department is not filled, an employee must be shifted from another department, or a supervisor must cover the job, even if the work in other areas may suffer.

Hardison, like other employees at the Kansas City base, was subject to a seniority system contained in a collective-bargaining agreement that TWA maintains with petitioner International Association of Machinists and Aerospace Workers (IAM). The seniority system is implemented by the union steward through a system of bidding by employees for particular shift assignments as they become available. The most senior employees have first choice for job and shift assignments, and the most junior employees are required to work when the union steward is unable to find enough people willing to work at a particular time or in a particular job to fill TWA's needs....

[After being hired,] Hardison began to study the religion known as the Worldwide Church of God. One of the tenets of that religion is that one must observe the Sabbath by refraining from performing any work from sunset on Friday until sunset on Saturday. The religion also proscribes work on certain specified religious holidays....

[Hardison informed management of his religious beliefs, and asked that his schedule be arranged to accommodate them, but w]hen an accommodation was not reached, Hardison refused to report for work on Saturdays [and was discharged] .... [Hardison sued.—ed.] ...

[B.] The Court of Appeals found that TWA had committed an unlawful employment practice under ... 42 U.S.C. § 2000e-2(a)(1), which provides:

> It shall be ... unlawful ... for an employer .. to ... discriminate against any individual with respect to ... [hiring, discharge,] compensation, terms, conditions, or privileges of employment, because of such individual's race, color, religion, sex, or national origin.

The emphasis of both the language and the legislative history of the statute [as enacted in 1964] is on eliminating discrimination in employment; similarly situated employees are not to be treated differently solely because they differ with respect to race, color, religion, sex, or national origin.... The prohibition against religious discrimination soon raised the question of whether it was impermissible ... to discharge or refuse to hire a person who for religious reasons refused to work during the employer's normal work-week.... [In response,] Congress included the following definition of religion in its 1972 amendments to Title VII:

> The term "religion" includes all aspects of religious observance and practice, as well as belief, unless an employer demonstrates that he is unable to reasonably accommodate to an employee's or prospective employee's religious observance or practice without undue hardship on the conduct of the employer's business....

[This made] it an unlawful employment practice under [§ 2000e-2(a)(1)] for an employer not to make reasonable accommodations, short of undue hardship, for the religious practices of his employees and prospective employees. But ... the statute provides no guidance for determining the degree of accommodation that is required of an employer....

[C.] Collective bargaining, aimed at effecting workable and enforceable agreements between management and labor, lies at the core of our national labor policy, and seniority provisions are universally included in these contracts. Without a clear and express indication from Congress, we cannot agree with Hardison and the EEOC that an agreed-upon seniority system must give way when necessary to accommodate religious observances....

Any employer who, like TWA, conducts an around-the-clock operation is presented with the choice of allocating work schedules either in accordance with the preferences of its employees or by involuntary assignment. Insofar as the varying shift preferences of its employees complement each other,

TWA could meet its manpower needs through voluntary work scheduling. In the present case, for example, Hardison's supervisor foresaw little difficulty in giving Hardison his religious holidays off since they fell on days that most other employees preferred to work, while Hardison was willing to work on the traditional holidays that most other employees preferred to have off.

Whenever there are not enough employees who choose to work a particular shift, however, some employees must be assigned to that shift even though it is not their first choice. Such was evidently the case with regard to Saturday work; even though TWA cut back its weekend work force to a skeleton crew, not enough employees chose those days off to staff the Stores Department through voluntary scheduling. In these circumstances, TWA and IAM agreed to give first preference to employees who had worked in a particular department the longest.

Had TWA nevertheless circumvented the seniority system by relieving Hardison of Saturday work and ordering a senior employee to replace him, it would have denied the latter his shift preference so that Hardison could be given his. The senior employee would also have been deprived of his contractual rights under the collective-bargaining agreement ... at least in part because he did not adhere to a religion that observed the Saturday Sabbath.

Title VII does not contemplate such unequal treatment. The repeated, unequivocal emphasis of both the language and the legislative history of Title VII is on eliminating discrimination in employment, and such discrimination is proscribed when it is directed against majorities as well as minorities. Indeed, the foundation of Hardison's claim is that TWA and IAM engaged in religious *discrimination* in violation of [§ 2000e-2(a)(1)] when they failed to arrange for him to have Saturdays off. It would be anomalous to conclude that by "reasonable accommodation" Congress meant that an employer must deny the shift and job preference of some employees, as well as deprive them of their contractual rights, in order to accommodate or prefer the religious needs of others, and we conclude that Title VII does not require an employer to go that far....

Our conclusion is supported by the fact that seniority systems are afforded special treatment under Title VII itself ...: "Notwithstanding any other provision of this subchapter, it shall not be an unlawful employment practice for an employer to apply different standards of compensation, or different terms, conditions, or privileges of employment pursuant to a bona fide seniority or merit system ... provided that such differences are not the result of an intention to discriminate because of race, color, religion, sex, or national origin ...." [Details omitted.—ed.] ...

[D.] The Court of Appeals also suggested that TWA could have permitted Hardison to work a four-day week if necessary in order to avoid working on his Sabbath. Recognizing that this might have left TWA short-handed on the one shift each week that Hardison did not work, the court still concluded that TWA would suffer no undue hardship if it were required to replace Hardison either with supervisory personnel or with qualified personnel from other departments. Alternatively, the Court of Appeals suggested that

TWA could have replaced Hardison on his Saturday shift with other available employees through the payment of premium wages.

Both of these alternatives would involve costs to TWA, either in the form of lost efficiency in other jobs or higher wages. To require TWA to bear more than a *de minimis* cost in order to give Hardison Saturdays off is an undue hardship. Like abandonment of the seniority system, to require TWA to bear additional costs when no such costs are incurred to give other employees the days off that they want would involve unequal treatment of employees on the basis of their religion. {The dissent argues that "the costs to TWA of either paying overtime or not replacing respondent would [not] have been more than *de minimis*." This ignores, however, the express finding of the District Court that "[b]oth of these solutions would have created an undue burden on the conduct of TWA's business," and it fails to take account of the likelihood that a company as large as TWA may have many employees whose religious observances, like Hardison's, prohibit them from working on Saturdays or Sundays.}

By suggesting that TWA should incur certain costs in order to give Hardison Saturdays off the Court of Appeals would in effect require TWA to finance an additional Saturday off and then to choose the employee who will enjoy it on the basis of his religious beliefs. While incurring extra costs to secure a replacement for Hardison might remove the necessity of compelling another employee to work involuntarily in Hardison's place, it would not change the fact that the privilege of having Saturdays off would be allocated according to religious beliefs.

As we have seen, the paramount concern of Congress in enacting Title VII was the elimination of discrimination in employment. In the absence of clear statutory language or legislative history to the contrary, we will not readily construe the statute to require an employer to discriminate against some employees in order to enable others to observe their Sabbath....

Justice Marshall, with whom Justice Brennan joins, dissenting....

An employer, the Court concludes, need not grant even the most minor special privilege to religious observers to enable them to follow their faith. As a question of social policy, this result is deeply troubling, for a society that truly values religious pluralism cannot compel adherents of minority religions to make the cruel choice of surrendering their religion or their job. And as a matter of law today's result is intolerable, for the Court adopts the very position that Congress expressly rejected in 1972 ....

[A.] With respect to each of the proposed accommodations to respondent Hardison's religious observances that the Court discusses, it ultimately notes that the accommodation would have required "unequal treatment" in favor of the religious observer. That is quite true. But if an accommodation can be rejected simply because it involves preferential treatment, then the regulation and the statute, while brimming with "sound and fury," ultimately "signif[y] nothing."

The accommodation issue by definition arises only when a neutral rule of general applicability conflicts with the religious practices of a particular employee. In some of the reported cases, the rule in question has governed work attire; in other cases it has required attendance at some religious function; in still other instances, it has compelled membership in a union; and in the largest class of cases, it has concerned work schedules.... [In each case, exempting the employee will] result in a privilege being "allocated according to religious beliefs," unless the employer gratuitously decides to repeal the rule *in toto*. What the statute says, in plain words, is that such allocations are required unless "undue hardship" would result....

Assume[, for instance,] that an employer requires all employees to wear a particular type of hat at work in order to make the employees readily identifiable to customers.... [If] an employee ..., for religious reasons, insisted on wearing over her hair a tightly fitted scarf which was visible through the hat[,] ... the employer could accommodate this religious practice without undue hardship—or any hardship at all. Yet as I understand the Court's analysis ... the accommodation would not be required because it would afford the privilege of wearing scarfs to a select few based on their religious beliefs. The employee thus would have to give up either the religious practice or the job. This, I submit, makes a mockery of the statute....

[W]hile important constitutional questions would be posed by interpreting the law to compel employers (or fellow employees) to incur substantial costs to aid the religious observer, not all accommodations are costly, and the constitutionality of the statute is not placed in serious doubt simply because it sometimes requires an exemption from a work rule. Indeed, this Court has repeatedly found no Establishment Clause problems in exempting religious observers from state-imposed duties, *e.g., Wisconsin v. Yoder*; *Sherbert v. Verner*, even when the exemption was in no way compelled by the Free Exercise Clause, *e.g., Gillette v. United States*.

{The exemption here, like those we have upheld, can be claimed by any religious practitioner, a term that the EEOC has sensibly defined to include atheists and persons not belonging to any organized sect but who hold "[a] sincere and meaningful belief which occupies in the life of its possessor a place parallel to that filled by the God of those admittedly qualifying for the exemption." The purpose and primary effect of requiring such exemptions is the wholly secular one of securing equal economic opportunity to members of minority religions. And the mere fact that the law sometimes requires special treatment of religious practitioners does not present the dangers of "sponsorship, financial support, and active involvement of the sovereign in religious activity," against which the Establishment Clause is principally aimed.}

If the State does not establish religion over nonreligion by excusing religious practitioners from obligations owed the State, I do not see how the State can be said to establish religion by requiring employers to do the same with respect to obligations owed the employer. Thus, I think it beyond dispute that the Act does—and, consistently with the First Amendment, can—require employers to grant privileges to religious observers as part of the accommodation process. {Because of the view I take of the facts, I find it unnecessary to decide how much cost an employer must bear before he incurs "undue hardship." ...}

[B.] Once it is determined that the duty to accommodate sometimes requires that an employee be exempted from an otherwise valid work requirement, the only remaining question is whether this is such a case: Did TWA prove that it exhausted all reasonable accommodations, and that the only remaining alternatives would have caused undue hardship on TWA's business? To pose the question is to answer it, for all that the District Court found TWA had done to accommodate respondent's Sabbath observance was that it "held several meetings with [respondent] ... [and] authorized the union steward to search for someone who would swap shifts." To conclude that TWA, one of the largest air carriers in the Nation, would have suffered undue hardship had it done anything more defies both reason and common sense.

The Court implicitly assumes that the only means of accommodation open to TWA were to compel an unwilling employee to replace Hardison; to pay premium wages to a voluntary substitute; or to employ one less person during respondent's Sabbath shift. Based on this assumption, the Court seemingly finds that each alternative would have involved undue hardship not only because Hardison would have been given a special privilege, but also because either another employee would have been deprived of rights under the collective-bargaining agreement, or because "more than a *de minimis* cost" would have been imposed on TWA. But the Court's myopic view of the available options is not supported by either the District Court's findings or the evidence adduced at trial.... [Factual details omitted.—ed.]

{I [also] seriously question whether simple English usage permits "undue hardship" to be interpreted to mean "more than *de minimis* cost," especially when the examples the guidelines give of possible undue hardship is the absence of a qualified substitute. I therefore believe that in the appropriate case we would be compelled to confront the constitutionality of requiring employers to bear more than *de minimis* costs. The issue need not be faced here, however, since an almost cost-free accommodation was possible.}

To begin with, the record simply does not support the Court's assertion, made without accompanying citations, that "[t]here were no volunteers to relieve Hardison on Saturdays." [TWA and union representatives] ... testified that [they] had made no effort to find volunteers .... Thus, respondent's religious observance might have been accommodated by a simple trade of days or shifts without necessarily depriving any employee of his or her contractual rights and without imposing significant costs on TWA.... [T]he burden ... is on TWA to establish that a reasonable accommodation was not possible. Because it failed either to explore the possibility of a voluntary trade or to assure that its delegate, the union steward, did so, TWA was unable to meet its burden.

Nor was a voluntary trade the only option open to TWA that the Court ignores .... First, TWA could have paid overtime to a voluntary replacement for respondent—assuming that someone would have been willing to work Saturdays for premium pay—and passed on the cost to respondent. In fact, one accommodation Hardison suggested would have done just that by requiring Hardison to work overtime when needed at regular pay. Under this plan, the total overtime cost to the employer—and the total number of overtime hours available for other employees—would not have reflected Hardison's Sabbath absences. Alternatively, TWA could have transferred respondent back to his previous department where he had accumulated substantial seniority, as respondent also suggested.

Admittedly, both options would have violated the collective-bargaining agreement; the former because the agreement required that employees working over 40 hours per week receive premium pay, and the latter because the agreement prohibited employees from transferring departments more than once every six months. But neither accommodation would have deprived any other employee of rights under the contract or violated the seniority system in any way. {The accommodations would have disadvantaged respondent to some extent, but since he suggested both options I do not consider whether an employer would satisfy his duty to accommodate by offering these choices to an unwilling employee. Cf. *Draper v. United States Pipe & Foundry Co.*, 527 F.2d 515 (6th Cir. 1975) (employer does not discharge his duty to accommodate by offering to transfer an electrician to an unskilled position).} Plainly an employer cannot avoid his duty to accommodate by signing a contract that precludes all reasonable accommodations ....

Thus I do not believe it can be even seriously argued that TWA would have suffered "undue hardship" to its business had it required respondent to pay the extra costs of his replacement, or had it transferred respondent to his former department. {Of course, the accommodations discussed in the text would have imposed some administrative inconvenience on TWA. [But this does not make] the statute violative of the Establishment Clause.... [We have in the past sustained] have placed not inconsiderable burdens on private parties. For example, the effect of excusing conscientious objectors from military conscription is to require a nonobjector to serve instead, yet we have repeatedly upheld this exemption.}

What makes today's decision most tragic, however, is not that respondent Hardison has been needlessly deprived of his livelihood simply because he chose to follow the dictates of his conscience. Nor is the tragedy exhausted by the impact it will have on thousands of Americans like Hardison who could be forced to live on welfare as the price they must pay for worshiping their God. The ultimate tragedy is that despite Congress' best efforts, one of this Nation's pillars of strength—our hospitality to religious diversity—has been seriously eroded....

INDEX